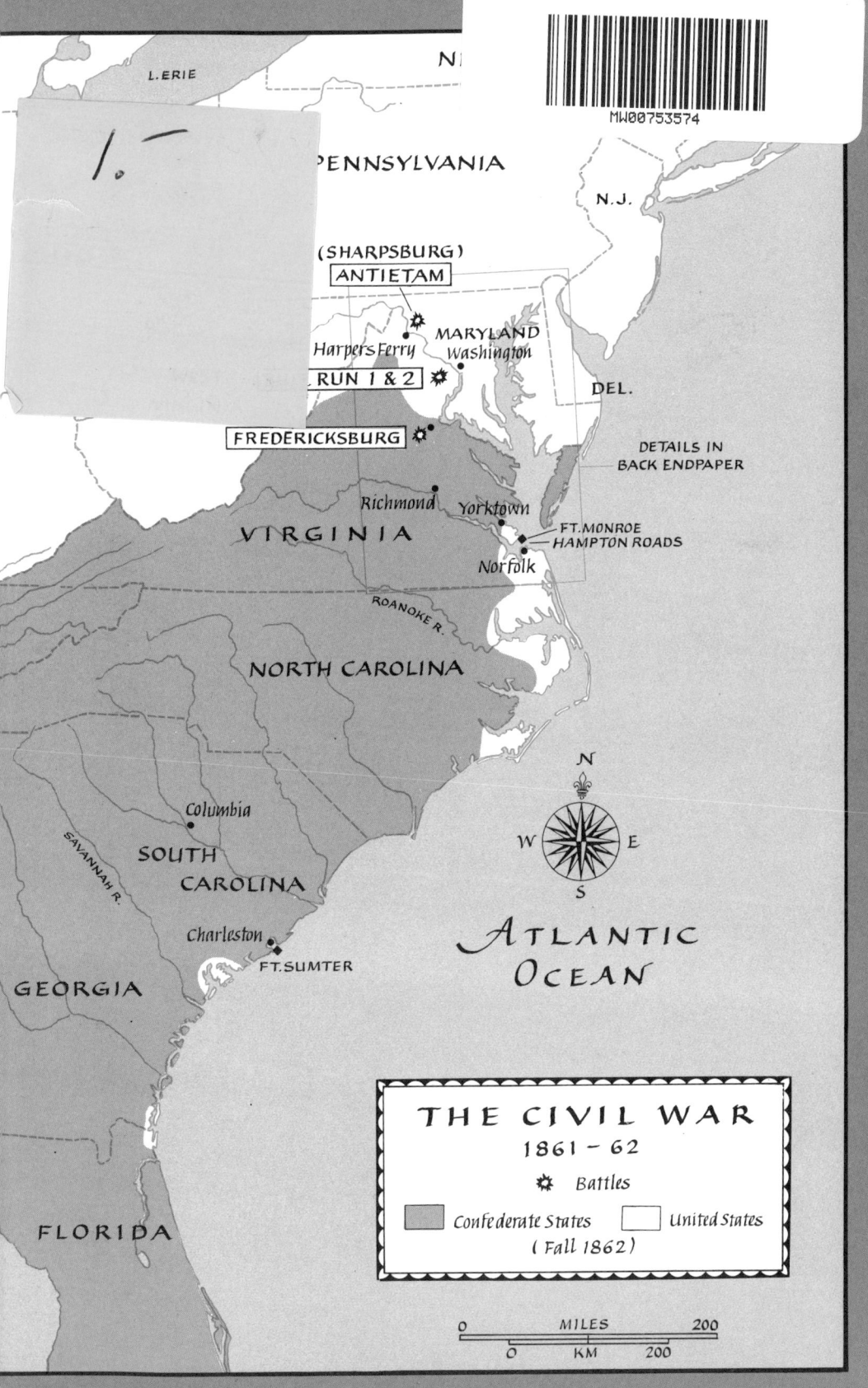

L. ERIE

PENNSYLVANIA

N.J.

(SHARPSBURG)
ANTIETAM

Harpers Ferry
MARYLAND
Washington

. RUN 1 & 2

DEL.

FREDERICKSBURG

DETAILS IN
BACK ENDPAPER

Richmond
Yorktown

VIRGINIA

FT. MONROE
HAMPTON ROADS

Norfolk

ROANOKE R.

NORTH CAROLINA

N

Columbia

W   E

SOUTH
CAROLINA

S

Charleston

ATLANTIC
OCEAN

FT. SUMTER

GEORGIA

SAVANNAH R.

FLORIDA

THE CIVIL WAR
1861 – 62

✿ Battles

Confederate States   United States
(Fall 1862)

0   MILES   200

0   KM   200

FREEDOM

By William Safire

Language

SAFIRE'S POLITICAL DICTIONARY:
THE NEW LANGUAGE OF POLITICS

ON LANGUAGE

WHAT'S THE GOOD WORD?

I STAND CORRECTED

TAKE MY WORD FOR IT

Politics

BEFORE THE FALL

SAFIRE'S WASHINGTON

Fiction

FULL DISCLOSURE

FREEDOM

FREEDOM

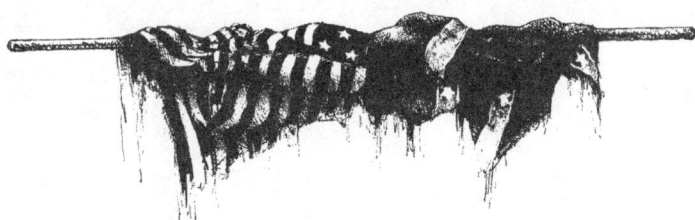

William Safire

DOUBLEDAY & COMPANY, INC.
GARDEN CITY, NEW YORK
1987

Library of Congress Cataloging-in-Publication Data

Safire, William, 1929–
Freedom.

1. Lincoln, Abraham, 1809–1865—Fiction.
2. United States—History—Civil War, 1861–1865—Fiction.
I. Title.
PS3569.A283F7   1987   813'.54   86-29254
ISBN 0-385-15903-X

To the memory of my father, Oliver C. Safir

In memory of my father, Oliver Owen

CONTENTS

NOTE TO THE READER

If you want to look over the author's shoulder, consult "Sources and Commentary" in the back of the book. That underbook separates fact from fiction and makes judgments on the historical controversies raised.

In general, the credibility quotient is this: if the scene deals with war or politics, it is fact; if it has to do with romance, it is fiction; if it is outrageously and obviously fictional, it is fact.

PROLOGUE

"When will they come?" The man who had taken the presidential oath six weeks before heard himself repeating aloud: "When will they come?"

The capital was besieged and its connection with all the states cut off. The continued existence of the Union depended on the appearance, and quickly, of troops to hold off the expected Confederate assault. Lincoln peered out the second-story window of the Mansion. He scanned the Potomac River for signs of a ship supposed to be bearing the Eighth Massachusetts regiment under Ben Butler, bolstered by the Seventh New York and perhaps the Rhode Islanders that Governor Sprague had promised. Only with those reinforcements could any sort of serious fight be waged to save the nation's capital.

"Sir, General Scott is downstairs," said an officer at the door. It was Colonel Stone, in charge of the city's ragtag militia. Lincoln knew his force was made up of thirty-three companies of part-time soldiers and a Home Guard of elderly veterans of the War of 1812. The only company considered a fighting force was a National Rifles company of Marylanders, but that was a hotbed of disloyalty. In Georgetown, the Potomac Light Infantry had just disbanded, prompting the derisive toast "invincible in peace, invisible in war." But Colonel Stone was doing the best he could until troops from the north arrived. "Shall I ask him to come up?"

Lincoln shook his head and followed the colonel downstairs to the front portico. General Scott weighed three hundred pounds and was almost disabled; climbing stairs would be painful for him.

"They are closing their coils around us, Mr. President," said the commanding general of the army that did not exist. Scott reviewed the three military disasters that had befallen the government of the United States in the past three days since the secession of Virginia: the burning of the Harpers Ferry arsenal, the abandonment of the Norfolk Navy Yard with all its ships, and worst, the destruction of the railroad bridges leading from the capital to the north. The general then turned to Colonel Stone to ask how he planned to defend the city of Washington if the rebels came across the Potomac.

"We will resist at three points," said Stone, "the Capitol, the Post Office, and here at Executive Square."

"No," said Scott immediately. "You don't have the troops for three centers. Concentrate what forces you have on holding this area right here."

Lincoln nodded vigorously; it was essential to hold the Mansion until reinforcements came, if they ever did. He assumed that General Scott, hero of the War of 1812, remembered the national ignominy when President Madison had to flee this house and allow it to be burned by the British; if that were to happen now, the war would be over before it began.

"Barricade every entrance to the Treasury," Scott ordered, pointing to the building across the street. "That will be the citadel."

"We can build breastworks there with sandbags," the colonel agreed. "It has a good supply of water and two thousand barrels of flour in the basement."

Apparently flour was important in a siege; Lincoln had been told that flour had doubled in price to fifteen dollars a barrel. At least they would have bread to sustain them, if there was a bakery in the Treasury Building. He would be sorry to see the presidential mansion surrendered, but the government would not be so humiliated if it chose to make its stand in the more fortlike Treasury.

Lincoln thought he heard the boom of cannon. Rebel artillery? Had the assault commenced? Scott and Stone said they heard nothing. Lincoln left them and hurried back upstairs, not knowing whether he had taken to hearing things or his commanders were deaf. Outside his office was a delegation of wounded soldiers, men of the Sixth Massachusetts who had been injured in rioting in Baltimore.

"I don't believe there is any North," he told the handful of men who had proved their loyalty. "The Seventh Regiment is a myth. Rhode Island is not known in our geography any longer. You men here are the only Northern realities."

Lincoln saw that his bitter words caused concern on the faces of the New Englanders standing awkwardly in the presence of their commander in chief. He realized it was unseemly for him to reveal his own doubts to loyal boys who had come to the capital through a barrage of rocks. The President composed himself and asked their leader how he and his men had been injured.

"We left Boston a week ago, right after you called for the militia," the sergeant said. "Train came down through New York and Philadelphia fine, but in Baltimore there was a terrible brawl. We had to shift cars, and the crowd of plug-uglies hit us when our railroad cars were being drawn by horses from one depot to the other on the far side of town."

Baltimore, the only rail link north, was steeped in secession sentiment. The month before, on his own trip from Springfield to Washington to take the Inaugural oath, Lincoln had been forced to sneak through the city of Baltimore in disguise. That had angered him; no President of the United States should be forced to undergo such indignity. He asked about casualties to the Union soldiers.

"We heard a pistol shot and fired back at the mob. Killed about ten or so, I think—four of our men were killed in the wild rush. Maybe thirty hurt, like us here."

Lincoln could imagine the scene: an infuriated crowd, rocks thrown at the frightened recruits, perhaps a shot fired in the air or at someone, and the undisciplined soldiers responding in panic by blazing away into the mob. Blood, fury, hatred, everyone at fault and nobody to blame. After that riot, the Mayor of Baltimore and the Governor of Maryland had sealed off the state from the further passage of troops. Theirs was a selfish and craven act. Coming so soon after the secession of Virginia, the closing of the bridges meant that the capital of the Union was isolated from the North.

Then the telegraph wires to the North had been cut. Washington was out of all touch with its supporters, if indeed the national government had any supporters. The last batch of New York newspapers to come through last week had been filled with glorious expressions of war spirit and news of enlistment parades. But where were those parading soldiers? Panic's contagion did not find him immune; the sudden desertion of the city left Lincoln shaken.

He had not expected it to be this way at all. The bold steps he had taken—to provision Fort Sumter, to call out the militia, to resist secession, to spend great sums of unappropriated money—seemed to lose all force or meaning as the local citizens packed their belongings, nailed shut the doors to their homes and commercial establishments, and ran. The black freedmen disappeared as well, presumably fearful of being newly enslaved. Those citizens who stayed included the Southern sympathizers, of which Washington had so many, waiting to welcome the conquering Confederates.

Lincoln sent the wounded men out with a few reassuring words and resumed his vigil at the window, troubled to have to admit to himself that the cannon sound he could have sworn he had heard had been only in his imagination. Reinforcements were not forty miles away. Why did they have to wait to rebuild the rail track, or wait for a ship—why couldn't they start walking? Ward Hill Lamon, his trusted friend from Illinois—a Virginian of powerful build and blind loyalty who had appointed himself presidential bodyguard—remained at the door, pistols at the ready, posing as a last line of defense in a helpless city.

When would they come? If General Beauregard's Virginia troops moved before the Union ship or train arrived, the secession would be successful. England and France would promptly recognize the political force that had captured the Union capital, overrun the Treasury redoubt, and seized the President and his Cabinet. He was certain no Northerner would then come forward to rally his countrymen to the cause of Union; on the contrary, the pressure from nervous Republicans, not to mention fretful Democrats, to let the Southern states depart the Union peacefully would be irresistible.

"One good thing about being surrounded and cut off," said young John Hay, the second secretary, "is that you can throw a rock down the hall and not hit an office seeker. First time it's been quiet in this place." Lincoln did not feel up to responding to the attempt at cheer. "I was at Willard's last night," Milton Hay's nephew continued, "and the hotel was deserted. Nobody at all in the dining room. Eerie feeling."

Lincoln hated to have to depend on General Ben Butler, of all politicians, for the nation's deliverance. In the past election, the Massachusetts Democrat had been a Breckinridge man, and the abolitionists in Boston were angry at Butler for supporting the candidate the slavocrats preferred. Butler was a maverick, said to be tempestuous, arrogant, with a reputation for acting before thinking. In this extremity, however, just that sort of action by a blustering politician in a general's uniform was what Lincoln needed.

He craned his neck forward; what was that activity on the river? "Hill, go down to the Navy Yard and see what's happening." Butler might have landed his men in Annapolis, against local orders and state laws, and marched his men to Washington. Or he might have steamed around. Or this might be a boatload of secessionists.

Hill Lamon passed the order to Hay: "John, you run down there. I'll stay with the President." Lincoln did not object; Hay would probably be quicker anyway.

The wait was agonizing. Lincoln assumed that if the vessel contained a rebel regiment, General Scott would make a brief but symbolic stand at Treasury, then begin negotiations for surrender. Perhaps the general would try to slip the President and Cabinet out of the city on horseback to Annapolis or by fast boat that night. If faced by that prospect, what should he do? Run for it, of course. Perhaps he could rally the country from Philadelphia or New York; each of the two cities had been the capital at one time.

What had he done wrong? Against the advice of his Cabinet—all but the strong-willed Montgomery Blair, a West Pointer—Lincoln had decided to wage war rather than permit the Southern malcontents to break up the government. Even now, he was absolutely certain that had been the right decision. The secession had presented one stark question: whether a democracy could maintain its territorial integrity against its internal foes. The answer, in his mind, could not be clearer: a government could not be so tender about the rights of its citizens that it lost the power to maintain its existence.

No; the mistake he had made was military. He had counted, foolishly it now seemed, on the existence of a North—of armed forces in being—prepared to march and sail down to defend the capital. He had thought Maryland, a slave state, would be neutralized by the sight of thousands of Federal troops passing through. To those rebellious souls who threatened him with "peaceful dissolution or blood," he hoped to have the troops on hand to give his answer: blood, or no dissolution.

He heard rapid footsteps. Hay appeared at the door with a breathless "It's General Butler and the Eighth Massachusetts, sir, and the Seventh New York, and Sprague and his men. They're forming up to march down Pennsylvania Avenue."

Lincoln picked up his hat and went down to the front porch to see for himself that there really was a North. General Scott wheezed his way from the War Department across the street to join him. He could hear a drumbeat in the distance.

"Mr. President, the Maryland legislature is meeting tomorrow to vote on secession. General Butler asks permission to bag the whole nest of traitorous Maryland legislators, and to bring them in triumph here," the old hero of the Mexican War announced. "I told him that was a political decision for you to make."

For the first time Lincoln realized he had the military power to prevent a state from seceding. But did he have the legal authority? The arrest of whole legislatures had never been contemplated by the men who had formed a union of states. Lincoln was not bothered by punctilio: he had already summoned a militia and imposed a blockade without permission of Congress, which was being called despotism. Of course, Lincoln rejected such charges, but he had decided weeks ago that he would do better without the Congress breathing down his neck until the crisis was over. He had set the date for convening Congress at July 4, more than two months from now. It would hardly help the cause of Union to have the politicians from all over the country in town, in session and in his hair. To get the war properly begun, he needed a breathing spell, the freedom of action to put down the rebellion without the intervention of the institution that reserved for itself so much of the power he needed.

"I think it would not be justifiable," he replied to Scott about the arrest of the Marylanders. "We cannot know in advance that their action will not be lawful or peaceful."

"We could simply disperse them," offered the general. "No arrests."

"They'd immediately assemble someplace else." Residents were beginning to appear along the street—some cheering, others sullen, most just waiting for the parade. "No, let's watch and wait. If they take up arms against us, you can bombard their cities." At least for now, Lincoln would resist the temptation to arrest a state government.

"General Butler is a lawyer, sir, which I am not. He says he must have the power to suspend habeas corpus."

He winced. There it was: the demand for military rule. The success of the plug-uglies of Baltimore in choking off the capital's line of communication and supply made necessary, at least according to Butler, the application of unprecedented power. He hesitated. "I'll have to mull that over."

Down Pennsylvania Avenue from the Capitol, raising the dust from the hard dirt of the wide boulevard, came the most welcome sight of his life: well-formed ranks of soldiers of the Union, flags fluttering, the chirruping, booming sound of a splendid regimental band heralding their arrival.

"That's the Seventh New York," said Scott, squinting at the flags. Across the street, the whole Blair family turned out on the porch of their house, waving a large flag. The citizens of Washington came out of hiding and lined the avenue in front of the President's house to cheer. Lincoln breathed easier, feeling the spirit and power of liberty embodied by men in blue uniforms surging into the capital of the nation.

The next day, as the Federal troops were bivouacked in the House of Representatives, the President read and reread a draft of an order that would take him into waters that the Constitution had only sketchily charted.

The pigeonholes of his rolltop desk contained the accumulation of his brief time in the presidency. Some were already stuffed full, like the one marked "Greeley," containing editorials from the *New York Tribune,* with covering letters from the editor exhorting him to smash the rebels who had dared to fire on Sumter; others held only a single item, like the slot for Thurlow Weed, the Albany editor and notorious wirepuller, who had written asking for the juiciest patronage plum in New York.

On the writing surface of the desk was a sheet of paper, the words on it awaiting only a date and signature to take on the force of law. Lincoln picked up the order to his commanding general, considered it, put it down again unsigned. Succinct enough, limited to the area of greatest danger, surely necessary.

He rose, placed the knuckles of his large hands on either side of the paper, and read:

"To General Scott: You are engaged in suppressing an insurrection against the laws of the United States. If at any point between the city of Philadelphia and the city of Washington, you find resistance which renders it necessary to suspend the writ of habeas corpus for the public safety, you personally, or the officer in command at the point at which resistance occurs, are authorized to suspend that writ."

If this were signed, any lieutenant serving under Ben Butler could arrest any person he thought suspicious, clap him in jail, and all but throw away the key. The lawyer in Lincoln came in conflict with the commander in chief. Of all the freedoms wrested over the centuries from kings and tyrants, the privilege of the writ of habeas corpus was fundamental. "Produce the body" was the Latin command, the demand of an independent judiciary that anyone arrested by the government be brought before a court of law to see whether his arrest was legal and proper. Under habeas corpus, both the rulers and the ruled agreed to subject themselves to the rule of law; without habeas corpus, the courts were powerless to determine whether a citizen was arrested for cause. Where that writ did not run, no society could call itself free—any soldier or policeman could break into any house, grab the occupant, throw him into prison, and the person would have no recourse. The word for government without habeas corpus was tyranny—martial law, the age-old route to absolute power by dictators. In this case temporary, of course, rooted in necessity for survival, but that was the way most permanent tyrannies began.

William Seward entered the President's office as airily as if it were his own, which he and many people thought it should have been. Lincoln always admired the way the Secretary of State carried himself: all grace and nobility, a commanding presence made piquant by trace of world-weariness. "Billy Bowlegs" was the tallest short man Lincoln had ever met.

Seward glanced at the document on the table and said, "Yes, that's it—sign it. What are you squeamish about? There's a war on." When Lincoln explained that the suspension of habeas corpus was not a precedent to be lightly set, Seward brushed aside his reservations about the abridgment of liberty. "It's right there in the Constitution. Didn't your eminent Attorney General explain it to you?"

Lincoln was quite familiar with Article I, section nine, paragraph two, and recited it aloud: "The privilege of the writ of habeas corpus shall not be suspended, unless when in cases of rebellion or invasion the public safety may require it."

"Well, there you have it. That means the writ may indeed be suspended when, in case of rebellion, the public safety does require it. Which is now, so sign." Seward tapped the top of the paper. "Put today's date up in the space provided—it's the twenty-seventh."

Lincoln reminded him that some lawyers were saying that the founders had put the suspension in the section of the Constitution dealing with the powers of Congress, and that the legislative branch alone, not the Executive, was vested with that power.

"That reminds me of a story," said Seward, mimicking Lincoln's technique of argument. "Your campaign manager in Chicago made a horrendous political deal at the convention, promising that old thief Simon Cameron a Cabinet post if Pennsylvania would desert me and support you. However, you sent a telegram to your manager, saying with some sanctimony, 'Make no deals in my name.' And your manager said loud and clear, 'We're here and he's not' and the dirty deed was done. The point is, we are here and Congress is not."

Lincoln appreciated the story. "More rogues than honest men find shelter under habeas corpus."

"If you want company on this, let the responsibility for the arrests be mine. We cannot suppress an insurrection while observing all the constitutional niceties."

Lincoln took up his pen. "Old Roger Taney isn't going to like this one bit."

"To blazes with the Chief Justice. It was his own damned decision in the Dred Scott case that brought on the war."

If Seward had no compunctions, Lincoln asked himself, why should he be afflicted with them? Chief Magistrates of great nations were supposed to be the way William Henry Seward was at this moment: decisive, firm, single-minded, purposeful.

Lincoln thought of the rowdies in Baltimore, how their criminal agitation had caused the deaths of innocent civilians as well as sturdy young soldiers. Would it not be wiser to arrest such men before their troublemaking led to death, and before their terrorizing could cause the state to isolate the nation's capital?

He wrote in "27" after "April," which already appeared across the top, and signed his name. Seward snatched up the document and handed it to a secretary to rush to the War Department. Lincoln was aware that he had just clothed himself with more power than had ever been possessed by George Washington or Andrew Jackson. Environed by treason, he did not feel uncomfortable about it.

John Cabell Breckinridge

BOOK ONE

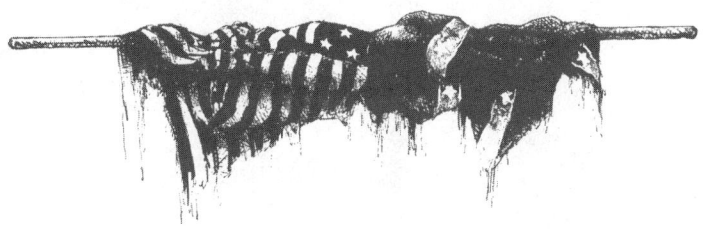

John Cabell
Breckinridge

CHAPTER 1

JUDICIAL DEFIANCE

Getting up the steps to the bench was a problem. Irritated at his own infirmity, Roger Taney waved aside the bailiff's offer of help. The oaf had mispronounced his name in calling the court to order—Taney should be said to sound like "tawny"—and the Chief Justice wanted no assistance up the stairs from the likes of him.

The Chief Justice of the United States was one year older than the nation. At eighty-four, after thirty-six years of service as John Marshall's successor at the head of the Supreme Court, Roger Taney was aware that he had been preparing for a lifetime to take the action likely to cause his arrest and imprisonment. The old man had told his daughter as much that morning, instructing her what clothes and books to bring him at Fort McHenry's military jail.

He pulled himself up the railing next to the steps, taking his seat behind the bench with an angry grunt. The prospect of dying while incarcerated held no terrors for him; that sort of martyrdom would help him make his point.

The point that Taney was determined to drive home to the nation on the broiling day in late May in Baltimore was that the Constitution could not rightly be defended by unconstitutional means. If the Union could not be maintained lawfully, with a proper regard to the civil liberties of its citizens during its greatest test, then it was the Chief Justice's opinion that a peaceful separation of the slaveholding states should be permitted.

Not that he approved of secession—on the contrary, Taney believed that the Southerners were mistaken in their intent to dismember the Union. But he never let his personal views determine his decisions: his job, his mission in life, was to stick to the law as written. No law, no word in the Constitution, prohibited a state from withdrawing from the Union, and every power not expressly given to the national government belonged to the states and the people. The founders had established a federal system, not a national system, and nothing that this arrogant new President said in his Inaugural about an oath "to preserve the Union" could change that. Taney had to give Lincoln credit for being a clever lawyer; interpreting the union of states as indissoluble on the basis of his understanding of the oath of office was creative. But it was not the law, nor was it for the President to decide what was the law. Roger Taney and his Court would do that.

He ignored the gavel in front of him; a judge should be able to quiet a courtroom by the force of his gaze, with no help from pounding wood on wood. Not that this was much of a court, he observed; the old Masonic Hall served as a district court because the citizens of the rowdy city of Baltimore were too cheap to build a courthouse.

Each of the nine members of the Supreme Court was expected to ride circuit, as he was today, sitting as an individual judge in a designated area. Taney's assigned area included the state of Maryland, where the first casualties of a civil war had taken place. He had seized the opportunity to come to

Baltimore and try the case that would hold the new President to the rule of law.

The bailiff, although he could not pronounce a name properly, had been properly instructed to cry out Taney's national title—Chief Justice of the United States of America—and not judge of the federal circuit court, sitting as a local jurist. Taney was determined to issue his order as Chief Justice of a nation, just as Chief Justice Marshall had done in the time of Thomas Jefferson, establishing the court's authority to decide what is constitutional and what is not.

Not since he had issued his decision on the runaway slave, Dred Scott, holding that a negro in this country had no rights which the white man was bound to respect, had Taney felt as exhilarated. He looked around the courtroom for black faces; there were a few, and he could feel their hostility. Pity about that. They would never understand he held no animosity toward the blacks, had freed his own slaves fifty years ago, and had said in open court that slavery was a blot on the national character. But it was not for a judge to write law, merely to interpret it as its writers intended.

Robed and ready, comfortable in the law and secure in the rightness of his cause, the Chief Justice surveyed the other faces in his courtroom. Word had evidently spread, as he had hoped, that this would be a day of confrontation between the national executive and the national judiciary, between the force of arms and the rule of law. Taney's eyes, still sharp enough to read footnotes in agate type in printed opinions, spotted some familiar faces at a table set aside for members of the press. The correspondents of the Northern radical press were there in full strength, poised to brand him "traitor" for daring to uphold the authority of due process. The man from Horace Greeley's *New York Tribune*, along with the man from Henry Raymond's *New York Times*, were certain to support their radical Lincoln in any of his dictatorial acts aimed at punishing the seceding Southerners. The other side was there, as well: a reporter from the *Louisville Courier* was present, a man Taney had spoken to several times, and from whom he expected a fair report on the day's proceedings. Kentucky was as important as Maryland these days, and both those internally divided border states were more important than New York.

Looking at the seats beyond the table of reporters and defendants, the old man could make out the strong features of the face of another Kentuckian: Senator John Breckinridge. Taney nodded in his direction. Breckinridge, until a few months ago, had served as Vice President of the United States in the Buchanan administration, and many thought he was more responsible than any other man for Lincoln's election. By running for President as a Peace Democrat, Breckinridge had split the vote of War Democrat Stephen Douglas, helping Lincoln to win the presidency with fewer than four votes out of ten cast. After the national election, the legislature of Kentucky had immediately sent the popular Breckinridge back to Washington as senator.

Why was Breckinridge in court here in Baltimore? Taney surmised that the Kentuckian wanted to receive instruction on the limitation of the war powers of the President. The Chief Justice would give him that, and more, all to be used as ammunition in the Senate to curb a runaway Chief Executive.

Taney's eyes followed Breckinridge as the tall man changed his seat to put himself next to Anna Ella Carroll, who had positioned herself in the first row behind the reporters' table. Taney knew Miss Carroll, too, just as everyone of any influence seemed to; he was friendly with her father, the former governor of Maryland. In Maryland, the Carrolls were as influential as the Blairs, though not as wealthy. This daughter had surprised everyone by turning out to be a writer, a pamphleteer and publicist for the railroads. Taney considered her an attractively vivacious, if somewhat assertive, young woman. Not so young anymore—he estimated her to be fortyish now—and blessed with a keen mind. Would likely have made a good lawyer, had she been born a man.

The large family that sat together at the defendants' table, looking more indignant than worried, was the kin of John Merryman, the man seized by Union troops after the outbreak of violence and the subject of the day's hearing. Taney did not see Merryman himself in the courtroom. That meant that the government was refusing to "produce the body" and was prepared to show its contempt of the court. The Chief Justice called on Merryman's lawyer to begin.

"Being at home, in his own domicile," the lawyer read from notes, "petitioner John Merryman was aroused from his bed about two o'clock in the morning of May 25, 1861, by an armed force and deprived of his liberty."

Taney nodded and prompted him. "The writ."

"He has been imprisoned without any process or color of law whatsoever. The person now detaining him at Fort McHenry is General George Cadwallader."

"The writ, the writ," Taney snapped, wishing the lawyer knew how to present evidence in proper order.

"We promptly came before you in this court to pray that a writ of habeas corpus be issued, directed to the said George Cadwallader commanding him to produce your petitioner before you with the cause, if any, for his arrest and detention."

"Upon my order, the writ was issued," Taney said. "Clerk will read it."

"The United States of America to General George Cadwallader, Greeting," the clerk called out. Taney wondered if the characters in this drama realized the constitutional import of their roles. "You are hereby commanded to be and appear before the Honorable Roger B. Taney, Chief Justice of the United States, in the U.S. Courtroom in the Masonic Hall and that you have with you the body of John Merryman—"

Taney cut him short and pointed at the U.S. Marshal, a portly fellow standing alongside a man in uniform. "Did the court's marshal serve the writ?"

"I served the writ on the general, Your Honor," the marshal's voice boomed, "who sends this court his aide, Colonel Lee, in reply. So answers Washington Bonifant, U.S. Marshal for the District of Maryland."

Taney glared down at the military aide; for the general to send a flunky added insult to constitutional injury. "What is the general's response to the lawful writ issued by this court?"

"The prisoner is charged with various acts of treason," replied the colonel coolly, "and with avowing his purpose of armed hostility against the government."

"That is no answer to the writ."

"General Cadwallader has further to inform you," the officer went on, unperturbed, "that he is duly authorized by the President of the United States, in such cases, to suspend the writ of habeas corpus for the public safety." He began to offer a legal argument. "In times of civil strife, errors, if any, should be on the side of the safety of the country, and—"

Taney would have none of that, from a person with no standing before this court. He wanted to keep the issue clear. "Have you brought with you the body of John Merryman?"

"No."

"The General has acted in disobedience to the writ," Taney declared, "and it is ordered that an attachment forthwith issue against him for a contempt, returnable before me here at two P.M. today. Marshal, do your duty."

The Chief Justice took lunch alone in what passed for his chambers, a dingy room upstairs where he spooned down an obligatory bowl of Maryland she-crab soup. He wondered if it would be his last meal as a free man, and whether it was possible to bring on a heart attack through willpower. He could also refuse to eat. The death of a Chief Justice in jail would surely create a furor, setting a precedent that might protect other judges in a time that presidents liked to call "necessity."

He pondered the power of precedent. When his predecessor, John Marshall, in *Marbury vs. Madison*, affirmed the right of the Supreme Court to decide whether laws passed by the Congress were constitutional, neither the Congress nor President Jefferson took issue with him. That lack of challenge set the precedent that gave the Court its power as an equal branch. Now here was Lincoln, seizing a war power reserved to the Congress. If nobody challenged him, the precedent would be set, and the presidency would assume a power that could not be taken back. The worst part of that dark prospect was that this war power—arbitrary arrest, the ability to set aside the due process of law—was at the core of what had caused the American colonies to rebel against the English king.

Did Lincoln realize this? Taney was of the opinion that the new President was not the country bumpkin, the rail-splitter, the baboon soon to be taken into camp by his betters in the Cabinet, that his detractors were saying he was. The Chief Justice thought Lincoln knew precisely what he was doing. First, he had begun the war without the necessary declaration by the Congress, which was not in session. Then he had usurped the power of the absent Congress to raise armies and pay them. Finally, today, he was snatching from the legislative branch the power to suspend the writ of habeas corpus, which was the citizen's basic protection against dictatorship. The President's motive was obscure, but the pattern could not be more clear.

Taney asked himself, as he finished the lumpy soup, what he would do next if he were in Lincoln's shoes and wanted to make permanent this seizure of power. He didn't know Lincoln, but he had known Andy Jackson—indeed, had written President Jackson's farewell address, warning of North-South divisions—and prided himself on reading the minds of strong-willed presidents. Jackson would confront the opposition, as he did the banks, spoiling for a public brawl. What about Lincoln? His style seemed different, deceptively self-deprecating, as he made huge incursions into the power of the Congress. Perhaps he would not accept the invitation of the judiciary branch to have it out right here and now. Perhaps he would be cagey enough to avoid the trap Taney was setting. But Taney did not see a way out for Lincoln: either he would have to back down, setting the precedent that would forbid any future President from assuming the power to suspend the writ, or he would have to arrest the Chief Justice for treason.

Court convened promptly at two. Taney called for the marshal's report.

"I proceeded to Fort McHenry for the purpose of serving the writ," intoned the marshal, half facing the judge, half the press table. "I sent in my name at the outer gate. The messenger returned with the reply that there was no answer to my card."

Taney leaned forward. "Were those the exact words?"

"No answer to my card. I was not permitted to enter the gate. Therefore, I could not serve the writ. So answers Washington Bonifant, U.S. Marshal."

So that was Lincoln's tactic: neither specific refusal nor permission to enter. Taney nodded in grim understanding: Lincoln had decided neither to flout the law nor to obey the law. He would simply try to ignore the law by refusing to confront the judge.

"You have the legal power to summon out a *posse comitatus,*" Taney told the marshal, "to seize and bring into court the party named in the contempt attachment." A look of horror crossed the marshal's face at the prospect of leading a posse into the military camp. "But it is apparent you would be resisted in the discharge of that duty by a force notoriously superior to the posse." He could hear Washington Bonifant let out his breath.

"Under these circumstances," Taney continued, frustrated by the Lincoln refusal to engage or disengage, "I can only call on the President of the United States to carry out his constitutional duty to enforce the law; in other words, to enforce the process of this court."

The old man could feel his heart racing as he laid the legal base for the impeachment of the President. Taney forced himself to slow down and to let his gaze roam over the people in his courtroom: the so-answering marshal, the angry family of the arrested man, Breckinridge whispering to Miss Carroll, the excited reporters, a few of the plug-uglies who had chased the first contingent of Union troops out of Baltimore.

History, Taney assumed, would either judge the President to be a usurper or the Chief Justice to be a traitor. Perhaps the Almighty had preserved him to this age and brought him to the place and moment to draw the issue. He took his weapon in hand—a written opinion, prepared as the case ripened in anticipation of this constitutional impasse—titled *Ex Parte Merryman.*

"The opinion which I shall read," he began, looking at Breckinridge, "is that of the Chief Justice of the United States." As the leader of the judiciary branch, he would use every shred of his legal authority and intellectual skill to stop the encroachment of military despotism. He was certain that the greatest threat his countrymen faced was not, as Lincoln thought, separation into two nations, but the loss of freedom in the name of protecting freedom.

CHAPTER 2

PRESERVED FOR THIS OCCASION

"Brave old man," said John Breckinridge.

"Damned traitor," the woman next to him whispered back.

The senator from Kentucky looked at Anna Carroll first in disapproval, then back again in wonderment. Did she mean that, or did she enjoy being outrageous?

"The President not only claims the right," Justice Taney was saying from the bench, "to suspend the writ of habeas corpus himself, at his discretion, but to delegate it to a military officer. No official notice has been given to the courts of justice or to the public that the President claimed this power."

"Now they know," Anna Carroll said under her breath, for Breckinridge to hear. "No proclamation was needed. Taney wants Lincoln to submit to the court's jurisdiction on this, so the court can deny him his war power. But Lincoln's no fool."

"I certainly listened to this claim with some surprise," Taney read his opinion, "for I had supposed it to be one of those points of constitutional law upon which there was no difference of opinion—that the privilege of the writ could not be suspended except by Act of Congress."

Breckinridge looked to the small, intense woman at his side for her response. "Congress isn't in session," she murmured with less assurance than before, "it had to be done immediately."

The Kentucky senator shook his head at that. She might be ahead of him on the war powers of the President versus the Congress as expressed in the Constitution, but he was squarely in the middle of the tug-of-war that was going on in Washington today. He knew that Lincoln could easily have called Congress into session back in April, when the crisis over Fort Sumter arose. "Wrong," he told his companion. "Lincoln doesn't want us there in session in Washington, not until he has his war under way."

She shrugged that off, which niggled him. He had known Anna Carroll for ten years, since he first came to Washington from Lexington to represent Kentucky. She had been a close friend of his Uncle Bob's, the preacher Breckinridge, who headed the society that bought up slaves, set them free, and shipped them off to the new state of Liberia in Africa. The Reverend Robert Breckinridge had taken a profound interest in being the spiritual guide of the young woman, and had commended her to his nephew, a stranger in an unfriendly city, as an intellectual companion and source of new political friendships. That Anna had surely been to the young senator, and for the first few years, no more than that; but she was an attractive lady, demanding as well as giving, and one thing had led to another. Their need for each other in Washington made it awkward for both to see much of Uncle Bob, and that relationship with the avuncular guide ended for both: the preacher Breckinridge would not have approved a love affair between the young woman who looked to him for moral teaching and his nephew, whose wife was raising three sons for him back in Kentucky. John Breckinridge did not approve of it either, but the months away from family on official business were long, and it was impossible for him to separate his need for the stimulus of this particular woman's unique mind from their mutual need for more. So they had what they had, and he decided it helped them without hurting anybody, and tomorrow would take care of itself.

Taney, meticulously building his case against Lincoln, cited the precedent of President Jefferson's restraint in the matter of rebellious Aaron Burr; in that instance, the President had deferred to Congress on a suspension of the writ of habeas corpus. Breckinridge was familiar with that case; his grandfather had been Jefferson's Attorney General, which instilled a familial interest in the precedent Taney was citing. Nodding in agreement, he listened to the aged jurist's analysis of the passage in the Constitution that permitted the suspension of the writ in case of rebellion: the clause appeared in the enumeration of the powers of Congress, and did not appear in a separate article listing the powers of the President. He looked at Anna, who did not turn her head; she had no answer to that.

Taney then plunged into the history of the great writ in English common law. He showed why it was a legislative rather than an executive prerogative: the Parliament, suspicious of the power of a king to arrest arbitrarily one of his subjects, made certain that any temporary suspension of the most elemental political freedom required a legislative action.

"I can see no ground whatever," said the judge in his piping voice, "for supposing that the President, in any emergency, can arrest a citizen except in aid of the judicial power. He certainly does not"—here Taney looked up and laid stress on the next few words—"faithfully execute the laws," and looked down, continuing, "if he takes upon himself legislative power by suspending the writ of habeas corpus, and if he takes upon himself the judicial power also by arresting and imprisoning a person without due process of law."

"That lays the basis for an impeachment," Breckinridge whispered to Anna Carroll.

"No chance," she replied. "The votes for that walked out of the Congress a month ago."

He had to admit she was right. Six weeks from now, on July 4, Congress would convene, but the representatives from the Southern states would not be there. The secession, which Lincoln did not recognize as valid, would remove most congressional constraints from Lincoln. When the Southern representatives walked out, the man elected by a minority of the people would have a majority of the votes in the Congress.

Breckinridge realized he would be one of a handful of senators, from the border states, left to hold out for peace amid a flock of warhawks. In the current atmosphere, peace did not have many defenders, North or South, but he believed that some time remained for reasonable men to avert a bloody war. Fort Sumter was a mere skirmish; no real battles had yet been fought. Despite the firebrand oratory of the Rhetts and Yanceys in the South, and the Bakers and Wades in the North, and despite the symbolic action at Fort Sumter, the war fever was not yet a disease. It could be cooled; military men knew that war had not yet begun.

Taney applied what, to the lawyer in Breckinridge, seemed to be the crush-

ing argument about who held the constitutional power, in case of invasion or
rebellion, to permit arbitrary arrest. "Chief Justice Marshall," said the judge
who succeeded to his position, "used this decisive language: 'If at any time,
the public safety should require the suspension of the powers vested by this
act in the courts, it is for the legislature to say so. That question depends on
political considerations, on which the legislature is to decide; until the legislative will be expressed, this court can only see its duty, and must obey the
laws.' I can add nothing," Taney said triumphantly, "to these clear and
emphatic words of my great predecessor."

Anna Carroll was ready for that. "Marshall's opinion was an obiter dictum," she said quickly, "only his personal opinion, made in passing on an
unrelated matter."

"You've researched that closely," Breckinridge noticed.

"Marshall's obiter dictum was not part of the Court's decision, and doesn't
count as precedent," she insisted. "That troublemaker on the bench knows
it."

He knew, and was aware that Anna knew, that John Marshall's opinion on
whether a President had the right to suspend habeas corpus would count
heavily with anyone concerned with the rule of law. That was why she was so
quick to try to minimize its importance. Breckinridge wondered why she was
so well informed, and repeated his question more directly. "You've been
working on one of your pamphlets?"

She nodded. He could see she was torn between protecting a confidence
and boasting of her assignment. He knew his friend well enough to wait until
her craving for recognition did its work. "I'm helping the Attorney General a
little. Old Bates doesn't have much of a staff."

"Just a little research in the library, then."

That assumption of insignificance nettled her. "Actually, I'm drafting the
Attorney General's memorial to the President on war powers. If Lincoln
agrees with my argument, then I'll put the memorial in a pamphlet form, in
language that people can understand."

Breckinridge knew what that meant: a fiery broadside, certain to be reprinted by newspapers across the North, demolishing in the most fervid terms
the legal argument being set forth in musty detail by Taney. Anna was superb
at persuasive writing, and had taught Breckinridge a thing or two about
rhetoric in his own speeches. But the trouble with her writing, in his view,
was in the way that she could persuade herself to adopt, without reservation,
positions that served the interests of her client. Lawyers found means to serve
clients' ends all the time, he acknowledged, but she did not have a lawyer's
credentials.

"You really believe," he asked, "that Lincoln has the legal authority to
wage war, to raise and pay troops, and to arrest anybody for no reason—all
by himself?"

She glared at him, then patted his hand and smiled. "This is a war to stop
treason. Get used to it. Don't stand on ceremony."

Her ready acquiescence to what struck him as a clear case of constitutional
outrage troubled him. Here was a woman of intellect, with a solid background in business and politics, and with the Tidewater good sense that had
kept him out of trouble many times. If Taney's arguments about the limits of

the war power could not persuade Anna Carroll, what chance did peacemakers have against less intelligent Northerners spoiling for a fight? Turning it the other way, what chance did peace-seeking unionists have against secessionists spoiling for separation and independence?

"Great and fundamental laws have been disregarded," Taney was saying. "If judicial authority may thus be usurped by the military power, the people of the United States are no longer living under a government of laws." The Kentucky senator felt the frustration and sorrow in the Chief Justice's words. The old man's voice weakened in his conclusion. "I have exercised all the power which the Constitution confers upon me, but that power has been resisted by a force too strong for me to overcome."

Except for the buzzing of the flies, the Masonic Hall was silent for the judge's order about the writ he could not serve. "I shall, therefore, direct the clerk to transmit a copy of my order, under seal, to the President of the United States. It will then remain for that high officer, in fulfillment of his constitutional obligation, 'to take care that the laws be faithfully executed.' "

"That's a personal slap," Anna Carroll said. "It was Taney who swore Lincoln in two months ago, and he's reminding him of the words of the oath."

"Good words to remember."

"Lincoln was also sworn to defend the Union."

"No," Breckinridge said carefully, remembering the oaths he had taken as senator and Vice President, "he swore only to preserve, protect, and defend the Constitution. Not the Union. The Constitution remains the same when new states come in or old states go out." She shrugged that off; he suspected the next time he brought it up, she would have a well-researched answer.

Taney was not a gavel-banger; court was adjourned when he rose and the bailiff called out for all to rise. Breckinridge saw Taney's grandson come forward to help the old man down the stairs.

"I want to see him, Anna, and tell him he's a brave man. Will you come with me?"

She shook her head. "I don't want to have to testify in a conspiracy trial."

He looked down at her, more amused than disturbed. "You really think it could come to that? That Lincoln would arrest the Chief Justice for high treason? Or send his soldiers to arrest the duly elected senator from Kentucky?"

"You just be careful what you say to him. I'll wait for you here; I need some help getting home."

Breckinridge strode to the stairs behind the bench to shake the judge's hand, and of course the old man recognized him. The last time they had talked was at the 1856 inaugural ceremony at the Capitol, when Buchanan and Breckinridge were sworn to the nation's highest offices. He recalled that Taney had said something tart at the time about Breckinridge being the youngest Vice President in the nation's history.

"Ah, Breckinridge," Taney said warmly, "I am an old man, a very old man, but perhaps I was preserved for this occasion."

"The nation is fortunate that you were."

The Chief Justice waved his grandson away, took the senator's arm and motioned ahead toward the room serving as his chambers. "It's like a delir-

ium, this passion the country is in. I grieve to say that hate sweeps everything
before it. Too violent to last long, I hope. You will stay in the Senate?"

"For as long as I can," Breckinridge assured him, certain that the majority
in pro-slavery Kentucky opposed secession, "to speak both against secession
and against war."

Taney stopped to catch his breath. "It may be hard to remain adamant
against both. A peaceful separation, with free institutions in each section—
that would be better than the union of the present states under a military
government and a reign of terror."

"I always thought that secession would be a mistake."

"A peaceful separation," repeated Taney, evidently preferring that phrase
to "secession," "would be better than a civil war that will prove as ruinous to
the victor as the vanquished."

The old man, Breckinridge judged, was not dealing with political reality. In
the 1860 election, Breckinridge had run for President in the moderate posture
of a man opposing abolitionism forthrightly and secession quietly; as a result,
he had won most of his votes in the South. It was true that his campaign was
taken over by the firebrands eager for secession, but secession had never been
his platform. "Secession means war," he told Taney. "The radicals up North
like Greeley, and out West like Ben Wade, will never let Lincoln agree to
peaceful separation. They want to subjugate the South."

"Don't be so sure," Taney argued. "Lincoln may sound like a radical, but
he may not be—he didn't put a Blair in his Cabinet for nothing. Lincoln and
Blair may be personally unsympathetic to slavery, as am I, but they are surely
not for abolition. The new President may turn out to be more reasonable than
he seems."

Breckinridge was surprised. "How can you say that, after the opinion you
just read?"

The judge squinted up at the senator and observed, "I'm not under arrest,
am I?"

"The country would never stand for that."

"For a politician, Breckinridge, you don't know much about the popular
will. If Abe Lincoln were to clap me in jail this minute, the whole North
would applaud, except for a few constitutionalists and they don't count." He
began walking forward. "I wish with all my heart that Lincoln would react to
my order with an arrest. Then I would die on him and drive my message
home. But he's too damn shrewd for that."

"You're a brave man, judge."

"Get to eighty-four and you see how easy it is to be brave. Remember Chief
Justice Coke, the high judge of England? The king asked Coke what he would
do if a case came to him involving the royal prerogative, and Coke told him,
'When the case happens, I shall do that which shall be fit for a judge to do.' If
you're not ready to do what's fit, you shouldn't be a judge. Or a senator."

The Kentuckian thought about that. If and when the time came to decide
between secession and war, what would be fit for him to do? Should he follow
his Kentucky constituency, which was split but leaned toward union? Or
follow his conscience, which was sending him confused signals? He could in
all good conscience oppose secession in principle, but in practice, could he
support a war that would force the South to remain in a union its people

despised? How fine Taney's term, "peaceful separation," sounded, with its application of a cool intellect to a time of great passion. But Lincoln would permit no separation without war. The choice, which had been union or peaceful disunion, had been changed; Lincoln had forced the choice of union or war.

"What happens to Merryman?" he asked Taney.

"Who?"

"The fellow in the stockade. Lincoln won't hand him over to you. Can the President get some other court to try him for treason?"

"Ah, Lincoln and Bates probably think they can. They'll try to bring this fellow Merryman before a district judge here and make an example out of him. The man did burn the railroad bridge to the North in wartime; that's a fairly treasonous act."

"And the courts cannot stop the President. What's becoming of this country?"

"Cool down," said the old man. "Lincoln cannot get any court here to try Merryman for treason and hang him legally."

"Why not?"

Taney's wizened face took on its cagiest look. "I'll tell the district judge that all capital cases must be referred to me for trial. And I'll be too sick and infirm for the next year or so to come to Baltimore, so no treason case will be tried here for as long as I live." The Chief Justice dug his birdlike fingers into Breckinridge's arm. "I may be powerless to free that man, but I can damn well make certain that Lincoln will never have the legal power to hang him."

CHAPTER 3

THE PLUG-UGLIES

Anna Carroll watched the old man take Breckinridge's arm and walk off with him alone. Their private get-together did not trouble her; with no witnesses to their conversation, no damaging testimony was likely to be taken if Lincoln decided to round up Taney and all the other anti-Union judges.

She engaged some of the reporters in conversation, as Attorney General Bates had urged her to do, and as befitted the only woman whose name was well known in the area as a political pamphleteer. Anna provided some of the journalists, who knew so little about the great issues they were covering, with arguments exposing some of the weaknesses in the Chief Justice's decision. She had read Madison's journals of the constitutional convention, and doubted that the men who wrote the Constitution had ever debated where to place the right to suspend habeas corpus; it had been merely the decision of the committee on style to put that power to make arbitrary arrests among the legislative powers rather than under the President's powers. Who were John Marshall and Roger Taney to invest that minor decision with such far-reaching significance?

The man from the *New York Tribune*, Horace Greeley's abolitionist paper, noted her point and showed her the lead sentence of his story: "The Chief

Chief Justice Roger B. Taney

Justice today took sides with traitors, throwing about them the sheltering protection of the ermine." She admired that and told him so.

She took issue with Washington's *National Intelligencer* story. The writer for that anti-abolition daily—which Mr. Lincoln was known to read every day—defended Taney's decision as "able and lucid." At Anna's urging, the reporter added that "Lincoln's action resulted from what he believes such an impervious public necessity as is held to justify him in transcending the letter of the Constitution." She especially liked the use of "transcending" rather than "transgressing"; as she saw it, the President was reaching over and beyond the Constitution, stretching its reach but not challenging its authority.

Even as she dealt with these men as her writing equals, Anna hated to admit that she felt the need for the physical protection of a man for the next few hours. She was afraid of the plug-uglies. In a moment of panic, Maryland's wavering governor—an old friend of the Carroll family, and her father's successor—had destroyed all the railroad bridges between Baltimore and Washington. That was supposed to keep Maryland out of the way of belligerents, but it effectively isolated the nation's capital while making travel in Maryland unsafe for anyone. The plug-uglies roamed the streets of Baltimore and the roads to Washington, waylaying travelers who would ordinarily choose safe rail travel. Their name came from their plug hats as well as from the spikes studded in the front of their boots, worn by the hoodlums to do greater injury with a kick.

Anna had come to the courtroom from Washington's Ebbitt House in the company of a troop of returning Maryland militiamen, and had a note from General Winfield Scott that would requisition a military escort for her return. But she wanted to stop at her father's plantation on the way back for a personal mission that meant a great deal to her, and the presence of a troop of soldiers would be awkward. The less her family knew of her political activities, the better; she wanted no lectures about a woman's place from those who her activities were supporting. That meant she needed a man, strong and armed, to accompany her; otherwise, she was certain she would be attacked, beaten, humiliated, raped, robbed, and murdered. She had frequently imagined that sequence in detail.

Breckinridge returned from his talk with Taney and, to her relief, offered her a ride in his carriage to Washington.

"Are you armed?"

"Of course not, Anna. I'm a politician. Haven't carried a musket since the Mexican War."

"We'll stop at my father's farm and pick up a shotgun," she said with finality. "It's on the way, and I have something to do there." She knew he would not object; his way was to give in on all the little things. On the great issues, she knew, he worked out his own way, not always taking good advice. She was determined to keep him from making more of a pariah out of himself in the Senate.

In the carriage, they said little at first. The road to Annapolis was deeply rutted and Breck let the horse pick his way. As the Kentuckian stared straight ahead, concentrating on the horse and road, she looked at his profile: pugnacious yet aristocratic, an odd combination, making him not so much handsome as magnetic. Perhaps that was the secret of his attraction as an orator, on the stump or on the Senate floor; he was a big man who seemed unconscious of his size, slow to decide but hard to budge after having made his decision, not especially talkative in an armchair but eloquent on his feet. The defeated candidate for President left Anna the clear impression that he was in quiet command of himself even when he was unsure of his position. Breck was at his most persuasive, she had found, when he seemed to be working things out for himself, aloud, and carried his audience to his own conclusion.

That was not her way at all; she knew what she thought, or at least what she was supposed to think, and she said it or wrote it without the usual coyness expected of a lady. That was true in almost all things, but when it came to this man, her sustaining certainty slipped away. She never knew quite how to feel about him.

The men in her life had always been men to admire. Her governor-father, her political mentors, the railroaders who directed lobby-agent business her way, the Reverend Bob Breckinridge, even that two-timing hypocrite President Fillmore and the gentle bachelor President Buchanan—all were men of substance and stability, secure enough in their success not to resent her independence. Like them, Breck moved confidently in the most exalted company; he had almost reached the very pinnacle of power while a youth, and was in her mind the most presidential non-President in the country today, but her attraction to him was a mystery to her. She loved him and could use him, both of which were important, but he was the only man she looked up to that she worried about.

John Breckinridge struck her as a strong man who lacked the inclination to protect himself; he showed too little interest in striking back at his detractors. That curious deficiency drew strange impulses from a woman who rejected the usual motherly or wifely traits. Because he did not weigh the personal consequences of his political stands, he was especially vulnerable. She had often vowed to straighten him out on that. If he was to be President one day, as she hoped and suspected he would, he would have to learn to protect his back.

She was glad he was happily married. Anna had never wanted to be held down by marriage and motherhood, and felt only contempt for men who found it necessary to be unhappy with their wives to be her friend. Friendship was what counted, on rare occasions a complete and sexually satisfying friendship, building those lifelong loyalties best achieved with a man whose family life was secure and whose family was far away. She took the interest of a maiden aunt in Breck's sons, especially the rebellious eldest, Cabell, and delighted in dispensing the sound advice on upbringing that only an objective non-parent could give.

Maiden aunt. Did Breck ever think of her that way? Anna Carroll, at forty-one, saw herself as a vivacious redhead with a magnificent complexion and a fine if petite figure, and had never looked or felt better in her life. The drive and sparkle that had attracted two presidents and a handful of the most powerful men in America were undiminished, and the fierce loyalty and talent that had resulted in lifetime friendships with families as politically diverse as the Wades and the Blairs were increasing in her maturity. She could help a man like Breck, and not just in arranging Know-Nothing support for his campaigns, as she had in the past. She was convinced that she could help him count mightily in the future of the country, if she could prevent him from making a terrible mistake about secession and the war.

"Forget about that shotgun, Anna," he said out of nowhere. "I can talk our way out of any trouble."

"If you won't carry it, I will. I'm not worried about getting raped," she added, enjoying the way he winced whenever she used a taboo word, "I just don't want you getting robbed."

She trusted him, and knew just how much he trusted her: ever since the first stirrings of secession, nearly a decade ago, he had given her for safekeeping the correspondence between many of the Southern leaders. She knew it was then all a lot of fire-eater talk—absurd plans for a Southern nation that would absorb Cuba and Mexico, extending clear down through tropical America—but fascinating to any student of politics. Someday, after the current trouble was over, she would write about these early roots of rebellion. But not now; Jefferson Davis, for example, might be a traitor, but he had been Anna's loyal supporter in business and politics. She had worked on assignments from him to promote the Memphis-to-Charleston railway that linked South to West.

Thank God for all those railroaders. To a man, they needed political information: whom to support, who could win, who could be reached on rights-of-way. They hungered for access to power, introductions to landowners and financiers. Those connections could best be provided by someone with social standing and a hearty sense of politics, saucy and sensible, and Anna felt comfortable in that role. She spoke their language and took their money and felt good about both.

She needed those earnings. Her father, the former governor who had spurned the legislature's offer of a Senate seat, could never come to grips with the economic operation of a large plantation. Her fees as a pamphleteer and purveyor of entrée to men of influence supported him, four of her six sisters who were not yet married, and herself. Anna did not treat this as a great burden; she had been given a good education and a curious gift.

The carriage wheel hit a rock and nearly pitched her out. She grabbed for Breck, then poked him in the arm and told him to be more careful, and did not release her grip on his arm. The curious gift, uncommon among women in her set or any set, was her talent in expressing outrage on paper. She considered herself as persuasive a pamphleteer as the Revolution's Tom Paine, nearly as powerful in her prose as the mutton-fisted Englishman William Cobbett. Writing with zeal and toughness was her special knack; so was spinning out a long, scholarly argument on paper. The only time she wished she had been born a man was when she thought of how much more money she could have made.

The road was deserted after they left Baltimore's outskirts. It was still light in the summer evening, but Anna wished they had that shotgun. On the other hand, Breck might be right; if accosted, perhaps it would be safest to hand over some money and go their way.

"You still in touch with your old political friends?" he asked. He meant the Know-Nothings, a group that Anna had allied herself with a decade ago, after the Whig Party broke up and before the Republicans got organized. They styled themselves the Native American Party, and called themselves the "Sams," after Uncle Sam; the anti-foreigner feeling was easy to exploit, and the support of the frankly bigoted Sams was quietly sought by many a politician too queasy to make the blatant anti-immigrant appeals directly. She had steered Breck some Know-Nothing help in his campaign; her old friends were not proper political company for right-thinking people, but they had their uses.

Anna smiled and gave the silent signal: one finger up, then touching the side of the nose, then an "o" with the thumb and forefinger. "I Nose Nothing." The secretive party had provided the margin of victory in many elections; she was proud, in a way, to have been one of the founders when she was a young woman. But then the Native American Party was taken over by the pro-slavery gang, and she left it for the Republicans.

"You didn't mean it, did you," he asked, "when you called Justice Taney a traitor?"

She was not going to give him any reassurance. "That evil old man knows exactly what he's doing. He's trying to make it impossible for Lincoln to crack down on treason, which is all around us, and that puts him in league with the traitors."

"Those are hanging words, Anna. You throw them around too easily."

"That mob in Baltimore killed four Union soldiers," she told him, "and the soldiers killed a dozen of the rioters, the friends of that thug Merryman. That's not just debates in the Senate, Breck, that's blood being spilled."

"Is it better to have more bloodshed—to try to hold together two parts of the country that want to go their separate ways?"

He was just baiting her, she figured; Breck was no disunionist, never had been, even though the Southerners dominated his presidential campaign. "There are some things important enough to spill blood over," she replied.

"What if the violence goes beyond a few people killed in riots," he asked, "beyond a few hundred casualties in skirmishes. What if this war becomes a real war—hundreds of thousands dead, orphans, hunger, cities on fire—would holding those states in the Union be worth it then?"

That was not a question to be answered when everyone knew the insurrection would be put down before the winter. "Just say what you want to say."

"I don't know, Anna, I haven't decided. Sometimes a good thing is too costly. Nobody is thinking about the price, in lives and in misery, of forcing the South back into the Union."

She felt a constriction in her chest. "You can preach peaceful separation in the Senate all you like, that's your right as Kentucky senator. But nobody's going to listen." She thought a moment. "You're not going to try to take Kentucky out, are you?"

"That would be treason, wouldn't it?"

She wondered if he could actually be entertaining the thought. Why? He hated war, that was fine, so did she, so did everybody, but the war had become a fact. At that point, even the pacifists had to think about their futures. "Yes, that would be treason. Don't let them use you again, Breck."

"Again?"

"The secessionists used you in the last election to split the Democratic vote for Douglas and to elect Lincoln. You know the secesh wanted Lincoln to win so they could walk out on him. You know you were used. Don't let them use you again."

He shook his head, guiding the horses out of a rut. "No, I won't try to take Kentucky out. Kentucky will cling to the Union while a shard of it remains. Bluegrass people will stay loyal as long as the abolitionists don't take over in Washington."

"Lincoln is no abolitionist."

"I wish I could be sure. I get the feeling, sometimes, that he means to reach into the South and free every slave there."

"That's scare talk, and you know it! Lincoln is against the extension of slavery out West, and so am I—but there is nothing abolitionist in being a Free-Soiler."

"That's what Lincoln says now, and repeated in the Inaugural—he would not strike at slavery where it exists," Breckinridge said. "But let's see what he does when your friend Wade gets after him."

Ohio senator Ben Wade, a leader of the radical Republicans, made no bones about his abolitionist intent. "Ben is my friend," Anna said carefully, "and Carolyn Wade is my best friend. But even they know they're a tiny minority in the country, and it would be foolish, even unconstitutional, to strike at slavery where it exists."

"Abolition is what this fight is really about, Anna."

"Wrong!" She saw through his strategy: he would pretend the fight was not about the preservation of the Union, nor even about the extension of slavery into the territories; instead, he would change the issue to the one that appealed to the extreme men on both sides—slavery itself. "Lincoln is not threatening to take away anybody's slaves, you know that. Abolition is a scare, that's all, and you're using it to make secession look right."

"I can understand," Breck said in a reasonable tone, "an abolitionist fighting to 'save the Union,' because he's passionate about his cause—to establish a Union that does away with the slave property of the South. But you, Anna —you and Lincoln and all the conservative Republicans willing to abide slavery where it exists—why do you insist on a bloody war? Just to hold some territory intact?"

"You swore an oath when you became Vice President," she reminded him, "to preserve the United States. You would break that oath?"

"I swore to preserve the Constitution, and it doesn't matter whether that sacred document covers thirteen states or thirty." She frowned at that; the oath was one of Lincoln's favorite arguments, binding the most upright to his side. "If the sections cannot live together in peace," he went on, "it may be better that they live apart. There is no excuse in American history or geography for brother killing brother in war."

She took off her hat, put it in her lap, and let the wind whip her hair. She quoted to him, in derision, the slogan of the peace crowd: "Erring sisters, depart in peace."

Breck smiled. "Horace Greeley wrote that in his *Tribune*, but Lincoln's friends turned him around in a hurry. The *Tribune* changed its tune. Now it's 'On to Richmond!' "

Anna was aware that Lincoln and Seward, recognizing Greeley's importance in keeping up pro-union spirit, had sent Thurlow Weed to the New York editor to straighten him out about the erring sisters. There was to be no easy secession; the sister states would not be allowed to depart without war.

"How many slaves do you own, Anna?"

"Twenty."

"You inherited them, of course."

"I bought them with my own money," she said abruptly. "Four hundred dollars a head."

He grunted surprise and said no more. Quietly, she began to seethe. What did this ill-used border state politician know about the ownership of slaves in a Southern state economy? She was especially glad he was with her on this visit to her home. He would learn something about Southerners and slavery.

Within an hour, Breck's carriage drew up in front of Castle Haven, the Carroll farm. The house and scrubby land were a far cry from Kingston Hall, the family estate where she had been raised; that had been lost long ago under the auctioneer's gavel, and the small farm was all that was left. Anna, who had not been home in six months, winced at the way the farmhouse and grounds had continued to run down. She had been promised they would paint this year, and cut away some of the rampant creeper. Too cavernous to be modest, the house looked hugely disreputable. She confronted her dismay and turned it around: with her companion in mind, she was glad her home looked that way. Part of his lesson.

Thomas Carroll, a political man when in his prime, had turned reclusive in his old age; he saw them from the porch and went inside to his room. Two of her sisters came running to greet them.

"We won't be staying for dinner," Anna told them after an embrace, "Senator Breckinridge has to be in Washington. But I have to see the girls, every one of them, in the parlor right now."

The senator looked puzzled. He accepted a tall glass of mint tea offered by an elderly slave, and when he was alone again in the parlor with Anna, asked, "What 'girls'?"

"You think I'm a hypocrite, buying slaves myself while I side with the North." She cut off his courteous protest. "You've been a soldier and a politician, and you may have practiced law for a few months, but you've never been in the business world. Let me show you something about the slave business."

She took out a ledger and laid it on the desk. "We have sixty acres of land here. Corn, potatoes, a peach orchard. We have one hundred and fifty slaves." She waited for his question.

"Isn't that a lot of slaves for a farm this size?"

"About a hundred more than we need. Now if we were smart business people, we'd sell off our surplus slaves. At eighteen hundred dollars a head for a strong field hand, about half that for a house slave, that would give us capital to work with. We could buy some decent livestock, a few strong horses for plowing, maybe build a barn to replace the one that burned."

"Bring down your expenses, too," he added helpfully.

She nodded at his quick grasp of the economics. "Absolutely. Our operating expenses would come down if we had only fifty mouths to feed. We could even show a profit, take good care of Papa." She perched on the edge of the desk and crossed her arms. "The problem is, we cannot sell a slave. Papa doesn't believe in splitting up families."

"You could sell a whole family," he offered.

"Into what? The negroes on this farm grew up with us, and they're accustomed to decent treatment. When you put a family on the block, that may be fine for your conscience, but the next slave trader will break up that family on a strictly business basis. You know what some of those plantations are like downriver, and how they drive their slaves. Could you sell a family, knowing they'd be split up, and used like animals?"

"No."

"Neither could we. So our slaves kept breeding like damn rabbits, and growing up and needing more food, while we had to sell off our land until we were broke." She slammed the ledger shut and tossed it on the desk. "I know how the reporter for your *Louisville Courier* says how the 'peculiar institution' is essential to the Southern way of life, but to people like us, slavery is a burden. It's ruined my father and disinherited my sisters. We're stuck with our slaves, and it's made no more than slaves out of us."

When he said nothing, she went on: "Now you should ask why we didn't simply free our slaves, the ones we couldn't use to work the farm."

"I'm aware of the laws of Maryland," the senator said. "No slave can be set loose here. Anybody who frees a slave must ship him to Liberia."

"That was the law up till last month," she snapped, irritated that he stepped on her point. "And I wouldn't send my worst enemy back to Africa. Your Uncle Bob is a sweet and kind man, but that colonization society of his is a disaster. Liberia is a hellhole."

"There were ways to get around that law."

"Sure, sell them to New Yorkers who would free them up there," she said quickly. "And that would mean that they would starve and freeze. Who would take in a freed slave? White workers hate 'em, they undercut their wages, and they hound them out. The abolitionists are all for freeing slaves in the South, so long as they don't come up North."

"It was a dilemma, I know."

He did not begin to know, but she would educate him. Some of her girls began to slip into the parlor, tentatively, each worried about being part of some formal occasion, which could be harsh news. Mostly house blacks, their ages ranged between sixteen and thirty. Almost all were tall, many were unusually attractive.

"The debtors began to close in on this farm about seven years ago," she told him. "There's a glut of field hands around the Eastern shore, but the slave traders have a ready market for prostitutes, and they had their eyes on these girls. Look at them, Breck." He was looking, all right. "They're beautiful, nubile, highly desirable as prostitutes or for some rich man's private stock. Every time we went four hundred dollars deeper into debt, the slavers had the legal right to claim one of these girls."

The room was filled with the slaves, who were eyeing their owner and her friend with curiosity. The girls were well behaved, but not unusually shy or in any way beaten down. Anna knew each one well and was proud of the lot.

"So I went to one of my railroad men and took out a mortgage loan on the lot of twenty slaves. I used that mortgage money to buy the slaves from Papa.

At that point, the farm's creditors couldn't touch a one of them, because they were my personal property—as long as I could come up with four hundred dollars a month to service my mortgage debt."

She was tempted to recount the wheedling she had to employ on visits to New York and Philadelphia, scratching up writing assignments from rail-roaders, supplemented by loans from abolitionists sympathetic with the cause of keeping a score of black girls from the life the slavers had in store. She had pleaded, dramatized, persuaded, wept on cue; the one period in her life that she really abased herself, setting all pride aside, was to find that four hundred dollars a month above her own needs. She held back from telling him all that; such pleading was out of the independent character she wanted to be in his eyes. Suffice it for Breck to know that she had good reason to put a high fee on her writing skill and her politico-social services to railroaders.

"Thanks to you," she said instead, "the Douglas vote was split, Lincoln was elected, and the slavers walked out of the Congress. That made it possible to free slaves in Maryland today without condemning them to shipment to Africa or starvation up North. And that's what I'm going to do right now."

Flushed with excitement at the consummation of her work in front of the border-stater most respected by the South, Anna addressed her property for the last time.

"I don't want anyone to be frightened at this, because it is good news," she began. "You're free. All of you. Free. I have a letter of manumission for each of you, with each of your names on it. Come up here as I call your name and take it. You're nobody's property anymore."

Anna called out the names one by one, handed out the letters, shaking each former slave's hand. Breckinridge, standing alongside, extended his congratulations to each with a handshake of his own, because it seemed the appropriate thing for a visiting politician to do. He whispered to Anna, "How do your mortgage holders feel about your giving away their collateral?"

"They know I'm good for the money." She had no idea where she would get the eight thousand dollars to pay off the chattel mortgage. She would manage; it was enough that the girls were out of reach of the slavers.

"Miss Carroll," one wanted to know, "where we gonna go? What if we don't want to leave?"

"You have to go," she said firmly. "You're free. If you want to marry one of the hands, fine, Papa will free him and you can go away together. But you have to go." Anna did not want to face the paradox of the cruelty involved in the manumission. She hugged one of the girls who had been especially close to her, wrote out addresses in Frederick and Annapolis where some might find work, and ran upstairs to say good-bye to Papa and find the shotgun for the journey.

In the carriage, riding southwest after sunset, when she could trust herself to speak, she said, "What a goddamned relief."

Breck looked at her as if he had never heard a woman of any social standing use profanity before. Anna assumed he had not and it would be good for his soul.

"They're free, but you're not," he said, jiggling the reins loosely as the horse made his way along the darkening road. "You still have the debt service on your slave-purchase mortgage."

"I can handle four hundred a month," she said almost merrily, glad he understood the extent of her sacrifice, "and someday I'll raise the whole eight thousand."

Breckinridge shook his head. "A senator makes three thousand dollars a year. Sounds like a lot of money to me."

Anna knew how much of a mountain it would be to climb, and how small the likelihood of climbing it before her old age, but she had no regrets. "Twenty virtuous women saved from a fate worse than death," she said lightly; "I'd do it again."

"Emancipation is wonderful," he replied, "so long as somebody pays for the property and the seller is willing."

"I had dinner the other night with Rose Greenhow," she changed the subject, "in that marvelous home of hers. Rose and I never see eye to eye on politics, but she's well informed—"

"Stay away from Rose Greenhow."

She glared at him. Who was he to tell her to stay away from anybody? "I'll see whoever I like."

"Just stay away from Rose. I like her, too, and I can think of a half-dozen senators who are crazy about her, but she's trouble."

She thought that over. Rose O'Neal Greenhow, a widow of Anna's age and social standing, was outspokenly pro-Southern but had never been in political trouble. Her brick home on Lafayette Square, a short walk from the President's house, had become a salon for many of the most interesting leaders and soldiers in the capital. If there was any woman Anna envied, it was the "Wild Rose"; she wished she had her height, her striking facial features, and her rich dead husband's home for dinner parties of wild pigeon and old Madeira.

"What sort of trouble?" she wondered aloud, she hoped idly.

"Wouldn't be good for your business." He was vague about it; she suspected he might be having an affair with Rose and was worrying about the two women comparing notes about him. Anna smiled at that as they rode in silence for a couple of miles.

On the high road to Washington, not far from the Silver Spring estate of the Blair family, the carriage lurched and splashed thin mud. Breck reined in the horse and then relaxed the reins, letting the horse pick his way through a series of what Anna presumed to be puddles in the road.

A lantern flashed in the blackness ahead. Two horsemen appeared, blocking the roadway. The horse and carriage stopped. Anna heard a voice to the side, in the darkness behind a bush, say, "Where you nice folks coming from?"

"All of us are coming from Baltimore," Breck said, his voice steady. "I guess we're a couple minutes ahead of the others."

Another voice behind them said, "Nobody's following them. 'Cept me."

"Get out of the carriage and hand over your money," one of the men in front said. The voice was low and authoritative; Anna, in her terror, assumed that was the leader.

"Whatever you say," Breckinridge said. Anna was slightly relieved. They were surrounded; this was no time for heroics. It could be all they wanted was money and the horse and carriage. She started to rise and felt her companion's hand firmly on her arm, pushing her back down. With the same deliberate movement, he reached behind him for the shotgun. She wanted to tell him to leave it alone, she didn't mind walking, it made no sense getting killed, but the words stuck in her throat.

"Get out and lie down by the side of the road," said the voice up front. "There's four guns aimed right at your heads."

"I have only one gun aimed at you," Breckinridge said in the direction of the voice. "But it's a shotgun. At this range, it won't miss you. And the second barrel should take care of the man next to you before you kill us."

The damn fool was going to start a bloodbath, Anna thought. She said nothing, holding her breath.

"He's bluffin', Alvin," said the man behind them.

"Hold the lantern up high, Alvin," said Breckinridge. His voice, she noted, had assumed his stump-speaking tone, resonant and commanding. "You'll see the barrel pointed at you. Your friend back there can afford to be brave, he'll get your share afterward."

"Don't move that damn light," Alvin hissed at the man at his side, "he wants a target."

"I'll take two of you with me," Breckinridge said, his voice more menacing than the highwayman's. "The boy here with me may or may not be armed; you can't know until the shooting starts."

"All we want is your money," the voice at the side said, negotiating. "You can keep the carriage. Just throw down the money in your pocket."

"If you don't get out of the way, Alvin," Breckinridge replied, making the most of his knowledge of the plug-ugly's name, "I'll blow your head off. I'm a soldier and I shoot straight and I'm prepared to die. Are you?"

The leader of the group was silent. The man at the side said, "Who you soldiering for? Federals?"

"We're headed South," Anna croaked in as low a voice as she could muster, hoping to give the plug-uglies an excuse to withdraw without appearing to be cowards.

"Say hello to General Beauregard," said the man who answered to the name of Alvin, and the pack turned and rode away.

Anna, her stomach in spasm, bent forward and moaned. She felt the carriage begin to move ahead in the mud's softness. She did not trust herself to speak.

When the knot in her stomach began to relax and her hands stopped shaking, she ventured a comment. "All they wanted was money."

"To tell the truth," he said cheerfully, pleased with his reaction to the emergency, "I never was faced with a challenge of that kind. Always wondered what I'd do. Strange, no fear at all."

"You could have gotten yourself killed. For nothing." That did not seem to trouble him. "You could have gotten me killed."

"I knew that if I laid my life on the line, the gang leader would back off." He was not thinking of the danger to her at all. "I had to do what was fit for a man to do."

"Oh for God's sake," she exploded, "did you swallow all that pap from

Judge Taney? He quotes Coke and the King of England at every dinner party he goes to, and to every pompous ass who'll listen." She straightened up. "Listen, Senator Breckinridge, you can take your life in your hands all you like, but when you take my life too, I want to have a say in it."

"I never thought of it that way, but of course you're right. Didn't think you'd look at it that way." He was still analyzing his own foolhardiness, which he surely took for bravery. "You know, Anna, there's no telling what those men would have done."

"They'd have robbed us and let us go. If they started tearing my clothes off and raping me, then you could have grabbed a gun and been a hero. But not over a few dollars."

"He really quotes Lord Coke to everybody?" He was missing her point. She had a right to participate in a life-or-death decision.

"What are you, Senator, one of those fire-eaters? Do you live for violence?" Now that the danger was past, she was getting her natural voice back. She could hear herself prattling in the darkness, clenched fist jabbing into his leg, at once proud of his quickness of mind and cool nerves and determined not to act the damsel saved from distress. He had leveled that shotgun with great authority; she could not comprehend his fatalism in lazily assuring the thieves that death, while not a friend, held no terror for him. As her confidence returned, and the gaslights of Washington's streets brought at least the illusion of safety, she stopped hectoring and took his muscled arm in her two hands. She thought of Fillmore, the weakling, and of Buchanan, the vacillator, and of Lincoln, about whom she knew little. This man in her hands, even if all too pleased with himself at the moment, possessed a character and intelligence probably superior to all of theirs. If he did not throw his future away on some mistaken notion of peace-above-all, he could one day grace the highest office.

She was being offered a drink of corn whiskey from his flask. She shook her head. He tilted his head back and started gurgling; after a while, she said, "Leave a little for me." He stopped, swallowed hard, and handed the flask to her. She finished the remainder.

"You said we were going South," he observed.

"I lied. One of us needed to show some sense. You're not going South, nor is Kentucky." She swore to bend every effort to keep her Maryland loyal and hold her favorite reckless Kentuckian in the Union as well.

CHAPTER 4

JOHN HAY'S DIARY
JUNE 29, 1861

Hallelujah, the long faces of May and June are lifting. (If sad faces are long, why are happy faces not described as short?) The Tycoon is in a fine whack, no longer pacing the Mansion as if he wanted to kick the cat. When A. Lincoln wants to look miserable, nobody alive can out-melancholy him, but he has reason to be perkier these days.

Not only is he well served by his two secretaries—George Nicolay of the furrowed brow, and mustachioed me, John Hay of the short face—but the Prsdt has good news in the public prints.

Old Roger Taney got his comeuppance. Henry Raymond of the *New York Times*—a good egg, friend of the Tycoon's—denounced the jurist who supported the plug-ugly Merryman as "the man destined to go through history as the Judge who draggled his official robes in the pollutions of treason." ("Draggled"? Does the editor of the *Times* mean "dragged" or an active form of "bedraggled"? As a putative poet, I have the obligation to ask these questions.)

From Illinois, the land to which I shall one day return, burdened with honors, after my years of faithful service to the greatest American since Henry Clay, came this blast: "When Judge Taney delivered the Dred Scott decision he was already in his dotage," wrote the *Chicago Tribune*, which always supports us, "and the Merryman decision was evidence that in the intervening years his faculties have brightened none whatsoever." Horace Greeley, in the *New York Tribune*, who blows hot and cold, blew hot on this issue: "When Treason stalks abroad in arms, let decrepit judges give place to men capable of detecting and crushing it."

My employer—to whom I shall refer in the pages of this most secret diary as The Tycoon (after the potentate of Japan) or the Ancient of Days (displaying my affection for the poet Blake)—went over these cuttings with delight. I did not bother to show him the *Louisville Courier*, which would have lowered his spirits. Mr. Seward wants to shut the rag down, and we have to do that soon, as its editors are poisoning the minds of the too-neutral Kentuckians.

Hill Lamon, my cousin from Illinois who has appointed himself the Prsdt's bodyguard, has been walking around for the past month with what some say is permission in his pocket to arrest the Chief Justice. I would love to see the old recreant sitting in a military prison cell, issuing meaningless writs of habeas corpus for himself, but no such drastic remedy as arrest seems necessary. Nobody much cares about Taney's Merryman opinion, and so the Prsdt has decided to ignore it. It must be lying around here somewhere, but Nico has conveniently lost it. That's what democratic government is about: if the courts don't have public sentiment behind them, then the President rules the roost. Why should Lincoln make a martyr out of Taney by jailing the old man? Since there has been no uproar, we'll just file and forget his opinion and replace him with a more amenable judge when he finally gives up the ghost.

Then there is the good news about Maryland. With all the Union troops pouring down from Boston, New York, and Philadelphia, the riotous city of Baltimore is calm again. Whiff of the grape was what those plug-uglies needed. Now the capital in Washington is no longer surrounded and we can get the newspapers again. There *is* a North!

The other morning I went in to give the Prsdt a selection of the correspondence that has come in urging that we enlist slaves in our army. General Ben Butler, he of the large paunch and crossed eye, has the notion that he should retain such fugitive slaves as come within his lines, arm them, and aim them at their former masters.

The Prsdt was looking downriver through his telescope. He tilts his chair back, rests his stocking feet on the windowsill, and perches his telescope on his toes. Butler is down there somewhere, at Fort Monroe, all hot for arming slaves and abolishing slavery like most of his fellow politicians from Massachusetts.

"Some of our Northerners seem bewildered and dazzled by the excitement of the hour," the Tycoon observed. "They seem inclined to think that this war is to result in the entire abolition of slavery."

That, of course, is not the case. Although brother Butler has come up with the legally creative idea of declaring runaway slaves "contraband of war," seizing them as enemy property, we have told him to merely hire them and keep a record of their services.

"The central idea pervading this struggle," he told me, still looking through the spyglass, "is the necessity of proving that popular government is not an absurdity."

That struck me as rather an important item to record. I snatched the quill up, dipped it quickly in the well on the Prsdt's desk, and jotted it down; the Tycoon likes it when I do that. I read it over and asked him what he was getting at.

"We must settle this question now," he replied, bringing his feet down and turning toward his desk, "whether in a free government the minority have the right to break up the government whenever they choose."

"And if we fail?" I asked, Macbeth-like.

"It will go far to prove the incapability of the people to govern themselves."

Frankly, the idea of majority rule seems rather an academic notion to fight a war about, and I hope he can whip up some excitement in the message to Congress he's been working on. Congress will convene in about a month, and will be asked to ratify all the war moves we've made so far. It had better; we've been playing a bit fast and loose with the Constitution. Taney may be wrong about disloyalty, but we've been spending money for the army that the Congress never appropriated, and a blockade is an act of war that Congress is supposed to declare.

The Tycoon thinks the war might drag on until the end of the year, but that seems unduly pessimistic. I fail to see why it should continue past the fall. General-in-Chief Scott is whipping the army into shape, and the Army of the Potomac should make its big push in June, before Congress convenes.

The war that worries me more is the war in the Lincoln Cabinet. The Ancient may have thought it a good idea at the time to appoint all his chief rivals for the presidency to his Cabinet, but the result is the fiercest kind of backbiting. Seward at State—old "Billy Bowlegs"—has been brought to heel, and realizes finally that Lincoln was the one elected, but that éminence grise of his, Thurlow Weed, gives me the willies. Pure politician, perhaps sticky fingers. Seward and Weed, in their turn, get their creeps from our Mr. Money-bags, Salmon Chase at the Treasury. I do not trust Mr. Chase. The Ancient of Days says he needs him, and Chase may be eminently qualified to help finance the war, but unlike Seward, he has not given up his designs on the presidency. I hear his daughter Kate is worth a look.

The only thing Seward at State and Chase at Treasury have in common is their distrust of the Blairs. I rather admire our Postmaster General, Montgomery Blair, and the Tycoon certainly respects his father, Old Man Blair. That cagey old Jacksonian surely helped deliver Maryland, saving this capital from isolation and evacuation. Now that I think of it, Seward and Chase and the Blairs have something else in common: belief in the profound corruption of Simon Cameron, our Secretary of War. The Lincoln Cabinet is not a happy family.

Even so, today it managed to hold a real council of war. The President summoned General-in-Chief Winfield Scott to present his plan. Wheezing, ponderous, and enormously fat, that old hero they call "Old Fuss and Feathers" thinks our troops are too raw for battle and suggests an expedition down the Mississippi to try to cut off the South and starve it into submission. Not well received. General McDowell presented his plan for attacking the rebels under Beauregard at Manassas, a stone's throw across the Potomac from Washington. That was more like it. The Prsdt said that further delay might cool Northern ardor, and the public wanted action. So beware, Beauregard and all you rebels: Manassas will be the site of the battle that wins the war.

Juicy gossip abounds in this hotbed of intrigue. A word from the Wise tells me that the English Ambassador's valet has just caused Mrs. Emory's maid to become *enceinte*, and that Miss Carroll of Baltimore was raped by a negro last month on her way back from that rowdy town. Wise's only question was "How did she appear to like it?" Cannot vouch for authenticity; small incidents often get exaggerated, but it's all very titillating.

Enough; I have in my hand a product of the calligrapher's art, in the form of a formal invitation to a reception a few weeks hence at the Blairs' house across the street. I am told that their home is not so elegant as the house in Arlington we snatched from the disloyal Colonel Lee, but reportedly better furnished than this old, slightly dilapidated presidential mansion. Why is a lowly secretary like me invited to rub elbows with the likes of the Blairs? Not because of my intellect or good looks, I fear, but because I am that delicious oddity: a single man. Unattached men of twenty-one, university graduates, are coveted by hostesses in this city. Perhaps Kate Chase will be there. She is reputed to be a redhead.

CHAPTER 5

FAMILY MAN

The old man arose before any of his family. He shuddered; the morning was surprisingly cool for the Fourth of July in Washington. Francis P. Blair dressed hurriedly in his usual black outfit—silently, to avoid awakening his wife—wrapped a black sash around his neck in lieu of a tie, and trotted down the narrow stairs to the sitting room. He ordered a black manservant to light the parlor fireplace.

"Use the *New York Tribune*," he told the servant, pointing to a stack of newspapers, "not the *Globe*." The *Globe* was his paper, a specialized sheet that reported the official proceedings in both houses of Congress. Old Man Blair knew how to get his hands on an institution of supreme importance to Washington's politicians. The *Globe* was only one of his publications; the others were in Maryland and Missouri, the states in which he had a political interest.

The servant had forgotten to open the flue and the fire belched black smoke into the room. Blair muttered a low curse, pushed the man aside, and reached up into the chimney to snatch at the lever that controlled the opening. The day was not starting well for him. He reminded himself that he was in the Pennsylvania Avenue home he had given to his son Montgomery, and not out at his own estate in Silver Spring. The old man drew a deep breath and briskly apologized to the servant, reminded him to expect a visitor before 7 A.M., and called for a large pot of tea in the formal silver service. Waiting, he exposed his back to the heat of the fire, coughing angrily at the smell of smoke remaining in the room. When the tray came, he blew on his cup of tea and brooded over the state of the nation and his family until the fluid and the fire warmed his bones.

Francis Preston Blair, at seventy, considered himself the last remaining link of the government in Washington to the days of Andrew Jackson, with the possible exception of Roger Taney. He had a right to that claim: nobody else was alive and active on the scene in the capital who had been a member of President Jackson's "kitchen Cabinet," the tight circle of advisers who shaped the direction of the country while lesser men ran the departments. The rambunctious Andy Jackson, the general from common people's Western stock who had snatched the presidency from the aristocrats of the Adams dynasty in Massachusetts, had burned into Blair an idea that was held—then and now—by only a minority of Americans: that the Union was more than the sum of the states. The Jackson men, Blair among the fiercest of them, had refused to go along with the prevailing Jeffersonian notion that the nation was like a gentlemen's club, some unbound association of sovereignties that states could be resigned from at will. That looseness of confederation guaranteed only weakness, invited disunity, and was the reason the founders had scrapped the Articles of Confederation for a tightly binding Constitution. No;

Blair was certain that once you were in, you were in. No second thoughts allowed.

That was why Blair felt that he and his sons could claim a good share of the credit for the unrelenting refusal to bow to the disunionism that had brought on this war. Without the urgent persuasion and political support of the Blair family, Lincoln would never have defended Fort Sumter.

The Old Man sipped his tea loudly and nodded agreement with his conclusion. Only the Blairs had counseled armed resistance to secession. Seward, that double-dealing sneak, had sent word South that the seizure of the Federal fort would not be a casus belli, and that secession would be met with acquiescence; the Secretary of State had been airily certain that the Southern states would come back after the ardor for independence had cooled. Same with General Winfield Scott, who had offered the President his judgment that the forts were not defendable, and urged him to permit peaceable secession. Same with all the Cabinet, including the slippery Chase, who managed to come down on both sides of that choice. Only Montgomery Blair, after a family council of war, had risen to urge Lincoln to hold and possess all Federal property. Lincoln had listened, and Old Man Blair had taken him aside afterward to tell him what Jackson would have done. No secession without war. And the war had come, if war is what you could call the silly horn-tooting and fist-shaking that was going on this summer.

Come the first substantial spilling of blood, and the sudden realization that the war might drag on for months, perhaps even a year, would the war spirit of Northern workingmen remain in support of some vague political theory called "union"? Not in the border states, where it counted, Blair concluded. Not in Maryland, his home state, whose politics he sometimes dominated. Not out in Missouri, where he had emplanted a son and bought a newspaper. Not in Kentucky, the pivotal state, the native state of Abraham Lincoln and Jefferson Davis; it was Blair's view that if Kentucky went South, the war would be over before it was fairly started, with the Union sundered.

Kentucky made him think of the Breckinridges, especially cousin John. The Blairs and Breckinridges were not close kin, but a distant blood connection was strengthened by the ties of family affection. Eliza Blair, still sleeping upstairs, had assumed the job of nursing John Breckinridge's father in the last week of his life when he was afflicted by the fever ravaging Washington. John was only two years old at the time, and Blair's daughter Lizzie, only a few years older, had taken charge of the child; that affection lasted to this day. All the Breckinridge men seemed to die young, Blair recalled, thinking of John's father and his grandfather, Jefferson's Attorney General. Great careers cut off in their thirties. Not one of them had the robust health or political potential of the young man coming to breakfast on his way to the opening of the Senate. The old man had his heart set on the presidency for Frank, his younger son, but if that boisterous Blair was forced to bide his time, then the Old Man's second choice was cousin John.

"Merry Christmas, Father Blair." The tall form of Breckinridge filled the doorway to the small sitting room, his eyes looking quizzically at the fire.

The damned fire that morning was not one of his best ideas, the Old Man conceded to himself, but he would brazen it out. "Had to burn some papers," he said mysteriously, "and besides, it was a little chilly before sunup."

Francis Preston Blair

His visitor shrugged amiably and took a seat on the far side of the room. "I had breakfast already, across the street with my cousin Mary, but these muffins look good." Breckinridge plunged into a plate of them, washing the cakes down with a glass of milk he poured from the silver pitcher. "Cousin Mary," Blair knew, was Mary Todd Lincoln, across the street in the Mansion; all these Kentucky people were related, it seemed. It was good, however, that Senator Breckinridge was spending some time with the Lincolns. The new President, Blair had learned, could be persuasive and was almost Jacksonian when he made up his mind.

"John Cabell Breckinridge," he called out ominously, "do you trust me?"

"Father Blair," said the former Vice President without hesitation, "I trust you almost as much as I trust your wife, whom every Breckinridge knows to be a saint." Good political answer, the old man noted; it said nothing. Any protestation of complete trust would have been a lie. Nobody wholly trusted a Blair except another Blair.

"Why did you let Jeff Davis talk you into running for President last year?" Blair asked, testing the young man further. "You must have known it would split the Democrats, make it impossible for Judge Douglas to beat Lincoln."

The senator nodded, pointing to his cheek full of muffin as an excuse for saying nothing.

"You knew that you were guaranteeing the election of the Republican," Blair went on. "And you knew, as we all did, that the election of Lincoln would be the excuse for the fire-eaters in the South to secede. Yet you ran and split the party and got Lincoln elected. Why?"

The senator swallowed and said, "I made one speech in that campaign and it was for the Union. Against secession."

"Yet the effect of your candidacy was anti-Union," Blair pressed, knowing the answer. "You received 900,000 Democratic votes, Douglas 1,200,000 Democratic votes, and Lincoln about 1,900,000 Republicans. Your candidacy practically guaranteed the election of the man you knew would bring about disunion. Why?"

"I have never answered that," Breckinridge said, "because it would cast doubt on the honor of men I respect."

Blair was not having any of that evasion. "Tell me what happened when Jeff Davis and Robert Toombs came to you before the Baltimore convention with a certain proposal," Blair said, tipping his hand a little. Surely the young man wanted to tell someone the real story; it would help if Breck knew that the Blairs suspected the truth that made him look like less of an unpatriotic ass.

"They told me I was the only one who could unite the Northern and Southern factions of the Democratic Party," he said, as if glad to spill what had been dammed inside. "Douglas was unacceptable to the Southerners. I was against secession, and acceptable to Northern Democrats, but not against slavery's extension west, and therefore acceptable to the Southerners. Especially the pro-Union South, the Southern people without slaves. There are a lot of them, you know. They voted for me."

"What did Davis and Toombs offer you?"

"They said if I accepted the nomination of their faction, they would go to Senator Douglas and use that to get him to withdraw. With me in the race,

Douglas would know he could not win. Then I, too, would withdraw and we would pick a compromise candidate that would hold the Democratic Party together."

Blair could picture Davis and Toombs, the two high-minded Southerners, probably filled with a desire to establish an independent state, dangling this proposal before the young Vice President. They had persuaded him that only with his public acceptance, with the fait accompli of a Breckinridge candidacy, could they force Douglas to withdraw and bring about a party reconciliation.

"But the 'Little Giant' wouldn't go for that, would he?" Blair asked. Of course not; it had all been a ruse to split the party.

Breckinridge shook his head. "Jeff Davis came back to tell me that the man's ambition was greater than his patriotism. Douglas was determined to run, with or without the Southern Democrats. It was Douglas who split the party, with his unreasonable refusal to compromise. That's what they reported to me."

Blair shook his head in grudging admiration of the political skill with which Jeff Davis had entrapped the innocent Breckinridge. "And when Douglas refused to compromise, why did you hang in to the bitter end? Why didn't you face reality and graciously withdraw?"

"You know the answer to that, Father Blair," the senator said, misery in his eyes. "I had publicly announced. I was a formal candidate, the choice of the states that had been unfairly driven out of the regular Democratic convention. I would have looked the fool to knuckle under to the ambition of Stephen Douglas. It would have been the end of me, which is not so important, but it would have let down all those who had nominated me." The moment was evidently painful for him. "Men are sometimes placed in a position," he said finally, "where they are reluctant to act and expose themselves to censure they do not merit."

Blair waited a moment for the young man to listen to the echo of his defensive words. "You understand, of course, that you were ill-used. You were tricked by a cabal that wanted only to see elected the man who was anathema to their region, and then divide the Union."

Breckinridge looked into the fire, apparently still unwilling to accept as fact his own suspicions of the motives of the men who had induced him to declare as a candidate. "It could be that they were sincere, and thought truly that my candidacy would drive Douglas out. I want to believe that. I have no good cause to believe otherwise, except—"

"Except that the internal logic of the situation suggests that you were cruelly manipulated," Blair snapped, "and tricked into doing a terrible disservice to your country. The trouble with you, my dear young distant kinsman, is that you're so goddamned honorable yourself that you fail to see dishonor and deceit in others."

"Maybe you're right," Breckinridge said, suddenly brightening at the appearance of Lizzie Blair, the Old Man's daughter, in the sitting room. "And maybe not. Lizzie, do you think I have been cruelly manipulated?"

"If Father says you have been, you have been," she affirmed, "because he knows more about that than anybody."

The Old Man glared a warning at her; this was no time for her to hint at

his objection to her marrying that swashbuckling sailor. At least her husband's seafaring ways made it possible for her to live at home with the Blairs.
Because Lizzie and Breckinridge had always been close, the elder Blair had
arranged for her to drop in at the end of the breakfast to lend her support to
his plea. She was more of an independent-minded woman than he had
planned, however—had less judgment than her brother Monty, far more
good sense than her younger brother Frank. He hoped she remembered she
had been invited to breakfast for a reason. In hammering home the lesson of
last year's candidacy, with all its troublesome consequences, Blair was telling
Breckinridge not to let his concern for constitutional rights get in the way of
the overriding need to hold the country together. But the young man was
obstinate; Blair had to be subtle. He hoped he had not been too subtle, which
was where his daughter could help.

"The Congress convenes this morning," she said dutifully. "John, whose
side are you going to be on?"

"The Constitution's."

"I knew there was going to be trouble," the old man growled. Anna Ella
Carroll, a Maryland ally, had told him of the Kentuckian's fervent belief in
the rightness of Judge Taney's ridiculous defense of the plug-uglies in Baltimore. "What Lizzie means is—are you going to make a lot of unnecessary
enemies in this session of the Senate, or are you going to think about your
future?"

"What Lizzie means," interrupted Lizzie, "is that we expect that you'll do
whatever your conscience tells you to do. It's just that you're inclined to be a
man of moderation, John, and these days there isn't too much sentiment for
moderation."

"I commend to you Henry the Fifth," the elder Blair added. " 'In peace
there's nothing so becomes a man as modest stillness and humility, but when
the blast of war blows in our ears—' "

"There is no war. Just a lot of parading around, getting ready." Breckinridge was respectful, still affectionate, but unyielding. "There need be no
war."

"Now we're to the point of why I asked you to stop by," Blair said. "You
have to realize that secession means war. Jackson said it, Lincoln is saying it,
and that's the way it is, no matter how silent the Constitution may be. If you
stay on the right side of that, you can criticize the government all you like for
arbitrary arrests. But just cross over, try to argue that the South can secede
without war, and you'll throw away your future. Worse, even."

Breckinridge nodded his understanding and rose to go. Did he really grasp
the import of opposing the prevailing sentiment? Blair wondered if he knew
how easy it would be for men who felt strongly about the secession to impute
treason to opposition—no matter how principled or right-minded or loyal
that opposition—that abetted treason.

Lizzie embraced him, saying, "What Father means is that whatever you do,
you can count on the Blairs to stick up for you, right up to the point where it
begins to hurt Frank's chances. Then we don't know you. Nobody will know
you, except the same people who trapped you before. Don't let it come to
that, John."

After he left, she turned to her father and said, "How are you going to persuade anybody to do the sensible thing when you light the fireplace on the Fourth of July? That smell of smoke will be with us all summer."

Blair didn't care. He thought he made his point, and his politically sage daughter had helped him make it. She was a Blair, all right, as practical as she was loyal. "You manipulated your cousin cruelly," he said, pleased with her and himself, almost certain the young man would take the right path. Blair picked up a poker and jabbed at the fire, breaking up the logs so the damn thing would flame up and burn itself out before his wife came downstairs.

"I worry about that man," Lizzie said, and revealed more about her cousin than her father had known. "Last year's campaign tore him apart—he wasn't running for office, he was enduring an ordeal, and for the first time in his life he knows what it is like to be hated. He lives here in the capital and his wife and sons live down in Lexington. He's seeing too much of Anna Carroll, I think, and they say he sees Rose Greenhow too." She sighed profoundly. "And they say he's drinking."

Blair thought of Andrew Jackson and how all the scandals never harmed him politically. He allowed himself to wonder what Rose O'Neal Greenhow, the "Wild Rose," would be like in bed. "Breck shouldn't drink," was all he said to his daughter.

CHAPTER 6

I RISE IN OPPOSITION

The best policy for Kentucky, Breckinridge decided, was armed neutrality. The state would not join the secession, nor join those Union fire-eaters like the Blairs who pushed Lincoln into warring on the separated states. Kentucky would sit this war out, letting the ardor on both sides burn until it became obvious that neither side could impose its will.

Mediation at this early stage seemed hopeless, though he would continue to search for a suitable compromise before the fighting became serious. If some major battlefield bloodletting did take place, then no mediation could proceed as the popular demand for vengeance rose, but in time neutral Kentucky, as the only state that could treat with both powers evenhandedly, might provide the bridge to bring the parties together. And John Cabell Breckinridge, the apostle of moderation in the moderate state, would be the most trusted peacemaker.

Like most other senators, he had doffed his coat on the sweltering July day. In the cloakroom, the Washington humidity was especially oppressive. The usual lobby agents were not present, since the Senate was considering a motion to make legal all the unconstitutional acts Lincoln had committed before calling Congress back into session. That sort of legislation provided benefits to none and was certain of passage.

John Forney, sometime newsman, now clerk of the Senate, had called him out to talk to Anna Carroll before his speech.

"Miss Carroll here thinks you are liable to make a damn fool of yourself this afternoon," Forney drawled as he brought them together, "and she'd like to save you from yourself. Like everybody does, even Wade and Baker. Never saw so many people so worried about one senator's stand."

"He's right," Breckinridge said to the woman he was so glad to see. "I am quite aware that nothing I can utter here will have the slightest effect."

"Not true," she said, dismissing Forney with a nod and a quick smile. "You could do great harm to the cause of the Union, Breck, and I know you don't want to do that."

Two nights before, in her rooms at the Ebbitt House, they had stayed up through the dawn arguing the details of the President's war power. She had been prepared for the discussion far better than he; the senator suspected she had helped the Attorney General help Lincoln prepare his long July 4 message to the convening Congress, asking for blanket approval of waging his undeclared war. They must have gone at the argument for nine or ten hours, never bothering to eat and stopping only once to make love. She had not permitted him to bring a bottle of whiskey.

Anna had attempted to persuade him to accept the argument of necessity. In war, much must be sacrificed to necessity, and he had granted that not all the legal niceties could be observed near the front, but in this case there was no necessity for war. A political union, much like the marriage of a man and woman, had to be based on comity and shared beliefs; a union with one section forced to belong was tyranny. The terrible acts required to enforce control of one section by another, he had argued, would infect the rest of the government and end all hope of democracy. Anna Carroll had refused to see that an unconstitutional war would corrupt the North and ruin what union remained. Obstinate woman, irritating in her tenacity, but adorable even when not adoring, and helpful in putting him through the arguments he would face on the Senate floor.

"That was not my purpose," she said grimly in the Senate cloakroom, when he thanked her for preparing him for his speech this day. "I am trying to save your life in politics."

"There comes a time—" he began, squaring his shoulders, but stopped when she reached up and banged her fist on his upper arm.

"There comes a time in life when a man should learn to shut up," she said. "This is such a time. If you don't agree on the war powers, abstain. Go have tea with Lizzie Blair, who loves you more than that silly sailor of hers, or go pay a secret visit to the Wild Rose, I don't care. Just don't make an ass of yourself in the Senate on the burning issue of the day."

An auburn tendril had spilled over her forehead; he pushed it back automatically. Men who denied themselves the friendship of older women, it occurred to him, were missing much in life. He remembered her from ten years ago, when she was Uncle Bob's wide-eyed spiritual ward, and she had never been in such full bloom as a publicist or a woman. Lizzie, too, was more attractive to him now, but he had never had a love affair with Old Man Blair's daughter; just friends, always the unresolved tensions. It was better to make love and have that a part of it all, not a distraction because of its presence or absence. The Wild Rose was a different story; she brought passions out of men they never knew they possessed, but Rose was a hater, not a thinker, too relentlessly stimulating to be anybody's companion.

Did all that make him a libertine and a hypocrite? He thought not, although he had to allow for the moral possibility. Mary Cyrene Breckinridge had never wanted to share the part of his life that centered on the District of Columbia, preferring to raise the children and be a good companion to him at home in Lexington. An upright, loyal wife—come to think of it, he could not recall Mary's opinion about peaceful separation of the states, although she made no secret she despised slavery—deserving of a loyal, respectful husband, which he was whenever they were together.

Breckinridge knew that his vice, as far as the public was concerned, was supposed to be a fondness for corn whiskey; he did not think that much of a vice, especially for a politician from the state that produced the product, and in an odd way it protected him in a way from talk about womanizing that might have worried Mary. She did not worry about his drinking because she knew he could put it aside whenever he had to. She did not worry about other women because he gave her no reason to worry. His only problem at home was his son, Cabell, who was sixteen and looked older and liked to talk of war. Breckinridge did not know where the boy got that from. Mary looked young to have a boy that age, and was much more innocent in the ways of the world than the woman who was punching his shoulder again.

"You're not listening. Here is a memorial of the points I made, with citations from Justice Marshall, and a precis of the nullification debate. It shows how President Jackson was right and Senator Calhoun didn't understand the Constitution."

He took the paper and nodded his thanks, assuming she had been told of the nullification precedent by Old Man Blair, whose hatred of Calhoun never abated. Her writing, as always, was a hurried scrawl, evidence of her vigor and haste. It would be a useful checklist, if any senator wanted to argue the law after his speech. He hoped there would be no debate today. His purpose was to plant the seed of doubt in some minds already set on war, and angry ripostes would not advance that aim.

"Senator Baker isn't here today," she told him, "so you won't be provoked. Ben Wade is, but I've talked to him and told him the best way to handle you is to ignore you."

Breckinridge frowned at her mothering, the main drawback of older women. Senator Edward Baker of Oregon, the Eddie Baker from Illinois who used to be his good friend in the House years ago, was the closest to Lincoln of any man now in the Senate. Lincoln's first son, who died in infancy, had been named Edward Baker Lincoln. Now Baker was a colonel in the Union Army, dividing his time between the Virginia front and the Senate floor. The Kentuckian knew there had to be a clash in the Senate with Baker, who was foolishly spoiling for war and was all too ready to vote Lincoln the powers of a dictator. And Ben Wade, who wanted a war to wipe out slavery, was a man Breckinridge looked forward to debating one day. But not today, not yet; he fought down his irritation and was glad that she had arranged for that temporary protection.

"Wade expects me to make a Confederate speech, doesn't he?"

"You'd damn well better not," she snapped. When he glared back, she softened: "A great many important people are hoping I'm right about you.

I've told them that you'll suffer in silence, and not let your love of the form of the Constitution undermine the union cause."

He knew that, all right; she had surely told Ben Wade, probably told the Blairs, and possibly even Lincoln that she could take him into the pro-union, pro-war camp. Or at the least, get him to be quiet, enabling the pro-union Kentuckians to carry the day. By speaking out, he would also damage her career, he supposed; he regretted that.

They shook hands solemnly. He strode to his desk on the Democratic side of the aisle. She climbed to the gallery to watch.

Vice President Hannibal Hamlin, presiding, recognized the junior senator from Kentucky.

"I rise in opposition," Breckinridge said to a full chamber, "to the Republican resolution to grant approval to all the extraordinary acts taken by the President since his inauguration."

That caught everyone's attention. Briskly, and without the full-throated oratorical flourishes he was noted for, the Kentuckian mentioned the raising of armies without sanction of the legislature, the imposition of a blockade of Southern ports as an act of war without proper declaration by the Congress, unlawful searches and seizures, and, most important, Lincoln's usurpation of Congress's power to suspend the privilege of habeas corpus.

"The fact that the Republicans are eager to pass this resolution," he deduced, "is a bald admission that President Lincoln has been operating in gross violation of the Constitution and the laws he is sworn to execute."

"Fudge," came a loud growl from Benjamin Wade of Ohio. As a mere ejaculation, without recognition from the Chair, the Wade remark could be ignored. Breckinridge was not seeking a confrontation; he did not demand that Wade's word be "taken down" and the offender forced to remain quiet for the rest of the day. Breckinridge sailed on, unperturbed.

"Moreover, we of the Congress cannot indemnify the illegal actions of another branch. If we could do that, then we could set aside the Constitution at will. If we could alter the Constitution by mere passage of a resolution, then that document is meaningless. As all here know, the power to amend the Constitution is reserved to the States."

The law was on his side, he knew. It was vital that he stick to the law, in a quietly judicious tone, to persuade any of his fellow senators to open their minds to the possibility of temporary, peaceful separation. A little doubt at a time was all he could sow; not too much in one speech; and always in a spirit of loyal Democratic opposition, conscious that he was lighting his candles in a room filled with the spirit of war, where almost all the men were waiting for him to say something bordering on treason.

"In raising an army and navy, in blockading ports, in imprisoning loyal Americans who dared only to disagree publicly with his policies," the Kentuckian argued, "Mr. Lincoln has drawn to himself not only his own executive powers, but those of the Congress and the Supreme Court. The President decides who is to be arrested and who is to be jailed. In every age of the world, this has been the very definition of despotism."

Should he have used the word "despotism"? He was testing the outer perimeter of loyalty, but nobody else in this chamber was saying what had to be said. The tension after the word "despotism" was palpable. With the

Senate expecting him to defend the Confederacy, it was time to back away a little.

"I do not deny the authority of this body, together with the Executive, to wage war to preserve the Union under the Constitution. But let us be certain that we do so in a strictly constitutional manner, as we have waged other wars. Let us take care not to use this war as an occasion to change the nature of our government."

He thought of Edward Baker's pernicious suggestion to wipe out all state divisions entirely, replacing the identity of Pennsylvanians and Virginians with a new national consciousness as Americans. He thought, too, of Baker's proposal to subjugate the Southern states and treat them later as territories.

Not now; the time was not ripe to take that on. Not with Baker in the field, in uniform; the time would come to debate these extreme notions after they had been shown to be the logical extension of today's rubber-stamp resolution.

He moved to safer ground. "Another resolution before the Senate is 'a bill to suppress the slaveholder's rebellion.' I submit to you that this bill is in effect a scheme to emancipate all slaves in those states in rebellion." He looked toward Wade and the other Republican radicals, a distinct minority within their own party in favor of outright abolition. "This resolution even implies that we should employ these freed slaves in our army, a suggestion that will repel many of our Northern countrymen. It is an open invitation to servile rebellion, to rapine and murder throughout the South. Its passage would foment hatred here at home for the next century, and would be seen as a monstrous act before the world."

He had the black Republicans there; only a handful of senators were bloody-minded enough to follow Wade, Chandler, Baker, and Sumner into the morass of inciting a slave rebellion. "If Congress could legislate this unconstitutional seizure, and if Congress could make legal the murder of masters by slaves, then Congress would have the absolute power to overthrow all our rights, personal and political."

By linking the two resolutions, he made the point that a vote to ratify Lincoln's illegal acts on such as habeas corpus would surely lead all the way to abolition of all slave property everywhere, including that in loyal states. The majority of Republicans could, with Lincoln, reasonably oppose the extension of slavery into the West, but only a few firebrands insisted on seizing slave property and turning the freed slaves on their masters.

The speech, as he had hoped, left the Senate distinctly uncomfortable. Conservative Lincoln Republicans called for recognition to make clear that the resolution to make legal the President's emergency acts, which had wide support, was in no way associated with the emancipation resolution, which was not supported by the President.

The vote on the resolution to ratify the President's war actions passed overwhelmingly, as Breckinridge fully expected. He had registered his protest in a rational manner; he had troubled a few consciences. When the moment came for mediation and moderation, Breckinridge would be available.

He looked up to the gallery. Anna Carroll, looking intense and angry, was walking out. Nobody came around to talk to him after the speech. On the way out, John Forney came up to him, shaking his head. "Sophistry, John.

Your friends down South fired on Sumter and started a war. The Congress could not abandon the President in fighting back."

Breckinridge shrugged. "You think anyone will pay attention to my dissent?"

"Sure. Miss Carroll did, made notes like crazy, and will probably start writing to all the newspapers. She was sore as a bear. I told her you were making your point of principle, and now you had it out of your system, you could sit tight. Was I right?"

Breckinridge shrugged, feeling bad about Anna, who now had to hurry to protect her own interests. Forney's mention of the press reminded him of an important item about his speech. "Did the Associated Press send a copy to all the newspapers that asked for it? Especially in Kentucky and Maryland?"

"The reporter undoubtedly intended to," Forney replied ruefully. "But the War Department refuses to send your speech over the telegraph wires."

"But that was a speech by a duly elected senator, on the Senate floor. Nobody could impute disloyalty to that dissent. Where does the Secretary of War get the right to decide what the people can read about?"

It was Forney's turn to shrug. "War power, I guess. Don't get the idea you can talk over the Administration's head to the people, Senator. You're lucky to be able to talk to the men in that room."

CHAPTER 7

SUNDAY IS NOT THE BEST TIME

"I had to throw John Breckinridge off the Military Affairs Committee today."

Rose Greenhow steadily poured the tea into the cup held out by Senator Henry Wilson. The cup shook slightly; the senator was nervous. Rose knew just what was bothering him and offered no assistance.

"After that speech he made about Lincoln being a despot," the senator added, "I had to. Frankly, we were prepared to arrest Breck if he said anything outright treasonable, but he held back just short of that. Enough tea, Rose. You know I hate the stuff."

Rose had been told of the plan to arrest Breckinridge, if he went too far, by several of the abolitionists. She had warned her Kentucky friend of his peril, and he said he would reword his speech with that in mind; evidently he had, and the Republican radicals were foiled. "I thought that Breck was one of the few senators with military experience," she allowed, deliberately filling the cup to the brim, "as a major leading the Kentuckians in the Mexican War."

"Can't take a chance," said Wilson. "He's a risk to go South. He could reveal all our plans."

"I'm glad we have plans, Henry." She plopped a lump of sugar into his teacup, causing the liquid to spill into the saucer. She knew that in his agitated state, he would put up with anything. "I was beginning to think this war is all pronouncements and parades."

He slurped at the tea to stop it from spilling as his hand shook. "Our troops under McDowell will be on the move one of these days. They'll smash the rebel army in Virginia."

That vague "one-of-these-days" was not good enough. She raised her hand with what she felt was the appropriate languor. "Please, no military secrets, Henry. You tell me what everybody in our set in Washington knows already, and you act as if you were confiding the most sensitive information in the Republic. Spare me."

"Rose, do you suppose we can go upstairs now?"

The poor fellow was in a state; Rose concealed her contempt, shaking her head as if sorry not to be able to accommodate his passion. "You are beginning to treat me as your plaything, Senator. I am nobody's plaything. I am more of a lady than anyone you know."

She let him assure her of his abiding respect, and confess to her his terrible weakness. This was their routine; he liked to be treated shabbily, and she was experienced in taking a man much farther down that demeaning road.

As the wife of a State Department librarian, Rose had been denied the social distinction she craved. Defeated, the Greenhows moved to San Francisco where Rose had an incredible run of luck: when her husband was killed by a fall into an open sewer, she sued the city and was awarded a large sum from an amorous judge. She had been able to return to Washington on her own terms: a woman of wealth and independence, with still enough good looks and charm to establish a salon of the powerful.

Mrs. Greenhow now traveled in the incestuous circle of political privilege, more sought-after than seeking. Political figures, men of wealth, and now high military officers came to her fine brick home for social or political connection. She knew that she retained much of her beauty, and knew how to use all that was left of it; more than that, she understood how certain men in positions of power needed to be dominated by a woman. For nearly twenty years, she had savored the underlife of this Southern city, and now that she had been recruited by the Confederacy as a spy, she felt fulfilled as never before. Her breeding, her inclinations and her hatreds came together in this time of war to give her life purpose. The woman once known merely as the Wild Rose gloried in having a mission at last: to conspire against and to crush the men and women she had come to despise.

Rose nodded coldly at Henry Wilson's long apology, calculating the possibility of getting one useful fact out of him. Despite his tendency to turn into sexual jelly, the man was no fool and was reluctant to pass along what he knew. She used him mainly for confirmation of what she gleaned elsewhere. Rose had established a sexual liaison with a clerk on the Military Affairs Committee who probably knew more of the detail of the strength of McDowell's forces than the committee chairman knew. She had already arranged with a colonel on Confederate general Beauregard's staff a simple code and method of delivering messages across the lines. The general had been informed, by a message wrapped in the tresses of a young woman who worked for Rose, that the likely direction of the Federal attack would be from Arlington Heights to Centreville and on to Manassas. She was certain, from her infatuated clerk and two other sources, that McDowell had thirty-five thousand men in his command, almost double the Beauregard strength.

One fact she had not yet been able to send through to Confederate headquarters: the timing of the Yankee attack. Her contact on Beauregard's staff, an attractive young colonel who went by the name of Jordan, had pleaded for this specific information: it was vital because a Confederate force of twelve thousand under Joe Johnston was protecting the entrance to the Shenandoah Valley, a possible Yankee route to Richmond. If the South could find out what day the Federal movement was to begin toward Bull Run Creek, Johnston's force could quietly disengage and slip through the Manassas Gap, without concern about leaving the valley undefended, and consolidate with Beauregard in time to meet the Union advance into Virginia.

When would McDowell move? Johnston's Army of the Shenandoah could not pull out of position defending the valley until the Federals committed themselves to an assault toward Manassas. If McDowell had the benefit of surprise in his timing, the Confederates could not unite forces in time for the battle and could be beaten in detail.

"When, Rose?" That startled her; the word "when" had been in her mind. "When can we go upstairs? It's been a week."

She breathed deeply and let her stern face appear to soften. "I'm still in mourning, you know." Her older daughter had died months ago; she was alone in the world with her eight-year-old now. Rose wore black, and draped a few of the windows suitably, but did not ache for her long-sickly elder daughter; she had been like her late husband. The eight-year-old, Little Rose, was more her mother's daughter.

Henry Wilson's expression was a cross between sympathy and frustration, an odd mixture of passion and compassion that did not suit him. Rose did not have much time for subtlety in questioning; the courier was in the basement and had to leave before nightfall to get across the Long Bridge. Perhaps she could find out in the unguarded moments after sex.

She relieved the senator of the teacup and took his hand. They would dispense with the elaborate preliminaries.

Rose led the way downstairs, disappointed and irritated. She had probed indirectly at first, using his opening about keeping information from the likes of Breckinridge; nothing there. At one point, both staring at ceiling, she wondered directly about when the city would be stripped of its defenders. His only reply had been deep, satisfied breathing. She had rolled him out of bed and handed him his pants, saying something about expecting visitors.

"Who's coming over now?" he wanted to know, following her down the staircase.

"My other friendships are no business of yours, Henry," she snapped, adding, "actually, it's just my cook. I'm planning a reception here Sunday."

"In competition with the one at the Blairs'?"

She had forgotten about the Blairs. "It's just a whim of mine, to have an intimate party on a moment's notice. Not everybody will want to get in that crush at Monty Blair's. Perhaps General McDowell will prefer a visit here."

The senator hesitated and she said nothing. At the door, he took his hat and kissed her cheek, telling her he adored her.

"You're invited," she said. "I'll have Addie Douglas over. She's sick of being in mourning, and so am I."

"Look, Rose, I can't say why, but this Sunday is not the best time for a party. As of tomorrow morning, McDowell will be gone. And on Sunday, some of us are planning a carriage ride over the bridge to watch the end of the war." A worried look crossed his face. "I only hope the Lord does not chastise us for fighting on the Sabbath."

"It wouldn't be much of a reception without the general," she said, trying to look stupid.

"He'll have his hands full cutting the Manassas Gap railroad," the senator blurted, halfway out the door. "Postpone it a week and make it a victory celebration. Your Southern friends will be upset, but they'll need you to intercede on their behalf with a lot of angry Lincoln men."

"That's a good idea," she said, waving. "I'll wait a week."

She slowly closed the front door, then rushed down to the courier in the basement. They coded a message: "Order issued for McDowell to move on to Manassas tonight. Intend to cut Manassas Gap railroad to prevent Johnston joining Beauregard. R.O.G."

The man slipped out the back. Rose went to the upstairs bedroom window, looking west into the sunset across the Potomac, her heart pounding. All the Yankees who had used her and insulted her through the years would pay. She told herself that the surge of emotion she felt was neither hatred nor vengeance but only the purest patriotism.

CHAPTER 8
_____

FAMILY COUNCIL OF WAR

The clan had been busy on several fronts; time for the first wartime Blair council of war.

Lizzie no longer had to demand to be included in the political sessions during these ingatherings at Silver Spring. With her husband, Phillips Lee, at sea most of the time, she had become her father's confidential secretary, drafting his most important correspondence and keeping track of the family's far-flung financial commitments.

When the businessman-son, James, died a decade ago, Father Blair had prevailed on his widow to raise the grandchildren in a house on the Silver Spring compound. Lizzie had felt that parental pressure, too, and had resisted at first, using part of her ten-thousand-dollar stake from her father to build a house flush up against the Blair house in town on Pennsylvania Avenue. Then Father gave his original house, so convenient to the Executive Mansion across the street, to Montgomery, the oldest surviving son, and the parents proceeded to make Lizzie's house their in-town home.

Lizzie liked that arrangement. The Blair-Lee houses were almost a single unit, kept from complete amalgamation only by the sniffiness of Montgomery's second wife, and nobody with an interest in the nation's affairs could be lonely there. It was a lively place; in the front parlor of the Blair house, only a couple of months ago, Father and General Scott had offered the field command of the Union Army to Colonel Robert Lee, who turned them down and went South.

In this council of the clan, around the dining-room table of the great three-story house, Lizzie sat on the firm wooden arm of the chair of Frank, the family's favorite. He was a black-mustachioed man, enthusiastic and impetuous and not oppressively intelligent, who had adopted Western ways when he took charge of family newspapers and businesses in Missouri. Frank was the politician-son, the most immediately likable of all the Blairs; he was already a factor in Congress, and was destined by the clan's common consent to be President one day. Lizzie was pleased that Montgomery, just turned fifty, who now sat as Postmaster General in Lincoln's Cabinet, never showed the slightest jealousy at the family's choice of his brother, ten years his junior, to be the family candidate for Chief Executive. Montgomery, a fine lawyer whom Lincoln liked to call "the judge," had the intellect, but Frank had the ability to lead, if he could keep from tripping over his big feet.

To Lizzie's left, in a straight-backed chair directly across the circle from her husband, sat the woman Washington society called the Lioness. Mother spoke up, defended her brood against all comers, and counted for much at family decision time. She had been like a daughter to Henry Clay, co-edited the Jackson-supporting *Globe*, and through her extensive family, the Gists, extended the Blair family influence throughout the South and West. She had more than doubled her husband's reach; the clan had blood connections throughout the nation.

"You could have had your head shot off at that arsenal, Frank," Mother said.

A month before, with nobody's authority, Frank had enlisted a detachment of troops in St. Louis, appointed himself their leader, and seized the city arsenal in the name of the Union. This daring act prevented the secession-minded governor from turning over a great store of arms to the South.

"We had to shoot into the mob," Frank reported proudly, "killed about twenty, lost only a handful of my men." Lizzie ostentatiously patted him on the back on behalf of the clan. "That's what the Federal commander should have done in Baltimore when the mob took over."

"The Baltimore riots called for different handling," Montgomery, whose base was the state of Maryland, countered. "We had the votes in the state legislature to defeat secession, so we just kept moving the legislature around, out to Frederick, so the mob couldn't influence the members. Not as dramatic, but it worked."

Frank shrugged. "You're the Cabinet member. I'm not even Speaker of the House."

"Don't complain," Father said to the younger son. "The speakership had to go to Pennsylvania. It was part of my deal to make Monty Postmaster General."

Frank pretended to look put out, then grinned up at Lizzie. "Always glad to lay down my career for my brother. Which reminds me, Monty, I'm broke."

"You're worse than that," Montgomery replied, "you're bankrupt. I had to send an accountant out West to bail you out. How do you lose so much money on a newspaper?"

"In a good cause," Father interceded. "I don't mind losing money on the papers for a while, if they promote our cause. Remember those two reporters

Frank hired last year out of Lincoln's law office in Springfield? Nicolay, the serious one, and the young lady-killer fresh out of the college in Rhode Island? They're the President's secretaries now, and they owe their start to the Blairs."

"The word is around Washington, Father," said Frank, "that you're the one who has Lincoln's ear. True? Were you really the only one to see the Inaugural Address before he delivered it?"

"Seward and I," his father nodded. "Men who have the destiny of great nations in their hands never hear the truth; I am trying in this instance to make Lincoln an exception. I told him he had to put in the part about not abolishing slavery where it exists. Seward added that folderol at the end about the better angels of our nature."

"If the Blairs are in so close, Preston," said Mother, "how come Billy Bowlegs carries so much weight? He's hated all the Blairs from the start."

"That's the way Lincoln operates," the oldest Blair explained. "He balances forces, keeping us all at each other's throats, so that no faction gets the upper hand. But don't say that Seward hates us, Eliza. He offered Frank the vice presidency last year."

Frank looked up sharply, as did Monty. "Seward offered me what?"

Lizzie, alone of the children, knew the secret, and was glad it was out. The old man relished telling the story.

"You will recall at the Republican convention last year, Seward of New York was the strongest candidate. Bates of Missouri was second, Lincoln of Illinois third. The rest was split between Chase of Ohio and Cameron of Pennyslvania."

"And we supported Bates," said Frank impatiently. "We even got Horace Greeley to desert Seward and swing his support to Bates. We controlled the Bates support at the convention. I forget why we were so high on Bates."

"Because," Lizzie put in, "only a border-stater like Edward Bates, who was no abolitionist, could keep the South from seceding. Father was right about that. When Simon Cameron double-crossed everyone and threw Pennsylvania to Lincoln, old Abe got the nomination and we've got a war."

"What has that got to do with me and the vice presidency?" Frank, though not the shrewdest of them, had his eye on the main chance.

"Thurlow Weed came to me on behalf of his longtime partner, William Seward," said the elder Blair. "As you know, Mr. Weed and I detest each other, but business is business. In his desperation, after Pennsylvania had defected to Lincoln, Thurlow Weed offered the vice presidency to you, Frank, on a Seward ticket—if I would deliver the Bates support to Seward on the next ballot."

"And you turned him down?" asked the youngest son weakly.

"I turned him down, and as a result, Lincoln won the Republican nomination. With Breckinridge splitting the Democrats, it meant that our decision put Lincoln where he is today."

"Our decision? This is the first I heard of it." Frank was genuinely put out.

"It would have been unfair of me to put the offer to you at the time. You would have jumped at it, and Seward would have taken the nomination and the presidency, with you as his vice president." The elder Blair paused before making his point: "And William Seward, that damnable weakling and coward, would have let the Southern states secede." He shot a look at Montgomery. "Am I right about that, Monty?"

"Seward was not prepared to fight to keep the Southern states in the Union," his older son confirmed. "All his talk years ago of an 'irreconcilable conflict' was just so much talk. I'll never forget that Cabinet meeting—if Seward had been President when they fired on Sumter, we would be two nations now."

"I suppose, Father," Frank said gloomily, "we got something at the convention in return for standing fast for Bates and blocking Seward."

"Yes, of course. I traded our refusal to help Seward for a post in the Lincoln Cabinet for Monty. And for the Blair family's influence in this administration."

Monty spoke up. "I really think, Father, that a choice as far-reaching as that should have been made by all of us. Or at least with the consultation of the two of us most directly affected. We've been grown men for some time now, and nobody's puppets, not even yours."

"You're wrong." The Lioness spoke for the first time. "In a clash of your futures, it's better if your Father decides. That way, the two of you remain allies."

"Come on, Mother," Lizzie said, "tell them the real reason. Good politics comes before family sentiment."

Her mother looked at her with surprise, then smiled. "Another reason is that Frank is the Blair destined to be President. Everything we do, all of us, is toward that end."

"Then what was wrong with the vice presidency?" Frank asked. "It seems like a step in the right direction."

"The vice presidency leads nowhere," said the Old Man. "Look at your cousin John Breckinridge—the vice presidency saddled him with all the mistakes of the fool Buchanan. Only Martin Van Buren made it, and that was despite the vice presidency."

"Sometimes vice presidents succeed to the office," Monty put in mildly.

"Twice in sixteen times," Lizzie said. She remembered when her father had asked her to look it up; Seward's offer had not been rejected out of hand.

"I don't like those odds," said Francis Preston Blair. "And waiting for somebody to die is no way for an honorable man to aim for the top. More important, I wanted to have nothing to do with a deal that would result in the dismemberment of the Union."

After a silence, Mother said, "I think it might be nice if the boys were to ratify their father's decision."

Frank broke into a smile. "Father—tell Thurlow Weed to go to hell! I would rather labor in the vineyards of the Lord, than—"

"You'll labor in the United States Army," snapped the Old Man, who, Lizzie could see, felt better. "We're in a war, such as it is, and the President after Lincoln is going to be a war hero. A general. That's what you're going to be, Frank."

The clan chewed that over. After a moment, Frank put forward a problem: "Frémont. He's a Missourian, a famous soldier, the first candidate of the Republican Party for President, in fifty-six. They're sure to make him the commanding general in St. Louis, and you know John Frémont—he thinks he's God. Where does that leave me?"

"That leaves you in Congress for the time being," his father said, "until the world can see Frémont making an idiot of himself, like he always does."

"But the war will be over soon."

The Old Man shook his head. "That's what everybody thinks. It's what Lincoln thinks, he's told me as much, and he's counting on a big victory this weekend. He thinks the war is about the preservation of the Union, that's all he talks about. But Lincoln is wrong. The schemers who are taking over his party—Wade, Stevens, Baker, Greeley, the lot of them—will make slavery the issue. That would push the border states, which are slave states, into Southern hands. And all the South will fight to the death against abolition, which means a long war, maybe two or three years. General Scott agrees with me."

"I disagree." The family's eyes swung to Monty. "I don't think Jeff Davis speaks for the masses of people in the South. I think a group of conspirators have got control down there, and as soon as we get into that territory, the people—most of them don't own slaves, you know—the Southerners will come over to us. Scott's plan to blockade the South, to seize the Mississippi and starve them out, is crazy. All it will take is one sharp blow to put down Davis's band of plunderers."

Father Blair waved at that theory in disgust, causing his wife to say, "He's the only one here who went to West Point, Preston. Maybe he learned something there you don't know."

"Wait," Frank said, trying to figure out his plans. "In case Father is right, and there is a long war, who would win?"

"If the radicals get Lincoln to fight this war over the abolition of slavery, the South will win." The Old Man had thought it through. "The North will just get tired and tell the South to take their slavery and go away. But if we Republicans with enough sense to see that abolition will lose us the war—if we can hold Lincoln to his promise not to interfere with slavery where it exists, and just to oppose its extension to the West—then the North will win and the Union will be saved. The Southerners will get tired of fighting for slavery out in Kansas so long as they can keep their damn institution at home."

When this was digested, Frank asked the traditional question: "So what's the family plan?"

"We've got to beat the radicals in our party so Lincoln can win the war. You, Frank, will have to undercut Thaddeus Stevens in the House. That mean old bastard—you know, he lives with a black woman—will be the power behind the Speaker, and he lives for abolition. I'll make it my job to work on the Senate, I have Orville Browning there to counter Ben Wade. Maybe I'll have Breckinridge, too, if Kentucky stays in the Union—which it better, or there's hell to pay."

Lizzie saw Montgomery being quiet, so she said, "The big fight is inside the Cabinet."

Her brother nodded, eyes closed, as if going around the Cabinet table. "Attorney General Bates is with us, a border-state man, a Whig, no abolitionist. Seward, I don't know—"

"Seward will give the appearance of siding with the radicals," said his

Representative Frank Blair

father, "to hold his New York constituency and to keep Horace Greeley quiet. But in a pinch, Billy Bowlegs will be as conservative as any of us."

"Simon Cameron?" Lizzie asked Monty.

"The Secretary of War will go whichever way the wind blows. He seems to be influenced most by Chase."

"Salmon Portland Chase," said Frank, rolling the name around on his tongue. "I'll never figure out why a senator from Ohio, with the best chance of anybody of becoming the next Republican candidate for President, took the thankless job of Secretary of the Treasury. He's a pompous coot, I know, but—"

"Great dignity," the elder Blair cut him off. "Never underestimate him. Serious man, wants to be President, thinks he should be President right now, finds it hard to conceal his contempt for Lincoln. Ohio is shot through with abolitionism, and Chase will be working with Wade in the Senate to push every damn radical idea."

"Wade and Chase despise each other personally," Mother explained to Frank, "like Seward and us. You learn to swallow your dislikes in this world. What counts is what side you're on."

"I'll keep my eye on Chase," Monty promised. "My Post Office Department, by the way, is more than just a good source of the patronage. It's helpful in keeping track of all sorts of information, holding up certain newspaper deliveries."

"Not as good as the War Department," said Father. "That controls the telegraph service. Remember, boys, never send a telegram, even in code, that you don't want Cameron or Chase to read."

Frank shook his head in wonderment. "We have more enemies on our side than on the other side."

"Another idea," said the Old Man, rising slowly as the clan council came to an end. "Anna Carroll will be helpful in learning what Chase is doing. You remember, she did a lot of writing work for Bates, who can't put a sentence together. She and Chase are good friends, but she shares an interest with us."

Lizzie presumed that cryptic reference meant that Father had Anna Carroll on his payroll somewhere. Lizzie liked Miss Carroll; there was talk about her having a romantic liaison with Millard Fillmore some years ago, after she had arranged Know-Nothing support for his attempted comeback, but the former President had treated her shabbily. Man's world, politics.

"I'll ask her to the Sunday reception, Father."

"You still think we ought to have a big party," Frank cautioned, "with a battle coming on?"

"The Secretary of War thinks it will be a great way to celebrate the victory," Monty replied. "Cameron ought to know."

CHAPTER 9

JOHN HAY'S DIARY
JULY 18, 1861

The Hellcat's Southern kin are causing no end of snide comment. A sister of Mrs. L. from Alabama imposed on the Lincoln hospitality long enough to supply the rebel forces with a load of desperately needed quinine, slipping it through the lines with a pass from the President and then crowing loudly about how she had outwitted "brother Lincoln."

The Tycoon, however, seems not to take notice of the sly digs and instead insists that his wife's Southern affiliations might actually do some good in cementing border-state affections. He has said he would like to have God on his side, but he *must* have Kentucky.

Frankly, I find it hard to see how a state can be both pro-slavery and anti-secession, as persnickety Kentucky seems to be, but the Ancient is willing to take the most egregious abuse from the abolitionist Jacobins among the Republicans rather than offend the peace Democrats who still profess to be loyal.

Fortunately, "Mrs. President"—I hate it when she makes people call her that—has one of her Western kin, rather than her Southern kin, living at the President's house. Her favorite cousin, Elizabeth Todd Grimsley of the sainted state of Illinois, is her constant companion even as our forces are massing in Virginia to crush General Beauregard at Manassas. Mrs. Grimsley is about as deep-rooted a family guest as can be found: she was a bridesmaid at the Lincoln-Todd wedding lo these almost twenty years ago, both as a cousin of the bride and a good friend of the groom. The Tycoon likes her—not only for her common sense, but because she is very tall—and this kins-woman from Springfield is one of the only women in the world that he can talk to at a levee without his wife seething with jealousy.

Mrs. Grimsley has a relative, maybe through marriage to her Kentucky husband, named John C. Breckinridge. That wavering senator is also a dis-tant cousin of the Hellcat, or so they call each other; Kentucky stock all runs together, it seems. He came to tea today. That cousinly gathering struck me as highly nervy of all of them, since the senator earlier this week had been denouncing the Prsdt as a despot for being beastly to the traitors in our midst.

The Tycoon took it, however, not as nervy but as a good opportunity to win over the most influential man in the most worrisome state. When I mentioned to the Tycoon that the ladies were entertaining Breckinridge down the hall he suddenly developed a yearning for tea and cookies. We loafed into the upstairs dining room (the entire downstairs is taken up with hordes of office-seekers and contract-grubbers) and the Hellcat immediately exploded with "This poor man, my own flesh and blood, has been under attack all day by that boor from Ohio, Ben Wade."

"Wade has been after me, too," the Prsdt said to Breckinridge, while deliv-ering a peck on the cheek to Grimsley, to whom he must be grateful because she takes up so much of the Hellcat's time. "Says I don't have the proper abolitionist zeal."

"People in the South respect 'Bluff Ben' Wade," the senator responded, to general surprise. "He says what he thinks. There was that time a couple years ago, after Sumner was beaten with a club in his Senate seat—"

"Dastardly act," Mrs. L. put in, "Charles was crippled in that bully's attack." She likes the vain Sumner, who butters her up outrageously.

"Wade invited one of the Southerners who applauded the attack to challenge him to a duel," Breckinridge recounted. "When Bob Toombs of Georgia made the mistake of taking him up on it, that meant Wade got to name the weapons. Ben chose squirrel rifles at twenty paces, each man to wear a white target patch over his heart, and if they missed on the first shot, they were to advance a couple paces closer and shoot again until one or the other was dead. That scared hell out of Senator Toombs, who only wanted to shoot off a popgun in the meadow from a mile apart for honor's sake. He came over to Wade's desk and asked, 'What's the use of two grown men making damned fools of themselves?' They're friends now."

Lincoln had a good laugh out of that, and the Tycoon laughing is something to see. He leans over in his chair, grabs his knobby knees, rocking back and forth, his high voice hollering, "Hee, hee, hee!" This embarrasses Mrs. L., whose expression of merriment is a short snort.

"I like the time," said the Prsdt, who never lets a funny story go unswapped, "when they were arguing the Kansas-Nebraska bill that denied slavery in that territory. Some old Southern senator asked, 'You mean when I go to settle in Nebraska, I can't take my old black mammy with me?' And Ben Wade shot back at him: 'No objection to taking your old black mammy to Nebraska, Senator, what we object to is your selling her when you get her there!"

More general rocking-back-and-forth by the men, a laugh from Mrs. Grimsley and a snort from the Hellcat. After recovery, at a nod from the Prsdt, Mrs. L. rose and said to her visiting kinswoman, "I must show you the new chandelier in the dining room downstairs. I bought it in New York."

When they bustled off, the Prsdt said to me, "Did the bill come in on that yet?"

I had it my pocket. "One hundred sixty-six dollars."

He winced and asked Breckinridge what his senatorial salary amounted to each week. The senator told him sixty dollars and Lincoln allowed as how about three weeks' work was now hanging over the dining room table. Then they got down to business.

"Is there a plot afoot, John, to take Kentucky out of the Union?"

"Probably. But Kentucky will stay in, if you let us stay neutral. If you invade, or try to raise troops to fight in your war, you'll push Kentucky into secession."

"No state has a right to secede," said the Prsdt, and the fat was in the fire.

"Every state has always been a sovereign entity," the Kentuckian disagreed. "They came together voluntarily. The individual states granted the federal government certain powers, and reserved all other powers not specifically enumerated to themselves. Nowhere in the Constitution does it say that the bond is permanent, or that the national government can force a state to remain when it decides it has just cause to secede."

"That is sophistry," Lincoln said flatly, "sugar-coating rebellion. Southern leaders have been drugging the public mind of their section with that for more than thirty years."

"So says a President elected by 40 percent of the people," Breckinridge replied, forcefully but not disagreeably. "Your saying so, and Andy Jackson having said so, does not change the Constitution. The Framers were dealing with sovereign states, doling out a small portion of their sovereignty to a central government."

"The word 'sovereignty' is not in the national Constitution," Lincoln argued, moving from name-calling to lawyering, "nor in any of the state constitutions. Except for Texas, which gave up its independent character when it chose to come into the Union, no state has ever been a state *out* of the Union."

Breckinridge started to challenge that, but Lincoln had his facts straight. "The original states passed into the Union *before* they cast off their British colonial dependence. Having never been states, either in substance or in name, outside of the Union, whence this magical omnipotence of 'state rights,' asserting a claim of power to destroy the Union itself?"

"You and Jackson are the only presidents to make such an attack on the rights of the states that considered themselves sovereign when they formed the Union." Breckinridge leaned forward, pushing the tea plates and cookies out of the way. "Read the accounts of the debates of 1776: they called themselves 'states' before they united—not colonies, not lands, not territories— and they put that sovereign word in the union they formed, United *States*. Words meant something to the Founders, if not to you." Breckinridge shook his head, as if overwhelmed by the absurdity of Lincoln's attack on Jeffersonian beliefs. "Your reach for national power is not bottomed on constitutional law. You must have been talking to my cousins, the Blairs."

Lincoln did not deny that. "If the Founders had meant to make the Union a temporary arrangement, subject to a walkout by a minority, they would have provided such means of dissolution in the document. Besides, be practical," said the Prsdt. "If one state may secede, so may another; and when all have seceded, none is left to pay the national debt. Is that fair to creditors?"

"You would seriously use such a penny-pinching argument to launch a bloody fratricidal war? The colonies did not concern themselves with England's national debt when they declared their independence and named themselves 'united.' " He added, "And if all you are worried about is the debt left behind by the seceding states, I will volunteer to lead a delegation to negotiate a just settlement of obligations left behind." (I fear he got the best of that point, and Lincoln did not raise it again.)

"I did not launch this war," Lincoln responded, never letting that accusation go unanswered. "By the affair at Sumter, the rebels forced upon the country the distinct issue: 'immediate dissolution, or blood.' "

"You created that incident to lay the blame on them," Breckinridge came right back, "and it worked in igniting the war spirit of the North. But you are obscuring reality: The seceding states want to leave in peace. They are not making war on the North. Only you insist on war. Right at this moment, it's no secret, senators are renting carriages to ride out to Manassas Sunday to see the great victory. Your troops are invading Virginia. Virginia is not invading you."

This fellow is a better debater than we thought. The Prsdt, I think, decided about then to stop trying to make points and to start trying to persuade a member of a jury. He did, after all, want to win this man over.

"Our popular government is an experiment, John. Two points in it, our people have already settled—the successful *establishing*, and the successful *administering* of it. One point still remains: its successful *maintenance* against a formidable effort to overthrow it."

Breckinridge started to object that nobody was out to overthrow the government in Washington, but Lincoln held up his hand and continued his line of reasoning. "It is now for us to demonstrate to the world that those who can fairly carry an election can also suppress a rebellion. We must demonstrate that when ballots have fairly, and constitutionally, decided, there can be no successful appeal back to bullets—that there can be no successful appeal except to ballots themselves at succeeding elections. If we fail to demonstrate that the majority rules, then the great experiment in democracy that is this republic will have failed." He let that terrible prospect sink in, rubbing his hands slowly on his knees, adding, "Such will be a great lesson of peace. It will teach men that what they cannot take by an election, neither can they take by war."

"I understand and respect that, Mr. President. I believe in this experiment in personal freedom as fervently as my grandfather did, serving in Jefferson's Cabinet." (That's where he gets his fear of a strong central government, I guess.) "But no majority can long rule over a beaten minority and remain a democracy. The sections are in a state of profound disagreement, and the hotheads are in the saddle, North and South. But we are not yet really at war. There has been no vast bloodletting in battle, no terrible hatred generated yet. There is still time for compromise."

"Compromises are often proper," said the master of them, "but no popular government can long survive a marked precedent, that those that carry an election can only save the government from immediate destruction by giving up the main point of the election. Only the people, and not their servants, can reverse their own deliberate decisions."

A look of pain crossed the Kentuckian's face; I believe the man was actually suffering, in his inability to sway the resolute President. He is surely not one of those arrogant fire-eaters that usually do the arguing for the secesh— more of a Hamlet, this one is, which is why the Tycoon is spending the time to save his soul from political perdition. "Do not recognize the Confederacy," Breckinridge suggested, "recognize only the need for a period to cool off. During a period of peaceful separation, the natural bonds that you spoke of so eloquently in your Inaugural will have a chance to rebind."

When Lincoln did not immediately rebut, the Kentuckian went on: "Nothing will separate us more permanently than war. And it will be a long war, Lincoln—don't believe what the Blairs tell you about the unionist Southern masses rising against the few conspirators. I know the South better than Father Blair, or Monty or Frank. If you attack and try to conquer those states, you will force the people of the South to rally together, to fight you and to hate you."

"Follow your peaceful secession argument to its conclusion," Lincoln countered. "The Southern states secede. Then there is further disagreement and Georgia secedes from the Confederacy, and then a section of Georgia secedes from that state. That way is anarchy, not democracy. If the experiment that is our nation is to succeed, the dissatisfied elements must submit to the will of the majority."

"By carrying any idea to an extreme, you make it absurd," Breckinridge answered. "It is true that the people of the North and South are brethren. I know that in my own family, and you in yours. But the South has become distinct. It is not so much a section of the whole as it is a world of its own, with a way of life different from the cities of the North, with different commercial interests and crops and social patterns—slavery, for example. To most Southerners, Yankees are more foreign than Englishmen." He drew a deep breath. "And when a people become distinct from their brethren, they deserve a distinct national identity as well."

He was quoting Benjamin Franklin on that, which the Prsdt must have known. "When it comes to slavery," Lincoln promised, as he always has, "I have no purpose, direct or indirect, to interfere with the institution of slavery where it exists. I have no lawful right to do so and I have no inclination to do so." It was Lincoln's turn to sigh, because I suspect he feared he was losing his case. He added only, "You have become a disunionist, then."

"I have resisted every pressure to support secession, you know that. For the past year, I have opposed disunion. Now, on the very eve of battle, I want to avoid the permanent disunion that comes from war. If you insist on war, Lincoln, you will sow the seeds of hatred that will divide this continent for a century. But if you permit peaceful separation now, the people, in time, will come back together, as their commercial and social intercourse increases."

Lincoln slowly shook his head. "I have no moral right to shrink from my duty to preserve this Union. And you, John, have no right to pursue a policy of 'armed neutrality' for Kentucky. You would be building an impassable wall along the line of separation, and this would be disunion completed."

"If the people of a state choose not to fight," the Kentucky senator replied, "no national power can force them to fight. By our example of remaining at peace, of offering men of goodwill an honest broker, perhaps we can save you from yourselves."

"No. That would take all the trouble off the hands of secession. Your notion of neutrality recognizes no fidelity to the Constitution, no obligation to maintain the Union." Lincoln paused, sat straight, and looked directly at his man. "While many who favor it are, doubtless, loyal citizens like yourself, it is, in effect, treason."

That word lay between them like a grenade. To ameliorate it, the Tycoon added, "My wife calls you 'Cousin John,' and I wouldn't be surprised if you and I were Kentucky kin as well. In a larger sense, we are all the same family, and if you could use your great influence with the border-state men to win the war before it gets worse, you would do your kin and mine a service that our common native state would never forget." The Tycoon always likes to remind Kentuckians he was born in their state.

The ladies returned, Miss Grimsley nattering about the beautiful chandelier, which caused the Ancient to roll his eyes heavenward, or chandelier-ward.

"I hope you will come back again soon, Cousin John," the Prsdt said warmly. "Cousin Lizzie here is to be our guest for at least six months, clear through to Christmas."

"Cousin Lizzie, I would not like you to be disappointed in your expected stay at the White House," said the gallant Kentuckian, adding a shocker: "So I will now invite you to remain here as a guest if the Confederacy takes possession."

"We will be only too glad to entertain her until that time, Senator," said the Hellcat, obviously troubled at the touch of bitterness that underlay the Breckinridge charm. But when the possibility of treason is raised, even in the nicest way, I suppose it tends to make a person think of ropes.

"Perhaps when next we see each other," the senator said in shaking hands with the President, "we can discuss the suspension of the writ of habeas corpus."

"I'll be around," said Lincoln, not giving an inch on principle, but not giving up on Kentucky or its favorite son.

CHAPTER 10

PICTURE OF WAR

"Pack a picnic lunch," Mathew Brady told his assistants, Alex and Tim, quickly amending his directive to "pack enough food for two of us for two days. Nothing that will spoil."

"Who are you taking with?" Alexander Gardner asked.

"Tim." Brady had decided that the day before. He judged Alex to be more adept at developing and printing, always difficult in the field, but considered Tim O'Sullivan to have the edge in preparing the wet plates quickly. Besides, Tim was physically stronger than Alex, which would be important on a battlefield, handling the mules drawing the photographic wagon-darkroom and lugging the heavy glass plates in and out of the wagon. "You're my second-in-command, Alex, your job is here in the gallery. The customers know you." What he meant was that Gardner had a sharp Scotsman's eye for money, a talent that neither Brady nor O'Sullivan shared; it was for the studio manager to remain behind.

"We are going on an historic mission," Brady felt called upon to say to his men. He was not one inclined toward dramatic statements, nor did he permit his photographic subjects to assume flamboyant or romantic poses, but surely the mission he had planned was historic.

"How many plates?" Gardner asked dryly.

"This will be the first time that a photograph will be taken of a battle in progress," Brady continued, gripped by a sense of the occasion.

"Twenty plates," Gardner decided. "The subjects are likely to move, and you could spoil half the plates right there." Brady nodded agreement. "You want to take both cameras?"

"We'll just take the big one," Brady replied, putting his hand on the Anthony & Company camera. One camera would do, even for making history; the stereoscope was too expensive to risk out of doors, and taking it would strip the studio naked of cameras. The stereoscopic slides were all the rage in Washington and New York, surpassing in sales even the *cartes de visite*, his illustrated calling cards.

"If anything happens to the big camera," O'Sullivan put in, "there goes the history. We may never get another battle in this war, at least not near here."

"Timmy's right, Mr. Brady," said Gardner. "Everybody's saying, 'On to Richmond!' which is where the next fight is likely to be. That's a long way in a bouncy wagon for the glass plates."

Brady tugged his goatee in thought and then acceded to their wishes. The risk was not so much to the cameras, it was to the history of his infant profession if one camera failed and the battle went unrecorded on colloidal plate. He did not try to conceal his excitement from his operators on this Sunday morning: the light was excellent, the tension of battle was in the air, the city was alive with spectators preparing to rush to the front to witness the decisive blow for the Union.

"You're sure they won't stop you at the battlefield?" Gardner worried.

Brady, looking closely in the long mirror to see if his top hat was on properly and his doeskin pants were neatly pressed, smiled as he took a letter from his jacket pocket. Three days before, as soon as he heard that the Union troops were on the move toward Manassas, he had obtained a pass signed by General McDowell from the only officer who was his superior. Gardner read it quickly—lucky fellow, he did not have to squint through thick spectacles to make out the words, as Brady did—and wondered how his employer had managed it.

Brady smiled. "The naked general remembered his friend." Only a week before, the aging, ponderous General Winfield Scott—"Old Fuss and Feathers"—had been in the Brady studio. A sculptor had been commissioned to produce a statue of the General-in-Chief to be placed in Scott Square, and the artist needed a photograph of his subject stripped to the waist. While Scott was posing with his shirt off, an English actress entered for her photographic appointment and Brady had quickly stepped in front of the general, saving the day by preserving his modesty. When Brady called on him to present his photograph, at no cost, the general could not turn down his request to photograph the battlefield.

"Winfield Scott is a grand old man," Brady pronounced, although the hero of the Mexican War was hardly the man for these times. That marvelously wrinkled old face would probably be replaced soon by Irvin McDowell, after the victory, or if the victor at Manassas suffered too many casualties, by George McClellan, who had gained recognition after several skirmishes in the West. Brady made a mental note to be sure to approach both generals for a sitting; a tidy profit was to be made out of selling pictures of heroes. "McDowell had said he did not want photographers and spectators cluttering up his field," Brady told his assistants, "but Scott told him that photography might become useful for military topography."

The provisioning of the wagon was complete in an hour. The assistants carried the 16 × 20 Anthony camera out of the studio and into the mobile laboratory, with Brady carrying the 4 × 4 stereo camera. Gardner remembered the oats for Guerro, the mule, which Brady had forgotten.

"I feel like Euphorion," the photographer remarked as he climbed onto the front of the wagon, letting O'Sullivan take the reins. "Destiny guides my feet."

"Who's going to pay for these pictures?" Gardner was moved to ask, Brady thought with typical lack of imagination.

"Destiny," Brady replied, nudging O'Sullivan to start. Guerro—a name Brady had chosen this week as appropriate to the first combat photographer's mule—lurched forward and the adventure was begun.

In the end, Brady mused as they rolled down rutted Pennsylvania Avenue, Posterity would pay. The War Department would need official records of the battle that smashed the slavocracy, and there was good reason to suggest that photographs could be part of the official record. Brady would have to induce Simon Cameron, Secretary of War, to visit the gallery; it was said that he was a man always ready to do business. A series of portraits of Cameron and his family might do the trick.

The wagon left the two-story house on the corner of Seventh Street and Pennsylvania Avenue, passed the fashionable National Hotel, where the photographer was staying while he debated whether to make his personal headquarters in New York or Washington. The gallery here was in good hands with Gardner, and the emporium in New York did not have a capable manager he could trust: good business sense suggested that Brady keep his eye on the store in New York. Yet Washington, despite the stench from the sewer in the summer, was sure to be the center of the war, the place where most of the history was to be made, or at least observed from. The art and science of photography could best be advanced from here for the next few months at least.

Traffic on the avenue this Sunday morning reminded him more of the congestion of New York's narrow streets than the usual freedom of the capital's wide boulevards. Carriages containing just about every congressman, reporter, and social butterfly jammed the streets, crawling toward the bridge leading to the battlefield. A troop of cavalry, single file, pranced past the carriages and men on mules and horses. As his wagon passed the President's house, Brady saw for the first time a platoon of rebel prisoners, looking properly dispirited, coming back from the Virginia front. No time to stop for a picture; after the main battle, there would be plenty of time for shots of captured rebels.

Nearing Long Bridge, O'Sullivan and Brady were forced to wait in a half-mile line behind what seemed to be every hack, gig, and wagon available in Washington. In one elegant carriage directly in front of them, its fine horse ridden by a negro boy, was a passenger Brady recognized as William Howard Russell of the *London Times*. The famous reporter, whose writings were notably hostile to the North, as suited British officialdom, was dressed for India.

"Brady!" he called over his shoulder. "Are you going to get the two armies to hold still for a picture?"

Brady, who secretly wished that such a moment could be arranged, merely shrugged. As an Irishman and a staunch Union man, he instinctively disliked the British Southern sympathizer. It made the photographer feel good to be on the way to record the end of the insurrection.

"Tell me, Brady, they've been skirmishing for two days—do you know if they've chosen the spot for the grand battle?"

"Follow the traffic to Manassas," Brady told him, feeling it no breach of trust to repeat the directions Scott had given him, since the crowd seemed to know the way, "about two hours' drive. Look for the signs to Centreville, it overlooks Bull Run." He could hear the rumble of artillery in the distance, across the Potomac. "And follow the sound of the guns." He felt like an old soldier giving advice to a recruit.

Twenty miles into Virginia, the cannon thunder lost its rolling character and became sharper and, to Brady, more menacing. Yet the festive air prevailed on the roadway, the congressmen and other civilians hailing each other on the way to catch a safe whiff of war. A military man rode up behind with whiskers Brady found familiar. Colonel Ambrose Burnside's beard ran down his cheeks but instead of continuing to the chin swept up into his mustache, which was a variation on the fashion in facial hair. He had been in for a photograph a few days before. Brady hailed him, and the colonel slowed his black horse to a walk beside the wagon.

"You'll have a problem with the smoke," Burnside advised, "if you try to take pictures out there. I was at Bull Run yesterday, when the artillery opened fire, and by afternoon it gets hard to see the movement of troops."

"Are we winning?" O'Sullivan inquired. Brady wished his assistant would not ask stupid questions about the battle but would direct his concern to the problems of light and position.

"Of course," Burnside replied. "McDowell has only sixteen hundred regular army troops to season all his recruits, but Beauregard's men are green, too, and he can't have half as many." The colonel looked northwestward, striking what seemed to Brady a most impressive pose. "Another rebel force, under Joe Johnston, is about a day's march away in Winchester, but they can't make it to the battle because we have them tied down defending the valley."

That was fortunate, Brady thought; by outnumbering the rebels two to one, the Union Army should have little trouble scoring a decisive victory. He wondered aloud at the appearance of a column of Union soldiers, dark blue uniforms relatively clean and muskets slung casually across their backs, coming back from the front.

"That's a sight to make any patriot furious," said Burnside. "Damned ninety-day men."

The sergeant on a mule alongside the column pulled up to throw a desultory salute at Burnside. The colonel scorned the mockery of discipline and asked, "Couldn't stand the noise?"

The sergeant shrugged. "These men signed up for ninety days. Enlistment ran out yesterday, and we're going back to Pennsylvania. We enlisted early— about half the army has another week to go."

"You mean," asked Brady, "you're going to miss the victory? What will you tell people when you get home?"

"We'll tell 'em we stood on our rights. If you like being a sorefoot soldier, mister, you join the army."

"If you can remember back to your military life," Burnside said acidly, "what did the battle look like in the position you left just now?"

"Couple of our divisions crossed Bull Run Creek, flanked the rebs," the retiring sergeant reported. "Planning to make a charge at Colonel Jackson's Virginians at the stone house. We seem disorganized as hell, though."

"Why so?"

"Been a long march out here, most of the men ate their rations early. When our boys hear the damn cannon, they forget how to load their muskets. And that secesh cavalry scares hell out of our gunners."

"You recognize the danger, and in the face of the enemy, you and your men are going home," said Burnside. "No shame at all?"

"You're talking to a civilian, soldier-boy," said the former sergeant. "Now why don't you get your fat ass up to the front and fight like we hire you to do!"

Burnside cursed and spurred his horse, kicking up dust as he passed the column of smiling men. The photographer assumed they would go back and call themselves veterans of the campaign that won the war and saved the Union.

"I suppose that was the main reason Lincoln pushed his generals into fighting this soon," Brady observed to O'Sullivan; "most of the army will fade away in a few weeks as the enlistments run out."

"Should we get them to pose along the roadside?" his assistant asked.

"Let's get on to the battle," Brady decided, "before the war's over."

The photographer's wagon reached Centreville in a half hour. It squeezed through the bottleneck of Cub Run Bridge, past the carriages of spectators, wagons loaded with food and ammunition, stray soldiers on foot and a few on mounts.

"Make for the high ground," Brady ordered, uncertain of their position in relation to the battle line. The smoke was worse than Burnside had predicted, stinging Brady's weak eyes and irritating his throat. He worried that the smoke would befog the lenses. The noise of the crowds on the roads mingled with the cannonading and Brady felt a frisson of fear. He stole a look at Timmy O'Sullivan, who had his hands full with the frightened mule. Brady pointed to a side road and O'Sullivan headed the mule in that direction up a hill, through a stand of trees.

That was when Brady saw his first dead body. The crumpled form of what had been a human in gray uniform lay face up alongside the narrow path. No time to stop—the photographer wanted to find a place that would give him a panoramic view of the battlefield—but he made a mental note to come back for a picture of that body if possible.

Guerro picked his way up the hill, through the brambles that grew across the path, and out of the woods onto a rising slope. The mule stopped and refused to move ahead. O'Sullivan scrambled down to get him a bucket of water.

They were in the open. Below, the wooded countryside was dotted with cleared fields and patches of green. A line of purple ridges led up the far hills into what he assumed were the Blue Ridge Mountains. The battle smoke

swept in on them in great black clouds and Brady succumbed to a fit of
coughing. He heard the shouts of soldiers, the pops of musketry amid the
booming cannon. He put his handkerchief over his nose and mouth and
stopped coughing. The voices shouting sounded unlike the cadences of men
from New York. He squinted to see the soldiers in gray uniforms racing
across the hilltop, setting up a battery of artillery.

He was seized with the terrible realization that he was on the wrong side of
the battlefield. The men nearest him were fighting for the Confederacy, determined to kill as many bluecoats as they could. His dismay at being behind
enemy lines grew when he remembered that the great Union attack would
soon be aimed at these men in this position, which meant at him and his
assistant and his mule and his cameras and darkroom-wagon. The thought
entered his mind for the first time that it was entirely possible to be killed in
this engagement. He would be remembered in history only as the first man to
be shot dead while trying to photograph a war. It would be not only a
personal disaster, but also a setback for the science.

"Turn around and get out of here," he told O'Sullivan.

"You want to take a picture first?"

If his young assistant was going to make a test of bravery out of it, Brady
would not be found lacking in courage. The thought occurred also that it
might be less dangerous to get busy, and look busy, than to appear to the
soldiers in gray all around to be running away, perhaps as Union spies. The
photographer climbed out of the wagon and ordered O'Sullivan to tie up the
mule to a tree stump and set up the large camera.

A Confederate officer on horseback, in the gray and blue uniform that
Brady took to mark him as a general, waved his sword to rally his men, not
thirty yards away. The men were wandering about, or running back and
forth, in a most unmilitary way and to no seeming purpose. The officer
shouted at the men to reform their lines and charged at a group of laggards.
All this was moving too fast for a picture, and Brady could not very well ask
them to stop and hold still for a minute under these circumstances. The rebels
milled about, looking for some place to form a line.

The mounted officer wheeled his horse toward Brady's wagon, shot a puzzled look in the photographer's direction at the two men working on their
contraption in front of the mule, then wheeled again toward his men.
"Alabamans!" he called out, pointing to a ridge that seemed to offer a shelter
from the intense firing. "There stands Jackson like a stone wall—rally round
the Virginians!"

Their patch of open land was soon deserted as the Alabama regiment ran
to the high ridge.

Brady pointed the camera toward the field of battle. He did not much care
if the brave Southerner was complaining about a man named Jackson for not
moving forward in support or was praising him for holding his own position.
He ducked his head down under the shadowing fabric and tried to look
through the lens.

Nothing. He could not see clear objects well under good conditions, and in
all the smoke, he could see nothing at all. No massed armies, as he had long
envisioned, in grand array, bayonets at the ready, with generals at the head of
the columns, swords raised, standing still; instead, blurs and smoke and con-

Mathew B. Brady

fusion. Maybe his eyes had completely failed; he told O'Sullivan to take a look. The assistant did, and came up saying he would not waste a plate on that.

The sound of the cannon from the ridge where Jackson was standing like a stone wall was giving him a headache, especially now that it was mixed with the screams of soldiers in blue coming under the withering fire from that hill. He could make out the general in the distance, pressing his stragglers forward to the new position on the ridge, and saw him lurch forward suddenly and slide off his horse.

"We need a better position," he told O'Sullivan, who was ready to leave also, and carried the camera back to the wagon instantly. They guided Guerro down the hill into the woods, past the familiar dead body—no time for a picture—all the way back to the Centreville Road.

Only an hour before, the traffic had all been one-way toward the battlefront; now it was two-way. As O'Sullivan maneuvered the wagon into a left turn, toward the front but this time behind the Union lines, frightened men came past them, suggesting to Brady that all was not well up ahead. The returning ambulances were to be expected, sure sign of battle, but too many soldiers were coming back without muskets, leaderless; others trudged back with their coats hung over their firelocks, with a look of men who had something important to do elsewhere. The road was littered with evidence of lightened packs: canteens, knapsacks, cartridge boxes, and blankets lay in the dirt.

Russell of the *Times* drew up, on his way to the rear. "Have you seen what it's like, Brady? Can you believe the ineptitude?"

"We've been lost," O'Sullivan started to say and Brady shot an elbow to his arm.

"We've been at the center of the battle," Brady said, "saw Jackson standing like a stone wall, as they said. What news have you?"

"It's a disaster for the Union," the Englishman called out, not in appropriate distress, "the Federal army isn't an army at all, rather a mass of men milling aimlessly, not knowing how to fight or where to go. McDowell must be an idiot, going into battle so unprepared."

"You're leaving? Is the battle over?"

"I can tell which way it's going," the portly correspondent snapped, as if Brady had questioned his courage, which in a way he had. "Your artillery batteries were moved forward without infantry cover, and the Confederates captured them. Fear of the cavalry is rampant—I've heard prodigious nonsense, describing batteries tier over tier, and ambuscades, and blood running knee-deep. This road will be under fire in a very short time. Move aside!"

O'Sullivan let the man from the *Times* pass. Russell was quickly followed by a group of picnickers in three carriages who had lost their taste for the afternoon outing. The road was becoming more congested than at any place since Long Bridge. An ammunition cart came past them, loaded with explosives. It occurred to Brady that a full load should be headed in the opposite direction. A red-faced officer on the cart, with an empty scabbard dangling from his side, said, "Turn back! We are whipped."

"I don't like this," O'Sullivan said. "You can smell the panic."

"Think about capturing it on a wet plate," Brady replied. Even if this turned out to be a standoff, or at worst a defeat, the War Department would want pictures. He had not been able to find a photographable scene.

By midafternoon of a day with hot sun burning through the haze of smoke and choking dust, no observer, military or amateur, could doubt that a rout was under way. Men in blue uniforms were running down the main road to Centreville, throwing their muskets by the roadside, desperate to get away from the sound of the guns. Occasionally a lone officer would shout at them to stop, and Brady saw a senator he knew, Ben Wade, a pistol in each hand, threatening to shoot deserters but being ignored in the general exodus from a scene of confusion and destruction. As far as the photographer could learn, no order of retreat had been given by General McDowell. His army had simply decided to go home.

They unloaded the camera at a vantage point below the smoke, close enough to a stream for washing, facing up a hill looking toward a stone house. Brady could hardly believe his dim eyes: there must have been four hundred dead bodies lying up the long slope. With the sound of bullets whining and smacking nearby, O'Sullivan began the process of sensitizing the plates. In this heat, the coating, exposing, and developing would have to be completed within ten minutes.

Brady looked nervously up the hill as his assistant washed the plate in the collodion solution, a mixture of guncotton and sulfuric ether and alcohol. When the plate flowed with collodion, O'Sullivan laid on the chemical excitants—bromide and iodide of potassium—and, when that turned properly tacky, lifted it into a tub containing nitrate of silver and iodized water. It remained in the darkness inside the wagon for four minutes. Sullivan then lifted it out, drained the plate, placed it in the lightproof holder, and carried it, dripping, to the camera.

Brady ducked his head under and looked; he could make out forms on the ground, little else. He walked forward to make certain they were rebel dead; at least the body in the foreground was, and the others could be called that as well. The Northern public, he was sure, was not ready for pictures of Union dead.

O'Sullivan had the camera loaded. He focused it, as the nearsighted Brady could not, moved it slightly to get the form in the foreground in focus, and grunted. Brady lifted the lens cap, counted to thirty, and ended the exposure. O'Sullivan pulled out the holder, raced back into the wagon and began the delicate business of dipping it into the developer of acids and soda. In two minutes, he ran out to the stream and held the plate under water. Brady prayed there would be no mud to stick to the still-gummy surface.

An image appeared. The dead rebel in the foreground would be frozen in history as he was frozen in death. Brady could feel his heart pounding as the science so few now appreciated passed a milestone. "Photograph by Brady" of a nation at war. He told O'Sullivan to take the plate inside the wagon quickly and to bring out the stereo camera. The assistant hefted the plate gleefully, saw his employer's warning frown, and carried his developed image inside. Brady was glad he had chosen O'Sullivan, who followed orders and never so much as breathed on the sensitive plates.

The young Irishman was taking the next Brady photograph of the dead bodies when he suddenly let out a cry and dropped the little camera. Brady rushed over and picked up the instrument, which fortunately had landed on a cast-off blanket; aside from the smearing of blood over one of the lenses, it appeared to be unbroken.

O'Sullivan was staring at his left hand, which was dripping blood. Both of them were apparently in the line of enemy musket fire. They ran into the wagon, which offered little cover, and Brady took the reins while O'Sullivan fashioned a makeshift tourniquet out of a lenscloth. In moments, Guerro had them on the road back toward Centreville.

Almost all the traffic was headed away from the front by this time, but one rider that Brady recognized was making his way forward. It was Breckin-ridge, the Kentucky senator who had steadily ignored Brady's letters of invi-tation to be photographed.

"Great day for Southern sympathizers," the photographer said coldly.

The rider shook his head in what struck Brady as genuine sadness. "A terrible day for all of us." He seemed the only calm presence in the spreading panic.

"McDowell's fault?" Brady wanted to get home in a hurry, and did not want O'Sullivan fainting from loss of blood, but he remembered that Breckin-ridge had once been a military man and probably had some idea of what was going on. Brady was amazed that he could be at the very vortex of a battle and not have the foggiest notion about the movement of the troops, although anybody could tell that the side that was running away was losing.

"Lincoln's fault," the senator answered, "but the general will get the blame. Lincoln wanted this fight, here and now, before his ninety-day men had the chance to go home. McDowell had thousands of soldiers, but no army. Look over there."

Brady looked over his shoulder and shuddered at the sight of a force of rebel cavalry sweeping down a far hill, hacking at running blue infantry. All too fast in motion, no chance for a picture.

"Those are Joe Johnston's men," the Kentuckian explained, moving his horse out of the way of an ambulance wagon. "They must have come down from Winchester on the Manassas Gap railway and joined Beauregard's army. That's what the Federals thought could never happen." He spotted a fellow senator, whose name slipped Brady's mind, who was urging his car-riage away from the firing. "Ah, Henry, what does it look like?"

His Senate colleague struggled by in his gig, not speaking. Wilson of Mas-sachusetts, Brady remembered, the Military Committee. Good that he was getting a firsthand look, because some great changes would have to be made immediately.

They left the Kentuckian surveying the road and the field. Although the Centreville Road had become a slow river of vehicles and stumbling men and crying women sightseers, it was the only way back. And as Russell of the *Times* had warned, the jammed road was coming under fire from Confederate artillery.

Nearing the stone bridge at Cub Run, Brady saw his first big explosion: a shell hit the bridge ahead of them; he could hear the whoosh of fire, then the blast, and the bridge had disappeared. A score of people crammed on the bridge were obliterated. Amid the screaming and whinnying, with the line that had been waiting to get on the bridge now spreading out along the stream preparing to swim, wade, or float across, Brady felt a wave of resignation come over him.

"We will stop here," he told O'Sullivan, "and take a photograph of the place where the bridge used to be. Are you up to it?"

O'Sullivan held up his bandaged fist and grinned. Brady turned the wagon off the road and stopped. He unloaded the big camera and watched O'Sullivan, one-handed, apply the colloidal wash and prepare the plate. He helped his assistant carry the heavy plateholder to the camera and told him to aim at the scene of the devastated bridge. He took off the lens cap, waited, put it back. O'Sullivan went through the developing process, washing the plate in the creek that they had just photographed.

"That should come out," Brady announced. "Good light, not much smoke. Not exactly two armies clashing in vast array, but at least we can prove we were here."

He took the two exposed and developed glass plates in his arms. O'Sullivan picked up both cameras and carried them high on his back. Together, they kicked and shouted at Guerro, who finally got the idea he was to drag the emptied wagon though the water. The two men, and the mule with the wagon, made it across the stream, with the water never higher than Brady's knees.

The thumping of the cannons sounded louder as they neared the Union long-range artillery hurling shells at the pursuing rebels. Then the sound was pierced by a bloodcurdling scream that Brady knew he would remember in his nightmares—the rebel yell, the battle cry of the cavalry swooping down on batteries and fleeing bystanders. The yell achieved the desired effect, sending terror through the routed ranks, with the gunners abandoning their fieldpieces, every man for himself.

Brady knew he could not leave his equipment behind without leaving his whole life's meaning with it. At the same time, he was aware that he was profoundly afraid. He tried to speak several times and finally was able to choke out instructions to Timmy O'Sullivan to be calm. The young man was loading the cameras on the wagon and reached down for the plates in Brady's arms. The photographer gave up his burden, adjusted his top hat, and climbed up.

A man whose gray uniform was bloodstained across the neck and shoulder called up to him. He was propped against a tree by the side of the road, face white, unable to move. Here was the victor, the photographer thought grimly, Johnny Reb on his day of triumph over an overconfident Union Army. He considered whether to tell O'Sullivan to set up the equipment again to take a picture or just to take the wounded man along.

Timmy must have read his thoughts because the young man jumped off the wagon and lifted the wounded rebel, carrying him into the rear of the wagon. Brady did not argue. The man was more of a sorry object than a good subject, but might do them some good if the rebel army in pursuit caught up with them. He hoped that would not happen. He hoped their generals would not learn of the extent of the rout until too late and would not carry their triumph at Manassas into an undefended Washington.

CHAPTER 11

THE WAKE OF BULL RUN

Montgomery Blair decided to go ahead with the reception. Although casualties could be expected in the Virginia campaign, and enemies of the Blair family were ready to criticize any party-giving in the midst of war, he thought it important to show confidence in the country and unconcern about criticism.

By six o'clock on that sun-drenched, humid Sunday afternoon, he was delighted that he had gone ahead with the gathering: all the reports from those returning early from Manassas had hailed the Union victory. Across the street, at the telegraph office of the War Department, the dispatches from the front had been more than encouraging. The Postmaster General's home was no farther from that communications center than was Lincoln's office, on the opposite side of Pennsylvania Avenue, and Monty Blair had checked an hour before. McDowell, attacking, was confident of success against Beauregard's smaller force; the other Confederate army in the area was well out of the action, tied down in Winchester. Here in the District of Columbia, General-in-Chief Scott had gone to take his afternoon nap.

Standing on the porch, Blair could see President Lincoln, unmistakable in his stovepipe hat, long legs hanging down the horse's sides, going out for his late-afternoon ride. Blair waved; the horseman returned the salute. If Lincoln was relaxed enough about the word from the front to take his customary outing, Blair was not about to worry about the outcome of the battle or the mood at his party.

Lincoln looked odd on a horse, Blair observed. The President rode well, and must have had plenty of equestrian experience as a lawyer riding circuit, but he did not sit a horse well. A man of the President's height and angularity would find it difficult to appear graceful in any position. The Postmaster General caught himself thinking of Lincoln as the President, and was amused by that subtle acceptance of the new man in the post. It had been so hard to push him into acting like a President, into overruling Seward and the others on Sumter, into drawing the line that separation had to mean war. Father had worked on Lincoln in private, using the Jackson precedents, and Monty had himself worked on Lincoln in Cabinet, stressing his duty never to give up federal authority anywhere, an idea to which the new Chief Executive, happily for the Union, seemed almost mystically attached.

The Blair house, then, deserved to be the scene of the victory celebration because this battle was largely the Blairs' doing. General Scott had waffled and wavered, claiming the army was unready; Seward had been fearful, as usual, seeking some settlement. Only Lincoln had understood the political necessity of a sharp, early, decisive blow. Delay was purely military advice; what the President had needed was political advice urging him to marshal the war spirit on which military strength depended.

His sister Lizzie came over from the adjoining house to help him greet the guests. A political enemy, Thurlow Weed, was the first to arrive: Seward's alter ego, editor of the *Albany Union,* and a notorious wirepuller known in New York as "the wizard of the lobby." The white-maned politician was alone, his usually serene face flushed and worried-looking. "Any news from Manassas?"

"The signs are good," his host reported. "The President was just out riding."

Weed shook his head. "I was standing on the corner in front of Willard's and Colonel Burnside came riding by. You know him, fellow with muttonchop whiskers that kind of run under his nose and up his cheeks?"

Blair nodded; Ambrose Burnside was a born failure, an inventor of a breech-loading rifle whose company went bankrupt a year ago. George McClellan, a born winner in military and commercial affairs, had given him a job at the Illinois Central. When Lincoln called for troops, McClellan was given command of the Department of the Ohio and his unsuccessful friend found a regiment of Rhode Island Volunteers to lead.

"Burnside was too mad to talk," Weed said. "Ran inside and had a drink at the bar, seemed all riled up to me."

As other guests arrived after seven o'clock, the signs grew more ominous. The guests who had loaded their buggies with champagne and box lunches and departed for a festive occasion came directly to Blair's house looking shaken, talking of retreat, some even talking of a rout. Outside, silent crowds had gathered in front of the Executive Mansion, the War and Treasury departments. Pennsylvania Avenue was becoming a thoroughfare of retreat, as returning spectators in carriages, officers on horseback, foot soldiers, and wagons of wounded jostled each other to leave the confusion in Virginia far behind.

"I think we'd better send our guests home," said Lizzie, soon after sunset. Brother Frank agreed.

"Go across the street, Frank," Monty told him. "See what news is coming into the telegraph office. Let's not lose our heads—the first to come back from a battle are never the fighting troops."

"What if Lincoln's there?"

"Say, 'Hello, Mr. President,' and tell him that most of his Cabinet will be right here if he needs us." The younger Blair bolted out.

With the exception of Secretary of State Seward, all Cabinet members and their wives were in the Blair house, nibbling nervously at the Maryland crab claws, worrying aloud with the assembled editors, congressmen, and financiers. A messenger came from the War Department, asking to see Secretary Cameron alone; Lizzie took the messenger and the Secretary upstairs, and came down with the sad report that Cameron's brother, a colonel, had been killed in the action. Monty Blair noticed that nobody from the White House had yet arrived; he knew how eager the young Hay had been to come, and his absence was troubling.

"Calamity!" From the hallway leading to the main parlor, Blair heard that word hissed from the small sitting room near the front door. He stood still and listened. "This is what comes of Lincoln's running the machine for five months. Right this moment, Lincoln and Scott are disputing who's to blame."

"You despair for the Republic, then, Mr. Stanton." Blair recognized the voice of Adams Hill, the *New York Tribune* man in Washington.

"No, if our people can bear with this Cabinet, they will prove able to support a great many disasters."

Stanton was a Democrat, a holdover from Buchanan's administration. Simon Cameron had given him an important job in the War Department, as general counsel, on the strange-for-Cameron reason that organizational merit should count over political affiliation. Blair made a mental note to warn Cameron about Stanton's evident duplicity, but not tonight, in the War Secretary's bereavement.

Kate Chase, on the arm of Lord Lyons, the English ambassador, interrupted his eavesdropping. She was both radiant and intense, and Blair felt his gloom begin to lift as she brought the two men together.

"The ambassador has heard that the Confederacy has gained a crushing victory," she said, "and I don't believe him."

Blair asked Lord Lyons the source of his report.

"William Russell of the *Times,*" was the reply. "He borrowed my carriage to go to the front, and that's the last I shall see of that buggy. He returned just now, on a horse I presume he purchased after my carriage was destroyed in the mad rush. He's off writing his dispatch, but I take it the capital is in danger of capture by Beauregard. And your General Scott is distraught."

Father Blair joined their circle with the heavily bearded Gideon Welles, the Navy Secretary. "None of this is Scott's fault," said Welles. "He cautioned us against putting our green troops in the field, against a possibly superior force."

"Nonsense." Only the elder Blair could speak to a Cabinet member that way. "We outnumbered the rebels two to one. Our defeat, if that is what it was, is inexcusable. Scott may not be up to this war."

"No recriminations," rumbled the Navy Secretary that Lincoln liked to call "Neptune." Monty Blair caught his father's wry look; that remark meant that recriminations for the surprise defeat would come thick and fast, and the Blairs—who had pressed for this battle—would be on the receiving end.

"If the rebels are coming tomorrow," asked Kate Chase, Blair thought quite sensibly, "shouldn't we all be preparing to defend the city? Barricades, and that sort of thing?"

Thurlow Weed thought not. "It could be that the rebels are as tired and disorganized as we are. And have you looked out the window in the past few minutes? It's pouring rain. I doubt whether either army will be ready to fight again tomorrow."

The front door opened and Senator Ben Wade burst into the room, dripping wet, a black look across his normally ferocious face, followed by a subdued Senator Henry Wilson. "Goddamn incompetence!" Wade announced, pulling off his hat and shaking the water on the floor. "Goddamn cowardice! I was out there at Long Bridge and I damn near shot the deserters as they ran across. Should have, treason everywhere, not one general officer who knows what the hell he's doing. Any telegraph news from Centreville?"

Frank had not returned with fresh news; Monty hoped he was with Lincoln. He sensed an opening in what Wade had just said to deflect some of the blame from the Blairs. "You believe our generalship fell short?"

"Nobody could even find McDowell at the front," Wade growled. "And Scott can't get up off his duff. We need a real general, and right away."

"You may be right, Ben," said the elder Blair. "If it's a defeat. We don't know yet, it may just look bad from here."

Frank Blair returned, holding an umbrella for William Seward. The hawk-faced Secretary of State looked haggard. "The battle is lost," he said quietly, a telegram in his hand. He looked at some of the newspapermen who closed in around the Cabinet members. "I speak in total confidence, of course. The telegraph from McDowell says that he is in full retreat—flight, I suppose is the more accurate word—and he calls on General Scott to rally the troops here to save the capital."

"What does the telegraph message say?" The voice was Salmon Chase's; Blair knew that a defeat would make it infinitely harder for the Secretary of the Treasury to raise the money to finance a war.

" 'The day is lost,' he says. 'The routed troops will not re-form. Save Washington and the remnants of this army.' I take that message to be definitive," Seward said wearily. "The President wishes the Cabinet to meet with him tonight, immediately, in General Scott's office."

As they drew on coats and shawls, Adams Hill of the *Tribune* said, "I thought this was supposed to be a thirty-day war."

"That could still be," replied Thurlow Weed, "but with a different result than we thought. I can hear your employer, Horace Greeley, changing 'On to Richmond' to 'Erring sisters, depart in peace.' "

Seward shook his head, put his hand on his friend Weed's arm, and said to Hill, "We will all have to prevail on Horace to be stalwart."

"That son-of-a-bitch Breckinridge will be crowing in the Senate tomorrow," muttered Wade. "We ought to clap him in the Old Capitol Prison in the morning."

The deflated partygoers quickly dispersed into the rain. On the porch, the three Blair men huddled.

"We were not wrong to press for an early victory," said the father, laying down the family line. "Scott, the old fool, moved too slowly, and McDowell was incompetent. Maybe George McClellan is our man. If Seward says I-told-you-so in the Cabinet tonight, Monty, or if Scott tries to blame us for pushing him—hit them hard for cowardice and incompetence."

Monty Blair nodded agreement. He did not know how Lincoln would react to this setback, and assumed the President would need strong supporters to stiffen his backbone. He ran to catch up to Seward, who was wading across the sea of mud with Cameron and Bates.

The Cabinet members had to stop in the pelting rain to wait for a strange procession to pass in front of them: Senator Breckinridge on a horse, looking not in the least triumphant or anything but wet and miserable, followed by a mule dragging a wagon driven by Mathew Brady, the photographer. The top and one side of the wagon was knocked out, and three wounded soldiers lay exposed to the rain, two in blue uniforms, one in gray.

CHAPTER 12

WHAT DRIVES THE MAN?

Breckinridge brought the Confederate soldier with the musket ball in his thigh to the Old Capitol Prison. About two hundred other captured Southerners were cramped into the receiving room there, a third of them in need of medical attention. The Federal military hospital had turned those wounded away; because too many Union soldiers were forced to go without beds, no hospital chief was inclined to put rebels in hospital beds or even in cots that crowded the hallways.

At the Old Capitol, however, a medical team made up of Southern sympathizers had been organized. Nobody stopped them from bringing scarce bandages and supplies to attend the Confederate injured; Breckinridge assumed this was as much because of the impending invasion by the victorious Southern troops as for any humanitarian concern.

"He's from Kentucky," Senator Breckinridge, Democrat of Kentucky, said to the doctor taking the man off his hands, loud enough for the Federal guards to hear. The wounded man was originally from the Bluegrass state but had moved to Virginia, where he joined up with Jackson's brigade. The senator wanted it clearly understood that the wounded man was his constituent; Breckinridge would face censure on the Senate floor for visiting the Southern soldiers after the battle, and needed an excuse. Taking care of a wounded constituent was an action no other senator could easily condemn.

"You're the only member of the Yankee Congress who had the courage to come."

Rose Greenhow's husky voice was a pleasure for the senator to hear in that hostility-filled old building. She had brought her personal physician and two of the girls who worked for her to the prison and set up a medical unit in one of the larger cells. Breckinridge admired the Wild Rose: her commanding presence, eyes that could be fierce or mocking, expressive mouth, the sense of abandon in the way she moved. He had always enjoyed her hospitality, though rarely taking advantage of her available favors; in Washington, Anna Carroll's companionship was more than enough for him.

"If my Kentucky friend were a Union casualty," Breckinridge said, still in that stentorian voice he used on the Senate floor, "I would be with him in a Federal hospital." Unlike Rose, he did not take unnecessary chances; she took entirely too many, which suggested to him that she relished danger.

She took his arm, steered him out into the prison corridor, past the jam of cots and benches containing the wounded or the sullen, to a supply closet room where they could speak alone. "We've won, John!" She put her hands on his shoulders and shook him. "We beat the Yankees at Manassas, and I had a big hand in it."

"You're telling me something I don't want to know about," he cautioned. He long suspected—in truth, he had to admit he knew—that Rose was a Confederate spy. The spacious brick house on Sixteenth Street, so convenient to James Buchanan when that bachelor had occupied the White House, was more than ever the place where politicians and generals gathered. The reckless Rose sometimes modified but never concealed her contempt for the abolitionists. That was still socially and politically acceptable—in fact, most of the Republican radicals were considered a dangerous minority—but Rose probed the outer limits of sympathy for the rebellion. It would be natural for her to share what she learned in the Union capital with her friends in the Confederate capital, and she would be automatically suspect in a city where the word "treason" was being bandied about. Why, in that circumstance, was she not much more circumspect? Calculated recklessness, he supposed; dangerous flirtations attracted her.

"I'll tell you what I please, Breck, because I trust you," she said, her strong grip moving down from his shoulders, along his arms, to his hands. "Do you know how Beauregard knew when the Yankees moved out? From me. You know how we knew the whole plan of attack, with Joe Johnston supposed to be held down in Winchester by that old idiot Patterson, so he couldn't reinforce Beauregard? From me, from a message I braided into Bettie Duval's beautiful long hair."

He looked over her shoulder into the crowded hallway for the appearance of Federal guards. "That's your secret, Rose. I won't be a party to espionage, not while I sit in the Senate."

"The entire battle plan," she persevered, "the map with the red dotted lines on it showing the Yankee troop movements—can you imagine the advantage that gave us?"

So that was why the Union suffered such unexpected disaster at Bull Run; she had given Johnston the signal to slip away from the force supposedly tying him down. That was no mean feat of spying. Against his better judgment, he asked, "Where did you get the information, Rose?"

"The chairman of the Military Affairs Committee of the Senate, who banished you from the committee because you were a risk to the security of the Union." A look of pure malice mixed with the delight and triumph in her eyes.

"I can't believe that about Henry." He meant that; Senator Wilson was a patriot, and no fool. He suspected that Rose might be spreading rumors about her Senate lover to mislead the world about her true source.

"Your dear friend Henry Wilson is a slave to sex. I have given him a new sexual life beyond his wildest dreams."

Breckinridge winced at that. "You sure say what you mean."

"I am a patriot first and a lady second. I am prepared to put everything that God has endowed me with in the service of the Cause." In case that did not make her point, she added, "I would prostitute myself for my country."

He shook his head at her certitude about the Cause, whatever it was, and at her blunt language. "Henry Wilson handed you that map in bed?"

"Senator Wilson has some strange desires," she said. "One is to set the slaves free. Another is to be a slave himself. I do what I can to accommodate him. The Wild Rose can get fairly wild, if you really want to know."

"As I said, I don't really want to know."

"I want to talk to you about Anna Ella Carroll," she said, veering to business. "I've seen the two of you together in my house, trying to act as if you met there by accident. Doesn't fool anybody. We could use her. She knows everybody, even Lincoln, especially Bates—"

"Forget her," he advised. "Pro-Union all the way." That was more than true; he did not add that he had spent the previous evening in her room, listening to her read to him the text of the speech made in Lexington, Kentucky by the Reverend Robert Breckinridge on the moral wrong of secession, complete with gestures and inflections taken from the lecture-hall style of Uncle Bob. Secession was immoral, in his thesis, because it invalidated the grandest contribution of modern times to the progress of civilization, the Constitution, which had given validity to the natural right of men to change or abolish their government by voting.

No pledge of his to read the Union pamphlet with great care would stop her; she had to stand there, on the footstool in her bare feet, reading the tract for an hour and a half. When her visitor was drawn into making a point in rebuttal—that the Constitution would remain in effect for those states that subscribed to it—she had launched into a long recitation of a paper she was drafting called *A Reply to John C. Breckinridge*. They wound up with three hours' sleep, and he was off to watch the battle the next morning.

Rose did not accept his head-shaking about Anna Carroll. "She's from Southern stock, with slaves of her own. And she may not be so pro-Union after today. Lots of people are going to go with the winners, and Anna was a power in the Know-Nothings—she's not above buttering her bread on both sides."

"You're mistaken about her, Rose—forget it."

He must have spoken too sharply, because she flared: "She loves you, you damn fool, and you can take advantage of it for the Cause. She gets around. She's attractive, if you like 'em small, but she uses her head more than her body to get things out of men."

He did not like that and set his jaw to say nothing; she saw the facial gesture and softened. "We could use her, Breck. You may not realize it, but she would do anything for you, no matter what she says now." She looked over her shoulder, a touch too dramatically. "The Yankees may be on to me before long."

To change the subject, he picked that up: "You ought to be more careful, Rose, especially the way you talk at your parties. This prison is no place for a woman, as a prisoner. Or her daughter." He knew Rose's surviving daughter was too young to be separated from her mother, and would probably accompany her to prison. Rose had to be worried about that, love of danger or not.

"Who would suspect that I would speak up for the South and spy for the South? Most spies try to hide their true beliefs."

"Don't outsmart yourself. Pinkerton is just dumb enough to suspect somebody who's suspicious."

"And you're protecting Anna Carroll. It's your duty to recruit her."

"It's my duty to try to end this war before it gets any bloodier, right here where I can be most useful, in the United States Senate."

"You see your duty wrong. You're wasting your time here in Washington. It's a cryin' shame seeing you haggling with these Yankees like a damn lawyer when you should be serving your country in Richmond."

That troubled him; were they saying in Richmond that his lonely vigil for civil liberty in the Senate made him untrustworthy? A guard passed the closet and looked in; Rose took a length of bandage off a shelf, rolled it up, and handed it out to the man, who shrugged and took it away. Breckinridge asked her the politician's question: "What are they saying about me?"

"You know Mary Chesnut in Richmond, Breck—she likes you."

He nodded. Vivacious, politically keen, his age, well-connected, the former Mary Boykin reminded him of Anna.

"She tells my friends that you could have been Vice President, or Secretary of War, or general-in-chief, if you had come down in the early summer, when the Confederacy was getting organized. Mary says every day you spend up here is a day that your political future gets worse."

He nodded again; Mary Chesnut's assessment was probably right, and every day spent in the middle of the opposing forces eroded his opportunity for leadership on either side. "I don't care about that, Rose. All I want to do is stop this horrible fratricidal contest."

"Idiot!" she hissed, hammering her fist on his shoulder. "Whose side are you on? Don't you see we need this war?"

"To teach the Yankees a lesson?"

"To make the Confederacy a nation, the way the Revolution did a hundred years ago, and to show the Westerners that they should join us. For God's sake, Breck, we can't just creep out of the Union in peace—we have to show the world who's master on this continent."

His head was shaking no, as she spoke, and he told her when she finished that no reponsible Southern leader wanted anything but to depart in peace.

"That's what they say, but that's not what everybody thinks. No wonder you're stuck halfway and can't see your duty clear, Senator, you believe what politicians say. Wake up! All those talks with that baboon in the White House have put you to sleep."

"He's no baboon," he said. Just as Rose underestimated Lincoln in her mixture of hatred and patriotism, it was possible that Lincoln did not properly gauge the degree of determination in the secession spirit. "He's a very stubborn man, a little on the arrogant side, who thought he could hold the Union together at not too great a cost. It doesn't help to call him a baboon, Rose. He's shrewd, and knows how to argue, but he has this blind spot."

She turned her head as if to indicate she would not listen, then said in a low voice: "I hate him because he represents all the grubby foreigners in those factories up there who think they can grind us down to their way of life. They're ugly, and he's ugly, and that's why he's a baboon."

"He is not ugly, and there is no reason to fear him, or them."

"What does he want from us, then? What drives the man?"

"It's just that blind spot of his, Rose. Lincoln doesn't want to compromise, he wants to win. In that way, and in no other, he's like you."

She appeared not to hear, and leaned close to impart some intelligence. "I hear that Jeff Davis is coming up from Richmond to hold a council of war with Beauregard and Johnston tonight." She did not say how she knew, nor did he ask, but he assumed her information was accurate. "I hope to hell they march on Washington tomorrow, because this city has no defense at all. If we come across the Long Bridge in the morning, your baboon friend will be spending the night in this prison."

Breck thought he would almost welcome that, if only to put an end to the war before the lust for vengeance caused the North to mobilize hundreds of thousands of men and appoint some real generals. But the Confederates at Bull Run seemed to him almost as disorganized and amateurish as the Union's civilians in uniform, and they might fail to press their advantage. In that case, how would Lincoln react to a battlefield humiliation? Breckinridge guessed he would shift the blame to his generals and grow more obstinate than ever, settling in for a long war. Such a war could last until both sides quit from exhaustion, bled white, and all for nothing—for Lincoln's strange need for national dominion and the Southern leaders' imagined need to protect slavery.

To Rose Greenhow, he said only, "Don't get too confident. And don't worry about my career in the Confederacy because I may never get there. It may be Kentucky's destiny to be neutral, the peacemaker."

"You're a fool. The Yankees will arrest you in the middle of one of your mealymouthed speeches in the Senate and hang you for treason." Her prediction, he knew, was not so farfetched, though he did not foresee hanging. Dishonor, prison—perhaps this very prison, or Fort Lafayette—and, worst of all, enforced silence in the midst of despotism. But Rose's solution, to take up arms in the South against the government he had served and the Constitution he revered, held no appeal for the grandson of Jefferson's lawyer.

"The next Senate speech I make will not be mealymouthed," he said. "It should offend everyone. You're invited to the gallery."

"I'll bring something I can throw," she said, suddenly putting her hand behind his head, drawing him forward to kiss him flush on the mouth. He offered no resistance because he did not want her to think he feared being observed by the guards. "Beats having to bend down to kiss a woman, doesn't it?" she teased, then became serious. "Recruit her for us, and leave her. Anna's accustomed to being left by men. Make your damn speech and go South, where you belong."

CHAPTER 13

OLD FUSS AND FEATHERS

Winfield Scott, feeling every bit of his seventy-five years and nearly three hundred pounds, managed to rise when the President entered, then sat back heavily in his leather armchair. He motioned for his aide-de-camp to take Lincoln's wet cape and hat.

The general-in-chief's office was filled with memorabilia of the man who liked to say that, like Roger Taney, he was "one year older than the Constitution"—captured flags and surrendered swords from the Mexican War, the fading colors of regiments he had commanded in the War of 1812, when the British sacked Washington—and mounted on the wall was his pride and joy, a leather bag containing a dozen bullets.

Under Scott's direction, the U.S. Army in 1849 had adopted the muzzle-loading gun capable of firing the Minié bullet—popularly known as a "minnie ball"—named after French Army captain Claude Étienne Minié. The lead projectile was shaped quite differently from the old musket ball: this was cylindrical, conical in front and hollow at the back. When its sides were forced by the explosive charge against the rifling on the inside of the gun barrel, the bullet was sent spinning out of the barrel with a degree of accuracy and a range that greatly improved small-arms fire and, the general had long been certain, would revolutionize infantry tactics. The new weapon and its ammunition gave entrenched defenders an advantage over any attacking force, whether infantry or cavalry. In Scott's opinion, it effectively ended the Napoleonic era of massed assaults.

"General, it appears we are undone," the President was saying, as he thrust a handful of the latest dispatches from the War Department telegraph office into Scott's hands.

In a few moments, Secretary Seward led the Cabinet into the office. General Scott surveyed the group. The Secretary of War was the picture of personal despair. Half of them—Attorney General Bates, Cameron of War, and Seward of State—were obviously in their sixties. Welles, Montgomery Blair, Chase of Treasury, and Caleb Smith of Interior were in their late- or mid-fifties, and Lincoln, whom Scott knew to be fifty-two, was the youngest of the lot.

Curious that he should surround himself with older men; a good sign, Scott thought. Perhaps the older heads, his own included, could restrain Lincoln from his less judicious inclinations. The general recalled clearly—but would not mention, of course—that when Scott was in his fifties, carrying the flag down to the Rio Grande, then-Congressman Lincoln had been privately assailing "Polk's war." As President himself, Lincoln better understood what internal resistance had to be overcome to wage a war—especially one to carry out his belief that the Union could not be dissolved.

Scott read the later reports from the front in silence, and in immediate understanding of the source of the disaster. What had changed the nature of the battle was the presence of General Johnston's rebel force at Manassas, which should have been engaged at Winchester by General Patterson. That old Irishman had served with Scott in 1812 and in Mexico; he had always followed orders. Patterson had assured him that he would tie Johnston down. He had failed, and as a result McDowell faced combined rebel armies that had the advantage of a defensive position. When the green Union troops met resistance, they broke and ran.

"General Scott," Attorney General Bates asked, "does this mean that the capital is in danger?"

Lincoln sharpened the question. "To what degree is Washington in danger of capture?"

Scott did not want to contribute to their dismay, and pointed out that the reports did not show close pursuit by the rebels. "It may be that they are not fully aware we have abandoned the field."

"Can't you do something about rounding up the troops wandering through the streets," asked Montgomery Blair, "to mount some sort of defense? Can't we close the bridges and force our men coming back to stand and fight in Arlington? The ineptitude we have seen this afternoon seems to be continuing."

General Winfield Scott

The general glared at the man whose bad advice had pushed them into this mess and allowed as how he would order a general roundup of stragglers immediately. He looked around the group, expecting someone to remind the Postmaster General that the impetus for this ill-fated engagement came not from the old soldier who commanded the army, but from the young politician who ran the country.

Seward handled it obliquely. "The strategy the general preferred is well known to us, Montgomery. We all agreed that the political need of a sharp and decisive blow right away outweighed his purely military advice of caution."

But Blair pressed the point. "I, for one, would never have been in favor of any bold military advance if we had known that our army was no army at all, but a mob in fancy uniforms."

That triggered Scott's fury. He heaved forward in his chair to do rhetorical battle. Neither Blair nor Lincoln were going to make him, or his raw recruits, the goat of this disaster. The Scott recommendation after the secession was no secret: to let the seceding states go in peace, since an attack on interior lines in an age of defense was impractical. When that advice was spurned, Scott had made his military recommendation to win the war: to seize the forts along the Mississippi down to Memphis and then to New Orleans, to blockade the Atlantic ports, and thus to starve the South into submission.

This sound strategy had been ridiculed in the press as his "anaconda plan," after the snake that squeezed its victims to death, and was dismissed by impatient politicians as overly timid, but it was not his job to satisfy the "On to Richmond!" zealots. The task of the General-in-Chief, once the civilian authority had made its decision to fight, was to recommend the best way to win. When his judgment was set aside by the President, he had gone along with his superior officer's decision—and now was being accused of being the cause of the defeat.

"I must be the greatest coward in America," he said, startling them all. "Do you want to know why, Mr. Blair? Because I permitted this battle to be fought against my better judgment."

"Your bravery has never been at issue," Blair began to backtrack, but Scott plunged ahead, his patience at an end. Blair was his ostensible target, but what he had to say was intended for Lincoln.

"The President ought to remove me today for moral cowardice. As God is my judge, after my superiors had deemed it necessary to fight this battle, I did all in my power to carry out their orders. I deserve to be cashiered because I failed to stand up for what I believed to be true. I did not rise up and protest, when my army was obviously in no condition to fight, and resist the political pressure to the last."

He stared Blair down, then looked over to the man who had ordered the engagement on the grounds that the country needed the news of a victory to stir up its war spirit. Lincoln had a look of pain on his sallow face approaching desperation.

"You seem to imply, General Scott," the President was moved to say, "that I forced you to fight this battle."

The sight of the stricken visage of the President gave the general pause. The harried and uncertain Lincoln did not need to be pushed into accepting responsibility at this point; rather, the man was in terrible need of support. That placed Winfield Scott in a dilemma: he would have to choose between his public reputation and his self-respect. In order to exonerate himself, he would have to embarrass his commander in chief. At this moment, with the nation stunned and its capital in danger of falling, any further humiliation of the President would weaken the government and could well affect the outcome of the war.

Scott enjoyed his longtime hero's reputation. He was proud to be the only American other than George Washington to hold the rank of lieutenant general. His only defeat in life was political, when he ran for President as a Whig in 1852 as that party was nearing its final stage of disintegration. He had posed willingly, even eagerly, for that picture in Brady's studio, to be used as the model for the statue in Scott Square that would stand for centuries. He did not want anyone to hang a sign beneath that statue that read "Perpetrator of the Rout at Bull Run."

But he was first and last a soldier, and would go into retirement soon as a good soldier. "I have never served a president, Mr. Lincoln, who has been kinder to me than you have been." He hoped that would be enough to be taken as an assertion that he meant no imputation of blame to his commander. More would be an outright lie, since Scott had persuaded himself that he had indeed been forced to fight this battle.

"If there is a good possibility that the city will fall," said Chase, changing the subject to a more practical one, "I think we ought to concentrate on that. We have to get the gold out of here. We should think about evacuation."

Lincoln, the blame-laying past, was making notes on a pad. "General, what must be done now to defend the city?"

Scott focused on the immediate problem and knew exactly what had to be done. "Round up all available troops here in the city and send them to McDowell's support. Close the bridges across the Potomac, blow them up if necessary—no more retreat, the men can stay in the encampments they used in Virginia last week. Put Baltimore on the alert in case we have to fall back. Telegraph the recruiting stations of the nearest states to send all organized regiments to Washington."

Lincoln, nodding approval, made notes with his pencil. Scott reluctantly added a thought that he knew would have command consequences. The only Union general with any recent success was George McClellan, whose well-organized operations in the West, while not all that significant militarily, had made him the darling of the press and had helped Northern morale. "And order McClellan to come down to the Shenandoah Valley," Scott said, "with such troops as can be spared from western Virginia."

"I hear he's very good," said Chase. "They call him the young Napoleon."

That's the trouble with McClellan, Scott recalled. At thirty-five, he was young for major command; it occurred to Scott that he had been given departmental command at age twenty-eight, but that was in an era when the nation itself was new and experienced hands were few. In Mexico, George's troops always liked him, usually a good sign, but there was evidence of an unwillingness to take casualties. Had an unfortunate habit of appointing cronies to key positions; Burnside, a hack, found a place on his staff in civilian life. Scott forced himself to admit his chief concern about the man: McClellan was a born commander, and that type often tended to challenge the authority of any soldier above him.

Recognizing his own bias, Scott considered the qualities of the officer who would, in these circumstances, be hailed as the man of the hour and be subjected to the heady wine of national adulation. Second in his class at the Point. Good combat experience in Mexico. Creative mind for an engineer, invented a comfortable saddle the horsemen swore by and even the horses seemed to prefer. Good family man, having taken that girl away from Powell Hill in a long romantic struggle that was the talk of the officer corps. Most important, McClellan exuded success: bored by the peacetime army, he made a career in railroading, and was said to earn ten thousand dollars a year running the Illinois Central. Scott assumed McClellan had met Lincoln, too, who had been a lawyer for the railroad.

"What about McClellan, General?" asked Blair.

"Good organizer."

"Let's get him here, then," Blair said to Lincoln. "Put him in charge of organizing the defense of Washington. Tonight."

"Wait a second," Welles of the Navy, who seldom spoke, put in. "Is he the best?"

Seward cautioned, "He's a Democrat."

"But he's a Douglas Democrat," said Attorney General Bates. Scott prided himself on being above politics, at least ever since that unfortunate trouncing at the hands of Frank Pierce in the campaign of '52. But he knew the difference between a follower of the late Stephen Douglas, a Democrat who supported the war, and a follower of John Breckinridge, the Democrat who opposed it. Republicans in Congress were furious at the military commands going to Douglas war Democrats—three to one over Republicans, it was charged—but nothing infuriated them like the advancement of Breckinridge Democrats. Scott had approved John Dix, of Buchanan's Cabinet, to be the general in Baltimore, and Benjamin Butler of Massachusetts, another Breckinridge Democrat, to take charge of the vital post in Fortress Monroe. At least George McClellan had a history of being a Douglas Democrat.

"And he's too comfortable with pop sov," added Lincoln, who had campaigned against Douglas's popular-sovereignty argument on the extension of slavery into the territories, "but I need an organizer. Someone to stop the panic."

"Pity the best West Pointers went South," Blair observed. "Can't blame Robert Lee, I guess, he's a Virginian."

"I'm a Virginian too," General Scott said icily, remembering how he had offered the command of Union troops to Lee in Blair's parlor. "Lee could have done his duty to his country. That's why his country sent him to West Point."

Lincoln took a watch out of his pocket and flipped open the lid. "Let's meet again in a half hour over in the Mansion," he told the Cabinet members. "I'll be along directly." He remained with Scott after the others left. Alone, the President said to the general: "I appreciate that. What you said about my not forcing you into battle. You are a patriot."

"I have never evaded responsibility, sir."

"Well, I have and you just saw me. You and McDowell are going to have to stand a lot of gaff for a while, because I cannot afford to."

"I did not want to say this in front of the others, Mr. President, but I suspect that the rebels had our plans. Someone in a position of trust, perhaps even in the Cabinet, may have betrayed that trust."

Lincoln shook his head; that was evidently too hard to take, on top of unexpected defeat and the prospect of the loss of the capital. He walked to Scott's window and watched the group crossing the street. "Seward thinks he should be President. And yet if he had been, the Union would have been dissolved."

Scott frowned, and decided to be totally honest with the President young enough to be his son. "I, too, have favored peaceful separation. Neither the North nor the South has the power to conquer the other quickly, and the section defending its own territory has an enormous advantage. Your only hope is what they call the anaconda, slow strangulation by blockade, but I doubt that the North has the patience for that. It would take years."

Lincoln continued to watch the men walking off in the rain and Scott did not know if he had listened to the essence of his strategy. No time like now, in the shock of defeat, to make a major reassessment. But the President's thoughts seemed to be elsewhere: "Chase is despairing. Thinks he should be President, too, but he doesn't see the central idea. He's with the radicals, wants to strike at slavery where it exists."

"That is how to lose the war promptly," said Scott without doubt. On that point, political and military tactics intersected. If abolitionist rabble-rousing drove the slave states on the border into secession, the North would soon have to sue for peace.

Lincoln pointed to the receding back of the man Scott had warned him would be another way to lose the war. "What a mistake," he said about Simon Cameron. "Utterly ignorant, and obnoxious to the country. Incapable either of organizing details or conceiving and executing general plans. Is the Secretary of War a great trouble to you?"

"The military contracts go to his friends." General Scott did not want to learn much more about that subject, or to pass on what he did know to the President, who might be safer not knowing about low-level corruption. The general said only, "Cameron may be more trouble for your administration than for the army." Scott had taken to going to Chase at Treasury for many of the decisions about raising troops and financing the army that would ordinarily be in the purview of the Secretary of War.

"Bates is a fair lawyer," Lincoln said, needing to confide, which was not like him. "Caleb Smith is a cipher at Interior, I'm afraid, but Welles turned out to be surprisingly good at Navy."

"That leaves Montgomery Blair." Scott thought the Blairs were a dangerous family with all too much influence on the President.

"I like the judge. Admire his father, too—trust his political judgment more than anybody's. Father Blair goes clear back to Jackson, like you do." He veered off the subject. "Hasn't been a two-term President since Andy Jackson." He veered back. "The Blairs know how much I need Maryland and Missouri, and Kentucky. We lose Kentucky and the bottom is out of the tub."

Because the President had been sharing his most intimate judgments with him, Scott felt called upon to blurt out the truth: "What I said about being a coward, sir, was true. I should never have allowed you to go into this battle. I should have threatened to resign. That would have stopped you."

"I wish you had, General, but that's behind us." Lincoln dug his fingers in his hair and almost cried out the question, "What will the people say?" In a moment, he gave a kind of answer: "Sinners will call the righteous to repentance."

The President came back from the window and sat at Scott's desk, his pencil notes set before him. "Here is what I think we have to do. See what you think."

Scott thought that the young President's willingness to come back and confront his new difficulties offered some hope for his success. A leader had to be capable of rallying his own mental forces in the midst of confusion and despair.

"Let the forces late before Manassas," Lincoln said of the routed troops, "be reorganized as rapidly as possible in their camps here and about Arlington."

"Except the three-month men," Scott amended, "they're a bad influence on the others. If they won't sign for the duration, discharge them."

Lincoln nodded, making the change in his notes. "Let the force under Patterson—" He stopped, uncertain.

Scott finished the thought for him: "Patterson, or whoever we replace him with, maybe Banks, be strengthened and made secure in its position. We'll need Harpers Ferry."

The President nodded. "Let the volunteer forces at Fortress Monroe, under General Butler, be brought—"

Scott shook his head. "I don't know about Butler, he's one of your politician generals, and his men aren't ready to fight."

"Let them be constantly drilled, disciplined, and instructed," noted Lincoln, amending his order immediately. "Let Baltimore be held as now. Let the forces in western Virginia—" He looked up.

"Tell McClellan to tell them what to do, he'll be coming from there." Scott knew McClellan's recall to Washington was inevitable, because there was nobody else with his energy or experience or support in the press. McDowell was finished, at least for a while, and Scott could not ride a horse; Lincoln needed a man who could take charge in the field. The young man would want to take charge at headquarters as well, but that was tomorrow's worry.

"What else?" said Lincoln. "Blockade," he answered himself, jotting that down at the bottom.

"Let the plan for making the blockade effective be pushed forward with all possible dispatch," Scott dictated, adding, "Make that the first item."

Lincoln wrote that down, circled it, and drew an arrow to the top of the page. To show he understood the anaconda plan—now even Scott thought of his strategy in that term—the President added its Mississippi dimension: "Let General Frémont push forward in the West, giving rather special attention to Missouri. This done, a joint movement from Cairo down to Memphis, and from Cincinnati on East Tennessee."

Scott nodded; the President had finally adopted his strategy. Lincoln then pushed the general's inkwell and quill toward him. "Write out the order bringing McClellan here right away. I'll take it down to the telegraph office."

The general looked sternly at him: the President as messenger did not sit well. "Don't take on too many details," he advised, "they'll eat you up."

"The details are what count," Lincoln said grimly. "From now on, I want to know everything." That did not sit well with the general, either. Scott saw a President distrustful of his Cabinet colleagues, putting together a command structure with one man's strategy and another man as executor, trying to decide everything himself without being certain of himself.

As the one man who had carried the burden of military leadership from the years following the Revolution to this civil war, Scott felt he had much cause to worry about the man who would now have to shoulder that burden as well as the political weight. He knew that he could not remain in command of a long war, as this would have to be—his infirmities made that impossible—but the general did not know if Lincoln would be strong enough in execution of the vital details to sustain the strength of what he kept calling the "central idea." The only thing Lincoln was certain about was the absolute necessity of preserving the Union as it was, and Scott disagreed with his judgment on that.

Not good. The general hoped Lincoln would learn to delegate authority later, if the Northern public and the Southern forces gave him the time, and if men capable of handling the details appeared. At least the President would no longer be overconfident; give the shock of Bull Run credit for that. The President was a shaken man and was not through this crisis yet, but at least he gave signs of being shaken in the direction of becoming realistic, not of giving up.

In a strong hand, Scott wrote out the order commanding the "young Napoleon" to come to Washington immediately to undertake the defense of the capital. He handed it to the President, who thrust it inside his coat, grabbed his cape, and hurried out the door to what would surely be the longest night of his life.

CHAPTER 14

JOHN HAY'S DIARY
JULY 21 AND 22, 1861

July 21, 2 A.M.

Hasn't been a night like this in the President's house since the British put the place to the torch in 1812.

Anybody who takes the trouble to drop in tonight, any Sunday picnicker on the way back from the obliteration of our army, gets to see a President of the United States lying on the couch in his office. He won't let me close the door and the stream of irate visitors and told-you-soers is likely to last all night.

The parade began after the Cabinet left. That was a sad mess, with Blair and Chase at each other's throats, everybody looking for a scapegoat. After they went scuttling home in the rain, everybody and his brother came troop-ing in. Lincoln just lies there, stretched out, sick at heart, ready to see every-body who has a report of the battle, and that includes plain soldiers, bitter generals, the sightseers who took a picnic lunch to Bull Run, and the con-gressmen. Wade and Chandler were the worst.

"McDowell is useless," Wade snarled, "and that old windbag Winfield Scott is still fighting the Mexican War—you ought to sack him tonight."

"Who will lead the troops?" came the weary voice from the couch. I wish he would get up, or let me close the door.

"Anybody!"

"That'll do for you, but not for me. I must have somebody."

"McClellan, then," Chandler offered, in that slurred speech that comes either from liquor or a Michigan dialect, it's hard for me to tell which. "Young and vigorous. He's won some fights."

"You think he'll do?" he asked Wade, seemingly uncertain. That struck me as encouraging; we had already sent for McClellan, and Lincoln knew that Wade's radicals were distrustful of McClellan's Democratic connections and wishy-washy position on slavery. Even in his supine state, he was trying to get Wade committed to participation in the selection of the commanding general. That would make it harder for the senator to criticize for at least a week.

But Bluff Ben Wade would not take the bait. He stood there, looking down at Lincoln with something approaching contempt, the natural lines of his mouth making him look like a dog ready to go for the jugular.

Zachariah Chandler finally said what was on my mind. "You better snap out of it, Lincoln. You ought to go to that desk and write out an order to the states to enroll half a million men right now, at once."

Wade nodded his agreement and the President slowly rolled to a sitting position. "You have to show the country and the rebels that the government is not discouraged," Wade said.

"That you're just beginning to get mad," Chandler added.

General Scott arrived at that point, wheezing mightily from the walk up-stairs, and asked to see the President in private. The senators left. Credit them with getting Lincoln off his couch.

4 A.M., same night.

Dramatic episode involving the Hellcat. Mrs. Lincoln's stubbornness turns out to be of some value. General Scott walked Lincoln over to the oak Cabi-net table and sat him at the head, then put the latest cables from the War office in front of him. I stood with my back to the door, keeping it closed and the nocturnal visitors out.

"No organized army stands between the capital and the rebels," old Scott said. He said it calmly, seeming to gain dignity in defeat. "I want you to know —you need to know this—that this house is in danger of being taken by the enemy tomorrow."

Lincoln nodded, saying nothing.

"That would mean internment," the general went on, "assuming, as I do, that the Union would pursue the war from a new capital in Philadelphia or New York. Internment of the President would be a fresh defeat, and could affect the outcome of the war. You could consider—"

"I'm staying here," said Lincoln. If he were captured and interned, it would be possible for an infuriated North to fight on; but if the Prsdt were to leave the capital and it did not fall, he would be the laughingstock of the nation.

He had already been made to look the fool when he first came to Washington from Illinois to take the oath of office. Pinkerton, the detective for the railroad, claimed to have discovered an assassination plot. They slipped Lincoln into the nation's capital wearing a felt hat with the brim over his eyes and his coat collar turned up. The entire episode was ludicrous, and a stupidly coded telegram from Pinkerton made it worse. Lincoln likes to be considered an informal man, plain of speech and dress, but he is fierce about presidential dignity. I knew there would be no running out of town, not unless the rebels were banging on the front door of the Mansion, and maybe not then.

"I recommend, sir," Scott said formally, accepting his previous decision without question, "that you let me evacuate Mrs. Lincoln and your sons."

Lincoln thought about that. Neither Scott nor I said anything. I knew that Mrs. L., with her chronic headaches and her sometimes really unsettled mind, would not take military confinement well. Robert, the oldest boy, on the remote side, would be all right; Tad was sickly; Willie, the apple of the Prsdt's eye, would make life in prison more bearable for the family. Hard choice.

"The decision is Mrs. Lincoln's to make," the Prsdt said finally. "Fetch her, will you, John?"

Luckily, Lizzie Keckley, the negro modiste who works for the Hellcat, was sitting there in the hallway in case she could be useful on this terrible night. She's a good egg, and not a sneak about information or a petty thief like some of the staff that madam has befriended. Lizzie is a handsome, statuesque freedwoman, curiously self-assured, who made the ballgowns for half the famous ladies in Washington. She can handle the President's wife even in her worst rages, or when she is weirdly afflicted by the specter of ultimate poverty. I sent Lizzie to fetch Mrs. Lincoln.

Who, to my amazement, turned in a finer moment than anybody who knew her would have expected. The lady is not my favorite person, and to my mind that marriage is the worst personal mistake the Tycoon ever made. My Uncle Milton in Springfield, who has known them both well for years, says he is "an old poke-easy" who has been relentlessly "henpecked." Her jealousy of other women, totally unwarranted so far as I can see, and her testiness are a great burden to her already burdened husband; her Southern relationships are a source of attack from his critics who claim she's a secret rebel sympathizer. On this night, however, as she stood in her nightdress and robe in the doorway, I could find no fault with her conduct.

"Mother," the President said, (why must he always call her that?) "General Scott here thinks you and the boys would be safer for the next few weeks out of the capital."

"Long Branch, in New Jersey," I suggested, to take the sting out of the evacuation. That is the fashionable watering place—racing, gambling, the baths—surpassing Newport and Saratoga in the gossip of Washingtonians, and I knew the Hellcat wanted to visit it. Frankly, so do I, and will as soon as the current unpleasantness passes.

"The family should stay together at a time like this," she said without a second thought. She looked more serene and supporting, in her plain face and robe and slippers, than she usually did in her rouge and powders and insistent décolletage.

"If the President is imprisoned," Scott said, putting it straight, "he might have more peace of mind knowing that his family is safe and free."

"You do not know my husband, General. His family is a source of strength to him, as he is to us."

The Tycoon smiled for the first time this awful night. "That's your answer, General Scott. Good night, Mother. Look in on Willie if you can; all the noise may be keeping him up."

"You're not coming to sleep?"

"I'll see." He guided her to the door, passed her on to me, and I passed her on to Lizzie Keckley. The night's only good moment had come and gone; after Scott left, the stream of angry and puzzled visitors went on and on.

6 A.M.
I am exhausted and fear we have lost the war. The Prsdt has not slept and is standing at the window looking out at Pennsylvania Avenue and the Parade.

A rain-soaked mob is staggering down the street, eastward, away from the rebels, half in uniform and half not. That is our army, salvation of the Union, home from Manassas and not an army anymore. The avenue is a slow river of mud, and from where we look, the soldiers in the early light seem like wooden figures in a logjam. Lincoln is sighing deeply and often, as if he cannot get enough air in his lungs. Now the day begins that may end in the surrender of this house for the second time in our history.

July 22, 6:30 P.M.
Wrong about the last night's final entry. Mustn't let myself get so glum. The rebels are still just over the river, but they have not moved against us to follow up their victory. Scott says they're just as green as our men, and General Beauregard cannot be certain that we are defenseless. God knows, there are plenty of Union soldiers around Washington, mainly in the bars or sitting in the streets getting drunk. General McClellan is on the scene at last, and I must say looks like a general, commanding presence and all, riding about with his twenty-man escort, shouting orders and putting up a good front.

Horace Greeley, he of the "On to Richmond!" headlines, sent a letter to the Tycoon after the Bull Run disaster. Lincoln opened it before I could, then tucked it away in his Greeley cubbyhole, but I saw it anyhow.

"If the Union is irrevocably gone," writes the intrepid Uncle Horace, "an armistice ought at once to be proposed. I do not consider myself at present a judge of anything but the public sentiment. That seems to be everywhere deepening against further prosecution of the war."

Can you imagine? That pusillanimous outpouring comes from the guiding spirit of the radical cause, the beacon of the Jacobins hooraying for abolition. In one quick battle, he has gone from On-to-Richmond to On-to-surrender.

The Ancient knows what power Greeley of the *Tribune* holds in the formation of Northern public sentiment and he is sick at heart about that lily-livered letter. He is well off the couch and out of his yesterday's daze, however, and has asked for books on military strategy. General Scott sent over the book by General Henry Halleck: "Old Fuss and Feathers" evidently likes the work of "Old Brains." (Why are so many generals bedecked with sobriquets beginning with "Old"? At least McClellan is the "Young" Napoleon.)

Lincoln had a curious reaction to Horace Greeley's spinelessness. After his loss of faith in his field generals as well as in his own political-military judgment, that craven abandonment by the editor who was abolition's chief proponent seemed to be the last straw. Instead of collapsing into despair, as I was fully prepared to do, the Ancient perked up and counted his blessings.

The rebel army had not advanced into the capital, as it so easily could have done, which meant that the other side had its lapses of judgment too. And the defeat at Bull Run decisively awakened the North with more of a stinging slap than a stunning blow. Not everyone fell apart like Greeley and read the public mood as panic-stricken. Many of the Republicans got mad, just as Wade and Chandler did, and they led the call for 400,000 "duration" troops. That was more than the "three hundred thousand more" that Lincoln had asked for in story and song, so he cheered up.

"Cheered" is not quite the right word. He is not a cheerful person. He is a congenitally melancholy person who looks for reasons to smile occasionally. I am the one who has cheered up.

The Tycoon is determined to see the war through, even if it takes to the end of the year. I am with him all the way, even when the duty is onerous, as when I missed the chance to meet Kate Chase at the Blair party, or more accurately the Blair wake, last night after Bull Run. My chance will come.

CHAPTER 15

THE PRESIDENT'S BEST FRIEND

She even slept independently. Most women, in his experience, slept in constant contact with him, no matter what size the bed. They would wriggle their behinds into his midsection or, if his back was turned, would make a chair with their knees and fit themselves against him. He did not mind that, unless the night was oppressively hot, which this night was not; in fact, Breckinridge rather liked having the need for his physical presence shown by his partner in the bed.

Anna Carroll, however, most often slept face up, arms at her sides, as if at attention on the hard mattress. When she was sleeping deeply, her face seemed to shed twenty years. He liked to study her in that horizontal profile: perfect nose, long eyelashes, sensuous lower lip, the long red hair covering her naked shoulders. When she went to bed worried, he had noted, the supine-attention stance was abandoned. Then she lay on her stomach, fighting the pillow until it found a niche between her substantial breasts and the tip of her chin. Her head hung forward over the pillow, a frown on her face, an occasional blurred word barked in her sleep.

At no time in either position did the unconscious Anna seek physical contact; unlike most of the women he had known, she was no snuggler. In fact, in the first year he knew her, she would instinctively draw away when he touched her. That had changed this year; he could touch her anywhere in sleep now, and she would sleepily return the pressure. If that did not lead to intercourse—which it usually did, and at greater length and intensity than with any woman he had ever known—she would return to her deep-sleep posture of horizontal attention or worried pillow-wrestling. She had become accessible, in body and mind, welcoming without searching. He had never told her how much he appreciated that, assuming she would prefer not to be watched in her sleep.

He slid the sheet down to look at her in the pulsing light of the gas lamp outside and just below her corner rooms at Ebbitt House. Nose and toes straight up, ankles together, breasts spilling toward her arms, hands at her sides, skin luminescent; for a woman who relied on animation and wit for her attractiveness, she was more beautiful in repose than she knew. Breck had not realized before how necessary it was for him to have her close, hands meshing and minds lightly touching, at such a critical moment in his life. For the past month, he had been standing almost alone for the preservation of the rights in the Constitution against men who claimed to stand for the preservation of a sundered Union. The next day, in the Senate, one grim week after the first awakening bloodshed, he would probe further into the cause of the war. He would frame the issue of what lay behind what seemed to him Lincoln's implacable belligerence.

It would have been hard to face this night-before alone. Colonel Ned Baker's troops at Bladensburg, earlier that evening, had jeered at him cruelly; he had managed to turn that around with a politician's trick, but found it troubling that the booing came from good men, patriotic Americans, whose deep resentment of his flirtation with reason probably presaged the response from the Senate gallery tomorrow.

Cool air stirred the thin window drapery and Anna pulled the sheet back to cover her legs. He eased his long body out of bed—a hard bed, because she had come to the uncomfortable belief that resilient mattreses were bad for the back—and sat on the arm of the armchair near the window facing west. The Executive Mansion's white walls struck him as splendid in the half-moon's light. Not a year ago, as part of "Buck and Breck," he had been a breath away from residence in that house. He had taken pride in the presidential palace then, and looked proudly on it now—not three blocks from Anna's window—wondering if Lincoln was having trouble sleeping that night. He judged, from his brief visit only six hours before, that the President of a nation at war had finally found some means of repose.

He had never seen Lincoln more relaxed. Breckinridge had to smile at the picture etched in his memory that afternoon of Ned Baker, flat on his back, head cushioned by his rolled-up uniform jacket, with his feet up against the trunk of the great magnolia tree on the long lawn northeast of the President's house. Lincoln had been sitting on the grass with his back against the same tree, in a shirt with the tie untied and the collar open, jacket folded neatly next to him, shoes unlaced. With his huge feet drawn back, Lincoln's knees were at his eye level; he balanced his tall hat on his knees as he passed the time of day with a good friend. His son Willie, born long after the child christened Edward Baker Lincoln had died, was kicking a ball nearby. A pleasant and peaceful sight on a late afternoon in midsummer, only a week after the capital had come so close to capture and the United States to military humiliation.

The Kentuckian had handed his horse's reins to the stolid Marshal Lamon, who was minding the mounts about fifty yards from the tree, and walked to the two men. Half in jest, Breck asked if they were plotting a dictatorship. Lincoln scowled at that but Baker smiled.

"Dictator is what the country needs," Baker said, rearranging his feet on the tree trunk, "with men like you in the Senate. You know what this big galunk did last week, Lincoln? He blocked Senate approval of your right to suspend habeas corpus."

"They approved everything else," Breckinridge remembered having replied, "blockade, calling up the troops, waging war, all the illegal spending." The Senate would have gone along with Lincoln's seizure of its power to make wartime arbitrary arrests, but the senators paused when Breckinridge reminded them that it was their own constitutionally given power they would be handing over forever. Protecting the institutional powers of the Senate had more of an appeal as an argument than any appeal to individual liberty, so the use of habeas corpus was left out of the resolution of approval of all Lincoln's warring acts. No outright disapproval, of course, and the President could continue to use his despotic power, but the argument about who held the power was postponed until the emergency was over. A small victory, but enough to give Breckinridge some hope that his continued presence in the Senate would do the Republic some good.

"Lucky they did," Baker yawned, picking up and pulling a long piece of leather near Lincoln's coat to change the subject. "This a new whip crack?"

"Cost a quarter at the harness maker's," Lincoln said. "Take it if you need one, Ned."

"I will." Baker pulled his feet back, rolled, grunted as he rose. He smacked the whip against his boot, satisfied with the sound. "I invited Breck to see my regiment in Bladensburg, have dinner out there tonight. Want some tips on training from an old Mexican War veteran."

"I was an army lawyer in Mexico," Breckinridge confessed. "You were the 'hero of Cerro Gordo.'" The Kentuckian remembered that episode as a foolish and potentially costly assault uphill against a fort, but carried by Colonel Baker with help of a couple of junior officers, a Captain Lee and Lieutenant Grant. A famous victory, but in retrospect it was clear that Baker and his inexperienced commanders took too great a chance of major defeat.

"Least you weren't in Congress, Breck, giving the President a hard time about fighting a war of conquest on some false pretext." Baker smiled. Lincoln merely winced. Breck knew that few others could make the painful reference to Congressman Lincoln's opposition to President Polk's war without drawing the ire of the present warring President. Evidently Baker was supremely secure in his friendship with Lincoln; Breck hoped Lincoln was not wholly influenced by the passion of his friend to conquer and punish the South. "Subjugate" was the word Baker took a perverse delight in using.

They bade farewell to the President, who did not rise from his post at the tree trunk, and left him massaging his aching feet in the shade. On the road to the Maryland town where the California and Oregon troops were billeted, Baker made no effort to argue his guest out of strongly held views. Breck liked that about the combined senator and colonel. Baker had one of those departmented minds that had a place for political argument, which was the floor of the Senate, and a place for personal talk, which was at the base of a tree or a ride out to his regiment.

Ned Baker was Lincoln's age, a decade older than Breckinridge. Thinning gray hair brought him the sobriquet of the "Gray Eagle," but Baker exuded an ingratiating optimism that seemed to the Kentuckian to belong to a much younger man. Perhaps that inclination of Baker's to see life in primary colors, rejecting the grays of moral issues, had to do with his decision in middle life to become a Far Westerner, moving from Illinois to represent the Oregon pioneers, ultimately opening a law practice in San Francisco. If any man could be said to "run" most of the west coast of the continent, that man was Senator Edward Baker. Certainly his influence and vigorous campaigning had much to do with swinging Oregon away from Breckinridge to Lincoln in the 1860 campaign.

Breck saw some of his own proudest characteristics in Baker: informal to all, convivial with a few, and, above all, loyal to those who had shown loyalty to him. As Breck was faithful to the Constitution, Baker's fidelity ran to the Union and to his friends, especially his friend Lincoln. Breck assumed Baker would do anything for Lincoln, and grant him any power he needed, because he trusted the President he knew so well to use even the wrong means to pursue the right ends. The Kentuckian could understand that sense of loyalty in a friend, but had often tried to make Baker see that a President was more than a man—he was one of a line of men that could one day include a tyrant. Evil means, used with good intent, had an insidious way of corrupting the best of ends.

"I should tell you I'm making a long speech in the Senate tomorrow, Ned," he called to the horseman on his left.

"Despotism again? That dog won't hunt. Lincoln doesn't want to be dictator, he wants to get re-elected."

"Purposes of the war. Need to stop it now. And your goal of 'subjugation.' " And much more; Breck suspected that the loss at Bull Run had made Lincoln a captive of Wade and Chase, the outraged radical wing of his party, who were now pushing him into a war for abolitionism, against all his promises. If this suspicion was well founded, then Lincoln, under the rubric of Union, was secretly plotting abolition, which to Breck meant not only permanent disunion, but two hostile powers on the same continent.

"I'll be there this time," his companion had said. "Just try me on subjugation of the rebels." Baker, Breck knew, blamed himself for not being present when the Senate was talked out of approving Lincoln's use of arbitrary arrest. Breck wanted him there this time. Ned Baker was widely known to be Lincoln's man in the Senate; moreover, the fiercely honest Far Westerner would hold nothing back in arguing Lincoln's side. Perhaps he would modify or

even change Breck's views on some points; that was a point of pride in the
Kentuckian, that he could make concessions in debate when the other debater
had a better argument. Breckinridge dearly wanted reasons to stay in the
Senate, to believe that his presence saved that body from the excesses of war
fever. The thought of renouncing the Constitution, as Jefferson Davis and the
others did, was more repugnant to Breckinridge than any sacrilege. Let the
radical Republicans say he was heading South; Breckinridge planned to stand
rooted in his place in the United States Senate as long as a majority of
Kentuckians, or at least enough Kentuckians, went along with his view of a
need for a third force in the divided nation.

"I'll be there," Baker repeated, "but don't get on your feet too early. I have
to inspect and drill the troops in the morning."

"McClellan makes a big point of that, I hear."

"He's just a boy, like you, likes parades." They rode a bit, and Baker
added, "Beware a general who's crazy in love with his wife, it makes him
cautious. About tomorrow—as soon as I get to the Senate, Breck, I'll rip your
speech to shreds. Then I'll give you a few minutes for rebuttal, because I feel
sorry for a loner."

They reached camp in Bladensburg in time for the retreat ceremony. With
the sixteen hundred men of his regiment drawn up in front of the flagpole,
Colonel Baker announced with some pride "a distinguished visitor, our former Vice President and now the senator from Kentucky, John Cabell Breckinridge."

A loud groan went up from the ranks, followed by booing and catcalls. The
men had read the newspapers, and knew John Breckinridge to be the one who
led the Senate opposition to the war. Breck, stung, showed no emotion, murmuring only "Not many votes in this crowd" to Baker, who was red-faced at
the rude reception.

"Captain," Colonel Baker ordered in a ringing voice, "you will apologize
on behalf of the officers of the California regiment for this insulting behavior
to a guest."

A captain rode up, snapped a salute, and expressed his regret. Baker called
for the sergeant major, who did a better job: "Senator Breckinridge, on behalf
of the noncommissioned officers, I want to apologize for this breach of discipline, and assure you the regiment will be punished for this discourtesy to a
guest of the colonel."

Breck turned to Baker and used a bit of tradition that always made a hit
with the cadets at West Point. "Do you offer guests the privilege of amnesty?"

Baker, suppressing a smile, nodded.

"Then I request that the infraction be forgiven forthwith," said the visitor
solemnly, "and that soldiers under restriction for other minor offenses be
relieved of such restriction."

"Granted," snapped Baker loudly, adding under his breath, "You should
have been in politics."

The sergeant major led three cheers for the visiting senator, and ranks were
broken for dinner. After sunset, Baker broke out the best Tennessee corn
whiskey and the two men told stories of Lincoln's days in Congress opposing
Polk's Mexican War. Breck counseled his host to choose soon between the
army and the Senate, because a straddle would diminish his capacity to fight

and some—Breckinridge among them—would object to a military uniform on the floor of the Senate. Baker confided that a concern for that problem led him to turn down a general's commission; as an officer of lesser rank, he thought, he could remain in the Senate to support Lincoln during this crucial session. After it ended, he would stop straddling. He had made the decision to resign from the Senate to fight the war, and Lincoln would soon make him a major general of volunteers. He would be the President's trusted man in the army; if the war lasted until the next year, as Breck expected, and if McClellan fell short of expectations or proved to be politically unsound, Baker would be a good bet for a high command.

Breck rode back from Bladensburg to Washington alone, wondering how such a good politician and soldier, with such a keen lawyer's mind, could be so monumentally wrong about the burning issue of his time.

How could he seriously believe that one half of a country could conquer and subjugate the other half, and still maintain the pretence of being a democracy? Wasn't it all predicated on the consent of the governed? Even if conquest were possible, what sort of country would emerge, half oppressive occupier and half embittered occupied? Didn't Baker see the quagmire ahead, and the certain failure even if his most bloody-minded hopes of crushing conquest were realized? When Baker talked of subjugation, he reminded Breck of Rose Greenhow: both partizans refused to see that the survival of democracy in such a nation would be impossible.

Breck pushed the question further: did Baker speak for Lincoln? Where the President was cagey, Baker was forthright; where Lincoln kept his counsel and balanced his support, Baker made no bones about the object of the war. The Kentuckian suspected that the two best friends saw eye to eye, which offered the bleakest of prospects.

Breck's horse delivered him to his dark home near the Capitol, but he could not make himself go inside. Instead, he had directed the animal toward Ebbitt House and Anna.

The possibility that she might not be alone had not occurred to him until he was halfway up the stairs. He stopped, considered the chances that she had another guest, thought of the embarrassment and awkwardness of such a moment, and then continued his climb. There was no way of sending a note ahead. He would take for granted that she slept alone when he was otherwise engaged, though she had never made any such commitment to him. If another man was there, the politician in Breckinridge would think of something to say; he would be walking more of a tightrope in the Senate the next day, and he needed to be with the only person who knew fully what was going on in his mind. As he approached her hallway door, he found himself biting down on the toothache in his mind of her possible infidelity, if it could be called that. The married Breckinridge reminded himself that it could not.

She had been working on a pamphlet and the delight on her face at his surprise visit had warmed him. Now—seated on the arm of the chair at the window, looking past the Mansion toward the Potomac and the battle lines—he savored the recollection of the way she gulped down the news of his moment with Lincoln and evening with Baker.

A Reply to Breckinridge was the title of the pamphlet she had been working on, which struck him as a little presumptuous, playing as it did on Daniel Webster's immortal *Reply to Hayne*, when those giants of Massachusetts and South Carolina had addressed today's issue in their own time. However, as the only pamphleteer who fully understood the import of his attack on the war power of the President, and as the only woman he knew with a grasp of the ideas embodied in the Constitution, Anna was entitled to some degree of presumption.

Before the lovemaking, as she turned down the light she had warned him against getting hot under the collar in debate the next day, because every word he said was being taken down and could be used in expulsion proceedings against him. Debates, especially vigorous sallies against men whose opinion you respect, did suck a speaker into saying more than he planned. He was determined that that would not be the case with him tomorrow. He hoped Ned Baker would commit some degree of excess, giving him the opening he needed to expose the iron fist of conquest in Lincoln's velvet glove. At the same time, he hoped Ned's passion would not take him to the point of personal political threats. That would be a source of trouble. Not everybody realized that personal friendship could survive political enmity, or that mutual respect in debate could make civilized discourse possible even in the most barbaric of times. Baker had the power, as no other senator did, to fan into a blaze the resentments that smoldered around Breckinridge; the Kentuckian hoped his opponent would not assume that his colleagues would be as filled with the spirit of comity after intellectual combat as Baker was himself.

The east wall of the Mansion was picking up the first light. It had been James Madison's notion to paint the dull sandstone of the Mansion a brilliant white, in the reconstruction of the President's house after the British had burned it in the War of 1812. Breck put that down as a good idea: the white house seemed to awaken the neighborhood in the dawn. White suggested purity and honor, he mused, as well as cold and death; the Roman senators wore white togas, and the Roman legions laid white lilies on soldiers' graves. He allowed his mind to dwell on such morbid thoughts for a time, then broke off abruptly as Anna stirred beneath her sheet. He thought then of the moral compromises he had so readily made to open the way to this unique love, and of the political compromises he was finding it so difficult to make to become again a contender for the white Mansion across the way. His conscience was becoming dangerously selective. It occurred to him, as the sun's rays struck the President's house and the city sounds rose, that a little less fervor and a little more caution would be the best course in debating the President's best friend on the subject of constitutional compromises needed to put down an armed rebellion.

Senator Edward Dickinson Baker

CHAPTER 16

I HAVE READ WITH PAIN

Anna loosened her hold on the pillow underneath her and reached out for Breck. He wasn't there. She could have sworn that he had come to her late in the night. It was not like her to have those dreams of a phantom presence in an empty bed; she had long ago come to terms with the single life. A woman had to stand in her own shoes and not be dependent on a man's help in life or his form next to her through the night.

She arched her back and twisted her head around. Breck was seated by the window, in the bathrobe she had given him to leave in her rooms, reading in the morning light the draft of her latest pamphlet, the one Attorney General Bates had asked her to write, *A Reply to Breckinridge.*

This was the first time in all the nights they had spent together—at least twice a week for nearly a year, excepting his visits to Kentucky—that he had risen first. She returned to the pillow and lay still, turning that thought over. Sex in the morning enervated her, ruining the morning for work, and the morning was when she did her best writing; that was why she always rose first, meeting his outstretched hand with a mug of coffee and giving him a smiling face that did not betray too many of the wrinkles of a woman on the far side of forty. Except when he was drinking, Breck was always ready when it came to sex—always respectful, but always ready, night and morning—and she liked to complain that he needed a younger woman. They both knew he already had a younger woman, his wife at home in Lexington, and Anna suspected that he had the worship and perhaps companionship of Lizzie Blair, also in her mid-thirties. She also wondered about Breck and Rose Greenhow, who was her age, but would never ask him about other women, because she had made the point to Breck that neither had any claim on the other. Still, he had shown up unannounced last night, as if he assumed she would be sleeping alone. That was true, and she was glad he made that assumption, although it would be a mistake to compromise her independence by confirming it verbally.

Why his sudden visit, and why the early awakening this morning? He must have been lonely and worried. Anna slipped out of bed, jammed her feet into slippers, hunched into her robe and, without saying good morning, hurried down the hall. First to the water closet, then the washroom, then the hotel kitchen for a tray of cakes and coffee. She took a small pot and enough cake for one, because she did not want talk among the kitchen help; her reputation as a stern and virtuous maiden lady was important to her.

" 'I have read with pain,' " he read aloud when she returned, " 'the speech of the Honorable John C. Breckinridge, and now I see him descending from his high position as a senator and come to Maryland for the purpose of stimulating and strengthening the Confederate rebellion.' "

"I'm surprised you can read my handwriting," she said, ashamed of her masculine scrawl, pleased that he was studying her work.

"You write like you make love," he said, and did not elaborate. She would be damned if she would ask what he meant by that. That she wrote and made love at great length, or oblivious to any distraction, or with great satisfaction, blazing climaxes, and no pecuniary benefit? All true, but that subject was not for light banter; to Anna, lovemaking was something to do with a full heart and the gaslight on, and near a large mirror if the man was so inclined, but never to talk about; it was one thing to be free, quite another to be brazen.

"Did you get to the Jefferson citation? That was hard to find, Breck, but it was meant for you."

He nodded, poked through the pages on the table, and read aloud: " 'To lose our country by a scrupulous adherence to written law would be to lose the law itself . . . thus absurdly sacrificing the end to the means.' Good quote, but I'd have to see the context. And it doesn't answer my argument, Anna. I'm not a stickler for the letter of the law. I want Lincoln to adhere to the spirit of the Constitution. George Washington conducted the Revolution of the thirteen colonies without martial law."

"You don't know what you're talking about," she told the senator from Kentucky. "He ordered the Tory prisoners held in New York, including the mayor, removed to Connecticut—no trial, no hearing. There was nothing but martial law all during the Revolution."

He shook his head. "Never like this. Never closing down newspapers who dare to criticize. Never ignoring the courts, seizing property nowhere near a war zone. All this is what we conducted the Revolution against."

She felt the bile of hot argument rise in her throat and fought it down. There was a time to argue with this man and a time to find out what was troubling him. He did not come to her last night, as he had on other nights, to use her mind for a sharpening stone and her body for release. He needed something else, something that he had never sought from her before. She was eager to give him what he needed, as he had so often given her, if she could figure out what it was.

She stabbed in the dark: "Everything all right at home?"

He took several deep breaths and said, "My son Cabell, the sixteen-year-old. He's run away. Mary thinks he went South and joined the rebel army."

Anna could think of nothing to say. She had met young Cabell on the day the electoral votes were counted and his father, as president of the Senate, had officially declared Lincoln the victor. Despite the divisive campaign and the dividing Union, the executive power had passed in dignity, with no rancor. Uncle Bob had introduced her to his grandnephew in the gallery and the boy had impressed her as the sort of son she would have liked to have: sturdy, thoughtful, potentially rebellious. She had pressed his hand and hurried on, not wanting to meet the rest of the Breckinridge family.

Breck shook his head, as if to get out of his mind the picture of his son in uniform, carrying a musket. "I've been against the war in principle," he said, "but there's something about having your child in the line of fire that lends a certain urgency to the position."

"Will they use that against you in the Senate, evidence of rebel sympathy?"

He did not seem to care. "I had dinner with Ned Baker last night. We're going to have at each other today in the Senate."

That was why he had come. Anna knew Senator Edward Baker to be one of the best debaters in that body, a passionate and sometimes savage orator, faster on his feet in debate and far more eloquent than Ben Wade or any of the other radical Republicans. Baker was master of the art of the cutting question, and would stack his questions, shortening them as he went on, until the audience could not bear the tension. She admired that technique, and knew that his reputation as a fighting officer added to his stature as a political speaker. The "Gray Eagle" knew how to soar and when to swoop. Anna suspected that Breck was troubled by the prospect of doing rhetorical battle with him and would not admit it to himself.

"You know, Breck, opposing the war is like beating a dead horse. Peace is that dead horse, and there's nothing you can say to bring it to life. It only makes you sound—" She avoided words like "traitorous" or "treasonable" and chose "unpatriotic."

"One man could stop this war overnight," he replied. "Lincoln tries to make us believe it wasn't his decision to bring on the war. 'In your hands, my dissatisfied fellow citizens,' " he mimicked, " 'and not in mine, is the decision of peace or war.' What a lie. He knows the South wants only to depart in peace. Lincoln's advisers all told him that peaceful separation was preferable to a war that will create hatred on this continent for a century. Isn't that true, Anna? You know them. That's a fact, isn't it?"

She nodded. Only Blair, of all the Cabinet, had backed Lincoln's decision for war. She did not add that Tom Scott in the War Department had told her that Winfield Scott himself had made it clear to Lincoln that an invasion of the South would not be successful. On that point, Breck was right: had it not been for one man, the stubborn A. Lincoln, the war would not have come. Two nations would exist, one slave, one free.

"That's no longer the question," she replied obliquely. "The war is here. Bull Run has been fought, the South won, and the capital in Washington did not fall. Now you have to choose sides." She said that gently, she hoped, not argumentatively.

"Peace is still a side," he replied, shaking his head, "and that is the side I am on. Lincoln once said the nation could not exist half slave and half free, and he believes that, no matter what he says now about not striking at slavery where it exists. I believe that no nation can exist half victor and half vanquished."

That sort of talk, at this stage, was going to get him in trouble. After the loss at Bull Run, the senators would not take kindly to any position that smacked of cowardice or disloyalty. She wanted him to restrain himself, to stop well short of giving his political opponents the ammunition to disgrace or arrest him.

"That's a powerful line for a debate, Breck, and I know there's principle in your position, but you're going to be President of these United States one day. Probably three years from now, when the war is just a memory. There is no doubt in your mind who is going to win the war, is there?"

"The Union outnumbers the Confederacy two to one," he said without hesitation, "and has all the industrial resources. If the people don't get weary of bloodshed, the North should win. But Anna—such a United States will be a hate-filled nation, without liberty in the North, and denying liberty to the South it subjugates."

"You're making that speech again," she said evenly.

"I said something like that in the Senate," he admitted. "Baker is vulnerable on 'subjugation.' It's a word he's used often, and it goes too far."

She decided he needed a shock. "Breck, are you thinking of going over to the rebels? Joining your son?"

"Of course not. I'm going to keep Kentucky neutral."

"People are saying that your plan is to go South. They say you're staying in the Senate as long as you can obstruct the war, and then you'll take a place in Jeff Davis's Cabinet."

"They say that because they can't stand to listen to the truth. They want blood, and they want to believe that anybody who doesn't want blood is a traitor."

"Breck, you know I love you, and I have your best interests at heart." She had never mentioned to him or to herself that she loved him, which she realized was true, and she just threw it out in passing. "You're a politician, and you have to be practical. Let's examine the possibilities." She ticked them off. "If you do go South—I know, but let's just assume that you talk yourself into it—and the state of Kentucky doesn't follow you, then your career is finished no matter who wins the war."

He nodded agreement, adding, "The senators in the seceded states would at least be honored at home, if the South loses. I would be a pariah at home and a traitor in the North." He obviously had done some thinking along those lines.

"Will Kentucky go South?" she asked, knowing the answer was no.

"Kentuckians will split, like the Breckinridge family. Brother against brother, son against father. The state won't leave the Union unless Lincoln tries to free the slaves."

"Which I have heard him say a dozen times he would not do," she added. "So Kentucky stays in. Let's assume you stay in with your state, and you lay low in the Senate. You can be the conscience at times, and do your duty as you see it on habeas corpus, but by and large show your loyalty to the Constitution, and smite the radicals like my friend Ben Wade when they try to turn this into a war for abolition."

"That is what all my friends in the Senate suggest, Anna. John Forney has told me that a hundred times. What then? What about the rivers of blood that nobody raised a hand to stop?"

She knew Forney, a Pennsylvania newspaperman who badgered Simon Cameron into getting him the juicy plum of Secretary of the Senate. Sharp mind, good soul, excellent connections, but a drunkard. He was not a good influence on Breck, who could hold his whiskey with any man, but no ordinary hard drinker could hold his own with an experienced drunk.

"Here is what then," she said. "No war lasts forever. This war may drag on for a year, and neither side will be the winner. The South will be exhausted, no shoes for the soldiers. In the North, nobody, especially not Lincoln, is going to hold together the Douglas Democrats, the Breckinridge Democrats, the radical Republicans, and the conservative Republicans. I mean, it just cannot happen. That's the moment for a peacemaker."

"You think the nation must 'lay me down and bleed awhile.' "

"Lincoln was born in Kentucky," she said. "Jeff Davis was born in Kentucky. More than any part of the country, more than my Maryland even, that state is half North and half South, half slave and half free. When the moment comes for peacemaking, you're from the state that understands, the home of Henry Clay, the great conciliator. And the man who makes the peace will be the next President."

She drew herself to her full height, certain she was right. She would never have this man as husband, but she would have him in more important ways: political partner, conspirator, sharer of power. She could help him in ways that suited her experience. She had helped Millard Fillmore by enlisting the legions of Know-Nothings in his cause, only to be disappointed by that pusillanimous ingrate. She had provided political support to "Buck" Buchanan, until that confirmed bachelor withdrew behind the palisades of power. Breck was more secure as a man and as a politician than either of those presidents, and indeed had attacked her Know-Nothing crowd at its zenith, when even Lincoln was being cautious about offending the powerful "Sams." Anna wanted to be there when he made it to the top, and she was certain that this time, this once, she would not be disappointed. She was so tired of dealing with men in power's place who changed radically from the same men on power's path.

"I have a lot to think about," Breck said, riffling the pages of her pamphlet, not committing himself to discretion. "I see you kept all the family secrets to yourself."

Anna nodded solemnly. He referred to the notes and letters in her possession of many of the Southern leaders, who had been plotting secession for more than a dozen years. As a power in the Native American Party, she was privy to many of the secession movement secrets, but had taken care to keep a certain distance, never to expose herself as a member of any conspiracy. She could write some stunning revelations of a decade of treasonable conspiracy if she chose to, but this was not the time, and she did not want to embitter her *Reply to Breckinridge* with suggestions of treason. With proper bounds, their disagreement would serve them both well, and certainly remove any suspicion about their relationship.

"You're going to walk to the Hill, so you can think about ways to stop the sedition bill without coming out for secession?" she suggested. She wanted his horse.

"Good idea. You can take my horse, it's in the back. I assume you're coming."

"I'll be in the gallery. Wouldn't miss Ned Baker in debate with anybody. Don't, for God's sake, let him bait you into saying anything good about secession."

CHAPTER 17

POLISHED TREASON

The dome of the Capitol was not yet half finished. It seemed to John Forney, Secretary of the Senate, that the home of the national legislature stood out on the Hill like a tooth that had been drilled but not yet filled—a great, empty molar with raw nerve exposed.

Forney took up the bill referred by the Judiciary Committee to the Senate acting as a Committee of the Whole, to be considered that morning: S. 33, "A bill to suppress Insurrection and Sedition."

Henry Anthony, senator from Rhode Island and owner of its *Providence Journal*, was the presiding officer that morning. At a nod from the senator, Forney rose, cleared his throat, and took a sip of water. Most of the senators thought he was sipping gin, which he sometimes did on a dull day with nothing to read but interminable amendments, but he never linked arms with John Barleycorn on historic occasions.

Which this session surely would be. The bill under consideration was nothing short of nationwide martial law. Stung by the defeat at Bull Run, the Republican war hawks proposed to empower military commanders to seize and hold as prisoners any civilians "aiding or abetting" the rebellion, to ignore the civil courts and to try them by court-martial. The military commander could execute those found guilty.

The legislation superseding the authority of civil courts, which also required loyalty oaths of all suspects, struck Forney as kind of sweeping, but the Senate had already approved a great many stunning actions undertaken by the President. What made this morning's session interesting, potentially dramatic, was the rumor that there was to be a clash between the two most articulate, and most diametrically opposed, men in the Senate: Breckinridge and Baker.

That packed the galleries. As Forney droned his way through the ten sections of the bill, he glanced up at the press section, which was jammed. Forney nodded to Adams Hill, of the *New York Tribune*, and his correspondent, George Smalley, in whose arms Forney had gratefully passed out after a tenth round of drinks the night before. The section reserved for important visitors was packed as well: guests included the entire Blair family, it seemed, from the old man to his daughter Lizzie; Addie Douglas, the senator's widow, was sitting with her cousin Rose Greenhow, presenting what Forney knew to be the most socially prominent pair of unattached women in Washington. One of the President's secretaries, Hay, whom Forney had found to be a bit of a snob with his college-boy airs and graces, was accompanying a woman related to the President's wife who was living at the Mansion. Next to them, Anna Ella Carroll, the Maryland political lady Forney knew to be Lincoln's agent in keeping Maryland's Governor Hicks in line for the Union. At the last moment, Kate Chase had made her entrance with Lord Lyons.

Breckinridge had asked the president pro tem for a delay to allow Baker to arrive, and another piece of legislation, to authorize a national loan, had been taken up first. Still no Ned Baker. It was assumed his military duties in the field had taken priority, and the insurrection-sedition bill was brought up. Senator Lyman Trumbull of Illinois, a Lincoln ally and the bill's author, then spoke in its favor. "Let me tell you, senators," he assured his colleagues, "it is no new feature for courts-martial in times of rebellion, insurrection, and civil war to bring men before them, sentence them, and shoot them, without the intervention of any kind of grand or petit jurors."

The Chair recognized Breckinridge of Kentucky. Forney wondered why this man kept coming back every day to ram his head against the wall of resentment. The giants of the South had left the Senate and were creating their own government in Richmond. With no deep-Southern votes in the United States Senate to restrain them, the remaining senators could not only pass legislation the South had blocked for generations, but take up measures to crush the rebellion and punish the rebels.

Only Breckinridge remained behind, a voice from the Senate's divided past, seeking vainly to obstruct the near-united will of the people of the North. The traditions of the Senate gave him full hearing, and with Anthony in the Chair this morning he would have no difficulty gaining recognition, but rumblings had been heard that more than a limit to patience was involved: the Kentuckian inveighing against war was seen to be speaking for the South, and in wartime such advocacy smacked of a high crime.

The word "treason" was muttered but never spoken on the Senate floor. Breckinridge, even when accusing Wade and Chandler of plotting to precipitate the war in order to abolish slavery, took care not to step beyond the limits of toleration. The week before, the sentiment whipped up by Breckinridge in Kentucky had caused his fellow senator from Kentucky, the venerable and strongly pro-Union Crittenden, to propose a resolution limiting the purpose of the war: "Resolved, that this war is not waged for any purpose of overthrowing or interfering with the rights or established institutions of any states, but to preserve the Union with all the dignity, equality, and rights of the several states unimpaired." Crittenden's anti-abolition compromise had passed, thirty to five, to the outrage of radical Ben Wade and his watercarrier, Henry Wilson, who called it "a complete surrender to the demands of slave propagandism." The passage of such a resolution, mollifying the loyal slave owners of the border states, proved that the presence of Breckinridge still had an effect.

The presiding officer recognized the junior senator from Kentucky. "This bill, sir," said Breckinridge in a mild tone of voice, "provides for the destruction of political and personal rights everywhere, and would operate as harshly on nonseceded as seceded states. I wish it were published in every newspaper in the United States. I believe if that were done, it would meet the universal condemnation of the people."

Orville Browning, the junior senator from Illinois and a man Forney knew to be nearly as intimate a friend of the Lincolns as Baker, asked if the speaker would yield for a moment, which Breckinridge did.

"The senator from Kentucky has assailed the conduct of the Chief Executive in the chamber for the past week with a vehemence that borders on malignity," said Browning. "I would caution him to speak with respect of our commander in chief at such a perilous moment in our nation's history."

Breckinridge would not accept that. "I have criticized, with the freedom that belongs to the representative of a sovereign state and the people, the conduct of the Executive. Towards that distinguished officer, I cherish no personal animosity. I deem him to be personally an honest man, and I believe that he is trampling on the Constitution every day, with probable good motives."

"Your sarcasm does you no honor, Senator."

Breckinridge bridled. "I am quite aware that all I say is received with a sneer of incredulity in this body. But let the future determine who was right and who was wrong. We are making our record here; I, my humble one, amid the aversion of nearly all who surround me. I have forgotten what an approving voice sounds like, and am surrounded by scowls."

Forney heard a sound in the rear and looked toward the eastern entrance to the chamber. Senator Edward Baker, in the blue uniform and fatigue cap of a United States Army colonel, dust-covered from hard riding, entered and walked down the aisle to his seat. He laid his officer's sword on his desk and sat down, the clanking heard by everyone in the room. Forney was ambivalent about the appearance of Baker: glad to have a champion of the President who could take on Breckinridge in debate, uncomfortable about his appearance on the Senate floor in uniform. The soldier-senator made martial law, an abstract term, seem vividly martial.

"What is this bill," Breckinridge continued, warming to his task, "but vesting first in the discretion of the President, to be by him detailed to a subaltern military commander, the authority to enter the commonwealth of Kentucky, to abolish the state, to abolish the judiciary, and to substitute just such rules as that military commander may choose. This bill contains provisions conferring authority which never was exercised in the worst days of Rome, by the worst of her dictators."

"That son of a bitch is asking for it," Forney heard Ben Wade mutter.

"I have wondered why this bill was introduced," said Breckinridge. "Possibly to prevent the expression of that reaction which is now evidently going on in the public mind against these procedures so fatal to constitutional liberty. The army may be used, perhaps, to collect the enormous direct taxes to come to finance the war."

Forney held his breath; he wished he had gin in the water glass. The Kentuckian was sticking this bill down Northern throats.

"Mr. President," Breckinridge told the Chair, "gentlemen here talk about the Union as if it was an end instead of a means. Take care that in pursuing one idea you do not destroy not only the Constitution of your country, but sever what remains of the federal union."

"A question," said Senator Baker.

"I prefer no interruptions," said the Kentuckian; "the senator from California will have the floor later."

"Oregon," said Baker.

"The senator seems to have charge of the whole Pacific coast," the Kentuckian said with a small smile, withdrawing his deliberate mistake, which Forney presumed was intended to cause some dissension in Western ranks. "Oregon, then." He became deadly serious again. "I desire the country to know this fact: that it is openly avowed upon this floor that the Constitution is put aside in a struggle like this. You are acting just as if there were two nations upon this continent, one arrayed against the other; some twenty million on one side, and some twelve million on the other as to whom the Constitution is naught, and the rules of war alone apply.

"The 'war power,' whatever that means, applies to external enemies only. I do not believe it applies to any of our political communities bound by the Constitution in this association. Nor do I believe that the founders ever contemplated the preservation of the Union of these states by one half the states warring on the other half.

"Mr. President, we are on the wrong tack; we have been from the beginning. The people begin to see it. Here we have been hurling gallant fellows on to death, and the blood of Americans has been shed—for what? To carry out principles that three fourths of them abhor; for the principles of despotism contained in this bill before us."

Senator Baker rose in his seat and remained standing, ostentatiously but patiently waiting his turn to speak.

"Nothing but ruin, utter ruin, to the North and South, to the East and West, will follow the prosecution of this contest," the Kentuckian continued, his outdoor stump-speaker voice growing in volume, resonating throughout the room like the doom he was prophesying. "You may look foward to innumerable armies. You may look forward to raising and borrowing vast treasures for the purpose of ravaging and desolating this continent. At the end, we will be just where we are now. Or if you are gloriously victorious, and succeed in ravaging the South, what will you do with it? Can you not see

John W. Forney

what is so plain to the world, that what you insist on seeing as a mere faction is a whole people, wanting to go its own way?

"To accomplish your purpose, it will be necessary to subjugate, to conquer, ay, to *exterminate*—nearly ten million people! Does anybody here not know that? Does anyone here hope vainly for conquest without carnage?"

His voice ceased its cannonade and dropped to a tone of reason. "Let us pause while there is still time for men of good will to draw back from hatred and bloodshed. Let the Congress of the United States respond here and now to the feeling, rising all over this land, in favor of peace."

He took his seat. Every eye in the chamber swung to Senator Baker.

"A few words as to the senator's predictions," Ned Baker began, as quietly and conversationally as his opponent had begun. "The senator from Kentucky stands up here in a manly way, in opposition to what he sees as the overwhelming sentiment of the Senate, and utters reproof, malediction, and prediction combined. Well, sir, it is not every prediction that is prophecy.

"What would have been thought," he went on, still conversationally, "if in another capitol, in another republic, in a yet more martial age, a senator as grave, not more eloquent or dignified than the senator from Kentucky, yet with the Roman purple flowing over his shoulders, had risen in his place, surrounded by all the illustrations of Roman glory, and declared that advancing Hannibal was just, and that Carthage ought to be dealt with in terms of peace?

"What would have been thought," Baker's voice rose, "if, after the battle of Cannae, a senator there had risen in his place and denounced every levy of the Roman people, every expenditure of its treasures, and every appeal to the old glories?"

Baker's rhetorical question was answered by a senator near him—Fessenden of Maine, Forney thought—equally versed in classical history. "He would have been hurled from the Tarpeian Rock!"

"Yes, a colleague more learned than I says that the speaker of such words would have been hurled from the Tarpeian Rock. It is a grand commentary on the American Constitution that we permit such words as spoken by the senator from Kentucky to be uttered here and now.

"But I ask the senator, what, save to send aid and comfort to the enemy, do these predictions of his amount to? Every word thus uttered falls as a note of inspiration upon every Confederate ear. Every sound thus spoken is a word— and from his lips a mighty word—of kindling and triumph to a foe that determines to advance.

"For me, amid temporary defeat, disaster, disgrace, it seems that my duty calls me to utter another word, and that word is, *war!* Bold, sudden, forward, determined war, according to the laws of war, by armies and by military commanders clothed with full power, advancing with all the past glories of the Republic urging them on to conquest.

"I do not stop to consider whether it is 'subjugation' or not. The senator animadverts to my use of 'subjugation.' Why play on words? We propose to subjugate rebellion into loyalty; we propose to subjugate insurrection into peace; we propose to subjugate Confederate anarchy into constitutional Union liberty.

"And when we subjugate South Carolina, what will we do? We shall compel its obedience to the Constitution of the United States; that is all. The senator knows that we propose no more. I yield for his reply."

Breckinridge had been angered, Forney knew, by that Tarpeian Rock business; although its significance eluded the Pennsylvania newsman, evidently it meant a great deal to senators who thought of themselves as linear descendants of the Roman lawgivers.

"By whose indulgence am I speaking?" The Kentuckian's voice was shaking as he sought to control his rage. "Not by any man's indulgence. I am speaking by the guarantees of that Constitution which seems to be here now so little respected.

"When the senator asked what would have been done with a Roman senator who had uttered such words as mine, a certain senator on this floor— whose courage has much risen of late"—the contempt in that last phrase was aimed at Charles Sumner, who, Breckinridge evidently thought, was his insulter—"replied in audible tones, 'He would have been hurled from the Tarpeian Rock.' Sir, if ever we find an American Tarpeian Rock, and a suitable victim is to be selected, the people will turn, not to me, but to that senator who has been the chief author of the public misfortunes.

"Let him remember, too, that while in ancient Rome the defenders of the public liberty were sometimes torn to pieces by the people, yet their memories

were cherished in grateful remembrance; while to be hurled from the Tarpeian Rock was ever the fate of usurpers and tyrants."

Forney nodded understanding; so that was the obscure reference that got
Breck's dander up; it was amazing what got under the skin of some of these
senators.

"I reply with just indignation," Breckinridge said, leveling a finger at Sumner, "at such an insult offered on the floor of the Senate Chamber to a senator
who is speaking in his place."

Forney wished he could send him a note that it was Fessenden, not Sumner, who had so learnedly insulted him, but that would not have made much
difference; Sumner of Massachusetts was the radical Republican Breckinridge
believed to be the instigator of Lincoln's punitive actions.

"War is separation," Breckinridge was saying, which Forney remembered
was a favorite phrase of John Calhoun's. "War is disunion, eternal and final
disunion. We have separation now; it is only made worse by war, and war will
extinguish all those sentiments of common interest and feeling which might
lead to a political reunion founded upon consent and upon a conviction of its
advantages.

"Let this war go on, however, you will see further separation. Let this war
go on, and the people of the West see the beautiful features of the old Confederacy beaten out of shape by the brutalizing hand of war, and they will turn
aside in disgust from the sickening spectacle and become a separate nation."

That was too much for Baker, who did represent most of the west coast.
"The Pacific states," he thundered back, clattering as he rose, "will be true to
the Union to the last of her blood and her treasure.

"I confess, Mr. President, that I would not have predicted three weeks ago
the disasters which have overtaken our arms. But I ask the senator from
Kentucky, will he tell me it is our duty to stay here, within fifteen miles of the
enemy seeking to advance upon us every hour, and talk about nice questions
of constitutional construction? Are we to stop and talk about rising sentiment
against the war in the North? Are we to predict evil and flinch from what we
predict? Is it not the manly part to go on as we have begun, to raise money, to
levy armies, to prepare to advance?"

Forney looked around the room at the rapt attention shown to the senator
in uniform; the Senate wanted him to speak for all of them in crushing the
fear and guilt raised by the Kentuckian.

"To talk to us about stopping is idle; we will never stop. Will the senator
yield to rebellion? Will he shrink from armed insurrection? Will his state
justify it? Shall we send a flag of truce? What would he have us do? Or would
he conduct the war so feebly, that the whole world would smile at us in
derision?

"What would he have us do?" Baker hammered home his series of questions like nails in the lid of a pine coffin. "Those speeches of his, sown broad-
cast over the land, what clear distinct meaning have they? Are they not meant
for disorganization in our very midst? Are they not intended to dull our
weapons? Are they not intended to destroy our zeal? Are they not intended to
animate our enemies? Sir—are they not words of brilliant, polished *treason?*"

The senators and the crowd in the gallery let out a roar. The dread word
had been said: Breckinridge, the secret spokesman for the rebellion in the

heart of the Union, had been branded a traitor to his face by the senator who stood closest to Abraham Lincoln.

After much gavel-pounding by Senator Anthony, the chamber quieted. The Chair recognized Breckinridge, whose response was delivered in a muted voice.

"The senator asks me, 'What would you have us do?' I have already indicated what I would have us do. I would have us stop the war.

"We can do it. There is none of that inexorable necessity to continue this war which the senator seems to suppose. I do not hold that constitutional liberty on this continent is bound up in this fratricidal, devastating, horrible contest. Upon the contrary, I fear it will find its grave in it."

Everyone heard, nobody listened. He continued in the same resigned, almost despairing tone. "The senator is mistaken in supposing that we can reunite these states by war. He is mistaken in supposing that if twenty million on one side subjugate twelve million on the other side, that you can restore constitutional government as our fathers made it."

Deep breath. "Sir, I would prefer to see these states all reunited upon true constitutional principles to any other object that could be offered me in life. But I infinitely prefer to see a peaceful separation of these states, than to see endless, aimless, devastating war, at the end of which I see the grave of public liberty and personal freedom."

Forney winced at the terrible admission: Breckinridge had finally come out for "peaceful separation"—for secession. That did it; he was on the record as being on the other side.

Baker rose again, a whip crack in his hand, that he lightly tapped against his boot. "The senator is right about the devastation ahead. There will be privation; there will be loss of luxury; there will be graves reeking with blood, watered with tears. When that is said, all is said. If we have the country, the whole country, the Union, the Constitution, free government—with these there will return all the blessings of a well-ordered civilization. The path of the whole country will be one of greatness and peace such as would have been ours today, if it had not been for the treason for which the senator from Kentucky too often seeks to apologize." Ned Baker was finished speaking; he laid the whip crack next to the sword lying across his desk and took his seat.

"You say that the opinions I express," replied Breckinridge, "are but brilliant treason. Mr. President, if I am speaking treason, I am not aware of it. I am speaking what I believe to be for the good of my country. If I am speaking treason, I am speaking it *in my place* in the Senate."

Forney caught Breck's legal points: first, he had no intent of committing the capital offense, and second, he spoke from his elected post of privilege, and could not be prosecuted for what he said from that place.

The senator stood in silence for a moment, considering what he was about to say with care. "If my opinions do not reflect the judgment of the people I represent," Breckinridge concluded, "I am not a man to cling to the emoluments of public life. If the commonwealth of Kentucky, instead of attempting to mediate as a neutral in this struggle, shall throw her energies into the strife on the side of what I believe to be a war of subjugation and annihilation, then she shall take her course. I am her son and will share her destiny, but she will be represented by some other man on the floor of this Senate."

CHAPTER 18

PEACE IS NOT THE GOAL

To demonstrate that the Senate firmly backed Lincoln's Ned Baker in that day's debate and stood foursquare against the "polished treason" of his opponent, an overwhelming majority of senators voted down a motion by a secession sympathizer to postpone consideration of Trumbull's bill.

Having voted officially not to postpone the anti-sedition bill, the senators then postponed it. At the quiet suggestion of Sumner of Massachusetts, the Senate proceeded to take up other business, leaving the "Bill to Suppress Insurrection and Sedition" for another day. Since the Senate was nearing the end of its special session, that meant the bill would not be taken up until December. Trumbull, supported only by the ever-vindictive Wade, was left sputtering and furious; Sumner, who read the mood of the senators after what was generally held to be a courageous stand by the lonely voice from Kentucky, wanted to avoid a vote on what Breckinridge had shown to be a seriously flawed piece of legislation.

"You really ought to apologize to Sumner," Breckinridge heard Forney saying to him, walking out of the chamber after the gavel fell. "He wasn't the one who brought up that rock that seems to bother you fellows, it was Fessenden. Sumner actually scuttled the bill. You ought to thank him."

Breckinridge shook his head; he wasn't apologizing to anybody who wanted to make war on sovereign states just to promote the immediate abolition of slavery, as Sumner had been doing for years. The vain senator from Massachusetts had been flattering and fussing over the friendless Mrs. Lincoln, thinking he could use her to influence her husband, a technique of advocacy that Breckinridge thought beneath contempt. If he had been wrong about the source of the insult on the Senate floor, so be it; Charles Sumner had escaped blame for many divisive things he did, and this minor injustice to him helped even the score.

At the posts behind the new Senate chamber, the tall Kentuckian craned his neck to see over others' heads, trying to spot Anna Carroll with his horse and an Ebbitt House carriage. He had to get home, pack, and get on the road to Kentucky that day. None of the other senators waiting for carriages spoke to him; he did not enjoy being a pariah, but understood their need for public distance. John Forney, his longtime drinking companion, remained beside him, looking gloomy.

Breckinridge knew that Forney owed his Senate job to Cameron and Lincoln, as a payoff for the enthusiastic editorials of his *Philadelphia Press*. Lincoln needed the support of War Democrats, the Douglas Dems who fought with the peace-seeking Breckinridge Democrats, and Forney helped the Republican administration reach them in Pennsylvania. But Forney was not the sort to burn his bridges to his fellow Democrats who did not support the war, and had done what he could to make life more comfortable for the tortured Kentuckians in the Senate.

"I'll see you in December, John," Breckinridge said to cheer up the politician-newsman.

Forney sadly disagreed. "This is farewell. You'll never again take your seat in the Senate of the United States, Breck."

Breckinridge looked at him sharply; had he shown weakness in that debate? "When I said I'd resign my seat if Kentucky didn't agree with me, I meant it—but that's why I'm going back now. I know I can get across the need for neutrality in Kentucky, John. I've run for the House, the Senate, and the Vice President there, and I've never lost. I won't lose Kentucky now." He had not carried Kentucky in his presidential race, but did not feel the need to point that out.

"My dear sir," Forney said formally, "you will follow your doctrine into the Confederate Army."

Breck resisted the impulse to shudder. "My doctrine leads to neither army. If I go over the lines, it will be to bring my son home."

They had heard no direct word about Cabell; a family friend said he thought the boy was in Tennessee with the rebels. Mary had written him that two of Uncle Bob's sons had gone South, which infuriated the preacher Breckinridge, while the other two signed up with the Federals. A niece, a frail favorite of his named Margaret Elizabeth, was trying to become a nurse in the Union's Sanitary Commission. He was saddened by the thought of his own family becoming a model for the dividing nation, but what he could not abide at all was the idea of the far-flung but close-knit Breckinridge clan—relatives who loved each other, helped each other, and were constantly going to each other's weddings and funerals—actually warring on each other.

He told Forney that this was the time for cool heads, especially in the one state where neutrality was possible and peacemaking could find fertile ground. Forney's assumption, which was probably that of most of the senators, was almost surely mistaken; Breckinridge intended to be back in December, to take his place speaking for the majority opinion he would help shape in Kentucky, providing the necessary neutral corridor to mediation of the dispute.

"If it's any consolation for giving up a great career," the Secretary of the Senate said in his Parthian shot, "I thought you won that debate with Ned Baker. He had the audience, you had the argument. All you lost was the presidency."

"We'll meet again, if we live, in the winter," Breckinridge called out, in a voice that carried past Forney to the others waiting. He often used that good-luck qualifier, "if we live," in his farewells; now, in what threatened to be wartime, the innocuous phrase sounded ominous, and he resolved not to use it again. "I hear you'll be starting a newspaper here in the capital."

Forney nodded yes.

"Lincoln money?"

The politician-newsman nodded again, looking guilty. "Some friends of the Administration," Forney admitted, "but some Democrats too." Because the leading newspaper in Washington, the *National Intelligencer*, was not sufficiently pro-Lincoln, the radical Republicans thought that a competing newspaper should be launched; Cameron and the War Department lawyer, Edwin Stanton, would see to it that government advertising would be available for its support. Breckinridge knew that Forney was being labeled "Lincoln's Dog" by many Democrats, especially newsmen, and thought that was needlessly cruel. "Politics is politics," Forney murmured, and the Kentuckian squeezed his arm in farewell.

Anna Carroll came up with the carriage and Breckinridge climbed in, expecting to drive her home. To his surprise, she handed over the reins without looking at him, turned away, and stepped down to the street. She almost ran toward Constitution Avenue, which led down the long hill toward her rooms.

His first thought was that she was being discreet, and he approved of that. Certainly no loyal Unionist eager to prove fervor for the anti-secession cause, as Anna surely was, would want to be seen with the likes of the senator who had been publicly tarred as the apologist for treason and the abettor of the conspiracy to dismember the Union. But there had been no secret signal in her movements, no whisper to reassure him or set a time to meet later.

He drove down from Capitol Hill along Independence Avenue, directing the horse's head toward the half spike jutting into the air that was intended to be a monument to George Washington. Great slabs of marble were stacked alongside the strange construction, with workmen who might be expected to be occupied building the city's defenses busy instead building the strange obelisk that would salute the nation's founder. Breckinridge wondered what Washington, were he alive now, would think of this great phallus aimed at the sky. He assumed the first President would be disappointed that his monument was not a heroic statue, but a huge stake poking at the sky; and that the rights of states like his native Virginia were being trampled on by one of his successors.

Breckinridge guided his horse around a mud puddle to turn right at Sixteenth Street, brooding about the roar of approval that greeted Baker's cry of "polished treason." His heart began to pound belatedly; with no more need for public self-control, he began to feel the strain of the long, tense debate. Phrases occurred to him that he should have used, points crowded in that had gone unmade. Of all the things he had said on the floor, however, the only remark he would have taken back was about public opinion in Kentucky. He should be showing confidence in his ability to lead opinion there and not suggesting he would meekly submit to the prevailing mood. Aside from that, he was satisfied with his presentation; he had said more than he had planned to say, but it was just as well that his support for peaceful separation was out in the open. Sooner or later, it would have had to be said, and the inflammatory words of peace were best uttered from his legally privileged place in the Senate.

Anna was probably disappointed. All her coaching on the war powers had gone for naught—indeed, had been used to ready him for strong rebuttal—and her pleas had been ignored, but he thought of her as a political professional; the fact of their public disagreement lent a certain piquancy to their private affair. He was certain she would forgive him for so vigorously espousing his minority view of how the Constitution should be read. Instead of drawing back slightly, as they had planned, he had plunged ahead to outright tolerance of secession. That might cause her to fret about the effect of his stand on his career, which did not worry him; in fact, the deep concern of a loving political ally about his future gave him a warm feeling. He was not totally surrounded by scowls.

His mind skipped to the likely reaction of other women in his life. At home in Lexington, Mary would probably be pleased at the Southern reports of the debate, if she took the time to read the newspaper in her sick-with-worry state about Cabell. Rose Greenhow? He was surprised she had not come to watch the debate from the gallery, as it seemed half the population of Washington's grand levees did, but perhaps the Wild Rose was otherwise occupied. He did not recall seeing Henry Wilson on the Senate floor that afternoon.

The spire of St. John's Church was ahead; he realized he was approaching the Greenhow house on Sixteenth Street. Rose was impatient with him for not racing South to lead the Confederate forces to glory, and she was still irritated that he would not try to enlist Anna Carroll in her intelligence network. He suspected that Rose also might be put out with him for not availing himself of the opportunity she offered of observing firsthand the charms that were the talk of the most powerful men in the town. The risk of entering a liaison with Rose, a woman with an undeniably arousing set of movements, was considerable, but a similar risk had not stopped him with Anna. It was just that Rose demanded so much at a time when his hands and heart were full. He did not think of himself as a greedy man; perhaps their friendship would take a physical turn in December, if she did not go South, or get herself caught here as a spy.

A large man trying to look small could be seen behind a tree on the corner. Breckinridge smiled at that, and stopped smiling when he saw a woman seated on a bench across the street closely eyeing him and every other passerby in the neighborhood of Rose Greenhow's house. He looked up at the second-story window of the house on Sixteenth Street. The blind was drawn down three quarters of the way, Rose's private signal to friends to stay away. Either that meant that she was occupied with a visitor, or it was a warning to messengers that the house was being watched by Union detectives. Breck drove his carriage right on by, looking straight ahead.

He was glad that Anna was not involved in any way with Rose. He could not leave for Kentucky for what might be months without saying good-bye to Anna, and the abrupt way they had just parted left him unsatisfied and troubled. He had a mission to perform at home, and its outlines were beginning to take shape in his mind. Peace meetings, small rallies held throughout the state to discuss and debate neutrality's many advantages might be followed by a peace convention drawn from all over the country. Louisville was a hotbed of unionism despite the *Courier;* would Lexington be the best site? On second thought, a conference at the capital at Frankfort would have the greatest effect on the Union-leaning legislators. If, as he hoped, a latent revulsion against war existed in many Northerners, a national peace movement was waiting to be mobilized. What it needed was a focal point, some event to plan for, talk about, hold, and then have friendly newspapers and pamphleteers hail as evidence of support for opposition to civil war throughout the nation.

At Ebbitt House, he turned in the rented carriage and arranged for the feeding of his horse. He sent up a boy with a note to Anna. The boy returned with a note in her angry scrawl: "Miss Carroll is indisposed." Frowning but not really worried, Breckinridge trotted up the three flights of stairs and rapped on her door.

She opened the door, eyes looking down and away to hide their redness, and let him in.

"You're angry at me, Anna?"

"Disappointed."

He told her he had to come because he was riding home that evening, and began to describe his ideas for a peace convention. She nodded dully, which was most unlike her; it was her custom to agree enthusiastically, to disagree forcefully, or to change the subject. She went to the closet and took out a small satchel and set it on the bed. Then she found and handed over his bathrobe, and, one by one, every item that he had left in her rooms.

"Why can't I leave these here? I'll be back before you know."

"You'll never be back. And if you do come back, please don't come back here."

He had evidently underestimated her displeasure. Slowly, giving himself time to adjust, he placed all the items she had handed him on the table in the middle of the room, atop her scattered papers. The Limoges shaving mug she had given him, which had belonged to her grandfather, he put alongside her inkpot. This gave him a moment to try to sort out what his reaction should be to her unexpected behavior. He began by confessing he did not understand why she was so upset.

"First," she said without passion, "you're a traitor to your country."

He controlled the surge of anger and said, "If enough of the Senate agrees, I'll be hanged from a gallows set up on the Capitol steps and that will be the end of it. But you say that's only the first thing. What else?"

"You've betrayed your friends, everybody who believed in you."

"Be honest with me, Anna. By 'friends,' you mean yourself. And by 'everybody,' you mean everybody you told that you would bring me around to Mr. Lincoln's view."

"Oh, go away," she said, sitting down at the window. "I don't want to argue. We've argued enough."

It struck him hard that she really did not want to engage. He drew up a stool and sat close to her. Her face was set in an expression of bleakness that rarely appeared there; the face he was accustomed to was heated in discussion's animation or cooled in sleep's repose. Anna had always been either onstage or offstage, never standing in the wings looking on in pain.

"It's possible for friends to disagree about the great issues and still remain friends," he said, he hoped gently. "The whole Breckinridge family is splitting North and South, and we're angry with each other, but we still love each other, we're still family."

"Don't you think I know that? It's never been *what* you think that attracted me, but how you think." She swallowed, balling her handkerchief between her palms. He waited for her unburdening.

"I didn't mind when you attacked my Know-Nothings, that you stood up for the immigrants who were ruining the country. People on both sides of that can still be close. But on the Union and the rebellion—that's not politics, that's life. When you decide where you stand on secession, you choose your whole future. And forgive me, I thought we would have sort of a future together—not publicly, not as man and wife—but as part of each other's lives, like we've been. Even more, as two friends on the way to doing great things, doing them together, neither one lonely anymore." She went back to rolling the handkerchief; he had never seen her close to tears, her voice choking its way through her throat.

"We agree about the Union and the Constitution," he argued, feeling awkward in using Senate-floor concepts in a situation so intimate, "but I don't believe war is a way to hold the Union together, and you do. I grant you that is a big disagreement, Anna—but it doesn't make me a traitor and you a patriot. Be reasonable. I don't want to lose you."

"You're thinking selfishly," she said, more in control of her voice now. "You're thinking like a child." He thought it best not to respond. "You're thinking only of today, this week, not of the future. A mature person thinks of consequences, to the country, to himself, to the people he loves."

Her point invited debate, but he had done enough debating that day.

"One of the things that holds us together," she continued, "and being together with you is important to me, is our careers. We are doing great things in historic times, and getting ready to do so much more. But in the Senate today, you threw your career away. You indulged your ego, you gloried in being the martyr in the arena full of lions, you gave no thought to the consequences, not to yourself, certainly not to us."

"I cannot believe that if I stand for my principles, even if it costs me my political future, you will think any the less of me."

"Well, guess what—I do, because your principle is stupid. The South knows there can be no secession without war. And thanks to Mr. Lincoln, the North knows that the only way to keep the Union, any Union at all, is to be willing to fight for it. Only you, only John C. Breckinridge, thinks everybody else is going to forget what they stand for and listen to what he thinks is sweet reason. You're a fool, and I'm a worse fool for thinking you would be the greatest man of our time."

Shaking her head bitterly, mortified at her weakness at not being able to force back tears, she looked away and wept.

He did not know how to deal with that. He had learned in life that the way to respond to most women's tears was with soothing sounds and tender holdings, and rocking back and forth, but he suspected that if he tried that approach to Anna Carroll's anguish, it would be like throwing oil on a fire.

After a time, when he felt she was ready to speak again, he offered a firm position: "Your judgment could be wrong, you know. There could be a stronger desire for peace than you realize. And even if I don't succeed in stopping the war from beginning in earnest, perhaps I can shorten it."

"The way you could end this war is to raise a Union army in Kentucky, smash down into Tennessee, and take the railheads at Nashville and Murfreesboro," she said with great certitude. "That would save lives in the long run, and you could accept the presidency of a grateful nation."

"It would go against everything I believe in."

"God save us from men convinced of their noble motives, because they deepen the rivers of blood." A chill went through his body at her words, cried as if from some Old Testament prophet. "Breck, get it through your head.

Peace is not the goal. Peace will have to wait. Democracy is the goal. The success of representative government is the goal. Lincoln sees that and he doesn't flinch."

"He is a despot and a hypocrite," he shot back. "Lincoln talks about freedom, and he rips away our most precious freedoms in the North. He talks about freedom, and he denies nine million of his fellow men in the South the freedom to start their own nation."

"He is stubborn and he is mean," she seemed to agree, "and all the nonsense about 'Honest Abe' is a terrible deceit. He will play one man against another, manipulate one interest to lacerate the next, and throw good men away when they have served their purpose. I've talked to Old Man Blair, who knows him, and held the head of his young secretary when he was in his cups."

"Then how can you—"

"Because Lincoln will do anything, go through anything, put us all through any horror, to reach his goal."

"And the goal is a Union with one half conqueror, the other half conquered. You think that a worthy goal?"

"His goal is majority rule. Breck, I know that sounds theoretical, and it won't rally most people round the flag, but that's what he is grimly determined to prove, once and for all. And he's like a man possessed about it. Nothing you do is going to stop him."

The notion that one man's obsession about a political theory should put a continent of brothers through a bath of blood—and that this normally intelligent woman should be resigned to follow him without question—was too much for Breck to tolerate. She had been wrong about her damned Know-Nothings, wrong about trusting Fillmore and Buchanan, wrong in her estimation of John C. Breckinridge, and he hoped to hell she was wrong about the brutal, bulldog tenacity of Abraham Lincoln.

"The great good sense of the American people will stop him. This country may go crazy for a while, but not for long. Anna, I'm leaving now, and I'm sorry it has to be this way. I miss you already."

"Go South," she said. "You belong there."

"I'm going to border-state Kentucky, where I belong, and I'll keep it neutral."

"I wish you well." She took a deep breath and let it out. "What I really wish is, I wish I had never met you."

He supposed that was a perverse expression of tenderness, coming from a woman who had given her love to few men, but he held his tongue. If peacemaking was to be his mission, he could not go to war with Anna Carroll.

"And I, on the contrary, will always be grateful I met you." He was human, and could not resist one bitter note: "I hope you enjoy your war and your war powers. Just don't confuse them with freedom."

She rose and lashed out at him. "Go South, with the other traitors, and see what kind of freedom you find. See what war does to your beloved states' rights, see what men are willing to do to the laws when they have to fight for survival. Goddammit, Breckinridge, war means fighting, and the men who fuss about the rules get pushed aside."

He put his belongings into the satchel. "I think there is something to be said for the law."

"How's your Latin, lawyer—*inter arma, silent leges.*" In time of war, the law falls silent. He did not correct her quotation of Cicero.

"I have always benefited from your instruction," was all he said, angry now, but more at Lincoln and the spirit of the times than at this misguided woman who meant more to him than any he had known. He did not want to hurt her, but he had by taking away her chance at participating in a great career. The career did not seem so important to him; she did.

Standing in the doorway, he took a last look at her. She faced the window, the bleakness across her face as if she had been abandoned again, but as Rose had told him about her, Anna had grown accustomed to being left by men. He closed the door behind him softly. The nation could not stay in this crazed state for long; the war fever, by its nature, would burn itself out. He could not be confident about his plans but tended to believe he would return to Washington, perhaps even to Anna, in December.

CHAPTER 19

SECOND-STORY MAN

"Plums arrived with Nuts this morning." That coded message was Allan Pinkerton's single most significant mistake—a trifle, he told himself often— but it had made him look the fool. No man who was persuaded that his destiny was to found a United States Secret Service could afford to let himself be thought a fool.

He sat under his round hat, behind his dead cigar, outside the War Department office of George Brinton McClellan. The general had been appointed a month before to defend the nation's capital from the expected attack by Beauregard, victor of Bull Run.

McClellan was making him wait. Pinkerton accepted the delay without question because he'd held the "Young Napoleon" in profound respect ever since he had first worked for him at the Illinois Central Railroad. McClellan had been the line's brisk and efficient treasurer and general manager, Pinkerton his chief of railroad detectives. The senior executive fairly exuded success: Pinkerton knew he had been offered, and turned down, ten thousand dollars a year to run a competing railroad. The detective did not consider his former boss a perfect executive, however. Mistakenly, out of friendship's sake, McClellan had hired and kept on as his company treasurer Ambrose Burnside, a dependent comrade who tinkered with inventions and paid little attention to the railroad's finances.

"Railroading is the best place for a military man in peacetime," Pinkerton remembered the civilian McClellan saying. The detective nodded vigorously at the recollection of the commanding voice of his longtime boss, now the leader of the army defending the capital. McClellan was only thirty-five, but age was no bar to high command—Napoleon himself won his greatest battles in his twenties. The detective was proud of McClellan's record: his renowned horsemanship, his business success, his proven concern for the welfare of his troops—all combined with a command presence that made him a born leader of troops. Railroading had been the perfect interim career. Logistics was at its core, communications was its key, and the training and organization of troops of workers was McClellan's favorite way of biding his time until the right war would call for his military talents.

"Plums arrived with Nuts this morning." Pinkerton reached behind his head and tipped his bowler farther down over his forehead. What had possessed him to come up with that code? The detective credited himself with a brilliant performance on his first assignment for the government, just six months ago. That feat of intelligence and protection not only impressed McClellan, but called the detective's good judgment to the attention of Abraham Lincoln—whose life Pinkerton was convinced he had saved—and to Thomas Scott, another former railroad man, whom Lincoln had appointed Undersecretary of War to manage the department while the Secretary, Simon Cameron, pulled political wires.

Pinkerton had been hired to ensure the safety of the trip of the President-elect from Springfield to Philadelphia to Baltimore to Washington. The detective's operatives in Baltimore had unearthed a plot by secessionists to assassinate Lincoln before the newly elected President could take the oath of office. Despite Lincoln's complaint that he did not want to appear to be "sneaking into the capital like a thief in the night," Pinkerton had prevailed upon Scott to reroute the train. After changing the President-elect's schedule clandestinely, Pinkerton had cut the telegraph wires from Harrisburg to Washington so that the plotters could not be informed of the change.

When the President-to-be arrived safely and silently in Washington, Pinkerton had wired the Lincoln supporters in Illinois and Pennsylvania a coded reassurance. Unfortunately, the detective brooded, waiting outside McClellan's door, when the message came to the attention of some sensationalist newspaper reporters, "Plums arrived with Nuts this morning" was taken to mean that Pinkerton had code-named Lincoln "Nuts"—he had given no thought to a double meaning—and this minor slip was the cause of much gleeful press derision.

The President-elect, a fellow Pinkerton had learned put great store by presidential dignity, had not been amused, since he was so abashed at having to slip into Washington in disguise anyway. A fine piece of undercover work and bodyguarding was thus spoiled by a mere oversight in nomenclature. Pinkerton glumly shifted his cigar and silently cursed the unpatriotic press.

McClellan greeted him from behind the desk with the words the detective wanted urgently to hear: "Pinkerton, I need you."

"I prefer you to use my code name, sir—E. J. Allen." He preferred any code name; "Pinkerton" always sounded effeminate to him, which was why he liked to substitute his first name for his last, with the spelling slightly changed to throw off suspicion. "My men and I are at your disposal. Women operatives too," he added.

"How do you feel about slavery, Pinkerton?"

That was a tricky question, the detective thought; what did slavery have to do with military intelligence? More to the point, what answer did McClellan want to hear? He knew the general had been a Douglas Democrat in the last election, so the detective stuck to popular sovereignty: "That's for local people to decide, sir."

"You're not an abolitionist, then."

"No, sir." Pinkerton sensed that was not enough. "I'm for the Union as it was, the Constitution as it is." That slogan, familiar to the followers of Stephen Douglas, came out foursquare against change, and it seemed to please the general. Pinkerton hoped the general did not know and would not learn of certain activities the detective had participated in a few years before in behalf of his good friend John Brown, before that abolitionist was hanged.

McClellan rose. The general was built stockily, giving the impression of being short without being small. "This war is not being fought about slavery, Pinkerton. On the contrary, it will be fought to keep the Union as it is, with each section free to make its own decisions. Abolitionism is no part of what we are fighting for. Are we quite clear about that?"

"Absolutely, sir. Union as it is. Be better if you called me 'Allen,' General."

"That would sound as if I were using your first name," said McClellan, obviously not a first-name man. "Might as well give you a code rank as well. How about colonel?"

"That sounds too important. Captain?"

"Nobody pays attention to captains," McClellan observed. "Make it major, then. Look at this, Major Allen." He pointed to a map on his desk of the fortifications around Washington. "Forty strong points, twenty of them operational right now. There were none—not one—only two weeks ago, when the remnants of McDowell's force were wandering drunkenly around this city. You will note how the most likely routes of attack can be swept by our cross fire. The remainder of the fortification will be accomplished in five days."

Pinkerton made the appropriate marveling noises, then frowned: "Who else has this map, sir?"

"President Lincoln has one; he knows nothing about warfare, but he keeps poking around with questions and having this map seemed to make him feel more secure. General Scott has another, because I am obliged to keep the old gentleman informed—"

"—for the time being." Pinkerton knew that although Winfield Scott had acquiesced in the choice of McClellan for the defense of Washington, the old soldier had been recommending another general—Henry Halleck, the military theoretician and writer called "Old Brains"—as a potential replacement of himself as General-in-Chief. That, in Pinkerton's estimation, would not do; the top job, when the wheezing Scott finally stepped down, should go to McClellan.

Certainly "Little Mac" had been earning it: in less than a month, the energetic and forceful McClellan had rejuvenated the Union army in Washington, turning the scared stragglers into cohesive regiments, organizing work parties to build battlements. Pinkerton knew that McClellan had also made it his business to seek out and cultivate some of the leading Republican radicals, especially Wade in the Senate and Chase in the Lincoln administration. The detective assumed that the general had withheld from them his private thoughts against abolition.

"Wonderful old man," McClellan was saying about Winfield Scott. "I served under him in Mexico, where he eclipsed the exploits of Cortés. But this is not his war. And the only other copy of this map—other than the one you see here—is in the hands of the Senate Military Committee. It's important to cultivate them, Pinkerton, that's how we'll raise the necessary troops."

"Major Allen, sir." The correction was automatic: Pinkerton was more concerned about the map in the hands of the Senate. He had been told of the Confederate knowledge of Union movements at Bull Run. Two of his men, along with one woman operative, were watching Rose O'Neal Greenhow's house at that moment. Some dramatic spy-catching coup would make his job easier: by reflecting well on McClellan's intelligence choice, it would please Lincoln and erase the memory of that unfortunate code message. More funds for operatives would follow, then the creation of a secret service worthy of the name, not only to find out troop strength facing McClellan—the most immediate purpose of military intelligence—but to send spies into Richmond to discover the secret plans of the rebel leaders.

"What's your assessment of Lincoln, Major Allen?" That seemed to Pinkerton a legitimate question for a military commander to his intelligence chief. The commander in the field had to know what sort of support he would get from the head man in the capital.

"I've only spent a few hours with him, sir, on that trip to Washington where we saved his life."

"I remember. 'Plums, Nuts'—"

"And my impression," the detective hurried on, "is that he's a bit weak. I happen to know that Edwin Stanton, the former Attorney General who did some legal business with him years ago, calls him an imbecile, though that strikes me as unduly harsh."

"An abolitionist, you think? That ever come up in conversation?"

Pinkerton thought that over, replying slowly. "Deep down, I think not. He keeps worrying about Kentucky and Missouri, losing them because of the radicals."

McClellan nodded, his head at an angle, not wholly satisfied. "But he appointed General Frémont in Missouri. Dangerous man. Fanatic abolitionist, and a sort who thinks he's the Messiah. Beware of politicians who think that pinning stars on their epaulets turn them into real generals, Major Allen."

"But not the other way around." The detective thought it was not improper to hint at all the talk about appointing a dictator if the military situation worsened.

McClellan caught his allusion. "I have no such aspiration," the general said seriously. "Mind you, a dictatorship would solve a lot of problems, but it is not what I have in mind. With Lincoln's help, I can do the job this way. Do you know what the men in my army call me?"

Pinkerton had heard everything from "Little Mac" to "McNapoleon," but did not know which the general preferred. He decided to treat the question as rhetorical and said nothing.

" 'Our George,' " McClellan answered himself with pride. "I am going to take good care of these men, for I believe they love me from the bottom of their hearts. I can see it in their faces when I pass among them." The general fingered his mustache. "I find myself in a new and strange position here:

President, Cabinet, General Scott, and all deferring to me." A boyish wonderment entered his voice: "By some strange operation of magic, I seem to have become the power of the land."

Pinkerton felt the conspiratorial thrill that made his chosen calling as undercover man so right for him. General McClellan was a leader, perhaps the ultimate leader that the country needed at this hour. Pinkerton was proud to be in his confidence.

When McClellan nodded dismissal, the detective took his leave without even working out the financial details of his employment. That was no cause for concern; the general had been a generous boss at the railroad, and Undersecretary Tom Scott would be the man to see about money.

He put on his hat and hurried out of the War Department, cutting across the lawn of the President's house across the street, making a mental note to suggest a fence around the grounds. He took his bearings on the steeple of St. John's and walked quickly toward the corner of Sixteenth and I streets. The gray sky was darkening. He did not want to get caught in the rain, which tended to come down in torrents in Washington on late afternoons in August.

Two of his men stood talking directly across from Rose Greenhow's elegant brick mansion, which was precisely the wrong place for them to be.

"Told you fellows to stay apart," Pinkerton gruffed, "and to stay out of sight." It was hard to find conscientious operatives; his best were in Virginia, trying to glean information on Confederate troop strength. Pinkerton had been confident that McClellan would want a secret service.

"Nobody's gone in all day," one of the men said.

"I wouldn't go in either, if I was a rebel spy and saw you two big goons loitering outside."

"Man came by in a carriage," reported one operative, "then speeded up after he looked up at the second-story window."

Pinkerton studied the house, a two-story edifice with basement, and a central stairs leading to a porch and entrance. On the second story, in the corner, was the window from which Rose probably flashed the all-clear signal; he noted that the blind was down at the moment, he assumed to discourage callers. Would Senator Breckinridge, who passed by the other day, have gone in if the blind had been up? He knew Breckinridge to be a Southern sympathizer—that was apparent from his public speeches—but doubted the senator was a spy, since he was no longer entrusted with military information. Still, the Kentuckian might be worth making the target of a "shadow man."

In the dusk, its darkness hurried by the heavy clouds, the Greenhow house showed no lights. Pinkerton, who had been keeping this place under close observation for nine long days and nights, determined to get a look at the layout inside. To the side of the front steps, some large boxwood bushes shadowed an area; above that was a window that looked in at the parlor on the first floor. He looked up and down Thirteenth Street. No pedestrians were in sight; only the woman on the bench, knitting, who worked for him. He motioned his two men to follow, ducked across the street, positioned them in the boxwood, and made ready to stand on their shoulders to get a look inside the house.

Large, plopping raindrops signaled an impending downpour. Pinkerton hesitated, the first drops bouncing off his hat. He hated getting wet in general, and he hated getting his derby hat soaked in particular; it was his favorite hat and was already on the tight side. The detective sighed and squared himself to the task: he removed his damp shoes and hoisted himself up on the shoulders of his operatives.

The wooden shutter was closed; Pinkerton twisted the slats to see inside, but before he could look, he could feel his foot being pulled in alarm. He scrambled down and the three men hid under the porch until a group of people ran past in the rain. The downpour, in its usual August force, filled his empty shoes with water, annoying him, but he was satisfied that the rain provided a distraction that prevented them from being observed.

He climbed back up, his stockinged feet slipping on the shoulders of his men, and looked through the shutters again. He saw a large parlor, expensively appointed, with a light in one corner where two people were seated on adjacent sides of a lace-covered table. Rose Greenhow, in a black dress, was one; the other was a man, sturdily built, well dressed, with a face that Pinkerton thought should be familiar to him. He could not quite place the man, but Rose's visitor was obviously a person of authority. He was leaning on the table, one knee on a chair, going over a large sheet of paper, talking animatedly to his hostess.

A shoulder supporting Pinkerton's foot suddenly shifted and the detective slipped, arms flailing, hands groping wildly for support, but too late—he landed in the mud. His men picked him up, tried to wipe him off, backed away at his hissed imprecations, and after letting some other passersby run past, hoisted him aloft again. By this time, the bulky visitor—"He's a congressman," Pinkerton muttered to himself—was folding the large paper, apparently a map. Rose received it from him when the folding was finished, took his hand, and led him to the central hall of the house. They passed beyond the detective's line of vision and were possibly headed toward the front door.

"He's coming out," Pinkerton told the men below. "Run for it." They raced across the street and around the corner. His chest heaving, the detective cursed his haste: he had left his shoes under the boxwood. They watched the house from a distance, waiting for the congressman to emerge.

He did not. Upstairs, a light came on in Rose's bedroom. The detective did not hesitate; his job was to learn what was going on up there.

"Need a ladder," said Pinkerton. He dispatched his men, on horses, to the construction site of the Washington Monument up Fourteenth Street, to steal a ladder high enough to get him a look inside that bedroom. Little danger of discovery while looking in, as long as the pelting rain continued.

In twenty minutes, Pinkerton, clenching his sodden cigar in his teeth and using his hat to keep the water out of his eyes, was able to look into the second-story window of Rose's house. This was far from his first Peeping-Tom activity, but the scene that came before his eyes made his jaw drop and he lost the cigar.

Rose Greenhow was naked, except for high-heeled shoes, black stockings, and a lace-trimmed garter belt. Her back was to the window, long black hair falling to her waist, her buttocks deliciously muscled. In her right hand was a riding crop. The congressman was totally unclothed, on his hands and knees in front of her, trembling like an animal in fear.

Pinkerton had read about such perversions in some novels published in England. He knew that flagellation was practiced in the expensive brothels across the Potomac in Great Falls but had never seen any such illicit activity in the flesh. He hung on to the ladder and stared, oblivious to the rain and no longer fearful of falling. No wonder she was known as the most exciting woman in Washington: her legs were long and perfectly shaped, her ass firm, her way of carrying herself at once imperious and sensuous. Pinkerton could not yet see her breasts, but assumed her front to be as lush as her rear.

The detective winced as the riding crop sliced through the air and caught the congressman on the side of his leg. Crawling forward, the man in thrall embraced her legs and buried his face between them. After a moment, Rose smacked him again, ordered him onto the bed on his back, and straddled him. Her breasts came into view, fuller than Pinkerton had imagined, the nipples erect and small and dark. He concluded those were the most impressive woman's breasts he had ever seen. The look on her face was a mixture of eagerness and contempt; the detective could not tell how much was sexual and how much political.

As Rose twisted her body in the direction of the window, Pinkerton ducked. He had seen enough and did not want to risk discovery. The awareness of the rain and the slippery ladder returned, and he climbed down with care. He estimated that it would take at least ten minutes for Rose to complete her fornication, and five minutes more to dress; that would leave him time for a daring counterespionage maneuver. If it worked, nobody in the Lincoln administration could doubt the need for a secret service.

"You sure look like you got an eyeful," said one of his operatives.

"She's occupied," Pinkerton snapped, "and she left the map downstairs on the desk."

He knew exactly what he had to do. Making an arrest would be a mistake. The immediate thing was to prevent the map from being sent from Rose to the rebels. Next was to shadow the congressman. Then the house could be used as a magnet for other Confederate spies, letting them be drawn in, arresting them as they came out.

"Force this window," he told his men. When the first-floor parlor window was sprung, he boosted himself on their shoulders again, and climbed into the parlor, dripping on the carpet but unconcerned about his wet footprints. He wiped his hands dry on the antimacassar covering the sofa and picked up the map and several documents on the desk. A copy of the *National Intelligencer* was nearby; he wrapped his gatherings in that newspaper to keep the incriminating documents dry, stuffed the package in his breast, and climbed back out the window.

"I'll shadow the traitor when he comes out," Pinkerton told them, grimacing as the water hit his hat. "You two let anybody in, but arrest them when they come out. We want as much of the ring as we can catch."

The downpour abated into a steady rain. Pinkerton and his two operatives waited, soaking. When the congressman emerged from the front door, Pinkerton trailed him for one block to the church nearby. There the congressman waited about twenty minutes. The rain stopped; it was dark but not yet night.

Two other men, one a clubfoot, joined the man who came out of the Greenhow house and the three walked down Sixteenth Street toward the

Executive Mansion. To the detective's dismay, the unidentified congressman went directly into the President's house with the others. Pinkerton could not go in—it would hardly do to make a scene trying to apprehend a suspected spy in the diplomatic reception room of the Mansion—but he had to find a way to identify his man.

He snapped his fingers, which, still moist, failed to make a satisfactory snapping sound. "Brady," he said aloud.

Every politician in Washington had a photographic calling card to hand to constituents. Somewhere in the files of Mathew Brady's gallery would be the *carte de visite* with a picture of his man. First, Pinkerton stopped by the War Department on Seventeenth Street to organize a raiding party of a half dozen of his men to pull in the spies who left Rose Greenhow's house, and to deposit the incriminating documents, which he worried might be getting soggy, in his safe. Without stopping to change clothes—no time for that, and it was a warm night, he would not catch a cold—the detective hurried to the photographer's studio.

CHAPTER 20

JOHN HAY'S DIARY
AUGUST 22, 1861

A long hiatus. The nights have been too busy for jottings. Then I was flat on my back with bilious fever for a week, and had a gay old delirium the other day, but am some better now.

Today a couple of Breckinridge's agents from Kentucky, claiming to be all for the Union but not to the extent of fighting for it, called on the Prsdt begging for permission of Kentucky's neutrality.

"Professed Unionists give me more trouble than rebels," he told them. He sees through their plot. Breck and the pro-secesh Kentucky governor want to put the responsibility of the first blow upon the gov't in Washington. If we "invade" a neutral Kentucky, it will be easier for Breck & Co. to rally the undecideds and take the state South. (That is substantially what we did in provisioning Fort Sumter, challenging the South to fire the first shot, which they foolishly did, helping us whip up the war spirit here. We know that trick.)

The Prsdt played what he likes to call "shut-pan" with them, telling them nothing. After I led them out, he told me why: "I cannot consent to what they ask, for Kentucky's neutrality won't last long. We want to go through that state."

He then looked out the window, peered more closely at a group approaching the Mansion, and proceeded to utter the last few words of a joke.

I could tell it was the ending of a story by his tone of voice. When Lincoln is speaking normally, his voice is slightly louder than that of most of us, perhaps from the needs of the courtroom, perhaps to make up for the unhappy fact that he is not blessed with a deep and resonant voice. When he is on the stump, that high-pitched voice of his carries well, almost rings out—

those debates with Douglas lasted for six, seven hours each, and the Lincoln words could be heard all day by the folks in the far reaches of the crowd.

When he is telling a story, however, the Tycoon's voice develops a kind of soft Western twang. When I hear that twang, I have no need for him to say "reminds me of a story," which he must do with strangers. Instead, I recognize the seemingly irrelevant remark as a joke's point, and if I do not ask him what the story is, he is a disappointed man.

"There comes them same damn three fellers again," was what he said, looking at the bustling trio of men.

Dutifully, I asked, "What same damn three fellers?"

"In a Kentucky school I attended as a boy," Lincoln said, in his rehearsed, storytelling twang, "we used to line up and read from the Bible, each in turn. One day we came to the passage about how the Israelites escaped the fiery furnace through divine intervention. The boy whose turn it was had to read the three difficult names, and he stumbled on Shadrach, floundered on Meshach, and went all to pieces on Abednego.

"The schoolmaster, kind of a mean man, cuffed the little boy and left him blubbering. Then we all took our turn reading. When it came his turn again, the boy looked at the part he had to read and let out a banshee wail: 'Lookie there, marster—there comes them same damn three fellers again!' "

I laughed out loud, not so much because it was a good story—though at least this was one I could relate at the Eameses' in mixed company—but because the Tycoon was chuckling away and needed company.

Besides, it lifts the heart to see what happens to his face when he laughs. From its natural, lugubrious, bloodhound-mournful look, it swings to high glee, especially when somebody joins in and bounces the laughter back and forth, at which point he winds up wiping his eyes and snuffling like somebody who has forced himself into a sneezing fit to snap out of a sadness spell.

I went to the window to see who I would be ushering in or blocking out. Sure enough, the same damn three fellers who show up whenever there is a whisper abroad of a lack of resolution in smiting the South—Ben Wade, Henry Wilson, and Tad Stevens, two senators and the smoldering power of the House. Senator Wade on the left, pounding along like he owned the earth, jaw jutting out, hands clenched into fists, ready to stop any retreating army that came his way. Senator Wilson in the middle, rotund, waddling and puffing, a Massachusetts abolitionist who was given the Military Affairs Committee when Jeff Davis headed South.

The third man I've never liked. He has the look of a dark cloud unable to rain. Thaddeus Stevens of Pennsylvania—clubfoot, the defender of fugitive slaves, the leading reb-hater and slavocracy-denouncer of all. In revolutionary France, he would have been among the bloodiest of the Jacobins, perhaps Robespierre himself. Unlike the pugnacious Wade, he does not have the saving grace of a sense of humor.

The radicals—that's what they proudly call themselves, and I must not let them catch me calling them Jacobins—had been enraged earlier this month by the Crittenden resolution. That was a much-needed expression by a loyal old Kentuckian in the House to disavow any intention of freeing the slaves, thereby stealing some of Breck's thunder among slave owners in that border state. Its ready passage showed how far the mood of the country is from abolition, though the radical minority swings some weight in the Republican Party.

To offset the Crittenden resolution, and to lean against the President's inaugural theme of not striking at slavery where it exists, the same-damn-three-fellers managed to pass the Confiscation Act. That strips rebels of their property, including slaves, when used in rebellion against the United States. They slipped it through as a get-even-with-the-rebels bill rather than an abolition bill, and the Tycoon reluctantly signed it to keep them on board his ship.

"Mr. President, you're murdering your country by inches," said brother Wade, in his usual subtle way, as soon as the trio barged in, "by the want of a distinct policy in regard to slavery. The South has got to pay for bringing on this war, and the payment is going to be giving up their 'peculiar institution.' "

Lincoln shook his head, no. "Wherever I go and whatever way I turn, you gentlemen are on my trail, and still in my heart, I have the deep conviction that the hour has not yet come."

His hint that the hour would one day come—a hint that he vouchsafed only to ultras—did not mollify Congressman Stevens. "Nothing approaching your present policy will subdue the rebels," the clubfoot growled. "You must gain the moral courage to treat this as a radical revolution. It will involve the desolation of the South as well as emancipation, and a repeopling of half the continent. I know this startles you, Lincoln."

It did. "You would upset our applecart altogether if you had your way," the Prsdt countered. "We'll fetch 'em; just give us a little time." That, of course, was not what Lincoln was telling our border-state friends or the War Democrats, but in politics everyone must be given some reason to hope his dream will come true, or so I am coming to understand.

Not fast enough for Wade. "I don't think you could be inspired to take action with a galvanic battery, Lincoln."

"We didn't go to war to put down slavery, but to put the flag back," the Tycoon replied evenly. "To act differently at this moment would not only weaken our cause, but smack of bad faith." He had been promising he would not strike at slavery at all, but the terrible trio refused to consider such pledges to the majority of the people of the North to be any kind of promise at all.

"Perhaps we could strengthen the Confiscation Act next session," Henry Wilson offered. He seemed more ill at ease than the others, but was at least being reasonable.

The Prsdt, who could not afford to associate himself with such abolition talk, also could not afford to shut the door on the radical wing of his party. "That thunderbolt will keep."

"Your damnable silk-glove treatment of the South will not work," Stevens pressed. "Unless you commit yourself to arming the free blacks, and freeing the slaves of the South to rise and rampage, I believe you are on the road to ignominious surrender."

"A president has not only to mean well," Wade instructed, "he must have force of character. You are surrounded by old fogies, more than half of whom are downright traitors and the other half sympathize with the South."

"Not so," said Lincoln. How can he put up with this? And yet he does. He cannot kick out the Congress.

"You must enlist slaves in the army, as a first step," Stevens insisted, glowering more darkly than ever. The man strikes me as almost a bit deranged on the subject. "You have to show some grasp of the revolution in store."

"You are inclined to think that this war is to result in the entire abolition of slavery," Lincoln said.

Wade exploded. "Inclined! My God, man, that's exactly what we do think, and that's what this war is about!"

"For my own part," the Prsdt went on doggedly, not mollifying anymore, "I consider the central idea pervading this struggle is the necessity to prove that popular government is not an absurdity." He made that same point in his talks with Breckinridge; he has this central idea quite clear in his mind. "We must settle this question now, whether in a free government, the minority have the right to break up the government whenever they choose. If we fail, it will go far to prove the incapability of the people to govern themselves."

Wade looked at his associates as if they were faced with a crazy theoretician in an ivory tower rather than a commander in chief in the Executive Mansion. I have to admit, our central idea lacks fire, and would not by itself rally many to the Union flag. Perhaps the Tycoon will find other ways to put it, or disguise it, or overlay his somewhat bookish notion with a more popular cause. Certainly the avoidance of absurdity did nothing for the same-damn-three.

"And while we're here," said Stevens, apparently too disgusted to pursue the President's central idea, "there's the matter of your Secretary of War." It is common knowledge that Thaddeus Stevens and Simon Cameron, both Pennsylvanians, despise each other.

"What about him?"

"He's a thief."

Lincoln glared hard at Stevens. "If you have proof of that charge, present it. If you do not, retract it." We have all heard rumors about Cameron and the contractors, but not a shred of evidence of wrongdoing had been presented. Honesty, personal financial honesty, is a very big thing with the Tycoon, and unfounded charges about it infuriate him.

"Perhaps Senator Wilson's Military Committee should exercise its power," Wade interjected, "to look into charges of corruption in the conduct of the war."

"Just send along whatever evidence you have," Lincoln came right back, "and we'll look into it right here."

Stevens spun around and, limping, started out. Lincoln evidently had second thoughts about offending them by being so abrupt, and called after Stevens, "You don't mean to say you think Cameron would actually steal?"

Stevens paused long enough to say dryly, "No, I don't think he would steal a red-hot stove." Wade roared with laughter and pounded Stevens on the arm. Lincoln thought that was pretty good, especially from Stevens.

I showed them out past the anteroom and found the bowler-hatted Mr. Pinkerton, the detective who works for General McClellan, sitting there patiently. On second look, I could see he was wet, soaked clear through, and a small puddle had formed on the floor under his chair. Only the cigar lodged permanently in the middle of his mouth was dry.

When I told the little detective the President was occupied with affairs of state, he refused to leave until he saw what he called "higher authority" than me. I could only pry out of him that he wanted to talk about a confidential matter concerning the loyalty and discretion of a member of Congress.

I carried his message to the Tycoon, suggesting that Plums let Nuts bolt, or whatever the silly detective code was. The Prsdt, looking out the window, said he was worried about that last remark of Wade's: could be this visit was a trap. Could be the Jacobins wanted a device to interfere with his conduct of the war.

What about spending some time with friend Pinkerton? The Ancient was inclined at first to see him, but on second thought decided it might be unwise to get directly involved on a matter about the discretion of a congressman, especially if it turned out to be a supporter.

"Send him to Seward," he said, and I started out. He stopped me. "No, Seward is on the severe side, send him to Judge Blair." He stopped me again. "Might be a good idea to keep it unofficial. Send him to Old Man Blair." That choice seemed apt: Francis Preston Blair, the keeper of the secrets of the wild and woolly Andrew Jackson private life, would know how to use the sort of embarrassing information a Pinkerton would unearth.

CHAPTER 21

TAKE IT TO BLA'AR

He could hear the frontier twang of Old Hickory saying. "Take it to Bla'ar." Not merely questions of patronage had been directed to Francis P. Blair by Andrew Jackson; the secrets of scandal were deposited in his hands by men in power, because Blair—then in his thirties, fresh from Kentucky—had learned at an early age how ambition could drive good men like John Quincy Adams and Henry Clay into corrupt bargains to deny the will of the majority of the electorate. Blair had learned, too, how indiscretions that the world considered sins could be used corruptly to emasculate the ability of good men like Andy Jackson to act as nationalists.

That reminded him of Jackson's wife, Rachel, a lifelong victim of the gleeful calumniators. Old Man Blair was ruminating about the stones cast by hypocrites at that good woman when Senator Henry Wilson, sent by Lincoln, entered the small sitting room in the house Blair provided for his daughter across from the Mansion.

The old man, still gripped in recollection, heard his daughter Lizzie's voice at the door introducing a visitor. He waved a worried-looking pudgy man to a chair.

Memory's train of thought was slow in leaving the stations of the past; Rachel had claimed to be divorced and free when she married Jackson, but that turned out not to be true. Her first husband, a miserable cur of a man, had then sued for dissolution of their marriage on grounds of desertion. After the divorce was granted, Jackson and the woman he had been living with went through a second marriage ceremony to make their union legal. All through his military and political life, that scandal of having been falsely married haunted Jackson and tormented his wife. As President, he came to despise gossips with a passion matched only by his hatred of bankers, and the young Blair of "King Andrew's kitchen Cabinet" had often been called upon to trade political favors to quash rumors, or to use his newspapers to attack the gossips.

And then, Blair recalled with a rush of nostalgia, there was the affair of Peggy O'Neale. There was a mouth-watering woman, much maligned, and to some extent deservedly so. Brought down the whole damn Cabinet and caused a switch in the succession to the presidency that changed the course of American history.

"You seem pensive, Mr. Blair."

The Old Man nodded slowly; ordinarily he proceeded to the business at hand with great crispness and celerity, lest a momentary lack of attention appear to be evidence of woolgathering in old age. But that concern did not apply in the case of Senator Henry Wilson's lapse in judgment, as described to Blair in delicious detail by that bottom-dwelling slug, the detective Pinkerton.

No, it was Blair's judgment that this sensitive interview with Wilson called for an ease of entry to the subject, leading to a slow but certain unraveling of his visitor's reserve, followed by a display of understanding possible only in an elder who has seen everything, and concluded by an implicit agreement of political control. Blair supposed that the only other political veteran who could handle this sort of assignment delicately but firmly—squeezing the political juice from the fruit of forgiveness without making the extraction seem like blackmail—was Thurlow Weed, the Albany wirepuller. But Seward's man Weed was a viper, not above twisting arms to advance his principal's ambition or his own greed, while Blair had always performed these delicate personal tasks for the benefit of his country.

"Do you know what Thurlow Weed had to say about me recently?" the Old Man asked, savoring both the possession of inside intelligence and the chance to indulge in irrelevancy. "He said that if I had lived in the days of Adam and Eve, the presence of a serpent would have been superfluous."

"An insult that well phrased is as good as a compliment," Wilson observed. Blair's respect for his visitor rose a notch; that was a perceptive thing to say. The senator had correctly noted one reason that the Old Man enjoyed giving currency to Weed's remark; another reason was Blair's desire to show to an abolitionist Republican like Wilson that the Blairs were no friends of radicals' most hated adversaries, Seward and Weed. The Blair family, which opposed the extension of slavery, was far from abolitionist; indeed, the Blairs saw abolition as harming the cause of the Union. But the Old Man knew that bridges were necessary between warily allied factions, and one bridge between the Blairs and the radicals was a shared revulsion toward the unprincipled Seward and his hatchet man, Weed.

"The President's secretary sent word," Wilson added, "that you wanted to talk to me unofficially, but he wouldn't say what about."

Blair nodded noncommittally; too soon for that. "What news about Frémont, in the West?"

"We may have made a terrible mistake about Frémont," said the Chairman
of the Senate Military Committee. "And I say 'we' advisedly, Mr. Blair. Your
son in the Cabinet joined Wade and me in urging the President to appoint
Frémont to head our forces in St. Louis."

Blair acknowledged the point. Explorer John Frémont, the "Pathfinder,"
was a man afflicted with an inflated sense of his own importance, but he was a
political ally of the Blairs in Missouri. In return for Blair support in this
appointment, the pompous old hero had agreed to take on Congressman
Frank Blair as second-in-command. A military reputation would help young
Frank gain the nomination for the next President.

"Back in fifty-six, when a few of us organized the Republican Party,"
Wilson went on, "I was all for John Frémont as our first presidential candidate. And politically, he's still one hundred percent—the slogan 'Free Soil,
Free Men, Frémont' still holds. But as a general, he spends most of his time
parading around making pronouncements, rather than fighting."

"My son Frank will provide the action when he gets out there," said Blair.
"But you fellows have to be sure that Frémont doesn't get it into his head to
start freeing slaves. That is not what this war is about."

"With all respect, we disagree about that, Mr. Blair. My friends and I think
that slavery is at the root of our troubles, and that the Union cannot exist, as
Lincoln once said, half slave and half free."

"Unlike Frémont, Lincoln stands for compromise," Blair explained to Wilson, whose expression was courteous and not yet troubled. "The split in the
Union is not between slavery and no-slavery, as your tiny minority would
have it, and as some of the Southern firebrands would have it. The argument
is about extension of slavery into the West. Most Democrats want popular
sovereignty—the decision to be made locally by the new states—and that's
not a crazy or unconstitutional position."

He held up his hand to prevent Wilson from interrupting before he made
his point: "The Blairs happen to disagree with pop sov, because we're nationalists like Andy Jackson. We think the federal government ought to decide
here in Washington whether slavery is extended West. Because we think slavery should not be extended West, and are willing to let slavery exist in the
South, that makes us compromisers—in other words, Lincoln Republicans."

"You completely ignore the moral element," said Wilson. "Human slavery
is wrong. The cruelty is immense."

"Yes, yes, my son Monty went into that when he defended the runaway
Dred Scott." Blair's purpose in arguing with Wilson was not to persuade this
fairly intelligent Massachusetts politician to abandon the opinion of most of
his constituents, but to lay the groundwork for his toleration of opposing
views later. "Morality," he sighed, "what sins are committed in thy name. I
remember what the Calhoun crowd tried to do to poor Peggy O'Neale."

"Who?" The name "O'Neale" sat Wilson up. Blair knew it was pure coincidence—Peggy O'Neale Eaton was probably not related to Rose O'Neal
Greenhow—but it would bring him around to the subject.

"Peggy O'Neale was probably the prettiest barmaid who ever worked here
in the city of Washington," said the old man, crossing his legs and steepling

his fingers. "A sweet girl, tall, dark curls, and a first-rate mind too—had a great many admirers, from sailors to senators." He stopped, lost in reverie; Peggy had once given him a big hug, just being friendly, and he never forgot it.

"And the barmaid?"

"She married a sailor, but he was away for long stretches. The gossip was that he killed himself when he returned, after a year, to find her preparing for a premature *accouchement*. I never believed that. Peggy was lonely, and she found companionship with Senator Eaton, but there was never a shred of evidence presented to substantiate the charge that she was whoring around. Poor girl was socially ostracized by the ladies of Washington society after she married Eaton."

"Eaton was in the Jackson Cabinet, wasn't he?" Like most politicians, Wilson was only vaguely aware of the scandal that had rocked the capital a generation before. Blair always felt like an institutional memory in a city of newcomers.

"Secretary of War. The Vice President at the time was John Calhoun, and his wife could not abide the thought of sharing a social evening with a woman she considered to be, if not a prostitute, a social inferior. Most of the wives in Jackson's Cabinet followed Mrs. Calhoun's lead, and it got to the point where Cabinet members were threatening to shoot each other. Made it hard to hold meetings."

"And the President?"

"Old Hickory, of course, supported Peggy Eaton all the way. He hated Washington society for what it did to his wife Rachel, with that false divorce. So he fired the whole damn Cabinet and let it be known that Calhoun was no longer his chosen successor. Some of us felt that Secretary of State Martin Van Buren got the vice presidency in the second term, and later became President, because he was the only member of the Jackson administration to befriend Peggy Eaton in her hour of need. John Calhoun was left to plot nullification and preach secession from the Senate."

After a moment, Henry Wilson said, "Somehow, I think you were reminded of that episode for a reason, Mr. Blair."

"The reason is that human weakness, which some bluenoses treat as terrible scandal, can have an effect, sometimes a considerable effect, on history."

Wilson nodded, waiting.

"Perhaps you would find it comforting, Senator, to confide in someone—an old man like me, who has reposed many a secret in his bosom—about a relationship that may be worrying you."

Wilson blinked and shook his head.

Blair pushed further. "Tell me about Rose Greenhow."

"My 'relationship,' as you call it," the senator replied coolly, "is the same as that of dozens of senators, generals, and the like. I've been to her home for dinner parties, teas, receptions. So have you. We all know she's a Southern sympathizer, of course, she makes no bones about it, but she doesn't do any harm."

"Senator, the Executive Mansion"—Blair used the name of the President's House rather than the President himself, to keep Lincoln completely clear of all this—"has been given some information about her activities, and your visits."

"Gossips have always abounded in this town," Wilson started to huff, but Blair cut him off.

"This has nothing to do with gossip. This has to do with espionage, and the needless death of Union soldiers."

Wilson's mouth worked and nothing came out. He rose, walked to the window, looked up and down Pennsylvania Avenue, returned to the chair and said, "I can't believe it. I mean, yes, I know Rose well, very well, but what I've done has nothing to do with spying. My God, that's treason. Are you accusing me of treason, is that the information you've been given?"

"Senator, I am not an officer of the law. I am not interrogating you. It may be that I can be helpful to you, but you will have to tell me everything."

Wilson began to rock back and forth in his chair. He tried to talk, failed, breathed heavily, and started to come apart before Blair's eyes. The round form pitched forward in the chair, gulping for air.

In a few moments, he gained control of himself and asked Blair, "How much do you know?"

Blair, who knew nothing beyond the detective Pinkerton's lurid report and attendant suspicions, said only, "You've been followed." He let that sink in, hoping a guilty conscience would do the rest. "Your friends in the Administration have asked me to discuss this with you before any action is taken. If you want to unburden yourself, here I am."

"I love the woman. No—Mr. Blair, I am enslaved by the woman. I don't know how to say this, it's been a nightmare, I've lost all dignity, all my self-respect."

In a torrent, Wilson confessed to sexual sinfulness, recounting in what seemed to Blair unnecessary but delicious detail all the interludes of passion and mornings of remorse. However, the senator said nothing about the passing of military information.

"Senator, what about the plans for Bull Run?"

Wilson looked up, red-eyed, and said, "What about them?"

"Rose Greenhow is a rebel spy."

"Yes. Yes, now I know."

Interesting. "How do you know?"

"Rose has the plans for the fortification of Washington, Mr. Blair. She showed them to me yesterday. They were identical to the plans submitted to the committee."

"Senator Wilson, are you saying that you did not give those plans to her?"

"Of course I didn't. My God, that would be treason."

Blair believed the man's disbelief at the enormity of the charge. "Then why, may I ask, were you going over the plans for the fortification of Washington with a rebel spy?"

"She wanted to verify them. She didn't know if the map that some army captain had given her was the real thing."

"And what did you tell her?"

"I lied. I said I couldn't be sure. I was shocked that she had them. I should have turned her in, but I couldn't. I wouldn't help her, but I couldn't betray her. I was trapped, I was tearing myself apart."

Blair let him weep silently for a while. If what he said was true, Wilson was a weak man but no traitor. That was fortunate. Blair had hoped to find a legitimate basis for forgiveness.

Wilson made an effort to compose himself. "Failing to report what she showed me yesterday," he breathed, "was, I suppose, a form of traitorous behavior. I should have gone to Secretary Cameron, or the committee, or McClellan, or somebody. But as God is my witness, Mr. Blair, I was not the one who gave her those plans. Nor was I the one who told her about Bull Run."

Blair had been willing to believe Pinkerton's charge that Wilson had been the source of the rebel knowledge of the plans for Bull Run; he was willing, too, to give credence to the eyewitness evidence that Wilson had gone over the map of Washington's fortifications with a spy. But now he could find a reasonable doubt in Allan Pinkerton's quick conclusions. Certainly Henry Wilson, in the grip of sexual obsession, was worthy of contempt for failure to report what he had learned about Rose's espionage, but Blair was inclined to believe the senator was more dupe than participant. His story was coherent; his manner of telling it revealed the self-revelation usually attendant to the truth, or at least what the teller believed to be the truth. Blair, who had dined in Rose's home frequently, had to assume the rebel spy with the wide-ranging salon had more than one Union source to tap; Pinkerton should be sent on the trail of the captain Wilson referred to.

"I wish I could tell you, Mr. Blair, how she drove me crazy. I did things I could never—"

"You were observed by a detective through the ground-floor window, going over the plans," Blair told him, because the man had the right to know. "And later, upstairs, through a second-story window by that same very determined fellow on a ladder."

The senator slumped back in his chair, defeated and profoundly ashamed. "Then you know the depths of my depravity."

"You sure popped that detective's eyes," Blair said cheerfully, calling up in his mind the description of Rose in high heels and with whip. Rose O'Neal Greenhow certainly outdid anything charged to Peggy O'Neale Eaton.

But it was no longer necessary to put Wilson through self-torture—although, Blair had to recall, flagellation was evidently an activity he enjoyed—nor would it serve the Republic to drag his name through the mud. Acting as judge and jury, Blair decided to forgive Wilson and to send Pinkerton off after the army officer, the real culprit; also to give the detective whatever he wanted for his secret service from the War Department. That would make it possible to turn to advantage what would otherwise be a scandal damaging to all Republicans, including the President.

"Rose Greenhow will be in the Old Capitol Prison very soon," said Blair, "and it may be necessary for you to visit her there, to keep her quiet about her relationships with loyal unionists. But I believe you to be a man who acted like a damn fool, and not like a traitor." He thought of a possible problem: "Will a search of her house turn up any letters from you?"

"I wrote letters," Wilson said numbly, "but I never signed my name."

"I'll recover them. The fewer specimens of your handwriting around town, Henry, the better." By using his first name, Blair hoped he got across a message of personal warmth; the man really had acted foolishly, dangerously so, but in the context of his whole life, he merited consideration, especially when his gratitude could be so useful. "You have a good record as a man and as a patriot," Blair assured him. "You started as a pauper, you succeeded in life, you founded the party, you've been a solid unionist. Consider this sordid business over. Devote your energies now to preserving the Union."

"You can depend on that, Mr. Blair," Wilson said, the beginning of hope in his face. "Please tell the President—"

"He knows nothing of this."

"Good. I would have difficulty looking him in the face if I thought he knew."

Blair now went to work. "Preserving the Union, Senator, is our common goal. Not abolition. Not conquest of the South, as some of your colleagues among the radicals seem to think."

When Wilson did not respond, the old man pressed: "Some of them— Wade, Chandler, Stevens—are privately scornful of the President, and consider him a man of no principle. There is talk of a cabal within the Republican Party which would like not only to determine the party policy, but wants to grab hold of the entire conduct of the war."

"The President is commander in chief," said Wilson. He was trying not to offend, but Blair noted he did not deny the existence of the cabal.

"I will be blunt, Henry, because I trust you." Blair uncrossed his legs, leaned forward in his chair, and glared straight at the senatorial specimen on the end of his pin. "You and your bunch are not politicians at all. You think of yourselves as men of principle, believers in the one true road, and what you seek is not settlement but victory. However, the majority of this country, and Mr. Lincoln, seek settlement of this conflict on terms that preserve the Union before we all kill each other."

Wilson nodded understanding, though not agreement. Blair felt not the slightest twinge of guilt in pressing a man not in a position to argue.

"Before the last election, you abolitionists lived in a state of perfect purity and bitterness. Pure because you were moral and everybody else was immoral; bitter because you had no chance whatever of amending the Constitution to end slavery." Blair saw the politics of this with what seemed to him perfect clarity: "You were a permanent minority, destined to nibble forever at the edge of power, able to indulge your moral superiority for generations— until those idiots in the South seceded. That changed the game. You're still a minority, but your slice of the pie stayed the same while the Union pie got smaller, making you much more important."

Wilson gave a small smile. "That's a colorful way of putting it, sir, but I wouldn't—"

"Bear with me. In the South's rebellion, you see the chance of a genuine revolution—your revolution, changing this nation to fit your high moral precepts. How do you get control? You'll never get the Democrats, but they're a minority in the North—the target of your revolution is the Republican Party, still in the grip of conservatives like Lincoln and the Blairs and the likes of Seward. Lincoln is your big obstacle. Overcome him, and you can change the purpose of the war from his 'Preserve the Union' to your 'Abolish slavery.' "

Senator Henry Wilson

"It is felt, Mr. Blair, that if Mr. Lincoln can be persuaded to follow his own best instincts about human freedom, this war can turn out to be a blessing for the country."

Blair slashed his hand through the air to cut through that nonsense. "Try that at the next election. Meanwhile, we're counting on you, Henry Wilson, to support the President who was elected to conduct this war in the way he sees fit." Wilson started to squirm, but Blair did not relent. "You are chairman of the Military Committee. Your advice and counsel will be welcome. Stay in charge of that committee. Don't let any other senators elbow you aside, or water down your authority. Above all, do not let Ben Wade seize control of jurisdiction over the War Department. That's yours."

"I have heard some talk about a joint committee—"

"Squelch it." Blair noticed the set of the senator's face harden at his order, and backed off a bit. "At any rate, do what you can to assert your committee's traditional prerogatives. The President can work with you. I don't know if anybody can work with the likes of Wade and that vindictive clubfoot in the House."

"I see what you mean, Mr. Blair, and I'll do all I can." He rose to go. "And I agree that the preservation of the Union should be our first concern."

Wilson might not be able to deliver on blocking Wade from grabbing Senate control of the war, the old man judged, but at least the shaken Lothario would be a voice of restraint in the radical camp.

"One other thing," Wilson said with some pain. "The detective at the window—"

"Pinkerton is going to work for McClellan, and will do what we say. He wants an appropriation for a secret service to send spies into the South, too— might be a good idea to accommodate him."

Wilson nodded vigorously. Blair walked him to the porch and put in a personal word for John Breckinridge, who Wilson had not known was a Blair kinsman. Blair considered that request to be a small fee of his own for doing the Administration's dirty work.

Watching the carriage pull away, Blair felt his arm taken by his daughter Lizzie. "Nice man," she said. "I like him better than the other senator from Massachusetts, Sumner. What brought him here?"

"Oh, he needed some lessons from the Jackson days."

"Did you tell him that Lincoln opposed the Jackson Democrats, and supported the Whig who ran against Van Buren?" His daughter always responded that way when he declined to confide in her.

"Lincoln is learning now that Old Hickory and he had a lot in common," was all he would say. Blair could see the face of John Calhoun before him now, furious at being replaced by Van Buren as Vice President and heir apparent; it served that South Carolina aristocrat right, with his pernicious notion of "concurrent majorities" and states' rights undermining the simple rule of the majority of the nation's people. "Did I ever tell you about Peggy O'Neale?"

"Mother did. Said that when the notorious Mrs. Eaton came into a room, you could never take your eyes off her."

Blair blinked; he had not known that his secret desire for that woman had been noticed. It never ceased to amaze him how the human element, especially in its sexual dimension, could stir politicians and affect the makeup of cabinets, the presidential succession—perhaps the fate of armies and the control of the conduct of wars.

"Remarkable woman, Mrs. Eaton. She even served a purpose today."

CHAPTER 22

"GENERAL JESSIE"

His father had never quite prepared him for Jessie Frémont. Frank Blair knew that John Frémont had delusions of omnipotence, but how does anyone deal with a highborn, power-bred lady who considers herself the partner, protector, and promoter of the greatest man on earth?

He faced Mrs. Frémont in one of the many sitting rooms of the palatial Grant house in St. Louis that the Frémonts had rented from a cousin at a cost of six thousand dollars to the government, giving rise to criticism of both lavish living and graft. Frank Blair, a colonel of the militia—the irregular command enabled him to keep his seat in Congress, which a regular army commission would not—was determined to reason with "General Jessie," as the wife of John Frémont was called. Frank, whose strong-willed mother ruled a powerful roost, was no stranger to outspoken and tough-minded women, but he had never come up against the combination of iron will and brassy voice that was Jessie Frémont.

A large gold ring flashed on the finger she leveled at him. "You're a mean, disloyal backstabber, young fellow, and if your father wasn't one of my life-long friends, I'd have you in military prison for the rest of the war!"

Frank knew that she never thought of herself merely as Mrs. John Charles Frémont, wife of the first senator from California, wife of the first Republican candidate for President in 1856, now wife of the commander of the Army of the West. She was, on the contrary, Jessie Benton Frémont, raised by her father, Missouri Senator Thomas Benton, to be a woman of the world. Her husband, whom she revered, was her equal partner. His reports from California, where his trailblazing created a territory for the nation and a personal fortune in gold for himself, were written by her. When Lincoln needed a radical Republican to satisfy Greeley and the anti-slavery North, he naturally turned to the team of "Pathfinder" John and "General" Jessie Frémont. They had both earned their sobriquets.

"You don't break the South by building fortifications, Mrs. Frémont," said the grim young congressman-named-general who had been placed under Frémont's Missouri command two weeks before. "I am not responsible for the stories in the newspaper that charge him with corruption—"

"Just because he wouldn't hire your corrupt political cronies!"

Frank bristled and could not resist adding "—and I'm not the source of the stories about his living like a potentate, in isolation and splendor, guarded by a bunch of Hungarian officers in European uniforms."

"Those lies get into print," said Jessie Frémont icily, "because the Blair family has an interest in spreading them. Why don't you admit it, Frank? You want my husband's job. You think you can organize an army overnight and win a great victory in the morning and next day run for President of the United States. That's your plan, isn't it?"

She had sent that shaft home; he fell silent, seething.

"As God is my witness," the young man gritted through teeth and black, flowing mustache, "I urged the President to appoint John Frémont as commander of the West, just as I urged him to appoint McClellan in the East. The Blairs were your biggest supporters."

"Not only that," said Jessie, smiling sweetly, "your father engineered my husband's nomination in fifty-six. You used to be our best friends. Now you've turned into our vilest enemies. Why?"

"Why? You're asking me why?" Southern sentiment was rampant in Missouri; if Frémont did not get his men out of camp and into the field, the rebels would soon take over. Just as bad, if no action took place in the West soon, the war would be won by McClellan in the East and the Blairs would have nothing to show in the way of heroism and triumph in the next election. But he could not say that; what could he say? He felt his face getting flushed.

"Try to get command of yourself, Frank. This isn't the floor of the Congress, where all the ladies in the galleries applaud every time you strike a pose."

That was too much for him. "I'm leaving," he said, "Get word to your husband, if you can get through the Imperial Court, that some of us are trying to fight and kill the rebel guerrillas in the areas he can't be bothered

with, while he draws up his crackbrained plans for a Grand Flotation down
the Mississippi."

"Tell him yourself. Why do you get so tongue-tied in the presence of John
Frémont?"

"Because, my dear lady—" He was at a loss for words, a rarity for any
Blair. Frank took a deep breath and started again. "Your husband refuses to
listen to political reason. He keeps making statements about abolition, and
that harms our cause here. Please tell him to stop."

"Nonsense. Slavery is what the war is about."

"Missouri is a slave state, Mrs. Frémont. So is Kentucky. Missouri and
Kentucky refused Lincoln's levy for troops. I was born and raised in Kentucky, I live here in Missouri and ran for Congress here five times. I know
these states, and I know how important they are to President Lincoln. Believe
me, it doesn't help put down the rebellion in Kentucky and Missouri when
the commander, from California, goes around threatening to snatch people's
property away from them."

Jessie Benton Frémont glared him down. She offered no good-bye as the
youngest and most vulnerable of the political Blairs buttoned his uniform
jacket and walked out of the house, probably headed to his headquarters in
what she presumed to be some ostentatiously ascetic tent.

She thought about his parting remark with bitterness. That had always
been the trouble with the Blairs: they lacked conviction. Her father, the
senator, had always warned her about that weakness in the elder Blair, which
he had discovered when they served together in the Andy Jackson days. Blair
and his entire clan were all too practical, too political, bereft of the fire of
idealism.

That night, before going to bed, she kissed her husband at his desk in the
library and warned him again about the Blairs. She reported her conversation
with Frank of the bristling mustache, and the lie that he was spreading that
John Frémont was avoiding decisive battles.

"War consists not only in battles," replied John Charles Frémont, "but in
well-considered movements which bring the same results." He spoke that
way, in aphorisms that could be recorded and remembered, and she remembered them. "Don't wait up for me, Jessie, I am working on something of
historic importance."

She retired. At dawn, when he had not yet come to bed, she went to look
for him. John Frémont was still at his desk, the glow of inspiration about his
fine head, the desktop littered with paper covered by his commanding scrawl.
He looked up and smiled at her; it was the beatific smile she remembered
from the time, twelve years before, he had preferred to accept a court-martial
rather than to compromise his principles.

"I face enemies in the field," he began, continuing his remarks of hours
before as if made a moment ago, "treason in the ranks, and—as you point out
to me in your invaluable way—insubordination or worse among my commanders. The moment requires a bold stroke, to confound opposition everywhere."

"You must punish the rebels and their sympathizers," she said.

"I must make treason costly," the Pathfinder agreed. Triumphantly, he took up the sheets he had written. "Here is my proclamation: 'Circumstances, in my opinion of sufficient urgency, render it necessary that the commanding general of this department should assume the administrative powers of the state.' "

She listened reverently as he read aloud. His proclamation declared martial law throughout Missouri, with all residents in certain areas to be court-martialed and shot if caught bearing arms. Beyond that, the property of all rebels was to be confiscated, "and their slaves, if any they have, are hereby declared freemen."

"A proclamation of emancipation," she breathed. "At last. John, this is a moment every free man in the world has been waiting for."

"And their slaves, if any they have," he repeated, intoning the words, "are hereby declared free men."

The declaration of freedom would surely be a flash of inspiration and illumination across the land. Her husband would be remembered in history not only as an explorer of the continent, but as the great emancipator of an oppressed race.

"What will the President say?"

"Lincoln can truthfully tell his timorous supporters that he had nothing to do with it. He can disclaim all responsibility and say it was a military decision made by a commander in the field."

"If he then asks you to rescind your proclamation?"

"I will refuse, of course. And there is nothing he can do about it, short of relieving me of my command."

"He could do that—"

"He could, but he would not. Lincoln is a follower, not a leader. He needs the example of a leader."

"What about the effect of this in Kentucky?" Her distasteful interview with Frank Blair had instructed her that Lincoln was most sensitive about his native state's pro-slavery majority. The Blairs and all the conservative Republicans and their ilk would have fits.

"The moment the Confederates in Tennessee make a move to send troops north into Kentucky, I have a general in Cairo, Illinois, with standing orders to cross the river into Kentucky and secure Paducah."

Jessie instantly grasped the military shrewdness in her husband's move, which she was certain had escaped Lincoln's narrow conception of strategy. If this historic emancipation provoked the South to violate Kentucky's neutrality, the Northern troops could move right in and save the state from a rebel invasion, real or anticipated.

"Who's your man for that position?" Her husband liked General John Pope, a daring and dashing officer in the Frémont mold.

"Sam Grant." When she said she never heard of him, he added, "Not a great general, but not a man given to self-elation, either. Persistent. He obeys orders without question or hesitation."

Nor would such a soldier be one to take credit away from his commander. "You're not worried your emancipation order will incite a slave revolt?" That was the frequent scare-tactic of pro-slavery forces—to warn of a servile rebellion, with black slaves raping and murdering white masters and mistresses, inciting primitive passions into unspeakable atrocities.

"The slavers wanted a revolution; let them feel the Terror."

"Hallelujah," she whispered. "History will never forget you for this, John. You're more than the Pathfinder. You're the Emancipator."

CHAPTER 23

JOHN HAY'S DIARY
SEPTEMBER 11, 1861

I have been reading the Southern mail with a new surprise and astonishment at the depth of degradation of which the human mind is capable. Nothing but the vilest folly and feculence, that might have simmered glimmeringly in the narrow brain of a chimpanzee, flows from the pens of our epistolary Southern brethren. I have seen rough company in the West and North, but never in the kennels of great cities or the wild license of flatboating on the Mississippi did I ever hear words that were not purity compared with the disgusting filtrations of the chivalric Southern mind.

The history of the world is leprous with thick scattered instances of national folly and crime, but it was reserved for the Southern states to exhibit an infamy to which other crimes show white as mother's milk, and a madness to which an actor's phrensy is sane.

Why do I thusly dip my private pen in vitriol? I have never seen the Tycoon so angry in the three years I have served by his side. That pompous ass Frémont, who thinks God is his junior partner, has gone and issued a proclamation of emancipation, completely befouling the works and harming the Union cause more than if he lost a dozen battles.

How do you suppose A. Lincoln, Prsdt of the U.S., the man whose War Secretary has an iron grip on the telegraph service and whose Postmaster General is in full control of the mails, found out that the slaves had been freed in the West? From his morning newspaper!

William Slade, the negro steward, was off that day. William usually opens the front door of the Mansion and takes the paper from the newsboy before breakfast, and brings it in to me or Nico, whoever is in the office first. That way, we can call the Tycoon's attention to anything we did not already know from reading the correspondents' dispatches in the telegraph office. But on this fine first of September, William Johnson, the boy who shaves the Prsdt, took the *National Intelligencer* directly in to him.

In a few moments came a holler from the Ancient of Days such as I have never heard before. "Did you see *this*? Does he know what he's *done*?"

When I had been apprised of the situation—I'll never again let anyone give him the morning paper without first showing it to me—I ran across the street to the telegraph office to see if Frémont had sent a draft to Washington that we had lost. Nothing. He just did it, with nary a word to a soul, except perhaps General Jessie.

"The Blairs were right," the Prsdt said, smacking his fist in his palm again and again. "They were right when they said Frémont would be the most popular choice, especially with the Germans in St. Louis, and they were right when they said they had made a terrible mistake."

He sat and stewed for a while, and then walked up and down, his carpet slippers flapping, talking to himself, muttering about politicians who think they are generals and generals who think they are politicians. He was less worried about Missouri than about the effect of the order on Kentuckians. Always Kentucky. "It will ruin our chances there."

Montgomery Blair came in, his father in tow, and commiserated with him. "With the set of scoundrels who have control of Frémont," said the Postmaster General, "this proclamation setting up the higher law is like a painted woman quoting Scripture."

The saying around town is "When the Blairs go in for a fight, they go in for a funeral," and, sure enough, they tried to get the Tycoon to fire Frémont forthwith. He resisted, though, figuring that would start a ruckus up North and bring the same damn three fellers back at his throat.

He tried to explain the problem to Frémont in a gentle letter, private and confidential. "I think there is great danger that liberating slaves of traitorous owners will alarm our Southern Union friends, and turn them against us— perhaps ruin our rather fair prospect for Kentucky." The Prsdt then, with great respect, asked Frémont to modify his proclamation to conform to the Confiscation Act of Congress, which Lincoln did not like but at least has signed. He closed with a mollifying "This letter is written in a spirit of caution and not of censure."

I have never seen the Tycoon, after being so angry, turn so obsequious. Why? The huge popularity of Frémont with the big German population in the West, which is largely abolitionist? Is he afraid of the talk about Frémont setting himself up as dictator out West, like a modern Aaron Burr? I can understand that a cool answer turneth away wrath, but this seems to me as too much self-abasement by the Chief Executive.

I was right. For the next week, the most horrendous cries came from our Union men in Kentucky. John Breckinridge, at his damn "picnics," has been using Frémont's proclamation as proof that Lincoln means to free the slaves, and is making great headway toward whipping up sentiment for neutrality. That's what we hear from the "good" Breckinridge, Robert the theologian, who is stumping the state against his nephew.

At that delicate moment, our friend Frémont deigns to send a reply that refuses to take the graceful way out. "Respecting the liberation of slaves," he writes to his commander in chief, "I have to ask that you will openly direct me to make the correction." The bloody cheek! If Lincoln wants to de-emancipate, then he has to be the one to do it personally, thereby bringing on his head all the abuse of the Jacobins.

But that was not the half of it. Frémont also sent General Jessie, in person, holding aloft another letter containing his grandiose military plans.

That was a bad night for everybody. Lincoln had been through one of his more strenuous days: he had gone with Cameron and McClellan to review the Pennsylvania troops in the morning, and then crossed Chain Bridge into Virginia to review the New York troops and listen to interminable speeches, arriving back to the White House after dark, where I gave him the insufferable, you-do-it-not-me letter from Frémont. He jammed his fingers through his coarse hair after reading it, and was thoroughly out of whack about the assault on his authority. The Ancient will put up with plenty, but I have noticed how ornery he gets when anybody tries to take any power from him.

Jessie got off the train from St. Louis about nine that evening and sent word from Willard's requesting an appointment with the President. Before she could wash her face or change her clothes—after two nights, probably sleepless, on the train, it might have been a courtesy to let her pull herself together—back went a peremptory note from the Tycoon: "Now, at once. A. Lincoln."

That was a summons from a hopping-mad President. I could tell a good fight was shaping up, so I stayed in the anteroom outside the Blue Room where he received the imperious emissary from the Western emancipator.

He didn't offer the tired lady a seat. All he said was, "Well?"

"The general wanted to be sure this letter reached you, so he sent me to deliver it. That's how important we think it is."

He waved that away, and got right to the point: "This was a war for a great national idea—the Union. General Frémont should never have dragged the negro into it."

"I am shocked, Mr. Lincoln, that you should say such a thing."

"He never would have dragged the negro into it," he snapped, "if he had consulted with Frank Blair. I sent Frank there to advise him."

"And now you've sent Montgomery Blair to St. Louis as well—why, to advise him? Or to further undermine his authority?"

As the wife of the man who was trying to usurp the President's prerogative, Jessie Frémont had some nerve to cry usurpation. "I assure you, my dear lady," Lincoln told her, "that the Blairs have never been your enemies."

"You're mistaken." Give her credit, General Jessie gave as good as she got; Lincoln had never been so hard on a woman in my memory, and she was just as hard right back. "Do you have any idea, Lincoln, what effect this emancipation proclamation will have in the West? For the first time, rebels realize what the cost of rebellion is. The general has placed fear in their traitors' hearts."

"He has no right to seize private property!" Lincoln fairly shouted, adding, "that's the action of a dictator." Ironic, hearing the Prsdt worrying about dictatorial power—that's what John Breckinridge is saying right now about Lincoln. Thanks to Frémont's untimely action, Breckinridge is killing us in Kentucky, stumping the state with this as proof of Lincoln's designs on everyone's slave property.

"You don't seem to understand, Lincoln, what effect this has already had in England and France." She stood there, feet planted about a foot apart, looking up at him and slugging it out. "The South is getting closer and closer to establishing diplomatic recognition. If they get that, and the trade begins between those nations and the South, and we sink a British ship running a blockade—they're in the war on the side of the South. If that happens, the South will win."

"You're quite a female politician." This said by Lincoln with much scorn.

"Female politician I may be," she snapped back, "but I know that our abolition of slavery will be met with great cheers among the working people of England. Lord Russell will never be able to support the South if the issue is slavery, not just Union."

"Political matters, madam, are for the President to decide. Not for field commanders."

"General Frémont has a political following, make no mistake about that," she warned. "If he decides to try conclusions with you, he could set up for himself."

That was insubordination of the highest order; a threat to take the West out of the Union. Then came Lincoln's stark calling of their bluff: "I'll just have to run that risk."

She held out the letter she carried, the second that Lincoln had received from General Frémont that day. Without a word he took it from her, walked to a spot under the chandelier and read it.

Weary, and without being asked, she sat down and waited for his response. He shook his head. "I've already answered this."

She drew herself to her feet. "The general feels he is at the great disadvantage of being opposed by people in whom you have every confidence."

"What do you mean? Can I not talk with persons holding different views from John Frémont?"

"I am given to believe, sir, that you have been sent a scurrilous letter from Frank Blair slandering my husband. I would like to see that letter now."

"I do not feel authorized to furnish you with copies of letters in my possession without the consent of the writers." He had received such a letter from Frank Blair; "scurrilous" was putting it mildly, but he had no intention of sharing its contents with her.

"You will discover, Mr. President," she said with all the hauteur she could muster, lashing at him where she knew it would hurt most, "that you cannot conquer by arms alone. You can only conquer with arms and an ideal."

That did it; the elected leader of the Union was not about to submit to a lecture on idealism from the scoundrels whose lust for popularity among the Jacobins had caused him so much practical grief. Her words apparently stung, however; Lincoln was too infuriated to let himself respond.

"Good night, Mrs. Frémont." Thus coldly and curtly dismissed, she turned and stalked out. Nobody shook hands. A bad night all around.

Next day—today, the eleventh—he wrote a public letter to the general, pretending "no general objection" to his proclamation, but noting that only the particular slavery clause—the heart of the whole mischievous thing— "appeared to me to be objectionable," adding tartly, "your letter, just received, expresses the preference on your part that I should make an open order for the modification, which I very cheerfully do." He preferred to use the word "modify" rather than the harsher "rescind," but rescind it was exactly what he did, and not in the least cheerfully.

That should help in Kentucky, and may even turn the tables on John Breckinridge, giving Robert—the good Breckinridge—the shield to ward off his nephew's attacks. Perhaps this evidence of the Prsdt's resolve will turn public sentiment back toward the Union and squelch the pernicious movement toward neutrality.

Gain at the border, lose in the North: Frémont's troublesome proclamation renewed the old explorer's heroic credentials with the radicals. Even that old fraud at the War Department, Simon Cameron, was going around praising Frémont's damnable action until I passed the word from on high to shut up. And Lincoln, as the villain who reenslaved the emancipated blacks, caught very hell from the furious Jacobins.

Horace Greeley excoriated the Tycoon in the *Tribune.* I have a stack of cuttings: James Russell Lowell, a pretty fair poet, asked, "How many times are we to save Kentucky and lose our self-respect?" Ben Wade blazed away with "Lincoln has done more injury to the cause of the Union by receding from the ground taken by Frémont than McDowell did by retreating from Bull Run." That Wade comment troubled the Tycoon; "Bluff Ben" dealt in real power, not in newspaper talk, and we suspect him capable of using this sort of presidential action to bite into the presidential war power. Lincoln sent for him, not so much to soothe his feelings as to feel out his intentions.

When the leader of the radicals came into the office this morning, Lincoln tried to finesse him by pretending he had merely been upholding the will of the Congress: "You astonish me, Wade. I was adhering to your confiscation law."

That was hogwash, not intended to be taken seriously, and the red-faced Ohioan gave the lame excuse short shrift: "Frémont's proclamation was entirely within the range of military necessity."

"No," argued Lincoln. "If a general finds the need to seize the farm of a private owner for a fortification, this is within military necessity. But to say the farm shall no longer belong to the owner, or his heirs, forever—that's purely political."

"We're talking about human beings in leg-irons, Lincoln, not 'property.' "

"If a general needs to make use of the labor of slaves, he can seize them and use them—but it is not for him to fix their permanent future. That must be settled by laws and not by military proclamations."

Wade waggled his wattles no. "A proclamation is all you need. With a stroke of the pen, you could set millions free."

"The proclamation by Frémont," said Lincoln, being the lawyer, "is simply 'dictatorship.' It assumes the general may do anything he pleases."

"For God's sake, man, wake up!" Wade exploded. "It is the only means of saving the government."

"On the contrary, it is itself the surrender of the government." Lincoln was quite controlled and precise. "Can it be pretended that it is any longer the government of the United States—any government of constitution and laws— wherein a general or a president may make permanent rules of property by proclamation?"

"That's very high-minded, Lincoln. I didn't notice that fine attention to constitutional principle when you snatched the power to suspend habeus corpus from the Congress. Our mutual friend, Miss Carroll, cooled me off on that with her pamphlet, but I'm keeping score." Miss Carroll is Mrs. Wade's closest friend; that channel is worth remembering.

"This proclamation was reckless," Lincoln said, "it would have surrendered the government."

"Come on, Lincoln, be practical," Wade said in his most ingratiatingly confrontational manner. "Wouldn't this have given a new impetus to the

North? Are you so blinded by expediency that you cannot recognize the real purpose of the war?"

Lincoln slid back in his chair, his favorite position when getting practical. He did not seem to resent the lecture, coming from Wade, who had earned his position with the legislature of Ohio and his colleagues in the Senate—no female politician, he. The Tycoon must find refreshing Wade's total lack of deviousness; when the man comes at you, he swings a huge ax at the center of your skull. In that, he is wholly different from his fellow Ohioan and fellow radical Republican, Secretary Chase; perhaps that is why those two purported political allies detest each other.

The heels of Lincoln's huge boots unlaced to give his corns some ease, went plunk, plunk on the desk, as he mildly observed: "No doubt the emancipation thing was popular in some quarters. But when the news came out, a whole company of our volunteers in Camp Robinson threw down their new arms and disbanded. The very arms we just furnished Kentucky—and I had promised not to send any arms into that state—might be turned against us."

"You are making too damn much of Kentucky."

Down came the Lincoln feet, in one big clomp. "To lose Kentucky is nearly the same as to lose the whole game. Kentucky gone, we cannot hold Missouri, nor, as I think, Maryland. These all against us, the job on our hands is too large for us. We might as well consent to separation at once, including the surrender of this capital."

"You're an alarmist," Wade snorted, "and you're beginning to believe you're a military genius. Disabuse yourself of that, Lincoln. If you can't act to defeat the insurrection, maybe we need a military dictator who can. Certainly we need a military committee in the Senate that will rally the nation."

"You already have a military committee."

"Henry Wilson has lost his zeal. With your latest provocation, snatching away emancipation, we'll need another way to light a fire under you."

He stormed out. That's the way Wade always leaves. Afterward, I asked Lincoln about the talk of the need for a dictator—temporary, as in Rome during its wars. That brought him back to his old self.

"Frémont a dictator?" The notion of that noble mind afflicted with the trials of real government tickled him. "Makes me think of the man whose horse kicked up and stuck his hoof through the stirrup. Man said to the horse, 'If you are going to get on, I will get off.'"

CHAPTER 24

TO SAVE THE CLAN

"Let me tell you a story of tyranny," the preacher heard his nephew cry to the torchlit throng. The crowd of ten thousand, massed on a hillside that formed a natural amphitheater, hushed in anticipation of the oratory of the best speaker Kentucky had yet produced. The speaker's uncle, Robert Jefferson Breckinridge, stood unnoticed with his companion and former ward at the fringe of the crowd. His bent-iron preacher's body was pitched forward, as if to help him listen intently.

"George Hubbell was a newsboy," John Breckinridge was saying, his powerful voice carrying a seemingly conversational tone in the sultry evening air. "He is a cripple, with a spinal deformity, but he hawks the *New York Daily News* on the streets and in the railroad stations because he is the sole support of his poor mother."

The orator held the crowd, largely Southern sympathizers, in rapt attention; everyone, the uncle realized, loved a story of human interest rather than some harangue about constitutional wrongdoing. John had that knack of using a story to get across an abstraction, which was why his nephew had beaten him at the polls when they ran against each other years ago for the legislature. Despite that embarrassment, the Reverend Robert Breckinridge had taken pride in his brother's son's amazing political career. He had marveled at the younger Breckinridge's God-given magnetism even as he took umbrage at just about everything the young man ever said. Despite the differences on policy, he had supported his nephew's presidential candidacy last year, assuming his kinsman would be pro-Union in the end; his nephew had been grateful for that support, though distancing himself from his uncle's anti-slavery views. The preacher, uncomfortable in this night's crowd of potential rebels, suspected that God had punished him for allowing family pride to come before moral principle. The gap had widened between the two Kentuckians since, and now the two Breckinridges represented neutrality vs. loyal Unionism in their divided native state.

"A United States marshal in Connecticut," the speaker for Kentucky's neutrality boomed out, "had ordered the selling of the *Daily News* stopped in railroads leading to his state, but the crippled newsboy did not heed the marshal's request. And so the marshal, clothed in all the self-righteousness that despotism uses to justify its rule, went to Simon Cameron, Lincoln's Secretary of War."

Sympathetic boos punctuated the oration at the scornful mention of Cameron. Widely accused of corruption, desperate for fresh political support, the War Secretary had lately been courting the anti-slavery radicals in the North. "And what was Simon Cameron's answer? He said, 'Arrest him—send the boy to Fort Lafayette!' I ask you, my friends, is there no depth to which the zealots of loyalty will not descend? Even Horace Greeley"—more boos and catcalls for the editor of the abolition-agitating *New York Tribune*—"even

Greeley, who has cravenly approved the arrest of editors who oppose the war, was moved to say this: 'When you descend to arresting newsboys, can the game be worth the ammunition?' "

The preacher did not expect his nephew to tell the end of that story—how Secretary Seward, nudged by a President sensitive to public sentiment, countermanded the Secretary of War's stupid order and released the newsboy.

"Only a little over a month ago, on August 8," the Kentucky senator went on, "Abraham Lincoln signed into law the loyalty-oath statute. Do you know what that does? It requires that every person who works for the central government sign a pledge—a sworn oath—of loyalty to the United States, the national government, and renouncing any contrary state resolution or statute. My friends, that changes the very nature of our government. No longer are we a free association of sovereign states, as our founders agreed—no, we are now a polity where states are mere districts, powerless fingers at the end of the central government's all-powerful arm."

"Here comes Jefferson," whispered the preacher's companion, squeezing his arm. "He never leaves that out, Reverend Bob."

The speaker's uncle nodded grimly. Jefferson was his own middle name, and the Breckinridge orators never failed to make the connection to the first John Cabell Breckinridge, who introduced the anti-Federalist Kentucky Resolutions defying the national government's infamous Sedition Act. Thomas Jefferson, fearful of being accused of sedition himself, had guided the hand of their forebear, and rewarded him in his own presidency with the post of Attorney General. That Breckinridge-Jefferson alliance had produced the first victory for what came to be known as states' rights, resisting a central tyranny.

The speaker surprised them by veering away from political theory and family history to concentrate on a national scandal reflected in a current local grievance. "One brave Kentuckian, a writer for the *Louisville Courier*, described that sort of assumption of power over Kentucky by the Lincoln regime as 'a usurpation which no citizen of Kentucky is bound to obey.' And you know what happened to him—he was dragged out of his bed in the dead of night by a Federal marshal, and, in defiance of a writ of habeas corpus, was shipped off to Fort Lafayette. Only God knows if we will ever see that brave man again. His great newspaper is in danger, at this very moment, of being silenced forever."

The orator used that incident to foster resentment at what he considered the termination of free speech that had taken place after the crackdown on press freedom throughout the North. In New York, the editor of the *Journal of Commerce* had rightly said, "There is now no Opposition press," as his outspoken daily was denied the use of the mails. In Brooklyn, the second largest city in America, the newspaper with the greatest circulation, the *Eagle*, was nearly driven out of business by Seward, who relented only after the editors agreed to stop publishing anti-war opinion. The only anti-Lincoln voice left in that state was the German-language *National Zeitung*, untouched only because Lincoln did not want to offend the largely pro-Union German community.

The litany of these encroachments on freedom had an effect on the crowd, which the preacher felt wanted help in justifying disloyalty. Reverend Breckinridge understood and despised the way his nephew was providing the crowd with a moral rationale for opposing the crusade against slavery, making it seem that it was cowardly to defend the Union against attack and courageous to refuse to become involved in the evil of war. Underneath these convoluted, high-sounding arguments of the intellect, the preacher Breckinridge believed, his nephew was appealing to the crowd's unspoken anger at abolition and fear of death.

"Damned sophistry," he muttered too loudly, and could immediately feel hostile eyes in the crowd turn toward him. His companion shushed him and pulled him farther back up the hill; this was neither the time nor the audience for a public debate between the Breckinridge men. He recognized that his nephew would have this crowd overwhelmingly on his side, and that the pro-rebel *Courier* account of any confrontation would make it appear that neutrality had carried the day, as it did only the other night at the opening of the Frankfort Peace Convention. Still, it rankled him to hear anyone turn truth on its head, as his nephew was doing with such effect.

The younger Breckinridge had for more than a week been exploiting the surge of anti-abolition sentiment in Kentucky caused by Frémont's untimely emancipation action; the preacher, who had split the Presbyterian Church by storming out when its synod would not endorse emancipation, thought the Pathmarker's blow to slavery was morally justified, but the timing could not have been worse for Kentucky Unionists. Lincoln's quickness in proving he was not in the radicals' pocket had turned that surge in the other direction; in speeches throughout the state, the elder, loyal Breckinridge had made the most of the President's reaffirmation of property rights and rejection of dictatorial powers. It was the preacher's assessment that the swift and decisive Lincoln reaction to Frémont's maneuver left the Union cause in Kentucky stronger than before.

"Hard upon us all, in Washington and here in Kentucky," his nephew was saying, "is crowding grim war, with death and devastation in train, with ruin for every interest, tragedy for many a hearthstone." He had been holding forth for nearly three hours—about the expected length for a major oration—and his uncle knew that the theme of the horrors of war would surely be his conclusion. Reverend Bob did not want to wait for the ending; he wanted to make a personal, familial, face-to-face appeal to his nephew at his hotel. As the speaker touched on what some were calling "the holocaust of lives" in store, Robert Breckinridge pressed Anna Carroll's hand on his arm and edged back up the hill and out of the fringe of the crowd.

The great, mellow voice followed them into the night. The preacher, his own speaking style now cramped by asthma, felt it inexplicably unfair that the Lord had denied him the gift of such an instrument of persuasion.

"Let other sections who call for war learn the horrors of war," the senator's voice could still be heard to say. "Let Kentucky stand for peace, peace at any price, and by our example show our sister states, North and South, that we need not destroy each other!"

His uncle walked forlornly down the other side of the hill toward the town of Lexington, Anna's grip a support. Twenty years before, she had been his spiritual ward, and he had lovingly shaped and guided her moral course, sternly protecting both her and himself from the natural attraction that had steadily grown until he had found it unbearable. After his return to the West, they had pursued their careers separately, but in curious unison: like him, she had fixed her thunder against the dangers of Popery and unbridled immigration, and led the Know-Nothing movement in Maryland as he had led it in Kentucky. Foreigners, Catholics, and slaveholders had been their common foe.

He was thankful that after all these years a concern for his disloyal kinsman had driven Anna to reestablish contact. Was there more to it than concern? The preacher refused to allow himself to speculate about the nature of the friendship between his nephew and his former ward—he knew the temptation that must be present, and prayed that no sin attached—and he did not intend to pry. It was enough that Anna had asked him to join forces to save his nephew from the gravest consequences of his political folly. All she had asked was that their joint plea be presented as his idea, a white lie apparently rooted in feminine modesty. He felt no compunctions about that, and indeed was pleased that Anna retained a certain personal shyness despite her career as crusading public pamphleteer.

Robert Breckinridge was even more pleased that his detailed argument against state sovereignty had been taken up by Lincoln in his most recent message to Congress (no state save Texas had ever been sovereign) and was flattered by the talk of his possible nomination, if he kept Kentucky in the Union, to replace the corrupt Cameron. A more profound motive existed, however, for his willingness to take the lead in petitioning his nephew and political rival at this crucial moment: his family was tearing itself apart. His nephew's young son, Cabell, had run away to fight for the South; his niece, Mary Elizabeth, had joined the Union nurses; closer to home, of his four sons of military age, two were leaning North, two actually thinking of fighting with the South. He could never forgive his boys if they turned traitor, and would cast them out forever; but they would be far less likely to rend his family and blight his old age if John C. could be persuaded to remain loyal.

"Neutrality," he told Anna Carroll, walking through the outskirts of town toward the Phoenix Hotel, "that's the key. It's John's idea, and that's how we can hold him."

"No possibility exists of any state remaining neutral," she said glumly.

"Of course not," he agreed. "But if John bases his decision on which side violates Kentucky neutrality, we may have him. President Lincoln has assured me that he will not send in his forces first." General Anderson, the Kentuckian who had been the hero of Fort Sumter, was under strict orders to sit tight with his men in Porkopolis, as Cincinnati was nicknamed, and Sam Grant was to make no move across the river from Cairo, Illinois.

"That's just not so, Reverend Bob. Lincoln has been quietly reinforcing Camp Robinson for the past month, and sending in arms."

He waved that off; she had not lost her unfortunate habit of being too literal and too ready to contradict. "Those are Kentuckians training in their own state. Neutrality would be violated only if an outstate army moves across the Kentucky frontier."

He knew that public opinion would be swayed by which side moved on Kentucky first. He prayed, for the sake of his state as well as of his immediate family, that the rebels would be the first to be drawn across the line.

The Reverend Robert Breckinridge

To the loyal Breckinridge, Kentucky's choice was not between war and neutrality, as his benighted nephew held, but between North and South, democracy and anarchy, right and wrong. His full, iron-gray beard quivered with righteousness: with the help of God, Lincoln, and this woman beside him—and counting on the stupidity and impatience of Leonidas Polk, the Episcopal bishop who was the general of the rebel troops to the south—he would bring his kinsman back from the brink of folly, treason, and eternal damnation.

CHAPTER 25

EVERY REBEL YOU KILL . . .

He swallowed a couple of times as he walked up the stairs, testing his throat after the oration, pleased that it felt in no way strained; after his three hours on the platform, only his feet hurt. On his speaking tours, Breck always traveled with a sack of salts in his valise, and looked forward now to lying down crosswise on his bed with his lower legs and feet dangling over into a bucket of hot foot-soak. After a Senate speech the previous year, Anna had surprised him by massaging his aching feet, an uncharacteristic gesture that introduced him to the notion that each toe was a separate, living thing, deserving individual attention. It had been a month since she had handed him his traveling bag, and he missed her.

As he put the large hotel key into the lock, Breck frowned at the light coming from under the door. He had left the Phoenix Hotel suite during the daytime.

He wished he had followed John Hunt Morgan's advice and armed himself. Morgan was a hothead whose arming of the sharpshooters called the Lexington Rifles would be seen as a warlike provocation, and Breck had spoken to him sharply about that, but the young horseman's suggestion about carrying a gun was probably sensible: a moderate form of self-protection might have been prudent for the man who was the object of Unionist hatred. Yet someone had to set the example for the principle of neutrality, and for the courage needed by peacemakers; besides, if some Yankee zealot was set on killing "the traitor Breckinridge," no weapon in his pocket would save him. If the rumors about plans to arrest neutralists were true and a Federal marshal awaited him, he would not shoot it out, even if armed; he had thought that through, and would attempt an escape on the way to Fort Lafayette. Under no circumstances would he spend the war as a prisoner, considered a fool in the South and a traitor in the North, and unable to be heard in behalf of any cause. He turned the key and pushed open the door.

An Old Testament prophet faced him from his armchair with a stern angel standing behind. Breck took a deep breath and stared, first at Anna Carroll, with whom he had shared a most unsatisfactory farewell, and then at his Uncle Robert, gnarled hands gripping the arms of the chair, cold eyes looking over the spectacles at the end of his bulbous nose, his half-gray, half-white beard flowing down to the middle of his chest.

"We told the man at the desk we were family," she explained, "and he let us in to wait for you."

He smiled, mock-angry. "You were here in Lexington and you missed my speech? I talked for three hours, settled everything."

"I know all your arguments," she said. Anna knew them as well as he did himself; in some cases, such as President Jefferson's latter-day switch to central supremacy, better.

"And they're all wrong," added his uncle. "Did you read her *Reply to Breckinridge* pamphlet? Destroys every one of your positions; Lincoln himself said so."

"The President sent word to me through Bates," she said chattily—she always spoke quickly and most self-assuredly when she was evading a show of emotion—"that they want ten thousand printed. I want to print fifty thousand, but I can't find the money."

"You'll find it," Breck said, drinking her in. He wished his uncle was not there. "Do you have a free copy for the actor in the title role?" She smiled tentatively, took a copy out of the bag in her hand and gave it to him. She seemed to want no evidence of warmth in front of his uncle, so he took it with a small bow of thanks.

"I asked Anna to join me in this visit," said the older man, "to verify in your own mind two most important facts that bear on your future, as well as that of our family and our country."

Breck had hoped the idea to come all the way from Washington to Kentucky to visit him was Anna's, but no matter; he was prepared to accept that whatever information the two of them conveyed was true. He offered them some of Jesse Wood's fine Old Crow bourbon whiskey, which Anna accepted and his uncle declined.

"I have this message from my friends in the War Department," said Anna. "They commend to you the example of your good friend, John McClernand. They seemed certain you would catch the significance of that."

Breck nodded. John McClernand had been born in Breckinridge County, Kentucky, and the families were friendly; he had moved to Springfield, Illinois, and become the Democratic representative from that district, serving in the Congress in a seat close to Breck's. The short, dapper Democrat was a political ally and drinking companion of Breck, but by choosing to remain loyal to the Union, he had reaped the political benefits: he was now a general in the Federal Army and was said to be a favorite of the President's, likely to lead the movement down the Mississippi denied to Frémont. High military command, influence at the top in Washington, receiving all the favor a Republican administration could bestow without losing the position of member of the loyal opposition, ultimately another clear opportunity at the presidency —it was all there for Breck to take, even after his sometimes strident criticism of the Lincoln administration. He was not surprised; he and Lincoln had argued strenuously, but had come to respect each other, and Breck had something important to offer at a crucial moment: a much more united Kentucky on the Union side.

"Together, you and I could make a difference in this war," said his uncle. "Opposed, the Breckinridges would be like paired senators, canceling each other out. Together—high field command for you, high civilian command for me—we can set an example for our children. Your son, my sons—they would follow the united family."

That filial consideration could not be ignored; his uncle had evoked a powerful argument. Breck was heartsick at the absence of Cabell, and knew that his uncle feared that his four boys might be forced into fighting each other—not merely serving on opposing sides, but actually shooting at each other in battle on Kentucky soil. That prospect of family unity, as well as the veiled offer of a high command—not to mention the resumption of his double life in Washington with Anna—weighed heavily in the scales.

"I'm not making a choice between North and South," he reminded them. "I'm choosing neutrality, with Kentucky the corridor through which peace can be made. At least one state has to keep its head amid all this craziness. I just spoke to ten thousand Kentuckians who agree."

"My audiences just as fervently disagree," said his uncle.

"How about a series of debates throughout the state?" Breck suggested, eager to get at those crowds reluctant to hear him now.

"No, my voice is physically no match for yours." Perhaps that was an excuse, but Breck knew the older man was not to be drawn into conflict on his nephew's terms. "John, neutrality is not an alternative. Neutrality is a position that only an independent nation can take in a foreign war, and Kentucky has never been an independent nation. It takes sovereignty to proclaim neutrality—"

"—and for any state to declare neutrality," Anna finished for him, "is just as much an assertion of sovereignty as it would be for that state to secede. An insurrection is going on, a civil war, and no part of the Union has the right to stand aside."

"A state proclamation of neutrality is an anti-Union act," the older Breckinridge added, "and you, John, have always spoken up for Unionism. That's why I could support you in last year's campaign, despite our disagreement about emancipation."

Breck believed such sovereignty to refuse war existed in each state, and that Kentucky's continued neutrality would ultimately contribute to a stronger freedom in a smaller Union, but saw no advantage to debating in private what his uncle was unwilling to debate before the citizens. As he listened, he leafed through Anna's pamphlet *A Reply to Breckinridge*, recalling the morning that he had first read a draft—their last time together, in her rooms at the Ebbitt House—when a name in it leaped off the page at him.

"You talk about General Quitman in here, Anna." He glanced further, surprised and alarmed. "My God, you have the Quitman papers, all the letters."

Breck had met John Anthony Quitman, Calhoun's nullification lawyer, in the Mexican War; in the early fifties, Calhoun, Quitman—then governor of Mississippi—and others plotted secession, to be sparked by forcing the federal government to reinforce a Southern fort to ignite a conflict, just as happened at Sumter in Charleston Harbor. The youthful Breckinridge had been on the fringes of that group, disagreeing with the plotters but never exposing them. But here, in Anna's pamphlet, was the damning story, with quotations from correspondence exchanged over a decade, demonstrating that the rebellion was far from a spontaneous reaction to Lincoln's election or a response to Northern provocation. Breck's heart sank. In cold print, the documents made what he considered merely correspondence among disgruntled but not disloyal Southerners appear to be a long-term plot to dismember the Union. In the context of *A Reply to Breckinridge*, the revelation of the secret history of the secession movement made him seem to be one of the central plotters.

"I didn't know you meant to destroy me," he said, stunned, "I thought you were writing a reply to my arguments." He turned a page, and winced at a letter urging the takeover of Cuba, Mexico, and all of tropical America. That was the sort of wholly impractical imagining that Calhoun's friends had tossed about, mainly to show to believers in a strong nation how a Southern Confederacy could grow to be more powerful than the current Union.

"The Quitman 'plot' was just a lot of talk," he added, "never meant anything. But this seems to give substance to all the nonsense you hear now about the Knights of the Golden Circle." That was the conspiracy scare that Lincoln men were currently using to stifle dissent and to whip up bitterness at men like him.

"When I go to war, I use all the ammunition I have," she said. Anna had been a repository of much of the correspondence, perhaps from her friend and railroad client Jefferson Davis, perhaps through her Know-Nothing activity. The plotters had been as much friends of hers as of Breck's, a fact not alluded to in her pamphlet. "When you left after that Senate speech, I was very angry."

And she was the wrong person to anger. The publication of this inflammatory material would be useful to those—not Ned Baker, but perhaps senators like Sumner and Wade—who were not content with calling him a traitor but were urging his arrest. Other elected advocates of peace like Representative Clem Vallandigham were being heavily criticized but were not considered such threats as to warrant the arrest of a duly elected public official; Breckinridge, in Kentucky at the knife's edge, was a threat that many felt had to be stopped.

"Have you heard of any plans to put me in Fort Lafayette?" he asked his uncle bluntly.

The older man sighed, looked up and back at Anna, and replied, "That is another reason for our being here. Just as there are those willing to make certain concessions to attract you to the cause, there are others, um . . ."

"Who want to hang you," she finished. "Seward is one. At the War Department, Cameron's lawyer, Stanton, says that as soon as the Kentucky legislature rejects neutrality, the Federal commander at Camp Robinson here would have the authority to arrest you without warrant or writ."

Breck nodded ruefully; that power was in a law he had fought against in the Senate. Although the Kentucky governor was foursquare for neutrality, the majority of Kentucky legislators favored joining the war on the side of the Union. Despite the Peace Convention and the picnics throughout the state, the legislature was likely to make its declaration any moment. Public opinion in Kentucky, he judged, went one third secession (like his son), one third loyal (like his uncle), and the controlling third neutral, like himself; if either North or South invaded, the neutral third would largely turn against whichever side was the invader. That is what Breck would be inclined to do, and he assumed that most others like-minded would be inclined the same way.

The only hope for neutrality was to keep the pro-Union legislature from acting, to keep pro-secession firebrands like Morgan from raiding arsenals, and to keep both North and South from invading; that way he could stay free and keep the state neutral. Breck was aware that his chances for success were slim, getting slimmer every day.

"I do not see," he said, fishing for more information, "in the light of the feeling against me in the Senate and the War Department, how there could be any serious bridges back."

His uncle hastened to assure him: "Anna here, who was remorseful after the publication of her pamphlet gave comfort to your detractors, made certain that your course of loyalty would be well received at the highest quarters."

This visit to Lexington had been Anna's idea, then; that made more sense, and made him feel better, too, about Anna's attachment to him. On that last day in the Senate, he had infuriated her—not only for speaking in favor of peaceful separation, but for jeopardizing his career—but he found it more acceptable, even satisfying, to have her angry and later forgiving than merely disgusted, as she had seemed at the time. He realized that Anna had reestablished contact with his uncle—whose influence she had broken away from years ago at an emotional cost—in order to reconciliate with his nephew. That displayed more contrition about her rejection of him, and regret for her bitterness in her pamphlet about him, than she could ever put into words.

"The old gentleman is on your side," she said, referring to Francis Blair, "and Mrs. Lincoln is not without influence."

Shouts from the crowd in the street below brought his uncle to his feet. He drew aside the drape, opened the window, and leaned out. Breck took that opportunity to tell Anna that he was grateful for her friendship and glad that his uncle had prevailed on her to come. Anna seemed relieved that he did not carry on about the Quitman exposure.

"Not all your partisans, back from the speech," Robert Breckinridge said, pulling back into the room. "Mixed crowd, could get ugly. I shall make arrangements, Anna, for us to take rooms here in the Phoenix for the night."

She nodded and looked at Breck. His hopes rose of being alone with Anna later. "What worries me most," she said, "is the possibility of the Federals violating Kentucky neutrality. We could lose you on that."

She knew him well. "It would be foolish, but it's tempting," he said. "You have Generals Anderson and Grant just across the Ohio River, in Cincinnati, and a brigade of McClernand's backing them up in Cairo. They must be dying to come across and grab Paducah."

"What is so signficant about Paducah?" his uncle asked.

"The Tennessee River is the key to the war. If the North takes Paducah," he explained, more for Anna's benefit, "and gets past Fort Henry, the Union forces would have a clear run down the Tennessee River to Pittsburg Landing, near the Alabama line." He knew it was not actually "down" river, since the Tennessee was one of the few waterways that quirkily flowed the other way, but it was in a southward direction and appeared "down" on a map, and most people who had not traveled the river said that. As a boy, he had taken a raft from Paducah, at the junction of the Ohio and Tennessee, south to Pittsburg Landing, pitching a tent alongside the old log Methodist meetinghouse that the parishioners had given the biblical name Shiloh Chapel.

Robert's Presbyterian preacher's bewhiskered face still wore a blank look; military strategy required some understanding of logistics, the science of supply lines, which Breck had picked up in the Mexican War. Anna Carroll, with her background in railroad promotion, quickly finished the obvious strategy: "If the Union took Pittsburg Landing, as far south as Alabama, we could supply the Federal army by water down the Tennessee River. Then the North would be able to turn right and pick off the great Mississippi River ports from the rear—Memphis, Port Hudson, Vicksburg."

"Couldn't take the Mississippi any other way," Breck said, distracted now by the noise from the street, "and who controls Big Muddy wins the war. 'Old Fuss and Feathers' is right about that." In addition, a fast river-thrust that far south would enable the North to sever the main east-west rail line that was the backbone of the Confederacy, but it occurred to him that some military strategy was better not vouchsafed to his pro-war uncle.

At a rapping on the door, Breck motioned to Anna to move to the side of the room, out of the line of any potential fire. He asked loudly who was there.

"My name is Haldeman," said a voice in the hallway. "I own the *Courier*. I have some news for you."

Breck opened the door briskly, extended his hand, and drew in the short, unarmed publisher. He recognized his staunchest supporter in the press. Walter Haldeman's *Courier* had beat the drum for Breckinridge in the presidential campaign, while the *Louisville Journal* had gone for Stephen Douglas, and the third paper, the *Democrat*, had taken up for John Bell, who carried the state. In recent weeks the pro-slavery *Courier* had supported Senator Breckinridge's neutrality crusade, on the theory that such a position would better help the South.

Breck told the publisher he could speak in front of his visitors, and Haldeman said in a flat voice: "General Leonidas Polk in Tennessee, anticipating a move by the Yankees on Paducah, has sent a Confederate force across our border." When the doom of neutrality had sunk in, he reported further: "He has occupied Columbus, Kentucky."

"Hallelujah," breathed Robert Breckinridge. "Serves the rebels right for trusting an Episcopal bishop at the head of an army. That idiot is delivering Kentucky into the bosom of the Union."

"You may be right, Reverend Breckinridge," the publisher said sourly. "The army that Lincoln outfitted outside Louisville, despite all those promises of neutrality, suppressed my newspaper this afternoon. Just marched in and arrested the editor and shut the paper down."

"Undoubtedly a wise decision," the preacher snapped. Breck could not blame him for that thoughtless reaction, because he knew how the *Courier* had savagely denounced his uncle's stand and reviled his emancipation activities. "War has come to Kentucky, and your damned treasonous rag has been aiding and abetting the enemy."

"You never gave a damn who got killed in this state," Haldeman retorted. "I remember when you and your Know-Nothings egged on the rabble to butcher the people of Louisville unfortunate enough to be immigrants."

Anna, no stranger to the Know-Nothing campaign against the foreign-born, changed the subject to a more immediate and personal one: "Breck, this means the rebels have violated Kentucky's neutrality. Your course should be clear now. You tried to keep the peace here, but the Confederate General Polk broke the peace with an invasion."

True. Breck, if he chose, could now go North with honor, although he knew that was far from Haldeman's purpose in bringing him the news. If that was to be his course, how to get word to Cabell? Perhaps he could get Mary Elizabeth, Uncle Bob's grandniece, to get in touch with a counterpart in the rebel ranks to bring the boy back—at his age, nothing he had done could be considered treason.

The publisher of the *Louisville Courier*, clearly uncomfortable about speaking in front of a political arch-enemy, broke into his thoughts with a request: "Senator, I have to see you alone. Right away, preferably downstairs." When Breck hesitated, Haldeman added, "There's more for you to know. It is private, secret, and—believe me—urgent."

Breck asked Anna and his uncle to wait in the room; it would not be good for either of them to be seen with him at that moment, particularly if Breck did not decide to go North, though the loyalist tug was unmistakable. He followed the publisher down the back stairs to a small room off the noisy hotel lobby.

"The other news is from the capital in Frankfort."

"The Peace Convention?" It had been meeting that day; he was scheduled to address it the next night.

"The Kentucky legislature has declared an end to neutrality and taken the side of the Union."

Bad news, but not as bad as the Confederacy's decision to invade Kentucky. "That's understandable," he said, "given Bishop Polk's move across our border."

"You don't understand, Breckinridge. It means that the Union troops right here at Camp Robinson—the same ones that closed down my paper this afternoon—can now make immediate arrests. And one of your uncle's flunkies in Frankfort, the Speaker of the House, put your name at the top of the arrest list."

He began to get a cornered feeling. "I can go to Frankfort and protest—"

"You seem to think you still have some kind of political choice," Haldeman said urgently. "The fact is that a detachment of troops left Camp Robinson a couple of hours ago for the sole purpose of taking you and me into custody. They should be here within an hour, maybe less. Whatever protesting you do, you'll do from inside a cell at Fort Lafayette."

All choice had been snatched from him. Circumstance had shut down what he imagined to be his alternative, like troops shutting down a printing press. Perhaps all thought of making a choice had always been a chimera, and his course opposing Lincoln, and before that in opposing Douglas, had been leading him inexorably into rebellion. The thought of self-entrapment pained him. He might have gone South on a matter of pride or principle, but now he would have to go as a matter of necessity. Forney had been right: John Breckinridge was not destined to return to the United States Senate.

Pain at his failure to control events, even to control his own personal decision, was followed by a kind of relief: If the choice had been made for him, at least he could make the most of it. He was not the only one sucked into the maelstrom of civil war, and already he could feel his resentment rising against the forces seeking to hunt him down and silence his voice.

"Mr. Haldeman, I want you to know how saddened, how outraged, I am about the suppression of your newspaper. It was the most courageous voice for peace in our state."

"Not dead yet," said Haldeman. "I'm headed out to Bowling Green. The western part of Kentucky will be impossible for the Federals to control, especially with a man like Sidney Johnston in command of all Confederate forces in the West. I'll publish there and smuggle copies up here. Ah, there's Morgan at last."

John Hunt Morgan, rifle slung and a pistol in his belt, eyes bright with excitement, led a crowd of his Lexington riflemen into the lobby. The noise died; arguments between the several hundred Kentuckians ceased in the presence of the hard-looking young men bearing arms.

"We raided the armory, Breck, and took some of those 'Lincoln guns,'" Morgan said. "We have horses for both of you—terrible old nags, but they'll have to do. I'd say we're a good half hour ahead of the regiment sent to get you. You want to say good-bye to this crowd for all of us?"

Breck did not know how to say no to a request for a speech. He stood on a chair and addressed the lobby crowd of his fellow Kentuckians, whom he judged to be evenly split between pro-Union and secesh. Should he send the publisher up to his room to fetch his uncle and Anna? It would be better, when the Federal troops came for him, that his friends and relatives be honestly surprised at his defection. He ached to have Anna hear his farewell, as she had heard so many of his speeches from her seat in the Senate gallery—especially, came the rueful afterthought, since this would necessarily be brief and pointed, the sort of oratorical style she kept encouraging him to adopt. But to bring her downstairs to the lobby to have her listen to him, in these times of hysteria, would be risking her pro-Union reputation, perhaps even her neck.

"My friends," he filled the room with his voice, "I have tried to stand for this state's wishes in Washington. I have opposed Lincoln's war policy at every step."

The crowd, as always in Kentucky since the time of Henry Clay, was made up of partisans of all stripes, interspersed this time with mountain men ready to go to war. The roomful of bluegrass citizens, abuzz with rumors of the impending arrests, quickly quieted to give him what he knew would be his last Kentucky hearing for a long time.

"I deny that I have committed any crimes, and I reject all charges that I have misrepresented my fellow Kentuckians.

"I resign my office for the most compelling of reasons," he told them with unfeigned sadness. "I resign because there is no place left where a Southern senator may sit in council with the senators of the North. In truth, within the meaning and spirit of the Constitution, there is no longer a Senate of the United States."

No boos or applause met his remarks; the crowd's members were either tearfully respectful or silently angry. "I am fleeing now, frankly, to avoid arrest. If I had any assurance that a trial by jury was possible, I would welcome arrest and would happily subject myself to the workings of a free judicial system. But that is not the sort of arrest in store for me, or for anyone who has dared to speak out against the usurpation of our rights as individual Americans, or our rights as citizens of sovereign states.

"Will Kentucky consent to these usurpations of Mr. Lincoln, to suffer her children to be imprisoned and exiled? Never—never, while thousands of her gallant sons like these men here have the will and the nerve to make the state sing to the music of their rifles."

That drew a cheer from a portion of the crowd, but he did not want to leave on a note of ordinary defiance. "I wanted peace and now have war. I wanted Union and now see a land permanently divided, because it would be wrong for either section to conquer and rule over the other. With my eyes open, I cast my lot with those who have been denied the protections and freedoms that are their birthright."

Morgan's raiders, he knew, were itching to run for the horses, but the departing senator was not quite finished talking to his constituents. Breck decided to be brutally honest about his choice, or lack of choice, in the decision to "go South."

"I have been forced to choose between arrest, exile, and resistance. I intend to resist. Therefore I now exchange, with proud satisfaction, a term of six years in the Senate of the United States for the musket of a soldier."

Later that night, after a regiment of Federal troops arrived to arrest the men who had fled not forty minutes before, Anna Carroll stood in a corner of the Phoenix lobby listening to Reverend Robert Breckinridge address the pro-Northern Kentuckians and the Union troops.

"How shall we deal with our traitorous brethren?" the preacher cried. "How can we pull the trigger, you will ask, at Kentuckians we know and have grown up with and love? Let me tell you how.

"When Simon de Montfort was slaughtering the Protestants in the South of France, he was appealed to by certain persons, declaring that his men were mistaken, that they were killing many who were good Catholics. To which he replied: *'Kill them all; God knows his own.'* And this is the way we should deal with our treasonous Kentucky brethren, even those whose hearts we think may not be in rebellion; treat them all alike, and if there are any among them who are not rebels at heart God will take care of them and save them at last.

"By every blow you strike," Robert Jefferson Breckinridge thundered at the armed men in front of him, "by every rebel you kill, by every battle you win—dreadful as it is to do it—you are adding, it may be a year, it may be a century, it may be ten centuries, to the life of your government and the freedom of your children."

The bloody-minded words made her shudder. Most of those present knew that among "every rebel you kill" might be the enraged preacher's nephew, and son-in-law, and two of his four sons.

Anna Ella Carroll

BOOK TWO

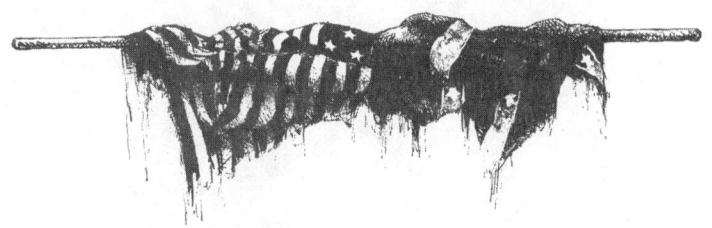

Anna Ella Carroll

CHAPTER 1

THE SHEEP FROM THE GOATS

Anna Ella Carroll held the proof in both hands that she was becoming a celebrated personage. In one hand was a note from Mathew Brady, the photographer: "I have read with pleasure your work, *A Reply to Breckinridge* and beg leave to tender you the courtesy which it has been my custom for many years to extend to the talented. Your portrait would be an interesting addition to my gallery." That meant the sitting would be free, enabling her to have her own *carte de visite* at no cost; it also meant he considered her picture salable to magazines and interested collectors of images of the famous. That was satisfying, after so many years of political labor behind the scenes. She would have to make an appointment with Brady as soon as she could afford a new dress and a modish haircut, and when she gained back some of the weight she had lost. She felt that at five feet four, her normal weight should be one hundred and twenty pounds; the worry of the last months had caused her to drop below that, and her arms and bosom were losing some of their plumpness.

In her other hand, she held a note marked "urgent" from Frederick Seward, the son of, and assistant to, the Secretary of State, inviting her to a visit that day to General Banks at his headquarters in the village of Rockville, Maryland. She was to be downstairs at the Ebbitt House at noon and to say nothing to anyone about the trip. Such importance was attached to it that young Seward hoped she could cancel all other plans.

After the shattering betrayal by John Breckinridge (she vowed never again to run after any man, even for reasons of state), these recognitions of her growing importance buoyed her spirit. She had been disappointed in his decision to go South, but was at a total loss to understand why Breck, who so prided himself on candor and honesty, would sneak off in the dead of night without so much as an explanation or a farewell. She assumed he had been too ashamed to face her and his uncle, and had taken the cowardly way out. That put Breck in the category of Millard Fillmore, another public man who had crept out of her life without an explanation or a thank-you. Never again. She was glad now she had put the damning Quitman papers in her pamphlet, which increased its newsworthiness and gave weight to the general condemnation of the traitorous Kentuckian. She was prepared at last to admit that her judgment of the character of men was seriously flawed; perhaps she would be better off without a regular male companion.

The only saving grace in that episode was that nobody in Washington knew of her failure to persuade Breck to take a stand for the Union. On the contrary, because the publication of her pamphlet coincided with his act of treason, her *Reply* was seen to be prescient, its reasoning made all the more unassailable by the defection of its target. Moreover, her political assignment from the Lincoln administration had never been in Kentucky, but in her native Maryland.

Until recently, Anna had credited herself with doing fairly well in frustrating the secession movement in Maryland. Her credentials for undertaking such an important effort were considerable: daughter and aide of the still-popular former governor, clear lineage to Charles Carroll of Revolutionary era fame, and, most of all, her political connection with the present governor, Thomas Hicks. Thanks in good part to Anna Ella Carroll's ardent sponsorship, Hicks had gained the American Party nomination for governor three years ago, and the Know-Nothings had delivered for him. The pro-slavery Hicks was not the most resolute of men, but he remembered who had put him in office and who might make him a senator after his term expired. This combination of gratitude and expectation kept him seemingly pro-Union in a state where the majority of the population leaned toward the Confederacy. Anna knew his present posture was not motived by any strong Union tie; rather, Hicks had some vague notion of staying out of the Confederacy only until its success might enable him to form a central confederation of border states. That was why Lincoln was so right about resisting any secession; once the principle was established that states could pull out, nobody could foretell where the subdividing would stop.

Maryland was on the knife edge, much as Kentucky had been until Bishop Polk blundered by sending his rebel troops up into Kentucky, ending Breck's dim hope for neutrality. The strategic difference between the two slave states was clear to her. Without Kentucky, the North could not win, and the war would end in stalemate; but without Maryland, the North could actually lose its capital in Washington, which would lead to intervention by England and France and a Southern victory. The riotous plug-ugly element in Baltimore had been forcibly suppressed by outstate Union troops, but the Maryland legislature remained adamantly secesh, its outright rebel supporters joining with the Peace Democrats who had carried the state of Maryland for Breckinridge in the presidential campaign the year before. (Breck had outpolled Lincoln in Maryland ten to one.) That legislature wanted to convene to vote secession, but Governor Hicks stood in the way: only he could call the legislature into session and, under pressure from Anna and her Know-Nothing friends, had flatly refused.

This week, over the governor's protest, the legislature had called itself into session. Governor Hicks responded by switching the place from the pro-rebel hotbed of Baltimore to the more neutral city of Frederick, requiring the most rebellion-minded to make a trek from Maryland's Eastern Shore. But Anna was worried. The session was scheduled to open in two days, and if the pro-South, anti-war majority passed a secession ordinance, the present Union "protection" of Maryland would turn into the violence-ridden occupation of enemy territory. She tried to think of some political lever to stop this move but could conjure none. Lincoln had been willing to defy Justice Taney on habeas corpus in this state, but if he wanted to prevent a vote of secession, he would have to expand his powers far beyond any ever considered in a democracy. Was Lincoln ready for such absolute repression of the will of the people of a state? If he was, would a display of despotism only add fuel to the fires of rebellion? Anna doubted if he had the gumption for a dictatorial coup, but could see no other way to force Marylanders into line.

The large, empty carriage arrived with Freddy Seward driving. She stepped in and sat with her back against his.

"First we'll pick up my father," he said. "Then we pick up the President at the Mansion."

When the young man concentrated on steering the horses up Fourteenth Street, she asked only, "How is the President?"

"Looks terrible. Maybe he has a chill, he keeps the fire burning in his office on warm days. Father gave him a couple of kittens yesterday to cheer him up."

At the Seward house on Lafayette Park, the Secretary of State climbed in and congratulated her on the pamphlet. He asked if it was being given heavy distribution in Maryland.

"As it happens, I received this letter from Governor Hicks this morning about that." She was proud to hand over the communication that not only reaffirmed her bona fides to the most powerful Cabinet member, but might help her in a practical, pecuniary way.

" 'Send me a couple of hundred copies of your *Reply to Breckinridge,*' " William Henry Seward read aloud, holding the paper at arm's length to see, " 'with bill of expenses for the same. I do not think it is right that you should furnish your publications gratis any longer.' Well, my dear lady, he's right about that. 'No money can ever pay for what you have done for the state and the country in this terrible crisis.' Ah, yes—the terrible crisis in Maryland is what we propose to resolve today."

He told her the plan, and the reason for her presence. They were to fetch the President, then stop by the McClellan house to pick up the new general and a small bodyguard of troops. "We will then drive to Georgetown Heights, and it will be a natural and reasonable conclusion on the part of the public and press that we are inspecting the camps and fortifications covering the hills in the direction of Tennallytown." However, after a few brief stops at fortifications, the official party would drive outside the military lines to the village of Rockville and rendezvous with General Nathaniel Banks, the former governor of Massachusetts who now commanded the small force keeping order and watching the river crossings in Annapolis, Maryland. "Once there, we will decide to do what has to be done. Your presence, Miss Carroll, has been requested in order to give the President, the generals, and myself the details of the political scene in the state where you and your family have such a benign influence."

The President came aboard looking preoccupied. Anna assumed, from a conversation the day before at the Blairs', that the Frémont affair was causing him no end of anguish. It seemed that Jessie Benton Frémont had ridden into town on her high horse and sorely tried the good man's patience, posing a Western secession threat if Lincoln interfered with Frémont's emancipation order, and blaming everything on misunderstandings caused by the duplicitous Blairs. Anna knew "General Jessie" to be one of those domineering women who made it so difficult for all women to succeed in public life; instinctively, she sided with the Blairs and Lincoln. Young Frank, serving under Frémont in St. Louis, would have his hands full.

"I see the kittens were a failure," said William Henry Seward.

Lincoln brightened for a moment. "They've been climbing all over me, and Willie loves them." That little byplay was fascinating to Anna. Seward, called "the Premier" at the start of the Administration, and considered a challenge to Lincoln's authority by virtue of his long preeminence in public life, was becoming a kind of courtier. She wondered if people had overestimated Seward or underestimated Lincoln.

The carriage stopped at the door of the headquarters of the Army of the Potomac. Presently, General McClellan came out and took the vacant seat. His score of troopers rode in front of and behind the carriage, with a horseman along either side, presumably to make it difficult for any would-be assassin to get a clear shot. This was the first time Anna had felt such protection, or the need for it, and she could not deny the thrill that accompanied it.

"General Banks will be expecting us, I reckon," the President observed to McClellan.

"Yes, sir," the general said, "I have telegraphed him. He will meet us at his headquarters at Rockville."

"Is that the best place for a meeting of this sort?" Seward asked.

"He will provide a quiet place for conference," the general said. "I agree, the headquarters would not be the most private."

"I regard General Banks as one of the best men in the army," the President said. "He makes me no trouble." Curious, thought Anna, that should be his criterion, but understandable considering the challenge of Frémont. She knew Banks from his Know-Nothing days a decade ago, when he was elected Speaker of the House of Representatives, before he became a Democrat.

"I suppose," queried McClellan, "that General Dix has already received his instructions?"

"Yes," Lincoln said. "Governor Seward went over to Baltimore a day or two ago and spent some hours with him at Fort McHenry. So he is fully informed."

Secretary Seward, who still preferred the title of Governor, nodded. John Dix was a War Democrat and good friend of Anna's; he had been Secretary of the Treasury in Buchanan's Cabinet, had been appointed major general of volunteers and placed in secessionist Baltimore because he could be trusted. In January, when the captain of a revenue cutter refused the Treasury Secretary's order to surrender to Federal authority in New Orleans, Dix gained some notoriety with his order: "Consider him a mutineer, and treat him accordingly. If anyone attempts to haul down the American flag, shoot him on the spot." Northern newspapers liked that.

"Can General Dix be counted on," asked McClellan, who did not know him, "to take care of the members in that part of the state?"

Seward gave him a small smile. "General Dix's views on the subject of hauling down the American flag are pretty well known. He can be depended upon." Seward, she noted, treated George McClellan with the same slight condescension he showed toward everyone except Lincoln. McClellan, on the contrary, seemed respectful without being deferential; like Breck, he carried with him the air of authority of youthful success. He was thirty-five; five years younger than Breck, fifteen years Lincoln's junior. She had heard that the "Young Napoleon" worshipped his young wife, and wrote to her every night they were parted; that spoke well of him, and Anna was prepared to like the military man on whom the nation now depended.

At Friendship Heights they held a perfunctory inspection, passing a few troops drawn up to see the celebrated leaders. McClellan saluted, Lincoln doffed his tall hat, Seward nodded, and the carriage continued on into Maryland. A half hour's ride over rutty roads took them from Tennallytown to Rockville. They stopped at a tavern that had been made a military headquarters, and General Banks started to usher them in. Rather than go inside, where conversation could be overheard by aides and squads of soldiers, Seward said loudly enough for onlookers, "It's a lovely day. Why don't we meet outdoors, in that grove." He pointed to a picnic area, with chairs and tables; nobody could approach within earshot without being seen. General Banks acted as if he had not selected the spot beforehand. When he drew out a pad to make notes, the President shook his head; not only was this too private for subordinates, evidently he did not think it wise to trust any of this to paper.

"The secessionists have not given up hope of dragging Maryland into the Confederacy," Seward began as the six were seated. "When their legislature meets on Monday, a move will be made to put forward an ordinance of secession."

"They have the tickets, I take it," said Lincoln.

Seward seemed unfamiliar with the Western expression, but caught the President's drift: "Yes, the traitors have the votes. The disunion sentiment in Maryland is considerable, and a majority of the state legislators are prepared to take the state out. Marylanders who now submit to Federal rule would then be called to active revolt."

"We cannot let that happen, Nat," Lincoln said to Banks. "Washington would soon be in rebel hands."

Anna had the impression that she and the Sewards were the outsiders in this group. Both Banks and McClellan had been vice presidents of the Illinois Central Railroad before the war, and lawyer Lincoln had been that railroad's counsel. Although McClellan and Lincoln had not been close—indeed, McClellan had traveled on the Stephen Douglas campaign train during his race for the Senate, helping to sober up the Little Giant between debates with Lincoln—they had learned the politics of railroading together, had spent nights talking after days of testimony in small towns, and spoke with the familiarity of men with shared roots. They knew each other to be successful men outside of politics.

"What about Governor Hicks?" asked Seward's son.

The Secretary answered, mainly for the generals' benefit, "We proceed on the thesis that Hicks is a loyal Union man." He did not repeat the suspicion that the governor had wanted to be part of a border-state confederation with Virginia and Kentucky, to form a third force between the United States and the Southern Confederacy, which Anna was certain would lead to anarchy. Thanks to the pressure of the Blairs and the Carrolls, Seward told them, and to the direct threat of bloodshed on his state's soil, Hicks had finally been pushed into an anti-secession position. "But Governor Hicks is unable to control the legislature."

General Banks posed a problem facing the loyalist legislators: "The pro-Union members of the legislature are uncertain about going to Frederick to fight the proposed ordinance, or staying away to try to block a quorum."

"We cannot afford to take that chance," said Seward, "because the secesh will fake a forum. I've seen that done often enough in Albany." Anna pre-

General Nathaniel P. Banks

sumed that Seward was taking the lead in this because Lincoln, whose presence at the meeting was required, did not want to dirty his hands with a matter that would not go down well with many high-minded congressmen. "General Dix in the eastern part of the state and, Banks, you here in the western part, will have to round up and arrest the secessionists before they get to the legislature."

Anna caught her breath. No wonder there was a need for absolute secrecy. No legal justification existed, in any Federal or state constitution, for arresting legislators on their way to a session. Not even the President's inherent war power, which she was prepared to stretch a long way, would stretch that far.

"How will we know which is which?" asked Banks.

"The views of each disunion member have been rather loudly proclaimed," said Lincoln, "so there should be little difficulty separating the sheep from the goats."

"I can give you a list," Anna added. "With addresses, and the likely road they would take to Frederick." It struck her that Governor Hicks's action to move the meeting across the state would make this sheep-from-goats plan possible. The idea of arresting the lawmakers before they could vote to secede had apparently been planned well in advance.

"Has to be done the same night, all at once, no court proceedings, above all no notice in the press," Seward directed.

"You should expect some protest," said McClellan. "There may be comparisons with Cromwell."

Anna knew that all present were aware that the new commander was a Democrat, the same as Banks and Dix, the political-military men chosen to carry out this precedent-shattering coup. Lincoln and Seward must feel that even War Democrats in the North would have some difficulty swallowing this. Anna assumed that the inclusion of McClellan in the plot showed how much Lincoln trusted the new commander, and also—by involving all these Democrats at the start—made difficult any subsequent criticism of dictatorial methods. McClellan had offered no objection, and surely must be thinking of the military problem of a Confederate Maryland interdicting his supply lines.

"To forcibly prevent a legislative body from exercising its functions," said Seward, speaking for Lincoln, "savours of despotism. Let us grant that it would generally be so regarded." He looked McClellan in the eye and gave him the overriding argument: "But when, departing from its legitimate functions, a legislature invites the public enemy to plunge the state into anarchy, its dissolution becomes commendable."

Anna promptly provided a quotation from Jefferson, patron saint of Breckinridge and all the defenders of civil liberty: "A strict observance of the written law is doubtless one of the highest duties of a good citizen, but it is not *the highest*. The laws of necessity, of self-preservation, of saving our country when in danger, are of higher obligation."

Seward smiled at her warmly for the first time. "I believe Mr. Jefferson said that, Miss Carroll, after, rather than before, he became President. Great men grow in power." He turned to Banks. "Absolute secrecy is vital. You, General Banks, on orders of General McClellan, are to watch the movements of all members of the legislature who are expected to respond to the summons to Frederick. Loyal Union members are not to be interfered with. They are free to come and go, perform their legislative duties, or stay away, just as they please."

"And the disunion members?" asked Banks.

"They are to be quietly turned back toward their homes."

"And if they don't go quietly?"

"Then you will be forced to arrest them."

That order hung in the summer air for a moment. Banks looked at McClellan, who said nothing. He looked again to Secretary Seward and said, "Governor, you know I'm quite prepared to do this, but when I arrest the mayor of Baltimore on his way to the legislative session, he's liable to ask about the grounds for his arrest. What do I tell him?"

Lincoln spoke up. "The public safety renders it necessary that the grounds of these arrests be withheld," he told Banks to say, "but at the proper time they will be made public."

"In a few weeks or months," added Seward, "when the danger is over, or when new legislators can be elected, we can release these men."

The generals understood. However, to Anna's surprise, Freddy Seward popped out with the unspoken question: "But people are going to be comparing President Lincoln with Oliver Cromwell in England, throwing out the

Parliament, and Napoleon throwing out the Assembly in France. I mean, it's never been done here, and you can just hear the press writing about high-handed usurpation. For the national military to stop a state legislature from the lawful—"

"Thank you, Freddy," said his father sharply. "This is not to be done in a Cromwellian or a Napoleonic manner. Just the opposite, nothing spectacular. As quietly as possible."

The President seemed to feel that the young man's point could not be brushed aside, and some more explanation had to be offered beyond a promise to reveal the reasons at the proper time. "Of one thing the people of Maryland may rest assured," he suggested the Marylanders be told, "that no arrest is being made, or will be made, not based on substantial and unmistakable complicity with those in armed rebellion against the Government of the United States."

"Then I'll say," said Banks, "that the general grounds for arrest are suspicion of—"

A shake of Lincoln's head cut him off. "In no case has an arrest been made on mere suspicion, or through personal or partisan animosities." The lawyer-President suggested the officers be most specific about intimating disloyalty while putting off the presentation of evidence until some later time: "In all cases the government is in possession of tangible and unmistakable evidence, which will, when made public, be satisfactory to every loyal citizen."

That sounded lawyerly, but everyone at the table knew it to be untrue: no such evidence existed in government hands at that moment, although in the next months perhaps some could be gathered for presentation at the proper time. The President added determinedly, "We will do everything we can to discriminate between true and false men."

God would know his own. Banks looked to McClellan, perhaps for a direct order; the commander of the Army of the Potomac merely nodded, in effect passing along the verbal order of the commander in chief. That was smart: nothing written down, nothing dramatic said. If this could be brought off gently, with a minimum of ammunition provided to the press, the public reaction to the clearly dictatorial action would be muted. This trick was to make this a fait accompli with no proclamation or order for even the Confederacy to make much noise about. Still, she could detect a feeling of unease amid the spoken determination.

"President Jackson," Lincoln said, as if changing the subject, and addressing himself to Freddy Seward. "After the battle of New Orleans and after a treaty of peace had been concluded, General Jackson still maintained martial law. Since the war was over, the howl against martial law grew more furious. A member of the Louisiana legislature denounced him in the newspaper. General Jackson arrested him. A lawyer got a judge to order a writ of habeus corpus. General Jackson arrested both the lawyer and the judge. When somebody called that 'a dirty trick,' General Jackson arrested him, too."

Anna had not been aware of this precedent, or of Lincoln's apparent need for one. The President must have been talking to Old Man Blair again about the Jackson days.

"After holding the judge in custody a few days," Lincoln continued, "the general sent him beyond the limits of his encampment and set him at liberty, with an order to remain away until the peace was formally announced or the British left the coast. After a few days, that happened, and in a few days more, the judge called General Jackson into his court and fined him a thousand dollars for having arrested him."

Lincoln rose and stretched. "The general paid the fine," he concluded, seeming to instruct young Freddy but making his point to the generals, "and there the matter rested for nearly thirty years. Then the Congress refunded principal and interest to Jackson's family. The permanent right of the people to public discussion suffered no detriment by that conduct of General Jackson, or its subsequent approval by the American Congress."

"General, do your duty," Seward said to Nathaniel Banks. "Not a word to anybody who does not need to know. And nothing on paper. And after the arrests, which you might call brief detainments— You have chosen discreet men to be guards?"

Banks smiled. "I have a Wisconsin unit for that. Swedish and German farm boys. Not a one of them speaks English."

CHAPTER 2

JOHN HAY'S DIARY
OCTOBER 25, 1861

"Oh, why should the spirit of mortal be proud!"

That is the concluding line of the Tycoon's favorite poem, "Mortality," by some anonymous Scotsman. The Prsdt has the entire four stanzas committed to memory. I have heard him declaim them all, with great solemnity, a dozen times. Not surprisingly, the bathos-drenched lines have stuck in my head, at least toward the dreary end:

> Yea! hope and despondency, pleasure and pain,
> Are mingled together in sun-shine and rain;
> And the smile and the tear, and the song and the dirge,
> Still follow each other, like surge upon surge.

Nor is that all. He stands, knuckles on the table, staring at the wall, reciting:

> 'Tis the wink of an eye, 'tis the draught of a breath,
> From the blossoms of health, to the paleness of death.
> From the gilded saloon, to the bier and the shroud.
> Oh, why should the spirit of mortal be proud!

It is a terrible poem. I cannot think of a more maudlin, banal, and weepy piece of poetry, and I speak as one who has no small ambition in the poetry line. Yet Abraham Lincoln told a newspaper friend of his the other day that he would give all he was worth, go into debt, to be able to write what he called "so fine a poem as I think that is."

Why do I refrain from telling this to the Tycoon every time he draws a deep sigh and begins to roll out the silly spirit of mortals? Because such impertinence would hurt his feelings, lessen me in his estimation, and sully one of his few sources of solace.

He probably knows it does not stand up to critical scrutiny because he is a good writer himself. Unfortunately, the cognoscenti, who wrongly equate flowery prose with good style, do not give him credit for that. My Uncle Milton gave me a cutting from the *Quincy Whig* of fifteen years ago, with a poem that Lincoln wrote about a boy he knew who went insane:

> *O death! Thou awe-inspiring prince*
> *That keepst the world in fear;*
> *Why dost thou tear more blest ones hence,*
> *And leave him ling'ring here?*

"Awe-inspiring" may be on the trite side, but Lincoln the young poet chose the right word in "ling'ring," and his dropping of the middle syllable, required by the rhythm, gives a nice effect on the page. A sad theme, but those moods overtake him. On occasion he lets the wave of melancholy overwhelm him, and when that hypo strikes, it makes any sympathetic soul miserable just to look at him. Only Willie can pull him out of those depressions of the spirit, and not even that sunny boy can do it right away.

The reason for these lugubrious observations is that Ned Baker is dead. The colonel died gallantly, at the head of his troops, storming the heights at Ball's Bluff crossing the Potomac into rebel territory in Virginia. Oregon has lost a great senator, the army a brave officer, and the President one of his friends. There is no denying the weight of the blow; casualty lists are always saddening, but when the scythe cuts down someone close to you, the terror of war comes home and sits next to you on the bed.

Mrs. Lincoln has retired to her room with only Lizzie Keckley for comfort, the Tycoon is disconsolate, and the boys are silent. Now even Uncle Ned, their dead brother Eddie's namesake, is gone. War is not all uniforms and parades and strutting around waving swords.

Anger is the reaction of most others. Senator Ben Wade of the ferocious countenance came pounding in here cursing John Breckinridge, whose recent role as bitter opponent in debate with our fallen hero has made him more hated than ever. That traitor senator has been reported to be in Richmond, and the Southern newspapers say he has been offered the choice of rebel Secretary of War or command of a brigade of Kentucky defectors in the field.

"We won't accept that bastard's resignation," Wade fumed to the mournful Tycoon. "At the first order of business in the winter session we'll expel him from the Senate for treason. The other senators who walked out followed their states, and can claim immunity in that, but not Breckinridge. When the war's over, that damn traitor will hang."

General McClellan was in the office at the time Wade roared in, and had been explaining to the Prsdt what had happened to Colonel Baker. At Lincoln's nod, with Wade standing there glowering, the general reported: "We've been sending heavy reconnaissances into Virginia, to find out the position of the enemy. I suggested to General Stone, Colonel Baker's superior officer,

that perhaps a slight demonstration on our part might cause an enemy movement that we could observe."

"A 'slight demonstration'?" said Wade in scorn. "We lost a thousand men
and the rebels lost a couple of dozen. Some goddamned slight demonstration!"

General McClellan went rigid in his chair. "I did not order General Stone
across the river. He informs me the troops under his direct command made a
careful probe, and that he did not order Colonel Baker to make a major
assault."

"So your story is that Ned Baker was rash and led his men into a trap, is
it?" When McClellan declined any intention of reaching such an extreme
conclusion, "Bluff Ben" lashed into him with what was the talk of the Jacobin
Club: "I hear different. I hear your General Stone is a disloyal Democrat who
wants to see slavery perpetuated and has had intercourse with known seces-
sionaries."

McClellan was stunned. "It's possible General Stone was unduly aggressive, but that seems to show that he wanted to fight the enemy—"

"That damn rebel sympathizer threw Ned Baker and his men across the
river with no way back and no reinforcements," stormed Wade. "He's one of
the pack of Democratic generals who want to lose. He sends back fugitive
slaves, he's challenged Sumner to a duel, and a lot of us have good reason to
think he's on the other side."

"The Fugitive Slave Act is the law, passed by the Congress," McClellan,
who was a Douglas Democrat, protested. Lincoln listened and said nothing.

"I say Stone killed Ned Baker and he ought to be impeached," Wade
blazed in his frustration and fury, and turned toward the President. "And if
you can't run this war any better, Lincoln, with this fellow here holding
parades with his two hundred thousand men and issuing bulletins about how
'the capital is safe' and defending traitor generals, then a joint committee of
the Congress will damn well run it for you."

That was his exit line, leaving the Young Napoleon quietly steaming.
"There is bad blood between Senator Sumner and General Stone over the
return of fugitive slaves, that's true," he said to the Prsdt, "but nobody sent
Colonel Baker and his brigade to their deaths on purpose. What kind of
officer corps can we have if every initiative that fails is called treason? Nobody is more determined to avoid unnecessary casualties than I am, Mr.
President—"

"I know. Wade is upset about the tragic loss of our friend Ned, and about
my reversal of Frémont on slavery to save Kentucky. I don't like the idea of a
joint committee, witnesses, testimony, second-guessing us all." That slicing
away of his power to conduct the war would not do. "Tell me the truth about
Ned, George. Did he act rashly?"

"Colonel Baker and his men fought nobly, and I would not hesitate to
testify to that," McClellan evaded. "That would be the extent of my testimony to any committee and it is true. Your friend was a brave man and a
patriot."

Lincoln gave him that level look that called for his military judgment of
what really happened at Ball's Bluff. McClellan took a deep breath and did
not equivocate: "He violated all military rules and precautions. Instead of

meeting the enemy with double their force and a good ferry behind him, Colonel Baker was outnumbered three to one and had no means of retreat. The result was a horrible butchery. A commander must never, never ignore the potential need for a way out."

The Prsdt closed his eyes. After a while, he walked to the window and looked out at the tree on the ellipse where he and his friend used to sit and talk. The mental picture of Ned on his back, feet up against the trunk of the tree, must remain vivid. He must have thought, too, of the colonel who was here on the scene last April, when the capital was all but undefended, when the President was saying "There is no North." That stalwart officer was Stone, now a general. Did he owe him nothing?

"General, go over to the Blairs' tonight after dinner. They're on your side in many ways." That was a veiled reference to the campaign by Montgomery Blair and the old gentleman to replace Winfield Scott with McClellan as General-in-Chief. Old General Scott, on the other hand, thinks McClellan is a damned upstart trying to get his job, which is true enough, but at the same time "Old Fuss and Feathers" is patriot enough to know he is too old and infirm for this war. Because of McClellan's impatience to get control of the whole army, Scott considers him an ingrate, and so has recommended that the Prsdt follow his inclination to appoint "Old Brains," General Henry Halleck, to be Scott's successor and the Young Napoleon's boss. Sobriquets abound in the military, as do jealousies.

Lincoln was also alluding to the Blairs' support of McClellan's desire to train his army rather than send it into the fray prematurely, for fear of bringing on another Bull Run. Building up against this caution is a sentiment that worries the Prsdt: the growing opinion of Republicans that McClellan is dawdling, unwilling to fight, while time is on the side of the enemy. It's hard to say right now who is right about that.

"Ben Wade and Zack Chandler will be there tonight, the old gentleman tells me," the Prsdt said. "It would be better for you to answer their questions privately than publicly." And to keep the Jacobin Club, which welcomed McClellan's appointment after Bull Run, on his side. If Wade, Chandler, and the rest of the abolitionists turn on him, especially after their darling Frémont was slapped down, much heat will be applied to the President by Jacobins who want to grab the reins. They cannot attack the President directly, but by finding reasons for disappointment in his surrogate, they can diminish Lincoln's power to decide what is the goal of the war.

McClellan nodded understanding, and brought up a pressing matter of the elections coming up in Maryland next week. "You will recall that the secession ordinance was not introduced last month," he said, looking toward me as if to wish me out of the room. "The chief of our Secret Service reports that several hundred Maryland disunionists have returned to their homes from visits to rebel headquarters in Virginia, and may interfere with the rights of suffrage of loyal citizens."

"What do you need?"

"Last month only sixteen legislators wouldn't listen to reason. The rest, who were stopped by Banks, agreed to turn around and go home. This time, considering reports to Mr. Pinkerton of secret arms shipments, there may have to be many more arrests, especially around the polling places. For the record, I'd like a written order from civilian authority."

"Get it from Seward," the Prsdt said. "He will authorize you to suspend the habeas corpus to make arrests of traitors and their confederates in your discretion." Lincoln hated to put that sort of thing in writing, but it didn't bother Seward a whit.

McClellan said he would go from the Executive Mansion to the Seward house immediately, then to the Blairs' after dinner. They were all within one block.

CHAPTER 3

THE YOUNG NAPOLEON

George McClellan, who sat a horse as well as any man in the United States Army, guided his steed to the top of a hill in Georgetown. The sun was disappearing behind the Virginia hills across the Potomac. One of his aides, the Comte de Paris—son of the pretender to the crown of France, a prestigious presence McClellan rather liked—handed him a spyglass.

On the rebel side of the river, heavy cannon emplacements threatened Union control of river traffic. Pinkerton, interviewing deserters, prisoners of war, and fugitive slaves—as well as running his own spies behind rebel lines—was estimating Southern strength in eastern Virginia at 98,400 men. McClellan had come to trust "Major Allen"; the little detective's warnings of enemy troop strength did not incline a general to rashness and the kind of hubris that led to defeats like Bull Run and Ball's Bluff.

McClellan's eye tracked his fortifications from Georgetown to Alexandria, south of the Potomac, in an arc about fourteen miles long. Spaced a mile apart, strongpoints with six heavy guns each defended against an attack from that southern flank; he had established another chain of forts to the west, across the river in Arlington; a third chain in Maryland defended the capital from attack from the north.

He swung the eyeglass back around the hills of Washington, their sides dotted with tents clustered around training centers. He had 152,051 men on his rolls. After deducting for absent, sick, and under arrest, and counting out the twelve thousand for whom arms had not yet been received—Chase had been slow getting the money—he had at least a hundred thousand men ready for action. His was the largest army ever assembled on this continent, and the great agglomeration was beginning to resemble a fighting unit.

The general permitted himself a satisfied smile. The troops were assembled in each area, the flag-lowering ceremony under way, honor guards marching about, military discipline and tradition being drilled into every soldier's mind. Three months ago, the men had been a mob; now they were the Army of the Potomac, McClellan's army, and he was becoming as proud of its men as he knew they were proud of the leader they called "Our George." Within a few months, after winter quarters, he was sure these green troops would be ready for the decisive battle that would win the war, or at least end the war with the Union preserved.

McClellan put down the spyglass and frowned. The night before, acting on Lincoln's suggestion, he had met with Wade and Chandler at the Blairs' house and promised a decisive battle before the winter. That assurance of early action had been necessary to enlist their support in the unseating of General Scott, and the blocking of Henry Halleck as replacement in the chair of general-in-chief.

"The name of Ball's Bluff must be wiped out," Wade had bawled, "by a decisive victory right away."

A victory was by no means certain using green troops, McClellan had told him honestly.

"I prefer an unsuccessful battle to further delay," the senator had said, incredibly, "since a defeat can be repaired easily by swarming recruits."

That was dismaying. Could any military man hope to succeed under the constant goading of such politicians? McClellan told him that he did not have men enough for a serious assault on the 220,000 Confederate soldiers facing him. They were behind fortifications stronger than he had observed in Sebastopol, when he was sent to Russia to learn about tactics used in the Crimean War. He much preferred to have a few new recruits before a victory than a swarm of recruits after a defeat. McClellan wanted these senators on his side in the campaign to replace old Winfield Scott, but he could not tell them exactly what they wanted to hear.

"What in hell is holding you back?" Zack Chandler, who was drunk as the hour approached midnight, had demanded. "Soldiering isn't all champagne and oyster dinners." Nellie's dinners were more elegant than the boorish Chandler would ever appreciate. Instead of defending himself, he took the offensive: "I am being stymied by General Scott. He is ever in my way. I am sure he does not desire effective action."

Wade had pushed him even farther: "You're the one surrounded by nearly two hundred thousand of your spit-and-polish paraders. You're the one issuing those stupid bulletins about how 'the capital is safe.' You claim that Scott is holding you back?"

"General Scott understands nothing and appreciates nothing," McClellan remembered replying with some heat. "I have to fight my way against him."

That was when the Blairs had come in strongly for his cause. Montgomery Blair, a West Pointer, said that Scott's choice of Halleck was proof of his lack of aggressiveness. "Old Brains" was notorious in the army for never leaving his maps to get out in the field. Wade, for all his bombast, showed himself to be shrewder than McClellan had originally thought. He told the Blairs to their faces that they were plotting to put "their" general, McClellan, in charge in the East while they snatched away authority from "his" general, Frémont, in the West.

That was an impressive reading of military-political affairs, McClellan had thought, who was then even more impressed by the way the old gentleman, Francis P. Blair, forced Wade to about-face on Cabinet influences. Senator Wade's abolitionist ally in the Cabinet was supposedly his fellow Ohioan, Secretary Chase, said Old Man Blair, but he had heard that Chase was plotting with Ohio friends to take Wade's Senate seat the following year, because it would provide the ambitious Chase a better springboard for the presidency in 1864. Ben Wade would be better off, the elder Blair told him, relying on the Blairs as his friends.

That political conniving, on top of McClellan's derogation of General Scott, did the trick. The senators left that night with a vague promise of early action in return for their support of McClellan as Scott's successor. To achieve supreme command, McClellan had learned, required distasteful participation in political dealings; once in charge, however, he was determined never to allow partisan politics to affect his military judgment. If postponing action until victory was likely angered Ben Wade and the radicals, so be it. It was Lincoln's job to keep the politicians in line while he fought the war.

Followed by his personal staff of about twenty officers and orderlies, General McClellan made his way down from the high ground to Pennsylvania Avenue and toward the Executive Mansion. The President had sent word that he would be pleased to receive the general at the end of the day.

Lincoln was a rare old bird, McClellan had to admit with respect. Undoubtedly, just as the President had arranged, Lincoln had been besieged by Wade and Chandler, probably with club-footed Thaddeus Stevens in tow, to get rid of the aging Scott and replace him with the vigorous McClellan as supreme commander. That was good generalship on Lincoln's part, in McClellan's judgment. A wise leader sometimes tried to get the adversary to entice him into doing what the leader wanted to do in the first place.

One of Lincoln's secretaries—a young man named Hay who, McClellan thought, should have been in uniform by now—led him in.

"Some wonderful inventions are in the works," said Lincoln. Evidently he was going to regale him with small talk before getting to the point. "There's this new repeating battery of rifled gun, shoots fifty balls a minute. Can you imagine? I've ordered ten of them. If you think it's proper, would you detail a corps of men to work on it?"

Such a marvel might be useful in a war a generation hence, thought McClellan, but he knew Lincoln was het up about inventions—had even taken out a patent himself for an ingenious method of lifting boats across river dams—so he promised to have someone look into the rapid-firing weapon immediately.

"And that's not all. Up in Long Island, they've laid the keel for an ironclad warship. I saw the inventor here myself a couple of months ago. As the girl said when she stuck her foot in the stocking, 'I think there's something in it.'"

McClellan dutifully smiled at the feeble attempt at humor, but he made no comment on what was being derided in naval circles as "the cheesebox on a raft." This war was not going to be won by naval eccentricities. The only invention that he thought might be helpful now was the hot-air balloon, the military application of which Lincoln, he was sure, had not yet considered. It would be good to get up high enough to see the enemy's order of battle.

"And this week, too"—Lincoln seemed to McClellan to be deliberately avoiding the subject of military command—"we've completed the transcontinental telegraph, the last leg from Denver to California. The war did that—would have taken years in peacetime." McClellan recognized the importance

of the telegraph east of the Mississippi, where the war was being fought, but
failed to see why it was so useful to be able to get the news from California.

"About the war, sir," McClellan said, reminding Lincoln.

"Yes. The Maryland Volunteers . . ." What did this man want to know
about a minor detachment of the Army of the Potomac? "Senator Reverdy
Johnson was in here asking that they be permitted to vote in the elections
next week in Maryland. Would you give them the time off? We need the
votes."

"It shall be done," he replied. McClellan thought that furloughing Union
supporters to vote was easier than arresting rebel supporters, but if in the
future he was going to have to send soldiers home to vote in the middle of a
battle, he was in for a long war.

"Wade and Chandler were in today. Hay here calls them the Jacobins.
They want to know why you haven't moved the army."

"Senator Wade told me last night that he so opposed delay that he would
prefer to have an unsuccessful battle. He said that a defeat could easily be
repaired by what he called the 'swarming recruits.' "

"And what did you say?"

"I told him," said McClellan, "I would rather have a few recruits before a
victory than a good many after a defeat."

"Good, good. No needless slaughter. Popular impatience is a dangerous
thing," offered Lincoln, adding, "at the same time, it's a reality. The popular
mood must be taken into account." When the general allowed himself to look
troubled at that, the President added, "At the same time, General, you must
not fight until you are ready."

"Don't let them hurry me, is all I ask."

"You'll have your own way in that matter, I assure you."

McClellan was dying to ask: In what capacity? As a field commander,
saddled with harassment from above, or as supreme commander, having to
answer only to the nation and to history? He restrained himself, of course,
but did not want to leave the matter of "hurrying" at that. Lincoln had to
understand that there would never be a problem of lack of personal bravery at
the highest level. He was prepared to lay down his life at the head of his
troops, but he was determined that it be in a well-planned, victorious engagement. If he was anything in his life, he was a success. "I have everything—my
whole life—at stake," McClellan said earnestly. "If I fail, I will not see you
again. Or anybody."

"I have a notion to go out in the field with you," said Lincoln, with one of
his deep sighs, "and stand or fall with the battle." The general recognized
that to be a kind of standoff; physical courage was not limited to the military.

Finally Lincoln set aside his woolgathering look and assumed an air of
authority. "I have to make some changes in military command. What do you
think of General Henry Halleck?"

McClellan's heart sank; Scott's revenge. McClellan would have rid himself
of a superior officer only to have him replaced by another. "He's written a
book," he replied dully. "I don't know how much practical action he has
seen."

"I've been reading that book right here—*Elements of Military Art and
Science.*" Lincoln picked it up, hefted the tome in his huge hand, put it back

on the desk. "I'm thinking of replacing Frémont in the West with Halleck, as the Blairs suggest. What do you think, George?"

The familiar "George" registered, along with the question, as evidence that he was to be named General-in-Chief. "I think that's an excellent choice," adding, "Mr. President."

"But will Frémont hold still for it?" The question came from Lincoln's young secretary, who McClellan considered hardly deserved the right to speak up on such affairs of military high command, but the President did not seem to mind. "There's talk that if President Lincoln relieves him, he might try to set up for himself, refuse to cede his authority. Or else go out West and organize a new nation."

Now the general saw a good reason for an interest in a transcontinental telegraph. He also surmised that Lincoln, through his aide, was testing McClellan's reaction to possible military challenge to control by civilians; in times like these, a dictatorship was a real possibility.

"Frémont is a patriot," he said decisively. "He's a terrible general, and that wrongheaded abolition move of his made it impossible for him to maintain complete control in Missouri, maybe for the rest of the war. But he knows that a President is the commander in chief. He will take a direct order and step down. To do anything else would be the act of a traitor, which John Frémont is not."

That was evidently what Lincoln wanted to hear. "I have in mind, further, that you should succeed General Scott as General-in-Chief. That, in addition to your command of the Army of the Potomac."

McClellan swallowed and stood erect.

"This is a vast increase of responsibility," Lincoln continued. "In addition to your present command, the supreme command of the army will entail a vast labor on you." He seemed to want reassurance.

"I can do it all," McClellan said with certainty.

"Well. Call on me for all the sense I have, and all the information."

McClellan understood that the President—an uncertain leader, feeling his way, fearful of delegating responsibility—wanted to be sure that his advice would be considered. "I am now in close contact with you and with the Secretary of War," said the new General-in-Chief. "I want you to know, sir, that I would not be in the least embarrassed by your intervention with your ideas at any time."

"Good. Then it's done. General Scott, of course, knows." He did not say "approves." "You'll want to talk to Wade and his friends again, maybe cool them off a little about Frémont."

Lincoln had involved Wade, Chandler, and Stevens in the making of the McClellan appointment, and now wanted "their" man to mollify their fury at the replacement of Frémont. Smart politics, McClellan thought, with an edge of contempt for it all.

"And I wouldn't spend too much of your time with the Secretary of War. At the War Department, there's Tom Scott—you must know him from your own railroad days"—McClellan nodded; Scott had run the Pennsy when McClellan headed the Illinois Central—"and Edward Stanton, a War Democrat like you, that I used to argue law cases with in the old days. Simon Cameron—well, deal directly with me on anything you need."

McClellan nodded; he knew from Greeley's *New York Tribune* that Cameron was Secretary of War only because Lincoln did not trust him to be Secretary of the Treasury, the post he had been promised in return for the support that delivered to Lincoln the Republican nomination. Politics again. He was glad that was Lincoln's profession, not his; if Lincoln would fight off the politicians in Washington, McClellan was certain he could defeat the enemy in the field, at a time and place of his own choosing.

CHAPTER 4

IT FLOWS THE OTHER WAY

"Get me outa here!"

"You'll be out soon enough," Anna Carroll told Frank Blair, visiting the caged congressman, now the only Union colonel in jail for insubordination, in his large cell at the military prison in St. Louis. "Frémont is to be replaced by Halleck in a few days, and meantime David Hunter will be in command. He'll let you out first thing."

"Frémont is a madman," the youngest of the Blair clan gritted. "First he gets some of my closest friends needlessly killed. Then when my newspaper criticizes him, he closes it down. Then when I point out the corruption in military contracts and demand a court-martial for those friends of his who are stealing us blind, he claps me in jail."

"Maybe you shouldn't have called him an opium-eater," she suggested.

"It's the only explanation for the way he acts," he muttered, "and he said I was a drunk. I drink all right, but I'm like your friend Breckinridge—I can hold my booze."

She changed the subject. "I think Jessie put him up to arresting you."

"That crazy woman! You know what she once told me? She said she modeled herself on the role of the Empress Josephine, who helped Napoleon overthrow the French Directory. Thanks to her, I've been rotting here for days, instead of fighting rebels, while that posturing maniac who thinks he's Julius Caesar reincarnate is out losing the war!"

"It's your own fault, Frank," she told him. "You pushed him until he lost his temper. Now the rebels are in control of large parts of this state at night. Your damn feud was bad for the Blairs, bad for the Union cause in Missouri, bad for the country."

He sat down on the bunk next to her, still puffy with rage, but slightly subdued. She liked him; immature, pugnacious, emotionally volatile, even a bit spoilt, but a brave man with the right political instincts. Moreover, the Blairs were her allies in Maryland and Washington.

"I'll take that from you, Anna," he growled, "because you're like family. Besides, you're the first woman they've let come in here. How did you manage?"

She displayed her military pass signed by Colonel Tom Scott, Assistant Secretary of War. The credential, entitling her to a military escort, had taken her into a dozen army camps between Washington and Missouri, along the route of the Baltimore and Ohio, up to Chicago, then down to St. Louis. She had been sent at Attorney General Bates's request to reconnoiter for Lincoln. She had observed the state of troop training, studied the condition of readiness of the generals, and made copious notes on the logistical support for planned movements. Most people talked freely to her, assuming her to be only a woman who would not understand.

"I've talked to Cump Sherman. He's John's brother, you know. He wants you out and back in action," she said. General William Sherman's middle name was Tecumseh, and she did not know him well enough to call him "Cump" to his face, but she liked to show her familiarity with these fellows. "He says that Sam Grant, in Cairo, wants you out too."

That cheered the prisoner. "I'll be surprised if Frémont steps down without a fuss."

She grinned and laid a hand on his hairy arm. "He's not making it easy. His camp is on the lookout for messengers from Washington. Frémont must figure if he doesn't actually receive an order to relieve him, he can go looking for a battle to win one of these days. I know the order has been cut, but Lincoln's man may have to dress up like a farmer, sneak through to his tent, and hand him his orders."

Blair roared with laughter and as quickly subsided. "But you think that puffed-up popinjay will obey?"

"With grace and dignity," she predicted. "He'll tell all the hotheads around him to go to work for the next commander. Give Frémont credit, he's a patriot."

"I'll give him nothing. If Jessie is with him when the order arrives, he'll lead a revolt."

She rose and clapped him on the shoulder. "You cool off and we'll get you out. Strong language now can ruin your chances later." Everybody knew the family had big plans for him.

She had an appointment at the Mercantile Library with the chief librarian, an old friend who was the brother of the Confederate general in Tennessee. That was where she was to research her war powers pamphlet, and, while she was at it, to get some idea of the order of battle of the contending armies.

Before she left the cell, Anna remembered a sad chore she had to carry out for Lizzie Keckley, the black modiste who made her dresses—and Mrs. Lincoln's—in Washington. "What went wrong at the battle of Wilson's Creek, Frank?"

He leaned his head into his hands and rubbed his temples, as if to blot out the memory. "General Nat Lyon took five thousand men to Springfield to stop a rebel force of twice that size. Frémont wouldn't back him up. Lyon might have brought it off, but he got killed and his men ran. Disaster because there were no reserves. Cost us thirteen hundred casualties, and half the state of Missouri. Nat was my best friend."

"I'm sorry. A friend of mine's son was killed there. All she saw was his name on the casualty list—Keckley, killed in action. She asked me to find out what I could."

He looked up. "Keckley. Big, strapping, redheaded kid. Worked around headquarters. I remember him."

She shook her head. "Couldn't be him."

"The Keckley I recall was a freckle-faced redhead. Anyhow, tell your friend that her son died a hero, trying to save General Lyon's life. Nobody knows. It'll make her happy, and I'll back it up."

"What will you do when you get out, Frank?"

"Take a command with Sherman, if he'll have me, or Grant, if Halleck doesn't run him out of the army. Congress doesn't convene for two months."

"What should the Army of the West be doing?"

"Driving right down the Mississippi Valley," the colonel-congressman said with no hesitation. "Take Columbus, storm Vicksburg—that's not going to be easy—and go right down to New Orleans. Cut the rebels off from guns and ammunition coming up now through Mexico, and from Texas food. Scare away the British and French, who might recognize the rebels if we don't move soon. When we reduce all those Mississippi forts, the secesh will wither away. Why are you shaking your head?"

Frank had been describing Scott's "anaconda plan" to slowly squeeze the South into submission. That notion had already been derided in Congress and the press for taking too long. Now General Scott was out and McClellan was in, and the new man—younger than Frank Blair, but a born commander—was known to believe the war was to be won in the East. Anna said only, "That relies on gunboats to reduce the Mississippi forts. You're building gunboats every day. Have you ever been on a gunboat?"

"No. You?"

She held up her pass. "I have a date to visit the boatyard tomorrow." She pulled his long mustache to one side and kissed his cheek. "But I'll camp in the commanding general's office until you're released, I promise."

Outside the prison, she changed her plans and made a beeline for the boatyard. The walk took forty minutes, but the War Department had not provided carriage expenses, and the November air was crisp and the walkways hard and dry. The pamphlet she had been asked to write on the war powers of the President was a piece of difficult work and she would get around to it soon enough. More troubling was the military strategy that seemed to be taking shape. It struck her as a recipe for defeat.

Who was she, as military men suggested testily, to be "dabbling in military affairs"? Such life-and-death matters were strictly for bewhiskered West Pointers, for students of Napoleon like "Old Brains" Halleck—not for amateurs, and least of all for ladies. But with similar condescension, offended males often also said that the law was for learned counsel, and she had discovered that eminent attorneys—Bates, for example—would turn to her to do legal research, to think through a legal position, to talk it over with a lawyer or two, and then to write it in persuasive form. After a while, she had stopped clearing matters with lawyers; in the case of the habeas corpus memo, and the *Reply to Breckinridge*, and now the war powers memo, she was on her own. The lawyers would then pick at it, change it a little, but treat it with the reverence that the printed word commanded. They all agreed that, had she not been a woman, she "would have made a fine lawyer." But, in fact, she acted as a fine lawyer.

Military strategy attracted Anna Carroll for the same reason. It was not war—no blood, no privation, no bravery—rather, strategy was a study of power relationships, based on geography and logistics. Her years of experience promoting railroads steeped her in more logistics than most military men studied in a lifetime. With Jefferson Davis and Bob Walker five years ago, she had written tracts and presentations for the Memphis & Charleston, showing how the financing of this cross-Southern railroad—linking Memphis on the Mississippi with Charleston on the Atlantic—could give impetus to the industrialization of the South and form the basis for a southern-route transcontinental railroad. Jeff Davis had a fine mind, she judged, and had been a good client: he had often called that railway "the spine of the South." She knew every inch of that line, and how it supplied Atlanta, Montgomery, Nashville, even Richmond. She wondered if any of the Union generals, most so recently civilians, knew how important that transportation system was in the movement of armies and supplies. Anna assumed that some did; but of the generals she had spoken to in the past two weeks, almost all had eyes fixed on a Mississippi campaign, down the most heavily fortified river in the world. Never an element of surprise. Worse, the success of such a Mississippi River campaign rested on gunboats, with which most generals had little experience.

At the shipbuilder's, Anna flashed her impressive War Department credentials. The yard boss, obviously wondering why he was required to show the construction of the latest machines of war to a lady, pointed out the two boats in preparation. One was a wooden ship, the other partially ironclad; almost all the guns were located forward, few aft.

"How fast are they?"

He shook his head at the stupidity of the question. "These are like barges, lady. Not built for speed. Built to take weight, to carry heavy artillery to match the guns of the river forts, and not to sink so quick when hit by enemy cannonballs. The whole idea is to float slowly toward and past a river port blazing away."

"How slow are they, then?"

"Seven knots, eight if you push it."

She nodded. "River pilots," she said. "Where do they eat?"

The amused shipyard man told her of a restaurant-bar along the wharf and added a suggestion that she not go there alone. She agreed, thanked him, and headed for her hotel, the Everett House. Coming down to St. Louis from Chicago, Anna had met a river pilot's wife, a chatty, frumpy woman, who said she would also be staying at the Everett.

Mrs. Charles Scott was her name. Why was it, Anna wondered, that so many people in her life were named Scott? Winfield Scott, who would come to her father's house and discuss military tactics after the Mexican War; Thomas Scott, who had hired her for pamphleteering and some influence with state legislators when he was with the Pennsylvania Railroad, and who as Assistant Secretary of War had signed her pass; and now this Charles Scott.

The river pilot's wife, gabbing amiably about the way the rebels had stolen her husband's boat, agreed to search for him at his favorite restaurant on the wharf. With Mrs. Scott in tow, Anna hired a carriage and headed the horses down to the Mississippi docks.

Charles Scott did not appreciate the visit; he was quietly and privately drinking the afternoon away. "I got nothing to tell you," he glared, "you may be secesh." He glanced only briefly at her credentials; Anna suspected he could not read.

"You'll be helping the Federals when they go down the river to take Vicksburg, won't you?"

He grunted. "Prob'ly get a cannonball down our throats. You been downriver? Rebs are expectin' visitors."

She ordered a beer and said nothing. She was accustomed to dealing with this sort, who resisted all questions asked, and would answer only unasked questions. After a while, and some hard looks between husband and wife, Mrs. Scott volunteered, "My Charlie's done some work for one of the Union generals."

Anna made a face to indicate she didn't believe her husband was that important.

"Grant," said the river pilot. "I work part-time for him, showing him the forts down around Cairo, sometimes drawing fire to see where the guns are. Commander Foote's boat, the *Essex*, you heard of it? Dangerous work."

"The Mississippi's current gets pretty fast down there," Anna offered. Right or wrong, it would keep him talking.

"No," said the pilot. "Current stays pretty steady seven knots all the way south, to Memphis, Vicksburg, New Orleans. You don't know much about the river, ma'am."

"A gunboat floats down past those forts on a current of seven knots," she calculated aloud. "If you put on the engines, you can add seven more knots. That's fourteen knots passing the forts. Does anybody hit anything?"

The pilot had to laugh. "Not at that speed, the current plus the engine speed. No, you go as slow as the river lets you when you fire your artillery into the fort. You cut engines, or reverse engines, and slug it out."

"And what about coming back?"

"That's the problem." Long pause. Anna did not ask what the problem was. "Gettin' back."

"If the gunboats don't reduce the fort on the way downriver, the boats must fight the current coming back," she said. "At best, you get one or two knots of relative speed."

"And you've been under fire from the shore batteries," the river pilot sighed, "most likely damaged, and you can't offset the current's speed of seven knots. So you hang there, dead in the water, and then you get carried back by the current, floating downstream until you're captured by Johnny Reb and spend the war in a prison camp."

"No wonder General Frémont didn't launch a big attack down the Mississippi," Mrs. Scott piped up. "Pity the Big Muddy doesn't run the other way. Then we could do our fighting and, if we didn't win, we could float back and try again later."

"Mississippi runs south," said the river pilot with some contempt. "Rivers have a way of doing that on this continent."

"I haven't met Sam Grant," Anna said. "Some say he drinks."

"They say I do, too," growled the pilot, "and I say the hell with them. Grant's a fighter, if the powers that be ever give him a decent command. He's not happy about the talk about Old Brains coming out here next month. There's some bad blood between him and Halleck."

Anna sipped her beer and tried a new tack. "If I wanted to ship a load of coal to Charleston, over on the Atlantic coast, from here in St. Louis, how would I go about it?"

"Barge halfway down the Mississippi to Memphis, Tennessee, then by rail straight across to Charleston. That's why they call that railroad the Memphis & Charleston, lady."

"But there's a war on, Captain. Can't use the Mississippi."

Scott frowned; she was asking him to think. "There's a couple of other rivers southeast from Paducah. You could ship the coal on the Cumberland River to Nashville, and then overland to the Atlantic." He thought that over and rejected it. "No—best bet would be up the Tennessee River to Pittsburg Landing, where it crosses the Memphis-to-Charleston line, and then use the railroad clear across the country to Charleston Harbor."

That last formulation confused her. Anna tried to remember something about the Tennessee River that Breckinridge had told her, but the thought was elusive. The river ran southward on the map from Kentucky down through Tennessee, paralleling the Mississippi River for a time, then jogged east across northern Alabama. It offered a military strategist an alternative way to cut the central east-west rail line of the South. But war was not all the business of cutting enemy supply lines, it was establishing lines of your own. If the Confederacy could keep the Mississippi closed to shipping from Missouri, Ohio, and Illinois, those Union states of the West would soon bring pressure on Lincoln to end the war. She looked for a new outlet to the sea: "What if I want to ship through New Orleans from here?"

"You couldn't, the Mississippi's closed. Best you could do is"—he stopped for a moment, an idea forming in his mind—"the same as before, take the Tennessee River to Pittsburg Landing, right where the Tennessee joins with Alabama and Mississippi. Then you cart the coal overland just a couple of miles—hell, I've walked it a hundred times—to the Tombigbee River, and straight on down Alabama to Mobile on the Gulf. Just as good a port as New Orleans."

"Navigable all the way?"

"Not by the kind of ships that work the Mississippi, but medium-sized ships—sure. There's just that little jump overland, from river to river, where you'd have to unload and switch ships. But I thought your destination was the Atlantic coast, not the Gulf."

"The Gulf ships sail to Europe too," said Anna Carroll, putting down a nickel for her beer.

That night, at the Everett House, the sheets of foolscap about the war powers of the President pushed aside on her desk, Anna traced an idea for a troop movement down the Tennessee River. Paducah, Kentucky, at the top of the Tennessee River, was already in Union hands. The musings of Breck in Lexington a month before flooded back to her memory: "*If the North takes Paducah, and gets past Fort Henry, the Union forces will have a clear run down the Tennessee River to Pittsburg Landing.*"

That was why General Sidney Johnston, best of the Southern strategists, had strengthened Fort Henry, on the river near Paducah. If the South could not stop them there, the Union forces would be in a perfect position: Grant and Sherman would have the choice of turning right to pick off the great Mississippi strongpoints like Vicksburg from the rear, or turn left and march clear across the South to the sea. That was why Kentucky had been so crucial: if Breck had held it neutral, the North would be denied the use of the Tennessee River. It was a lucky thing that the impatient rebel General Polk had blundered by invading Kentucky, giving Grant the excuse to grab Paducah and pose his threat to Fort Henry.

Anna was startled by a rap on her hotel door. She looked at her clock: the time was past 11 P.M. Perhaps Frank Blair had been freed. She called through the bolted door to see who it was at that hour. A slurred voice answered. Her curiosity overcame her fear.

River pilot Scott was standing in the hallway, in a robe, looking troubled and slightly drunk. "I have to talk to you, ma'am."

She let him in, motioning to the chair, but he did not sit down. "About your load of coal. There's something I suppose you ought to know. My wife says you're a good Union lady, and you even know Lincoln, so I suppose you ought to know about it."

She said nothing, looking interested.

"It's not like a secret, or anything—I mean, everybody who ever worked the rivers around here knows it and never even thinks about it."

Anna nodded.

"You were askin' about how fast the currents went, and I was tellin' you how the gunboats couldn't get back up the Mississippi if they got shot up." He sat down on the edge of the desk chair, blinking. "The Tennessee River? There's one big difference about it. It flows the other way."

Anna could feel her chest constrict. "It flows north?"

"Kind of a freak. It starts in the east, and then comes up north toward us. When the Tennessee parallels the Big Muddy, it's flowing the other way. Toward the north."

The gunboats could get back. If disabled after engaging the shore batteries, they would not float into enemy hands. "That's why Sidney Johnston is building Fort Henry, near Paducah?"

"Yeah. Fort Donaldson, too, on the Cumberland. I guess he figures we'd think of coming up the Tennessee to Pittsburg Landing one of these days. Makes a lot of sense."

That was it, the incongruence that had been nagging her mind. "Up" the Tennessee River current meant "down" on a map, southward.

"Maybe I better tell Grant about it," the pilot mused sleepily. "He's not hard to get to, not like Frémont."

"Do that. But don't tell anybody else."

"It's so obvious."

"Sooner or later, it'll occur to everybody," she agreed. The important thing for her was to be sooner, and to be the one who brought this plan to Lincoln.

"You could grab Vicksburg from the rear too," the river pilot said, other advantages of the strategy unfolding for him. "All its fixed guns point west, toward the Mississippi."

"And the Tennessee is navigable clear down to Pittsburg Landing?" she repeated, making certain.

"That's what we call that landing," said the pilot. "The Rebs down there call it by the name of the chapel up on the bluff—Shiloh."

CHAPTER 5

FLUB-DUBS

Ashes of roses was the color of the silk, with a wavy, moiré antique pattern. Elizabeth Keckley was seated on the Lincolns' bed, needle plunging expertly in and out of the material, raising the hem an inch because the President's wife had directed that the gown show more arm and bust. Lizzie had to drop the whole dress, which was a few hours' work, but Mrs. Lincoln was right; she knew what looked good on her. The material was the best, from France, the color just coming into fashion. Not even Kate Chase had been seen in it yet.

She thought of her son again and had to stop sewing. She took the letter from Miss Carroll out of her bag and read it once more. The letter, just received from St. Louis on Everett House stationery, was a comfort. "I have it from no less an authority than General Blair, who was General Lyon's closest friend and who looked closely into the history of the action at Wilson's Creek on August 10, that your son, James Keckley, died a hero in the glorious cause of the preservation of the Union." Miss Carroll's letter went on into considerable detail about Private Keckley's heroism in holding "Bloody Ridge" from sustained rebel attack, his succor for his dying general, and finally his own quick and painless death. She would keep that forever. She folded the pages into the envelope, tucked it away, and resumed her sewing.

Jim had been a strong boy—six feet three, nearly as tall as Mr. Lincoln— with the red hair and green eyes of his father, the white man who raped her twenty years ago. She knew she would have lost him, in any event, whether or not he survived the war. Her son had been determined to pass for white. She had seen slave families broken up and sold in her youth and was resigned to the breakup of her tie to her only son when the time came to cast off the past. James Keckley lived and died a free man; his mother had seen to that. She had bought her freedom and his fourteen years before, for twelve hundred dollars, the money borrowed from the St. Louis ladies who appreciated her talents as a seamstress.

"Seamstress" no more; "modiste" was the word, chosen because it meant she designed her own patterns, cut the material, and made no two dresses the same. Lizzie Keckley was not the sort to boast, but carried with her always the certainty that she was the best in the city of Washington at what she did. Her select clientele agreed; Varina Davis, who had been a good customer, made sure Mrs. Lincoln knew of Lizzie's abilities before she had to leave for Richmond with her husband, the former senator. Mrs. Keckley opposed the central element that the Confederacy stood for, but she was prepared to grant

Elizabeth Keckley

the slaveholders had shown good sense in electing a gentleman like Jefferson Davis as their President for the next six years, if the rebellion succeeded.

"Where's Mother?" Willie Lincoln, eleven, followed as usual by Tad, two years younger, burst in the room. She liked the boys, especially the spunky Willie, who reminded her of her own free-spirited Jim at that age. Both Willie and Tad were spoiled by their parents, but not seriously so. They called her "Mrs. Keckley" rather than "Lizzie" at the direction of their father, who insisted they show respect to a free negress. The President had called her that, too, until she suggested "Lisabeth," which she felt was a good compromise between undue formality and disrespectful familiarity.

"Your mother is with Major French, down in the Green Room," she told them. Mrs. Lincoln was with the Commissioner of Public Buildings, summoned to help the "First Lady of the Land," as a newspaper reporter liked to call her, solve a terrible problem. "You'd better stay away. Especially with your face looking that way."

"What's wrong with my face?" Willie's face, with its nice hint of mischief, was obviously unwashed. Tad's face was neither as sweet nor as sparkling; the younger boy's head was large for his body, which was why, as a baby, he had been called "Tad," for "tadpole." He was afflicted with a badly formed palate, causing him to speak with difficulty. Good boy, though, who worshipped his brother. She handed Willie a hand mirror.

He looked and nodded. "Mrs. Keckley," he announced gravely, "that is a very dirty face in the mirror. Boy ought to wash. But"—he chucked the mirror back merrily—"my pony will never notice!" He ran out with a clatter, followed by Tad.

Would William Lincoln grow up to be like his father? She judged not. A basic cheerfulness to his character made him different from Mr. Lincoln. She had seen the President one night come down the hall to see whose light was on, so he could read aloud from one of Bill Nye's humorous passages, but Abraham Lincoln seemed to her to be a melancholy man, steeped in a lifetime of sorrows. When she was sitting on one of the hallway chairs, with the casualty list containing Jim's name in her hand, he had come by and sat with her saying nothing for a while. They grieved together, with no tears. Then this ordinarily shut-mouthed man had opened his soul to her about his mother's coffin, in their house for three days, and his sister's coffin when she died in childbirth, and the time he had the hypo after a young woman he had known died in the winter of '35. He described to her the little coffin of Eddie, his second son, aged four, named after the man who had been killed at Ball's Bluff. Like her, he felt what he called "the intensity of death." Death was never far from him.

Strange man, in many ways. His eldest son, Robert, was away at Harvard; whenever that boy came home, Lisabeth Keckley could notice the coolness between father and son. Robert was remote—"Mary's boy," in contrast with Willie, his father's boy—and seemed to resent Mr. Lincoln. She could understand the jealousy of Robert for the much-adored Willie, and his anger at his father's favoritism, but then Lisabeth had heard from one of the President's former law partners, sitting in the waiting room one day, about Mr. Lincoln's strange relationship to his own father. Hated him, this strange little man claimed. When she said she didn't believe that, the lawyer said that when

Thomas Lincoln was dying, only sixty miles from Springfield, Illinois, his son Abraham refused to go and visit him. Later on, he refused to attend the funeral. There has to be a lot of bad blood between father and son if one doesn't go to the other's funeral. If what the lawyer said was true, Mr. Lincoln knew what it was like to be the son with an anger festering against the father; didn't he see what it was like for Robert Lincoln now?

She picked up her needle and thread and sewed until the hem was almost finished. She could hear voices coming up the stairs: an almost tearful whine of Mrs. Lincoln's, and the tut-tutting of Major French.

"Mr. Lincoln will not approve it! No, Willie, not now—and wash your face! It's sixty-seven hundred dollars over." She swept into the bedroom, saw the modiste, and barked at her, "Tell him how expensive everything is! What do men know?"

Mrs. Keckley nodded solemnly to the harried commissioner of public buildings, whose job she knew it was to make certain that expenditures did not exceed appropriations. She handed the gown to Mrs. Lincoln and joined the major in the hall while the first Lady dressed.

"It's this bill from Carryl & Brother in Philadelphia," he explained. "We had a budget of $20,000 to refurbish the Mansion, and this comes to $26,700."

"Didn't you tell the store what the limit was, Major?"

"Oh, they knew the limit all right. But Mrs. Lincoln kept adding items—draperies, a better grade of carpeting, repairing the chandelier in the East Room—and the cost kept going up."

Mrs. Lincoln put her head out the door, still wriggling into her dress. "Mr. Lincoln will never approve, Major. Go see him right now, he's just down the hall. Tell him how common it is to overrun appropriations."

"That's not always—"

"Tell him how much it costs to refurbish. He doesn't realize . . . He'll want to pay for it out of his own pocket." Mrs. Lincoln started to cry, real tears, not for effect. "You know, Major, he cannot afford that, he ought not to do it. You've got to get me out of this!"

"I'll ask for an appointment."

"He's just down the hall, you can go now. Lisabeth, dear, go with him—you know what fabrics cost, how they've gone up. It's the war, the blockade, our own blockade." She sniffed away her tears and looked at him squarely. "Major, if you get me out of this, I will always be governed by you henceforth, I will not spend a cent without consulting you. Go both of you, together, please—right now. Don't let him know you've seen me!" She shut the door.

The major looked down at the bill in his hand. "I'll go in if you come with me, Mrs. Keckley. He may not go through the roof if you're there."

She accompanied him down the hall to the secretaries' office. George Nicolay looked up, smiled faintly, and waved them into the President's office without asking questions. Lincoln was holding a book and comparing a map on one page with a map spread across his desk.

"Halleck on military strategy," the President explained. "I'm trying to see how to apply what he learned from Napoleon to our own situation in the West. Well, Major, how go the rugs?"

"I have called, Mr. President—" He began again: "I have been asked to come over, sir, on a matter of no official concern."

"A bill?" Lincoln looked sharply at him.

"For furnishing this house," the major replied. "It's some seven thousand dollars over the appropriation. Before I can pay it, I have to have your approval."

The President slammed his book shut. "It can never have my approval. I'll pay it out of my own pocket first."

"I really don't think that's necessary, sir, because many appropriations have not been enough to—"

"It would stink in the nostrils of the American people," said Mr. Lincoln, and it troubled Mrs. Keckley to see him getting so excited, "to have it said that the President of the United States had approved a bill overrunning an appropriation of twenty thousand dollars for—for flub-dubs! For flub-dubs for this damned old house, when the soldiers cannot have blankets!" She understood now the political reason for his anger and began to wonder if she was charging too much for Mrs. Lincoln's gowns. "Who is this furnisher, Carryl & Brother, and how came he to be employed?"

"I don't know, sir—first I heard of him, he brought me a large bill for room paper. Maybe your secretary knows."

Lincoln jerked a cord sharply and the steward William Slade opened the door. "Tell Nicolay to come here."

Both Nicolay and John Hay, the other secretary, appeared almost instantly. "Nicolay—how did this, this furnishings person, get into the house in the first place?"

"I don't know, sir."

"Who employed him?"

"Mrs. Lincoln, I suppose," John Hay volunteered. Mrs. Keckley had heard from Mrs. Lincoln that this young man continually got her into trouble with her husband. Mary Lincoln's suspicion was not misplaced; Mrs. Keckley had heard the young fellow refer to the President's wife as "the Hellcat, getting more Hell-cattical every day," which struck her as disrespectful in the extreme. She liked Nicolay, and the third man, Stoddard, but not Hay. Hay had too high an opinion of himself for Mrs. Keckley's taste; and why wasn't a man of his age in uniform, serving at the front?

"Well, if Mrs. Lincoln is to blame, let her bear the blame," the President almost shouted, "for I swear I won't! Where's the itemized order on this?"

Hay ran out to get the bill and brought it back, presenting it almost triumphantly. Lincoln looked at the offensive sheet, shaking his head, muttering " 'Elegant grand carpet, ten thousand dollars'—I should like to know where a carpet worth ten thousand dollars can be put."

"Probably in the East Room," suggested the major.

"A monstrous extravagance," said Lincoln. "It was all wrong to spend one cent at such a time. I never ought to have had a cent expended. The house was furnished well enough—better than any we ever lived in." It seemed to the modiste that the President was talking to himself. "If I had not been overwhelmed with other business, I would not have spent a nickel. What could I do? I couldn't attend to everything. I had other things on my mind."

He looked at her and frowned. "Lisabeth, why are you here?"

She was not about to concoct a story. "Mrs. Lincoln felt, sir, that if I came along with Major French, you might not lose your temper."

He nodded in grim understanding. "As you see, I have not lost my temper. This war is costing two million dollars a day, and Mr. Chase tells me we have no way of raising two million dollars a day. The nation is out of money, and I am out of money, and my wife is buying the grandest carpet in the world. Major—I will not approve that bill. Never. Never!" He waved them out.

"He'll have to approve the bill," the major told Nicolay and Hay. "The carpet is perfect for the East Room, which is a very big room and needs a lot of carpet. And he'd be crazy to pay it out of his own pocket."

Hay closed the door to the President's office. "Let it wait a few weeks," the young man advised. "It'll keep the Hellcat pinching the pennies for a change." Lisabeth Keckley glared at him, and he fell silent.

Nicolay had the answer. "I'll slip it in with a bunch of other items to approve, when he's in a good mood, or on a very busy day. Just make sure, Major, that the newspapers don't know about it."

"Flub-dubs!" She could hear the high voice of the President carry through the thick oak door. "For flub-dubs!"

CHAPTER 6

JOHN HAY'S DIARY, NOVEMBER 24, 1861

We won the election in Maryland, more by crook than by hook, and there are no longer those legislators sitting in Baltimore who can command a majority for secession. A couple of months ago, unbeknown to Nico or me or anybody, General Nat Lyon, acting on orders from Seward and McClellan, arrested a bunch of the pro-secesh lawmakers on their way to some Maryland mischief in Frederick. News of this has been largely suppressed, as it troubles some of the more fastidious defenders of democracy, but old "Bull Run" Russell of the *London Times* has bewailed in print the fact that "the news that twenty-two members of the Maryland legislature have been seized by the Federal authorities has not produced the smallest effect here." He takes this to mean that "all guarantees disappear in a revolution," which was the same tack taken by the traitor Breckinridge.

Maryland, threatening to sever our communication with the rest of the Union, is not our favorite state. The Tycoon calls it "a good state to move from," and tells the story of a witness on a stand who, on being asked his age, answers, "Sixty." Since it was apparent from his white beard and decrepitude that he was much older, the judge admonished him and demanded the truth. "Oh," said the witness, according to Lincoln, "you're thinking about that fifteen years I spent down on the Eastern Shore of Maryland. That was so much lost time, and it don't count." So much for the complaints from the plug-ugly state.

Russell's writings are more than annoying. The Prsdt differentiates between the *New York Times*—the "good" *Times*—and the *London Times*—the "bad" *Times*—and told Russell to his face "if the bad *Times* would go where we want them, good times would be sure to follow." But the bad *Times* is reporting that this is a war between the Southern yearning for independence and the Northern desire for empire, and that sort of twisted news encourages Her Majesty's Government to favor, perhaps even to recognize, the Confederacy.

As a result, Americans are getting fed up with England. The British are known to be plotting with the French and Spanish to take over Mexico, and at the same time have been sending troops to Canada and mobilizing them along our border. If the South prevails, the English would dearly like to take a bite out of our Northern tier. Seward has been ready to declare war on them for months, but the Tycoon, with an eye on our dwindling exchequer, keeps saying "one war at a time."

Money is a problem in little ways too.

The great uproar about the elegant grand carpet—who can ever forget the flub-dubs?—ended in the quiet payment by the government with nobody the wiser, and never approved by the President if anybody should ask. But the Lincoln family, with his healthy twenty-five thousand dollars a year salary, is not the only one with financial headaches.

I am getting fourteen hundred dollars a year, and that from the Interior Department because there is no authorization in the funds allotted to the President by a beneficent Congress for a second secretary. We recently hired a third secretary, Stoddard, to open the mail, which is mainly abusive, and to get the Hellcat out of our hair, but Nico hasn't figured out a way to pay him yet. Fourteen hundred a year is nothing; a mere congressman gets twice that. It's fortunate I get invited to dinner parties all the time or I would waste away to nothing.

Equally important, the Union is running out of money. The Tycoon was glooming on the way to the telegraph office this morning and I made a list of the things he complained about. Credit is gone at St. Louis now that Frémont is gone. Chase, the abolitionist in the Cabinet, professes unhappiness at the firing of Frémont but seems to be in genuine despair about the nation's overdraft, which is twelve million dollars. The Tycoon has to cram his head full of military strategy, so he leaves the raising of money totally to Chase, who worries about it. I worry about never meeting his daughter, who is said to have a dozen swains, each one of whom makes more than fourteen hundred a year. Lincoln is thankful Chase is at Treasury and not Cameron, who is utterly ignorant, selfish, and openly discourteous to the President, and a notorious crook.

I cannot understand why the Tycoon puts up with so many personal slights and even insults from the men who are supposedly working for him. Bates, our esteemed Attorney General, was in here complaining that the Lincoln administration was not an administration at all, but a separate and disjointed pack of Cabinet officers, each one ignorant of what his colleagues are doing. The Prsdt heard him out and promised to do better. Strange, that unconcern with presumption. Lincoln is neither a modest nor a humble man, stoutly resists any encroachments on his authority from any quarter. Yet when it comes to the formal showing of respect, to the proper deference to his position, he shrugs off social slights and even the most egregious insults. That is paradoxical. I think he makes a mistake in his willingness to "hold McClellan's horse, if need be," as he says; people assume if you let them take advantage of you in little ways, you will let them have a chunk of your power.

Here in Washington, the Army of the Potomac is now marching up and down, looking spiffier every day, and the Tycoon is beginning to get abuse for the Jacobins here and Greeley in the *Tribune* in New York for appointing a procrastinator as General-in-Chief. Wade especially is steaming—he thought the appointment of McClellan was a promise of action. The Tycoon is torn: he needs some successful action after Bull Run and Ball's Bluff to dissuade the Europeans from helping the South, but he cannot afford another defeat. He does not want to push McClellan into a disaster the way the "On to Richmond" set pushed Scott into Bull Run.

I wish here to record what I consider a portent of evil to come. The President, Governor Seward, and I went over to McClellan's house one night last week. The servant at the door said the general would soon return. We went in, and after we had waited about an hour, McC. came in and without paying any particular attention to the porter, who told him the President was waiting to see him, went upstairs, passing the door of the room where the President and Secretary of State were seated.

They waited about half an hour, and sent once more a servant to tell the general they were there, and the answer coolly came that the general had gone to bed.

I merely record this unparalleled insolence of epaulets without comment. It is the first indication I have yet seen of the threatened supremacy of the military authorities.

Coming home, I spoke to the President about the matter but he seemed not to have noticed it, specially, saying it was better at this time not to be making points of etiquette and personal dignity.

CHAPTER 7

THE THIRTEENTH PRESIDENT

Millard Fillmore was ambivalent about obeying Anna Carroll's summons "about gaslight, or any hour after, convenient to yourself." She wanted him to call at her room in the American Hotel in Buffalo, just as she had so often asked—demanded, really—that he pay court to her in the past, at hotel rooms in New York and Washington. She never had a proper home, where a gentleman could drop by without engendering gossip. Although Anna had the capacity to make life exciting, and certainly had the talent to make an association with her politically rewarding, she never succeeded in making anything convenient. "Always love me," her note said, "and feel for me the interest a daughter would give you."

Some daughter; although he was old enough to be her father, their secret liaison had illuminated his years in Washington, but all that was long over. He reminded himself, looking at the familiar, forward-leaning handwriting, that his curious relationship with this woman had not begun until 1853, just

President Millard Fillmore

after he had left the presidency and the year his first wife died. It concluded, at least as far as he was concerned, in 1858 when he remarried in his hometown in western New York. The breakup was as discreet as the affair itself—no thanks to the lady's unconcern about appearances, especially when it came to visits to hotels by a man whose face was instantly recognized—but he had to admit that he had not handled their last farewell gracefully. In fact, when she sent him a note in New York City on that day three years ago, asking him to her hotel at Eighth and Broadway, he had sent the messenger back with a curt verbal dismissal. Fillmore, just remarried, did not want to stir old passions and especially did not want anything else put in writing, and so he had just avoided all contact with her.

That cruel snub to a longtime political supporter and devoted friend, he now decided, had not been worthy of a man of his character. Fillmore felt more guilt about the manner of his breaking off the affair than about the nights of pleasure in her arms. He flicked her note with his fingers, remembering how she made love eagerly, happily, insisting only on being on top—she was tiny and he was then a powerful, big man. Still big, he thought, rubbing the belly he'd been acquiring. He was sixty-one now, which must put Anna in her early forties. He assumed she was as attractive and vivacious as before, with the perfect shoulders and bosom, and the incredible habit of sitting cross-legged on the bed after making love and insisting on talking about politics when he felt only the inclination to stare at the ceiling. She was freer than any woman he had known—Dorothea Dix crossed his mind, but that avid social reformer was a far cry from Anna Ella Carroll—and she had given herself to him without reservation or inhibition. Her refusal to acquiesce to the convention of male dominance in life was matched only by her eagerness to please in bed; he supposed there was some consistency in her sense of freedom in both areas. "Is there anything I do that you don't like," she had once asked him, sitting perkily cross-legged, her unforgettable breasts exposed to his gaze, "or is there anything I don't do that you'd like?" That was a crystal moment for him; her words had been sincere, well phrased, totally free of embarrassment, innocent in their abandon. Not even considering the political debt, he owed her more than a rude dismissal. Millard Fillmore, thirteenth President of the United States not a decade before, now a forgotten man, picked up a pen and responded graciously to Miss Carroll's kind invitation. He would be pleased to see her in one of the hotel's public rooms.

He spotted her in the salon having a glass of wine with a gray-haired man he did not know. He frowned; propriety was one thing, company another. She wore a yellow suit, which set off her red-gold hair, and stirred the old yearning in him. He shook off that thought and walked to their table.

Anna's face lit with a relaxed delight that assured him this was not going to be a difficult moment. He felt better about that, although unaccountably put out that he should feel deprived at the lack of tension. She introduced the man she was with: "This is Lemuel Evans, Mr. President, my friend and escort officer." After shaking hands, the man excused himself to make travel arrangements and took his leave.

"Escort officer? Sounds as if you're on a military mission."

"I am," she replied, as if that were a natural thing. "Captain Jones was assigned to me by the Secretary of War. We've been in St. Louis, looking at the river-war preparations and visiting Frank Blair. We're on our way back to Washington now. I couldn't come through Buffalo without seeing you again."

"Is he your lover?" Fillmore didn't know what made him blurt that out. He wished he could snatch back the jealous question.

"People sometimes ask me," she replied evenly, "if I ever had an affair with President Buchanan. Or if I was ever the mistress of Millard Fillmore."

"What do you answer?"

"How would you prefer that I answer?"

"With an unequivocal no, of course."

She smiled, not so warmly this time. "Captain Jones, then, is not my lover. Why did you ask, Millard? You have such an ingrained antipathy to any sort of gossip."

Fillmore shook his head. "Envy, I suppose. Anna, I came because I have an apology to make." She started to wave it off, but he pressed ahead: "When your note was handed to me in New York, I was exceedingly busy, and if my answer was not couched in polite language, I regret it and assure you that no disrespect was intended."

"You thought I had some pecuniary favor to ask," she said, with a sad smile, "but that was not true."

He said nothing because it was true. She always was short of money and could be almost as much a pest about that as she was about asking for jobs for her friends. He was glad she had some connection with the War Department now, to help pay her bills.

She changed the subject, asking brightly: "What do you think about your old friend Mason, being snatched off the British ship *Trent*? Did you think England will go to war if we don't give him back?"

Fillmore grunted—"your old friend" hit home. Jim Mason, the Virginian who was chairman of the House Foreign Affairs Committee for the three years Fillmore had stepped up from the vice presidency to fill out Zack Taylor's term, was author of the Fugitive Slave Act. Fillmore, over the protest of the anti-slavery Whigs, signed the bill forcing the return of escaped slaves to their owners, which cost Fillmore the Whig nomination in 1852. That act of compromise saved the nation from a civil war, or at least postponed it for a decade, but it was performed at the sacrifice of his political career. Fillmore felt entitled to feel sorry for himself about that.

Four years afterward, when the Whigs split into the anti-slavery Republicans and the Know-Nothings, Anna Ella Carroll had almost singlehandedly delivered to Millard Fillmore the nomination of the Know-Nothing Party. He had been in Europe pretending to have no interest in a political comeback, while Anna had been the one—"with no knowledge on the part of the world," as she discreetly put it at the time—to give him his last chance at regaining the presidency. Which he would have done, if the damned Free-Soilers among the Know-Nothings had not bolted to the Republican candidate, Frémont, thereby electing Buck and Breck. Fillmore owed this woman so much, and had returned so little; he luxuriated in his guilt at rejecting her.

"The *Trent* affair is the best thing that ever happened to the South," he said. That surprised her, which pleased him. "Mason and Slidell couldn't do the Confederacy much good in London and Paris—the Europeans know that Seward will declare war if they help the rebels. But this way, with the North crowing about insulting the British, and the British sure to demand satisfaction, there could be a war. And the South would benefit—the Union cannot fight the Europeans and the South at the same time."

"I didn't think of that," she said, nodding. "You're right, of course. What a waste, your being out of politics."

"Former presidents are nothing more than unwanted warts on the body politic," said Fillmore, glad to be appreciated again. "If you see the Wizard in Washington, tell him to tell Seward to avoid getting caught up in this foolish outburst of patriotic fervor." The "Wizard" was Thurlow Weed, widely known as the wizard of the Albany lobby, who had been Fillmore's political mentor, and the man who introduced him to Anna. The New York boss had more luck with Seward than with Fillmore as a candidate, though neither of his charges ever won a presidential nomination. Fillmore suspected that Weed and Anna Carroll, who had done business together in the past, were allies still.

"And what about you, Anna?" He was tempted to ask if she was still writing the anti-papacy diatribes and anti-immigration tracts that made her the darling of the Native Americans throughout the fifties, but he guessed she might be sensitive about that now. "What's this War Department assignment?"

"We're all doing what we can," she said offhandedly. "Dorothea Dix came down to Washington, now she's superintendent of nurses for the army."

He felt a sudden clutch of discomfort. Did Anna know about his long association with Miss Dix? If so, why had Anna never mentioned Dorothea throughout their years together; if not, why did Anna choose Dorothea Dix, out of all the women in public life, as her example? Both Anna and Dorothea had refused to return his letters, the social reformer because she felt them a part of history, the pamphleteer because she claimed to have already "consigned them to the flames." He bet she had not; Anna had improperly used one of his letters as a way of getting business for herself. He reminded himself that he had been single at the time of their affair. "Come now, Anna—what sent you to St. Louis with a military escort? An army pamphlet?"

"I have a plan," she said in all seriousness, "a plan to win the war." He did his best to keep a straight face. She had a deceptively keen mind, he was aware, and she thought like a businessman and wrote like a demagogue, but he doubted her abilities as a military strategist. "All the preparations in the West up to now," she said excitedly, "use the Mississippi River as the plan of attack. The rebels know that, and they've fortified the river."

He nodded solemnly, enjoying her enthusiasm, picturing her sitting cross-legged, naked, intensely talking politics, as they did in the old days.

"The heavy risk, and the casualties, can be avoided by using the Tennessee River," she stated, as if practicing a presentation. "This river is navigable for medium-sized boats to the foot of Muscle Shoals in Alabama, and is open to navigation all the year—and the distance is only two hundred and fifty miles, from Paducah in Kentucky, where the Tennessee meets the Ohio River, clear down to Alabama." He nodded again; her intensity, discussing men's business, was delicious.

"Another trouble with the Mississippi," Anna continued, taking a gulp of wine, "is that our gunboats, if crippled, would fall prey to the enemy by being swept downriver by the current. Now here's the best part. That trouble doesn't exist on the Tennessee River, because its current runs North. If our boats were crippled, they would drop back with the current and escape capture."

"Goes to the heart of the South, too, as I recall," said Fillmore, encouraging her. Obviously this must have occurred to the military men on the scene, but if Anna Carroll wanted to play military strategist, she should not be discouraged.

"Exactly. It would cut the enemy's main east-west supply line by intersecting the Charleston and Memphis railroad."

"That was the line you and Jeff Davis were promoting," he remembered, "the southern route to California."

"It would enable us to take the Mississippi forts from the rear," she added. "Vicksburg is impregnable from the river, but it can be taken from the east. That's my Tennessee River plan. Aren't you excited? The war could be over in three months."

"Strange that Frémont didn't try it," he mused. If it was so obvious, why hadn't it been done immediately? He had no love for John Frémont, and even less for Jessie, but they were no fools. They had known how to erode his strength in 1856 with that "Free Soil, Free Men, Frémont" slogan.

"That old windbag was too busy fighting Frank Blair. Come on, Millard—can you see anything wrong with my plan?"

Although he did not want to dampen her enthusiasm, he did not want her to suffer pain of ridicule. "It makes excellent sense, Anna. I see only one thing wrong with the plan. Its author."

When she did not register understanding, he explained gently: "No President, my dear, can afford to take military advice from a civilian—publicly, that is. And the notion of taking military advice from a woman is ludicrous. Not only would the military resent it, the public would laugh at it."

"That's wrong."

"I agree it's wrong, but that's life. That's the way things are in this world. Put military strategy out of your mind, Anna. In a few weeks, or a few months at most, a responsible general—Halleck, Grant, Sherman—will put it forward, and then it can be made to happen."

"Months! Do you realize how many lives can be lost in months? And do you have any idea of the carnage in store for our soldiers if they are sent down the Mississippi?" She seemed near tears; he had never seen her so furious. "It's so galling to hear you say that, Millard—that no military plan can be presented by a civilian and a woman. What if it happens to be a damn good idea?"

He backed away. "Let's assume the plan is a good one. Let's also assume that at least one or two of the generals are already considering it. And let's even assume Lincoln is too busy with McClellan and the Army of the Potomac, and with the *Trent* affair and war with England, to yet apprise himself of a Tennessee River plan. It's your responsibility to suggest it in a way that does not embarrass him. Who's your man at the War Department? Not Cameron, I hope."

"Tom Scott—he was superintendent of the Pennsy."

"Good man. Lay out the plan to him," Fillmore advised, knowing he was giving sound advice from his experience with the presidential office, "but not orally. Give him a written plan, with figures in it, and navigation charts, and mileages, and river speeds, and all the tedious detail. Sign it and date it and mark it secret. Then see if Scott can get it to the President's attention directly."

"I could write it on the train and have it in his hands by the thirtieth."

"Do that. None of your high-flown rhetoric, though—this isn't the *Reply to Breckinridge*." He could see she was glad he had read the pamphlet she had sent him. "Factual. Cold. Military. And secret."

"Yes, it's important the rebels not learn of the plan—"

He shook his head; she still did not understand. "It's not the rebels learning about it that's important, Anna, it's the public learning about who suggested it. Let the President give the generals the credit, if it works, and the blame, if it fails. Believe me, Anna, I sat in that office for three long years, I know how presidents think. Get your idea to him in a way that he can use it, and not in a way that precludes his using it."

She cocked her head, apparently impressed but not persuaded. Perhaps she needed to get the public credit; he could not know her private designs or suffragist desires. He asked her if she knew Lincoln.

She nodded thoughtfully. "I've met him several times at receptions, twice for a serious talk with Bates. He has me working on a war powers document. Don't believe that he goes around telling funny stories all the time—he's a serious man. But Lincoln has the same problem you had."

"Which was?"

"He's waiting for the country to lead him." Fillmore took umbrage at that but said nothing, since people who had never been President rarely understood how hard it was to do anything before the country was quite ready. Sometimes the greatest leadership was the ability to delay, as he had done, to the cost of his reputation as a leader. "His instincts are good," Anna continued, "—crack down on the traitors, but let slavery exist where it was—but Lincoln is too fearful of public sentiment. He's a compromiser."

"The party threw me out because I tried to compromise," the former President reminded her. She was quite wrong in her estimate of Lincoln; by refusing to compromise on the issue of secession, the Union President had brought on the war. "He's either going to have to let the South go in peace, or he's going to have to turn this into a war on slavery. There's no way to compromise union or disunion, there's no middle ground—and union is just not a big enough cause to fight a war over."

"That's what John Breckinridge used to tell me."

He studied her. "You and John Breckinridge too?"

"What do you expect me to say?"

He shook his head and allowed a smile of pain to show. That must have begun just as he was getting married in 1858. This was unfair of him; he had rejected this woman, and now felt a twinge of jealousy at her interest in other men.

Why had she come back through Buffalo? Not to see him growing old and fat while she remained involved and attractive; she may have been a pest at times, but it was not in her character to be cruel. To see him in the backwater of life, out of the public eye, while she was still in the mainstream, in contact with the powerful, having some minor but still measurable effect on history— some women would find that a sweet revenge, he supposed, but not Anna. He preferred to think that she had long ago forgiven him his social slights and pecuniary stinginess and had come to see him out of friendship and a need for mature political guidance. That thought comforted him.

Why had he answered her summons? Why did he feel the urge for her again, which he turned into a desire to make himself useful to her now that all he had to offer was his judgment? Fillmore told himself that his feeling of belatedness, of having failed to grasp an opportunity, was no mere sense of guilt at the way he had dismissed her when he had been in a position to return her many political and personal favors. He was not sorry for her anymore, or embarrassed at her importunings, or irritated at her pushiness; on the contrary, he realized, he was sorry for himself for not having invested more of himself in this woman, whose experience enabled her to flower in this crisis. He had come, too, because he missed the mystery of the center, and because he feared the loss of friendship with a woman who might no longer feel the old yearning for him.

Before they parted, he saw no harm in finding out what warmth remained in the embers. "Your last communication to me was a spirited one," he began.

"I know. I didn't like that remark about my being a 'Jeremy Diddler in petticoats.' " Fillmore winced; a Jeremy Diddler was one who borrowed money but did not pay it back, and he should never have passed along that judgment of her made by a political enemy. "Especially since I had openly," she continued, "before the world, done for you what no woman ever dared to do before for any man in America." He readily acknowledged that with a nod; she had delivered a national convention's nomination to him. "One of these days I may do a reminiscence," she said, looking at him levelly, "and I have the title: *Men as They Seem and as They Are.*"

He supposed he deserved that. "Whatever may be your opinion of me," he said, covering her hand with his, "I shall ever rejoice in your prosperity and fame."

CHAPTER 8

FIVE HUNDRED DOLLARS A HEAD

Old beaux are the worst, Anna Carroll decided. Back in Washington after her exhilarating trip West, with Congress beginning its second session and everyone eager to see how Lincoln would treat the *Trent* affair in next week's first annual message, she tucked the draft of her war powers pamphlet under the sleeve of her warmest coat—not new, but it would have to do—and headed for the President's house.

She could not help wondering what the world would be like if her American Party had been successful, and Millard Fillmore were President today. As an old-line Whig, he would probably have continued to straddle the slavery issue and argue for the Union, much as Lincoln did, but, unlike Lincoln, Fillmore would never have the gumption to actually fight the secession. Only a stubborn Lincoln would insist on Union or war. If all his Cabinet but one had advised him not to provision Fort Sumter, Fillmore would have gone along with the majority, and the continent would be shared by two nations: a Confederacy extending south to Panama or even farther, and a Union reaching up through Canada to the Arctic. Even so, Fillmore would not have escaped bloodshed: the Union would be at war with England now over a claim to the vast northern territory, a matter more fundamental to the fate of nations than the *Trent* issue of stopping ships at sea.

She grinned at the thought of the look on Fillmore's face when she had casually mentioned Dorothea Dix. Anna respected the woman—strong for prison reform, the first to show concern for better care for the feebleminded— but that torrid romance had been going on all the while Anna and Fillmore had been keeping secret company, right through the campaign of '56, and Anna had suspected as much. That half-strangled look on his face the other day confirmed it. Did the ex-President write Dorothea those stiltedly passionate letters too? Anna had dutifully destroyed all the nonpolitical mail; had her older rival done as much for him? She doubted it; let him worry.

That stop in Buffalo on her way back from St. Louis had been worthwhile. Not only had it satisfied her to see her unfaithful mentor and halfhearted champion on the sidelines while she was in the thick of events—he really had treated her shabbily, after all she did for him—but she had extracted some useful advice from him on how to deal with presidents.

She would accept half of that guidance. His suggestion to put her plan down on paper, in an official memorial to the War Department, was sound; a written record had permanence, and men's recollections tended to fade. She had started writing that memorial on the train down from Buffalo, attaching the notes on river speeds and navigability from the pilot. Fillmore's other notion, of remaining silent about her authorship, she would never accept. If it embarrassed the men of this Administration to accept a daring and ingenious military strategy from a civilian, and a woman, so be it. That was their problem, not hers.

The war powers pamphlet assigned to her by Lincoln, now in nearly final form, would be her means of access to the presidential ear. She nodded to the marine at the door of the President's house, went up the stairs toward Nicolay and Hay's office, and was struck by the sight of a long line of people in the hallway.

"You came in time for his 'public opinion bath,' " said Hay, his mustache slightly fuller than the one she remembered. He motioned at the crowd waiting to see the President—farmers, tradesmen, mothers seeking concessions for their army sons, politicians with a variety of complaints to make or secrets to confide. "Twice a week, the Tycoon does this. Can't stop him. Lasts three, four hours, everybody gets five minutes and no more."

"The President has more important things to do," she said. She carried two of the more important things under her arm.

Stoddard, the clerk opening the mail, put a word in: "The President doesn't think so. He thinks he gets a better idea of what the people are thinking from his public opinion bath than from the newspapers." He looked at a stack of newspapers on his table. "Mr. Lincoln doesn't get a whole lot of satisfaction from reading the newspapers."

Hay was unusually solicitous: "Is there anything I can do for you in the meantime, Miss Carroll?" There had to be a reason for that; perhaps the President had said something nice about her. She decided she liked the boy, and that the impression he sometimes left of arrogance was natural for anyone in his position at his age; if he wanted to treat her with the respect and affection customarily shown a favored aunt, that was all right with her.

"I have the war powers research he wanted," she said. "Perhaps I should take it to the Attorney General first."

"No, the President was talking about the war power this morning. When you returned from your sojourn in the West, I was supposed to show you a letter from Montgomery Blair about the government's power to confiscate slaves." He deftly extracted the letter out of a cardboard accordion file resting alongside his desk.

She scanned the letter from Postmaster General Blair, dated November 21, recommending that compensation be paid by the government to Union loyalists whose slaves were lost because of the operations of the war. But rebels he proposed to treat just the opposite: their land and houses would be confiscated to raise the money to pay the loyal Union men for their lost slaves. Blair's purpose was plainly to induce rebels to switch sides; by doing so, they would be paid for freeing their slaves, but by failing to switch, their slaves would be taken away without compensation.

"Not a good idea," she stated. "Compensation, fine; confiscation, no."

Hay raised his eyebrows at her decisiveness. Not everyone dismissed a Cabinet member's recommendation that quickly. "Why don't you just tell that to the President? I'll slip you in between a pardon-pleader and an office-seeker. But five minutes is all."

In a moment, as a satisfied, bemused man in overalls came out of the President's office, a note from Lincoln in hand, Anna Carroll was ushered in, her two documents at the ready. In five minutes, there would not be time for both; she would have to use her ticket, the pamphlet, and hold the Tennessee plan until later.

"My dear lady," Lincoln said, rising to greet her, waving Hay out.

"These public opinion baths tax your time," she offered.

"Gives me the atmosphere of the average of our whole people," he explained. "Every applicant for audience has to take his turn, as if waiting to be shaved in a barbershop."

"They must be exhausting."

He shook his head no. "Though they may not be pleasant in all particulars, the effect, as a whole, is renovating and invigorating."

She felt her allotted time slipping away and came directly to the point: "I have a draft of the war powers pamphlet."

"You saw Judge Blair's idea?"

"You have no power to confiscate property permanently," she said flatly, "for any reason, including treason. Blood attainder, unconstitutional."

He agreed. "But I can pay for property. Broach the idea, in your pamphlet, of compensated emancipation. I want to pay the loyal slave states—Delaware, your own Maryland, Kentucky, and Missouri—five hundred dollars a head for each slave the state buys from its citizens and frees."

Before she could respond, Hay poked his head in to say that General McClellan was there, and could he interrupt. The President nodded, handed Anna a draft for a state compensation bill to read outside, and told her to come back when the general had gone.

Seated outside the President's door, studying the draft of a Delaware law with Lincoln's comments in the margin, she let herself listen to the muffled voices. In fact, she strained to hear them, because McClellan's plans in the East would affect her own for the Western rivers.

"If it were determined to make a forward movement of the Army of the Potomac," Lincoln's voice was asking, "without awaiting further increase of numbers, or better drill or discipline, how much time would be required to actually get it in motion?"

"If the bridge trains are ready," McClellan estimated, talking more slowly, "two, three weeks—December fifteenth. Probably around the twenty-fifth, Christmas."

"How many troops could join the movement from southwest of the river?"

Long pause. "Seventy thousand."

Lincoln's high voice: "How many from northeast of the river?"

McClellan's low, reluctant voice: "Thirty thousand. Thirty-three, maybe." Taken together, she reckoned, such an advance against the rebel forces in Virginia would be the greatest troop movement in the history of the continent.

"Suppose, then—" Lincoln's voice fell, and, as far as she could make out, he was suggesting a plan to send the Union forces already across the river southward against the rebels, while the main Union force struck across the Potomac below and behind the battle, cutting off the rebel line of retreat. His idea, she presumed, was to capture the whole rebel army in Virginia, ending the war in a stroke.

"The enemy could meet us in front with nearly equal forces," McClellan's voice was saying, "and is anticipating just such an attack." She nodded imperceptibly; he was right. The attacking force had to outnumber the defenders, especially crossing a river. "I have my mind actively turned toward another plan of campaign."

More talk followed that she could not make out, but she hoped McClellan's reluctance to make such an audacious and dangerous strike across freezing water would prevail. The war could not be won in the East, at one stroke; she was convinced that the rebels could not be defeated in their heartland but would have to be broken from the West.

The general came out, turning smartly at the doorway and marching down the hall past the line of admiring visitors. At Hay's nod, Anna picked up her papers and went back in. Lincoln picked up his previous train of thought as if his General-in-Chief had not just dashed his hopes.

"We would offer seven hundred thousand dollars to the state of Delaware," he said in lawyerly fashion, "payable in six percent U.S. bonds over thirty years, for the state to purchase its slaves. All born after the passage of the act would be born free, all slaves over the age of thirty-five would become free right away, and all under thirty-five would become free on arriving at that age."

"That would end slavery completely," she calculated, "by the twentieth century."

"Even before—a cutoff in 1893, to coincide with the thirty-year payments. If a state desires the money sooner, let it advance the date of emancipation."

"How quickly—"

"Ten years. Ten payments, emancipation by 1872."

"It would be expensive," she cautioned, remembering the difficulty of buying and freeing her own slaves.

"That's why we could not finance it in less than ten years. But it would not be expensive," he explained, "in the long run. It would cost about a third of what it takes to support this war for a year."

Did he understand what a burden the manumitted slaves could be? "And the freed slaves," she asked, as if sure he had thought it through, "would go —where?"

He stopped, frowning. "Orville Browning raised that point. He says there must be a convenient place somewhere on the American continent."

She expected that. Browning was the senator appointed to fill Stephen Douglas's seat in Illinois, and she had been writing some of his speeches. He had asked her where the slaves could be shipped off to, and she had promised to work on that but had not known where to start.

Lincoln's slave-purchase scheme sounded eminently practical, had all the figures nicely lined up, and made much good sense compared to the cost of continued war. It had one small defect, in Anna's judgment: not one of the slave border states would accept the federal government's offer. Maryland and Delaware, she knew, did not want a method of ending slavery gradually; the people of those states wanted the system they had now. Lincoln was dreaming, and she was tempted to awaken him to political reality, but she decided against it. Let others, like McClellan, tell him what he could not do; she wanted to be an adviser who could tell him what he could do.

"I can add some material in this war powers pamphlet on your power to purchase property," she offered, "in the context of the absence of any power to permanently confiscate."

He nodded and went on to the next item on his mind. When Lincoln was pressed for time, he was systematic, no funny stories; she liked that. "You're a friend of the Wades."

"Yes. Carolyn Wade," she added, lest Lincoln think she had any improper interest in the radical Ohio senator, "is my best friend. I'm having dinner there tonight."

"Good. Excellent. He's starting a committee on the conduct of the war. It could be harmful to the presidential war power. Put in a passage, if you agree with me, Miss Carroll, about the primacy of the Executive branch in the conduct of military operations. He means well, I know what he's trying to do, but we must not work at cross purposes."

She agreed. He was already looking over her shoulder at the next visitor at the door; this was not the time to bring up the Tennessee River plan. She extended her hand, and he enfolded it in his own. She left, thinking oddly of the enormity of his hand, and started to make a beeline for the War Department across the street. Before she left the Mansion, however, John Hay came running after and caught up to her near the diplomatic entrance, where visiting envoys could contemplate the cows on the ellipse behind the Mansion.

"Miss Carroll, I understand you're to see Senator Wade tonight." She nodded, still walking; she had to get to Tom Scott, give him the memo on the Tennessee plan, and get him to endorse it and pass it on to Lincoln. At that point, John Hay's help would be important; she stopped and gave him her Maryland plantation smile, as if she had all the time in the world. "Secretary Chase will be at that dinner party too, Miss Carroll—they're all from Ohio, you know."

"I know. Both Secretary Chase and I will be able to work on Ben Wade."

That was obviously not what the young man had on his mind. He put his hands in his pockets and sauntered with her toward the War Department. She tried to draw him out: "I'm sure Governor Chase is loyal to the Administration, John." She used the title Chase preferred, rather than "Secretary," to show she knew him, which was true; before seeking the nomination in 1860, he had sought out her guidance. Although they were on different sides of the question of emancipation, they could do political business.

"Um," said John Hay. Since he evidently could not figure out a way to

express what was on his mind—unusual for him, an articulate young man—
and since she could not afford to dawdle, Anna decided on directness.

"John, let's be friends," she offered. "I like you and I want to help you.
What's bothering you?"

"Kate Chase," he said instantly, relief in his voice.

She caught herself in time and did not laugh. Instead, she said seriously,
"You have good taste. Not only a lovely girl, but she is becoming a social
force in this city. Worthy of you."

He was too naïve for her; she would eat him alive. On second thought, his
position would count in his favor. Kate Chase was her widowed father's
official hostess, and with the Secretary of State's wife a relative invalid, Kate
ranked as the second woman in the Administration. She had allowed herself
to become a social rival of Mrs. Lincoln, which Anna thought was a mistake,
but the girl was also known to be politically astute; through her friendship
with Lord Lyons, the British ambassador, she was educated in foreign affairs
as well. The center of attention at all the levees, the young woman rarely
spent time with young men purely for their social standing or graces, or even
to have a good time. Anna had only met Kate once, and that time briefly, but
came away impressed that her eye was solely on the furtherance of her father's career.

Anna remembered how it was to be the good-looking young daughter of a
famous political man, and how important it was for such ambitious women to
cultivate young men on the rise who could one day be useful. John Hay,
second secretary to the President, constantly at the presidential ear, trusted as
few men in Washington, privy to everything on and in the President's desk,
capable of promoting or hindering a cause with a nod or a wink or a moment's forgetfulness—John Hay would be a useful man for Kate Chase to
know. For that reason, a cat could look at a king, and a young secretary could
look at the reigning social queen.

"She's a purposeful and experienced young lady," she said. "Not the sort of
giggling young thing you bowl over with your new mustache at the parties at
Counselor Eames's." That was all the warning she would give him.

"I've seen her at receptions," he said. "She absolutely stuns me. Miss
Carroll—you're my friend now, and I have to talk to somebody about this—I
must get to know her. I'm a personable fellow, a graduate of Brown, and you
have apparently heard of the way I have been cutting a wide swath through
the eligible ladies of this city. That sounds conceited, but I really need the
comfort of conceit, because Miss Chase ties my tongue and renders me a
Springfield bumpkin."

She had a good laugh at that and squeezed his arm. "You have an ally in
me, John. I'll figure out a way to get you together, and I'll make sure she
knows how nice you are." She amended that: "How important you are."

"You're an admirable person, Miss Carroll. I know the President thinks so,
too, for what that's worth."

"Worth a lot." She became serious. "An alliance runs two ways. Right
now, I'm submitting some information to Assistant Secretary Scott. I'm sure
he'll want the President to see it—it's a plan for a Western campaign. When it
gets to Mr. Lincoln, it's important that he know it came from me."

He promised he'd see to that, pumped her hand warmly, and when she presented her cheek, kissed it with a satisfying smack. She hurried into the War Department, determined to deliver for him, certain he would deliver for her.

Thomas Scott was not his usual self. The head of the Pennsylvania Railroad, who had gone off the payroll to take the important number-two job in the War Department, still retained his nominal position at the Pennsy; a House committee on contracts had just denounced this arrangement as corrupt, since the War Department decided on freight rates. Scott had never before been accused of any wrongdoing; in the Cameron department, where bribery and shady dealing were reputed to be widespread, his desk was an island of integrity.

"I'm just trying to do a job, Anna," he complained. "And I want my job at the Pennsy back after the war is over. Is that so wrong? Does that make me a criminal?"

"I'm having dinner at Ben and Carolyn Wade's tonight," she assured him, using the invitation for all it was worth. "His new committee is the only one that counts. I'll see he knows the real story, and who's doing the work at this department." With that nicely smoothing her way, she took her memorial and map out of its envelope.

"Colonel"—she assumed he would prefer his military salutation, since he was under fire for being a civilian railroader benefiting his old cronies— "prepare to have your eyes opened to a glorious possibility in the West. You've been worried about the Mississippi forts. Stop worrying."

She went to the map on his wall; it was too high for her, so she borrowed his yardstick ruler and used it as her pointer.

He listened dully at first. After a few moments, he interrupted to dispute her information on the speed and vulnerability of the gunboats; the new ironclads soon to be delivered, he said, were more powerful. He wanted to know why the Tennessee River was so essential, why not the even more easily accessible Cumberland River, also leading south and east? As his questioning grew more pointed, she could feel his interest increase. He was posing questions she knew he would be asked by McClellan, Lincoln, Halleck, and others. As she answered, she decided not to hand over her memorial, and was especially glad not to have handed it prematurely to Lincoln; she could see holes in it now. Still, the essence of her plan was sound; most of it stood up under close examination, improved with criticism.

Scott came from behind his desk, his own newspaper troubles set aside now, to pinpoint Pittsburg Landing. "That's the spot, right near Corinth. It's like a chess game, where your knight threatens two enemy pieces at once. The rebels will have to choose to defend the rear of their Mississippi ports— Memphis and Vicksburg—or to defend against a thrust eastward, right through Atlanta to the sea. Brilliant. Better than brilliant—obvious."

"Sidney Johnston doesn't have the troops to defend both," she added. She had spent long hours in the Mercantile Library in St. Louis arguing with rebel General Johnston's brother, the chief librarian, who rose to her bait and explained how ingenious his rebel brother was in making his small force appear much larger. With her war powers research leading to this information, she felt that Fate was helping shape her Tennessee River plan. "Tom, my

Senator Benjamin F. Wade

plan may be obvious, but has anybody discussed using the Tennessee River for a major strike south with you till now?"

"No," he said frankly, "and I didn't know about the current flowing the other way. But I'm sure the rebs have thought of it—that's why they fortified the mouth of the Tennessee and the Cumberland, with forts here and here." He tapped Forts Henry and Donelson on the map. "And maybe General Grant has thought about it, which may be why he moved so quickly to take Paducah when Polk moved into Kentucky."

"Grant doesn't know about the river running the other way," she told him. "Most of my information comes from his pilot, who was never asked about this."

"Don't sell Grant short," Scott said, using what she vaguely recognized as a stock speculation term. "Halleck does, and your friend Wade distrusts him because Grant's a Democrat, and McClellan runs him down because he's not spit and polish, and he made a mess of his life outside the army. But Grant had good West Point training, and my guess is that he must have figured this out already and just hasn't told anybody about it."

"A lot of good that does," Anna snapped. "If the strategy isn't set at the top, nothing is going to happen. You know that from railroading."

He was forced to admit she was right. "Unless the information gets to where the decisions are made, it's all a lot of talk."

"So?"

"I'm thinking," said the Assistant Secretary of War. "I can't take this to McClellan, because he wants to forget about the West except for holding actions, concentrating on the war in the East. He wants to win this war personally."

And not with one quick battle, she knew, as Lincoln had suggested. "The Cabinet?"

"Cameron's closeted with his lawyer, Stanton, the holdover from Buchanan, on our addendum to the President's Message. I can't get to either of them with anything. They probably wouldn't understand, anyway, and Stanton's a McClellan man."

"This is awfully important, Colonel. If it's delayed in the bureaucracy for a month or two—"

"I'll take it to Lincoln. He's the commander in chief, and Bates keeps telling him to command. Do you have any of this on paper?"

She decided not to hand over her incomplete plan; if generals could find flaws in it, they could discredit the entire idea. She would submit it with all of Scott's questions answered. "I'll have it in a few days. But you ought to discuss it with the President now." She hesitated. "And be sure he knows who thought it up."

Scott smiled. "I'll never steal your credit, Anna. I'm sure the plan must be floating around in some other people's heads, but they're not here at the President's elbow when it counts." He promised to take the Tennessee River plan to Lincoln that very day. She told him to tell John Hay that it was about what she had hinted to him. Scott nodded; she could see he was genuinely impressed and excited, and would make her initial presentation better than she could.

She walked briskly back to her rooms to change for dinner at the Wades'.

Anna liked the position she was in: a close friend of Carolyn and Ben just at the time when Wade was becoming extremely important, perhaps even a challenge, to Lincoln and his men. At the same time, she agreed with Lincoln on the war powers, and could argue with Ben about keeping congressional hands off those powers. She also thought Ben and his abolitionist crowd were all wrong about trying to make this a war about slavery, and could represent Lincoln's views on gradual compensation to them, too, better than anyone.

Anna loved both Wades, and they knew it. She could get away with almost anything in arguing her views, and if this were witnessed by a Cabinet member like Chase, and reported back to Lincoln, she could be in a perfect bridge-building position. That was power, which women were traditionally denied in political Washington. If it were accompanied by some knowledge that her military plan was under consideration at the highest levels of the War Department, the power to build bridges would be buttressed.

Maybe, she thought while cinching her corset, in all this new power of hers, some way could be found to get paid enough to afford a new dress. Her out-to-dinner dress was practically falling apart, and she did not want to take up Lizzie Keckley's kind offer to make a new one on credit. She had to keep up appearances; power and poverty did not mix.

CHAPTER 9

THE DOUBLE CROSS

Twenty years before, Caroline Rosekrans of New York and Connecticut married Benjamin Franklin Wade of Ohio when she was thirty-five and he was forty. Both had expected to spend the rest of their lives single. She was independent-minded and admired that quality in him, especially because he admired it in her. Although Washington called him "Ben," "Old Ben," and "Bluff Ben"—and even, after he threatened to shoot deserters at Bull Run, "Two-Gun Ben"—she called him Frank.

Carolyn Wade had not intended to become a Washington hostess, but her "talking dinners" served her husband's political interests well and satisfied her own appetite for intrigue. She made no effort to match the champagne-and-oysters elegance of young Nellie McClellan's dinner parties, or to compete with Kate Chase's large and sparkling levees. In contrast, dinners at the Wades' were gatherings over simple, good food, where much political business took place to advance the causes of the radical Republicans, and suited the plain style and combative nature of the man who had become the driving force of the group fighting to end slavery now.

Before her guests arrived, she showed her husband how she planned to seat them. These were her decisions; he sometimes grumbled, but never overrode her preferences.

"Kate Chase is to your right, Frank," she told him, "because that's protocol, not because you need a young girl to turn your head."

"She hates my guts," said Wade. "I split the Ohio delegation support for her beloved papa at the convention that nominated Lincoln last year, and she remembers."

"But you enjoy her company, all the men do."

"Sure," he said, "but I like her for a different reason. She's a real hater."

"Anna Carroll is seated to your left."

"Good. I'll have somebody to talk to if the Chase girl freezes over. Did you see Anna's *Reply to Breckinridge*? She wiped up the floor with that blackhearted traitor. As soon as we're in session, I'll move to expel him from the Senate for treason."

Carolyn Wade knew all about the lovers-and-enemies relationship of John Breckinridge and her best friend, and did not think it was one of the items of information her husband or anybody else had to know. "I'm sure she'll appreciate that, Frank. On Anna's left is Chase."

"The Secretary of the Treasury," her husband opined, "and my esteemed predecessor as senator from the state of Ohio, is a pious blowhard and a pompous ass."

"Wrong," she said. Her husband was right to mistrust Chase, because he was so consumed with ambition to be President, but mistaken about the man's *gravitas*. "He has dignity. Big difference between real dignity and pomposity. Deeply religious, too, probably because of all that unhappiness in his life."

"I feel for any man who's had to bury three wives, but that doesn't make Chase any less a pompous ass."

"He's abolition's only voice in Lincoln's Cabinet, Frank."

"That's what so goddamn galling to me! The Blairs, damn their eyes, along with that oleaginous Seward, have cozened Lincoln over to their thinking that slavery's not so bad, and maybe we should gradually ease it out by the next century. Evil! And the only one to speak out against it in the highest councils is that holier-than-thou ass of a Salmon P. Chase!"

He was shouting out of habit, she knew, not because he was angry. That would come later, at dinner, if nobody thundered back at him, and instead yes-butted him. He appreciated worthy opponents, despised unworthy opponents, readily offended his political allies—Chase was a good example—and reserved a special hostility and contempt for yes-butters.

"Chase would prefer if you called him Governor."

"I have a mind to call him Salmon because it makes him furious. What the hell kind of a name is Salmon, anyway? A fishy name for a fishy fellow."

Carolyn Wade repressed a smile and indicated the chair to her right. "Lord Lyons, the British ambassador. Try not to start the war tonight. He's here because he's a bachelor and a friend of Kate's." She indicated the last two chairs: "Edwin Stanton and his wife Ellen. We never met her, but Kate Chase particularly asked that we invite them and you said yes. She's his second wife, a lot younger than Stanton is, I hear. Kate tells me he's a lawyer in the War Department now, quite a comedown from Attorney General."

"Edwin Stanton may just be the slimiest man in Washington," Ben Wade pronounced with relish. "You know why he's still got his job? Although he was Buchanan's Attorney General, he was secretly working with us all last winter."

She had not known that. "That's duplicity."

"Oh, he's one duplex fellow, this Stanton. Chase was his main channel to us, though some say he had a second channel to Seward. Stanton cozied up to the Southerners in the Buchanan Cabinet, and then told Lincoln's men the Southern plans for secession."

That was not the story she had heard. "The Blairs think Stanton actually supported secession," she reported, since she was the only one of the two of them who would speak to the Blairs. "They say that Stanton actually urged secession on the Mississippians."

Her husband shook his head vigorously. "He was just being sneaky, the way a spy has to be. Chase is high on Stanton, of course, wants him to replace Simon Cameron at the War Department."

"Could you support somebody like that—all slimy?"

"He's a Democrat, but he's not a crook, like Cameron." Her husband looked uncomfortable. "Personally honest and a good executive, they say. God knows we could use a little incorruptibility. Pity Stanton is such a double-crosser. We'll have a chance to look him over tonight. If he's right on slavery, and if he'll lay the whip to that two-timing son of a bitch McClellan, I'll help push him in the War Department."

At the dinner table, her husband stuffed a napkin in his collar and got right to the point: "Stanton, what's all this about your calling Abe Lincoln a gorilla?"

Stanton reddened and nearly choked. "That is a canard, Senator. Some years ago, I was chosen by the McCormick reaper company to be its counsel in a patent infringement case, and the company thought it wise to retain local counsel in Springfield, Illinois. Mr. Lincoln and I met very briefly in the courtroom. I did not utilize his undoubted legal talents and was, frankly, too busy to look at his brief, but I certainly did not snub him, as has been alleged. Nor did I ever use the term you mentioned."

"It wasn't a gorilla!" boomed the host, as if he had only half-heard the explanation. "It was a giraffe. You were supposed to have said—'If that giraffe appears in the case, I'll throw up my brief and leave!' Not true?"

"Not at all true." Stanton looked miserable, and Carolyn Wade worried that his wife might be moved to tears. Carolyn shot her a sympathetic glance and leaned across the table to pat his wife's hand.

"Damnation," Wade rolled on merrily, "I was prepared to like you, Stanton. If there's anything Abe Lincoln looks like more than a gorilla, it's a giraffe."

Chase came to Stanton's social rescue. "What's got you so riled up about Lincoln, Ben? You used to think pretty highly of him, especially at the Chicago convention."

"His 'House divided' speech appealed to me."

" 'A House divided against itself cannot stand,' " Anna Carroll quoted. " 'I believe this government cannot endure permanently half slave and half free.' "

"In those days," Wade said, "he sounded a lot more like an abolitionist than he does today."

"Unfair," said Anna. "He's always been against extension of slavery, not for abolition—and besides he wasn't courting the border states back then."

"What about our stalwart emancipator, William Seward?" Wade demanded. "Chase—you remember his 'irrepressible conflict'?" The host turned to Kate Chase, put on his most stentorian voice, and began to recite: " 'It is an irrepressible conflict between opposing and enduring forces; and it means that the United States must and will, sooner or later, become entirely a slaveholding nation or entirely a free-labor nation.' " He looked fiercely at her father. "Old Billy Bowlegs isn't talking that way now that he's our Prime Minister, is he?"

"No, he's not," Chase admitted, adding, "He's not the Prime Minister, either, though he tries to be."

"You're forgetting that Seward said 'sooner or later,' Ben," Anna Carroll put in. "If you try to turn this into a war about slavery, the Union will lose, and the traitors will go off setting up a nation including Mexico and Cuba."

"Bosh!" Wade sent an ostentatious glare at Anna, which Carolyn Wade did not worry about. The two of them had been through this before at their dinners, and it drew the others out. Her husband then turned to Stanton, who was recovering from the gorilla and the giraffe. "You agree with Miss Carroll, Stanton?"

All eyes swung to the lawyer with the scraggly beard. "I think the slavery issue is becoming ever more important," he said very carefully, "in the minds of the people who voted for Lincoln." That said nothing, thought Carolyn Wade. Stanton had probably voted for his fellow Democrat, Douglas, or even for Breckinridge. Now that he was in the lair of the radical Republicans, he leaned slightly toward abolition because he so desperately wanted to please. She wondered what he really thought.

"Well said, for a Democrat," Wade observed, not letting him get away with the evasion. "Do you realize that out of the one hundred and twenty generals in the United States Army, over eighty are Democrats, and Halleck out West is sending escaped slaves back to their masters in irons? How the hell are we going to fight a war against human slavery with generals who don't give a damn about slavery?"

"Some Democrats think slavery is wrong," said Stanton, more firmly now, "and some of us have been Union men in the midst of conspiracies for secession." He looked significantly at Chase, who chimed in with "Stanton's one of us, Ben."

"Good, good," said Wade, "and what do you think of McClellan, over there at the War Department?"

Carolyn, to give Stanton a moment to arrange his defenses, turned to Lord Lyons and explained, "Zack Chandler and Tad Stevens and my husband all urged Lincoln to appoint McClellan, over General Scott's objections. McClellan promised he would launch an immediate offensive, and he did not."

"Five goddamn weeks practicing bugle calls," Wade muttered.

"There's been no living with him," she added to the British ambassador.

"He double-crossed us! That slavery-loving bastard double-crossed us!"

Lord Lyons spoke up for the first time. "I'm not familiar with that expression."

"It's an American horse-racing term," Kate Chase explained. "When a corrupt jockey agrees to hold back his horse to let another horse win, he's a 'crosser'; but if he then races to win himself, breaking his agreement with the gamblers, he's called a '*double* crosser.' "

"I am astounded," said her father, who looked genuinely shocked, "at my own daughter's familiarity with the language of venality."

"You cannot protect her from life's harsh realities," Wade told him, then concluded to Stanton, "and one of those is that McClellan is a double-crossing bastard."

"Some of us are trying to urge him to action," Stanton said. "Unfortunately, Secretary Cameron lets him have his way."

"We'll soon put a stop to that," snapped Wade. "The Joint Committee on the Conduct of the War will soon be deciding which generals lead which armies. If they don't have their heart in the war, out they go. Only the Congress can declare war, under the Constitution, and only the Congress can decide how the war should be fought."

After a silence at the table, Anna Carroll put down her fork with a plunk and said, "You're mistaken, Senator."

Carolyn Wade noted how her husband gave her his most intimidating glower, and how Secretary Chase looked troubled at the way this little woman seemed to be putting her head on the block for the President. "I've been researching the war powers for the past month," Anna said, "ever since my Breckinridge pamphlet was sent out, and I can tell you that the President, as commander in chief, conducts the war in his own way and concludes the peace in his own time. And on his own terms. Congress has very little to say about it."

"The Congress raises the troops, and raises the money—"

"Congress was not in session when the war began, and the President did all that—which Congress later had to approve. You voted for that, Ben, remember?"

"I had no choice. At the time, I thought that Lincoln was exceeding his power, but in a just cause—"

Anna was pushing him further than Carolyn ever remembered, and she wondered if Anna was not going too far. "It was in Lincoln's power to suspend habeas corpus," her friend continued with animation, "it is in his power to arrest a sitting judge who obstructs the war effort, and it's in his power to arrest a legislature about to vote secession."

"It is not in his power to ignore the Congress," Wade told her.

"I happen to think," said Anna Carroll, "that it is in the power of the President, as commander in chief in wartime, to arrest and imprison, though not otherwise to punish, a member of Congress who interferes with the military conduct of the war."

Wade's jaw dropped. Chase harrumphed and said, "That's putting it a bit strongly, my dear lady." Stanton tried to make himself invisible and the British ambassador allowed his expressive eyebrows to rise.

"If I did not hold your intellect in the highest regard, Anna Carroll," said Wade finally, "and if you were not my wife's dearest friend, I would throw you right out of here."

Anna's reaction was to laugh, quickly and heartily, joined by a nervous Carolyn Wade and a delighted Kate Chase, which broke the tension. Lord Lyons took that opportunity to ask if Senator Wade thought the President had the power to stop neutral ships and seize Confederate agents. "—in effect, Senator, to take this nation into war."

"Only Congress can declare war," Wade told the Englishman, "but if England wants a war over those two rebels, she'll get it."

"Do not underestimate the unanimity of the American nation," Chase told the ambassador, "on the *Trent* affair. We are not going to hand over those rebels we took off your ship. Public sentiment will not permit it."

"Public opinion in England is equally aroused," Lord Lyons said quietly, "and getting more so every day. The American legation was attacked and burned, I am sorry to say. If this impasse is not resolved, our nations could very well be at war before the New Year."

"I think that's exactly what Lord Russell wants," said Wade, blunt as ever. "Your government wants the South to win, it's in your interest."

"Economic interests, which I grant would lead us to favor the South, do not always lead great nations into war."

"That's not what the senator means," said Stanton. "When the Union triumphs, it will be the greatest military power in the world. You don't want that. You want this continent divided into two nations, neither of which will be a threat to your sea power."

Carolyn caught the look of new respect on her husband's face; Stanton had scored.

"Even as we speak," said Lord Lyons evenly, "the President's envoy, Mr. Thurlow Weed, is meeting with my Foreign Office in London. I can only hope that his instructions are not as bellicose as the sentiment around this table."

Trouble; Carolyn shot Anna a look to stop her husband from saying what he thought about Seward's man Weed. Anna's interruption surprised her, though, because it departed from the points they had arranged beforehand.

"Excellency, I had a long talk with Lincoln yesterday," Anna said, always a good way to get the attention of the table. "He was working on his annual message, which of course will give us the answer on the *Trent* affair, and about which I can say nothing." Carolyn admired Anna's nerve; she knew Anna was not privy to any information about the Message, and had been squeezed into the President's office for a few moments.

"He takes a long view of some matters," she continued, "which is why I think you're wrong to be so impatient with him, Ben. He envisions that the youngest of us—you, Kate—will live to see a nation of two hundred and fifty million souls, more than all of Europe. And he says that the struggle of today is not altogether for today but is for a vast future also. I don't know. He may seem weak at times, but I've known a few presidents and I never heard one talk that way."

Carolyn marveled at the way her friend dared to convey admiration, even enthusiasm, for a President that everyone at the table had different reasons for holding in contempt. Because Chase was careful not to offend Wade, there was a space in the dinner conversation that needed filling, and Anna rose to the occasion. The only person at the table perceptibly cool to Anna was Kate Chase, who evidently did not like the way her father was raptly listening to an articulate and attractive woman near his own age. Carolyn weighed that; Kate was known to be passionately devoted to her father's career, perhaps unnaturally protective of her widower father's personal life. He was a good-looking man, Carolyn Wade thought, perhaps the most impressive-looking leader in politics today. Wealthy, too, she assumed. She watched the way Anna sparkled at Chase in selling her ideas, and at his fascinated reaction.

Her eyes met her husband's, and Ben Wade nodded too obviously. She could never get him to master the art of the imperceptible nod. She announced coffee in the parlor, and invited the ladies upstairs.

"Watch out for Chase's daughter," she murmured to Anna under her breath on the way upstairs. Anna nodded and murmured back, "Help me interest her in a young friend of mine—John Hay."

In front of the boudoir mirror, Carolyn asked in a normal voice, "However does the President manage, Anna? He must have a million things on his mind."

"He has wonderful assistants," Anna replied. "You know his secretary, John Hay? Remarkable young man."

"I've seen him at the Eameses' parties," Carolyn chatted back, trying to recall the face and not succeeding. She noticed that Kate Chase was trying to appear to be not listening. "Handsome fellow, hard to take that sort seriously."

"He really manages the President's office," Anna said, all seriousness. "The senior man, Nicolay, gets the credit, but the people inside know who has the President's ear. Keep your eye on him. Remember the name." She then murmured the name.

"Who?" Kate joined the conversation, looking in the mirror, curling back a strand of auburn hair. As Anna was small and buxom, she was tall and lissome; she had a graceful frame with shoulders that helped her carry clothes well, but she was too slender for the fashion.

"We were talking about a man who says good things about your father behind his back," said Anna.

"That's a novelty."

"Secretary Seward said or wrote something not altogether complimentary about Treasury, and John Hay spoke up to the President about it. Lincoln was most impressed. You don't know him?"

"We must have met at a reception."

Having baited the hook, Anna changed the subject. "You know what I'd like to do now, Carolyn? I'd like to break the iron discipline of tradition. I would like to go into the library and talk to the men."

"Oh," said a small voice from Ellen Stanton, "I don't think that's a very good idea."

"Miss Carroll—if you do, I will too." Kate Chase looked both mischievous and regal, a becoming combination.

Anna offered her arm solemnly, which Kate took, and they went off to take part in whatever brandied profundities marked the post-dinner political talk. Carolyn smiled after them: tall and short, twenty and forty, rich and poor, but both daughters of famous and powerful men, comfortable in the proximity of power, both headstrong, cunning, and vulnerably independent. She hoped they would be allies, for the two women had much to learn from each other. But so did opposing generals.

When Carolyn Wade went in to pour the coffee, she was pleased to see her library the scene of the closing of a deal. "Ohioans should stick together," her husband was saying, which Kate must have found bitterly amusing. "You went to Kenyon College in Gambier, Stanton? Chase's family gave that school its start." After some college reminiscences to establish a common bond, Wade took his coffee cup in hand and saluted Stanton: "The Joint Committee will look to you for complete cooperation on materials, especially telegraph cables, from pro-slavery generals."

"Unless Cameron or the President objects," amended Stanton, but in a way that sounded to Carolyn as a promise to get around such objections.

"And I want the scalp of the rebel sympathizer under McClellan who sent Ned Baker to his death at Ball's Bluff."

"I would want to know all about that too, Senator."

"In return, Stanton, you have our support if and when Cameron gets booted out," said Wade, deliberately unlawyerlike. "If you make it, I would like to put in a word right now for the continued success of Assistant Secretary Scott."

"He would have my complete confidence," promised Stanton.

"And I think you and he," continued Wade, giving his deal a final squeeze, "would do well to press a certain Tennessee River plan of Miss Carroll's. It makes a good deal of sense to me, and I would hate to see some pro-slavery general like 'Old Brains' out West drag a foot."

"This is something I want to look into immediately," Stanton said. Carolyn imagined he would promise anything else Wade had in mind.

"Just don't double-cross us," said her husband ominously, "the way McClellan double-crossed us about attacking the enemy before the winter set in. That little popinjay is going to spend a great deal of his time on parade in front of our committee."

Stanton wiped some coffee off his beard. "I think that would do the little popinjay a great deal of good."

Secretary of War Edwin M. Stanton

BOOK THREE

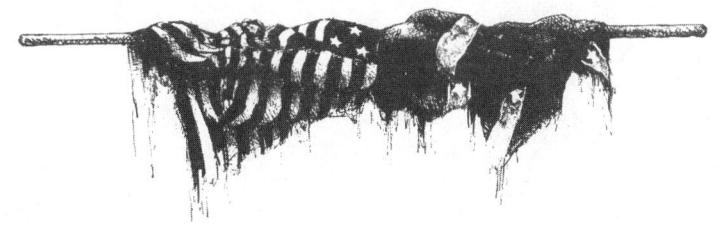

Edwin
McMasters
Stanton

CHAPTER 1

TO ORGANIZE VICTORY

No matter what duplicity was necessary, no matter what hypocrisy was called for, no matter what demeaning flattery or false promises were required of him, Edwin McMasters Stanton was determined to become a member of the Lincoln Cabinet. Not only a member, but the dominant member.

The Democratic lawyer had cultivated an acquaintance with Chase and Seward after Lincoln's election, despite the grumbling of some of his fellow Democrats who considered that a betrayal of President Buchanan. Stanton came to the conclusion that the men Lincoln had chosen were poseurs and dilettantes. The Blairs cared only for family power; Attorney General Bates he knew to be a poor lawyer, Cameron at War and Welles at Navy he considered hack politicians, and Caleb Smith at Interior he dismissed as a Hoosier joke. The war was being lost through sheer ineptitude. To save the nation, that collection of connivers and nonentities around Lincoln needed the invigoration of a man with organizational genius, unparalleled stamina, and a willingness to use power. Stanton, never devious with himself, was certain he was that man.

As a member of Buchanan's Cabinet, Stanton had watched that well-intentioned weakling temporize his way to the brink of national disaster. He had seen Lincoln creep into Washington in a slouch hat in the dead of night, and blunder into the ruination of all peaceful pursuits and into national bankruptcy under the malign influence of the Blairs. As Stanton had told friends, Du Chaillu, the explorer, was a fool to wander all the way to Africa in search of the giraffe or gorilla he so easily might have found in Springfield, Illinois. Pity that remark had been picked up; Ben Wade would probably spread it far and wide. The only way Stanton could think of to handle such an indiscretion was to deny categorically that he had ever made it.

Stanton had a clear idea of what it took to run the War Department in wartime. A man was required who would be capable of prodigious physical energy, ready to work twelve-hour days, seven days a week, driving and browbeating and shaming subordinates to work as hard; a man with a proven record of success, inspiring others to stretch themselves for a great goal. Stanton had been making fifty thousand dollars a year as a lawyer, more than any other attorney in the United States, and he was willing to toss it over for the eight-thousand-dollar salary of a department head, a fact that demonstrated both his past success and his dedication to his country.

Just as important, Edwin Stanton persuaded himself, the War Department needed a man unafraid to say no to the President, and the President's wife, and his cronies, and the other political bigwigs, on the thousands of petty favors that added up to the sense of favoritism and corruption. In his very first meeting as President Buchanan's Attorney General, in 1860, Stanton recalled vividly denouncing the then Secretary of War as a fraud and a thief, and warning the President that a move to withdraw the Union garrison at Fort Sumter would make him guilty of treason. Once in place, Stanton had shown he was unafraid to use his power.

What other criteria were required in one who would be the true organizer of victory? Stanton was ready with that answer too: the man would have to be willing to assume responsibility for internal security, and be ready to jail disloyalists and newspapermen when their snooping bordered on spying. He would have to understand the location of the real levers of power to seize control of the technology of rapid communication—the telegraph, the railroads, and the river systems.

The job of general manager of a civil war was a prodigious challenge, one never before met by any American. Its reward, he knew, was a guaranteed unpopularity, but that did not faze him; in fact, Stanton had always delighted in stimulating the indignation of the unworthy or the inept. He was ready for the appointment.

The trouble was, the President was not likely to turn to Stanton because he was not an agreeable politician. He had to be realistic about that. Therefore the power he sought would have to be derivative; no matter how much playing the courtier revolted him, he knew he would have to rule through another. Although the end did not always justify the means, he was firmly persuaded that when the end in sight was the end of America's nationhood, any means to avert that catastrophe would do. When treason was abetted by stupidity, venality, and petty bickering, he saw the patriot's duty as clear: to scratch and claw and connive one's way to the place where one's personal abilities could make the vital difference.

Stanton plotted his campaign to become Secretary of War with more meticulous care, strategic sweep, and attention to tactical detail than any general—certainly any general on the Union side—had planned a campaign in the field.

The position he now held was that of general counsel in the War Department, a trusted adviser to Simon Cameron. Stanton's previous service in the Buchanan Cabinet was, he was told, no longer held against him. To ingratiate himself at first, he had sought out and befriended Seward, Lincoln's choice for Secretary of State, immediately after the election; during the four months of the interregnum, Stanton had provided him with the details of all the deliberations of President Buchanan in his Cabinet. The conservative William Seward, Stanton assumed, was the key to Lincoln: the statesman of the East most trusted by the lawyer from the West. Then, hedging his bet on Seward, Stanton also fed tidbits to Chase and the radical Republicans.

"I want that message now," Stanton wheezed at his secretary—tension worsened his asthma. "Go down the hall and badger Cameron's secretary until he gives it to you. He can't fiddle with that document forever, and I don't want him showing it to every Philadelphia politician who wanders in."

The annual message of the Secretary of War, accompanying the President's State of the Union message to the Congress, was going to be Stanton's ticket of admission to the Lincoln Cabinet. He intended it to result in the removal of the bumbling Cameron and his replacement with the energetic War Democrat now being wasted in the menial role of general counsel.

Lincoln would never remove Simon Cameron for mere stupidity, inefficiency, or laziness, Stanton was certain. Such a removal would be an admission by the President that all the congressional charges of corruption and political favoritism in the purchase of supplies were well founded. Worse, firing Cameron would invite Senator Wade's new Joint Committee on the Conduct of the War to dominate the War Department.

Not that Lincoln held Cameron in high regard. On the contrary, Stanton had been told by Thurlow Weed how the President-elect tried to wriggle out of a promise made at the Republican convention the year before, for a Cabinet post to Cameron in return for the Pennsylvania votes for Lincoln. The new President felt obligated to offer the job to Cameron, but had pleaded with the man to turn it down. But Cameron had hungered for the glory of a job with vast patronage power.

Stanton wanted the War portfolio too, ached for the central assignment—but not, he assured himself, for vainglory. Just the opposite. He was determined to assume the War portfolio because the nation would surely founder without him. Only for that overriding reason would the leading lawyer in the United States have stooped to the series of subterfuges he had been forced to engage in over the past eighteen months.

The first step—an incredible misstep, he now admitted—had been to support Breckinridge for President because he had been far less abolitionist than either Douglas or Lincoln, and because Stanton knew and respected the Kentuckian. Then, as Lincoln's star rose, Stanton had to engage in furious backtracking, growing connective tissue to the pro-slavery radicals through that foppish Massachusetts Senator, Sumner. That was followed by his passing of private information from the Buchanan Cabinet meetings to Seward on Lincoln's conservative right and Chase on his abolitionist left. Little by little, Stanton had wormed his way into the confidence of both groups supporting the new President.

The final source of support was the most difficult for Stanton: holding on to his original base, the pro-slavery but fiercely pro-Union Democrats. General George McClellan was his key, a youthful mind susceptible to flattery, who despised the politicians in power and seemed not to mind hearing Stanton hint at the desirability of a military dictatorship in this time of trial. Stanton could envision McClellan, if he did well in the war, running for President in 1864 as a Democrat against the Republican choice—probably Chase, though possibly Lincoln might try again.

That was why the elegant Stanton home had become the hiding place for the impressionable General McClellan, the place where he could duck what he called "browsing presidents." Stanton had put the young man in touch with S.L.M. Barlow, the Democratic leader in New York City, who stood ready to become Stanton's law partner if the plot to replace Cameron did not succeed. Barlow had urged Stanton to drive a wedge into the already divided Lincoln Cabinet, to foster the personal bickering that would widen the political divisions—but to keep the General out of the machinations, so as to place young McClellan above the political battle until the time came to launch his presidential bid. Stanton had certainly done that, meanwhile telling the political innocent of the imbecility of Lincoln's administration.

The Young Napoleon was taking that instruction well, and showed signs of trusting Stanton's judgment completely. Only that morning, he had come for legal advice on the *Trent* affair: Lincoln had invited him to a Cabinet meeting to discuss the imminence of the war with England, and McClellan had been prepared to tell the President to admit that the American government was in the wrong and to get out of the scrape without taking on a huge new military and naval burden.

Stanton, the experienced lawyer, had promptly set the young man straight: that the seizure of the Confederates was fully justified by all the rules of international law, that the Union was fully in the right, and that it should be prepared to fight in a just cause. Any other course, Stanton persuaded him, would be seen as more Lincoln weakness and further dispirit the North. McClellan had gone to the Cabinet meeting with his original position completely reversed.

"If you cannot get me the information I need when I need it," Stanton shouted to his aide, "I will find someone who can!"

"Secretary Cameron is not finished with the message," Stanton's harried helper reported from the hallway. "He would only give me the first half."

"Let me see." Stanton snatched the sheets covered with the careful long-hand of Cameron's aide, tracked over with the Secretary's own markings, looking for the page Stanton had appended earlier. His urgently recommended insertion was not there; he assumed that his politically explosive section about the arming of slaves had probably been moved toward the end.

Stanton's plan was straightforward in its deviousness. Since Lincoln would never fire Cameron for toleration of corruption, or for executive ineptitude, what was needed was a more compelling reason for dismissal. Stanton's lips moved in the approximation of a smile when he contemplated that reason: Lincoln had shown himself to be highly sensitive to any attempt by anyone to wrest from him the authority to deal with the issue of slavery. The Frémont episode had been most instructive; Lincoln, when aroused on that sensitive subject, would throw a thunderbolt and be ready to take the consequences. If Cameron were to challenge the President, as Frémont had, on the one matter which Lincoln held closely to himself, then the way would be opened to the dismissal of Cameron and the appointment of a new Secretary of War.

The sheets of the first part of the war message in hand, Stanton hurried to Cameron's office. For a change, the general counsel noted wryly, the Pennsylvania political leader was on the job, in his office and not seeing contractors and office seekers and congressmen at his home. Stanton promised himself he would never conduct war business at home when he got the job.

"We have to get this thing to the printer," Stanton urged, "do you have the rest? Are you having second thoughts? I hope not—the entire course of the war hangs in the balance."

"As a matter of fact, Edwin, I am." Cameron was obviously uncomfortable, holding the packet of sheets in his hand lest somebody take them away against his will, walking up and down his office, dithering. "Lincoln's not going to like this one bit."

"Then the President will simply strike it out of your message," Stanton said soothingly. "If you believe in arming and using captured slaves in the army, then it is your responsibility to put it in your message. After that, the decision is up to the President. He's a lawyer, he can read."

Cameron wavered. Stanton went on, "I'll deliver it to his secretary myself, so the release can be co-ordinated at the Executive Mansion next week." The President's message to Congress would have to be delivered at the opening of the regular session, the first week in December. He assumed the President's decision on the seizure of the rebels off the British *Trent* would dominate, since defiance of England would be a good way of getting people's minds off the misconduct of the war. The President would pay little attention to the Secretary of War's accompanying message, at least in its preparation stage; that was what Stanton was counting on.

"You're sure it won't go out this way without his knowledge?"

Stanton let himself look cagey. "If Lincoln cuts your confiscation paragraph out—and I doubt if he will, since he certainly agrees with the philosophy—then it will come to the attention of a few of our radical friends that Simon Cameron at least tried to strike a blow against the slaveholders in rebellion."

"Greeley's the important one," said Cameron, "the President worries about the support of the *Tribune*. If Greeley knows that I'm the only one who's fighting for abolition in the Cabinet—well, me and Chase—then he'll have to stick with me. We can ride out this storm."

"Greeley will know," promised Stanton truthfully. He pointed to the final pages of the draft message on Cameron's desk. "Did you put the slave-arming paragraph in?"

"Well, I haven't decided yet." Dithering again; Stanton controlled his temper. "You know, Edwin, when Frémont tried to emancipate the slaves out West a couple of months ago, Lincoln humiliated him. Forced him to take it back. He sent me out West to fire Frémont finally, but that would have meant facing that hellion Jessie, so I had a messenger do it. Taking away slave property is a card the President likes to hold close to his vest."

"Frémont did not submit his proclamation to Lincoln first," Stanton told Cameron, "and you are. You've giving the President a method of carrying out last July's Confiscation Act in a quiet way. If Lincoln doesn't want to arm the slaves that are captured—"

"He won't. He's worried about servile insurrection in Kentucky and Missouri—"

"—Then he'll cut it out of your part of the message," Stanton assured him, "and Greeley and the other abolitionists will know that your heart was in the right place. If you don't keep those radicals closely behind you, Wade and Chandler will cut you to ribbons in their Joint Committee."

The threat of a Senate investigation ended the irresolution in Cameron. Stanton watched him poke nervously through the sheets on his desk to the paragraph that Stanton hoped would soon cause an uproar. "*If it shall be found,*" the words Stanton had drafted began, "*that the men who have been held by the rebels as slaves are capable of bearing arms and performing efficient military service, it is the right, and may become the duty of the government to arm and equip them, and employ their services against the rebels . . .*"

"Arming captured slaves," urged Stanton, "will send a shiver of fear throughout the South. Legally, Ben Butler's idea of confiscation of contraband is brilliant. By accepting the South's contention that slaves are property, we are able to apply the doctrine that property seized in war is contraband that can be seized and used against the enemy."

"Put it in," said Cameron impulsively, pressing the sheets on Stanton. "You're a better lawyer than Bates—be ready with a legal argument in case the Attorney General complains. Go ahead—get it printed and over to the Mansion. When Lincoln sees it in print and ready to go, he'll know it's the right thing to do."

Stanton's first rule in the courtroom was to stop arguing when the case was won. He nodded and walked quickly down the hallway of the War Department building, past the telegraph office where President Lincoln spent much of his time waiting for the results of losing battles, to his own cubicle where his messenger was waiting.

"Print it and mail it," he ordered, hoping that would take no longer than a few days. He added: "Send a copy to the President's secretary along with a stack of other reports. Be sure they're all wrapped together in a big bundle when you send them over."

As the man hurried off to the printer, Stanton stood tensely in his office, metal-rimmed glasses in hand, squinting across the street at the President's House, calculating his chances. He had no doubt that Lincoln would explode at Cameron's insubordination, and would take the Pennsylvania boss's action as the last straw. But what then? Could Stanton be sure the most important job in the nation, short of the Presidency itself, would then be his?

He had the trusting McClellan's full support; that counted for something with Lincoln, who wanted a War Department chief who could work in harmony with the army commander, and perhaps persuade him of the political imperatives of early military action. Only the day before, McClellan had told Stanton that Lincoln was thinking about replacing Cameron, and had asked who would be respected by the army's chiefs. McClellan had said he put in a word for Stanton. The attention, the flattery, the constant assurance that the commander would have a staunch representative in the Cabinet when he was in the field—all was paying off.

Stanton was satisfied, also, that McClellan and his pretty wife—the two were so blatantly in love it was embarrassing—had responded well to his candid derogations of Lincoln. "Imbecility" was the word he had hammered home, to McClellan's professed embarrassment; obviously neither Lincoln nor anyone in his Cabinet was capable of organizing an army or planning strategy. He could see that the young general agreed, though out of military decorum he refrained from joining in criticism of the President, and the point that so flattered the general had the added advantage of being true.

With his right flank protected, Stanton reminded himself to shore up his left: at that awful dinner at the Wades' the night before, he had reminded Carolyn Wade of his Ohio roots. Stanton assessed Wade to be a single-minded, purposeful black Republican, determined to expand his power at the expense of Lincoln.

McClellan, on Stanton's advice six weeks before, had promised Wade prompt military action, in return for radical support of his promotion to General-in-Chief; now Wade was pressing him to make good on the promise. Stanton would have to appear to be on Wade's side, but not so overtly that it would get back to McClellan, whose army was not ready for a major winter offensive.

Stanton's weak eyes could make out, across the street, the President's house being dusted with a cover of snow. The growing impatience with Lincoln, the pervasive feeling in the capital and in New York and Philadelphia that the job of running a war was too big for him, would be Stanton's key to power.

The radicals would direct their fire at McClellan, and McClellan and the Douglas Democrats would come to despise the abolitionist politicians in return; in that crossfire, Stanton would let each faction believe it could count on him. With that established, everyone would agree the time had come for a man of strength and intellect to take charge of Lincoln's war.

Across the way, the front door of the President's house opened. Stanton watched a short young man with a mustache come out on the porch, look at the snow, sniff the cold air, then duck back inside. Stanton recognized Lincoln's second secretary; on the expected inefficiency of young John Hay rested his hopes for the quick demise of Simon Cameron as Secretary of War.

CHAPTER 2

OF SLAVES AND GUNPOWDER

In his cubicle next to the vast office of Horace Greeley, managing editor Charles Dana went through the President's annual message, just received in the mail from Washington, for the third time. Nothing about the *Trent*. He shook his head in wonderment and carried the sheaf of papers into Greeley's corner office, with its grand view of Spruce and Nassau streets and the statue of Benjamin Franklin on the corner.

The editor was poring over the Secretary of War's message, which had been mailed separately; Dana was also surprised that his boss would turn first to what was so obviously the less important document.

"There's no lead to the story," said Dana. "The *Trent* affair is not even mentioned in the President's message."

Greeley did not look up.

"Here we are on the brink of war with England," Dana continued, "with harbors being fortified, and the British sending troops to Canada, and Lord Lyons about to issue an ultimatum or break off relations. And what does our President do? In his message to Congress on the state of the Union, with the whole world waiting, he says nothing. Nothing! It's as if Lincoln's in a world of his own."

"Less said the better," said Greeley, still reading through the printed message in his hands from the War Department. "Anything on war with England from our London correspondent?"

"Marx has sent in an excellent piece, for a change." The *Tribune* had arranged for a series of letters from London written by Karl Marx, a German observer there. Marx's writing was turgid, and Dana cut it mercilessly, but the dispatch just received on the *Trent* affair was filled with detail on the way the Palmerston government and its "slavish press" had been fanning the flames of resentment at the buccaneering Americans. "Includes this item," said Dana, pulling the piece out of his pocket. "General Winfield Scott, after retiring, happened to be in Europe during all the tension. He wrote a letter to the London papers predicting that the United States would cheerfully surrender the seized men if by so doing it would emancipate the commerce of the world. Marx says it had an important effect—'a beneficent reaction in public opinion, even on the London Stock Exchange.' I didn't think Old Fuss and Feathers was that smart."

"General Scott didn't write that letter himself," Greeley said, still not looking up. "Thurlow Weed wrote it for him. Probably made a few bucks on the Exchange while he was at it."

"That's unfair."

"That's Weed. I know the man, he and Seward and I were partners, and I tell you he's a conniving Albany wirepuller. He's over there to warn the British to forget about war, and he's probably setting up our surrender."

If Greeley despised him so, Dana figured, Weed must possess some good qualities. "I'll give the Marx piece a good display, then."

"He helps us with German readers," said Greeley, concerned as always with circulation; "pity he can't write in better English. And stop bothering me—I'm trying to find something in Cameron's message."

Dana bridled at the condescension. He had come to despise his boss, and knew his job was in jeopardy. Dana was for war to prevent disunion, Greeley was for war to stop slavery, which was enough of a disagreement, but it was compounded by Greeley's irrational urges to make peace, which would leave slavery in place. Lincoln was heard to say by Adams Hill, the *Tribune*'s man in Washington, that "Uncle Horace is with us four days out of seven." What kind of supporter was that? Dana wished he could get a job in Washington and shake free of this inconsistent tyrant.

To annoy the editor, Dana remained in the room. "There's one line in the President's message that's such an obvious lie that it must have made 'Honest Abe' gag to sign it," Dana said, wondering what it was in the Cameron message that Uncle Horace was searching for so intently. "In the part about the appointment of McClellan as general-in-chief replacing Scott, here's what Lincoln says: 'The retiring chief repeatedly expressed his judgment in favor of General McClellan for the position . . .' Everybody knows that's hogwash. General Scott hates McClellan—Scott wanted Halleck. Does Lincoln think the people are going to swallow that?"

"Here it is." Greeley, ignoring Dana, suddenly became agitated, smacking the pages on his desk in glee. "Hah! He did it. The old reprobate got away with it. What courage!" The editor circled a paragraph in red and Dana came around the desk to read it. "There's the lead for your story."

Dana read the buried paragraph and allowed himself to look impressed. "It is as clearly a right of the government to arm slaves," the Secretary of War had written, "when it may become necessary, as it is to use gunpowder taken from the enemy."

The decision to put deadly weapons in the hands of abused former slaves, bent on vengeance, would strike terror in the South, where so many plantations were now unguarded by men. The arming of freed slaves, a precedent sure to create a furor in the border states, was a victory for abolitionists and a break with Lincoln's previous policy. The President had evidently decided that the support of Republicans like Wade in the Senate and Greeley in the press was more important than the feelings of loyal slaveholders and Democrats.

That was indeed front-page news. Dana wondered who had tipped off Greeley to look for the paragraph. Somebody in the War Department—Tom Scott, Edwin Stanton, perhaps Cameron himself, currying favor with the radical Republicans? Weeks ago, Greeley had asked Dana to put together a story puffing Stanton as a man with a future, and had been irritated at him for not getting around to it. Perhaps James Gilmore, a correspondent assigned by Lincoln to pass advance news to Greeley in return for favorable treatment in the *Tribune*, was the source.

"Strange that the announcement should be in Cameron's message, not in Lincoln's," Dana said to Greeley, fishing. "The South will be furious about this—slave uprisings, rape of white women, all that." Next step would be drafting freed blacks to fight, and full-scale abolition could not be far behind. He thought Lincoln liked to keep these big decisions to himself.

A timid tap on the door suggested that a copyboy dared to intrude upon the two editors.

"I cannot be interrupted," Greeley said mildly. He usually barked or snapped that command, but he was apparently feeling very good.

"The Postmaster of New York is here, sir, and he says it is urgent, sir."

Without a moment's hesitation, Greeley rolled up the printed copy of the Secretary of War's report, took it to his closet, stuffed it down the sleeve of a coat hanging there, and locked the closet door. "Send the mailman in."

The postmaster, brandishing a telegram as if to ward off the evil spirits of the press, entered and stated his business. "I have received a telegram from Postmaster General Blair, informing me that the Secretary of War wishes to recover all copies of the message delivered this morning and to tell you, Mr. Greeley, that another, correct copy will be on its way tomorrow."

"I am the editor, not the mail clerk," said Greeley. "Anything else? I'm busy."

"A copy was delivered here this morning," the postmaster insisted. "In fact, Secretary Cameron's message was delivered along with the President's message, which I saw on the desk just outside your office."

"Does the Secretary of War want the President's message back too?"

"No, Mr. Greeley, just his own. It's here, and I really must have it."

"The message is not in this office," Greeley stated—technically truthfully, Dana noted. "If you wish to undertake a search, I will leave you here"—he went to his closet door—"and I will put on my coat, go to Washington, see President Lincoln, and demand that the Postmaster of New York be fired. No, more than that—arrested!"

The bureaucrat crumbled. "If you should find the Cameron message, Mr. Greeley, would you please return it?"

"Leave Mr. Blair's telegram with us," said Dana, taking it from the postmaster's hand as he ushered him out. "It will serve as a reminder."

Dana took a deep breath. "Are you going to run it, Mr. Greeley? Cameron's message has been officially withdrawn. They'll know that you deliberately disobeyed the War Department." Dana's heart began to race: Was this treason? Or was this press freedom in the tradition of John Peter Zenger?

Horace Greeley went to the closet, fished the document out of his coat sleeve, hefted it with a certain reverence, and handed it to his managing editor. "Publish," he said. "And if, tomorrow, we receive a new copy of the

Cameron message with some weaselly statement substituted by Lincoln, publish the Lincoln version next to the original version. Then we shall complain mightily about the way the President has edited Cameron à la Frémont and set back the cause of human freedom. I will write an editorial."

"The President will be extremely angry," Dana reminded him. "So will Seward. Remember what they did to the *Eagle*, and remember how the *Journal of Commerce* had to toe the mark."

"Those publications supported treason. The *Tribune* supports freedom." The editor, his agitation behind him, looked serene, his moon face beatific. "The President knows that if he touched the *Tribune*, the Republican Party would turn on him and demand abolition immediately or an end to the war. Lincoln will not dare to touch the *Tribune*."

"You're sure?"

"You forget, my dear Dana, I gave the Republican Party its name. I made Abraham Lincoln what he is today."

"Still, it's defiance of the government in wartime." Dana was prepared to go to Fort Lafayette, but wanted to be sure Greeley was in the cell next to him. "In the light of what's happened to some newspapers, it doesn't seem quite fair."

"One person may steal a horse with impunity," Greeley quoted a favorite proverb, "while another may be hanged for merely looking over a hedge."

Dana nodded slowly and went to the door, trying to figure out why Lincoln would permit Cameron to do what he had fired Frémont for doing. His hand on the doorknob, it occurred to him that the visit from the postmaster meant that Lincoln had not known what Cameron was up to, and that Greeley's decision to publish was the political death warrant for the Secretary of War. "This should force Cameron to resign, Mr. Greeley. The whole world will know how Lincoln rapped his knuckles, and if old Simon has any pride at all, he'll quit. Is that what you want?"

"That corrupt trimmer will be replaced by someone more sincere in his zeal for abolition. You handle the news, Charles, and I will deal with the politics." He began stirring the papers on his desk in preparation for editorializing. "By the way, I have accepted an invitation to speak to the Smithsonian Institution in Washington on January third. When next you are in touch with our man Gilmore, make sure he gets word to Lincoln of my appearance there. It would be nice, especially after all the fuss that this story is sure to cause, for the President to show his respect for the *Tribune*, and all it stands for, by attending my lecture."

CHAPTER 3

JOHN HAY'S DIARY
DECEMBER 4, 1861

The message disaster wasn't Nico's fault, it was all mine.

George Nicolay may be rapidly approaching thirty, and I have come to think of him as the elder brother I never wanted to have, but he is blameless in this fiasko.

When sturdy Stoddard came staggering in with his armloads from the War Department on that fateful annual message day, Nico pointed at me, and the heap was dumped on my desk. I should have gone through it all, including the draft message of the Secretary of War, but Cameron's message was not in draft form—on the contrary, it had already been set in type and printed, so it seemed to me to have been already approved. Even so, that's no excuse. I should have caught the wily Cameron's attempt to become the maker of policy on slavery.

Not until the bundles had been sent to the Postmaster General for transmission to his local postmasters, with special urgency to hand-deliver them to the press in New York, did the Tycoon himself come across the offending paragraph.

Big hullabalou. "This will never do! This is a question that belongs exclusively to me!" He had not been so furious since Frémont's emancipation proclamation; the President must think the entire war depends on the way he handles the slavery issue.

I ran over to Seward at State who rounded up the crew for a Cabinet meeting. Lincoln did not let his anger show at Cameron, who still commands legions of office seekers and sticky-fingered contractors who could cause the Administration great mischief. The Tycoon does not want Cameron doing to him what the powerful Pennsylvanian did to his predecessors, Buchanan and Fillmore.

Chase, who is firmly in Greeley's pocket, was the only one who stuck up for Cameron. "I believe it was unfortunate that it came out inadvertently," he boomed in that stentorian tone, "but we will soon have to come to the arming of freed slaves, and it might as well be now. The nation will applaud the Administration for this move. It might even buttress our effort to raise money to pay for the war, which desperately needs every support it can get."

Grandma Welles—that's what they call Father Neptune, but not to his face —gave wishy-washy backing to Cameron. Fortunately, Montgomery Blair was adamant that any move to free slaves was premature. That was a principled stand, because all knew that his father, old Francis Blair, was close to Cameron, and forcing the Secretary of War to eat his words publicly would cause the Pennsylvania dealmaker great embarrassment. Judge Blair, with Lincoln obviously on his side, carried the day. An innocuous paragraph was written by the President and given to Cameron to substitute, and Lincoln told Blair to retrieve all the copies with the offending policy.

That substitution turned out to be not such a good idea. I thought at the
time it showed how the Tycoon was growing more willing to take charge of
the Cabinet and let them know who is boss, but it showed just the opposite.
Uncle Horace let out a war whoop and printed both versions side by side,
embracing Cameron as the nation's savior and making Lincoln look like a
captain of a slave ship, and the rest of the press picked that up. The result is
that the Cabinet is in obvious public disarray and the President looks weaker
than ever. Add that to the "All quiet on the Potomac" news that is driving
the Jacobins wild, and you have a bleak winter scene here at the center of the
nation's miseries.

What comfort for the weary President in the midst of this mess? One ray of
sunshine is Willie, who marches into the Tycoon's office with scraps of poetry
or amusing stories that transfigure his father's normally gloomy face. I have
been dispatched to purchase a pony for the young fellow, the gift of his doting
parents, and now Willie can ride alongside Lincoln on those lonely late afternoon forays.

The Lincoln sons differ. Robert Lincoln strikes me as an upright and solid
lad, good college material, but he and his father never seem to find words to
say to each other. Tad is afflicted with an overly large head and a cleft palate,
and is treated tenderly, with hidden sadness. Willie, the middle one, is the joy.
He is spoiled, yet cannot be really spoiled because his character is generous.
He does more for his country than a division of fresh troops, because he can
lift the spirits of the man who must lift the spirit of the nation.

The boy has a serious side that complements his sunniness. Last month, he
sent off a poem to the editor of the *National Republican* with a note that said:
"I enclose you my first attempt at poetry." It was published, of course, and
wrung every heart around here:

> There was no patriot like Baker,
>　So noble and so true;
> He fell as a soldier on the field,
>　His face to the sky of blue.
> No squeamish notions filled his breast,
> 　The Union *was his* theme,
> "No surrender and no compromise"
> 　His day's thought and night's dream.

For a boy not yet eleven, that is not bad. It is better poetry than I was
turning out at that age. The thought of the boy playing on the lawn that
Sunday, Baker with his feet up against the big tree talking to his father, then
Ned buttoning his uniform, kissing the boy, and going off to review the troops
with Breckinridge—and then dying at Ball's Bluff is, without being sentimental, at least bittersweet.

Another cheerer-upper is the diplomatic mail. Not the letter from France,
which supported England on the *Trent* matter, or the communication from
Lord Lyons the other day just short of threatening war, but some of the
arcane things. I brought a letter from the King of Siam into the President's
office. He was taking a few press cuttings out of his hat and laying them on
the desk.

"Here's good news," I chirruped, "the King of Siam has come up with a way to help us win the war."

The Ancient of Days looked at the letter, seriously at first, then that grin spread all over his face. "Elephants," he noted. "His Majesty is offering us war elephants which, he says, when bred will develop into a herd of beasts that will solve all our transportation problems." He had a good laugh, took off his spectacles, and wiped his eyes. "John, how would I look on top of an elephant?"

"That's more General McClellan's style, sir."

He cackled a bit and wrote a few lines for Seward to prepare as a formal letter in reply. "I appreciate most highly Your Majesty's tender of good offices in forwarding to the Government a stock from which a supply of elephants might be raised on our own soil. Our political jurisdiction, however, does not reach a latitude so low as to favor the multiplication of the elephant . . ."

A more substantial uplift to the President's spirits came with a visit from Tom Scott. That efficient fellow—a rarity at the War Department these days —brought a map of the Mississippi Valley and the first daring idea for a military strategy we have seen in the West. The bright idea is to forget the plan to storm the Mississippi forts, and instead to use the Tennessee River, which I understand flows northward contrary to law.

Tom Scott's visit with a Tennessee plan of this sort had been predicted by Miss Carroll; true to my promise, I made certain the Tycoon knew that this remarkable lady had been the source of the plan. He told me to keep that information under my hat, since the military does not embrace suggestions from civilians, much less women, but he seemed interested in the idea and dispatched Scott out West to look into its possibilities. Anything to get things moving.

Then Ben Wade came booming in, unannounced. Colonel Scott must have discussed the plan with him, in cooperating with the new Joint Committee that was set up last week to cheer on antislavery generals and to nag McClellan. "I understand there is a plan," the Ohioan declared, "which, if executed with secrecy, would open the Tennessee, and save the national cause."

The Tycoon didn't want to show his hand, but did not want to get Wade's dander up. "Bluff Ben" has a dander very easily got up. The President mentioned that he had the plan, he liked the notion of taking the Mississippi forts from the rear as well as cutting the rebels' east-west railroad, but that some of his Cabinet officers wanted to pursue the route straight down the Mississippi.

"Sounds like Bates," gruffed Wade, right on target. "What in hell does he know about military strategy?"

"We want to be sure the views of General McClellan, and Halleck out West, are requested and considered."

"Sure, sure," Wade muttered, "McClellan doesn't think the West is important, and Halleck doesn't like any plan that wasn't dreamed up by Old Brains himself. They're both Democrats, remember. They are not out to crush the South. They get a kick out of sending fugitive slaves back into hell."

Lincoln, who I suspect privately agrees with Wade about that, would not say as much. He is putting down an insurrection, and does not want to let this conflict degenerate into a remorseless revolutionary struggle. His policy is to favor gradual, compensated emancipation, acceptable to all even if it takes until the year 1900 to complete, though he hopes for it to happen much before that. That was the point of his annual message, which did not get a very good reception anywhere.

"We are now in the last extremity," Wade said, and God knows that's true. "You have to choose between adopting and at once executing a plan which you believe to be the right one for saving the country, or deferring to those military bastards and losing the country."

Lincoln did not need to be told that. With McClellan sitting out the winter —and the general seems now to be coming down with a fever—the pressure is intense on Lincoln to get something going, somewhere, if not against the South, against the damned arrogant English.

The Tycoon did not flare up at Wade; he sees him as an honest sort, heart in the right place, and besides, that Joint Committee could cause all kinds of trouble if Wade wanted it to. It struck me that the President was sold on the Tennessee plan or at least some Western activity before Wade came in, and then acted doubtful so that Wade could sell him on doing what he'd already sent Tom Scott to suggest to Halleck and Grant to consider. That way, the Congress—at least the Jacobins—would have an investment in the plan. Just as they originally had in McClellan. That's the Tycoon's way, to push others out in front, and if disaster strikes, at least he is up there with company.

Everything seems to be coming to a head as this sad holiday season approaches. A sense of uncertainty pervades: War with England? Action on the Potomac before the money runs out? A thrust in the West? A way to keep the abolitionists from breaking up the North?

A shaft of sunlight in the gloom: coming out of the twice-a-week Cabinet meetings, Governor Chase placed his hand on Nico's shoulder and said confidently and mistakenly, "You're John Hay." My colleague dutifully denied that, and introduced the Secretary of the Treasury to the authentic John Hay. We have been introduced four times now; perhaps I could do something dramatic to fix myself in his memory.

"My daughter Kate," he said—my heart stopped—"tells me she hears what a fine job you are doing for your country. Perhaps you will accept an invitation to come to dinner one night soon."

I almost yelled at him, "When? Name the night!" but that would have been unrefined. How had Kate Chase come by this fine and accurate report of me? I suspect that the good Miss Carroll had done her work. Wonderful woman; brilliant military strategist too. Her Tennessee plan could win the war. I shall have to buy a suit.

I saw my favorite pamphleteer this afternoon in the Senate gallery. My mission was to carry the President's message over to the new session of Congress, which I did with appropriate pomp and handed the Senate's copy to the clerk, John Forney. He told me to go upstairs and watch a sadly historic moment. In the gallery, I saw Miss Carroll and took the seat next to her.

Like me, she was there to watch the public disgrace and well-deserved humiliation of the most dramatically disloyal member of the United States Senate. The chamber was unusually silent. Nothing like this had ever happened here before. The Southerners from the seceded states had left with the respect, mixed with sadness, of their longtime colleagues in the Union. Not one of them, not even Senator Jefferson Davis of Mississippi, was censured or condemned by their former Senate peers. But they had followed their states into insurrection; not so the junior senator from Kentucky. His state had remained loyal; his was a double betrayal, of his nation and his state.

Vice President Hamlin, presiding, recognized Senator Zack Chandler of Michigan.

"I offer the following resolution," said Chandler, weaving just a bit, "which I ask to have considered now. '*Resolved*, that John C. Breckinridge be, and is hereby, expelled from the Senate'."

The Chair recognized the other senator from Kentucky, who had supported Breckinridge in most of his fights with Sumner and Trumbull on habeas corpus and the like, but who remained loyal and kept his seat in the Senate.

"I will simply state to the Senate," said Lazarus Powell of Kentucky, "that I think Mr. Breckinridge has resigned his seat in the Senate. I have seen it so stated in the public papers reporting an address by Mr. Breckinridge, which I believe I have here." He fumbled with some newspapers on his desk.

"If the Senator from Kentucky will allow me," asked Lyman Trumbull of Illinois, like Chandler a radical ally of Ben Wade's, "has he not the same kind of evidence that Mr. Breckinridge is now in arms against the government he had sworn to support?"

"I will merely say to the senator," Powell replied, "that this address declares that he resigns his place in the Senate for the musket of a soldier."

"Then I will ask the senator," pressed Trumbull, whose bill to suppress insurrection I recall was frustrated in the previous session, "if he has not information of the same character as to his treason as to his resignation?"

"I have heard that Mr. Breckinridge is a brigadier general in the army of the Confederate states," said Powell matter-of-factly, "though I do not know the fact personally."

"Is it not a fact, sir, that he is in command of five thousand rebels who call themselves the First Kentucky Brigade, who are occupying the city of Bowling Green?" asked Trumbull. "Is it not a fact that the rebel general, Sidney Johnston, has been quoted in those same newspapers as saying Breckinridge was worth an entire division to the South, because his popularity and power of persuasion were such that he could recruit thousands more, and thereby use great sections of Kentucky to prevent our advance into Tennessee?"

That was a rhetorical question, and Powell did not feel he had to answer it. "I hold in my hand the address purporting to emanate from Mr. Breckinridge, and signed by him. At the close he says, 'And now I hereby return the trust to your hands.' That amounts to a declaration of resignation."

"A newspaper report is not a resignation."

"I would like the resolution to lie over," said the remaining Kentucky senator. "I think it entirely unnecessary to go through the form of expelling a man who is not a member of this body."

"Mr. President," Trumbull said to the Vice President, who is president of the Senate, "I desire to have the yeas and nays, and I offer the following as a substitute: 'Whereas John C. Breckinridge, a member of this body from the State of Kentucky, has joined the enemies of his country, and is now in arms against the Government he had sworn to support: Therefore, *Resolved*, that

Senator Zachariah Chandler

the said John C. Breckinridge, the traitor, be, and is hereby, expelled from the Senate.' "

That ringing "John C. Breckinridge, the traitor" brought the Senate to its feet, all but Powell. Ned Baker's death had gone unavenged; this would be a license for any general who captured Breckinridge to hang him. Vice President Hamlin asked Chandler if he accepted Trumbull's more stinging substitute.

"Yes, sir!" shouted Chandler.

The yeas and nays were called for. Senator Powell could not vote "yea" to expel a fellow Kentuckian, nor could he safely cast a "nay" vote to condone treason. He voted present. The final tally to expel Breckinridge, and condemn him as a traitor to his country, was 36 to 0.

I started to congratulate Miss Carroll, who had led the charge in print against the Senator's pernicious ideas, but held back when I noticed tears in her eyes. I proffered my handkerchief.

"I was remembering the moment," she said in a while, "when he stood there as Vice President and counted the electoral votes, and declared Lincoln to be President."

There had been talk of trouble that day by the Southerners, of demands from the Senate floor for removal of the Union troops, but Breckinridge had tolerated no tampering with the orderly transfer of power. He pronounced Lincoln's victory, and his own defeat, with equanimity; I suppose that was his finest moment in this chamber. Miss Carroll's emotion is understandable. It is sad to see any man fall such a long way.

CHAPTER 4

"FORT GREENHOW"

Allan Pinkerton was beside himself. "Superhuman powers," he muttered. Stogie clamped between his molars, holding his derby hat on his head against the January wind, the head of the small military intelligence organization he hoped would become a vast Secret Service was on his way from McClellan's sickbed to the War Department. "Damn woman must have superhuman powers."

He had personally attended to the incarceration of Rose O'Neal Greenhow. Pinkerton himself had turned her fashionable Sixteenth Street house, across Lafayette Square from the Seward home, into a detention center for spies and suspected traitors. His own men were on duty, supplemented by a thirty-man force drawn from the Sturgis Rifles, McClellan's bodyguard. The bedrooms had been stripped of furniture, then equipped with an easy-to-search bed, chair, and washstand. Rose and her daughter, eight, had been confined to a single room, with a board nailed across the door to an adjoining room and a guard at the only entry. All visitors had been examined; unless they were high military officials on business, they were searched before and after entry.

Even so, the "Wild Rose" was sprouting thorns. Pinkerton knew she was managing to gather vital military information and send it to Richmond. Documents found on other captured spies showed Rose's operation to be functioning still. How was this woman, confined to her room, guarded around the clock, getting information about General McClellan's plans? How did she manage to transmit secrets to Jefferson Davis?

The stealing and transmission of the secrets would have been bad enough had Allan Pinkerton been the only one who knew that Rose Greenhow had an open channel out of her prison home to the Confederate capital. But now, thanks to the publication of her letter, the whole world knew, and his fledgling Secret Service was being made a laughingstock.

"Laughingstock," he murmured aloud, barreling down the narrow corridor of the War Department, when he had to swerve to avoid running into Mathew Brady, who was plowing ahead with an armload of photographic prints under his arm. Brady did not recognize him. That was strange—Pinkerton's star had risen with McClellan's; everybody who knew where the power was recognized the head of military intelligence. "Brady! It's me, Major Allen."

"Who?" Brady fumbled for his glasses, drew them on, peered at the detective, and said, "Ah, it's you, Pinkerton."

"How can you see to take pictures," asked Pinkerton, "if you can't recognize a face two feet away?"

"I can see with my glasses on, and even better through a lens. You're becoming notorious, Pinkerton. You'll have to come by the studio for a portrait."

"Call me Major Allen." Why did Brady say "notorious" rather than "famous"? Had he heard about the damnable letter Rose had written to Seward? "I cannot let myself be photographed," Pinkerton said severely. "The nature of my work must remain secret."

"Maybe a photograph of you with McClellan in the field, conferring in his tent," the photographer persevered. "The front of the tent, where the flap opens, so there'll be light."

He thought over the photographer's offer. "I suppose it would be wrong for me to refuse to pose with my commander. We'll arrange it, if you promise not to sell it until I give the word."

"Done. You're going to see Stanton?"

"How do you know?" Pinkerton had told nobody, not even Gardner at the studio, that he was off to see the legal counsel to the Secretary of War.

"Seward must have jumped on Cameron, who jumped on Stanton, who's going to jump on you," Brady warned. "That was some letter of Rose's."

Pinkerton's heart sank. "They saw her letter in the Richmond papers?"

"Worse than that," said Brady, shifting his heavy plates to his other arm. "It's all over the *New York Herald.* James Gordon Bennett beat Greeley to it, and made Rose's triumph big news. Embarrassed Seward in his home state."

The detective slumped against the wall. Rose O'Neal Greenhow, the spy who supplied General Beauregard with the Union plans for Bull Run, and who had been at the center of a network of at least fifty spies in the capital, had written a letter of protest about her arrest to Secretary of State Seward. On top of that, as if to prove that her Union guards were a pack of incompetents, she smuggled a copy of her letter to the Richmond newspapers, which printed it in full, and now the New York press was reprinting that.

"The Wild Rose writes quite a letter," Brady observed, rubbing it in. "Her home entered without a warrant, herself arrested by you with no judicial authority, her property seized without due process. She's demanding that Seward cite the law all this was done under. You suppose she had legal advice?"

"Evil genius," Pinkerton breathed.

"I want to take a picture of her," Brady said. "Can you get me a pass to get into 'Fort Greenhow'?"

Pinkerton winced; they were calling the detention quarters "Fort Greenhow" because it was so easy to get in and out. "No!" he snapped. "Why don't you go back in the field? Gardner is doing all the work and you get the credit — he'll want to branch out for himself one day." Let the photographer worry about competition. With no farewell, Pinkerton hurried to Stanton's office.

Pinkerton had good reason to be certain of Stanton's personal regard for, and subservience to, General McClellan. The General was dining at his home with Admiral David Porter and the Prince de Joinville. As Porter recounted it to Pinkerton later, the sycophantic Stanton dropped by with some message and stood at the open door of the dining room. McClellan, who saw him, deliberately kept his visitor waiting, and finally motioned for him to come in. The War Department counsel was kept waiting there for five long minutes, standing while the others ate, until McClellan finally offered him some dinner. Stanton then sat and ate, but the general never introduced him to either of his other two guests at the table. Pinkerton knew precisely what McClellan had done: begrudged Stanton some status, but not enough to give him a swelled head.

Moreover, the detective knew that Stanton had been a frequent dinner companion of Rose O'Neal Greenhow during the Buchanan administration, and had visited her—along with a trusted McClellan aide-de-camp, Colonel Thomas Key, which made it all right—only the preceding week. The lawyer might have his own guilty memories about the Wild Rose.

With a show of casualness, the detective strolled into Stanton's office and said, "I understand the Secretary of State has been talking to you." Put them on the defensive, that was the way.

"You're well informed, Major Allen," said Stanton, "as always." Good man; none of this "Pinkerton" stuff. For privacy's sake the lawyer closed the door, which the detective appreciated. "Governor Seward is disturbed about the Greenhow matter," Stanton continued. "Not on the legal questions she raised in her letter—habeas corpus is suspended, and the President has given Seward the power to seize and jail anyone for any length of time. But the Secretary of State is troubled by the fact that she seems able to defy her captors. Do you have any idea how she was able to smuggle the copy of the letter to Richmond?"

"Do you have any idea," Pinkerton responded, hoping to turn the interrogatory table, "how often I have demanded that we stop being perfect gentlemen to these female spies? Why should Rose be permitted to live in her own house on Sixteenth Street, receiving a flock of visitors carrying who knows what information, and carrying away who knows what messages?" Stanton had been one of those visitors; Pinkerton hoped to put a little chill up his spine.

"You're absolutely right, Major Allen. I myself visited her not long ago, to discover some information about an old beau of hers. I noticed a certain familiarity between the prisoner and many of the guards. And I noticed several visitors waiting."

"You were acquainted with her?" Pinkerton had to admit that Stanton had scored a point by volunteering the information about his visit.

"Mrs. Stanton and I"—whenever a man was asked about the Wild Rose, he prefaced his answer with "Mrs. and I"—"went to her home often during the Buchanan administration. The President was a bachelor, and Rose a widow who entertained brilliantly—they saw a great deal of each other. Her home became a social center for Democrats of high rank."

"Many of whom became traitors," said Pinkerton ominously. "Did she ever speak to you of John Breckinridge?"

"I saw the Senator from Kentucky there from time to time, but it was his running mate—Joe Lane, the Senator from Oregon— that I suspected more. When he was running for Vice President on Breckinridge's slate, Lane was making a fool of himself over Rose."

That confirmed what the detective suspected. Pinkerton had confiscated a bundle of love letters from the departed Senator Lane, along with letters signed only "H"—probably Henry Wilson, the senator that Montgomery

Blair had told him to stop investigating. Rose was well connected. Her sister was married to Dolley Madison's nephew, and her niece was Mrs. Stephen Douglas. Rose could reach anybody.

"I will be frank with you," Pinkerton announced. McClellan had told him that Stanton was to be trusted, and was the general's candidate to replace the abolition-inclined Cameron. The likelihood of that taking place had intensified a week ago, when Cameron stupidly sent out a message declaring his policy to arm slaves, and Lincoln had humiliated him by forcing its withdrawal. Curiously, nothing happened to Cameron afterward; Lincoln had not moved to replace the powerful Pennsylvania political leader.

"In her present surroundings," Pinkerton said, "Mrs. Greenhow cannot be properly isolated." That was a nice way of putting her present ability to see and manipulate Washington's powerful. When Stanton had visited her, an informant told Pinkerton that she had breezily asked him for legal advice on habeas corpus. She probably used whatever he had told her in that damned letter to Seward, but the detective saw no need to embarrass the man McClellan said was his candidate for Secretary of War.

"To remedy that," asked Stanton, "what do you need to do?"

"Clap her in Old Capitol Prison." Pinkerton was blunt: "It's not a nice place to visit. And the guards are prison guards—hard men, not impressionable young soldiers."

"It's a depressing place," said Stanton, "and she has her child with her. How old is the girl—eight?"

Was Stanton about to go soft, too? The detective moved his cigar to the other side of his mouth.

"Do it," said Stanton crisply. "Take her there yourself, today. I'll send word to Wood, the prison warden."

"Whose authority?" He wanted the order in writing, lest Rose get ammunition for another letter, maybe to Lincoln himself next time.

"By the verbal order of the Secretary of State and the Secretary of War. You don't need any more authority than that."

Pinkerton accepted that, rather than lose the chance to shut down "Fort Greenhow." "She'll have no visitors, no writing paper," he promised. "I'll let her sew her tapestries to keep from going crazy, but that's it. You can expect complaints from powerful people that we're being cruel to a great lady and her dear little girl."

"Send them to me." End of subject. That was good—the high echelons could do with a man who so evidently relished saying no. "Your estimate of the rebel troops facing the Army of the Potomac is of special interest at this moment. You say two hundred thousand?"

Pinkerton had a rule of thumb for estimating enemy troop strength. He took the reports from deserters, prisoners of war, messages from Union loyal in Southern cities, and the nose counts of his spies working behind enemy lines in Virginia, and came up with his base estimate. Then he multiplied that by two. He knew the estimates he offered were probably on the high side, but better safe than sorry, and his general preferred them that way. As long as Allan Pinkerton was estimating the strength of the enemy, the Army of the Potomac would never go into battle against more rebels than expected.

"Two hundred thirteen thousand," he amended. "Latest information." Round numbers sounded like guesses; he preferred more precise estimates.

The detective rose to leave, relieved that his strategy had worked. He had not been reprimanded for permitting Rose to operate successfully despite her incarceration. His eyes, trained to read handwriting upside-down, swept Stanton's desk automatically; he saw a note in McClellan's fine penmanship.

"If you have a message for the general," he said smoothly, "that would better be communicated orally—"

"Yes. Tell him—tell him that there are powerful forces at work to unseat him." Stanton grew conspiratorial. "Certain senators—you and he know who they are—are insisting that McDowell take over the Army of the Potomac. That would leave McClellan, as General-in-Chief, with no troops. The President is wavering."

"The general will appreciate your warning," Pinkerton said in the inaudible voice he used for such occasions. "And he—and I—will remember his friends."

They clasped hands and Pinkerton darted out, glad that McClellan and he had a trustworthy ally in the War Department.

CHAPTER 5

CALHOUN'S ROOM

"Mother, there's a man standing at the door."

Rose Greenhow always sat facing away from the open door in what used to be her bedroom and was now her cell. The door was left open to insult her, the guard always able to peep in. By showing only her back to the door, she could force visitors to announce themselves. This one did not.

"Who is it, my dear? One of those Yankees who like to watch us undress?"

"It's an ugly man, with a beard and hat on and a cigar right in the middle of his face. I don't like him." Little Rose, eight and forthright, was at her best in the presence of Yankees. Alone with her mother, as she was all too often, the child was irritable and unhappy, but in the presence of others she joined with the "Wild Rose" in defiance and pride. The mother could not blame her for the peevishness in private because she could not do without her daughter's support against her jailers.

"Get your things together, Mrs. Greenhow," the rasping voice behind her said. "You've sent your last letter to Richmond."

She smiled and looked over her shoulder. "It's little Pinkerton," she told her daughter. "Isn't Pinkerton a pretty name for an ugly man?"

"Your airs and graces don't impress me, lady," the detective said. "It will go easier for you if you tell me how you got that letter out of here."

She turned back to her tapestry-making, the varicolored threads stretched in a circular frame in her hand, ignoring him, forcing him to walk into the room and stand facing her. He puffed on the cigar, deliberately spreading its odor through the room.

"You're going to be furious with yourself when I tell you," she replied, as if

Rose O'Neal Greenhow

on the verge of a confession. "I sent it out wrapped in one of your cigar butts," she replied. "Remember the last time you came by? You left your cigar behind. And everybody was so anxious to get rid of it—"

"You have five minutes to pack. One suitcase for the both of you. Or else you don't take anything."

"Are you sending us South?" her daughter asked. Rose was glad the girl piped up with that question; she did not want to deign to ask it herself. The purpose of her public letter, in addition to showing the Yankees how easy it was to make fools of them, had been to force Seward to send both imprisoned Greenhows to Richmond in an exchange. Her work in Washington was done; if she could arrange repatriation, she could catch a ship running the blockade and use her connections in London and Paris to encourage recognition of the Confederacy. Mason and Slidell, snatched off the *Trent*, were far more of a help to the cause in a Yankee jail than in England, which was incensed by the insult to the British flag; she had many friends in London, bankers especially, and could capitalize on the idiotic act of the Yankee captain. She had heard that Thurlow Weed was there now, to smooth things over; she could stir the English up beyond his powers to assuage, if only she could be freed.

Pinkerton waited for Rose to repeat her daughter's plaintive question. She did not, letting him know that she regarded him as unworthy of her attention. However, she did not want to travel without baggage. She went to the closet and quickly packed one change of clothes for herself—always black, as she had taken mourning clothes for her personal signature—and several changes for young Rose. When she finished, Pinkerton took the bag, unloaded its contents on the bed, and went through each item carefully before putting them back.

"You're not taking any soap?" he asked, which struck her as odd.

"There's plenty of soap in Richmond," she replied, fishing.

He grinned. "Take some. You'll thank me for it."

She ignored him. He shut the case—she hated to leave her dressing gown behind, but she would be damned if she would plead with this Peeping Tom for the favor of a second case—and signaled for a guard to pick it up.

Rose wearily took up her tapestry and the balls of thread: "Am I to be permitted to take this? You could hang it in your office as a souvenir captured from a rebel. You could pretend you were doing honorable work."

"Take your damn sewing," the detective gruffed.

"It's not sewing, of course," she said to her daughter, disdaining direct communication with Pinkerton. "Sewing is what we did when we took the tablecloth and made the Stars and Bars, and hung it out the window when the Yankees went by on parade."

"That made the men marching very angry," the girl grinned.

"Out," ordered Pinkerton.

"Wouldn't you like to take something to entertain yourself for the journey?" she asked her daughter. She had trained her what to answer, in case the situation arose. "It's two hours on the train, and then a long buggy ride."

Little Rose went to the desk and took a pencil and a drawing pad without hesitation. Pinkerton was not to be fooled; he grabbed them and snapped at the guard, "Who let them have writing materials? I left strict instructions!"

"The little girl wanted to draw a picture," the guard began, and the detective cut him off with a furious gesture. Rose began to worry; if their destination was Richmond, there would be little danger to the Union in taking writing materials.

Outside the house on Sixteenth Street, in the carriage surrounded by mounted guards, she was concerned when they started east, up toward Capitol Hill and the railroad station. The train would take them North; she was hoping for a boat South, to Fort Monroe on the Peninsula, near the Confederate lines. Then a flag of truce and an exchange.

She looked back at her brick house in Lafayette Square. Confined for nearly five months inside, she had almost forgotten how imposing it looked from the outside. "Fort Greenhow"—she liked that. Good times there; she recalled the dinner parties during Buchanan's administration, with the President making an ostentatious exit at 11 P.M. so the others could leave, and then sneaking back at midnight. She had trouble shooing out his Attorney General, Stanton, one night, before Old Buck came back. She smiled at the thought of Stanton's face recently, when she asked for advice on habeas corpus; the old conspirator quickly told her what points to make while vociferously denying her any aid.

The carriage left her house, and the old life, behind. She sat back and let the memories of other men and other nights at Sixteenth Street wash across her mind. In the 1860 campaign, only a year ago, John Breckinridge and his running mate, Joe Lane, had stayed up talking and drinking until dawn. She had been frustrated and angry when Breck left Senator Lane behind to sleep with her; Lane was a lovesick ass, but Breck was her idea of a man. Rose had heard that the drunken Zack Chandler had been the one to urge the Senate to eject him from that body as a traitor—a stupid act of spite. She had been relieved to learn that Breck, who had delayed his decision to go South longer than he should have, had been taken into the Confederate Army at a fitting level, second in command to Sidney Johnston in Tennessee. Johnston—she remembered him as Secretary of War of the Republic of Texas—was thought by many to be the best soldier the South could boast, had been offered a major general's commission by Lincoln, but chose to stay with Texas, which was, by treaty, an equal to the Union. Johnston and Breckinridge would make an undefeatable team in the West.

She missed Breck, whom she respected despite his infatuation with that two-faced Jezebel Anna Carroll. What must Breck think of Anna now that Lincoln had sent her pamphlet denouncing him all over the country? Served him right for trusting Millard Fillmore's scribbling plaything, a supposed daughter of Maryland who had impoverished herself on some fool plan to manumit her slaves; Rose had warned him.

The carriage left the house in the distance, but the images clung: Colonel Jordan, the Confederate officer who thought he had seduced her and then set up the spy network around her. Young Jordan was daring, though she liked him less when she discovered he had used his gallant talents in a similar manner with Mrs. Phillips, a willing spy but a vulgar woman—practically a prostitute. Different types of agents were needed for work at different levels, she supposed; still, it was demeaning to have such a slut confined at Fort Greenhow. She had not spoken to the woman once.

The carriage jolted along the frozen mud of Pennsylvania Avenue and headed up the hill, turning aside frequently to avoid the carcasses of horses. The many carcasses at first revolted Rose, then their significance pleased her: if Lincoln couldn't have the dead horses picked up off the main street of his capital, he must be desperately short of manpower. The guard next to her was dressed, like the men at Sixteenth Street, in a nondescript uniform made of shoddy, the cheap reprocessed wool that crumbled after a few washings— further proof that the Union army was in the hands of corrupt quartermasters and contractors. If the uniforms were made of shoddy, what about the rifles —were they the quality ordered? Good points to make when she met with Jeff Davis in Richmond; these were the little details that told much about a nation and an army.

Coming up toward First and A, Rose could see another building that had memories for her: the Old Capitol, built in 1815 as temporary quarters for the House and Senate after the British burned the Capitol in the War of 1812. When the House and Senate chambers were restored, the building at First and A was turned into a large roominghouse, and it was there—in a second-floor room overlooking the dismal courtyard—that Rose O'Neal had nursed the dying Senator John C. Calhoun in the last year of his life. The man she believed to be the very spirit of nullification, the fierce protector of Southern tradition, had inspired her to revere her section. Thanks to Calhoun, she had come to despise all those Yankees and abolitionists who schemed to centralize power in New York, Boston, and Washington.

Old Capitol was now a prison, primarily for prisoners of war, but also— Rose felt a chill as the carriage slowed—for deserters and soldiers of doubtful loyalty. She took her daughter's hand.

The carriage stopped. "Your new home," said Pinkerton, lifting his cigar out of his mouth and waving it at the dingy building, "for the rest of the war. No mail service to Richmond, I'm afraid."

"I was fully aware of your plans," she said as haughtily as she could.

"The hell you were," said the detective. "You would have taken soap."

Inside, Rose was led to Superintendent Wood, a short, muscular man who seemed sensible of the great honor that was being done his prison by the addition of the lady spy who had so recently embarrassed the Secretary of State. He signed the detective's receipt.

"She has superhuman powers," Pinkerton told the superintendent. "She is responsible for the deaths of thousands of our soldiers. Watch her as you watch no other prisoner."

Rose framed an acid comment about how that was the nicest thing a Yankee had ever said about her, but she held her tongue. The prison was frightening. Her daughter's hand clung tightly to her own.

"Stanton tells me she'll have a string of big shots at first," the smiling jailer replied. Rose did not like the sound of "at first"; this was no place for anybody of any repute to visit, and return visits would likely be few. Determined not to let her feelings of terror show, she drew herself up and said, "You may show us to our room."

"Follow me," Wood said cheerfully. She waited for him to pick up her bag. "Oh, allow me," he said, still pleased with his new charges. She turned her back on Pinkerton and followed him upstairs.

"This is no place for children," said Wood to her daughter.

"You have got one of the damnedest little rebels here that you ever saw," the little girl shot back. A surge of pride and pain brought Rose Greenhow close to tears, but she caught hold of herself. This was going to be a long war for mother and daughter.

On the second floor, the stench of urine and unwashed bodies assailed her nostrils. She recognized the boardinghouse rooms, and remembered the lay-out of the floor from all those years ago. It was like seeing, after too long, a face remembered as friendly that had turned hostile and ugly.

They stopped before a room especially familiar to her.

"They say this is the room where old John Calhoun died," Wood said. "Because of that, and because the window faces the courtyard and not the street, we've selected it for you. Stanton thought that was a nice touch."

"You know Edwin Stanton?"

"I was an expert witness once," the superintendent said, "in a case he was trying for the McCormick reaper people. Stanton owes me one. That's your bunk, with the one over it for your daughter. The table is for writing letters, but you won't get any paper. And a chair, all your own. Down the hall is the lavatory. You'll have to wait until it's empty, in case you're bashful. The mess is in Room 16—"

"I know," she said dully. Room 16 had been the boardinghouse dining room in the old days.

"Holler for a guard if any man makes advances," Wood said, she presumed for the record. "I don't approve of that." He looked at the little girl, started to say something, then shook his head.

"Where are the rebel prisoners?" little Rose wanted to know.

"Other side—you won't meet them," he said. "Here is strictly for disloyals. Come see me if you have anything to tell Pinkerton. People who help, with information or whatever, get extra rations."

When he left, Rose could not bear to sit in the room. She took her daughter to the mess in Room 16, and they had a cup of tepid coffee. A few of the men sauntered over to get acquainted; she froze, and immediately scanned the room for a protector. She spotted a heavyset, bearded man, eyes red-rimmed and slightly drunk—that meant he had access to privileges—sitting alone at one of the tables. She did not want to leave her daughter alone, but did not want her to hear what she was going to say. She told her to say nothing to anyone and to stare into her cup while she made some arrangements on the other side of the hall.

"You secesh?" she asked the bearded man, while keeping an eye on her daughter.

"Nope." He was obviously pleased at having a woman to talk to. "I'm from New York, the Zouaves. I got drunk one night at camp, started cussin' out old Billy Bowlegs, and the next thing you know I was here."

"You've been charged with treason?"

"Nobody gets charged with anything. Couple months ago, Lincoln arrested half the damn Maryland legislature. No charge, no trial, no nothing. They just sit around. Don't see many women, though. Never a kid. What'd you do?"

"I'm a spy." He looked impressed. She had to make a quick judgment. He was a drinker, but not a mean man. Strong; he'd do. "Look, I don't want the girl molested."

"I'm not a guard, lady; I'm one of the prisoners here."

"I'm in the last room on the A Street wing. Come along." She took him back with them. He sat on the chair while she opened her valise. She wished now she had taken the soap.

"Why you taking the stuff out?" he asked. "There's no closet." For some reason, that hit her as especially cruel. She drooped over the suitcase, closed it, sat on it.

"What else should I know?"

"You don't sleep in the bunks," the man said. "There's bedbugs drive you crazy."

"Where does one sleep?"

"On the table is best. No bugs. There's lice everywhere, nothing you can do about them, but the bedbugs are the trouble. They like the warmth of the bunks."

"I'll ask for another table."

"If you don't get it, try the floor, like most of us. Too cold for bugs, and you get used to it. Use a shakedown."

She put her hand on his arm. It was a muscled arm; she knew her hand was not the seductive hand that used to be, but it made up in experienced touch what it had lost in unveined good looks. She caressed the biceps. "I want you to take care of us. I'll be good to you. Here on the floor, or wherever you say, when my girl is asleep."

"I'm in with two other men," the man said, not reacting to her offer that once would have appealed to half the powerful men in the city. "One used to be a government worker, just a clerk, till the Potter Committee got to him. Accused him of being secesh, and that got his back up, and he wouldn't take the oath, so he's here. Other guy's just a thief, but he grabbed some ammo one night, and they put him in here."

She knew what he was getting at and did not want to face it right away. Stupid of the Yankees, she thought: if they kept arresting men on charges like failing to take the oath, Seward would breed thousands of Yankee-haters in the heart of the North. After a moment, she said, "The only thing I worry about is the girl. You take care of us, I'll take care of you."

He looked uncomfortable and rubbed his stubble beard. She breathed deeply. "And your two friends." Protection was costly. "One at a time, same time, makes no difference to me, but it has to be quietly." She was thinking about ways to put a curtain around the table where her daughter would sleep.

"A deal," said the bearded man. "If you got any money, I can probably get us some hootch."

She touched his cracked lips lightly with her fingertips. "If anybody touches the girl, I'll put a knife in your heart."

"That's why you rebs are gonna win the war," he smiled. "I shouldn't say that," he added, the smile disappearing. "They could put you in jail for saying that."

She sent him on his way for the time being and took out her tapestry. With her deal made, she felt better. The situation was not all bad for a spy. As men came into this jail, they would be bringing information; also, as prisoners of war entered the other wing, they would have information about the battle zone, of interest to Richmond. Even Superintendent Wood seemed well connected; Rose bet he had given false testimony in that case with Stanton, and was blackmailing him with it today. Visitors would come, she was certain of that, even to this dreary place: Henry Wilson, who loved punishment, could not stay away for long, and the charming Colonel Key on McClellan's staff who so liked to hold her hand during interrogations would surely be back. With Rose safely in jail, presumably cut off from the outside world, they would speak even more freely.

She sighed more in resolution than self-pity. Information would soon start flowing in toward her. Her problem then would be to find a way of getting it out of here, through the Federal lines; Colonel Jordan would soon help her see to that, as he had before.

What of encoding the information, and putting it in a form not likely to be intercepted by Pinkerton's men? She smiled at the detective's glee when he stopped little Rose from taking pencil and paper. That had been a ruse, to let him think he had denied her a means of putting information in a form that could be transmitted. In fact, her communications system was held openly in her hand: the tapestry's threads were a simple color code, memorized by Jordan and herself. When a message was ready to be sent, she could sew the information into an attractive fabric that would become a bookmark or glasses holder, which could be carried without suspicion by any courier.

She put her other dress on the table and helped her daughter climb on top to go to sleep. In the darkling cell, she sat against the wall, waiting for the gaslight in the hall to be turned off and for the men to come. War was war and she was not the only one who would suffer, she told herself stoutly, but the sound of her daughter scratching her head furiously at the first attack of lice made it hard. She wished again she had taken Pinkerton's advice about the soap.

CHAPTER 6

GUARDING THE SACRED INSTRUMENT

"I regret calling you all in on Christmas Day," Seward was saying to the Cabinet, "but Lord Lyons, the British Ambassador, has presented us with an ultimatum. Either we hand over the captured rebel emissaries, Mason and Slidell, or Great Britain will recall its diplomats and prepare for hostilities."

Simon Cameron felt uneasy. Just before this Cabinet meeting started, Lincoln had clapped him on the shoulder to wish him and his family a happy Christmas. Why had he been singled out for the President's good wishes? For the past three weeks, ever since the incident about the message, the Secretary of War believed himself to be the recipient of special kindnesses from the man who had so promptly repudiated his proposal to arm the freed slaves. Why was Lincoln being so damnably polite? Despite the uproar in the press about the disarray in the Cabinet, despite the charges of insubordination by anti-abolition congressmen, Simon Cameron had not been publicly or privately reprimanded by the President for the inflammatory paragraph in the annual message.

He was stuck with what he considered the worst job in the Cabinet. The strutting colonels and generals who raised their own armies expected to run their own shows. Bloodsucking contractors who saw the war as one great opportunity to make fortunes were attached to all the procurement offices. Every congressman who tried to get his favorite salesman an edge, and whom Cameron rightly refused, sought revenge by demanding an investigation into corruption, and the press made a great fuss about that.

Fortunately, Cameron mused, he had Tom Scott of the Pennsy to handle the business of transport, and Edwin Stanton, the Buchanan holdover, to guide him in the intricacies of the law. Stanton's language in the message had caused all the trouble, it was true, but Cameron was certain that was not the general counsel's fault—Lincoln's inefficient secretaries had never read the proposed draft. At least the War Department stand on arming the slaves had earned him the new respect of Chase and Wade, and even Greeley.

Perhaps their public support of Cameron explained Lincoln's odd friendliness, in circumstances that would ordinarily demand a resignation. Or perhaps Lincoln was still worried about what effect the firing of Cameron would have on support of the war in Pennsylvania. Or maybe Lincoln was waiting him out.

Seward cut into his thoughts with a brisk "Simon, are you with us?"

Cameron gave him a baleful look. "Why weren't we given these documents in advance?"

They were all looking at him. That was the damn trouble with being Secretary of War when somebody threatened war: Nobody wanted to be first to say "Surrender." Monty Blair, who had been the only one at first to resist the jingo spirit, looked troubled. Cameron offered an emotional way out: "I have been informed that the capture of the *Trent* was a plot by the British and the rebels."

That assertion startled Lincoln and the Cabinet. Cameron sat up, rather enjoying the role of detective. "Our man in Scotland," he told the group he knew to be looking for excuses to hand the men over, "writes that Mason and Slidell were seen in Havana just before the capture, talking to our Captain Wilkes. They arranged the capture to embarrass the United States, and to give the British reason to recognize the Confederacy and enter the war."

"Sounds like a lot of nonsense to me," Gideon Welles grumbled into his beard. Captain Wilkes was his man, and the press had been giving the Navy plaudits for stopping a British ship and seizing the rebel envoys.

Seward did not knock down the story. He asked permission to bring in Senator Charles Sumner, chairman of the Senate Foreign Relations Committee, to speak in behalf of surrendering the men. The radical Republican from Massachusetts, who had been savagely cane-whipped at his Senate desk by a fanatic Southerner years before, was too florid for Cameron's taste. The Secretary of War suspected that Sumner's airs did not impress the President, though it was said that Mrs. Lincoln was taken in by them.

Senator Sumner entered, read aloud two letters from England, written by noted friends of America—John Bright and Richard Cobden—that attested to the war fever sweeping the British isles at this outrage to their flag. Sumner

Secretary of War Simon Cameron

urged Lincoln to hand over the two captives, to avoid playing into the hands of the pro-Southern British aristocracy. That was smart of Lincoln, Cameron thought, to bring the chairman of Senate Foreign Relations in on this; it would provide political cover for the public disappointment to follow.

"What do you think, gentlemen?" Lincoln did not want advice, Cameron presumed; he wanted company in backing down.

"We don't have a leg to stand on," decided Blair. "Our seizure was illegal."

"It is gall and wormwood to me," intoned Chase. "Rather than consent to the liberation of these men, I would sacrifice everything I possess." They all waited for Chase to make his turnaround, because he was needed to quiet Greeley and help dampen public sentiment for a fight with the British. "But the technical right is undoubtedly with England," he sighed. "As contraband, the envoys could not rightfully be taken from the neutral ship until after the judicial condemnation of the ship itself, for receiving and carrying them."

Seward pointed out that Thurlow Weed's mission to London had been a success, and the unexpectedly gracious tone of the British ultimatum made it easier for the U.S. to cough up the rebel captives. He then offered a solution that would get the nation out of a war with England without making Americans feel like cowards, or losing the war spirit so vital in fighting the South. "We ought to declare a moral victory," Seward suggested. "We should declare that we are happy to see that England finally agrees with the United States on the rights of neutral vessels. Just as the British have been in the wrong for years, stopping our ships, we were in the wrong this time—and we are men enough to admit it."

"This reply to Lord Lyons's note," said Lincoln, tapping the Seward draft before him, "is pretty crafty. Not much on the law, but a clever way out."

"We take a stand on principle," said Seward, a man Cameron knew took principled stands only when they were expedient, "laid down by President Madison in his instructions to Secretary of State Monroe."

"The British want an apology," said Lincoln, "in addition to the prisoners."

"No apology," snapped Seward. "Captain Wilkes acted without government authorization, and when we make that clear, the British will interpret it as an apology. Besides, Thurlow Weed writes me that his British friends are prepared to overlook the need for an apology. We'll just say our man was wrong to adopt the British practice." He read the last line of his draft message: "They will be cheerfully liberated. Your lordship will please indicate a time and place for receiving them."

Lincoln looked relieved but unhappy. "I tried to frame an argument for the other side," he told Seward, "but I found I could not make one that would satisfy my own mind. That proves to me that your ground is the right one."

Cameron marveled at the way Lincoln had made Sumner and Seward the proponents of doing what Lincoln wanted to do. The President was striking the pose of being reluctantly dragged along. Cameron hurried to get on the side Lincoln wanted. "My man Stanton disagrees with you on the law—he thinks we have every right to seize the men—but I think Chase is right, and Seward offers us a good way out. Maybe we can spread the story of the rebel plot far and wide, make us look a little smarter."

"Sumner, your support on this in cooling down Wade and Chandler, not to mention Uncle Horace, would be appreciated," said Lincoln. "This is a pretty bitter pill to swallow, but after this war is over we'll be so powerful that we can call England to account for all the embarrassment she's inflicted on us. Reminds me of a story."

Charles Sumner rolled his eyes upward, those of Welles and Bates glazed over, and Chase's face took on a disapproving look, but Cameron actually enjoyed Lincoln's stories. They were invariably on the point, not funny so much as repeatable. The Secretary of War made a hit at dinner parties passing them along, though they lost flavor out of political context, and he sat forward to catch this one.

"I feel a good deal like the dying man in Illinois who was told he ought to make peace with his enemies," Lincoln said. "He said the man he hated worst of all was a fellow named Brown in the next village, and he was sent for. The sick man began to say, in a voice as meek as Moses, that he wanted to die at peace with all his fellow creatures, and he hoped that Brown would now shake hands. Brown had to get out his handkerchief and wipe the gathering tears from his eyes, and they had a regular love-feast.

"After a parting that would have softened the heart of a grindstone, Brown had about reached the room door when the sick man rose up on his elbow and said, 'But see here, Brown, if I *should* happen to get well, mind *that old grudge stands!*' "

Simon Cameron pounded the table and roared with laughter. The rest smiled.

"Averting this crisis is especially welcome," said Chase, "at a moment when we are at the brink of bankruptcy. I'm worried about meeting the army payroll."

Seward, a war with England avoided by what he would surely tell everyone was the diplomatic skill of his henchman and himself, tilted his chair back, took a pinch of snuff, sneezed heartily, and said, "Chase somehow always manages to scare his banker friends, and we muddle through."

"Six months ago," said Chase, obviously not appreciating Seward's breeziness, "the public debt was ninety million. Six months from now, it will be five hundred million. We have no way of raising that money."

"The banks?" asked Bates.

"I have coerced the state banks into lending us one hundred and fifty million dollars. I am starting a system of national banks, despite the objection of every governor in this land, that enables us to borrow on the faith of the United States Government in addition to the states."

"The bankers in Philadelphia are screaming," Cameron put in. "They say you threatened them."

"I am ashamed to say I did," Chase admitted. "When they told me there was no more to be lent, I told them that I would print paper money until it would wipe them all out and cost the average man one thousand dollars for a breakfast." Chase looked embarrassed and proud at the same time.

Lincoln made a face. "What about raising the money from the public?"

"The people of this country are not accustomed to taxation," Chase said. "Most of what revenue we have is from tariffs. That's why the end of the *Trent* affair will be a blessing—a British blockade would have cut off all our customs duties."

"The public bond subscription?" That was Blair; Cameron was glad at least one other Cabinet member was familiar with finances.

"With no victories," Chase said, "the public is unwilling to buy government war bonds. And we need that money from public subscription to repay the banks and roll over our short-term debt."

Lincoln leaned forward, elbows on the desk, and rubbed his head. "What are you going to do? You're running that end of the machine." The way he phrased it, Cameron noticed, put the question out of his ken—on monetary matters, Chase was as good as President.

"Tomorrow morning," Chase said with evident pain, "I am going to suspend payment in specie. We do not have the gold and silver to pay in coin. The nation will have to dishonor its promises."

Cameron could see what Lincoln wanted to ask next, and he asked it for him: "What will that do?"

"That means we are asking banks, and people, to rely on paper currency, not redeemable on demand in gold or silver. Bank notes. It's frightening."

"Napoleon did not fight his wars on hard money," said Blair, not worried at all. "Wars are fought on paper, and the winner redeems—the loser defaults."

Chase glared at the Postmaster General. "You're talking about making paper into legal tender."

"Why not?" Blair was confident; Cameron estimated that only Chase and Blair knew what they were talking about, but the rest of the men in the room were uncomfortably aware that the subject under discussion must be of great import.

"It flies in the face of the Constitution," answered Chase. "You cannot tell a free American that he must accept a piece of paper as payment for debts—good gold and silver coin that he made as a loan. That's stealing his property. The President here is not even willing to do that to slave owners."

"Can I make paper into legal tender?" asked Lincoln.

"Tad Stevens has a bill he's ready to introduce, giving you that power," Chase answered reluctantly. Lincoln looked to Blair, who nodded.

"Let him, quickly," said Lincoln. "I'll sign it."

"But it's unconstitutional," warned Chase. It seemed to Cameron that just as Lincoln had dumped a share of the blame for backing down on the *Trent* on others, Chase was being careful to place the full blame for doing the necessary but unpopular thing about money on Lincoln.

"I have that sacred instrument here in my desk," said Lincoln slowly, "and I am guarding it with great care." Chase shook his head in disapproval, which seemed to nettle the President. "Chase, down in Illinois I was held to be a pretty good lawyer, and I believe I could answer every constitutional point you raise, but I don't feel called upon to do it."

Nobody challenged that; it struck Cameron that Lincoln grew uncharacteristically testy when anyone suggested he was showing less than the proper respect for "that sacred instrument."

"Now what I want to know," said Lincoln, all business, "is whether, Constitution aside, the project of issuing notes will help us pay the soldiers and buy ammunition?"

"With the exception you make," Chase responded, "it is the only way open to us to raise money."

"Then let's do it right away."

With a resigned look, Chase nodded. "I will do my best to put it into immediate and practical operation. You know I think it is wrong."

"It will not help public confidence," the Postmaster General told the Treasury Secretary, "if you do it with a long face." Blair had him there, Cameron noted; Chase could not back into this, blaming Lincoln—not if he was to be seen as running that end of the machine.

"From this moment on," Chase said to the President, ignoring Blair but accepting the wisdom of his point, "in public or private, you will never hear from me any opposition on this subject."

The emergency Cabinet meeting broke up on that conciliatory note. Merry Christmases were exchanged and Blair said lightly, "Chase, you're a God-fearing man. Putting 'In God We Trust' on the coinage was your idea. What's to be the new motto for your paper money?"

Chase took that question seriously, and frowned in thought. Lincoln smiled and offered a suggestion: "Remember Peter and John? 'Silver and gold have I none, but such as I have give I thee.' "

Even Chase had a laugh at that. Cameron fancied himself as astute a judge of political horseflesh as anyone, and he had to say to himself that of all the men in the room, the most "presidential" was Chase: although a little on the stiff side, a serious man, a man of substance, even of majesty, and one whom people could trust on great affairs. Blair was too quickly decisive to be President, too much the peremptory executive, unwilling to let the people lead him until he could lead the people. Cameron thought Lincoln was good at misleading people into thinking they were leading him, but lacked Chase's presence and gravity. Seward, who had seemed only recently the first among equals, now seemed to the Pennsylvania politician to be slightly diminished—almost in Lincoln's shadow, instead of vice versa as everyone had assumed would be the case.

The Secretary of War took his time putting on his coat and wasted some more time, as the others left, putting together the papers Seward had strewn about. Alone with the President, he let Lincoln have the chance to mention the aborted move to arm the slaves, but Lincoln was ardently determined to play out his waiting game, and said nothing but friendly banalities.

"I don't know," said Cameron finally, "whether this job is the best one for my particular talents. If, at some propitious time, you should wish to make a change at the War Department, I would not be averse to another assignment."

Lincoln nodded solemnly. "Who would you recommend to replace you?"

Cameron thought about Tom Scott—loyal, efficient, honest, deeply knowledgeable about the operations of the army, but lacking in political experience, devoid of the necessary deviousness required of a major participant in power. "Stanton. He's obnoxious in some ways, and he's a bit of a courtier and flatterer, but he's a prodigious organizer. You may not like him, but you can rely on him."

The President said he would think about it, and murmured something that Cameron could not catch about a "major embassy." To show he was on top of his job, the Secretary of War took a crumpled letter out of his coat pocket.

"Something about one of our generals is bothering me." Cameron said ominously.

"McClellan? I've heard he is confined to bed. Is it the typhoid?"

"That's a troublesome prospect too, but I'm concerned about one of our men out West." He showed Lincoln the covering note from William Bross, editor of the *Chicago Tribune*, and an attached letter to the editor complaining about the Union general in Cairo, Illinois: "He was perfectly inebriate under a flag of truce with the rebels," the letter read. "Until we can secure pure men in habits and men without secesh wives with their own little slaves to wait upon them, which is a fact here in this camp with Mrs. Grant, our country is lost."

"Bross would not knowingly misrepresent," said Lincoln, who apparently knew and trusted the Illinois newspaperman. "General Grant was appointed chiefly on the recommendation of Congressman Washburne. Perhaps we should consult him."

"I'll look into it immediately." Cameron had heard the same rumor, from other sources, that Sam Grant was a drunkard.

"The generals in the West are going to be tested soon," Lincoln pressed, "perhaps very soon. Put my mind at ease on this."

His son Willie appeared, carrying one of the Seward pussycats by the nape of her neck, and the look of concern on the President's face was transformed into a smile of mock concern.

The chief executive must have a lot on his mind this Christmas Day, Cameron mused, stepping out on the porch of the Mansion into the bracing winter air. Avoiding one war while keeping up the national spirit for another war; finding the way to finance unprecedented expenditures by sticking the sacred instrument into the hole in the keel; pushing a possibly feverish general into action and worrying if he was pushing a drunken general into other action; and replacing his Secretary of War with an untried man.

The Paris and London embassies were in unfriendly territory, Cameron thought. Perhaps he could become ambassador to Spain or Germany. Or Russia, where our Minister, Cassius Clay of Kentucky, had allowed himself to become involved in a love affair with a ballerina, which would ordinarily have been ignored except that the girl was the mistress of the Tsar. That absolute monarch not long ago had freed the Russian serfs; Cameron allowed himself to wonder if the Tsar's War Minister had stimulated that historic act by suggesting they be armed.

CHAPTER 7

TURNING BACK THE CLOCK

"Read this!"

Never before had the Secretary of War come to Thomas Scott's rooms at night, pounding on the door, flinging himself into a chair as if the war had been lost. Simon Cameron brandished a sheet of paper, demanding that Scott read it, but not giving him the opportunity.

They were all Pennsylvanians: Scott, the railroad man trying to run the War Department under Cameron; his guest that evening, A. K. McClure, politician and journalist; and Scott's boss at the War Department, Cameron, a personal friend but longtime political adversary of McClure.

Cameron, the paper trembling in his hand, turned to McClure. "This is more than a political affair. This is personal degradation." The Secretary of War started to sob. Scott did not know what to do. He fetched a brandy, which Cameron swallowed, crying, "A personal affront, a shameful business —God, he's ruined me!"

McClure reached over and took the sheet of paper from Cameron's hand. He read it aloud to Scott, the Assistant Secretary: "It's in Lincoln's hand. 'To Simon Cameron. Dear Mr. Secretary: I have this day nominated Hon. Edwin B. Stanton to be Secretary of War and you to be Minister Plenipotentiary to Russia. Very truly yours, A. Lincoln.' "

That started Cameron off again in a fresh outbreak of sobbing. "Can you imagine," he choked, "anything so insulting? Like a pail of ice water, as if he believes all those lies about me. There hasn't been a Cabinet dismissal like this ever—never, never. I'm finished, and all I ever did was to get Lincoln the nomination. If it weren't for me, Seward would be President today, and what do I get? This!"

Scott took the paper from McClure and looked at the President's handwriting: it was indeed a curt and cruel dismissal. Scott found that curious; if Lincoln had been so icily furious with Cameron for last month's insubordination on the arming of slaves, why hadn't he fired him then? On the other hand, if Lincoln wanted to make an example out of Cameron, affronting the Secretary's new abolitionist friends and pleasing the anti-corruption crusaders, why give him the Russian post?

Scott drew McClure aside, hoping that Cameron, left alone for a moment, would compose himself. "This makes no sense," Scott told the publisher. "Lincoln isn't like this, unless he has a reason. And I don't think he has a reason."

"It's a terrible letter," McClure agreed. "I've opposed Simon in politics— the truth is, Colonel, I think the man's a thief, and I told Lincoln that before the appointment. But when it comes to the patronage, Lincoln is the most political animal alive."

"Do you think Cameron deserves this?"

McClure hesitated. "I've been told by one of my reporters that Thurlow Weed gets five percent of all contracts his friends get at the War Department, and he kicks back half of that to Simon. Is that true?"

"No. I'm right there and I would know. There's surely corruption down the line, but it doesn't go to Simon." Scott felt that the man who had resigned a Senate seat to take this job was being given a raw deal. He was the wrong man to be Secretary of War, but his removal had to be handled in a way that would not reflect discredit on him for the rest of his life.

"Look, I've always fought him, but I'm not a killer," McClure said. "This cold dismissal finishes him. It will be taken as saying that all the accusations of fraud are true."

Cameron came in to them for solace. "He's been so nice to me all month," Cameron protested. "Lincoln knows I hinted that I'd accept another post. I made it easy for him. I could have made it very difficult. Why? Why?"

Scott cut the wailing short. "Who gave you this letter? How was it delivered?"

"Chase gave it to me, in a sealed envelope. Said Lincoln asked him to deliver it, and he did not know what was in it."

"Chase doesn't lie," observed McClure. "He thinks he's God, and God isn't the lying sort."

Scott began to figure a way to back the train away from the wreckage. It was midnight, too late to go to the White House, but he had an idea. "I'll see Lincoln first thing in the morning," he told Cameron. "You start writing a letter of resignation as if nothing had happened. Pretend this letter never was delivered, that you received the kind of letter that you deserve instead."

Scott presented himself at the White House next morning before Nicolay or Hay was in the office. Lincoln was in the hallway of the second floor, in dressing gown and carpet slippers, carrying a cup of tea. Seeing Scott's expression, he put on a defensive look: "What have I done wrong?"

"The letter you sent to Cameron—through Chase—deeply distressed the Secretary of War, sir. I cannot believe you intended to be cruel to a loyal supporter."

"I did not," the President said immediately. "Did it come out that way? I had my mind on something else."

"He showed it to McClure and me. It reads like a slap in the face. When the papers get it, they'll ruin him in Pennsylvania." Scott paused before adding, "Where he still has friends."

Lincoln closed his eyes and shook his head. "I just wrote it out, signed and sealed it, and gave it to Chase to give him. I shouldn't do that. I forget what I wrote."

Scott showed him his letter. Lincoln looked at it bleakly, nodding as he gulped his tea. "I didn't mean it to sound the way it does."

"But it's retrievable, sir."

"How do you retrieve the irretrievable?" Lincoln wanted to know. "This letter was delivered by Chase's hand. Simon got it. If he's sore, and I guess old Simon has a right to be, he can cause all kinds of trouble. I don't want half of Pennsylvania all riled up against me."

"No, Mr. President. I didn't think you did."

"And the truth is," said the distraught Lincoln, "I cozied him along for a month so nobody would think I had eased him out because of corruption, which nobody has proved, or that message business."

"Let's just turn back the clock," suggested Scott. "The letter you wrote, you never wrote. Why don't you sit down now and write a more cordial note, one more in your usual style, and date it two days ago, January 11?"

The President thought about that. He looked at his letter, tore it up, and wrote instead: "As you have more than once expressed a desire for a change of position, I can now gratify you consistently with my view of the public interest. I therefore propose nominating you to the Senate next Monday as minister to Russia. Very sincerely, your friend, A. Lincoln."

Scott read that, nodded, then handed Lincoln another letter: "Now here's his reply to that, dated yesterday." Cameron's letter, written with Scott and McClure late the night before, acknowledged "the kind and generous tone" of the President's letter, adding, "I thank you for the expression of your confidence in my ability, patriotism, and fidelity to public trust."

"Getting a little thick there," said Lincoln, over his spectacles.

"I propose you make it even thicker," said the railroader. "Give him another, private letter, that he can show at the court of the Czar, in case anybody needs to know how he stands with you."

"He could use a letter like that in Pennsylvania," Lincoln said, quickly grasping the harmless subterfuge, "but I write it with no political intent—just to help him with the Czar."

"Exactly. Instead of having an unnecessary political enemy, you'll have a lifelong ally. And you will have righted an unintentional wrong." Scott added that last because it was not for a former superintendent of the Pennsylvania Railroad to tell the President of the United States how to play politics.

Lincoln grinned and nearly went overboard on the next backdated letter:

"I have been only unwilling to consent to a change at a time and under circumstances which might give occasion to misconstruction . . . you bear with you the assurance of my undiminished confidence, of my affectionate esteem . . ." It went on like that. This encomium, Scott noted to himself, was about the man who had been forced down Lincoln's throat at the convention, who had failed him in office, and who was now being shipped as far away as possible to keep him from causing more trouble. And it was all backdated, part of a grand political charade. But a white lie or two was for the best, Scott assumed, if it undid harm.

"That smooths out the track," said Scott. "The passengers will never be able to hear the noise."

"I like the way you turned back the clock," said Lincoln with what seemed to Scott to be genuine admiration. "I wish we could do that on so many things."

This approval emboldened Scott: now was the moment for Lincoln to cut the rest of the deadwood out of his Cabinet, including Bates at Justice and Caleb Smith at Interior. "Sir, it's generally talked about, in the press and all over, that the Cabinet is in disarray. I'm a manager and a businessman, and in a case like that I'd try to solve more than one problem at a time."

He did not have to draw a diagram. Not only were Bates and Smith dead weight, but Seward and Chase were at each other's throats, with Blair against both. Disarray was a mild word—the Cabinet had not been so rent with dissension since Jackson's day. Now was the time, with the nation displeased with the administration and the war, for the President to reshuffle the whole deck.

"There was a farmer, in the far West," Lincoln began, his drawl deepening for the story, "whose fields were infested with skunks. So he set a trap and caught nine. He killed the first, but that made such an infernal stink that he thought he'd better let the rest go."

Scott laughed dutifully, disappointed at the answer, and made to leave. Lincoln clopped down the hall in his carpet slippers, limping a little, complaining about his corns, and put his hand on the railroader's shoulder.

"You'll have to live with Stanton for a while, Scott, so it's good for you to know what happened here. Chase is certain that Stanton got the job on Chase's recommendation. Seward is just as sure that I took Seward's advice, because he's been pushing for Stanton with nobody else knowing. Most important, McClellan wants Stanton, even goes to ground in Stanton's house, which none of the others know. And in the Senate, Wade and Chandler want Stanton too. Stanton is everybody's man—especially McClellan's—and so he's my choice, too. I need somebody that everyone thinks he has a piece of."

Scott shook his head; at least Lincoln recognized his Cabinet problem, and instead of cleaning house, hoped to find a catalyst for it. But Scott had come to know the devious Stanton well from working alongside him, and could see the underside of the man's ability to get all factions to recommend him. Scott also knew he could not work under him for more than a few months. Obsequious to superiors and tyrannical to subordinates, Stanton was a man whose personal honesty was exceeded only by a coldly impersonal duplicity. But Scott saw no use in objecting; the President's decision had been made, and

Lincoln was delighted with himself for making it seem to each faction that he was following its advice.

"It draws the Cabinet together for the first time, at a crucial time," Lincoln said. "I need that now. The people are impatient; Chase has no money and he tells me he can raise no more; the General of the Army has typhoid fever. The bottom is out of the tub."

Scott felt the giant hand squeeze and release his shoulder. He left for the War Department across the street, glad that his backdating chicanery had served some national purpose. He had saved Lincoln from a minor blunder with Cameron; as in the *Trent* affair, Lincoln was prepared to be surprisingly flexible in order to avoid big and little wars that would detract from his main purpose. Everything, in strategy and in the tactics of finding men who could best help him, was subsidiary to his central idea of being the glue for the Union, of using any means to achieve one great end. The railroader wondered if he should have put forward his fears about Stanton.

CHAPTER 8

"LITTLE MAC"

George McClellan pulled back the coverlet, put his legs over the side of the bed and felt his feet touch the carpet. He pushed up with his strong arms and came to attention. The room seemed to move around him, the face of Colonel Key became a blur, and he had to lower himself to a seated position on the bed. He closed his eyes and tried rising again.

"Are you sure you're ready for this, General?" Thomas Key, a dependable older man, looked worried. "The doctor says you're too weak to receive visitors. The fever has taken a great deal of strength out of you."

A moment before, Key had told him that Lincoln had sent word that Edwin Stanton had been named Secretary of War, and that Stanton was downstairs to pay his respects.

"I'll see Stanton." That appointment was good news. Simon Cameron had not interfered in the conduct of the war, and for that reason McClellan had not joined the chorus of those seeking to oust him, but Cameron's recent flirtation with abolition had been disturbing. None of that with Stanton, he had been assured. Stanton would trust the general-in-chief's judgment in conducting the war, and McClellan wanted to welcome him.

"You wouldn't want to pass out right in front of him, General," Key's voice said. "You haven't let anyone in the Administration know the extent of the fever's effect."

Of course not—the impatient fools would try to replace him. The typhoid had struck him as Christmas had come on, and the doctors said it might have another week to run. The fever killed the weak, but those with strong constitutions could shake it after four or five weeks. Lincoln, he knew, was worried to the point of alarm, but the disease would run its course soon enough, and no time was being wasted: the recruits needed the training in the new equipment. Basic training could not be rushed.

The general remained standing on this try, and glared at his chief aide. Key's iron-gray head became less of a blur. McClellan felt for the chair near the bed and began to dress; he had already been shaved. He asked his aide what day this was; Key said "Sunday." Then he added "Sunday, the twelfth of January." McClellan frowned; his closest men were not sure he was aware what month it was.

The general took his time; Stanton would wait. With his jacket on, though still unbuttoned, he sent Key to get the Secretary-designate.

This was good news, he repeated to himself, waiting, the perspiration beginning to run under his blouse. Cameron could no longer be of help in calming the radical politicians, who wanted another battle immediately no matter what the cost. Stanton, who was understanding and judicial, despite his rude private attacks on the President, could better keep them at bay until McClellan was ready to unveil his grand strategy.

Stanton arrived, did not dwell long on concerns about the fever—McClellan appreciated that—and announced that Lincoln had sent his name to the Senate for confirmation as Secretary of War.

"I have come, General, to confer with you as to my acceptance of this post."

McClellan asked what reason would stop him from accepting it.

"It would involve very great personal sacrifices on my part," he said. "The only possible inducement would be that I might have it in my power to aid you in the work of putting down the rebellion." At McClellan's nod, he went on: "I am ready to devote all my time, intellect, and energy to your assistance. If you wish me to accept I will do so, but only on your account. I have come to ascertain your wishes and will act accordingly."

"Accept the position," McClellan told him. He could see Stanton's face nodding. "I'll be myself again in a week, don't worry. It will be good to work together with you."

"Your improving health will not come as good news to your many enemies," said Stanton confidentially. "Even as we speak, they are counting on your death, and are already dividing among themselves your military goods and chattels."

When McClellan did not react quickly enough, Colonel Key asked for him, "In what way? Who? Where?" The general was glad Key was at his side.

"Two blocks from this spot."

McClellan's home was on the corner of Fifteenth and H; two blocks meant the White House.

"The radicals are representing to the President that you are the only person who knows the exact condition of the Army," Stanton said. "They have persuaded him that your malady may terminate fatally, and if so, it would cause great confusion and alarm. For that reason, they have caused a secret examination to take place today, this morning, of your leading commanders."

In the face of this challenge, McClellan felt a surge of anger; his mind became clearer. "Who have been summoned?"

"Franklin, because he knows most of your plans," Stanton answered, "Meigs, the quartermaster, and Irvin McDowell."

"I'm certain that General Franklin has been loyal to me."

"You're right, General. That's where I've been getting the information about Lincoln's meetings on your army, sir. He wants you to know that General McDowell—"

"That idiot almost lost the war at Bull Run." After that disaster, into which McDowell had permitted himself to be pushed by the political judgment of Lincoln and the unpardonable concurrence of General Scott, Irvin McDowell had been demoted. Now, McClellan assumed, this lickspittle general was trying to snatch back his command. He was probably telling Lincoln exactly what he wanted to hear.

"McDowell," continued Stanton, "is being consulted by Lincoln, Chase, and Seward. He's still under your command, but he's being asked what he would do if he were in your place."

"Lincoln has no excuse for undermining my authority that way." Then McClellan had a second thought: "Actually, he has a justification—he came by here the other night and I wouldn't see him. The guard told him I was sleeping." That was unfortunate; once before McClellan had sent the President and his young secretary, Hay, away without an audience, but that was to show them he was not at the President's beck and call. Other times he had taken refuge in Stanton's house to avoid the prowling President. This time he had been ill, not yet recovered from the critical period of the typhoid, which gave Lincoln the excuse to talk to other generals in his command about the Army of the Potomac. McClellan wished now that he had not insulted Lincoln by not seeing him the first time, but that was past.

"Yesterday Lincoln said to McDowell and Franklin"—Stanton lowered his voice and McClellan had to lean forward, which made his head hurt—"that if you weren't doing anything with your army in Virginia, he'd like to borrow it for a while."

"He used those words?"

"That's what Lincoln said. He's fairly distraught, I hear, what with the money problem, and the general depression over this *Trent* backdown, and the noise from the abolitionists in his own party."

"He's weak," said McClellan, swaying for a moment, regaining his balance by force of will. "Lincoln means well, but your assessment of him, I fear, is correct—he is putty in their hands. Hand me my sash."

Key buttoned his commander's jacket, draping the red sash over his shoulder and down across the decorations.

"Lincoln promised two months ago he would not hurry me," McClellan recalled. "He said he would help me move the Army at my own pace. Now he's showing panic in the face of political pressure, as you said he would."

"McDowell's a purely political general," Stanton agreed, "and a Republican. Wade wants him back. When slaves in Virginia come into the lines, McDowell frees them."

McClellan was relieved to have the astute lawyer's services available to him amidst the gaggle of geese that made up Lincoln's Cabinet. "Fugitive slaves, not working for hostile forces, should be returned to their owners," McClellan said firmly. "That was my order."

Which reminded the general of the singers. He turned to Key. "Did General McDowell let those damned singers come back?"

A bunch of young radicals calling themselves "the Hutchinson Family Singers," who entertained the Union troops, had been singing an abolitionist song composed by the poet Whittier, and McClellan had ordered them off all military bases. That had started a row with Wade and Chandler in the Congress: those abolitionists claimed that his expulsion of the radical singers was further proof McClellan was a "slave-catching general," out to prolong the war by not fighting it, until the North tired of the struggle.

"No sir, Fitz-John Porter has seen to it the singers will not be allowed near our men again."

McClellan regarded himself in the mirror, squaring his shoulders further. He hardly resembled his old self; he had lost twenty pounds and his face was unnaturally sallow, which was why Nellie had to fight back tears when she looked at him. He wished he had a shirt with a narrower collar to hide the weight loss. "What other mischief is McDowell up to?"

"He has recommended a general movement of the Army of the Potomac south and west toward Manassas," Stanton replied. "In your absence, he proposes to engage the rebels there, drive down to Richmond. Good railroad lines to supply a siege."

"Bull Run all over again!" McClellan exploded, then made a successful effort at controlling himself. McDowell, who was probably glorying in this "examination" he had to submit to, was not all that bad a soldier in the field, but had no grasp of strategy. To undertake an offensive against an enemy with superior numbers—over 200,000 to McClellan's 115,000, according to Pinkerton's estimates—in heavily wooded Virginia, as the worst cold of winter set in, was to invite another disaster. And to lose such a battle near the Union capital would tempt the victorious Confederates to seize Washington, as Beauregard should have done, the first time the Union was routed at Manassas.

Thinking ahead to the examination of his generals, especially Franklin, by the Lincoln Cabinet, McClellan was suddenly chilled by the possibility of the leakage of the most important military secret of all.

"Has anyone mentioned a plan about a different approach to Richmond?"

"Well—sort of, General." Stanton looked troubled. "General Franklin first said nothing should be done until you were consulted. Then, to head off the adoption of McDowell's offensive from Manassas, he told Lincoln there was another way."

"Did he say anything about the York River?"

"He mentioned it in passing, but that's what they are planning to ask him about today."

"Damn." McClellan had a brilliant strategy in mind, one that would avoid the high casualties of a grinding, yard-by-yard attack through Virginia. He envisioned putting the Army of the Potomac *on* the Potomac—on the river, in gunboats and other vessels, sailing silently down the Potomac to the Chesapeake, then up the York River to a landing point within short striking distance of Richmond. By such a daring maneuver, he could cut off the Confederate force at Yorktown and capture their entire garrison on the Peninsula. This plan would enable the Union forces to outflank Richmond's imposing fortifications and take the city from the rear. The plan was stunning, bold and imaginative, a raid on a vast scale worthy of a Napoleon.

There was risk: the presence of a Confederate army at Manassas would scare the politicians in Washington, since the capital would be relatively undefended, but he was certain that the Confederates at Manassas would be forced to withdraw when they heard that the decisive battle of the war was to be fought at Richmond. The Peninsula plan had the element of surprise, sure to be vitiated if the entire Cabinet and the political generals were let in on the secret. Lincoln would have to be informed; the others had no need to know.

"I have not been asked to be at the examination," Stanton was saying.

"Do I have a single defender in this cabal?"

"Blair, perhaps, but he's slippery," said Stanton. "It's most important that I be confirmed immediately, without any hearings, so I can work with you in averting another disaster."

McClellan would have to pass the word to the more sensible senators, who were in the majority in the Senate, to confirm Stanton immediately.

Blair was the only West Pointer in the lot, McClellan noted. It sickened him to think that the others were willing to see his great army, which he had almost brought up to fighting condition, cut to pieces, driven to rout and permanent defeat just to satisfy the impatience of a few abolitionist rabble-rousers. They had all kowtowed to McClellan only three months ago, when that army was in a shambles and no one else could rally them; now that the army was nearly in condition, almost up to strength, the same crowd was trying to grab the army and ruin it again. Feverish or not, McClellan would not permit that.

"You may have trouble with Chase," said Stanton. "He's been spending a lot of time with Wade and Chandler on that Joint Committee. They're after your hide."

"Not Chase—I've neutralized him." In early December, before the fever struck him down, the general had heard that Chase needed an infusion of confidence. McClellan undertook the necessary bolstering that helped that profoundly truthful man persuade New York and Philadelphia bankers to support the government with loans. Chase had been properly honored by the general's confidence when McClellan gave him the outline of his plan for a Peninsula campaign, seizing Richmond from the rear. He had sworn Chase to secrecy; as far as McClellan knew, that oath had been honored, but the Treasury Secretary was still a member of the radical crowd. McDowell would be "his" general, beholden to Chase for his return; McClellan assumed that one reason Stanton was alerting him to this White House meeting was to avert such a diminution of the power of the new Secretary of War.

McClellan could not afford to let his command authority be further undercut, or his plan spilled before the politicians. "Colonel, tell my groom to saddle Kentuck."

"I have a carriage right outside, General—"

"I can ride." If George Brinton McClellan could walk, he could ride. His problem was getting down the stairs, not climbing on his horse. Leaning on Key's arm, he maneuvered his way downstairs, stopping every few steps to slow the spinning, Stanton following behind. His army would fight for him; it would not fight for McDowell or the other politicians. He had whipped it into shape; the officers and men of the Army of the Potomac trusted him; he would not see them led to slaughter.

A cheer went up from his bodyguard—twenty mounted men—as their leader emerged from the house for the first time in too long. He smiled, then frowned them to attention.

Kentuck was brought forward; it made McClellan feel better to stroke the steed's neck, then to heave himself into the comfortable saddle he had designed. Astride his horse, he was relieved to find that his dizziness and weakness had passed. The general was prepared to defend his army from the insidious flanking movement of the politicians.

Montgomery Blair, picking his way across the frozen mud of Pennsylvania Avenue from his own house to the President's on that Sunday morning, was hailed by Thomas Scott, the Assistant Secretary of War.

"I'll be representing the War Department at this meeting," Scott told him. "Cameron is out and Stanton is not yet in."

"And McClellan is out, it seems, and McDowell is not yet back in," Blair replied. He trusted Scott—professional, straightforward, no political ambition—and would have advised Lincoln to put him at the head of the department instead of the treacherous Stanton. He found it troubling that Lincoln would not consult the Blairs on such a momentous decision. His father was certain the Stanton appointment was Seward's doing, and boded ill for the country.

"Stanton's going to be my new boss," Scott said cheerlessly, leaning into the January wind. "I hear you had some harsh things to say about him."

Only that he was a liar and a traitor, Blair thought, saying instead, "I hope I'm wrong. But he bears watching." It occurred to the Postmaster General that Lincoln, in selecting men as different as McClellan and Stanton to conduct the war, was prepared to make a great many personality allowances in order to get an effective army in the field. But perhaps the selection of Stanton meant the end of McClellan.

"Stanton's a hard worker, though, and decisive. God knows we need that." Scott pointed to a large van, drawn up to the side of the War Department across the street. "His appointment became public today, he doesn't take office till next week after the Senate approves, and he's already got his hands on the telegraph service."

The head of the postal service did not know that. "He just grabbed it?"

"Right out of McClellan's headquarters, before anybody could say boo. He's going to concentrate all the nation's telegraph service into one room adjacent to his office. Nobody in the Union will be able to send a wire without Stanton seeing it. He'll know what generals in the field are telling each other, as well as what they are reporting to us."

"Cabinet members—" he left the rest unsaid.

Scott shot him a wry smile. "If your brother in Missouri sends you a telegram, even in code, Stanton gets it first. Those are the orders."

Dangerous; control of communications was power. Blair would have to be careful Stanton did not poach on his preserve of the U.S. mail. "I imagine that telegraph office will be where Lincoln will be spending a lot of time," he noted. Stanton was doubly smart: proximity to power was also power.

In the Cabinet Room, Blair took his regular seat as Lincoln motioned Scott to the place left empty by the hapless Cameron. Seward and Chase were there, but not Welles or Smith or Bates; for some reason, Lincoln wanted this meeting small and unofficial. Three generals awaited interrogation, McDowell alone looking confident.

Montgomery Blair was ambivalent about Irvin McDowell. Six months before, the Blairs had joined in the urging of McDowell into action across the Potomac, and under that pressure the general did not hesitate. In retrospect, he should have hesitated; military commanders have an obligation to resist unsound civilian orders. Blair was angry at himself for being impatient, angrier at McDowell for not saving them all from that impatience. They were all guilty for Bull Run, but McDowell was guiltier than any.

Blair wondered why he had been invited to this stealthy replacement of McClellan. Presumably, Lincoln wanted a Blair present in these meetings as a counter to Chase and Seward, both of whom had already lost faith in McClellan: Chase had been persuaded that McClellan was a "slave-catcher" who did not want to pursue the war vigorously, and Seward was convinced that the commander was on the verge of death and would not soon be ready for action. But Blair felt uncomfortable at being there—he did not savor being part of a cabal operating behind a commanding general's back. McDowell, standing at a map on the wall, was pointing out how the rebels in Virginia could be attacked without jeopardizing Washington.

"What do you think, Judge?" Lincoln wanted an opinion from Blair about McDowell's plan to move in the next week, as Lincoln and the others—and the country—wanted the army to do.

"Before Judge Blair gives us the benefit of his military experience," Secretary Seward interrupted, "let me tell you something about enemy strength. An Englishman whom I consider reliable has just come to me from Richmond, Manassas, and Centreville. A military man. He said the rebel forces were in excellent condition—well shod, clothed, and fed—and that he estimated their number at one hundred thousand."

"*One* hundred thousand?" That was a surprise to Lincoln, who had been assured by McClellan, Pinkerton, and all the generals in the Army of the Potomac that the Confederate Army in Virginia numbered over two hundred thousand. "If that's true, we outnumber the enemy by three to two."

"*If* it's true," said Blair. "I think we are safer, and wiser, going by the Pinkerton estimate than by the unverified judgment of a single Englishman."

"Going by McClellan's estimate, then, what do you think?" Lincoln—a trifle more nervous and impatient than usual, Blair thought—wanted a firm opinion.

"I fear it may be Bull Run all over again," Blair said, to the open dismay of the men around the table, only General Franklin excluded. Blair began to explain why, and stopped abruptly.

General McDowell, face reddening, was staring toward the doorway. All eyes followed his to the form of a gaunt but resolute George McClellan. "Little Mac," the uninvited man, was present and would have to be accounted for.

Lincoln rose, went to the doorway, and clasped McClellan's hand. "Are you sure your health permits?" he asked in what seemed to Blair genuine solicitude. "We could not wait."

McClellan said nothing, just took his place at the Cabinet table and looked sourly at McDowell standing at the map of Virginia.

"I am presenting this plan at the President's direct order," explained Mc-Dowell to the general-in-chief, a note of apology or chagrin in his voice. McClellan remained impassive. McDowell, clearing his throat and looking for a glass of water, hesitated before going on. But at Lincoln's urging, he laid out his—and Lincoln's—plan for striking directly at the enemy strength across the Potomac, twenty miles from Washington, and then driving down toward Richmond. With his superior military officer now present, McDowell went into order-of-battle detail, stressing the logistical support of two railroad lines that could supply a train to enable the Army to lay siege to Richmond.

When the man at the map finished reviewing the plan, the President looked to McClellan for a response. The general did not respond. Blair thought that wise; his silence made everybody in the room nervous. McClellan was not without his high cards in this poker game. If the Young Napoleon blew up and stalked out, he could take a large part of his army with him—such was the control he had over his men.

"In my opinion," the unhappy McDowell concluded, "we will succeed, by repeated blows, in crushing out the force in our front, even if it is our equal in numbers and strength."

Blair believed that judgment to be militarily unsound; with equal forces, the dug-in defense in home territory had the great advantage. Although the new breech-loading rifles made it possible for attackers to reload rapidly, that increased firepower had been more than offset by the rifling of the musket barrels—the defense could now shoot a ball three times as far and with more accuracy. When defenders were shooting at men coming across an open field, the difference between a two-hundred-yard range and a five-hundred-yard range was the difference between defeat and victory.

"And in my opinion," McDowell concluded, "the time is ripe for such an attack." He was no longer looking toward Lincoln, but seeking some assurance from his commanding general.

After a long pause, McClellan said only, "You're entitled to have any opinion you please." He added nothing to that. If he wanted to show scorn for his subordinate's attempt to curry favor with civilians to dislodge him from command, Blair thought he had succeeded.

The silence became painful. "I made this presentation," McDowell said lamely, "because of the critical nature of your illness."

"I have regained my health. This examination may now cease."

Chase leaned over toward Lincoln, whispered something, and then spoke up. "The purpose of this meeting is to determine the military plans in detail, for our approval or disapproval. General McClellan, proceed."

McClellan slowly shook his head. "The purpose you express is entirely new to me. I do not recognize the Secretary of the Treasury in any way as my official superior, and I deny your right to question me on the military affairs in my charge."

Chase leaned his head forward and his big voice filled the room. "I want to ask you a direct question, General. I speak as one with the responsibility to raise the money to finance this army—which, by the way, is not your army, but the United States's army. My question is this: What do you intend doing with the Army of the Potomac, and when do you intend doing it?"

"The President and the Secretary of War alone have the right to interrogate me."

Chase set his face hard, turned and whispered to the President again.

After a moment Lincoln said, "General Franklin here says there might be another approach to Richmond, by water down the Potomac. Perhaps he will make that more specific for us."

General Franklin was most uncomfortable. "I raised that possibility only because I knew it was in General McClellan's mind. If the general-in-chief wishes to discuss it, he's here."

Again McClellan said nothing. Blair, on McClellan's side in this unexpected confrontation, wished he would lay out his plan for a bold water-and-land assault on Richmond by way of the James River. The idea struck him as infinitely more effective, and far less costly in casualties, than a grinding overland campaign beginning at Manassas. But the young general remained mute.

Lincoln filled the silence with some nervous talk about details of the McDowell plan, but Blair felt for the first time that the President was not in charge of the meeting. Lincoln's voice ran on and dribbled to a stop.

"The case is so clear," said McClellan finally, "that a blind man could see it. First, I need to know how many additional forces are to be placed under my command in a general advance."

Blair knew what he was getting at. Lincoln had held back some forces from McClellan's Army of the Potomac, putting them under Generals Burnside and Butler, who operated best alone, and whose presence in the vicinity gave the capital's residents more confidence. McClellan, under attack by his political foes, was defending his position by taking the offense, using the occasion to gather more forces under his direct command.

Lincoln temporized, and Blair assumed the President did not want to make a decision or a promise to McClellan without knowing whether the general was going to adopt the plan to strike through Manassas and on to Richmond. Seward fidgeted in his chair. Tom Scott was hunched forward, arms on the table, apparently amazed that the management of the war had come to this impasse.

Blair managed to catch McClellan's eye and shook his head imperceptibly to warn him about insubordination. The general could not stand mute, not if the President wanted him to speak.

"I would like," said the general-in-chief, "to see some diversionary action in the West. Kentucky. Or Missouri." That, Blair knew, was something, but not good enough. McClellan closed his eyes for a moment, as if to steady himself, and then said what was on his mind: "I am very unwilling to reveal my plans to this gathering. In military matters, the fewer people who know about them, the better."

"I am the Secretary of the Treasury, responsible for financing the war," said Chase. "This is the Secretary of State, and the Postmaster General is here because of his military background. Here, at the head of the table, is the President of the United States. Which one of us do you think should not be trusted with knowledge of your plans?"

"I will reveal my plans," said McClellan coolly, "and thereby endanger the security of my army, only if I receive a direct order to do so. A written order."

"If that is your decision," warned Chase, "you are a ruined man." He resumed his private talking to the President.

Blair thought McClellan had overstepped; Chase thus abused would be his implacable enemy, and the demand for a direct order, especially in writing, was an insult to the President. The Quartermaster General, Meigs, drew his chair around to McClellan's and spoke to him quietly and urgently. Blair could not hear their conversation clearly, but Meigs was saying something about being "not respectful" and McClellan was murmuring, "Can't keep a secret . . . I don't want my plans in the *Tribune* tomorrow morning."

Eyes swung to the only man in the room capable of giving the order to force McClellan's hand. Blair knew that Lincoln needed a way out: he had been embarrassed by McClellan's unexpected presence in a series of meetings that had been intended to goad him to action or take over his command. Now Chase and McClellan had put it up to the President: Who was in charge of the army? Blair considered interrupting to deflect the challenge, but then decided to see how Lincoln would handle it.

"Well, General," said Lincoln after the caucusing, "I think you had better tell us what your plans are."

"Sir, if you have any confidence in me, you will not find it necessary to entrust my designs to the judgment of others. If your confidence is so slight as to require that my opinions be fortified by those of other persons, it would be wiser to replace me with someone"—he looked toward Irvin McDowell—"fully possessing your confidence."

Tom Scott broke that tension with a practical note, spoken in a friendly way to a fellow former railroad executive. "George, everybody in this room knows in general terms about your Peninsula idea. It's no big secret here."

"My point exactly," said McClellan. "The President knows the direction of my thinking, and so does the Secretary of the Treasury. Why should it be necessary to set forth details that would soon be spread all over Washington and become known to the enemy?"

Seward stood up, buttoned his coat, and said almost merrily, "Well, Mr. President, I think the meeting had better break up. We're not likely to make much out of General McClellan." Blair looked at the man with a mixture of amazement and disgust: it was all a game to him.

"Wait a moment," Lincoln said to Seward, who promptly sat down. "General, answer me this. Do you have, in your own mind, some particular time fixed when a movement will be commenced?"

When the general just stared at him, the President amended his question. "I am not asking you to reveal what that time is, but I want to know if you have a fixed time in your mind."

"I have."

"Then," rejoined the President, trying to look as if he had asserted his authority, "I shall adjourn the meeting."

Score one for the Young Napoleon, thought Blair. As all rose, Blair noticed that McClellan, who was next to him at the table, staggered. Casually, Blair put an arm around the general's shoulders, as if in a collegial way, but supporting him under his arm. The general's body was trembling. Blair engaged him in idle conversation, doing most of the talking, and helped him through the front door of the President's house and onto his horse, urging him to hurry home. Rivulets of sweat were pouring down his face, and the cold air would not do him any good.

Blair and Scott stopped at the corner of Seventeenth and Pennsylvania, puffing vapors into the air. "Judge, there's something we can do to help the President," Scott said. "He and McClellan are going to be arguing for weeks over which route to take to Richmond. That's what Little Mac wants, to delay till spring, when he thinks his men will be in shape."

"That's too late."

"Right," said Scott. "If we don't win, we lose. Now at today's meeting, you remember Little Mac said he wanted a Western diversion. I have a plan in hand that may turn out to be much more than that. The idea is to ignore the fortified Mississippi River; instead, to send a force to Ohio to take Forts Henry and Donelson, and then invade the South down the Tennessee River."

Blair knew all about the Tennessee plan—Anna Carroll had gone over it with the Blairs, and probably others, asking them to press for its adoption with Lincoln. He had not; Miss Carroll was a persuasive pamphleteer with wide-ranging political connections, but it struck him as absurd to consider any woman to be a military strategist. "You think it makes sense?"

"It makes a lot more sense to me," said Scott, "than McClellan's notion of leaving Washington undefended while he sails down the river and up the Peninsula to Richmond."

Blair did not agree—he preferred taking Richmond by maneuver, before defenses could be constructed—but Scott had a point: a Western diversion was a worthy idea. "Then urge it on Halleck out there—or on his generals, Grant and Sherman," Blair said. "We need some success soon."

"It needs more serious backing than mine," Scott hinted. Blair caught his meaning.

"If it's your judgment that the Tennessee plan has merit, I'll talk to the President. Meanwhile, you plant it in Stanton's head and make it his idea. I don't think Halleck out West will like it, but McClellan won't object—it takes the pressure off him."

Scott agreed. "You'll never believe who came up with the Tennessee plan first. Of course, the idea is obvious—the only thing is, nobody else put it before the President."

"Don't underestimate the daughters of Maryland, Colonel."

Scott grinned. "Don't send any telegrams you don't want Stanton to read."

They parted, Scott to the War Department, Blair across the street to his house. Anna Carroll had helped get Frank Blair out of jail when Frémont lost his temper; the Blairs would help her press her plan, now that a sensible fellow like Scott had judged it to be sound. The focus of attention out West would give McClellan a month or two, which he needed, and would prevent another McDowell blunder at Bull Run.

Little Mac was much abused by the radical faction these days, and Blair feared his challenge to Chase today would worsen the enmity. McClellan surely had the confidence of his men, who would follow him to hell, but the problem was that he was reluctant to lead them there. A cautious man—

necessarily so, considering that another major military blunder could lose the war for the Union—but with one noticeable drawback: vanity, which combined with political ambition, could lead to trouble. As his conduct at today's meeting showed, McClellan combined personal courage with congenital stubbornness. He showed he could storm a citadel and take the high ground, but Blair wished he had shown the maturity to win over the men he had forced to back away. The general had every right to be furious at the way Lincoln had gone around him to his field commanders, but had no right to treat the President and Chase as his equals. Blair charitably attributed that lack of judgment to the fact that the man was fighting for his position while concealing a raging fever.

At least McClellan was accepted throughout the nation for what he was: a first-class military man, top of his class at the Point, author of a brilliant report on the Crimean War and its lessons for the U.S. Army, and a leader capable of inspiring the kind of devotion that common soldiers reposited only in a Napoleon. He was "the man of the hour" because no other military man came a close second. Blair hoped the generals out West, now under "Old Brains" Halleck, were as soldierly. One of them, Sam Grant, was a West Pointer, but it was widely reported he drank, and had been pushed out of the army for cause; on top of that, he was a failure in civilian life. The other, William Sherman, had been a successful enough banker in California, ran a military academy in Louisiana, and was sustained politically by his brother in the U.S. Senate; but Sherman had not shown much leadership under McDowell at Bull Run; he had an obsession about the press, and the reporters were fond of hinting in print that he was slightly deranged. Not much of a group to rest the fate of a nation on, especially with Halleck known to be a jealous, small-minded man with a minimum of battlefield experience.

The Union generals were up against Sidney Johnston, the former Secretary of War of the Republic of Texas, and thought by most West Pointers, Blair included, to be the best all-round soldier in America. Like Robert Lee, whom Blair thought overrated, Sidney Johnston had been offered high command of the Union armies by Lincoln, but he had turned down the offer as Winfield Scott's second-in-command and chosen instead the Confederate Western command. As expected, Sidney Johnston had easily trounced Frémont, and was now fighting Halleck's superior forces to a standstill. If the war did not end soon, Blair feared that Albert Sidney Johnston would be named supreme commander of the Southern forces, and his theories of the "offensive defensive" in modern warfare would be devastating to the kind of invasion Lincoln had in mind.

Blair knocked the dirty snow off his boots on the stand outside his door and pulled out his key. At that moment a man with a sack on his back came up to the door and asked, "Is this number 1601?" Blair said it was. "You ought to put the number on the door, mister, it'll make it easier for us. We've begun regular delivery of the mail."

"You mean," Blair smiled, "we don't have to pick it up at the post office anymore?"

"That's right," said the postman, handing over a couple of letters. "You may want to put a box out here for it; they have them in the stores now."

Postmaster General Blair nodded, took the letters and went inside. The war was stalemated, the Northern spirit was sagging, the Union general was sick and refused to admit it, the Cabinet was divided and would soon be afflicted with a manipulative War Secretary, and the President was not sure of himself. But amidst it all the nation had instituted mail service right to the addressee's door, and on a daily basis. Not a major event in a country in such straits, but some little progress that made Blair feel his long days were not for naught.

CHAPTER 9

A NOSE SLIGHTLY PUG

The brick Chase mansion on Sixth and E looked imposing to John Hay. He flipped the brass knocker and waited in the cold, turning his fur hat over in his hands, his thoughts of the tense session with McClellan fading in anticipation of a private meeting with the most adored and envied young woman in Washington. He reminded himself not to let his ill feelings about Mrs. Lincoln show to her younger social rival—no "Her Satanic Majesty" cracks in Miss Chase's presence. Not even "La Reine," as Nicolay called her; only "Mrs. Lincoln," or at most, with the slightest shade of irony, "Madame."

This long-sought rendezvous had been arranged, of all places, at the Smithsonian Institution after that terrible blowhard speech by Horace Greeley. The President was in attendance, sitting on the platform showing the greatest respect to the editor of the *New York Tribune*. That hot-and-cold patriot who, Hay remembered, had been willing to surrender the cause of the Union after Bull Run, was at his abolitionist peak as Stanton came to power. "By condoning slavery," the editor had publicly wagged a finger at Lincoln, "we cherish the viper which has its fangs now fastened in the national breast."

After the lecture, Hay had gone up to the platform to have the President introduce him to the famed editor, who might be an inconsistent political supporter but who could one day help a fledgling poet. Lincoln was explaining to Greeley that he hoped his plan of compensated, gradual emancipation could be presented to the border states persuasively, not menacingly, and the editor was shaking his head, no.

"What a wonderful man," Hay had heard spoken behind him, and turned to look at the most level set of challenging gray-green eyes that had ever set his loins contracting.

"I have felt that about the President," Hay responded, "ever since I went to work for him."

"Him, too," was all she said. He had seized his chance to invite her to Willard's for a glass of champagne, and she countered with an invitation to tea at the Chase house. The date had been postponed twice—both times by her—but the time had come.

He lifted and released the cold brass knocker again.

She opened the door herself, which surprised him; two servants were in the background. His poet's heart leaped at her guarded smile and the incredible, fresh beauty that she wore so casually, then as suddenly sank when he real-

ized she was too tall. Maybe she was wearing higher heels especially for this
occasion—or perhaps, the crazy thought struck him, he was getting shorter.

"I'm overdressed for our meeting," she said easily, reaching for his arm
and drawing him in. She was in a stiff white silk gown with a sprig of jasmine
on the shoulder. "We have guests coming at eight, and I didn't want to take
time from our tea to dress."

He liked that. Why didn't she invite him for dinner?

"You're invited to stay, of course," she said, "if you like a dreary group of
bankers from Philadelphia." Good; such a gathering would not show him in
his best light, and it would be gauche to appear too eager. He declined, saying
the President expected him back for some early evening work.

"Tea, or sherry, or whiskey?"

He would have preferred a hot cup of tea—he had walked from the White
House, ten blocks across the frozen mud—but that would not have been
manly. He told the butler he would have whiskey.

"Bourbon and branch water for two," she ordered, saying confidentially to
him, "It gets my color up—better than using rouge." Hay liked her quick
intimacy. "That was some confrontation with the Young Napoleon," she said,
cutting quickly to the core of his life. "Father said McClellan acted abomina-
bly. How could he do that? Does Little Mac think he's going to be dictator?"

She was going a little fast for him. Hay had been outside the Cabinet Room
all weekend, overhearing what he could of the secret examination, and then
he and Nicolay had talked it over afterward with Lincoln. Lincoln said he
had thought McClellan—whose surprising arrival, Hay knew, had embarrassed the President terribly—had acted like a man.

With Kate looking right at him, expecting an intelligent answer, Hay
stalled. "Do you think we need a dictator?"

"Might not be such a bad idea," she said offhandedly. "That's what the
Romans did when the nation was in danger. But not McClellan. He dithers
too much to be a dictator."

"His men swear by him. Wasn't for him, we wouldn't have an army at all."
That was the defense Lincoln put forward to others, even when privately
upset with the general's refusal to grasp the political damage of military
delay, or when the general-in-chief failed to take the commander in chief fully
into his confidence. Lincoln liked to hear the fine details of military plans,
down to regimental placements and types of bridges; it gave him the sense
that the planner was serious.

"Do you always say the safe thing, Mr. Hay?"

That shaft went home; he had been saying the safe thing ever since he
finished his studies at Brown, certainly since he had come to the District of
Columbia. Working in the President's mansion put a young man in the safe-
thing habit.

"I do not know you well enough," he replied, "to say the unsafe. I am,
after all, the keeper of the President's conscience."

She affected a deep sigh; in her tight dress her breasts, not large, became
noticeable for a moment. Hay had come to Washington at twenty-two, a
virgin—maybe. The maybe was the girl in Springfield who claimed he had
penetrated her during their passionate farewell, but he could not be certain
that she was not just being kind. In a year in the nation's capital, with ready

Kate Chase

access to the maidens at counselor Eames's parties, and with the power drawn from his proximity to the President to appear mysterious and secretive, John Hay had cut a swath. He liked the phrase. He wished desperately he could engage in swath-cutting with Kate Chase and knew the first step required him to say something daring but not indiscreet.

She leaned forward and put both hands on his knees, a movement that he had never experienced before. "How old are you, John Hay?"

"Twenty-three," he said. He almost added "and a half," but that might not be taken as humorous.

"Almost my age. We are, both of us, very young to be doing what we're doing. I am the hostess and political confidante of the Secretary of the Treasury, the man who represents the most enlightened and progressive elements of the Republican Party. You are the private secretary of the most powerful man in the nation, if he only knew how to use his power."

"He knows," Hay interrupted, to say something daring, "but he has to maneuver the country ahead of him." How could he tell her what he really knew of Lincoln? Not the Honest Abe of the cartoons, or the timorous procrastinator of today's meeting in the Cabinet room—but the detached, remote man, hiding in his melancholia, supremely confident of his own destiny and privately a bit amused by the "great men" with whom he had surrounded himself, Kate Chase's father emphatically included. Lincoln cultivated his modest nature and mocked all pretension, but Hay thought it absurd to call him a modest man. No great man was ever modest. Lincoln's easygoing intellectual arrogance and unconscious assumption of superiority confounded men like Chase and Sumner, but the patent-leather, kid-glove set knew no more of Lincoln than an owl knew of a comet blazing into its blinking eyes.

Kate Chase, who inspired him to such stunning images, was obviously trying to knife through his defenses. "Look, John Hay, you and I are in the same boat. I want to be your friend and your ally. We could help each other. Am I being too direct? Do you prefer women who wait for you to take the lead?"

"No," he said truthfully, "I like straight dealing. I admire that." The "admire" was better—why couldn't he be as quick with the right words in his conversation as in his diary?

"You're not accustomed to it," she teased. "You like the fluttering eyelashes of those girls at the Eameses', the pouting and the wide eyes and the giggling. I don't giggle."

"Never?"

That stopped her. "I suppose I giggle when I'm tickled," she said seriously, "but I don't waste a lot of time flirting or making small talk. If that sort of thing is what you're looking for—"

"Everything I tell you," he assured her, beginning to enjoy himself, "will be pregnant with meaning. Unfortunately, you already know all the state secrets I know."

"You're being silly. Here's your drink." She was a touch on the serious side, but perhaps her earnestness would be leavened with time. "Why do you call Mrs. Lincoln 'the Hellcat?' "

She had waited until he was in the middle of his first swallow of bourbon and he almost coughed it up. "Who said I said that?"

"Let's never ask each other a question like that, John—we both hear a great deal. I don't expect you to admit what you said about Mrs. Lincoln, but it shows you have good judgment."

Must have been Stoddard, the third secretary, who tattled; the damned little clerk was always buttering up the Hellcat. Hay made a mental note to watch what he said around Stoddard, and to warn Nico to do the same. "In my youthful exuberance—" he began, and Kate cut him off.

"She's a disgrace and we both know it. My heart goes out to the President, encumbered with a Southern sympathizer in the midst of a rebellion." That was putting in plain words what people only hinted at: Mrs. Lincoln's Southern relatives, enlisted in the Confederate Army, were a source of embarrassment more profound than her inclination to go into debt on wardrobe and furnishings and "flub-dubs," as all the carpets were now called. "I trust you, John Hay. I wouldn't say something like that to anybody else."

He began to feel a bit manipulated; there was such a thing as being too direct about being direct. Yet she could be a valuable ally, and perhaps he and she could bridge some gaps between Chase and Lincoln—on compensation for slave owners, for example—and being allies could lead to becoming friends, which in turn could lead to becoming who-knew-what. Could he hope to compete with a man of the world like Lord Lyons? More to the point, could he trust a woman of the radical world like Kate Chase? He decided to set a small trap to see if she would tell him the truth on a more substantive matter.

"You were wrong about McClellan in the meeting today," he confided. "It was important that he take charge. That's what generals are for. His alternative plan is worth thinking about." Hay was fishing; did she know about the Peninsula plan, the inland sea route that would avoid the casualties of a direct strike through Manassas?

"My father had to drag it out of him," Kate said. "Was Lincoln told before this of a Peninsula plan?"

"Of course," said Hay, and slipped the test question in naturally. "Did your father know?"

"No, today was the first he knew of it. And it was important he know, because he would have to finance the purchase of the extra barges."

Kate Chase was lying. He was surprised; she lied as easily as sipping bourbon. Chase had known of McClellan's plans as early as a month ago, back when Wade and Chandler and the other radicals were still high on McClellan. That was certain: Montgomery Blair had come back to the Mansion that afternoon to tell the President how he had helped the feverish and trembling McClellan onto his horse, and to pass on the information that McClellan was furious at Chase for pretending he had not been informed a month before of McClellan's Peninsula plan. Chase was following the abolitionist signals to dump Little Mac, who was insufficiently anti-slavery, even if it required concealing his foreknowledge of McClellan's plans. And Kate lied about it with the greatest of ease. Some ally.

"What does your father think of the Peninsula plan?"

"I don't know," she lied again. "He hasn't had a chance to think about it." Or to talk it over again with Ben Wade and perhaps Horace Greeley. "I can tell you a plan he won't like, however. Anna Carroll—do you know her, the little woman who writes for money?—has been in to see Father several times about some notion she has to send an army down the Tennessee River."

Hay feigned ignorance; Assistant Secretary Scott had been espousing Miss Carroll's idea, complete with memorials and maps, for more than a month. Considering McClellan's new interest in a Western diversion, Lincoln was coming around to the idea, if General Halleck in the West, along with his two unreliable commanders, Grant and Sherman, could be sold on it.

"It's all a plot by the Blairs," Kate said, "to take the pressure off McClellan. If they can focus attention on the West—Missouri, where the Blair family is powerful—that will let McNapoleon sit here all winter. They pay Anna Carroll's room bill at the Ebbitt House—she's not to be trusted."

He had not yet heard the "McNapoleon" derogation; it was cutting. "And yet I have heard your father praising Miss Carroll to the President," Hay said. Secretary Chase liked Miss Carroll, he knew—was this not-to-be-trusted view really the Treasury Secretary's, or was it the result of some jealousy or possessiveness on the part of his daughter? On the other hand, could something be going on between the ultra-dignified and ostentatiously pious Salmon P. Chase and the passionate little pamphleteer? If so, did Kate consider it a threat of some kind?

Hay put in another barb, just for fun: "Miss Carroll just came back from an assignment in St. Louis, probably about the plan you're talking about. I don't know what it is about her—most of the men in the Cabinet really like her. The President, too. And they say Buchanan, and Fillmore—"

"She must have been attractive when young," Kate said coolly. "Until very recently, she was a slave owner. She and Rose O'Neal Greenhow used to go to the same parties."

"Now there's a rebel," said Hay, pleased to be able to change the subject, "with the courage of her convictions. The Wild Rose drove poor Pinkerton crazy and she's still stirring up trouble at the Old Capitol Prison. Smuggled a letter out to the Richmond newspapers complaining to Seward about her treatment and there's been hell to pay."

"They ought to hang her—she's a spy." Hay assumed that Kate felt roughly the same about Anna Carroll. All these powerful women were somewhat on the severe and unforgiving side.

"Brady, the photographer, wants to take a picture of Mrs. Greenhow and her daughter in prison," he offered. "Kind of before-and-after. The President will send him over to Stanton." It was good for Kate to understand that he knew what the President would do.

"Edwin Stanton will let him," she said with certainty. "I suspect Rose may have something on Stanton. What do you think of our new Secretary of War?"

Both Chase and Seward thought they were the sole sponsor of Stanton; that was one of Lincoln's tricks. Instead of responding, Hay looked at his watch, which had stopped—he had misplaced the key.

"I'm glad we made this alliance," he said, extending his hand. To his surprise, she put her hands on his shoulders, looked him straight in the eyes —about the same level as hers, unfortunately—then placed her cheek next to his for a moment in a kind of kiss. Her nose, he had heard, was slightly inclined to pug; up close, it was deliciously tilted and fit her face as few noses he had ever observed.

"I don't know whether I'll invite you to a *soirée conversable* or a *matinée dansante*," she seemed to be ruminating aloud. Hay liked the afternoon dancing parties that were in vogue, with drapes drawn and candles lit, but ever since Daniel Webster had declared a perfect dinner to be the highest consummation of civilization, most serious men said they preferred the smaller evening dinners.

"Invite me to both."

She laughed easily. "I'll see you at the Hellcat's big *musicale*," she said.

He frowned; that party, the Hellcat's surprise bid for social dominance, had not only not been announced, it was not even bruited about; that ranked with the Peninsula plan and the Tennessee plan in the level of secrecy around the President's house. In the past, the White House entertaining had been dinner parties known for their intimacy, Daniel Webster style; it was Mrs. Lincoln's notion that tickets should be issued to seven hundred guests for a musical *grande levée*, adding a note of culture to the proceedings.

"It will be an innovation," he heard himself saying, "complete with a President's March, and a polka composed by Francis Scala himself."

"Mrs. Lincoln's polka," Kate breathed. "Everyone will be so pleased. And a guest list of a thousand."

"Seven hundred." He began to think that was why he had been invited for a glass of bourbon, and lest she pry more out of him, he mock-saluted and bade her farewell. The thought raced through his mind that he would like to tear the clothes off this scheming belle, and then leave her—disheveled red hair cascading down naked shoulders—to await her dinner guests. With that heartening thought firmly in mind, he stepped out onto the frozen mud and skipped and whistled his way back to the President's house.

CHAPTER 10

THE TEXAS RANGER

"Your son is not in the Tennessee Volunteers," Simon Buckner told him. "At least not under his own name."

General Breckinridge nodded his thanks. Buckner and he carried the same rank of brigadier, but he readily acknowledged the short, sturdy man facing him in the Bowling Green headquarters building to be the more professional soldier. Not yet forty, Simon Bolivar Buckner had taught philosophy at West Point, distinguished himself in the Mexican War, quit the army to make a fortune in Chicago real estate, and returned to Kentucky to take charge of its militia and to work with Breckinridge to keep their home state neutral. When the Confederates under General "Bishop" Polk moved across Kentucky's border—Breckinridge winced at the thought of how that well-meaning cleric gave the Federals under Sam Grant the opportunity to grab strategic Paducah —Kentucky's neutrality ended, and Buckner had to choose which side's commission to accept. The young namesake of "El Libertador" chose to report to

General Albert Sidney Johnston, commanding the Confederate forces in the West.

"We know of a Margaret Elizabeth Breckinridge," Buckner continued, eager to be helpful to the worried father, "with the Sanitary Commission traveling with the Union Army near St. Louis."

"My Uncle Bob's granddaughter. I didn't know she was a nurse." Breck ached at the memory of the comely, intense face of cousin Maggie at family weddings and funerals. Cabell, when he was eight or ten, headstrong and rebellious to his parents, would follow after Margaret Elizabeth doing whatever she asked. She was the sort to involve herself passionately in the war, as were her three uncles—two of whom went South and one North—and her father, who went North. Breck knew that the preacher Breckinridge, with his offspring on opposite sides and the potential of fratricide in battle more than an abstraction, must be undergoing the tortures he often told his parishioners were reserved for the damned. "How did we get that information, Simon?"

Buckner had made a face at the mention of Robert Breckinridge, who had done as much as any Kentuckian to keep that slave state in the Union. "We're all in each other's pockets in Missouri," Buckner replied; "no secrets up there. The general's cousin runs the mercantile library in St. Louis."

That was one reason Sidney Johnston had been able to intimidate the new Union commander, Henry Halleck. Johnston anticipated Federal troop movements and feinted at the Union strongholds. He placed stories in the *Louisville Courier* about the way his ranks were being swelled by recruitment, and how General Beauregard was coming to join his command at the head of 20,000 fresh troops. That was a palpable lie, but Beauregard was passing through and his presence was useful for the rumor factory. Johnston's bluff and bravado kept two stronger Union forces off balance.

"I'll keep an eye out for your boy," Buckner said. "Hell, at sixteen, he's bound to brag to somebody that his father got a million votes for President."

"Which cut into Douglas's vote and helped elect Lincoln," Breckinridge said ruefully. "I never thought old Abe would be so hell-bent for war." He recalled in some bitterness how inflexible Lincoln had been, in their White House talks, about peaceful secession.

"Button up," said Buckner, rising and reaching for his tunic. "We're to see the general at ten sharp."

"Is Sidney all that Jeff Davis cracks him up to be?" The new General Breckinridge, who did not know Sidney Johnston well, had learned to be skeptical about men with big reputations. Born in Kentucky and trained at West Point, Johnston had become a legend in the American officer corps: he had enlisted as a private in the army of the Republic of Texas and rose to be its Secretary of War. After annexation, the states'-rights Southerner in Johnston led to an angry falling-out with General Sam Houston, an ardent Union Democrat. But at the outbreak of the Mexican War, General Zack Taylor had chosen Johnston to head the Texas Volunteers, an outfit that gained a reputation for valor and mobility.

Before secession, Johnston was colonel, and Robert Lee lieutenant colonel, of what Breck had heard was the best cavalry regiment in the U.S. Army. In April of 1861, General Winfield Scott had offered Albert Sidney Johnston the post of second-in-command of all Union land forces; like the Virginian Lee, the Texan Johnston sadly turned Scott down, choosing to go with his state rather than his country. Jefferson Davis, a close friend of both men, kept Lee in the east and sent Johnston west. In Richmond, Breck had heard it said that choice was made because the defense of the Southwest without an adequate army was infinitely more difficult, and Davis considered Johnston to be the most skillful general on the American continent.

"He's the best we have," Buckner snapped, "the best anyone has, and you should not call him Sidney. He's not a general like you and me, he's 'the General.' You know how the Yankee newspapers try to compare McClellan to Napoleon? Well, Albert Sidney Johnston has the sort of mind and character that put him in rank with Napoleon. Daring but calculating at the same time. More of a Texan than a Kentuckian."

They walked down the hall of the large Bowling Green headquarters building to the commanding general's suite. In the anteroom, Breckinridge saw a familiar face: Walter Haldeman, editor of the on-the-run *Louisville Courier*, which was being printed in Confederate-held Bowling Green.

Haldeman pretended to be impressed by the star on his fellow escapee's collar, fingering it reverently. Buttoning the top button on Breckinridge's tunic, lest the new general be dressed imperfectly at his first meeting with the real General, the publisher told his two Kentucky compatriots, "Sidney's thinking about pulling out of Kentucky. Don't you let him. Your whole Kentucky Brigade will desert, and I'll have to close down the only voice for our cause on the border."

Breck thanked Haldeman for the warning. He remembered to express his appreciation for the favorable stories in the *Courier* about his appointment— not everyone in Confederate headquarters thought latecomers deserved high rank—and followed Buckner into his first encounter with the hope of the Confederate Army.

Not as tall as I am, thought Breck, extending a hand rather than saluting, but tall enough and ramrod-straight. Silver-haired at fifty-eight, booted for his morning ride on Fire-eater (it occurred to Breck that generals named their horses for qualities they wanted to exhibit or wished they had), Sidney Johnston exuded what Breck had to admit was a command presence, without the pomp or mysticism of a Frémont, even though his Utah explorations rivaled those of the Pathmaker. A commanding figure, surely, but not a political commander: Americans seemed to prefer the pretensions of humility of a Lincoln or the dazzle of a Douglas to the crisp authority of military men like the Texan before him.

"I admired your eloquent statement," the general said to him, "about exchanging the term in the Senate for the musket of a soldier." After Breck's pleased nod, Johnston added a barb: "Took you long enough in Richmond to find that musket."

"You know how it is to deal with Judah Benjamin," Breck replied. As Johnston would know, that was an allusion to the Confederate Secretary of War's reluctance to part with any weapons for the Western theater. Judah Benjamin in Richmond had rebuked General Johnston for accepting the enlistments of "one-year men," rather than those who would agree to sign up for the duration, and had refused to provide the short-termers with any weapons. Since he had arrived in Bowling Green, Breck had quickly sided with

Johnston in the dispute with Benjamin, who seemed incapable of badgering the Southern manufacturers or blockade-runners into providing enough small arms. In such a fix, any general would accept a man who walked into camp with a gun on his shoulder for any length of time he would sign up. Theoretically the Secretary of War was correct, but in the field, the general needed recruits.

"We're going to send you on some skirmishes with a small force to get you blooded, Breckinridge," said the commander, getting right to the point, "and if you hold up the way Simon here promises, the Army of the West can use you." Breck took a breath to make a proper response, but Sidney Johnston went on: "In our particular fix, the qualities of a politician can be of great use. We need generals who can make us appear much more than we are." He waved them to seats and strode to the wall map.

"Halleck's up over here," he said, pointing to Illinois, "thinking about coming down the Mississippi River and cutting us off from Texas and the world. He's got, say, twenty-five thousand troops under Grant and Sherman and Smith." He tapped the center of the map, near Kentucky. "Don Carlos Buell is in the middle, with 20,000 men, with orders to come down the Cumberland Gap and take Nashville and join up with Halleck's army." He waved at the East. "And McClellan's over there in the sector of least consequence at the moment."

"Why is the war in Virginia inconsequential, General?" (Breck agreed that "Sidney" would be out of place.)

"McClellan won't try an overland winter offensive—the Union Army isn't ready. And the Confederate advantage is in defense, so we won't move. But since they're near the capitals, Washington and Richmond, the War Department of each country gives it the most attention and the most weapons."

He returned to the West. "The basic problem with our army," he took a breath, "is that we don't have an army. We have to position our small force— I have fewer than 22,000 at present, Simon, as you know—between the Union force under Halleck and Grant in Illinois and their force under Buell in Kentucky. We are required to fight defensively, along a four hundred and thirty-mile front, never committing all our forces to one area or the other. That is how to defend an area; however, it is not how to win a war."

Breck could see the logic in that; if Johnston attacked either Union force, the other would be free to knife southward. Jeff Davis's strategy was to delay the war in the West and concentrate on the East: if the South could invade Pennsylvania and Maryland, perhaps the Yankees would become war-weary and Lincoln would lose his source of men and money. As a politician, Breck could count the numbers—nearly twenty million in the North against eight million whites in the South—but it was felt that one well-trained Confederate soldier, experienced with a rifle and defending his way of life, was worth a dozen city boys drafted into the army in the North to fight in an alien land, or to fight for somebody else's freedom. The commanding general seemed to want to be questioned about his last remark, so Breck obliged: "How do we win the war?"

"With a surprise attack on a large concentration of their troops. Territory is unimportant. We have to defeat the Union Army."

"Where?"

Johnston hesitated, then decided not to answer. "For the moment I have to keep moving between Halleck and Buell until Richmond realizes that the West is where the war will be won or lost, and sends us an army."

"Are you confident, General," Breck asked, "that our forts along the Mississippi are secure?" Simon Buckner shot him a warning glance; Breck was not being properly reverential.

Johnston, smiling, put his fancily booted feet on the desk. "I pray for the day that 'Old Brains' puts his troops on a flotilla and floats down within range of our shore batteries. Don't tell me about the success of Allied ironclads against the Russians in the Crimea—I read McClellan's report from there, but I assure you our placed guns could destroy a flotilla with ease. We could defeat the Union on the Mississippi."

Breck pointed to the map. "There are a couple of other rivers into the South." Buckner started to interrupt, but Johnston motioned him silent and looked to Breck to continue. "The Cumberland, and the Tennessee."

"Obvious, isn't it?" Johnston seemed pleased at the question. "If I were the Union commander, I would strike down the Tennessee—it flows northward, as you know, which would turn their gunboats into a real threat—down toward Alabama." His hand dropped from Kentucky to Tennessee. "We would have to fall back to avoid being captured, abandoning Nashville without a fight."

Nashville, Tennessee, was the Confederacy's central supply depot in the West, and a strongpoint indispensable to a defense against invasion, and here was the South's commander suggesting that the Union could take it by maneuver.

Breck asked the inescapable question: "If it's so obvious a strategy, why haven't they adopted it?"

"Ah. One reason could be that they have not thought of it yet, because Halleck is so mesmerized with the Mississippi."

"That can't last," Buckner put in.

"Agreed. I know you Kentuckians were furious at Bishop Polk for violating your precious neutrality by grabbing Columbus, but the one hundred and twenty big guns in that city effectively close off the Mississippi. That forces Halleck to look elsewhere. My cousin in St. Louis, the librarian, reports that a woman carrying a pass from Secretary Stanton himself has spent a week in his library, studying maps and currents of the Tennessee River."

Breck's heart sank. "They know what to do," he said dully. "Lincoln knows exactly what to do." If Halleck, the general who wrote the book on military strategy, had not already comprehended the South's vulnerability, surely Anna Carroll would be calling it to Lincoln's attention.

"To discourage them, we've built a couple of forts," said Johnston, "at the place the two rivers separate from the Mississippi. Here—Henry and Donelson."

"Fort Henry is a joke," said Buckner instantly. "It is in a swamp and the batteries will never fire effectively. At Fort Donelson, we have a chance—and if we turn them back there at the Cumberland, the likelihood is that they won't have the strength to come down the Tennessee."

Johnston did not agree. "Donelson was built to discourage an attack. It was not built to resist an attack by any capable general."

"Don't count it out," pressed Buckner, eager to defend Kentucky. "If you commit troops to its defense, we can hurt the Yankees and scare them off. They don't know our vulnerability. If we can beat them at Fort Donelson, they'll forget the Tennessee River and go back to trying the Mississippi, and we can punish them forever."

"It would take a pretty bad general to fail to take Donelson," said Johnston, who apparently knew exactly how to take it.

"We can rely on bad Union generals," said Buckner. "Halleck won't take the field—he's never left his armchair. That leaves three possibilities. One is Sherman, who taught school in Louisiana and has his job only because his brother is a senator. The New York papers say he's unstable, even crazy, gets terrible moods. No reason to think he can carry off a sustained campaign."

"But there's Baldy Smith," said Johnston, ticking off a second brigadier under Halleck, "West Point. I had him under me in Utah, and he moved and maneuvered his men so fast we never had to shoot a Mormon. Hell of a soldier."

"Agreed," said Buckner, "but Halleck has him under Sam Grant. The likeliest choice to lead the attack on Donelson is Grant, and if he's the one, we can beat him."

"You know him? They say he drinks, but that may be jealous talk."

"I more than know him, I've been saddled with him as a friend all my life," Buckner told him eagerly. "We were in the same class at West Point. The man has failure written all over him. He does drink—that is why he was cashiered. He tried to go into business in Cairo and that failed. He was selling firewood on the streets of St. Louis only a couple of years ago, wearing his army overcoat to try to keep warm—pitiful. He came to me and borrowed two hundred dollars to keep his family alive. If it hadn't been for this war, and some political pull that got him back in the army, Sam Grant would be destitute."

"Did he ever pay you back?" Johnston wanted to know.

"No, but if he'd had the money he would have. He's honest—as I say, he's my friend—but it's just that he's a born failure. I'll never see that money; I consider the loan pure charity."

Breck recalled that Sam Grant had led a small force down the Mississippi on a raid a month before. "How did he conduct himself at Belmont, Simon?"

"He stumbled into a fight, let his men run wild, took a lot of unnecessary casualties, and just made it back to his boat in time. Grant was the last to board, and he showed his bravery with that, but he botched the operation and Halleck was furious with him."

"Sounds like he fights, though," Johnston offered. "Not all of them are ready to spill blood."

"He'll take terrible casualties because he's afraid to be a failure again," Buckner said. "Believe me: Sam Grant is not a general, he's a butcher. He's afraid to retreat, and he doesn't have the courage to admit failure by surrendering—he could sacrifice a whole army."

That settled it for Johnston. "The men we have in charge of Forts Henry and Donelson are not military men," he said. "Floyd and Pillow, a couple of politicians. I'll send you there, Simon, with a detachment of four thousand men and Nat Forrest's cavalry. That'll be fourteen thousand total, all I can afford, against at least forty thousand, plus their navy. I hope you're right about Grant, and you're not facing Baldy Smith."

That was encouraging to Breck. At least the South would put up a fight for Kentucky, justifying the faith of those Kentuckians who were branded traitors for their decision to stand with the South. Buckner had put his case on the quality of generalship, which carried weight with West Pointers, but it seemed to John Breckinridge, the newest general, that the man with the best military credentials in America was reluctantly agreeing to defend an area he believed to be ultimately indefensible. Breck reminded himself that most of his own choices in the past year had been between the lesser of evils.

Johnston's assessment of the Confederate generals now at Donelson had been guarded but was on the right track: General Floyd was known to everyone in the Buck-and-Breck administration to be a rascal as Secretary of War in the Buchanan Cabinet, and General Gideon Pillow was an equally bad appointment: in the Mexican War, Breck had been Pillow's lawyer in a dispute with Winfield Scott, and had come to have a high regard for Scott and a low opinion of his client. Simon Buckner would be the only real soldier on the scene at Donelson, and he would not be in command.

"Hold the fort, Simon," were his instructions from Johnston, "but if that is not possible, hold your force intact and a route out open. Go now, and entrench. Do not lose a moment. Work all night. If you must withdraw, we'll meet in Nashville."

General Johnston sent Buckner out to give the editor, Haldeman, a story about reinforcements on the way to him through Georgia, to mislead the Union commands in St. Louis and Ohio. The newspaper would probably be read avidly by Lincoln and Stanton in Washington. Breck found it curious about Stanton's being named Secretary of War; his reports on that man were contradictory. In the Buchanan Cabinet, Stanton had talked for the Union but had secretly consorted with some secessionists; in the election of 1860 Stanton had voted for Breckinridge, telling friends it was the only hope of preserving the Union. What had inspired Lincoln to pick Stanton for the most important post in the Cabinet? Ruthlessness and the capacity for guile, Breck supposed, along with sheer, fierce impatience with anyone who stood in his way. Those were exactly the qualities—and qualities they became in wartime—lacking in his counterpart, Judah Benjamin, who could not find the guns for Sidney Johnston's troops.

The general crossed his arms and looked hard at Breck, who assumed that Johnston's arrangement for the two of them to be alone meant talk of politics. "I didn't vote for you, Breckinridge," he announced.

"You voted for Bell," Breck guessed.

"You say that because you saw what you assume to be my slave outside. I manumitted Randolph years ago. No, I never voted for anybody other than Zack Taylor, and that because he was my friend."

Now Johnston was in his bailiwick and Breck no longer felt in the least intimidated. "You say that to show how nonpolitical you are, General, but I happen to know you were approached in 1858 to run for President by the same Democrats who later came to me."

"I said no." The question implicit in that was: Why didn't you say no, too?

"I'm a political man, not a military man," said Breck, "so I said yes. I thought I could prevent this war. I was mistaken."

"I should have voted for you, then, but I didn't know if you could make up your mind," said the Texan. "This is going to be the worst kind of war. A seven-year war, unless we can swallow up their army."

Johnston made statements designed to trigger questions, as if testing his visitor's attention. Breck made up his mind not to play that game, and remained silent.

"Let me tell you about generalship, young man." Johnston sat on the edge of his desk, arms still half locked, at ease. "You've been senator and Vice President, you're well aware what leadership is—the ability to speak on the stump, to appear trustworthy, to play one faction against another. All that will be useful to you now, but it's not generalship."

Breck was vaguely aware of that; he also knew that Johnston's lack of political finesse in Richmond had cost him command of the main forces in the East and might be the cause of his exaggeration of the strategic importance of the West. He awaited the generalship lesson.

"The nature of war is changing. The seizure of territory is insignificant—that is settled afterward. What counts now is the destruction of the enemy's army, the removal of the enemy population's will to fight, and ultimately its ability to fight. By your expression, Breckinridge, I take it you think that is barbaric."

When his listener did not react, Sidney Johnston went on. "Lincoln and Stanton want General McClellan to go and 'take' Richmond, but they're fearful that with the Union Army off on that expedition, Lee or Jackson will 'take' Washington, so they won't give the Little Mac all the troops he needs. The same fencing-match philosophy afflicts President Davis and General Lee. Each side is fighting battles for territory, hoping the other side will get tired. That's the way it was in the old days, and the side that was less exhausted won."

He rose from his chair to pace, which reminded Breck of Lincoln, who hated to talk while seated. "But a revolutionary war, which is what this is, is a war of a whole nation against a whole nation, and that takes a different kind of fighting. The enemy army must be gathered, enticed to fight to a decision, and destroyed or captured. Remember, when you hear criticism of us for losing vast territories—no battle is 'won' if the enemy is not destroyed or captured."

"I'm told, General—and you should be aware of the criticism in Richmond —that you are the one avoiding battle."

"Of course. Because if I massed my ill-armed little force against two larger Union armies, where each soldier has a rifled musket, I would lose. My 'Army of the West' as we grandly call it, would be destroyed, and the war would be over. I must husband my resources, wait for a moment and a place to surprise the enemy when we are on a nearly equal footing, and then strike with everything. No quarter."

"Where will that be?"

"I know precisely where the great battle of this war will take place," said Johnston slowly, "and when you cross over from politician to general, you will know too. Frankly, it should not be hard to figure out."

Breck refused to take the test and asked about the war in the East. Johnston relaxed, uncrossed his arms and walked to the window, his boots sounding sharply on the uncarpeted floor. "McClellan hates to take casualties, so he'll probably slip down the Potomac by boat and try to strike at Richmond up the Peninsula, up the James and York rivers. Frankly, that's what I would do—not to take Richmond, which means nothing, but to cut off the Army of Virginia and destroy it."

"How do we counter that move, if he makes it?" Breck had not thought of that approach, but suspected that McClellan, a trained strategist, had.

"If Bobby Lee remembers what I taught him, he'll advise Jeff Davis to resist the screaming from his nervous Cabinet to come scurrying down to defend Richmond, and to strike immediately at Washington instead."

"I thought you said that territory, capitals, mean nothing."

"You're learning, but Lincoln won't. At the slightest threat to his capital, he will hold back the troops McClellan needs to smash our army in front of Richmond. All that chess-playing will mean nothing, because the object is not to take the king, but to wipe out the other side of the board. The war will go on until a general takes charge who understands the need to destroy armies." He turned to face his student. "If I shock you, it is because I want to change you from a leader of people to a leader of troops. We deal in death."

"This is your business, General," Breck sighed; "I'll try to learn it." He asked himself whether a willingness to accept huge casualties, to order death and mutilation to your enemy and your own troops as well, was really at the core of generalship. If so, the South, outnumbered nearly three to one, was doomed. He sensed a contradiction in what Johnston had said about U. S. Grant, and asked the general directly: "If Grant is the butcher that Simon Buckner says he is, why do you hope for Grant at Fort Donelson?"

"Time is not on our side. With a Grant, we could win decisively. The worst that can happen is that we lose, and run away. I suppose we have to try to defend the rivers from those forts; we cannot fall back without any show of resistance, and you can never tell in battle—generals do stupid things. But that battle is not likely to be decisive. Buckner does not have the instinct for destruction."

"Nor do I. Who does?"

"On our side? I do. Bobby Lee, Braxton Bragg. Here in my command, Pat Cleburne, the Irishman. Not Joe Johnston, not Beauregard, certainly—that little Creole already lost his opportunity to destroy the Union Army after Bull Run. On their side, it's hard to say. McClellan is the best they have, but he fights battles, not wars. Grant, maybe, from what Buckner says of him. Certainly not Halleck."

General Breckinridge, staring at the map, thought he had figured it out. Restraining his excitement, drawling to display calm, he said, "I hope to have the honor of being one of your commanders, sir, at the Battle of Corinth."

"Close." General Sidney Johnston smiled at him warmly for the first time, and Breck could feel why this man inspired such confidence in his commanders and respect from political superiors. "You grasp the strategy of an offensive defense, but not the tactical detail.

"Here. This is not a matter I want you to discuss with Simon Buckner, because I do not want his morale to suffer in any way. Let us assume Fort

Henry falls, as it must, and he cannot hold Donelson, which is probable. He is then to march his men to Nashville, joining our retrograde movement."

"You mean a retreat South."

"Thank you for that, Breckinridge; I should not flinch from the hard word 'retreat.' With the Tennessee and Cumberland rivers in their hands, we cannot hold Nashville or Bowling Green, or we would soon be cut off from behind. We will have to fall back, back, back."

"My God, General, you are talking about giving up the rest of Kentucky and all of Tennessee." The enormity of the unfolding trauma of defeat, only hinted at by the publisher Haldeman, struck him with force. What about his brigade of Kentuckians? How would they react to retreat from their native soil, without so much as a fight? What had they enlisted for, if not to defend their state—could he keep them from deserting?

What about all the Tennessee troops, the backbone of the western army, such as it was? The newspapers would be calling for Johnston's scalp, his replacement with a fighting general, as would all the sponsors of General Beauregard in Richmond. Jeff Davis was Johnston's friend, and liked to say to critics, "If Albert Sidney Johnston is no general, then we have no generals," but not even the President's support was bottomless, given the resistance from the governors of Georgia and South Carolina building against his centralization of authority.

"I have pondered this step well," said the general. "It is a step that no man would take if he did not know he was right." When Breck shook his head he added, "I anticipate a popular clamor. But the clamor of today is converted into the praises of tomorrow by a single great success."

Breck kept shaking his head, not so much in disagreement as wonderment. Lincoln liked to say that if the end brought him out right, all would be well, but that if it brought him out wrong, ten angels swearing he was right would make no difference. Johnston here was saying the same thing, that the end would justify all, but both men were betting that public support would stay with them through terrible trials, until they could show how right they were. But that was not the way of democracies. No political or military leader—not Lincoln, not Johnston—could long afford to defy public sentiment.

"Assume that their plan is to use the Tennessee River from up here at the Kentucky line," the general was explaining, "come down through all of Tennessee and aim for Corinth, in Mississippi just over the Tennessee line. That's where they want to cut the Memphis to Charleston railway. Then they can strike west to Memphis and down the Mississippi to Vicksburg and Port Hudson."

That prospect seemed dreary to Breck, but Johnston saw it differently. "The deeper they penetrate, the more triumphant they feel, and the more vulnerable they become. Our object is to destroy Grant's army before it can be joined by Buell's army, and then to destroy Buell's army. Destroy. Obliterate. Kill 'em all, except those who surrender. The shock to the North of the loss of a hundred thousand men, just when victory seemed assured, will end the war."

Breck got up to examine the point on the map that was the place where passengers on boats debarked to go to Corinth, Mississippi, before the Tennessee River veered east.

"We hit them just after they debark, with the river to their back, from the heights overlooking Pittsburg Landing," said Johnston. "They give up or drown. Then Buell comes to the rescue with his army, and we do the same to them."

The general was coldly certain of the intelligence of his adversary, of the inexorability of the campaign, and of the victory of the defense over a force twice its size. He was the only man Breck had met in the past year who knew how to win a war. How much depended on circumstance, how much on the wisdom of his strategy, how much on the human element? Did one man, on either side, count that much in a clash of huge armies?

Breck put his finger on the spot of the river landing.

"That's it, exactly," said Sidney Johnston, "where the great battle of the southwest will be fought, and the war won."

The engineer who drew up the map had written the name of a local landmark above the location of the landing. Breck squinted and read aloud, "Shiloh Church."

"I want you with me there, Breck."

"God willing, I'll be there, General."

Walter Haldeman, the *Courier*'s publisher, read with distaste a copy of his competition, the *Louisville Journal*, while he waited for General Breckinridge. That pro-Union sheet was especially abusive of certain members of one famous Kentucky family: it was noted that Robert Breckinridge, son of the loyal reverend, had been appointed captain in one of the six regiments making up the brigade commanded by his cousin, John C., "the only senator to be expelled as a traitor." The story noted that the Reverend Robert had disowned his son, denounced him for his treason, and the writer—Haldeman knew him, a liar and a cheat—gratuitously added that John C. had been observed drunk on the streets of Richmond after receiving his general's commission from Jeff Davis. That was below the belt; Haldeman knew Breck to enjoy a glass of bourbon as much as any man, but not to be a drunkard by any means. Now the Kentuckian would have to be especially careful about every drink he took in public, lest his reputation grow as the Southern counterpart to Sam Grant's.

Breck came out of Sidney Johnston's office with the look of most men who spent time with the man reputed to be the best soldier in America: inspired, uplifted, determined. He was dressed in his "Kentucky jeans," a blue-jacketed departure from the Confederate butternut gray, but each brigade could choose its uniform. The publisher noted that Breck, who had been clean-shaven as senator and as Vice President, was now growing a mustache.

Haldeman threw the paper aside. "Are we going to defend Kentucky? Simon Buckner wants me to write that Beauregard brought reinforcements. I will, of course, but—"

"Sidney took what you said to heart. Grant will have a fight on his hands at Fort Donelson."

The publisher felt the surge of pride that came with influencing great events; he was certain that one day soon his exiled *Courier* would be published in Louisville again, and he looked forward to front-paging a story about the demise of the *Journal*.

"You ought to know something that's bothering the men in B company, second regiment," the publisher told the general.

"Cousin Bob's company?"

Haldeman nodded. "He ordered a private to sweep out the captain's tent, and the private—you know how these Kentucky kids are—he told the captain to go to hell. So the captain put him in the regimental guardhouse. Troops are sore about that."

"Damn!" The general pulled off his slouch hat and slapped it against his knee. Haldeman followed him out of the headquarters building into the frigid February air. Breck took his horse from the orderly, mounted, and whipped the horse with his hat, the publisher riding hard on his own mount to keep up.

At Company B, the general dismounted and stormed into his cousin's tent. The facts of the incident were as Haldeman had described.

"But he told me to go to hell, John," the captain said, "what was I going to do? There's such a thing as discipline."

"When you can't get a private to volunteer to sweep out your tent," the general told him, "you do it yourself. There are no menials in the Kentucky Brigade."

"Do you sweep out your own tent?"

"Damn right I do! Kentuckians are gentlemen, and neither you nor I have the right to command any one of them to do a menial service. Now you come with me to the guardhouse and apologize to the soldier you have insulted, or so help me, Captain Breck, you'll take his place in that cell."

The three men marched about a hundred yards to the large tent that served as a guardhouse. Haldeman and the general waited outside while the captain went in to fetch the rebellious rebel.

The prisoner, a boy having difficulty getting his jacket buttoned, appeared soon and saluted, holding the salute.

"I told the private my command was out of order," the captain said, "and released him."

"You mustn't go around telling your officers to go to hell," said General Breckinridge to the boy. "If you think an order is wrong, argue about it with respect." He returned the salute and the soldier scampered off. Haldeman was sure the boy's story would spread quickly through the brigade, endearing the general to his men as never before. The fact that the general had not hesitated to embarrass his own kinsman in protecting the dignity of Kentuckians would add piquancy to the telling.

"Cousin Bob, I'm sorry I had to do that, but these men are especially touchy these days, and recruiting—"

The captain cut him off. "Forget that. There's a kid in that tent, the bunk next to the private from my company, came in two days ago from Tennessee. Got throwed in the guardhouse for stealing a farmer's fence rail to use as firewood. Stay right here."

Breck's cousin ducked back into the tent and appeared a moment later with a tall, good-looking boy who bore a striking resemblance to the general.

"Thank you, Cousin Bob. Hello, Father."

After what seemed to Haldeman to be a heartbreaking pause, the general said, "You call him Captain, and me General. This is the Confederate Army."

"Yes, sir."

"You're familiar with the regulations about stealing the property of the people of this area, your fellow Kentuckians, whose lives and property you are in the service of protecting?"

"Now I am. It was cold, sir."

"You ever want to get out of that guardhouse?" The boy nodded vigorously. "Then what I would do," said his father, "is to volunteer, of your own free will, to sweep out the tent of the captain here every day for a month. And to do any latrine digging or any other menial task that no man in this brigade, including you, is required to do."

"I volunteer, General."

When the general found it difficult to say anything more, Captain Breckinridge said, "You can go back to your quarters now, Cabell. The regulation is against taking whole fence rails. Pieces of fence rail, however, can be used for firewood. Soldiers around here know that two halves of a fence rail are considered pieces."

The boy turned, turned back, saluted clumsily, and grunted when his father grabbed him by the shoulders and pulled him close. Haldeman walked off with Captain Breckinridge, who apparently was profoundly moved by the reunion. It occurred to the publisher that the men Breck called "Uncle Bob" and "Cousin Bob"—Robert Breckinridge, father and son—were on different sides of the war and were not likely to embrace again.

CHAPTER 11

NERVE CENTER

Anna Carroll was startled at the change of scene in the offices of the Secretary of War. Two weeks before, with Cameron in charge, the place had been nearly deserted most of the time, as the politician from Pennsylvania preferred to do his confidential army business at home, in private. Today a crowd of a hundred people was jammed into Stanton's reception room, spilling out into the hallway in front of the newly installed telegraph office.

It made no sense, Anna decided, to try to see the Secretary on a matter so secret as the Tennessee plan in front of that mob. Instead of trying to elbow her way in, she walked authoritatively into the telegraph office across the hall, asked for the officer in charge, and used Tom Scott's name to make an acquaintance.

"The chief of the telegraph service is over in the Secretary of War's office," said a sallow young man in front of a machine feeding paper out, "along with everybody else."

"That means you're in charge," she replied, looking impressed. "You're very young to have such a responsible position."

"I'm Homer Bates," he said, pleased, "and I've seen your name in a couple of messages, Miss Carroll."

"About what?"

"I'm not at liberty to say, but they were to St. Louis. A lot of this work is very secret. It's no wonder that Secretary Stanton moved us over here from the McClellan headquarters first thing."

"You're at the nerve center of the entire war," she told him.

Bates nodded delightedly. "The President himself came in last night. He calls me Homer. You can, too, if you like."

A chatty young fellow to be at the nerve center, she thought. "What a complicated machine," she said. "Does it take many years to learn telegraphy?"

Homer Bates shook his head, trying to be modest. "You have to have a knack for it. The fast fist. And then you have to learn the ciphers. The message about you yesterday," he volunteered suddenly, "was from Scott to Old Brains in St. Louis. He wanted to know about the progress of the iron-clad gunboats for your Tennessee plan."

She did not ask directly about the reply. "Can replies come back the same day on the machine?"

"Oh, within an hour sometimes. When a telegraph tent is near a general's tent, the message can go back and forth in minutes." Because he did not volunteer any information about a reply about the gunboats from General Halleck, she assumed no reply was received. Rather than arouse his suspicion that he was being cultivated as a source, Anna chatted briefly about her own war work, letting the young man know of her closeness to Senator Wade, chairman of the Committee on the Conduct of the War, and exaggerating her own acquaintance with the President. At the proper moment she turned the conversation to his career.

Her new friend Homer responded like a grateful puppy. In the return of confidence that flowed from her interest, she gleaned a couple of curious bits of information: that if one Cabinet minister communicated with another over the wire by secret code, Stanton had left standing orders that the message be deciphered and communicated to him. And that was not the most intimate intrusion: whenever General McClellan telegraphed his wife from the front, Stanton was to know the contents of the dispatch immediately, endearments and all.

"There's a side entrance to the Secretary's reception room," he told her. "Shall I slip you in?"

She nodded eagerly and gave him her most conspiratorial smile: Homer was a young man she would make it a point to know better. "Why does he have so many people in at once?"

"Efficiency. He can go through two hundred people in a day that way. You should see him make decisions, Miss Carroll, it's amazing. And best of all, it's in public view—no secret deals with contractors. They say that was the trouble with his predecessor," he confided, "but I don't know that for a fact."

"The place does seem changed."

"Like day and night, the old-timers tell me, Miss Carroll. No more 'improvised war'; somebody's finally organizing a victory. Go ahead, see for yourself." He pushed open the connecting door and slipped her inside.

Edwin Stanton was standing behind a high desk at the end of the large room. His scraggly beard, with its white streak down the middle, pointed toward his chest as he peered angrily over his steel-rimmed spectacles at the crowd.

"Step forward," he said to one after another; "state your business." Soldiers were recognized first; enlisted men received more courtesy than officers from the gruff Secretary, but even they were dealt with summarily. A well-dressed man stepped forward bearing what he said was a card from President Lincoln's wife and asked for a commissary's appointment. Stanton's temper flared; he tore the card in half and threw the pieces up in the air.

"The fact that you bring me such a card would prevent me from giving you any appointment," Stanton snapped, loudly enough for all to hear. "Politics no longer have any place in army appointments. Out!"

Anna watched a parade of favor seekers pass through; almost all were rudely turned down and went away angry. Occasionally a request would make sense to Stanton, and he would tug a cord hanging from the ceiling. A messenger would run in, be given a slip of paper in Stanton's writing, and run out. Sometimes the messenger ducked across the hall to the telegraph office to get quick action in the field.

Senator Ben Wade strode in, spotted Anna on the side of the room, and motioned her over. "Hell of a way to do business, isn't it?" he boomed admiringly.

Stanton's demeanor immediately changed at the sight of the senator. He hurried out from behind his desk to make an exception by greeting him. "Give us five minutes in private," Wade said to him, adding for all to hear, "it's not about a damn contract."

Wade pulled Anna along with him to the window facing the Executive Mansion and said to the Secretary, "Her business first, Stanton. Remember, this little woman damn near saved Maryland for us all by herself." Stanton nodded and looked squarely at her.

She had to be brief. "Two items. The first is to press my Tennessee plan." She did not mention Colonel Scott's support since Scott was out West, on a final tour of the battlefronts, and was soon to be replaced by someone personally close to the new Secretary, possibly Stanton's brother-in-law. "My report shows the best time to move on Donelson and down into Tennessee is now, in February. Johnston would have to split his forces in half to defend—"

"I know all about the Tennessee plan, my dear lady," said Stanton, "but that's entirely up to General Halleck. Frankly, what's happening out West is not at the center of our concerns at the moment. The first thing is to get McClellan moving right here." He turned to Wade. "I went around McClellan to his ten division commanders and asked them about a move right away against the rebels at Manassas. You know what we have? Ten generals afraid to fight."

She bit her lip; he did not understand that the war could be won, and at infinitely less cost, in the West. No time to argue it now; he would turn against the plan if she nagged him.

Wade picked up the slap at McClellan. "That's what you and I think about McNapoleon, but what about Lincoln? Is he still defending that slave-catcher's delays?"

"You will be pleased to learn," Stanton whispered, "that I had a heart-to-heart with the President this morning about the general's protracted inactivity. He agrees! My opinion of Lincoln, I must say, has risen considerably."

"Not such a dumb gorilla, now that he agrees with you," Wade said, not quietly enough.

Stanton looked horrified for a moment, then took his visitors into his confidence: "I mentioned to Lincoln a way to get our general-in-chief away from his elegant dinners and out into the field. A special war order directly from the President—never been done before, I think. I'm letting him work on it by himself, because it would be wrong for me to confront McClellan directly so soon. But your committee will be pleased, Senator."

Anna saw an opening and spoke up. "My second point is to urge you to take control of actions against the seditionists."

Seward had been heavy-handed with the arrests of dissenters, she explained quickly, and the Peace Democrats were making a big issue of it in New York and Baltimore. Stanton's seizure of the telegraph office, and the way he was reading everyone's messages, told Anna that the new War Secretary had power ambitions; such a switch of Cabinet authority on arbitrary arrests would fit into Stanton's mode of operation, and she wanted him to be aware that her influence with the Blairs and Wade might make it easier for him to extend his power. She assumed he wanted the suggestion to come from someone other than himself, and pamphleteer Anna Ella Carroll was known and well regarded in the President's circle for her war powers study. In return, she figured, Stanton might press for her Tennessee plan, and ultimately would help her gain the recognition that should flow to its author.

"It might be a good idea for me to start with a general amnesty," Stanton said slowly, showing that he had already been thinking about moving into Seward's domain. "Ask for an oath not to talk treason, and empty out the jails. Later, if we need to tighten up on the press or the copperheads, this act of amnesty would demonstrate our fairness. What do you think, Ben?"

"Hold on to the worst ones, like the Wild Rose," Wade replied, "and as for that traitor of a general who killed my friend Ned Baker, throw the key away."

Stanton nodded eagerly. "I'd want your advice on that. Miss Carroll, your thought about seditionists has merit, as of course all your thoughts do."

"Look, here's my business," Wade stated. "I want a commission for your nephew."

"Impossible. Precisely because he is my nephew."

"But for God's sake, man, he qualifies, and he's a friend of mine. It's a hardship to place him on any worse ground because he's related to you. You're being absurd."

"I'm being the Secretary of War, and the answer is no." Bluff Ben began to redden; Anna knew the senator must have assured the young man he could deliver the commission. "Before you make life miserable for me before your committee," Stanton said, "look at this."

He took an envelope out of his inside pocket. On the back, in Lincoln's handwriting, was this message: "Benjamin Tappan wishes to be a lieutenant in the regular army; and if the Secretary of War knows no objection to him except that he is a relative of his, let him be appointed on my responsibility." The Secretary of War pointed to a notation below, in his own writing: "The Secretary of War declines to make the appointment desired by his nephew Benjamin Tappan because it would be a violation of a rule made by the

Secretary against appointments to the regular army except by promotion for meritorious service from the ranks of the regular service."

Wade shook his head and quoted Scripture: "Stand not next to me, for I am holier than thou."

"I have to be. I have the hardest job in the world, and I cannot afford to let any taint of influence touch me. Or touch Lincoln. As a matter of fact, as soon as I clear this mob out of the reception room, I will go across the street to let Mrs. Lincoln know that she has overstepped the bounds of propriety several times this week."

Wade looked at Anna and shrugged. "We better get out of here before he throws us out."

Stanton took her hand and bid her the most gracious farewell: "I know all you have done for your country, my dear lady. You are doing great work, even if it makes others famous." She assumed at first he was referring to her war powers memorandum for the Attorney General, but then wondered if he meant that Halleck would be jealous about anyone else getting credit for her Tennessee River plan.

A man in an officer's uniform appeared at the office door. "I am the arsenal officer, Mr. Secretary, and I am in receipt of your telegram ordering heavy guns to Harpers Ferry."

"I sent that telegram yesterday," Stanton growled, motioning for Anna and Wade to stay and hear.

"It was not convenient, sir," said the officer, "to dispatch those guns yesterday. It was Sunday. But if you think it is at all urgent, I will attend to it at once this morning."

Stanton bit off his words: "I ordered you to send those guns out yesterday, which I was well aware was Sunday. When you did not do so, I went down to the arsenal at the hour it opened, helped to drag those infernal guns out myself. I went with them in the wagons to the railway. I made certain they were on the midnight train to Harpers Ferry."

The officer listened to this bureaucratic heresy with his mouth open.

"The guns are at this moment in place facing a rebel attack," Stanton continued with relish, "and you, sir, are no longer in the service of the United States Government. Out. Out!"

Stanton, obviously pleased with himself, took Anna's hand and squeezed it firmly in farewell. She led Wade out past the thunderstruck quartermaster, briefly introduced the senator to the telegraph operator across the hall—"my friend, Homer Bates, who is doing vital and secret work," a description she knew would mightily satisfy the young man—and walked out the Seventeenth Street exit of the War Department.

"Stanton enjoys his new power," said Wade.

"He wallows in it." She amended that at once: "Certainly Mr. Lincoln needed a man like that"—she searched for the word—"that fierce, to get some energy in the prosecution of the war."

"Old Abe needs him, all right," boomed Wade. "The question all of us are asking is—does Stanton need Lincoln?"

CHAPTER 12

JOHN HAY'S DIARY
JANUARY 27, 1862

"The little black terrier," as Judge Blair calls Stanton with no little contempt, came barreling in this afternoon demanding to see the Hellcat. I could not resist the prospect of a confrontation between the indefatigable new Secretary of War and the quite fatigable Mrs. Lincoln, and took him to the family quarters myself.

Lizzie Keckley, who must have been fitting Madame for some outrageously expensive outfit, came to the bedroom door. I said, somewhat merrily, "Lizzie, would you tell Mrs. Lincoln that the Secretary of War attends her pleasure." When that brought a puzzled frown to her handsome black face, I amended it to plain English: "Mr. Stanton here would like to see her."

Lizzie looked him in the eye and then nodded, closing the door in our faces. There is a remarkable composure in that statuesque woman, who seems freed not just from slavery but from any lingering attitude of servitude; frankly, I would as soon visit a smallpox hospital as cross the fearsome Stanton, but Lizzie treats him like just another enemy of her friend and customer.

In a moment, Her Satanic Majesty appeared, took us into the yellow oval sitting room, and motioned for Stanton to sit down. He did not.

"I have in my heart the one single object of overcoming the rebellion," went his little speech, "and restoring the authority of the government in time to save the nation from the horrible gulf of bankruptcy." Did he know about the money she was spending? That remark took the hard look out of her face and put a trace of fear there. "I must also restore the integrity of the Department of War, which has been in the clutch of the most corrupt politics. Favoritism and nepotism have been rife." As she caught the drift of his complaint—not money, but meddling—she seemed to relax a little.

An interruption: Willie came running through the room in his pajamas, face flushed, evidently on his way to the kitchen. "Go to bed," his mother ordered. "You have a fever; you mustn't run around that way or you'll catch your death."

"But I'm thirsty, and I've been in my room all day, and I'm getting better." He cast an eye on Stanton, standing in the middle of the room, hand in jacket, midway through his prepared presentation. "Hello, sir—did you just grow that beard? It's not very bushy yet."

At last, Edwin McMasters Stanton, organizer of victory and scourge of timorous generals, met someone he could not intimidate. William Lincoln— "Willie" is not longer suitable, in my eyes, for such a brave lad—hugged his mother and beat a path to his room, leaving Stanton touching his wispy beard with some embarrassment and groping for a way to resume his remonstrance.

"Favoritism is the enemy of public trust," he intoned, sounding a little like the pious Chase, "and without realizing it, madam, you have allowed yourself to be used by unscrupulous people. Twice this week, men have come to me with your card asking for favors, and now one has presented a letter from you, on Executive Mansion stationery, with a formal request for an army commission. I have said no. I will continue to say no. This interference with my office must stop."

"You are entirely right, Mr. Secretary."

"You have a duty to your nation and to your husband—" He stopped, evidently unprepared for her immediate surrender.

"I thank you for reminding me of it," she said humbly, giving the lie to my sobriquet of Hellcat. I never saw her so much the pussycat; perhaps the Tycoon had spoken to her about his inability to prevent the new Secretary of War from exacting terrible vengeance for any interference.

"I will never trouble you again with improper requests," she said in farewell. She returned to her room clothed in dignity, which is at least less expensive than some of her other raiment, leaving Stanton, Lizzie, and me standing there.

What makes the former Hellcat so devoid of claws, so mild, even penitent? I suppose it is the result of those accusations of spendthriftiness flying all over town. The other accusation—of harboring secret Southern sympathies—is beneath contempt, probably based on her having all those relatives in the Confederate Army. But the charge of foolish and tasteless ostentation in wartime holds water. Stoddard has got her visiting hospitals to improve her reputation, but the press remains hopelessly down on her. Kate Chase never visits hospitals, and also spends money like water, and the press treats her like an angel. Perhaps it helps to look like an angel.

The Hellcat must feel guilty about the big levee planned for next week. Six hundred people invited to the first musicale to be held in the Mansion in years. I deposited the Prsdt's January salary check for $2,000 the other day, and that's not going to cover the half of it. She didn't invite the press— Stoddard was remiss—and everybody else not invited is predicting it will be a great bore. Ben Wade sent back his invitation with a furious note demanding to know if the President's wife was aware there was a Civil War on. As a result, it will be a sit-down musicale, the first "ball" ever held without dancing. I fear we are in for a disaster of a party, and the same fear is moderating the Hellcat's behavior.

The War Secretary, his speech delivered and Madam in full retreat, started to cough. Little coughs at first, then big wheezes into his handkerchief, shaking his glasses off his face. He had great difficulty catching his breath. Lizzie eased him into a chair and ran to the pantry around the corner for a glass of water. I picked up his spectacles and tried to pat him on the back, which he resisted.

"Asthma," he choked to me. I didn't know what to do except look sympathetic. Lizzie came back with water and a jar of honey and ministered to him until his coughing fit passed. As he was recovering, I introduced them.

"Lizzie, this is Secretary of War Stanton. Mr. Secretary, this is Lizzie Keckley, Mrs. Lincoln's modiste."

"I'm grateful to you, Mrs. Keckley." That made me feel small; by ostentatiously giving a negress a proper honorific, he was reducing me in her eyes. Then he startled us both by asking her an odd question: "Do you think negroes should be enlisted in the army?"

I had to step into the silence that followed. "Mrs. Keckley's son did not appear to be black, Mr. Stanton. He enlisted and was killed at Bloody Ridge last summer."

"A hero," she added, reaching in her dress for a wrinkled envelope. "Miss Carroll wrote me the details."

Stanton read it through and was visibly moved. By that I mean there were tears in his eyes. I excused myself to fix some tea in the pantry. I am not an eavesdropper by nature, but the conversation was clearly audible and is the sort of thing I should transcribe.

"Do you have other children, Mrs. Keckley?"

"No, the one was killed was all I had."

"Your husband?"

"Gone long ago."

Pause. "I am no stranger to the death of loved ones, my good woman. I lost one daughter in the cradle. I kept her ashes in my room for a year. Another died in her teens. My dear wife died a few years ago; I've since taken another. My elder son is in college in Ohio. He wants to join the army. I cannot interfere but I dread the day."

"The President's son at Harvard, Robert, wants to join up," she said, "but Mrs. Lincoln won't let him."

"Not only that," Stanton was saying, caught up in his account of death and woe in his own family, "but my infant, not two months old, has been afflicted with the most terrible sores since his vaccination. I fear for its life, and my dear young wife is always at his bedside, and I cannot get home because of the demands of this job. I tell no one of this."

"Are you a religious man, Mr. Stanton?"

"I am, profoundly."

"I will pray for you," Lizzie promised. "It is good, in a way, that you and death are no strangers. There is so much death ahead in your war." She took a breath and I could hear her exhale. "Mr. Lincoln sometimes reads the Bible, but he finds no comfort in religion. He lost a young boy, years ago. Name was Eddie, after Senator Baker, who was killed last year. Nobody around here can pull him out of it when the hypo gets to him, except maybe Willie. Mr. Lincoln is no stranger to death either, Mr. Stanton. I suppose we all have a kinship in that."

Long pause, Stanton having trouble with his breathing. Then: "I am in favor of abolition, Mrs. Keckley. I look forward to the day when the President agrees."

"He wants to set my people free," she said, "but he thinks it would be best if we were sent away."

"Colonization," he said, getting official again. "First compensated emancipation, then colonization, perhaps in Haiti or Panama or some other congenial climate. That will be hard to sell to the Congress."

"I don't want to go. Even with all the troubles, I want to stay here. I bought my freedom, I want to be free to stay."

"Colonization would be voluntary, Mrs. Keckley. Nobody would be forced to leave."

"I know you mean that, but things happen. No white man in the North is going to want a free nigger taking his job. I've seen that."

"Mrs. Keckley, rest assured I am on your side. So is Governor Chase. I wish I could say as much for the rest of them. As for McClellan, he's pro-slavery clear through." After a pause, he pressed that home. "Be sure Mrs. Lincoln knows that—she could be influential. We have to get rid of him."

Since Stanton was back to his old tricks, I reentered with my tea in hand and reminded him about the Prsdt's big activity of the day—War Order No. 1, a better reason for Mars to visit the Prsdt's house than to bawl out the Hellcat or commiserate with her modiste.

Stanton huffed his way down the hall of the Mansion, me following a respectable three paces behind, working his dander up again before seeing the Tycoon. The War Order should have been the first order of business, but the black terrier had a different order on his mind. Lincoln wanted to let certain prisoners of war, who had taken the loyalty oath and wanted to join the Union ranks, enlist—and to credit that enlistment to the quota for certain districts that had special political significance. The Prsdt had to think of his support in key districts that could not be pushed too hard.

Lincoln was lying on the couch. "You got my prisoner-of-war order, Stanton?"

Stanton shook his head. "You must know, Lincoln, your order cannot be executed."

That brought the Prsdt to his feet, the long, roundabout way, and in a tone I can only call unusually peremptory for him, replied, "Mr. Secretary, I reckon you'll have to execute the order."

"Mr. President, I cannot do it. The order is an improper one, and I cannot execute it."

In a manner that forbade all further dispute, President Lincoln said: "Mr. Secretary, it will have to be done."

Stanton stood stock still for a moment, then walked to my office outside and said to Stoddard, who was sitting there, "Go across the street and tell Provost General Fry to execute the order I have been holding on prisoner-of-war enlistments. Tell him I gave him a verbal order to do it immediately, watch him do it, and then come back here and tell me it was done."

Then Jupiter and Mars got down to the business of the day. The Tycoon opened a drawer and pulled out a sheet of paper. (I'm glad he didn't take it out of his hat, as he does with so many other papers. There is something un-presidential about filing your papers in your hat.)

"General War Order Number One," he said. "See what you think. I have to get the armies moving. McClellan's got the slows."

For the past two weeks, ever since that terrible meeting with the stubborn McClellan and his craven generals in the Cabinet Room, the Prsdt has been at his wit's end. The country demands action, the press is critical, the Congress is driven by Wade's committee to grab control of the war, and all we hear is "all quiet on the Potomac." He remembers what McClellan did in protecting Washington from capture after Bull Run, and the Prsdt is not one to forget a favor—and I think he genuinely likes the insufferable Young Napoleon, despite the slights—but the South is getting stronger every day and the war is slipping away. That's why he appointed Stanton, I think: The President wanted someone he respected to tell him to do what he wanted to do all along—which was to rescind that promise to McClellan to let him fight the war without political pressure.

Stanton read aloud: " 'Ordered that the 22nd day of February, 1862, be the day for a general movement of the Land and Naval forces of the United States against the insurgent forces.' " He looked up. "Why Washington's birthday?"

"It has a certain significance," Lincoln said. "The President is commander in chief."

"The order is good as far as it goes," said Stanton. "Our generals out West might take it seriously, but it doesn't light any fires under McClellan."

The Tycoon was disappointed; I know he had set great store by that order and deliberately associated himself with General Washington in its timing. "It's a General War Order, pronouncing military policy. I'll follow it in a few days with specific orders to McClellan to engage the enemy at Manassas and seize the railroad there."

"That's more like it," Stanton replied. "Be sure and put in that he should leave enough troops in Washington for the defense of the capital. A direct, written order should flush him out." He was fairly rubbing his hands at the thought of the generals out-generaled, then looked up sharply. "You're not still thinking of taking field command yourself, are you?"

Lincoln shrugged that off; I knew the thought had crossed his mind weeks ago, and if matters reach a desperate state, he well might. Still, the Tycoon was reluctant to place his military judgment—or Stanton's—above that of men steeped in military affairs all their lives. He was coming to understand military strategy, but errors in tactics could cost God knows how many lives.

"You were pretty high on McClellan a month ago, Mars"—the Prsdt liked to call Stanton "Mars," which he did to his face, but he never called Welles "Father Neptune" except in private—"what do you think of him now?"

"I'm afraid he's afraid to fight. We have had no war, we have not even been playing war."

Lincoln looked pained. Stanton went on, "Besides which, he is a pompous, overbearing, power-hungry, arrogant conniver. God! I don't know why we should have to put up with this!"

Stanton ranted on for a while, then picked up his copy of the order from Stoddard and charged out to work all night or whatever he does. (Actually, I'm told he goes shopping. Three mornings a week, very early, before going to the Department, he visits the city market to shop for vegetables, meats, everything. A manservant pays for his purchases and carries the packages home. Strange form of relaxation for a man.)

I sense a chilling side to Stanton. He will stop at nothing, except a direct order from the Prsdt, and I suppose we're lucky to have such an energetic and brilliant man at the helm of the war machine, to mix a metaphor. He is not someone I want to cross; one of these days I may want a commission myself, because it may not be good for my career to spend this war as a civilian, even here in the White House. Young men not in uniform get suspicious looks in Washington—I know how Robert Lincoln must feel—and I suspect that even Kate Chase wonders about my courage. I will have to puzzle out where Duty lies, here or in the field. More fun here. There may be no dancing at the musicale next week, but all of glittering Washington will be there, including Kate, and I would hate to read about it coming in from a cold and lonely patrol.

After Stanton had bustled out, I told the Tycoon about his interview with Madam, which rather pleased him. I said he had hired an opinionated, impolitic, and highly excitable man as his Secretary of War.

Reminded him, etc. "Some Westerners had a Methodist preacher who got himself all worked up," said the Prsdt, "hellfire-and-brimstone, exhorting them at the top of his lungs, jumping up and down in the pulpit. Finally they came up with a solution to the fervent preaching—they put bricks in his pockets. We may have to do that with old Mars, but I guess we'll let him jump awhile first."

CHAPTER 13

THE BALL WITH NO DANCING

Kate Chase descended the stairway in their home, ten blocks from the Executive Mansion, looking as dazzling as she knew how. Her dress, bought for the occasion at A. Stewart in Philadelphia, was café-au-lait lace; she intended the buttons high to her neck to de-emphasize her lack of bosom and call attention to her graceful neck. The hoop in her skirt was smaller than the fashion, but she asked for it that way because she wanted to move closer to people. Kate Chase went to parties not to be an island but a metropolis, not to be circled by admirers but to extend her father's network of influence.

As she neared the bottom of the stairs, she could hear her father speaking sternly to Jay Cooke, the financier, in the library. "If they can't come up with fifty million this week, I'll print paper money until it costs a thousand dollars to buy breakfast!"

He used that threat often, but rarely to Mr. Cooke, the Philadelphian he had chosen to be chief financier of the war. Jay Cooke was a man Kate admired—dynamic, shrewd, unafraid to admit to his financial ambitions—and he would, she was sure, be helpful in raising the money for a future Chase presidential campaign. The ball gown she was wearing had been purchased through Cooke—actually by Cooke, since he had been thoughtful enough not to send the bill. That was a small confidence the two of them did not feel the need to share with her father. The Secretary of the Treasury was almost ostentatiously stiff about accepting favors from anyone, setting a standard for Stanton to follow, but Kate, who did the Chase family bookkeeping, was more aware than her father of the low state of their funds at the moment. The Chases were almost as broke as the country, which struck her as fitting. Perhaps, if the nation's affairs reached a state where it cost a thousand dollars for breakfast, it would be easier to pay off their overdue bills.

"You mustn't use that tone of voice to Mr. Cooke, Father," she said, entering modestly, deliberately not sweeping in as her younger sister would. "I'm sure he's doing his best."

"You ought to listen to her, Chase," Cooke said. The banker looked at her with obvious delight: "Look at her, too. Wish my daughter looked like that."

Cooke was forty, like an uncle to her, and because he was not a beau, she felt she could accept the gown.

"Stanton wrote a draft for two hundred and fifty thousand dollars to Indiana's militia today, my dear," her father told her, "and the United States Treasury doesn't have the money to cover it. To use the vernacular of the banking system, that check will bounce as if made of rubber. I am hoping our friend Jay will pass on to his banker friends the urgency of the nation's need for a loan."

"Rest assured I shall drive home that point," Cooke said, still looking at the girl in the gown he had secretly bought for her, "And also the fact that you now have the ability to print United States notes, thanks to the Legal Tender Act."

"That too, I suppose," Chase said heavily, in the tone she recognized from their Sundays in church when he was called upon to accept the inevitable. "I am ashamed to be associated with that betrayal of the public trust."

Kate took his arm and drew him down for a kiss. He really did lose sleep over the country's danger. She took the arm of both men and pleased them by saying no woman in Washington had handsomer escorts to the ball.

Mary Todd Lincoln pulled the sleeves down a little farther, helping the dress accentuate her fine shoulders and breasts. She had chosen white satin overlaid with black lace, and a flounce of black lace on one shoulder. Nobody wore black and white these days—this was the year for pinks and shades of purple—but because Queen Victoria's consort, Prince Albert, had recently died, and because Thurlow Weed had written that the Prince had been so influential in averting a war with Britain, Mary thought it would be appropriate for at least part of the wardrobe of the President's lady to acknowledge the British Government's official mourning. She made a mental note to tell that to Mr. Russell, the awful *London Times* man, and to Lord Lyons, the nice ambassador. That is, if she could find Lyons at the party; he was a bachelor and would probably be giving his attention to Kate Chase, like the rest of them.

"Whew!" her husband exclaimed, "our cat has a long tail tonight." Lincoln, in his plain black suit, raised his eyebrows at her dress's elegant train, and then at the near-bareness of his wife's bosom. She did not deign to reply. "Mother, it is my opinion, if some of that tail was nearer the head, it would be in better style."

What did Abraham Lincoln know about style? It was all she could do to get him to keep his shoes on in the daytime. The residue of the Todd family's disapproval of her match lingered even now: they were all convinced she had married beneath her station. She had seen strength and dignity where others had seen awkwardness and boorishness, and tonight, at her first White House *grande levée*, she would show all the Todds and their friends, North and South, that she had been right in her choice, and she would show the world that her husband had the foremost lady in the nation on his arm.

"I have arranged for Lisabeth to stay in Willie's room this evening," she said, examining in the mirror the striking headdress of natural white roses in her hair. Willie's fever had not abated; she remembered her lost Eddie, and she worried. Willie, more than any of them, was the joy of her life;

Mary Todd Lincoln

Abraham's too. Taddie was loved in a different way; he was to be protected. She hoped he would not catch Willie's fever, but could not keep the boys apart.

"Maybe we should have called this party off," he said, the melancholy look crossing his face.

"Not at the last minute. Washington society hates me enough as it is." The idea for a great reception like this, a musicale and midnight supper, had been her break with tradition: up to now, entertaining at the Executive Mansion had been limited to small dinners, or to huge receptions open to all comers on New Year's Day or the Fourth of July. Here was Mary Todd Lincoln's innovation, an invited grand reception with music, which would have been a ball had it not been for the war and Ben Wade's nasty letter. The ladies of Washington—those matrons remaining after the leaders of Southern society had been forced out of town—were waiting for Mrs. Lincoln to prove their gossip right. They said she was a Western bumpkin, wife of a man amusingly cartooned as a baboon, incapable of entertaining in high style. She would show them; she had redecorated the Mansion—at too great expense, perhaps, but with great taste—and her parties would prove that she was as elegant as any of them. She would be a conscientious mother, too, visiting Willie frequently through the evening.

"Well, Mother, who must I talk to tonight—shall it be Mrs. Douglas?" She knew he enjoyed the company of the widow of his former political rival.

"That deceitful woman! No, you shall not listen to her flattery." Addie Douglas, with her syrupy voice and languorous eyes, told him everything he wanted to hear. Mary Lincoln pinned a diamond brooch on the sleeve opposite the flounce of lace, and nodded; that went well with the pearl bracelet. Were the diamond earrings too much? She thought not.

"What do you say to Miss Chase?" he asked, she thought mischievously. "She is too young and handsome to practice deceit."

"You know well enough, Mr. Lincoln, that I do not approve of your flirtations with silly women, just as if you were a beardless boy, fresh from school."

He was trying to get his huge hand into a white glove, with an expression of mock gravity. "I insist I must talk to somebody," he said, pushing her patience further. "I can't stand around like a simpleton and say nothing."

"Anybody you like, just not Mrs. Douglas or Miss Chase. I detest them both." She did not want to hear the next day that the daughter of the Secretary of the Treasury had captivated the President. This was to be Mary Lincoln's night, the center stage shared with nobody else.

"Very well, Mother. Now that we have settled the question to your satisfaction"—he proffered his arm, which she took, "—we will go downstairs."

Robert Lincoln, home from Harvard, waited for his parents to come out so that he could walk downstairs with them. It was hard to get a minute to talk, what with the concern about Willie and the preparations for the big party. On the subject troubling him, the eldest son was eager to speak to both parents together: talking to Father alone was hard, and he could never pry a decision out of Mother alone. Getting them together was not easy; he could not go to them early in the morning, because they never slept in the same room, and lately his father had taken to sleeping with Taddie on the end of his bed. Robert repressed the tug of jealousy; that sort of intimacy had never been shown to him.

"I have to tell you an incident that happened on the way down from Cambridge," he began, hoping to break the ice.

"Have you looked in on your brother?" his father said. "Willie's not been well."

"I will." Always Willie. "Mother, you look lovely. Anyway, I was buying my sleeping car reservations from the conductor on the platform just where you board the train in Boston. There's a space between the platform and the train, do you know? The crowd started to push, and I guess I wasn't looking, and I stepped into that crack and started to drop. Really, I was helpless. Then I could feel my coat collar grabbed and somebody pulled me up out of danger. You know who the man who saved me was? It was Edwin Booth, the famous actor."

"I've seen him perform," said his father. "You should send him a note. Look in on Willie now, he needs cheering up."

Time was slipping away; they were at the stairs leading to the crowded party. Robert breathed deep and blurted it all at once: "Now that I have you both here, I want to talk to you about joining the army. Sixteen of my classmates at Harvard have volunteered, and at age twenty it just isn't seemly for anyone, especially me, to be in college during a war. If I—"

"Not now," said his father, irritated.

"I couldn't bear it," said his mother. "I know you're being manly and noble, my darling, and I want you to do what you think is best, but I'm so frightened you may never come back to us."

"Father?"

"This is not the time."

It was never the time. Coming into public view at the beginning of a big reception was hardly the best time for a discussion of his future, Robert granted, but he had no alternative. There was no good time to bring this up: Father was still angry with him for asking if his roommate could have a commission, to the point of threatening to pull him out of college if Robert sought political favor for anyone again. He had been ashamed of himself later for that, but unashamed about wanting to serve in the army and not wanting to be called a shirker. Mother was a worrier and had always been overly protective, but Father should be on his side about this. He followed a few steps behind them into the public eye, trying to conceal his disappointment by making his face a mask.

The new Secretary of War knew that the way to suborn a newspaper editor was to take him into his confidence. Charles Dana was the key to Horace Greeley, who controlled—or at least, in Stanton's opinion, had an inordinate effect upon—Lincoln's attitudes on slavery and the use of negroes as soldiers. With the backing of Greeley's *Tribune,* Stanton would not have to worry about Bennett's irksome *Herald* or bother with Raymond's stolidly loyal *Times.*

"I want you to know how grateful I am for your editorial column upon my appointment," he told Dana, "but you must be careful—praise makes me vulnerable to jealousy." He looked over toward George McClellan, who was holding forth to a group of officers. He was pale, but obviously on the mend.

"You have enemies," Dana told him, "and some of them have ways to reach Greeley."

Stanton sensed an opening: perhaps Greeley had a less than enthusiastic supporter in his own chief lieutenant. "As soon as I get the machinery of this office working," he assured the editor, "I shall move. First I have to get the rats cleared out and the rat holes stopped."

"We hear the Army of the Potomac is going to sit out the winter," Dana told him. He was correctly informed.

"This army has got to fight or run away," Stanton promised. "While men are striving nobly in the West, the champagne and oysters on the Potomac must be stopped." That was a direct slap at the elegant parties McClellan liked to attend, and an indirect derogation of tonight's affair, as much as Stanton dared.

"I hear that there is movement out West, even as we speak," said the editor. "Our correspondent reports that Admiral Foote and General Grant are already moving boats and men toward the forts protecting the Tennessee River."

"You haven't printed that yet, have you?" Stanton was alarmed; perhaps Halleck and the command out West was taking Lincoln's General War Order No. 1 seriously. Why hadn't Stanton been informed? Why should newspapermen know more about the conduct of the war than the Secretary of War? "Dana, you appear to me to be a patriot and I shall take you into my trust. Tomorrow I intend to take an action that will have every newspaper in the country furious at me."

"Censorship," said Dana, not surprised. "About time."

Stanton was thunderstruck. Whose side was Dana on, that of the press or the government?

"Greeley and Raymond won't like it," Dana went on. "James Gordon Bennett will be especially angry because he has the best men in the field. But I think you're right—the rebels should not learn our plans by just reading our newspapers. I figured that was what you had in mind by taking over the telegraph lines."

"Dana, if you can calm Greeley down on this, you will be doing the cause of the war a great service."

"I may have my troubles with Greeley," Dana said circumspectly. Stanton wondered what he was getting at—was there more than minor friction at the *Tribune?* Could Dana be used now, perhaps be detached from journalism and then used by the government in another capacity?

"Whatever troubles you have in keeping Greeley aggressive," Stanton said with care, "and whatever your patriotism costs you in your career, that will be carefully considered here." As Dana nodded, Stanton decided to make the offer more specific. "One day you might want to serve your country here, right across the street. At the propitious moment, say the word."

Dana nodded again. Stanton felt sure he had him.

"Cloth is hot."

Elizabeth Keckley removed the wet cloth from Willie's brow, immersed it in the pan of cool water, wrung it out, and replaced it on the fevered forehead of the President's middle son. The bilious fever, which had lasted for over a month, had wasted the boy, and showed no signs of abating. It should have passed by now, she calculated; it was probably the same fever that struck General McClellan, and he was up and around. Some people were better able to throw it off than others.

"My pony?"

"He's fine. Your father and Tad go over to the stable every night." That was no story; Lincoln and his youngest son made sure Willie's pony was taken care of, and reported to Willie that the animal missed him.

The modiste sat silently in the dark, listening to the boy's breathing and the sounds of the party below. Twice tonight the President had come in, said a few words of comfort to his son, felt his hot hand, and returned to his guests. Mrs. Lincoln had come in briefly with her son Robert; in the shaft of light spilling from the open hall door Lizzie could see Willie smile at his older brother. It was said that Robert favored his mother, and it was true that his face resembled hers, but he had his father's remoteness. Willie had his father's swings in mood, from inexplicable sadness to sudden laughter and the urge to share the humor with everybody, and in her judgment was the one through whom Lincoln saw his spirit living on.

The party below was not a good idea, the negro woman decided. Mrs. Lincoln had staked too much on it, and in her mind had irrationally linked the ball, which could not be canceled, and her son's fever, which no bed rest or cool bath could long control. Mrs. Lincoln seemed to her friend the modiste always on the edge of breaking. She could not join in the general hatred of the South, where her relatives lived, but she was a loyal enough Unionist with no desire to protect slavery. She was worried almost to distraction about Willie, having lost one boy to illness already, and refused to let Robert go near danger. President Lincoln was in a fix about that, Mrs. Keckley knew, torn between the boy's desire to enlist and his wife's need for him not to enlist. Besides, there was the talk of favoritism, keeping the boy out of uniform. Lincoln, she felt sure, would put up with the criticism and Robert's pleading in order to keep his wife from losing her mind.

Was "losing her mind" too strong? Lizzie Keckley thought no; Mrs. Lincoln was a good woman in more trouble, with more pressing down on her, than anybody knew. She dipped the cloth in the pan and wrung it out again.

"The wallpaper was worth it," Major French said to George Nicolay, who was helping himself to the champagne punch in the Japanese bowl at the center of the State Dining Room.

"Sixty-seven hundred dollars' worth?"

"It comes all the way from Paris," the major argued, hoping to win an ally close to the President. The walls were really beautiful, French was certain, far nicer than the Executive Mansion had ever seen, a mark of good taste directly attributable to Mrs. Lincoln. The new carpet, too, and the silver service; why should the palace of the American President be a shabby place, ridiculed by the European diplomats? "It's going into an appropriation for sundry civil expenses." The Congress had better go along, the major thought—eight hundred dollars of the advance for the wallpaper had come out of his own pocket.

That was when Mr. Lincoln flatly refused to pay for what he kept calling "flub-dubs."

"Who laid out this feast?" Nicolay asked. The musicale portion of the evening had ended, and when the doors of the East Room were opened, the guests were led to a giant punch bowl in the central hall. Waiters passed through the crowd dispensing what French had been told were "finger sandwiches." He quickly admonished Nicolay to ignore the sandwiches and save his appetite for the display of exotic foods served at the midnight supper.

"Maillard's of New York. Come through here." Major French had ordered a ton of game: partridge, pheasant, and venison were laid out on the tables of the State Dining Room, along with the usual ham and turkey and duck. On a table of dressed game, the confectioner had created a sugar model of Fort Sumter. Plunk in the middle of the venison, a model of the frigate *Union* was in full sail on a stand supported by cherubs and draped in the flag. Charlotte russes ran out of a sugar beehive, and water nymphs made of nougat supported a fountain. Nothing like that, Major French was certain, had ever graced the Mansion before.

"My God, what's that?" breathed Nicolay.

French smiled proudly. "That's Fort Pickens, done to exact scale, and stuffed with quail eggs. Wait till you try a quail egg, Nicolay. Put your hand right through the front of the fort."

The President's first secretary declined. "Good thing you didn't send to Paris for the food," said Nicolay, breaking a piece of nougat off one of the parapets of Fort Sumter. The fellow was obviously a Philistine when it came to elegant parties. French knew that the presidential secretary's younger colleague, Hay, was more socially adept, and hoped he would be suitably impressed.

"You see that fillet of beef over there? It's called Chateaubriand, the supreme achievement of the gastronomic art," Major French instructed him. "I've already heard this function compared to the Duchess of Richmond's ball in Brussels."

"I read about that ball," nodded Nicolay, swallowing the nougat and heading to the Chateaubriand table before the crowd, "in the history books. Night before Waterloo."

Lord Lyons, the British Ambassador, waited his turn to greet the President's Lady. An American senator was ahead of him.

"I just met your son, Mrs. Lincoln," he heard the senator say sourly. "Fine, strapping lad. He should be in uniform."

"He wants to go, Senator Harris, but I just cannot bear the thought at the moment."

The senator said pointedly, "My only son is in the army."

She looked stunned and Lyons rescued her. "I note that part of your gown is black, Mrs. Lincoln," he interrupted, easing the senator out of the way, "and I will include that in my report to Her Majesty. I know Queen Victoria will be grateful for your most appropriate expression of condolence." The President's wife quickly recovered her composure, and Lincoln looked relieved.

The ruddy, hearty Englishman, cheeks fringed with whiskers, had come to respect Lincoln during the *Trent* affair. Lyons was no longer as certain as some of his countrymen, including the Foreign Secretary, that the South would win its independence.

General McClellan had done a remarkable job in rebuilding a defeated army in a short time, according to the military experts Lyons trusted most. Moreover, the British Ambassador had learned from one of McClellan's more impetuous aides that the General-in-Chief had just sent a force under General Burnside to seize Roanoke Island, which gave the Federals a first-rate base off North Carolina to enforce the blockade. Lyons had also heard from some Southern friends that seizure of the offshore island provided a clue to McClellan's intentions: he might be planning to approach Richmond by water, maneuvering the Confederates out of their positions near Washington. In addition, McClellan had authorized Halleck and Grant to begin operations against the forts guarding the Tennessee River in the West.

Some heard only the foolish complaints of the press and the radicals in Congress, but Lord Lyons also listened to the well-considered worries of the Southerners as well. With McClellan gathering his forces for a surprise attack, and refusing to be hounded by amateurs into a premature midwinter advance, Her Majesty's envoy now considered British neutrality a wiser course than intervention, Southern cotton or no.

Having done his diplomatic duty to the Lincolns, the bachelor British envoy went in search of his favorite Washingtonian. Most of the evening, Kate Chase had resisted holding a small levee of her own, preferring to dart in and out of conversations, but now she was surrounded by admirers, including Sprague, the Governor of Rhode Island, inebriated as usual, as well as Congressman Roscoe Conkling from New York, an officer from Ohio named Garfield, and one of Mr. Lincoln's younger secretaries. Lord Lyons sighed and joined the group.

Anna Carroll took Salmon Chase aside. "I must see you a moment in private."

"For you, my dear lady, I am always available." He was such a fine-looking man, a tower of strength; she thought it a pity about his unwavering, sometimes excessive, dignity. The Wades insisted that Chase was the only man in the Cabinet of presidential stature, a political assessment that included and then rejected Seward; Anna was inclined to agree. Chase looked and moved like a President—more so than Lincoln, surely. He was surrounded by an aura of probity, almost nobility. She shared in the general trust of Chase, and saw an opportunity to do a favor for him.

"This is none of my business," she began, pleased at the way he inclined his majestic head down to hear her low voice, "but I noticed when you came in and greeted the Lincolns, your daughter said something that was less than kind to the President's wife."

He winced. "Kate is headstrong. I didn't hear what was said, I was talking to the President."

"I overheard it," she said, "Kate said something—a little too sweetly, if you ask me—about Mrs. Lincoln being far more experienced than she, and the President's wife took it as a reflection on her age."

"Ah." He looked helpless; Anna was glad she had spoken up.

"Here's what you should tell your daughter," she said, presenting the solution immediately after stating the problem, which she liked to do. "The Lincolns' son, William, is upstairs with a fever. It may be the same typhoid fever that killed Prince Albert, and almost killed General McClellan. Mrs. Lincoln is upset, worried sick, trying not to show it."

"My God. And my daughter was—"

"It's not something that Kate would have said, I'm sure, if she had known about the boy." She put her hand on his arm and took a deep breath, showing her concern and her bosom. "Tell her to go back to Mrs. Lincoln and offer her sympathy. Be good for the both of them."

"I'll do that immediately. Miss Carroll—"

"Anna."

"Anna, I know better than most what it is to be in fear of losing a loved one." Anna was aware that he had lost three wives and five of his seven children to disease; death was a frequent visitor to this strong, magnetic, probably lonely man. "I will be certain that my daughter expresses the profound understanding of the Chase family. She and I are in your debt."

Anna squeezed his arm and sent him on his way. Why did he make her think of Breck? Probably because of his height and deep voice, and the pull of his personality. She found herself afflicted by the thought of Breck for a moment, until Brady, the photographer, came up to her. He peered at her through thick spectacles, recognized her face, and urged her to drop into his shop for a portrait soon. She begged off for the moment; a photographic portrait required a new dress and she would have to make a decision about the length of her hair.

It was after 1 A.M. and the party was at its peak—surely a first, Anna figured, for this early-retiring Southern city. She was flushed with its excitement: People were doing business, diplomats were doing each other in, generals were taking the opportunity to mend fences with politicians, and social Washington had to be impressed with the ability of the Lincolns to entertain royally even in the midst of war. Everyone had gasped at the display of viands in the banquet hall. Anna judged that the big party ws not a lapse of taste, but an expression of Union confidence in a dark time; the Wades had been wrong to stay away.

She looked for Stanton; before dinner was served, she had seen him talking intently to the man from the *Tribune,* but the Secretary of War had apparently slipped out while the party was in full swing.

Anna guessed that he would have gone across the street to the War Department before going home; Stanton was the sort who would like it to be known that he had been too busy with official cares to partake of the midnight feast. He would also wonder what he had missed. She seized the opportunity: in a moment, she was in the kitchen with Major French, putting together a basket of game and delicious victuals from Maillard's for the Secretary of War. She also obtained a small package of cakes and nougat icing for young Homer Bates and whoever else might be in the telegraph office at this hour, listening to the sounds of revelry across the street.

Anna was convinced that the moment had come for the Union Army in the West to strike. The Tennessee River was at high water and Fort Henry was probably half inundated, and Federal gunboats under Admiral Foote were out of the boatyards and in operation at last. Was anybody following her plan? Tom Scott was out there, on a survey for Stanton—surely he would be urging the movement on the generals in the field, telegraphing his recommendations back to the War Department.

She drew her cape around her—one day, when she received recognition and recompense, she would be able to afford fur—gripped the basket in her ungloved hand and scurried across the street to the building that she hoped had become the nerve center of the war.

"My dear lady, you are like a visiting angel," Stanton said, pleased that someone would report his selfless presence at his post. He was also glad to have the food. His wife, at home with their ailing infant, would want to know about the party; at least he would have something to give her from there without the indignity of asking Major French, surely a wastrel and probably a thief, for a packet to bring home. "Take the cakes to Eckert and his men across the hall right away, they'll bless you for it. And come right back."

Even as the President's wife was stuffing her guests with expensive game, the War Secretary knew that the navy had undertaken to reduce Fort Henry. That rebel installation at the head of the Tennessee River was under attack by some of Halleck's command under Congressman Washburne's protégé, General Grant. Halleck was worried about Grant: unstable. If he took Fort Henry and continued on to the seriously defended Fort Donelson, Grant could get himself cut off and be forced to surrender fifteen thousand men. The Union could not afford another defeat, and Stanton's spotless reputation as organizer of victory would be immediately besmirched. Was it worth the effort?

Assistant Secretary Scott was all for the movement. Scott was a sound executive and honest, but a Pennsylvania Cameron man; he would have to go. Only men absolutely beholden to Stanton could work at the top echelons of the War Department. This little lady who claimed to have conceived the idea was urging it on all and sundry, and her closeness to Wade meant that Stanton would show her at least the courtesy of consideration. Stanton had resolved to leave that military decision to Halleck; if it failed, he could fire Halleck, court-martial Grant, and blame the defeat on the navy. The West was not important anyway; this war would be settled in the East, if ever he could get McClellan to move. The caution he saw as an asset in Halleck was a liability in McClellan. He, too, would have to go; Stanton would put in his own man to run the war in the field. He thought of how he had been forced to stand like a beggar at McClellan's dinner table, awaiting the great general's notice, and the memory of that studied slight made him burn.

"You will be pleased to learn," he told Miss Carroll on her return, "that all political prisoners arrested under authority of the Secretary of State will be released upon taking a loyalty oath." That would display Union confidence and appeal to Democrats who had been making a fuss about civil liberties.

"Spies, too?"

"John Dix will determine who will or will not be exempted," he replied. He could count on Dix, a Democrat who had served with him in the Buchanan Cabinet, to make certain Rose Greenhow would be properly oathed and sent South before she made any more trouble.

"And if habeas corpus requires suspension again?"

She was an astute little woman. "Extraordinary arrests will hereafter be made," he smiled, "under the direction of the military authorities alone." Seward was out of it, his prisoners given amnesty; now the power was Stanton's.

"Good," the little woman said. "A war power belongs in the war office."

He impulsively pushed a stack of deciphered cables toward her, withholding only the one expressing Halleck's concerns about Grant's "bad habits" to McClellan. "Senator Wade will be interested to know that the Tennessee River campaign that you and he suggested is under way."

Let her think it was all her idea; that would involve Wade, protecting Stanton from criticism from the Joint Committee if the attack on Forts Henry and Donelson failed. If it succeeded, credit would devolve on Halleck and the generals in the West, and of course on the new Secretary of War.

"The purpose of this war is to attack, pursue, and destroy a rebellious enemy," he said. He was certain that George Brinton McClellan was no destroyer; the general probably harbored some notions of a negotiated peace after some good days on a battlefield, which made McClellan more of an enemy to the Union cause than any rebel soldier. He would have to be broken, his place taken by a general of Stanton's choosing.

The parading around was over; he would make heroes of the generals who accepted the need for mutual slaughter. The North could afford the lives, the South could not. After Miss Carroll left, Stanton wrapped up the expensive food and took it home to his wife.

General Ulysses S. Grant

BOOK FOUR

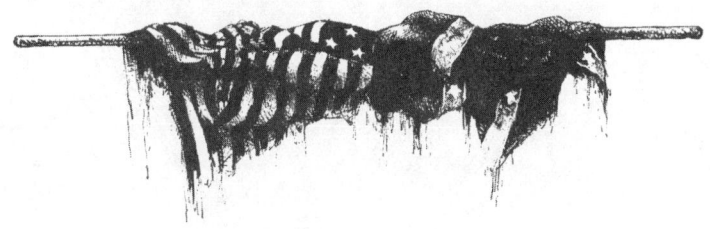

Ulysses
Simpson
Grant

CHAPTER 1

Unconditional Surrender

Sam Grant, hatless, blue uniform blouse unbuttoned despite the unexpected cold, sat on a keg on the snow-covered bank of the Cumberland River to watch the navy's gunboats attack Fort Donelson.

He answered to the name "Sam" because that was what they had called him—"Uncle Sam"—at the military academy, thanks to his initials, U. S. Some clerk had mixed up his name on his West Point application, changing Hiram Ulysses to Ulysses Simpson, and he never bothered to correct it: U.S.G. got him called "Sam," and H.U.G. would have earned him "Hug" so he let it alone.

If he failed in this expedition, Grant knew, he would be a failure for the rest of his life, just as he had been a failure in everything up to now. Only a remote political connection—his Galena, Illinois, congressman, Elihu Washburne—had given him this second chance; there would be no third. Grant was sorry he had not been able to get to see George McClellan when the "Young Napoleon" had a command in the West. He was acquainted with Mac from the Military Academy—Grant had been in his fourth year at the Point when McClellan was in his first—and Grant still thought he would make a fine cavalry brigade commander in Mac's Army of the Potomac.

No gunboats yet in sight. He took out a knife and began to whittle a stick. Attacking Forts Henry and Donelson this way was sensible, because it seemed plain enough to him that the way to break the back of the rebellion in the West was to take men on gunboats down toward Corinth via the Tennessee River, outflanking the forts on the Mississippi. But last month, when he went to General Halleck with the plan, "Old Brains" just stared at him as if Grant were drunk or crazy. Wouldn't respond at all, just treated the idea with contempt.

Was Grant's plan so preposterous? He didn't think so, but Halleck had written the book on strategy, and Grant had to wonder about his own military judgment. All he had ever done was to fight in Mexico—creditably; that was the high point of his life, in retrospect—but he took no real satisfaction in that either, because it was an unjust war: a strong nation had fought a weak one just to grab some territory. Grant thought the nation was paying now in blood and treasure for the sin of that conquest of Mexico.

No matter; this was a good war and he felt comfortable in it. He disagreed with all the harangues in the public press about this being a war against slavery. His inclination was to whip the rebellion into submission, preserving all property rights, and if the South could not be beaten in any other way than a war against slavery, only then let it come to that legitimately. If slavery had to go in order to keep the Union in existence, then let slavery go; that was his position. But Grant thought that Greeley—and the rest of the press trying to whip up an anti-slavery war—were as great enemies to their country as if they were open and avowed secessionists.

Grant thought Lincoln had the war goals about right: defeat the rebs, save the Union, let slavery take care of itself. Grant himself had not been eligible to vote in the last election, having just moved to Galena, Illinois, which was just as well because he had pledged his support to the Democrat Douglas. That election was essentially Breckinridge versus Lincoln, minority rights against majority rule; he was glad Lincoln had won. Lincoln's War Order No. 1 was aimed mainly at McClellan in the East, where the war would be decided, but Grant took that as his license to go hunting, and without really asking permission from Halleck, had plotted with Admiral Foote to grab Fort Henry.

That ill-situated fort had been easy pickings. Strange bird, Foote—an old salt sailing little ironclad gunboats on fresh water, fulminating all the time about the two worst evils in the world, slavery and whiskey. Grant was not fighting this war for the slaves—his wife, Julia, used to own some when she lived in style, before she became the wife of a born failure—and he was certainly not fighting this war to exorcise Demon Rum. Old Foote was a hellfire preacher, though, and even got the navy to cancel the traditional rum ration, which cost him more than a few sailors.

The river navy didn't need a full complement to take Fort Henry; at high tide, the Tennessee flooded half the fort's batteries and the place was practically defenseless. With the advantage of the river's freak northward current, the river fleet leveled the fort. After two hours of shelling from the gunboats —enough time for most of the fort's defenders to slip out and head for Donelson twelve miles away—the rebel commander climbed into a boat, was rowed out to Foote's *Carondelet,* and asked for terms. Foote framed a pretty ringing response, Grant thought—no terms at all, just "unconditional surrender."

Grant squinted into the mist and made out four gunboats steaming around the point, and heard the guns of Donelson roar. Fort Donelson was not Fort Henry: 128-pounders had been placed high atop its bluffs, and were now firing down at the sloping iron sides of Foote's fleet. The sides of the boats were angled to make shots aimed at the same level carom off, but the cannons high on the bluff fired down, the balls slamming into the gunships head-on, shuddering them on impact, the clang of iron ball on iron armor echoing in the frozen hills around.

Foote kept coming, blazing back at the fort, his boats supported far behind, by long-range artillery from wooden ships too fragile to risk the batteries on the bluff. On the bluff, one rebel 128-pounder fell silent, hit by naval fire or spiked by its own crew, but at 500 yards the fire from the fort's short-range, 32-pound carronades was devastating to the Union fleet. Grant watched the fort's cannonballs rip the armor off the ships like shucking corn, and the admiral's flagship took a solid shot that tore away the pilothouse.

Grant wondered whether that last shot had killed Foote. The *Carondelet* took advantage of the river's northward flow and drifted back to safety. The other three ships in the ironclad fleet limped after her. As Fort Henry had shown what ironclad gunboats could do, Fort Donelson had shown what they could not do.

"Siege," Grant said aloud. He had 24,000 men, not enough to storm a garrison of 18,000. He needed a three-to-one advantage to storm a fort successfully, according to the book, even if he was willing to take heavy casualties. He took out a pencil and began writing a message to Halleck: "I fear the result of an attempt to carry the place by storm with raw troops." Halleck would like that; Old Brains always wanted to be careful. Still, Grant's superior officer had to be pleased with last week's capture of Henry, and was probably claiming great credit for himself in telegrams to Stanton and McClellan. Grant would have to write a letter to Congressman Washburne, in hopes he could show it to Lincoln.

"I feel great confidence in ultimately reducing the place," Grant wrote in the pad on his knee. No bravado; it was true. Grant had been informed that his opposition at Donelson was badly led. The fort commander, General Floyd, had been Secretary of War in Buchanan's Cabinet and was run out of Washington for stealing Union stores. Floyd was all politician, no soldier, and he would rely for guidance on his deputy, Gideon Pillow. General Pillow was a walking military disaster, Grant recalled—flamboyant, foolishly eager for combat, a braggart who had been censured for laying claim to exploits not his own in Mexico. With Pillow running the rebel show, and notorious for failing to reconnoiter, Grant was certain that any Union force, no matter how small, could march up to within gunshot range of any entrenchments Pillow was given to hold.

Grant tried to figure out why rebel General Sidney Johnston had not come to take personal command; that seemed a mistake. Against a first-class military mind like Johnston's, this would be a tough campaign, perhaps impossible, but he was certain Floyd and Pillow would panic under siege. The weather was on the rebel side, Grant acknowledged, mounting his horse to see whether Foote was alive. Ten-degree cold was harder on the attacker than on the dug-in defender, especially when the Union men had discarded their overcoats two days before, when the weather appeared summery. Grant was aware that he and his men were exposed, and Halleck was warning that a swift move by the rebels in Bowling Green could cut them off. Too much depended on Foote's gunboats.

Private J. Cabell Breckinridge, a proud member of the Second Kentucky Brigade just assigned to join in the defense of Donelson, considered himself lucky. Sweeping out tents and boiling the lice out of clothes, his major activities in Bowling Green headquarters, was not the sort of war he had in mind. He had joined the only rebel unit from a state still in the Union last year, when he was sixteen, but he was big, and had lied about his age and used his middle name for his last. Cabell had seen action at Mill Creek and escaped with his life from that disaster, having shown his comrades that he would not run under fire. His gun didn't go off during a charge but that wasn't his fault, and he was almost shot by a Mississippi outfit that mistook his Kentucky jeans for a blue Yankee uniform.

He knew his mother and father had been upset with him for running away to fight, especially when his father was still engaged in a hopeless effort to hold the Union together in the Senate. Now that his father was a general in the Confederate Army, Cabell was determined not to serve too close to him. Being the son of top brass troubled him: in school, he had always been "Senator Breckinridge's son," and then "Vice President Breckinridge's son." He was better off fighting this war without that burden.

Nor did his father, for all his political experience, seem to understand what this fight was really about. Throughout his early teens, Cabell had listened to tedious lectures from his father about the danger of disunion. Compromise was sheer foolishness, and the Vice President should have known it; Cabell could have told him he would lose the election for President, but it was not a son's place to say that to his father.

Cabell's way of thinking, supported by all his young friends in Lexington, was that the Northern abolitionists were out to strike at the power and the way of life of the South. They were not content to limit the territorial expansion of slavery, as Lincoln and other moderates pretended, but were determined to disrupt Southern life. Toward that selfish end, the abolitionists intended to incite servile insurrections—with all the rape and murder of whites that entailed—with offers of "freedom" to chattel property who were far better off under the paternal hand of their masters than they would be in the grip of Northern factory owners. The real intent of the abolitionists, Cabell was certain, was not to save the Little Eva of Harriet Beecher Stowe's novel, but to enslave the whites of the South.

Cabell felt lucky, too, because he was sent north to fight at Donelson rather than south to get all fixed to retreat from Kentucky. What was wrong with General Johnston, anyway? The greatest general of the Confederacy was forever falling back. The sergeants said these retreats were a trap for the Yankees, to be followed by some glorious battle that would decide the war. He hoped so; the soldier life had been exciting these past few months, except for those scary moments at Mill Creek, but he'd just as soon go back to school soon. He imagined the envious faces of the boys when he would tell of his personal experiences in the War for Southern Independence.

His best luck had been to be chosen as General Buckner's orderly. It happened back in Bowling Green when the corporal sent a detail to the general's tent to pack up headquarters equipment. Buckner looked at Private Cabell, looked closer, and asked, "Your unit coming with me to Donelson?" Cabell said yes, and he sure would like to get out of sweep-up duty to a fighting job. "You look like a Breckinridge," Buckner said. Cabell could not deny it, because Buckner had been a frequent guest at family gatherings. The general then assigned him on the spot to be his orderly, working with a Kentucky corporal, which was not quite the front-line duty he had in mind but was better than his current condition. They had marched into Donelson a few hours ago and heard the booming of the guns on the river.

"We whupped 'em," the corporal said gleefully, chucking a handful of coals into the stove. "Same damn Yankee ships that pounded Fort Henry down last week. This place be a tougher nut to crack, you bet. You see those entrenchments? How'd you like to be a Yankee on the other side of them, comin' up the hill?"

"Rather be this side," Cabell replied, "if our guns work."

In the morning the corporal was less cheerful, reporting to the general that Yankee troops had invested the area close to the fortifications during the night. Buckner was coldly furious; Cabell followed the general over to the command bunker where he confronted Generals Floyd and Pillow.

"Where were your pickets?" Buckner demanded, as if he were not the junior officer present. "The Federals should have paid for every yard outside the lines. We had a clear field of fire. Now they're on top of us and you haven't fired a shot."

"It was ten degrees last night," Pillow said glumly, "and the pickets were inside celebrating the victory."

When Buckner cursed, Floyd said, "I don't like your attitude, General. I am in command here and you are insubordinate." Cabell, standing at attention back in the corner, wondered if this was how general officers usually ran their councils of war.

"Begging your pardon, General Floyd," Buckner said through tight lips, "but what is your plan?"

The politician turned to his companion. "Pillow?"

"Our plan is to hold this place for three days," said the swarthy general, "protecting Johnston's general withdrawal from Kentucky. Then we'll cut our way out and join him in Tennessee."

"During the siege, we can inflict heavy casualties on the assaulting troops," Floyd added, not too sure of himself, "and then really smash them when we cut our way out. Grant will be in no shape to pursue."

Buckner shook his head but said nothing. Cabell hoped the other generals knew what they were talking about; this "council of war" didn't seem like much of a meeting to him.

Grant's wounded were freezing to death. The general surveyed his three-mile line around the fort and was less confident than his telegram to Halleck had suggested. For three days his assaults had been inconclusive; the heavy snow covered each day's casualties, giving him the feeling that he was fighting a new battle every day.

From his command post in Mrs. Crisp's boardinghouse, where only the kitchen was heated, the general waited for the pressure to cause one side or another to crack. Flag-officer Foote was alive, although injured, and kept a steady bombardment on the fort from a distance. Halleck had sent in several thousand reinforcements, all he said he could spare.

A messenger appeared with a rebel knapsack in his hand. "The enemy is attacking McClernand's position, sir, and in force. We took some prisoners and they were all wearing these. Seems the rebs expect their offensive to last."

Grant opened the rebel knapsack to find provisions for three days. More food than ammunition. That meant this attack was no foray; these rebels were trying to escape, to break the siege. It could be that the whole army at Donelson was trying to cut its way out.

"The one who attacks now will be victorious," Grant told the other officers in the kitchen, "and the enemy will have to be in a hurry if he gets ahead of me."

He hurried outside, climbed on his horse and rode hard on the icy road to McClernand's division, finding men standing in groups, leaderless and confused. "Fill your cartridge boxes, quick, and get into line," he called, "the enemy is trying to escape."

General McClernand came up and began a long-winded explanation of his ideas about withdrawing out of the range of Confederate fire. Grant knew that McClernand had strong political connections in Illinois that reached into Lincoln's White House, but he could not permit the man's dawdling to cost him the garrison at Donelson.

"That road must be recovered before night," he told McClernand, controlling his anger. "I will go to see Baldy Smith now. At the sound of your fire, he will support you with an attack on his side."

Grant sent a courier to Admiral Foote asking the gunboats to make a lot of noise. He rode to Baldy Smith, an old regular army man who had been his teacher at West Point, to tell him to counterattack immediately. He watched Smith lead his men to breach the rebel entrenchments and lodge themselves on a ridge where artillery could fire into the fort. In that way the defenses could soon be broken. No escape; Grant had the rebels where he wanted them. The trick, he knew almost instinctively, was to hit hard when everyone was exhausted, when nobody wanted to hit or be hit. Your enemy never had to know how weak or demoralized your men were; you had to be the one less disgusted and disheartened by war.

Cabell stood guard, at General Buckner's order, at the door of the Confederate generals' council. It was two in the morning. A white-faced Floyd asked, "What is best now to be done?"

"We'll fight 'em to the death," vowed General Pillow dramatically. Cabell frowned as he overheard that. In the heat of the attempt to break out a few hours before, when Buckner wanted to press the attack, it had been Pillow, now talking so tough, who had folded at the first sign of Union resistance and insisted they return to the fort. Victory had been so close—the soldiers knew it; for no reason, it seemed, the officers had given back the field so hard won.

"No, not now, not anymore," said Buckner wearily. "Their troops are fresh, our men are exhausted. Grant will attack at daylight and I will not be able to hold my position half an hour."

"Yes, you can!" Pillow shouted.

"The Second Kentucky is as good a regiment as we have in the service," said Buckner in a tired voice, and Cabell silently agreed. "An hour ago, before I could rally and form them, I had to take at least twenty men by the shoulders and pull them into line."

"We can still cut our way out," insisted Pillow; "fight the Yankees to their death."

"Where the hell were you a couple of hours ago?" Buckner said bitterly. "Another attempt would cost us three quarters of our men. No commander has that right."

"I will never surrender. I will die first." It struck Cabell that Pillow seemed eager to show a fierceness in council that he had not shown in the field.

"I cannot and will not surrender," said Floyd. "But I confess personal reasons control me." Cabell and everybody in the fort knew what Floyd's personal fears were: the Federals would probably try him for treason and hang him. Why wasn't Sidney Johnston here, in command where and when it counted? Cabell had heard from the corporal that Johnston would never have folded yesterday.

"If the command of the army is turned over to me," Buckner said, "I will surrender the army and share its fate."

"If I place you in command," asked Floyd, "will you allow me to get out?"

"I will," said Buckner.

"Then, sir, I turn over the command to General Pillow."

General Pillow immediately blurted, "I pass it."

General Simon Bolivar Buckner, C.S.A.

"I assume it," said Buckner dutifully. "Give me pen and ink and paper and send for a bugler. I will ask for terms."

The cavalry colonel in the corner, Nathan Bedford Forrest, spoke out. "There's more fight in my men than you suppose. I will take out my command, no matter what the cost."

"You don't have the right to sacrifice five hundred men," said Buckner.

"I'll ask for volunteers," growled Colonel Forrest. Cabell had heard of Forrest, a slave trader and all-around fearsome fellow.

"Let him cut his way out if he wants," said Pillow to Buckner. "Floyd and I will go with him, unless the steamer is safer."

"There's no need to surrender," Forrest insisted. "I just sent two men up the bank of the river and they didn't run into any Federal forces."

"The Federals' campfires are all lit," said Buckner.

"Those are old campfires. There's a high wind," reported Forrest, "so they're blazing. You could walk two thirds of this garrison out to fight again, and they'd never run into a Federal soldier."

Buckner was weary. "Colonel Forrest, take the cavalry out with you, those who choose to go. And take Floyd and Pillow. I assure you, Colonel, I do not look forward to spending the rest of the war in a prison camp, but I am in command here."

"You know Grant; he's an old friend of yours," said Forrest. "Do you suppose he would surrender, in your shoes?"

"Maybe Grant would sacrifice his army if he were in my shoes right now,"

Colonel Nathan Bedford Forrest, C.S.A.

Buckner replied evenly, "but I am a soldier, not a butcher. I will not give up the lives of fifteen thousand men so that one or two thousand can escape."

"I came to fight, not to surrender," Forrest said. Cabell liked that attitude. He assessed Floyd as a coward, Pillow as someone not to be trusted, Buckner as honorable—at least he would go to prison camp with his men—but as an officer and a gentleman, too much the gentleman and not enough the officer. Forrest, however, knew what this war was about. Cabell could claim no knowledge of military tactics, but it occurred to him that neither could the trio of generals here. Common sense suggested that the South did not have enough men in uniform to be able to surrender a whole army. Besides, you could never tell in a battle—strange things happened; maybe the defenders could cut their way out without huge casualties, or even drive off the attackers.

Cabell, standing rigidly at the door, wondered what his father would do in these circumstances? He liked to think that General Breckinridge would fight; but Father had a habit of trying the peaceful way. Cabell would fight, if he had his way. Now, for the first time, the prospect of surrender's personal effect occurred to him: the rest of Private Cabell's war would be spent in a Yankee prison.

Grant showed Buckner's letter asking for terms to Baldy Smith. "It's not Floyd or Pillow in command, it's Simon Bolivar Buckner," Grant said. Could Buckner have been in charge all along? If so, Grant would never have taken the chances he had; he'd thought he was fighting a couple of amateurs. Maybe Floyd and Pillow were just sticking Buckner with the humiliation. Grant remembered when Buckner had lent him the two hundred dollars when he was down and out. "What should I say?"

"No terms to armed rebels," barked old soldier Smith. "Tell them what Foote told them: immediate and unconditional surrender."

That was a good way of putting it. Ben Butler had demanded "full capitulation" when he took Fort Hatteras in North Carolina last summer, but Foote's phrase sounded more final. Laboriously, with papers spread out on the kitchen table, Grant wrote the note to his old acquaintance from West Point: "No terms except unconditional and immediate surrender can be accepted. I propose to move immediately upon your works." Two "immediates" sounded awkward, but no mind, it was written. He added a closing which he hoped Buckner would realize was meant for him: "I am, sir, very respectfully, your obedient servant, U. S. Grant, Brigadier General, Commanding."

In the telegraph office at the War Department, Homer Bates looked up to see the President come in. The telegrapher was handed a message to send from Lincoln to General Halleck: "You have Fort Donelson safe, unless Grant shall be overwhelmed from outside. Our success or failure at Fort Donelson is vastly important, and I beg you to put your soul into the effort."

"How is your boy, sir?" Everyone in government knew of the President's worry about his son Willie.

"I fear for him, Bates. I had another boy, Eddie, who had that same raspy sound in his throat the last night. You'll send this right away?"

"The bastard," said Buckner: Grant, a failure in civilian life, was a failure in military honor. No great or inspired generalship had earned Grant this victory, Buckner was certain; it had been plain perseverance and luck in the face of floundering and cowardice by the two politicians skulking aboard a steamer leaving the dock at that very moment.

Reluctantly, Buckner wrote his reply: "The distribution of the forces under my command, incident to an unexpected change of commanders, and the overwhelming force under your command, compel me, notwithstanding the brilliant success of the Confederate arms yesterday, to accept the ungenerous and unchivalrous terms which you propose." He believed that duty and honor required this first surrender of a Confederate army; the alternative, with Grant, was prolonged butchery.

Buckner looked at the Breckinridge boy. "Orderly, take this to the messenger for General Grant."

"Yes, sir. After that, can I make a break with Colonel Forrest? He's letting every cavalryman take a foot soldier on the same horse."

Buckner was torn. He had told General Breckinridge he would look out for his boy and not let him do anything foolish. Surrender, prison, perhaps ultimate exchange—none of that was foolish, dreary though it would surely be and, with the disease in the Federal camps, not devoid of danger. On the other hand, perhaps Forrest was right and the campfires were misleading; it would be foolish to give up. Buckner had already made his choice, protecting the lives entrusted to him; he could not make it for Breck's boy, who knew what he wanted to do.

"Take my horse, Breckinridge," he told the boy; "I won't be needing it. You ride, don't you? All right, take my horse to Colonel Forrest and tell him I ordered you to follow him out of here with as many as he can safely manage."

"I'm grateful to you, sir."

"You're sure that's what you want? A lot of men will be killed trying to break out. It is in no way dishonorable to remain for the surrender."

"I'll make a run for it with the cavalry."

"Report to General Breckinridge when you can," nodded Buckner. He was childless, but hoped one day to have a son as courageous. "Tell him I tried to keep my word."

CHAPTER 2

ENFORCED ANONYMITY

Anna Carroll wished Thurlow Weed would get back from Europe. She needed writing assignments from railroad or banking interests that would pay her enough to dine at Willard's once in a while. The government payment for the war powers pamphlet was shamefully low—$1,200, including printing—and the attack on Breckinridge had brought even less, although she had supplemented the meager fee with a kickback from the printer. The interest on the loan she had taken to help pay for the slaves she had bought and freed last year was a constant worry.

When so much of importance cried out to be done, it was exasperating to have to think about subsistence. She started to admit to herself there might be something to be said for getting married, but then remembered Fillmore and his complaints about a lack of pension to ex-presidents. She was better off poor and free than half-poor and compromised.

Chase, a widower and obviously wealthy, would be something else—a man to discuss great issues with, to share the play of power. She remembered Kate and put it out of her mind. She was not about to compete with a child.

A crowd had gathered around the newsstand in front of Willard's. She waited until the jostling let up—no small woman could compete in a crowd—and then bought a paper. The *Intelligencer* headline made her catch her breath: "REBEL ARMY CAPTURED!" She gulped down the details of the Union victory in the West: nearly twenty thousand rebels taken, the first crushing defeat of Confederate arms, the heroism of the gunboats under Admiral Foote, and especially the emergence of a victorious general, U. S.—for "Unconditional Surrender"—Grant. The strategic significance of the capture of the mouth of the Tennessee and Cumberland was beyond the ken of the correspondents in the field, but columns of praise appeared for Grant, extolling the ease with which he had routed the rebels. Scorn was heaped on the traitors Floyd and Pillow, slinking away from their command to avoid justice.

Anna felt a surge of triumph, vindication of all she had been through to persuade obstinate men of the wisdom of her strategy. Her Tennessee plan was in operation. The success of her river strategy's first stage, even to the inundation of Fort Henry's guns at high tide, was evidence of what imagination and daring could do to transform the war. Let the commanders in the East issue their ridiculous bulletins of "All Quiet on the Potomac"; now the Army of the West was on the march, or on the boats, cutting into the heart of the South.

Who would share this moment with her? The Wades, who had helped her press the plan with Lincoln, were all involved with what seemed to Anna inconsequential domestic affairs: the Homestead Act, selling up to 160 acres of Western land to settlers for $2.50 an acre, and the bill that Wade and Justin Morrill of Vermont had been pushing to give away public land to agricultural and vocational colleges. It irritated her that Ben Wade would take time away from the prosecution of the war to provide for federal aid to hardscrabble farmers and visionary educators.

Tom Scott was the one who had placed her memo of November 30 before Lincoln, and again before Stanton after that scary man had taken over the War Department. Scott was the friend for her to see and savor this moment with; Anna guessed he would be at the office now, after supper. He was near the telegraph office as well; Lincoln or Stanton might be there.

She hurried the three blocks across Washington's frozen mud past the President's house to the War Department. Discipline had broken down at the telegraph office; the mood in that usually somber place was frenzied delight. Someone had broken out champagne; Grant's name, along with that of Halleck's, was toasted time and again. Messengers on their way to the President, clutching telegrams from Halleck, were stopping to read them in the halls to everyone who came by. Stanton was not on the scene.

Curiously, Tom Scott was not especially excited. He sat alone in his office, tossing the contents of his desk into a packing crate.

"Tom, it worked—my plan, it worked!"

"You have a right to be very proud, Anna."

"What's all this?" She pointed to the crates. "You're being sent out West again? Another report?"

"No, I'm going home. War's over for me." He seemed relieved. "Glad to leave on a note of victory."

"Stanton?"

Scott nodded. "He's a wild man. I can't work for him."

Anna's heart sank. Tom Scott was one of the few who knew her part in conceiving and detailing the Tennessee plan, and one of the few men close to the President that she trusted. It occurred to her that Scott, as a railroader, would be a source of consultant fees again, but that was not as important as ensuring that her plan was carried out clear down to the rail junction at Corinth, as well as getting her fair recognition as its author.

"You can't go. Lincoln knows you. You brought him down here past the assassins in Baltimore—"

"Stanton, the 'organizer of victory,' wants his own man."

"Who?"

"His brother-in-law for the time being, but I suspect the one he has in mind is the newspaperman Dana, Horace Greeley's right arm. Stanton and Dana have been exchanging secret messages for months."

That was why Stanton was so quickly welcomed by the radicals, despite the initial belief that he was a Seward man; the *Tribune* in New York always took Stanton's side. The switch of assistants made political sense, Anna quickly figured; she kicked herself for not having cultivated Dana at the recent White House reception.

She knew Scott well enough to put her own concerns to him directly. "Look, Tom, you're my best friend here. Who else knows how hard I worked to get this campaign in the West under way?"

"Stanton," Scott said mildly, "and the kid in the telegraph room. Maybe Halleck, maybe not. Maybe Grant."

"What do you mean, 'Maybe Grant'? He has to have the plan, and my name is on the memorandum to Lincoln about it. I spoke at length with Grant's river pilot in Cairo—"

Scott shook his head slowly. "You're no stranger to politics, Anna. Everybody's fighting for credit for this win at Donelson. Last month, Old Brains Halleck brushed me off when I went over it with him, pretended I was stupid. Then when Grant came up with the same idea—I mean, basically, it jumps out at you when you look at the map—I hear Halleck threw him out of his office."

Anna gave him an icy look. "It didn't jump out at anybody until November, when I wrote it all down."

"It was your plan, Anna, but I'm telling you not to count on credit." He stopped packing and looked directly at her. "Halleck despises Grant, thinks he's a drunk. He only grudgingly gave Grant permission to help the navy move on the forts when Lincoln sent the general order. Now Old Brains is out to grab all the credit for Donelson—wants Lincoln and McClellan to name him commander in the West over Buell's army too."

She concluded that Scott did not grasp the pressure of public sentiment. "All the papers are making Grant the hero. Halleck wasn't near the action. He never gets off his—out of his chair."

"McClellan may agree with Halleck. Little Mac doesn't want any big heroes making him look like number two. He knows Halleck is no threat."

"Ah, Miss Carroll." The rasping voice was Stanton's. "It's fitting that you are here. Colonel Scott, would you try to bring some order to this chaos in the halls? Must I be present at every moment? Come with me, dear lady." He led the way to his office and motioned her to a chair beside his desk.

"Congratulations, Mr. Secretary," she took the lead, "on a great victory.

We would never have turned the tide in the West were it not for your leadership. I believe this is the turning point of the war."

"It was your plan, Miss Carroll," he said. She relaxed a bit; that was gratifying. When Stanton went on to say, "You will see how the Tennessee River strategy develops exactly as you worked it out," she sighed in relief. She should have known better than to panic at the suggestion of a man, even an old friend like Scott, who was bitter about being replaced. With Stanton's acknowledgment, as well as that of Chairman Wade of the Committee on the Conduct of the War, proper credit to the woman who had put forward the plan to invade the South down the Tennessee River was assured. A place in history was hers, as well as financial security, and beyond that, greater respect for women generally. Not to mention a quicker end to the war. She smiled at Stanton, she hoped modestly.

"I want to ask you for a further contribution to your country," Stanton said, pulling at the white part of his beard. Another assignment? "I want you to keep secret the planning of the Tennessee and Cumberland action. Completely secret."

She said nothing.

"For the time being," the Secretary of War continued, "we must give the credit where it is not quite due—either to Halleck or Grant, depending on which one best suits the President's and the nation's interests. Say nothing, my dear lady."

"Why?"

"First, because the plan is hardly begun, and it should remain a secret until we take control in Corinth and cut the Memphis to Charleston railroad. And secondly"—he walked to the window—"how shall I put this? The nation needs military heroes. It would hardly do if any of the conception of this strategy were attributed to a civilian."

By "a civilian," he meant "a woman." She swallowed and remained silent.

"Let the military men be seen as the great geniuses. We all know that the character and strategy of this war will come from here, in the War Department, and not from the officers in the field. Certainly not from our spit-and-polish General-in-Chief. I have great difficulties with McClellan, my dear lady. I need your help with him."

She decided quickly she had no alternative but to go along; when it suited Stanton to diminish Halleck or Grant, she might get recognition. "I know how to keep a secret, Secretary Stanton. Trust me, as I trust you." She added, for insurance, "And Senator Wade."

"Create your own writing assignments," Stanton said grandly, "for which there will be proper recompense, of course. I'll arrange that with Scott."

He pulled the cord that summoned an aide and sent for the departing Assistant Secretary of War. "Miss Carroll will continue to submit military studies," he snapped, "and you will arrange for approval of expenses for time and travel. Do that before you go, will you, Scott? And where is my amnesty order?"

"It's the President's executive order," Scott corrected him. "I sent it across the street."

Stanton's irritation showed. "All political prisoners will be released," he told Anna, "when they subscribe to a parole that they will give no further aid and comfort to the enemy. What sort of a reaction to this act of conciliation do you suppose we can expect in the press?"

"The Peace Democrats will see it as an act of mercy long overdue," she said, "but the black Republicans will think Lincoln is going soft."

"If I tap that bell over there," Stanton said mildly, "I can send anybody in the country to a place where they will never hear the dogs bark. We are not going soft on traitors, Miss Carroll, and I would be grateful if you would get that word to your many influential friends."

"What about the captain of the slave ship, sentenced to be hanged?" The abolitionists in New York were eager to hang their first slave-ship captain.

"Nathaniel Gordon hangs tomorrow," Stanton said, relishing the words. "No clemency from here."

"Rose Greenhow?"

Stanton frowned. "I would like to get rid of her presence one way or the other. In jail, she made an ass of Seward, and she is driving Pinkerton crazy. Devilish woman. Will she sign a parole?"

"She'd die first," Anna told him. Rose O'Neal Greenhow was not the type of person to promise to spend the war doing nothing for the Confederacy.

"We'll put her on trial, then." Stanton looked uncomfortable at that prospect. "I just wish I had a spy like her working for us in Richmond."

On their way out of the War Department, Scott and Carroll met a distraught John Hay hurrying in to see Stanton.

"Isn't it exciting," Anna began, setting aside Stanton's request for her silence, "just as we hoped in that plan I wrote back in November—"

"Is Stanton upstairs?"

Scott said yes.

"Get him to disperse the crowds outside, making all that noise," ordered Hay, "and for God's sake, shut up that band on Pennsylvania Avenue."

"Come on, now, Hay, this is their first real victory."

"Willie just died."

Anna winced. "How is the President taking it?"

"He came staggering into our office," said Hay, "and said, 'He's gone, my boy is actually gone,' and burst into tears. Never saw him so upset."

"And the boy's mother?"

"She let out a long wail," said the secretary, "that was as terrifying a sound as I've ever heard. And there's no stopping her hysterics. Scott, for God's sake, get some soldiers and make them stop that noise outside, will you?"

CHAPTER 3

JOHN HAY'S DIARY
FEBRUARY 28, 1862

A passage in the opening of the new Dickens novel describes the mood of the Mansion this week. "It was the best of times, it was the worst of times . . . the spring of hope . . . the winter of despair."

We barely had time to savor the great news of the capture of the rebel army at Donelson when a blanket of gloom descended with the death of Willie. At one point, all I could hear was the sound of revelry outside and the screams of the Hellcat down the hall.

Thank God for Lizzie Keckley. If it weren't for her calming effect on the Prsdt's wife, Madame's hysteria would never let up. Maybe it's because of Lizzie's recent loss of her own son, or the fact that she suffered through slavery, or some inner source of strength that makes itself felt in a mystic way —whatever it is, the Hellcat clings to Lizzie and sobs and cries for hours on end until she passes out.

Willie's body lay in state in the Green Room downstairs, and thousands of people trooped through. Mrs. Lincoln could not leave her bed even for the funeral. That was just as well, because too many of the visitors made snide comments about the way she threw a splendid ball when her boy lay dying. Unfair; why do they hate her so, even now? I've never been her champion, and fear that her state of mind is becoming another great burden for the Prsdt, but she's not evil.

They buried Willie in the Carroll family vault at Oak Hill cemetery. Senator Orville Browning, the Lincoln family's closest friend now that Ned Baker is gone, made the funeral arrangements. Browning spoke to Anna Carroll about the proper place to bury the boy and she put him in touch with her remote Washington kin, and that solved the interment problem.

Then we all had another scare when Tad came down with a fever, and the Prsdt sat in his room one terrible night, but it wasn't the typhoid that struck Willie, and Tad is better now. He has taken to sleeping regularly in his father's bed.

This paralysis cannot go on. Too much is pressing in. I have urgent requests for appointments with Senator Wade, who wants to reprimand Generals Halleck and McClellan for allowing slaveholders to search for fugitive slaves on army posts, and with Senator Sumner, who wants to know if Lincoln will oppose a bill abolishing slavery in the District of Columbia. The radical Republicans are going too fast, and forgetting the plan Lincoln and old Blair worked out for paying states to gradually buy slaves their freedom.

I think I'll try to get Lizzie to get the Prsdt to focus on this. He cannot grieve for his boy or fret about his wife's temporary derangement for long. This is not the only house in the nation draped in mourning.

CHAPTER 4

SOURCE OF STRENGTH

"Madam Elizabeth," Mr. Lincoln said, "I want to bring Mother here by the window."

Lizzie Keckley did not think that was such a good idea. She put her arm behind Mary Lincoln's back, supporting her weight as she helped the President's wife out of bed. The modiste could feel her uncontrollable trembling. After one of her hysterical fits, screams piercing the Mansion walls, the poor woman would lie shaking for about a half hour.

"Mother, do you see that large white building on the hill yonder?"

Mary Lincoln looked and her trembling increased.

"Try and control your grief," the President said sternly. He pointed to a white building that Keckley knew to be the lunatic asylum. "Control your grief, or it will drive you mad, and we may have to send you there."

That was a terrifying threat. The modiste thought Mr. Lincoln was cruelly wrong to remind his wife of the insanity in her family and where that distraction was likely to put her. At the same time, Mrs. Lincoln's black friend could see how badly the President wanted to force a limit to his wife's unhealthy reaction to the loss of their beloved Willie.

Mrs. Lincoln had to pull herself together. The Mansion could not long continue to be draped in black. Nor could the President's wife be permitted to reach out to spiritualists, because they could not bring the boy back. Mrs. Keckley, a religious woman, would have no truck with the conjurers. Last night, Mrs. Lincoln had arranged a seance with a spiritualist and had all but physically dragged her husband along. That troubled the modiste: the President of the United States should not be sitting at a seance, listening to thuds and whispers in the darkness, even to humor his wife who refused to accept God's will in the reality of her loss.

After that strange session, and after Mrs. Lincoln had sobbed for an hour before collapsing in exhaustion, Mrs. Keckley made ready to leave the bedroom. The President motioned for her to sit in one of the chairs near the bed. "It's a wonder you're not exhausted, Madam Elizabeth. I don't see how you do it."

She did not mention that she would spend much of the remainder of the night sewing in her room. The dress orders had to be filled, the needed money to be earned. She was now supporting six jobless black freedmen who were wondering if freedom meant the freedom to starve. Mr. Lincoln did not want to be alone, obviously, and people at sad times like this had a way of unburdening their souls to her. She never knew why; she rarely asked a question. She assumed that because she did not seek confidences, people—important white people, especially—confided in her.

The President started to speak of his dead boy. When he came to the words "Willie was too good for this world," the tall man hunched forward and broke into sobs. She let him cry silently for a while, then rose and stroked his head. The hair was stiff, uncombed, unwashed. He leaned his forehead against her hip, took some deep breaths, and tried to compose himself. She saw him fumbling in his pocket for a handkerchief that was not there. She went to the bureau and brought back the piece of white cloth and he wiped his eyes and blew his nose. She also handed him her Bible.

When he could talk again, he told her that he did not read the Bible often, but when he did, he found the most interest in the Book of Job. She found that curious: in all of Scripture, she found the story of Job, with his defiant questioning of God, to be almost blasphemous. Job kept demanding to know why the wicked could triumph and the good die young if God was just, until God finally had to tell Job to stop bothering Him.

The melancholy man wondered aloud if he had been unkind to point out the asylum to his wife. The modiste was glad he felt bad about that. He admitted to his own lifelong experience with "the hypo," those moods of deep melancholy that gripped him for days on end, when he could not think straight, hardly work at all. The first time the hypo struck, he told her, was after the death of a young girl he knew in New Salem. Brain fever. He had been a boarder at Rutledge's Tavern, and the girl was engaged to another man in Salem, but she was nineteen and dear to him. The inexplicable cutting short of her life recalled to his mind the death of his mother, Nancy Hanks Lincoln—he remembered her withered features and want of teeth—and his sister Sarah's death in childbirth at twenty-one, she who had mothered him as well.

Ever since, he told the black freedwoman, obviously taking some comfort in the telling, he had suffered periods in which a dark cloud overtook him and all he could think of was death and loss and emptiness, and, of late, rivers of the blood of war. That was why he had to force himself and his wife to shake off the corrosive sadness surrounding the loss of their favorite child.

He said all this with his head in his huge hands, looking down at the floor in the darkness, alternating stretches of revelation with periods of silence. She struck a match and lit a lamp.

He looked up. "There is a poem that expresses my feelings," he said. He proceeded to recite verses that ended with the line, "Why Should the Spirit of Mortal Be Proud?" It took five minutes, and he recited with an actor's expression. She liked the poem. It spoke of humility in a proud way.

He changed the subject, seeming a bit perkier after the recitation. "I'm not the only one around here who gets this way."

One night in the telegraph office, he related, Secretary of War Stanton had told him that he had been inconsolable after the death of a baby daughter, and could not leave his dead wife's grave for a month. Further, Stanton had told Lincoln about his brother's committing suicide, and his own morbid desire to do the same when he heard the news. Yet Stanton was a strong man and a successful lawyer, Lincoln told her, the best in the country. The hypo grabs a person sometimes for days, even weeks, but it goes away by itself, or is driven away in time by a force of will. He insisted it was not a sign of weakness, citing Stanton as his evidence.

She did not see the similarity but said nothing. She had heard that Stanton flew off the handle, even went into the most terrible rages, and then could cry like a child, but his despair was not like Lincoln's. The President, she had

observed, could be seized by gloom, remembering how death was so much a
part of his life, and it was a weakness, all right, but never a cause for panic.
Stanton, she had observed, was brilliant and all, but he lived at the edge of
panic, as if he were never sure he would remain in control. She judged that
there was great sadness in Lincoln, but real fear and rage in Stanton, who
reminded her a bit of her late husband.

"I saw a slave in chains once," the President said, "when I was sailing
down the Ohio with Josh Speed. There were twelve slaves on the river
steamer, all chained together like so many fish upon a trotline. I asked about
them. They were from Kentucky, my home state, torn from family and
friends on their way to the Deep South."

"The life is different there," said Elizabeth Keckley. "In Virginia I had a
kind master, never beat me except when I was bad. Then times got bad and
he sold me South."

"How old were you?"

"Eighteen. Were there any girls on the chain you saw?"

"No," Lincoln said, looking into the past, closing his eyes, "all young men.
One had a fiddle, and he played while the others sang and danced, as well as
they could in the chains, and joked and played card games. I suppose God
tempers the wind to the shorn lamb."

"That means—?"

"He renders the worst of the human condition tolerable, while He permits
the best to be no better than tolerable." He looked over at the sleeping form
of his troubled wife. "I still think of that spectacle," he said; "it's a torment to
me. Slavery has the power of making me miserable."

"No, God does not always temper the wind," said the black woman. That
one look at the men in chains was this man's only exposure to the reality of
slavery. How could he have any idea what it was like? He had seen the blacks
on the river joke and dance, and assumed they were happy. Why did he
believe that blacks had some special protection from God that numbed their
misery?

She had never spoken of her youth to any man, black or white, but here
and now, in the midst of his anguish, she felt it had a place and was the time.
And maybe she had been called upon to help him feel the way it was.

"The wife of my new master in Carolina thought I was uppity. I did my
work and more, but I wouldn't cringe and scrape, and she complained about
my stubborn pride. So one day he called me in and told me to take down my
dress and said he was going to flog me."

She could see that man's face as clearly as Lincoln's. "I said no, not without a reason. He got a rope and tied my hands behind me. I fought as hard as
I could and he tore the dress from my back." She could not stop telling it now
if she wanted to. "Then he picked up a rawhide and began to beat me. He'd
nerve himself for a blow and then smash down on my flesh, cut my skin—I
could feel the blood running down into my skirt. I didn't scream. I stood like
a statue."

She drew herself tall. "When he finished, I asked him what I had done
wrong, and he picked up a chair and hit me over the head with that.

"Next day he sent for me again, and I saw he was prepared with a new rope
and a new cowhide. I told him I was ready to die but he could not conquer

me. In the fight with him, I bit his finger, and he hit me with a heavy stick until I was dizzy. A couple days later Mr. Bingham again tried to conquer me, and we struggled and I caught it in the head again, but when I woke up he was crying. As I lay there bleeding, I saw that my suffering had subdued his hard heart. He asked my forgiveness. He said he would never hit me again, and he kept his word."

"Thank God," said Lincoln.

"That was not the worst," she continued. "I was young and considered fair, and I was sold to a man who had evil designs on me. One day he bid me take down my clothes, and I refused. He tied me, too, but this time tried to have his way with my body, and I fought and scratched him. Then he beat the backs of my legs with a horsewhip until I couldn't move for a week. I still have those marks, and I have walked slowly ever since." She had heard her customers say that her walk gave her dignity; if she walked any faster, she would be in pain.

"The next time he came at me, I did not have the strength left to defend myself. He took me that way whenever he wanted for four years. That was the real suffering, worse than the beatings, knowing I was a toy he could play with whenever he wanted. Mr. Lincoln, it's like not being a person. That's what a slave is—not a human being anymore. Just an animal that's used to give a mean mistress satisfaction or to give a master pleasure."

She was breathing heavily and put her hand on her chest to catch her breath. Once it started to come out there was no stopping. "Finally he stopped having me when he saw I was to become a mother. I brought a boy into the world, and if he suffered humiliation because he was the son of a slave, it was not my fault. My boy looked white. He got his freedom when I bought mine. And then, passing for white, he joined the Union Army."

"Where is he now?" asked the President.

"Safe in his grave," she replied. "Miss Carroll found out all about the battle that killed him, and wrote me he died a hero." She patted the letter in her bosom but did not take it out. "That's why I can feel for Mrs. Lincoln. When your boy dies, it makes you feel like there is nothing to stand on, nothing comes after you, all your life's been a waste."

"No, no, never a waste," said Lincoln. They sat in silence for a long time. Had she struck the right note? Had she made him see that the political subject he had debated about all his life was more than a mere matter of right and wrong? She was vaguely dissatisfied; the pride that burned inside her, so harshly beaten down for so long, was important for him to understand. The moment would not come again, and nobody who was black might ever have the chance to make him know the living hell of slavery.

"It is not just the cruelty," she added. "It's the no hope. Do you know Senator Davis?"

"I never met Jeff Davis."

"I made all Mrs. Davis's dresses. I lived in their home for a while. He is a fine man, kind, in many ways like you." Not quite true—Mr. Davis was distant; she could never have had a talk like this with him. "Not so easy to talk to, maybe, but a good man. He'd never raise his hand to a black man, not cruel in any way. But he doesn't know what it is like to have no hope, to never be yourself." She felt inadequate, disappointed because of her inability

to show that slavery was infinitely more cruel to the mind than to the body.
Maybe it was better to appeal on the basis of the pain of the lash; anybody
could testify to that. The need for dignity was hard to explain to anyone who
had always been free.

"You're a good judge of people, Madam Elizabeth," Lincoln's voice was
stronger now. "What sort is Jeff Davis? If you lived in their house—"

"A gentleman," she said. "Honorable. God-fearing." She thought about it.
"Strong," she added. "He sticks with the people he trusts. It don't matter
what people say or what the papers write, he'll do what he thinks is right.
Even if it's wrong." She thought of the Davises' many kindnesses, and wanted
to end on a note of special truth. "He's not a man who hates anybody. I can't
hate him."

They sat for a long time in silence. Mrs. Lincoln's breathing was labored,
but she was not crying out as on other nights. The President seemed to fall
asleep in his chair, and she moved quietly to the door.

As she left, she heard him say, partly to her, more to himself, "I'll see
Wade and Sumner tomorrow, but I cannot do what they want about abolition
in the District. Too soon. It's too soon."

CHAPTER 5

EDGE OF THE CROWBAR

George Nicolay let his assistant, Hay, have the day off to see his secret
ladylove. Nicolay, at thirty, was six years Hay's senior, and had for years
been in awe of the young man's talent, *joie de vivre,* and self-confidence.

They had met in Pittsfield, an Illinois prairie village where the fatherless
Nicolay had been eking out a living as a printer's devil on the *Pike County
Free Press* and the well-to-do Hay had been preparing to go to Brown College
back East. Nicolay had hoped to join his younger friend at the college, but
had neither the money for the expensive school nor the physical stamina for
the trip. Instead, the newspaper and the local political headquarters became
the Bavarian-born Nicolay's college, and his introduction to the lawyer and
politician Abraham Lincoln.

As Nicolay studied law at night, he ran Lincoln's political errands, provided him with election tabulations, and made himself useful: when Lincoln
needed to make his peace with the Know-Nothings in 1860, it was Nicolay he
sent to their leader in Terre Haute with the written instructions, explicit in
their vagueness, "tell him my motto is 'Fairness to all' but commit me to
nothing." By that time Hay was back from college and found a job on the
Blairs' newspaper, and then, through his Uncle Milton, to Lincoln's inner
circle in Springfield, where Nicolay welcomed his only real friend's high
spirits and his help.

On occasion, Nicolay felt about Hay the way Robert Lincoln probably used
to feel about Willie: envy at his natural charm and his easy intimacy with
Lincoln, tempered by affection engendered by the irresistible youngster. Hay
never challenged Nicolay's preeminence in the office—partly, Nicolay sus-

John George Nicolay, Abraham Lincoln, John Hay

pected, because he did not want the heavy responsibility. Hay had a mischievous streak and a sense of fun which put him in special tune with Lincoln in an area where Nicolay could never hope to compete: it was Hay, not the first assistant, that Lincoln sought out at night, carpet slippers flapping, to swap funny stories.

If there was anything that worried Nicolay about his junior partner, it was Hay's ease at manipulation: he had a genius for jollying people along, and an immature way of shaping the facts to fit his positions. They had agreed to join in the writing of a history of the Lincoln administration; Nicolay felt the responsibility of writing history with accuracy, and worried that Hay would use the chance to get even with those who had stood in Lincoln's way. He hoped his assistant was keeping his diary with fidelity, but doubted it.

Nicolay, who had always been sickly, worried about the way Hay, who had always been robust, abused his health. How could anyone, he asked himself, stagger home at 3 A.M. and be ready for a day's work at nine? In addition to the usual carousing, Hay had been putting in eighteen-hour days in the two weeks since the tumultuous period of the *grande levée*, the victory at Fort Donelson, and the death of Willie. He also showed the mooning signs of falling in love. Nicolay, faithful to his Therena at home in Illinois, took vicarious pleasure in Hay's romantic escapades, as did Lincoln, but Nicolay noted that he seemed flushed this morning, and ordered him to bed; the young man accepted and gratefully collapsed.

Nicolay sent his second assistant, the studious Stoddard, to fetch Ben Wade, whose chairmanship of the Joint Committee on the Conduct of the War was rapidly making him the most important man in Congress. Nicolay considered that to be a remarkable achievement for a leader of what was, after all, only a minority faction of abolitionists.

"What in hell do you mean, 'too soon'?" roared the senator as soon as he and the President squared off.

Nicolay knew that Lincoln would take no offense at the bluster, because that was the way the fellow addressed everybody.

"The time is not yet ripe," said Lincoln, on his feet, walking around the office as usual.

"You've been saying 'too soon, too soon,' since the day after Bull Run." Wade mocked. "Remember? Chandler and Sumner and I were in here telling you that you should proclaim emancipation or, at the very least, announce that the end of slavery was the supreme object of this war. But all you pleaded then was 'Kentucky, Kentucky.' Now we have Kentucky. After Donelson surrendered, Sidney Johnston skedaddled out of Kentucky, and Nashville, Tennessee, is about to fall in our lap. You don't have your old border-state excuse anymore."

"Abolition is too big a lick," said Lincoln. "We're recruiting soldiers in Kentucky, and in Maryland and Missouri, and while they'll fight for the Union, they won't join up to fight for abolition. Most people are for 'the Union as it was'—with slavery where it is, but no extension into the territories. Ben, slavery cannot exist for long if all the new states are free states, you know that."

"What you lack, Lincoln, is backbone." Nicolay, in the back of the room, wondered if Lincoln's temper would flare at that. It did not; evidently the

President was aware of that charge and preferred to have it hurled directly at him than spoken behind his back. "You know this war is about slavery. You're afraid to admit it."

"I'm going to name Senator Andrew Johnson to be military governor of Tennessee," the President said coolly, showing some backbone by deliberately offending the radical Republicans: Johnson was a War Democrat and a native Tennessean who would attract support in that newly liberated state. Wade and his crowd—which, Nicolay noted, now had two Cabinet members in its ranks, with Stanton joining Chase—had demanded an abolitionist in that post.

"We'll fight him in the Senate," said Wade. "And to show we mean business, we'll pass a confiscation bill. Not symbolic, like last year, but one with teeth in it."

"That's not needed," said Lincoln quickly.

"Every rebel is an outlaw," boomed Wade, rising and sinking on his toes as he did on the Senate floor. "I am for inflicting all the consequences of defeat on a fallen foe that started an unjust war. I am for confiscating the property of rebels—taking every slave from every damn rebel, thereby making the slave owners pay the cost of this rebellion."

"What good will that do? A confiscation bill would only hurt us in the border states and make the South fight all the harder."

"God! You must be listening to Seward again, and the Blairs. Not even a galvanic battery could inspire any action in your Cabinet."

"We didn't go into the war to put down slavery," Lincoln said, giving not an inch, "but to put the flag back."

"Times have changed."

Lincoln did not agree. "To act differently at this moment would, I have no doubt, not only weaken our cause but smack of bad faith. Your thunderbolt will keep."

Wade seated himself, which Nicolay took as the prelude to dickering. A confiscation act was too extreme to have any hope of passage; Wade had just thrown that out to open the negotiation.

"You can expect to see a fugitive-slave bill on your desk soon," Wade predicted, putting forward a step toward abolition that had wider appeal, "to keep your damned pro-slavery Democratic generals like McClellan and Halleck from turning over slaves that are running away from rebel owners. Try to veto that."

Nicolay knew that Lincoln did not want to face the need to veto that, and the President's attitude became more conciliatory.

"Just last night," he said, a shadow of sadness crossing his face, "I began to think that this terrible war was a great movement by God to end slavery. And that the man would be a fool who should stand in the way." Wade waited for more. "The other day I was telling Sumner that the only difference between him and me on this subject is a difference of a month or six weeks in time."

"He told me you said that," Wade shot back. "Only it wasn't the other day, it was a month or six weeks ago." A telling point, Nicolay conceded.

"Too big a lick right now. But how's this—" Lincoln reached in his drawer and came up with a few lines in his handwriting scrawled on a piece of paper. He handed it to Senator Wade.

The Ohioan squinted at it and read aloud: "I recommend the adoption of a Joint Resolution by your honorable bodies: 'Resolved that the United States ought to cooperate with any state which may adopt gradual abolishment of slavery, giving to such state pecuniary aid, to be used by such state in its discretion to compensate for the evils public and private, produced by such a change of system.' " Wade read it again silently, lips moving.

"It's the initiation of emancipation," Nicolay dared to put in.

"Thin milk-and-water gruel," snorted Wade, shooting the young man a withering glance, but holding on to the paper. "It would take a hundred years your way."

"In my judgment," said the President carefully, "gradual and not sudden emancipation is better for all. Not all the slave states will undertake it, but as the loyal slave states do—Kentucky, for example—it will become apparent to the Deep South that no hope exists for border states to join the Confederacy when peace comes."

"This is the best you can do?" asked Wade, dissatisfied but apparently unwilling to let this first, tentative move by the President toward abolition go unsupported.

"It is a start," said Lincoln.

The senator passed the paper back, motioning to Lincoln to make a change. "I don't know why you say 'abolishment' when you mean 'abolition.' " Nicolay was surprised that Wade caught that; Lincoln deliberately had sought to avoid the more incendiary word. "And you don't mean 'evils,' you mean 'inconveniences.' No move toward freedom can be evil."

Lincoln acknowledged that the latter was true and made the change. Wade was not one to be taken into camp by minor adjustments, however, and made to leave with a firm, "It's not enough. You cannot buy your way out of slavery, and you know it. This is just a palliative."

When Lincoln did not contradict him, but just looked quizzical, Wade made a suggestion: "Abolish slavery just in the District of Columbia. No states-rights argument works here, Lincoln—this is a federal city. Now, that would be a start."

"I once introduced a bill to that effect when I was a congressman in the forties," the President said mildly, in what Nicolay knew to be his horse-trading voice. "It hasn't been expedient to put it forward recently, but my opinion hasn't changed."

"I'll go for your waste-of-time resolution to pay off the border-state slave owners," offered Wade, "if you'll send us a bill rooting out the evil in the District."

"I won't send it to you," Lincoln countered, "but if you pass one and send it to me, I'll sign it. Provided it includes compensation to the owners."

"That's a bargain," snapped Wade, going up to Lincoln and pumping his hand once to put a seal on it. "We'll pass your thin gruel, and mark my words, the loyal slave states will laugh at you. The border states people won't sell their slaves—they like the damnable institution. But we'll put the fear of God in those bastards by freeing the slaves in the District."

"You initiate abolishment in the District, I'll sign it," said Lincoln, "but it has to include compensation. And my resolution about gradual emancipation comes first."

"Done." He went to the door. "Remember, Lincoln"—a Parthian shot—
"the word is *abolition!*"

A week later, with Lincoln's proposed joint resolution sent to Congress,
followed by a March 6 message on gradual emancipation issued by the President—but with the second step of abolishing slavery in the District not yet
taken—Nicolay ushered in Henry Raymond, editor of the *New York Times,*
whose closeness to William Seward and Thurlow Weed was well known after
their falling-out with Horace Greeley. Raymond had been summoned by
Lincoln; the *Times* was not as influential as Greeley's *Tribune,* and neither
had the circulation of Bennett's *Herald,* but it was one of the only three eight-
page dailies in the United States and had been a loyal supporter of Lincoln.

"I'm just reading some of the New York journals, Henry," Lincoln began.
Actually, Nicolay had been reading those newspapers to him that morning,
starting out with the praise, as Lincoln liked, but including later some of the
criticism. Nicolay had noted the surprise defection of the *Times* and the
President would have none of that.

"Here's the *Tribune,* the *World,* the *Evening Post*"—Lincoln pushed them
all forward—"all have written excellent editorials about my message on gradual, compensated emancipation."

"I've seen those, sir, yes," said Raymond. "I think I know what you're
getting at."

"And here's the *New York Times,* the one paper I thought I could count
on, saying that my proposal is 'well intentioned, but must fail on the score of
expense.' Did you write this?"

"Actually, it was done by one of my editors." The editor squirmed. "If you
figure slaves at four hundred dollars a head, and that there must be at least
three or four million slaves, you get into astronomical numbers."

"Have you stopped to figure," said Lincoln severely, "that less than one
half-day's cost of this war would pay for all the slaves in Delaware, at four
hundred dollars a head? That eighty-seven days' cost of this war would pay
for all in Delaware, Maryland, District of Columbia, Kentucky, and Missouri
at the same price?"

"I hadn't looked at it that way, Mr. President."

"Were those states to take the step I suggest, do you doubt that it would
shorten the war more than eighty-seven days, and thus be an actual saving of
expense?"

"You're absolutely right, Mr. Lincoln."

"Think about it, then, and let there be another article in the *Times.*"

"I will telegraph my office to sustain your message without qualifications or
cavil, sir." Nicolay was glad that Lincoln had not had to put on greater
pressure, which he had readily available. Stanton had just issued an order
putting military censorship into effect, forbidding publication of intelligence
about military operations on pain of losing all access to the telegraph.

Lincoln put his arm around the editor, who had state political ambitions of
his own, and walked him to the door. "It is important that the *Times* be on
the right side of this."

"I regard your message as a masterpiece of practical wisdom," said Raymond as he disappeared down the hall, "and of sound policy."

Nicolay smiled; the editor had felt the heat and seen the light.

"Nicolay," Lincoln said, "what's the commotion out there?"

Running toward him was one of Stanton's new assistants.

Nicolay took the message, a dispatch from General Wool in Fort Monroe in Hampton Roads. That was the port where the Union fleet was massing to help McClellan begin his Peninsula campaign to take Richmond by the water route. Nicolay saw its urgency and hurried to Lincoln, who read the telegram aloud:

" 'The *Merrimack* is loose. It has sunk the *Cumberland,* compelled the *Congress* to surrender, and forced the *Minnesota* aground. No wooden ship can stop the iron monster.' "

CHAPTER 6

TIN CAN ON A SHINGLE

"Father Neptune" (Navy Secretary Gideon Welles knew that was what Lincoln called him behind his back) arrived at the Cabinet room in time to watch a panic stricken "Mars" (the Secretary of War, whom Welles was quickly coming to despise) make a spectacle of himself.

"Calamitous!" cried Stanton, refusing to sit at the table with Lincoln, Seward, General-in-Chief McClellan, and Welles, choosing instead to pace like a caged lion. No, "caged lion" implied a creature of courage; in this case, not even "cornered rat" was apt. The Secretary of War, in Welles's judgment, was a man seized by fear, and his loss of nerve was rattling the President. Welles had never been more certain that his own resistance to Stanton's reach for control of the entire war was wise; the navy was the equal of the army in every traditional respect, and Stanton was dangerously wrong to try to treat the United States Navy as some sort of appendage to the War Department's power. The only victory the Union could claim in the war was the naval victory at Forts Henry and Donelson by Admiral Foote, despite the attempt by Stanton to grab the credit for Halleck and Grant.

"Do you realize what the rebel navy has done?" Stanton was hollering at him. "They've broken the blockade!"

Taking his seat solemnly, the Navy Secretary said, "Such a judgment is premature."

Stanton rolled his eyes heavenward. "What good is your precious navy with this iron crocodile swallowing up its ships? Look at these telegraphic messages from your own man down there in Hampton Roads, for God's sake —any ship that comes near the *Merrimack* is doomed! The *Cumberland,* sunk. The *Congress,* the *Minnesota* and the *St. Lawrence,* run aground and helpless."

"I am as aware as you of our losses."

"That floating battery will destroy, *seriatim,* every naval vessel we have," Stanton went on, to Welles's mounting disgust. "The blockade of the South is finished; guns and munitions will start flowing in from England—who knows, this may mean Britain will recognize the Confederacy. How do you like that?"

"There is no cause for panic," Welles said slowly. He was resolved to maintain his calm, if only to offset Stanton's flailing of arms and corrosive despair, but he could not set aside the possibility that there was genuine cause for alarm. Perhaps the mauling of the Union fleet by the rebel ironclad meant that every great wooden ship of the line in all the world's navies was obsolete.

Certainly there had been tragic losses down in Hampton Roads. When Welles learned of the sinking of the *Cumberland* an hour before, he stopped on his way to the Mansion at Saint John's Church, where he knew Commodore Joseph Smith would be attending services. Smith's son was captain of the ship rammed and sunk by "the monster." When Welles told him of the way the battle had gone, the wooden ship helplessly bouncing shot off the impervious hull of the *Merrimack,* the commodore had said, "Then Joe is dead." Welles suspected that was true. It made him especially angry at the shrill Stanton's contempt for his service.

Obviously the President needed the steadying of someone, because Stanton's outburst evidently shook him; Lincoln was looking out the window down the Potomac, cracking his knuckles nervously, as if expecting to see the *Merrimack* appear any moment.

"What do we know of the *Merrimack?*" the worried Lincoln asked the Navy Secretary.

"She was one of our ships that was sunk in Hampton Roads, near Norfolk, last year," Welles replied. "The Confederates refloated her, pumped out the mud, renamed her the *Virginia,* and cut her hull down to the water's edge. Then they covered her over, down to two feet below the waterline, with two-inch overlapping armor plate. Ten guns, mostly nine-inch smoothbores. An iron ram-beak on her prow."

"If you knew so much about her, why didn't you tell me?" Stanton demanded. "Maybe General McClellan here would have sent some soldiers into their base to do something about it. Something! Anything!"

"Pinkerton tells me," said McClellan, "that you had a spy in their naval yard, Mr. Welles."

"Yes, we've known about this," said the Navy Secretary, "and we have sent an ironclad of our own to engage her. Ours is a much smaller vessel, and it must be slowly towed in heavy seas or it will capsize, but—"

"Oh, God," wailed Stanton, "you mean that little boat they call the 'tin can on a shingle'—or the 'cheesebox on a raft'? How many guns?"

"The *Monitor* has only two guns in its turret," Welles admitted, "and we are not certain she is seaworthy. But the President encouraged us to press on with her construction. The contractors have disappointed us with their delays."

"Pipe dreams," said Stanton, pacing again. "That monster can come steaming up the Potomac any time it likes—do you realize that while you're sitting there, this very mansion could be under fire from the *Merrimack?* A cannonball or a shell could be crashing through this Cabinet room before night falls!"

There was silence. Lincoln asked, "Is there danger of that, Welles?"

"The *Merrimack* has a 22-foot draft because the armor makes it so heavy. I do not think she would be able to pass the shallow portion of the Potomac at Kettle Bottom Shoals."

"You don't *think*," Stanton derided, "that's not enough. What do you *know?*"

"In a sense, I would welcome her appearance in the Potomac," Welles replied, "because that would give the navy an opportunity to destroy her. I believe General McClellan also has some shore batteries in position."

"He doesn't understand," Stanton said to Lincoln, as if Welles were a backward child who had just failed his lesson, "that shells just bounce off the sides of the *Merrimack.*"

"Every shot that hits is felt," Welles countered, not certain about how many direct hits could be taken by the first ironclad ship of the line in America.

"That's nice, so we sit here and do nothing," Stanton taunted. "McClellan, get somebody over to the Navy Yard and commandeer every canal barge you can lay your hands on. Load them with rocks, gravel, whatever is heavy, and get the navy to take them down to those shoals and sink them there. Maybe we can block the monster before it gets here."

That was a naval operation, and General McClellan had the decency, in Welles's eyes, to say, "That's a naval matter, isn't it?"

"If that unsinkable battery of guns is allowed the run of Norfolk-Newport News-Hampton Roads area," Stanton rasped, "then it's good-bye to your beloved movement down the Potomac to the Peninsula and then to Richmond. That rebel monster will sink every troop transport you have, and there is nothing we can do to stop her. You'll have to change your plans in a hurry and go overland, through Manassas."

"No, that's the bloodiest way," said McClellan quickly. More directly concerned with his own operation in jeopardy, he looked at Welles. "With your permission, I'd be happy to confer with your commander at the Navy Yard—"

"I'm going down to the Navy Yard," said Lincoln, rising. "I want to see what Admiral Dahlgren says. Is there any danger to New York and Philadelphia, Welles?"

"The *Merrimack* is capable of reaching New York and shelling the city," the Navy Secretary admitted dutifully, "but in that case she would hardly be on duty to sink our troop transports in Chesapeake Bay. There can only be one danger at a time."

"You're blind, blind," Stanton said savagely. Still pacing, he proceeded to cross-examine Welles as he would a hostile witness, using sarcasm and derision to discredit the witness just as he had done as a famous litigator. Welles stood his ground, giving factual answers as far as he knew them, refusing to be stampeded.

Apparently exasperated at the iciness of his witness, Stanton resorted to shouting. "Do you have any idea what would happen if the *Merrimack* stood in New York Harbor and demanded that the city surrender and pay millions of dollars to save itself? New York would give up in one minute! Every New York regiment would be pulled out of the war, and every New York bank would stop lending us money, and we couldn't pay anybody and the whole damned army would desert!"

He slumped in a chair, exhausted, until another apprehension took over. "What if she goes out to sea and attacks Annapolis and destroys all our stores? There go all our supplies!"

Senator Orville Browning walked in the room at that point, paying a social Sunday morning call, and Welles was glad the President seized that opportunity to get out of the roomful of acrimonious advisers. Lincoln reached for his hat, told Browning to come along, and left for the Navy Yard without asking any of his Cabinet to accompany him.

Secretary of State Seward, who had been silent through all Stanton's tirades, put in after the President left: "This really could be quite serious, Welles. If the *Merrimack* comes upriver and reduces the public buildings in the nation's capital, or forces New York to pay tribute—or even makes possible an end to the blockade, which it seems to have done already—then we may see foreign intervention on the side of the South."

"Let's see what the *Monitor* can do," Welles maintained. He was confident that Commander Dahlgren at the Navy Yard, an ordnance expert highly regarded by Lincoln, would not do anything to put the service in a role subservient to the army. Lincoln often entrusted the details of army plans to Dahlgren, who would pass them on to the Navy Secretary, which was the only way Welles could find out what the War Department was doing. In return, Welles had planned an expedition to take the port of New Orleans with a naval force without informing Stanton. Let him find out about that operation from Lincoln.

Welles was not as confident as he made himself appear. Perhaps the small, untried craft could do little or nothing to stop the carnage in Hampton Roads; perhaps it would be rammed and sunk as soon as it tried to give battle; worse, perhaps the *Monitor* would sink before it even reached the scene. Aware of these dire possibilities, the Navy Secretary could only hope for the best, but he was certain that hair-tearing would do no good. Stanton, the Navy Secretary was certain, was a tyrant to those beneath him and obsequious to those above him, and Welles was his equal in rank. He would not serve the country or his President by permitting Stanton to bullyrag him.

Welles had assumed the rebels would take the *Merrimack* on a trial run, enabling Union spies to calculate its seaworthiness and speed, but the trial run turned out to be a surprise attack. The ship, he knew, was under the command of Commodore Franklin Buchanan, an excellent sailor, the founder and first superintendent of the Naval Academy at Annapolis, and the fact that the Confederacy entrusted this command to him demonstrated the seriousness of their endeavor. Several newspapers, especially Frank Leslie's *Illustrated Weekly*, had reported the rebel work on the raised ship and wondered why the Union had no similar iron-cladding going on. Welles had sent a message only the other day to the Brooklyn yard, where the *Monitor* was being rushed to complete its trials, countermanding the order to hurry down to Hampton Bays and ordering her instead to the Potomac for the defense of Washington, which the President always considered paramount. Evidently Welles's message had arrived too late, and the "tin can on a shingle" of designer Ericsson was on its way to the battle scene.

"Ram," said Stanton, lurching out of his chair to resume his pacing. "If our shells bounce off her armor, the *Merrimack* could still be rammed and sunk, the way she rammed the *Cumberland.*"

"We have no ship with an iron prow and rammer," Welles began, but Stanton interrupted with "Then build an iron rammer on the front of the biggest, heaviest ship you have! Do it today!"

When Welles looked disdainful, Seward put in, "Maybe there's merit in that suggestion, Mr. Secretary. We have to try."

"I have already ordered the *Vanderbilt* be fitted with such equipment," said Welles.

"Where is it?" A flicker of hope showed in Stanton's face.

"It will be ready in two weeks."

"Two weeks!" Stanton repeated, with the same sarcasm he had used for "two guns" on the *Monitor.* He went to the door. "I have to warn the governors. I've imposed tight military censorship on everything coming out of Fort Monroe, and we're the only outsiders who know of the *Merrimack*'s rampage. Now the damned telegraph lines are down and we can't find out anything ourselves. But I'm going to tell our coastal cities to get ready to defend themselves. Maybe they can place obstructions at the mouth of their harbors. We cannot just sit here and do nothing!"

He ran out to the telegraph office, to send, Welles was sure, terrified and terrifying messages to the governors of coastal states and to the mayors of Baltimore, Philadelphia, New York, and Boston.

Two tense hours later, Lincoln returned from the Navy Yard looking dispirited. "I have frightful news," he said, relating some more details he had picked up of the *Merrimack*'s rampage. "Dahlgren doesn't know any more about what to do than we do," he reported. "While I was there, the commander received an order from Stanton to load sixty barges and sink them at Kettle Bottom Shoals, to block the passage up the Potomac."

"I know," Welles said. "Dahlgren has since sent me a message asking if Stanton's order was by my authority. I told him no."

General McClellan nodded agreement. "Blocking the river would isolate us from Hampton Roads," he said sensibly, "but it would also isolate our operations in and around Richmond from support from here."

"First let's see what the *Monitor* can do," repeated Welles, gambling on an unproved vessel in an unknown type of war. He hoped that his animosity toward Stanton had not affected his naval judgment. He was a Connecticut newspaper editor, and had never claimed to be an expert in naval warfare. But if the age of the wooden warships was ended, there were no experts in naval warfare.

Lincoln, caught in the crossfire of conflicting military advice, temporized. "I'll tell Dahlgren to get the barges and load them up," said the President, "but not to sink them on the shoals unless he sees the *Merrimack* approaching."

"I trust that will come out of the army's budget," said Welles.

Lincoln opened his mouth to say something, then shut it, closed his eyes and nodded.

Jack Worden felt sick. He had joined the United States Navy at sixteen, served twenty-eight years waiting for action, but when the war started he had been captured on land trying to run secret dispatches. He had spent seven months in a rebel prison, was exchanged, and on his return to duty as a lieutenant was given a ship to command that no senior officer wanted: the small experimental ironclad *Monitor*.

One week after it was commissioned at Brooklyn, a tug started dragging it down to Chesapeake Bay. Sitting low in the water, the low-slung craft did not hold up well in rough seas. Water cascaded down the blower pipes into the engine room; for forty-eight hours the sixty-man crew was hand-pumping water and trying to keep the vessel afloat.

Nobody had slept during the two days and nights of that ordeal, but that was a fight with the elements that sailors had to expect. What sickened Worden now was the sight at Hampton Roads as the *Monitor* was dragged around Cape Henry.

Carnage had overtaken the Union Navy. He could see the remains of the ruined *Cumberland*, the *Congress* and the crippled *Minnesota* run aground and sitting prey for the marauding *Merrimack* in the morning. Hundreds of sailors were dead and dying, burning in the hulks or drowned trying to swim away. Worden climbed out the top of the turret down to the iron deck, nearly at sea level, and looked for the largest ship afloat. That was the frigate *Roanoke*. It had sent out a boat to bring him aboard.

The captain of the *Roanoke,* John Marston, tried to express the horror of the day and could not. "We couldn't run," he said a few times. "The *Cumberland* gave her a broadside, and we could see the shots bouncing off the armor."

"Damage her at all?" Even an ironclad, Worden had been warned, could feel the impact of a shell.

"Maybe a little. When the *Merrimack* rammed the *Cumberland* and sank her, the iron rammer broke off, so she can't do that again."

"Captain Smith?" Worden knew him.

"Dead; shell blew his head off. They never had a chance. And then when she ran the *Congress* aground and started raking her," Marston reported, "the *Congress* gunners may have knocked out a couple of guns through the *Merrimack*'s portholes. But she's a deadly machine. The navy will never be the same. It's not fair this way."

"The *Merrimack* can't hurt the *Monitor,*" Worden told him with more confidence than he felt. He might be David facing Goliath, but this time Goliath had an advantage in the number of slingshots. Luckily, the *Merrimack*'s ram was broken; that meant the *Monitor* could move in close and slug it out.

The captain of the wooden frigate looked over the rail toward Worden's little ship and did not seem impressed. "You the only ironclad coming? Don't we have a ship the size of theirs?"

Worden ignored that. "Where will the *Merrimack* attack tomorrow morning?"

"At the *Minnesota,* ready for the kill," the pilot said with certainty. "She's stuck aground and can't move. She can't fight the monster off, and the *Minnesota* won't strike her flag."

Worden decided to slip alongside the *Minnesota* to await the attack. He had no concern about running aground; the *Monitor* drew only ten feet of water and could maneuver anywhere. A large wave might sink her, but she was undeniably maneuverable, and Ericsson's invention of a revolving turret made it possible to fire its 11-inch guns in any direction at any time. Lying alongside the crippled *Minnesota,* he would surprise the *Merrimack.*

Marston then surprised him by saying he had a packet of orders to deliver to the captain of the *Monitor* from the Secretary of the Navy. Worden took the packet, started to read, and could not believe his eyes. Gideon Welles was ordering him up the Potomac to defend Washington.

According to the orders, the commander of naval forces in Hampton Roads—that was now Captain Marston—had been directed by the Secretary of the Navy not to let the experimental ship engage the *Merrimack* "except for some pressing emergency." Worden shook his head: Here, with the United States Navy half destroyed, on the verge of total destruction, the only ship that might save the day was being ordered away from the scene of battle— why? Worden knew the answer: because the politicians in Washington were fearful of an attack on the capital.

"The Secretary could not have given this order," said Worden, "knowing what's going on down here." One of the messages had been sent to Brooklyn to stop the tug from taking the *Monitor* down to Hampton Roads, and apparently arrived hours after Worden had left. He was thankful for that.

"You might want to decide that a 'pressing emergency' may exist," said Marston. "The *Minnesota* is about to be destroyed with all its sailors aboard. So you might feel your duty is to ignore the secretary's orders and fight it out here. But it's up to you."

Twenty-eight years in the navy. These were the first orders Worden had ever received, or was ever likely to receive, from the secretary himself. What was the course of duty? Maybe Gideon Welles had learned something about the weakness of the *Monitor,* or some hidden strength of the *Merrimack,* that Worden did not know; maybe grand strategic purpose lay behind the order, unbeknownst to the men on the firing line. On the other hand, maybe some people at headquarters were panicked at the prospect of the "monster" moving north; if so, the place to stop the *Merrimack* was here and now. If it could not stop the slaughter of the men on the *Minnesota* here at Hampton Roads, the *Monitor* would not be able to stop the capture of Washington by the *Merrimack* steaming up the Potomac.

He felt the need to write a brief farewell to his wife. Marston took him into his cabin and waited. Worden sealed it, handed it to Marston to deliver if Worden were killed and Marston were not. "A pressing emergency causes me to disregard the secretary's orders," he said, in case of a court-martial.

"I agree," said the commander of what was left of the Union fleet.

At 7:30 A.M., First Officer Greene took his eye from the sighting hole in the *Monitor* turret to announce, "It's coming. And Jesus, it does look like an iron crocodile."

Worden looked and swallowed: the U.S.S. *Merrimack,* renamed the C.S.S. *Virginia,* was an immensely ugly ship, black, smokestacks billowing, stubby guns poking out of holes in the sides, moving like a turtle on land with none of a turtle's grace in the water. Before the black ship could draw within range of the *Minnesota,* Worden took the *Monitor* out to make his challenge.

The *Monitor* fired first, slamming its 180-pound solid cannonballs into the railroad iron on the side of the *Merrimack*. Worden looked for signs of damage; he could see none, and wished that Commander Dahlgren and his damned Bureau of Ordnance had allowed designer Ericsson to use a powder charge twice as strong. But if ever a ship could look surprised, that was the appearance of the Confederate ironclad, slowing, turning, trying to lower the level of its guns to point at the small annoyance in its way.

A blast from ten guns roared at Worden, who stepped back from the peephole to receive damage. The *Merrimack,* expecting to meet the wooden *Minnesota,* had brought explosive shells, which banged harmlessly against the round armored turret and low deck of the *Monitor;* Worden was glad his enemy had not loaded up with solid cannonballs, which his ship could probably have taken but which might have caused more damage.

"Return fire," he commanded; "fire at will."

The two ships poured shot at each other, neither appearing to do damage. The *Merrimack* captain, frustrated at the ineffectiveness of his shells, and despite the absence of an iron ram, attempted a ramming maneuver. But the big ship was ponderous; Worden easily turned aside his hull and let the giant slip by, blazing at the rear as it passed, trying for a lucky hit in its steering mechanism. He circled his opponent, pounding away like a cooper with a hammer going round a cask. Worden did not know if any ship, even an ironclad, could take so many direct hits from solid shot without being profoundly damaged; even the few explosive shells that hit the *Monitor* caused screw heads to fly off and spin about the inside of his ship.

A new danger: Worden saw the *Merrimack* come alongside with intent to board. If an enemy force could land on top of his ship, they could stop up the chimney and, armed with crowbars, pry open the hatch. Or they could set rags afire and drop them down the air vents, or pour water in. Here, in a new era of naval war, the rebels were trying a technique as old as any fighting at sea. Worden gave them encouragement: he let them come temptingly close, then he slipped quickly away.

The fight went on for four hours, neither adversary gaining an advantage, with the obsolete wooden warships far in the distance, looking on, daring no intervention in a battle of ironclads. The *Monitor's* sailors, stripped to the waist, were blackened by powder.

"Aim near the waterline," Worden told First Officer Greene, "if we can get two shots on top of each other, we can break through the armor and sink her." The *Monitor* was delivering two shots every six minutes, but never two near the same spot on the *Merrimack.*

"She's closing in again," said his first officer, at the peephole, "slower this time. Having engine trouble."

"Let me see." Worden stepped up to the sighting tube and was surprised to see the black armor of the *Merrimack* not ten yards away. He started to draw back from the viewer but not quickly enough: a 9-inch shell fired point-blank exploded against his turret, and it was as if fire were pouring through the peephole. Blinded, his beard afire, Worden screamed in agony, rubbing his hands against his beard, smearing his blood against the burning gunpowder. "Sheer off!" he yelled.

When he could feel a wet towel being applied to his seared face—he hoped he had not been unconscious long—Worden croaked out the word, "Damage?"

"That last shot lifted our turret a few inches," said Greene's voice, "and we made it to the shallows. The *Merrimack* crew is cheering as if their ship won the battle, but we're seaworthy. Shall I take her out again?"

"No," said Worden, hoping he would see again, "not unless she's moving on the *Minnesota*. Did we save the *Minnesota*?"

"Yes. The *Merrimack* is out of range, and the ebb tide is running. The *Minnesota* is safe," said his exec.

The three hundred sailors aboard the *Minnesota* were saved from execution. Worden counted that a fair day's work, even if not a victory. With the *Merrimack* parading up and down, Southerners might claim triumph over the smaller craft, which had retreated out of range to shallow water, but the *Monitor*'s job had been to stop the *Merrimack*, not sink her. The *Minnesota* was saved. The blockade of the Southern ports was still on.

"She's pulling away," reported Greene. "I think she's headed back toward Norfolk. Should I follow her out? Make it look more like we were chasing her home? I hate to think the rebs will claim a victory."

"Let her be; she might turn on us and we're not in such good shape," Worden said before he passed out.

The surface under Worden was solid and soft, not pitching; he was on land. His face was in bandages, a wet cloth across his eyes. A woman's voice said, "President Lincoln is here to visit you," and removed the cloth. Worden's vision was clouded, but he was not blind. He thanked God for that. He could see the outline of the bearded face at his bedside, and he struggled up to lean on an elbow in a kind of attention.

"You do me great honor," he whispered to the commander in chief.

"Not so," said the voice, higher-pitched than he would have imagined. "It is you who honor me and your country."

"Where is my ship?"

"Where you left it, at Newport News," said President Lincoln. "I told the Secretary of the Navy there was too much danger to your vessel to send it after the *Merrimack*."

"Good," said Worden. "Don't let them go skylarking up to Norfolk, unless"—he reached for the phrase—"there's a pressing emergency."

"I'll tell him that. You should know that the *Merrimack* caused us great anxiety in Washington. Even now, we have a fleet of barges at Kettle Bottom Shoals, just in case she makes a run north."

"She couldn't do it with those engines," Worden told him. "Underneath the iron, it's just an old, raised, wooden ship." He wondered if Lincoln had known of the order to bring the *Monitor* up to Washington rather than engage the *Merrimack*, but it was not for him to ask.

"Then 'Stanton's navy'—that's what they're calling it," said Lincoln, "and Mars doesn't think it is very funny—will have little to do. Welles was opposed to the scheme of sinking the barges in the shallows, and it seems Neptune was right."

Lincoln sat on the edge of the bed. "Stanton's navy will be as useless as the paps of a man to a suckling child. There may be some show to amuse the child, but they are good for nothing for service."

Worden's bandages kept him from smiling, so he said "Heh-heh."

He felt his hand taken in a pair of big hands. "I'm recommending that you be promoted to captain. You're a brave man."

"I wish I'd given you a real victory."

"When we don't lose, we win," said the President. "When they don't win, they lose. So you could call this a victory."

CHAPTER 7

COST OF LIVING

At the request of the cook, Kate Chase went to the tradesman's entrance of the imposing brick house on Sixth and E to have a chat with the greengrocer.

She knew what was on his mind. The ten thousand dollars her father had borrowed from Hiram Barney for personal expenses had run out. The Secretary of the Treasury did not want to borrow further from his own appointee, the Collector of the Port of New York, but the real estate slump made it impossible to sell the Chase house in Columbus, Ohio. That left the Chases short on cash, with barely enough to pay the staff of six needed to maintain the Washington mansion in the style demanded by a Treasury Secretary, and Kate had to contend with irate tradesmen. She was becoming good at it; a natural bent toward imperiousness helped.

"What seems to be the matter?" she asked.

"It's my bill, ma'am." The greengrocer was nervous. "It's past due for three months now, and I would never trouble you—"

"I should hope not. I put your bills aside because I noticed your prices have become outrageous." She went on the attack. "The lettuce that cost five cents a head when we came here last year is now eight cents. You're charging nearly twice as much for potatoes. Explain that, if you please."

"It costs me more, ma'am. I don't grow it myself, the farmers who sell it to me can get more selling it to the army, so they raised their prices to me."

"Profiteering," she said sternly.

"Not me!" The tradesman obviously knew who Chase was, and Kate knew he must be worried about what an angry government official could do to his business. When she reminded him that her father was personally occupied with keeping the *Merrimack* from shelling the food stores near the docks, he hastily apologized for bothering her; backing away, he hoped she would get around to his bill when it suited her.

She told the cook that Secretary Chase would be going to New York today, and that she wanted a dinner for only four: Colonel James Garfield, a dark-eyed Ohio legislator who now commanded a regiment here, and his homely wife, and John Hay. Colonel Garfield, her father judged, had a good future in Ohio politics and could be helpful against the Wade Ohio forces at the 1864 presidential convention; Kate agreed, enjoyed a flirtation with him, and had made him her confidant. She had already arranged for the colonel to send the

Garfields' regrets at the last minute, to leave her alone with Hay. It was time, she decided after the ball at the Executive Mansion, where the young man had cut quite a figure, for them to be alone together.

In the breakfast room, her father was staring glumly at the two-day-old *New York Tribune*. The Treasury Secretary looked up at her, smiled bravely, kissed her extended cheek, and announced, "I fear we cannot pay our bills."

She concealed her alarm; had any of the tradesmen reached him directly? The keeping of the Chase household books was her responsibility, which she took seriously. The servants had been admonished never to let a complaining supplier of any kind see Secretary Chase. If he saw how deeply in the red they were, he would either sell his property in Ohio at distress prices, a prospect intolerable to Kate, or would cut back on their style of living in Washington, which would be unseemly for a potential President.

"Has anyone complained, Father?"

"Horace Greeley, for one," he replied.

That puzzled her. They did not subscribe to the *New York Tribune;* her father brought it home from the office.

"Here is what he says," he said, shaking the paper: " 'The Treasury has been virtually empty for a month; at least one hundred millions of dollars are this moment due to people who need their pay and ought to have it; among them are thousands of volunteers who have suffered and dared for thirteen dollars a month'—that's how much a private soldier receives in pay, my dear —'and whose families are suffering for the two, three, four, and even five months' pay which the country promised them and of which they have not yet received one cent.' "

"What a terrible thing to publish." She sighed in relief. It was the Treasury of the United States that could not pay the bills.

"The terrible part is, Greeley's right," Chase said. "The Treasury is empty. It's bad enough that I cannot pay the soldiers in the field, which is terrible for morale. But I cannot pay the government's suppliers and contractors."

"Pay them with your new paper money."

"Yes, the infamous Legal Tender Act enables me to do that. But the new green paper won't be ready until April. Payment in gold and silver coin was suspended at the beginning of the year, and my demand notes were not declared legal tender until last week." He leaned back in his chair, awed at the financial crisis over which he was presiding. "That means for three months no lawful money has been circulating."

She sat down and spooned some honey onto a piece of toast. "What do people do? How do people manage without money?"

"That's the amazing thing," her father said. "Bank checks and notes are being accepted by people, despite the fact the notes and checks are not good for gold, and no paper money yet exists. By all rights there should be a panic, but there's not. Everybody seems to think I'll straighten it all out in a little while."

"They have faith in you," she said, meaning it, "and so do I."

"So does Lincoln—too much at times. He doesn't want to bother his head with any of these monumental problems and leaves it entirely to me. For example, he doesn't know the first thing about gold."

"Gold doesn't seem to be so important now, does it?"

"True," he said. "We don't need gold because people know we don't need gold. We're mining plenty in California. And because of the war and the tariff, we're not buying from overseas, while we're still selling to Europe. That means no gold is going overseas, and there's no panic. You only need gold when you need gold—does that make sense?"

"Confidence is everything," she replied. Garfield had explained that to her. "But what's worrying you?"

"First, I cannot pay the current bills. Second, the printing of paper money, untied to gold, will surely lead to the inflation of the currency."

She remembered his reference to thousand-dollar breakfasts in his talk with Jay Cooke. "Wouldn't the war bring the inflation even with gold coins in use?"

He looked at her in surprise turning to admiration. "I do not know the answer to that, my dear. And the fact that I do not is another reason to worry. However, yours is a profound question. I will put it to the bankers in New York."

She changed the subject. "Father, whose picture will appear on the paper money?"

"I'm being given the honor of appearing on the thousand-dollar-bill. The President will appear on the lower-denomination notes." He paused at her frown. "Do you think that will cause criticism?"

"I think it's a mistake," she decided. "Let Lincoln have the honor of being on the big bills, the ones the banks use. Your face should be on the ones and fives and tens, the money people will use every day. Think of 1864."

"I try not to think about the next presidential election," he said immediately, and then caught her skeptical look. "Of course you're right, Kate. We'll give the President the honor of being on the big notes. I'll be in the people's pockets."

"No President since Jackson has been reelected," she said, warming to her favorite subject, "and Lincoln will not even be renominated."

"Don't be so sure," he said. "We underestimated him last time, Seward and I. If Lincoln and McClellan go along this way, taking their time on fighting the war, avoiding the abolition of slavery, then there is a good chance we'll have peace next year—the Union preserved, slavery intact in the South. And then Lincoln would be unbeatable."

"That would be a disaster."

"Stanton's my only ally in the Cabinet," he said, examining political assets and liabilities with her, as they often did, "and he's a War Democrat. Among the Republicans, the Blairs despise me as I do them. Seward is now completely in Lincoln's pocket—an amazing transformation of that man. If Lincoln cannot win the Republican nomination, he and Thurlow Weed will connive to deliver the nomination to Seward."

Kate went to the window, arms crossed, thinking. She stared at the half-built monument to Washington. Why was Lincoln protecting McClellan, who was so notoriously pro-slavery? Why did Lincoln not side with Wade and the Republican radicals in the abolition cause?

Because, she concluded, Lincoln wanted to occupy the middle ground and stay where majority opinion was likely to be: "the Union as it was," reunited, with slavery allowed to continue in the South but prohibited extension into new states, combined with a freedom-purchase scheme buying freedom for negroes in the South over the next thirty or forty years. Smart reelection politics, staying in the midstream of the majority.

What would be an effective way to head that off? She had discussed that with both Garfield and Roscoe Conkling, a New York congressman and would-be beau. First, it would be necessary to break off Lincoln's support from War Democrats; that meant a wedge had to be driven between Lincoln and McClellan. General McClellan had to go; Stanton, a War Democrat himself, would be the man to bring McClellan down, which would cost Lincoln the support of conservatives and soldiers, who adored the Young Napoleon. It was also important to crush McClellan before he won the war, which would catapult him into the presidency.

Next, her father would have to be sure that he, and not Lincoln, received the credit for the smashing of slavery. Slavery was not the issue in the whole North, but slavery was the central issue in the Republican Party, and that was the group that was to deliver the nomination. Alongside Wade in the Senate and Stevens in the House, Chase—and not Lincoln—could be identified as the leader of the anti-slavery cause in the Executive Branch.

The political course became obvious: to use pro-slavery McClellan to discredit Lincoln in Republican eyes. Stanton was an ally in this, along with Republican radicals Wade and Greeley; conservatives Seward and the Blairs were the enemy.

Despite the niggling money worries, despite the dangers of the untested legal tender, she was more than ever convinced that Salmon Portland Chase's day as President would not be denied. Kate Chase would be a worthy "first Lady of the land," in the phrase Russell of the *London Times* was applying to Mary Lincoln. Kate knew she could be the best first Lady yet, bringing style and elegance, intellect and youth, to a place that had been occupied by a series of frumpy old wives or simpering presidential daughters. The nation deserved more.

And it would be fun. The war would be over, the gaiety returned, no more dreary restraints on great levees and sparkling balls. She would give the nation a presidential house it needed after the tragic years, helping to lift the spirit of her countrymen. When the moment came for her to wed, she would have the grandest wedding Washington had ever seen, turning the East Room into a bower of white flowers. Not least of all, there would be no more money worries; presidents, Kate assumed, had great secret sources of funds, and first Ladies did not have to deal with bill collectors.

CHAPTER 8

JOHN HAY'S DIARY
MARCH 15, 1862

Everybody except Father Neptune looks a little sheepish this week. Nobody wants to talk about the way Stanton treated the attack of the *Merrimack* as the end of the world, and frankly, the way the Tycoon kept getting up to look out the window for the oncoming iron monster was nothing he can be proud about, either. In retrospect, our reaction was *alarmiste,* but at the time, frankly, the situation was pretty scary.

One result of the success of the *Monitor* is the new respect everyone is paying what seemed up to now to be crackbrained schemes. Pinkerton has a woman spy down in Richmond who reports that the rebels are working on a sub-marine, a ship that goes under water and shoots projectiles they call torpedoes. That seemed a pipe dream, but after the *Merrimack,* who knows what the rebels have up their sleeves? Our ordnance is working on a gun wheel proposed by Mr. Gatling that fires God knows how many rounds a minute and would give a two-man crew the firing power of a company. Then there is a plan for the use of hot-air balloons for reconnaissance, but since General Fitz-John Porter, McClellan's favorite, almost got blown into the enemy camp trying one out, there's been a go-slow on balloon ascensions.

The other result of the scare is that the Ancient of Days is personally going to make damn well certain that the nation's capital is not left undefended. Just as the *Monitor* was told not to go skylarking after the *Merrimack* in Norfolk, the troops needed to defend Washington are not going to be sent skylarking down to Richmond. No matter what McClellan wants or says he needs.

The Prsdt has split his difference with Little Napoleon. He has grudgingly approved McC's plan to sail down the Potomac and Chesapeake Bay to the Peninsula between the James and York rivers and to attack Richmond from the east. At the same time, he has removed McClellan's title as General-in-Chief and set up a board of Republican generals, in four army corps nominally under him, to watch what Little Mac does.

The fig leaf offered Little Mac for his removal as overall commander of the war is that he will now be too busy in the field, as head of the Army of the Potomac, taking Richmond, to direct the war in the West. Actually, it's a trade: McClellan gets his way and can invade the South the easy way, by water, and Lincoln punishes him for dawdling throughout the winter by taking away his cherished title.

What makes the Prsdt uncomfortable about the Peninsula expedition is that it leaves Washington relatively naked of defenders. On the overland route to Richmond, via Bull Run, we would at all times have our army between the rebels and our capital. Let all the generals talk about the wisdom of this river maneuver, Lincoln still remembers how it was here in Washington only a year ago, cut off from the North—"There is no North"—and even how it was right after the debacle at Bull Run. No more of that.

So, instead of giving McClellan all the men he wants for a swing down the river, the Prsdt will send General McDowell, no fan of McClellan's, by the direct route overland toward Richmond with another army—that way, there will be a defending army between the rebels and Washington at all times. If this leaves Little Mac believing he is being pushed into battle with one hand tied behind his back, so be it. He wasn't here when a cavalry foray could have captured the President and Cabinet.

Some funny business is going on between Halleck and Grant out West. Courtesy of Mars, who monitors all the messages between generals, I have a telegram from Halleck to McClellan that reads: "A rumor has reached me that since the taking of Fort Donelson General Grant has resumed his former bad habits." That means drunkenness. "If so, it will account for his neglect of my oft-repeated orders. I do not deem it advisable to arrest him at present, but have placed General Smith in command of the expedition up the Tennessee." Mac then replied to the effect that if Grant is drunk, arrest him.

Jealous military backstabbing is what Grant's patron saint, Congressman Washburne, has been insisting is at the root of the rumors, and he has been in with his assurances that all the stuff about drinking is slander. Hence Halleck was given overall command in the West, but Grant was singled out for promotion to major general. Lincoln likes Grant because "he fights," which is his tacit way of goading the Young Napoleon, who takes his time preparing to execute some grand maneuver. But hell would be to pay if Grant goes into battle with a sword in one hand and a bottle in another.

Old Man Blair, who backs McClellan, told me that Lincoln is learning how to use certain unpopular people as criticism-absorbers—that's why he has Stanton, to be the hated disciplinarian while Lincoln signs the pardons. Is the Tycoon really that devious? A year ago, I would not have thought so; now, I don't know.

I have a rendezvous tonight. I shall not reveal the identity of my companion lest this diary fall into enemy hands. But how can a man be simultaneously smitten and distrustful? All my life, through all my conquests, triumphs, glories, spoils, I have assumed that love and trust, like liberty and union, were one and inseparable. Now the one I love most is the one I trust least. Strange. Is she like McClellan, or will she fight?

CHAPTER 9

HAYLOFT

"The Garfields could not come," she told him at the door. "We're dining alone."

John Hay professed a look of alarm.

"The house is full of servants," she added. "Your honor will not be endangered."

"Send them all home," he said bravely.

"They live here."

"Ah. I brought you these," he said, handing her a bouquet of violets wrapped in a government document. "They're done up in the Legal Tender Act."

"You're thoughtful, Mr. Hay."

"If you'll be legal, I'll be tender."

"Now you're out of prepared remarks."

"True. From here on, I'm on my own. Did that moment really happen after the ball?"

Kate Chase knew she was going to enjoy the evening. Mainly on impulse, only partly with calculation, on the night of the ball, a freakishly warm winter evening, she had accepted his invitation to a stroll in the small garden behind the President's house and told him he was an exciting man and kissed him. That was not the sort of thing she usually did, but John Hay was a man —not quite a man; a youth, really—quite different from the men who escorted her or trailed after her. He was a poet who traipsed through tropes, as he put it, at the center of power. She liked the way he asserted, rather than admitted, his pretensions as a poet. He was also a fountain of good conversation, a source of inside information, and a channel to the mind of her father's present superior but ultimate adversary. Time flirting with this young man was not wasted.

And he was attractive. Roscoe Conkling, the congressman from New York, was a package of ambition and purposefulness who wanted too much from her; Governor Sprague had all the money she would ever need, spoiled her outrageously, followed her around like a puppy, and ran out of things to say; Lord Lyons never ran out of things to say, stimulated her mind elegantly, but was nobody to dare anything with. Those men were her father's contemporaries; Hay was the only young man she found to stir more than one interest. She tried to think of him as a useful diversion, but John was more than a little diverting.

After their intimate dinner, over coffee, she said, "Now all the girls you dazzle at Counselor Eames's parties get to this moment and say, 'Tell me about Mr. Lincoln. What is he really like?' What do you tell them?"

"As cunning as Seward, as incorruptible as Stanton, as honorable as Chase, as wily as Weed, as funny as Petroleum V. Nasby—"

"Honorable?" The comparison with Chase was the interesting one to her. It was curious that John should pick that one trait, perhaps playing the innocent, using the word "honorable" maliciously, as Marc Antony had about Brutus. Why not "wise" or "efficient" or "ambitious"? Did he suspect the beginnings of the radical move within the party to replace Lincoln?

"Nothing wrong with honor," he said. "I think of your father as laden with probity. Reverent. Self-disciplined, principled . . ." She waited. ". . . a little on the stuffy side, which hurts him with the voters, but a great appointed official."

"He won his race for governor." She wanted to kick herself for being on the defensive. "Why do you worship Lincoln so?"

"I revere him," said the young man lightly. "Worship is not the word. Worship is the word for the way men, especially older men, feel about you."

She would not let him turn the conversation back to her. "What makes you revere him?"

"He's a poet, like me, only better than I am. That surprises you? Good, I enjoy surprising you, Kate Chase. So few of your wide coterie do."

Oh, this young man was good at ending his statements with an arrow pointing to a discussion of one's weaknesses. "Lincoln a poet?" she scoffed. "Come, now."

"Not the way he thinks," he admitted. "He thinks poetry is 'Why Should the Spirit of Mortal Be Proud?' God, if I hear that gloomy, sentimental pap once more, I may regurgitate all over his carpet slippers. Nor is it Shakespeare—he does a pretty fair Macbeth seeing Banquo's ghost. No, Lincoln's poetry is imagery. He talks in phrases that call up pictures."

She gave him her skeptical look.

"The other day, when McClellan asked for more troops again," he explained, "the Tycoon said that sending men to McClellan was like trying to shovel fleas across the floor: a lot of them get lost on the way."

"That's poetry?"

"Of course. Metaphor; most specifically, simile. It's as if I were to equate your eyes or your hair to something in nature."

"Not fleas, I hope."

"Not 'limpid pools,' either. Nothing is trite about you, and you're like me —you have a lust for originality." He looked at her directly, saying nothing for a moment, thinking, she assumed, of an appropriate simile. Sure enough, he said, "Your eyes flash bright and cold, like icicles in the sun."

He impressed her with that, and she did not try to hide it. Bright and cold was the way she tried to appear, and the way she feared she might really turn out to be. She thought about his figure of speech for a moment, then asked, "What happens to an icicle in the sun?"

"It melts."

Time to break the contact off. "I'd like to take a walk in the fresh air."

"It's a lovely night," he agreed. "Except for a little freezing rain, which is hardening the mud underfoot. We could pretend there are stars in the sky. Do you have galoshes?"

"What I really mean is, I'd like to take you to my room." She had not meant to say that but was glad it was out. She wanted to hold him close, and needed also to shut him up. He had the good grace to follow her upstairs in silence.

She closed the door behind them. The gas lamp on the street outside was the only illumination, and they let their eyes become accustomed to the darkness in the room.

Her young man stood in silence, not knowing what to do next. She gently pushed him into a chair and sat across from him on the edge of the bed. Kate had been planning this interlude of intimacy all day, but she had not known how she would feel. She had taken men to her room before for moments of almost-abandonment—experienced men, aroused but never out of control—who had shown her how to satisfy their desires by hand, without risking the dangers of a loss of virginity. She liked to play at passion, to feel their hands explore her, but knew where to draw the line; she would never let the possibility of pregnancy endanger her future.

But never had she teased a man of her own age in this room in this house, and never felt such a yearning to open herself completely. For all John's pretenses of experience, and his reputation with the young ladies, and the availability of local prostitutes, she could not be sure that he was not a virgin himself.

"Something is troubling you, Kate."

She changed her mind. "I want to hold you and kiss you, John Hay," she said. "That's all. Will you understand?" She slipped out of her dress; still covered neck to knee with underclothes, she sat on his lap. He was hard, which pleased her, but he did not put her hand on him and she would not make the first advance. Innocent sparking would suffice; if their time to love ever came, she did not want him to think of her as wanton or brazen.

He smelled young—no tobacco, no liquor, good teeth. "Legal tender," she whispered, and they kissed for a long time. He was surprisingly gentle and did not grope at her. When he grew up, she decided, he would be quite a man.

"You can touch me, if it pleases you," she said, and he obediently put his hand on her breast. "I don't have much of a bosom. Always envied women like Anna Carroll or Rose Greenhow, even Mary Lincoln."

He exhaled. "You just went past three very different women, each of whom would dearly love to be as beautiful and as young as you."

"Not Anna. Do you suppose she's interested in my father?" She noted he was concentrating on cupping her breast and did not hear the question. "I think she is. They have a lot to talk about, the way we do. That's important. I can't let her get close to him," she said, going on more than she usually did. "He needs to focus all his energies on being a great man. We're a team, my father and I."

"Can you be on more than one team at a time?"

"No," she said firmly, and softened it to "not likely. We're too much alike." She kissed him long and hard on the mouth, darting her tongue between his lips, and then quickly moved off his lap, pushing him back in the chair, sitting on the edge of the bed again. "By that I mean we both want to go to the top. You want to be—I don't know, a senator or Cabinet member one day, maybe a poet besides. I want to be the most important woman in the country. We can't do that together. You and I can watch each other, and help each other, but we have to go our own way."

"You've thought about this too much," he said. "Remember how you feel. Don't deny your feelings."

"I don't, that's why we're here."

"We can't go to my place," he said mournfully; "the President lives there."

She laughed. "We'll continue to be acquaintances in public, and we'll see each other like this in private, and after a while it may be difficult for me to want to stop you. But I trust you to remember, John, we go our own way. We pledge each other nothing." She had not meant to be this honest with him, but she could not help herself. She trusted in him not to believe her.

He rose, took her in his arms, and held her tightly for a long moment. She responded, safe in the farewell embrace, with pressure of her thighs against him.

"You're a bit too tall," he observed. He was right; she slipped out of her shoes instantly and they were exactly the same height. "Major Garfield says you have a pug nose, and he's wrong. You have a nice nose."

He kissed her again, toe to toe, hip to hip, mouth to mouth, perfect fit. She was certain she could make love to him beautifully, better than with anyone else she knew, experienced men like Conkling and Garfield or fumblers like Sprague.

"The important thing to have is a kindred soul in an alien world," he said, in a more serious tone. "Strangers are everywhere. Don't foreclose the future, Kate." He was mistaken; he would be hurt. She had warned him.

She pulled away, slipped on her unrumpled dress, and led him out of the bedroom. She liked the way his face was flushed and knew she looked at least as excited.

After she sent him out into the freezing rain in his galoshes, Kate looked at herself in the hallway mirror with some satisfaction. The violets in the Legal Tender Act were lying on the table, and she arranged them in a small vase; her father would like the thought. She turned her head to fix her hair, catching what she could of her profile out of the corner of her eye. Garfield was right about the pug nose, but some men found it attractive.

CHAPTER 10

THE FAMILY LINE

"The important thing in life is to know who you're for," Francis P. Blair instructed his sons and daughter, gathered in conclave at the estate in Silver Spring. "Right now we're for McClellan. That's because we're about the only ones around who are loyal to Lincoln."

Frank, whose mustache his father thought was getting out of hand, frowned at the seeming anomaly. "But Lincoln is always complaining about McClellan. Says he's got the slows. Took away his title of General-in-Chief and let him read about it in the newspapers. I don't think they're close, Father."

"That's for public consumption," said Monty, supporting the elder Blair's viewpoint. "In the Cabinet meetings, Lincoln backs up McClellan most of the time. Chase and Stanton are out to stab him in the back, and Welles and Bates are leaning their way. Only Lincoln remembers it was McClellan who saved the army after Bull Run."

"Make no mistake," the old man told Frank, who had had trouble grasping the finer points of political machinations since he was a boy, "McClellan is not personally loyal to Lincoln, the way we are. He wants to set up for himself—as dictator maybe, or surely as Democratic candidate in sixty-four."

"If Stanton doesn't beat him to that," Monty put in.

Lizzie waved that off. "Stanton couldn't get elected assistant paymaster," she pointed out, as her father nodded vigorously. "Chase is the one fixing to grab the Republican nomination away from Lincoln, with the help of Horace Greeley. But right now, McClellan is useful to Lincoln because he's the only general the President has got that the army will follow. And Lincoln must know that the radicals out to get McClellan are also out to get Lincoln."

"He knows, all right," added her father. "I told him."

Frank, frowning, thought about that. "Why are the Blairs for Lincoln?"

The elder Blair started to express his exasperation and then reminded himself that what Frank lacked in political sagacity, he made up for in personal likability. He was the only likable Blair, the only one with voter appeal, except for daughter Lizzie, but a woman was not electable to anything.

"Good question, son. We're for Lincoln, first, because he's for us and he's shown it. And second, because he knows what is best for the country. The time is coming—Jefferson foresaw this, and I could never get Jackson to see it—when the extermination or deportation of the African race from among us will be inevitable."

"Don't say deportation, Father," Lizzie cautioned. "We say colonization."

"She's right." Monty sounded judicial. " 'Colonization' implies that it is voluntary. You cannot deport four million people against their will."

"Of course not. Stop trying to teach an old man how to suck eggs." The elder Blair respected his older son's judgment, and was glad he had been able to place him in the Cabinet, protecting family interests, but "the Judge" tended to forget who had taught him all he knew. "It's Lincoln's plan, which I've been helping him work out for the past year, to buy back the slaves from their owners. Then, when they see how horrible the caste system will be here, with whites treating blacks like dirt, the Africans will want to find a congenial place to go. Liberia, maybe, but most won't want to go back to Africa. Haiti is better—hot climate, not far away. Best of all, Panama. Vast deposits of coal."

"Here comes the vision," Lizzie smiled at him. He would take that irreverence from her.

"The blacks could be the advance agents of American empire," he declaimed, largely for Frank's benefit. "The Southerners, not the firebrands but cousin John Breckinridge and the smart ones, know all about the importance of Central America. They'll take it over if the South wins this war—and so should we when we do. It's my plan to populate Central America with our four million blacks, speaking English, not Spanish, and friendly to us—dependent on us, in a lot of ways. We'll do in Central America and the Caribbean what the British have done in India. The colored race will be happy down there, and we'll have far more power in the world."

"They're not going to want to go," said Frank. "They like it here. It's hot as hell down there, snakes, jungles—"

"They will prefer colonization soon enough," the elder Blair said with confidence. "Look at the irreconcilable castes in Spain—the Spaniards and the Moors are an abhorrent mixture in the same peninsula. Mixing does not work, and slavery is a vicious institution that imbues a brother's hand in a brother's blood. That means we have to find a good place for negroes to go." He strove to make it simple, easy to remember. "Compensation, followed by colonization, that's the ticket—an end to slavery and an end to the caste problem. Buy 'em up and ship 'em out."

Frank, hungry as always, cut a piece of cheese from the elegant service before them and looked up at his brother Monty. "How did your get-together in the President's office with the border state congressmen go? They tell me it was a flop."

"Frank is right about that, Father. I turned out all the men from Kentucky and Maryland who could respond to Lincoln's compensation offer. The President argued with them, reasoned with them, finally beseeched them. I never saw him work so hard on a delegation."

"And they turned him down flat," said Frank. "Nobody in the loyal slave states wants to sell slaves. If the North wins, the value of slaves in the border states will go up, and if the South wins, the notes of the federal government paying for the slaves will be worthless. So the slave owners loyal to the Union are sitting tight and shouting down the abolitionists. Wade and Stevens and the rest of the radicals make a lot of noise, but the sentiment of the majority in Congress is against abolition. I know—I'm right there on the floor every day."

"Damn fools," said old Blair. "They'll wind up without their money and without their slaves."

"If compensated emancipation is such a losing proposition, Father," said Lizzie, "why are you and Lincoln pressing it so hard? According to Monty, the President was begging them to accept. He could get turned down—humiliated, even. And you always used to say, when you know you can't win, back off before you lose."

Blair smiled cannily. At least, after he died, his brain would go on calculating and conniving inside her skull. "Lays the groundwork. The President made them the offer in good faith, it's their choice. Later on, the border states won't be able to blame Lincoln if all the slaves are freed by amendment. Next step is emancipation here in the District."

"Henry Wilson's bill. I'm for it, right?" Frank, who alternated between serving in Congress and serving as an officer in the field, when he wasn't in jail for insubordination, had a grasp on the voting basics. The old man nodded, yes.

Which reminded the elder Blair; he took his watch out of his pocket and consulted it. "I'm expecting Miss Carroll in a few minutes," he announced. "She turned out to be right about that Tennessee River plan of hers, contrary to what you thought, Monty. The Donelson victory is the only thing that's given the banks confidence in the new greenbacks. She knows her railroads, something most generals don't seem to understand." He did not add that she was on his payroll; some things the boys did not need to know. She did good writing work cheaply and he liked her. "Montgomery, what have you been doing, besides failing to deliver the border states to their own salvation?"

"The Post Office department is turning around," reported his elder son with some pride. "Lost six million dollars last year, should break even next year. And that's without collecting anything from the receiver of letters."

"You're on the lookout for fraud?" the old man said sharply. The enemies of the Blairs would like to find some small thievery to blacken the family name.

"We're using a new indelible ink on cancellation to cut out the fraudulent reuse of stamps," Monty assured him, "and I've started a money order system to stop the theft of money in the mail. Here's the exciting part: we're sorting the mail on the railroad cars on its way to delivery. Saves two days, and—"

The elder Blair shrugged all that off and let his natural testiness show. "It's nice that you're running the department, but you're in Lincoln's Cabinet for bigger things than delivering the damn mail."

"It's a big job in itself, Father," Monty protested, and then shut up. The elder Blair wished his older son would understand that Postmasters General were not supposed to fuss with the mail; if that became their job, they would lose Cabinet rank.

"Think first about winning the war and getting Frank, here, elected President," the old man told him. "And about helping Lincoln in that snakepit of a Cabinet."

"Sometimes I wish Lincoln were more like your old friend Jackson," said Frank, who liked things clear and direct.

"Not the time for a Jackson," snapped his father, "time for a Lincoln. Man who can get together a group of men who all think they're his betters and make them work for him. Man who can accept insults without rancor, tack this way and that because he knows his destination."

He looked hard at his younger son, who knew it was a test.

"And that destination is"—Frank took a guess—"abolition?"

"No, dammit! Get it through your thick skull that it's Union, Union, Union. Slavery is a side issue, Frank—if abolition helps him, he'll use it; if it hinders him, he won't!"

"Try not to get too excited, Father," said Lizzie. "Frank needs to know when that train is going to leave the station, so he can be in position to jump on. If he jumps too soon, he'll never be President."

The elder Blair stomped around the room and sat down. He took a few deep breaths. If only Lizzie were a man. He explained patiently: "Learn from Lincoln, who never gets too far ahead of public sentiment. He knows he can't do a thing about slavery in the loyal states—it would take a constitutional amendment to take away a loyal citizen's property. Abolition can be used as a device to hurt the traitors, Frank, and to satisfy the Northern radicals—but never anything to make some sort of moral crusade out of in the border states, where national elections are won."

"So do we ever become abolitionists?"

"Not soon," said his father. "Never say a word in favor of slavery, Frank, but don't join up with the radicals. They're against us and for Frémont, and now Chase. That crowd hates us, always will. That's why the Blairs are for McClellan—he'll make it possible for Lincoln to reunite this country."

The elder Blair walked out to his gardens, one of the beauties of Silver Spring. Now that March was here and summer approached, Lincoln would begin to spend weekends at the Soldiers' Home, on high ground west of the Mansion, and would visit the Blairs more often. The President, the old man knew, liked to handle the fine books in the library and to partake of the delicious breakfasts on the terrace and the sense of gracious solitude of the grounds of the Blair estate. Silver Spring was a good place for reflection, and the solidity and grace of his physical establishment counted for something in Blair's influence with this and other presidents.

The old man plucked a few rose blooms from the top of their stems until he had a handful of colors, and returned to the house to float them in a silver dish. His wife liked to see that when she came in from riding.

CHAPTER 11

IN DURANCE VILE

Alexander Gardner was mystified. His boss, Mathew Brady, had been trying to arrange to take a photograph of Rose O'Neal Greenhow in Old Capitol Prison for months. Allan Pinkerton, the Secret Service chief who had made it possible for photographers to pass through to the front lines of McClellan's battles, such as they were, had resolutely refused permission for Brady to see her. Obviously, with the Wild Rose still smuggling mail and messages out of the tightest security the Union could contrive, Pinkerton wanted to block further publicity for the figure that the Southern newspapers had so dramatized.

Yet when Gardner had mentioned to Charles Dana, the former *Tribune* editor who was Stanton's new assistant, that he hoped to pose Mrs. Greenhow and her daughter, word came back the same day that he would be issued a pass to Old Capitol Prison. That was an unexpected turn of fortune; it was the first time Gardner had seen what a personal political connection could do in business.

Brady would not like it. The assistant hurried about Brady's studio, getting together the cameras and plates he would need inside the prison. Up to now, all the connections had been Brady's; the famous photographer catered to the celebrated, gave too many free sittings to the political great, and used those associations to cadge passes to the scenes of war. Gardner, the inside man, knew nobody; Brady saw to it that all the credit for photographs taken by Gardner and the others went to the owner of the gallery, and nobody raised his eyebrows in recognition when Gardner's name was mentioned. Only Mathew Brady was to be famous. The Scotsman thought that was unfair; he knew Brady could ill afford to pay a decent wage, since the gallery was not making money, and the least the boss could do was to let recognition fall on his fellow workers. He suspected that Brady did not want a competitor.

But now Alexander Gardner, who did not make friends easily, had a connection to a man in power. Charles Dana was famous as a newspaper editor, but Gardner had met him a dozen years before when both were young idealists trying to live by the socialist teachings of the utopian Welshman Robert Owen. Gardner had made two trips to America from his native Glasgow, where Owens's dream first took hold, and brought over members of his workingmen's reform party to found a settlement called Clydesdale, in Iowa, on the Mississippi River.

The thought of the tragedy of Clydesdale made him rest the heavy plates on a counter and lower his head. "Galloping consumption" had been the name of the disease that crushed that community, the cause of the death of so many of the sturdy Scot families that Gardner had accompanied to America.

Gardner had gone home to Scotland on his final round trip to gather up his family and bring them with him to the American oasis of education and opportunity, and instead had found death and devastation. He had hurried them back to New York City and, using his knowledge of chemistry, had applied for employment with Brady. The famous photographer looked at Gardner's pictures of Iowa's Indians, questioned him about his knowledge of bookkeeping, and hired him. Gardner set aside his dream of being a business-man in a community interested in the welfare and education of all, and became a photographer. He was not sorry; photography was not a good business, but it was an interesting occupation.

Brady was out of the gallery and in the field, across the Potomac, leading Tim O'Sullivan and Gardner's younger brother James in shooting the fortifi-cations that the rebels had recently abandoned. Washington was agog about the embarrassing discovery that some of those dread fortifications were "Quaker guns"—big logs set up to resemble cannon—that had fooled and terrified the McClellan commanders for a year. That would make an eye-popping picture, published as a woodcut in *Harper's Weekly* or *Frank Leslie's Illustrated Newspaper,* and perhaps sour Brady's relations for a while with Pinkerton, who had been taken in by the rebel trick. Gardner had to give his boss credit: when a picture cried out to be made, Brady stopped at nothing to make it.

His employer's absence, Dana's intercession, and Stanton's sudden ap-proval gave Gardner the chance to enter the prison alone. Since Brady had been getting credit in the magazines for all the pictures Gardner and the other assistants were taking, the young Scot felt no twinge of conscience at grabbing the opportunity; the name on the picture would be Brady's anyway. Maybe, one day, he would ask for the copyright in lieu of salary; his time would come. Gardner did not know quite how to tell Brady, but he had heard from the President's junior secretary that Mr. Lincoln preferred the young Scot's work to that of the famous photographer; Lincoln had taken to show-ing up at the studio when Gardner, not Brady, was behind the lens.

He left Foons, the free black, in charge of the gallery with instructions to clean out and straighten out the Indian headdresses and leather outfits stored for their visits. Whenever the Indian chiefs came to Washington to meet with the Great White Father, they tried to look like white men, in jackets and pants, but Brady insisted they be photographed in full-feathered regalia be-cause nobody would buy a picture of an Indian without feathers. It meant a dozen outfits had to be kept on hand, which cluttered up the studio.

He drove the small wagon up to the Old Capitol alone. Gardner first stopped to take an exterior view of the prison, a place of historic and photo-graphic interest. Whitewash coated the lower floor, presumably to silhouette anyone making furtive entry or exit. The upper two stories were dreary black, windows heavily draped to prevent prisoners from signaling to passersby. Gardner placed a wet colloidal negative in the camera, estimated a thirty-second exposure in the strong early April daylight, and quickly removed the slide that allowed light to spill onto the glass. That one exposure would have to do; Brady rarely approved taking only one shot of any scene, but Gardner wanted to save his negatives for his primary subject.

Waiting in the lobby of the prison for a Lieutenant Nelson to approve his pass, amidst slovenly guards and a noisome atmosphere of filth and decrepitude, Gardner let his mind dwell on his personal dream: to leave Brady, the showman-promoter-pioneer of photography, to start a business with his brother James. Unlike Brady, who was obsessed with controlling the photographic coverage of the war, and kept talking of some grandiose mission to record history and advance the art of photography, Gardner would have a bookkeeper to collect his receivables and pay his bills. In a month or two he could have enough business to hire Tim O'Sullivan, the assistant who was probably the best picture taker of them all, and who also chafed under the "Photo by Brady" credit on all his work.

Gardner shifted his foot to crush a roach marching near his bench. Of the one thousand photographers working in the United States, Brady's name was the only one widely known, and the nearsighted pioneer was evidently determined to dominate the field for as long as he lived. Gardner could not accept that; he credited Brady with the vision to make photography a part of the war, and not a mere collection of *cartes de visite* by the wealthy, but he would not credit Brady with the pictures Alexander Gardner took. Not for long.

"The superintendent wants to see you," said a burly lieutenant. Equipment in his arms, Gardner went into the office on the ground floor marked "Superintendent Wood."

"I don't know how you got this pass," said Wood, a short man hunched over a desk, examining the War Department credential, "and I don't think it is a good idea."

"Secretary Stanton signed it himself," Gardner said helpfully. He did not know Stanton's reason either; it hardly seemed in the interests of the government to permit photographs of this pesthole.

"She can do anything," Wood said, as if to himself. "She can arrange for her own protection—we found a loaded gun in her cell a week ago. She can write a note and get a senator to visit her—Henry Wilson was in here this morning. And now she can get Stanton to turn this prison into a photography studio."

"I'll only be an hour or so."

"God knows what's next. I have her in solitary confinement, with her daughter, and you know what she did? She ripped up a plank in the closet and has been handing the girl down to the rebel prisoners of war on the floor below. They feed the kid because the captured soldiers have better food than the prisoners of state."

"If you know about the closet, why don't you seal it up?"

The superintendent glared. "I'm not cruel, no matter what she tells you. It means I have to search every one of those fellows every night to make sure she's not slipping out messages that way. Her little girl is sick, too, but the hifalutin Mrs. Greenhow won't let the prison doctor near her. Hates him, calls him a poisoner, gets him all upset. 'The Wild Rose' is more trouble than any dozen prisoners in this jail."

"Does she know I'm coming to her cell?" Gardner especially wanted her to pose in the room in which she was confined, to show the contrast between her surroundings as a queen of society and now.

"You're not getting near that floor. I'll clear the niggers out of the courtyard, and you can do your work against a wall. Your wall's being washed right now. You turn your camera on anything else and I'll arrest you as a spy and you can spend the rest of the war taking pictures of Rose."

Gardner was taken through the lobby by the lieutenant, past a room with triple-deck bunks cramming thirty people into a space for four, and noticed the main activity of the inmates was tracking and burning vermin. He had not been inside fifteen minutes and he wanted to take a bath.

"What are their crimes?" he asked mildly. Gardner was a reformer at heart, and even now, his dream of a socialist settlement gone, he found time to work with the philanthropist Amos Kendall in his school for the deaf, dumb, and blind. He held no brief for traitors; still, there seemed to be many more "prisoners of state" than he expected.

"Speaking out against the President," the lieutenant listed the farrago of crimes, "publishing incitement to desertion. Suspicion of treason. Brokering draft substitutions."

"Wasn't there an amnesty declared a month ago?"

The lieutenant smiled grimly. "Yeah, we had no room for any more, had to clear a bunch out. But that's just Mr. Stanton getting rid of Mr. Seward's arrests. He'll cram this place with his own before long. You know the Greenhow woman?"

"No, we've never met. I've been out in the field working for the army." The photographer thought it was a good idea to reaffirm his loyalty.

"Impossible bitch. We gave her a few candles and some matches to burn a few of the graybacks off her walls," said the lieutenant. "You know what she did? The night the *Merrimack* was causing all that fuss, she took down the window drape and burned a candle in the window. When a guard on the street warned her he'd shoot it out, she lit all the candles at once, made a bloody celebration, singing 'Dixie' and all. She had her door bolted and we had to break it to blow out the damn candles."

Gardner liked the woman already. One of his photo subjects last month, General John Dix, who had been Treasury Secretary under Buchanan, knew Rose well and had described her to him: black hair, white skin, flashing dark eyes, a look of hauteur or passion depending on her mood, and above all, according to General Dix, a talent for beguilement. Powerful effect on men. Gardner suspected that Dix had been one of her many lovers. Would such a woman's qualities be capturable on film?

In the prison courtyard, he set up a chair with a headrest in back so that she could hold a pose for thirty seconds without movement. The child would be a problem—kids were hard to hold still—but he wanted her in the photograph too. He got behind his camera, threw the cloth over his head, and looked through the lens at the chair.

Behind him a woman's imperious voice said, "I would like to know why Mr. Mathew Brady could not come himself."

Gardner turned to look at the ravaged remains of what might once have been a handsome face. Rose Greenhow's eyes were haggard, skin pocked with insect bites and gray-pale, the mouth set in a hard line. Her hair, obviously unwashed but tied back tightly, was turning iron-gray. She was dressed in mourning, as Gardner was told she always dressed, in memory of a baby daughter who had died the year before; that recent loss was why, he supposed, she could not part with her eight-year-old.

"I am Alexander Gardner, manager of the Brady gallery." He presented his only credential: "I have photographed President Lincoln twice, at his request."

"That's no recommendation," she said. "Have you photographed a gentleman? Or a statesman?"

"General Scott?" No reaction. He thought fast. "Secretary Stanton?" He racked his brains for a rebel. "Senator Breckinridge?"

Her face softened. "I saw the photograph that was John Breckinridge's *carte de visite*. You did that? It said 'Photo by Brady.'"

"They all say that. I took the picture."

"General Breckinridge is a great man. Do you know where he is right now?"

"In the Western theater, I understand, with General Sidney Johnston." He had read that the traitor senator was on the run clear down to Alabama, and that Halleck had reinstated Grant to go deep into the Southwest with General Sherman to finish off what was left of the rebel army down there.

She nodded in approval, introduced her daughter, and took a seat in the chair in front of the camera. He hoped it would not be insulting to offer her a chance to improve her looks for history: "Here is a comb and hand mirror, ma'am, if you want to straighten your daughter's hair just a bit."

She took the mirror, looked at herself, and put it down in pain. She sighed, picked it up again, and did what she could with herself, then handed both to her daughter. He explained the posing requirements and looked through the lens. The white wall in the background was too bright; the cleanup squad had done its job too well. He moved the chair over toward a window, which broke up the background. As he was doing this, she asked idly if he had been photographing in the field recently.

"Yes, only yesterday, just across the Potomac at Winchester."

"General McDowell? A nice fellow, if an incompetent. I knew him some years ago—"

"No, General Banks."

"McDowell wouldn't pose? He's usually so vain—"

"He and his men are well past Manassas, ma'am. Brady's down there with them."

"Your employer likes to be in the thick of action."

"The main action will be down in the Peninsula," he said, and then shut up. He had been telling her the disposition of some of the Union forces, which she might be able to put together with reports from incoming rebel prisoners. He reminded himself she was a spy capable of getting information out of the prison. He said, "Hold it now—breathe deep, hold your breath while I count to thirty, don't move an eyelash—" He let the light into the aperture and waited for the image to impress itself on the colloid. "One more," he said. "Without the child."

"Don't hurry," she said. "This is the first time they've let us into the courtyard. We haven't felt sunshine on our cheeks in over a month."

"That's terrible," he said. But was she telling the truth? He decided she was; their pallid faces showed uninterrupted indoor incarceration.

"You're from Scotland?" Since his accent was unmistakable, Gardner figured it was safe to say yes. "I have many friends in England," Rose Greenhow chatted. "They're just waiting the proper moment to enter the war on the side of the Confederacy. Have you photographed Lord Lyons, the British Ambassador?"

"No."

"He told me he met with Mr. Seward one day, and the Yankee Secretary of State said the most remarkable thing to him." In her dramatic voice, she mimicked Seward: " 'My Lord, I can touch a bell on my right hand, and order the arrest of a citizen of Ohio. I can touch the bell again, and order the arrest of a citizen of New York. Can the Queen of England, in her dominions, do as much?' "

Gardner had heard about that boast; the Peace Democrats had made much of it months before, when they were trying to whip up sentiment against arbitrary arrests. The photographer busied himself with his equipment, aware he was under close scrutiny by the guards across the courtyard, but not hurrying with the actual picture taking. He wanted to let the little girl and her mother have as much fresh air as his visit allowed.

"Perhaps you are wondering," she said, "why I permit our picture to be taken."

"Historical record," he offered.

"My purpose is to shame all my friends here in Washington, and my relatives, too, who fear to visit or to help me. I know how I look, Mr. Gardner. I used to be a famous beauty, and I am one no longer."

"We have artists who will touch up the negative," he assured her, not knowing what to say. "We enhance the reality as a matter of course, much as portrait painters emphasize the more positive—"

"Let your camera tell the truth," she told him. "No artist's brush. Promise me not to touch out a wrinkle of care, or to put a smile where there is a look of hardship. I want people North and South to know what life is like in this hellhole, how the proud and mighty Yankees can devote time and energy to breaking the spirit of one woman. But they will never break me, Mr. Gardner."

"Or me," added her daughter. Gardner had a son, fourteen, a sensitive boy who did not want to look at the war pictures. He had a fleeting and depressing thought about what life would be like with him in a rebel jail.

"The person who arranged for your pass," Rose Greenhow said, changing the subject, "did he say anything about our release? Or about a trial?"

"No," Gardner said promptly. But why had the approval for the photograph come through so suddenly? And through Stanton, not through McClellan or Pinkerton? He suspected there could be a difference of opinion between Stanton and McClellan about releasing the mother and daughter. "To tell the truth, I've heard rumors of a trial. Maybe if you confessed and signed a parole of honor, they'd release you to go South."

She set her mouth. "I would never give the tyrants that satisfaction. If Stanton's man asks you, tell him that. In fact, tell him that whether he asks you or not. Would you do that for us?"

That was none of his business. "Hold it—breathe deep, listen to my count for thirty, press your head back against the rest—" He let in the light. She

Rose O'Neal Greenhow and daughter, Rose; photograph by Gardner, Brady Studio.

held her expression: dignity, determination, disdain, resignation, the faintest touch of hope. He could hardly wait to get the plate into the wagon, back to the gallery and into the darkroom.

CHAPTER 12

WHITE RABBITS

Lincoln rolled off the office couch and stood up. He had been allowing himself to think about the inevitability of this war, and that was never profitable. Was this, as Seward had once said, an "irrepressible conflict," with great subterranean strains and pressures building up for a century that necessitated some terrible earthquake, or could a wise President have averted the war, keeping the Union intact with compromises? He had not given the matter deep thought at the time, when events led him to the decisions that had seemed so painfully plain, but now—thousands of deaths later, with the killing just beginning in earnest—he found himself examining paths not taken. But at a time that Union armies, East and West, were finally on the move, such second-thinking was weakening, enthralling; he put all that out of his mind and walked to the door.

His hand on the doorknob to his secretaries' room, Lincoln stopped; a mental picture of Willie hanging on that doorknob, swinging the door open, suddenly afflicted him. He shut his eyes and waited for the memory to shudder past. Through the oak door, he could hear the voices of Hay and Stoddard.

"The Hellcat is in a 'state of mind' about the steward's salary," Hay was saying. "Her Satanic Majesty thinks she will blackguard me into giving her the money, and I won't."

Lincoln winced, then smiled, at "Her Satanic Majesty." Hay had a nice sense of exaggeration.

"Isn't that properly Nicolay's decision?" Stoddard asked.

"Nico is off to see the fair Therena back home," said Hay. Lincoln nodded to himself; he had sent Nicolay west to check up on the rumors about Grant's drinking and Halleck's desire to arrest him, and to test the local political waters on the idea of using Treasury funds to buy up all the slaves. He did not trust the opinions in the newspapers to accurately reflect the public sentiment. Apparently Nicolay had told nobody, not even his assistant, about his mission; that was sensible. Lincoln loved Hay as he wished he could love his son Robert, but he trusted Nicolay. He turned the doorknob noisily and entered with his customary "What news?"

"Hill Lamon seems to be taking his title as marshal too seriously," Hay said promptly. "Surprised us all by indicting Horace Greeley criminally for libel. Says he's going to New York to arrest him and bring him to jail down here."

Lincoln did not need that added burden. Ward Hill Lamon was not the smartest of his old Illinois friends, but he was intensely loyal and a strong physical presence to have around; accordingly, Lincoln had appointed him

U.S. Marshal for the District of Columbia, which paid the salary of the President's bodyguard.

At Lincoln's pained expression, Hay said, "His best friends cannot persuade him to drop it. I tried—he's my cousin—but Hill says it's a point of honor." Hill could be marvelously stubborn. Lincoln would have to pass word to the judge that the President would not be offended if he threw out the case.

"On top of that, sir," Stoddard added, "Secretary Stanton has arrested a *New York Tribune* correspondent in the field, and he's tapping the wire of the *Tribune* to see what other reports are being sent over the telegraph by reporters who learn too much about military movements."

Neither Hill Lamon, in his foolish pride, nor Edwin Stanton, in all his fierce caginess, seemed to understand how much store Lincoln set in the power of Uncle Horace. He would have to talk to Stanton about that; perhaps it was a case of his new assistant, Dana, getting even with his old boss at the *Tribune*. That harassment would have to stop; let an example be set with other newspapers, not the *Tribune*.

Lincoln had just written a letter to Greeley saying he was in favor of urging compensated emancipation "persuasively, not menacingly" upon the South. It was not that he expected Greeley's support, or even the editor's acquiescence in keeping the focus of the war on preserving the Union rather than on freeing the slaves. His object was to use Uncle Horace as a foil in assuring the border states, and the conservative majority in his Republican Party, that A. Lincoln had not suddenly become an abolitionist. If emancipation should then be needed as a weapon, a military device, the world would know that was his legitimate reason to break the compact on slavery made by the nation's founders. If abolishment became needed to coerce the South or invigorate the North, such an extreme action could best be taken by a President who did not seem to want to free the slaves on moral or sentimental grounds. The appearance of military necessity was central; reluctance rather than fervor would have to be the posture. He would conceal his anti-slavery feelings.

He would have to argue with Greeley, gently and publicly, putting distance between himself and Wade's radical crowd, but not an unbridgeable distance. He might have to accede to some of the abolitionists' wishes one day, to serve his own larger purpose. An approach to the molding of public sentiment began to shape in his mind, making use of a respectful disagreement with Greeley. First, this harassment of the *Tribune* with libel suits and threats of arrest would have to be stopped.

"Stod, the President has had enough troubling news," Hay announced. "Get the box."

At Hay's direction, Stoddard went over to the corner of the room and lifted a large cardboard box with holes poked in it. The secretaries trooped into the President's office and placed the box on the table with the maps.

Lincoln heard scurrying inside and lifted the lid. Two white rabbits, pink noses twitching rapidly, looked at him in terror.

"Get Tad, quick," he told Stoddard. Grinning, he lifted the rabbits, one in each hand, out of the box and set them on the floor. They scampered under the desk. When Tad walked in, Lincoln told the boy to look for a present somewhere in the room. In a moment, Tad had both white rabbits in his arms and a look of sweet wonderment on his face. The secretaries left and the President, his son, and the rabbits had a great romp.

That respite from care lasted until Stanton came in, and the rabbits almost escaped between his legs. The Secretary of War stopped, looked, started to say something, then clamped his mouth shut in disapproval. Lincoln was tempted to put one of the rabbits in Stanton's arms, but held himself back; Mars might drop the creature. He told Tad to put them in the box and wrote a quick note to the sender: "Thank you in behalf of my little son for your present of White Rabbits. He is very pleased with them." That was an understatement. He wondered if they were a male and a female. At a nod, the boy lugged the big box out of the office, to take them to his mother, who Lincoln hoped would not be too surprised.

"Everybody thinks he's a great military strategist," said Stanton, brandishing a copy of the *Tribune*. "Here's Greeley with one of his pompous editorials, which he calls 'The Expected Blow.' "

"And where does Uncle Horace expect the blow?" Lincoln inquired.

"Not in the East, of course, where all the troops are and the action is. The great military mind thinks we should be on our guard for a great secessionist offensive in the West."

Lincoln frowned. Halleck and Grant had the rebel general, Sidney Johnston, on the run in the West, pursuing the Tennessee River plan that Lincoln had recommended. What was Greeley's cause for concern?

"A lot of alarmist talk," Stanton assured him. "I read the wires from the *Tribune* man in the field who is with Grant's troops on the Tennessee River. The correspondent foresees a new Bull Run disaster ahead, and that talk could hamper our enlistments, especially in New York. I've censored the dispatch, of course. Wish I could suppress the damned editorial."

Lincoln inquired whether Grant knew about the rumors.

"Of course, and it's the usual thing that frightens only generals like McClellan." Stanton handed him a copy of a telegram from Grant near Pittsburg Landing to Halleck at headquarters. Grant had wired: "I have scarcely the faintest idea of an attack being made upon us, but will be prepared should such a thing take place."

"Good man, Grant," said Stanton. "Steady, fearless—not like the Little Napoleon, seeing hordes of secesh behind every tree."

Lincoln knew that Stanton had countersigned McClellan's direction to Halleck to arrest Grant if he resumed the habits that had caused him to quit the army years before. That was the natural response of the army leadership to one of its generals—in this case, Halleck—who needed support on a matter of discipline in the field. Grant was a man Lincoln had heard was experienced in personal failure, having once been reduced to selling firewood. McClellan, on the contrary, was experienced in success, as manager of a large railroad. Lincoln needed, above all, a man who would bring success to Union arms.

Caution, however, which was McClellan's hallmark, was not always the route to success. "I hear he fights," was all he said to Stanton about Grant.

"Congress has passed the bill freeing the slaves in the District of Columbia," Stanton said suddenly. "You'll sign it?"

"I understand it purchases the slaves from loyal citizens for no more than three hundred dollars a head," he corrected the lawyer. "I want to think about it." Wade had promised to pass a Joint Resolution first, putting forward Lincoln's plan for gradual, compensated emancipation, which the radicals hated to swallow.

"The Joint Resolution you asked about is on your desk," said John Hay, reading his mind, "unless the rabbits ate it."

"Then I will sign the bill," Lincoln told Stanton. Senator Wade had been as good as his word; with his conservative price met, the President allowed himself to be drawn a radical step forward. He picked up a treaty, forcing his attention toward an agreement with the Potowatomi Indians of Kansas, hoping General McClellan would be bold and General Grant would be careful.

CHAPTER 13

THE IRREPRESSIBLE CONFLICT

"You're a political man, Breck, " said Sidney Johnston. "Did this war have to happen? Could it have been avoided?"

On the eve of battle, the general liked to think large thoughts, of the sweeps of history rather than the worries of the morrow. The notion of Henry V in Shakespeare's play, walking incognito among his men before striking the French at Agincourt, appealed to the Texan, but he chose instead to spend the evening before the decisive battle jousting with the most political of his subordinates.

"This is the most unnecessary war of the century," Breckinridge replied, hunched forward on a cot in the tent, bourbon in hand. That was the reaction Johnston expected from the disappointed peacemaker. Wrong, of course, but challenging.

He had come to like Breckinridge more than any of his other commanders, not because he was the best soldier—Hardee was more dependable, ran a disciplined headquarters—but because the Kentuckian's mind, like his own, delved into the roots of the war. Breck was the classic example of the right man in the wrong place at the wrong time. Hardee was stolid, "Bishop" Polk too gregarious, Bragg a martinet subject to debilitating headaches, and Beauregard a temperamental tactician with no notion of grand designs. Pat Cleburne, the fierce and funny Irishman, was a talented general with the most potential and, if the war dragged on, would be his candidate for commander in the West when the time came for Johnston to step up to supreme command.

Breckinridge, though, was his choice for mutual rumination just before a major event, and Johnston believed the attack at Pittsburg Landing would be the turning point in the war. He thought of Breck as an honorable politician with his fundaments eroded, through no fault of his own—a good man who had not slipped his moorings as much as one whose moorings had slipped him. He worked hard, drank harder but not on duty, obeyed orders and inspired his "Orphan Brigade" of homeless Kentuckians to resist the temptation to desert. Johnston counted him among those generals who was doing his duty but not fulfilling himself in the war—caught up in neither the spirit of the South's revolution nor the cause of his own advancement.

"Seward once called it 'an irrepressible conflict between opposing and enduring forces,' " Breck went on, "and he was dead wrong. No reason these sectional differences could not have been compromised, as they always were by our forefathers. We were driven into this war by foolish, irrational, hot-headed men."

"Lincoln's fault?"

"Partly. His speech a few years ago—that the Union could not endure half slave and half free, that it had to become all one or all the other—talk like that helped bring on the war. But Lincoln wasn't the only one. It was the fault of the whole blundering generation, Southerners definitely included."

The Texan drew him further on. "You don't think the issue of slavery was that important, then."

"It became important, when demagogues—abolitionists and Republicans, mainly, followed by the firebrand Southerners—whipped up the public into a frenzy about it."

"Um. But one section thinks that slavery is immoral, cruel, un-Christian, and the other thinks not," Johnston mused. "Pretty basic difference on a matter that stirs emotions."

Breck rose and stood in the center of the tent, holding the pole, in an attitude that Johnston assumed was a vestige of his Senate days. "That same difference existed between Virginia and Massachusetts during the American Revolution. Same difference in the Jackson days, when Calhoun nullified. Same deep split later on, when we defeated the Wilmot Proviso and passed the Missouri Compromise and worked out the Chittenden resolution. The issue of slavery did not change, but the nature of the men who dealt with that issue changed for the worse. Peaceful men were shunted aside, and the would-be warriors took over."

"Issue wouldn't go away, though, would it? Kept coming back, getting more divisive."

"That's where you're wrong," Breckinridge pounced. "Slavery was a dying issue, because slavery had reached its natural limits. You can't raise cotton profitably in the South without slavery, but you cannot grow cotton up North or out West."

Johnston let himself be pushed back further. "The whole fight about the extension of slavery into the territories, then, the subject of the Lincoln-Douglas debates—"

"All a false issue!" Breckinridge boomed. "Slavery, and cotton, had already reached its natural frontier. Stephen Douglas was right—popular sovereignty would have killed slavery in the territories, because the West is free soil in its nature. Slavery would have stayed in the South, and ultimately died there."

"Why?" He put out skirmishers. "My family had slaves, first in Kentucky, then in Texas, pretty far west. Made good money for us."

"The institution of slavery ultimately must crumble in the South because it is wrong and makes good people morally sick." Breckinridge appeared absolutely certain of his position, and though a border state man, without any doubt about his ability to read the mind of the South. "Forget all that sentimental pap in *Uncle Tom's Cabin,* the stories of torture that inflamed the

North. Sure, discipline is necessary sometimes, but nobody with any sense really abuses his slaves, because you don't destroy your own property or encourage it to run away. But the fact is, keeping people in slavery is wrong, corrupting to the soul, no matter how well you treat them. Didn't you feel guilty about having slaves?"

Johnston nodded yes, urging Breckinridge to commit the reserves of his argument.

"Washington did, too, and Jefferson. Manumission was a growing movement until all this happened, and public opinion was shifting against the ownership of human beings, because the great majority of Southerners do not own slaves. Our peculiar institution would have steadily disappeared if the blunderers hadn't taken over, if the fanatics up North hadn't whipped up the zealots down South."

"Let's assume you're right. Say that slavery would not have extended into the West, and it would have died out in the South," Johnston posited. "Still, that's a long time to wait. Four million people would be living in slavery for at least two generations. That's a lot of broken families, a lot of whipping, a lot of rape, a lot of misery, you must agree. Your preacher uncle would call it a mountain of evil."

Breckinridge let go the center pole and leaned forward, resting his big hands on his knees. "You don't think what we're going to do tomorrow is evil? If all goes as you've planned it, we're going to send our boys into their camp to stick our bayonets into sleeping Americans. You don't want merely victory in the battle, you want the utter destruction of Grant's army, followed by the annihilation a day later of Buell's army. How many dead—twenty, thirty thousand?"

"That should do it," said Johnston coolly. It could come to that; war was death.

"Multiply that a hundred times, to get an idea of the evil of this war. How many dead will both sides count if this war drags on—half a million men? That's one dead soldier for every six slaves to be freed. Killing innocent young men is evil, too, General. You not only snuff out their lives, but you deny life to the children they would have had. You don't eradicate evil by committing a greater evil."

Johnston admired the passion and conviction in his argument, and held up his palm in a motion to sit down.

"I disagree. I do not see this war as the blunder of a generation of agitators, as you do." The general, who considered himself more a man of decision than of oratory, liked to make his points march in quiet order. "I do not think this conflict could have been avoided by leaders of goodwill. Even if you Democrats had not split in 1860 and John Breckinridge had been elected President, this war would have come."

"I watched Buchanan try to keep the peace," Breckinridge broke in, "and he did, though everything started to unravel toward the end. I would have kept the nation together and let the slavery issue cool down, and the war fever would have died. It's a damn tragedy we got Lincoln and war."

Johnston hoped to open the other man's mind a crack to another point of view, perhaps to lessen his bitterness in having been denied a chance to save his countrymen from their holocaust of lives. The general knew that his friend Jeff Davis had in the back of his mind the appointment of Breckinridge as his Secretary of War. The replacement of Judah Benjamin with the Kentuckian who understood the vast military opportunity in the West would make life in the field much more productive for Albert Sidney Johnston. If Breck could be made to see the inevitability of the struggle, perhaps he would find it a worthier cause for his unique political talent. As a general, Breckinridge was offering the Confederacy his life, but was by no means giving his all.

"This is not, as you would have it, an accidental or unnecessary war, the work of fanatics," Johnston observed. "Jeff Davis had it right: there has been for a generation a persistent and organized system of hostile measures devised by Northern congressmen to strike down the tenure of property in slaves. Breck, that amounts to thousands of millions of dollars. No people anywhere, ever in history, voluntarily gave up near that value of property."

His companion, apparently remembering the decorum of floor debate, held his fire.

"Your specific assumptions about the mind of the South are inaccurate," Johnston told him. "Manumission has been steadily decreasing, not increasing, because slavery is more profitable than ever. The proof of that is easy: you know that the price of slaves is rising."

"There are voices—"

The general shook his head. "No Southern antislavery movement exists that I know of, and nobody in the South is calling for making the rape of a black woman a crime. And if you think the people of the South were led unwilling into secession by a few noisy politicians, come to Texas. We're the only state that held a referendum on that. The people voted three to one to secede."

"You're saying that the divisions are deep-seated," the Kentuckian acknowledged, "and I don't deny that. But these disagreements existed in 1830, and in 1850, and we didn't start killing each other."

"Our people have grown apart in that time, from competing sections into two opposing nations," Johnston answered. "Different customs, different ways of doing business, and a wholly different idea about what is right and wrong. The North has come to see the South as the world's last outpost of the most degrading economic system invented, threatening free labor everywhere. And the South, as we know, has come to see the North as aggressive and domineering, the masters of capital seeking to plunder the tillers of the soil. We see the abolition radicals demanding huge, wrenching changes in Southern society at no cost to them."

"It's only the leaders of each side who are convinced of their rectitude," Breckinridge argued, "and those blundering politicians cannot see how the two economies complement each other. United, we can compete with the world; divided, both sections will be exploited by the world. That's why the British want us apart."

In danger of being outflanked, the general launched his central attack: "More important, each side, each very different culture, is persuaded that the other is in fundamental antagonism. It is much different from a generation ago, or from Calhoun's time. You're quite mistaken, Breck, about this desire to disengage being the product of a few rabble-rousers and newspaper editors. The two peoples have grown apart, and one side or the other must dominate.

With two strong-minded male dogs in the same house, only one can be top dog. That's the way of the world."

It was Johnston's turn to rise and hold the center pole. "If the South is not to be subjugated, it must go its own way. In life, in war, in national destinies, timing is everything, as you will see in battle tomorrow. A century ago, it was natural and right for these colonies to separate from England; today, it has become just as natural for these two sections that don't belong together to separate again."

"Rather than plunge the country into war," Breckinridge said, "I was prepared to accept that proposition. But Lincoln wouldn't hear of it."

"Of course not, neither would I," said Johnston, enjoying the look of puzzlement on his adversary's face. "To resist that separation is natural, too. Lincoln is doing what I would do, refusing to recognize the natural division, insisting that we fight for our freedom as Americans did a century ago. No national leader worthy of his calling can stand by and watch the dismemberment of his country. War was inevitable, irrepressible. It was Lincoln's duty to force the South to fight, and the South's duty to take up the challenge."

Breck held his ground. "It was his duty, back in the campaign, to run for President in such a way as to be able to hold the country together without war. He failed to do that."

General Johnston pressed his point: "These are great tides, huge and fundamental moral and economic forces, Senator Breckinridge,"—he purposely used the political, not the military, title—"and there comes a time in a nation's history when fundamental debate turns from the political forum to the military field."

"I have heard that pernicious argument expressed another way, General, by Mr. Lincoln. He says that if you have an elephant on a string and the elephant wants to run, better let him run. He puts it more colorfully than you do, but both of you are wrong. The elephant of destruction must be stopped at any cost. War is never right, enormous bloodshed is never justified, unless a nation is resisting invasion." Breck stopped, took a swallow of bourbon, and added glumly, "and now the South is resisting invasion. That is why I am down here, not up there. But sometimes I wish I were still in the middle, where my poor Kentucky tried to be, trying to stop this waste of American lives."

Johnston felt a surge of frustration at having a better position but, facing a more experienced opponent, not being able to win the argument. He tried his own metaphor: "Have you ever seen a huge logjam, Breckinridge, a river clogged impossibly, the logs backing up forever? The only way you can get the river flowing is by blowing up a section with a huge charge of gunpowder. We have come to the moment when only a violent shock can save us."

Breckinridge rose to face him; Johnston was tall, but his guest was about three inches taller. "I suppose that is why you are a general, Sidney Johnston, and I am a politician, and always will be. To me, violence is always failure. Rage is the mask of weakness. No war was ever worth its cost."

"The War of Independence was," Johnston countered immediately. "For the South, if we win, we will have made a nation by spilling the blood it always seems to take, and this war of independence will be well worth the cost." The General thought about it from the other side, as good generals

General Albert Sidney Johnston, C.S.A.

always tried to do. "And for the Union, if Grant and Sherman are not surprised tomorrow and we are defeated, this war will bring an end to the fissure that has weakened this nation in the world. Not all wars are worth the cost, I will agree to that—but this one is."

The general expressed confidence in Breckinridge as a soldier, and told him that as commander of the reserve division, he and his Kentuckians would be committed to the hottest sector at the most critical moment. The subordinate general saluted and retired.

Johnston sat on his cot for a few more moments, thinking about Sam Grant and "Cump" Sherman—inexperienced, overconfident young commanders, his military juniors in every way—and about the peaceful independence that would follow victory. His final thought as he let sleep overtake him was that the smell of the peach blossoms on this April night was deliciously overpowering.

CHAPTER 14

AMERICAN WATERLOO:
SHILOH

"Where'd you learn to make Kentucky ashcakes, rich boy?"

Cabell did not take offense, but he could never figure out why his buddies assumed he came from a slave-owning family. Maybe it was the way he talked, more Lexington than upcountry, the big words he sometimes used that he'd unconsciously picked up from his old man.

He mixed the cornmeal with some water, pinched on some salt, and wrapped the mixture in the cabbage leaves. He had staked out a cabbage patch for some rabbits, shot two, and brought back both the meat and the makings. His buddy Albin put the pieces of rabbit on a spit and rotated them over the fire until Cabell put the ashcakes in the embers to cook.

"Learned how at Donelson," he told his new friend.

"S'pose a big battle's shapin' up? Folks comin' in from all over. Never seen so many generals. Breckinridge from up home, even Sidney Johnston hisself."

Johnston hisself. Cabell was down on Johnston: the general was a retreater. He was the highest-ranking field commander in the Confederate Army, and it was surely an honor to be near him, but after Donelson, nobody but Jeff Davis rated Johnston a big hero. The Kentuckians were especially bitter, because he had given up Kentucky without a fight. Tennesseeans remembered how he'd abandoned Nashville after the fall of Donelson, moving back South, worried about the Yankee boats using the Tennessee River to get behind him.

Fortunately, Cabell was with Forrest and his Tennesseeans, who'd fought their way out of Donelson (well, they really walked, but would have fought if they had run into any of Grant's troops) and struggled to get supplies out of Nashville after General Pillow had run out of there. When crowds began looting the Confederate stores, Forrest's men, on horses, had to charge a jeering mob to get ammunition stores aboard the last train South. They hightailed it out of Nashville before Yankee general Don Carlos Buell arrived, and spent the next two weeks raiding, harassing Buell, keeping track of his movements. Cabell knew that one of Forrest's forays yielded prisoners who revealed Buell's plans: to march overland through Tennessee to join Grant and Sherman at or near Pittsburg Landing. The goal after that, so the prisoners said, was to march twenty miles from the Landing—on the west side of the Tennessee River where Tennessee's border meets Alabama and Mississippi—to Corinth. That would cut the Memphis-to-Charleston railway. Corinth was the railhead where the Yankees figured Johnston would stand and fight.

Cabell enjoyed the riding and reconnaissance. He thrilled at killing himself a Yank, which gave him a kind of eerie feeling: the man in blue was two hundred yards away, just a tiny figure at the end of a gun barrel, and Cabell could see him drop clean. The young soldier doubted that it would be much fun to kill anybody nearer; he would hate to see the look on the other fellow's face up close.

Should he report to his father, now that both of them were in the same area? Cabell loved his old man, missed him, and wanted to see him soon—but not yet. He knew that John Breckinridge would bring him to headquarters, take care of him, make sure he didn't get himself killed. Maybe later. It would be a nice surprise.

Albin was a Kentucky boy, a member of the "Orphan Brigade," so called because they were a Kentucky bunch fighting for the South while their state was still in the Union. Cabell and Albin were thrown together on picket duty, as Forrest's cavalry and Breckinridge's infantry were melded into lookouts.

The first indication that a passel of Nationals were near came with the rabbits. Not the one on the spit, but the ones running in the thick underbrush from the sounds of people. Albin and he threw dirt on the fire—pity about dinner—and took positions behind shallow entrenchments they had dug earlier. Must be a lot of rabbits in these woods, Cabell thought, what with the Tennessee River rising in the spring, pushing back its banks and flooding the countryside. Nice place, too; peach trees and dogwoods in blossom, birds chirping away, not many people around. Albin whistled to the picket on his left, and Cabell alerted the man to his right.

Five Yanks, fairly close together, came crashing through the woods not thirty yards from them, and Albin opened fire. Cabell shot at a face he could see and missed. It would take him two minutes to load and fire again if he hurried. He bit off the cartridge cap, poured the powder into the breech, and pushed the ball in with the ramrod. By the time Cabell was ready to fire again, four of the Yankees had fled to a clump of trees for shelter; the fifth, Albin's target, was holding one arm up in the air to surrender. He had taken a shot in the other arm. Cabell was surprised at the way the Yankee was dressed: not in Union blue, but in the same jeans material that the Kentuckians in the Orphan Brigade wore. Hard to tell Yank and rebel apart. The men in the clump of trees were not shooting, in order that their comrade surrendering in no-man's-land could be safely received. He came forward, pain on his face, and Cabell heard Albin let out a holler.

"Linwood, is that you?"

"Albin?"

"Come on ahead, Linwood, you silly-ass fool, you coulda got yourself killed. Nobody shoot him, he's my brother."

Cabell had heard of this happening but thought it was just newspaper talk. But it should not be so surprising among Kentuckians; he thought of his cousin Margaret, a nurse for the Federals on one of their hospital ships, and Uncle Bob's sons split two and two.

Albin was embarrassed to have taken his brother prisoner. "You take him back to Colonel Forrest, Cabell, like he told us. See he gets his arm fixed up. I'll stay here." As Cabell started to take the prisoner to the rear, Albin resumed his position and aimed at the sound of gunfire that began again. The prisoner wheeled around and yelled, "Hold on, Albin, don't shoot at those trees, that's Father!"

Linwood turned out to be a useful capture. "I ain't gonna tell your people a thang," he announced, but he was willing to chat with Cabell on their way to Colonel Forrest. "Grant must have, oh, 'bout twenty, twenty-five thousand troops here. Six, seven more up on Crump's Landing under General Wallace."

"Any more on the way?"

Linwood grew cagey. "You're here from Corinth, aren't you? How come you're over this close to the river?"

"We got lost. You know Albin."

"Lucky thang he never larned to shoot."

"You ever see General Grant himself?"

"Naw, he doesn't even camp here. Sleeps warm and dry up in a house seven miles upriver. Sherman's the one in charge here. Mean little runt, nervous. Grant sets a big store by him, though. Gonna hit you folks hard in Corinth, after Buell's army gets here."

"Buell won't be here for a week," said Cabell, fishing.

"What you talkin' about? He's two days away at the most. Twenty thousand men. You better start runnin'."

General Breckinridge was afflicted with "the Tennessee quickstep." He vowed not to swallow any more water in this area, but if thirsty would turn to reliably sanitary whiskey.

He lay on his back on a blanket in the late afternoon sun, knees up to reduce the pain in his belly. Standing at the edge of the blanket was Colonel Forrest, the blunt cavalryman assigned to Breckinridge's Reserve Corps. Forrest was reporting what he had learned from his pickets, one of whom had brought in a talkative prisoner. Listening around the blanket's edges were General Sidney Johnston and his chief lieutenants: "Bishop" Polk, Braxton Bragg, and the hero of Fort Sumter and Bull Run, General P.G.T. Beauregard. "Old Bory" had been sent by Jeff Davis to inspirit the army under Sidney Johnston's much criticized command. This meeting, Breckinridge assumed, was a kind of council of war. Since it was his first, he wished he could comfortably stand; there was some ignominy in being flat on his back with the Tennessee quickstep.

"There's twenty-five thousand Federals with Sherman this side of the Tennessee River," reported Forrest, "plus Lew Wallace's bunch six miles away, with seven thousand or so."

"Where is Buell's army?" Johnston asked. The Federal plan had become apparent: to have Buell's army of 40,000 join Grant's army of 35,000 men at

Pittsburg Landing, and then march together to smash the Confederate forces expected to defend the railhead at Corinth.

"Buell's advance guard is just t'other side of the river," Forrest said. "Main body is two days' march away."

"Why so slow?" Johnston asked.

Breckinridge could have told him: to march troops through wet terrain in the first week of April was damnably slow work. His Kentuckians, among the fastest marchers in the army, had lost a day slogging over washed-out roads, laying logs in mud to haul guns. The rest of the Confederate forces, coming up from New Orleans and down from Murfreesboro, had also been delayed. The Johnston plan had been to surprise Grant with an attack this morning, but there had been no getting the Confederate force assembled in time.

"Cap'n Morgan's been driving Buell's army crazy," Forrest told Johnston proudly. "Cavalry harassing 'em, slowing 'em down." Breckinridge remembered John Morgan as a hot-tempered young fellow who took too many chances, and was glad he'd found an outlet for his wildness as a cavalry raider in this campaign. Delaying Buell's force was crucial: if those 40,000 bluecoats were to arrive before Johnston's attack on Grant's army was complete, the combined Federals would outnumber the Confederates two to one.

"Do you think Grant knows we're here, Forrest?"

"I don't think so, leastways not in force. He's spending his nights in Savannah instead of with his men this side of the river."

Breckinridge wondered how Forrest had learned that. More to the point was the import of the information: Was Grant drinking again? Why wasn't he with his troops? Did he have a woman up there? Grant must be unhappy about Halleck's stern treatment of him after Donelson—the rebuff and temporary relief from command had been in the newspapers—but could any general be so confident not to need to be encamped with his own army? Perhaps Grant was trying to emulate "Old Brains" Halleck in staying far from the scene of action, or perhaps he wanted his friend Sherman to be in sole command of his men.

"I don't believe it," said Beauregard. "How could Grant not know that our force of forty thousand men is not two miles away? Our men are mostly green, and they haven't been exactly quiet, shooting rabbits for food. Grant knows we're here, all right."

"Why does he go upriver to sleep?" Johnston asked. Forrest had brought in a puzzling piece of information.

"He's left Major General Sherman in charge, right in the middle of things at the Shiloh church," Beauregard said testily, his voice constricted. "Sherman's not a lunatic, as the newspapers claim. He's probably got his men entrenched up to their eyeballs, waiting for us. It's a trap."

"My men had a fairly rough skirmish with the Nationals about noontime," General Polk, the Episcopal bishop, put in. "They've got to know they're not alone here. I would agree that we lack the element of surprise. Even so, I say we should attack."

"We'll be slaughtered," insisted Beauregard. Breckinridge was surprised at his reaction: caution was Johnston's reputation, not Beauregard's. "Look." The short Creole drew with a stick in the mud. "Put yourself in Grant and Sherman's shoes. You've established a camp with twenty-five thousand men this side of the river, with men and supplies coming in from a good landing behind you. On your right flank, to the North, you have Snake Creek—unfordable, natural protection. On your left flank, Lick Creek, also flowing into the Tennessee River, also a natural barrier to attack. Water on three sides. That leaves one simple line of defense, here, facing us to the West. Sidney, I think it utterly inconceivable that Grant not order his men to entrench along that line until Buell's men arrive. It's plain common sense. That gives him an unassailable position."

"If he has dug in. If he knows we're here." Johnston weighed the alternative. "What is it you recommend, Bory?"

Beauregard coughed, coughed again, spit out some phlegm; Breckinridge hoped his chest infection had not debilitated him. "I recommend we give our exhausted men a rest tonight—most marched through the night last night, you know. Then we slip back to Corinth in the morning and get busy building defenses. When Buell gets here day after tomorrow, if that soon, he'll have to cross to this side of the river in boats. That will give us time to get ready. When Grant and Buell attack us in Corinth, we'll be in position behind barricades. Grant will keep coming at us—that's his way, I hear—and we will be able to wear down and destroy his army."

"Thank you, General." Johnston looked down at Breckinridge. "Your corps ready to move? The reserves will have to do some fast marching, right or left of the line, no telling which."

Breckinridge rolled to one side and struggled to his feet. "My men are amply provisioned, they can move. Kentucky men want to fight right here." If another retreat should be ordered, this time to Corinth, he didn't know how much of his force would melt away and go home.

"Gentlemen," said Johnston, "we attack at daylight tomorrow." He made a fist. "I intend to hammer 'em. We're going to hammer 'em hard."

Beauregard shook his head in disbelief, then quickly nodded, accepting the decision of his superior. The other generals went with him back to their commands to prepare for the onslaught in the morning. Johnston walked slowly down the muddy road with Breckinridge.

"I would fight them if they were a million," Johnston, wanting to talk, told him. "They can present no greater front between those two creeks than we can. The more they crowd in there, the worse we can make it for them."

"Horatius at the bridge," said Breckinridge, hoping he had his Greek history right. He was concerned, now that he was to go into his first major battle, that he knew so little of classical military tactics. He assumed that was why he had been placed in charge of the Reserve Corps, which would be the last to engage.

"I am not going to string my army out on a line," Johnston explained. "I will use Napoleon's order of battle—line each corps behind the other and hit the enemy in waves."

That was total offensive commitment, a form of near-suicidal assault that Breckinridge doubted had yet been tried in this war. If the Federals were surprised, their army would suffer terrible casualties; if Grant was not surprised, but had his men entrenched and waiting, the loss of Confederate life would be horrendous.

Johnston caught Breckinridge's worried expression. "You'll do fine, Breck.

Just control your own men, rally them when they fall back, and lead them back to take whatever position you see is important. Late in the attack, when everybody wants to regroup and rest, don't let them. That is the critical moment, and victory will go to the side that keeps hammering. God! The South can win this war tomorrow."

When Breckinridge did not respond to his elation, Johnston said, "Don't you see what's at stake here? Forty thousand men— all we have here now—is all the Confederacy has been able to scrape up to fight in the West. In two days Grant's army will be double ours in size, and if we retreat to Corinth he'll drive us out of there or kill us all. But at this moment we face Grant with a force no bigger than our own, and with his back to the river, hemmed in. We can stick that demand of 'unconditional surrender' down his throat, and when he refuses, destroy them all."

"Surely he'd surrender in that case—"

"Why should he? I wouldn't. In his shoes, I'd fight like hell till Buell came and saved what was left." When Breckinridge shuddered, his commander added: "Breck, don't be a McClellan. Don't be a Beauregard or a Buckner, arranging always to fight another day, under circumstances that will reduce your losses. Never forget: war is not tactics. War is death."

In the silence that followed, Johnston reached up and tore a small branch off a peach tree. He sniffed at the blossoms. "Grant understands that. I made a mistake about Fort Donelson; I should have been there myself and I would have beaten him there. This Tennessee River is the key to the war, don't you see? If we fail here, they'll cut our railroad west to east at Corinth and there goes our lifeline. If we fail here, 'Old Brains' will know the next step—to send Grant to attack our Mississippi forts from the rear, and take Memphis and finally Vicksburg. That's the end of the war for us."

"You paint a black picture."

Johnston shook his head and grinned. "Ah, but if I smash Grant and Sherman here—not just defeat them, but obliterate the Union Army, that's the important thing—then I can reverse the course of the war."

"A victory would do great things for morale in Richmond," Breckinridge agreed, recalling the demands for Johnston's scalp, and Jeff Davis's persistent refusals to remove the man he insisted was his best commander.

"Forget morale. Bull Run boosted our morale so high it almost ruined us. Destruction or capture of armies is all that counts. Territory is unimportant; we'll go back to Nashville and clear on up to Fort Donelson whenever we want, if we destroy Grant's army now." Johnston stopped; Breck used that moment to lean forward and take the pressure off his cramping stomach. "Tomorrow, our aim is not merely to win a battle; we're out to win a war against a population four times our size. When they are made to see how costly war can be, the people of the North will desert Lincoln. If we lose—" he shrugged.

"McClellan in the East will have clear sailing," Breck finished for him.

"Either that, or Grant will grind the South into sausage."

They walked on into the gathering darkness. The commanding general seemed reluctant to let his political general go until he understood his strategy. Perhaps, Breckinridge reasoned, Johnston was apologizing in advance for heavy casualties.

"McClellan is the most brilliant organizer and tactician on either side," Johnston continued, "but when it comes to the strategy of destruction, Lincoln is right and McClellan is wrong. The Union should be fighting overland to Richmond—not to take Richmond, but to attack and destroy our army. Grant must know that. He's a crude tactician—and we see here right now that he's a stupid general not to anticipate an attack—but he knows that war is death."

He looked hard at his junior officer, obviously eager to get through to the born civilian decked out in a general's uniform. Breck had been impressed with Beauregard's reservations at the council of war, and was uncertain about Johnston's wisdom in counting on surprise.

Johnston pressed: "Robert Lee understands. He was my regimental deputy in Texas, and before I left to put down the Mormon Rebellion, I drilled it into him—destroy armies, destroy the other side's will to fight. He's not as skilled in the field as McClellan, and he drives you crazy with all his talk about God, but at least Lee's not in love with his army, the way McClellan seems to be. A general has to spend lives—that's what an army is for."

Breckinridge straightened and said without enthusiasm, "We're ready. I'm ready."

"Mark my words, we'll decide the War Between the States on this field tomorrow." Johnston looked at the sky, where stars had begun to show, and at the hundreds of pup tents in the fields, the woods, and the bloom-laden orchards nearby. With less certainty, he added, "I only wish we had been ready to hammer 'em today."

William Tecumseh Sherman sat with Grant at the kitchen table. They were in the home that Grant had commandeered to await Buell's arrival, to join forces for the march on Corinth.

"Getting dark. I better get upriver," Sherman said, reminding himself that "upriver" meant "south" on the Tennessee. "Why are you smoking those stogies all the time? You never used to smoke cigars."

Grant looked at the end of his cigar, pleased. "Somebody sent me a couple of boxes after Donelson. Not bad. Takes my mind off my leg."

Sherman, who lived with teeth clenched on a cigar butt, sympathized with his fellow general: Grant had been riding in the rain a few nights before, and his horse stumbled and fell on his rider's leg. Grant's ankle swelled; the surgeon had to cut the boot off and put him on crutches. That accident came on top of the genuinely foul mood he had been in following Halleck's unaccountable irritation after the Donelson victory.

"I think I'm going to tuck it in, Cump. After Corinth, I'm going to ask for leave to go home."

Sherman had been afraid of that. "Why? War's just getting started."

"I'm just in the way here," Grant said, disquieted. "I've endured it as long as I can, but I can't put up with all this stuff any more." He went to the kitchen cabinet and pulled out a bottle of whiskey and two glasses. "Halleck says I'm drinking again. Want a shot?"

Sherman nodded. He could hold his liquor better than Grant. Two stiff shots and Grant's voice slurred; that, in his friend Sherman's view, and not an excessive intake of alcohol, explained his growing reputation for drunkenness.

General William Tecumseh Sherman

"McClellan sends word to put me under arrest. Why? Because I went up to Nashville and that was supposed to be outside my command, and I didn't report in to Halleck. Can you imagine that? Arrested?"

"Halleck was worried you'd be promoted over him."

"Maybe not—Old Brains claims it was McClellan's doing. I don't know. Nothing I do ever goes right." He moved his foot, winced, and swallowed the whiskey, pouring another shot. Sherman signaled no more for himself. He would have stopped Grant, but the whiskey was the best medicine for the throbbing pain in his foot.

"Donelson went right. 'Unconditional Surrender' Grant."

"You know what was good about that?" Grant cheered up for a moment. "I had a chance to pay Buckner back what I owed him. Part of it, anyway—a hundred and fifty, I still owe him fifty. When I took Simon aside after the surrender and handed him the money, he couldn't believe it."

"You were a little rough on Buck. That 'unconditional surrender' demand appealed to the damned newspaper writers, but it humiliated the rebel general, a West Pointer and a gentleman who had not deserved such treatment."

"You know why I asked for surrender in such a hurry? Because I was afraid that Halleck would do something to change my plans, pulling me back before I could take the fort."

That made Sherman feel better; such insulting behavior, especially to a friend and benefactor, hardly seemed like Sam Grant.

"Since then," said Grant, reverting to gloom, "they've all been after me— you must hear the talk."

Sherman held up a hand for silence; a courier was at the kitchen door. "Sir, should the men be ordered to entrench?"

"No need." Some regimental commander always wanted to show how he could run his command by the book.

"General Prentiss says—"

"Tell him we'll be out of here in a day or two," Sherman snapped. "There's no sense wearing out the men digging holes in the ground when what they need is sleep. Besides, we're on the offensive, let's not take the edge off that spirit." He waved him off.

"Help me put this foot up," said Grant. Sherman lifted the bandaged foot onto the kitchen table. Grant had another slow sip of the same glass of whiskey; Sherman was glad he was making it last, and it seemed to be relieving the pain. "Old Brains will be coming down here to take personal command next week, for the attack on Corinth."

"The Ohio regiment keeps reporting reb skirmishers at Pittsburg Landing."

"There will be no fight at Pittsburg Landing," Grant assured him. "We will have to go to Corinth, where the rebels are fortified." He took a deep drag on the cigar, the way a neophyte cigar smoker does, and coughed it out. "After that, he won't want me around, not the way the newspaper scribblers are after me. Let Halleck be the hero—I'm going to St. Louis."

"You got business in St. Louis?"

"Not a bit."

Sherman scratched his head hard. He kept his red hair short to avoid cooties in the field. He wanted to keep his friend, who had never been a success in business, from going back to work with his no-good father Jesse. Sherman had heard that Grant's father was doing some shady business right now with the Jew peddlers following the army, perhaps peddling his supposed influence with his son; since Sam Grant could not bring himself to castigate his father, he often directed his private fury against all Jew peddlers. Sherman understood; Grant had come to feel about Jews the way Sherman felt about newspaper correspondents. Quitting the army would be a mistake for Grant; it was his only chance for improving his lot in life.

"Sam, a couple months ago I felt the same way. The damn papers were saying I was a lunatic, remember? Just for telling Buell I needed two hundred thousand men, and for taking off after that pain-in-the-ass correspondent? They weren't going to put me in jail, like you—nothing so respectable. I was set for the loony bin."

He steamed again, just thinking about it: the writer who signed his dispatches "Agate" had called him a monomaniac, and the *New York Times* reported he had been relieved six months ago for a mental disorder. That had led McClellan to dispatch his aide, Colonel Thomas Key to examine Sherman, and the distraught general was certain that Key had reported his mind was too unsteady for command; how else would Assistant Secretary Scott have come to the conclusion that Sherman was "gone in the head"?

To make his point, Sherman fished in his wallet for the crowning clipping, from *Frank Leslie's Illustrated Newspaper*: "Here, Sam, listen to this: 'General Sherman, who lately commanded in Kentucky, is said to be insane. It is charitable to think so.' My wife and children, my brother the senator, must have been so ashamed. I tell you the truth, I thought about killing myself." But suicide was the route of a madman, and he did not want to give the damned scribblers the satisfaction. He had been transferred west, and Grant had given him another chance at command. He owed this man the same stout support he had received from him.

"Well, time passes;" he told Grant. "Things change. Here I am, back in high feather again. It was a good thing I didn't kick it all in. I was thinking about it, though, like you now."

Another man at the doorway. "Colonel Appler, sir, wants to be sure the general knows that his Ohio Regiment has been fired upon by what appeared to be a picket line of men in butternut clothes."

"Tell Colonel Appler," Sherman exploded, "to take his goddamn regiment back to Ohio! There's no enemy nearer than Corinth." The man left.

Sherman rose to return upriver to camp. "You think they'll be ready for us in Corinth?"

"They know we're coming," said Grant. "Sidney Johnston has to make a stand somewhere, and he might as well fight for that railroad line. We'll lick 'em. Halleck will be made general-in-chief."

"If that happens, you'd wind up top commander in the West. Lincoln will stick by a fighter, and that's you." Sherman, seeking a command post, had met Lincoln once, early in the war. The interview had gone badly, and it caused Sherman pain to think about it, knowing that the President probably gave credence now to all the stories about Sherman's being unstable. It was better for Grant, who never made much of a first impression, never to have met Lincoln. His deeds would speak better than he could. "I'll see you tomor-

row," Sherman told him. "Rest your foot and come over for Sunday lunch."
He poured Grant a last drink, and took the bottle with him. No sense letting
more stories get around. Grant leaned forward, took the bottle back, and
handed Sherman one of his gift cigars.

The steamer *Tigress* took about forty-five minutes for the trip to Pittsburg
Landing; it was dark when Sherman docked. He slept well, hoping he had
talked Grant—not a cultured man, but a good soldier—into staying in the
army. Sherman thought of himself as more intelligent than Grant, and he
knew more about war, military history, strategy, and grand tactics than
Grant did; he was Grant's superior in organization, supply, and administration. But his friend had one quality that Sherman knew he lacked himself: he
did not give a damn about what the enemy did when out of his sight. Sherman tended to march one way and countermarch the other, trying to outsmart what he thought were the enemy's shifting movements; Grant held his
ground, issued his orders, and never got nervous. Sherman determined to
emulate that resolute quality in the battle at Corinth.

Next morning, stepping outside the Shiloh meetinghouse soon after dawn,
the banker-lawyer-educator turned general was struck by the beauty of the
scene: peach trees in full bloom on what the early light promised to be a fine
April Sunday. Shiloh, Sherman knew, was the biblical site of the Ark of the
Covenant; odd that such a place would turn out to be a conquering general's
headquarters.

Odder to him, though, was the sudden proliferation of rabbits and squir-
rels. They were scampering across the meetinghouse clearing, always the
same direction, west to east, by the score. Curious; rabbits did not act that
way in his boyhood home in Ohio, or at the Louisiana military academy on
the Red River, where he had been superintendent when the war came. Maybe
the small animals in this neck of the woods migrated in the mornings to the
Tennessee River for a drink. Sherman watched a deer blink at the sunrise,
then dart across the clearing with the rabbits. The general shook his head in
amused wonderment, and went back to his headquarters in the church for a
good breakfast.

About 7:30 A.M. on the morning of April 6, Grant limped off the boat onto
Pittsburg Landing. He had hastened to the *Tigress* as soon as he heard the
thunder of cannon.

For the better part of an hour, chugging up the river, he was heartsick at
the realization that the Southerners had not waited for him to choose the
place and time of attack. He had grown so accustomed to Sidney Johnston's
skillful retreating that he had forgotten that the man was, like him, a fighter.
He recalled Sherman's contempt at entrenchment, and his own tacit approval
of the failure to anticipate an attack. The grim Grant estimated Johnston's
strength at eighty thousand men, and supposed the firing was a flank attack at
the Union soldiers under Wallace at Crump's Landing. He was almost certain
it could not be a direct, frontal assault by the whole Confederate Army on his
main camp. That was something he might do, but not Johnston.

A newspaperman who had clambered aboard the *Tigress* at Crump's Landing asked to see Grant; it was Whitelaw Reid of the *Cincinnati Gazette*, the

"Agate" who had made Sherman out to be a maniac. Grant declined, expecting nothing good to be reported about the forthcoming battle, and having no credible answer about why he was not with the troops.

As the boat pulled up to Pittsburg Landing, Grant could see the stream of Union deserters and stragglers coming down the hill in the first sign of a rout. The sound of a major battle was unmistakable. Rifle fire, shots mingled with screams, the boom of artillery; the smell of smoke and powder; the dismaying sight of the frightened green troops huddling for cover near the landing, hoping for a boat to take them away from the savage surprise attack.

Grant proceeded to do the immediate job at the scene at the dock. The men up front taking the attack on the heights would need ammunition; he organized an ammunition train to supply cartridges from the warehouse near the landing. Hobbling over quickly to a confused-looking colonel standing by, he said, "I am General Grant. Get that detachment over there to arrest the stragglers and organize them into a reserve. Then move them up the hill."

His foot pulsing pain, Grant was assisted onto a horse, and sent an aide downriver to order Lew Wallace, on nearby Crump's Landing, to bring his seven thousand men immediately to the defense of the main body of troops. He sent a message to Buell, whose army was still some forty miles away, estimating the attacking force at one hundred thousand and urging him to hurry. He ordered Buell's advance division across the river into the fight, regretting the casual way he had let them stay up near Savannah the night before, but the time for feeling guilty was not now. He rode up the bluff for the camp of his second-in-command, Sherman.

He was encouraged to see his friend cool under the withering fire. When asked how he was doing, the embattled Sherman, biting his own cigar, said, "Not bad," and asked only for more ammunition. Grant moved on, glad that Sherman did not need him. He looked for General Prentiss, an argumentative sort who had crossed Grant on matters of seniority throughout their army careers. His division of raw troops was in the center of the line and taking the most punishment, slowly falling back toward a defensible patch of woods.

"You'll have to hold them here at all costs," Grant told Prentiss. He repeated, "At all costs." Prentiss nodded; Grant could not trust him in army politics, but figured the man was enough of a soldier to understand the need to take whatever losses were necessary to hang on to a key position.

Grant looked up through the trees; what sounded like rain was bullets ripping through leaves. He wanted a place that would enable him to observe more of the battlefield, but no commanding view was available. He rode with six members of his staff along the sagging Union line, buoyed by the thrill of battle and troubled at the wholesale defections from ranks—men were running away faster than they could be rounded up and thrown back into line. He halted in an exposed position.

"General, we must leave this place," said one of his staff. "It isn't necessary to stay here. If we do, we'll all be dead in five minutes."

"I guess so," Grant told him, and slowly moved away. His Union force was in great trouble; the attackers were inflicting more casualties than they were taking, reversing the usual casualty rate in battle. Should have dug in. Johnston had twice as many men, Grant figured, and could push him back into the river by nightfall. Grant would never surrender, but faced the prospect of losing his entire army. He had the feeling of being in a slugfest, where finesse didn't count and no military orders would be carried out on either side. Both his flanks were falling back, exposing Prentiss and his men in the center. He rode back and told Prentiss to hold on, not to fall back in any attempt to straighten the line, but to fight it out in what the soldiers were calling the "Hornets' Nest."

General Buell arrived on his horse, without his army: hearing the cannonade, he had taken a steamer upriver, and was shocked at the five thousand Union stragglers cowering at the landing.

"My men are a hard day's march away," Grant heard Buell say. "We can cover your retreat, if you can get across the river."

"I still think we can win," said Grant, but when he saw the disbelief in Buell's face, he added: "Bring your artillery up fast to cover a bridge of boats in case we need it." Grant went back up to the front to view what he could of the carnage: a rebel battery had been pulled alongside the Union line, turning its flank, and was pouring canister into the line of bluecoats, who were screaming and dying, or screaming and running. Grant knew he had no good reason for the confidence he showed to Buell. He might need that line of boats across the river.

Breckinridge could not believe this pandemonium was an organized battle; it was more like a swarm of individual fights, with no military tactics involved and no understanding of what was happening outside your own small world of fire. He received an order from Johnston to bring his Reserve Corps to the left; they marched forward and toward the left. Another order came to cancel the previous movement, the reserves were needed more on the right; picking their way through the bodies of fallen Federals, they traversed the brigades to the right. The constant booming made it hard to think.

A Federal battery on his left roared out at his men, cutting down three soldiers and giving the others their first sight of comrades falling. A minute later the gun roared again, this time with canister decimating the ranks of Kentuckians moving forward in line. The Confederate line broke; Breckinridge thought it might be smarter to let the men move forward their own way, not in line, but he remembered the tactic book that stressed the power of men moving shoulder-to-shoulder. He yelled at the men to form a line, but they didn't listen; he rode to his left, to General Bragg, and asked for help against the Union cannon.

"I'm too heavily engaged," shouted Bragg; "charge it yourself."

Breckinridge rode back to his brigade, pulled together a single company of Kentuckians, pointed to the high ground where the flashing and booming had been coming from, and dismounted. The white faces looking at him, he sensed, could be moved to take or destroy the gun.

General Breckinridge had never ordered a charge before. He pointed ahead, drew his sword, and yelled "Charge!" Nobody moved. Breckinridge said quietly to one lieutenant, "Follow me, then," and the two of them ran forward into a ravine, then up the hill. He looked back at men walking forward. "Kentucky!" he yelled at the top of his lungs, and that word triggered it—more than a hundred men broke into a run, with rebel yells, and passed him in the charge up the hill.

When they arrived, breathless, at the crest, they found no gun. The Federal battery had already retreated. Everybody around him looked pleased; nobody was dead, and they had charged on command as soldiers should. Behind the ridge was what was left of an enemy camp, which the Kentuckians invested to find a dozen wounded and a dazed medical officer. Breckinridge waved his men forward; the hundred on the ridge passed the signal to the three thousand behind. Facing sporadic resistance, the Reserve Corps moved forward three quarters of a mile. The battle could be won, and maybe the war, he found himself thinking, breathing the smoke. He mounted his horse to get a better look over the brush.

Abrupt stop. Heavy fire was coming from a Federal line along a sunken wagon trail running across their front. The Union men had taken advantage of a strong natural barrier and were fighting back a regiment of men in gray. Breckinridge sucked in his breath; bodies were everywhere, lying in grotesque positions, and some of the wounded were trying to crawl back toward him. A general officer on a horse approached. It was General Johnston, excited, flushed, radiating confidence; Breckinridge felt better seeing him.

"Charge the Hornets' Nest," Johnston ordered, "that's the center of the Union line. I'll bring up another brigade to support you. Get the Tennesseeans in line with the Kentuckians."

Breckinridge, more certain of his ability to lead troops now, ordered his captains to form for a general charge on the center of the Federal line. He ran forward to get a better look—the haze of smoke hung low in the woods under the midday sun, and it was hard to make out the line—and saw, twenty yards in front of him, a boy pitch his shotgun ahead of him and fall. A tall boy, in Kentucky jeans. Breckinridge, taken by the irrational notion that it might be Cabell, ran forward and turned the body over. The boy's face was shot away, but a silver tooth gleamed in what was left of the mouth. Cabell had no false tooth.

The Kentuckians went in, were bloodily repulsed, and Breckinridge called for the Tennesseeans. Those green troops would stand behind trees and shoot long-range, but would not be ordered into running over the bodies against a withering fire from the wagon trail. Breckinridge was stymied; would it not be better to slip around this pocket of resistance? He rode along the line looking for General Johnston.

"No," said Johnston firmly, "we take 'em or kill 'em." Isham Harris, the former Governor of Tennessee, was with him; the general directed him to go with Breckinridge to get the Tennesseeans to break the line.

Harris managed to get his fellow Volunteers into line, but neither he nor Breckinridge could mount a charge. The carnage was sickening; the number of dead near the Hornets' Nest presented a sight to discourage any but fanatic soldiers, and the Tennesseeans were no fanatics. For two hours Breckinridge poured shell and shot into the redoubt; a captured Federal battery was turned on the Union soldiers but they would not give, nor did their ammunition give out. Breckinridge felt dull inside; the headiness was gone. The business of facing and dealing death numbed him.

He went back to Sidney Johnston and said he could not get the brigade to charge into certain death. "I think you can," Johnston replied, and Breckinridge shot back, "I tried, I failed. Why don't we go around them?"

"I'll help you," said Johnston. "Be calm, Breck—you'll see, we'll water our horses in the Tennessee River tonight."

"My men need rest. They're exhausted."

"No rest until we win this battle, and we must win it today." Johnston was relentless, to Breck inhuman. "Beauregard is sick, he's in Sherman's head-quarters in Shiloh church, out of action. Sherman and Grant have their backs to the river. I want that Hornets' Nest to surrender. That will start the surrender of the rest of the Union Army. Come on!"

Johnston rode to the front of the 45th Tennessee Regiment, exhorting the men along the line to fix bayonets and ready themselves. He stationed Breck-inridge at the left of the line, took the right himself, raised his sword and spurred his horse into the enemy front. "Charge them, Tennessee, charge!" Breckinridge shouted, breathed deep and rode forward into what he assumed would be his death. It was a noble cause, sort of. It was his free choice, and it was time; he was with his people and one way or another it would lead toward the conclusion of the war.

Four thousand reluctant Southerners moved ahead in a ragged line, sweep-ing down a short slope that gave them momentum, through a ravine and into the Hornets' Nest. Breckinridge's horse fell and he continued on foot, shout-ing at the top of his lungs, waving his sword like a crazy man, as the Confed-erates overran the Union front line and broke through to a scene more heart-stopping than any the Kentuckian had yet seen. Bodies were lying on top of one another; over nearly an acre, it was impossible to walk across the forest floor without treading on human flesh.

A gray-faced Union officer introduced himself as General Prentiss and announced he was prepared to surrender.

Johnston rode over, his horse picking its way through the dead. "How many do you have?"

"I had a force of five thousand. We may have a couple thousand left. I was ordered by Grant to hold at all costs. All costs." Prentiss had a mariner's beard, red-rimmed eyes; blood ran down his hand. His division had stopped the Confederate advance for four hours.

"Send a message to Grant that you've surrendered," said Johnston quickly. "Leave a burial detail. March your men to my rear. And don't be dispirited, General, we'll swap you for Simon Buckner."

Breckinridge noticed a red stain on Johnston's leg, just above his boot. "You're wounded, General."

"Just a nick. Press on here, Breckinridge, straight through to the Landing. No rest. Win today." Johnston spotted a lieutenant nearby taking a briar pipe out of the knapsack of a dead Union officer. "None of that!" he called out, and the officer hurriedly dropped the pipe. Johnston spurred his horse over to the subaltern and said, "We're not here for plunder." He leaned down and picked up a tin cup from the table used by Sherman's staff. "Let this be my share of the spoils today."

He rode out of the center of killing, his horse shying from a stream that was running thickly red, then plunged ahead, splattering the nearby leaves with the mixture of water and gore. Breckinridge retched and sank to his knees; Prentiss helped him up.

Sidney Johnston knew the day was won, his reputation repaired, the cause of the South rejuvenated. Grant might fight on all afternoon, then try to get some of his men across the river that night. Probably the seven thousand from up on Crump's Landing, which never did get to the fighting on time, would cut its way back across the river, too, but Grant's army was no more. Twenty-five, perhaps thirty thousand men killed, wounded, captured: that would be a shattering blow to the North, especially to families in Ohio, Illinois, Iowa. They would learn the meaning of Lincoln's invasion of the South—not parades, not newspaper dispatches, but death. The pressure to let the South secede in peace would become intense.

And the captured equipment. Johnston's army had been fighting with a ragtag collection of old muskets, ancient imports, and hunting guns—few of the new rifles and Minié balls. He reached down to his leg, where a Minié ball had penetrated his boot; no pain, but his foot was squishing in the shoe. He would have to have it seen to, during a lull. But there must not be a lull—delay worked for Grant, with Buell's army on the way.

This was exactly as he had planned: to beat the Union armies in detail. First this army, with the stores Johnston needed so badly to equip his troops; then Buell's army across the river, the same size as his, but leaderless and demoralized. That would be the real test, Johnston thought, knowing how Beauregard would insist that the men needed rest. Bragg and Breckinridge, too, thinking of the comfort of their men, would counsel remaining in position on Pittsburg Landing. But these generals did not understand the new meaning of war: the side that rose from exhaustion to fight on was the side that won, and the defeated army that is allowed to escape is the army that ultimately defeats you.

Johnston would take his tired men across the Tennessee River, confront Buell's forty thousand—equally tired from their days of forced marching—whip them, and capture their equipment, too. With that, he would return up through Tennessee to Kentucky, restoring those states to the Confederacy. With Kentucky in hand—both Davis and Lincoln knew how important that state was—Johnston would link forces with his longtime subordinate, Robert Lee, and defeat McClellan. End of the war. The prospect was dizzying. Jeff Davis had already hinted that he wanted Johnston to succeed to the presidency of the Confederacy; that would be worthwhile, the general thought, but for only one term. After that, back to California.

Johnston, suddenly unexpectedly weak, felt a twinge of guilt. He had done nothing for the wounded among the thousands of Union prisoners. Using his souvenir tin cup rather than his sword as a pointer—a nice touch, he thought; that was how to direct a battle—he ordered his staff surgeon to the rear to arrange for care of the prisoners. "And after that, Doctor, check General Beauregard in his ambulance cot—he's burning with fever." The surgeon rode off to the captured headquarters. Johnston, his throat suddenly dry, thought of lying down a moment himself. No Federal artillery could be seen; Johnston guessed that Grant had drawn the guns back to the bluffs for a final stand. Grant would not need boats or pontoons for more than ten thousand men, because he would not have ten thousand left.

"Your horse has been shot," Governor Harris told him. "Blood running down its flank." Johnston looked over and felt terribly dizzy. "General, it's not your horse," said the governor, alarmed; "that's you that's bleeding."

Johnston held out his hands toward the blurring face and collapsed into the arms of his friend. He felt himself slowly lowered to the ground and his boot being pulled off, filled with blood. It had not hurt at all. It was a minor wound, he should have had it seen to; he was angry with himself as consciousness slipped away and the cup rolled out of his hand.

Breckinridge, with Bragg's help, helped Beauregard out of the ambulance and into the Shiloh meetinghouse, which had been Sherman's headquarters until its capture that morning. When his coughing subsided, the ranking officer sat up to hear the news.

"General Johnston is dead," Breckinridge told him. "Bled to death. Anybody could have saved him with a tourniquet, but nobody knew what to do and he'd sent the surgeon away."

"I assume command," Beauregard said immediately. "What is the situation?"

"We cannot get half our men up on the line," said Bragg angrily, "but Grant's in worse shape. A third of his force is on the Landing trying to get out. He's setting up an artillery semicircle, backed up by his gunboats on the river."

"Our infantry?"

"Slowly advancing, as we have all day. Polk says he can turn the left flank."

"Don't drive them into the Landing," said Beauregard sensibly. "Don't let them get to the Landing. Keep Sidney's death a secret. How much more daylight?"

"It's four o'clock," said Breckinridge. "More than three hours. We're winning, Bory."

"The battle might as well go on, then." That struck Breck as a curious thing for a general to say. The little Creole went into a coughing spasm but would not return to the ambulance.

One man could not make all that difference, Breckinridge told himself. This battle was not in the hands of the generals, but was up to the sergeants, who would win or lose the thousands of life-and-death engagements all along the front. The South's officers had no more than a vague idea of what was going on, only that the general movement was forward. Units had drifted apart. Some men deserted, others mingled with unfamiliar units.

Breckinridge found his Orphan Brigade swarming through a warehouse of enemy supplies, throwing away their old guns for the Union weapons, putting on leather shoes, stuffing rations into their knapsacks. The Kentuckians were delighted, refreshed, ready for the victorious finish of the fight. He led them to a small glade and gave them a brief talk about the plan to carry through to the river tonight, saying nothing about Johnston's death. In a few minutes, at 5:30, Breckinridge was given an additional division of Polk's corps, as Bragg, acting on Beauregard's authority, ordered a general advance.

Breck took his troops striking down the main road to the Landing, pursuing the Federals hard, reaching a commanding hill less than a mile from the river. He felt himself at the foremost point of the Southern attack, the most advanced Confederate thrust of the day, and found that position exhilarating. He could see, four hundred yards down the road, a clump of Federal flags behind a semicircle of artillery pieces that were blazing away at Bragg's men. He thought he could make out Grant and another general—stubbly red hair —to the left rear of the big guns. The combined batteries were not heavily defended by infantry. Backs to the river's wall.

An artillery captain right behind him was ordering his gun unlimbered to return the shelling from the Union batteries. The nearby booming of the battery, and the river shelling from the gunboats—aimed over the heads of the Union men into Confederate ranks—showed how heavily Grant depended on his artillery for a last-ditch defense.

"Hold your fire," Breckinridge shouted to the artillery officer. "I'm going to charge those batteries."

"If you're going to charge," came the reply, "now's the time."

Breckinridge ordered his men into line for the final assault. About six thousand of his men would run at the Union guns from an angle, with fewer than half the semicircled guns able to shoot directly at the charge. He sent word to Bragg, somewhere on his right, that he was going in, but could not be sure the messenger would reach Bragg. It was a tremendous gamble to take on his own responsibility, and if he was wrong he would live in shame the rest of his life, but there—less than 500 yards away, a ten-minute charge—were the heart and brains of the Union Army of the West.

A courier came up with an order from Beauregard. "Break off all engagements and retire to shelter and safety. Prepare for engagement at daylight."

"This is a mistake," Breckinridge said. "Stay in position." He rode hard to the Shiloh church a mile away. Bragg was already there, arguing with Beauregard.

"Our troops are tired and disorganized," Beauregard was saying, shaking his head. "Darkness is close at hand. We cannot hope to finish now. The men need food and rest."

"We still have over an hour of daylight," Bragg urged. "So what if we're not in order? The enemy is worse off."

"What about Buell's army across the river?" Breckinridge asked. "If that swarm of Yankees gets here tomorrow, we could lose everything."

"We have information that they are still more than a day's march away," Beauregard replied. That was wishful thinking. Breckinridge knew that part of Buell's army was the Kentucky Federal infantry, with Bill Nelson of Maysville in charge. Nelson, an old friend, was the type to close quickly on a fight; he could get here to help the Union sooner than that.

"Your information could be wrong," Breckinridge began.

"So could yours," snapped Beauregard. "And I am in command."

"Nobody disputes that, General," Breckinridge argued, "but Sidney Johnston said only this morning that the side that keeps fighting past exhaustion will win. He said this is not the normal kind of war, we could demand more of men—"

"General Johnston is dead." Beauregard did not seem overly saddened at the fact. "I thought a battle at this time and at this place would be a mistake, and I said so. Since the battle was in progress, and it is not good to quit the field at midday, I permitted it to continue. At least a third of our army is wandering about the field, plundering Union supplies, and your Kentuckians are among the worst offenders, Breckinridge. Get them in hand. Tomorrow, rested and reformed, we can defeat the Federals."

"We got here fust with the most," said a voice in the back of Sherman's captured headquarters. Colonel Forrest, who had no right to speak in a generals' council, said, "We oughta beat 'em now."

"Thank you for your advice," said Beauregard icily. "Stand down and bivouac where you are. As it happens, I expect reinforcement tomorrow from General Van Dorn to the west. Be ready for an attack at daylight."

Sherman was satisfied with himself, though mostly in negatives. He had not panicked; he had not gone crazy; he had not made a mistake after his initial, unforgivable failure to entrench; he had comported himself honorably in the hottest fire, four horses shot from under him.

Now, midnight, was the time to retreat from the field of defeat in good order. The night was filled with the sound of gunfire from the Union riverboats, lobbing cannonballs over the precarious Federal position into the enemy camp. Buell's army was arriving on the other side of the river. Led by Nelson's division of Union Kentuckians, it would form a potent force to restrain the victorious rebels if they chose to try to cross the river in pursuit of the defeated Federals.

Sherman assumed he and Grant would have plenty of explaining to do at having been taken by surprise, and the terrible casualties of half-awake men bayoneted in their tents would evoke a great outcry in some newspapers, but to Sherman the escape of the main body of the Union Army was the important thing. They would fight again another day.

A storm had rolled in from the west, pouring rain on the blood, thunder adding to the noise of the river guns. Sherman looked for Grant at the log house near the Landing that was headquarters, but that large room was filled with groaning wounded.

He was directed to a large tree on the hill overlooking the Landing, where Grant was standing, water dripping from his hat, in the warm rain. He was holding a lantern, resting his weight on his good foot, staring at the steamers bringing Buell's troops over to the Landing.

Sherman was moved by a sudden instinct not to ask about the details of what he had assumed until that moment would be the night's retreat across the makeshift bridges. "Been a devil of a day, Grant, hasn't it?"

"Yes." Grant took the wet, unlit cigar out of his mouth and repeated, "Yes. Lick 'em tomorrow, though." He put the dripping cigar back and chomped hard on it. No despair showed in his face; doggedness was the expression. He was not going to run. If Sidney Johnston was going to come after him, so be it; it occurred to Sherman that the rebel commander should have followed up his advantage tonight, because Grant was determined put up a hell of a battle the next day. It was a stupendous gamble, risking the loss of the entire army on what Sidney Johnston liked to call "the iron dice of war"; Sherman hoped Grant knew what he was doing.

Sherman watched the incoming troops with Grant for a while, then started back up to his command post to get ready to counterattack on Monday morning. He stopped when he thought he heard Grant talking to him. He went back and heard Grant muttering to himself, "Not beaten by a damn sight."

Cabell hoped he would never have to live through a day like Monday at Shiloh again. Nobody had slept the night before, what with the rain and the thunder, and the guns on the river and shells in camp, and the bodies all around, some dead, others wishing they were. He got up more tired than he had lain down.

The day started all wrong, with the Federals firing and yelling and coming back through the peach orchard. Now he knew how the Union soldiers had felt the morning before, surprised by an attack. Nobody was giving any orders, so Cabell picked up his things and started to head back away from the firing with a bunch of others. He suspected that was wrong, and stopped to look for an officer. Colonel Forrest had taken the horses to the rear for the night, and Cabell was with a group of twenty cavalrymen without their mounts.

They tried not to step on the dead on the way to the rear. Coming forward the day before, the bodies had all been Federals, and he had rushed past them in his enthusiasm, but now he could see that over one in three was a Confederate. Would they have a chance to come back and bury them? Did anybody care?

"Stay behind trees or walk low," Albin called to him; "those are Kentuckians. Crittenden's men, and they can shoot."

Cabel remembered Thomas Crittenden, old Senator Crittenden's son, as one of his father's closest friends, who had been in their house a hundred times. He used to bring Cabell a birthday present every year. The scouting knife, the one on his belt, was a gift from the Crittendens.

Cabell moved faster toward the rear, broke into a run. Yesterday they had walked over this mile of woods firing every three minutes, paying a terrible enough cost in blood, and now he was racing back over it trying not to step on anybody. He had heard Sidney Johnston was dead and couldn't be blamed for the retreat. Who was calling for the retreat, he wondered, Beauregard? Bragg? His father?

Ahead of him, a large tree hit by the Union battery back near the river collapsed on the running soldiers. Cabell stopped to pull a comrade out from under the branches and then hurried on. Nobody was going the other way; nobody was stopping the retreat. There did not appear to be any officers around. How could a battle turn so completely? Was yesterday a complete waste of time and blood? He wished he were on a horse. This was not what he had joined up for.

"You men, stop! Turn around, reform behind that big tree that fell." It was Colonel Forrest on his horse, and Cabell suddenly felt ashamed. Unhesitatingly he whipped around and took a position behind the tree trunk, hurriedly reloading his Union rifle with the Union Minié balls he had taken at the warehouse near Shiloh church. Others in gray came up beside him, and he felt better. He had to be careful not to shoot his own men running toward him, and it was hard to distinguish the Confederates in Kentucky jeans from the Federals. What would his father say to his panic of a moment before? Was his father still alive? He presumed so; the troops heard about it when a general was killed. He wished now he had looked in on his father, because if the Federals overran this position, Cabell and all the others would be buried in a mass grave and nobody in his family would know if he was alive or dead. Proving bravery and independence no longer seemed so important to Cabell. The sweet victory of yesterday had soured to awful disaster today, and this was a good time to be near kin.

They were coming, Crittenden's Union Kentuckians, through the forest in a ragged line—hundreds of them, surely followed by thousands more of Buell's army from across the river. They must have poured in overnight.

He took aim at one man striding forward fifty yards away, hoped the charge in his gun hadn't been too damp, and pulled the trigger. The cartridge worked and the man dropped. He started to reload but knew he had no chance to be ready with another shot before the Federals were upon him. He looked behind him; Forrest was there, urging more men into the line. Were they stopping them? Was it disaster everywhere? All he could know was that the battle, the war, was this line of men coming at him, one officer pushing them forward, one officer keeping him in line.

He could see the expression on the face of the man in blue coming directly at him, pulling away the branches, gleam of bayonet on the end of a gun that was as unloaded as his own. The man was going to stick the knife in him if he didn't do something. Cabell took his own gun by the barrel and tried to smash the butt over the man's head. He missed, crashing it onto the soldier's shoulder and knocking him down.

He could hear the scream of Albin to his left as a bayonet reached him. Cabell pulled his scouting knife from his belt and leaped on the man who had charged him, stabbed him five, six times, left the bloody knife in him and turned to recover his gun. He was crying, and his pants were wet. This was not how it was yesterday, or how it was supposed to be. He vomited on his victim, shook his head, found his ramrod and started to reload. He looked for the next man coming at him, but the Union charge had failed. Did Forrest expect him to leave the tree trunk and go after the Federals? He didn't want to leave the tree. He wanted to stay right where he was for the rest of the war.

"Fall back on the horses," Forrest was calling, and he was glad to be able to turn and run back without being a coward in retreat. War was better on a horse.

The day was lost, General Breckinridge knew, as he had known it would be from the moment of decision the evening before. As Beauregard had not known the time to strike the day before, Bragg had not known when to stop striking after the reinforced Union turned the tide: the little martinet had sent Pat Cleburne's brigade into the Union center on what was surely a suicide mission. Cleburne, the Irishman who had lost two thirds of his brigade the day before, had objected to a charge without support and into a position where he would be outflanked; told to obey the order by the implacable Bragg, Cleburne had plunged in, losing most of the rest of his command for no good reason.

As Breck saw it, victory at Shiloh died with Sidney Johnston, who foolishly failed to take care of a minor wound. With his death died the hopes of defeating the Union Army in detail, recapturing Tennessee and Kentucky, smashing the Tennessee plan, retaking Donelson, and making the defeat of the Confederacy difficult if not impossible. For one glorious moment the possibility of victory in the war had been within grasp; now all that remained was the long avoidance of defeat. Breckinridge was heartsick, not only at the human carnage around him, but also at the lost chance of soon ending the bloodletting. The simple, obvious Tennessee River plan had worked; at Corinth in a few days, Grant's advancing army would cut the Memphis-to-Charleston railroad, an artery as important to the heart of the South as the artery on Sidney Johnston's leg cut by the Minié ball was to the Battle of Shiloh.

Time now to prolong the agonies of both nations. As soon as it became apparent that Van Dorn was not coming to help him at Shiloh, Beauregard fled with the remainder of his army toward Corinth. Artillery was being abandoned along the road. The tables of the previous day had been turned: a determined push by Grant would now destroy or capture the bulk of the defeated Southern army, and the benumbed Breckinridge could see no reason for Grant not to press his advantage.

The Kentuckian, with his Orphan Brigade and Forrest's cavalry, was assigned the rear guard. The brigade of Tennesseeans that he had personally led for the past two days had suffered such casualties as had never before been seen in war on this continent. The men remaining hoped for the exhaustion of the Federal forces to save them; little else stood between Grant and the annihilation of the less than thirty thousand Southern troops left of the more than forty thousand that had surprised their enemy at Shiloh.

Breckinridge was prepared to sacrifice the rear guard to save that army, which was what he supposed rear guards were for. He was prepared, too, to be killed or captured—killed, he thought, might be better than tried for treason, since the Senate had already branded him a traitor.

"I told that idiot Frenchy twice't, goddammit," Forrest was saying, "that we should either attack last night or pull the hell out. I sent scouts dressed in Federal overcoats down to the landing last night as Buell's army began to cross. That was the moment to hit or to run."

"What did you do with that information?" Breck asked dully.

"Couldn't find Bory all night. His headquarters at the church he made into a hospital, and he didn't set up a headquarters of his own. Couldn't find his tent. Two o'clock in the morning I knew we would face two armies instead of one, and I had no commander to tell it to."

Breckinridge did not want to hear more of what could have been; he discussed with Forrest the best place for a series of delaying skirmishes and retreats, to be followed by a last stand before the infuriated Sherman pounced.

"Hell with that," growled Forrest. "Let's hit him from the flank. Sherman thinks we're all running."

Breckinridge pondered that. Grant, like Sidney Johnston, understood that a victory was nothing without the destruction of the enemy army. His deputy, Sherman, in hot pursuit of the beaten Southerners, had shown he could be taken by surprise.

"Do you have enough men to hit him hard along Lick Creek?"

"Couple hundred Texas Rangers, Morgan's cavalry and my own. Maybe a thousand men."

Not many to string out on a line in defense, but potent if concentrated in an attack. Sudden punishment might discourage Sherman from following further, at least overnight. Forty-eight hours before, Breckinridge would have hesitated before ordering a thousand men to undertake what might be a suicidal charge, but now daring was all they had in the way of strategy. His rearguard infantry was worn out and might throw down their guns after the first volley.

"Hit them at dusk," he said. "I'll make a lot of noise with the artillery we have. Make it look like a full-scale counterattack. After the first strike, get some of your men off their horses to act like infantry. I'll move on their skirmishers from here."

Breckinridge waited while Forrest went into action. The massed Union infantry could make mincemeat out of cavalry, outnumbering them twenty to one, but not at any one point. Concentration of numbers in a salient made the difference—"fust with the most," as Forrest liked to say. At dusk, when he heard the rebel yells and the firing, Breckinridge opened with his few artillery pieces and sent a thousand men on foot into the oncoming Federal skirmishers.

Waiting, lantern in hand, in the middle of the road of retreat, he hoped Tom Crittenden and Bill Nelson would live through all this. He thought about his son, who might be anywhere on the road to Corinth, if he was not dead on the field.

Two cavalrymen brought Forrest back in a stretcher on a cart. Breckinridge shined the lantern on the figure. The colonel, his face twisted in pain, gritted, "We turned the bastard around," before passing out.

"He has a ball in his back," a voice said in the darkness. "He overran the charge, went right into the enemy infantry's second line. Shot his way out with a pistol before they got him, but he stayed on his horse."

Forrest was the last casualty of Shiloh, Breck hoped, the last blood shed on the bloodiest day that the American continent had ever seen. "And what about Sherman?"

"He's digging in for the night," a second man said. "Building entrenchments. Learned his lesson, I guess. They won't be coming after us."

The voice of the second man was deeper than he remembered but was familiar. He lifted the lantern to look into the bleak, dust-caked face of his son. He slowly put down the light, and the two men leaned on each other for a long moment in the middle of the road.

CHAPTER 15

JOHN HAY'S DIARY
APRIL 10, 1862

"I tell you, Lincoln, the nation demands that Grant not only be relieved of command, but dismissed from the army!"

Those were the words I heard emanating from the Cabinet Room half past midnight last night, as I was creeping back from my rendezvous at the house on Sixth Street.

The piping voice was recognizable as that of Alexander K. McClure, the Pennsylvania politician. He is one of the handful of men—Old Man Blair, David Davis, Leonard Swett, Hill Lamon—who can say almost anything to Lincoln, and the Tycoon will never take it amiss because he trusts them absolutely. He had been right about Simon Cameron from the start, too; good judgment. One of us.

Tonight McClure has been inveighing against the man everyone is calling "the butcher of Pittsburg Landing," who only recently was known as "the hero of Fort Donelson."

The papers have dubbed the battle of Shiloh "the American Waterloo," because it has become known as a battle with only villains, no heroes, unless you count Don Carlos Buell, whose rescuing troops arrived in time to keep the secesh from applying the *coup de grâce* to Grant's reeling army. Horace Greeley, whose *Tribune* had so aptly warned of an expected rebel blow in the West, now looks as astute as Grant and Sherman look foolish.

Our side took thirteen thousand casualties, the rebels maybe half that, and Grant was as wrong about rebel strength across the Tennessee River as McClellan has been about the rebels across the Potomac. Our man in the West was overconfident, while our man in the East has been underconfident.

I brought a pot of tea and a couple of cups into the Prsdt and McClure and tried to act as if I'd been assiduously on duty all evening. Lincoln was sitting in front of the fire, his feet in carpet slippers up against the marble mantel, looking as morose as only he can, while McClure was pacing back and forth. I don't know why those two chose the Cabinet Room; perhaps the Prsdt wants a change of scene from his office.

"You know I have nothing against Grant," the Pennsylvania pol said. "I've never met the man. Neither have you, so there can be nothing personal. But I tell you, Lincoln, the clamor for his dismissal is unprecedented in all American history."

Lincoln grunted to show he was listening. People who do not know him take that grunt for assent, but it means only "keep talking."

"Have you read the dispatches from the *Cincinnati Gazette*'s Whitelaw Reid?" The Prsdt had; I clipped them for his agonized perusal all last week. Every paper in the country had picked up and printed those damning dispatches, none with more vitriolic accompaniment than Bennett's *New York Herald*, the big supporter of Breckinridge for President two years ago. Reid, who styles himself "Agate," was on the scene at Pittsburg Landing, and described the bloodletting in the tents of the Union Army when it was taken by surprise. Blamed Grant for all the bungling—not Sherman, who turns out not to be crazy after all, but rather brave under fire.

Those "Agate" articles, taken up and resonated by the other papers, have started all the stories about Grant's drinking again. Winners can drink, as we learned after Fort Donelson, but generals who are surprised and who take the worst casualties in anybody's memory have to be cold sober. Grant wasn't in camp where he belonged, that is certain; I wonder if he was drunk, or with a lady. So must the Prsdt wonder. The most noble and patriotic of men succumb to temptation at times, as I can testify.

"He's been denounced as incompetent by the public journals of every party," McClure went on. "He's been repudiated in the Congress by every leader without regard to political faith."

"Not by Elihu Washburne," Lincoln interposed. He picked up a marked copy of the *Globe*, with Congressman Washburne's impassioned defense of his constituent and protégé: "Listen: 'There is no more temperate man in the army than General Grant. He never indulges in the use of intoxicating liquors at all.' Man knows him better than you or me."

"You believe that, Lincoln?"

"Washburne says that Falsehood will travel from Maine to Georgia while Truth is still putting on its boots. What he says about rumors is true enough."

"His hometown congressman defends him," conceded McClure. "But Washburne's the one who has been pushing Grant for years—getting his commission, assuring you that the stories about his drinking are not true. 'Never indulges'—hogwash! Everybody else in the Congress and the country is furious with a general too besotted to tell his troops to entrench."

"You think that hurts the Administration, McClure."

"I think the universal revulsion with Grant hurts you, Mr. President. If you try to sustain Grant," McClure said very slowly, "I am convinced you will not be able to sustain yourself. And I'm not the only one with your interest at heart who thinks that way; there's Swett and Lamon—"

"I know, I know." Both had spoken to him about the way Grant's unpopularity would rub off on Lincoln, and how the storm of protest needed some sacrifice to permit it to abate.

"It's your interest we're thinking about, yours and the country's." When Lincoln stared at the fire without response, McClure added, "I don't have any pet general who might benefit by Grant's overthrow. But I do know that the tide of resentment is so overwhelming that you must yield to it or go down with him."

Lincoln shifted his feet and continued to stare at the fire. I went outside and continued hearing McClure's voice making excellent sense. "You above all, Lincoln, are the one man who never allows himself to appear as wantonly defying public sentiment." True; I had not known anyone else was walking around with that insight. "Yet that is what you are doing in this instance. Why? You owe Grant nothing. Why should you associate yourself with his unpopularity? Let the bereaved mothers hate him, not hate you."

Long silence.

"We've been through a long winter of terrible strain with McClellan and the Army of the Potomac," the Tycoon remarked at last, which struck me as off the point. He was agitated; McClure had shaken him. "In the East, nearly every day brings some new and perplexing military complication. And from the day that Grant started on this Southern expedition until now, we've had little else than jarring and confusion among the generals in the West." He did not go into detail about Halleck's getting McClellan to order the arrest of Grant; his visitor didn't know the half of it.

"All right, if I'm oppressing you, I'll drop it," said McClure.

"No, no, you have no ax to grind in this." If his visitor that night had been Father Blair, who is prejudiced in favor of McClellan, the Prsdt's distress would not have been so acute. But McClure is a straight shooter, his main concern the ability of Lincoln to lead the North. In the phrase I have heard him use a hundred times, Lincoln called for a specific recommendation: "What, then, is to be done?"

"Remove Grant at once. He's been cashiered before—this time do it based on his reckless exposure of his army and be done with it. That will put you on the side of the people who are justifiably angry, and you will ride out the storm."

In the ensuing silence, and to help McClure make his point, I took in the New York newspapers; the two men looked at the front-page lists of casualties.

"This is only New York," McClure said, "which did not bear the brunt. Believe me, when those casualty lists are finally posted in Ohio and Illinois and Iowa, where the losses were worst, there is going to be a wave of fury the likes of which you've never seen."

The Prsdt's feet came down from the mantel and hit the floor. That was usually indicative of a decision.

In a strained, pained voice, with an earnestness I have never heard before, Lincoln said to McClure, "I can't spare this man; he fights."

Wisely, McClure shut up. The nearest I can explain this apparent willingness to go down with Grant's ship is this: Lincoln had spent the winter trying to get McClellan off his bemedaled butt, and he was not about to join in the bedevilment of a general who was willing to engage in battle.

"But you're right about not defying public sentiment, McClure," Lincoln added after a while. "I cannot do nothing."

"Maybe a reprimand—"

"No." Here was to come, I could tell, a plot from the master of indirection. "A reprimand would not satisfy his critics and would destroy Grant. The object is to remove him from command temporarily, which would appease his critics, until such time as he can do battle again. And to do that in a way that does not insult or demean Grant as a military officer."

So that was why he had made "Old Brains" Halleck the overall commander in the West a few weeks ago. I began to see the plan in the Prsdt's mind; we were both far ahead of the normally astute McClure.

"I have ordered Halleck to leave St. Louis and go to Pittsburg Landing," Lincoln continued.

"That means he will automatically supersede Grant as commander of the army there," said McClure, comprehending. "That should take some of the pressure off. The trick is to remove Grant from command right now. The people demand that."

"At the same time, there is no insult to Grant in Halleck's joining the army in the field," said Lincoln. "It could be that the public anger will subside with another in command. Perhaps General Grant is being unjustly accused, and this odium will be lifted, or perhaps another event will occupy the public mind." He turned that thought over in his head, adding, "If need be, to give him confidence, I could publicly appoint Grant second in command."

"That is what he would be anyway," said the logical McClure, "with Halleck there."

"Nobody has ever appointed anybody second in command," I put in. "Whoever is next in line down the chain of command is that automatically."

"I know that, John. But an official appointment would be encouraging," said the Prsdt, "and would tell the people in the army—where there is plenty of politics, McClure—that I'm behind him."

"That's a fairly sagacious way of handling it," McClure allowed, "if you feel you cannot spare him."

"He fights," the Tycoon repeated. Evidently that has become a more important quality in a general than anyone realizes. We cannot know for certain if Grant is a drunk, or an incompetent, or worse; all Lincoln can be sure of is that the man inflicts terrible punishment, and anyone who does that for him must be protected at all costs.

When McClure had left after one in the morning—they had been talking, I guess, for over two hours—I told the Prsdt I knew how he could return Grant to field command, since Halleck was an armchair general.

"It will be easy," I said. "You have just removed McClellan as General-in-Chief." Ostensibly that had been done to free Little Mac for his field campaign around the Peninsula to Richmond, but in reality it had been to mollify the radicals who wanted McClellan fired entirely for failing to show the proper abolitionist fervor. "After the hubbub over Grant subsides," went my analysis, "you bring Halleck back to Washington and make him General-in-Chief. At that point, second-in-command Grant gets his army back."

"You're too young a man to think like that," said the Tycoon, pleased at my precocity, the deviousness learned at his knee. "I might not do that at all, especially if McClellan wins a great victory in the Peninsula. But such a series of moves," he granted, "would appease public sentiment, and at the same time give me a general out West who fights."

General and Mrs. George Brinton McClellan

BOOK FIVE

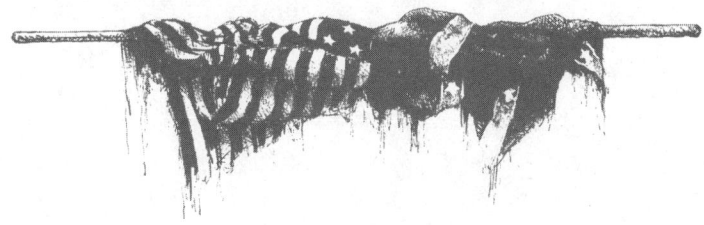

George Brinton McClellan

CHAPTER 1

MUCH LIKE TREASON

George McClellan was in good spirits. A few moments before, at 7:30 A.M., he had received word that the President wanted to see him alone, immediately. No need to keep Lincoln waiting; he swallowed one piece of toast, gulped his tea, and checked his uniform in the full-length hall mirror. His aide, Lieutenant Custer, was holding his overcoat at the front door but the general motioned him to wait. He bounded up the stairs to the nursery.

Nellie was feeding the baby, and the sight of his robust, sleepy-eyed son at the breast of the woman he loved moved him to silently thank God for his good fortune. She motioned for him to come in and lifted her face. He kissed her lips with all the tenderness in his heart—none of this cheek-kissing so common to husbands and wives in this sink of iniquity of a city—and stopped as he drew back because the baby had taken hold of one of his tunic buttons. The general smiled at his son's demanding nature: one of his small hands grasped at his mother's nipple and the other at his father's button. He pried the fingers loose, nuzzled the back of his wife's graceful neck, and slipped out.

"You want to get a haircut, Custer," he told his aide, a youth too much taken with his long blond locks. They walked in a brisk cadence to the President's house three blocks from the McClellan home. His staff insisted that the general not walk the streets of the capital alone at any time, and he had acceded to this wish; Pinkerton had information that McClellan was a likely target for an assassination attempt. At the door of the President's house, he shed his overcoat and handed it to Custer, instructing him to be ready with horses when the interview with Lincoln was over.

He was pleased that Stanton would not be present. The Secretary of War had managed to prevent frequent personal interviews between the President and the commander of the Army of the Potomac. McClellan was certain he could deal with Lincoln far better without the double-dealing Stanton's inhibiting presence; perhaps Lincoln was awakening to that as well. The President was not a bad sort, in the general's judgment, but he was too easily influenced.

Lincoln did not rise from his chair, as he customarily did, nor did he look his general-in-chief in the eye. That, thought McClellan, augured ill. He did not like something in the President's manner; it seemed to be that of a man about to do something of which he was ashamed.

"I wish to talk to you about a very ugly matter."

McClellan took his seat and entrenched for the assault. "What is that?"

Lincoln hesitated, fiddling with the spectacles in his hands.

"On ugly matters," said the general briskly, "the sooner and more directly such things are approached, the better. Speak frankly."

"I suggested a movement that would make the capital safer," Lincoln began. McClellan suspected what was coming: an unfair criticism of his move across the Potomac to open the Baltimore and Ohio railroad. The plan had been to bring canalboats through the locks at Harpers Ferry and to use them as a pontoon bridge to enable McClellan's force to cross the river. Everyone from the President on down had agreed to the brilliance of the planned maneuver, which would have saved the months it would take to construct a permanent bridge. Unfortunately, nobody had measured the width of the canal locks, and it turned out that the canalboats were six inches too wide. He could not fault the army engineers, who had relied on the assurances of experienced railroad employees. The operation had to be abandoned, stimulating criticism that no activity was under way against the rebel forces.

"The Harpers Ferry episode?" McClellan said, urging Lincoln on.

"Why in tarnation," Lincoln demanded, "couldn't you have known whether a boat would go through that lift-lock before spending a million dollars getting them there?"

"I am not a naval officer, and had to rely—"

"Neither am I," Lincoln said with more asperity than McClellan had seen before, "but it seems to me that if I wished to know whether a boat would go through a hole or lock, common sense would teach me to go and measure it. I am almost despairing at these results. Everything seems to fail."

"I explained the matter in detail to the Secretary of War—"

The President was not finished. "The impression is daily gaining ground that you do not intend to do anything." He looked directly at his guest for the first time that morning. "You know what Chase said about the fiasco at the lock? He said your heralded expedition died of lockjaw."

"I'm sure you enjoyed that joke, Mr. Lincoln." This President was known for crude witticisms at the most serious moments.

"Well, we don't get many jokes out of Chase. But really, how could you let this happen? The country is crying out for action, for movement against an enemy sitting comfortably a few miles from Washington, and the reports all say 'All quiet on the Potomac.' " When the general decided not to dignify that with a response, Lincoln went on. "Well, George, I will say this: for organizing an army, for preparing an army for the field, for fighting a defensive campaign, I will back you against any general of modern times. I don't know but of ancient times, either. But I begin to believe that you will never get ready to go forward."

With the President's tirade tapering off, the general felt the time ripe for a response. "I have been deceived," he stated.

"What and who has been deceiving you?"

"Two weeks ago, I sent you a memorandum explaining what happened at Harpers Ferry. Did you receive it?"

"No." Lincoln's puzzlement seemed sincere.

"Stanton assured me he would give it to you personally. He told me, a day or two afterward, that he had done so, and that you were entirely satisfied with my conduct. He desired me not to mention the subject to you. I was foolish enough to believe him."

"Maybe it's here in my papers," the President murmured.

"We are moving on Winchester independently of the bridge, and in such force that may cause the Confederates to withdraw from the Potomac heights, where their big guns endanger the boats moving our troops down for the Peninsula campaign against Richmond." McClellan let that sink in, hoping the President would comprehend the military situation. "The purpose of the move was to take Winchester, not to build a bridge of canalboats."

"I wish you would tell me these things," Lincoln said irritably. "I would be better able to sustain you if you would take me into your confidence."

"I tried to, and your Secretary of War intercepted my communication."

"You say the rebels may pull back from the Potomac embattlements? That would be good news, well received."

Unfortunately, Lincoln was obsessed with the safety of Washington, D.C.; he could not understand, the general felt, the dictum of Swiss General Antoine Henri Jomini: that an offensive was the best defense. But McClellan assumed it would serve no useful purpose to argue with a civilian about fears that had no military rationale. Lincoln did not grasp the strategy that would draw the enemy troops southward and out of striking distance of the capital. The President remained fearful, and could be satisfied only by the presence of nearby Union troops; no military man could ever talk him out of it. Therefore, the general would leave a token force behind to allay those fears while he maneuvered the main Confederate strength away from Washington with his attack on Richmond from the east, up the peninsula formed by the York and James rivers.

Why would Lincoln and Stanton never admit to the brilliance of his bold maneuver? A Peninsula campaign would minimize casualties. Perhaps they were willing to grind up the army in a step-by-step overland battle only to make the politicians feel secure in Washington; he was not.

"I hope I have disposed of what you called 'an ugly matter,' " said McClellan in a gesture of conciliation.

"No, that's not the half of it." The President took a deep breath, more of a sigh, and plunged in. "It has been represented to me that your plan of campaign was conceived with traitorous intent."

McClellan was too thunderstruck to answer. Traitor? Could the President be serious?

"I've been told that your plan, by removing defenders from Washington, is intended to give over the capital to the enemy." Lincoln met McClellan's stare for a moment and added, "It does look to me much like treason."

The general rose out of his chair. "Take that back, Lincoln. Damn your eyes, take it back! Nobody can mention my name in the same breath with the word 'treason.' "

That shook the President, who backed away from endorsing the charge. "It's not my idea," said Lincoln, much agitated, rising to face the general across his desk, "I'm just repeating to you what has been represented to me."

"And you believe that abominable slander."

"No, no, I don't believe a word of it." A moment before, he had been saying it sounded much like treason to him. "It is what others are saying, and you should know about it."

"What others? Stanton? Wade? I demand to know."

"Men like that, I shouldn't say exactly who," he evaded. "But I don't believe them."

"Then you ought to damn well watch your language. You gave me the distinct impression that you believe those slanders to be well founded."

"Then I was wrong and I apologize." The President sat down again. "It is not my purpose to impugn your motives, only to give you an idea of the depth of feeling that exists about leaving Washington defenseless—"

McClellan could not get over it. "Treason!" He paced to the window and back and laid his hand on Lincoln's desk. "I'll tell you about treason. It is in the minds of those men who don't want me to succeed. My plan is bold and brilliant and will win a smashing victory and end the war in a month. But that's not what your Stanton wants, or what Wade wants, or what Chase wants. That cabal doesn't want me to win this war this spring, because they want to launch a crusade against slavery. They don't want the South to sue for peace terms; they want the South crushed and bloodied and punished for what they think is some great national sin that only blood can expiate." He jabbed his finger at the President's chest. "Your radical Republican friends want a long war, Lincoln, with plenty of casualties on both sides, and they're poisoning your mind about me to get their way."

"No, you're all wrong," Lincoln said, in a soothing voice. "Please sit down. I can understand how you feel, but don't start impugning their motives."

"I'm fighting a two-front war," added McClellan with relish, his enemies on the run; "the rebels on the one side, and the abolitionists and other scoundrels on the other."

"You have it all upside down," the President said. "Ben Wade and Zack Chandler and the committee are not calling for inaction. They, and I, are urging you to act—to get the army, your army, fighting the enemy. We all want the war over with as soon as you can finish it."

"No. You don't understand. They want hand-to-hand combat between here and Richmond, at an exorbitant cost in lives," said McClellan, now determined to make the most of the President's indiscretion in passing along the gossip of his malicious aides. "We do not have to destroy our army or the Southern army to win this war. Follow my plan. Trust me, as you promised you would. Jeff Davis will be in flight from Richmond in a month, and the secession will be over."

It was Lincoln's turn to walk around his office. "I will follow your Peninsula plan," he said finally, "on this condition: that you leave such force at Manassas as shall make it entirely certain that the enemy shall not repossess himself of that position. We cannot let him sack Washington."

"Done," agreed McClellan. In his mind, the small force under General Banks in Virginia was adequate, backed up by the Washington constabulary behind the solid entrenchments that McClellan had built. He needed every other man he could muster—at least a hundred and fifty thousand—to face the horde that Pinkerton had informed him the Confederates had assembled to defend Richmond.

"You are sure," said Lincoln, still doubtful, "the roads down there in the Peninsula near Richmond are passable this time of year?"

"I am," said the general. Pity that Lincoln never made a clean decision, but accompanied it with hedges and doubts.

"You were sure about the canalboats fitting through the locks," said the President sorrowfully and, the general felt, unnecessarily. "But let me not discourage you. Be bold. Bring us victories."

Riding back to his house, McClellan said nothing to his escort of officers. Custer started to make conversation, but a nod cut him short. The general, seething, was determined not to show his emotions to anyone. Any display of irritation after a visit to the Mansion would start rumors buzzing that he was in disfavor with Lincoln.

"Major Allen seems to want a word with you, sir," Custer said, pointing to Pinkerton pacing in front of the McClellan home. The scowling detective, under his derby hat and with the cigar sticking out of his face, cut an almost comic figure, but McClellan valued him. His reports of enemy strength justified a caution that many of the firebrands around Lincoln did not feel.

Pinkerton signaled not to dismount; McClellan tensed his legs around the horse's flanks and leaned down to get his message.

"Couple of men in your parlor, General, waiting to see you," the detective whispered urgently. "Came unannounced; I'd avoid 'em."

"Why not just send them away, then?"

Pinkerton shook his head. "One is Fernando Wood, the Mayor of New York. Used to be head of Tammany Hall and not a man to be trusted, in my opinion, sir. The other is Horatio Seymour, used to be governor, may run for governor again. These two are very big Peace Democrats."

"Ah." McClellan straightened in his saddle, thinking about that. Wood, he had heard, was a wild man who talked of having New York City secede from the Union. Seymour was another matter: respectable, a proven vote-getter, and—according to Seward, a former Governor of New York, who ought to know—a man who had become a concern to Lincoln men in New York. If Seymour and his Peace Democrats took New York's governorship in the fall, they would put a stop to recruitment in the Union's biggest state.

"I don't think you should talk to them," Pinkerton murmured, his voice at his peak pitch, slightly above his whisper. "Rather, you should not be seen talking to them. Feed right into the cabal's hands, giving them evidence about what they call your 'disloyalty.' "

McClellan nodded, Lincoln's repetition of the slander of his "traitorous intent" fresh in mind. He guessed that Seymour and the rest of the loyal political opposition were worried about McClellan's being replaced by a radical; if that took place, then the abolitionists would be in control of both the Cabinet and the army, with no hope for a negotiated peace.

It struck McClellan as not beyond the realm of possibility that Seymour might also be carrying a message from New York Democrats about a presidential nomination of McClellan in 1864. That was two long years away; it was much too soon to give an indication about, or even think about, a future in politics. But perhaps it would be a good idea to find out what support there was in the North for a negotiated peace on the basis of "the Union as it was" —preserving the Union and limiting slavery to the Southern states.

"I'm going on to camp," he announced. "Tell Seymour, and only Seymour, that it is always a good idea for a former governor to visit men of his state serving in the army here. If he comes to camp and drops by my tent, it would be most natural for me to see him."

Pinkerton smiled and winked. McClellan wished he wouldn't do that; it made the general feel part of some conspiracy. He had already given the lie to that, to Lincoln's face. Curiously, the election of Democrats in New York might even strengthen Lincoln's hand in dealing with the likes of Wade and Stanton and Chase, who were dragging him toward a fight-to-the-finish abolition policy. Abolition might well bring the armies of England and France on to the field against the Union, and New Yorkers had to worry about an invasion by British forces in Canada. In all his expressed concern for border states, Lincoln forgot that New York was a border state too.

He twitched the bridle lightly, and Kentuck responded; the saddle was his own design, much more comfortable for the animal than the formal saddles of the past; the McClellan saddle was being adopted throughout the U.S. Army. In the general's mind, cruelty was always unnecessary, and the prolongation of the war was beyond cruelty, it was savagery. He would see Seymour in private and listen to what he had to say.

He hoped the New Yorker would not broach the "dictator" idea that young Custer kept bringing up, because that struck him as unseemly at the moment; still, the notion of the ancient Roman solution helped soothe the rankling in his breast at the thought of Lincoln's giving credence to the charge of "traitorous intent." What kind of commander-in-chief would countenance such slander against the man who had already saved the Union from sure defeat, and was on the verge of a great campaign to subdue the enemy? Why couldn't the man back up his military leaders when they came under political fire?

CHAPTER 2

LADY MINE

"The President is an idiot."

She shook her head, no; it was wrong for George to talk that way.

"I went to the White House directly after tea," her husband continued, poking a long match into the wadded newspaper under the fire logs, "where I found the Original Gorilla about as intelligent as ever." His hand holding the match was shaking, he was so angry. "What a specimen to be at the head of our affairs now!"

"What did he say that upset you so?"

George McClellan watched the fire start, not answering her right away. "Oh, I was of course much edified by his anecdotes, ever apropos, and ever unworthy of one holding his high position. I suppose he's honest and he means well."

Ellen Marcy McClellan did not press him. Whatever had passed between Lincoln and her husband must have been so odious that he considered it would hurt her too much to relate. George confided almost everything to her, as she to him, holding back only out of kindness.

"I have a lot of scamps to deal with," he said, "unscrupulous and false. They throw whatever blame there is on my shoulders." He rose and watched the flames leap up. "I do not intend to be sacrificed by such people. It is perfectly sickening to see the fate of the nation in such hands."

"God's will," she reminded him.

"I trust that the all-wise Creator, in His own good time, will return us to His favor. I trust there is a limit to His wrath, and that ere long, we will begin to experience His mercy."

She knew George McClellan was a God-fearing man, a profound believer determined to observe the Sabbath even in planning battles, who struggled against his tendency to let bitterness spill over.

"But it is terrible to stand by and see the cowardice of the President," he continued, "and the vileness of Seward. Welles is an old woman and Bates an old fool. The only man of courage in the Cabinet is Blair, and I don't altogether fancy him."

"Remember, you were wrong about Stanton."

"I was at first, and I should have listened to you. You saw through that viper from the start." He put his hands on her shoulders and looked directly at her with that sudden burst of boyish respect that never failed to move her. "Who am I wrong about now?"

"The President. He's been through the fires with the loss of his boy," she told him, "you should allow for that. Stanton is poisoning his mind against you all the time. Lincoln makes mistakes, and he reads one book and thinks that makes him a general, but he's not an idiot, and you must stop calling him a gorilla. Somebody will hear."

"That was Stanton's description, remember, when that conniver was ingratiating himself with us. With me." He brightened a bit, as usual after the bouts of bitterness at the forces arrayed against him on his own side. George liked to denounce his foes with fierce words, she knew, and to exaggerate the cabals and conspiracies of politicians that were constantly being formed to frustrate him and to sacrifice his beloved troops. But he was not one who hated those who stood in his way, and was always ready to repair relations with people angry with him. Powell Hill, for example. "All right. I am sure I will win in the end in spite of all the rascality. History will present a sad record of these traitors who are willing to sacrifice the country and its army for personal spite and personal aims. The people will soon understand the whole matter, and then—woe betide the guilty ones."

He announced that he was going upstairs to play with the baby, a good sign that the pain of his interview with the President was wearing off. She remained at the fireplace, thinking about, of all people, "L'il Powell"—Ambrose Powell Hill, the dashing Virginian who had, in the most tempestuous period of her unmarried life, taken her away from Captain George McClellan.

"Miss Nellie," as the youthful set in Washington had called her six years ago, had been seeing "Little Mac" with some regularity. Her army father approved, especially since the widely respected captain intended to resign from the army and pursue a lucrative career as an executive with the Illinois Central. George duly proposed, but she rebuffed him because she had fallen under the spell of his close friend, the moody, vulnerable, attractive Lieutenant Hill, then with the Coast Survey Office in Washington.

Powell and Nellie became engaged. Her father, at his post in Laredo, Texas, was not merely disappointed, but furious. She would not forget his letter: "Abandon all communication with Mr. Hill. If you do not comply with my wishes in this respect, I fear my ardent affection would turn to hate. Choose between me and him."

She fought for Hill, who was able to show her father a worth of ten thousand dollars, but then her mother came to her with a rumor that the young man was afflicted with a social disease. When Nellie told this to her young man, he wanted to fight a duel with whoever started the canard, and even her father sided with the wronged young man on this issue, but by this time her parents' concern—and the steady, forgiving, loving presence of Captain Mc-Clellan—had bred second thoughts. Powell was afflicted with sick headaches and sometimes disappeared for days at a time, when she most needed him. She broke the engagement, to her father's relief, and resumed seeing the faithful George, with Powell angry at what he must have felt was betrayal by both of them.

George wrote a beautiful letter to Powell when Nellie accepted his proposal, and the rejected suitor could not resist McClellan's frankness and eagerness to repair a shattered friendship. "My ticket is Douglas for President and McClellan for Secretary of War," Powell replied in 1860, reporting that he, too, had married—the lovely sister of their mutual friend, John Hunt Morgan, in Lexington, Kentucky, and over the objections of her parents.

The two men in her life were now warm friends again, but George was taking the Army of the Potomac into action against the Army of Virginia, which included a division under General A. P. Hill. Powell's commander was Joseph E. Johnston—not Sidney Johnston, who had just been killed at Shiloh, but George's lifelong friend who addressed his letters "Beloved McC—." She felt heartsick about the fate that pitted her husband against two of his closest friends in army life. Like Roman gladiators, they were pledged to kill each other but were not required to hate each other.

The orderly entered to say that Francis Preston Blair was at the front door. She sent the soldier to fetch George and greeted the old man warmly; he would not stay, just wanted to deliver a message to the general before he began his expedition.

"I was just telling Nellie," George said as he welcomed Blair, "that your son's was the only courageous voice in the Cabinet."

"Welles isn't bad," Father Blair replied. "Sounds like an old woman, but stands up to Stanton, that damned two-face. Look, I'm here for a reason." The wizened face squinted its eyes at the general. "There is a prodigious cry of 'On to Richmond' among the carpet knights of our city, who will not be shedding their own blood to get there."

"I am aware of their zeal," said her husband.

"I am one of those who wish to see you lead a triumph in the capital of the Old Dominion," said the old man, "but am not so eager as to befoul it by hurrying on too fast."

"You're the first one to say that," said Nellie. "Everybody else, from the President on down, is berating my husband for not storming Richmond in the dead of winter, or when the roads were a mess of mud."

"The veterans of Waterloo filled the trenches of General Jackson with their bodies and their blood," said the old man, a living link to the military heroes of earlier generations. "If you can accomplish your objective of reaching Richmond by a slower process than storming redoubts and batteries in earthworks, the country will applaud the achievement. It will give success to its arms with the greatest parsimony of the blood of its children."

"I'll be satisfied with bloodless victories, my venerable friend."

"The envious Charles Lee denounced his superior, General Washington, as gifted too much with that 'rascally virtue *prudence.'* Exert it and deserve his fame."

Blair hunched his cape around him and left without a farewell. Nellie could see how welcome the rare words of caution had been to her husband. She took his arm at the doorway and watched the carriage draw away. On the morrow, her husband and her father—General Marcy was now George Mc-Clellan's chief of staff—would leave on a daring campaign on boats down the Potomac to the James River, and on to the battle of Richmond. An army wife and daughter, who had done her duty to her father and been rewarded by a wonderful marriage to a good and loving man, she knew better than to tell her husband to be careful or to avoid enemy fire. She was glad that his goal was the victory that would lead to a negotiated peace, and was not destruction of an enemy and subjugation of people who were friends.

"I will not fight for the abolitionists," he said, moved by Blair's visit, "but when I think of some of the features of slavery I cannot help shuddering. Try to realize, Nellie, that at the will of some brutal master, you and I might be separated forever." She tightened her grasp on his arm; in the separation that was the lot of soldiers and their wives in war, there was at least hope of return. "Slavery is horrible, Nellie. I do think that some of the rights of humanity ought to be secured to the negroes. There should be no power to separate families, and the right of marriage ought to be secured to them."

She led him upstairs to see the child and to spend the last night together before a long string of lonely nights. He would write every night without fail, as he had in the field before, and she would save his letters for her memories and for history, but she was as worried as any wife of any soldier in the departing Army of the Potomac.

"Some generals, in the field," he said, "like to sleep in houses." He might be thinking of Grant, sleeping in comfort as his men were attacked. "I prefer a tent. Next time I sleep in a real bed in a house, lady mine, it will be right here."

CHAPTER 3

SOME LAWFUL PURPOSE

Thurlow Weed liked the idea that he could add to his longtime sobriquet "Wizard of the Lobby" the self-mocking phrase "international wirepuller." He was no longer a mere Albany publisher and lobby agent; fresh from six months in England and France as Lincoln's personal emissary, Weed was satisfied that he had put a lifetime's experience in political maneuvering to work in a noble cause of averting what some feared would become "a war of the world."

He took the roomiest overstuffed chair in the Secretary of State's office and sank his large bulk into it. "William Henry," he said to Seward, his longtime political partner from New York, "I am proud to say that I have served my country well."

"Our ambassador to London agrees. Henry Adams says you are the only unofficial envoy who did a job of work for us."

"That *Trent* affair made it touch and go." Weed shook his white mane at the recollection. "England was ready to go to war. Troops ready to sail for Canada, ships ready to break the blockade of Southern ports, such as it is. Perfect opportunity for Lord Russell, the old bastard, to whip up public sentiment to do what he really wants to do—come into the war on the side of the South and reestablish the cotton trade."

"As soon as I received your letters—you must have written every day, old fellow—I shifted my position. As the President said, 'one war at a time.' "

"Lincoln getting any better at it?"

"We underestimated him, Thurlow."

Weed nodded ruefully; at Weed's urging, Seward had started out a year ago with a memorandum suggesting that he be made de facto prime minister, with Lincoln more or less of a figurehead, but the President slapped him down skillfully. Lincoln, with all his homespun posturing, was no bumpkin when it came to accumulating and defending his power.

"Lincoln is growing in the job, I'm glad to say," Seward said. "Leaves diplomatic affairs completely to me. Puts up with the most terrible abuse from Stanton and McClellan—I'd never stand for such impertinence—but he says he'd hold McClellan's horse for him if he brought back victories. I suppose that takes a certain inner strength."

Weed frowned; his partner apparently did not understand the political subtleties in the prosecution of the war. Perhaps Seward was too close to the center to see the whole.

"McClellan is launching his campaign with an eye to ultimate reunion," he explained to the Secretary of State. "That is what infuriates the radicals, who want only destruction of the South—subjugation, abolition, conquest."

"We are, after all, engaged in a war, Thurlow. A general must smite the foe."

His friend really did not understand. "Wars come to an end. How they are ended is central to who governs the nation in the peace that follows." Enough of abstraction: to the patronage, the stuff of politics that both of them thoroughly understood. "Lincoln has unwisely given the job of Collector of the Port of New York to a Greeley man. That means twelve hundred jobs, all of which contribute a part of their salaries to the radical faction. That money, and those votes, will go to further the cause of abolition and conquest. I need hardly tell you whom that strengthens for the next national campaign."

"Chase."

Weed nodded. "At the same time, Lincoln is putting all other patronage in New York through me and mine."

"That's his way," Seward said, "Balance, counterbalance—does it all the time."

"That is not always wise. The radicals will never settle for balance with conservatives like thee and me. They want it all."

"Fear not, Lincoln will never succumb to that. I am here."

Weed, who had made the arrangements that put Seward where he was, nodded thankfully but made his point: "The next canvass will be won not by the radical Republicans, nor by the peace wing of the Democrats, but by a

Thurlow Weed

convergence of the center, a Union party. That is where we must make sure Lincoln is. That is where we must be. If the abolitionists take over our party, and demand a fight to the finish, we must abandon them for a standard-bearer who can reunite the nation."

"You think the next few presidents will be generals."

Weed nodded; it was a kind way of indicating that the Seward quest was over for good. The slogan "vote as you shot" was already being bruited about; military service would be a must, and generals who took good care of their troops and did not treat the opposition cruelly would be sought after by all political parties. "That is why so many Democrats—Seymour, Wood, Sam Barlow—are looking at McClellan, who seems to understand that the task is to end the rebellion and restore the Union, not to conquer and occupy a hostile region."

"He had better not try to make peace on his own," Seward warned. "Lincoln is very jealous of his prerogatives and refuses to show weakness in any way. And I think he understands the political necessities, Thurlow, which is why you have been summoned."

"Yes. What do you make of this?" Weed leaned forward and tossed a telegram onto the Secretary's desk. All it said was: "Thurlow Weed, Albany. Can you be here tomorrow morning? Answer. Nicolay."

"I know what it is about," Seward said curtly, and said no more. Curious. Seward had few secrets from Weed.

"Of course, I hurried down here on the train last night, arrived at six this morning, came straight here. I suppose," Weed said, fishing, "Lincoln wants a report on my conversations with the Duc de Morny at the French court. I told him we would soon seize some of the cotton areas of the South ourselves, and would be able to supply some cotton."

"That, too." Seward did not look comfortable. "It's primarily a money matter."

Weed felt a twinge of conscience; was his perfectly legal speculation in the markets over there, based on his inside *Trent* information, known here? Weed had made a small fortune in England on this trip, and at no expense to the American war effort; how and when those well-deserved earnings were accumulated was nobody's business but his own.

"Tell me what I should know, William. There are no secrets between us."

"Connecticut politics, I think," said Seward. "There's a problem in Hartford that requires money, quietly raised, quickly produced, no questions asked. I told Lincoln to see you about it."

That made Weed cautious. "I would rather do it through you, as always, Governor."

"Better this way. Let Lincoln be beholden to you directly; it might help in that balance of patronage in New York you were talking about."

Weed nodded and heaved himself out of the chair. Good for Seward, to let him deal directly with the President on a delicate matter. Patronage in New York State ought really to be weaned away from the venal Hiram Barney, Collector of the Port so close to Chase and Stanton, and this would be helpful. Weed was less bashful at pressing for returns for favors rendered than Seward. Credit Lincoln with being shrewd about patronage; probably old man Blair, who all but invented the game in Andrew Jackson's day, had been tutoring him.

"Your London sojourn achieved great results, Thurlow," Seward said in parting, "with the English press. For the first time since this war began, they printed your letters, and others, explaining the Northern point of view. How'd you do it?"

"Bribery!" boomed Weed cheerfully. "The money you gave me to suborn the journalists was well invested."

"Don't tell Lincoln about that," cautioned Seward. "Let him credit your powers of persuasion."

Weed laughed and pounded his frail friend on the back. Weed never told him about his previous experience with Lincoln on the subject of expenses. He took himself off to the President's house.

A short, mustachioed young fellow rose to greet him, and seemed surprised when the senior secretary, Nicolay, who had sent the telegram summoning Weed, abruptly took him into Lincoln's office and shut the door. The place was cluttered, the furniture old and the upholstery faded; evidently it had escaped Mrs. Lincoln's extensive redecoration. Weed noted that the dark green wallpaper did not show the dirt, however, and the green rug showed no sign of wear. Maps covered the walls; bundles of papers, mail, and newspapers littered the tables, and two large wicker wastebaskets held the refuse. A working office, suitably unpretentious. Nicolay left the room, closing the door, and Weed was alone with Lincoln.

"Weed, what effect would abolishment have on the English Government?"

That startled him; was that really in the forefront of Lincoln's mind these days? Or did the President want to begin with a respectable subject? The New Yorker was prepared with an answer.

"The English Government wants the South to win the war. Then it would have a supplier of cotton for its mills, and a weakened North as an industrial competitor."

"I know that. You didn't answer the question."

"I am just getting started, Lincoln," Weed told him. "Only one thing keeps the English Government from extending diplomatic recognition to the South. That is the sentiment of the English workingman, who sees human slavery to be a moral abomination and, probably, a threat to his job. Nothing else keeps England neutral."

"There's that to be said for the prospect of abolition, then." Lincoln, after six months, seemed to Weed more careworn, yet more direct; no funny stories to begin.

"Weed, we're in a tight place," the President said briskly. "Some money for a legitimate war purpose is needed immediately. There is no appropriation from which it can be lawfully taken." Lincoln cleared his throat and moved some items around on his desk. "In this perplexity the Secretary of War suggested that you should be sent for. Can you help us to fifteen thousand dollars?"

"Yes, sir." Weed was not shocked; in May of 1860, when he visited Lincoln in Springfield after the man from Illinois had won the nomination, he had made a contribution to Lincoln's campaign that the victor probably deposited in his personal bank account. Men in public life needed money, as Weed well knew, all the more when they were honest. Few friends could be trusted to raise and give funds discreetly, and he was pleased that Lincoln thought of him that way. "But as you say you need the money immediately, the matter could be hastened by giving me two lines to that effect."

He made a scribbling motion with his fingers. None of his big-money friends in New York would give that sort of money to Weed without some kind of indication that it would be passed on directly to Lincoln. But with any sort of note from Lincoln, even an obscure one, Weed's solicitation would be buttressed; most of the top money men in New York would be honored to be the President's benefactor in a secret donation. The fact that Weed had been chosen as the trusted intermediary would be especially useful in foiling some of Greeley's plots with Hiram Barney at the Port office.

Lincoln turned to his desk, hesitated, then took out a sheet of stationery with "Executive Mansion" printed on the top. His pen scratched across the paper.

What did the President need fifteen thousand dollars for? That was a lot of money, five times the yearly salary of a congressman, well over half a year's presidential salary. And why had Lincoln tried to tie it to a war purpose, one suggested by Secretary Stanton, when Seward had told him it was for a political purpose, and suggested by him? Had Mrs. Lincoln gone overboard on expenses? Was the President in debt? On the other hand, was it legitimate politics—payoffs required in Connecticut that would help the Republicans turn back the Peace Democrats? That would be quasi-legitimate war purpose, growing out of a purely political purpose. Or was the money needed to help the War Democrats like Stanton repel the onslaught of the copperheads like Clem Vallandigham?

Weed, the discreet soldier, asked no questions; if Lincoln had wanted him to know, he would have told him. The Albany editor showed absolutely no hesitancy, which would have troubled the asker, as if Weed might have had some ethical compunctions. He blandly watched the President fold the sheet of notepaper and search for an envelope—obviously Lincoln did not want this matter examined by his secretaries. After some awkward clerical groping about, the President stuffed the note into an envelope and handed it to Weed. They shook hands cordially—the publisher always marveled how his own large hand seemed lost in Lincoln's—and Weed hurried for the train to New York.

Aboard the train, he took out the President's cryptic note, read it and shook his head in political admiration; Lincoln had used the perfect degree of circumspection, and was just specific enough without being embarrassingly specific. Under the letterhead of "Executive Mansion, Washington," the note read: "Mr. T. Weed: Dear Sir: The matters I spoke to you about are important, & I hope you will not neglect them. A. Lincoln."

His carriage driver had rarely been so busy, skipping lunch, taking him through the rainy streets to different offices near the financial center all afternoon. By 3 P.M. Weed had visited sixteen prominent New York businessmen. Each had been suitably impressed by Weed's solicitation when backed up by the President's urgent note. Each man who gave one thousand dollars—Aspinwall, Vanderbilt, A. T. Stewart, and the rest—had signed his name at the bottom of Lincoln's note. The last man, Russell Sturgis, could only get up five hundred dollars, and so he added Henry Hubbell for another five hundred; Weed thought it would have been tidier for fifteen men to have given a thousand apiece, but time was of the essence, so he lumped the final two together as joint donors of a thousand.

By that evening, fifteen thousand dollars in banknotes, including some of the new greenbacks—the bills with Mr. Lincoln's face on them, not the low-denomination bills with Chase's picture, which Weed thought might not have set well, and which would have made too bulky a package—was on its way to John Nicolay at the Executive Mansion, ready for deposit or transfer first thing the next morning. Weed did not write a covering note; Weed always believed that prompt action spoke louder than well-drafted letters, and the less put on paper about these matters, the better.

He held on to the discreet note written in the President's hand, countersigned with the names of each of the contributors. Perhaps he would mention their names to the President, as he had faithfully promised each, perhaps not; he would think about that. The document was valuable in itself; it occurred to Weed that he would hold on to the page of autographs of eminent men for some years and then, long after it could stimulate any controversy, offer it for sale for the benefit of some meritorious charity.

CHAPTER 4

JOHN HAY'S DIARY
APRIL 9, 1862

Stanton came in this morning in the highest dudgeon, fuming about McClellan, who has finally taken his army out of Washington and landed it on the Virginia peninsula near Richmond. Mars was brandishing one of Mr. Brady's photographs.

"Will you look at this? These are the fearsome 'guns' that have been intimidating our intrepid commander," he sputtered. "This is what has been pointing at us across the Potomac."

The Prsdt looked, first with great dismay, then with a sad smile. He let me look. Brady had captured the scene of the "Quaker guns"—logs rolled into position by the canny rebels and made to look like cannon.

"Wooden guns," fulminated the Secy of War, pacing, "and who knows how much of the vaunted rebel army of two hundred thousand, supposedly menacing us all winter, was a figment of Pinkerton's imagination."

"Their strength was exaggerated," the Prsdt allowed, "but still, a rebel army was there." He never liked to let Stanton heap abuse on McClellan without some reproof.

"If that blathering incompetent had attacked when I ordered him to," snapped Stanton, referring to the Prsdt's War Order, "we would have been in Richmond a month ago. Right through Manassas. None of this brilliant maneuvering around Chesapeake Bay, boats, all that complicated tactical folderol."

Lincoln, of course, agreed wholeheartedly, but put forward McClellan's excuse: "It's supposed to reduce casualties."

"Mark my word, Lincoln, now that he's down on the Peninsula in force—with one hundred thousand men, facing half that number—McClellan will do the same as he did all winter here in Washington. He'll find excuses to dig in. He'll call for more men. He'll blame the weather. He'll never fight."

"Well, he's in the field at last."

"But he's not in earnest," Stanton insisted. "He cannot emancipate himself from the influence of Jeff Davis. I fear he is not willing to do anything calculated greatly to damage the cause of secession."

Lincoln does not go that far. "When I took leave of him at the wharf in Alexandria, he shed tears when speaking of the cruel imputations upon his loyalty."

Stanton then produced his evidence of intended delay, in the form of a telegraph message from the front. "Listen: 'The enemy are in our front in large force and being reinforced daily. I beg that you will reconsider the order detaching the first corps from my command.' It's the same old story."

Lincoln sighed in what I suspect was reluctant agreement. "Let's send him a message." He wrote it out: "I think you better break the enemy's line from Yorktown to Warwick River, at once. They will probably use time as advantageously as you can." Stanton looked at it, nodded, and went to send it himself before I had a chance to fix the grammar.

Later that day, Postmaster General Blair came in. The Prsdt was glad to see him; all three Blairs, father and two sons, were at work on a speech, to be given by Frank on the floor of Congress, promoting gradual, compensated abolition, followed by colonization. At a time when the radicals were claiming the Prsdt had "no policy," Lincoln wanted some powerful voices in the Congress (and Frank is chairman of the House Military Committee) to ring out with his policy.

Lincoln does not want to spell out his buy-them-and-colonize-them policy all by himself, without support. His object is to prevent loyal slaveholders from becoming rebels. Monty Blair goes even further: he thinks that plenty of white Southerners who own no slaves are secretly loyal, and are ready for a peace within the Union if no attack is made on the South's peculiar institution.

"I'm concerned about your treatment of General McClellan," the Postmaster General said. The Blairs are good eggs, but they do tend to take up the cause of the Little Napoleon. "He read about being relieved of his overall command in the newspapers. Perhaps you should have discussed it with him before he went into the Peninsula campaign."

Easy to say. I would hate to be the one to tell the rank-sensitive McClellan to his face that he was being demoted; he may not fight the enemy in the field, but he fights him gloriously in the office.

"Did you see this?" The Tycoon picked up the Brady photograph of the Quaker guns and handed it to him. "That's the sort of thing that was worrying McClellan for months, delaying any action. Wooden guns!"

"There were plenty of real guns, too, as we discovered at Bull Run," Blair came back. "I hope you won't get caught up in this anti-McClellan hysteria, Mr. President. The radicals are after him in full cry because the general returns fugitive slaves, which happens to be the law of the land. And he says openly that this is a war to save the Union and not to abolish slavery—which is your position too. The abolitionists can't get at you directly, at least not easily, so they direct their fire at you through McClellan."

To be fair, which I in no way intend to be, that is true enough; Ben Wade had demanded a meeting with the Prsdt before his Joint Committee on the Conduct of the War, and the Tycoon defused that constitutional challenge by inviting them over to the Mansion the other night. All we heard were complaints about McClellan and the Democratic generals, and demands that Washington be defended by Republican, anti-slavery generals. The Prsdt quieted Wade & Co. a bit by giving General Frémont, the old blowhard, a command in Tennessee, which infuriated the Blairs.

It was at this moment that a messenger came in from the telegraph office in Stanton's domain with Little Mac's reply to Lincoln's suggestion to move. The Tycoon told me to read it aloud to both of them.

"He says, 'My entire force for duty amounts to about eighty-five thousand men. Since my arrangements were made for this campaign, at least fifty thousand men have been taken from my command.' "

"Is that true?" Blair interrupted.

"By Stanton's count, McClellan has one hundred and eight thousand men. There's a discrepancy of twenty-three thousand men. Like shoveling fleas," Lincoln added, which must have struck Blair as mysterious.

"And did you take fifty thousand from his command?" Blair asked. "My God, that's more than a third of his force."

"Finish reading," Lincoln told me.

" 'Here is to be fought the great battle that is to decide the existing contest,' the general says. 'I shall do all in my power to carry the enemy's works, but to do this I require the whole of McDowell's First Corps.' "

The Prsdt laid his hand across his forehead. "That's George McClellan for you. His dispatches complaining that he is not properly sustained, while they do not offend me, do pain me very much."

"If he started the campaign with those troops assured to him—" Blair, the former West Pointer, began, but the Tycoon cut him short.

"After he embarked on his expedition," said the exasperated Lincoln, "I ascertained that less than twenty thousand unorganized men, without a single field battery, was all that was left here to defend Washington."

The Prsdt was speaking slowly, and I could tell he was more than a little angry. The defense of McClellan that he had shown to Stanton was absent in his discourse with Blair. "This presented—or would present, if I let McDowell go with McClellan—a great temptation to the enemy to turn back from the Rappahannock and sack Washington." He did not have to tell Blair what the capture of the federal capital might mean: recognition of the Confederacy by France and Britain, a sinking of the national spirit of the North, pressure for peace with secession.

"As soon as McClellan moved toward the Peninsula," Blair pointed out, "the Virginians were forced to leave the vicinity of Washington, to fall back to be available for a defense of Richmond. His plan is masterly, and it has been working. I would hate for you to deny him the capacity to bring it off."

"My explicit order," said the Prsdt, in his most executive tone, "was that Washington should be left secure. That order was disobeyed."

"Neglected, perhaps. Or interpreted in a way that seems disobedient to you but not to him."

"Neglected, then." Lincoln is not one to turn aside a gentler word. "That was what drove me to detain McDowell's corps. Do you really think, Judge, that I should permit this city to be entirely open, except what resistance can be offered by twenty thousand disorganized troops, the dregs of the army?"

"But we have another thirty-five thousand with Banks in the Shenandoah Valley," Blair reminded him. "McClellan must have considered them part of the defense of Washington, which they are."

"That's not here." The Prsdt must have been thinking of the time, only a year ago, when the city was helpless and he used to say that it seemed there was no North.

Blair hesitated. "To commit the full force would be a risk. There is another risk, however—of not giving your main commander the troops he needs for victory. If he fails, we're in great trouble. If McClellan's army is destroyed, nothing can stop the rebels from moving North again and taking Washington. They would outnumber McDowell and the dregs, as you call them."

"There is that danger," Lincoln conceded, "but I cannot believe that a soldier of McClellan's caliber would lose an entire army. I reckon he would retreat in better order than any man alive." Lincoln picked at the mole on his cheek. "No. I will not gamble with the capital. Fifty-five thousand men must stay here, as Stanton says all the army corps commanders agree with me is needed. And McClellan, down there, must move."

"You have given him an excuse for delay."

"No. I always insisted," the Prsdt reminded the Blair family representative, "that going down by Chesapeake Bay in search of a field, instead of fighting at or near Manassas, was only shifting, and not surmounting, a difficulty. We would find the same enemy and the same entrenchments at either place. The country will note that the delay is the same."

I stepped forward to ask if he had a reply to McClellan's complaint, to be sent to the general near Yorktown, where his troops had landed and were standing around. It is disgraceful to think how the little squad of rebels at Yorktown keeps him at bay.

The Prsdt dictated to me: "It is time for you to strike a blow. It is indispensable to *you* that you strike a blow. *I* am powerless to help this." He stopped to remark to Blair: "George must understand the pressures here. Fortunately, he thinks in personal terms." He continued dictating: "I have never written you in greater kindness of feeling than now, nor with a fuller purpose to sustain you, so far in my most anxious judgment I consistently can. But you must act." He laid great emphasis on the last four words.

After reading it back to him, I could not help vouchsafing, "Little Napoleon ought to get the point."

"Too much so, you think?" the Prsdt, suddenly more solicitous, asked Blair. "Perhaps you should write him a letter. Make my case to him as you made his case to me, Judge. You'll do it far better than I can. Tell him that what disturbs me is his lack of confidence."

Blair smiled. "I'll do it, and hope you can find some extra troops somewhere to reinforce him. Perhaps strip Frémont's command, which won't be doing anything."

"Or I'll send McDowell's corps, all forty thousand men, if I think Washington is safe. But tell George to do what he can with what he has."

"I wish he had taken Frank with him," said Blair. "My brother volunteered for a field command on the Peninsula, but McClellan turned him down."

"Try Grant, if Frank wants to fight," said Lincoln. "We'll miss him in Congress, but I can understand."

I took the but-you-must-act missive over to the telegrapher across the street, a nice chap named Bates who is terrified of Stanton and insisted on showing it to Mars before putting it in cipher.

The Secretary of War glared at my writing on the piece of paper and sniffed, "Kid gloves." The message seemed fairly bareknuckled to me, and I said so, but the Secretary of War is a stern fellow.

"I have discovered who McClellan's evil genius is," he said with the certitude of a man who reads all the messages. "Colonel Thomas Key, the former judge and Democratic legislator in Ohio, now his judge-advocate and confidant, and—" this added darkly, "Democratic political adviser. Key has a brother here in the War Department, too." He quickly added that not all Democrats were suspect, that he was a Democrat himself, and that he had great faith in General John Dix, who had served with him in the Buchanan Cabinet. "I'm trusting Dix with the Rose Greenhow problem," he added, presumably to try, hang, or exchange her. "But not all Democratic generals can be trusted."

I know this is a strange and possibly disloyal thought, but I cannot get it out of my head that Stanton would be displeased by a McC victory. Perhaps because of his sick, probably dying baby, covered horribly with skin eruptions, and the terrible toll the impending tragedy is taking on his young wife, Stanton is undergoing some kind of spiritual transformation. He has commenced church attendance, implores divine aid at the drop of a hat, and identifies the Union with morality and the secesh as the embodiment of evil. He fears that McC is maneuvering more with an eye to reunion and reconciliation than fighting for victory, and would exploit his popularity to drain the final peace of its moral content.

That is the only reason I can find for Stanton's Order No. 33 this week to stop all recruiting, to reassign all recruiting officers, and to sell the recruiting office property to the highest bidder. Overconfidence? I think not; Stanton is sending McClellan and his political backers the message that no more troops will be available to him, which must feed McC's delusions that the Administration is planning to abandon his army by refusing to reinforce it.

That is where Stanton and Lincoln are so different; the Prsdt may be exasperated by the insolence of epaulets, but would be the first to wave his tall hat at McNapoleon if he came back at the head of a victory parade. Mars, contrariwise, would sulk if the wrong man turned out to be the hero.

CHAPTER 5

FOR SERVICES RENDERED

"The President paid you a very handsome compliment in the Cabinet meeting," Attorney General Bates told Anna Carroll over lunch at Willard's. They had a window table looking out at the purple-and-white magnolia blossoms. "Said how useful you were to the country."

She beamed at him; Edward Bates was not much of a lawyer, but he was a dear man who never missed an opportunity to report anything good said about her in high places. She had buttressed him in her *War Powers of the President* pamphlet and took care never to upstage him; she knew the Missouri politician appreciated that.

"Please go on," she said. "What brought my name into the highest council of state?" She had already been alerted to the subject of the discussion: at Father Blair's suggestion, Lincoln had asked her to write an analysis of the prospects for colonization of freed negroes. After consultation with the Blairs, she had dismissed Liberia and Haiti as likely homes for former slaves, pressing instead the virtues and opportunities of Panama.

It was not the climate that caused her to reject Africa and choose instead the strip of land that connected North and South America. The reason was purely imperial: Anna was aware of the elder Blair's secret design for an American empire in Central America, ruled by friendly blacks. To disguise that purpose, she directed her argument to the economic opportunity presented by the likely presence of coal. Since the narrow strip of land separated the Atlantic and Pacific oceans, ports on each coast of Panama, with a rail link, might save transportation costs and transform the backward area into a valuable land.

"The memorial you wrote to him on colonization, of course," said Bates. "Lincoln handed the paper with your views on colonization, and on the proper place to initiate the colony, to Secretary Smith. The President said you had given him a better insight into the whole problem than anyone."

Caleb Smith, the Secretary of the Interior, was a man Anna considered a political zero, but he did have something to say about railroads in the West, and Anna thought he would be a useful politician to know. What better way to approach a Cabinet officer than to have the President himself make the appointment?

"He told Smith that you thought the Interior Department the proper agency to look after the matter," Bates added, consulting the large Willard menu, "and advised the Secretary to get into communication with you." He paused. "The fish is always good here. Caleb Smith was happy about your recommendation; nobody pays much attention to him."

"Any reaction from Treasury?"

"Chase agreed, but said deportation had to be voluntary."

Listening to him, she flicked her eyes around the dining room, hoping the right people would see her with a Cabinet officer, even if only the Attorney

Attorney General Edward Bates

General. Thurlow Weed was in his accustomed corner table, with a couple of *New York Tribune* men, Adams Hill and the new correspondent, a dapper young man named George Smalley. Adele Douglas, accompanied by some young man, caught her eye; Anna nodded, as if to confirm that both were doing well that day, and wondered if she had summoned up the courage to visit her cousin Rose Greenhow in jail.

"My dear lady," Bates was saying, "what else are you doing for your country?"

She told him of her latest work for the War Department. It had been six weeks since the Army of the Potomac had embarked on its Peninsula campaign, two weeks since the fall of the rebel stronghold of Yorktown, where Joe Johnston had withdrawn without a fight after McClellan finally managed to place his siege guns into position. Despite all the press attention being paid to McClellan's drive on Richmond—and the panic that had gripped Washington the week before when Stonewall Jackson roared up the Shenandoah and successfully diverted McDowell's corps from the attack on Richmond—Anna was determined to get across the need for a vigorous follow-up to Shiloh in the West.

"Nobody is thinking of what we should be doing now that Halleck has taken Corinth," she said, warming to her favorite subject. "Beauregard will probably send a large rebel column into Texas, where wheat and beef abound, to hold that country for subsistence of the South. We should stop him with gunboats on the Yazoo River, and by moving quickly on Vicksburg. We can cut off rebel commerce at Vicksburg, and their army will wither on the vine."

Bates blinked at this outburst of military strategy; it was evidently not his subject. "Are you as optimistic as the Cabinet is? Even Lincoln, who is not as enthusiastic as Stanton, thinks the war can be ended this summer. That's why he is concentrating on compensated emancipation—if peace negotiations develop, the sale of slaves might be the answer for a great many Southerners. Pay the states to buy and free many of the slaves and send them home, or to wherever." He peered at the menu. "Of all the fish, the rockfish is best."

"I'm a Marylander, General—we have rockfish and crabs all the time. I think I'll have the roast beef." She was hungry; this was her first Willard's meal in longer than she cared to remember.

Here she was, discussing high military policy, listening to compliments from the President in Cabinet relayed by the President's own legal adviser, but without the money to buy an elegant dinner. The few dollars from the elder Blair went for rent; her bill to the War Department for the Tennessee plan, as well as her bill approved by Tom Scott for her War Powers pamphlet, was languishing in some bureaucratic limbo. She had laid out the last of her money for printer's bills, distributing her pro-Lincoln pamphlets to congressmen and editors. Anna was broke and tired of it. She ordered enough lunch for a famished soldier.

"I take it, Miss Carroll," Bates said, "you approved of the President's message countermanding the emancipation order of General Hunter."

"No," she said, "it should have been much stronger. Lincoln was almost apologetic about it. When any general takes it into his head to free the slaves —Frémont, Hunter, whoever—he ought to be fired forthwith."

The waiter brought an appetizer of fried oysters, a Willard's specialty, and she dug in as she spoke. "Mistake number one was signing the D.C. emancipation bill; I wrote the President about that last month. Yes, I know he proposed it twenty years ago and couldn't go back on that, but it only whetted abolitionist appetites. Mistake number two will come when he signs the bill abolishing slavery in the territories—"

"But that's Republican dogma, the issue of the debates with Douglas—"

"The message to the South will be clear," she reminded him. "The abolitionists are on the march in the Congress. The Congress is taking power away from the President. The next step is total confiscation."

The Attorney General tucked his napkin under his beard and shook his head, no. He was not what she considered politically alert.

"Don't you see? If we let the abolitionists make slavery the issue, my dear General, the war will go on and on. Only the ultras, North and South, want to talk slavery, because they want a fight to the finish."

"I don't know . . . 'unconditional surrender' did a lot for Grant, at least until that unfortunate episode at Shiloh."

"That phrase was a mistake." The man really did need educating. "Do we really want the South to fight to the last man? The worst traitors in Richmond are delighted with the radicals up here—the abolitionists in the North are putting the fear of slave uprisings in the South. That's what holds the Confederacy together."

"You have strong feelings, then, about the Confiscation bill." Now he was getting to the point. The nice news about the President's compliment, the indirect probing, the good food—he was leaving half his oysters, but she could not very well switch plates with him—all were leading to a new assignment. Provided her responses were in line with Lincoln's thinking.

"The Confiscation bill is a constitutional abomination," she stated.

It was his turn to beam. "The President thinks so too, and has asked me to begin thinking about a veto message."

She raised her eyebrows and tilted her head. Lincoln had not yet vetoed any act of Congress; this veto of confiscation would create a furor, set back abolition, encourage the Blair conservatives, enhance Unionist sentiment in the South.

"I was thinking," Bates suggested, "just as in the war powers controversy, it would be good if you were to do a pamphlet first, for wide distribution, that would lay the groundwork for others to support the Lincoln position."

She assumed he meant he needed her to do the legal research for him, put it in the form of a persuasive brief, and anticipate the opposing arguments. Then he could tell the President, who was a far better lawyer than his Attorney General, what the most vulnerable legal points of the proposed Act would be. Anna decided immediately to do it, but felt she could get away with adding a condition. "It would be useful to get some preliminary thinking from the President on this," she said, as if thinking it over. "I don't mind taking on Senator Sumner, but before getting into an argument with Ben and Caroline Wade . . ." She let her reservation dangle.

"Come to the Executive Mansion this afternoon at five," he said. "We have an appointment with Mr. Lincoln. Here is a copy of the Confiscation bill, as proposed by Senator Trumbull."

Anna knew she would have only three hours to run up to the Library of

Congress to see what Judge Story had written about penalties for treason and bills of attainder. She finished her brandied peach pie and left him in the restaurant. The lobby of Willard's was hectic with the confluence of contractors and government officials, officers and ladies, Washington society and visitors from the big cities. Willard's was where Lincoln had stayed before his Inauguration, meeting his new Cabinet members in Parlor 6. The hotel was authentically American in the way it permitted a noisy milling-around in its large public rooms; British visitors, accustomed to quiet dignity in their hotels, hated it. She spotted Orville Browning, a Senator from Illinois, an intimate of Lincoln's, for whom she had helped make arrangements for the burial of Willie in the Carroll family mortuary. He was a good old friend, a practical man, and she needed some fast, practical advice.

"Orville, I have an appointment with the President and the Attorney General at five. You have to help me."

"You want your friend Tom Scott to be appointed Collector of the Port of New Orleans." The Senator smiled. "Wade told me. I'll do everything I can."

"No—I mean yes, that too, but this is personal. Come over in the corner." She showed him a thick dossier: the memorandum of the Tennessee plan, the *War Powers* pamphlet, the *Reply to Breckinridge* pamphlet, assorted assignments done for the War and Justice departments. She showed him bills, expense accounts for her trip West, invoices from typesetters and printers, and time sheets detailing her own long hours researching and writing for the past year. "I have a commitment to be paid five thousand dollars for the *War Powers* alone from the Assistant Secretary of War, who is cleaning out his desk as we speak. Orville, how much should I ask for?"

Senator Browning flipped through the documents and offered some counsel: "You're right to go to the top on this, because it was all done for Lincoln or at his request. But don't ask for pay for yourself—that embarrasses everybody. Ask for an appropriation for the distribution of millions of these pamphlets. They are obviously war expenses, and nobody doubts that printing costs money. Ask for, say, fifty thousand dollars for everything—distribution and printing and preparation of these, and maybe your next one too."

Fifty thousand seemed like a lot. "Will you back me up on that?"

"You hand these to the President in person. Afterward I'll avail myself of the opportunity to converse with him about it." He looked around the room. "Compared to the sums being discussed all over this room at this moment, it's not such a significant amount. And it has been money well spent."

"I'll do it. By the way, where do you stand on the Confiscation bill?"

"I'm with the President—against such a punitive measure. But if the war takes a turn for the worse, and McClellan fails to take Richmond, Trumbull and Wade and Sumner will get it passed."

After two hours of burrowing through books on treason at the library near the Capitol, Anna Ella Carroll presented herself at the Pennsylvania Avenue entrance of the President's house.

John Hay met her at the top of the stairs. "Bates won't be with you," he said with a grin. "The President wants his legal counsel undiluted."

The central hall, which used to be jammed with office seekers and visitors, was empty; she was glad Lincoln had finally stopped seeing people all day long.

Lincoln was cordial; he took her hand, led her to a chair, and then stretched his lanky frame out on the couch. From her petite perspective, he seemed a grotesquely long man. "Good news from the West," he said. "Memphis is ours. I'm thinking of bringing Halleck back here."

That meant Grant would be in command in the West. "Send Grant after Vicksburg next," she said. "That controls the Mississippi now."

He frowned, got up, went to a map on the table, peered down, nodded, came back and sat down behind his desk. "The Confiscation bill. I'm told you don't like it."

"It would give the South a new incentive to fight," she said. "By unconstitutional means, it takes everything away from every rebel, even Southerners who may not want to be rebels. It is an invitation to more war."

"When you extinguish hope, you create desperation," Lincoln agreed. "We would be wise to leave misguided men some motive for returning to the Union. But why do you say it's unconstitutional?"

"This is nothing more than a bill of attainder," she said, non-lawyer to lawyer, "an act of punishment by the Legislature, usurping the powers of the courts. Do you know what Sumner and Tad Stevens want to do? They're not content with the abolition of slavery; they want to take the land from all the rebels and break it up and give it to what Sumner calls the poor and the homeless."

"Well, why not?" Lincoln, she knew, was baiting her, as in a courtroom.

"The Constitution is why not. Sumner knows that if he tries rebels the lawful way, in courts, local juries will never convict neighbors as traitors. So he ignores due process and treats the South as a conquered foreign province."

"Where is it in the Constitution—"

"Right here." She reached for the copy of Jefferson's *Manual* on his desk, flipped quickly to a familiar passage, and read: " 'The Congress shall have power to declare punishment of treason, but no attainder of treason shall work corruption of blood or forfeiture, except during the life of the person attainted.' "

"Wonderful old English language," said Lincoln.

"Despots have a habit of accusing a man of treason in order to get his property," she said with satisfying certitude, having just researched the subject. "To make certain that no accusation of treason could be made to gain plunder from the victim, the authors of the Constitution absolutely prohibited the confiscation of the estate of the traitor to the government, leaving it free to pass to his heirs."

"And the bill is ex post facto law to boot," said the President, who was evidently familiar with the forfeiture prohibition. "I could never sign such a bill."

"You have refused to permit secession. That means you do not recognize the Confederacy as a foreign country. That means all the Southerners are still citizens of the United States."

"Exactly," said Lincoln.

"When a nation cannot protect any portion of its territory, the inhabitants must yield obedience to the de facto government, the rebel government," she explained. "The nation cannot hold the local people responsible, as individuals, for any act they may commit while under the pressure of a usurping power. Neither the Congress nor the President can punish Southerners as a class, by legislative or executive fiat."

He nodded agreement.

"Only individual acts can be punished," she said, "after due process in courts, because the people of the South have all the protection of United States citizenship. And no property can be taken away from a traitor's family."

"You've been talking about real estate, land," said Lincoln. "That's the meaning of the English law in this country, as I see it. But what about slaves? Since they're considered property, it was Ben Butler's idea to seize them as contraband of war. Would you say they can be taken away by the Congress? Or by the President?"

"No," she said with finality. "Not unless you amend the Constitution to do it. The Constitution specifically acknowledges slavery as it stands, you know that."

"Well, I don't know about that. Under the war power, and last year's sort of mild Confiscation Act, we can seize a rebel's munitions, and any slaves he uses for war purposes. I reckon a field hand harvesting food that ultimately feeds soldiers is serving a war purpose." He was arguing in favor of the bill, searching out her arguments against.

"But this bill is much more sweeping," she countered. "You can justify confiscating property that is being used against you in war—we've been doing that for a year. But this bill means total abolition of slavery as an institution. Listen." She read a portion of the bill she had underlined. " 'All slaves of persons who shall hereafter be engaged in rebellion against the United States, or who shall in any way give aid thereto . . . shall be forever free.' That's emancipation, plain and simple."

"You skipped a line," he said.

True, but she had deliberately left out insignificant words. Anna felt less certain in the presence of a real lawyer. She went back and read the words she had left out: " 'or who shall in any way give aid thereto *being within any place occupied by rebel forces and afterwards occupied by the forces of the United States* shall be forever free.' What's your point?"

"That Confiscation bill would free the slaves only in those areas controlled by the rebels, which we take, and not the slaves in the loyal border states," Lincoln pointed out. "It frees only their slaves, not ours; it does not abolish the institution."

"Trumbull framed it that way to pick up some border-state votes for confiscation," she said, "but he won't. The border-state congressmen—and I know, I'm from Maryland—all recognize this for what it is. Abolition."

"Read the fine print, Miss Carroll," the President replied, instructing her in the legal argument. "You're a good lawyer, though you don't claim to be. The section on confiscation is imperfectly drawn. No procedure is specified as to how emancipation is to be effected. It is not enforceable legislation."

She gave him a hard look, turning from legalisms to politics. "It tells the South that if they lose the war, slavery is finished. It would be proof that the hotheads and firebrands have been right all along, that this is not a war 'for the Union' at all, but a war to abolish slavery." The thought struck her that Bates might be wrong, and Lincoln was not merely seeking arguments to help him veto the bill. "Are you seriously thinking of signing this?"

"It might not pass," said Lincoln, avoiding a decision until the last moment, a habit of every President she ever met, "and if it does, I want to have a veto ready. Here." He made a smaller decision. "Do a pamphlet, Miss Carroll, along the lines of your *Reply to Breckinridge*. Only this time aim it at some of our more radical friends—or, rather, their overly enthusiastic ideas."

"Not Wade," she said. "Perhaps *A Reply to Sumner*. I could do it in a week, show you the draft, and have it printed and in every congressman's hands by the first of July. All the newspapers, too."

"Leave out the slavery part," he directed. "Concentrate on the unconstitutionality of a bill of attainder, and ex post facto." He rose slowly.

"There's something else," she said, "while I'm here." He sat again, not hurrying her. "I hate to bring this up to you, but nobody else seems to understand. You were a practicing lawyer; you'll know what I mean. It's about money."

He looked surprised and not amused. She began by explaining how she had been the one to create the Tennessee River plan, which caused him to frown. That was a mistake, she realized, making it look as if she were putting a price on the plan itself.

"Isn't this something you want to discuss with Stanton?"

She had not made her deal with Stanton, only a part of it with Assistant Secretary Scott, who would soon be gone. The crispness of her presentation, which she had written out beforehand, wilted in her embarrassment, but she was bound to see it through. She read aloud from her memorandum. She listed the items she had been working on, her time expended, the expenses of travel; the more she read, the more irritated he looked and the more nervous she became.

"And how much is it you want?" he interrupted.

She forgot the approach Orville Browning had recommended about putting her work together with a printing and distribution project and remembered only the fee: "Fifty thousand dollars."

He looked at her as if she had gone out of her mind. "Did you say—fifty thousand dollars?"

She swallowed and nodded.

"Your proposition," he said, rising to his feet, "is the most outrageous one ever made to any government on earth."

"We differ, sir, on the value of intellectual labor."

"Fifty thousand dollars!" Lincoln took his tall hat off the corner of the desk and threw it on the floor. "Fifty!"

She looked at the black hat rolling on the green carpet. She took a deep breath, forced back her tears, and said, "If that is too high, the error is not mine, but that of friends of yours and the country. I will not bother you about this further. I do not think you comprehend me."

"I reckon I comprehend only too well."

She could say no more about it. She brushed past young Hay on the way out and went back to her flat to be alone.

CHAPTER 6

NOT BY STRATEGY ALONE

Lincoln retrieved his hat from the floor and threw it on the couch. Steaming, he sat on his desk, facing the Pennsylvania Avenue window. Fifty thousand dollars. That was two years' salary for the President of the United States. For a pitiful fifteen thousand dollars, he had been forced to all but sell his soul to Thurlow Weed, and that for no personal profit. He still had to pay for Mother's flub-dubs out of his own pocket. The disproportion of it all galled him. Miss Carroll was useful—she shored up Bates on the law, and had helped keep the wavering Governor of Maryland in line—but such a display of greed was intolerable.

He stiffened his arms, hands flat on the desktop, and slid forward to rest his feet on the floor. The pain in his toes caused him to sit on the desk again. He reached down to undo the laces, pulled off the shoes and kneaded the ball of his right foot below the aching corns. Seward, who had the same problem, said that a man grew to bear the steady throbbing. Maybe so, but Seward was a much smaller man, and not so much weight rested on his feet. One of the worst things about the nagging pain was that the ailment was considered so common as to be ludicrous, and corn sufferers found that their wincing drew smiles. The only respite came when all the weight or pressure was removed, and he resolved to do less walking and to wear slippers instead of shoes, no matter what his wife said.

In his stocking feet, he went over to the map on the table. McClellan, like Lincoln a Westerner, thought he was going to win by strategy, and the army officers took on the same notion. They had no idea that the war had to be carried on, and put through, by tough, hard fighting; that it would hurt somebody; that no headway could be made while the delusion of bloodless strategic advance lasted.

Lincoln hoped that all that kept McClellan from smashing the enemy head-on was a natural excess of caution, or a regard for the lives of his men, or a belief that one man's military genius could determine what happened in the fiery trial of war. If that were all, the President as commander in chief could put up with it, urging him on, passing along the pressure from the radicals in ameliorated form.

But what, he asked himself, if the delays were caused by more than innate caution, more than a reluctance to face the need for butchery, more than the dictates of all the books on strategy? What if George McClellan held a different view of the purpose of the war?

No, that was not the central question. Of course George saw the war differently—he was a Stephen Douglas Democrat, and according to Mars was under the political influence of his closest staff aide, Colonel Thomas Key, a leading Ohio Democratic politician. They were not quite Peace Democrats, but these politicians in uniform, who saw eye to eye with so many of the professional officer corps out of West Point, were prepared to offer their friends and classmates of the South "pop sov"—extension of slavery into the

West, as if the election of 1860 had not settled all that once and for all. The people had spoken; never mind that he was a minority President, he had been elected on the square, and he would be damned before he would reward the secession leaders with the sort of victory they could not gain at the polls.

McClellan and all the believers in compromise could hold their beliefs—it was a free country; that did not bother him. The issue boiled down to this: could the Democratic generals and the officer corps impose their view of a negotiated peace on the elected leadership of the nation? Put more bluntly, was George taking orders about the way war was to be fought, or had he set up shop for himself?

Lincoln would not let himself be rushed into a conclusion about this. One reason for restraint was that he had nobody of stature to replace McClellan at the head of an army that loved "Little Mac"; another was that he knew George to be a patriot and a good soldier, who had proved his loyalty and ability after the Bull Run debacle. Others, like Chase and Stanton, were quick to forget; Lincoln prided himself on remembering those who had stuck by him in the Union's darkest hour.

And yet—rumors had reached him that some of the officers dreamed of dictatorship. He had heard, too, of approaches made to McClellan by Democrats in New York about heading their party in the election after the war. That sort of talk would be very tempting to an ambitious young man, and George was no less ambitious than Lincoln had been at age thirty-five.

It occurred to him that most of his time was taken up with keeping his friends and potential rivals from nibbling away the little actual power he had.

Inside the Cabinet, that nibbling had begun right at the start with Seward's attempt to establish himself as Premier, and now Chase was beginning to complain that the Cabinet did not have enough authority. Lincoln had struck a balance of power between Chase and Stanton on one hand, Blair and Seward on the other; he wondered how long that would last.

In the Congress, the conservative Republicans still outnumbered the radicals, but Ben Wade and Thaddeus Stevens were gaining strength, and would probably press the slavery issue to seize control of the war from the Executive branch. He saw that as a serious threat to the central idea of representative government: nobody believed more strongly than Lincoln that the secession had to be crushed and the South defeated decisively enough to stamp out any idea of secession to the latest generation, but he also was persuaded that the Southern states had to be drawn back into the Union and not treated as a conquered province by the abolitionists after surrender. That was why his reelection, in the Andy Jackson style, was so necessary—why he would gladly use the furlough power to help put the soldier vote in the Republican column, why he would employ Thurlow Weed to squeeze funds from financiers.

The Cabinet, the Congress, the military: he had struck a precarious balance of forces within the first two, leaving himself the master; now he had to apply the same technique to the military, and needed to find a general to counterbalance a successful McClellan.

The President stretched out on the couch and thought about that. After Shiloh, Grant would not do, at least for a long while. Halleck had been named General-in-Chief, but he was more a buffer than a balancer; there was a lack of magnetism to the man that would likely cause him to be dominated

in the commanding presence of McClellan. John Pope, the hero of Island No.
Ten out West, was a possibility; Chase and Stanton were high on him. Most
likely, Lincoln judged, the best man was McDowell, a good Republican who
was not really to blame for Bull Run.

The trouble with McDowell was that he sided with McClellan on the most
troublesome area of disagreement between the President and his foremost
field commander. As Lincoln saw it, the trick was not so much taking Richmond, it was taking the capital of the Confederacy without losing the capital
of the Union.

George could not get it through his head that the city of Washington had to
be defended from a raid and a sacking at all costs. The capture of the federal
city, even for a short while, would dishearten the North and bring the foreign
powers in on the side of the South. That was why a sizable Union army—the
forty thousand under McDowell—had to remain between the rebels and
Washington. If such an interposition meant that the strategy of McClellan to
take Richmond by water would come to naught because of a division of
Union forces, so be it.

Incredibly, however, McDowell agreed with McClellan, a man he despised,
on this central decision. To the President's dismay, McDowell had argued
that it was foolish to allow the enemy to paralyze his large force with a small
one under Stonewall Jackson in the Shenandoah Valley. Both Union generals
agreed that the threat to Washington was minimal, that the North should not
be deterred by a feint, that the only way to take Richmond was to combine
the Union forces for an assault. Washington, they assured him, would be safe
because the rebels would need every available man to save Richmond. Sure.
You and I know the dog won't bite, but does the dog know he won't bite?

Nicolay knocked and put his head in to say that a group of congressmen,
Wade included, was expected soon to be present for the signing of the Homestead Act. Lincoln sat up, nodded, and began to fit his tender toes into his
shoes.

If McClellan was so cautious, the thought struck him, why was he being so
bold about stripping the capital to throw everything against Richmond?
Could there be something to that charge of treasonous intent that Stanton
had made? Lincoln put that distasteful thought out of his mind, remembering
the convincing reaction of the general when the charge was put to him in a
friendly way.

No; George wanted to win, but to win the least costly way, covering himself with glory but not with blood. He probably thought that if the enemy in
Richmond saw themselves impossibly outnumbered, they would withdraw
without a fight, much as they had done recently at Yorktown. Lincoln
thought the opposite, that Jefferson Davis would fight for every street in
Richmond, just as he would in Davis's shoes.

He decided, tentatively, to send McDowell's army to connect with McClellan's forces to close on the rebel capital. To withhold the power that might
make the difference would be a terrible display of timidity. But he would send
them overland, keeping one Union army between Stonewall Jackson and
Washington. If that took longer—which it would, in this spring's unprecedented downpours of rain—George would not really mind. He was in no
hurry to attack.

Lincoln rose to meet the congressional delegation that had enacted legislation to give 160 acres of land out West to anyone who would settle it for five years. He took a deep breath and let it out slowly, silently cursing all corns. McClellan was his chosen general, and Lincoln was stuck with a plan of action his man favored. But he could not help thinking that the rebels would never be whipped by strategic moves, only by the cruelest kind of bloodletting. He would support his general so long as he acted as a general, but would withdraw that support, no matter what the cost, if ever the military leader presumed to act like a President.

CHAPTER 7

THE GATES OF RICHMOND

Mathew Brady's "Whatizzit Wagon" was stuck in the Virginia mud.

He had loaded it with the ingredients for collodion—guncotton, sulphuric ether, alcohol—and the necessary chemical excitants, along with a covered vat of silver nitrate solution in which to bathe each plate before loading it into the camera. With Alexander Gardner's help, and ignoring his assistant's complaints about being left behind to tend to the studio, Brady had packed the camera securely under the wagon seat. He had then overseen the wagon's loading onto a gunboat at the Navy Yard in Washington, and followed the water path of McClellan's army down the Potomac to the peninsula leading to Richmond.

The photographer, his wagon, and his horse had disembarked at Yorktown, recently surrendered by the slowly retreating rebels. He soon caught up to the Union Army, only to get his wagon bogged down axle-deep near the tents of McClellan's headquarters, next to a sign reading "Richmond, six miles." He cocked his head forward past Foons, the black man driving, and peered around; from the looks of the caissons and the curses of nearby artillerymen, it seemed to Brady that the same mud that stopped his Whatizzit Wagon had stopped the heavy cannons of the Army of the Potomac.

"We thought you'd never get here," said Pinkerton. The detective's boots made sucking sounds as he rocked back and forth in the mud. "The general's been asking about you. Too busy making money in the nation's capital?"

Brady wiped his hands on his well-smudged white linen smock, put his eyeglasses on—his eyesight, sadly, was getting steadily worse—and regarded the detective. Pinkerton, under a derby hat and flicking ashes from a cigar, looked especially smug on this warm, rainy morning in late May.

"Don't talk to me about money," the photographer snapped back. "This war is ruining the Brady Gallery. As soon as I pay Gardner his back wages, the man will quit. That's why I won't pay him."

"I see you managed to get your man Gardner in to see Rose Greenhow in the Old Capitol Prison," Pinkerton said, in an offhand way that Brady thought was too casual by half. "How'd you manage that?"

That touched a sore nerve. Brady decided to cross up Pinkerton by telling the truth: "Gardner did that on his own, last month when I was in the field."

"But weren't the Wild Rose and her sniveling litle brat supposed to be your subjects? You'd been after me to get to them since last September."

"I was a little irritated with Gardner about that," Brady admitted. More than a little; he had taken a historic picture, one of great human interest. "But he said that all of a sudden, Stanton gave him a pass."

Pinkerton smashed his fist in his palm. "I figured it was Stanton. He's trying to pull a fast one." Brady waited for the detective to tell the rest. "The Douglas widow got to him, I think, or Senator Wilson. Stanton wants to ship her back to Jeff Davis, get her out of our hair. But I won't let him. McClellan will personally object."

"What's it to McClellan if they let her go?"

"It matters to me. My best spy, Timothy Webster, was caught in Richmond. They're going to hang him. But maybe we can swap him for Rose." He pointed his cigar in the general direction of Richmond. "I want the damned secesh to know that if they hang our spy, we'll hang that spying bitch of theirs."

Brady shuddered; although Pinkerton sometimes gave the impression of being a caricature of a secret agent, it could not be denied that the man dealt in a grisly business. The photographer had learned, however, that he gained an advantage over the detective by refusing to take him seriously. If Pinkerton did not intimidate you, you intimidated him.

"Well, Gardner got his photograph," Brady gloomed, "and he'll probably sell a lot of them when he sets up for himself. He'll probably steal Timmy O'Sullivan as well—thirty-five dollars a week isn't good enough for him. That leaves me with the likes of Foons." He waved toward A. B. Foons, a freed negro who drove the wagon. Foons took fairly good pictures, too, but Brady was loath to admit to anyone that a good number of his photographs were the product of a camera operated by a black man. Magazines wanted the war pictures as the factual basis for their engravings, although everyone else with money to spend on images wanted little portraits on *cartes de visite*. Brady had popularized them but thought they were cheapening the art of photography.

"We're making history here," Pinkerton said expansively. "By sheer brilliant generalship, this army has been brought within shouting distance of Richmond with hardly any casualties."

"That's good," said Brady. He was not looking forward to taking more images of rows of dead bodies.

"That's strategy," said Pinkerton. "We bring up the artillery—takes a while—dig in to protect the guns, lay siege, and the rebs fall back toward Richmond. If we had gone Lincoln's way, overland from Manassas, frontal assaults all the way, there's no telling how many men we would have lost. Strategy, not butchery, that's McClellan's way."

Pinkerton ordered a few soldiers to assist Foons in freeing the Whatizzit Wagon and led the photographer to the telegraph tent. "We're in constant touch with Washington," he announced, then added in a worried voice, "what's the mood up there? We cannot trust what they tell us."

"I'll tell you, Pinkerton—" Brady began, but the detective winced and cut him off.

"Allen," he whispered.

"I try not to be familiar," Brady said, "by using first names, Allan, but if you—"

"Major E. J. Allen. That's what I go by, you know that."

"How is changing your name going to help your business after the war?"

"Never mind that, dammit, don't you realize this is a war zone? Secesh everywhere."

"Seems pretty quiet, actually."

"If you start with that 'all quiet on the Potomac' stuff, Brady," the detective gritted through his cigar, "I'll see to it that your contraption over there never gets out of the mud."

"The feeling in Washington is that we're winning the war," said Brady quickly. "Admiral Farragut and General Butler took New Orleans. Halleck finally used Grant's army to take Corinth. General Hunter captured Fort Pulaski down the coast, near the mouth of the Savannah. But as for McClellan—people are saying McClellan has the slows."

"I am aware of that figure of speech, Mr. Brady," said a deep voice at the entrance to the tent. George Brinton McClellan, silhouetted by the light behind him, a hand resting on the sword at his side, looked to the squinting Brady to be positively Napoleonic. " 'The slows' seems to be Mr. Lincoln's favorite expression. And yet here, with the spires of the enemy capital in sight, the decisive battle of the war is about to be fought."

"My report of the Washington mood is accurate, General," Brady told him. "I mean no disrespect, but you're expected to take Richmond any day now, reinforcements or not." Another thought, triggered by the general's words about the spires of the enemy capital, stirred his imagination. "Can you see Richmond from some high point around here?"

"Yes, from Mechanicsville. But soon as General McDowell's army arrives —forty thousand men, promised by the President to be here tomorrow—you, Mr. Brady, will be able to capture scenes inside Richmond."

"Will the city be put to the torch?" He wondered if a huge conflagration would provide enough light for a picture. Brady had not had much luck with nighttime photography.

McClellan glared. "Of course not—we're not barbarians. The object of this war, sir, is not to destroy the people and the homes of the South, but to reunite the Union. I think the President would agree, though much depends on who talks to him last." He turned to Pinkerton. "Any word from prisoners on enemy strength, Captain Allen?"

"Major Allen, sir. General Lee has one hundred and eighty thousand men to defend Richmond," said Pinkerton without hesitation. "During our assault on the city, General Jackson can be expected to move down from the Shenandoah with thirty-five thousand more."

"I have a hundred thousand men present for duty," McClellan told Brady. "You can see how important it is for McDowell's army to join me."

Brady discounted Pinkerton's estimates, which everybody knew had proved high in the past, and figured it would be a pretty even fight if both McDowell and Jackson arrived on schedule. Across the tent, a telegraph key started to chatter.

"If you were a military man," said McClellan, "you would be asking me

why I have my army straddling both sides of this confounded Chickahominy
River."

Brady went along: "Why is that, sir?"

"The position is terrible. We are extraordinarily vulnerable. But I have no
other choice." He pulled at his mustache in irritation. "The great military
minds up in Washington have ordered me to extend my right wing to the
north of Richmond, so as to hook up with McDowell's left wing when he
marches down from Manassas. On a map, it looks logical; but here on the
ground, as anyone can see, it incurs a senseless risk. Nobody thought this
stream would swell into a river."

"It hasn't rained this way down here for twenty years," Pinkerton added.

Brady heard the telegraph chatter. After a moment, the operator took a
message to the cipher man; while it was being decoded, McClellan waited
silently.

"Maybe this will be news of McDowell's arrival," Brady said hopefully. He
could pose "the two Mc's" right here; it was common knowledge that they
were rivals, and the picture of the two on the eve of a great victory would be
historic.

The message was handed to McClellan. He read it once, blanched, and
crumpled the paper in his hand. "It's from Lincoln. He has stopped McDowell and turned him around to help Banks go chasing after Jackson near Washington."

"Lincoln lost his nerve," said Pinkerton.

McClellan's face, at first unnaturally pale, began to redden. "Heaven save a
country governed by such counsels!"

"The President is said to be concerned," Brady said cautiously, "that
Stonewall Jackson might run up the Valley and sack Washington while we're
all down here."

"That imbecile cannot get it through his head that the entire purpose of
Jackson's movement is to make Lincoln panic and do exactly what he is
doing." The photographer blinked at that insubordination. "He is falling into
Jackson's trap!" the general choked. "Lincoln is denying me the means to
take Richmond and end the war."

The general fumed, paced about for a couple of minutes, then checked his
anger long enough to dictate a message to the President: "The object of
Jackson's movement is to prevent reinforcements being sent to me. All the
information from balloons, deserters, prisoners, and contrabands agrees—"
Pinkerton nodded vigorously—"that the mass of the rebel troops are still in
the immediate vicinity of Richmond, ready to defend it."

Brady presumed that Lincoln and Stanton were at the telegraph office in
the War Department. Although McClellan had often been accused of not
keeping Lincoln informed of his plans, Brady observed that the telegraph link
between the President and the field was remarkably close on this campaign.

In a few moments, the President wired back a description of the havoc
Jackson and his "foot cavalry" were wreaking on the Union forces in the
Shenandoah. The message from Lincoln added: "If McDowell's force was
now beyond our reach we should be entirely helpless. Apprehensions of something like this, and no unwillingness to sustain you, has always been my

reason for withholding McDowell's forces from you. Please understand this, and do the best you can with the forces you have."

"Idiots! Imbeciles!" McClellan shouted. He checked his outrage, stared at the ground for a moment, then asked, "Where's Lieutenant Custer?" His aide-de-camp with the flowing blond mustache appeared immediately. "Armstrong, you're always spoiling for action: take a detachment of cavalry across the Chickahominy at New Bridge. Draw fire, see if you can find out where they plan to come at us."

"The stream is still rising, sir—"

"I know that, but I know Joe Johnston—he will attack my force on the Richmond side as soon as he learns that Jackson's feint has succeeded and my reinforcements are not coming."

The telegraph operator showed him a communication from McDowell forwarded through the War Department. "Even McDowell!" the distraught general cried. "Look"—he showed Brady—"the good Republican, the radicals' pet, even Irvin McDowell thinks Lincoln is sending him on a wild-goose chase after Jackson. He calls Lincoln's order 'a crushing blow to us all.' Give him credit for being a military man—McDowell is enough of a general to know a feint when he sees one. But there's such panic in Washington that they won't even listen to him!"

Brady was astounded at the persistence and ferocity of McClellan in arguing with his commander in chief. The next message sent by McClellan to Lincoln contained more than a hint of future recrimination: "A desperate battle is before us; if any regiments of good troops remain unemployed it will be an irreparable fault committed."

Lincoln fired back: "I think the time is near when you must either attack Richmond or give up the job and come to the defense of Washington."

That sharp riposte stung the general; with ridicule in his voice, he read aloud the President's parting request: "Can you get near enough to throw shells into the city?"

No pleading by McClellan could induce Lincoln to grant him the reinforcing army he was certain was needed to take Richmond. Brady, knowing Lincoln to be a photographic subject who resisted directions to pose from the camera operator (only Gardner could wheedle him into assuming a less formal expression), tried to envision the furor on the other end of the telegraph line. The radicals were all insisting, certainly, that McClellan was a traitor willing to expose Washington to capture—or a coward unwilling to take the offensive against Richmond with the army on hand. Brady was no military man, but he had learned enough in the past year about military tactics to know that no general now tried to attack entrenched positions without at least equal numbers, and most insisted on a three-to-two edge.

Moreover, Brady had quickly learned that nobody here on the scene imagined that McDowell had the remotest chance of catching Stonewall Jackson —that harsh, lemon-sucking "bay'nets and grape" religious fanatic who whipped his rebel troops into a frenzy of quickstep marching. If Lincoln was wrong and McClellan right, the President's military misjudgment could cost the Union tens of thousands of lives—perhaps years of war.

"He is doing his best to sacrifice this army," McClellan said bitterly. Brady wished he were not there to hear such near-traitorous remarks, in case of a court-martial. "It is perfectly sickening to deal with such people. If Lincoln wants to storm Richmond with half an army, let him come and do it himself."

The general then took command of his disappointment. "Pinkerton, round up the staff for a picture in front of the headquarters tent. Mr. Brady, remember this as a moment of calm at the front during another panic back at the Executive Mansion." McClellan buttoned his tunic, ruminating aloud, "I witnessed that same cowardice in Washington not long ago when the *Merrimack* attacked us. Stanton and Lincoln lost their minds. But last week I outflanked the rebels at Norfolk and forced them to scuttle the *Merrimack*—so much for hysteria in high places."

In a controlled voice, he gave orders for his army to defend itself as best it could in its exposed position straddling the swollen stream. Brady noticed that McClellan, at work in his profession, appeared to know the exact disposition of his troops and their capabilities. When he was not embittered and insubordinate, the general seemed to Brady to be a confident commander.

"You really think," Pinkerton said, in a less than military way, "that Joe Johnston will stop falling back, and attack us?"

"He will because, for the first time, he's been given the chance." McClellan explained concisely how the Confederate commander had been forced to retreat steadily, unable to attack the inexorably advancing guns because the Union forces were constantly entrenched, and unable to hold his line because the superior artillery pounded him back. As in a chess match, Joe Johnston had no choice but to give up ground or he would lose his army. But now, with the Union force separated by the swollen stream in anticipation of linkage with an army that Lincoln had suddenly decided not to send, the rebel commander would surely see the Union vulnerability and launch an attack.

"Unless, of course," Brady said, overstepping himself but unable to stop, "you attack first." By risking all, McClellan might win; of course, if he lost, taking huge casualties in a vain assault at a superior force, the rebel army could then walk up to Washington relatively unopposed and end the war. Brady was glad the decision was not his.

McClellan shook his head slowly. "I dare not risk this army; I intend to make a sure thing of the capture of Richmond. And I will do it in my own time."

He turned to another aide, whose short gray hair contrasted with the slim, tall Custer's blond ringlets, and said crisply, "The mission you suggested is approved." To Brady, the general said, "I want you to copy a detailed map of an area north of the James River, in case I have to make a change of base."

That would have to be some maneuver, swinging a hundred-thousand-man army through the mud and across a river, around to a position that still menaced Richmond but was defensible and well supplied from the North. The civilian Brady could sense the danger of having an army destroyed in the middle of such a move.

The photographer had an assignment. He went outside the headquarters tent to see if he should set up his camera; the rain had stopped, but it was still too dark for clear pictures. He handed the map back to Pinkerton for safekeeping, arranging to take the picture of it midmorning of the next day. A photographer's ability to copy a map exactly made him welcome to generals in the field; certainly vanity played a part in most officers' willingness to put up with a civilian at headquarters, but the map-duplicating ability provided the military reason.

"You might want to look at the captured guns," Pinkerton called after him; "they're real guns." Evidently the detective recalled the Brady photographs of the "Quaker guns," logs made up to look like cannon, after the rebels abandoned the Potomac defenses. The photographer noted that people in government never forgot an embarrassment.

The older aide, who introduced himself as Colonel Key, approached him with a Brady *carte de visite*. "Do you recognize this man? This was taken in your studio."

Brady examined the picture and nodded. "Howell Cobb, of Georgia. I took that in my Broadway gallery about ten years ago, when he was Speaker of the House. There's a later picture, too, I think Gardner took in my Washington studio, when Cobb was Buchanan's Secretary of the Treasury."

Colonel Key nodded his thanks. "I want to be sure I'm dealing with the right man."

That struck Brady as curious. Howell Cobb had quit Buchanan to go South and organize the first congress of the Confederacy. He was very nearly selected to hold the post given to Jeff Davis, and was now a general in the rebel army. Brady handed back the old *carte de visite* and asked no questions.

CHAPTER 8

SUBMISSION AND AMNESTY

"Jeb Stuart's cavalry rode all the way around us, clear around the whole damn Army of the Potomac."

Colonel Thomas Key, moving at a slow trot toward his rendezvous with the Confederate representative near Mechanicsville, nodded silently to Lieutenant George Armstrong Custer, chief of the cavalry unit accompanying him.

"Colonel, do you have any idea what that cavalry ride does for the rebel army, even their infantry?"

"Gives their spirit a boost," Key allowed. "And I suppose it told them something about our weakness to the north. But now we know they know."

"Sir, it means that their new general, Lee, made us look like a pack of fools. We can't deny it was an act of courage." The young man was evidently heartsick. "Where was our cavalry?"

"It wasn't commanded by Lieutenant Custer," the colonel grinned at the rider at his side. Never let the blond ringlets fool you, Key told himself, the impetuous boy was also a brave man. On his first combat assignment, leading a small force of cavalry on a reconnaissance mission across the Chickahominy north of McClellan's headquarters, Custer had been first across the stream, first to open fire at enemy skirmishers, and last to leave the field. His probing helped alert the Federal forces to the attack by rebels at Seven Pines, south of the swollen stream. That short engagement was hailed by McClellan as a

victory for the North because the attack was repelled; it was notable for the
wounding of rebel General Joe Johnston, and his replacement by Robert Lee
commanding the Army of Northern Virginia.

Key was ready to forgive Custer his record of having been graduated last in
his West Point class the year before. Needed now was courage in cavalrymen,
such as that shown by the rebel Jeb Stuart in his swing clear around the
Union Army. Custer, in his baptism of fire, had proved he possessed that
requisite combination of recklessness, cunning, and luck; he would become a
good cavalry leader, if he didn't get himself killed before he turned twenty-
three.

The colonel could understand why George McClellan wanted the young
man at his side as one of the aides-de-camp: he was from an Ohio family,
suitably worshipful of the commander, and would carry out any order in the
heat of battle. McClellan's other aides—the Prince de Joinville and the
Comte de Paris—added panache and international depth to the headquarters
staff, although the presence of titled Frenchmen around the general was much
derided by the radicals in Congress. McClellan also was fortunate to have
Nellie Marcy McClellan's father, a regular army veteran, as chief of staff, and
—Key was realistic—to have Thomas Key, an experienced Ohio Democratic
political leader and judge, as his adviser on matters political. Such counsel
was indispensable to a future President. Key saw McClellan as following in
the footsteps of Washington, Jackson, and "Tippecanoe" Harrison: "vote as
you shot" was a slogan with wide appeal to veterans, and veterans would cast
the largest bloc of votes in the election of 1864.

"Pinkerton says that General Lee sent his son and his nephew to ride with
Stuart," said Custer gloomily. "That was a show of contempt for us, and a
display of faith by Lee. They're not calling him the 'King of Spades' or
'Evacuating Lee' anymore."

Key knew that General Lee, though a personal favorite of Jeff Davis, was
unpopular with troops, perhaps because he forced them to do "nigger work"
entrenching and building barricades. His record in the first year of this war
had been undistinguished. Would he be maneuvered out of Richmond, as Joe
Johnston would, when McClellan's big siege guns drew close enough to shell
the city to smithereens? Or would he throw his troops against the well-
entrenched Federals first, taking fearsome casualties and risking the war on a
single battle?

"I'm afraid Mac was too kindhearted about the rest of Lee's family," said
the colonel. Lee's wife and daughter had been cut off from the rebel forces
when Union troops overran the Lee family home, White House, and had
requested permission to return to Richmond. Against Key's better judgment,
McClellan ordered the women passed through, with a display of cordiality to
the rebel officer escorting them, an old army friend. That sort of chumminess
with the enemy did not set well with the radicals in Washington; the courtesy
was a political mistake, giving ammunition to those who suspected McClellan
of being a secret rebel sympathizer. But Mac would not think twice about
reuniting the Lee family, perhaps because he was naturally gallant, more
likely because he missed his own wife and child a bit too extravagantly.

"No, we're not at war with women and children," said Custer. "The general was right about that. It's just that—" he fiddled with his reins, appar-

ently uncomfortable at what he was about to say. "We did spend a hell of a lot of time in front of Yorktown. I sometimes wish we'd get on with the war."

The colonel shot him a sharp glance and laid down the policy: "The McClellan plan was to turn Yorktown immediately by the movement of McDowell's corps on the north bank of the York river. Lincoln's vacillation destroyed that plan, forced us to spend a month on the Peninsula uselessly, and kept us from taking Richmond in May."

"Yes, Colonel."

"Before General McClellan was absent from the intrigues of Washington for forty-eight hours," Key continued slowly, so that the young man would never forget if the Peninsula campaign was not successful, "his largest corps, commanded by his second-in-command McDowell, containing more than one forth of his army, assigned to a service which was vital to the success of his campaign, was detached from his command without consultation with him and without his knowledge. That was the first great crime of this war, and we can only hope that the nation will not be punished brutally for it."

He spurred to a gallop and his escort followed. Custer's doubts nettled him; Key had heard from his younger brother John, a major who worked in the War Department, that Stanton wanted this expedition to fail, and would do all in his power to see that the war was won another way by another, more radical general. The President's loss of patience, shown in his telegraph messages, was not so much the product of the slow advance as of the constant badgering from the radicals around him.

Key did not fool himself about McClellan, who erred, when he did, always on the side of caution. Such a general might not always win, but he rarely lost a battle, and such avoidance of mistakes won wars. Stanton's hatred was not irrational: McClellan's conduct of the war matched his political aim in the war, which was quite different from Lincoln's. McClellan wanted peaceful reunion, and it was hard for Key to tell now exactly what Lincoln wanted— perhaps total victory, with slavery abolished and the South occupied, breaking every promise he had made. Accordingly, McClellan sought to maneuver the rebels to surrender, by superior strategy while Lincoln wanted to bludgeon the rebels until they collapsed with some great lesson learned. Yet the two men, Lincoln and McClellan, were both sides of the same preserve-the-Union coin, and Key thought the combination promised a compromise in the war's goals.

The mud had hardened under the mid-June sun; it was not yet dry enough for the horsemen to raise dust, but the improving condition of the roads augured well for the movement of heavy artillery. At Gaines's gristmill, the riders passed men of the 16th New York picking and shucking ears of corn on that sunny Sunday morning. The work was for their own dinner; in an army led by George McClellan, the Sabbath was observed.

"There's Richmond!" Custer shouted, pointing to the spires visible through the trees. Down a long slope, the road led for five miles into the city. The land alongside the road was studdéd with thick mounds of earth protecting cannon; Lee, the King of Spades, had been at work. They rode into Mechanicsville, a country crossroads of a town turned into an army camp, garrisoned by the 4th New Jersey Volunteers, overlooking the swamped bed of the Chickahominy.

Key drew to a halt, brought out a white cloth that would serve as a flag, and knotted it to a broom handle. Feeling an exhilarating tightness in his chest—this could be a turning point in the nation's history, and much might depend on Thomas Key's political sense—the colonel told Custer and the escort to wait where they stood. He guided his horse down to the broken bridge agreed upon as the meeting site, dismounted, and planted his white flag in front of a shanty a few feet from the Union side. He ordered the two Union pickets inside to leave.

As he watched, a figure approached, carrying a white flag. His face soon was recognizable as the man in Mathew Brady's *carte de visite*, with a heavy brown beard added. General Howell Cobb paused for his escort to lay a plank across the hole in the bridge, then walked to the shanty alone.

Cobb and Key shook hands and went inside. Before their talk could begin, it was interrupted by a knock and the opening of the shack door.

"Colonel Simpson, Fourth New Jersey, charge of pickets," the officer announced. Key had not made advance arrangements with the local commander, hoping to lessen the possibility of an advance report to Washington that might trigger an order canceling his plans; he counted on his headquarters cavalry escort to be evidence of his credentials.

"Colonel Key, of General McClellan's staff," he said to the New Jersey man. "I am here holding a conversation with General Howell Cobb. Permit me to introduce you."

The colonel in charge of pickets peered at the face of the Confederate general and surprised him by asking, "The former Secretary of the Treasury?"

"Yes." Cobb smiled. "I once held that position in the United States Government."

"I used to see you in Washington, where I had business with your office. You've become so metamorphosed by that beard, I'd hardly know you."

"We all seem to be fighting under masked faces," said Cobb, which Key thought a singular thing to say, as if the Southern leader doubted the sincerity of the men espousing the issues behind the war.

"We are discussing an exchange of prisoners," Key told the inquiring officer, who plainly did not like being surprised by a truce parley on his watch, "under the authority of General Dix." The name of the Union general in charge of prisoner exchanges satisfied him, and the picket colonel withdrew.

"Dix succeeded me at Treasury," Cobb observed affably. "Fine man, good Democrat. Better than most in that woebegone Buchanan Cabinet."

"President Buchanan wanted you to run for the Democratic nomination to succeed him, didn't he?" Key had studied Cobb's background: fighter against the Calhoun secessionists in 1849, compromise Speaker of the House, pro-Union Governor of Georgia, a Southerner who left the Union with a heavy heart to organize the Confederacy. Admired and trusted by many old friends in Washington, and now stationed with the rebel leaders in Richmond, Howell Cobb was the perfect man with whom to explore peace negotiations.

"Buck was for any Democrat who could beat Stephen Douglas. Breckinridge had the better chance, so we both backed him." He shook his beard. "Seems like so long ago. What's on your mind? Not just prisoners, I take it."

"Permanent peace."

"You could have that within half an hour," Cobb replied instantly. "Take your army and go home."

Key carefully disclaimed any representation of an official character, pretending to be holding a private conversation after a discussion of prisoner exchange; for the record, Cobb did the same, noting that it would then be possible for each of them to report the entire conversation to the commanding generals. His heart beating fast, Key then went to the heart of the matter: with a Union army within six miles of the rebel capital, under what circumstances would the South agree to a cessation of hostilities?

"A treaty of peace could be agreed on at once," said Cobb more formally, "but reunion? Only by subjugation or extermination of the South. Your invasion has created in the Southern mind such feelings of animosity, such a spirit of resistance, that reunion could only be effected by permanent military occupation."

"Your statement surprises and grieves me, sir." Key had not expected a more forthcoming response; they had to feel their way, neither showing weakness. "I had hoped that you, at least, would be impressed by a sense of the hopelessness of the struggle. The contest is unequal: the North has the greater numbers, wealth, credit and resources of all kinds. The border states, on which you based such hope, have established their loyalty. Union sentiment still exists throughout the South—"

"Stop there," Cobb said. "Outside the foreign element in New Orleans, no Union sentiment is left anywhere in the planting region of the South. The slaves have never been so tractable as now. The military strength of the Confederacy is unbroken, and you have not the power to force entrance into Richmond."

"You will fight to hold Richmond? The city will be destroyed."

"Personally, I am opposed to defending the town," said Cobb with frankness that surprised Key, "but my superiors are determined to do so. But what does it mean if you take Richmond, and every other major city in the South? You would gain nothing—organized military resistance will never be suppressed. You would be compelled to hold the country by occupation, and every military position would be surrounded and harassed by a hostile population."

Key refused to accept that. "I do not believe the free white citizens of the South are opposed to the United States Government. I believe secession is the scheme of a class of men who arrogated to themselves superior social position in order to grasp and hold political power." It had not been his intention to get this hard this quickly, but Key plunged ahead. "If your view of the future holds, we will have to disorganize the condition of society that gives rise to that class of men, and to raise up an order of laboring men and middle-class white men who would be loyal to the Union."

"You will never, damn your eyes, find men in any of the seceding states who will be made into a loyal class."

"Then we will find some to move there on our invitation."

"You've made my point, Colonel Key. You can only reunify by military occupation, which, believe me, will be a bloody business for a generation."

Stymied, Key drew a deep breath and tried again. "Sir. Your intelligent people know that they are fighting their friends. Neither the President, the

Army nor the people of the loyal states have any wish to subjugate the Southern states or diminish their constitutional rights."

"Really? Talk to John Breckinridge."

"Our soldiers exhibit little animosity toward yours," Key pressed on. "On both sides, the men fight only because it is their duty. On what grounds can you justify continuance of this bloodletting between brothers?"

"The election of a sectional President, whose views on slavery were known to be objectionable to the whole South," snapped Cobb. "How about those for grounds?"

"But the slavery question has been settled! It is abolished in the District and excluded from the territories. As an element of dissension, slavery cannot again enter into our national politics." Key could sense interest in his interlocutor and developed the position. "The President has never gone beyond this in any expression of his views. He has always recognized the obligation of the constitutional provision as to fugitive slaves, and that slavery within and between the slave states is beyond congressional intervention."

"Our papers say Lincoln is preparing a declaration of radical views on slavery," the Georgian observed, apparently looking for some common ground.

"Toleration of slavery where it exists is the political creed of the great body of the Republican Party. No political organization in the North of respectable numbers would propose violation of the Constitution on slavery."

Cobb thought about that. "Judge—that is, Colonel Key," he said, appearing to slip, "I have every respect for the three centers of political power you have referred to: the President, the Army, and the people of the North. Speaking just as a reasonable man, and with the clear understanding that no official representation is being made or considered, do you have a specific suggestion in mind?"

"Submission and amnesty," Key said, having discussed the proposal with General McClellan. "Proclamations to that effect by Mr. Davis and Mr. Lincoln would be sustained by the great mass of the whole nation."

Cobb sighed. "No Confederate leader could openly advocate such a position and continue to live. The moment he uttered it, he would be slain." He rose to go. "The South cannot now return to the Union without degradation. The blood that has been shed has washed out all feelings of brotherhood. We must now become independent or conquered."

At the broken bridge, Cobb remarked to Key on the world of difference between Union generals: how Butler in New Orleans offended every notion of Southern womanhood with his abusive orders, and how McClellan had graciously offered his protection to the wife and daughter of General Lee. Key replied he was glad to be serving under McClellan.

Although Lieutenant Custer was dying to know what had gone on in the shanty, Key told him nothing on the ride back to headquarters. Alone with the general, he summarized the meeting that had shaken his confidence in their ability to shape the peace: "First, the rebels are in great force at Richmond, and mean to fight a general battle in defense of it."

"I shall make the first battle mainly an artillery combat, push them in upon Richmond, then bring up my heavy guns, shell the city, and carry it by assault."

Key nodded, hoping the rebels would wait until the Army of the Potomac was ready. "Second, the Confederate leaders do not have the power to control the secession movement they launched," he reported, thinking of Cobb's prediction of death to any leader who proposed submission and amnesty. "Finally, there is little hope of peace and reconstruction so long as the rebels have a large army in the field anywhere."

McClellan nodded grimly. "You assured him of my views on abolition? That they should have no fears of loss of property?"

Key surprised himself with his next conclusion: "In particular states, I now think it may be necessary to destroy the class that created this rebellion—and the only way to do that will be to destroy the institution of slavery."

The general looked puzzled—Key had never spoken with such pessimism before—then shook his head. "That kind of talk, or any such declaration by Lincoln, would make peace negotiations impossible. Never forget, Judge, our goal is to force a settlement of this conflict in a way that reunites the nation. Let's see what they say after we take Richmond. Write a report of your meeting and I'll send it to Stanton to give the President."

"I don't think that would be such a good idea," said Key. Did McClellan fully realize what they had done, in approaching the Confederacy about peace terms without prior approval from the President? Lincoln had not hesitated to humiliate Generals Hunter and Frémont for overreaching his authority in declaring captured slaves "forever free" and prolonging the war; what would he do to a general and his aide-de-camp for overreaching in the other direction?

"I am not in the least ashamed of trying to end this war without further bloodshed," said the general. "Nor can the President legitimately object. I must save the country, and cannot respect anything that stands in the way. Write your report, Judge. I'll make sure Stanton shows it to Lincoln."

CHAPTER 9

ROSE ON TRIAL

General John Dix considered this assignment the most odious since the arrest of the Maryland legislators on their way to Frederick to vote for secession. He was to preside at a "commission hearing"—an official but extralegal trial—designed to extract from Rose O'Neal Greenhow, his longtime close friend, a confession of treason.

Secretary Stanton, with whom Dix had served in the Buchanan Cabinet—Stanton Attorney General, Dix at Treasury—had made the stakes clear.

"McClellan and that idiot detective Pinkerton, who has created whole armies of nonexistent rebels," Stanton had told him, waving his spectacles in agitation, "want to hold her hostage for one of Pinkerton's spies caught in Richmond. If they do hang the Pinkerton man, I don't want to have to hang Rose. I would prefer to ship her down to her traitor friends in Richmond."

"She would have a lot to say about a great many important people, stand-

General John Adams Dix

ing there on the gallows," Dix agreed, and was not surprised when Stanton shuddered at both ends of that grisly thought.

"But she has to cooperate," Stanton had said. "I'm leaving that to you. You knew her as well as I did—or do. Mrs. Stanton and I were no strangers to her home." Dix suspected that Mrs. Stanton, like Mrs. Dix, had rarely accompanied her husband to Rose's salon in the old days. "Get her to confess, Dix, and if that fails, at least to promise not to engage in further anti-Union activity. Get something from her, anything, that will give me an argument against McClellan. We don't want to keep her, we don't want to hang her."

Extracting a face-saving confession from the Wild Rose would not be easy. Dix knew the time urgency as well as Stanton; Pinkerton and Colonel Thomas Key of McClellan's staff had come up from headquarters in the Peninsula to urge Dix, as the man in charge of prisoner exchanges, to intercede with Richmond for the life of Timothy Webster, sentenced to hang as a spy in Richmond. That was a major request, since prisoner exchanges, except for high officers or political figures, were frowned on by Lincoln: the North had more men to spare than the South. But Colonel Key was persuasive in showing how Webster's case was unique, and Dix, concerned about pressure that would surely come to hang Rose Greenhow in retaliation for any extreme punishment meted out to Pinkerton's man, sought the approval of the President and his Cabinet.

Stanton had pushed through the plea to avert future agitation from Pinkerton and radicals alike to hang Rose; accordingly, Dix had sent a message to the rebels that leniency toward Pinkerton's man would be matched in dealing with Confederate spies caught in the North. Now, if the rebels would be reasonable, and if the undefeated Rose would come down off her high horse, John Dix could carry out his government's wishes and his own. Two big "ifs."

Rose's trial, called a hearing, was held in one of the elegant old houses of Washington, now converted to government use. The irony of the setting was not lost on Dix: Rose and he—and Buck and Breck, and the Stantons and the Cobbs—had attended many parties in this mansion, home of a former California senator, where secession had been a topic of heated after-dinner debate among friends. He'd had his share of arguments here with Rose and others, but always as members of a civilized society distressed by the chasm opening between them.

Now a soldier stood guard where a black butler had once greeted guests. Other men in uniform lounged and talked idly in rooms that had once sparkled with laughter, good wine, and better conversation. He noticed that the furnishings were showing signs of wear; a long velvet drape had been removed to let in more light, revealing paint scars on the walls.

Dix sat at a table with Edwards Pierrepont, a civil judge and ardent abolitionist present for appearance's sake, and a court reporter. He sent for Mrs. Greenhow, who had been held in a room upstairs. When she appeared, Dix's heart sank: she was dressed in ruffled black, still in mourning, a lace snood holding graying hair in place, her face haggard but set in defiance. The Wild Rose had changed almost as much as their world had. He stood and looked at her in sadness.

"Gentlemen, resume your seats," she said. "I recognize the embarrassment of your position. This is a mimic court, and I shall answer or not, according to my own discretion."

Dix wanted the record to show that no special treatment had been granted the accused, nor any acquiescence given to her rebellious statements. "Madam, you are charged with treason."

"I deny it, sir, most emphatically." She sat straight in the wooden chair, looking at him squarely. "You are the minister of a President who has violated the Constitution, destroyed the personal rights of every citizen, and inaugurated and provoked revolution."

"You are charged with providing military information to the enemy in wartime," Dix said, not to be put on the defensive. He held up a letter to a Confederate officer that had been seized in her home, which detailed the disposition of troops quartered around Washington. Dix knew it to be accurate, down to the exact location of his headquarters on the Maryland side. "Do you deny writing this?"

She examined the document and tossed it back on the table. "That is not my writing. Guests come to my house; they may leave things behind. I cannot be held responsible."

"The charge," Judge Pierrepont put in, "is not that you wrote this in your hand, but that you caused it to be transmitted through your agency to a rebel general."

"I am nobody's agent," she said firmly, evading the question. She looked at the man taking notes and demanded to know why he was there. "Is this to be given to the newspapers? Am I to be made a spectacle of?"

Dix knew she was hoping these proceedings would be made public, and a spectacle was precisely what she wanted to be. He ached to be able to tell her she did not understand the danger she was in, that her defiance might make headlines but might also hang her.

"Your testimony is being taken down for the War Department," he said, "and may be used in convicting you of treason. Do you understand that?" Dix was no pettifogging lawyer; when arresting rebel sympathizers on Election Day six months before, he had felt no qualms in declaring the reason for his action "to prevent the ballot-boxes from being polluted by treasonable votes," but today's use of the military power to coerce a prisoner, even a spy, distressed him.

Rose seemed to sense that. "How pleasant a duty you gentlemen have to perform."

"The evidence is incontrovertible, madam," Dix told her, "that you have been holding communication with the enemy. It is here in front of me, stacks of it." Pinkerton had intercepted most, though not all, of her mail.

"If it were true," she said, admitting nothing, "you could not be surprised at it. I am a Southern woman. Everyone I have known and respected has been driven from this city by a ruthless despotism. It would be natural for me to be in touch with those you call the enemy."

"How is it, madam, in spite of the vigilance exercised over you, that you have managed to communicate with the enemy?"

"That is my secret, sir. If it be any satisfaction to you to know it, I shall, in the next forty-eight hours, make a report to my government at Richmond of this farcical trial for treason."

Judge Pierrepont interrupted his questioning. "Thousands of young men lost their lives as a result of the information you supplied to those in armed rebellion. There is no more serious offense in law, Mrs. Greenhow. This trial today is no farce."

"The South has caused no loss of life, sir. The South seceded from this Union peaceably. All we want is our independence from the tyranny of abolitionists, who have told us we cannot continue under the Constitution as it was. We are declaring our independence just as our grandfathers did when English tyranny became unbearable."

She leaned forward, speaking slowly as if repeating an explanation she had given her young daughter. "We are not invading the North; the North is invading the South. We are not pillaging your cities; you are pillaging ours.

We want to be left alone; you want to conquer and destroy. The blood of soldiers at Bull Run is on your hands, gentlemen, not on mine."

"Do not assume a position of high morality, madam," Judge Pierrepont shot back. "The South wants to break the compact that binds this nation for the most reprehensible of reasons—to preserve and extend human slavery, which is the most degrading cause any group of selfish zealots ever fought for."

"There you are," Rose said triumphantly, "the basis of the attack on the South—not to 'preserve the Union,' as you keep pretending, but to abolish our way of life. What do you know, sir, about the treatment of Africans in the South? You believe those horror stories that Mrs. Stowe writes to sell her books. Our colored servants are well cared for—we have good reason to care for them, they are valuable property. What do you offer them?"

"Freedom," said the judge.

Dix wished Pierrepont had not allowed himself to be drawn into this. Their job was not to get Rose angry or get her to incriminate herself; their purpose was to work out an arrangement that would give the government some satisfaction with her penitence, and to grant the clemency that would send her into exile.

"With white Southern men at the front," Rose flashed, the familiar throaty power returning to her voice, "you offer black slaves the temptation to rise up and attack women and children. Do you have any idea of the horror and carnage your talk of 'freedom' is sure to bring on?"

Dix held up his hand, but he knew there was no stopping her short of physical restraint.

"And if you should conquer us, which God forbid, what will you do with your four million Africans? Will you take them into your Northern cities, welcome them, let them have the jobs that white workers want and need? No —your kindly abolitionists will be the first to try to ship them off somewhere, back to Africa, down to the hell of Santo Domingo. Or you'll try to hold them in the South, uncared for, incapable of fending for themselves, ruining their lives just as you want to crush out the honor of every Southerner."

"Don't talk to us about honor—" Pierrepont began, but Rose stood up and stared him down.

"That's your 'freedom,' " she flung at him. "Freedom to starve, or freedom to be driven away from home and loved ones. Why do you suppose the vast majority of blacks in the South support our armies, and turn a deaf ear to the blandishments of abolitionists? Because they know they are better off with us than with your 'freedom.' "

"How can you, a mother, tolerate a slave auction that tears families apart, treats children like animals—"

"Lies! Have you ever seen the way slave families live, and are bred, in the South? You're the one who will break up families, driving the women into poorhouses and brothels, the men from city to city looking for jobs you'll never let them have. Don't talk to me about families—with Lincoln's invasion, you've broken up more homes in a few months than happened in a hundred years of slavery!"

"I don't think we can settle that argument here, Rose," Dix said wearily.

After a long silence marked by Pierrepont's angry stare and Rose's labored breathing, he approached the central point.

"I would like to be able to recommend clemency, if proper admission is made and penitence is shown." He could see her hackles rising and hurried on, setting aside the requirement for a penitence that would never come. "If we were to offer you the opportunity to go South, would you be willing to sign a confession and declaration that you will undertake no further disloyal acts against this government?"

"I have never been disloyal to the Constitution of the United States," Rose Greenhow said. "I will sign nothing that admits to having been a traitor."

"It's called a 'parole of honor,' " Dix tried, modifying and prettifying the offer. "Confederate soldiers, to be exchanged, sign a parole of honor not to fight again—"

"I will not swear an oath knowing I will violate it. When I am free of the cruel and inhuman imprisonment inflicted upon me, I will do all in my power to help the Confederate states gain their lawful independence."

Dix slumped back in his chair; the stubborn woman was putting her neck in a noose.

Judge Pierrepont turned to Dix, and signaled the stenographer to stop taking notes. "General, you know this woman. Why don't you talk to her privately?"

Dix took Rose to a room upstairs. "For God's sake, Rose, you're killing yourself. And you're ruining your daughter's life. Be sensible—"

She sat down and looked at him, chest beginning to heave, hot tears in her eyes.

"You think I want to stay in that hellhole? Do you know what it's like? Do you have any idea what I have to go through just to keep their filthy hands off my darling girl?"

Dix gave her his handkerchief and walked around the room as she composed herself. After a while, she said, "I'm not a martyr. I want to get out. I just cannot sign anything that makes a mockery of everything I believe in. I will not let you defeat me."

"Rose, this is me, John Dix, remember? I'm not trying to defeat you."

"I don't mean you, John, you're a good and kind man. I mean Stanton and Pinkerton."

"Stanton is trying to help you."

"Watch out for him, John, he's not like you, he's an evil man. I know him, better than you do, better than most people. There is something wrong in his head—no, not like Henry Wilson, but wrong in another way—he has always frightened me. A man like him should never be in power."

"For whatever reason, I assure you he's trying to get you out. Others want to hang you, Rose. I mean that. Hang you."

Her figure sagged in her chair. He was sorry he had to put the fear of execution in her, but it was better that she know the danger she faced.

"I don't want to die," she said. "And I can't take much more of that jail, John. The prisoner who protected me at nights was killed by a sentry last week. For no reason—he was standing by the window, singing, and they shot him dead. Then they took the lock off my door."

"Sign a parole, Rose."

"No!" She flared and then relented. "How can I get out without signing anything?"

He picked that up. "Will you go South immediately? Will you"—he reached for a way to put it delicately—"continue to be discreet about those who tried to help you?"

She nodded. "Just don't make me sign anything or promise anything."

"You're not making it easy, Rose." He sought some opening. "If not a confession, some expression of regret at the loss of life—"

She seemed not to hear him. "Remember this house, John? The parties, the people. Only a year or so ago."

"That whole world is gone."

"Christmas last year, before the war, I walked around this very room, candle in hand, caroling. I walk around the prison room now, with a candle, burning the bugs off the walls." She stood up. "General Dix, I must return to my daughter. I will admit to no treason but I am willing to leave my home, this center of tyranny, at the earliest moment. If they cannot get me out right away, tell Stanton and Wilson and my pretty niece Addie Douglas to come and visit me in the prison. It intimidates the superintendent."

"You're not helping me to help you, Mrs. Greenhow." Dix had to add, "I cannot find it in myself to threaten you, but believe me, you're in danger. I don't want to see a woman like you on the gallows."

"Used to be quite a belle," she smiled, touching his cheek and leading the way downstairs.

At the foot of the stairs, before reentering the drawing room being used as a courtroom, she shook his hand formally and used that moment to say: "I will never swear to stop fighting for the Confederacy. If you can send me South without your damned parole, I will go. Whatever you do, I suggest you move quickly."

Dix started to say he could imagine how terrible prison life was for a woman and daughter, but Rose waved that aside. "A new prisoner came in this morning," she whispered, "captured in a skirmish on the Peninsula. He was in Richmond a few days ago. Pinkerton's man Webster, who was trying to find out the Confederate troop strength, was hanged as a spy."

CHAPTER 10

John Hay's Diary
June 19, 1862

An auspicious if unnoticed day: the Prsdt signed the bill abolishing slavery in the U.S. territories. I took the document in to him when the messenger from the Congress arrived, and the Tycoon looked at it and shook his head and said nothing.

He must have thought back to all the debates with Stephen Douglas over "popular sovereignty," or the so-called right of new states to adopt slavery, versus "no extension," the position that lost Lincoln the '58 senatorial election in Illinois. Everyone agrees now that it won him a national position in the Republican party, but we did not do any celebrating at the time.

He used a good figure of speech in those days, equating slavery with a snake. If a snake were in the bed with children, he could not strike at it; but it made no sense to put a snake in a bed with children. That is, he could not abolish slavery in the South, where it already existed, but we should prevent its spread to new states in the West.

So today he signed it quietly, and now the argument is over: "pop sov" is dead—no snakes in the territories. Thanks to the war, the argument has now become whether to strike the snake in the bed with the children of the South.

Senator Sumner came in, not to say thanks for taking this step, but to make a case for reconsecrating the Fourth of July with a presidential declaration of general emancipation.

"Too big a lick now," said the Tycoon.

"It is a time for big licks," Sumner insisted. "People in the North are losing heart about an endless war for no higher moral aim than to stick together. Do it, Lincoln!"

Lincoln told him: "I would do it if I were not afraid that half the officers would fling down their arms."

Exit Sumner with his usual dramatic tossing of the locks. He doesn't realize that we have just had a communication from one of McClellan's politician-officers, a Colonel Key, in which he proudly recounts his unauthorized attempt to make peace on the basis of the Democrats' "Union as it was."

This fellow Key, who they say is McClellan's "evil genius," has the audacity, or gall—again, the insolence of epaulets—to write of the sources of power in this republic as "the President, the Army, and the people." That's McNapoleon and his coterie for you. The Prsdt told Stanton to answer coldly that such peace discussions were not the business of the army.

A sinking sensation is being felt all around. The euphoria of this spring, with Grant on the march in the West and McClellan finally on the way to Richmond, has given way to a vast disillusionment. Shiloh was a bloody standoff, followed by Halleck's mile-a-day creep into Corinth and the escape of Beauregard's army. Now Little Mac is encamped in front of Richmond, demanding reinforcements before he will budge, trying to make peace instead of war. Meanwhile, a rebel army under Stonewall Jackson has been scaring Washington half to death, and the Tycoon cannot release McDowell's army to play McClellan's game.

So the feeling has set in that the war may not be over this summer after all. Pessimism pervades. The only action taken so far against General Lee has been to seize his house across the river here in Arlington, which he inherited from General Washington's son. We have turned it into a Union hospital.

Stanton came in around noontime, with Senators Wade and Chandler in tow, to belabor the Tycoon about the man who is failing to take the rebel capital.

"McClellan, the damn traitor," said Ben Wade, "refuses to assault Richmond. Instead, he's trying to strip Washington of defenses so Jackson can grab and sack this city."

"Damn right," said Chandler. "And the chairman of the Democratic committee up in New York has been sending McClellan telegrams."

"McClellan is being urged to disregard interference by the Administration in army matters," said Stanton, who gets to read private telegrams, "and to act on his own judgment. Said he would be sustained by the people of the North, tired of having military affairs directed by civilians in Washington."

"A man isn't responsible for messages that are sent to him," Lincoln said mildly, having received quite a few about Wade himself.

"We need a general who will fight rebels," said Wade, "and who will fight slavery."

"Who do you have in mind?"

Instead of saying "anybody," to which Lincoln always replies, "I must have somebody," Wade said, "John Pope. Hero of the capture of Island Number Ten." That victory was mainly the navy's. "With Halleck at Corinth in the West. A proven fighter, and a hater of slavery."

"I like his dispatches," said Chandler. "Datelines say, 'Headquarters in the saddle.' Man on the move, action, all that."

The Prsdt chewed that over. "If Pope's headquarters are in the saddle," said Lincoln, "then he's got his hindquarters where his headquarters ought to be."

Nobody laughed but me; the joke wasn't original, but I thought it was pretty funny.

"There has to be an end to this kid-glove warfare," said Wade. "We're going to give you a new Confiscation Act that will strike some fear in traitor hearts. And a Militia Act to enroll negroes for any war service in which they may be competent, and that means as soldiers."

The Tycoon countered with his litany: abolition had to be gradual, even if it took until 1900, though better much sooner; accompanied by due compensation; and finally, joined to a scheme of colonization.

"That's what you say," replied Wade, "and that's what your man Browning keeps haranguing us with in the Senate. But the notion that you and you alone will decide the issue is illegitimate and unconstitutional. The Congress will decide how and when the slaves will be freed."

When the senators marched out, Zack Chandler weaving a little, Stanton suggested that arming negroes might not be a bad idea. "General Hunter was doing it—without my knowledge, of course."

Somehow that little disclaimer made me suspect that Stanton knew beforehand of Hunter's intent to free the Africans in his area. Does the Tycoon suspect this also? He seems like such a trusting soul, but that is what he wants to seem like.

"How is your sick baby?" Lincoln asked Stanton.

"Not getting better."

The Tycoon never ceases to amaze me. Here is the Secretary of War as much as advertising that he was lying about not knowing about Hunter's embarrassing proclamation freeing the slaves; and there is Lincoln, who had to write an order countermanding that military proclamation so as to keep the issue tightly in his own hands, inquiring about a matter weighing on Stanton's mind, the illness of his baby.

Which reminds me: Tad is not sleeping on the couch in the office during the evenings anymore, to be carried off to bed when the Tycoon finishes, because the family is now spending the summer in the Soldiers' Home. Cooler there than here in the District, where the miasma from Foggy Bottom reaches into everybody's brain during the summer.

That move to Silver Spring led to another problem: everyone grumpily accepted the Hellcat's prohibition against the Marine Band performing at the White House during her mourning for Willie, but now that she is away, she still insists the band not play. The locals objected, as well they might, and I suggested a compromise: having the band give evening concerts in Lafayette Park across the avenue. The first Lady grumbled, but her husband did not want to have her even less popular than she is with the people. So the band will play.

After Stanton left, Bates came bumbling along with what he described to me as a draft of a pamphlet by Miss Carroll denouncing the Confiscation bill that Wade, Chandler & Co. seemed determined to place on our desks.

I was glad to hear that: she was in here last week, saw the Tycoon, and went past me in departing like the proverbial bat out of hell. He was more than a little upset himself; probably spoke to her the way he did to Jessie Frémont, another woman not easily beaten down. One thing about the Tycoon, he is not courtly when it comes to women; to put a good face on it, as one day I will be called on to do, he treats them like the equals of men.

At any rate, Miss Carroll's draft means that Bates will not have to cook up a veto message by himself, which the Prsdt was worried about. He needs a persuasive argument, not a dusty legal tome. I mean, if the army's officer corps is going to make the decisions about enlisting slaves (McClellan against, Hunter for), and our most illustrious warrior turns out to be a political peacemaker, and the Congress is going to arrogate emancipation policy to itself, then what's a President for?

The Attorney General came out with a note from Lincoln addressed to Miss Carroll; Bates wrote a covering note and asked me to dispatch the letter immediately.

I read it. "Dear Miss Carroll," the Prsdt wrote, "Like everything else that comes from you, I have read the address to Maryland with a great deal of pleasure and interest. It is just what is needed now, and you were the one to do it."

That should cool her ire. She can wave the Prsdt's praise around and pick up some railroad pamphleteering business, I hope. The nation needs her, and more to the point, on a matter that I am too pressed to go into now, I need her, too.

CHAPTER 11

COUNTERATTACK

Breckinridge hefted his traveling bag and stepped off the train at Richmond, a city without a unified train depot. Instead of a union station, five individual lines each had a small siding to discharge riders. Breck had heard one passenger say ruefully that the only agreement between the lines was that one train left before the competition's arrived, which made connections impossible.

He looked in vain for a carriage to take him to the Fenlon Hotel near the Executive Mansion. It was shift-for-yourself in the besieged capital. General Breckinridge supposed that every military wagon had been pressed into service supplying the city's defenders four miles east, and he set out on foot. The city was familiar to him, but war had changed Richmond drastically: pedestrians were hurrying, dust permeated clothes and lungs, and the charming prewar town had acquired an ugly look of transience as war more than doubled its population.

Jefferson Davis had sent for him but had not given any reason. Breck knew the President of the Confederate States from their years of service together in the U.S. Senate, and thought more highly of his character than of his political skill. Not only did Davis lack the common touch, but he could not spellbind a crowd from a stump; in private, his cadaverous face made him seem more severe than he was. But the Kentuckian considered Davis a loyal ally who would not desert friends when political fortunes changed or when the press turned vicious. Breckinridge remembered the Davis reaction to complaints that the retreating Sidney Johnston was no general: "If Sidney Johnston is not a general, then we have no generals."

Shifting his bag to his other arm, stepping around a dead horse in the street —both capitals had those rotting landmarks in common, he noted—Breck recalled Davis's kindnesses to Anna Carroll when that woman was starting to develop her connections in the railroad industry. Breckinridge hoped she was gaining the recognition she sought; he knew the Tennessee River plan had been all too successful.

In the ten weeks since Shiloh, Breckinridge had developed a curious lethargy, rooted in his unhappy conviction that the South was going to lose the war. The loss of his own life in it did not seem so earthshaking to him; because of this, and because he became angrily resentful of the death of men who served under his command, the Kentuckian took more chances under fire than a wise general should. That had gained him a reputation for personal bravery at Shiloh and on the slow retreat to Corinth, and had earned him the promotion that he supposed brought him to Richmond.

He was careful not to let his numbness toward personal survival infect his son; Breck was ready at any time to make a deal with the God of war to meet a Minié ball anywhere if he could be assured that Cabell would live through the war. After the boy's escape from Donelson, Breck assigned him to be his

aide-de-camp, determined to let him see the action that would satisfy him
without gettting himself killed.

Now the Orphan Brigade of Kentuckians, the only brigade of volunteers
from a state that had not seceded from the Union, was to join in the fight to
deny the use of the Mississippi River to the Federal forces. Memphis had
fallen; Island No. 10 had fallen; New Orleans had surrendered without a
fight. Only the guns of Vicksburg remained as an obstacle to the Federal
seizure of the great western waterway. He belonged with them in Vicksburg
now, but President Davis wanted him in Richmond for a few days, ostensibly
to personally award him the stars of a major general. No other politician had
received such a promotion.

A sergeant driving what had once been an elegant carriage but was now a
makeshift ambulance spotted the brigadier's star on his uniform, saluted, and
invited him up. "Where from, sir?"

"Out West." He shielded his eyes from the dust. When the sergeant said
Richmond was his home, Breckinridge put an odd question to him: "Why do
you suppose we make our capital so close to the front? Wouldn't the Confederacy have been better off in Montgomery, or Atlanta?"

The sergeant chewed that over, as if being tested on a matter of strategy.
He answered, "Works both ways. Concentrating our forces here keeps the
Yankees worried about Washington. Besides, if we lost the Iron Works yonder, and the iron mills all around here, it'd all be over quick. Lose Richmond,
lose the war."

Breckinridge shook his head. "That's not what I hear. I hear that Robert
Lee said he would be willing to swap queens."

"You mean, run up and grab Washington while McClellan takes Richmond?" The sergeant laughed. "That's what we say to scare Lincoln. Works,
too—he's split the Yankee army, and that's why McClellan has to creep up on
us, slow-like."

"What do you hear from the front?"

"McClellan's been sittin' tight for three weeks, sir, ever since we hit him on
the Chicahominy. Slick bastard, he maneuvered himself out of that when I
thought we had 'em."

His sentence was punctuated by the sound of cannon fire. "Hear that?
That's them on the move again, but tomorrow we're fixin' to go after 'em.
You know General Lee? Took over for Joe Johnston when he got wounded?"

"I haven't met him yet." All Breck knew about Robert Lee was from a
mutual friend who said Lee had voted for him in 1860. That was a start. But
so had "Beast" Ben Butler, the Yankee general now occupying New Orleans;
politicians from Kentucky often attracted a wide range of support.

"Now we can gamble on holding Richmond with a small force, y'see, like
Magruder did at Yorktown, while the rest of the army moves out and takes
McClellan by surprise. We'll do it, now that Stonewall Jackson's back. Here's
your hotel, general."

Some surprise, if every sergeant knew about it; Breck hoped he would find
out from President Davis if Lee intended to put up a fight inside the city or
evacuate before McClellan's artillery came within range. It would be a desperate gamble, almost suicidal, for Lee to attack well-entrenched superior

forces covered by artillery and commanded by an experienced officer like McClellan.

Breckinridge thanked the driver and checked into the hotel. He spent a long time in the deep bathtub, soaking his bones in the cool water after months in the field and a morning in the Richmond heat. He brushed his gray uniform, glad he'd left his Kentucky blue jeans uniform behind; blue showed the dust, and he did look more like a Confederate general in gray and gold. Ready to do political or military business, he walked down the street to the Mansion.

"It's as if the Government of the United States anticipates the failure of McClellan's expedition," Jeff Davis told him right out. The Confederate President, who had lost weight since Breckinridge had seen him the preceding October, struck Breck as strangely optimistic for a man whose capital was under siege. "Lincoln has just created a new army under John Pope. McDowell's Corps, Banks' and Frémont's men, are now under Pope—and all denied to McClellan! You know, we owe a great deal to Thomas Jackson."

Breckinridge knew that the erratic Jackson—"Stonewall" of Bull Run fame—had been giving the Yankees fits in the Shenandoah Valley. "His diversion is working? But I heard Jackson was back here in Richmond—"

"Just arrived, but the Federals don't know that yet. Lincoln is evidently panic-stricken," Davis said. "If McDowell's forty-five thousand Federals were added to McClellan's army, we would be hopelessly outnumbered here, while still unable to mount a serious attack on Washington. On the likelihood of the two Union armies joining here, I prepared to evacuate the capital. The gold and the archives have been loaded on railroad cars."

Breck was surprised at Lincoln's military timidity. The radical press in the North was calling McClellan overcautious, but in fact his Peninsula strategy was daring—only Lincoln's fears, his strategic hesitancy, and his interference with his general kept the Union forces from forcing the Confederacy out of its capital.

"Our spies in Washington say McClellan thinks we have two hundred thousand men here," Davis added. "In truth, we will have less than eighty-five thousand, including Jackson's men."

"We have a new general."

"I want you to meet Robert Lee, Breck. He reminds me, in a way, of Sidney Johnston. What a tragedy his loss has been."

Breckinridge nodded and did not ask why he had been summoned. Having dealt with President Buchanan for four years, and to some extent with Lincoln only last year, he had come to know that presidents get to the point in their own time.

"What about Beauregard?" Davis wanted to know.

"You were wise to relieve him. Bory is a sick man, and his spirit is broken —he cost us the victory at Shiloh. I'm not too sure Braxton Bragg was a wise choice—he's a martinet, and the last thing our men need is spit and polish."

"What do they say out West about Lincoln's new favorite, John Pope?"

"I think he's a lot of talk. Grant and Sherman are butchers, but at least they're quiet about it. Halleck showed himself to be no general at all—I had a rear guard of five thousand men, and made Halleck fairly crawl to Corinth. We held him to less than a mile a day."

"You distinguished yourself, Breck, and now you're both a military and political leader. The Senate confirmed your nomination as major general in three days, record time."

Judah Benjamin walked in without knocking; Davis and he evidently had that sort of relationship. The soft-spoken man had been the Confederacy's first Attorney General, then stepped in as Secretary of War when Davis's first choice had turned out to be almost as bad as Lincoln's Cameron; Benjamin now served as Secretary of State.

"Let me tell you how the war is going, General," Benjamin said after the amenities. "We're broke. We cannot replace equipment. We've suffered enormous losses in the West, and the enemy is at our throat here." He smiled. "I think we're going to win."

Breckinridge began to wonder if he had been wrong to dismiss the information from the sergeant. Was a counterattack actually in the works? An air of expectancy and urgency was everywhere; military couriers were bustling about and all the traffic was headed east and north. It seemed that everyone in Richmond knew about the movement and was heartened by the prospect of seizing the initiative.

Breckinridge knew Benjamin from the mid-fifties, when they had served in the Congress together. He admired the ease with which the Jew, born in the West Indies, dealt with Davis, the Baptist turned Episcopalian from Kentucky. The controversial politician was no stranger to attack: years before, while Benjamin was representing Louisiana in the U.S. Senate, Ben Wade had characterized him as "an Israelite with Egyptian principles" because of his defense of slavery.

"Our greatest mistake," the urbane lawyer was saying, "—a really monstrous mistake—was to think we could force England and France into recognizing the Confederacy with our cotton embargo last year." Judah Benjamin looked at Davis, who had been blamed for the mistake. "As a result, we reduced cotton production from five million bales to five hundred thousand. Having a cotton bonfire was considered the patriotic thing to do."

Breck was surprised by the admission that the economic distress of the Confederacy was a self-inflicted wound. Like most, he assumed that the Yankee blockade was to blame for the shortages of money and equipment.

"What about the Yankee blockade?"

The smile that usually played around Benjamin's lips disappeared. "Purely paper. The United States Navy had three ships to blockade a thirty-five-hundred-mile coast. No, it wasn't the Lincoln blockade that crippled our economy—it was our own foolish embargo."

"Explain to me, then," said Breckinridge, "how we're going to win." He was not swept up in the counterattack euphoria.

"Assume for the moment," said Benjamin, more to Davis than to him, "that General Lee, with Lincoln's help, is able to lift the siege of Richmond. Now make a second assumption. Let us say that General Lee is able to drive McClellan all the way back down the Peninsula to where he originally landed, cutting his army to pieces as he retreats. That would lead to the Union Army's capitulation."

Breckinridge remembered how close Sidney Johnston had come to demolishing the enemy army at Shiloh, nearly driving Grant's force into a river. If

Confederate Secretary of State Judah P. Benjamin

the Confederate counterattack here was successful—if—then it might be possible for Lee to destroy McClellan's hundred thousand in retreat from Richmond. If McClellan were forced to retreat, he would have to be a military genius to shift his base in a flank march while under attack; it was unlikely that he could remain anywhere near Richmond in some secure position, still able to menace the capital and tie down Lee's army. Unable to change base and set up a secure line of supply, went the Confederate hope, McClellan would be forced to surrender to save his army from slaughter.

"Such an event would shatter Northern morale, which expects victory any day," Benjamin continued. "I can read Greeley's headline now—'Erring sisters, depart in peace.' The pressure on Lincoln to stop the killing and settle the war would be irresistible."

"Lincoln is a harder man than you think," said Breckinridge, recalling his talks in the President's house in Washington.

"The only thing holding back recognition by England," said Benjamin, "is the anti-slavery sentiment among the working people, and a smashing Confederate victory at Richmond now would vitiate that sentiment."

Breckinridge was amazed at the way intelligent, ordinarily realistic politicians could build a towering house of cards on a single premise: that their untried general, with an outnumbered army, could assault the enemy in his works and not only lift the siege of Richmond, but destroy or capture the entire Federal expedition. All their dreams were based on that hope. If that could be done, then it would follow that the British would recognize the government at Richmond, and trade and loans would flow and the war would be sustained until the North gave up hope of conquest.

"It's important for my purposes for Breck to meet Lee," said Davis, rising and picking up his hat. "Come along. I visit him at the front every day."

"This may not be the best day," Benjamin offered.

"Nonsense. He seeks my military judgment." Davis was a West Pointer, Breck knew, and that sort always thought of themselves as soldiers first. "Unlike his predecessor, Robert Lee shares everything with me."

That told Breck something about the command structure: Joe Johnston, probably like George McClellan, did not like the civilian authority to know everything; apparently Lee felt it necessary to take Jeff Davis into his confidence.

Nine Mile Road, leading to General Lee's headquarters near the front, was clogged with wagons and soldiers moving up for the offensive. The troops, glad to be out of their bulwarks and trenches, delighted at not having to fall back and wait for the Yankee artillery onslaught, shouted and waved at them. Other politicians and civilians quickly joined the President's party, and by the time they approached the headquarters after a brief ride, the group had swollen to thirty.

"Our main force, under Powell Hill," Davis explained, "is to strike at the Union troops under Porter north of the Chickahominy. Jackson's troops will move down at the same time to threaten McClellan's supply line. Lee thinks that McClellan, to avoid being cut off so far from home, will fall back."

"What if he doesn't?" The obvious occurred to Breck. "What if his force south of the Chickahominy just walks into Richmond? You don't have that many defenders left."

"I know that," said Davis, elated. "It's a great chance we're taking. But if McClellan makes that move, Lee assures me that those of us defending the city will just have to hang on a few hours until he gets back. I'm not Lincoln, I'll take that chance." In a few moments, he added, "McClellan's an engineer, so is Lee. He thinks McClellan will worry about logistics first."

On that judgment Lee apparently was ready to gamble the capital. Breckinridge noted that Lee's headquarters was hardly a model of military efficiency. Eight pole tents, pitched with their backs to a stake fence, were situated on rocky ground. Three wagons were drawn up in front of the tents, and untethered horses wandered about the field. Breckinridge looked for sentries or at least aides-de-camp; none were visible. A large farmhouse stood nearby, the obvious choice for a general's residence, but Lee, evidently determined to set an example of respecting civilian property, lived in a tent.

As a politician, Breckinridge was curious about the touted and deprecated son of "Light-Horse Harry" Lee, the Revolutionary hero who died a debt-ridden exile. The South's new commander was a soldier who had distinguished himself as a captain in the Mexican War under Winfield Scott, but that was a lifetime ago; what had he done since to justify his growing reputation? Yet Scott had offered him command of the Union Army; Jeff Davis, after watching Lee flail about with no special distinction in the opening months of the war in western Virginia, brought him in to be his personal military adviser and now—with Sidney Johnston dead, Joe Johnston injured, and Beauregard sick and discredited—to be defender of Richmond.

Why such trust in the man? To some, the aura of trust was created by Lee's marriage to the granddaughter of George Washington's adopted son. They lived in a good Washington family home in Arlington; to them, Lee had become the living spirit of Washington. Breckinridge, who had profited from his own distinguished lineage, granted that Lee had a fine background for a military leader of a new American revolution, but his record in battle so far was nothing to justify all the faith placed in him now.

The general, a severe look in his eyes, rode toward them, drew up, and saluted frigidly. He pointed to the entourage with Davis.

"Mr. President," Lee asked, "who is all this army and what is it doing here?"

Davis looked around at his crowd of followers. "It is not my army, General."

"It is certainly not my army, Mr. President, and this is no place for it."

Davis appeared stunned. "Well, General, if I withdraw, perhaps they will follow me."

The President turned his mount. Breckinridge, like the others, turned to follow him, but Lee caught the eye of the man with two shiny new stars on both shoulders and beckoned him to come with him. Breck assumed that getting to know Lee was what the President wanted him to do, and trailed Lee's white horse to the headquarters tent.

Lee's tent looked like the others—there was safety in anonymity, Breckinridge supposed. The commander offered Breckinridge a firm, gentle hand, and covered it over with his other hand as he looked into his caller's eyes. Breckinridge, three inches taller than Lee, looked downward at a man older than he expected. His graying hair and stiff white beard and, more than that, his gravity and bearing gave the impression of a man who had long passed his mid-fifties.

"You were with Sidney Johnston at Pittsburg Landing," said Robert Lee. "A good man and a great soldier. He must have been an inspiration to you, as he was to me."

Lee struck Breckinridge as wholly different from Johnston—serene instead of vital, dignified rather than dashing. "Had he lived," the Kentuckian agreed, "we would not have lost to Grant at Shiloh."

"What sort of general is Grant?" Lee asked. "Our paths never crossed in the army."

"Sloppy. No interest in maneuver. Willing to take impossible losses. A butcher. That was the word Sidney Johnston used about him—butcher."

"The opposite of McClellan," Lee observed. He looked toward the front. "A careful general, inexorable in his advance. To his credit, he cares about his troops. They all have shoes." He sighed and said, "I mean no disrespect to our War Department, but it is disconcerting, after a fight, to watch our men remove the shoes of the dead."

Breck said he had been shown Lee's General War Order No. 75, and asked about the plan of attack.

"My object is to draw McClellan out of his works to defend his line of communications. Ultimately, the object is to disrupt his prearrangements and thereby change the character of the war."

"But if Porter's division holds, and McClellan then moves on Richmond?" Breckinridge had become expert in the movement of reserve corps.

Lee shook his head. "I'm depending on him to follow the pattern he has set. McClellan is overcautious and Lincoln is overanxious, and between them we should be able to save this city. That, and the spirit of our men, and the help of Providence."

"We have had some trouble with discipline in the West," said Breckinridge. How did Lee handle the deserter problem? Bragg was shooting too many of his men.

"Our men have a certain natural aggressiveness that is a military asset," Lee said. "Discipline is not the problem. When men are defending their homes, the job of a leader is to give them a sense of direction and unity. These are Virginians, fighting for their native land. They do not need drill. They need a sense of unconquerability."

That stopped and impressed Breckinridge; he had not heard this approach from the generals he worked with.

"They say you put a great deal of faith in your commanders," Breckinridge offered, thinking of how Halleck had hamstrung Grant and Sherman.

"My interference in battle would do more harm than good," Lee replied. "I have to rely on my brigade and division commanders. I think and work with all my power to bring the troops to the right place at the right time; then I have done my duty. As soon as I order them forward into battle, I leave my army in the hands of God."

More, Breckinridge said to himself, in the hands of his division commanders. If Stonewall Jackson's "foot cavalry" did not strike at precisely the right moment tomorrow at the Union supply lines, the battle could turn into a disaster. Lee's hands-off philosophy of battle sounded good, but Breck remembered how Sidney Johnston had saved the Tennessee Brigade by personally leading a charge. Then he thought of how the battle was lost by the absence of a general who had exposed himself unnecessarily.

Breck sought to ascertain Lee's political views. "It looks as if Lincoln is moving toward abolition," Breckinridge said. "You heard about the Confiscation Act? What effect—"

"If the slaves of the South were mine," said Lee fervently, "I would surrender them all without a struggle, to end this war." He caught himself. "But that is a political matter. I must not wander into politics, a subject I carefully avoid. And you, Breckinridge—what brings you East?"

"I wish I knew. President Davis sent for me without a word of explanation." He shrugged. "I should get back with my Orphan Brigade, where I belong. Frankly, General, I wish I could be as optimistic as Secretary Benjamin, or even as"—he searched for the word—"serene as you. But since Shiloh, something has gone out of me. I thank God I found my son. I fear there is not much more good that will come out of this war."

"Nearly a hundred years ago," said Lee, standing erect and looking over the wagons toward stacked arms, "there was a day of remarkable gloom and darkness, a day still known in Connecticut as 'the Dark Day'—a day when the light of the sun was slowly extinguished as if by an eclipse."

Breckinridge had to lean forward to hear.

"The legislature of Connecticut was in session," Lee continued, "and as its members saw the unexpected and unaccountable darkness coming on, they shared in the general awe and terror. It was supposed by many that the Day of Judgment had come. Someone moved an adjournment."

Lee signaled to an aide for his horse, Traveller, and went on with his story. "There arose an old Puritan legislator, Davenport of Stamford, who said that if the Last Day had come, he desired to be found at his place doing his duty, and therefore moved that candles be brought in, so that the House could proceed with its work.

"There was quietness in that man's mind," Lee concluded. "The quietness of heavenly wisdom and inflexible willingness to do present duty. You will do your duty, General Breckinridge; you cannot do more. You should never wish to do less."

The horse was brought around, not shying at the sudden sound of artillery in the distance, and Lee swung easily into the saddle. A rider came in to say that A. P. Hill had engaged the enemy at Mechanicsville, but Jackson's troops were not yet in place.

"Are we going to win?" Breckinridge asked.

"I'm not concerned with results," said Lee surprisingly. "God's will ought to be our aim. I'm contented that His designs should be accomplished and not mine. I hope we meet again, Breckinridge. I'd like to have the chance to vote for you again."

The Kentuckian did not move for a moment or two after the Virginian left. The man's words seemed unduly reverent in a military camp, but Lee's voice resonated with sincerity, and brought to the chaos of war a certain quietude and certainty. This general would not agonize over decisions. Breckinridge found himself concluding that there was indeed something of General Washington about Lee—the leader in battle and yet above the battle, with the remoteness that created a sense of mystery; sure of himself and his destiny and unshakable in his fundamentalist faith. Not fierce or fanatic, the way they said Jackson was, but secure, perhaps too secure for a man whose decisions determined the death of thousands. He deserved the aura that was forming around him; despite a concern about Lee's detachment, Breck felt some of his own listlessness lift.

Now all Lee had to do was win; only winners become heroes, and fathers of countries. For the first time since his arguments with the implacable Lincoln, Breckinridge felt the stirrings of hope. He knew a good deal about the qualities of leadership, and the man he had just met was a leader.

The army of the new nation—and Benjamin had pointed out that the British leader, Gladstone, had told Parliament that the Confederacy had indeed "made a nation"—was not led only by the dashing Johnston, the fainthearted Beauregard, the bullheaded Bragg, the acquiescent Buckner, the reckless Morgan, the doubting Breckinridge. The man selected to conduct the war had what the Quakers liked to call peace at his center.

Breck found President Davis not far from headquarters, watching the troops come up to the line, giving them awkward words of encouragement. He did not seem put out by the dismissal from the field by his commander, nor had he left the field. Breckinridge remarked on the essential goodness of character that General Lee impressed on him.

"Unusually calm and well-balanced judgment," added Davis, "and he is

General Robert E. Lee

instinctively averse to retiring from his enemy. He may turn out to be a great * general, though he tends to think only of this army in Virginia rather than the total war."

"I like the way he calls it the Army of *Northern* Virginia," observed Breck. He advertised his intent to carry the war to Yankee territory in the name of his army, which seemed a paradox in a man who so exemplified humility.

Together in the carriage on the road back to the capital, passing tobacco warehouses that had been converted to hospitals, Davis came around to the reason for his summons. "You're doing well in the field, Breck, but your talent is that of political leader. I'm having difficulty finding a suitable Secretary of War. Judah upset everybody last year, and now George Randolph has been trying to act without taking me into his confidence."

Here it was: Life in the capital, at the "heart of Secessia," as the Federals called it, with a return to the political life on the grand scale. But Secretary of War in the Davis Cabinet was a winless proposition: Jeff Davis was his own Secretary of War, as three men in the past two years had discovered. Now the military judgment was also in the hands of a general who, if he beat McClellan, would soon be General-in-Chief. To be War Minister in Richmond would be the same as being Vice President in Buchanan's Cabinet in Washington—a man waiting to profit when something terrible happened. He knew that Jeff Davis did not want, and could not abide, a Stanton, or anyone else who would try to take charge; Lincoln was willing to put up with a great deal to get an efficient organizer, and Jefferson Davis was not.

"I'll try to make a good suggestion, Mr. President. It's an important post. Not for me, of course—"

"Why 'of course'?"

Breckinridge could not say his reason for denial was that he wanted to get lost in the army, or that he wanted only to protect his boy until it was over and then to quit politics forever, or that he wanted no part of being a figurehead in an administration that had a President acting as Secretary of War.

He said instead, "I'll do my duty, whatever it is. I'll never wish to do less. But I think my duty is in the field." He added an afterthought: "I have a plan to recapture Baton Rouge, which should take some of the pressure off Vicksburg."

Davis sighed. "I'll stick with Randolph awhile. Jefferson's grandson, you know. Let's discuss Baton Rouge when we get back." They drove in silence for a time. "If I need you here, Breck—"

Breckinridge remembered Lee's departing words, and replied, "I'll do my duty."

CHAPTER 12

THE NEWSPAPER WAR

Adams Hill, second in command of the *New York Tribune*'s Washington office, was well aware that he was no favorite of Horace Greeley. Scrawny, nervous, nearsighted, the newsman was unable to turn out the soaring prose or biting political commentary that Greeley expected his Washington correspondents to mix into their news reports.

Instead, the studious Hill cultivated his acquaintance with men like young Stoddard, third secretary at the Mansion; General Grant's sponsor, Washburne, in the House; McClellan's advocates, Thomas Key at headquarters and his brother John in the War Department; Count Gurowski, a Seward-hating translator at the State Department; the innocent Homer Bates at the telegraph office, and the conspiratorial Sumner in the Senate. These were among his wellsprings of information, and while the reporter could not please the boss with readable copy, he could provide the newspaper with the stuff of news—sometimes, even better, the background on which news judgments could later be made.

Senator Sumner, only a few days before, had told Hill about his talk with the President, urging him to make July 4, 1862, Emancipation Day, and the Lincoln answer, "too big a lick." The reporter had passed that on by letter to New York in strictest confidence, knowing it would be of great interest to Greeley. He included, for verisimilitude, Sumner's characterization of Lincoln's idea that such a decree of freedom would be a *brutum fulmen*. Hill enjoyed adding that the Latin phrase meant "futile threat." That was not dramatic copy, worthy of initials of the reporter added to the end of the story, but it was "inside" stuff. Hill's concession to the need for drama in newspapering was in setting aside a small room in the *Tribune*'s cramped quarters in Washington for what he told the managing editor was "secret copying of documents and stolen interviews."

Hill dreaded Greeley. He dealt only with Sydney Gay, who had replaced Charles Dana as the *Tribune*'s managing editor, and never with Greeley himself. Hill reported only what happened, or what he had learned was about to happen—but never what should be happening, as the top editor wished. In addition, he had offended Uncle Horace, who had a habit of treating the word "news" as plural. When Greeley once telegraphed, "What are the news?" Hill had innocently cabled back, "Not a new." Since then, Hill had been dealing only with Gay.

With Sam Wilkeson, chief of the *Tribune*'s Washington office, off to the Peninsula with McClellan's troops, Hill was in charge of the office. Wilkeson was the star reporter whose initials almost always appeared at the end of his stories, and he liked to call the office "the Washington bureau," but Hill, behind his back, thought of it as the office. When Wilkeson wired from the field demanding another man on the battle scene to match the competition—Henry Raymond of the *Times* was down there himself with six reporters, and

Bennett's *Herald* team outnumbered them all—Adams Hill took a chance, hired a clerk in the Auditor's Office of the War Department who was aching to be a war correspondent, bought him a bay horse, and sent him down to help out.

"The last assistant you sent," Wilkeson had cabled from the front on a dull news day in June, "came to me with his lifeless drawling whine about the impossibility of getting accommodations and buying forage for his horse. Enough! This work needs first-class men: men of physical courage, intelligence, tact, patience, endurance, DEVOTION."

The new man was doing better: Charles Page went into action on June 27 at Mechanicsville, dodging Minié balls with notebook in hand, teaming up with the artist for *Harper's Weekly*, Winslow Homer, to give the color that Greeley liked while Wilkeson filed the news of McClellan's victory, or defeat, or whatever was happening—it was hard for Hill to tell.

Hill, reading copies of the telegrams his newest reporter was sending on to Gay in New York, liked Page's eye and ear. "There are both cheers and yells," the young man had written, "for our men *cheer* and their men *yell*." That was perceptive; Hill had never seen that observation about the shouting qualities of each side made before, and he hoped the editors in New York would not cut it out. Another line of Page's that impressed Hill was this macabre report: "During the stampede to the rear, for a moment the attention of hundreds was attracted to a horse galloping around carrying a man's leg in the stirrup—the left leg, booted and spurred. It was a splendid horse, gaily caparisoned." Hill admired that, since he could not write that kind of copy himself, and urged Gay to run the young reporter's initials after his dispatches.

The trouble was, that was the last dispatch anybody had received out of the Peninsula. Hill wished Page had put a little more news in the story: which army was stampeding to the rear, Union or rebel? That was the trouble with new men, they tended to get wrapped up in the gory details without bothering to mention who was winning.

The telegraph wire from Fort Monroe had been cut; for two solid days, nobody—not even Stanton's War Department—had any word from the front. The city of Washington was ready to root in its garbage cans for news. The President was said to be having fits, and worse, Greeley kept sending messages to Hill through Gay to find out what was happening to General McClellan. Had Richmond finally fallen? Was it time for the great celebration? Not a new.

At last the telegraph in the *Tribune*'s Washington office on that night of June 29 clacked with a message from Baltimore. Hill hurried to the machine; the message was from C. C. Fulton, editor of the *Baltimore American,* and an agent for the Associated Press, who sometimes went into the field himself. Hill read each word as an editor's advisory came over the wire:

"I am writing for the American a detailed account of events before Richmond and on the Peninsula during the last four days . . ."

Fulton had the story: Hill felt his heart palpitating and closed his eyes for a few moments, taking deep breaths, relieved that Fulton was writing for the AP and not one of the *Tribune*'s competitors. Greeley did not like to rely on the service set up by all the newspapers, but he did not demand that heads roll as he did whenever the *Tribune* was beaten by Raymond's *Times* or Bennett's *Herald.*

". . . including facts obtained from Washington," Fulton continued, "having been sent for by special train to communicate with the President. If you desire it, I will send it to you. It should make four or five thousand words." The AP agent added a sentence to make every Northern heart not only cheer, but yell: "We have the grandest military triumph over the enemy, and Richmond must fall."

That was a first-class scoop. Not only had Fulton been the first to return from the fighting with the story, but the President—as much in the dark about developments as anybody—had apparently sent a special train for the AP's man to report to him directly about the battle. Now the reporter had two stories—the victory of McClellan at Richmond, and the only firsthand account of the reaction of President Lincoln.

Hill fidgeted, waiting for Fulton's accounts to come over the ticker. No story emerged. Hours passed, Hill staring at the machine.

Finally, the machine chattered: "The Secretary of War decides that nothing can be telegraphed relative to affairs on the Peninsula. Have tried our best to get it off."

That was ominous; why should Stanton suddenly impose censorship on this story? McClellan's Richmond campaign was to be a grand triumph, according to Fulton; was his first flash mistaken? Had anything happened at the front since Fulton's return to Baltimore that made his conclusion misleading?

A copy of a telegram to the President from the AP agent came in that made Hill's jaw drop: "Sir—I find myself under arrest and on my way to Fort McHenry. I appeal to you for a hearing and prompt release. Respectfully, C. C. Fulton."

With that troubling development weighing on his mind, Hill hurried over to the War Department and went straight to Stanton's telegraph office. He spotted Homer Bates running down the hall and stopped him.

"Why was Fulton arrested? What's happening on the Peninsula?"

"Our line is still out, we don't know," said the distraught young man. "And I'm not supposed to say anything about Fulton. You better ask Colonel Sanford about him. The colonel is the one who saw the President."

Hill went looking for Sanford, superintendent of the military telegraph, and found him surrounded by the competition. The colonel posted a telegram he had sent to Fulton that Hill copied: "Your arrest was not made for publishing the statement, but upon your statement that you were preparing a detailed account of facts obtained from Washington. This is regarded by the President and the War Department as a flagrant violation of confidence. Publication of such facts is a high military crime."

"Is this order from Stanton," Hill asked, "or from Lincoln?"

"I am authorized to send it," the colonel replied carefully.

"On whose authority?"

"The highest."

Hill took that to mean that Lincoln himself wanted the editor jailed. The *Tribune* man hustled across the street and found Stoddard, the third secretary, working in the President's outer office with Nicolay and Hay. Hill motioned urgently for him to come outside into the hallway.

"Why did Lincoln arrest the man with the news? For God's sake, Fulton is the only Union-screaming editor in Baltimore."

"The President hit the ceiling when Stanton showed him that message," Stoddard said, looking over his shoulder. "Lincoln didn't talk to Fulton to give him an interview, he talked to him to find out what was going on. So when Fulton sent that telegram about facts obtained from Washington, he told Stanton to clap him in jail."

"Was Fulton's story about what he saw on the Peninsula wrong?" That was what counted, not the arrest of a newspaperman. "Does Lincoln have contrary news?"

Stoddard, nervous, grew circumspect. "Stanton thinks Fulton got his news from McClellan, and left before the battle was over."

"Well, are we advancing on Richmond, or what?"

"We started to, and took some strongpoint at a place called Oak Grove, but then there was something about a counterattack. McClellan thinks Jackson's army has come down from the valley and threatens his rear." Once Stoddard started talking, as Hill knew, he could not stop. "Before the line went out, McClellan had been demanding reinforcements to get him out of a dangerous position."

"So will he get them? McDowell is just standing around—"

"No, the President can't send them—I'm getting up an order right now, calling for three hundred thousand more three-year men. We just don't have the troops. Can't tell you any more. Stay out of jail yourself."

Hill knew he had one big story, about the call-up of more men, which would come as a blow to Northern hopes after Stanton had stopped recruitment earlier. But the demand from New York, the starvation for news everywhere, was for word about what had happened to McClellan's big push on Richmond.

Hill had a hunch that Stanton had more than a hunch that the general was retreating. He ducked back over to the War Department and found telegrapher Bates having a cup of coffee downstairs.

"Your Colonel Sanford is an idiot," he told the earnest young man, "arresting the only loyal editor in Maryland. That is a blunder he will pay for the rest of his life. Going to cause a hell of a stink in Baltimore. I'll bet Sanford did it on his own."

Bates did not rise to the bait. Sipping his coffee, he said only, "The colonel is a good man. Saved McClellan from being tried for treason."

"Go on. How so?"

Bates took out a telegram. "You won't print this?"

"Promise."

"Here's the telegram we got from McClellan a half hour ago, just as the wire came back on from Fort Monroe," said Bates, who would not let Hill read it for himself. "Says, 'I have seen too many dead and wounded comrades to feel otherwise than that the government has not sustained this army. If you do not do so now, the game is lost.'"

"He's in retreat," Hill said.

"Sure, but listen to this," said the telegrapher, "coming from a general to

Adams Hill

his commander in chief: 'If I save this army now, I tell you plainly that I owe no thanks to you or any person in Washington. You have done your best to sacrifice this army.' "

"McClellan sent that to the President?" Such insubordination was hard to imagine, unless it came from a man overwhelmed by bitter disappointment. "What did the President reply?"

"The President doesn't know about the last two lines," Bates confided. "Colonel Sanford said it was infamous and treasonable, and was meant to reach the public as a means of shifting the blame for defeat. So the colonel just cut those two lines out. We never gave it to the cipher operator, and nobody knows, and you better not say or you'll be in the jugheap too."

Hill did not let the story of the insubordinate lines sidetrack him, since everybody knew what McClellan thought of Lincoln; the big news was what was happening in the Peninsula battle. "What did the President reply?"

Bates felt in his pocket and took out the cipher. " 'Save your army, at all events. Will send reinforcements as fast as we can. We protected Washington and the enemy concentrated on you. Had we stripped Washington, he would have been upon us.' That's all Lincoln sent—I wonder what he would have said if he'd known what McClellan accused him of."

"Yes, that's pretty mild," Hill said, to reassure the telegrapher. "No news. Maybe you can give me a story someday."

"Sorry," the young man said. "I have to keep these confidences, or I'll get in trouble." He went for more coffee.

Hill had the guidance he could give to New York, although he could not put it in a news story: McClellan in defeat, Lincoln promising reinforcements to help save the army from annihilation. He decided to ignore the part about McClellan's insubordination, because he did not want to wind up as Fulton's cellmate, or dry up a source in Bates.

The *Tribune* man checked upstairs at the telegraph office, and was shown the official statement from Stanton: "Nothing has been received to warrant the belief of any serious disaster." That confirmed it: the use of the adjective "serious" meant that there had been a little, non-serious disaster, which would likely turn out to be pretty damned serious.

He hurried back to the *Tribune* office to get off what he could that would get past Stanton's telegraph censorship, and to await a copy of the report from Wilkeson in the field to New York—or from young Page, if he had not panicked and run. Hill scribbled a private note to Gay and sent it up to New York by overnight train, informing him that no matter what anybody else was saying, or any newspaper was headlining, this was "the bluest day since Bull Run."

In the *Tribune* building on the corner of Nassau and Spruce streets in New York, Sydney Gay did not know which way to go with the Peninsula story. For two days, fragmentary reports from the front had been contradictory; nobody knew what was really going on. Apparently this was not one grand battle, but a series of daily battles that might last a week.

He would not ask Greeley for his judgment; when Charles Dana left to become Stanton's spy in the West, Gay had made it clear that the news operation on the *Tribune* was to be his own. Greeley, as editor-in-chief, had the right to criticize, but the "managing" editor—Dana's original title—was in charge of the news operation of the paper. That left Greeley time to write editorials, to travel and lecture and politick.

At the moment the old man was closeted with James Gilmore, a shadowy character with a close connection to Lincoln—probably through Robert Walker, the railroad man. Gay suspected that Gilmore was the go-between for both Greeley and Lincoln, with the President trying to influence public sentiment and the editor trying to influence public policy. Better Gilmore, a writer, than Thurlow Weed, Gay thought. Getting in bed with the likes of Weed led to no good; Greeley had once prevailed on Weed to pass a law requiring the placement of state banking department statements in one paper, which became a nice source of advertising income until the political world turned, Weed and Greeley fell out, and a new banking commissioner steered the money to Greeley's former assistant, Henry Raymond at the *Times*.

Gay looked out the window, to draw his daily inspiration from the statue of Ben Franklin. A crowd was gathering on the Nassau Street side of the building, reading the latest newsless bulletins in the *Tribune* window, waiting for the casualty lists. It was nearing the moment to make his decision on the front-page headline and to put the paper to bed.

The early edition of the *Times* was already out, spread on Gay's desk. Henry Raymond had whipped his correspondent Bill Church, still lame from a leg wound a month before, into a report on a series of battles near Richmond that covered the entire front page. To judge from the account in the *Times,* which Gay studied again, McClellan had backed into a great victory.

"General McClellan and his staff all agree," the *Times* story ran, "that the present position of our army is far more advantageous as a base of operations against Richmond than that hitherto occupied." That was putting a good face on a retreat; Harrison's Landing, where McClellan's army now rested, was on the bank of the James River, about ten miles farther from Richmond than at the start of the fighting. "In spite of all that the army peddlers and other skedaddling croakers have to say, the terrific battle which has been raging for the past week has exhibited the most masterly strategy on the part of McClellan and bravery in himself, his officers and men."

Maybe so. Gay took a hard look at the competition's headline: "Immense Losses on Both Sides/Gen. McClellan Safe and Confident in his New Position." He assumed that the *Herald,* which was anti-Lincoln and had been hinting at a McClellan run for the presidency, would be similarly positive. Raymond was being patriotic and letting that color his dispatches, and James Gordon Bennett's *Herald* would be partisan but would come out the same way.

Against the weight of that opinion molding, Gay had to place the message from Adams Hill about the bluest day since Bull Run and the ominous tip about the new call-up of troops. Tomorrow was the Fourth of July; the people of the North needed a lift. Could the *Tribune* carry a wet-blanket story while the other papers were hailing McClellan's victory? The editor wondered how much to trust the judgment of Adams Hill, who was nowhere near the scene of the fighting.

"Do we have a good night or anything from Wilkeson?" Gay asked the copy boy, and was told no, the correspondent had not filed, nor had the assistant, Page. Gay could use an AP story and fill with a rewrite of the *Times,* hailing a costly victory, but Adams Hill's pessimistic judgment nagged.

The chief of his telegraph room burst in. "It's like a dam is breaking. This fellow Page is filing three days of dispatches that were held up by McClellan or Stanton. Going to be eight thousand words, too much to use, and he's still writing."

"Headquarters reports, or eyewitness?"

"He was right in the thick of it, and the first page of the first report—that was five days ago—is about McClellan's retreat, the burning of stores, panic among the Pennsylvanian regiments—"

He would go directly against the play of the story in the competition. "Bring it to me, page by page," Gay said. "We're going to run it all, seriatim. As soon as I get his most recent dispatch, I'll write the headlines for the whole paper."

"We have a Washington dispatch, too," said the telegrapher. "From Hill, passing along a War Department statement that we beat the enemy badly. That doesn't seem to fit with what Page is sending us from the field."

The managing editor paused: Maybe Page had seen a losing skirmish and extrapolated it into a false story of the battle; the *Tribune* had to be careful. "Anything else from Fort Monroe? If Page could file, so could others."

"An Associated Press story dated last night, saying we lost twenty thousand men."

"And the rebel losses?"

"Don't know yet."

Gay winced; almost as bad as Shiloh, and without Shiloh's tail-end redemption. "We'll lead with the AP figures and the War Department claims." That would take care of the Fourth of July spirit, and keep Stanton from getting after Greeley. "Then run all of Page."

The makeup man shook his head. "That would take the whole front page, and a jump. And the kid hasn't stopped writing."

"Set it all," said Gay. "Give me half the first column for headlines." He would play the story down the middle, between the government claims and the truth, in direct defiance of the *Herald* and the *Times*. He had a responsibility not to cause panic in the North, and would balance the stark, bad news with brave statements of the damage inflicted on the enemy.

As they brought in Page's copy and the AP reports, Sidney Gay wrote the headlines: "From General McClellan's Army. The Enemy Still Press On. Our Gunboats Repulse Them. The Rebels Retreat in Disorder. Remarkable Endurance of Our Troops. Our Right Wing Swung Round Thirty Miles. 185,000 Rebels Against 95,000 Union Troops. Great Slaughter on Both Sides. The Work of Evacuation."

He paused at one page of copy by Page from the landing on the James River, seventeen miles below Richmond, to which McClellan had retreated.

"Huddled among the wagons were 10,000 stragglers"—that would tell any reader of the extent of the Union disaster—"for the credit of the nation be it said that four fifths of them were wounded, sick, or utterly exhausted, and could not have stirred but for the dread of the tobacco warehouses of the South." Those were the hellhole hospitals and prisons. Page's copy went on in the style Greeley was looking for, and in this case, that Gay agreed was needed: "The confusion of this herd of men and mules, wagons and wounded, men on horse, men on foot, men by the roadside, men perched on wagons, men searching for water, men famishing for food, men lame and bleeding, men with ghostly eyes looking out between bloody bandages that hid the face —turn to some vivid account of the most pitiful part of Napoleon's retreat from Russia, and fill out the picture—the grim, gaunt, bloody picture of war in its most terrible features."

Gay swallowed, and at the bottom of the four days' dispatches added the reporter's initials: C. A. P.

CHAPTER 13

JOHN HAY'S DIARY
JULY 4, 1862

McClellan has failed. Lee has lifted the siege of Richmond, and our army has scurried for shelter beneath the naval guns on the James River. The Tycoon and all here are heartsick.

The largest army ever assembled on the North American continent, over 100,000 men, better equipped than any army in the history of the world, trained and drilled and practiced to a fare-thee-well, has been turned away from the gates of Richmond by a ragtag army of rebels who attacked and outfought the Union forces over seven grueling days, took our new guns and stole the shoes off our dead.

The Young Napoleon's apologists are talking about "a change of base" and "a strategic withdrawal," claiming the greatest shift of base in the history of warfare. Some of the papers are loyally swallowing that, but the fact is that McClellan retreated and Lee advanced. With all Mac's brilliant maneuvering —and everybody agrees it was brilliant, saving the army and all that—Robert Lee drove him away from his object: the enemy capital.

Now Pinkerton and Key and that bunch are putting out the word it was all Lincoln's fault. How those lickspittles to a popinjay can claim a victory in retreat, and in the next breath put the blame on the Tycoon for McClellan's own cowardly failing to storm Richmond is hard to grasp.

General Randolph Marcy, McClellan's chief of staff and father-in-law (we don't know which title makes him more important) came in this morning from the front to beg for more reinforcements. He does not realize that only yesterday I took a message from Lincoln over to the telegraph office to Governor Morgan of New York asking for more troops in a hurry: "If I had 50,000 additional troops here now," the Prsdt pleaded, "I believe I could substantially close the war in two weeks. But time is every-thing." The defeat on the Peninsula, coming so soon after Stanton's confident ending of all recruitment, embarrasses us terribly.

"Unless you give us more men, and soon," Marcy told the Prsdt, who has not been sleeping the past few nights and looks terrible, "I would not be astonished if the army were obliged to capitulate."

"General," Lincoln said, as coldly furious as I've ever seen him, " 'capitulate' is not a word to be used in connection with our army."

When McNapoleon's father-in-law apologized, the Prsdt told him, "I repeat what I have twice before said to your commander: 'save the army, at all events.' Is that clear?"

"Yes, sir. But you have at least fifty thousand men you do not need in this area, and with that number the general can retrieve our fortunes. Sent at once, they would enable us to resume the offensive."

"You surely labor under some gross mistake of fact," the Tycoon said. "I have not seventy-five thousand men east of the mountains. The idea of sending you fifty thousand is simply absurd."

Marcy could not challenge that without being insubordinate. He lowered his head and looked miserable.

Lincoln then relented and said, "If in the general's frequent mention of responsibility, he has the impression that I blame him for not doing more than he can, please be relieved of such impression." That was a mild reaction to an offensive telegraph message from the front. "I only beg than in like manner, he will not ask impossibilities of me."

"We recognize, Mr. President, that you have ordered some reinforcements sent to us from Burnside and Hunter," Marcy responded in kind, "and General McClellan will do the best he can with the force he has."

"I do not see how I can send you another man within a month," Lincoln told Marcy, the cold edge gone from his voice now that the dread word "capitulation"—which would mean the loss of the war, and charges of treason—was no longer in the air. "Under these circumstances the defensive, for the present, must be your only care. Save the army—first where you are, if you *can;* and secondly by removal, if you must. But I repeat—save the army, at all events."

McClellan's man said he thought they could stay put with safety, pending reinforcements for a new assault on Richmond. Marcy also offered the President the cold comfort that in the seven days of battles, Confederate casualties had outnumbered our own significantly—twenty thousand to fifteen thousand was his guess. That was because Lee was doing the attacking. (Ordinarily, such a terrifying exchange was exactly what Lincoln wanted; engagements that bled the South would bring the war to an end, considering our over three-to-one advantage in population. McClellan did not want to exchange heavy casualties, but was forced to; Lincoln was ready to trade the suffering though he would never admit it publicly, and yet is unsatisfied with the result. I see an irony there.)

To cheer up McClellan, whose latest dispatches have been almost incoherent with grief, Lincoln handed Marcy a copy of a telegraph message just received from one of our people in Fredericksburg, where the *Richmond Examiner* is still distributed. "It censures the confederate generals severely," the President said, "for failing to capture General McClellan and his army. And here, he'll like this: the rebel paper pronounces McClellan's whole movement a 'masterpiece of strategy'."

As Marcy took his leave to return to the front, the Prsdt added a postscript: "If, at any time, you feel able to take the offensive, you are not restrained from doing so."

In the midst of this misery, we had a caller on the other great topic on everyone's lips these days, the Confiscation bill. Miss Anna Ella Carroll arrived with a great sheaf of papers under her arm, to discover Lincoln half under the desk, rubbing some blacking on his boots. He had gone out looking for a newspaper early that morning, and the mud of Pennsylvania Avenue has a special way of clinging to leather.

"Why, Mr. President," she said, ostensibly shocked, "do you black your own boots?"

"Whose boots did you think I blacked?" Lincoln shot back.

Miss Carroll was in the process of writing a pamphlet entitled "A Reply to Sumner"—she likes titles like that—demolishing his position on the Confiscation bill, with no little encouragement from us. Nico and I knew it was this lady's research and legal arguments that were the basis of the Attorney General's withdrawal from the world for the past few days, to sweat over a veto message—Lincoln's first, but the decision to veto is not final.

"Thank you for your note," were her first words to the Tycoon. "I interpreted it as an apology."

"I shouldn't wonder," he replied. (I have often wondered about that frequent locution of his: what does "I shouldn't wonder" mean? He uses it whenever he wants to make a noise that sounds like a response but is not, and it is for the listener to read whatever he wants into it.) He motioned her to a chair, which is more than he ever did for Jessie Frémont.

"I'm here to urge you to veto the Confiscation bill. It will be passed any day now, I'm told on good authority—"

"Wade?"

"Yes."

"Then he has the tickets. This setback of our army on the Peninsula will help him."

"If you sign that abolition bill," she declared, giving "confiscation" its real name, "it will be as if you added fifty thousand men or more to the rebel army."

"Tell me why," the Prsdt asked. "Sumner was just in here telling me it would reinvigorate the North, put the war on a high moral plane—"

"Rubbish. It will unite the South as it has not been united before, and will protract the struggle indefinitely. That means the European powers will recognize the South—they must, they need the cotton—in which event, the ocean will swarm with rebel privateers. France will help Mexico regain Texas—"

"Seward is sending money, quietly, to Benito Juárez," Lincoln said quickly, referring to the revolutionary who was giving fits to the Emperor of Mexico. "We want Maximilian off balance."

"Mr. President, I wonder if you realize that Senator Sumner"—she pronounced his name to give the impression she thought he was an oleaginous blowhard—"is telling one and all that he has been assured by you that you will act out the will of the abolitionists."

"He's saying that, is he?"

"You have to do something to antagonize the abolitionists. A veto here would give heart to the moderates."

She is a purposeful woman, Miss Carroll, and she has the good of the Prsdt and the Union at heart. Lincoln is unhappy with this Confiscation bill, and with the way the Congress is trying to snatch back the war power to free the slaves, but he is not in a strong position these days. He may have to throw McClellan to the Jacobin wolves, or else sign their cherished Confiscation bill.

"I understand your reasons for signing the D.C. emancipation," she conceded. "You have been in favor of that since you came to Congress as a Henry Clay Whig. As for signing the bill for abolition in the territories, you took that side in your debates with Douglas."

The Prsdt nodded; he is always pleased when somebody remembers his record on slavery.

"But now you have to tack the other way," she said. "Otherwise, you will change the whole moral tone of the war—away from preservation of the Union, and toward the subjugation of the Southern states. I cannot believe you intend to destroy the social system of the South, to go back on your pledged word and the platform of the Republican Party."

"Circumstances change," he said, but not decisively—just keeping the door open.

"You would make Davis and his co-traitors look like patriots struggling for constitutional liberty against a revengeful government. If you approved Confiscation, you would make yourself look like George the Third."

"Hold on, now—"

"Where in the world are you going to send four million Africans?" Now she had him on the weak point. "You know that on no other condition than colonization can they be made free. If you free them and leave them in the South, you will confer no benefit on them, but incalculable injury."

I asked what she meant by that. "John, you're from Illinois. You know there aren't a quarter million blacks in the entire North, a population of nineteen million. Not one person in a hundred in the North is black, because the North won't have them—and if abolition came, the South would never be able to afford to hire them."

She stood up, dropping a few of her papers, which I retrieved. "The blacks are human beings, and they may be docile now, but they won't starve in silence—they'll riot and rebel. And Abraham Lincoln and the Confiscation Act will be blamed rightly." She let that sink in, and it did. "But by your veto, the Republic may yet be saved."

"You make a case, Miss Carroll." His face took on that melancholy look. I am concerned that the losses in the Peninsula, the dashing of his hopes to end the war quickly, have put him in danger of getting an attack of the hypo. "I'm to see the border state congressmen next week, to try again on gradual, compensated emancipation, which you and I favor. Perhaps we can get our radical friends to change the worst parts of the bill, so I won't have to use the veto."

"That is all I ask. Either a clear veto, which the Senate will surely sustain, or some threat from you to get the bill moderated, which would be seen as a defeat for the radicals. Or as John Hay calls them, the Jacobins."

I thought it would be a good time to put in an argument for Miss Carroll to shoot down. "There's some logic to confiscation," I offered. "It was General Ben Butler's idea, and it was ingenious. He said that he was already empowered to seize the enemy's ammunition, uniforms, food, every bit of military property. Then he said that the enemy considered its slaves to be property, too, and he happily agreed—so he could seize them too. And since he wasn't in the slaveholding business, he could set them free."

"Slaves used by rebels to build fortifications or carry weapons are legitimate contraband of war," Miss Carroll said, ready for that. "But this bill goes further. This reaches behind the lines, into civilian areas, using powers to take away property. No Congress or no executive has ever claimed that power on this continent."

"I liked your war powers pamphlet," Lincoln put in. "A little expensive," he could not resist adding.

"But there are limits to the war powers," she said with some passion. "Just as there are limits to war. It is one thing to destroy the enemy on the battlefield, or even to strike behind the lines at his military supplies. It is something else entirely to treat his civilian population as if it were part of the army. That's what this unbridled confiscation does; that's what abolition does. If all slaves are contraband of war, how about all other property? How about food —are you prepared to burn farms, on the theory that some of the food goes to rebel soldiers? Are you ready to call for a slave uprising, with murder and pillage? Are you prepared to shell hospitals, set fire to entire cities, deliberately kill women, children—"

Lincoln was shaking his head; such totality of war was uncivilized, unthinkable. He would never let it come to that.

She pressed her point. "That's what this bill is a long step toward—a kind of war the world has never seen—not just armies against armies, but a nation against a nation. Are you prepared to take this Union into such an orgy of destruction?"

With a look of pain, Lincoln rose to his feet. He managed a wan smile: "Say, Miss Carroll, do you work over Ben Wade and Zack Chandler like this? I hope so."

"They are both patriots, and my close friends," she replied seriously, "but they are hopelessly wrong. Their radical policy would destroy the Union. Your current policy will save it."

This time, on the way out, she took my arm and we walked down the stairs together. She was thoughtful, probably going over in her head all the things she did not say. We who have the Prsdt's ear all day long forget that others must make each moment count.

"I hope he doesn't think I'm in favor of slavery," she said. "I'm not."

I assured her he knew about her manumission of her own slaves, and the financial sacrifices she made to pay for that purchase of freedom for others.

"I wasn't too pushy, was I?" Fascinating, the sudden change in her; in Lincoln's office she was totally in control of her arguments; afterward, selfdoubt takes over and she responds to all compliments and reassurances with "I hope so." Frankly, I like her better this way. I told her I could not abide pushy women, and she immediately smiled and said, "You're having your troubles with Kate."

"How do you know?"

"The governor told me."

Aha. It's no longer "Secretary Chase"; it's "the governor."

"Be careful, John. She may be using you."

"I wish she'd try," I said. "One day she can't get enough of me, the next month she won't see me, she's too busy with her drunken Governor of Rhode Island, or Roscoe Conkling in the House. Both in their mid-thirties, old men."

"The governor tells me—in absolute confidence—that she's genuinely attracted to you, John. He says her affection for you is causing her great difficulty."

"You believe that?"

"I believe what he tells me." She paused. "I don't know that I believe what she tells him. Well, go after Kate, if it's important to you. But remember, her loyalty runs to Chase, not to Lincoln; don't get caught in a conflict of loyalty." When I said that could never happen, she added, still with that beguilingly doubtful expression, "I suppose that goes for me, too."

I returned to the office upstairs two steps at a time. Nico was fretting, looking for me. It seems that Lincoln does not like this business of dealing with McClellan through intermediaries, and cannot abide this warring-by-telegraph, which makes a record but no progress.

He has decided to sail down to Harrison's Landing, the new base on the James River, Stanton in tow, to survey the military situation for himself. It is intolerable that McClellan's 100,000 could have been stopped by a force of fifty it's size. If need be, he will confront the general whose political ambition, or lack of soldierly heart, has lengthened the war. Either he will reinforce the man and approve a new offensive to take Richmond from there, or he will tell him to pack up his army and its vast herd of cattle and come back to Washington, where a more sensible campaign can be once again launched, this time without gambling the loss of Washington. Such a campaign would be commanded by John Pope, he of the portable headquarters, not by George McClellan, who in avoiding decisive defeat gives up the hope of great victory.

I was going over the details of the trip with Hill Lamon, the marshal-bodyguard, when the Tycoon came out of the inner office. Thank God, with a physical movement in store, his haggard aspect and gloomy demeanor had been replaced by his reminds-me-of-a-story look.

"Seems to me McClellan was wandering around and got lost," he said. "He's been hollering for help ever since he went south—wants somebody to come to his deliverance and get him out of the place he's got into.

"He reminds me of the Illinois man who visited the state penitentiary. He wandered everywhere on the tour and got separated from his friends and couldn't find his way out. He came to a place where he saw a convict behind the bars of his cell door, and he said to the convict, 'Say! How do you get out of this place?' "

HELL OF A FIZZLE

Edwin Stanton felt secure: Harrison's Landing, a tiny river port on the James less than twenty miles from Richmond, was now fortified by the presence of a hundred thousand Federal troops, under the further protection of naval batteries. The USS *Ariel* had conveyed the presidential party down the Potomac first to Fort Monroe and a visit with General Dix, and overnight to the estate that had been the property of President William Henry Harrison. Now this site of great Virginia plantations had become the impregnable fortress of the Army of the Potomac, with abundant bathing and recreational facilities; a good place for weary soldiers to rest after a hellish week of fighting, and as good a place as any, in Stanton's view, for Lincoln to decide to rid himself of the scoundrel-general who stood in the way of an aggressive prosecution of the war against the slavocracy.

The Secretary of War made it a point to see McClellan privately before the general and the President met alone. Stanton did not want McClellan worrying Lincoln with tales of the perfidy of his War Secretary. He assumed it would be typical of the whining McClellan to complain that Stanton had kept vital messages from the President or had otherwise undercut or demoralized generals in the field.

"I meant to send a personal message to you by General Marcy," Stanton told McClellan, "but I was in the country that morning." The War Secretary put on his most mournful expression. "I wanted to be with Mrs. Stanton to see one of our children dying."

The general, who had been cool, was instantly sympathetic. "I trust your baby's illness may not prove fatal."

Stanton felt a rush of emotion that added sincerity to what he was about to say. "In this brief moment, I can only say that there is no cause in my heart for the cloud between us."

As he said the words, Stanton almost believed them himself; that had happened to him before juries, when he was suddenly swept away in the emotion of pressing his client's case. "That cloud of suspicion was raised by wicked men for their own base purposes. No man had a truer friend, General, than I have been to you."

McClellan was taken aback. "When you were appointed, I considered you my intimate friend and confidential adviser."

"I was and am."

"But your concurrence in withholding a large portion of my force," said the general, still puzzled, "which spelled the difference between victory and defeat, led me to believe your mind was warped by a bitter personal prejudice against me."

"Wholly untrue," Stanton assured him. "I have been ready to make any sacrifice to aid you. I have been praying to Almighty God to deliver you and your army from all peril." His own words brought tears to his eyes.

"Well, I'm relieved. Obviously I've been mistaken about your real feelings. As you used to say, together we can save the country."

Stanton, choked up, nodded vigorously. The general would believe anything; no wonder he had been so easily fooled by Lee, unless it was McClellan's own traitorous inclinations that stopped him short of Richmond.

"Last summer," McClellan said in a confidential tone, "you and I talked over the way the war should be fought, and the ends to be achieved. I have put those views on paper, in a confidential letter to the President. I cannot show it to anyone, but I am sure the President will discuss it with you. My critics might say it goes somewhat beyond my purview as a general, but we cannot disconnect military means from political goals."

"On to victory," Stanton said, grasping the general's strong arm and squeezing it hard. For a moment, he felt a wave of genuine affection for the beleaguered soldier. That wave receded when Stanton considered how the deployment of this huge army in this backwater left Washington undefended from assault by the bulk of the Confederate Army. McClellan would be finished soon, if Stanton had his way and Lincoln could see the light; the right general to win the war was John Pope.

Together, they joined the President for a review of ten thousand of McClellan's men: hardy, healthy, well-equipped soldiers, who Stanton thought must be amused at the sight of Lincoln's long legs dangling from a horse in contrast to their general's impeccable bearing. Stanton did not like military reviews; he thought the men should be fighting rather than parading.

Lincoln, ever the politician in Stanton's eyes, could not resist dismounting, climbing up on a rail fence, and addressing the troops.

"Be of good cheer," he called out in his high, piercing stump-voice, "all is well. You have, like heroes, endured, and fought, and conquered. Yes, I say conquered; for though apparently checked once, you conquered afterward and secured the position of your choice. You shall be strengthened and rewarded. God bless you all!"

Stanton supposed that hogwash went down well; Lincoln needed to say something to compete for the love this army displayed toward its conservative commander. Then the Washington group got down to what Stanton considered the business of the visit: preparing the way for a transfer of the army from this spot back to the fortifications around Washington.

In a meeting with McClellan and his staff—including the "Dukes and Princes," several foreign-born dignitaries the Young Napoleon liked to have near him—Lincoln, notebook in hand, closely questioned the military men on the army's current position. "What amount of force have you now?"

"About eighty thousand," said the general.

"What is likely to be your condition as to health in this camp?"

"Better than any since we left for the Peninsula," McClellan reported stoutly; Stanton knew he wanted to stay in this spot to fight again.

"Where is the enemy now?"

"About five miles from here. No force in our vicinity—they suffered terrible losses in their last attack."

"If you desired, could you remove the army safely?" That was the crucial question; if Lincoln ordered McClellan to remove his army from the Peninsula, that would be the end of the campaign, and the general's career would be finished. Stanton knew that Pope, a favorite of Chase and Wade, was prepared to take over McClellan's army and add it to his own force near Washington.

"It would be a delicate and very difficult matter," McClellan told the President, putting on him the danger of an attack during an evacuation.

"Is the army secure in its present position?"

"Perfectly so, in my judgment," McClellan said. "Gentlemen, do you agree?"

Most of the other generals, even two of the anti-slavery men that Stanton had put in McClellan's camp, agreed. One of the generals, Fitz-John Porter, whom Stanton considered a McClellan sycophant, added, "Not only are we secure, but we are ready to move forward on Richmond."

"With adequate reinforcements," the commanding general added.

Lincoln, making notes, made no decision, and it became apparent that the President intended to take under advisement whether to order an end to the campaign.

"Right here, in front of Richmond," McClellan argued, "this is where we can win the war. My army is ready to fight. We have punished the enemy in the Seven Days and shown that Lee and Jackson can be beaten. It would be a terrible mistake to remove the army, a tremendous blow to morale."

"Move the army and ruin the country," added Porter. Stanton made a mental note to cashier him the moment McClellan was out of the way.

McClellan asked to see the President in private; the generals left but Stanton stayed.

"Mr. President, my private letter to you is in your hand, but let me tell you and the Secretary what is uppermost in my mind." He looked at Stanton, who made an effort to return his glance with some sympathy.

"We are not fighting a war looking to the subjugation of any state. This should be a war against armed forces, not civilian populations."

Lincoln listened, noncommittal.

"Neither confiscation of property, nor political executions, nor forcible abolition of slavery should be contemplated."

Stanton was secretly delighted at the general's presumption; this was certain to offend the President. Ben Butler's iron rule in New Orleans, John Pope's somewhat excessive order aimed at rebel guerrillas, and David Hunter's emancipation were what McClellan obviously had in mind; this was one general criticizing what other military officers were doing, but that was Lincoln's prerogative, not his.

"All private property taken for military use should be paid or receipted for," McClellan went on; "pillage and waste should be treated as high crimes; military arrests should not be tolerated except in places where actual hostilities exist."

Stanton suppressed a smile; McClellan was proposing a kid-gloves war, implicitly criticizing the "abuses" that congressional Democrats so often decried. He was writing the 1864 Democratic platform, and Lincoln would see through that in a minute.

"I mean this respectfully, sir. I believe you understand the impact the political climate has on the raising and holding of troops."

"By my count," said Lincoln, "nearly fifty thousand of your men have simply disappeared."

"Morale affects defections." McClellan took a deep breath. "Sir, I am convinced that a declaration of radical views, especially upon slavery, would rapidly disintegrate our present armies."

Stanton glowered, but in fact could hardly contain his glee; he was persuaded that the general had, in that last statement, ended his military career.

"You need a General-in-Chief who possesses your confidence," McClellan concluded. "I do not ask for that place for myself. I am willing to serve you in such position as you may assign me, and I will do so as faithfully as ever subordinate served superior."

The President said only "All right," and the meeting was over.

On the boat back to Washington, Stanton played on Lincoln's considerable pride. How dare this young upstart, who could not mount an offensive against an inferior force, tell the civilian leadership of the nation what the policy should be on slavery!

The political threat was real. Stanton had recently been in touch with

Samuel Barlow, the Democratic leader in New York. No longer was Stanton being thought of as a potential Democratic candidate in 1864; he had been informed politely that George McClellan, whose views on "the Union as it was" were closer to the thinking of most Democrats of all factions, was the likely candidate.

Worse, with Lincoln's compromising approach, there was always the chance that the President might bring the popular Nathaniel Banks in to head the War Department, or worse yet, bring McClellan into the Cabinet in Stanton's place, as a uniformed Secretary of War. Little Mac might not be much of a fighter, but he was indisputably the nation's best army organizer. And Stanton was accumulating enemies, particularly in the Blair-Seward set; he had to beat them or be beaten.

The Secretary of War leaned on the railing of the gunboat and studied the Potomac shore. Passing Kettle Bottom Shoals he could see the canalboats loaded with stone, waiting to be sunk to prevent the *Merrimack*—since scuttled—from coming upriver. That was an unwelcome reminder of Stanton's overreaction to the rebel threat; why didn't some idiot send the canalboats back where they belonged?

"They call them 'Stanton's navy,' " said the President, standing alongside.

"Very funny. I wonder if you have grasped the degree of insubordination we have just witnessed?"

"He did get a little into our business," Lincoln allowed.

"That letter he gave you, supposedly private. I know all about it; there are copies everywhere. It's the future Democratic platform."

Lincoln looked perturbed at that. Stanton's accusation was untrue—McClellan apparently intended to keep the letter private—but Stanton exploited the opening. "He doesn't want to stay down there to take Richmond; he'll never attack Richmond unless we send him the whole population of the North. He only wants to be down there with all the troops who love him to expose Washington to Lee's attack." The Secretary of War decided to go all the way. "It is in McClellan's interest for us to lose the war. He's either a coward or a traitor, and I don't think he's a coward."

"That's a lot to say." Lincoln was playing what he liked to call "shut-pan," and Stanton hated that. "This letter is platform-ish. You think we ought to bring the army back?"

"Under John Pope," Stanton promised, "that army will fight. And take Richmond without jeopardizing Washington."

Lincoln said he wanted to hear what General Burnside had to say: they would dine with him on the steamer back to Washington that afternoon. A long silence, then, "Reminds me of a story."

Stanton closed his eyes in pain; another one of those interminable, unfunny anecdotes that required the listener to laugh heartily at the conclusion and tell the world of its pertinence and profundity.

Lincoln launched into a dreary tale of an Illinois blacksmith who heated a piece of soft iron in a forge and tried to make it into a claw hammer. But the iron wasn't small enough, so he heated it again and tried to make an ax, but that didn't work—Stanton became convinced that the story would never end —so the blacksmith took a forgeful of coal, pumped the bellows and made a tremendous blast, bringing the iron to white heat, and then lifted it high with a tongs and threw the glowing iron into a tub of water, exclaiming, "If I can't make anything else out of you, I'll make a hell of a fizzle, anyway!"

Since Lincoln's point was that McClellan had made a great fizzle of the Peninsula campaign, Stanton drew his lips back and made chuckling noises. He was ready and willing to play the courtier, to contort his face at anything that cast derision on the soldier he had come to despise with heart and soul.

A terrible scraping noise roared through the gunboat, soon followed by gongs and bells, followed by a red-faced captain explaining that they had misjudged the depth of the shoals and were aground. Told that they would be delayed two hours until the tide lifted the ship off the river bottom, Stanton growled, "Damned navy."

Lincoln reacted quite differently; capriciously, he said that it was a hot day and a perfect time for a swim. He borrowed the captain's bathing suit and led a small detachment down the boat's side into the fresh water. Stanton remained at the rail, sweltering but clothed in dignity, frowning at the sight of the incredibly lanky Chief Executive splashing and cavorting at a time of grievous difficulty.

Then it struck the War Secretary that Lincoln was acting like a man who had put a decision behind him and didn't want to think about it anymore. Stanton wished he could be sure that the President's decision was to dump McClellan and bring the army back to Washington.

George McClellan, with the presidential party gone, sat down at his desk late that night and took pen in hand to confide his thoughts about Lincoln's visit to Nellie.

"His Excellency was here and found the army anything but demoralized or dispirited—in excellent spirits." Lincoln and Stanton wanted to find an army beaten and at bay, McClellan was certain, to remove at once back to Washington to begin all over again with a more savage and abolitionist commander. But this was a newly confident and battle-tested army, which took the worst the rebels could throw at them; an army that was victorious at Malvern Hill, the final battle of the Seven Days, and would be ready to take Richmond soon with a modest number of reinforcements.

"I do not know to what extent he has profited by his visit," the general wrote the woman he loved, "—not much, I fear, for he really seems quite incapable of rising to the magnitude of this crisis. I enclose a copy of a letter I handed to him. Preserve it carefully."

He was proud of that letter, so closely reasoned beforehand with Thomas Key, but written mostly by himself. True, it was political, but the talk of the officers and men of his army was political, and if they believed the Union cause had been replaced by abolition, the effect on morale—the desertions en masse—would have a most military result. McClellan was glad he had added a point urging the manumission of slaves in the border states, after proper compensation. The slavery interests would not like that, but it made good political and military sense for the government to buy slaves in loyal states to employ for war work.

Strange, how Lincoln had not reacted at all to the letter, couched in the most respectful terms. He had said only "All right" and put it in his pocket.

Perhaps he was ultrasensitive to his political prerogatives. That was the mark of a small man and an insecure leader.

"I did not like the President's manner," he wrote. "It seemed that of a man about to do something of which he was much ashamed." It reminded him of that day when Lincoln all but accused him of treason. "I do not know what pretty trick the administration will play next. A few days will show it, and I do not much care what the result will be. I feel that I have always done enough to prove in history that I am a general, and that the causes of my want of success are so apparent that no one except the Chandler Committee can blame me hereafter."

That was untrue, and Nellie would know it. "I have not done splendidly at all," he admitted, looking at the words he had written and knowing them, as Nellie would, to be the truth. "I have only tried to do my duty and God has helped me, or rather He has helped my army and our country and we are safe."

But why had God denied him victory? An answer came to him and he hurried to share it with his wife. "I think I begin to see His wise purpose in all this. If I had succeeded in taking Richmond now, the fanatics of the North might have been too powerful, and reunion would be impossible."

Colonel Key pulled back the flap of the tent—McClellan, after his pledge to Nellie, would not sleep in the large brick house—and entered, followed by Lieutenant Custer. The young lieutenant clutched a sheaf of papers.

"General," the young man said tightly, "we have commenced receiving letters from the North urging you to march on Washington and assume the government."

"Put those away," Colonel Key told him, annoyed, "they're from a bunch of troublemakers. General, you should know what I have heard from people around Secretary Stanton."

Key's brother worked at the War Department. McClellan motioned for Custer to put the letters on the table, where he would look them over at his leisure for his amusement, and said to Key, "His attitude seemed to change toward me. Perhaps the illness of his child—"

"He has said that your private letter was an act of insubordination, a political platform from which you intend to oppose the President."

The general controlled his anger for a moment; then, among his closest aides, he let it out. "That man is the most unmitigated scoundrel I ever knew, heard of or read of. I do not wish to be irreverent, gentlemen, but had our Secretary of War lived at the time of the Savior, Judas Iscariot would have remained a respected member of the fraternity of the apostles, and the rascality of Edwin M. Stanton would have caused Judas to have raised his arms in holy horror and unaffected wonder!"

That explosion was not like him, but it made him feel better. With awe on the face of young Custer at the display of irreverence and insubordination, McClellan went on, "I hate to think that humanity could sink so low. He has deceived me once—twice; he never will again. Enough of the creature—it makes me sick to think of him! Faugh!"

His aides bid him good night and left. The general of the largest army ever assembled on the North American continent thought for a moment of Marshal Jomini, the great military tactician whose works were studied by both

Lee and himself. Jomini, McClellan judged, had turned out to be mistaken in his scorn of earthworks—a not very good soldier, well dug in, backed by some artillery, and armed with a gun with a rifled musket, could hold off three times his number—but Jomini was surely right about the nature of war. Battles were to be fought by soldiers against soldiers, commanded by professionals—not fought by a people against a people, with hatreds whipped up by bloodthirsty politicians.

He had done the best he could with the army at his command. Though he had no faith in this administration, he had served it honestly. Now he suspected Lincoln would deprive him of the means of winning and then dismiss him for failing to attack.

He was convinced that history would judge McClellan right and Lincoln wrong, that here was where the great battle would have to be fought, not all the way overland from Washington through ninety miles of hostile territory. Perhaps—the thought crossed his mind for the first time—he should have taken the President more into his confidence from the start, won his support away from Stanton and Chase and the other radicals. If he had built political earthworks in his rear, perhaps God would not have had to deny him the capture of Richmond while the radicals held sway in Washington.

Now it was up to the President, to win the war or to extend it, until some other general with Lincoln's trust put forward McClellan's plan. It was up to Lincoln to resist the pressure for abolition that would make peaceful reunion impossible; at least he had been warned of its effect on the army. McClellan would have to think about writing his financier friend Aspinwall for a job in industry, and passing the word through Key to Horatio Seymour and Fernando Wood about his interest in Democratic affairs.

He picked up the pen. "In this weary world, I have seen but little happiness save what I have enjoyed with you," he wrote Nell, finding his greatest comfort in his correspondence. "So the baby has more teeth! When will she begin to say a word or two? I suppose when I come back home I will find her handling a knife and fork . . ."

CHAPTER 15

FIRST DRAFT

Homer Bates gave up his desk to Major Eckert, who had given up his larger desk in the telegraph office to the President, just returned from a visit to the Richmond front. Bates was familiar with the regular procedure for a presidential visit: when Mr. Lincoln chose to spend time near the flow of cables, the desk under the Maltese Cross on the wall, with a chair at one of the windows that looked out on Pennsylvania Avenue, was made available to Mr. Lincoln.

But the presidential presence in the telegraph office was expected only when a battle was imminent or under way. Bates, working on his ciphers on a makeshift desk in his lap, knew of no major engagement going on at the moment. In Kentucky, rebel cavalry raider John Hunt Morgan was causing trouble, as he often did. A flurry of cables had gone back and forth when Lincoln appointed Halleck General-in-Chief, putting Grant in command out West and subordinating both Pope and McClellan in the East to "Old Brains," but no urgent military activity had taken place since the end of the Seven Days' battles. That was over a week ago.

Lincoln asked Eckert for paper. The major procured some foolscap and handed it to him, along with a small barrel-pen made by Gillot, such as were supplied to cipher operators. Lincoln had begun these visits to work on some writing project just after the Seven Days, before he went down to see McClellan at Harrison's Landing. The President had explained then that he was interrupted too often at the White House—that's what people had taken to calling the Mansion—and he thought the telegraph office would be a good place to work undisturbed, without being out of touch.

Bates watched him look out the window for a while. Lincoln then put pen to paper, not writing much at once. He would think a bit, put down a line or two, then sit quietly for a few minutes. Apparently he was in no hurry to finish this particular piece of writing, which Bates presumed was some message to Congress.

The key began clattering. When the fresh dispatch had been received and deciphered, the young operator took it over to the President: Nathan Bedford Forrest and his rebel raiders had captured a Union garrison at Murfreesboro, near Nashville. General Lee was reported by one of Pinkerton's men to be moving some of his men away from Richmond and up the valley toward Washington; that could be trouble.

Stoddard, the President's third secretary, who was a man Bates called a friend, came from across the street to get Mr. Lincoln's signature on an act carrying into effect a treaty made with Great Britain for the suppression of the African slave trade. The President signed the measure and went back to looking out the window; Bates assumed the act just signed into law could not have been all that historic.

What struck Bates as an overly long message moved on the wire from General Pope, announcing to his new troops, "I have come to you from the West where we have always seen the backs of our enemies." That would not sit so well, in the telegraph operator's judgment, with the Union's Eastern soldiers. "I hear constantly of 'lines of retreat' and of 'bases of supplies'," went Pope's odd greeting. "Let us discard such ideas. Success and glory are in the advance, disaster and shame lurk in the rear."

Bates grinned; he suspected that Stanton himself might have written that bombastic message, to take a poke at McClellan, and the unintended result would be that Pope was going to be a laughingstock among the men. Bates thought of showing the Stanton-Pope pronouncement to the President but decided against it; Mr. Lincoln came to the telegraph office to work on his writing, not to be interrupted with minor business.

"Big spiderweb," said the President idly.

The major had left for a moment, so Bates answered. "You noticed, sir. That's an institution of the cipher room." The large web stretched from the lintel of the portico to the side of the outer windowsill. "Please don't open that window," he told the President, "you'll destroy the web. In a while, you may get to see Major Eckert's lieutenants."

Lincoln put down his pen and looked closely. "Where are they?"

"The lieutenants will soon report and pay their respects. They always do."

In a few moments, a large spider appeared at the crossroads of the web and tapped several times on the strands. That brought five or six other, smaller spiders—the lieutenants—out from different directions.

"There seems to be a great confabulation taking place," reported Lincoln delightedly. "Now they're all going back. How often do they do this?"

"Now and then," said Bates.

Lincoln went back to work for a while, writing a line or two. The major returned with some work for Bates to get started on, which he promptly did. It felt good working in the same room as the President. After a half hour or so, Lincoln looked at the clock on the wall and rose. Eckert was back and stood at attention, but Bates remained seated because his lap was full.

"Take charge of this," the President said to the major, handing him the single sheet of paper. "Put it with the others, and don't let anyone see it." He added he had more to do on it, but was not pressed for time.

"With pleasure, sir. I won't even read it myself."

"Well, I should be glad to know that no one will see it," Lincoln said mildly, "although there is no objection to your looking at it, Major, or you, Bates. Keep it locked up until I call for it tomorrow."

"I'll lock it here in the safe, Mr. Lincoln. Either Bates or I will have the key. One or the other of us is always here, or sleeping down the hall."

"Good. I have to go see some border-state congressmen, now. Judge Blair's got them all lined up in the office, and I have to sell them my way of thinking."

"Compensated emancipation," Bates piped up. "Four hundred dollars a head."

"That's the best way," the President nodded, with that sad smile that made Bates feel he was family. "I do not speak of emancipation at once, but of a decision at once to emancipate gradually."

"Where you going to put 'em all, sir?" Bates asked. "That's what my folks always ask."

"Room in South America for colonization," the President replied, as if practicing his lines for the border-state men, "can be obtained cheaply, and in abundance. And when numbers shall be large enough to be company and encouragement for one another, the freed people will not be so reluctant to go."

He made it sound so simple; Bates assumed that if the President said so, that was the way it would be.

Lincoln bent down and tapped lightly at the window in farewell to Eckert's lieutenants.

"That's the best way," he repeated. "But not the only way."

Treasury Secretary Salmon P. Chase

BOOK SIX

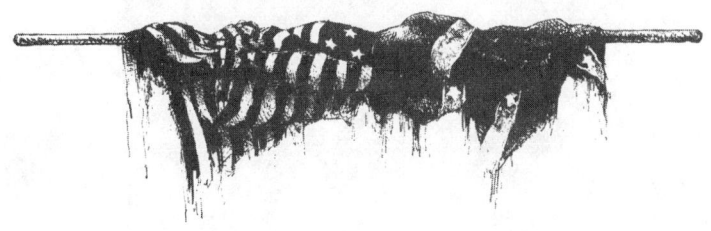

Salmon
Portland
Chase

CHAPTER 1

SMALL CHANGE

"Do you have change for a dollar, Father? I want to pay the boy for the *Intelligencer.*"

"Not you too, Kate," Chase muttered in irritation. "I've had enough of that today."

His daughter looked at him in genuine surprise. "What do you mean?"

Chase instantly felt guilty at his reaction. Kate, despite the education he had given her in the finances of government, could have no inkling of what the failure of McClellan's Peninsula campaign had done to the value of government paper; suddenly everyone was demanding payment in specie. As confidence in a Northern victory ebbed, the price of gold and silver had spurted upward, and the value of the greenback against gold declined. The silver in coins was now worth more than the face value of the coin, which was why small change seemingly disappeared.

"Tell the boy to come back when you owe him a dollar," the Secretary of the Treasury said, "and then pay him with a greenback. The whole country is out of small change."

She sent the boy away and returned. "What are you going to do about it?"

"The first thing is to issue paper bills for ten cents, a quarter, and a half dollar."

She looked at him quizzically. "Ten-cent bills?"

"We'll call them stamps, but people won't use them to stick on letters; they'll use them for change. We'll make them directly convertible to greenbacks."

He watched his official hostess—no longer his little girl—think that over, and waited for the inevitable question.

"Why won't people use them for stamps, Father?"

"No glue on the back," he said triumphantly. That had been one of the more practical ideas to come out of the Treasury staff.

His daughter looked dubious, and Chase could not blame her; the Treasury Secretary himself did not like the idea of paper change, but it was either that temporary expedient or coining zinc and other cheap metals, which would make the nation seem permanently penniless.

"That's the easy part of my problem," he told her. "The hard part is paying the new soldiers. I had the accounts more or less current after we went to paper money. We were all set to win the war this summer; Stanton stopped recruiting. Now it looks like a longer war, the President has called for three hundred thousand men, and I can't find the money to pay them."

"Raise taxes?"

He gave her a stern look; she was not putting to good use the long hours he had spent explaining finance to her. "The people are paying three percent of their income to taxes already. I went along with the tax on incomes last year as a war measure, but it would be madness to be associated with raising it further."

"You'll have to borrow it, then."

He swallowed. "Yes." He did not like to consider the possibility of failing to sell the government's bonds. "Either borrow, or issue more greenbacks."

"But that would lead to inflation of the currency, panic, collapse—" She was smiling. That was what he had said a year before. Kate had an unfortunate ability to remember everything a man said, and a tendency to turn it back at him, which he suspected would not help her in life.

"I've been surprised by the success of the greenbacks," he admitted. "I thought people would act sensibly—I expected them to use the greenbacks, which draw no interest, to buy government bonds, which pay six percent. Instead, they just hold on to the greenbacks." He shook his head in wonderment at the ignorance of the people. "The government has a hundred million dollars in greenbacks in circulation out there, and we don't have to pay any interest. It's amazing. The private banks used to do that, issuing paper notes, and they must have made a fortune."

"I hope you don't say that in Cabinet, Father. The Blairs would use it against you."

He smiled his thanks at her political protectiveness, then turned serious again. "It is amazing how little we know about the political arithmetic, or what they call 'economics' now. This war is costing a million dollars a day; we are going deeper and deeper into debt; by all rights, the credit should be drying up. But somehow, because we're acting as one nation—not as a collection of states and local banks—there doesn't seem to be a bottom to the well. Extraordinary what we can do, acting as a nation, in borrowing money. Pity it took a war to teach us."

"Do you suppose Lincoln understands any of that?"

"Of course not. He keeps talking about 'the Union' as if it had some mystical influence, but I don't think he has the foggiest notion about what this war is demonstrating in terms of national power."

Vast changes, it seemed to him, were taking place without anybody thinking them through. Chase suspected that Stanton's demand for national control of the telegraph was overreaching, and he had even more doubt about the constitutionality of the government's takeover of the railroads, which was a seizure of private property from loyal citizens in "the public's" interest. His own Western faction in Congress, led by Ben Wade, put over the Homestead Act, granting free soil to settlers and guaranteeing the stretching westward of the nation's labor force; the Easterners countered with passage of the land grant to set up agricultural colleges, by which the national government threatened to replace sectarian churches in the sponsorship of higher education. Would all this centralization lead to monarchism? Chase hoped that federalist principles would emerge, with states running the new institutions being set up by the national government, but nobody could be sure. It was all happening so fast.

"Are you saying, Father," Kate's voice drifted to him, "that we should create one central bank and control the money from here?"

"In a way, yes." He struggled with the power and the danger of his own contribution to the great new changes. "Yes. I should have the power to charter all banks. I should be able to tell them what their reserves should be, how much should be lent to the federal treasury. I suppose we could run the entire country from right here in Washington."

"Will Lincoln go along? Will the Congress?"

"Who knows?" he shrugged, although he would not admit such ignorance to anyone but his daughter. "There are no experts in this. Plain paper seems to be as good as gold. I think we can get a national bank. We can get anything, provided we get McClellan out and a general in who restores the people's confidence."

"So that's why Bill Sprague had to go to Corinth to see Halleck," she said, "to put more pressure on Lincoln to kick out McClellan."

Chase liked the way her mind leaped ahead, but it troubled him that his daughter's quick intelligence was too willing to attribute some ignoble motive to his actions.

"Exactly," he told his daughter. "The President has unfortunately committed the management of the war almost exclusively to his political opponents. If this continues, the public confidence that supports the paper money will disappear—nobody will take greenbacks, nobody will lend us gold, and we will not be able to pay the contractors or the troops. I've explained all that to Sprague."

"Yes, the boy governor told me."

Such a display of personal disrespect toward Sprague, her lovesick beau, and her admission that she had wheedled the most confidential information out of him with such ease, troubled the Treasury Secretary.

"There is nobody in this world I trust more than you, Kate, but I wish you would not wring every last secret out of Governor Sprague, who is torn by his obligation to confidence and his love for you."

"He was drunk," she replied with the sort of insouciance that irritated him more, "and he would have told anybody anything."

He ignored that. Sprague was the wealthiest man in New England, said to be worth $25 million, and had followed his purchase of a regiment by buying a Senate seat for next year. He would make a superb son-in-law and a useful supporter in a race for the presidential nomination. Chase checked himself; such thoughts, in combination, were unworthy of a dutiful father.

He noted the frown on his daughter's lovely face. Perhaps he should not burden her with the problems of high finance; it was not one of the subjects taught at Miss Haines's school in New York. "But don't bother your head with the financial ramifications of military politics, my dear," he sighed.

Still frowning, she gave him a sharp look. "I'm bothering my head, as you put it, wondering how we can make some money to meet the household bills out of all this. Thurlow Weed would know how to turn a profit out of what we know."

"Don't talk to that man," he ordered. "Weed is a scoundrel, a wirepuller, no sense of the public morality at all. Does Seward's dirty work, and he'll be conniving against us at the next convention. Stay away from him." Seward and Blair, probably with Gideon Welles, were forming a conservative clique in the Cabinet and might soon dominate the vacillating Lincoln. Chase pictured Weed at the center of such an intrigue.

"John Hay says that Lincoln keeps a special cubbyhole in his desk just for communications with Thurlow Weed," she replied, ignoring his advice in her headstrong way.

"Hay is another one you're seeing too much of," Chase told her. Kate had claimed originally she was cultivating a contact close to Lincoln, to learn what could be useful, but Chase knew she was attracted to the young man. Young Hay struck him as a high-living and a sharp-witted fellow who could turn the tables on Kate's use of him. Chase did not want the President to know of plans to garner support for Chase's candidacy, or of Chase's widely expressed low opinion of the way Lincoln failed to use his Cabinet: In this Administration, a Cabinet session had degenerated to nothing more than a meeting of department heads. The Treasury Secretary deplored both the lack of central direction and the sense of moral fervor. In addition, as a father, Chase had the obligation to warn his daughter of the occasion of sin, which the mustachioed bachelor so obviously presented.

"I will see whom I please when I please," she flashed. "Who are you to tell me whom to go out with?"

"I am your father," he replied, with what he thought was eloquent simplicity.

"When it's convenient."

"And what is that supposed to mean?"

"I suppose you've forgotten that you sent me away for eleven years," she blazed with what he feared was a reversion to the tantrums of her childhood. She had been four years old when her mother died, and he had remarried quickly—too quickly for the child, who had refused to speak to her step-mother. That was when he sent her to Miss Haines's school in New York. "From five to sixteen, I did very well alone," she said, defiance growing.

"Mind your tongue, young lady."

"You never visited me," she went on, stinging him, "or wanted me home at Easter or Christmas. Finally, when you needed a respectable hostess again, after you buried your third wife, you saw that you had a beautiful, well-bred daughter. Suddenly I fit in. And now—you dare to tell me whom I cannot see?"

"I did not leave you destitute for eleven years, as you seem to think." He was furious, as only Kate could make him, and felt his self-control slip from him. "What ingratitude! You could not bear to be at home with your new mother, who was a fine and loving woman, and I had to go without proper clothes to make it possible for you to learn your fine ways in New York."

"How you must have suffered, Father."

"Do you remember a bill for three hundred and five dollars for new clothes that you sent me one day?" He had a picture of that invoice in his mind's eye. "As governor of Ohio, I was making eighteen hundred dollars a year—that little extravagance of yours was nearly three months' pay. And I paid the bill without a word."

"There is more to raising a daughter than paying bills."

"There is more to being a daughter than running around with corrupt lobby agents and handsome young men who are your father's political enemies," he thundered, hating himself for losing his temper, which he rarely did. Only she could bring out the rage in him. All her life, the girl had been afflicted with an unreasoning jealousy—rooted in jealousy for her father, he understood—but she had an insidious way of making him, the most upright of husbands three times over, seem almost unfaithful.

Chase was certain Kate's jealousy was none of his doing; his younger daughter, Nettie, was sweetly dutiful, proving that the fault lay in some strange dark urges in Kate wholly unrelated to any heritage of his. Now that he had given her all she wanted—an education that enabled her to flirt with the British ambassador, an official position in Washington society second only to the wife of the President—Kate was as headstrong as when she spat at her stepmother, rest that woman's saintly soul.

Now that it was her turn to repay some of her debt to him for her high station in life, Chase was determined to call her to account. "I am going to the office," he announced. "When I return, we will discuss your obvious need to leave this city for a time." That assertion of parental authority seemed to bring her up short; he could still control her physical whereabouts. "Perhaps this is the time for a trip to Buttermilk Falls—you can use the simple farm life; it's good for a short temper."

"I am planning to dine tonight with Roscoe Conkling," she said icily, "the congressman who introduced the confiscation bill in the House. Tomorrow I shall go riding with your good friend Major Garfield of Ohio. Is their company politically suitable for me?"

"Conkling is an adventurer and Major Garfield is married," he replied, ignoring her sarcasm. "Neither has much of a future. Start looking to the future." He took a deep breath and made a show of searching for his hat. "I refuse to continue this discussion. I confess that you have made me profoundly angry."

"Go to the office, then, where you can get your mail."

That was a low blow; he felt a new surge of anger mingled with guilt. Against his better judgment, he was impelled to ask again: "And what does that mean?"

"The postman who brings the mail, thanks to Postmaster General Blair, tells me you have directed him to deliver the mail that comes here from your lady friends to the Treasury Department."

He did not let himself express his outrage.

"Dear Father, I don't mind your correspondence with Adele Douglas, a cultivated lady and respectable widow," she said, as if the subject was any of her business, "even though she is Rose Greenhow's sister-in-law, and suspected of trying to help that spy avoid the hanging she deserves. And Carlotta Eastman worships you, an attitude you especially admire in your women friends—you left one of her letters lying on the table in the den, probably for my edification."

She was getting the better of this discussion. Chase wished he had not been irritable or so easily provoked, but he could not back down now. "Your blessing is appreciated. I take it," he said, "that there is one correspondent to whom you do object. I wish you would get to the point."

"Anna Carroll is the one you're seeing too much of," she said, in what he saw was a deliberate parallel to his stricture against John Hay.

He rose to go. "And what makes Miss Carroll especially offensive to you, my dear daughter?"

"Certainly not her figger, which would delight a voluptuary," Kate said, putting a suggestive hand to her own somewhat meager bosom. "No, my objection is purely political. She's a Know-Nothing at heart, and on record as one of their leaders. She's pro-slavery, anti-confiscation, against everything you stand for, and probably in the pay of the Blairs. Your association with her is a political embarrassment."

"Miss Carroll has made no secret of her views," he answered slowly, "and her recent pamphlet, which I commend to you, unfortunately makes a fool out of Sumner."

He put in that dig at Charles Sumner because the Massachusetts senator had made frequent trips to New York while Kate was at Miss Haines's, befriending the girl, who had undoubtedly professed her loneliness; Sumner still retained what he claimed to be an avuncular affection, which Kate reciprocated. The foppish senator from Boston was a fellow radical in the Republican ranks, but his manner put Chase off. Too often he had seemed to be willing to make Chase feel inadequate as a father.

Chase had a subtler reason for reminding his ungrateful daughter about her friendship with the senator who flattered her at all the best parties. If the Senate radicals succeeded in getting Lincoln around to abolition, Sumner and Wade would remove Chase's key moral issue in wresting the nomination from the inadequate President. However, if Anna Carroll, in her obscure alliance with the Blairs and Seward, succeeded in blocking an opportunistic shift toward abolition by Lincoln, Chase would be well positioned to make his move on an anti-slavery platform in 1864.

That was a political thought that Chase considered unworthy of greatness; he felt a twinge of guilt in thinking it, and assured himself that its intricacy escaped his daughter. He assuaged the twinge with the conviction that in the long run a Chase presidency would be best for both the nation and the slaves.

"Miss Carroll is a spinster in her late forties," his daughter went on, now on weaker ground, "and she has been rejected by two presidents—Fillmore and Buchanan. She's damaged goods and would make you a laughingstock."

"I am fifty-six," he replied. He had always been pleased to be in Anna Carroll's company, stimulated by her strong mind and—he grudgingly admitted it—attracted by her delectable figure, but had not until this moment given any serious thought to romance. Certainly she would bring him political support where he was weakest, among the party's conservatives. He admired her self-reliance. Stanton had told him the modest little lady was the originator of the Tennessee River plan, which if true—you could never tell with Stanton—led to the Donelson victory and the successful flotation of the bond issue in April. If Kate suspected she was more than a political ally, let his jealous daughter think it. The shift in Kate's accusation from emotionally abused daughter to unjustly competitive woman lessened his sense of guilt. He could now feel better about her odious outburst; it was none of his doing. He looked forward to Sunday and the cleansing of his soul.

With even more than his usual dignity, Chase put on his hat and walked out into the July humidity. He did not deign to bid his daughter farewell. He could hear Kate's parting shot: "And worst of all, she's smarter than you!" That stung him.

CHAPTER 2

John Hay's Diary
July 12, 1862

Everything seems to be coming apart.

The Prsdt has the hypo. The black mood started to descend three days ago, when he came back from Harrison's Landing.

The obvious reason is the military debacle of our Little Napoleon, pushed back from Richmond when the rebel capital was in his grasp.

The less obvious reason is the political box the Prsdt finds himself in. The defeat of McClellan in the Seven Days battles gave a lift to Wade and the rest of the Jacobins in Congress. This session will end in four days, on the sixteenth of this month, but it will not be soon enough for us. The Jacobins are pushing hard for abolition, which bids fair to break up the Republican Party and totally divide the North. The confiscation bill must be headed off at all costs, and I must confess that a note of desperation has attended our efforts.

This morning, a suffocating Saturday, the Prsdt made his plea to the border-state congressmen. The meeting did not go as he had hoped.

"I do not speak of emancipation at once," he told the twenty or so congressmen who packed into the office, "but of a decision at once to emancipate gradually. If you all had voted for this last March, the war would now be substantially ended."

That told-you-so did not set well; I could see, from the back of the room, how Lincoln's implicit charge that they had prolonged the war angered some of the Kentuckians.

"Chase can't get the money to pay contractors for uniforms," one snorted, "much less raise four hundred dollars a head to buy thousands of slaves."

The Tycoon has faith in the ability of Kate Chase's father to come up with money miraculously, and he persevered. "How much better for you, as seller, and the nation as buyer, to sell out and buy out slavery—rather than to cut one another's throats."

But we could all tell that the majority of border-staters in that room was hostile. When a few of them fretted that compensated emancipation would solidify the spirit of rebellion in the South and fan the fires of secession in their states, the Prsdt played his last card: the threat of growing pressure from the abolitionists.

"I am pressed with a difficulty not yet mentioned," he broached it at last; "an instance of it is known to you."

"If you're talking about General Hunter's misbegotten declaration of emancipation," one of them said hotly, "that almost kicked my district into secession. If you hadn't disavowed that abolitionist trick, Lincoln, most of us wouldn't be here listening to you today—"

"General Hunter is an honest man," Lincoln said of the persnickety Republican general who pulled a fast one on him a few months ago. Hunter had forced the Prsdt to slap him down, as the Prsdt did to Frémont when that popinjay also took it on himself to free the slaves. "He proclaimed all men free within certain states, and I repudiated the proclamation. Yet in repudiating it, I gave dissatisfaction, if not offense, to many whose support the country cannot afford to lose."

"Horace Greeley, and Wendell Phillips, and Ben Wade and that whole crazy bunch," said a man from Maryland, with what I had to privately admit was uncanny accuracy. "To hell with them."

"The pressure, from that direction, is still upon me," Lincoln insisted, pacing behind his desk, knowing he was losing his jury, "and is increasing. By conceding what I now ask—selling your slaves at a fair price—you can relieve me, you can relieve the country, in this important point."

"Not so," said the Marylander. "Once you give in to them on this buy-out of slaves in the loyal states, the abolitionists will want the whole thing. They'll demand you free the four million slaves in the rebel states, and this will be a war not against the rebellion but against slavery. And my folks are for Union, but not for abolition. So are you, Mr. President."

The Prsdt had no good answer to that; so, like a good lawyer, he flattered them and appealed to their love of country. "You are patriots and statesmen," he said, laying it on a little thick, "and as such, I pray you, consider this proposition. To you, the privilege is given to assure this nation's happy future, and to link your own names with it forever."

I suppose he felt he had to give compensated emancipation one last try, but the appeal to patriotism fell flat. The Kentucky man mumbled he would send a written reply from the delegation, but everybody there knew what the answer would be: thanks, but the loyal people in our border states prefer their slaves to stay slaves. No sale.

John Crisfield, a Marylander but a good Union man, was going out with the glum group, and Lincoln detained him. They had served together as Whigs in Congress back in the forties. Crisfield was a member of a House committee assigned to write a report on compensated emancipation, which Lincoln knew would not likely be produced.

"Well, Crisfield, how are you getting along with your report? Have you written it yet?"

"No." The finality of that suggested to me that not even Lincoln's old friends among the border-staters could be counted on to offer payment for slaves.

"You had better come to an agreement," Lincoln said doggedly, as if he refused to grant he was losing. "Niggers will never be higher."

Crisfield shrugged; maybe he thinks Marylanders want their peculiar institution untouched, or maybe he thinks the price of negroes will continue to be bid up by the federal government. He's probably wrong; they're all wrong; the Prsdt is more likely to close down the game than to raise the ante.

Tonight the Tycoon ate alone at his desk. Mrs. Lincoln and son Robert are up in New York, on the way to West Point. I brought in a bill for him to sign creating a Medal of Honor for soldiers who have acted with incredible heroism. He reviewed some of those cases, and the heartrending stories in the citations made him feel worse. He pushed his plate away.

I went across the street with him to the telegraph office in the War Department. There, Stanton told him McClellan's troop figures were cockeyed—our

Little Napoleon is claiming to have only half the army we know he has. Stanton wanted to freeze the rebels on prisoner exchange, but Lincoln wants General Prentice, hero of Shiloh, back from prison: he directed Mars to authorize General Dix to trade Simon Buckner (the non-hero of Fort Donelson) for Prentice. Dix wants to know what to do with Rose Greenhow, in the light of the hanging of our spy in Richmond, and nobody knows what to tell him. That's not a cheery thought, either. The Prsdt said he wanted to work on some writing in the telegraph office—I suppose it's his veto message on the confiscation bill—and told me to go out to a party, which I did.

No solace in parties for me, however, even at the Eameses'; Miss Chase, who blows hot and cold, has left suddenly for a farm in upstate New York. Not a word of farewell to me—I found out about her abrupt departure from Lord Lyons at the party. Strange girl. Close, so close—then gone. It may be that she is fearful of her own feelings toward me.

Tomorrow, Sunday, is not going to be any better. Stanton's baby died, which is a mercy in a way, after a short life of horrible boils, and the funeral is tomorrow. That is bound to be a crusher to the Prsdt's spirits, a terrible reminder to him of the loss of Willie. I know he will come back from that dreary interlude with an indescribable look of sadness on his face—he really can look sadder than any man alive—and spend an hour perusing an album of war heroes that his own dead Willie had prepared. He does that now and then, usually with Senator Browning, just leafing the pages, with Tad asleep on the couch.

CHAPTER 3

THE TIME HAS ARRIVED

A white coach with a white coffin, symbolizing the purity of an infant, led the way. The reins of the black horses were held by undertakers in tall black hats. The coach of the Stanton family followed, and behind that was the coach of the President. A dozen coaches of Cabinet members, family, and friends formed the funeral cortege for James Hutchison Stanton, son of the Secretary of War, who died before he reached his ninth month.

William Henry Seward sat next to Lincoln in the President's carriage, facing forward. Opposite them sat Seward's daughter-in-law, her dark blue dress decorated with the single white carnation that all the women had been asked to wear that morning. Jammed into the seat next to her was "Father Neptune," Gideon Welles, the Secretary of the Navy. It occurred to Seward that the gray-white beard of "Father Neptune" kept getting bushier and longer.

Seward knew when not to talk to Lincoln. As the cortege wound its solemn way toward the cemetery north of Georgetown, the Secretary of State assumed that the President was reliving the anguish of the burial six months before of his beloved Willie. There had been no thought of having Mrs. Lincoln attend this funeral, for fear of a relapse into extended hysteria. The President, under his tall hat, was silent, lost in thought.

Although he never held any affection for the Secretary of War in the carriage ahead, Seward could feel a genuine sympathy for Stanton as a bereaved father. The long-expected loss of his baby seemed to crush Stanton just at the moment his many conservative Republican enemies, along with the Peace Democrats, had made him the target of their most furious attacks. As he had been hailed as "the organizer of victory" a few months before, Stanton was now being denounced as a primary cause of defeat. Seward had undergone the vicissitudes of politics as much as any man who had come within an eyelash of the presidency, and knew how hard it was to bear those shifts in public opinion when overlaid by personal tragedy.

He was glad that the Blairs had not told him beforehand of their campaign to discredit Stanton. Newspaper friends of the Blair family, especially at the *New York World,* had pinned McClellan's defeat squarely on Stanton's refusal to reinforce him with McDowell's army. Lincoln was not the press's target; Stanton drew the lightning. Even Horace Greeley's *Tribune* had printed a dispatch from Wilkeson, its chief correspondent in the Peninsula, praising McClellan and castigating the Secretary of War for throwing away the chance to capture Richmond and end the war.

Seward could sympathize with anybody, even Stanton, who was the target of Uncle Horace's personal fickleness and political infidelity; still, even on this sad day for the Secretary of War, he found himself siding with the Blairs against Stanton and Chase. Seward thought it curious: from a start as Lincoln's greatest rival in the party, William Henry Seward, of all people, had become a "Lincoln man," more than any of his colleagues, who were still representing factions of the party in the Cabinet.

"Good work with the governors," Lincoln said unexpectedly.

Seward bobbed his head in acknowledgment. He had been sent to his home state of New York the week before, to induce a group of the governors meeting there to raise additional troops, now that the realization struck that the war was not going to be over in two weeks. Seward was well aware he had performed at his ex-gubernatorial best, persuading his former fellow state executives that the impetus for further recruitment must appear to come from them rather than from the President.

As a result, the governors, led by Morgan of New York (Seward made a mental note to get him a commission as major general of volunteers when his term ended), had "volunteered" three hundred thousand men. A rousing song was concocted: "We are coming, Father Abraham, three hundred thousand more." If those volunteers did not come, a military draft would be needed; Seward could envision the riots that forced conscription would bring in New York City, hotbed of copperheads' agitation about the necessary arrests of traitors.

"I spoke to the border-state congressmen yesterday," Lincoln, ready to talk, reported. "You saw my speech. I wrote it out because I wanted a record of it. Gradual, compensated emancipation. I really beseeched them, told them my proposal acted not the Pharisee."

"No takers?"

"Oh, Crisfield says maybe a third of the delegation will go along," the President said. "The others say it would be too expensive, or that we promised the war was for the Union and not against slavery. They just cannot read the signs of the times."

Seward caught Lincoln's biblical allusion to the prophet's denunciation of hypocrites; one of those "signs of the times" was the passage in Congress two days before of a bill to educate the children of the freed slaves in the District of Columbia. Six months before, nobody would have thought to appropriate money to raise up black children.

Seward remarked that if the border states had not been moved by the reaction to McClellan's defeat, they were never likely to take up Lincoln's offer of buying back slaves at four hundred dollars a head.

"If the rebels do not cease to persist in this war against the government," said Lincoln, "and I see no evidence that they will, maybe it will be necessary to emancipate the slaves by proclamation."

Secretary Welles, who had been leaning back in his seat, arms crossed, suddenly leaned forward; what was that the President said?

Seward, too, was surprised at Lincoln's statement. Whenever the subject of abolition had been raised before, the President had given it short shrift, pointing to three loyal states that would probably throw down their Union arms. Up to this moment, Republican dogma held that slavery—which could no longer be extended to the territories—was a matter to be decided upon by each of the present states. Seward immediately sensed the scope of the change in the President's thinking. Evidently the rejection by the border-state men of his proposal yesterday had quite an effect on Lincoln; or perhaps the Union reverses on the Peninsula, and the public's growing war-weariness, were driving him to desperate measures.

"I've been giving a lot of thought to it," Lincoln continued, "and I've about come to the conclusion that it is a military necessity. It may be absolutely essential for the salvation of the Union. We must free the slaves or be ourselves subdued."

Now Seward was thunderstruck; this was no idle thought uttered aloud. Lincoln, after behaving so sensibly in the face of radical Republican cries to "arm the slaves," and after having braved the Greeley onslaughts by countermanding military orders declaring captured slaves "forever free," was now showing signs of panic. His alternative to abolition—"or be ourselves subdued"—was more than a bit excessive; Seward was sure the North was in no danger of losing the war, only of losing heart.

"This is the first occasion I've mentioned the subject to anyone," the President confided. "Tell me, frankly, how the proposition strikes you."

Seward knew Lincoln well enough by now not to underestimate his political cunning. The radicals' confiscation bill, which was given no chance of passage when Trumbull and Conkling introduced it six months before, had taken on new life with the bitter Peninsula disappointments of July. If confiscation passed in the coming week and Lincoln vetoed it, the radicals might take over the Republican Party—or take the cause of abolition right out of the party. If the bill passed and Lincoln could not avoid signing it, the issue of slavery—which Lincoln, at Seward's constant urging, had kept in his own hands—would be wrested away from him by the Congress. Wade's radicals would then be emboldened to take over the direction of the war and the resolution of the peace. That would be a disaster, Seward felt, a recipe for sectional hatred for a century; evidently Lincoln felt the same way.

On the other hand, a proclamation issued without the ability to enforce it might cause a servile rebellion and provide Lord Palmerston with the excuse to send English troops to prevent anarchy in a cotton supplier. It would also remove all possibility of negotiation for peace. The Secretary of State had to think fast. Perhaps a limited military proclamation, basing an obviously unconstitutional act on the President's claim of war power, would turn aside Ben Wade's challenge.

"This subject involves consequences so vast and momentous," Seward tried to hedge, "that I want to give it my mature reflection."

Lincoln, however, wanted a reaction then and there. "Of course," the President pressed, "but how does it strike you?"

"The measure might be justifiable on military grounds," said Seward, not wanting to make a mistake, confining his reaction to the legalities. "You might use words like 'expedient,' and 'necessary.' " The English might understand that.

"Those are my views as well," said Welles when Lincoln looked toward him. "The reverses before Richmond impel us to adopt extraordinary measures to preserve the national existence."

"Give it your special and deliberate attention," Lincoln directed, adding carefully to Seward's daughter-in-law, "Not a word to anyone."

Seward nodded firmly to his son's wife, who because his own wife had been ill was present at a moment of great import. In a way it was fortunate, Seward thought, that Frances was not there: she would have let peal a great hallelujah at the thought of eradicating what she kept calling "this great moral evil." And if emancipation were presented as some great moral decision, rather than a military necessity forced on a grudging government, the majority of the north would rebel.

They rode on, each turning the matter over in his mind. Welles adverted to it again before they reached the cemetery, and when Seward suggested it needed much more deliberation, Lincoln said only, "Something must be done."

Seward set aside the politics for a moment to weigh the foreign-policy effect of such a move. In England, most workingmen would embrace American abolition and perhaps block the government's inclination to aid the Confederacy now that a long war seemed assured. On the other hand, people in England and France would be repelled by anything that smacked of a call for slave uprisings, and the rape of white women by rampaging blacks. He would need Thurlow Weed's reading of the Europeans on that.

Weed would also want to know why Lincoln had chosen Seward and Welles to discuss it with first. Why not Father Blair? Seward looked around; none of the Blairs was present at this funeral, perhaps because of an aversion to hypocrisy; they all hated Stanton. But the Blairs would not be consulted first on emancipation, Seward assumed, because the conservative element, which included Attorney General Bates, would likely oppose the proposition. On the other hand, Lincoln would not likely turn to Chase first, because that ally of the radicals would undoubtedly be for it, to the extent of letting one and all know he was bringing it about. Same with abolitionist Stanton, though he would be more circumspect.

No; Seward and Welles were the men in the center of this Cabinet to whom Lincoln would turn for unbiased judgment. This was no sudden, emotional idea that occurred on the way to a burial; the President was looking for a way to counter his military disappointment and respond to the radicals without roiling his own conservative center.

"You're not thinking of arming the slaves, are you?" Welles asked.

"Not at present," the President answered. "Arming former slaves would produce dangerous, perhaps fatal, dissatisfaction in our army, and do more injury than good."

Seward noted the "not at present"—even the most extreme of radical proposals was not beyond possibility in time. He tested to see how deeply the President had thought this through: "What if this proclamation brings thousands of Africans into our lines?"

"No negroes taken and escaping during the war should be returned to slavery," Lincoln said, tempering that rejection of old fugitive-slave laws with "but no inducements are to be held out to them to come into our lines. They already come faster than we can provide for them and are becoming an embarrassment to the government."

Seward noted Lincoln's care in shifting his earlier positions, and concluded he must have been chewing it over since his return from Harrison's Landing. Had McClellan said or done anything there to trigger this move of Lincoln's now? Seward knew from the Blairs that General McClellan felt strongly it would be a mistake to tamper with slavery where it exists. However, if McClellan was a military loser, his political strategy would lose as well.

"Think about it," Lincoln repeated as they neared the cemetery. "The time has arrived when we must determine whether the slave element should be for or against us."

That puzzled Seward. Did Lincoln think that the slaves in the South would withhold their labor on the plantations and thereby cripple the Confederacy? Or was he unaware of the terrors of a slave rebellion, shocking and revolting the civilized world, thereby giving the leaders of England and France the chance they were looking for to come to the aid of the South?

The Secretary of State feared that Lincoln, buffeted by the failures of the military and the storming of the radicals, was moving too far ahead of national sentiment. "Not a word to anyone," he agreed aloud, repeating the President's admonition, hoping Lincoln would keep this thought to himself lest some monumental mistake be made.

The procession was at the cemetery. Seward motioned Lincoln to go on ahead. The President, walking alone, followed Stanton behind the white coffin to the grave.

CHAPTER 4

DYING SOMETIME

Before breakfast on Monday morning—before the week really began—Orville Browning paid a call on Anna Carroll. The senator told himself the purpose of his visit was to drop off his latest speeches, which she had helped prepare, but he knew she would be available to discuss political strategy in the waning days of the session.

"Will your friend Lincoln veto the bill?" she asked, handing him a cup of coffee. He sipped gratefully at first, then more slowly. It tasted terrible; Miss Carroll was no cook.

"He says he's leaning that way," Browning said. "But he doesn't want to split the party."

"You told him about our idea for a Union party?"

"I did, and he seemed to like it." In reality, Lincoln had not shown more than modest interest in the idea, but certainly it made sense to put together the conservative Republicans, the war Democrats, and Miss Carroll's old Know-Nothing friends under the rubric of a Union party. Such a coalition would freeze out the radical Republicans bent on abolition and a long war of subjugation.

"Orville, never forget—most people in this country today are in favor of the Union as it was, the Constitution as it is. They're against this confiscation bill, taking away property, arming the freed slaves."

Browning agreed. He admired Miss Carroll, though she was too strictly business when it came to politics. Most men resented her. He could see how Lincoln could become irritated with Miss Carroll's damnable persistence but would admire her withal. Not many people—and very few women—could be so helpful in figuring out legal arguments, then writing and circulating them far and wide. He took a swallow of coffee and grimaced; no wonder she never married.

"There is only one remedy for the evils upon us," she continued, in that way he found so didactically charming. "Only one way to save the country. That is, by antagonizing the abolitionists, by some unequivocal, unmistakable act. He has to veto confiscation, and force his Cabinet, Chase and Stanton included, to go along."

"I told Lincoln that this decision would be either his victory over the radicals or his defeat by them," Browning reported. "And I'll tell him that again in a few minutes, if he hasn't decided. It's one way or the other: sign or veto."

"I wonder." She put her face in her hands, elbows on the kitchen table, and pondered. She rose and fetched a piece of white biscuit. "This is hardtack, what the soldiers eat. Have you tried it? Stays fresh forever. Watch your teeth."

"What did you mean, 'I wonder'? The President is boxed in; he must either go one way or the other, Anna. This is the moment of decision."

Senator Orville Hickman Browning

"Senator Fessenden has been talking to Chase," she informed him. "You know the Senate far better than I do, Orville, but I hear they're looking for a way out."

It bothered Browning that this woman knew more about the maneuverings of the senators than he did. Bill Fessenden of Maine headed the committee that kept an eye on the Treasury; he was an anti-slavery man, but considered one of the more reasonable radicals. Browning knew that Fessenden would have preferred no confiscation legislation at all; like him, the senator from Maine thought that should be left to Union generals in the field. He could understand Fessenden searching for a way to avoid forcing Lincoln to veto the legislation, but where did Chase fit in this?

"I thought Chase was an abolitionist," he said to the lady, and tentatively took a nibble of the biscuit. It was like stone. "I should have thought he'd be urging Lincoln to sign the bill, and urging Wade and the others to fight for it."

"Well, Chase is not altogether disloyal to the President," she said. When Browning gave her a funny look, she laughed and said, "I suppose he has his own reasons, but whatever they are, Chase wants a compromise here."

"Too late for that, the bill's been passed. Seward and Weed favor a veto," Browning told her, "and so do the Blairs, and Bates. And so does Lincoln's best friend—namely, me. I don't see how he can wriggle out of this one."

"The President loses either way," she said, cocking her head analytically. "If he signs that bill to abolish slavery wherever the Union army goes, Lincoln hands over his control of the slavery issue to the Congress. Ben Wade would effectively represent the North, and the South would become a distinct people resisting an invader. Jeff Davis, Breckinridge, all those traitors would be seen down there as patriots."

"He must not sign that bill." Browning was certain of that.

"On the other hand, if Lincoln vetoes the confiscation bill, he splits the Republican Party just before this fall's elections." She shook her head. "That's not like Lincoln. He'd prefer to keep the issue to himself and keep the party together at the same time."

Browning pulled back his cheek and tried to crack the rocklike hardtack with his molars. "Our soldiers exist on these biscuits? God help them. I think you're mistaken, Anna—the Congress goes home tomorrow. No time left for a compromise. We cannot change the bill, nor can Lincoln—it's up or down."

"Could you sustain his veto in the Senate?"

"Yes. And if that is in doubt, Lincoln just has to put the bill in his pocket and let the Congress go home without signing it. It won't become law." The pocket veto might be the best strategy, even if it drove Ben Wade to heights of fury until December, when the Congress came back in session.

She pulled some papers out of the cabinet and pushed them across the table. "Here are a few thoughts for your speeches," she said modestly. The Senator looked them over hungrily for what could be used in that day's debate about the admission of West Virginia as a new free state. He forgave her for the hardtack and coffee.

Twenty minutes later, Browning was at the Executive Mansion. Lincoln was not in his office. Young Hay told him the President was alone in his library, writing, and had left orders to deny entry to everybody, but of course that did not apply to Senator Browning. The senator went down the hallway and looked in on his friend. The President was at a map, peering at the markings of forces arrayed on the Peninsula, and seemed pleased at the distraction.

Browning handed him the copy of the confiscation bill passed by the Senate. "Lincoln, this is a violation of the Constitution and ought to be vetoed."

Lincoln read the bill as if for the first time, frowning.

"Your course on this bill will determine whether you are to control the radicals," Browning told his friend, "or they are to control you. There is a tide in the affairs of men—"

"Taken at the flood," Lincoln murmured, showing he caught the Shakespearean allusion, "shallows and miseries."

"By vetoing abolition, you will raise a storm of enthusiasm for the cause of union in the border states worth a hundred thousand muskets." Browning could tell that Lincoln was not impressed with that prospect; the attitude of the border-state men the other day had depressed him. "If you approve it, on the other hand, I fear our friends in Kentucky will no longer sustain the Union cause."

"McClellan says that about the army," Lincoln observed.

Lincoln always reacted better to incentives than threats. "A veto would secure a unity of sentiment and purpose," Browning assured him, "that will bring to our support every loyal Democrat and consolidate all truly loyal men in one party—the Union party."

"I want to think about that, Orville." He dropped the bill on a table. "I promise I'll give it the most profound consideration."

"You look careworn, Lincoln. How are you?"

"Tolerably well." He did not look well, tolerably or otherwise. Browning was troubled by the President's appearance; Lincoln's complexion was normally sallow, but today the skin was almost gray.

"I've never seen you look this way, my friend." Browning went around the library table, reached up and laid a hand on the bony shoulder. "With all these troubles crowding in, I fear your health is suffering."

Lincoln took his hand, pressed it, and surprised his friend with a tenderly spoken "Browning, I must die sometime."

"Your fortunes, Mr. President, are bound up with those of the country." He had to shake Lincoln out of this mood, and patriotism was the most logical route. "Disaster to one would be disaster to the other."

"I don't know about that," Lincoln said, sadness in his voice. He sat down with a profound sigh.

Browning, seeing the suffering in his friend's eyes, could not bring himself to talk further about the veto or any other Senate business. "Do all you can to preserve your health," the senator said. He reached out and took Lincoln by his shoulders and squeezed hard, the way he had when Willie died and the numbed and shattered father seemed to need physical contact with humanity. The two men parted, tears in their eyes.

"Sir." Hay, the second secretary, was speaking to him. Browning blinked, wiped his eyes, and looked at a letter and an attachment Hay was handing him. "If you're going to the Senate now, would you present these to the president pro tem?"

He looked at the attachment first. "It looks like a bill." Presidents did not submit legislation to the Congress. He read it warily, then brightened. "This is a rehash of the compensated emancipation measure that never went anywhere." Lincoln's idea was apparently to make a nice gesture by sending a substitute for the bill he was going to veto. "I get it. Okay, I'll give it to Solomon Foot, the president pro tem. He'll bury it."

Browning then looked at the letter, which he found puzzling.

"It's an official request that the Senate stay in session one extra day," explained Hay. "I'll bring an identical letter to the Speaker of the House."

Browning still did not fathom Lincoln's motive, but did not want to go back at that moment to ask why the President needed the Congress in session an extra day. Perhaps Lincoln was too steeped in melancholy to face any decisions that morning.

CHAPTER 5

NOT SO FAR TRUST ME

Senator Benjamin Franklin Wade sensed a move to head off his plan to force
Lincoln to free the rebels' slaves.

In the Capitol, on the Senate floor, Solomon Foot of Vermont—President
pro tem of the Senate—accepted a letter handed to him by Orville Browning,
looked at it, frowned, and signaled to Ben Wade to meet him in the cloakroom.

Wade walked back, tapping Zack Chandler and Henry Wilson on the way;
with the confiscation bill finally passed in both houses, Wade suspected Lincoln would come up with some last-minute trick to cheat the Congress of the
honor of striking down slavery. The sniveling substitute bill sent up to the
Hill by the man in the Executive Mansion, delivered by his pet horse, Browning, was speared by Wade and promptly tabled. Trust Lincoln to try to set a
precedent with a presidential introduction of a bill in Congress; the man's
arrogance was infuriating. Wade was determined to prevent Lincoln's half
measure of buying up slaves from now till Doomsday from ever coming to a
vote; now, at long last, after the defeat of the cowardly McClellan by a ragtag
bunch of rebels, Wade was certain the North was ready for serious anti-
slavery legislation.

Arms folded, Wade awaited Foot, who came hurrying up with letter in
hand. "Message from the President, an informal request," said the president
pro tem. Foot read it to them: " 'Sir: Please inform the Senate that I shall be
obliged if they will postpone the adjournment at least one day beyond the
time which I understand to be now fixed for it.' "

"That's all?" Chandler asked.

" 'Your obedient servant, Abraham Lincoln,' " Foot added.

"I smell a rat," said Wade. The President's request, without a reason, was
disrespectful on its face. Lincoln had something up his sleeve. "He thinks the
Congress comes and goes at his whim. Tell the President to go to hell. I'll get
Tad Stevens over in the other body to tell him the same." Wade could count
on Thaddeus Stevens, the power of the House of Representatives, to strike
back hard at any attempt by Lincoln to water down the dispossession of
slaveholders passed by Congress.

"Maybe it would be better to smoke him out," Solomon Foot observed.
"I'll ask Lincoln what he has in mind."

"He has in mind making us appear to be his goddamn handmaidens,"
snorted Chandler.

Wade, on second thought, decided to go along with Foot's suggestion,
provided the Senate letter was sufficiently surly. He took out his pad and
pencil and drafted a reply.

Senator Foot read Wade's draft aloud to the others: " 'I am advised that it
will be exceedingly difficult, if not impossible, to postpone the adjournment

unless some senator can say *it is necessary*. To this end, several senators desire me to ask that you will state the ground or reason of such necessity.' "

"That'll show him," said Chandler.

Within an hour, a messenger brought back Lincoln's response. The four senators gathered to go over it.

Foot handed the note, in Lincoln's tight handwriting, to Wade, who looked it over first and growled, "Our friend downtown is getting a little testy." He read: " 'I am sorry senators could not so far trust me as to believe I had some real cause for wishing them to remain.' "

"Maybe my note was a little harsh," Foot worried.

"Shut up," snapped Chandler. "Keep reading what that baboon has to say, Ben."

" 'I am considering a bill which came to me only late in the day yesterday, and the subject of which has perplexed Congress for more than half a year.' "

"Confiscation," said Henry Wilson, "couldn't come as a surprise to him."

"He's threatening a veto," Wade told them. He read: " 'I may return it with objections; and if I should, I wish Congress to have the opportunity of obviating the objections, or of passing it into a law notwithstanding them. That is all.' "

"Did he say, 'That is all,' " asked Wilson, "or is that you saying it, Ben?"

"He wrote it, right here. 'That is all.' Damnation, it's enough."

"He's going to veto the confiscation bill," said Foot.

Wade glumly added, "and blame us for not making the changes he needed to sign it."

"Unless we make those changes," Fessenden interjected. Wade considered the Maine senator a flaccid ally in the anti-slavery fight, like Wilson, who voted right but did not have the passion to punish the slaveholders. Fessenden had softened the bill already, removing the death penalty for treason, making it impossible to suitably punish the slavocrats who had plunged the country into bloody war.

"I would make the bill stronger if I could," Wade fumed. "When I have brought a traitor who is seeking my life and my property to terms—and when I go bankrupt trying to put him down—I have no scruples about taking his property to indemnify myself. Including his slaves."

"Lincoln's inviting us to make a few changes," Fessenden pressed, "to keep him from having to veto it."

"For God's sake, the bill's been passed! Congress has worked its will! Who does he think he is?" Wade saw this clearly as Lincoln's latest attempt to usurp the power of the Congress.

"He is, after all, the President," Fessenden began, but Wade cut him off with contempt.

"The President cannot lay down and fix the principles upon which a war shall be conducted," he told Fessenden. "It's for Congress to lay down the rules and regulations by which the Executive shall be governed in conducting a war."

"Thinks he's a goddamn dictator," added Chandler.

"Saying that may make you feel better, Zack," said Fessenden, "but it isn't going to free any slaves. Lincoln wants to deal. I say let's deal."

Wade was sure Lincoln wanted more than to deal. Now, finally, with public sentiment turning against the go-slow, pro-slavery generals Lincoln had put in command, and with more of the people beginning to realize that the war was about slavery and not merely Union, Lincoln wanted to appear to be leading the Congress.

The legalistic President had been dragging his feet against abolition all along, Wade thought bitterly, up to this very morning; with defeat of his pusillanimity staring at him, the man in the Mansion was suddenly seeking to appear to be the Great Abolitionist.

"I'll stand for no mousing around the President," he told Fessenden, "no crawling before the White House throne."

"I don't like your insinuation, Senator—"

"Maybe we ought to have a committee on vetoes," Wade baited him with sarcasm. "We ought to have a committee to wait on the President whenever we send him a bill, to know what his royal pleasure is. You've been faint-hearted on this bill from the start."

"I have a right to my convictions," Fessenden flared, "and no man has a right to call me to account for them."

"The people of your state of Maine want an end to slavery—"

"And no man has a right to threaten me with the judgment of the people of Maine," Fessenden shot back. "I damned near had a son killed at Shiloh, Wade, and, what's more, when General Hunter challenged the President with an emancipation decree a few months ago, another son of mine formed a regiment of negro soldiers. The Fessenden family doesn't have to answer to you or anybody else about our dedication to the Union or to the cause of ending human slavery. If you want to call what I do in that cause 'mousing around,' you can make your impotent speeches in the Senate until you're blue in the face. I will try to find a way to get a bill signed into law."

Wade had to admire the man from Maine for that outburst, but he would give no ground: "Fessenden, you're missing the point of Lincoln's little trick. If emancipation comes from the Congress, as it surely does right now, it sets a precedent—gives us the supremacy that surely belongs to the Congress over the conduct of the war."

"And after the war too," added Chandler, correctly. Only if Congress dominated postwar policy would the South be treated as a conquered province, and would former slaves be given their full rights as human beings. Wade was sure of this: If the Democrats, or the Republican Blairs and their ilk, took over reconstruction, the blacks would be downtrodden for a century.

"You do what you like; I answer only to the people of Maine," Fessenden said. "I'll see what Lincoln wants changed."

"We don't have to give him everything," Foot put in.

Wade stared down at his shoes. Last year, before Congress was in session, Lincoln had assumed the war powers that properly belonged to the Congress. Now, as this session of Congress was ending, Lincoln was moving to gain total control of the slavery issue. What was he going to demand be cut out of the confiscation act? Anna Carroll, in her *Reply to Sumner* pamphlet, had made a fuss about the provision confiscating the property of people in rebellion before the passage of the act, complaining it would be ex post facto law. Of course, it was—served the traitors right for killing tens of thousands of loyal troops—and the Constitution would have to bend a little, as it had been bent when Lincoln took it on himself to suspend habeas corpus. What else?

"If he tries to take out the forfeiture provision," he told Fessenden, "tell him it's no deal. The traitors give up their property, homes and all, for all time—we don't give it back to traitors' heirs. We'll use that confiscated property to pay for the war."

"I still don't see how we can amend the bill at this stage," Henry Wilson wondered. "It's been passed. We don't have time to pass another. He can't veto parts of it, that's not the system; it's all or nothing."

"He wants control of the slavery issue," Wade warned. "We've taken it away from him, and he wants it back. And if he gets it, Congress will have no control of the war."

"Or the peace," added Chandler. "Lincoln isn't going to ship four million Africans back to Africa, no matter what he says. And the North won't take them. Those poor black souls will just sit in the South, supposedly free, but hungry and ignorant and in worse chains than ever."

Solomon Foot left to see the Speaker of the House about granting Lincoln the extra day. Wade could not stop Fessenden from going to sound out the President's desires, but it galled him to be bluffed out of a position so laboriously won.

This session of Congress, no thanks to Lincoln, had changed the very character of the country. Wade and his following—not just radicals, either—had won four great victories that Southerners had been blocking in Congress for generations. He had rammed through the Homestead Act, opening the West to settlers over the protests of some Eastern industrialists who wanted cheap labor close to home. Wade then turned against Westerners and the churches and pushed through the land-grant college bill, establishing the idea that the nation as a whole had a stake in higher education. Wade of Ohio had followed that with the Pacific Railroad Act, recognizing that private capital could not do the job of cutting through an uninhabited continent. These were the acts of a nation, not a committee of states, and he knew that Benjamin Franklin Wade, not Abraham Lincoln, was the guiding genius of this national transformation; now, at the moment of triumph, when the greatest act of the session was at stake and the issue of slavery was to be settled forever, he suspected that the President was pulling a fast one to weaken and cheapen the triumph.

Worse yet, Wade had a hunch that Lincoln would try something once Congress was out of session to overwhelm and nullify the Confiscation Act. Lincoln was showing himself to be the sort who would try to seize absolute control of the war clear through to the return of Congress in early December. Either the President was a shrewder politician than Wade had first thought, or else that baboon from Illinois had learned a lot in the past year.

CHAPTER 6

THE VETO THAT WAS NOT

"Stroke of genius," said Old Man Blair. He and Lincoln were on their horses, riding slowly up to the Capitol on a hazy Thursday morning, followed only by Marshal Lamon. Blair was delighted that the President had asked him to accompany him on his foray to the Congress on the final day of the session. It would be good for the radicals to see that the Blairs were in the saddle with Lincoln at a crucial moment. He had alerted Frank to leave his seat in the House and to wait for them in the little room that was the President's official office at the Capitol, near the rotunda. The office was a courtesy provided the Executive branch by the Congress, primarily to show that the center of governmental power was on Capitol Hill.

"I thought you'd appreciate it," Lincoln said, grinning. He sat tall in his saddle, legs dangling to low stirrups, stovepipe hat firmly on his head, and seemed to Blair to be about two feet taller than he was. "Fessenden turned out to be helpful. He and Orville Browning and I had breakfast this morning, and they went on ahead."

It was 9:30 A.M. on the last day of the session, the extra day the President had requested. Lincoln told the Blairs he wanted the Senate and House to convene and pass a joint resolution "explaining" the confiscation bill. The President would be on the spot to sign the Act then and there. The ingeniousness of the Lincoln tactic was its amendment of the act without actually amending it. The accompanying explanation would be treated by the President as part of the bill itself, shaping it to presidential specifications. Never had a President so thoroughly interjected himself into the lawmaking process, going beyond the mere threat of a veto.

"You got out the ex post facto impediment?"

Lincoln nodded. "Yes, there'll be no confiscation until every rebel has had fair warning. And no blood attainder, either—Tad Stevens, I hear, had a hard time swallowing that."

Blair approved. Property seized from rebels would be returned to their families after their deaths, as the Constitution provided, in the wisdom drawn from protection against the plundering of kings. Anna Carroll had made that point about a "blood attainder" in her work on the veto message for Bates.

The old man made a political calculation. This meant that the losers' property could not be used to pay the costs of the war. Who, then, would pay? Surely not the winners; it would have to be the next generation. He resolved to let the world know it was Chase, the conniving bastard, who had come up with the unpopular idea of an income tax—but to be paid later, long after the war ended, by generations that would profit from the sacrifices of these years, not by the generation that fought and bled.

Blair wondered if Lincoln had forced the radicals to the wall. "What about the enlistment of Africans as soldiers?" Blair called up to the man riding by his side. "Ben Wade and Tad Stevens wanted that badly."

"I went along on that. Maybe it's time. We don't have to arm them right away."

Blair liked the way the action had been cloaked. It would not seem to be Lincoln's doing. The President appeared to be merely going along with the will of Congress, forcing the hotheads to concede on some of their more outrageous demands, and helping recruitment, which was suffering in the wake of the summer's defeats.

Stanton had blundered badly on the suspension of recruitment, Blair was pleased to recall. He had canceled recruitment when it was brisk, and was now forced to plead with governors for troops, threatening to arrest young men heading up to Canada to evade service. The patriarch of the Blair clan marveled at the way Lincoln had positioned himself alongside, just a little behind, public sentiment: drifting toward abolition, not too fast, strictly on military necessity, able to step back from it if the war turned in the Union's favor or if Northern sentiment reacted sharply against the radicals.

"Frankly, I thought you were going to veto the bill," he said to Lincoln. Andy Jackson probably would have done that just to show Congress who was boss.

"Still can," the President said, tapping his stovepipe, where he evidently had stashed his veto message, "if the resolution explaining the bill doesn't pass."

They dismounted at the Capitol steps, handing the horses to Lamon. Blair's son Frank was at the entrance, eagerly awaiting them.

"The Senate has just acted, Mr. President," said Congressman Blair. "The explanation resolution has passed. The House will be voting in a few minutes."

"Did you make a speech, Frank?" the old man asked him.

"No."

"Good." The boy was learning to think ahead. Blair, himself steadfastly against the folly of abolition, wanted his son Frank to go with the tide of public sentiment and not allow himself later to be portrayed as having been a party to any weakening of abolition measures. Blair could see what Lincoln liked to call "the signs of the times." In a few years, maybe in '68, Frank would be the Blair running for President, and by then anybody who had opposed freedom for the slaves during the war would have a difficult time getting the Republican nomination.

When the Blairs and Lincoln came to the President's office in the Capitol, the elder Blair signaled Frank to leave them alone. The young man went back to the House chamber. The President made himself at home in the room that the Congress had kindly provided the leader of the sister branch of government.

Lincoln took off his hat, pulled out what Blair assumed to be his veto message, and put both hat and paper on the desk. It was nearly 10 A.M. The President sat down to await the action of the House. Blair sat in a corner, steepled his fingers, and remained quiet. Ten minutes passed, and nothing was said.

The old man spent the time trying to figure out a way to damage Chase in Lincoln's eyes. The rebels were the immediate enemy of the nation, but Salmon P. Chase was the ultimate enemy of the Blairs. Chase's man, Jay

Cooke—the Philadelphia financier who was making too much money out of his favored position in the financing of the war—was buying newspapers in Missouri. That meant Chase would try to undermine Frank Blair in his home base.

Stanton had turned out to be no bargain, either, undercutting Montgomery Blair in the Cabinet and undermining McClellan in the field. Chase and Stanton were thick as thieves these days, the old man mused, meeting with the radicals and joining them in calling the Blairs and other sensible men "Philistines." The old man was coming to cordially despise the Treasury Secretary: Chase was a man who thought the country owed him the presidency and, in his supreme arrogance, was willing to do anything to bring it about.

A clumping sound could be heard in the hallway outside. In a moment, the door, left invitingly ajar, was pushed open. The brooding face and crippled form of Thaddeus Stevens appeared in the doorway.

The light was slashing in from the window behind Lincoln, into the radical congressman's eyes; he blinked and held his hand before his face. "That you, Lincoln? I've got this damned weaseling explanation you extorted from us."

Blair looked at the President, who nodded politely to the power of the House and said nothing.

Stevens dropped his hand and came forward, seeming to the old man to slam down purposely on his clubfoot, and laid the joint resolution on the desk. "We now construe this bill to mean that nobody is to be punished for any act committed in the rebellion before the bill's passage," the congressman said. "That's what you wanted, is it? To let all the traitors off scot-free?"

"I shouldn't wonder," said Lincoln vaguely.

"I got eighty-four votes for confiscation," said Stevens of the darkened brow. "We passed it eighty-four to forty-two. A year ago, I couldn't muster fifty votes to free the slaves of traitors. We've come a long way, no thanks to you."

"It's the war," said Lincoln. "I'm grateful to Senator Fessenden for—"

"Fessenden has too much of the vile ingredient called conservatism," Stevens interrupted, "which is worse than secession." He turned to Blair. "Oh, for six months' resurrection in the flesh of your stern old Jackson! He would abolish slavery as the cause and the support of the insurrection; he would arm the free people of color, as he did at New Orleans; he would march into the heart of slavedom to put weapons into every free man's hands. Do you deny that, old man?"

"Andy Jackson wouldn't put up with such impudence from the likes of you," Blair snapped. He disliked the haters, almost to the point of hating them, and Thaddeus Stevens was the quintessential hater; the old man thought him obsessed with his need for revenge on all slaveholders, possessed with some perverse notion that the black race deserved not merely tolerance and freedom, but actual equality with whites. God help the cause of patching together a Union if such as Stevens wrested power from Lincoln.

"We are doing only what is needed to end the war," Lincoln offered mildly.

"Our object," Stevens said bitterly, "should be not only to end this war now, but to prevent its recurrence." Across the desk from the President, continuing to stand while Lincoln sat, the man seeking to be scourge of the

Representative Thaddeus Stevens

South put his hand on the desk and leaned forward. "You know that slavery is the cause of this war. So long as it exists we cannot have a solid Union. Patch up a compromise now and leave this germ of evil, it would soon again override the whole South, even if you freed three fourths of the slaves."

"How I wish the border states would accept my proposition," Lincoln replied evenly, referring to the substitute bill he had sent up that all agreed had no hope of passage. "Then you, Stevens, and all of us, would not have lived in vain. The labor of your life would be crowned with success—you would live to see the end of slavery."

"Forty more years of hell for four million people," Stevens spat back, "and you call that 'gradual emancipation'? I call it ignominious surrender to the South."

"What are you suggesting?"

"Don't just confiscate and liberate the slaves of rebels, Lincoln. Go beyond this bill, with its pusillanimous explanation—liberate the slaves of all, right now."

Blair sensed that Lincoln did not want to clash with Stevens on his extreme abolitionism; the purpose of this visit to the Hill was to get and sign the watering-down resolution and bill. He put in, "What of the loyal slave states? Should we break faith with them?"

"The real patriots who are still loyal to the Union," Stevens told him, "would willingly lay the sacrifice of their property on the altar of their country."

"It's a terrible weapon," Blair said for Lincoln, "asking for a black uprising, three or four millions of them—"

"Instruments of war are not selected on account of their harmlessness," Stevens interrupted. "You choose the cannon that has the longest range. You throw the shell that will kill the most men by its explosion. You grind your bayonet to the sharpest edge." Stevens was pale, shaking with conviction. Blair was worried that the man would have a heart seizure on the spot.

"You're trying to turn this war for the Union into a second revolution," Blair told him. Up to now, Blair had assumed Stevens was radical but reasonable. When Lincoln saw to it that a rider had been tacked on to the bill freeing the slaves in D.C. and providing them steamship tickets to Liberia or Haiti, Stevens had added a half million dollars on the appropriation. He was a good friend of colonization. But now Stevens was showing himself to be worse than Wade. His black concubine must be driving him to such a lust for vengeance.

"Nothing approaching the present policy will subdue the rebels," Stevens said slowly. "Whether we shall find anybody with a sufficient grasp of mind, and sufficient moral courage, to treat this war as a radical revolution and remodel our institutions, I doubt."

"That would involve the desolation of the South," Blair began.

The congressmen seized on his words. "Yes, exactly that, Blair—desolation as well as emancipation, and a re-peopling of half the continent. This ought to be done, now."

"I am going to sign the confiscation bill and the joint resolution together," said Lincoln, turning to business, "since they are substantially one." He seemed to debate with himself for a moment, then reached inside his hat and took out a copy of the draft veto message. "Before I was informed of the passage of the explanatory resolution, Stevens, I prepared a draft of a message stating my objections."

Blair was puzzled. What did the President have in mind? He'd won. The Congress had backed off and met his objections. Did Lincoln plan some form of congressional humiliation? Surely he would not now make public his veto message, since he was signing the bill.

Lincoln signed both the bill and his veto message and handed both documents to Stevens with the cool and official words, "I am transmitting a copy herewith."

Stevens, white-faced, looked at the long veto message in Lincoln's neat script. "All your lawyer's reasons why the bill is no good," he choked. "What colossal gall. You're for it and against it at the same time."

The President was impassive. Stevens turned to the door, papers clenched in a fist, and spun round on his crippled leg before he left. "I'll have your damned message read to the House, as I must. But I'll lead the members out during the reading, and I'll be damned if anybody will offer a resolution to so much as print it. Wade is right—the country is going to hell with you in the White House!"

When the clubfoot dragged himself out, Blair rose from his seat in the corner, picked up Lincoln's hat, and handed it to the President. "That's what Jackson would have done," he told him. "Rubbed their noses in it." He could not resist sending a final shaft: "That viper Stevens is your man Chase's closest political ally. Watch your back."

Lincoln shrugged that off and picked up his hat, not smiling. Blair assumed he was worried about whether he had gone too far in setting forth his non-veto veto message.

As they walked out into the July sun, Blair observed that there would surely be an exodus from the city on the weekend, with the adjournment of Congress. He suggested that the wifeless President come out to Silver Spring.

The tall man sighed, no, he had a delegation of senators coming—Sumner, Wilson, Trumbull—"the same damned three fellers again," with some substitutions, to work out an order based on the Confiscation Act. General Dix was coming in on Saturday, too, Lincoln mentioned, to get instructions about his prisoner exchange.

The elder Blair frowned. The notion struck him that Lincoln would not ordinarily let appointments like that keep him from spending the weekend away from the heat and smell in the low-lying Mansion. What else did Lincoln have up his sleeve? The President, it seemed to Blair, was inclined to keep his own counsel these days. A year ago, he would not have been so remote; now he liked to play a lone hand. That was not good for the Blair influence, but the old man could not think of much he could do about it.

"I think I'll get the whole family together for a few days," Blair told him as they mounted their horses. "You won't miss Montgomery on Monday, will you?"

Lincoln thought about that. "It would be helpful to have the judge at the Cabinet meeting Monday," he said at last. "And Tuesday, the twenty-second, especially."

"He'll try to be there." The old man fished for the reason.

"Tell him it could be important."

Blair gave up fishing. "Montgomery will be there."

CHAPTER 7

AN INSIDE SOURCE

"He's up to something," Greeley said to his managing editor. They were reading the telegraphed text of Lincoln's halfhearted approval of the Confiscation Act, following the strangely backtracking joint resolution by the Congress. "I do not trust that man, Sydney. He's like Seward. Quicksilver."

Sydney Gay did not wholly trust Lincoln's dedication to abolition, either, but the newsman was more concerned with what the President was likely to do than what he should do. Great moral guidance for the nation was

Greeley's affair; it was Gay's job to make sure *Tribune* readers knew what was really going on. And on emancipation, Gay was not sure; Adams Hill was the best reporter in Washington, but all these machinations about the Confiscation Act had taken the *Tribune*'s Washington office by surprise too.

"Lincoln is dragging his feet," pronounced Greeley. "I predict a faithless, insincere, grudging"—the editor groped for an expressive word—*"higgling* execution of the Confiscation Act, which is a most righteous and vital measure."

"Still," offered Gay, "if he permits generals to enlist and arm negroes, as this new act permits, that'll be a big step—"

"He won't," said Greeley with certitude. "I have that from both Chase and Stanton, who want him to arm the blacks. Lincoln keeps telling them no."

"You trust their word, Mr. Greeley?"

"More than Lincoln's," said the man in the white round-brimmed hat. "You'll see, Lincoln won't carry out this act. He'll tell his generals to hire negroes as laborers or something. Anything to avoid antagonizing the traitors. He'll see to it that this Confiscation Act is not worth a damaged Delmonico shinplaster."

The editor rose and strode around the room. Gay remained in his chair in the center of the huge corner office, twisting his body to keep his boss in view.

"I'm going to demand that he write a brief, frank, stirring proclamation," Greeley said, composing an editorial aloud, "recognizing the Confiscation-Emancipation Act as the law of the land and the basis of a new war policy. And no more of this flimflam from half the army officers who are more or less in sympathy with the rebellion. Lincoln must instruct each of them to rigorously enforce the Confiscation Act's provisions." He sliced the air: "Enough of this McClellanite foot-dragging! We need more moral giants in uniform, and we need this law backed up with an official proclamation."

"Have you considered the possibility," Gay asked, "that Mr. Lincoln may be going in that direction? Toward abolition?"

"I know more about Lincoln's private plans than you, Sydney, and he's not. Seward is whispering in his ear that it would cause the blacks to rise up and attack every white woman in the South, horrifying the world."

Gay thought the possibility of a Lincoln move toward abolition had to be considered. "Did you read the *Times* this morning?" He produced a copy, with a Washington dispatch from one of Henry Raymond's men reporting the rejection of Lincoln's plea by border-state congressmen. He read a line that troubled him: " 'It seems not improbable that the President considers the time near at hand when slavery must go to the wall.' "

"What the hell does Henry Raymond and the *Times* know?" scorned Greeley. "Sycophants. They had McClellan winning a great victory in the Peninsula when my man Page knew that coward was running away from Richmond."

Gay recalled how he had to press Greeley to run "my man Page's" report that day, but said only: "I would hate for the *Tribune* to be caught complaining about no action, if there's big doings in the works."

"What are you getting at, Sydney? I'm a busy man."

"I think we need an inside informant in the White House."

"Adams Hill is not getting the news? Dismiss him."

Horace Greeley

"No, he's a good reporter. But we need more than a reporter, if we're to beat Raymond, with his Lincoln connections. We need an intermediary."

"You mean your friend Gilmore," said Greeley. "I won't have it. Lincoln does not set the editorial policy of the *Tribune.*"

James Gilmore, whose novel about life in the deep South had caught Lincoln's fancy, was a friend of Gay's. Soon after Gay had taken over from Charles Dana as *Tribune* managing editor, Gilmore had approached the new managing editor with a remarkable offer. It seemed that through the good offices of Robert Walker, the railroader and former Kansas governor who was a behind-the-scenes power in Washington, Gilmore had proposed to Lincoln that he be the go-between for the White House and the *New York Tribune*—whose support Lincoln readily asserted was worth a hundred thousand soldiers to the Union cause. According to Gilmore, Lincoln had assented to the proposed arrangement, promising to provide the *Tribune* with advance tidbits of news. Greeley had warily consented to Gilmore's scheme, but when the go-between acted mainly as an apologist for Lincoln's delays on emancipation, Greeley ordered Gay to ignore him.

Gay had not obeyed his boss's order. Privately, away from the offices of the *Tribune,* he had arranged to see the Lincoln intermediary whenever Gilmore came up to New York. Gay had paid for the tidbits with assurances to Gilmore that he would assuage Greeley's wrath about the foot-dragging Lincoln, which the managing editor was sure Gilmore passed on to Walker and perhaps the President. Keeping the channel open cost nothing and might pay off one day.

"I'd like to use him, Mr. Greeley. We need a direct connection to the White House. It would give us an edge over Raymond, and we could kill Bennett and the *Herald.*"

Greeley was obviously torn. He wanted to beat his rivals, yet did not want to be charged with compromising the integrity of the *Tribune*'s editorials. "I won't trim my position," he said grudgingly, which Gay took with a grain of salt, since Greeley had trimmed more than his share to get ahead in politics.

"You needn't, sir. All we'll tell Gilmore is that if Lincoln enforces the Confiscation Act vigorously—including arming the negroes—the *Tribune* will vigorously support Lincoln's conduct of the war. Which we will anyway."

"That much you can say," Greeley agreed, looking out the window at the statue of Benjamin Franklin. "Don't bring Gilmore in here to the *Tribune* offices, though. You go down to Washington," the editor ordered, adding, "or continue to see him in the saloon down the street."

CHAPTER 8

SURPRISE SUPPORT

"General Hunter down in Hilton Head wants fifty thousand pairs of scarlet pantaloons," said Stanton to his visitor from New York. "You know what for? He wants to arm the slaves who come into his lines and send them into action against the rebels."

"Dressed in scarlet pantaloons?"

That puzzled Stanton too. "I guess he wants them to stand out on the battlefield. Or maybe blacks like colorful uniforms. Anyhow, Lincoln won't let me do it."

It distressed the Secretary of War that the President, now that he had the congressional authority to enlist escaped slaves, still hung back. Foolish waste of a potential asset, Stanton thought; the use of slaves propped up the rebel army. The Africans tilled the Southern soil and manned the rebel factories, freeing every able-bodied white to fight in the Confederate Army, while the North had to divert its manpower to such supporting tasks. If only he could send the word South that escaped blacks would be welcomed into the Northern ranks, Stanton was certain an exodus would begin, stripping the rebel generals of their advantage.

"General Hunter tried to emancipate the slaves all by himself a few months ago," his visitor reminded him. "No wonder Lincoln worries about him."

"We had to slap Hunter down on that," the Secretary of War said hastily. "I didn't know about it beforehand, no matter what they say." He assumed his visitor from New York had heard the rumors of his complicity in embarrassing the President. "I countersigned the countermanding order along with Lincoln."

"Come now, Stanton," his visitor said. "You and I are good Democrats, and I'm for you. And for Hunter."

Stanton, feeling more isolated than ever before in his life, needed to trust someone. In the nine days since the funeral of his baby, Stanton had plunged into work, turning the Western command over to Grant, bringing Halleck East, disputing McClellan's estimates of how many troops were present for duty, supporting General John Pope—the fiery leader the army needed—in Pope's stern warning to rebel civilians in Virginia that terrible retribution would follow any guerrilla harassment. During this critical time, Lincoln had been silent, remote, curiously detached. The President had spent long hours in the telegraph office next door, mulling over some papers at Major Eckert's desk, and had not come in to consult with the Secretary of War. That made Stanton suspicious. Why was Lincoln being so secretive? Was he cooking something up with the Blairs? Why had Lincoln been so insistent that Stanton be present at the Cabinet meeting set for later in the day?

He impulsively decided to trust the lawyer in his office. Francis Brockholst Cutting had been a pro-slavery Democrat, but he was a good War Democrat from New York and a Stanton ally in that state where Seward and Weed and

Greeley held sway among Republicans, and where Sam Barlow and Fernando Wood were the Democrats trying to make use of McClellan.

"Listen to this letter from General Hunter, Cutting." Stanton pulled it out of the center drawer of his desk. "He says, 'Please let me have my way on the subject of slavery. You can censure me, arrest me, dismiss me, hang me if you will, but permit me to make my mark.' Do you blame me for wanting to send Hunter his scarlet pantaloons?"

"In the *Herald,*" his visitor observed, "Bennett says that you and Chase have been conniving with General Hunter on arming the fugitive slaves, trying to force Lincoln's hand."

"I've already covered that with Lincoln," Stanton said instantly. In the same folder with the Hunter plea was a copy of a letter from the President to editor Bennett, which Stanton also read aloud: " 'Stanton mixes no politics with his duties; knew nothing of General Hunter's proclamation;'—this is in Lincoln's hand, mind you—'and he and I alone got up the counter-proclamation.' "

Cutting, who, Stanton saw, was a born conspirator, smiled. "You manipulate the President that easily? Do you have Lincoln believing that?"

"He believes what he wants to believe," snapped the Secretary of War, "the way he believes he can deport all the slaves that are freed to some congenial clime back in Africa or someplace. It's comfortable to believe, and has the practical advantage of cooling off some of the hotheads in Illinois." Stanton had no doubt that the President had the knack of avoiding worry by constructing certain fancies. "Lincoln trusts me, Cutting, because he knows I'm not running against him for the Republican nomination, like Chase, or dreaming of a military dictatorship, like McClellan."

"Will Chase stand firm with you on arming the slaves? I know McClellan is against that."

Stanton nodded yes; Chase was rock-solid on anything to free the negro so long as it was done by military commanders, and so long as Lincoln got no credit for it among anti-slavery Republicans. In the brief Cabinet meeting the day before—the first one in weeks—he and Chase had plumped for letting the generals outfit fugitive Africans with guns and uniforms, but Lincoln would go no further than employing them as laborers. The President, timorous as usual about the border states' attitude, suggested an order promoting colonization in Haiti, as provided in the Confiscation Act, but backed away when Chase argued against it. Lincoln struck Stanton as being secretive; why had the President asked about Montgomery Blair's absence, and called another Cabinet meeting for this afternoon? Did he have some surprise in store that required conservative backing? Was he asking to be persuaded to put guns in black hands? Seward and Welles seemed especially smug; Stanton worried that they might know something he did not know.

In the light of Lincoln's reluctance to use his new power to arm escaped slaves, Stanton doubted the President would move decisively to punish the South politically for its resistance before Richmond. Stanton resolved to keep up the pressure. Tentatively, he asked Cutting, "You and the other party people still out to protect the peculiar institution, even now?"

Cutting surprised him with his answer: "Some Democrats have come around to thinking that the North's only hope is to get behind the anti-slavery movement. Shouldn't be just the Republicans."

Stanton looked at him sharply: "That just your personal idea?"

"No, the sentiment is spreading. Most Democrats still oppose abolition, the way I did," Cutting allowed, "but the war's really about slavery, and we might as well face it. I think it may be a good idea for you to let Hunter have his scarlet pantaloons."

Stanton looked at the man hard. Cutting represented a small force that Lincoln did not know existed: War Democrats moving unexpectedly toward abolition, not out of any love for Africans but as a practical matter of winning the war.

"Have you ever met Lincoln?"

"No."

"I'm taking you over to see him right now," the War Secretary announced. "We have about two hours before the Cabinet meeting. Blair wasn't there yesterday, and he won't be here today, so we could get something accomplished." Stanton did not say that he had assured Blair that nothing of substance was to be discussed. "You'll tell him Democrats support the arming of fugitive slaves, but now go further: Why do you think our generals in the field should be able to set free all slaves in their area of battle?"

Cutting put forward a cautious argument. "I think it would deter England and France from recognizing the Confederacy. The leaders of those countries could not go so strongly against popular—"

Stanton made a face; Seward would sweep that argument aside.

Cutting stopped. "What is it you want me to say?"

"You're a politician, talk politics. Talk about his beloved border states. Lincoln thinks that Democrats will go over to the secesh if our generals, on military necessity, free slaves." Stanton walked to the window, looked across the street, and talked fast, lawyer to lawyer. "Make the case that Kentucky and Tennessee are disloyal at heart, can never be counted on—their congressmen insulted the President last week when he begged them to come along on compensated manumission. So to hell with them—we keep them in the way we kept Maryland in, by brute force. Arrest the disloyal legislators if necessary. The loyal Democrats up North won't scream. Assure him of that, because it's a new development; that's a shift in public sentiment he does not know about. You ready?"

He led Cutting across the street to the Mansion, and into the secretaries' office. Stanton knew that Nicolay would be there, with Hay off chasing some lady love up in New York. Stanton strode through to Lincoln's office, where the President was hunched over his desk, putting the finishing touches on some document.

"Here's a man you want to see," announced the Secretary of War. "A Democrat who may surprise you." He left Cutting in the President's office.

Two hours later, Stanton returned for the Cabinet meeting. He was pleased to see that Postmaster General Blair was not in the Cabinet Room, and surprised to see Cutting just coming out of the President's office. That must have been a long, lawyerly session. Cutting signaled for Stanton to step out into the hall.

"You hit him on the border states?" Stanton asked.

"Yes. Also the foreign intervention. Also the shifting opinion in New York, general weariness with the war, need to do something dramatic to turn the tide. He knows how important New York is, both for recruitment and for money, and the split in Democratic ranks got him excited. Did you know he's concerned with workers in the West worried about blacks taking their jobs? I said deportation was the answer—ship all four million back where the climate is suitable."

"Sure, sure," Stanton nodded. If Lincoln had the need to think mass deportation would solve everything, fine for now; he could be disabused later. "Is he turning around on arming the slaves?"

Cutting shrugged. "Be ready for more than that. I think he wanted to be persuaded to go all the way, so we talked about the support of Democrats on that."

"About what?"

"About support on a proclamation."

Stanton could feel his excitement mount; Lincoln was on the verge of permitting the right generals to do the right thing. "Hunter would, and Pope," he whispered, "but not McClellan—"

"No, not the generals. Lincoln himself. A presidential proclamation of emancipation."

Stanton, shaking his head in disbelief, hurried into the Cabinet Room.

CHAPTER 9

THENCEFORWARD AND FOREVER

Chase was prompt. At precisely 2 P.M., that July 22 of 1862, he took his seat and awaited the others.

The Treasury Secretary looked toward the head of the small Cabinet table, at the chair that would one day, God willing, be rightfully his own. Chase had long been appalled at the way Lincoln demeaned the great office, not merely with his coarse language and vulgar stories, but by making it the center of brokerage for political patronage—worse than in Jackson's time, when the spoils system was said to bloom. At the moment when the nation was in desperate need of an infusion of moral authority, the United States was afflicted with the non-leadership of a sometimes sly, sometimes buffoonish country lawyer with no sense of the grandeur and majesty that should emanate from the office of the nation's Chief Executive.

He felt vaguely apprehensive. Daughter Kate had gone off in a huff to Saratoga, hinting of a romance with someone other than Governor Sprague. Chase worried, too, about Lincoln's scheme for gradual, compensated emancipation. Even if that plan were to take a generation to accomplish abolition, the Treasury Secretary did not know where he could come up with the money to begin to finance the purchase of the slaves.

Chase was also fearful of impending military disaster. After the retreat of the Seven Days, the two Union armies of McClellan and Pope were split a hundred miles apart, headed by generals whose temperament and political outlook were even more widely divergent. At dinner the night before, General Pope had told him that if he ever were to need support from McClellan's army, he could not expect it of his fellow Union general because McClellan was incompetent and indisposed to move.

This very morning, Chase had come to the Mansion to press again for McClellan's removal. The President would not take action. Chase judged he did not grasp the financial ramifications of a rise in public sentiment about hopes for victory. However, Chase did shake Lincoln that morning with a letter he had received from Colonel Thomas Key, a fellow Ohioan on McClellan's staff. Key informed Chase that he had reason to believe that if General McClellan found he could not otherwise sustain himself in Virginia—if he were not reinforced, and found his army in extremis—he would declare the liberation of the slaves. Lincoln, of course, found that amazing. Frémont and Hunter were abolitionists and such a move had been in character for them, but McClellan! Chase shared Lincoln's dismay, and characterized the Key letter as a form of political blackmail, especially since the colonel wrote that the President would not dare to interfere with a McClellan emancipation order. The general and his staff were obviously disloyal and had to be dismissed; why did Lincoln delay?

The others arrived, Stanton looking more agitated than usual, Welles impassive behind his huge beard, Seward exuding his oppressive sprightliness, Attorney General Bates laboriously drawing on his glasses, Caleb Smith fretting. Blair was absent again. Chase marshaled his thoughts to support the arming of fugitive slaves, the best part of the Confiscation Act, and to oppose the deportation of freed blacks, the worst part of that legislation.

Lincoln looked around for the Postmaster General, shrugged, and began. "We have a few orders here, which we discussed yesterday, respecting military action and slavery."

Chase leaned forward, determined to block Lincoln's order colonizing freed slaves. It was impractical and inhumane, and Wade and Sumner were against it; opposition by Chase would add to the proof that there existed a clear distance between himself and Lincoln on the handling of the negro.

"The first gives authority to commanders to subsist their troops in hostile territory," said Lincoln.

"We only hope that some of our generals try to find out what hostile territory is like," murmured Stanton, in a reference to McClellan.

Next, the President read his proposed order to give commanders authority to recruit negroes as laborers. "I think we should go much further than that," said Stanton, and Chase nodded his support; they had agreed to press for arming the fugitive slaves. Lincoln said that was another matter, and the Cabinet agreed to the issuance of the order.

Lincoln also proposed an order requiring commanders to keep good accounts, so that compensation could be paid where slaves were taken from their masters.

"I doubt the expediency of keeping accounts for the rebels," Chase put in. "Our men in the field have more important things to do than to make certain that traitors get paid." But it was felt that an attempt at accounting would appeal to the border-state men, make it seem that the Union was being fair; the Cabinet wanted to go along, and Chase did not disagree.

"Now as to your colonization order," Chase began, preparing himself for eloquent evocation of the distress of blacks faced with deportation, his own experience with the failure of previous colonization schemes, and the depressant effect on slaves in the South who would otherwise be embracing the Northern cause.

"I'm willing to put that aside," agreed Lincoln unexpectedly, pushing the colonization order he had drafted under some other papers. With this surprising victory, Chase moved to the offensive on the arming of fugitive slaves.

"I wish to advocate," Chase began again, "with all the warmth and sincerity at my disposal, the step that is clearly intended in the Confiscation Act—namely, the arming of those Africans who come across the lines to our side."

Stanton murmured assent; Blair was not there to disagree; Seward looked uncomfortable; Bates was noncommittal; Caleb Smith stared at the ceiling. Chase thought that argument could bring Gideon Welles of the Navy, over to his side; because there was bad blood between Stanton and Welles, the presentation of reasons to arm the blacks could not be made by Stanton.

But Lincoln appeared not to be listening. That was a departure for the President, who was ordinarily quite solicitous of advice when he finally got around to calling a Cabinet meeting. Chase wished the man would concentrate on the job at hand.

"I'm unwilling to adopt the arming of slaves at this time," Lincoln said, without waiting for the rest of the Cabinet to comment. He pushed aside his set of orders and placed another document in front of him. Chase was miffed; recruitment of fugitive slaves was hardly a matter to be decided with no discussion.

Lincoln took a deep breath and said, as if he had been rehearsing the line, "I feel we've reached the end of our rope on the plan of operations we've been pursuing."

Chase looked at Stanton. This was a new tack, not a continuation of yesterday's Cabinet meeting. What was the President's game? Would he replace McClellan with Pope? Stanton did not meet his glance.

Lincoln took a long sheet of paper out of his jacket pocket. "I am determined upon the adoption of an emancipation policy."

Into the stunned silence, Lincoln went on: "I have resolved upon this step. I have not called you together to ask your advice"—Chase choked back his protest at this breach of protocol, not to say common courtesy—"but to lay the subject matter of a proclamation before you. Suggestions will be in order after you have heard it read."

Ponderously, the President began reading the draft he had written of a legal document, beginning with reference to section six of the Confiscation Act—a warning to all rebels to cease rebellion forthwith on pain of the forfeitures and seizures within the act.

The Treasury Secretary, piqued at the President's insult to his Cabinet at the commencement of the reading, began to realize what the President had been up to. The canny politician was leapfrogging the radical position, putting aside the controversy about arming the slaves, to go directly to the action that the most extreme radicals had been vainly calling for from the start—abolition of the institution of slavery.

"And I hereby make it known that it is my purpose," Lincoln droned on, reading his detailed and legalistic proclamation, "upon the next meeting of Congress, to again recommend the adoption of a practical measure for tendering pecuniary aid to the free choice of any and all states . . . which may then have voluntarily adopted . . . gradual abolishment of slavery."

There he goes again, threatening to break the United States Treasury by bribing slaveholders. Chase began to relax a little, since this was Lincoln's familiar position, but then he stiffened as the President took the plunge:

"And as a fit and a necessary military measure for effecting this object, I, as commander in chief of the Army and Navy of the United States, do order and declare that on the first day of January, in the year of our Lord one thousand eight hundred and sixty-three, all persons held as slaves within any state or states wherein the constitutional authority of the United States shall not then be practically recognized, submitted to, and maintained, shall then, thenceforward and forever be free."

Chase was thunderstruck. In a single stroke, the previously conservative Lincoln was gathering to himself the credit for all that the radical Republicans had long been fighting for. He was effectively removing the main basis on which Chase could challenge him for the Republican nomination in 1864. Lincoln was doing to Chase what McClellan had just threatened to do to Lincoln: steal his emancipation clothing.

But as the most anti-slavery member of the Cabinet, what was the Chase reaction to be? How could he dissuade Lincoln, the eternal compromiser with an infernal sense of timing, to refrain from doing what Chase's faction had so long espoused? Notes would be made of everyone's expressed opinion this afternoon—he was certain he was not the only Cabinet member keeping a diary, and Stanton was openly making notes at that moment—and the press would one day be informed of the stand each man took.

The Treasury Secretary steepled his fingers and appeared lost in thought, waiting for others to speak.

Seward, wearing his best poker face, wondered what the hell had become of Blair. His only ally in the Cabinet capable of making the political and military arguments against Lincoln's extreme action was absent. Was this a trick of the Blairs? The Secretary of State decided to put that possibility out of his mind; it was one of those unworthy thoughts that came to a man too long associated with the duplicitous Stanton and the ever-so-pious Chase.

He then wondered what had caused the cautious Abraham Lincoln to suggest this reckless action. The man was no radical; granted, McClellan's retreat in the Peninsula had made him impatient, and the President had raised the possibility of an emancipation edict at the Stanton baby's funeral a few days after that, but Seward thought his own coolness at that time had chilled Lincoln's ardor for dramatic action.

Only the other night, the President had dropped in at the Seward house and the Secretary of State had introduced his sister-in-law, Lazette, as a radical. When Lazette demurred at that label, and claimed she was no ultra, Lincoln had told a little story. During the War of 1812, it was the fashion for sweethearts of soldiers to make belts with mottoes sewn into them, and one young lady asked her soldier if he wanted his belt emblazoned with "Liberty or Death!" To which the soldier replied that was a little strong, how about just "Liberty or Be Crippled"?

That was the quintessential Lincoln speaking—never a radical. Why, then, this sudden turn? Thurlow Weed might know; luckily, the Albany editor was in Washington after his sojourn in London. Seward resolved to see him immediately after Cabinet.

"I see no reason to rush into this," Seward told his colleagues briskly. "Of course, I share with the President—we all do—his wish that slavery be ended one day." Nobody could go on record as opposing the President's move, least of all Seward, who had been denied the Republican nomination because he was seen to be too willing to welcome the "irreconcilable conflict," as the phrase went that had been hung around his neck in 1860. "But is it wise to do it in this manner, at this time?"

"The President has the war power to do this, I think," said Bates.

"I do not doubt for an instant that it would be legal," granted Seward to the Missouri lawyer who so offhandedly made sweeping constitutional decisions, "or could be made so in due course, when the Congress gets around to it. But it is, let us not deny it, a coup d'état. There's no telling right now where it all might lead."

"A servile insurrection, you mean," said Bates. "A slave uprising."

"What, in God's name, would be so bad about that?" demanded Stanton. "We could use a good uprising down there. It's about time."

Seward gave Stanton what he hoped was a withering look. "If this proclamation causes the Africans to turn on their masters, with all the pillage and rapine that would entail, the civilized world would look upon our action with horror. The British would enter the war on the side of the South."

"The British workingman," Stanton held, "would never permit British troops to be used to uphold slavery. Palmerston's government would fall first."

Seward looked at the navy's Welles, who was familiar with Stanton's overreaching. "Perhaps Mars here should be given the State Department portfolio too."

Lincoln allowed as how he would be interested in what Weed had to say about British reaction, and Seward replied that he would send him around that evening. Then Seward saw a second point to his barb about a slave uprising: "Mr. President, consider the fact that this terrible war will not last forever. After the war, assuming we are victorious and the Union remains whole, there will be the challenge of a harmonious restoration of the Union. How could we heal the wounds if we had incited the negroes to murder their masters?"

Nobody spoke while that thought sank in. Stanton looked to Chase, the leading radical in the Cabinet, who had been silent. Seward was confident that Chase would straddle, so he looked expectantly toward the Secretary of the Treasury.

Unable to preserve his silence any longer, Chase spoke cautiously: "Of course, I should give to any such measure my cordial support, but—well, first, I should prefer that no new expression on the subject of compensation be made. We simply cannot afford it."

"But what of the substance of the Proclamation?" Lincoln asked.

"This is a military measure," Chase said slowly. "You are basing it on military necessity and on nothing else. You are using your power as commander in chief of the armed forces." He paused, thinking, and the others let him. "Should not a measure of emancipation—which of course I cordially support—be more properly issued by our generals in the field? As a military measure to meet a military exigency, it should in my judgment be suffered to stand upon the responsibility of the generals who make it."

Seward repressed a smile. The amalgam of pretension and ambition and dogged shrewdness in Chase had given the Treasury Secretary an out.

"General Hunter—indeed, General Frémont—have already led the way," Chase continued. "Public sentiment is prepared for military men to arm fugitive slaves, and to encourage slaves to run away by promising them freedom. We could proceed much more quietly—avoiding depraved actions and massacres—by letting a military measure of emancipation be undertaken by military men. And our generals would be in a better position to know how and when to issue orders of emancipation, depending on local circumstances. They could balance the avoidance of massacre with the support given the insurgents by the slaves in any given area."

Stanton started to say something but stopped himself. Bates offered only, "I support the President on this, provided that the deportation of the colored race be made coincident with emancipation." Chase looked at the Attorney General in disgust.

"Time seems to be getting short," said Lincoln glumly. Seward read that to mean that the military setbacks and the prospect of difficulty in the fall elections had made the President willing to do anything to reverse the trend of the war.

Stanton said flatly, "I need to strike terror in the hearts of the rebel generals. Their fear of insurrection back home would do that. What's more, I need to get those negroes off the farms and out of the rebel military camps—right now, they're freeing white men to fight. I don't care who issues a proclamation of emancipation"—that, Seward noted with amusement, was a shot across Chase's bow—"as long as it is issued, and right away." He banged on the Cabinet table. "That's what the people of the North want."

"Even among extreme men," said a voice in the doorway, "there is no public sentiment in the North which now demands an emancipation proclamation." Montgomery Blair came in and took his seat. "I have just come from Senator Sumner. He tells me that the anti-slavery men would be satisfied with the enforcement of the laws of Congress as they stand."

The Secretary of State breathed easier. He would no longer have to face his wife and sister-in-law, abolitionists both, with the news that William Henry Seward alone had saved the Union from an act of desperation which would have ensured the loss of the war, followed by generations of hatred and disunity. Besides, Seward was never at his best as a leading advocate; his influence was best brought to bear when he could play the role of mediator, coming in at the end with a satisfying synthesis. Montgomery Blair was the one to make the argument that would turn Lincoln back from the precipice.

The proposed proclamation was poor politics, and the Blairs had Lincoln's confidence on the subject of politics.

Lincoln seemed awfully determined, however. Seward found his informal preamble about not wanting Cabinet advice on the wisdom of this matter to be harsher than usual. Blair, at least, had not heard the admonition and was not constrained by it. The trick was to delay the President this afternoon, avert any decision, and give Thurlow Weed time to work on Lincoln's good political sense tonight.

Seward, seated at Lincoln's right hand, reached in front of the President and pushed the draft proclamation across the table for Blair to read. He gave him time by turning to Chase and asking, "What do you suppose your friend Sumner meant by that?"

Blair was furious at Stanton for misleading him about the importance of today's meeting. The Postmaster General was more angry with himself for ignoring the instruction of his father to be present; it was just that Lincoln seemed to have lost interest in the Cabinet as an institution, and Blair thought other meetings more urgent. Senator Sumner, on Capitol Hill, and a *New York Times* reporter had asked Blair questions about emancipation that had sped Blair belatedly to the Cabinet session. He read down the two pages of the document in the President's handwriting, as Chase intoned his answer.

"I imagine that such an action by the President, rather than by generals in the field," said the Treasury Secretary, "might be construed as an attempt to evade the provisions of the Confiscation Act." Blair, reading, listened with half an ear; it seemed that the Cabinet's resident radical was not being so radical when the chips were down. Chase was making good sense. "The Act calls for action now, whereas the President's suggested proclamation would be announced now but not go into effect until January first of next year," Chase continued. "That effectively delays the process of confiscation, and arming of negroes, for almost six months. I don't think that would sit well in Congress. I imagine Thaddeus Stevens and Ben Wade would not appreciate the President's motives, and might even see this as some sort of trick. You know, the publication of the planned veto message did not endear the President to them."

" 'Forever be free,' " said Blair aloud, reading the last words of the Lincoln draft in his hand. He looked across the table directly at the President. "This is abolition. Total abolition."

"No," Bates interposed, "the slaves in the loyal border states are exempted. This would free only the slaves in those states in rebellion."

"On what basis do you make that distinction?"

Bates looked to Lincoln, the author. The President replied, "I base this on military necessity. It is a war measure, designed to reduce the ability of states in rebellion to sustain their war. It cannot, on that reasoning, be applied in loyal states."

"You may impress lawyers with that," said Chase, "but it flies in the face of common sense. You can purport to manumit the slaves in rebellious states, yet its operations will in fact be universal. Nobody will suppose that slavery can still exist in the border states after it is abolished farther South."

"I think it is an error to exempt the border states from the proclamation,"

Postmaster General Montgomery Blair

said Welles from behind his beard. "Any separation of regions, for any reason, undermines the integrity of the Union. Chase is right. This document dooms slavery in the border states as well; why not recognize it? Why treat them differently?"

"Because the slaves in the border states," Lincoln answered with what Blair saw was some logic, "as well as those in areas controlled by Union troops, are not supporting the rebellion." The President did not add, Blair noted, that loyal Kentuckians now endangered by Confederate General Braxton Bragg's latest movements might just decide to defect to the South if the war's aim was changed from pro-Union to anti-slavery.

The Postmaster General saw that it would be up to him—the defender of runaway slave Dred Scott before the court of Chief Justice Taney—to save the President from the terrible mistake of premature emancipation. Lincoln was a lawyer, who respected sensible arguments; Blair set out to do his job rationally.

"The purpose of this proclamation is to affect the behavior of blacks in the South," he began, "to intimidate the secessionists, and to affect the sentiment of whites in the North. Am I correct?"

"Yes, Judge," Lincoln nodded.

"Take the blacks first. We are already giving freedom to all those who join us. Their masters have been telling them for years that abolition is our intent. Publishing it in this new form gives them no new information." Blair rose; he felt better on his feet in arguing his case.

He stood behind his chair. "It was confidently expected by the people of the North, in the early stages of the rebellion, that when our armies reached the negro regions, insurrections would follow their advent."

"But experience has not verified this expectation," said Seward, who, Blair recognized, wanted to lend a hand.

"On the contrary," Blair argued to Lincoln, "the able men who stimulated the rebellion did so despite the presence in the South of four million blacks. They did not believe the negro was a source of danger to them. As events proved, they were right."

Stanton, as Blair had hoped, took the bait. "How can you say that? Look at what happened on Hispaniola—that was about the bloodiest rebellion the world has seen. The overthrow of the whites in Hayti proves—"

"Proves nothing," countered Blair. "You are in the grip of a false analogy. In Hayti, the contest was one of race, and for supremacy—and the climate was on the side of the negro. Here the contest is between divisions of the white race, and though one division offers personal freedom to the negro, we do not offer supremacy to the race. And we cannot do it because the climate is not his and never can be. The negro has neither the motives to join in the fight, nor the physical superiority in the heat to give him the success he had in Hayti."

"Freedom is not a motive?"

"He has that motive indeed, calculated to incline him to our cause," Blair replied, "but he has not the fury imparted by the instinct of dominion in his natural clime. The conduct of the blacks in our war—their docility, if you will—justified the opinions formed of them by those Southerners most familiar with them. Their passivity is natural, in my judgment, and will not be altered by any proclamation of the President."

As he was making the point, which was not refuted by any Cabinet member, Blair realized from the expression on Lincoln's face that he was undermining his own case. Despite the military rationale given the proclamation, Lincoln did not want a slave insurrection, with the horror and possible foreign intervention it entailed; he wanted merely to deny the slaveholders labor. Any assurances from Blair that North-South hatred would not be abetted by his proclamation were welcome to Lincoln. Blair changed his tack.

"Consider now the effect on whites. First, in the South. The way this proclamation is drawn"—Blair tapped the document on the table—"it gives the states in rebellion nearly six months to comply. The object of this postponement is only that it may terrify the secessionists into submission. I cannot think it will be in the least operative in that way."

Nor did the others at the Cabinet table, Blair knew; the notion that this ultimatum would faze the Southern leaders was absurd. "The controlling minds among them have long since been convinced that slavery must stand or fall with the rebellion. This proclamation will only confirm what they have been saying from the beginning."

Blair looked toward Chase, then Stanton, for any refutation; there was none. Lincoln did not appear pleased, but Blair was not in the Cabinet to please the President.

"Among whites in the South, then, this measure will only stiffen resistance. Now, in the North—"

"There is a general weariness of the war," snapped Stanton. "We can tell that in recruitment. And the bankers are not exactly falling all over Chase, here, to finance us."

"I have already reported to you my conversation with Senator Sumner of Massachusetts," Blair retorted, "a leader of the radicals, who is content with the Confiscation measures taken so far. The governor of Iowa, who has an appointment with you this afternoon, Mr. President, will tell you—as he has told me—that the people of his state would be satisfied with the orders you were supposed to issue this week."

"We just approved them," said Chase, "before you came in. Except for colonization."

"Good." He would argue for colonization some other time. "I disagree with Stanton, Mr. President, this proclamation is not needed to recruit our army. I see no reason to suspect a want of ardor in the support of the war at present."

"I do," said Lincoln. "That 'want of ardor' is impressed upon me every day."

"Our military reverses have saddened our people, surely," Blair conceded, "and impaired our financial strength. But what people in the North want this sort of proclamation? A small portion of the people—the radicals, a few politicians, and a few newspapers. Not the effective partizans in the war."

"You're mistaken," Stanton said. "The President and I have received reports only recently that even Democrats are beginning to swing over to the need for some bold, decisive action about slavery."

"This proclamation is your idea?"

"No," said Stanton quickly. Blair did not believe him.

"You, Chase?"

The Treasury Secretary looked pained. "It would surely lead to universal emancipation, and it is a measure of great danger."

Silence in the room. Blair gently pushed for more. "Is it your recommendation, Chase, to do this?"

"The measure"—Chase, cornered, groped for words—"goes beyond anything I have recommended." Chase's backtracking caused Stanton to twist in his seat and redden; the Treasury Secretary did not look Stanton's way. Blair was glad to note that those two radical thieves had fallen out.

"The idea is mine," Lincoln confessed. "I feel that we have played our last card and must change our tactics or lose the game."

"We are already changing our tactics," Blair argued, "with the Confiscation Act, with the orders you are issuing today. But by going all the way to abolition, you introduce a note of desperation. You will be seen to be counting on insurrection of the slaves, which is the only military aid we can hope for from it." He saw a way to turn that point to his advantage. "And I am not sure that a slave uprising would not damage our cause rather than aid it." He looked to Seward for help on that.

Seward nodded sagely and said, "I've spoken of that already. But what are the politics of this, Judge? Will this help us or harm us in the congressional elections this fall?"

Blair recognized the Seward touch. He would come in at the end, acting as a judge alongside Lincoln, rather than as an advocate against the proclamation. "If I am right in this," Blair responded, "it follows that abolition would endanger our power in Congress. It would put power in the next House of Representatives in the hands of those opposed to the war, or at least opposed to our mode of carrying it out." His brother Frank could even be toppled from his seat in Missouri if whites there lashed back at the sudden change in the very basis for the fighting.

A voice not often heard in Cabinet councils spoke up. "Dithathter," lisped Caleb Smith, the Interior Secretary.

The Indiana politician, forced on Lincoln as payoff for the votes of Indiana at the Chicago convention, was not as embarrassing a legacy as Simon Cameron had been, but the rotund Interior Secretary was a disappointment as a Cabinet member. Blair was not sure if his support was helpful in any matter, but nodded at him to continue.

"The Democrats will kill us with it. I can't imagine how I could ever support it."

Was Smith threatening to resign? Blair knew that Lincoln would dearly love Caleb Smith to quit, making room for his capable Assistant Secretary, John Usher. Lest this welcome opportunity weigh in the balance for an emancipation proclamation, Blair motioned Smith to be silent; his support for delay was worse than opposition.

Lincoln, slumped deep in his chair, pulled himself up and abruptly walked to the window. He looked south down the Potomac, his large hands clenching and loosening. In that interim, with nobody saying anything, Blair wondered if he had gone too far. His father had warned him to block any radical moves proposed by Chase or Stanton, but this document was in Lincoln's handwriting. And if Frank Blair was to be a candidate for President one day, it might not be helpful for the Blairs to be on record as having blocked negro freedom.

"Suppose you were my lawyer, Judge," Lincoln said, coming back to the table and sitting down. Blair sat as well. "If I went ahead with this thing, what do you think would be the best way to sell it to the country—so that it does the least damage among your friends and mine in the North, and in the border states?"

Blair struggled with that. He was an advocate for a cause: the gradual, compensated manumission of slaves, justly and legally, over the course of the next generation, with colonies established to receive them offering jobs and dignity. In that way, North and South could reunite and build a great continental nation. He opposed the opposite cause, immediate abolition, because he was certain that would lead to Republican election defeat, a peace settlement on a basis of disunion, and the perpetuation of slavery.

At the same time, in a narrower sense, he was the appointee of the President of the United States, duty-bound to give him the best advice when it was requested. Lincoln needed the argumentation of a trained lawyer to help him examine his own judgment; Bates could not do that and Stanton had become too passionately involved. Blair decided to construe his role narrowly, being as helpful as the President wanted him to be, arguing against his own cause.

"The only reason that would be satisfactory to the country for this abolition measure," he replied with certainty, "would be its necessity to prevent foreign intervention."

Seward frowned. Blair knew that the Secretary of State felt betrayed, with the Postmaster General using foreign affairs to make the case that Lincoln wanted made. But the President was entitled to support from even a non-supporter.

"The political damage in the North would be lessened," Blair continued, "if the measure were to be explained as a means of drawing the slavery issue between the governments of Europe and their people. Our people here would then hail the measure to be judicious, if it served to keep England and France from entering the war on the side of the South." Having done his duty, Blair tried to turn it to an argument for delay: "I therefore hope that you will reserve the emancipation measure to meet that contingency."

Since Lincoln was his client, he might as well warn him of another way to avoid danger in implementing the wrong course: "By the way, you should change the scope of your proclamation. Do not limit it to the states in rebellion—include the border states as well. If you do not, our enemies abroad will say—not with truth, but with effect nevertheless—that the federal government still maintains slavery. They'll go further and say that it will be reestablished in the South when the rebellion is put down."

Lincoln half-nodded, seeing the point but not accepting the argument. Blair, while he was at it, could not resist fixing the document further: "Whenever such a decree is made, and I trust it will not be soon, it should go into immediate effect."

"Fairness requires notice," said Lincoln.

"Only if we were acting judicially." As the only former judge in the group, Blair felt he was on solid ground. "But we are not. The law under which we act is necessity. Our right to put forth such an order is derived solely from the duty to resort to any measure to save the state. This implies that the emergency is upon us at the date—right now—and that now the public safety does not admit of a different line of conduct."

"I see no harm," Attorney General Bates put in, "and much equity, in giving the rebels time to comply, say, by January first of next year."

Blair shut his eyes for a moment; the nation's chief law officer did not understand the law. "The law under which we profess to act, by its very emergency nature, restricts us to deal with the present, not the future. It is only the law of necessity under which we can act; we cannot logically make a decree operative in the future, because it cannot be said that any such necessity will exist in the future." Blair had him; Bates shut up.

Seward cleared his throat. Blair hoped that Billy Bowlegs had some sort of crushing argument to appeal to Lincoln to delay this decree. Blair was all but certain it would lose the border states and cost the Republicans governorships in New York and New Jersey at least, with all that meant to recruiting. It would cause dismay in the army ranks; the boys were not fighting for black freedom, but to save the Union. Blair was convinced that the cause of black freedom would be set back for generations by this premature decree.

"We are not sure, then," said the Secretary of State, as if summing up for Lincoln, "if this measure would cause an uprising or not, and we are not sure we want one. We are not sure," he went on, "that it should exempt the border states, because we run the risk of losing them to the rebels if we free their slaves, and run the risk of seeming to the world to be hypocrites on slavery if we permit it to continue where we have the ability to strike it down now.

"We are not sure if we should emancipate immediately," Seward continued, "which we have the legal authority to do under military necessity, or try to coerce our Southern brethren with a six-month delay which will undergo some challenge in the courts."

"I have considered those arguments," Lincoln said, shaking his head, "and settled in my own mind what to do."

"Then it is not a question of if," said Seward smoothly, as if Lincoln had agreed with him, "but when. I think we all concur that the matter of timing is crucial. I wonder if its immediate promulgation would not be extremely unwise. The depression of the public mind, consequent upon our repeated reverses, is so great that I fear the effect of so important a step." He paused for effect. "It may be viewed as the last measure of an exhausted government, a cry for help; the government stretching forth its hands to Ethiopia, instead of Ethiopia stretching forth her hands to the government."

"Your idea," said the President, "is that it would be considered the last shriek on the retreat?"

"Precisely," said Seward. "Now, while I approve the measure, I suggest, sir, that you postpone its issue, until you can give it to the country supported by military success, instead of issuing it, as would be the case now, upon the greatest disasters of the war."

Lincoln wavered; both Blair and Seward had made the point about the appearance of desperation, and it evidently registered with him.

"I'll think about it some more," Lincoln said, folding the document and putting it in his pocket. Blair suppressed a sigh of relief. "Mars, what else do you have?"

"I want to talk about drafting fifty thousand additional men," said Stanton.

"Not to serve under that incompetent, McClellan," said Chase.

As the meeting continued through the long midsummer afternoon, Blair reached the conclusion that Lincoln had been only momentarily sidetracked. More pressure had to be put on, right away, that night, lest Lincoln launch by himself the proclamation that he had drafted by himself. Stanton probably had a stream of abolitionists ready to pressure the President.

The politics of this thing was the key. Blair asked himself: Whose judgment, besides Father Blair's, did Lincoln trust most on politics, especially New York politics? Not Seward's; that player in the power game did not believe in the reality of the passions his positions excited, because he felt none himself. But Seward's alter ego, Thurlow Weed, was both more impassioned and more devious. Montgomery Blair hoped that Seward had primed Thurlow Weed on the task that remained to be done because the emancipation decision could still go either way.

CHAPTER 10

SECOND THOUGHTS

Anna Carroll stepped into Chase's study in the house at Sixth and E streets, not far from her Ebbitt House rooms, and was struck by the contrast of the two portraits on the wall. One, recently done, was of Charles Sumner, an abolitionist ally with whom Chase had served in the Senate. The other must have been painted nearly seventy years before, around the turn of the century: Charles Carroll of Carrollton, signer of the Declaration of Independence, first senator from Maryland.

"He was a relative of yours, Anna—a great-uncle?"

"A cousin of my grandfather's."

"A great man," the governor said. "One of the founders of the Catholic Church in America, as you know. I visited him in my youth, because I wanted to meet the last surviving signer of the Declaration of Independence."

Anna assumed that Chase would be impressed by that branch of her genealogy. Anna's side of the family was firmly Protestant, and had long been estranged from the Catholic Carrolls. She had taken a certain family delight in her espousal of the Know-Nothing cause, with its vigorous anti-Catholic, anti-immigrant bias, but that was not a matter to be discussed with Salmon Portland Chase.

"He was probably the richest man in America," she observed, which impressed her more about her remote forebear. "The Sprague of his time." She could not resist that dig; it was the talk of Washington that the Chases, father and his elder daughter, were making much of the dissolute Governor Sprague of Rhode Island. The thought of a woman seeking the courtship of a drunkard for his vast monetary resources was repugnant to her; on the other hand, a liaison with a man of intellect and character who also happened to be a man of financial substance—such as Chase—was another matter. Wealth was hardly a drawback. "And where are your daughters tonight?"

"Kate was suffering from an attack of immaturity," the tall man said, stumbling over the word "immaturity"; Chase had a slight speech impediment that manifested itself when he was agitated. It had kept him, she heard, from being much of an oratorical force in the Senate. "Sometimes Nettie, who's only fourteen, seems more grown up. I sent them both to New York for a couple of weeks, to some old friends on an estate near Troy. I suppose they were just as glad to get out of this Washington heat."

Anna put two and two together: John Hay's sudden leave from the Executive Mansion coincided with Kate's brief exile, and it was an absence that the two young people at the center of power had probably coordinated. She said nothing, wishing she had done more of that at Kate's age.

"Lincoln has not become desperate enough to get rid of McClellan," he said, fiddling with his glass, moving his silverware around fussily, adjusting the napkin on his lap. "That was some campaign in the Peninsula—fifty days, fifty miles, fifty million dollars. And his failure has driven the value of the dollar down to eighty-seven cents."

She had heard the dollar was falling against the price of gold, evidence of lack of confidence in a Union victory. That meant more difficulty in borrowing and less money for war supplies; Chase's antipathy to the "Young Napoleon" was based on more than his radical politics.

"The President won't budge when it comes to firing that incompetent," Chase was saying, "but he is desperate enough to take the most radical of measures on emancipation. Beyond anything I have recommended."

"I was surprised when he signed the Confiscation Act," Anna replied carefully. "I sent him a memorial opposing it."

She found talking politics with Chase was both easy and hard: easy because they were both so well informed, hard because they were on different sides of the abolition issue. An added complication was their web of friendships: Ben Wade, for example, who had said he would drop by Chase's house to take her home later, was the man she trusted most in the world, and was a radical like Chase; yet Wade and Chase, both Ohio Republicans, cordially disliked each other. Chase had told her he thought Ben Wade had cheated him out of a unanimous Ohio delegation at the Chicago Wigwam in the 1860 convention, and Wade once told her, "Chase is all right, only his theology is wrong: he thinks there is a fourth person in the Trinity." So often, she had found the people she agreed with most were the least appealing; the other way around, too—she had argued with Breckinridge on Union and with Chase on abolition. The intruding thought of Breck saddened her; she had no reports about him since the bloodletting at Shiloh.

"The Confiscation Act is as nothing," said Chase, "to what he's thinking of doing now." He did not say what it was, muttering only "dangerous, dangerous. Too soon." Anna knew she had no need to pry; Chase could not keep this to himself, and with his daughter gone, Anna was his natural confidante. She let herself look puzzled, which was easy enough. What could Lincoln be up to that went further than arming the fugitive slaves?

"Lincoln was positively insulting in Cabinet today," the Treasury Secretary complained. "I, though charged with the responsibility of providing for the enormous expenses entailed upon the country, have no control over—no voice even in deciding on—the measures by which the necessity for them is created."

She nodded sympathetically, pouring them both some wine from his crystal decanter. She liked wine with a meal, it made her merry, though she was careful to limit her gaiety tonight. "Lincoln can be stubborn," she said from experience.

"Anna, you shared your confidence with me about your unfortunate interview with the President, when he acted so boorishly about your hard-earned fee. I think it only right to take you into my confidence now."

She wished he would get to the point. If ever the two of them got together, she could help him on that. She leaned forward, low-cut dinner dress exhibiting her fine bosom, chin in hand, ready for the revelation of Cabinet deliberations.

"He wants to threaten publicly to abolish slavery in the states in rebellion," Chase said heavily. "An invitation to an uprising. Stanton's behind it."

"Lincoln wants this?"

"Well, today he does. Tomorrow, I don't know. But he had a proclamation all drafted. It put me in a most embarrassing position."

She saw that right away. If Lincoln went overboard to the radicals, Chase would lose his constituency. But that was insignificant compared to the import of the President's inexplicable shift. She feared its consequence: the end of the Union, done in the name of the Union. "Did anybody stop him?"

"I could not, obviously. The position I took was to urge that local emancipation take place by commanders in the field. It is galling to admit this, even to myself, but I was glad that Blair and Seward were there to restrain him."

Anna was torn between delight at this measure of confidence from a lonely man in the nation's highest council and her consternation at the awkwardness of his position. When a conservative like Lincoln outradicaled the radicals, what was a lukewarm radical like Chase to do? Should he go along with the new, abolitionist Lincoln, for consistency's sake—or seek to restrain him for Chase's personal political gain? She foresaw another complication. If Chase counseled delay, it would soon become known that he had not been an enthusiastic backer of the President's change of heart. When that got out, Ohio's favorite son would be hurt among his own radical faction.

"You're in danger, Governor, of being outflanked." The military metaphor was apt. Lincoln's lunge leftward would undoubtedly please the radicals, reducing their need for an alternative to Lincoln at the next convention.

Anna was about to give Chase some good personal political advice on how to delay emancipation without appearing to do so when she stopped herself. That was the mistake she had made with Fillmore and the others. She had always been too free with her advice, making it the less valuable, and her help had too often been interpreted as bossiness. Moreover, she was curious to see how Chase would come out of this by himself. Would he put principle above all, and encourage Lincoln? Or put long-term political advantage first, and seek to stop him? Trickiest of all—would he see the danger in putting political advantage first, and take a principled stand for fear of being caught off political base?

She relished these possibilities, and was grateful to Chase for the chance to see the play of power in Lincoln's Cabinet. To Chase, the war now offered a way to abolition, and to Lincoln, abolition now offered a way to win the war. She thought both were wrong. Abolition was a way to lose the war, and only if the war were won would slavery ultimately be ended. Anna resolved to restrain her impulse to tell a political leader what to do.

"What if this threat of abolition at year's end did cause the loyal slave owners to sell their slaves to the government?" Chase asked aloud, finding another chink in Lincoln's proposal. "Where would I get the money for that? The spigot in Uncle Abe's barrel is twice as big as the bunghole."

That turn of phrase was uncharacteristic. "Excuse me, Governor—what did you just say?"

Chase looked at her, surprised and pleased with his own figure of speech. "The President may have been a good flatboatman and rail-splitter, but he never learned the true science of coopering. The bunghole in a barrel is where the air—in this case, the money—comes in. It has to be bigger than the spigot." He coughed nervously. "Perhaps that's an undignified way to talk—"

"Oh, no, Governor—talk that way, by all means. Too many people take your normal manner as, um—" Was he ready for this? She took the plunge: "—stuffy. Lincoln is criticized for his coarseness, and rightly so, but many voters appreciate a leader who speaks colorfully. I wish the public could see you as I do, and hear you talk about the spigot and the bunghole."

He beamed at her, then caught himself and frowned. "Frederick Douglass, the freedmen's leader, speaks often of the 'image' of a public man. I fear mine hardly reflects the man I really am." When she did not contradict him, he added ruefully, "I wish there were something I could do about this perception of my—what you call 'stuffiness.' I'm really not, you know. Not at all."

She reached over and squeezed his hand, then withdrew her own. "There's a newspaperman I want you to meet," she said. "Whitelaw Reid. Writes under the name of 'Agate.' He's asked me if he can be helpful to you in any way, and I was thinking, maybe he can do some pieces on the 'real' Governor Chase. Or even help you with some of your speeches, when you don't have time to work on them because of the press of other affairs." She was not about to volunteer for that assignment herself and wanted to shunt Chase off on someone else before the need for such help occurred to him. Senator Browning demanded enough nonpaid writing for now, along with Bates and the others.

A black servant knocked and entered. "The Secretary of War is here, sir, with another gentleman. He says they not expected but must see you right away quick."

Chase motioned for Anna to remain seated, adding, "I have no secrets from you on this, Miss Carroll. And if Stanton brought a witness, perhaps I should have one too."

Stanton and a tall, thin man who was introduced as "Cutting, a Democrat from New York" were ushered in. She reached up to shake Cutting's hand, squinted at him, and took a chance: "Did you not serve in Congress some years ago?"

"Almost a decade ago, Miss Carroll," the New Yorker said, pleased to be recognized. "I came here at the end of the Fillmore administration. We met at a White House reception."

She remembered Francis Brockholst Cutting better than he knew. John Breckinridge had told her of the time Cutting and the other "Hards" in New York had joined with him in pushing a bill to repeal the Missouri Compromise and bring in Kansas and Nebraska as states with "pop sov"—free to decide for themselves about the extension of slavery. When the abolitionists in New York got wind of the deal, Cutting was forced to renege; then Breck denounced the double cross on the floor, and Cutting claimed to have secretly financed the Breckinridge campaign. When Breck called him a liar to his face, Cutting challenged him to a duel. Breck accepted the challenge, named the weapons—rifles at sixty paces—and Cutting, through some skillful seconds, backed down. Breck had good reason to distrust Cutting politically and to despise him personally.

"Look, Chase, we have a damned crisis on our hands," the agitated Stanton said, ignoring amenities. "Victory is in our grasp, and Blair and Seward and that sneaky lobby-agent Weed are trying to snatch it away."

Cutting looked at Stanton sharply and raised an eyebrow, taking note of the presence of an outsider. Stanton dismissed his caution with "This lady does the work that makes others famous." Anna liked the way he paid her the compliment of not fawning over her. "Miss Carroll, I rely, as always, on your absolute discretion." Stanton drew on his glasses. "No time to beat around the bush—thanks to Cutting here, Lincoln has proposed to emancipate the slaves in rebel states. Happened this morning in Cabinet."

"I was not aware of your role," Chase said to the New York lawyer. Anna was glad the focus had shifted from her; she did not want Chase put in the position of admitting he told her about it or, worse, of having to cut her out of the conversation.

"Cutting here was with Lincoln for two solid hours before the meeting," Stanton said. "Give Chase the gist," he ordered.

"I argued in substance that the emancipation of the slaves would produce very important and beneficial effects on our relations with foreign powers," Cutting reported. "After we struck off the shackles of the bondsmen, foreign governments would not dare to take sides in favor of their masters."

"That's what Blair said was the best argument for, but Seward doesn't agree," said Chase, "and Lincoln trusts Seward in foreign relations. Did you talk politics?"

"I dwelt on the importance of encouraging that rapidly increasing demand of our loyal citizens," said Cutting, "who eagerly wish for the destruction of slavery."

"This fellow is a New York Democrat," Stanton said, slicing through the man's verbiage. "When those fellows start turning on abolition, that has to be important to Lincoln."

"Did the President show any concern about the effect of his emancipation order on the border states?" Anna put in.

"Oh, yes," the lawyer assured her. "That was his main difficulty with the idea."

"Cutting hit that very hard," said Stanton, excited. "Tell them what you told Lincoln."

"That we had already sacrificed too much to a vain attempt to conciliate these people," Cutting replied. "At heart, most of them are disloyal, as the inaction of a committee of them meeting with the President had shown. To hesitate to confer freedom on human beings merely because it would be distasteful to slave dealers in Kentucky and Maryland would be to reject the claims of justice."

Anna bridled at the effrontery of the New Yorker, who had probably never met a slave. She held her temper: "And did the politics come up?"

"I told the President that a dramatic emancipation would infuse the hearts of our loyal Democrats with additional fortitude." Anna took that to mean that Cutting had not warned of the reaction of voters at the polls this fall.

"It had great effect, Miss Carroll," said Stanton, "so much that these arguments caused Lincoln to move on a document he has evidently been working on since the Seven Days defeat."

"You think he'll issue it?" Chase looked worried. "Tomorrow?"

"I think so," said Cutting. "He's ready."

"He said he was going to think it over," Chase countered. "He said Seward had a point about his looking desperate, a last shriek on a retreat—" Anna wondered what that meant.

"Lincoln is damn well going to issue that proclamation tomorrow," Stanton said with determination, "and I'll have it on every telegraph wire in the country before he has a chance to change his mind again." If Lincoln was so sure to sign the proclamation, Anna wondered, why was Stanton here? Why was Chase's support necessary now?

"It is a larger step than I ever contemplated," said Chase. "I had in mind that the generals in the field—"

"Dammit, Chase, I thought we could depend on you," Stanton said, rising. "You were awfully silent in that meeting at the critical moment."

"You know that my sympathies are—"

"I don't need your sympathies, I need your heart and hand in this!" Anna had never seen the Secretary of War this upset. "You sat in that Cabinet Room today, when human slavery could have been dealt a death blow, and you said nothing. Nothing!"

"That is untrue, Edwin Stanton." Chase rose and glared at his guest. "I ask you to withdraw that remark, sir."

Anna's eyes darted back and forth between the men in confrontation. Chase was on the spot. If Lincoln listened to Seward and Blair and put aside the proclamation, Stanton and this man Cutting would let it be known to Horace Greeley and other radicals that Chase was the man who failed them. On the other hand, if Lincoln went ahead and issued the abolition order in the morning, Chase might be even worse off politically—standing on the platform after the abolition train had left the station. Anna was enjoying this.

"I mean no offense"—Stanton seemed to back down, but immediately bored in again—"but don't you see how it will look tomorrow, with the proclamation issued over what some people may think is your objection?"

"You'll be ruined," said Cutting. Anna was certain he and Stanton had rehearsed their argument.

"Then those are the consequences I am prepared to suffer," said Chase solemnly. Good for him, Anna thought. "I give my advice in Cabinet on principle, and not with any thought to political advancement." Sometime, she decided, his stuffiness was endearing, if he meant it.

"Spoken like a patriot," said Cutting, motioning Stanton to sit down. Apparently the New York lawyer would try another tack, since Chase would not be stampeded. "If this golden moment passes, there are surely many who will say that you, Mr. Chase, must be held responsible for delaying or defeating the greatest act of justice, statesmanship, and civilization of the last four thousand years. I shall surely not join them. I fully recognize your commitment to emancipation, done in a more orderly—more soldierly—way." Cutting paused to let that sink in; he was a good trial lawyer.

"It is a most dramatic step," Chase said. "I know that Stanton here wants an uprising, but to think of four million Africans on a rampage against the women and children of the South, with white husbands and fathers away at the front—it's too terrible to contemplate."

Stanton started to speak but Cutting motioned him silent. "Forget the political implications of failing to be behind the President when he takes his historic action," said the New York Democrat smoothly. "Consider only the principle. There comes a moment in a nation's history that great issues turn on a single person's advice. We are at that moment now. The war is being lost by the North, we all know it; emancipation is truly an act of desperation, of military necessity. If Lincoln acts now, slavery can be made the issue of the war, and struck dead if the North should win."

"And if he does not act—" Anna was drawn into the flow of the lawyer's presentation.

"Suppose there should be a military success next month," Cutting posited. "Suppose Lee's rebel army disengages from McClellan and comes to challenge John Pope here outside of Washington, and Pope smashes Lee and the Union wins the war. What pressure then will be on Lincoln to free the slaves? None."

Chase was silent; the man had a point.

"The President, as you know far better than I," Cutting added, "is not the sort of man to take chances. He is fundamentally conservative. If he begins to win, Lincoln will stick to the cause of the Union and forget about abolition. And the moment to end slavery now, in our lifetimes, will have come and gone."

Chase took a deep breath and exhaled. Anna admired the presentation: Cutting had changed the situation in Chase's mind from one in which he was a reluctant follower to one in which he could be the central figure. But what about Chase's convictions?

"Come with us to see Lincoln in the morning," said Stanton, controlling his agitation. "We need you. Human freedom rests in the balance. Your silence today will be forgotten, your voice tomorrow will be remembered forever. Are you with us?"

Anna took a handkerchief and patted her face and chest while they waited. God, it was hot in Washington in July.

"I want to think it over," Chase said finally. "Let's ride to the Mansion together in the morning."

"We'll be here at seven," said Stanton, now sure of his man. "Miss Carroll, if the Secretary of the Treasury has any doubts about the President's war power in this matter, I know you are prepared to elucidate."

As they rose to leave, Cutting said to Anna, "I admired your pamphlet tearing apart that scoundrel Breckinridge."

"He spoke of you often," she replied, not especially seeking this man's friendship. "Rifles at sixty paces, wasn't it?"

The New Yorker blanched and followed Stanton to the door. After they departed, Chase looked at her directly. "What do you think I should do, Anna?"

"Do what your conscience directs," she replied, not helping him a bit. She should have done the same with Fillmore and Buchanan; if Chase had no political judgment or moral backbone, it was time she learned about it.

"I have no real choice," he said at last. "This proclamation at this time, and in this way, may be a terrible mistake. It is surely more than I contemplated." He sighed deeply. "But I cannot afford to appear to be inconsistent, which is what further opposition to a presidential proclamation would seem to be."

She nodded sagely, in understanding rather than in agreement; he was getting set to cave in.

"Tomorrow morning," he announced as if to an assemblage, "I shall go with them to the presidential Mansion and give my unqualified approval to emancipation. And I know, my dear lady, that I can depend on you to make it clear to your friend and mine, Ben Wade, that at the decisive moment it was Salmon Portland Chase who turned the tide."

"I feel I know you much better now, Governor," she said with feeling.

"I am glad," he said. "Your good opinion, Anna, means more to me than I can now permit myself to say." Responding to his carefulness, she said nothing.

He rose, took her hand, and led her to the library adjacent to the dining room. She permitted herself to be ushered along, marveling at the way he had decided, with no discernible anguish, to risk the lives of millions of white women and children rather than risk his place in the pantheon of radicals.

She respected the Chase taste in good living, that was certain. The polished, leather-bound books were warmly inviting because each was an individual copy, not part of matching sets; his desk was suitably stacked with work taken home; the tea table was probably Sheraton, and the fire irons were the sought-after old double lemon-tops made in Boston during the Revolution. A bottle of old Madeira was on the tea table, which he carefully decanted before pouring two servings into heavy crystal goblets. The man knew how to live, in a way that reminded her of the Carroll home when her father was governor.

Anna knew she was not about to live that way again short of marriage to a man like Chase. She was three thousand dollars in debt—not a huge amount, but one that always seemed more than she could get a handle on. The chosen life of a spinster, with all its independence and privacy, was no longer so satisfying. And there was place for pride, along with some derivative power, in being what they were calling "First" Lady. Still, the need to keep her opinions to herself rankled; she did not know if she could restrain herself for very long.

"What troubles you most about the proclamation, Governor?"

He answered as if he were still addressing a meeting. "Arming slaves that come across the lines, in small numbers, under local military control, is a good thing, and I have been pressing for it. But a proclamation aimed at the slaves on undefended plantations, far from military control of any sort, is incitement to uprising. Pillage, carnage . . ." He groped for another word ending with "age."

"Serve the traitors right," she could not help saying.

He looked closely at her and stopped talking to the whole room. "Do you know what you're saying, Anna? The women and children at home are not traitors. The children are not responsible for the rebellion. The people who will suffer are the innocents, not the real traitors, who are surrounded by soldiers."

She wondered if that concern was really what motivated him. "You want to know what I think?"

He took a deep breath and said, "No." She looked up, more surprised than annoyed, but ready soon to become annoyed.

"I hope you will not tell me what you think, Anna, because I fear that you have a set of reasons, brilliantly marshaled, that will make me feel even worse about what I am determined to do. I do not need reasoning that makes me feel like a hypocrite. At this moment I would appreciate, instead, your support."

Anna chewed that over. After a moment, she decided the challenge went to the heart of the sort of person she was, and wanted to be. She would do what she could to minimize her bossiness, but she was not going to become somebody's abject supporter at this stage in her life. She pushed her chair back and stood up.

"I won't wait for Ben Wade to come by and get me," she announced. "I'll walk home. I live only a few blocks away."

He motioned for her to sit down. "I knew you'd take it that way. I really wish you would not."

"You've been living with your daughters for too long," she told him. "You don't need a woman friend, you want an audience. I'm not that way." When he said nothing, she went on: "So I'll say what I think, whether you like it or not." Why didn't he argue? He merely looked defeated, which made her feel bad; when she went into intellectual combat, she expected, needed, resistance. "Are you listening?"

He rose to his full height and looked sternly at her. Chase was a very big man; at times like these, she wished she had the physical stature of a Breckinridge or a Sumner. At any rate, she had gained his full attention, and she pressed on.

"You know where I stand on the war power," she told him. Stanton's parting remark had contributed to her bona fides on that. "I think a President in wartime may arrest a legislature, the way Lincoln did in Maryland. I think he can defy the Supreme Court's decision on habeus corpus, the way he did with Taney. I would even go further: as commander in chief, the President has the right to put down rebellion or repel invasion by assuming dictatorial power. I'm no weak sister on executive authority, the way F'nandy Wood's copperheads in New York are."

Chase nodded. "Your position on the war power is well known."

"The President's expanded power comes from his constitutional obligation to strike at the enemy," she said. "Now, who is the enemy? The Confederate States of America?"

"We do not recognize the Confederacy," Chase answered correctly. "Our opponents are merely insurgents, not another nation."

"Those states in rebellion—are they the enemy?"

Chase hesitated, then said: "No. We hold that secession is unlawful. No matter what the rebel leaders say, it remains our position that the states of the South are still in the Union. This is not a war between the states and the nation, it is an insurrection by rebels against the legitimate government."

He had it right, and she had him. "Then individual rebels may be punished for acts of treason, but not entire states—right?"

His brow clouded; she could tell he could finally see where she was leading him. "True."

"Then it is permissible to punish individual rebels who use their slaves to wage war, by declaring the slaves contraband—as Butler did—and freeing them. And it is permissible to punish rebels further, in the Confiscation Act as explained in the resolution, by seizing slaves of all traitors supporting the rebellion. In those cases, you are striking at the property of individual rebels, who collectively make up 'the enemy.' "

"Make your point, Anna."

"But if Lincoln declared all slaves within a state to be free, he would be making war on that state *as a state*. He would be punishing all its slaveholders, whether or not they were taking part in the rebellion. With no compensation, that's a blood attainder and unconstitutional—but, worse, it says that the federal government has the right to take property from all the citizens of one of its states without regard to individual crime or liability."

"But isn't that war?"

She sagged; he had missed her point. "That's not war, that's revolution. Don't you see? If Lincoln issues that proclamation, *he* becomes the revolutionary. The Southern leaders can say, with absolute justification, that they are the ones upholding the Constitution and Lincoln is the one who has turned war into revolution. And by treating 'the enemy' as whole states, and not as individual traitors within those states, Lincoln would inform the world he is fighting a legitimate nation."

Chase sat down, comprehending. Anna sat beside him. "My own plan of emancipation," he said, "was to have local commanders in the field free the slaves in the areas they occupied."

"That has a legal base in martial law," she said approvingly, "which operates only in areas subject to military occupation. The military can appropriate property in land it has won, call it contraband or whatever, and free individual slaves—but neither the military nor the President with all his war power can legally abolish slavery itself. That would take a constitutional amendment. And you certainly have no right in international law to seize property in areas you do not occupy."

"My own plan, then," said Chase with growing satisfaction, "is not merely the practical way, it has the advantage of being constitutionally sound. And it does not confer sovereignty on the states in rebellion."

"The rebel leaders," she told him, "are in rebellion, not the states. This is not a war between the states, as the Southerners like to call it, this is merely an insurrection of individual rebels. Only if Lincoln issues that emancipation proclamation does he practice revolution and elevate the rebellion to a war between the states."

Chase beamed at her. "Why didn't Blair think of that?"

Her mind raced ahead to consequences months from now. "Lincoln had better be prepared to be a complete despot, if he goes for his proclamation. I take it recruitment is falling off?"

Chase nodded. "Stanton is preparing for a draft."

"Then you can expect riots, especially if young men are being sent to fight for an unpopular cause like abolition. Agitators will urge resistance to the draft, and Lincoln will have to put them all in jail. He'll need more power to do that than he has now, power on a grand scale."

She had not thought this through before, but the natural consequences of such a proclamation quickly occurred to her, especially with Congress not in session. "If he issues this abolition proclamation, he'd better be ready to have another proclamation ready simultaneously, asserting his authority to clap every objector in jail. Vallandigham and the lot. Otherwise, we'll lose the war."

Chase shook his head; he did not want to think about that. "Tomorrow, Anna, I shall accompany the Secretary of War to the President and once again urge my approach to emancipate and arm slaves on a local-commander basis."

"If Lincoln persists in his own way?"

He sighed profoundly. "Then I will give my heart and hand to a war between the states," he said wearily. "I cannot oppose him on emancipation in any form."

She put her small hand on his large one. His was not as large as Lincoln's, which was huge, but it was a substantial man's hand, knuckled and impressively veined. "Get right with your constituency, if you have to," she advised. She hated to see a man go against his conscience, and she felt small in offering no objection to his doing it, but she was satisfied in having had her say. She stood in her own shoes; he was too preoccupied with gaining power to stand in his.

"We won't wait for the Wades," he said. "I'll walk you home."

Her rooms were a mess; she would bid him a firm good night at the door. "I would appreciate your support," she said solemnly.

Chase did not catch that reference to her reaction to his earlier announcement at first, but in a moment it registered, and he smiled back with warmth. She hoped that the prospect of ending her own loneliness was not causing her to give him too much the benefit of the doubt. Chase was not a quick-minded man, and not a deeply principled man, but she judged him to be a good man, or at least a good-enough man, better than most presidents she had known. Anna resolved to find an excuse to come back to this house before his daughters returned.

Negro soldiers

BOOK SEVEN

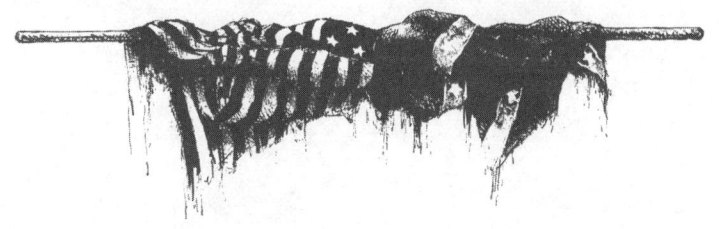

The Negro

CHAPTER 1

WIZARD OF THE LOBBY

In front of Willard's, nodding to acquaintances entering the great hotel for dinner, Thurlow Weed awaited William Seward. A late afternoon thunderstorm had broken the heat, leaving Washington humid but tolerable. On the corner of Fourteenth Street, Weed could look up Pennsylvania Avenue to the half-built Capitol dome. As carriages approached, he stepped far back on the wooden sidewalk to escape the splash of mud.

Seward had sent a messenger with a curt note, telling his longtime political partner to stand by for a meeting with Lincoln after dinner, that the President was on the verge of a coup d'état. What did that mean? How could a President be accused of taking over his own government?

The Secretary of State came rolling up in his carriage at about nine o'clock and signaled Weed to climb in.

"I'm taking you to the Mansion and setting you on Lincoln alone," he said with no preamble. "I've delayed him for a few hours, but I cannot handle him on this. It will be up to you, Thurlow, to save him from losing the war in a single stroke."

No mere matter of the patronage, this. "What's all this about a coup, Governor? Has Lincoln taken it into his head to be President again?"

"He's written a proclamation freeing the slaves," Seward said. "Just like that—abolition in less than six months if the South doesn't give up."

Weed said little, listening to his alter ego's analysis of that day's Cabinet meeting. His first reaction was sorrow that the President evidently felt that the war was lost. Weed's second thought was more in line with his natural instincts for political combat: "Where is Chase in all this?"

Seward's hawklike face flashed a smile. "He's embarrassed. Floundering about. This is Stanton's play, and he'll bring Chase around in the morning to carry the radical banner. Meanwhile, I have bought the time for you to do the job. Stop the proclamation before it splits the North."

Weed could see the white Mansion a block ahead. "Why does Lincoln suddenly want to issue a proclamation on this?" If Lincoln felt so strongly about freeing and arming the slaves, to stir up a servile insurrection behind rebel lines, he had the Confiscation Act.

"Ah, proclamations," said his partner. "You know the story of the man after the Revolution who couldn't rest until his village raised a liberty pole. When his neighbors asked if he didn't feel as free without it as with it, the man always answered, 'What is liberty without a liberty pole?' And what's a war without proclamations?"

Weed nodded in appreciation at the jest but knew there was more to Lincoln's move than a need to give the appearance of leadership. Either Lincoln was using emancipation to reverse the tide of war, or he was doing just the opposite—using the war emergency to do something about slavery. "Is Lincoln dead set against slavery? More than he lets on?"

"No more than you or I," said Seward with his customary certainty. "He's

influenced in this precipitate pronouncement by the notion that the common
people in foreign nations expect us to be against slavery."

"He's right about popular sentiment abroad," Weed said, remembering the
distaste felt by the cotton-hungry English leaders at the workingman's aversion to American slavery. "Even the Tsar is freeing the serfs."

"The people in England and France, my dear Thurlow, do not understand
that this war, if successful, will ultimately end slavery here. But if we try to
end slavery during the war, we'll lose. There'll be riots in New York City,
abetted by its contemptible mayor. Can you imagine drafting white Irishmen
to fight and die for the freedom of the Africans?"

"I want John Dix for governor on the Republican ticket," Weed said,
turning to a matter closer to home. "Greeley won't take him—Dix is a Democrat. But if we don't put up a good War Democrat like Dix in New York, the
Peace Democrats will beat us, especially if the Democrats prevail on Horatio
Seymour to run."

"Don't bring that up tonight," Seward told him, as the carriage wheels
oozed to a stop in the mud outside the White House. "You're reputed to be
the Wizard of the Lobby. Concentrate on one great lobbying goal: stop that
proclamation."

Weed did not get out immediately. "Henry, it's a good thing your good wife
can't hear you say that."

Seward slumped in his seat. "I had a letter from Frances today. She said
that I had advocated liberty for forty years, and she cannot understand how I
can tell her now that the preservation of republican institutions is more important than the abolition of slavery. She thinks, as I used to think, that
Union and slavery are incompatible." He was silent a moment. "She said that
this was the first time in my life that I had spent an entire year without
writing a line in defense of human liberty."

"If Lincoln goes through with it, the name of Seward would be on that
paper, alongside Lincoln's," Weed reminded him. "The Secretary of State
countersigns proclamations."

Seward winced. "I know that. But abolition now is a mistake. Thurlow,
I've told you what to do, but I haven't asked what you thought. Are you with
me on this? Is my judgment sound?"

Weed squeezed his friend's bony leg and climbed down. "We think alike.
But I wish I knew what's driving Lincoln on this."

"I can't say for sure what, but I can tell you who. Stanton brought in our
old friend Cutting." Seward made a face.

"The professional switcher?"

"And he has switched again, from pro-slavery to abolition. I fear this has
unduly influenced the President. You're the antidote to that poison."

Weed nodded farewell, rapped on the front door with his knuckle, and a
black servant he remembered from Frank Pierce's day showed him inside.
The President's son, the little boy with the large head and cleft palate, raced
down the stairs to say that his father was in the telegraph office across the
street and that Mr. Weed was to wait in the small sitting room next to the
bedroom upstairs.

The Albany editor followed the boy upstairs and awaited the President. He
knew that the man would not be as easy to turn around as he had been a year

ago; Lincoln of late had become more confident of his own political judgment.

Lincoln came in moments later with an expression that changed from melancholy to cheerful at seeing a fellow politician he liked. Then he went back to a worried look: "Morgan's raiders are storming all over Kentucky, and we can't get a firm handle on the state. Weed, I hate to say it, but the bottom's out of the tub."

Weed knew better than to be drawn into a serious discussion about the war right away. He complimented Lincoln on the way his boy was growing up, meeting people cheerfully, handling himself well. The gangling President mellowed immediately—his mood swings were remarkable, and not at all insincere—and soon was telling a story that Weed had long ago told Seward. They laughed together, and Weed announced that Lincoln could relax, he had not come to press him about the New York patronage.

"Justice to all," said the President benevolently, which was a code phrase meaning an even split in New York between the Weed and Greeley factions. Weed dearly wished he could tell Lincoln what he knew about Chase's appointee at the Port, Hiram Barney, surreptitiously lending money to the Secretary of the Treasury, but he knew that would be out of place.

"You surprised them in the Cabinet today."

Lincoln removed his shoes and massaged one of his feet. "Surprised, eh? What did you hear?"

"Your abolition plan. Big meeting at Chase's tonight, with Stanton twisting Chase's arm to get you to go through with your proclamation tomorrow."

"I think I will," said the President. "Wrote it myself, no help from anyone in the Cabinet." He kept working on his sore foot. Weed had no foot problems himself, but knew how Seward suffered all his life from corns, and could sympathize silently. Weed would never lobby a politician who did not ask to be lobbied; he had no need to fill up the silence. That was the trouble with people who met with presidents; they felt they had to use every moment to get a point across.

"You were in London last month, Weed. How will they take emancipation? Judge Blair says that's the best argument for it."

"The public in England and France will approve," Weed allowed, "although that won't be decisive in keeping those nations out of the war. If the negroes rise up in the South, and there's carnage on the plantations, you can count on a revulsion all over the civilized world. I supported you on the Confiscation Act—"

"I saw those editorials in your *Evening Journal;* they were very good—"

"—and most of our readers go along with refusing to return slaves that come into our lines, and with using them as laborers." Weed put on his most somber look. "But to change the whole purpose of the war? To go from preserving the Union to freeing the slaves down South?" He shook his head. "If you issue that proclamation, Lincoln, I promise you that the Peace Democrats will win this fall. You won't get any more troops out of New York."

Lincoln did not flinch at that. "We're thinking of conscription, if we have to."

"A draft might work to defend the Union, maybe—not to free the slaves.

You'll have riots, huge mobs in the streets. And not only the mayor but the next governor on the side of the rioters."

Lincoln drew a deep breath. "If that's true in New York—"

"It would hold for New Jersey, too, and most of Pennsylvania." Weed could count and so could Lincoln. "You'd win in Massachusetts and lose the border states, of course. You'd lose Ohio." Weed was pretty sure that in Illinois, Lincoln's convention manager and old friend, Leonard Swett, would go down to defeat, but thought it impolitic to tell that to the man from Springfield. He phrased it delicately: "I wouldn't know about Illinois, maybe Leonard Swett could squeak by—"

"We could have trouble in Illinois," Lincoln admitted. "Depends on the state of the war." He threw up his huge hands. "Well, it's the people's business—the election is in their hands. If they turn their backs to the fire and get scorched in the rear, they'll find they have got to sit on the blister."

Weed shook his head no; the way to approach the most important election in America's history was with neither fatalism nor stubbornness. He had to induce the President to face the adverse political consequences of his proclamation. "I know what you're trying to do," said Weed helpfully. "You're trying to put new spirit in the North, to capture a great moral fervor after the awful letdown in front of Richmond. But in my political judgment, a proclamation would do much more harm than good. On the stump, the issue would turn on equality, not abolition."

Lincoln looked up sharply. "What do you mean?"

"The first question, in a political race, would be: Do you believe blacks and white should be equal?"

"I answered that back in fifty-eight, in the debates," said Lincoln. "I said then I had no purpose to introduce political and social equality between the white and the black races, but I held then and hold now that there is no reason in the world why the negro is not entitled to all the natural rights enumerated in the Declaration of Independence."

"Think politics, now," Weed pressed.

"Free the slaves, and make them politically and socially our equals?" Weed could see Lincoln bristling at being forced to make again the disclaimers he had made in his debates with Douglas. "No. A universal feeling, whether well- or ill-founded, cannot be safely disregarded, Weed. You know that as well as I do. We cannot make them our equals."

Weed noted Lincoln's disclaimer within the disclaimer—"whether well- or ill-founded"—which was characteristic of the man. Weed had made a study of Lincoln's statements on the negro, and while nobody fearful of social equality could find fault with what Lincoln said, there was usually some little twist or qualifier that made his anti-equality position seem grudging. In his heart, he probably leaned toward equality.

"People up in New York are worried about the practical effect of abolition," he told the President, sticking to politics. "Take this step now, and you take another tomorrow toward intermarriage, mongrelization . . ."

"Counterfeit logic," snapped Lincoln. "I won't accept an argument that says that because I do not want a black woman for a slave, I must necessarily want her for a wife." He glared across the sitting room. "I need not have her for either. Hell, Weed, I can just leave her alone!"

"You're making debating points," the New Yorker told him, "and I'm talking public sentiment. Remember the Frémont campaign in fifty-six."

He did not have to spell that out for Lincoln; everyone who had tried to help John Frémont in that first Republican campaign for President remembered the anti-black undercurrent that swept away so many votes and made it possible for Buchanan and Breckinridge to win.

Lincoln raised both feet and brought them crashing down on the floor. "Negro equality! Fudge! How long, in a government of a God great enough to make and maintain this universe, shall there continue knaves to vend, and fools to gulp, so low a piece of demagoguism as this?"

The bugaboo of social equality, Weed knew, was the greatest riposte any politician could offer to appeals for abolition. A proclamation along the lines of the one in the President's pocket, he was certain, would raise the equality issue and elect governors and congressmen who would settle the war on the South's terms. If slavery were ever to be ended in America, it could not be accomplished under an abolition standard or by a firebrand like Wade or Stevens. The trick was to persuade Lincoln not to exaggerate the abolition sentiment in the North; it was noisy, but abolition did not win elections. Weed pondered the best way to get this simple point across to the complex man before him; Lincoln was at once melancholy and droll, familiar and reserved, easy enough to cajole but very hard to push. He probably saw this as a military blow that coincided with his party's drift and his personal wishes. Weed saw the proclamation as a military nullity that would harm his party at the polls, ultimately defeating his personal hopes for emancipation by losing support for the war.

"Forgive me, Weed. Here"—he took a sheet of paper out of his coat pocket —"read it. What will the effect be? I hope for greater gain than loss, but I'm not entirely confident."

That was frank; Lincoln was offering an opening. The editor perused the document. Only two paragraphs. The first simply asserted the provisions of the Confiscation Act passed last week, threatening to seize the property of rebels. The second began by announcing an intention to submit another bill proposing compensation for slave owners in all loyal states. Nothing startling about that.

Then came the final sentence, concluding with "shall then, thenceforward, and forever, be free."

Weed read the last line again. "This means you promise to free the slaves where you have no power to free them, and not to free them where you can."

Lincoln acknowledged there would be charges of hypocrisy. "But I act out of military necessity, and there is no military necessity to free the slaves in loyal states."

Weed raised a large eyebrow. Military necessity seemed to him more of an excuse than a reason.

Lincoln read his mind: "If I take this step without the argument of military necessity, I do so without any argument at all. Should I say the measure is politically expedient, or morally right? If I did that, I would give up all footing on Constitution or law."

That explained why the proclamation was dry and legalistic, with no soaring prose. Weed said: "It will infuriate the South, and discredit any Unionists still there."

"What would you do in my position? Would you drop the war where it is?" The President became sarcastic: "Or would you prosecute it in future with elder-stalk squirts charged with rose water?"

Weed put the paper on the low table between them. "Do you act out of military necessity? Or political necessity?" When Lincoln did not immediately answer, Weed answered for him. "I think you're acting out of what you think is political necessity—that if you can't keep the radical Republicans behind you, you won't be able to keep your troops at the front. I think that's a mistake."

"Man came in here this morning, friend of Stanton's, Democrat from New York. Cutting—you know him? Says sentiment is changing, that the War Democrats will go for abolition now."

"Frank Cutting couldn't get elected dogcatcher in Brooklyn," said Weed, glad to get in a poke at a Greeley supporter. He wondered why Stanton, up to now a moderate on abolition, was taking the lead, even ahead of Chase, to push Lincoln to this extreme. But Weed put first things first: to undermine Cutting's obvious credibility in Lincoln's judgment. "Frank's a pretty good lawyer, I suppose, but you remember that duel business with Breckinridge— he tends to change his mind a lot. He served one term in Congress and couldn't get renominated." Weed suddenly remembered that some said that was true of Lincoln, too, and added, "because he is out of touch with the common people. Abolition is fashionable among the well-to-do, but to the man in the trolley cars, the negro represents a threat to his job."

"You disagree with Greeley on that."

"Uncle Horace," sighed Weed, on familiar ground with Lincoln, "reports as fact what he wishes were true. What does his man Dana say?" Seward had told Weed that Charles Dana, who deserted Greeley to go to work for Stanton in the War Department, was advising against this proclamation because it would go so strongly against popular opinion in New York City.

"Dana agrees with you," said Lincoln.

Weed nodded. "This is not a political necessity. Strange, I thought Stanton had a good political mind—"

Lincoln smiled. "He thinks it is a *military* necessity."

Weed could understand why Stanton, never a firebrand on abolition, had become a radical, out-Chasing Chase. The Secretary of War wanted a slave uprising to undermine rebel troop morale. And he wanted black soldiers in the Union Army, because enlistments were falling off amid the general decline in Northern spirit. Weed wondered, too, if Stanton had a personal political motive. Why should the Democratic nomination in 1864 automatically go to a conservative; why not to the Democrat who was the organizer of victory in the war? "You believe this is a political necessity," he summed up, "which you can cloak as a military necessity. Stanton sees this as a military necessity, and is selling it to you as a political necessity. And you, in this document here, are putting it to the people as a military necessity."

Lincoln smiled in a mysterious way, probably pleased that somebody else understood it so well. "It's the only way I can do this. I have no power to take property away from people for all time. It is justifiable only as a war power, to confiscate rebel property. And as Judge Blair says, to keep the Europeans out."

Weed marveled at the President's willingness to rise to the heights of deception in what he considered a just cause. He had to admire the man for that; Seward might have balked, in such a spot. The problem was that Lincoln's political assessment was unsound; he underestimated the voters' resentment.

"You have asked me my political judgment," Weed said, limiting his role and avoiding the sort of presumption that always had a bad effect on Lincoln. "I'm not equipped to argue the law—I assume you can justify this legally, or maybe, when old Taney dies—" He groped for the proper legal phrase.

Lincoln helped him: "When measures, otherwise unconstitutional, might become lawful."

"However you work it out. Or Congress can pass a law later legalizing what you've done, the way they did last summer. On the military side, I defer to Stanton, although McClellan, I know, believes that a proclamation like this would goad the Southern troops to new levels of fierceness."

He steepled his fingers and pronounced political judgment. "First, I think the effect would be to dismay most of the Republicans and almost all the War Democrats, who fight for the Union and not for the slaves. It would bring on a terrible defeat in the fall elections, and enormous pressure to settle the war short of victory.

"Second, any uprising on the plantations, and slaughter of innocents, would give Lord Palmerston an excuse to bring England into the war to save the South, soon followed by the Emperor of France.

"Third, the passions this would arouse would defeat your ultimate purpose —a reconciliation of North and South after the war."

Lincoln said nothing.

"I know how you feel about slavery," Weed added softly.

"It is a monstrous injustice," said Lincoln. "If slavery is not wrong, then nothing is wrong."

"You have to judge whether this proclamation emancipates the slaves eventually, or dooms them to slavery if the North will not follow you."

Lincoln nodded. "I hate it, too, because it deprives our republican example of its just influence in the world."

Weed nodded pious agreement. "If we win this war, slavery is surely dead. If we do not—" He left his thought unfinished. "I don't envy you the responsibility to history of a rash decision." After a moment, he added, "What's the hurry? Why do you have to lead public sentiment on this? Why not simply encourage it along?"

"I confess that I have not shaped events," said the President, "but events have shaped my policy."

"Let them push you into this," suggested Weed, who thought Lincoln was being less than candid. "Be reluctant to do what you ultimately want to do. Let a majority develop, if it is to develop."

"Seward suggested I await a victory."

"And if we win a great victory, if this fellow Pope turns out to be our savior, you may not need the proclamation at all. It will cease to be either a political or military necessity. Or you may want to let the commanders in the field arm fugitive slaves, like Ben Butler in New Orleans, as Chase suggests—"

"No," Lincoln said abruptly. "If it is done, it will be on my authority."

"You're right, absolutely." With Lincoln coming over, it was wise to keep agreeing with him. Weed picked up the document again and read it over. He saw an opportunity to press his advantage. "You know, this first paragraph could stand by itself," he said. "It promulgates the Confiscation Act and warns the rebels that they stand a chance of losing their all. You could hold the second paragraph until the time is ripe, and go ahead with this."

Lincoln picked up the paper, considered the first paragraph alone, and nodded. He seemed to feel better, since he would proclaim something right away, and not leave the last word on slavery with the Congress.

Weed took his leave, certain that the issuance of the first, harmless half of the proclamation would satisfy Lincoln's hunger for personal action this week. He wished he could tell Lincoln Seward's liberty pole story: What's a war without proclamations?

Having saved Lincoln from the folly of abolition, the bulky New Yorker walked down the hallway with the tall, lanky President, debating with himself whether to broach the subject of patronage. He knew he should not, but it was impossible for him to resist.

"John Dix," he said. "Loyal War Democrat. You like him?"

Lincoln nodded. "He has taken on some difficult chores."

That was putting it mildly. "I want him to be our candidate for New York governor. Greeley wants an abolitionist. If Uncle Horace gets his way, the Republican ticket will lose to Horatio Seymour, who's a copperhead for certain. A word from you—"

The President shook his head. "That's for you two to fight out. Justice to all."

Weed sighed; it had been worth a try. But it had not been a wasted evening. At least he had saved the party and the Union from the folly of sudden, uncompensated abolition.

CHAPTER 2

PHOTOGRAPH BY BRADY

Mathew Brady left his Whatizzit Wagon outside his studio on Pennsylvania Avenue between Sixth and Seventh streets. The ground floor was occupied by Gilman's drugstore and the banking house of Sweeney, Rittenhouse, and Fant, but the top four floors—as the huge sign hanging from the balcony proclaimed—made up "Brady's National Photographic Art Gallery." The sign had cost enough, but he had to dominate a street already too crowded with photographers, especially John Plumb's establishment a few steps from his own. The competition to sell *cartes de visite* was keen, but Brady was preeminent in the field coverage of the war; unfortunately, the money was to be made in the little pictures of celebrated people.

He parked the wagon out front for a purpose. The mud-spattered conveyance from the field of battle served as an eye-catcher to passersby. Although few people bought prints of war pictures, most would find it creditable that at least one photographer—the intrepid Brady, not the commercial Plumb—was doing his bit for the Union at war.

Business was terrible. The boom in *cartes de visite* had not ended, but thousands of photographers around the country were turning them out more cheaply than Brady. Alexander Gardner made it possible for Brady to compete by ordering four-lens cameras that made four exposures on a single plate of glass, quadrupling efficiency, but even so, the proliferation of photographers was killing his trade.

Brady arched his back to regard the giant Imperiales high on the walls of his reception room on the second floor. Webster, Clay, and Calhoun, blurred in his vision, looked back at him, their oil portraits made from glass-negative copies of daguerreotypes taken by Brady in the days when he could see clearly. The negatives had been projected on sheets of canvas, with the images then colored in oil paint, resulting in startlingly lifelike portraits.

The Imperiales were Gardner's idea, Brady admitted to himself—his intense little employee was a wizard at chemicals—and were still a Brady Studio exclusive, but the cost was too high for all but the wealthiest. Then there was the root reason for the falloff in trade: Brady was rarely on hand at his studio. As at a restaurant, the customers wanted the man whose name was on the door to serve them, or at least to greet them. Brady had chosen to go into the war fronts for weeks at a time, spending much of his remaining time badgering the War Department, to fulfill what he considered his destiny. Brady was determined to make photography a respected profession, an adjunct to the written record of history; this noble determination was bankrupting him.

Time was short for that destiny. McClellan, he was sure, would not be reinforced for another assault on Richmond, and the new commander from the West, John Pope, so beloved of Secretary Chase, struck Brady as a blowhard. Two days before, Lincoln had issued a proclamation putting the Confiscation Act into effect, threatening to seize property of rebels, which seemed to betray a certain desperation; there had even been rumors the President had considered outright abolition, the telltale sign of a war being lost, until Seward and Weed and Blair talked him out of it. So many images of war to be recorded, Brady thought, so little war left.

"O'Sullivan, are these quills sharp?" He tested one on his fingertip. It was ready for service.

Tim O'Sullivan was the best camera operator working for him. Gardner was irreplaceable in the darkroom, and had organized an operation on the roof to print pictures by means of bright sunlight, but it was O'Sullivan who managed to bring in the best war pictures, the ones that the engravers sought for the illustrated magazines. O'Sullivan looked to the freedman, Foons, and asked if he had sharpened them. The black nodded. "Go ahead and use them, Mr. Brady," O'Sullivan said. "I hope you're doing the books, so we can get paid."

Brady sighed, not only for the days of his Broadway studio when a hired bookkeeper did the nasty work, but for the time long ago when he could see the point of a pen. Now everything more than two feet away was a blur. With his thick glasses on, he put his face down toward a piece of stationery, taken from a local hotel, and proceeded to write a promotional letter.

"I'm doing this to get in Judas goats," he informed his staff, who, he was sure, would never get the hang of the sales end of the business. The Brady studio, to remain celebrated, needed celebrated subjects—generals, senators, entertainment personages, the President. Lincoln was scheduled to come in this afternoon for the first time in six months, but not even the occasional presence of the President was enough. People of power and influence should be coming every day, even when he was in the field and a man of lesser personality, like Gardner, was in charge.

Brady's invitations usually drew a favorable response. When he had written to Harriet Beecher Stowe, the novelist had come into the studio and her visit generated considerable business afterward. Same with Anna Elizabeth Dickinson, the youthful lecturer. Women were an untapped source of revenue for most studios; individuals and newspapers would buy pictures of famous or notorious women. He was glad Gardner had caught Rose Greenhow before she was sent South, which was to be any day now, though Brady wished he could have supervised that one himself, using one of his minor assistants to focus and uncap the lens. No matter; it was still a "Photograph by Brady." Only Brady's name would appear on any picture taken in his studio or by his men in the field. Though he relied on their eyesight to operate the cameras, the new vista of war coverage was Brady's vision.

He wrote "Brady's Gallery" across the top of the hotel stationery, and then "Miss Anna E. Carroll. Dear Madam, A friend of yours has been kind enough to tell me of your interest in photography"—he always used that opening; everyone had some friend curious about photography—"and I suggest that your portrait would be an interesting addition to my Gallery." He picked up a book, not Miss Carroll's latest work but the only one he had been able to find in the library, and personalized his letter further: "As I have read with exceeding pleasure your work *A Warning to America and Americans,* I beg leave to tender you the courtesy which it has been my custom for many years to extend to the talented and distinguished." That meant the sitting would be free, unless the talented wanted extra prints, which they always did. "Yours respectfully, M. B. Brady." He checked Miss Carroll off his list and was proceeding to Kate Chase, next in alphabetical order, when Gardner asked to see him for a moment.

"You can see I'm busy," Brady told him. Brady's burly, bright-eyed Scottish import was an annoyance, when he wasn't making amazing positives from seemingly lost negatives. Gardner was a Mason, and Brady distrusted the Masonic order: do-gooders in secret. Moreover, he suspected Gardner was a socialist; the man had brought his entire family from Scotland to Iowa, and now the uncles and aunts and cousins were engaged in a strange communal organization seeking to prove the universal goodness of mankind, even while the immigrants were falling like flies from some unknown disease. Gardner, Brady freely admitted, was an honest manager of the studio, and Brady was glad to have paid the man's passage from Scotland, but Gardner was too liberal with promises of wage increases and too inclined to spend money for experimental devices.

"All of us would like to talk to you now, Mr. Brady," Gardner said ominously. Brady squinted at the group. Behind the manager, in a semicircle, were Gardner's younger brother, Jim, and Tim O'Sullivan, along with three other photographers: Guy Foux, David Woodbury, and George Barnard. Only the black freedman was not with them; apparently he had slipped out, frightened of a confrontation.

"You'll get paid when we get some money in here," Brady said testily. "The War Department is a notoriously slow payer. I'm planning to see Stanton about it tomorrow." He went to the cash box and spilled the greenbacks on the desk. "There's thirty dollars here, or so. Share it among you."

"It isn't only the money," said Gardner, obviously the ringleader. "It's the credit—the photographic credit. It isn't right for you to put your name on our work."

"You're using Brady cameras," said Brady slowly. "Brady chemicals, Brady plates. You're using the world-renowned Brady studio, the famous Brady Whatizzit Wagon. That means the pictures are Brady pictures. I own them, I sell them, I put my name on them."

"Photography is not just a mechanical, chemical process," Gardner came back stubbornly. "It is an art, like painting or sculpture. Someday people will understand that. And nobody has the right to put his name on another man's art."

Brady drew his white smock around him and glowered in Gardner's direction. "The fact that it is a Brady photograph enhances its value. Why do you suppose we can charge so much for an Imperiale?"

"I invented the Imperiale, Mr. Brady. I do all the retouching and the painting. My name should be on my work."

"That idea was mine!" Brady exploded. He vividly remembered telling Gardner what he wanted, and the Scotsman had merely accommodated him on the technical details. "Same with the *cartes de visite*, and the stereotypes—not the technical part, but the idea."

"The technical part *is* the idea," replied Gardner. "Why do you deny me—all of us—our due? What does it cost you?"

In Brady's view, these ungrateful hired hands were attacking his dream of making photography a respected profession. They could never understand how necessary it was to act as merchants, to sell under one respected name, to use the fame of an individual to spread the word of the entire new field.

"I can understand your impatience in not being paid," Brady said, controlling his temper, "but I cannot understand your objecting to 'Photograph by Brady.' It does not mean by me as an individual, it means by my organization."

"There is no such thing as a photograph by Brady," O'Sullivan put in.

"Never mind that, Tim, " said Gardner.

"What does he mean?" Brady wanted to know.

"I mean," said O'Sullivan, despite what Brady took to be Gardner's reluctance, "that you have not taken a photograph in years. There hasn't been a true 'photograph by Brady' since the war began."

Brady threw down his quill pen. "That's a damn lie and you know it. Get out of my sight!"

"You have no sight to get out of," O'Sullivan shot back. "You can't look through a lens and focus. Face it, Mathew Brady, you're damn near blind.

Alexander Gardner

You're not a photographer at all, anymore. You're the employer of photographers, the exploiter—"

"Shut up, Tim," said Gardner.

"I took you out of the gutter," Brady seethed, "I taught you everything you know about this business. You call yourself a great war photographer now, don't you? That's because you're too stupid to get out of the way when the guns are firing. Too blind to take a picture, am I—you scum! Out! You're fired!"

The massive O'Sullivan stepped toward Brady to throttle him when Gardner interceded. "Look, you two, this is not what I meant to do. I mean to work out a compromise."

"Never," said Brady. "You all think that a photographer is somebody who merely sticks his head behind the camera and uncovers the lens." He waited for the pounding of his heart to slow before continuing. "I'll tell you what a photographer is. He understands the subject. He composes the picture the way a musician composes music. He pours the light the way a painter strokes on the paint. He waits for the moment, no matter how long it takes, and then freezes his subject and makes the moment immortal. That's what I do, poor eyes and all. If I want, I can hire six teamsters off the street to do my focusing. And a couple more blacks to make the prints. I don't need any of you. You can all march to hell out of here right now."

"Mr. Lincoln will be here in a little while," Gardner reminded him. The manager did not have to add that Lincoln preferred Gardner to take the picture.

"I will take the President's picture myself," Brady told them. "I was taking pictures of great men before any of you ever saw a daguerreotype, when you, Gardner, were a miserable jeweler. Now get to work or get out."

"I'll get out when I get the two thousand, three hundred dollars you owe me," said Gardner. "You owe the others another fifteen hundred."

"I'll pay you one day. I don't want you hanging around the studio with your hands out, scaring off the customers. You're a bunch of deserters, no better than any who run away from the enemy. You're deserting your duty to history by running away from the photography of this war." Brady liked that point; he believed it, and it stung them.

"We'll have our own wagon in the field," said Gardner, "but we want our money, or something equally as valuable, right now."

Brady instantly knew what he was getting at. "You cannot have the negatives," he said, really worried for the first time. "Those are mine. I intend to present them to the government after the war."

"I am taking every single plate with me that belongs to me," said Gardner. "That means every photograph that I have taken."

"And I, mine," said O'Sullivan. "And if you want to call the police, I'll haul you into court and blacken your damn name as a cheat and a bankrupt forever."

Brady knew he had no real defense; they could even take his wagon for back wages if they wanted. He sagged in his chair and took off his glasses.

"You do not know what you are doing, breaking up the collection," he pleaded. "Gardner, think of the profession. You think you're an artist, think of the collection—"

"There does not have to be only one collection," Gardner said. "I will protect my plates just as fiercely as you protect yours." He offered a concession. "We'll leave behind with you the plates that were taken by operators who just passed through the studio."

Brady thanked God for the rapid turnover of personnel in the past that would leave him with the bulk of the collection. After a long silence, he agreed to negotiate, plate by plate, through his entire collection, with the right to keep one positive print of the plates the others took with them.

Gardner and his crew did not immediately quit; they walked out together to think over the crisis. Brady, still seated, trembling with rage, hand on his chest, felt a new fear. What would happen when the President arrived? O'Sullivan, damn his soul, was right: Brady could not take a photograph. After a few moments, Brady walked upstairs to the third floor, the finishing and mounting rooms, where the women touched up the photographs and operated the presses that sealed the bond between images and backings of *cartes de visite*. He found A. B. Foons, the negro who drove the wagon, cleaned the studio, and occasionally operated a camera when everyone else was out, and told the free black to follow him upstairs to the fourth-floor studio.

An hour later, when President Lincoln arrived, Brady was ready. Hill Lamon, who accompanied the President, inquired about Gardner's whereabouts and Brady shrugged off the question.

"I want to pose Mr. Lincoln myself today," said Brady, as the President took his accustomed seat in Brady's famous chair with the wooden arms. Brady had borrowed that chair from the House of Representatives in 1859 and never got around to returning it. The photographer arranged his favorite props on the table: the leather-bound copy of the annals of Congress, the inkwell. He decided against the clock with his name on the face, stopped as always at eleven fifty-two, because a clock would make the picture too busy.

Brady went behind the camera, threw the cloth over his head, pretended to focus, and then stepped to the side of the camera. "Foons, uncap the lens when I say," he said to the black, as planned. Foons went under and focused the lens on the President's face.

Brady looked at Lincoln, who was sitting stiffly in the chair as usual, neck pressed against the brace hidden from camera view, never smiling, expression frozen, presenting to the lens only what he thought should be a portrait of a President. "Put your right hand on the arm of the chair," he told the subject. Lincoln complied. "The left hand, put it to your chin. As if in thought."

The President shook his head no; that was not a gesture natural to him, or it was not the photo he had in mind. Brady found it regrettable that Lincoln was so stubborn, because in his desire to maintain his dignity, the President appeared stiff.

"Then lean forward a little, and just leave your left hand up there," Brady urged, adding, "where it's natural, the way you often do."

Lincoln, frowning a little at Brady's instructions—evidently Gardner and the others did not direct him how to pose so specifically—kept his hand near his chin, thumb to forefinger, which made him appear to be feeling his way. Brady liked the expression and the pose, as well as he could tell through his thick spectacles, but he knew the picture's composition was not in balance.

President Abraham Lincoln

On an inspiration, he went to Lamon, who was holding the President's silk hat, took the hat, and put it on the end of the table.

Foons moved the camera back a few inches to get in the hat, refocused while Lincoln remained still, and when Brady said "now," uncapped the lens, and when Brady said "cover," capped it again.

During the wait to make another for safety's sake, the President's bodyguard made conversation about the Southern resentment of the employment of freed slaves by the Union Army, especially by the hated General Ben Butler in New Orleans. Lincoln replied, "I am a patient man, Hill, but it may as well be understood, once for all, I shall not surrender this game leaving any available card unplayed." Brady, glad that his little deception about the focusing had not been noticed, did not intrude on their conversation; he hoped, however, that all this talk about using blacks against the South did not give Foons ideas.

When the President and his bodyguard left, he said to the black man who took the pictures, "Remember, Foons, anybody can aim a camera, and any careful hand can develop and print. The single most important element in making a picture is composition. That's what makes a 'Photograph by Brady.'"

CHAPTER 3

MAN OF AUDACITY

John Adams Dix, summoned from his headquarters at Fort Monroe, sleeked back his silver hair, squared his shoulders as befitted a political figure acting as a general, and marched into the President's office. The late July night was stifling; Lincoln was in his shirt sleeves behind his desk, his son Tad sleeping on the couch.

The President rose and pumped his hand cordially. Ever since the episode a year ago, when Dix and Nat Lyon stretched the law to prevent the meeting of the seceding Maryland legislators, the New York Democrat felt that he was among Lincoln's most trusted political generals. Dix's service in the Buchanan Cabinet and as Postmaster of New York City had not been held against him. He knew how valuable a good War Democrat was to the Republican administration, especially one with political roots in New York, where Democrats had come under the domination of Mayor Fernando Wood and Horatio Seymour of the peace wing.

"How go the negotiations?" the President asked directly. A year ago, Lincoln might have bandied about a bit at first. Dix wondered at the reason for the new crispness; it could not be the progress of the war.

"I met my counterpart at Aiken's Landing, up the James River," Dix reported, laying a paper on the President's desk. "Here is the tentative cartel we drew up."

Lincoln put on his spectacles and began to read the exchange document. Almost at once, after the first few lines, he said, "Good. I was worried, as you know, about anything that might imply recognition of the Confederacy. This is fine, calling yourselves 'the authorities they respectively represent.' Never call them the Confederacy," he said sternly, adding, "as I just did. We're having enough trouble delaying the prize cases from coming before Taney's court."

Dix understood. Last year, by declaring a blockade of Southern ports, Lincoln had treated the South as an independent power. In cases involving blockade runners that had been seized, the rebel owners argued that if the North was not acting against a belligerent nation, the laws of prize capture did not apply. The rebels' trick was to force the federal government either to release the ships or to treat the South as a separate nation at war, which would help the Confederacy gain the recognition of foreign powers. Taney's Supreme Court would probably stick to the law and recognize the South. Dix muttered: "That old man just won't die, will he?"

Lincoln shook his head in frustration as he continued to read Dix's draft of a cartel document. Dix knew that the Supreme Court, as presently sitting, had only one Lincoln appointee, with two vacancies. The fight for the two jobs was fierce—David Davis, Lincoln's campaign manager in 1860 and best friend (but for Herndon) in Illinois, was pitted against Orville Browning, the President's best friend in Washington, for one of them. With both empty seats filled, Lincoln might have a majority, if a couple of the earlier appointees came over to Lincoln's side.

Dix also knew Lincoln had an ace up his sleeve. If old Chief Justice Taney did not behave, the President would press for a tenth judicial circuit, and a tenth judge on the Supreme Court. If it followed that an even number resulted in split decisions and judicial paralysis, he could logically ask Congress for an eleventh judge, and appoint him too. Lincoln's threat to the court was unmistakable, but evidently he did not want to tangle with Taney, preferring a strategy of delay, ignoring the court as he did after Taney's habeas corpus challenge.

"Sign it," said Lincoln, nodding approval as he finished. "At the moment, we need the cartel more than they do."

"There's a hitch," Dix reported. "General Pope's orders. They're infuriating the leadership in Richmond."

"Harsh," Lincoln acknowledged, "but Stanton says they're needed. He wants the rebels to know they're not just fighting McClellan anymore. Wouldn't be surprised if Mars had a hand in Pope's orders himself."

"It's not only the Pope order telling our Army of the Potomac to subsist on the Virginia countryside," Dix argued, "which is a license for looting. It's his order that holds the local civilians responsible for damage by guerrillas, forcing them to repair any disruption of roads or telegraphs"—Dix now came to a delicate point—"and any man captured who was firing on Union soldiers to be shot without civil process. That's some order, Mr. President. Does it have your approval?"

Lincoln turned and fished a paper out of one of the cubbyholes behind his table. "Pope says: 'I find it impossible to make any movement without having it immediately communicated to the enemy. Constant correspondence between the enemy's forces and the so-called peaceful citizens in the rear of this army is carried on which can in no other way be interrupted.' That's what he says, and he's the general on the scene."

Dix was surprised and disturbed at the President's willingness to go along with such a barbarous policy of executing civilians, especially in light of the state of negotiations about prisoners of war. Dix granted that Pope was angry at the way some civilians behind his lines shot at Union stragglers; he granted that Stanton and Pope wanted to show the rebels a new, get-tough attitude after the too-gentlemanly war between Lee and McClellan—still, was that cause to go to the outer limits of the rules of civilized warfare?

"Mr. President, surely you cannot be aware of Pope's Order No. 11 issued day before yesterday." The rebel general who was Dix's counterpart on prisoner exchanges, already complaining about reaction to the earlier orders of Pope, might break off negotiations entirely when word reached him of No. 11. "Pope requires officers to arrest all disloyal citizens of Virginia, give them a choice of a loyalty oath or deportation South. And then Pope's order declares that any who return to their homes and violate the loyalty oath can be shot without a trial."

"I'm aware of it," said Lincoln, leaving it at that.

"Sir, that—" Dix was about to say that such an order was barbaric, but thought better of such insubordination. "That invites retaliation by the rebels. They can hang our men, too."

"Proceed with your negotiations, General. Perhaps there won't be cause for retaliation."

Dix took that to mean that Lincoln went along with the fire-eating oratory in the orders but had some quiet understanding with Pope or Stanton that the threats would not be carried out.

As if to ameliorate Dix's concern about presidential willingness to tolerate Pope's blustering barbarity, Lincoln added, "Henry Halleck has arrived from the West to take over as General-in-Chief. 'Old Brains' agrees with you about Pope's orders—and, of course, McClellan is hopping mad about them. But there is something to be said for a man of audacity."

Dix half-rose to leave, but Lincoln motioned for him to sit down—he had a story he used to tell an old law partner about an audacious man. Dix crossed his legs and relaxed, pleased to be passing the time of night with the President and his sleeping child. It was a far cry from working for the stiff old bachelor Buchanan.

"There was a party once, not far from Springfield," Lincoln began, enjoying the tale, "and among the crowd was one of those men who had audacity. Cheeky, quick-witted, never off guard on any occasion. The audacious man, chosen to be the carver of the turkey at the dinner table, whetted his great carving knife and got down to business carving the bird." The President made carving motions.

"The man of audacity expended too much force," continued the President, "and let a fart, a loud fart, so that all the people heard it distinctly. It shocked all. A deep silence reigned.

"However, the audacious man was entirely self-possessed. He pulled off his coat, rolled up his sleeves, spat on his hands, whetted the carving knife again, never cracking a smile or moving a muscle on his face. It became a wonder in the minds of all the men and women how the fellow was to get out of his dilemma."

Lincoln leaned forward, and so did Dix. "He squared himself and said loudly and distinctly, 'Now, by God, I'll see if I can't cut up this turkey without farting!' "

Dix threw his head back and roared with laughter, joined by Lincoln, who liked his own story. The New Yorker knew it was a gem he could use at military and political gatherings, evidence of his closeness to the President. He would not tell it to McClellan or his staff, however; it was too well known that Lincoln thought his general in front of Richmond lacked the audacity of the man carving the turkey. Dix had the clear impression that McClellan's star was setting, Pope's was rising; that meant the Union Army would soon be pulled out of the Peninsula. He guessed that something fundamental had gone wrong between the President and his commander during their meeting at Harrison's Landing.

As Dix was leaving, he was surprised to see about twenty men standing in the hallway, awaiting admittance to the President's office. It was past 10 P.M. Lincoln came out behind Dix, drawing on his jacket, his good mood changing; the President said somewhat testily to the men who wanted to see him: "It is a matter of no importance to me whether I spend my time with half a dozen of you, or with the whole of you, but it is of importance to you. Therefore, when each of you comes in, don't stay long."

Before Dix could make his way through the crowd, Lincoln put a hand on his shoulder. Not caring if he was overheard, the President asked what Dix thought of Horatio Seymour, who Weed said might be hard to beat for Governor of New York. Dix, who hoped to get the Republican nomination to oppose Seymour, put the Peace candidate's position in a nutshell: "Union as it was, Constitution as it is." Seymour—and a large body of opinion in the North—wanted the war ended and the Union preserved even if it meant the continuance of slavery in the South.

"People in rebellion states must understand," said Lincoln, "that they cannot experiment for ten years trying to destroy the government and, if they fail, still come back into the Union unhurt. If they expect to ever have 'the Union as it was,' I say, 'Now is the time.' " Unspoken was the alternative. If the Southerners failed to return soon, the Constitution would be altered to abolish slavery.

Dix headed toward Seward's house across the square, to find out more about Weed's visit. Next morning, he would stop at Old Capitol Prison to pick up Rose Greenhow and her daughter, to sweeten the atmosphere with the Confederate exchange negotiator. After the predations of Pope in Virginia and the treatment being shown the women of New Orleans, rebel tempers would be high.

CHAPTER 4

FAIR EXCHANGE

Rose O'Neal Greenhow leaned on the rail of the Union gunboat taking John Dix and his two female prisoners, herself and her daughter, up the James River, past the site of what she knew to be the glorious defense of Richmond during the Seven Days battles on the Peninsula. She strained to see if she could spot Aiken's Landing, the official point of contact between the two nations.

Her daughter was in a sulk since General Dix and his party awakened them the night before. Young Rose flatly refused to believe she would soon be free, after all those false starts throughout the spring, the assurances by Stanton, the threats from Pinkerton, the handwringing visits from Senator Wilson. The girl, just turned nine, sat in the back of the boat, looking at the water churned by the engines, frowning her fear of more disappointment. Rose was thankful the girl's dark hair and pouting mouth showed signs of her own good looks; in a vindictive world, her daughter would need them.

"It's not far now, is it, John?"

"Ten minutes or so, Rose. Don't lean so far out, you'll fall overboard and I'll be blamed for pushing you."

"That would make you a hero in some quarters." She smiled at him. "Most of your friends would love to see me dead."

"Not most," said Dix. "A few. Pinkerton wanted to see you hanged, but that was because the kind souls in Richmond strung up his man, Timothy Webster."

"In retaliation for the valiant ship's captain, Nathaniel Gordon, you hanged as a slave trader," Rose reminded him. The thought of the detective Pinkerton, cause of so much of the misery inflicted in the past year, oppressed her. "That miserable little German Jew," she muttered.

"Pinkerton? He's a Scot from Glasgow. Protestant, I think." The handsome general—he was aging gracefully, she thought, and looked fine in his uniform—had a hearty laugh at the thought. "You ought to hear him and the other Scot, Brady's man Gardner, hoot-monning each other."

"He only puts that on as a disguise, John. He's a German Jew named Pincus." Rose had nothing whatever to base that on, but it pleased her to plant a seed of suspicion; she would spread that rumor in the book she would write to raise her suffering to patriotic martyrdom. "He may enjoy his work as a Peeping Tom, but your man Pinkerton is not much of a spy."

"McClellan thinks highly of him."

She smiled with satisfaction. "The little sneak came to my cell back in March, trying to find out, in his heavy-handed way, what I knew of our troop strength around Richmond." She smiled at the thought; it was good to smile again. "At the time, all that stood between McClellan's hundred and fifty thousand troops and the gates of Richmond was Magruder's force—eight or ten thousand Confederates who were marching and countermarching to give the impression of being ten times as many. With that tiny force, General Magruder kept your 'Young Napoleon' and the whole Yankee army in check for nearly two months."

A pained look crossed Dix's face, which pleased her. "I aided in the mystification," she added, "by 'inadvertently' supposing our force on the Peninsula to be not less than two hundred thousand strong. Pinkerton swallowed it all."

"You not only stole information," Dix said sadly, "you fed back wrong information."

"Part of the job, overlooked by most who presume to call themselves spies." A surge of anger mixed with her pride. "That German Jew is not the only one who wanted me dead. There's also the Honorable Henry Wilson—he's terrified that I'll talk."

"You could hurt a lot of people, Rose," the general sighed. "But you couldn't limit the damage to Yankees, could you? Once that story began unraveling, it would touch your family, the Breckinridge family, a few men in Jefferson Davis's Cabinet—it's not the sort of thing you would want to be remembered for." He looked aft. "Nor to have little Rose know about."

He was making a case she knew far better than he; in newspaper interviews and in her memoirs, she planned to hint at the liaison with Wilson, but no more, because such tidbits of truth invited trouble and would make legitimate the calumny heaped upon her by the savage Northern press. She was determined to be remembered as a patriot, not as a whore.

"Stanton, too, I suppose," he said, fishing. Not even John Dix, her old friend, was above interest in Rose's affairs.

"In the worst times," she replied slowly, "when the candle went out and I could not burn the vermin off the walls, when the paws of those men reaching out for my girl might have made me lose my mind, Edwin Stanton made it possible for certain people to have access to me." She owed Stanton her freedom, and would not betray him.

"Strange fellow," he mused.

"He has his demons," she agreed. "Soft and deferential in his manners, to the point of servility when it suits him—insolent and arrogant to those placed in his power, though that is tempered by a certain degree of prudence. Like Seward, he is physically a coward." That was all she would tell Dix, or anyone.

"See the work of your *Merrimack*," Dix said, pointing to the wreck of three ships near the shore.

"Hooray!" she shouted, drawing surly glances from the crew of the gunboat. "Cheers for the gallant *Virginia!*" She ran back to the stern, showing her daughter the damage inflicted on the wooden Federal ships by the Confederate ironclad. The queer-looking black *Monitor* lay low in the water nearby. Rose recounted the tale of the glorious series of victories, skipping the final standoff. The glum little girl did not react; she left to take another bath. It worried Rose that her daughter felt the urge to bathe every couple of hours.

Rose strolled down the deck and struck up a conversation with a seaman, hoping to find out if McClellan's troops were to stay down here on the Peninsula or withdraw northward toward Manassas, where Pope's army had been making threatening noises. Two other seamen came and led their comrade away.

Rose returned to Dix, evidently the only person on the boat authorized to have communication with her. He was cagey, but his kindly nature made him a potential source; she was soon to be in Richmond, and wanted some verification of her suspicion—and some intelligence—that Halleck had ordered McClellan to move his troops north, to reinforce Pope.

"John, you are the only gentleman in Abolitiondom," she observed. "I thank God Lincoln has no other agent like you."

"You know we're not fighting for abolition, Rose."

"No? Then what was that Confiscation Act all about? The newspapers say that Abraham the First issued a proclamation putting it into effect."

"Stop that 'Abraham the First' stuff. I don't want to hear it."

"You don't think he's a dictator? A man who can clap any person he dislikes into prison, without a trial, without so much as a charge?"

"The Constitution allows him to suspend habeas corpus in times of rebellion," Dix said grimly.

"There was a man who used to protect me in prison, John. He tried to bribe a guard to let him out in the yard—he just wanted to get some air, away from the stench of the effluvium that poisoned the atmosphere. The guard took the money, and when my friend went into the yard, the guard shot him dead, claimed he had been trying to escape. The guard who took the bribes was promoted to corporal. Do you know what my friend was in prison for? He was in jail for saying something favorable about secession."

Dix looked across the water and said nothing.

"Your Ben Butler," Rose continued. "The Beast of New Orleans." The thought that New Orleans had been given up without a fight infuriated her. "He issued an order, approved by Abraham the First, that any Southern ladies who refused to have any truck with Yankee soldiers were to be treated like common prostitutes."

"Some women were spitting at the troops," Dix said. "And then one of them emptied a slop jar out a window and it hit Admiral Farragut."

"Is that a reason to insult every lady in an occupied city? Come now, General Dix, doesn't that touch your conscience? General Butler's order fairly invited his men to have their way with any woman who offended them. And the execution of a citizen of New Orleans last month, for daring to haul down the Yankee flag from the mint—do you go along with that sort of justice?"

That spear went home, as she knew it would; Dix had become famous early in the war for his "shoot him on the spot" message, directed at anyone who hauled down the Union flag, but he had never actually ordered a human being to be put to death for such an act. That blustering order of Dix's was a threat to rally support, to cow resistance—but she doubted he ever intended it to be carried out.

"I have warned as much myself, Rose."

"But you never killed a civilian for an act of patriotism. And the man who was later shot made his glorious gesture *before* the city was occupied. Your Butler is nothing but a beast and a murderer, and Lincoln loves him for it."

"Butler may be worried about a counterattack at Baton Rouge by your friend Breckinridge," Dix said defensively. "Fear makes a general do terrible things. Killing civilians is not government policy."

John Breckinridge was considered a threat to Butler; she would remember that bit of news. "I can recall the day when Breck was a good friend of yours as well," she reminded him. Dix and Breck had been close in the Buchanan administration.

"I felt for Breck," he said, "torturing himself last year, trying to find a middle way. But in a war for the nationality of the country, there can be but two sides. The neutral clogs the movement of the government by his dead weight, as the *vis inertiae* of matter impedes its motion."

She interrupted before he slipped further into Latin; in his spare time, Dix translated Latin love poetry, and in the past she had tried to look interested when he started to declaim his dreary exercise. "And all the orders from John Pope to take hostages and shoot innocent men if Southern farmers threaten his soldiers? Are you trying to tell me that's not Lincoln's policy either?"

"That was a mistake by one of Pope's officers," Dix explained wearily. "Some rebels, not in uniform, were bushwhacking stragglers—that's a form of murder, and it sometimes calls for summary treatment."

"No trial? Just catch them and shoot them?"

"Damnit, Rose, stop trying to make Lincoln look like a monster. You're trying to make a pattern of dictatorship out of a few isolated instances."

"Like closing newspapers that dare to challenge the government position—"

"Consider what he has *not* done, in the midst of a rebellion. A dictator would suppress the legislature and rule without it—but the Congress sits and argues and investigates and—"

"Not the Maryland legislature, you took care of them."

He did not stop to wince. "A dictator would quell all political opposition, and Lincoln has not. He's the most publicly abused man in the North. There is no Lincoln party, no party emblem substituting for the flag, no secret criminal violence to intimidate people, no systematic crackdown on the press, no national policy to crush dissenters—"

"What?" She would not let him get away with a defense of the indefensible. "You saw what went on at Fort Lafayette—that's where they threw the people who dared to say out loud, or write in a newspaper, what they thought of the edicts of Abraham the First. I've spoken to former prisoners there—they told me they thought the Old Capitol, with all its stench and filth, was an improvement."

"There were a few mistakes until Stanton took over internal security from Seward," Dix argued, in his stubbornly reasonable way. "I went to Fort Lafayette this spring with Judge Pierrepont, and we held sessions with ten prisoners a day until most of the political prisoners were released." He raised his hand to stop her interruption. "They shouldn't have been there in the first place, I know, but there was panic when the war began, and Lincoln could not be expected to stand against the popular demand for suppression."

"It was Stanton's man, Watson," she recalled, "who said, 'Let them prove themselves innocent and they will be discharged.'"

"A mistake. We rectified it. Fort Lafayette is half empty now and you see how your own release has come through. There aren't many dissenters in jail at the moment."

His relentless defense of wrongdoing infuriated her. "Don't you see that you don't have to imprison everybody who disagrees—just enough of them to serve as an example to everybody else?"

"No, I wouldn't," he said, holding his ground. "There's no attempt to hinder the elections this fall. They'll be free elections, freer than anywhere, and smack in the middle of a civil war—that's unheard of. That's not the action of a dictator. It may be in the next month or so," he added, "the President will have to issue a couple of proclamations that may seem especially harsh to the fainthearted in the North, but we're at a difficult moment."

"How can you stand there, John Adams Dix, and defend what you know to be despotism?"

"The Constitution may be violated in some cases, and stretched in others, but there it stands. Besides, who are advocates of human slavery to talk about freedom?"

That was a low blow. She narrowed her eyes and hissed, "Go give your pretty speeches in a Union jail! Suffer the most obscene indignities because you dare to speak out for your country, and then talk to me about 'democracy' and 'Constitution'!"

They stared at each other, breathing hard, hopelessly split. She turned toward the water after a moment and thanked God, honestly this time, that Lincoln had so few men as Dix as agents to undermine the hatred that sustained her.

"When you negotiate your prisoner exchange cartel," she said when she was in control of herself again, "remember what horrible cages prisons can be. And when you hear talk of abolition, remember that no white men are left on the farms in the South, only the slaves, who need very little to go out and fulfill their dreams of raping every white woman they can lay their hands on."

"If emancipation comes, the South will have brought it on itself." He did not give an inch; if this good man would not see, who in the North would? "We're near the landing, Rose. Better get your child."

Heart pounding, but with her voice controlled, she said, "I want to repay your many kindnesses, John."

"I prefer to think it was I who repaid your past kindnesses."

"Don't be gallant, be serious. I know something that might help you. I know, from someone in Lincoln's highest councils, that you will *not* receive the nomination to oppose Seymour for governor of New York. If you are planning on it, forget it, your hopes will be dashed. Something—I don't know what—is in the works that will make the convention take the abolition candidate and not you."

Dix was paying close attention to what she said. "This is not the sort of trick you played on Pinkerton?"

She permitted herself a small smile. "I would not mislead you, John, on a personal matter." The boat's engine slowed perceptibly and the foghorn blew. "And I hope your command in Fort Monroe will not shrink to insignificance when our Peninsula loses its foreign residents."

"Don't worry about that, Rose. I'll have plenty to do in the next campaign." That was what she needed to know: the Peninsula campaign of Mc-

Clellan was over, and his troops would be moved back North away from Richmond for the next campaign. That meant that General Lee was free to move north and smash the barbarian Pope. Dix's unthinking verification would have to be conveyed to President Davis immediately.

"Now that we are here, and you cannot change your mind," she added soberly, "let me tell you what I hear about your mission this week. I have not been totally out of touch with President Davis. Unless Pope's uncivilized orders are changed, and until the Beast of New Orleans is brought to justice for his murder of that innocent patriot, your prisoner cartel is doomed. So long as you think you can kill our people you hold captive, your prisoners of war will rot in Southern camps. We won't kill them, but the smallpox will."

She fetched her daughter, but before debarking delivered a message to Little Rose in the hearing of some of the sailors and General Dix. "You have shared the hardship of my prison life, my darling, and suffered all the evils which a vulgar despotism could inflict."

Her daughter shook her head, resisting; the first words she spoke that day were, "I don't want to think about that." But Rose wanted to drive the lesson home to the listening sailors.

"Let the memory of that never pass from your mind," she said loudly, "else you may be inclined to forget how merciful Providence has been—in severing us from such a people."

An officer from the *Monitor* came on board and transferred the former spy and her daughter to another, smaller boat, which took them toward City Point. As she approached the soil of her country, Rose turned to the ship that took her out of captivity, determined to make a last gesture of defiance that would surely be reported back to the tyrant and his minions who had made her life miserable the past year.

While in the hellhole of Old Capitol Prison, she had laboriously and secretly stitched together a Confederate battle flag for presentation to General Beauregard, and concealed it as the lining of her shawl. She gave one end of the shawl to her daughter and told her to hold it high. The girl obeyed. Rose faced the Union vessel, saw that General Dix and the Federal sailors were lined up at the railing watching them, and unfurled her glorious Stars and Bars.

Mother and daughter waved and jeered, little Rose releasing her emotion in delighted shrieks. In the distance, she could see her friend and enemy, John Dix, shaking his head. Let him tell Abraham the First and all his sycophants that the spirit of the South was unconquerable.

CHAPTER 5

JOHN HAY'S DIARY
AUGUST 1, 1862

I suppose I'm fairly spoony about her. Up to now I have been languidly appreciative, but a diary is a place to be honest: Kate Chase and I have reached the point of outright spooniness.

Six hours on the train to New York City. Inhale fumes for an hour, changing trains, then on to Albany. In the station, peruse Thurlow Weed's *Albany Evening Journal*, with its gobs of loyal worrying about General Pope's army —could it be that Weed harbors distrust of the audacious Pope and affection for the craven McClellan? Story in the paper about Secretary Chase plumping for enlisting negroes in the army; how little the correspondents know about what really is going on. The other day, the Tycoon had me bring in a detailed map of the Mississippi, and showed Browning how the counties on each side of the river from Memphis down averaged four to one blacks to whites. "I am determined to open the Mississippi," said the Prsdt, "and if necessary will take all these negroes to open it and keep it open." When the time comes to use blacks, he won't need urging from the likes of Chase.

Hired a horse in Albany, no easy matter, and then over the hills and down the dales to Buttermilk Falls. What won't a poet do to fasten his eyes on the object of his delight?

There is an actual falls in Buttermilk Falls. Kate and I strolled out after dinner to a small glen where the creek pitched its water about four feet down, making a nice small roar, and causing much evanescence from the turbulent waters. Late dusk, rising moon, balmy air, no bugs. I wished I had time to take a bath after the trip, but no matter. We took off our shoes, kissed long and sweetly, and splashed our toes in the brook. The war was on another planet.

Kate is a first-class woman in every way but she cannot detach herself, as I can, from the world's hurly-burly.

"Nothing is happening in Washington," I assured her. It is true that the Tycoon was tense and secretive last week, but nothing of import is likely to happen until Pope takes the offensive. His firm treatment of rebel bushwhackers has upset the prisoner cartel that John Dix had worked out last week; Jeff Davis lost his head about Pope's taking of hostages and the threat to shoot them, and has ordered that officers from Pope's army be treated as felons rather than prisoners of war. Obviously the secesh have grown too accustomed to McClellan's soft war. Poor old Dix is crushed, though—he really wanted to get our men out of the tobacco warehouses where they're being maltreated.

Kate did not accept my assurance of inactivity. "You think the condition of the nation is something I shouldn't bother my little head about," she said with an edge in her voice. Nice, well-modulated voice, genuine edge.

Not so, I explained, but there was a time and a place for everything. This

John Hay

was the time for romance, and I tried to kiss her again, but she turned away. I don't like it when a girl turns away. It is taking advantage, it is insulting, and I said so.

She looked straight at me, took my shoulders in her surprisingly strong hands, and explained, as if to a younger brother, what she thought was wrong between us. "You don't trust me and I don't trust you. That's because you think my father wants Lincoln's job, and I think you're trying to find out what my father is up to."

True enough, as far as it went. "Lincoln tells the story of the chin fly," I said. "Farmer tells his farmhand not to knock the chin fly off the horse, because that's the only thing that makes him go. Same thing about Chase's presidential aspirations."

"Cut it out, John. Deal with reality." She turned pensive suddenly—the changes in mood are immediately reflected in her face, especially her mouth, and are quite stunning—and decided to confide in me. "Here's something I never told anybody about my father. He's deathly afraid of women. He really fears that women will dominate him, and he cannot face up to it."

I did not have to search hard for something equally revealing about Lincoln. "He couldn't face his father's death, you know. Wouldn't go to see him on his deathbed, even though it was only sixty miles away, and wouldn't attend the funeral. Still talks about doing something about the grave marker, but he never will."

"Now something about me," she said, as if to herself. I was glad we were getting away from revelations about our principals and on to ourselves, because, the truth is, I do not always like to face the truth about Mr. Lincoln. I respect him, I admire him, I even love him, and it will be my goal in life to make certain the world knows what a great man he is, but I also know he is neither the lovable Lincoln of the funny stories and Western ways, nor the hateful dictator-baboon of the newspaper legends. He is a hardened man who gives in at the edges but will not give an inch on his central idea, who knows how to say no, who puts the fervor of the Declaration of Independence ahead of the compromises of the Constitution, and who is looking for a general who is willing to take and inflict heavy casualties to save the Union. And there is a dark side to his brain that has him worried all the time about death and madness, in those around him and in himself. I like to think he is a man of balance, using the weight of others' arguments to pitch his own forward, but I suspect he is frightened of the imbalances within himself.

Kate derides his modesty, but it is absurd to call A. Lincoln a modest man. As I have asserted before, no great man was ever modest. It was his intellectual arrogance and unconscious assumption of superiority that men like Chase and Sumner never could forgive. He scarcely ever looks into a newspaper unless I call his attention to an article on some special subject, and frequently says, "I know more about that than any of them." And when I give him a cutting that extolls his vision to the heights, he carefully puts it in his wallet and carries it around for months.

Never has there been such a prestidigitator of men and events. He manipulates others by seeming to get them to manipulate him. The woods are crawling with politicians who think they have taken him into camp, and who never realize that their camp is where he wants them to think he is at that moment. I know this is nothing I ever want to discuss with anyone, least of all with Chase's delicious daughter. Nor is this a side of Lincoln to appear in any history.

Kate was telling me something about herself that I knew and did not want to hear: "I'm too ambitious for you, John. Sometimes all I can think about is the way it is going to be when I can tell everybody to do what I want them to do. Including you. That's unattractive, isn't it? That's not what they taught us to say at Miss Haines's school."

"Nothing wrong with ambition," I told her. "What I'm saying is that you mustn't let it permeate your whole life. Go ahead, dare to be first Lady, or whatever—but don't let that get hold of your whole being." I enjoy lecturing to her. "You know what you should be afraid of? You should worry about drying up inside, of growing cold, of toughening inside the way you would never let your skin toughen on the outside. If you're a success in only one thing, you're a failure." That's a dandy aphorism; Kate brings out the best in me. It was not, however, the right thing to say.

"What do you know about my life?" she flared. "Who are you to judge? If I can get the one big thing, everything else will follow, and if I can't have it, all the rest means nothing."

"Children, husband, home," I said coolly. "Music, art, philosophy, civilization—you don't care. You think if you're the Queen of Washington, all that will come to you? You'll miss it all, you'll die lonely."

"And poor," she said, goading me, eyes glittering.

"Spiritually poor. You're driving yourself single-mindedly straight to hell.

You'll be celebrated, envied, bejeweled—miserable." It made me feel good to tell her this, I am ashamed to say.

"That's enough," she said. "Talking this way is a mistake. You're really talking about yourself, you know. You're the one who's the moth circling the flame, in that big white house. Everyone dances around you, you don't have to put on a—" She stopped.

"Uniform," I finished for her. "I think about that a lot. So does the President's son, at Harvard. Give us a chance, we'll get a whiff of grapeshot before this is over."

"I didn't mean that."

"Sure you did. You and I like to hurt each other. Why?"

"We're good at it."

I laughed bitterly. I have a superb bitter laugh, which I have been practicing in my mind for many years, and the occasion to use it had at last arisen. "You're wrong about me, Kate, my love. I am going to be a complete man. First, after this war, I'm going to be a great poet. And then, if I can master my French, I will be a great diplomat, and maybe a really grand historian if there's time."

She thought about that in silence. When she responded finally, her question took me off guard. "You're not going to run for office?"

"That depends on the woman with me," I said on impulse. Suddenly she was all over me, laughing, biting, yelping, carrying on in a manner that her finishing school mistress could never have had in mind. Then, as suddenly, she sat up.

"You have to know a few things. That I am truly fond of you, and that I am a virgin and intend to remain so until my wedding night."

I told her that only the first item was of concern to me, but that was not true. I am a romantic and she is a flirt. I came here prepared for a genuine romance, but Kate, I fear, has in mind merely an innocent flirtation. So be it; my time will come.

One purpose of a diary is to make a record of what might otherwise be forgotten, especially the significant detail or illuminating offhand remark so vital to historians. I do that when I can. Another purpose, more central to the poet, is to give stereoscopic depth to the turning points of youth, much as Brady's special camera does, because as the moving moments are recorded, the diarist knows that an older self will be receiving the letter and judging the writer.

I will need no record to remind me of my night in Buttermilk Falls, and I will surely relive its poignance a thousand times. Toward that more central purpose, I must remember to be more than a camera, but to take the time— when there is the time—to be a portraitist. As I put the pictures of tonight's closeness on paper, I wonder: Did I miss a message? Was Kate telling me about herself, or about our future, in her supreme practicality? Am I missing a warning? Or, as is more likely, is she concerned about being too old for me, and is she protecting herself from the pain of what she sees is a young man's passing fancy? I shall have to reassure her about that.

Back to Washington in the morning. Contrary to some mawkish poetry spouted all too often by a man of otherwise good taste, the Spirit of Mortal sometimes has good reason to be proud.

CHAPTER 6

BATTLE OF BATON ROUGE

"Didn't you once tell me, Father, that Ben Butler was a big supporter of yours?"

"Long ago. This is no time to talk about it." General Breckinridge had made his advanced command post the balcony of a saloon on the main street of town, where he could best see the street fighting and hear the sound of the naval guns on the river.

"You said he was one of the most astute political leaders of the North," his son persisted. "I remember that because you made me look up 'astute' in Webster's."

As far as the general could tell, the hand-to-hand fighting in the streets of Baton Rouge was over. Breckinridge's "Orphan Brigade" of Kentuckians, along with ragtag regiments from Mississippi, Alabama, and an undisciplined collection that called itself the Louisiana Partizan Rangers, had retaken the capital of Louisiana—at least for a few hours. The shelling from the Federal gunboats under Admiral Farragut in the Mississippi River would surely make Baton Rouge impossible for Confederate forces to hold for long, but General Breckinridge had hopes that a surprise was in store for the Yankee fleet.

The former Vice President of the United States rarely talked about the political days before the war. But he could hardly begrudge his son and aide, Cabell, an answer, and there was little to do until the surprise attacker came downriver to stop the Federal naval barrage. "The Democratic Party split in '60 over the nomination of Senator Douglas," Breckinridge recounted. "Ben Butler of Massachusetts and a bunch of other Northern men came to see me about joining the Southern Democratic Party, provided I was against secession. I was."

"How come the Massachusetts men weren't for Lincoln, Father?"

"I told you to call me General when you're in uniform, Cabell." The uniform consisted of Kentucky jeans, but Breck felt even that semblance of dress called for a military attitude. "Butler knew that Lincoln's election meant the South would secede. So Ben and his Northern friends supported me, figuring I could have prevented secession."

"You didn't even carry Kentucky," the boy observed.

"Neither did Lincoln. Run over to General Ruggles and see if there's any word from the *Arkansas.*"

The boy sped off. He was nearly eighteen now, tall and broad as his father, and so much a look-alike that the general had grown a mustache in amused defense of his identity. Father and son had agreed to fight the war together, recognizing the need not to do anything that would cause the other to flinch from danger. It was painful at first for the General to send his son on a messenger mission that might result in his death or capture, and he granted it must be hard for the boy to watch his father expose himself leading a charge, but both decided it was better to stay close through the war, even though that proximity did not mean they could always protect each other.

Breck looked across the rooftops to the clock on the tower of the state-house, still in Union hands; it showed ten o'clock. From that tower, he knew, a Union naval observer was directing fire, the gunboat shells arching over the city into Confederate lines. The morning fog had finally lifted; in the early morning darkness, when Breckinridge had attacked, it had been impossible to see twenty yards ahead. The fog kept casualties down on both sides, which was especially fortunate because on the march down from Vicksburg the heat and polluted water had cost Breckinridge nearly a third of his original force of forty-five hundred. He was aware that the Federals had their disease problems, too, perhaps from the yellow fever the newspapers said had broken out in New Orleans. Many of the Union soldiers firing from the houses were wearing hospital gowns, a stranger uniform than jeans.

The *Arkansas* had been due at dawn. The ironclad Confederate ram, a rebuilt riverboat, had already lifted Southern hearts by chasing the Union gunboats from the waters around Vicksburg. Now the pride of the South's river navy was taking on a more daring assignment: to combine with land forces in striking southward through Baton Rouge toward New Orleans, dispersing Farragut's gunboats that had made possible the Federal occupation of much of Louisiana.

Breck's part of this first Confederate joint land-sea operation had been to march his force downriver fifty miles from Vicksburg. Through heat and swamp and despite all the straggling, that had been done. Regrouped, that was the force now attacking the garrison that Ben Butler sent up from his New Orleans command. The plan anticipated that the Federals would fall back to the protection of Farragut's gunboats to prepare a counterattack, which they were now doing. With superior numbers, the support of the gun-boat artillery, and interior lines, the Union would expect to carry the day.

That was where the surprise was to be in store. The ram *Arkansas* was set to steam on the scene, slam into the helpless Union gunboats, and make possible the capture of at least five thousand Union soldiers. Breck was certain that the recapture of a state capital, for the first time in the war, would lift Southern spirits, would force Grant, the new Union commander in the West, to divide his forces against Vicksburg. As a result, the Confederacy would reopen a needed supply line from the breadbaskets of Texas and Arkansas to the Southeast.

The Battle of Baton Rouge was not a major engagement, but it had strategic value, and was the first time John C. Breckinridge had been in complete command of a fight. Remembering the example of Sidney Johnston, he was determined not to take unnecessary personal chances. Breck also reminded himself to correct his own mistake at Shiloh, and to delegate more field authority to his brigade commanders.

To his knowledge, this was the first city street-fighting in the war. All previous engagements were fought on proper battlefields, away from civilians. But in this case, civilians were in the way, sometimes purposely; Breck swore when he watched Yankee soldiers force a man carrying an infant to pace up and down on a patio from which the Federals were firing. The fire from the Union gunboats into the buildings held by Breck's force was intense; no further advance was possible, and the position was becoming untenable. The *Arkansas* had to move those gunboats out soon.

Cabell came running back down the street and upstairs to the balcony headquarters. "Engine trouble on the *Arkansas,*" he panted. "Only four miles upriver. They're trying to fix it now. And Ben Helm is dead, along with Alex Todd—an accident with the ammunition."

That was a blow; Helm was his only experienced brigade leader. Todd, Helm's aide, was Mary Lincoln's brother; there would be sadness in the White House, but no official mourning for a Confederate casualty.

"A prisoner says that Williams, the Union commander, is dead, too," Cabell added. "That's probably why there's been so much confusion in their ranks."

Breck knew Williams to be a martinet, almost as bad as their own Braxton Bragg, hated by his men but the most experienced general in Butler's command. That explained the initial quick success of the Confederate attack in the fog.

An uneasy feeling gripped Breck, and in a moment he realized it was caused by the silence; the barrage from the gunboats had stopped.

"They'll counterattack now," he told Cabell. He beckoned to his adjutant and told him to take over Helm's brigade, which would probably bear the brunt of the Federal charge.

The attack came, catching his Alabama unit out of ammunition. As boys came racing back down the streets, half of them in bare and bleeding feet, Breckinridge could see as well as sense the tide of battle shifting. He ran downstairs, mounted his horse, rode up the street, rallying the leaderless men, who cheered him and instantly turned.

"Fix bayonets!" he roared, saber high, taking courage from the need to show fearlessness. "Charge!"

The energized but powderless Alabamians surprised a Yankee regiment coming around a street corner with no time to stop and load weapons. With a rebel yell, they plunged into the Federals, sticking the blades into those who did not flee quickly enough. Breck had seen no uglier kind of fighting, with stabbers stripping the stabbed of ammunition and firing at the men bringing up the rear. He looked for Cabell, who was lost in the confusion of battle; Breck pressed on to his second brigade, which had withstood a lighter counterattack.

The rickety wooden buildings of Baton Rouge shook at the sound of a tremendous explosion. Soldiers on both sides stopped and looked around; such a blast could not have come from any cannon. Something terrible had happened on the river. After long moments of silence, the two sides disengaged. Ten minutes later, the Union's naval artillery barrage resumed; one large ball crashed into the saloon Breck had been using as his headquarters, setting it afire.

General Breckinridge sheathed his saber, turned his horse around, and ordered his troops out of Baton Rouge. Cabell came scrambling back to tell the general what he already knew: the *Arkansas* could not get its engines started. When the Federal gunboats threatened to capture the ship, the crew did what they had to do. They abandoned the *Arkansas* and blew it up.

Twenty-three days of glory on the Mississippi ended in a resounding bang. So much for the first Confederate combined land-water operation.

In a clearing in the woods on the outskirts of the city, outside the range of the naval guns, Breck assembled his remaining troops and made a casualty count: 84 dead, about 370 wounded. He was certain that at least as many casualties had been inflicted on the defenders, but the hellish march down and the street fighting was for naught. He stood on a caisson and made a little speech.

"You attacked a force that was well fed, well clothed, well armed," he told the red-rimmed eyes looking at him. "You have had indifferent food and no shelter, and half of you have no coats or shoes or socks; yet no troops ever behaved with greater gallantry."

Three thousand men, repelled but undefeated, hungry for pride, listened to him without a sound, and in the fierce attention of his audience the politician-general found inspiration for a moving address. His voice rolled out as on the stump so long ago, offering support to his supporters, comfort to his comrades, new spirit to men who wanted to find a meaning in the marching and killing and retreating. After he and they partook deeply of each other's solace and justification, he raised his voice and called out: "What can make this difference—unless it be the sublime courage inspired by a just cause?"

Cheers and huzzahs. His undiminished ability, after changing from a man of peace to man of war, to move a crowd to a roaring response exhilarated Breckinridge more than his ability to lead a charge. He put in a jab at the troops of Ben Butler who had so recently been insulting Southern womanhood: "You have given the enemy a severe and salutary lesson"—pause for more cheers, and then a taunt at the enemy—"and now those who so lately were ravaging and plundering this region do not dare to extend their pickets beyond the sight of their fleet."

Breckinridge was disappointed at not winning a smashing victory, yet he had not lost; he decided he had a right to be elated at the fact that he and his men had done their job well. He had held himself back as a commander should, until the moment when he had no choice but to take personal command, which had made personal intervention all the more effective. His Orphan Brigade had been bloodied again, and he was sure those who could walk would follow him anywhere.

He gathered six of his commanders around to explain his next objective and how it fit in with what he thought might be the scheme of the whole war. Farragut's Federal fleet could not stay and protect the city for long. Breckinridge figured his best strategy was to conserve his troop strength and wait until he could maneuver the Union troops out of Baton Rouge without a fight. He would go upriver a few miles and take a position at Port Hudson, whose high bluffs resembled those at Vicksburg, and thereby break the Federal grip on the southern Mississippi. With well-placed artillery, Breckinridge thought he could keep Farragut from assisting Grant in any further attacks on Vicksburg.

He remembered Anna Carroll's intensity about using the Tennessee River to break the South. The first phase of that strategy, whoever had conceived it, had been carried out by the Union, with the taking of Corinth and the severing of the South's east-west railroad. The second phase was under way now, to take the Father of Waters, the Mississippi River, denying the South the last chance of supply from the grainfields of northwest Louisiana and the cattle of Texas. Together with the blockade of the Eastern seaboard, the "anaconda" that old Winfield Scott spoke about at the start of the war would squeeze the South to death. But that grip would be loosened if General Butler could be scared into abandoning Baton Rouge and a sizable strip of the Big Muddy could be secured. That was the military value of Port Hudson; to the weary soldiers, the best news was that the target was only a few hours' march away.

In his tent that night, his son snoring nearby, the Confederate general lay in his uniform, staring up at the blackness, replaying his speech in his head. Was the cause as just as he had said? Yes, the defense of one's home against an invader was just; his former political supporter, Ben Butler, was demonstrating in New Orleans, largest city in the Confederacy, what Southern life would be like after the war under the heel of Yankee occupation.

The first task of Lee in the East and Bragg in the West was to get off the defensive. The cavalry raids of Morgan in Kentucky and Forrest in Tennessee had disrupted Yankee communications and given Southerners reason to take heart, but they were merely local raids. Far grander raids were called for, up through Kentucky, and simultaneously up through Virginia, carrying the terror of war north into Union homes, strengthening the forces of peace in New York and Ohio.

Breckinridge, at moments like these, worked at persuading himself he had been right to take the course he had taken, "throwing his life away," as Anna had put it, trying to avert the war. Now that Lincoln was turning out to be a despot, putting his own people in jail for daring to oppose the war, supporting Pope's barbarism and Butler's predations, Breck felt more secure in his early judgment. But the effect of the war on the South's liberties troubled him now. The draft was abusive, the newspaper suppression was almost as bad, and the central control of trade was even more rigid than in the North.

Perhaps, on second thought, "despot" was too strong to apply to Lincoln. That tower of relentlessness, as the general recalled from his arguments with him only a year ago, was a man driven by a single obsession about "union," but his actions were shaped by events much as Breck's had been. If backed into a corner, with his precious Union about to be defeated, would Lincoln stoop to the encitement of the blacks on the plantations to riot and rape? And if he did go through with abolition, would the millions of blacks rise and kill their masters and mistresses? In the aftermath of such savagery, what kind of nation would emerge?

Too terrible to contemplate. He wondered if the President, the Union President, had night thoughts as terrible as these. Lincoln was a man of the Declaration of Independence, with its radical "all men created equal," while Breck was a man of the Constitution, with its compromises, balances, and conservatism. Which was more American?

Breck considered writing Mrs. Lincoln a letter about her brother's death, and the death of Ben Helms. No, that might get her in trouble for corresponding with the enemy.

He thought of his own wife, Mary, back in Kentucky, living with relatives, uncomplaining. He never came home to her without feeling glad or left without being sorry. Perhaps they could be together for at least a time if he took an assignment in the central theater with Bragg, or took up Jeff Davis's offer of a Cabinet post in Richmond. He closed his eyes. No, not that, not yet. The bloodletting and bravery of the battlefield was easier to face now than the need to change the South in order to save it. Soldiering helped him avoid the wrenching paradoxes.

What would Anna Carroll think of his attack on Baton Rouge? In the darkness, his mind brightened at the thought of her reading his exploits in Washington's *Intelligencer*. She would see his strategy, of course, and warn Lincoln of Breckinridge's threat at Port Hudson to the coming siege of Vicksburg. He hoped that, like Cassandra, she would not be listened to. More likely, Anna's advice would be heeded and the source of it never mentioned.

Anna had been right about the importance of the Western theater. The North could win the war here, with long and painful squeezing, but the South could not win in the defense of the West, not after Johnston's great trap failed to spring at Shiloh. The hope of the South now was in striking northward, taking advantage of Lincoln's evident indecision after the Peninsula campaign's ambiguities. Davis and Lee would see that. The Confederacy could not win a war of attrition, but the North could. The answer to the weight of Northern numbers was to gamble all on a great raid into the North that would seem like an invasion.

Breckinridge knew the Union generals who had been in the West and were taking charge in the East. Halleck was a ditherer, Pope a fraud. On a Confederate thrust northward just before the fall elections, the only Union opponent worthy of Lee and Jackson was McClellan, and that capable defender was apparently being cast aside because he was insufficiently bloodthirsty. Breck thought of the charge that morning, the bayonets digging into flesh, the screams of their men and his, and, worse than today, the awful picking-through of the bodies by his horse at Shiloh.

"Father? General?"

He sat bolt upright. "What is it?"

"You all right? I thought you hollered."

"Wasn't me, I'm fine." After a moment he added, "When we're alone like this, son, in the middle of the night, you don't have to call me General."

A Southern liberation of Kentucky would depress Lincoln, perhaps shake that unshakable resolve, he thought, as he drifted off to sleep. And a victory in Maryland or Pennsylvania, threatening New York, would lead to a Peace Democrat landslide in November, and genuine fear in the crucial state of New York could lead to negotiations between the two nations. If that did not lead to ultimate reunion, at least it would offer hope for a neighborly sharing of a roomy continent.

CHAPTER 7

THE BEAST OF NEW ORLEANS

George Smalley knew that most of his comrades in the "Bohemian Brigade" —the rakish name that war correspondents covering the Army of the Potomac gave their loose association—thought him to be something of an aristocrat. On the dandyish side, the reporter, still a shade under thirty, did not discourage that impression. When some woman was interested in his good looks and sturdy physique, he let her know that he was the man who served as stroke on the first Yale crew to race Harvard on Lake Winnipesaukee.

However, Smalley knew better than to use his affectation of elegance in the presence of Major General Benjamin Franklin Butler. The "Beast of New Orleans," as Butler was known throughout the South and in the courts of Europe, was notoriously anti-aristocracy. He had imposed an onerous tax on all the best families of New Orleans to bear the burden of paying a small army of the poor to clean up the city streets. This strenuous and unprecedented effort at municipal sanitation was motivated less, Smalley had heard, to benefit the poor or to tidy the streets than to punish the wealthy. The leaders of society in this largest of Southern cities under Northern occupation were regarded by this Massachusetts politician in military uniform as the hated slavocracy. Ben Butler was said to have taken it upon himself to humiliate and break them, and thereby send a message of terror through all Southern leadership.

The correspondent, waiting in the anteroom of the commanding general's office, was more concerned than usual about his interview. Butler had put a *Boston Traveller* correspondent in ball and chains for ignoring military censorship. Worse, an *Evening Post* reporter—Norman Hudson, whom Smalley knew to be the mildest of chaplains and a Shakespearean scholar—had been put in a bullpen with Confederate prisoners and was later transferred to a manure-laden stable when he had the temerity to complain about Butler heavy-handedness.

But George Washburn Smalley represented the *New York Tribune* and Horace Greeley; that set him apart. Any general seeking radical credentials (especially one who had bolted the Douglas wing of the Democratic Party to support Breckinridge in the last election) would have to be careful with the leading radical journal, or so Smalley hoped. Sydney Gay, the *Tribune* managing editor, had assured the reporter that the sea voyage around Florida would do him good, and that Butler would receive him as a friendly correspondent. Smalley wanted to get back in time for Pope's campaign to smash Lee, and be there to cover the end of the war in Virginia. He was determined not to irritate this "beast" to the point of languishing in the steambox of a Louisiana cell through the rest of the summer.

"You're here to ask me about my woman order," Ben Butler announced without a greeting. The general was seated in a large chair in an enormous living room converted to office use. The man's uniform was wrinkled, his face

General Benjamin F. Butler

and body bloated. One eyelid drooped over a slightly crossed eye. Smalley observed that this man was probably the least dashing or attractive officer in the Union Army.

"I'm here to tell the *Tribune*'s readers the story of your unexpected military success," Smalley offered. He eyed a shiny pistol lying on the general's desk, presumably a warning to the many who threatened his life that the man was prepared to take care of himself. "Most people thought your expedition would fail. The capture of the port of New Orleans was a stunning surprise."

"Give Admiral Farragut credit for most of that," Butler said unexpectedly. "His ships forced the surrender. My men didn't have a rebel army to fight."

Smalley found that remarkably generous of Butler, in a war where generals invariably sought renown at the expense of colleagues. Butler added: "Although I brought the coal."

"The coal?" Smalley shifted his weight forward, as if stroking the Yale crew.

"The usual way of ballasting a ship is to fill it up with stones," Butler informed him. "But I learned that anthracite coal was rising in the market when I left from Boston, and I assumed that if I ballasted all my ships with coal, the ballast would be worth more when we got back than when I bought it." The general regarded him with irritation. "You'd better write this down, young man, I'm not going to repeat it."

Smalley began scribbling.

"When I got down here to meet Flag Officer Farragut at Ship Island before the attack," Butler continued, "the man was in despair. His coal had run out, and the Navy Department had forgotten about him. I told him I would let him have three thousand tons of the best anthracite coal—at no profit to me, mind you—and I would sail back later with dry sand as ballast. Farragut said, 'Why, this is almost providential.' And I said, 'Yes, I provided it.' You get that last part down? I said, 'I provided it.' "

"A play on words," Smalley noted without looking up. "You made nothing on the transaction, you say?"

Reports of widespread official corruption in New Orleans had reached the North. Butler, a canny criminal lawyer in civilian life, had chosen to associate with the worst elements of the underworld, and it was bruited about by Butler's many Massachusetts enemies that he and his top officers were making fortunes trading with the enemy. Those who did not call the general "Beast" called him "Spoons," suggesting that he was making off with the silver of his hosts.

"And my brother Andrew was not in on it, either," said General Butler, his voice hardening. "He's a colonel in the Union Army, and what he does is his own business, not mine. I am not responsible for any of his investments, and I take no part in them. He makes what he can and more power to him. Why are you so interested in my brother?"

"I'm not, General."

"Ask me about the woman order."

"What caused you to issue the woman order, sir?"

"The men of this city were set straight by the hanging of Mumford." General Butler referred, the correspondent knew, to the controversial show of harshness in executing a Southern patriot. "Farragut ordered the United States flag to be placed on the government buildings as a token of the surrender of the city. He warned that if the flag were taken down by some rebel, it would be a signal for him to bombard New Orleans. When somebody hauled down our flag, Farragut sent a small boarding party ashore, and it turned out this man Mumford, a gambler, had done it. We tried him, and I ordered him hanged."

"Nobody thought you would go through with it," Smalley put in.

"That was because nobody had been hanged in the state of Louisiana for eighteen years, and the abolishment of the death penalty resulted in crime rampant. I saw this as a question of which should govern—a mob, or law and order."

Smalley did not interrupt. The hanging of Mumford had been applauded by many in the North, including the *New York Tribune,* as a necessary symbolic act to show that no rebel could safely tear down the national flag. To Smalley, the punishment of death for such a gesture seemed excessive, but he did not say so.

"At the scaffold," Butler went on, reciting the story slowly enough for the reporter to get it down, "a swearing, whiskey-drinking mob assembled, their bottles and pistols sticking out from their pockets. They kept declaring that this was only a bluff on the part of old Butler, and threatened what the people would do if Mumford was hanged." The general waited.

"And did they riot?"

"At the appointed hour the drop fell, and as it did there was a universal hush," Butler said, relishing his words. "The bottles and pistols went out of sight, and the crowd separated quietly. And no scene approaching general disorder was ever afterwards witnessed in this city up to now." Butler sat back, satisfied; evidently the dramatic telling of this episode impressed all visitors.

"Is it true, sir, that you had a man arrested for dropping a single sheet of paper on the street?"

"Again a symbol. Every three years in this city, always in the summertime, there has been the scourge of yellow jack. You ever seen yellow fever, young fellow? I did, my father died of it. He served under Andy Jackson here, you know. Did you know?"

"Oh, yes, sir."

"Most of our doctors say that yellow jack comes from tropical lands and can be stopped by a quarantine. But we've seen that doesn't work. I learned from a book and map published after the last outbreak here where the disease had been worst. You know where?" He heaved himself out of his chair and went to a wall map. "Here, and here, and here—in those places that stank the most—the fish market, and the turning basin, which was covered with a thick growth of green scum, variegated with dead cats or dogs or the remains of dead mules. And it broke out near the open sewers—the people here were used to that stink in the summertime." He sat down again.

"Well, it's my theory that yellow jack comes from bad air," said Butler, "the way malaria is caused by the miasma rising from swamps. So I ordered a cleanup the likes of which this place has never seen before. The rebels resisted. I suspect they were relying on the yellow fever to clear out the Northern troops, since Yankees would usually be the first victims in any outbreak. I ordered the sewers flushed daily. I had the walls whitewashed with lime and salt. I put an end to dumping garbage in the streets. Infractions of my sanitary regulations are punishable by jail terms. Now in answer to your question."

Smalley, writing notes furiously, knowing he would not need this for his story, was glad Butler remembered the point.

"One rebel provided a test case by very patriotically throwing a piece of paper in front of a policeman," the general said. "I clapped him in jail for six months, and now nobody else is breaking the sanitary law. And you know what? This was supposed to be a big year for yellow fever, and there isn't all that much. My theory is right—no bad air, no yellow jack."

Smalley was thankful. Disease was the cause of more casualties on both sides than gunfire, and it was the danger correspondents feared most. A wound could be a badge of honor, but no glory attached to dying of a fever. Butler was undoubtedly dictatorial, but the correspondent allowed that good ends could sometimes be accomplished by evil means.

"You keep avoiding asking me about the woman order," said Butler. "It's important that such an episode be properly noted in the *New York Tribune*. The woman order shows that I'm stern but I'm just."

"I'm ready to take it down now, sir."

Butler groaned out of his chair, which creaked in relief, and went to a cabinet for a document. "After the Mumford hanging, the men of this city were under control. Not so the women of New Orleans. Whenever an officer would get onto a streetcar, the women would immediately get off with every sign of disgust, abhorrence, and aversion."

"And aversion," Smalley repeated.

"On the Sabbath, on the way to church, one of my officers withdrew to the outer side of the sidewalk to let two women by. As he did so, they both deliberately spit in his face. He came to me and said, 'I want to go home. I came here to fight the enemies of my country, not to be insulted and disgusted.' Can you imagine my reaction?" Butler frowned, which made his eyelid look more sinister. "And then there was the unfortunate incident with Admiral Farragut and the chamber pot, which I need not recount because it so pleases the traitors to talk about it."

The general paused in his narrative to let Smalley catch up on his notes. "How is this to be stopped?" Butler asked himself. "We have a very few troops in the midst of a hostile population of many thousands, including more than twice our number of paroled Confederate soldiers. Many of the women who do these vile acts are young, pretty, and ordinarily ladylike. Now, I know that a police officer in Boston can hardly arrest a drunken woman in the street without causing considerable commotion, which very quickly expands into something like a riot if she appeals for help. If Yankee soldiers were to arrest a woman for doing what these rebels consider patriotic, we would have the real danger of riot, possibly ripening into widespread insurrection."

Butler brandished the document he had taken from his file. "I once read an old English ordinance, which, *mutatis mutandis,* I saw might accomplish my purpose. Here it is."

Smalley listened to him declaim the brief order: "Headquarters Department of the Gulf, New Orleans, May 15, 1862. As the officers and soldiers of the United States have been subject to repeated insults from the women (calling themselves ladies) of New Orleans, in return for the most scrupulous non-interference and courtesy on our part, it is ordered that hereafter when any female shall, by word, gesture, or movement, insult or show contempt for any officer or soldier of the United States, she shall be regarded and held liable to be treated as a woman of the town plying her avocation. By command of Major General Butler."

"This order might lend itself to misunderstanding, General," Smalley said. "It would be a great scandal if even one of your men should act upon it in the wrong way—I mean, using your order as an excuse to force his attentions on an innocent woman."

"Let there be just one case of aggression on our side," said Butler quickly, "and I'll deal with that soldier in a way that it will never be repeated." Smalley thought of poor Mumford. "But since that order was issued," Butler said triumphantly, "not one case of insult by word or look has been reported. The order executed itself. No arrests have been made under it or because of it. You know why, young man?"

Smalley thought it best not to know why.

"I'll tell you why. All the fine ladies in New Orleans forbear to insult our troops because they don't want to be deemed common women, and all the common women—all the whores—forbear to insult our troops because they want to be deemed ladies. Hah! It's working: no insults, no arrests, no riots."

"The foreign consuls in this city don't quite see it that way—"

"Every little whippersnapper emissary from some government in Europe finds fault with everything I do," Butler barked. "Here I am cleaning the streets and feeding the poor and making the residents here pay for it at no cost to the North. Still, Lord Palmerston got up in Parliament and called my order 'unfit to be written in the English language.' Get this down, it will make a good story for you: I got the language of this order from an ordinance of the city of London!"

"One of the members of President Lincoln's official family," said Smalley carefully, to protect John Hay, his source, "called your women order 'indefensible as a matter of taste.'"

Butler smacked his open hand down on the desk. "It's one of those damned private secretaries of his! I don't carry on the war with rosewater, and I don't spend it loafing around the throne."

The general was getting his dander up, and Smalley did not know if it was such a good idea to annoy him further, but Butler had a few things on his mind. "That skedaddler Hay is also probably telling you I wasn't the man responsible for the theory of captured slaves being 'contraband of war.' I've heard that some people around Lincoln are trying to deny me my place in history."

Smalley nodded. The "contraband" idea was a brilliant legal maneuver, and it would be useful to know its origin.

"Last year, when I was in command at Fort Monroe, I wrote Assistant Secretary Scott asking what to do with slaves who came over to me across the lines. But neither Scott nor his boss, Cameron, was a lawyer. I'm a lawyer. I know something about the law of nations. At Fort Monroe, we had sixty thousand dollars' worth of slaves, including the slaves of loyal men. I argued that slaves being used by their masters in actual warfare became contraband when captured, subject to the capturer's disposal. I wanted the sanction of the government for my action, and I got it. No pasty-faced sycophant avoiding military service is going to rob me of my authorship of the contraband theory!"

"No, *sir*," said Smalley. "I'll make certain the world knows who conceived that legal theory."

"I have another idea along those lines," said Butler in a different tone of voice, suddenly dropping all bombast. Strange man, Smalley thought; brilliant and stupid, liberal and cruel, shrewd and childlike. His contraband idea was a tremendous legal contribution to the radical cause and had endeared Butler to Mr. Greeley; his iron rule in the captured Southern city also attracted radical applause—the "woman order" would be a great hit—but it troubled many conservative Republicans and most Democrats because it was being used by rebel leaders to whip up hatred of the North, and thus might prolong the war. When the time came after the war to reconstruct the states of the South, presuming the North won the war, the fierce occupation philosophy of Butler would augur a harsh era. Such a prospect might be encouraging Southerners to fight on.

"Has it anything to do with emancipation, General?" Mr. Greeley wanted Smalley to prod Butler on that; where Frémont and Hunter had failed, perhaps the shrewd political-legal mind of Butler could figure a way around Lincoln's edict reserving all emancipation matters to the President.

"You can't print this yet," he said, "but tell Mr. Greeley I have a plan for recruiting negroes to fight."

"You are forbidden to arm fugitive slaves—"

"I know that—who's the lawyer here, you or me?—but there are a great many *free* negroes in New Orleans." His face took on a cagey look. "They served under Andy Jackson in 1815, and even the Confederate governor last year allowed them to form up as a couple of regiments of 'native guards.' Those are legal precedents. I can call up those regiments of free negroes to fight on our side, and"—he lowered his voice—"who's going to inquire closely about the status of every man who joins that unit? That's for next week, so not a word. But tell Greeley it's a step forward, and tell him to remember who found a way to do it without embarrassing the President."

Smalley started to put his pencil away. "I suppose I should congratulate you, too, on the victory at Baton Rouge."

"It was a great victory. Breckinridge was driven off with terrible losses." Butler hesitated, looking uncomfortable for the first time in the interview. "Of course, that city is not important. As a matter of fact, we'll be withdrawing our forces from there. I've brought back here the city's statue of George Washington, and the important books from the state capitol library."

That struck Smalley as odd. If Baton Rouge was not important, why had it been defended so vigorously? Apparently Admiral Farragut could not station his boats there forever, and the rebels would take back their first state capital.

"I only held Baton Rouge because of the danger of yellow fever in New Orleans," Butler added unconvincingly, "in case I needed to move my men elsewhere. But New Orleans is now as healthy as Boston, and Baton Rouge is of no possible military importance. I want to concentrate my troops; let Breckinridge have the damn place."

"And Port Hudson?" Smalley had heard that Breckinridge's seizure of the bluffs upriver would facilitate rebel access to needed food supplies in the West.

"That's Grant's problem," said Butler, eyes narrowing, including the cock-eyed one, as if the correspondent knew too much. "He can take Port Hudson after he takes Vicksburg."

Smalley took his leave from Butler. The correspondent was determined to discuss the controversial commander with Smalley's friend, Ralph Waldo Emerson. That great moralist would be fascinated with Butler's contradictions: a genuinely unlikable fellow using his unpopularity to accomplish great goals of sanitation and freedom, and a politician not above letting his brother use his connections to make a million dollars. Butler was the sort to find ways to cut ethical corners both in accumulating money and in helping slaves to freedom. How is such a man to be judged? Smalley wondered if Lincoln knew of Butler's planned subterfuge in enlisting a black brigade; he might appreciate the cunning way around legal objections to arming blacks.

The *Tribune* reporter was glad to be out of Butler's conniving, domineering presence and on his way north to the Pope campaign against Jackson and perhaps Lee. Those soldiers were more his idea of generals. Smalley passed a delegation of negroes in the street outside, all wearing bright white shirts, presumably for an audience with the military commander. He said under his breath they were welcome to Benjamin Butler.

CHAPTER 8

NATIVE GUARD, COLORED

Correspondents were damned pests but Butler knew when one could be useful, even necessary. Horace Greeley's man was important. When the *Tribune* thundered, Lincoln would say, "there's meat in that," a favorite expression of his, and the President would try to go along or get along with Uncle Horace.

Benjamin Butler despised Greeley, with his white round hat, moon face, and pusillanimous nature. That disastrous slogan "On to Richmond!" had its origin in the half-addled brain of the editor, a man who had not strength enough to stand political defeat or military reversal. The general hoped that John Pope, arrived from the West to take over the army outside Washington, would not be rattled by the *Tribune*'s demands. Pope was the Union's best chance to save the nation from the likes of McClellan; Butler had heard the copperheads wanted to set him up as dictator. Meanwhile, some radicals wanted to set up John Frémont as dictator. Butler marveled at Lincoln's forbearance; if he were President, such treasonous talk about dictators would get certain generals slammed into Fort Lafayette.

The commander of New Orleans could probably count on the *Tribune* reporter to interpret properly the woman order and the sanitation crackdown, although radicals were queasy about the Mumford execution. Would this nervous snob Smalley write that General Butler had been driven out of Baton Rouge by Breckinridge, and catch the irony of the two former political allies now locked in combat? Butler hoped not; the *Tribune* would never again field a reporter in his department if such an embarrassing story were written. Butler nodded in grim satisfaction; he knew how to handle the press. When the publisher of the New Orleans *True Delta* had refused to print the general's proclamations, Butler immediately ordered the takeover of the paper. The publisher knuckled under soon enough.

"The Africans are here, sir."

"They're not Africans, they're American freedmen," he barked at his aide. "Tell them I'll see 'em in a minute."

He picked up a letter from Secretary Chase that had come from Washington on the same boat with the *Tribune*'s Smalley. Chase was closely apprised of Butler's interest in recruiting blacks, and the general's worry about being slapped down by Lincoln the way Hunter and Frémont had been. "The language of the President's revocation of Hunter's order," Chase wrote him, "clearly shows that his mind is not fully decided. It points to a contingency in which he may recognize the clear necessity of emancipation. My conviction is that that contingency will soon arise . . ."

Butler felt flattered by the personal attention of the Treasury Secretary. Chase probably wanted some Massachusetts political support someday, which was okay with Butler; he could use some radical help from Chase's friends in seeking the governorship of Massachusetts, especially if Chase wrested the Republican presidential nomination from Lincoln after the war.

He saw the advantage to Chase to have emancipation accomplished by military commanders rather than by presidential proclamation, and their political interests were parallel. The war would not last forever.

Chase's letter of July 31 contained an assertion that Butler liked: "We must either abandon the attempt to retain the Gulf states or we must give freedom to every slave within their limits. We cannot maintain the contest with the disadvantages of unacclimated troops." Right. Blacks could work and fight in this impossibly hot weather when whites, especially Northern whites, tended to drop in their tracks. That was another good reason for pushing Lincoln toward arming blacks.

"It will not escape your acute observation," Butler read, smiling, "that military emancipation in the Gulf states will settle the negro question in the free states. I am not myself afraid of the negroes. I have not the slightest objection to their contributing their industry to the prosperity of the state of which I am a citizen."

Butler frowned at that. Chase might be willing to see Ohio swamped with freed blacks, but there was no future in Massachusetts for a politician who stood for anything of the sort. "But I know that many honest men really think that negroes are not to be permitted to reside permanently in the Northern states," Chase wrote "and I believe myself that, if left free to choose, most of them would prefer warmer climes to ours." Butler nodded as he read the radical's point: "Let the South be opened to negro emigration by emancipation along the Gulf, and it seems pretty certain that the blacks of the North will go southward."

Butler agreed. Lincoln's notion about mass deportation was silly, but the idea of locating all the blacks in the South after the war made sense. That result would fulfill a Boston politician's dream: abolition of slavery without subsequent black competition for white jobs.

The first step was to find a way to arm the blacks in this area that would not force Lincoln to rebuke him. If Butler moved warily, in a way that did not directly challenge the President's authority, he could count on Chase to keep Lincoln from countermanding any Gulf states order. He signaled for his aide to send the negroes in.

Twenty freemen, selected because they were all former officers in the Confederates' "Native Guard, Colored," entered the office and formed a semicircle around his desk.

"You're an intelligent-looking set of men," Butler said, sliding back in his chair and looking up and around him. "Would you like to be organized again as a native guard, this time as part of the United States troops?"

In every group there is always a natural leader, Butler believed. Most of the men were of a very light shade of tan, reflecting the intermingling of the races in this area—slave owners must have used black women freely—but the purplish-black skin of the spokesman for the group was the mark of the pure African.

"General," the blackest negro asked before committing himself, "shall we be officers—leading our own men as we were before?"

Why not? Some Northern whites would take offense, but to hell with them. If the rebels had previously trusted the black leaders to hold the negro troops in line, Butler would too. "Yes. Every one of you who is fit to be an officer shall be."

The black leader looked at him steadily without responding. The man could obviously tell a qualifying clause when he heard one.

"Okay," Butler said, using Andy Jackson's word for "oll korrect," and waved his hand. He had no reason to be overcautious. "All the line officers will be colored men."

"How soon do you want us to be ready?"

"How soon can you twenty men give me two regiments of a thousand men each?" He added, "I won't be finicky about papers."

The black, whose name Butler had not caught and did not want to ask for because he did not want to get caught in a last-name requirement, answered immediately, "In ten days."

"Explain to me one thing," said Butler. He leaned back in his chair, arms crossed, and flung out the insult: "My officers believe that negroes won't fight."

Eager assurances from the entire group, all save the leader, filled the room. Butler observed the freedman's silence and felt his anger, and directed his remarks to him: "You know what this war is about. If the United States succeeds, it will put an end to slavery. Then tell me—why haven't some negroes, somewhere in the South, struck a blow of their own for freedom?"

The others looked to the black leader, who refused to answer. Butler went on, probing for the reason for the docility of Southern blacks, asking the question in the minds of so many whites in the North. "All over the South, the white men have been conscripted and driven away to the armies, leaving ten negroes in some districts to one white man. The war to end slavery is raging. But the colored men have simply gone on raising crops and taking care of the white women and children. Why? Are you afraid to fight? Are you happy in slavery?"

The black leader started to reply, then restrained himself. Finally he said, "You are the general here. I don't want to answer that and lose the chance you are offering us."

"Answer it honestly," Butler told him, meaning it, "and, I pledge you my honor, whatever your answer shall be, it will harm neither you nor any of your comrades."

The black leader thought that over. "Let me ask a question," he said at last. "Let's say we colored men had risen up to make war on our masters. Would it not be a war of all blacks against all whites? Would we not have to see all the whites as our enemies, and kill them all?"

"That's what a slave insurrection would lead to," Butler admitted.

"If the colored men had begun such a war as that, General Butler, which general of the United States Army should we have called on to help us fight our battles?"

While Butler mulled that over, the black pressed him: "If black men were slaughtering white men, and women and children, could we count on you, a white general, to come to our aid and help us kill the oppressing whites? Or would you have joined the whites to kill us?"

Butler, knowing the black's point to be well taken, changed the subject. "You haven't answered my question," he gruffed. "Why should we think you'll fight? You've been beaten down. You have servitude in your bones. You're afraid to lift a hand against the white man." He did not bring up the case of Hispaniola, where blacks had risen and murdered their masters. He baited them further: "Maybe you're just not fighters."

"We come of a fighting race," said the black, looking steadily at him. "Our fathers were brought here as slaves because they were captured in war. Not your kind of war, either, with guns that shoot men far away—but hand-to-hand." He held out his hands, huge and muscled, and made a slow, strangling motion so vivid that Butler could almost feel those hands squeezing the life out of him. He reached for the pistol lying on the desk and pretended to examine it.

"You ask if we have cowardly blood in our veins. I tell you, General—yes, we do." The dark-skinned black looked around at his light-skinned comrades. "But the only cowardly blood we have in our veins is the *white* blood."

Butler swallowed. "You are willing to fight?"

"As no other soldiers will, General, to break the chains of our people."

That was good enough for Ben Butler. "Recruit your men," he told them, rising. "Let them be mustered into the service of the United States on the City Hall steps two weeks from today at ten in the morning. I will meet you there. I will be proud to have you in my command."

They filed out, as proud and satisfied as he. Butler's heart was pounding. He had found a way to do what no other Union general could do, and what not even the President would dare to undo. Butler was sure the blacks would fight bravely, having more at stake than whites, and in the grim knowledge of what they would face if taken prisoner.

The events that would flow from this, he knew, were sure to include widespread emancipation. The armed freedmen of New Orleans—joined by many more fugitive slaves posing as freedmen—would lead the way to the arming of fugitive slaves wherever the contending forces clashed. And Butler was certain that no slave who fought for the Union could be denied permanent freedom, no matter what constitutional lawyers argued about property rights or blood attainders. Those who fought on the side that would preserve the Union could not later be denied full citizenship, with rights to vote and even with standing to sue in a court of law. Taney's decision in *Dred Scott* denying blacks their essential humanity would be a dead letter the moment a black man donned a blue uniform.

Let the captious slackers around Lincoln's throne try to take that away from him. Butler sat down to write a reply to his good friend and conspirator in freedom, Salmon Portland Chase. The key to abolition without divisiveness was in the fingers of military commanders in the field.

CHAPTER 9

BETTER THAT WE SEPARATE

"He's reading your memorial on colonization now," John Hay told Anna Carroll, motioning to the closed door between the President's office and the room for the three secretaries.

Anna noted that Nicolay was out. Hay, always more authoritative in the senior secretary's absence, was writing a letter that, he informed her, was for Lincoln's signature. She presumed he often drafted the President's correspondence, or at least wanted her to think so. The third secretary, Stoddard, was half-hidden behind a mound of mail.

"Caleb Smith sent it over from Interior with a covering stutter," Hay said with the irreverence that so often accompanies youthful proximity to power. "We expect a deputation of our African friends in a few minutes."

"There'll be no objection to my being there?" Anna was eager to see Lincoln in action on a subject she had researched for him. This would probably be the first time a group of blacks had met formally with any President of the United States in his office, and she did not want to appear to be intruding on a historic occasion. Lincoln was not the sort who would stand on ceremony, but she knew him to be ready to slap down anyone who overstepped.

Hay waved off her concern. "Sydney Gay of the *Tribune* was in the other day and arranged for a correspondent of his to be present. The *Washington Star* will have a man here as well, because we want the world to know the President's views on this. Sit in the back, scrunch down, nobody'll notice."

She nodded. It was not often that being small had its advantages. When Interior Secretary Smith asked her to prepare a paper on the shipment of negroes out of the United States, she had complied. Not for the pittance he offered in recompense, but because it was a subject that excited the interest of two rival Cabinet factions: the Blairs and Treasury Secretary Chase. The Blairs were avid supporters of colonization, Chase was resolutely against. Anna leaned toward the Blair position, remembering how hard it had been to find jobs for the slaves she manumitted herself, but a couple of questions about the deportation plan perturbed her.

She suspected that the Interior Secretary had some financial relationship to the promoters of the scheme to create a colony on the huge Chiriquí Tract in the Isthmus of Panama, which supposedly offered all part of New Grenada, which supposedly offered no objections. But the Navy Secretary—"Neptune" Welles, who struck Anna as stubbornly honest—made no secret of his opinion that the plan was a giant swindle aimed at bilking the government out of the half-million dollars appropriated by Congress for colonization in the Confiscation Act.

Moreover, nobody knew if the government of Guatemala would be willing to see the Isthmus crowded with freed slaves, and Honduras was distinctly unfriendly. It was certain that no refuge in Hayti was available, and the negroes that Caleb Smith had spoken to refused to go to Liberia, clear across the Atlantic.

Despite those drawbacks to the idea of colonization, Anna came down on the side of pressing ahead with the project because another matter was controlling: Lincoln, as Anna had learned from Chase, needed all the support he could muster for the proclamation of emancipation he was working on, and he would need the escape valve of colonization for the political pressure it was sure to cause. If active planning for the deportation of blacks were under way—or at least were openly reported to be under serious consideration in the White House—the conservative Northern fury at emancipation would be ameliorated. Anna reminded herself to use the word "colonization," which sounded less coercive than "deportation."

"I agree with Thurlow Weed, emancipation now would be a mistake," she told Hay, "but if the President is going to free the slaves, he'd better have a specific idea in mind about where to send them. People don't want them in New York or Philadelphia or Boston. Chiriquí in Panama seems best, though I wish I knew more about Brazil. At least Panama has coal, which they can dig and the Navy can buy." Only one part of the arrangement troubled her. "Are you sure the negroes will go along with this?"

"They'd better," said the President's younger secretary cheerfully, "or at least this delegation coming today had better. Reverend Jim Mitchell is bringing them, and he swears they'll hold still. That's why we have the reporters present, to show how willing the negroes are to go bother somebody else."

The deputation of blacks appeared, and were soon joined by the two reporters. Hay went into the President's office, and returned to say to the *Tribune* man, "Have you heard about the Sioux uprising in Minnesota? That's just what we needed now, Indians on the warpath killing settlers. Follow me, gentlemen, and Miss Carroll."

Lincoln looked sallower and more worn than on her last visit to his office. His wife should make him run a comb through that thicket of hair, she thought, and see that his coat is pressed every day as befits a President. Then she thought of an item in that morning's *Intelligencer* about the death of Mrs. Lincoln's rebel brother, and Anna softened. It must be hard not even to be able to mourn.

The President solemnly shook hands all around, said "my dear lady" to her, and motioned them to draw chairs into a semicircle around his leather couch. That was wise; the large desk would have been a barrier at a moment that required an ostentatious absence of barriers.

"We are here at your invitation, Mr. President," said the chairman of the free colored men's delegation, a light-colored man who had been introduced as E. M. Thomas, "to hear what you have to say to us." Evidently they had been invited to come to hear a plea, not to make one.

"A sum of money has been appropriated by Congress," Lincoln began, alluding to the half-million dollars Wade had put in the Colonization Act, "to aid the colonization of some country by people of African descent. That makes it my duty, as it has for a long time been my inclination, to favor the cause of colonization."

"Why should we leave this country?" The question seemed to pop out of the black leader, and he seemed embarrassed at having asked it.

"That is the first question for proper consideration," Lincoln assured him.

"Why should the people of your race be colonized," he repeated, and as if the answer were a foregone conclusion added, "and where?"

He plunged in, frequently checking his notes, obviously well prepared. "You and we are different races. Your race suffers very greatly living among us, while ours suffers from your presence. In a word, we suffer on each side. You are all freedmen?"

Thomas nodded yes, all present were freed slaves.

"Your race is suffering, in my judgment, the greatest wrong inflicted on any people," Lincoln told them, "but even when you cease to be slaves, you are yet far removed from being placed on an equality with the white race. You are cut off from many of the advantages which the other race enjoys. On this broad continent, not a single man of your race—free or slave—is made the equal of a single man of ours."

Anna noted the President's careful choice of words about the sensitive equality issue. He said they were not "placed on an equality," and not "made the equal," which avoided a statement that they were inherently unequal. Lincoln had thought through what he would say. "Go where you are treated the best," he continued, "and the ban is still upon you."

Thomas started to say something, but Lincoln held up his hand. "I do not propose to discuss this but to present it as a fact with which we have to deal. I believe in the general evil effects of slavery on the white race." He pointed to the map on the wall. "See our present condition—the country engaged in war —our white men cutting one another's throats. Then consider what we know to be the truth: but for your race among us there could not be war."

"Many men engaged on either side," said Thomas, "do not care for us one way or the other."

Lincoln readily agreed and pressed his point: "Without the institution of slavery and the colored race as a basis, the war could not exist. It is better for us both, therefore, to be separated."

Long silence, punctuated only by the scratching of reporters' pencils catching up to his remarks. "We are freedmen," another of the negroes finally countered. "Perhaps some of our race who are slaves might be inclined to go out of the country if that is the condition of their freedom—but we freedmen can live here as easily as in any foreign country."

"I speak in no unkind sense," said Lincoln, preparing, Anna assumed, to say something unkind in a kindly way, "but that is an extremely selfish view of the case. You ought to do something to help those who are not so fortunate as yourselves. If intelligent colored men, such as you, would move in this matter, you would open a wide door for many to be made free."

To his visitors' dismay, the President argued logically that slaves, with "their intellects clouded by slavery," offered poor prospects for a new colony, while free negroes "capable of thinking as white men"—such as those in the room—and who had not been systematically oppressed, would offer much greater chances of success.

"There is much to encourage you," he exhorted. "For the sake of your race, you should sacrifice something of your present comfort. In the American Revolutionary War, sacrifices were made by men engaged in it, but they were cheered by the future. General Washington himself endured greater physical hardships than if he had remained a British subject—yet he was a happy man, knowing he was benefiting his race."

His audience remained impassive. Lincoln added, "There is an unwillingness on the part of our people, harsh as it may be, for you free colored people to remain with us." The reporters noted that down.

He then swung away from the "why" to the "where." He touched on Liberia and as quickly dismissed it, observing that blacks born in America had a natural affinity for the country of their nativity, and came to the point: "The place I am thinking about having for a colony is in Central America— with great natural resources and similarity to the climate of Africa, thus being suited to your physical condition."

Lincoln then revealed a curious notion that Anna, in her analysis of the commercial future of Panama, had not envisioned.

"The particular place I have in view," he said, "is to be a great highway from the Atlantic to the Pacific Ocean." She wondered what the President had in mind for the narrow Isthmus: a railroad, a wide boulevard for carriages, some other kind of passage between the two great oceans? "On both sides there are harbors among the finest in the world," the President continued, as if he could see the area's development in his mind's eye. "And evidence of very rich coal mines, affording the inhabitants an opportunity for immediate employment till they get ready to settle permanently."

Was Lincoln trying to persuade the assembled blacks or to persuade himself? Anna knew that only the sketchiest evidence of "very rich coal mines" had been submitted by land speculators; she hoped that Gideon Welles had warned the President directly of the possibility of corruption between Caleb Smith and the promoters of the Chiriquí Tract.

"Whites as well as blacks look to their self-interest," Lincoln said, as if aware of the suspicions. "Everybody you trade with makes something. I shall, if I get a sufficient number of you engaged, have provisions made that you shall not be wronged."

He awaited a response; there was none. Lincoln hurried along: "The political affairs in Central America are not in quite as satisfactory condition as I wish." Anna blinked; Honduras was threatening to shoot blacks on arrival, and even the enthusiastic Blairs were aware of the need for treaties and armed protection.

"The practical thing I want to ascertain," said Lincoln, sitting up to make the sale, "is whether I can get a number of able-bodied men, with their wives and children, who are willing to go when I present evidence of encouragement and protection."

Anna was glad he was not accepting the point of view of Attorney General Bates that all the blacks must be deported, voluntarily or not; Lincoln was offering freedmen, at least, the choice of going or staying, and she assumed he would make the same offer to the slaves soon to be freed.

"Could I get a hundred tolerably intelligent men, with their wives and children, to 'cut their own fodder,' so to speak?" The President looked at the four men, and finally at E. M. Thomas, for a reply. The men looked at each other and did not speak.

"Can I have fifty?"

No answer. The President, with an edge of desperation in his high voice, fell back to his minimum plea: "If I could find twenty-five able-bodied men, with a mixture of women and children—good things in the family relation—I think I could make a successful commencement." Before they could fail to respond again, he went on: "Let me know whether this can be done or not. I ask you to consider seriously not pertaining to yourselves merely, nor to your race, and ours, for the present time—but as one of the things for the good of mankind, not confined to the present generation."

After a moment, the chairman of the delegation said, "We will hold a consultation and in a short time give an answer."

"Take your full time," replied the President. "No hurry at all."

They withdrew. Afterward, walking down the hallway with Hay, Anna concluded, "It's not going to work, you know."

The young man sighed. "He thinks it has logic on its side."

"On paper it may look perfectly logical," she told him, "and it may be what he thinks is the most humane and proper thing to do—just as I did—but it's all a delusion. He may or may not get twenty-five blacks with their families. But he won't get a few thousand. And he surely won't find this to be the answer for four million people. They just won't go, and if you try to force them to go, they'll hide. Or fight."

"It seemed like such a good idea," said Hay.

"But when you examine it closely, it falls apart." She began to regret her own part in it. "It is something to talk about, maybe, but it is nothing to do."

"He had about the same success with the border-state congressmen on compensated emancipation," Hay brooded.

She stopped. "He pleaded with Crisfield and the rest in order to say that he tried," she thought aloud. "And when they refused him, he signed the Confiscation Act. He begged them to take the money for their slaves, knowing he would be turned down. Why do you suppose he does that? Why does he make public offers of ideas he knows will be turned down?"

"Why, indeed?" said Hay, offering nothing.

"I suspect he knows this colonization idea is a lot of hogwash," Anna figured, "or at least he knows it after this meeting. But tomorrow it will be all over the newspapers, how he plans to send the Africans down to Central America, and how their leaders did not object. And a great many newspaper readers, especially in New York and Washington, are going to think that abolition will not mean blacks coming North for jobs."

"I think he still thinks colonization is feasible," Hay said loyally.

"Maybe." If Lincoln thought that, he would be a fool. If Lincoln knew otherwise, and was dangling colonization as a way out of facing the hard issue of competition for employment, he was a knave. Anna Carroll sighed with some satisfaction: she always preferred knaves to fools.

Lincoln, she concluded, had a more cunning mind than most politicians credited him with; he was never far ahead of public sentiment, but always catering to it, nudging it in devious ways. Here he was insulting the blacks, espousing the separation of the races—even as he prepared the ground for public acceptance of abolition of slavery. Where did he learn this trick of preparing the ground by getting rejected? Who was advising him—Thurlow Weed? But Weed was against abolition. Chase? No, Chase wanted no part of deportation, and did not have the type of mind that admitted such calculation as spreading the rumor to make abolition more acceptable. The Blairs? No—they really thought colonization would work. Not Bates; not shrewd enough. Maybe Stanton or Seward, both with conspiratorial minds. Or maybe nobody; the thought struck her that "honest Abe" might be devious enough to conceive the strategy himself.

General George Brinton McClellan

BOOK EIGHT

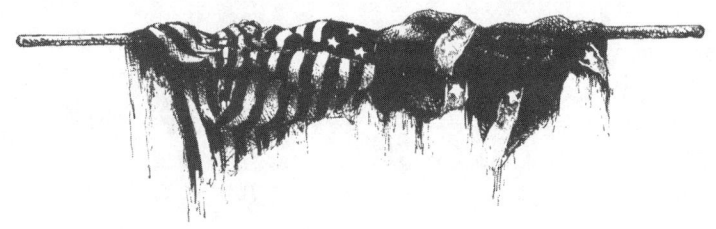

McClellan
Again

CHAPTER 1

FATAL ERROR

"Here, directly in front of this army," McClellan argued, tapping the map, "is the heart of the rebellion."

George McClellan was all but certain that the general across the table, sent down to the Peninsula from Washington, would not be blind to the military opportunity. How could anyone with any military training miss it? "It is here," he pressed, "within twenty-five miles of Richmond, that all our resources should be collected to strike the blow that will determine the fate of the nation."

The Army of the Potomac's field commander considered Henry Halleck to be his inferior in every way except rank. But the man listening to his plea was General-in-Chief and had to be reckoned with.

He wished "Old Brains" would comport himself more like a soldier and stop scratching his elbows. Halleck had come from the West, where his painstaking crawl toward Corinth after General Grant's curious debacle at Pittsburg Landing had made it possible for the Confederates to regroup and defend Vicksburg and the Mississippi. Now Halleck, having stumbled to the pinnacle of the nation's armed forces, was paying what McClellan presumed was a courtesy call on the army's most important field commander.

"I must take things as I find them," McClellan heard Halleck's whining voice say. "I find our forces divided, and I wish to unite them."

"Good, good," McClellan replied cordially. "Send me Burnside's men and McDowell's forces. That's all I need to take Richmond. I won't need Pope's men, they can stay to guard Washington."

Halleck looked uncomfortable. "You don't understand. Only one feasible plan has been presented for doing this—to move your army north to join Pope outside of Washington."

McClellan was thunderstruck at the thickheadedness of the man, but he kept his temper in check. "The more feasible plan," he said coolly, "is to send me the reinforcements I need to attack the rebel capital."

"A week ago," said Halleck, "I wired you that it had been determined to withdraw your army from the Peninsula to Aquia Creek. What have you been doing?"

McClellan sensed a trap. He could not let it appear that he was resisting a legitimate order. To show an intent to comply, he had been sending home his sick and wounded, delaying the retreat northward of his fighting force until he could prevail upon Lincoln and Stanton to do the militarily sensible thing: to send Burnside and McDowell to reinforce him, and not turn back the clock six months by going back to a static defense of Washington, followed by a long, bloody, interminable fight overland through Virginia to Richmond. That would be military madness, he was certain, war dictated by fearful politicians; and this grumpy military bureaucrat was apparently giving it his imprimatur.

"Your telegram caused me the greatest pain I have ever experienced," he said to the clerk with the general's stars. Even Lincoln was known to have described Halleck as "a first-rate clerk," and McClellan was unwilling to classify him as a first-rate anything. "I am convinced that the order to withdraw this army will prove disastrous to our cause. I have never done this before, General Halleck, but I entreat you—I beg you: Rescind that order."

"We have to consider the defense of Washington. General Lee has sent General Jackson and about twenty-five thousand men to strike at Pope."

That made McClellan wish fervently he had a President as daring as Jefferson Davis behind him. Evidently Lee had persuaded the Confederate President to risk the defense of Richmond—with McClellan's army still within a day's march of the capital—by sending Stonewall Jackson's brigade up to threaten Washington. The move could only be a feint but, incredibly, the Confederate strategy was working. Lincoln and Halleck were falling into the trap by ordering the withdrawal of the Army of the Potomac from its threatening position near Richmond. That retreat would free Lee to join Jackson and smash Pope up near Washington. And Pope was no match for either of those Confederate generals. McClellan considered Chase's choice for Union field leadership to be a civilian-killing savage who was more imbecile than general.

"The threat to Richmond is the true defense of Washington," McClellan pleaded. This man had written a respectable book on strategy. Why couldn't he see the obvious? "Here, on the banks of the James, the fate of the Union will be decided. The moment I begin to retreat—and it is a complex movement, as you are aware—Lee will streak north. His army will be on the attack, morale high—while this army will be demoralized and in retreat. Don't you see? This one wrong decision could cost us the war."

"The President expects you to carry out his instructions," Halleck insisted. McClellan felt only scorn for this uniformed errand boy, passing along political messages when he should be beseeching the President to act boldly as a commander in chief. So be it; neither reasoning nor begging would affect Halleck. McClellan rose, acknowledging defeat.

"If my counsel does not prevail, I will obey your orders," McClellan said carefully. He would give his enemies in Washington no ammunition to criticize him as mutinous.

"You cannot regret the order of withdrawal any more than I do the necessity of giving it," Halleck sighed. After a moment, the little eyes of the General-in-Chief grew cagey. "Are you certain you are not able to strike at Richmond without reinforcements?"

McClellan calculated quickly. Even without Stonewall Jackson's troops, now on the feint toward Washington, General Lee's force in front of Richmond remained formidable. He sensed a little give in Halleck's attitude. "Give me fifty thousand men, and I will win the war."

Halleck rubbed his chin and walked around. "I have no reinforcements to send you. But if somehow we were to find those fifty thousand, you would strike immediately? I should pass that on to Lincoln."

McClellan's hopes rose. They were negotiating with him after seeming to order him home. If he agreed to fifty thousand, they would cut it in half. He responded: "Make it a hundred thousand."

Halleck looked agonized. "That's just it. Lincoln says if he gave you two hundred thousand men, you would suddenly discover Lee had twice that many in front of Richmond. He had hoped that an attack on Richmond by your ninety thousand, in concert with an attack through northern Virginia by Pope and his forty-five thousand, would crack the Confederacy."

Rely on John Pope? That was absurd. If McClellan were to attack Lee's superior force in Richmond, depending upon the barbaric Pope to tie down Jackson near Washington, Pope would surely fail. The skillful Jackson would hold him off with a small rear guard and dash back to join Lee and overwhelm the Union attackers by sheer weight of numbers. Why couldn't Halleck see that and explain it to Lincoln?

Still holding his temper, McClellan said, "Lee has two hundred thousand men with him in Richmond right now, and the advantage of interior lines and friendly country. We know the number. Ask Pinkerton yourself. I have half that number ready for duty, but if I had reinforcements I could take Richmond. I could end the war in a single stroke, save all that bloodshed—"

"If it is true that Lee outnumbers you two to one," Halleck replied, "he could smash you here and then turn north and defeat Pope. By your own reckoning, we would be wiser to unite our forces near Washington."

There was superficial logic to that, but he had taught Lee at Malvern Hill that an army in a defensive posture under George McClellan could not be overwhelmed, even by superior numbers. Wearily, not wanting to give the ultras around Lincoln the satisfaction of cashiering him for insubordination, McClellan assured Halleck that he would use all his skill in maneuver and logistics to bring his men safely north, if that was the President's final decision.

After he put the uneasy Halleck on a boat back to Washington McClellan sought counsel with General Fitz-John Porter, his most trusted subordinate, the man whose troops had inflicted terrible losses on Lee during the Seven Days. Lee was said to be audacious, but McClellan judged him to be foolhardy, as the casualty figures proved; the Richmond newspapers pointed out that the South had lost more men than the North, which it could ill afford, and McClellan was still threatening the capital.

A late afternoon thunderstorm was brewing. A gust of wind swept through the wood-frame headquarters, blowing a tall desk over and smashing the "monkey," a pottery jug filled with water to cool the room by evaporation.

"There's a bad omen," said Porter, looking at the smashed jug. "They're getting ready to give you your walking papers."

"Maybe not." Halleck's tentative offer of some reinforcements made it possible Lincoln would change his mind. "The absurdity of Halleck's course in ordering the army away from here is that we cannot possibly reach Washington in time to do any good."

"Maybe Lee will attack us here," Porter offered. "We couldn't leave in that situation."

"Do everything you can to draw him on," McClellan ordered. "If we could only induce Lee to attack us now, I could beat him and follow through to Richmond—Lincoln would have to send reinforcements in that case." McClellan's spirits rose. "We could be ready to move tomorrow on Richmond while Jackson is lamming away at Pope."

"Lee is too smart to attack us now," Porter said sadly.

Reality closed in on McClellan. "I wish we could humbug him into it, but

General Henry W. Halleck

he must see the beginnings of a retreat. No, forget about an attack on Richmond. Lincoln and that incompetent fool Halleck are committing a fatal error in withdrawing me from here, and the future will show it."

"What do you see as the result of their machinations?"

"Pope will be badly thrashed within ten days, and then they'll be very glad to turn over the redemption of their affairs to me." That was part bravado, McClellan knew. He had already written to Aspinwall, the financier in New York, about a job after he was forced to leave the army. But if Pope failed, there would still be hope for McClellan and for the country. An eye-opening defeat could be the necessary precursor to ultimate victory.

Porter nodded. "Sometimes things have to get worse before they get better."

McClellan knew that Porter understood his position, and why they both had to speak circumspectly. It would be best for the Union, in the long run, for them to delay going to Pope's assistance, but such a maneuver had to be conducted with subtlety. What was patriotism in the long run might seem treason in the short.

"I presume Pope is being hard-pressed by Jackson," McClellan said slowly. "We cannot help him in time, as we don't have the means of transportation. The best way for Pope to handle Jackson in the Shenandoah Valley would be to send McDowell and Frémont after him—trap him at Harpers Ferry, cut up his force." That would never happen. McDowell was capable, but Frémont did not know the first thing about moving troops. It was important, however, for the written record to show that McClellan was struggling to get the means to move north. He would make that point in telegrams to the War Department. "I foresee," he told his favorite supporter, "that the government will try to throw upon me the blame for their own delays and blunders. So be it. I have learned to endure."

"But how unfair it is," the loyal Porter said angrily. "If you get Pope out of his stupid scrape, they'll all say how wise Lincoln was to bring you north. And if we don't get there in time to bail him out, Pope's defeat will be blamed on you. You can't win."

A fair assessment of the situation; Fitz was a good thinker. McClellan saw now that it was not primarily a personal animus that drove his Washington enemies. Stanton's hatred was to be expected, since their approaches to the war—and the peace that would follow—were diametrically opposed. Stanton, Chase, Greeley, that whole radical abolitionist crowd, wanted to kill the rebels, smash the South, conquer the territory, no matter what the casualties. But George Brinton McClellan—along with half the Republicans, the great majority of the Democrats, and most of the Army of the Potomac—wanted to capture Richmond and then offer generous terms for peace. Those terms would include, as Lincoln had repeatedly promised, preservation of the peculiar institution of slavery within Southern borders. That fundamental disagreement about goals was why McClellan could be certain that Stanton, Chase & Co. would go to any lengths to disgrace him.

The injustice was galling. Since they could not take him away from his army without great uproar from the troops, they would—piecemeal, corps by corps—take his army away from him. They would order him to fight here without reinforcements, and tell the world that he was a coward to wait for a full complement of troops. In the next breath, they would accuse him of treason for not racing north to save the reckless Pope. If the radicals now dominating Lincoln were so sure McClellan *could* win without reinforcements, he wondered, why were they so fearful Pope could *not* win without reinforcements?

"I want to strike square in the teeth of all of John Pope's infamous orders," he told Porter. "I want to give directly the reverse instructions to my army: forbid all pillaging and stealing, and take the highest Christian ground for the conduct of the war."

Porter grinned and nodded approval.

"Let Lincoln's government gainsay it if they dare," McClellan added. Lincoln, supposedly a lawyer, had never rescinded one of Pope's horrendous and unlawful orders ordering the hanging of rebellious civilians. "I will not permit my army to degenerate into a mob of thieves."

"I like that," said Porter, "but it will mean war to the knife with Stanton."

"And with Chase, and Wade, and all of them," McClellan added. "Their game is to humiliate me and force me to resign. Mine will be to force them to place me on leave of absence, so that when they begin to reap the whirlwind that they have sown, I may still be in a position to do something to save my country."

He trusted his right-hand man to conduct his portion of the withdrawal from the Peninsula with the utmost caution, despite all Stanton's and Halleck's demands for haste that might expose his Army of the Potomac to unnecessary danger. That was it; if Halleck dashed his hopes, McClellan would find good reason to protect his men in the process of safe withdrawal. Meanwhile, he and Porter would burn up the telegraph lines with cabled demands for more and better transportation. The Committee on the Conduct of the War would never be able to support a charge of deliberate delay; indeed, McClellan would contribute all his skill to a withdrawal—but by the book, with prudent regard to the safety of his men.

If the absence of Porter's force during Lee's attack meant difficulty for Pope, even his defeat, such were the fortunes of war. Lincoln and Halleck had placed their favorite new general in that scrape, and it was for them to get him out of it. He suspected that John Pope, manipulated by his sponsor Chase and the ever-duplicitous Stanton, was an instigator of the wrongheaded withdrawal from the Peninsula. He would never forgive that move, designed to ruin the McClellan reputation and ultimately sacrifice the splendid army he created.

In the midst of his frustration and humiliation, George McClellan sensed that his rival would fail, and knew when that happened his countrymen would turn to him again. Then the man they now called the "procrastinator" and the "coward" would have his day.

When Porter left, Lieutenant Custer came in with a fresh pot of ink and paper; it was time for the general to write home to Nellie.

"Armstrong," he told the aide—since they were both named George, the general had come to address the young man by his middle name—"with all their faults, I *do* love my countrymen." He sighed profoundly. "If I can save them, I will yet do so."

CHAPTER 2

JOHN HAY'S DIARY
AUGUST 19, 1862

These are halcyon days for me.

Kate and I grow in each other's mental and physical processes even as we observe the competition to come between our champions. Her father, of course, will fail in his desire to unhorse the Prsdt, but I shall be there to comfort her and perhaps provide a surprising substitute for her need for the proximity to power. The future, after the war, beckons us to become the most sought-after self-seeking couple in the nation.

Adding to my euphoria is the generally prevailing sense that something is finally to be done about the war. McClellan is finished, retreating in good order—he is really superb when it comes to retreats, there is no denying him that. Slow but sure, leaving not a matchstick behind. The man falls back as in the swoon of a great actress.

Burnside has already joined General John Pope in Maryland to mass for a grand attack down toward Richmond. A new start, a new leader, a new army —away with the taste of stagnation and defeat!

However, the army loves its soon-to-be-replaced leader with an embarrassing passion, which is why the Prsdt has been trying to paper over the differences between Stanton and McClellan in public. (Why shouldn't the rank and file love their Little Mac? He doesn't get them killed.) Last week, at a meeting in front of the Capitol, the Tycoon told the crowd that Stanton and McClellan were not nearly so deep in a quarrel as were some gossips who pretended to be their friends.

Everybody in the know knows that Stanton has triumphed and that Lincoln is only trying to salve the Little Napoleon's feelings, but I suppose it is a part of any President's job to blame dissension within the official family on second-level aides. Which brings me to the bothersome subject of the persnickety press, and especially Horace Greeley's *Tribune*. "Without public sentiment, nothing can succeed," Lincoln likes to say, especially to scribblers; "with it, nothing can fail." And public sentiment means the *Tribune*. In New York, Henry Raymond of the *Times*, who is in Seward-Weed's pocket, will do anything for us, and James Gordon Bennett of the *Herald* will do anything to embarrass us, and here in Washington, Jim Welling of the *Intelligencer* will run whatever we give him. But all across the nation, "public sentiment" means Uncle Horace's *Tribune*.

Sydney Gay was in here a few days ago. He's Greeley's right arm now that Charles Dana has become Stanton's right arm. Gay sent in a letter from some anonymous reader that really got under the Prsdt's skin. I have it here: "Can you enlighten the people in regard of the real object of the Administration in relation to the rebellion? The people begin to fear that we are being trifled with, that there is not and never has been any serious determination to put down the rebels. The President with full power to act hangs back, hesitates, and leaves the country to drift . . . does this mean he is ready to play conservative to the ruin of the Nation?"

The Tycoon's ire at that caused me to telegraph Gay in New York to come down and see the Prsdt. He did, after some delay about a death in his family, and A. Lincoln, commander in chief, gave him some broad hints about military action under Pope and about more use of fugitive slaves as laborers, which is catnip to the Jacobins. He hinted at emancipation but said nothing about arming the slaves, letting Gay persuade him to make more use of the Confiscation Act.

Then, yesterday, I brought in Robert Walker, the pro-Union former senator of Mississippi, and his partner in magazine publishing, James Gilmore. Gilmore wrote *Among the Pines,* a sentimental novel about Southern life that Lincoln likes, and is the fellow who is supposed to be our channel to Greeley.

"Well, Mr. Edmund Kirke," said the Prsdt, using Gilmore's pen name, "it is a long time since I beheld the light of your countenance. I infer from the recent tone of the *Tribune* that you are not always able to keep Brother Greeley in the traces."

"Any direct attempt to influence him has no effect," said Gilmore. "With Sydney Gay, I can be more direct, and he has softened Mr. Greeley's wrath on several occasions."

The Prsdt did not let on he had just seen Gay himself. "What is Greeley wrathy about?"

"The slow progress of the war," Gilmore reported, "and especially your neglect to make a direct attack on slavery. Mr. Gay tells me that Mr. Greeley is now meditating an appeal to the country which will force you to take a decided position."

Irritated that Gay had not told him about that plan, the Prsdt asked, "Why doesn't Uncle Horace come down here and have a talk with me?"

"Sir, Greeley says he objects to allowing the President to act as advisory editor of the *Tribune*."

The Tycoon put on his most innocent look. "I have no such desire. Does not that remark show an unfriendly spirit in Mr. Greeley?"

Robert Walker put in the answer: "I told Gilmore here that McClellan's tardiness and disobedience to your orders was the cause of that. I also told him, in strict secrecy, that a proclamation of emancipation had been drawn and was awaiting a favorable moment for publication. Shall he not be allowed to tell this to Mr. Greeley?"

Frankly, that was news to me; perhaps that explains the Prsdt's mysterious slipping-off to the telegraph office in July to be alone with his writing. Also all the secrecy about the Cabinet meeting last month and the reversal of some momentous decision after a late-night talk with Thurlow Weed.

"I fear only Greeley's passion for news," the Prsdt was saying. "Do you think, if you tell him, he will let no intimation of it get into his paper?"

"Not if he gave his word," Gilmore said hesitantly, "but he's absentminded about those things. I'll tell Gay instead, who can be trusted."

"Do that," the President told him.

"You have to tie emancipation with deportation," Walker said. "How are you coming on the Chiriquí plan? If that falls through, I have an idea about shipping them through Texas to Mexico."

Lincoln said he had put colonization to a deputation of free negroes a few days ago, but nobody wanted to be the first to go. He pressed the cunning idea of getting Gilmore to head off the abolitionist pressure from Greeley. We hardly needed more agitation from the radicals at a time when the conservatives were so skittish; the trick was to let the middle-roaders get comfortable with the idea of gradual, compensated emancipation, hurrying them a bit only with the argument of military necessity.

Unfortunately, the plan to head off Greeley was one day too late. Gilmore left last night, but this morning the New York *Tribune*'s front page is emblazoned with an editorial entitled "The Prayer of Twenty Millions."

I beat the Tycoon to work this morning, thanks to a tip from Kate that something big was afoot among the radicals. He came in with his shoes in his hand. As he massaged his feet before trying to insert them into their tight containers, I read him the radical diatribe.

"It starts out 'TO ABRAHAM LINCOLN, PRESIDENT OF THE UNITED STATES: A great proportion of those who triumphed in your election are sorely disappointed and deeply pained by the policy you seem to be pursuing with regard to the slaves of the rebels . . .' Shall I go on?"

Lincoln grunted yes.

" 'We require of you that you EXECUTE THE LAWS . . . We think you are

strangely and disastrously remiss in the discharge of your official and imperative duty with regard to the emancipating provisions of the new Confiscation
Act. They prescribe that men loyal to the Union, and willing to shed blood in
her behalf, shall no longer be held in bondage to persistent, malignant traitors.' "

"There goes Greeley arming the slaves," Lincoln said, jamming his foot
into the shoe.

"Says, 'We think you are unduly influenced by the menaces of certain fossil
politicians hailing from the border slave states.' "

"That's always safe to say."

He had to hear this, because "The Prayer of Twenty Millions" would
surely be hotly discussed across the nation. " 'The government cannot afford
to temporize with traitors, to bribe them to behave themselves nor make them
fair promises in the hope of disarming their causeless hostility. Had you
proclaimed at the outset that rebellion would strike the shackles from the
slaves of every traitor, the wealthy and the cautious in the South would have
been supplied with a powerful inducement to remain loyal. The rebels from
the first have been eager to confiscate, imprison, scourge, and kill. We have
fought wolves with the devices of sheep.' "

"The devices of sheep!" Lincoln exploded. The night before, he had been
looking at the long casualty lists. He took the *Tribune* out of my hand and
spread it on his desk, drawing on his spectacles, resting his knuckles on either
side of the editorial. "He calls compensated emancipation 'bribery,' " he muttered, taking up the reading-aloud himself.

" 'We complain that the Confiscation Act is habitually disregarded by your
generals. Frémont's proclamation and Hunter's order favoring emancipation
were promptly annulled by you. We complain that the officers of your armies
have habitually repelled rather than invited the approach of slaves; those
escaping have been brutally repulsed and often surrendered to be scourged,
maimed, and tortured by the ruffian traitors. A large proportion of our regular army officers evidence far more solicitude to uphold slavery than to put
down the rebellion.' "

His voice hardened; Greeley was accusing him of abetting the sins of Mc-
Clellan. " 'You, Mr. President, knowing well what an abomination slavery is,
seem never to interfere with these atrocities. The world will lay the blame on
you.' "

Greeley was getting personal; that was bad. Up to now, nobody with a
following had associated the President directly with the actions of some of his
field commanders. It had been part of Lincoln's way to remain detached from
what could be dismissed as mistakes under fire.

Greeley's "prayer"—more of a jeremiad—complained that the rebels were
using the anti-negro riots in the North to convince the slaves that they have
nothing to hope from a Union success. " 'If they impress this as a truth on
their ignorant and credulous bondsmen, the Union will never be restored.' "

The President, shaking his head at the power of the argument and the vigor
of the Greeley language—and estimating its likely effect—read the conclusion: " 'The loyal millions of your countrymen require of you a frank, declared, ungrudging execution of the Confiscation Act giving freedom to the

slaves coming within our lines. I entreat you to render unequivocal obedience to the law of the land.' "

We knew that Uncle Horace's philippic would be reprinted and debated in every home in the North, read from pulpits and pounded into the public consciousness. But—did it represent the public sentiment of most of the North? If it did not, would it swing much of the conservative sentiment over toward the radical view?

After reading it all the way through again, the Prsdt walked around his office and ours, repeating phrases like "the policy you *seem* to be pursuing." We have come a far piece from the old "my policy is to have no policy"; the Lincoln policy is clearly to save the Union, to solve the slavery issue through compensated and gradual emancipation and colonization. Not everybody likes that policy—indeed, very few people seem to be embracing it at the moment—but it is at least a recognizable policy. We are not drifting. Any other policy, from Greeley's previously defeatist "wayward sisters, depart in peace" to Greeley's present call to arm the slaves, would generate more opposition than the Lincoln way.

Then a curious thing happened. Instead of working himself into a fit of the hypo, complete with lugubrious poetry recitations, the Prsdt grew almost unnaturally calm. He lay down on the leather couch, propped his head under his arms, and pondered a bit. I started to step outside and close the door, but he beckoned me back.

"You notice," he said, " 'The Prayer of Twenty Millions' calls only for adherence to the Confiscation Act. Nothing in it about emancipation on a grand scale."

"But now, if you come out with an emancipation proclamation," I said, "it will seem to be in response to the radicals' demand."

He shrugged; that seemed unimportant to him. Evidently he was beginning to look at the Greeley letter not so much as an impertinent affront, which I think it was, but as an opportunity for him to use a device to prepare the public for his own coup. He hates to be seen leading, and much prefers to lead by shooing others out front. Can a great shooer be a great leader? I suppose so, if he gets the job done.

"I wouldn't give him the satisfaction of a reply," I advised. "The almighty editor of the *Tribune* didn't even send you an advance copy of his polemic; he just ran it in the paper. I would simply stand on my dignity and let people forget about it."

The Prsdt shook his head, smiling one of his this-is-too-good-to-pass-up smiles. He rolled off the couch and signaled for writing materials, which I brought, and he started scribbling a first draft as I looked over his shoulder.

"As to the policy I 'seem to be pursuing,' as you say," he wrote to Greeley, "I have not meant to leave anyone in doubt." Good way of handling an insult.

"I would save the Union. I would save it the shortest way under the Constitution. The sooner the national authority can be restored, the nearer the Union will be 'the Union as it was.' "

I grunted to show appreciation for the way he flung that phrase hated by abolitionists in Brother Greeley's teeth: "the Union as it was" is the rallying cry of those unionists who are willing to leave the South to its peculiar institution.

"Broken eggs can never be mended," he wrote, "and the longer the breaking process, the more will be broken."

"Do you really want to say that?" I ventured. "Doesn't sound presidential." He looked around at me with that expression he gets when he wonders if I spent too long at an Eastern university, but he neither argued nor acquiesced; he put a check mark against it, to think about it some more, and went on.

"If there be those who would not save the Union, unless they could at the same time save slavery, I do not agree with them." That put him against the Southern firebrands. "If there be those who would not save the Union unless they could at the same time *destroy* slavery, I do not agree with them." So much for the Northern radicals. He is now firmly in the center, inviting the ire of the extremes. I hope he is not alone in the center.

"My paramount object in this struggle *is* to save the Union, and is *not* either to save or to destroy slavery."

That was the sort of pithy line that could be used against him. "Do you really want to say that?"

He nodded firmly. That was his conviction, and not a matter of style up for discussion. He paused a long time before writing the next line.

"If I could save the Union without freeing any slave I would do it, and if I could save it by freeing *all* the slaves I would do it; and if I could save it by freeing some and leaving others alone I would also do that."

I had heard him say something like this to a friend earlier in the week; it was a thought he had been refining, until Greeley's letter gave him a chance to use it in finished form. I suspect that the last part—freeing some and leaving others alone—is what he has in mind, and he is getting people ready for what might seem like an outlandish or hypocritical compromise. He is just putting the notion out there the way a dramatist lays a knife on the table in the first act that he plans to use in the third act.

"What I do about slavery, and the colored race, I do because I believe it helps to save the Union; and what I forbear, I forbear because I do *not* believe it would help to save the Union. I shall do *less* whenever I shall believe what I am doing hurts the cause, and I shall do *more* whenever I shall believe doing more will help the cause." A perfectly balanced line; lucid, too, except that it seemed to put him a few long steps away from the anti-slavery Lincoln of the Douglas debates.

Perhaps he sensed that, too, because he added: "I have here stated my purpose according to my view of *official* duty, and I intend no modification of my oft-expressed *personal* wish that all men everywhere could be free."

Nice. Says his heart is with the radicals, but he can't let his heart rule his presidential head. They'll say they voted for his heart, but it's a fine position for him to take. Most important, it makes the arrangement for a reluctant conversion to emancipation later—telling conservatives that when he does emancipate, it will not be because of personal feelings but because it is the best practical course for the preservation of the Union.

"I still hate to see this in the form of a letter to Greeley," I advised, and Nico, who had come in to read it, agreed. Why let the man who insulted the

Prsdt sell his newspaper with a presidential response? It would put the editor on the same level as the Prsdt.

"Send for Welling," Lincoln said, referring to the editor of Washington's *Intelligencer*. I approved of that; if he was going to respond with a letter to Greeley, at least have it appear in another newspaper.

We sped Stoddard over to the editor's office, and he returned after the Prsdt had written the letter out on his Executive Mansion stationery. By that time, the salutation had been added:

"Hon. Horace Greely: Dear Sir—I have just read your letter addressed to myself through the New York *Tribune*. If there be perceptable in it an impatient and dictatorial tone, I waive it in deference to an old friend, whose heart I have always supposed to be right—"

That's pure Lincoln; he doesn't say he *believes* Greeley's heart is right, he only *supposes* so. He splits those hairs like the lawyer he is. I noticed that Lincoln misspelled Greeley's name, dropping the last "e," but thought that might be intentional and so said nothing; if it was a simple mistake, then I take pleasure in knowing it will cause that pompous old coot some discomfiture when he finally sees it. (Now that I examine my own copy, I see that the Prsdt spelled "perceptible" wrong, too; I should have caught that. Well, it's been a busy day.)

Jim Welling, who is a good egg, said he would get the reply in the paper the next morning, at least two days before Greeley could run it in the *Tribune*. And then—bless his sharp editorial eyes—he pointed to the line about the broken eggs and said, "Mr. Lincoln, this expression seems somewhat exceptionable."

The Prsdt did not like that. "Why so?"

"On rhetorical grounds," said the editor. "It seems out of place in a paper of such dignity."

With a sound that could fairly be compared to a growl, the Prsdt crossed out the line. I kept a straight face and said nothing.

CHAPTER 3

UNIVERSAL CHANGE OF FRONT

"It's not an answer to my 'Prayer,' " Horace Greeley stated, as he read the presidential reply in the *National Intelligencer* and the *Times*.

Sydney Gay, summoned into the editor's office from his desk in the middle of the newsroom, knew that Greeley was delighted to be at the center of attention; his front-page "Prayer of Twenty Millions" had turned out to be a journalistic masterstroke.

"Bennett at the *Herald* must be eating his heart out," he told his beaming employer.

Greeley's round face bobbed up and down. "Do you see, Sydney, what that proslavery knave Welling has to say?"

The managing editor had read Welling's editorial in the *Intelligencer* accompanying the President's reply to Greeley. "He says you had no right to speak on behalf of twenty millions in the North, Mr. Greeley, and that most of them would prefer Lincoln's position to your own."

Which, Gay added to himself, was true. When the managing editor visited Lincoln the week before, he had no idea that Greeley had this up his sleeve. He hoped the President did not think Gay had held back important information.

"Welling, that little toady, thinks I need a lesson in etiquette. Calls my editorial 'arrogant, dictatorial, and acrimonious.' Hah! I suppose that came straight from Lincoln, along with a copy of the letter to me." Greeley, the white round hat and white beard framing his cherubic face, was happy in his irritability. Gay knew he was feeling proud and defiant, and his complaining about the envious sniping of his competitors made him feel even better. Greeley had been unusually civil to the *Tribune*'s employees as he walked through the building earlier.

"Raymond of the *Times* is grumpy too," Gay offered.

"Yes, I have that right here." Greeley cheerfully read aloud: " 'Several days ago the President read to a friend a rough draft of what appears as a letter to Horace Greeley. He said that he had thought of getting before the public some such statement of his position on the slavery question, and the appearance of Greeley's "Prayer" gave him the opportunity.' Do you believe that, Sydney?"

"Yes," Gay dared reply. "Lincoln didn't just dash off that answer to your editorial. His line about freeing some of the slaves, and not others, struck me as very carefully prepared."

"I agree," the radical leader chirruped. "I have been used. How all the other ink-stained wretches wish they could be so used!" Gay was astounded at Greeley's willingness to be part of a political minuet. "The only pity is," Greeley added, growing serious, "that Lincoln refuses to budge—he won't put the Confiscation Act into operation. He won't arm the slaves, he won't force his Democratic generals to act like Hunter or Frémont or Pope. We have to keep pounding away at this, lest the North lose heart."

"You're not as angry at Lincoln as your 'Prayer' editorial suggested, then?"

"In my eyes, Sydney, he's a bad stick. The President really doesn't understand how weary people can get, how close we all are to quitting."

Greeley went to the large bookcase near the door and plucked out a book. Gay noted that the editor knew exactly where it was. "Look at the table of contents in this theological treatise." He jabbed a pudgy finger and the managing editor read: "Chapter I: Hell. Chapter II: Hell, continued."

"That's where we are in the war," Greeley said triumphantly. "In 'Hell, continued,' and no end in sight. Lincoln's reply shows he doesn't understand that only an attack on slavery can rejuvenate the Union cause."

"I don't know," said Gay, trying to assess Lincoln from his recent visit and this seemingly contradictory letter to Greeley. "I thought he was coming over your way. And Forney, in the *Philadelphia Press*, just went beyond the Confiscation Act clear to a call for emancipation."

"Forney has always been in the pocket of the conservatives," said Greeley, moved to wondering about that, "and he won't say boo without Lincoln's approval. Do you suppose it was a French whadyacallit?"

"A ballon d'essai?" The French had a method of weather observation that involved sending up balloons to see which way the wind was blowing, and this idea of "trial balloon" was a phrase Greeley chose for a political metaphor.

"Yes, that—do you suppose that Lincoln told the obsequious Forney to stick his toe in the water about abolition? If that's so, Sydney, I should be fully informed. The *Tribune* should not be the last to know if Lincoln has at last come around our way."

Sydney Gay shrugged. The President's emissary, Gilmore, was cooling his heels in the outer office, awaiting an audience with Greeley. "Ask Gilmore. He sees the President."

At the editor's nod, James Gilmore was brought in. The novelist-turned-magazine-editor seemed to Gay less cocksure this time; if Gilmore's job was to keep Greeley tied to Lincoln's wagon, he had not been doing so well.

"Well there, Gilmore," Greeley piped out delightedly, "what news from the inner sanctum? Was it true that my 'Prayer' was merely the forum for a statement heaping abuse on the cause of human freedom that Lincoln had previously prepared?"

"I have a piece of information for you, Mr. Greeley," the writer replied seriously, "but it cannot be bandied about, and certainly not used in your paper. Do I have your word? And yours, Sydney?"

Gay started to say no, but Greeley cut him short with "Out with it. I can keep a political confidence."

"Even before your editorial appeared, Mr. Greeley, the President prepared —and discussed privately with the Cabinet—the issuance of a proclamation of emancipation."

"Ah." Greeley stopped to chew that over; Gay did not believe it. "And what is keeping him from this necessary action?"

"He is only waiting a favorable time to publish it to the country."

"Then why," asked Gay, "does he give just the opposite impression in his reply to Horace Greeley? Lincoln's letter is the sort of answer that the Welling pro-slavery crowd at the *Intelligencer* cheered."

Gilmore shrugged. "I suppose the President has his reasons."

That answer struck Gay as honestly devious. The managing editor was coming around to the idea that Lincoln was a complex fellow, not at all the weakling or the hayseed he had been painted in the press of late.

"If Mr. Lincoln were not so cautious and reticent," said Greeley, folding his hands over his stomach and creaking back in his chair, "we should get along much better together. Tell him that, Gilmore, would you? I could forgive him a lot if he would infuse a little energy in affairs, dumping McClellan and his ilk. And I could forgive him everything if he'll issue that proclamation. Even this duplicitous reply. Did he say anything about arming the slaves?"

"No. Emancipation of all those in rebel hands, after proper warning."

"My, my, my." The watery eyes glittered; Gay wondered if the politician in Greeley was hailing the possibility of freedom, or relishing the fact that his timing had been perfect in leading the President. "Do you remember what Victor Hugo says of Waterloo—that it was not just a battle, but a change of front of the whole universe? That is what an emancipation act of Lincoln's would be—a change of front of the country. Henceforth we would be a free people."

Greeley turned to Gay, as if the tight-lipped editor were a blabbermouth. "Not a word to a soul about this, Sydney. The fact is more important than the news. Gilmore, tell the President it is time to fight with both hands now."

"I think he realized that, Mr. Greeley."

"And until he does," the emboldened editor went on, "just to be sure, the *Tribune* will urge him to carry out the will of Congress in the Confiscation Act—not in any grudging, halfway, underhand, equivocating, clandestine deference to it, but in an open, loyal, hearty, thorough recognition and execution of it."

Gay knew that Greeley did not trust Gilmore. Moreover, even if the intermediary spoke the truth about what Lincoln had told him on this occasion, Greeley did not in the least trust Lincoln. If the President could pretend to go one way while going the other, albeit to a great end, could not Lincoln also pretend to be an abolitionist, thereby to curb abolition? If Pope were to smash the rebel army assembling in front of him, and the South were to be forced to its knees, no military necessity would exist to require a proclamation of emancipation. In that case, Lincoln could then point to his reply to Greeley's "Prayer," willing to save the Union "as it was"—with slavery intact.

Gay hustled Gilmore out, thanked him for his efforts as an intermediary, and hurried back to Greeley's office.

"That corroborates Adam Hill's information," he told his boss excitedly, proud of his Washington chief. "He wrote us a week ago about a secret plan to emancipate the slaves. You ought to give him a raise."

"Or at least a commendation," Greeley mused. "Next time, I shall be more inclined to believe Adam's tips."

"He wrote that he heard it from two people—" Gay was eager to get across the value of the head of their Washington office. Greeley was too inclined to dismiss what Adam Hill had learned.

"Neither is a totally reliable source of information," Greeley reminded him. "Hill reported that Senator Sumner told him privately that a proclamation was in the works, but Sumner's been saying that since the Fourth of July."

"But Count Gurowski is right in the State Department working for Seward," Gay pressed. The grumpy Polish exile was a keen observer and a fountain of information. Why was Greeley so chary of giving credit? "And Gurowski hates Seward, so when Gurowski tells our man in Washington that Seward and Weed are trying to stop Lincoln from issuing a proclamation of emancipation, why don't you believe him?"

"Count Gurowski is a solid anti-slavery man," Greeley acknowledged, "and has the proper assessment of Seward and Weed. I think now that he told our man Hill the truth. But I had to be sure. I could not risk the chance of Lincoln's changing his mind. That is why I went ahead with 'The Prayer of Twenty Millions.' "

Why was Greeley being defensive? The truth began to dawn on Sydney Gay. Horace Greeley had not been in any doubt a week ago about Lincoln's intention to issue a proclamation. Greeley had believed Adam Hill's letters. But instead of running a story about the impending news event, Greeley played the politician. He demanded in a thundering editorial that Lincoln do what Greeley knew was about to be done.

If that was true—Gay's logical mind moved ahead to the next manipulation—Lincoln and Greeley were engaged in a complex game to use each other. Greeley was running out in front of Lincoln's emancipation parade, but if Lincoln should change his mind about parading in that direction, Greeley would be in a position to pull him along.

"Let me see if I understand, sir, what's been going on," Gay said slowly. "Lincoln had this emancipation proclamation planned, subject to some colonization scheme in Chiriquí being in place, and presented it to the Cabinet in the middle of July. Seward and Weed stopped it for the time being—"

"But not for long," said Greeley benignly, rocking back in his chair, "maybe just until the next victory in the field, if there ever is one."

"Knowing that, sir, you went ahead with your editorial demanding he carry out the Confiscation Act."

"Go on."

"Then Lincoln, not knowing that you know about his secret proclamation, puts out this letter to you—pouring cold water on the idea of such a proclamation. Lincoln is still fighting strictly for Union, not for abolition—or so he says. Meanwhile, he has his abolition order in his pocket."

"You could say there was a certain duplicity on his part," Greeley observed mildly. "In political life, one grows accustomed to that."

"Then Lincoln sends word to you through Gilmore not to take his written reply seriously," Gay went on, wondering which man—his President or his boss—was the more duplicitous. "Lincoln wants you to know that no matter what he says now in reply to your editorial, he means to do what you called for, or even more."

"Is there anything in this interchange that troubles you, Sydney?"

"I'm not sure." Gay did not want to lose his job; Charles Dana had been removed for crossing the boss. What did trouble him was the way Mr. Greeley had used his advance information: not to tell the readers that the great abolition day was fast approaching, but to take a noisy position that would make it seem that he deserved the credit for the change in Lincoln's policy. Gay mentally backtracked. It was true that Greeley and his radicals led Lincoln on this issue, but in this specific instance the editor was juggling events to make certain that history would give him credit.

Gay avoided stating that aspersion on Greeley's motives, but plunged ahead on current plans. "What troubles me, I guess, is what is to happen now. Emancipation of the slaves is news. I mean, it could be a very big story. What if Bennett gets it and runs it in the *Herald*. What if Lincoln gives it to Raymond to run in the *Times*? I think it would be better for the *Tribune* to be first."

"I hold great store in being first, as you know." Greeley put on a stern look. He had difficulty glowering; his round, completely white face, silken hair and beard, and pale blue eyes made him appear more cherubic than managerial. "On news from the front, Sydney, I insist that we be first. Is George Smalley with General Pope, by the way? That may be the victory we need to push Lincoln into doing his duty."

Gay had heard that their most intrepid and well-bred correspondent, Smalley the oarsman, had been denied access to the area as a correspondent but had resourcefully, if fraudulently, signed on as an aide-de-camp to a general. Gay thought it better that Mr. Greeley not know of the breaking of the rules. "Smalley's there," was all he said. If the decisive battle of the war was shaping up near Manassas, scene of last year's debacle at Bull Run, the *Tribune* could not afford to be denied access by some misguided penchant for military secrecy.

"Good. On the military news, I want to be first. But on great events, Sydney, I am a patriot first and an editor second. We shall keep our word to this fellow Gilmore, or Kirke, or whatever name he goes by. We shall not write about the imminence of a proclamation, lest we raise a storm that would make it difficult for Mr. Lincoln to carry it out."

Gay nodded, but inwardly he shook his head. Mr. Greeley had in mind to run for office again, and his "Prayer" with its ultimate proclamation "answer" would be his platform. No matter that the *Tribune* served Lincoln's purposes, and that Lincoln's temporary answer was a sham, misleading the people; Mr. Greeley would make Lincoln serve his own purpose, even at the cost of concealing the news.

"Lincoln is growing, you know," Greeley added, as if to justify the minuet being danced. "When I first met him in '48, he was a Whig representative in Washington, not quite forty, a genial, cheerful, rather comely man, the only Whig from Illinois—not remarkable otherwise."

It struck Gay as odd to hear the gangling President described as "comely," but he did not interrupt. He had not known Lincoln was the only Whig in the Congress from Illinois, which must have made him a Henry Clay maverick pressing for compromise.

"He did not vote for the resolution looking to the abolition of slavery in the federal district," Greeley recalled, "but instead introduced a counter-resolution of his own, looking to abolition by vote of the people—that is, the whites of the district—which seemed to me like submitting to a vote of the inmates of a penitentiary a proposition to double the length of their imprisonment."

Greeley rose and donned his white duster over his white linen suit, preparatory to a walk around the newspaper offices. "Then, after his election, when I said to him, 'Mr. President, do you know that you will have to *fight* for the place in which you sit?' he answered pleasantly, in words which intimated his disbelief that any fighting would be needed. And thus the precious early days of the conflict against slavery were surrendered, while he clung to the delusion that forbearance, and patience, and moderation, and soft words were all that were needed."

"What changed him, do you think?"

"Bull Run. After the wanton rout of that black day," Greeley opined, "Mr. Lincoln accepted war as a stern necessity and stood ready to fight it out to the bitter end. Never before have I seen a man so constantly and visibly grow since then. The Lincoln of 1862 is plainly a larger, broader, better man than he was in sixty-one."

Sydney Gay knew that many editorialists explained away their mistaken early notions about people by observing how they had grown. He reserved judgment on Lincoln's growth; it might be that Mr. Greeley was shrinking.

CHAPTER 4

OUT OF THE SCRAPE

"A cabal, that's what it is," whispered Allan Pinkerton urgently. "A cabal here in Washington determined to undermine the Army of the Potomac, to defeat McClellan, and to plunge the nation into years of bloody war!"

His listener, Mathew Brady, stared at him from behind thick eyeglass lenses. He seemed to be waiting for more information. Brady would have made an excellent spy, Pinkerton judged; well placed, canny, dour.

"A great battle is about to be waged on the very site of the Bull Run disaster," Pinkerton confided, keeping his voice down, although Brady's studio was strangely empty, "and the cabal in Washington is already conspiring to produce a defeat and to blame it on General McClellan."

"What would be their motive in that?"

Pinkerton edged closer. He trusted Brady—although, of course, nobody was to be completely trusted. "They hate McClellan because they know he wants to end the war without killing every man, woman, and child in the South," he said. "The cabal wants a harsh, brutal, bloody war, the South a conquered province, run by themselves and the negroes."

"Weren't you a big abolitionist once yourself, Allan?" The photographer took off his glasses and wiped them with a large lens cloth. "There's a picture of John Brown I've been trying to lay my hands on."

Pinkerton knew that Brady knew that Pinkerton had all but supplied railroad tickets for John Brown and his three sons, and their band of eighteen negro supporters in their bloody raid on the arsenal at Harpers Ferry. The hot-eyed Brown thought he could arouse the blacks in Virginia to join in a great rebellion against their slave masters, but the slaves were too frightened and a detachment of U.S. marines under Colonel Robert Lee, of all people, captured Brown and his band and turned them over to the courts for trial and execution. The detective kicked himself for having boasted to Brady of his part in that grand but foolish exploit before the war. He had put it out of his mind and hoped it had escaped the attention of everyone else.

"That was a lifetime ago," he snapped. "I'm still for abolition, but Lincoln's way—over time. Let it die out by itself. The general understands that—and that's why the cabal is out to get him no matter the cost."

"And who is this cabal?"

"I am not at liberty to say." But surely Brady already knew, so he confided in the photographer: "General Halleck, of course, he's their cat's-paw. And several members of the Senate, that drunk Chandler especially, and Wade. But the masterminds are in the President's Cabinet. Unbeknownst to Lincoln."

"Stanton and Chase, you mean?"

Pinkerton winced at the unauthorized mention of the names, then probed for information. "What do you hear, Matt? Chase was in your gallery not a week ago—did he say anything about Pope's plans?"

"Not a cabalist sound out of him," the photographer replied. "All our Treasury Secretary talked about was the unexpected success of legal tender. And he apologized for not bringing his daughters. I wish I could get a picture of the older one, Kate. I could sell a lot of those."

Kate Chase was of no interest to Allan Pinkerton. If his friend wanted to be uncommunicative, the detective knew how to get the photographer's dander up. Leaning back, he said in a normal, nonconspiratorial voice, "Why don't you go into 'spirit' photographs? I hear there's real money in those."

Brady scowled. "You mean that woman from Boston, the damned charlatan."

"You sit for your picture, with nary another soul in the room," Pinkerton said, recounting what he had heard from Smalley of the *Tribune*. "You get a clear portrait of yourself, by ordinary process, but lo!—standing beside you on the plate is the white, shadowy form of somebody who looks like a lost loved one. That's the spirit, the ghost. If you get a spirit on your portrait, the lady photographer charges you double."

"And are people really paying for that?"

Pinkerton nodded, rubbing it in. "Might be a good business, Mathew, things look a mite quiet around here."

"It's a humbug," Brady said, his voice rising. "She's a fraud. I can produce that 'ghost' in a minute without any supernatural assistance."

"So—?"

"It debases the art." Brady, distracted and furious, began stumbling about the room. "Photography is not a trick or an entertainment. It's not even a business, God knows. It's a way of using art and chemistry to show history. I have to wheedle with Stanton and show him how it helps make military maps, and I have to turn out these damned *cartes de visite* to make ends meet, and I have to fight with my own assistants to stick together and to use this war to launch the great new art—"

"You're getting all worked up, Mathew." Pinkerton feared that the photographer, who had turned pale and was now leaning against a wall, might be stricken with a heart attack.

"Gardner is gone," Brady continued, "and his brother too, the ingrates. I paid for their tickets here from Glasgow. And Tim O'Sullivan, my best man at the front—I hate him, the blackguard, but nobody alive can operate a camera in the field like O'Sullivan. And three of the others gone, hardly anybody left."

Pinkerton watched the anger seep out of the man, and feared for his friend because the anger was the only thing holding him up.

"The President was in here not long ago," Brady said, his voice breaking, "and it was all I could do to—"

He stopped speaking and wept. Pinkerton did the only thing he could think of, which was to look away until the photographer was himself again.

"We're not sentimental, Allan," Brady said after a while. "You and I are practical men. But did you never have a dream? I dream of assembling all the faces of our time—for these are historic times—as has never been done in all of history. I dream of using this new science, this new art, to show the war in all its glory and horror. I want people to see that war is not the brass bands and parades, but the faces of the haunted men, and the bodies of the dead turning stiff in positions of fear or grace. But now—even now, as the dream is turning true—my operators are leaving, my manager is gone. And the edges of my field of vision are fraying—it's as if my lenses are closing down and it's always too dark to make a picture."

Pinkerton did not know what to say to a man whose livelihood and life's purpose depended on light, as the darkness closed in. He tried to remember the name of the great music composer who went deaf, but it did not come to him.

Impelled to share a genuine confidence, the detective began to speak of the way he felt at the trial of John Brown. "I shouldn't have been there, at the sentencing, but I couldn't stay away. There was something magnetic about the man, the sort of pull I suppose you feel with a madman or a saint. They said he was crazy, and maybe he was, sacrificing his life and his three sons and all, but John Brown was so sure he saw something the rest of the world was missing."

For the first time in two years—time spent repositioning himself sensibly to be able to do his bit in the war and get ahead in life—Pinkerton let himself relive the scene in the courtroom. John Brown, haggard face, burning eyes—what a Brady photograph that would have been—standing at the prisoner's bar, listening to the sentence of death, responding with words that ennobled the abolition movement. "I see a book kissed," Brown had said, "which I suppose to be the Bible, which teaches me that all things whatsoever I would that men should do to me, I should do even so to them . . . to remember them that are in bonds, as bound with them."

Pinkerton, remembering, thought of the line in the letter McClellan delivered to Lincoln at Harrison's Bar that urged restraint on abolition, and felt a twinge of shame. Colonel Key had shown him a draft of that letter and the ex-abolitionist Pinkerton had not objected. "I believe that to have interfered as I have done is not wrong, but right," he could hear John Brown telling the judge who condemned him to death. "Now, if it is deemed necessary to mingle my blood with the blood of my children and the blood of millions in this slave country whose rights are disregarded by wicked, cruel, and unjust enactments, I say, let it be done."

"God, Brady, what a moment that was. The beginning of all the blood."

"And not a camera in the room."

While Brady went over to the sink to wash his face, the detective took out a batch of telegraph dispatches he had taken from the War Department and began shuffling through them. In a few moments, Brady asked about them. Pinkerton spread the dispatches out in sequence on the table Brady used in his photographs.

"You can see here what the cabal is trying to do," he said to his distraught friend, fixing on the matter at hand to snap them both out of their weak moment. "Here are the dispatches from yesterday, the twenty-ninth." He assumed Brady could no longer read, so he read aloud: "From Halleck to McClellan: *general battle imminent . . . Franklin's corps should move out by forced marches.* And McClellan replies: *I am not responsible for the past and cannot be for the future, unless I receive authority to dispose of the available troops according to my judgment.* And then Halleck tells him to send all his troops to Pope in Virginia, and McClellan replies: *We are not yet in condition* to move. Here's Halleck's immediate reply: *There must be no further delay in moving Franklin's corps toward Manassas, ready or not ready.* Can you imagine that? Halleck saying *You should have acted more promptly.*"

"Sounds like Halleck is making a record for a congressional investigation in case Pope loses," Brady said.

"Exactly. And realizing that, McClellan sent this telegram to Lincoln this morning: *I am clear that one of two courses should be adopted: first, to concentrate all our available forces to open communication with Pope; second, to leave Pope to get out of his scrape, and at once use all our means to make the capital perfectly safe. No middle ground will now do. I ask for nothing, but will obey whatever orders you give.*"

Brady frowned. "Lincoln's reply to that?"

"Here: *I think your first alternative—to wit, 'to concentrate all our available forces to open communication with Pope'—is the right one. But I wish not to control. That I now leave to General Halleck, aided by your counsels.*"

"Your man McClellan made a mistake," said Brady. "He should never have said he would 'leave Pope to get out of his scrape.' Sounds like he would just as soon have him lose the battle."

"But that was just an alternative," Pinkerton countered, alarmed. "And the second one at that. This shows how McClellan is willing to do anything, even send in unprepared troops."

"If there is a cabal, as you say," said Brady with new authority, "then your man McClellan is falling into its trap. You've come from the telegraph office —does Pope say he's winning?"

"Yes. All this Halleck paperwork, which was probably written by Stanton, is to show that Pope's victory—accomplished with McClellan's troops at the crucial point—is all Pope's doing, with no thanks to Mac."

Brady was not so optimistic. "Lee has been racing up from Richmond to join Jackson to defeat Pope today. If McClellan's army is not on hand to help Pope, I'll bet we'll lose. And they'll then court-martial McClellan."

"They wouldn't dare. The army would revolt."

"I'm telling you, Chase wants to shoot McClellan. Line him up against a wall and shoot him. He said as much, and he's a serious man, Chase."

"I'd better get over to the Mansion," said Pinkerton. Brady's opinion troubled him profoundly. "My friend Hay, the private secretary, is an excellent source for me. He's not part of the cabal."

Pinkerton put on his derby hat, headed for the door, then turned. "Mathew, look, my boss is out of power now. Instead of taking him away from his army, they've taken his army away from him, bit by bit. But when the panic comes, and Pope shows he's no general, my man will be back on top. And that's the time I'll see who gets passes to photograph the battlefield. Gardner will never get within miles of the place. O'Sullivan's out too. You'll be the chief photographer of the war, I'll see to that."

Brady surprised him with his gruff response. "Never do anything to keep any of those ungrateful bastards away from the front. And take care of your own backside. Be sure you're not sitting out the war in jail for helping McClellan let Pope 'get out of his scrape' by himself."

Pinkerton jammed down his derby and made haste for Sixteenth Street to see his friend Hay.

CHAPTER 5

SENDING OFF THE SILVER

"My friend Hay tells me that Lincoln is not part of the cabal," George McClellan heard Pinkerton report, "but that such a sinister plot exists is beyond all question. Hay has even heard, and vouchsafed to me in complete confidence, that Stanton and Chase are prepared to suffer the loss of the capital rather than see you ever returned to command."

McClellan, pacing the veranda of his Alexandria, Virginia, headquarters, nodded glumly. He was located just across the Potomac from Washington but might as well have been a thousand miles from the center of power. He could hear, not far from his small camp, the sound of cannon. Major General George Brinton McClellan was a general without a command; Stanton and Halleck had broken his army into pieces, and systematically parceled it out to John Pope.

He judged the cannon to be Pope firing at Jackson's fast-moving rebel "foot cavalry," if all was going well; or it could be Longstreet's artillery in Lee's army blazing at McClellan's own brigades now serving under the command of an incompetent Union general.

The general without an army, pacing the veranda with an unlighted cigar in hand, felt he had trained Lee and his lieutenants. He had taught them in the Seven Days the folly of attacking entrenched positions and had shown them the value of massed artillery on heights. He had, in effect, perfected the generalship of his opponents. Only he could outfox them now. McClellan was sure that John Pope, with his patched-together command of soldiers and generals who did not know each other, had no idea of the character or caliber of the enemy leadership he was facing: Robert Lee, still audacious but no longer foolhardy, supported by Jackson, Longstreet, and Hill, all men who now knew the way Lee would fight, all trained as a team just as much by George McClellan as by Robert Lee.

"I have just telegraphed very plainly to the President and Halleck what I think ought to be done," the general told his loyal intelligence officer.

"They won't listen, you know. The cabal has Lincoln's ear."

"I expect merely a contemptuous silence," McClellan agreed in pain. "Two of my corps will either save Pope or be sacrificed for the country." He did not add that he had also alerted Democratic friends in New York of the military-political malfeasance of the Republican leadership.

"There's a scare spreading in Washington," said Pinkerton, his hat still on. Wearing his derby at all times, even indoors, was an odd habit of the detective's; McClellan indulged him the idiosyncrasy. "A rumor got out that Lee was advancing on the Chain Bridge with one hundred and fifty thousand men. What a stampede! Chase ordered the government bullion placed on ships for escape to New York. The battle is shaping up near Manassas, and some people fear a second Bull Run."

"Are Lee's forces here?"

"I think so. What's scaring Halleck is that the secesh might have slipped in between Pope and the capital."

McClellan feared for his men on their way to support Pope. Lee had gambled intelligently in splitting his army, sending Stonewall Jackson up to strike Pope near Washington while the main Confederate force had remained to defend against McClellan near Richmond. Lee must have known that Lincoln would pull the Union forces off the Peninsula, freeing the main rebel army to move north.

If Pope had attacked Jackson last week, with the rest of Lee's army still near Richmond, the Union general would have crushed the rebels; or if McClellan had been permitted to remain on the Peninsula to threaten Richmond, Lee would never have been able to move north. But the imbeciles in Washington had thought otherwise, and now Lee and Jackson had combined to engage the Union forces under a rash commander like Pope, who probably did not know how dangerous his predicament was.

"Did you go to the telegraph office in the War Department? What news from Pope? Are my corps in place?"

"Pope seems to be out of communication with Washington," Pinkerton reported. "Fitz-John Porter is still trying to find him, to join forces. Halleck is screaming at him to get there in time for the battle, but Porter doesn't know exactly where Pope is."

"I never felt worse in my life," the general said, lighting his cigar, taking a few puffs, then stubbing it out on the porch railing in an expression of nervous frustration that he rarely exhibited to even his closest confidants. "They have taken all my troops from me. You see what's outside? A camp guard, a few orderlies. I've sent every man I have to save Pope. I feel like a fool here, sucking my thumbs and doing nothing that couldn't be done better by a junior officer."

"The men of the Army of the Potomac must feel abandoned," Pinkerton said.

McClellan did not want to hear that. He was torn. It was one thing to see Pope discredited, and it was valuable in the long run to show Lincoln that he could not trust Stanton and the cabal, but if such a necessary lesson meant the sacrifice of thousands of lives of men who trusted and loved him—that was hard to bear. That was why he had at first taken his time in the movement north, then changed his mind and sent orders to Porter to hurry to Pope, then held back Franklin's ten thousand men lest nobody be on hand to defend Washington.

Because he was of two minds, McClellan had to act ambiguously. He knew that seemed indecisive, never a good state for a commander of men, but he was being pulled in four directions: two ways by short-range obedience to orders and long-range duty to country, and two other ways between affection for his troops and love of his countrymen. Now that the battle was starting, however, he leaned toward selflessness, obedience, protection of his men; he wanted Pope to be supported even at the risk of helping him win. The best would be if he could share the sacrifices of his men and yet not be responsible for the command.

"I sent a telegraph an hour ago asking Halleck permission to be with my troops," he told Pinkerton. "Just to be on the scene with my men. They will fight none the worse for my being with them. Not to be in command—just to share their fate on the field of battle." That offer to brave the dangers of combat, sincerely made, salved his conscience at the risk to which he put the Union forces to prove the necessity of his return to ultimate command. "Do you know the reply? Here—Halleck says he would have to consult the President first!"

"Obviously General Pope doesn't want your help," said Pinkerton bitterly.

"I do not regard Washington as safe against the rebels. What does Burnside report?" Old Burn, a loyal friend, was a good brigade commander but was not to be trusted with great numbers of troops. Fortunately, he knew his limitations, and was truthful in his reports.

"Nothing from Burnside at the telegraph office," Pinkerton told him. "Pope reports a glorious victory, driving the enemy all day, expects to finish Jackson off tomorrow in detail. Says he has the rebel forces split."

"He does, does he?" McClellan's emotions collided. The thought of that idiot's triumph was almost as hard to swallow as the idea of his own troops' defeat. He guessed that Pope was being sucked into a trap by Lee, which was the reason for the Union commander's optimistic dispatches. The Virginian would take terrible chances, chances that McClellan would never take, and at Malvern Hill Lee had been made to pay dearly for one of his gambles. But now Lee knew he was no longer facing the prudent and experienced McClellan, and could count on the overconfidence of the unblooded Pope.

"I am going into Washington," McClellan said. That was against orders, which required special permission for such a movement from the War Department. He would see Lincoln if possible, Halleck if need be. He would not deign to speak with the cabal's leaders, Stanton and Chase, who were apparently ready to surrender the capital rather than entrust its defense to the only general in the army capable of rallying the Union troops and deploying them in a way to block Lee.

And while he was at it, McClellan reminded himself, he would drop into his own house, pack up the silver with Nellie, and send it off for safekeeping. If Chase could so protect the nation's treasures, and had that little confidence in Pope, then the McClellan family would do the same.

"I cannot express to you the pain and mortification," McClellan told Halleck—the President was not available to him—"of listening to the sound of firing on my men." McClellan contained his anger, since Halleck was merely the clerk, carrying out the orders of the cabal. "I respectfully ask that I be permitted to go to the scene of battle."

Halleck shook his head. "Pope is in command."

"Even if I cannot be permitted to command my own army, I simply ask to share their fate on the field of battle."

The General-in-Chief scratched his elbows and glowered. "You retain command of everything in this vicinity not belonging to Pope's army in the field."

"That's fewer than a hundred men!" McClellan shouted, then controlled himself again. "I am ready to afford you any assistance in my power, but my position is undefined. I have no right to give anybody orders. Believe me, in the field, I could be helpful."

Halleck pointed to a stack of telegraph cables on his desk. "Pope reports that he has Lee and Jackson split twenty miles apart, and he has seventy-five thousand Federal troops between them ready to strike. Your advice is welcome, General, but your presence on the field is not needed."

McClellan looked over the optimistic, bombastic cables from Pope and his heart sank. They were reports from a general out of touch with reality.

"I see the cavalry I sent—not prepared for battle—was captured." With a heavy heart, he added, "I have just come from Alexandria. The roads were filled with Union wagons and stragglers. I spoke to one of our sergeants, a man I know and trust. He says we were badly beaten yesterday, and that Pope's right is completely exposed."

Halleck's face sagged. McClellan knew he had brought "Old Brains" information direct from the field that he could not deny and had undoubtedly suspected might be true. That was why Halleck had been so panicky about getting Fitz-John Porter's men into line immediately. McClellan, reading Pope's cables, was able to discern the outlines of Lee's bold plan.

"To speak frankly," he told the general-in-chief, flirting with insult, "there appears to be a total absence of brains, and I fear the total destruction of the army." He walked to Halleck's wall map. "By this time, Lee will have occupied Fairfax Court House. Pope's forces will be cut off entirely unless he falls back tonight." He pointed out the likelihood of disaster, which any good general, even the deskbound Halleck, could see.

"I am fully aware of the gravity of the crisis," said Halleck, who had moments before been as certain of Pope's impending triumph, "and have been for weeks. That's why I kept urging you to get your men up here before Lee could reinforce Jackson."

He was covering up his mistakes, an old army game, but McClellan was not to be outmaneuvered. "I lost no time in moving the Army of the Potomac from the Peninsula to Pope's support," McClellan replied coolly.

"Not so! You dawdled in camp for more than ten days."

"After my arrival at Alexandria, I left nothing in my power undone," said McClellan, secure in the knowledge of his own difficulties on the scene, "to forward supplies and reinforcements to General Pope. I sent my personal escort out to guard his railway lines, leaving myself only with invalids and the members of the band."

He could see Halleck weakening in the battle of the cables, and pressed his advantage: "The impending disaster is not my fault. It is his fault and yours. And the fault of the men who would prefer to lose the capital than see me in command."

Halleck was staring at the map, no longer listening. Evidently even he could see, finally, the rebel strategy. "The enemy is retreating toward the mountains," Pope had overconfidently telegraphed. But now Halleck could see that the enemy, under Jackson, was obviously drawing the Union forces into a position where they could be slaughtered by the artillery of Lee's other commander, James Longstreet.

"What can we do?" he asked McClellan, a plea in his voice.

Not much to avert defeat; something to avert disaster and the surrender of the capital. McClellan did not hesitate: "Bring Burnside down from here and have him watch Pope's right. Tell Pope to fall back—tonight, if possible, and not a moment to be lost."

"I'll order Burnside up right away. But look"—Halleck showed a cable—
"I can't order a retreat, not on the basis of this, where Pope says he's all
right."

"He is not all right, he is losing not just a battle but the whole war. You
don't believe me?" McClellan put a blunt challenge to Halleck: "Go to the
front yourself, it's an hour's ride from here. See the true condition of affairs."

"Impossible. I'm too occupied with office duty, with keeping the President
informed—"

"What duty is more important than for the General-in-Chief to know the
condition of the chief army in the country? Your duty, Halleck, is to go out
and see for yourself how matters stand, and, if necessary, assume command in
person."

The man did not reply to this insult to his personal courage but grimly held
to the overriding importance of his presence in his office.

"At least send your chief of staff." McClellan, his concern increasing for
his men, pressed the point: "We could lose the war."

Halleck's chief of staff, a pale officer standing against the wall of the office,
shook his head; he did not want to go. McClellan, determined that the war
not be lost for lack of a reliable intelligence report putting the lie to Pope's
self-delusive reports, pointed next to Halleck's adjutant general. That soldier,
at least, saw his duty, and assented immediately.

"Don't just see Pope," McClellan told the man, assuming control if not
command from the hapless Halleck. "See his general officers, including Fitz-
John Porter, who should be there now. Talk to some of the sergeants in the
field, and anybody captured from Jackson's headquarters. Talk to all of them
privately, but don't waste time—get back tonight, and demand to see the
President. Tell Lincoln the truth, whatever it is. He needs to know."

The adjutant general—a man named Kelton, whom McClellan now remembered from West Point—did not even look to Halleck for confirmation
but whipped around and ran out.

McClellan was certain of his military judgments, confident of having them
confirmed by an independent observer, but was simultaneously filled with
dread. Not at the loss of the battle, or the capital, or even the war; not one of
those events need be a great tragedy. What McClellan dreaded was Pope's
foolish bravery, which might cause him to force his men to stay and fight
when he should sensibly fall back—or worse, fight to the bloodstained finish
when he should surrender. The tragedy would be the loss of the hundred
thousand men who were the cream of the North.

The Union's life was on the knife's edge. McClellan knew that the radical
cabal would blame him for Pope's defeat, but how much of the looming
disaster, he asked himself, was really his fault in not rushing north? Despite
the blame to come from men desperate to deny responsibility for their terrible
strategic blunder, would a Union in trouble turn to the man so often publicly
despised as "the procrastinator, the coward, the traitor"?

So much now depended on Lincoln. McClellan hated to admit it, but all his
hopes hinged on the possibility that the President could resist the drag of the
cabal and could defeat their plan to remove the Army of the Potomac from
the only man the troops trusted. He could not appeal to Lincoln directly; that
relationship had died at Harrison's Landing. Now Lincoln would have to act

alone, without advice, to save the army and the Union, at the cost of admitting a vast mistake. The young general did not know if the President was up to that.

CHAPTER 6

John Hay's Diary
September 1 and 2, 1862

September 1

Washington is not, at present, an alluring village. Everybody is out of town, and nobody cares for anybody that is here.

Yesterday I received a visit from Pinkerton, that polisher of McClellan's apples, who talks in a hushed voice as if to conceal something important from unseen listeners. He keeps referring to me as "my friend Hay." He never comes in when the President is around, only when he can waylay me and pump me for information to reassure his cowardly commander. This time, the man in the dirty derby hat imparted to me—in the strictest confidence, of course—news of a "cabal" to do in his idol. I refrained from telling him that if such existed, I would happily join it.

This morning, Sunday, I rode out to the country and turned in at the Soldiers' Home in Silver Spring, where the Tycoon and Hellcat are avoiding the heat. The Prsdt's horse was standing by the door, and in a moment the Prsdt appeared and we rode into town together. On the way in to the telegraph office, we talked about the state of things by Bull Run and Pope's prospect.

"General Halleck says the greatest battle of the century is now being fought," he said. "Seemed confident."

About time we had some good military news; Pope is a breath of fresh air after the Little Napoleon. (There is no fresh air in Washington. The stale and humid atmosphere has been sicklied o'er with the acrid smell of gunpowder; we could hear the cannon from where we were in Silver Spring.)

Here is what the Prsdt thinks about McClellan: "It really seems to me that McClellan wanted Pope defeated." Can you imagine? That's the insolence of epaulets run amok, but it was not for me to suggest a court-martial for treason, since the Secretary of War was busy drawing up the details for one.

"There's a dispatch to me from McClellan," the Tycoon went on, riding along, not angry, feeling pretty good about the news from the war front, "in which he proposed, as one plan of action, to 'leave Pope to get out of his own scrape, and devote ourselves to securing Washington.' That's really something."

"Don't forget his dreadful cowardice in the matter of Chain Bridge," I added, not to be outdone in McClellanophobia. "He ordered it blown up last night, but Halleck countermanded the order. Little Mac is the chief alarmist and grand marplot of the army."

The Prsdt had a topper: "George recalled Franklin's corps, and then when they had been sent ahead by Halleck's order, begged permission to recall them again. He only desisted when Halleck told him to push them ahead until they whipped something or got whipped themselves.''

I asked, "What do you suppose is wrong with Little Mac?"

The Prsdt made a circling motion with his finger near his ear; he seems to think McClellan a little crazy. He's being charitable, perhaps because of the demonstrated wisdom of his military policy; let us not forget that Lincoln argued all along against McNapoleon's cherished Peninsula campaign, and the Prsdt will be directly responsible for the coming triumph at Manassas.

When we reached the telegraph office, McClellan was there, trying to look gloomy about the war picture even in the face of the glowing dispatches coming in from Pope. The dread Stonewall Jackson, say the cables, is in full retreat and Pope is out looking for him to administer the coup de grâce.

Halleck was at the Telegraph office too, listening to McClellan explain away his tardiness in assisting in the victory and begging for a few more troops to be assigned to him for appearances' sake.

"We have reason to believe the Army of the Potomac has not been supporting General Pope properly," the Prsdt said to the new meek Mac, in a matter-of-fact way. "I have always been a friend of yours, George. Use your influence to correct matters."

Little Mac promptly wrote out a message to Fitz-John Porter asking him to make as his "last request" of the soldiers he led that they extend to General Pope the same support they always gave McClellan. Since the man had shown himself to be properly humbled, Halleck wrote out an order assigning the dribs and drabs of soldiers hanging around the city to McClellan's "command." But Mac's day is over; the republic is better off without him.

The Prsdt took me along to dinner at Mars's house, with young Mrs. Stanton as white and cold and motionless as marble, whose rare smiles seemed to pain her. Stanton was loud and unqualifiedly severe about the McC business.

"After this battle," Stanton boomed, "there should be one court-martial. Nothing but foul play could lose us this battle—it all rests with McClellan and that coterie around him. He did all he could to undermine Pope, who is the only real general the Union has had so far." The Prsdt agreed but, I know, is disinclined to go so far as a court-martial, especially after a victory. Little Mac may have saved what is left of his reputation by sending this afternoon's "last request" to his friends in the field.

And so, as Pepys wrote in his diary, to bed. Everything seems to be going well and hilarious for a change. I lay my head on the pillow expecting glad tidings at sunrise.

September 2

Forget all that about glad tidings. The dispatches from Pope turned out to be at best self-delusions.

Halleck, exercising excellent judgment on the need for firsthand information, sent his adjutant general to the front to check up on Pope, and the man came back with the accurate and tragic news. And Stod's brother Henry came racing in from the front, having commandeered a mule, to report personally to the Chief Magistrate of the nation news that some of the generals under Pope wanted the Prsdt to know—news that he might not get from Pope's rosy dispatches.

"Well, John, we are whipped again, I am afraid."

Lincoln had that indescribable look of sadness on his face. He came in my room as I was dressing and sat down on the bed. "The enemy reinforced on Pope and drove back his left wing, and he has retired to Centreville, where he says he will be able to hold his men. I don't like that expression. I don't like to hear him admit that his men need 'holding.' "

That, of course, was a veiled reference to McClellan and the hold he had on many of those same men. Our troops were bolting under Pope; the same men might stand and fight under McClellan. The President was in a particularly defiant tone of mind, despite his discouragement. "We must hurt this enemy before it gets away," he said, hammering his big hand on his knee.

"If we don't succeed in this battle," I said to calm him, "there will be others."

"No, Mr. Hay, we must whip these people now. Pope must fight them. If they are too strong for him, he can gradually retire to these fortifications around Washington."

"And if they don't hold?"

"If we are really whipped," he said, and changed his tense as his defiance collapsed, "if we are really to be whipped—we may as well stop fighting."

I had no cheery retort to that. The thought occurred to me, really for the first time, that the Confederacy could possibly win the war. Or at least occupy Washington, be recognized by England and France, and *then* win the war. Or then offer to make peace, with secession a fact. We would then be two nations, the Disunited States, with the North expanding west and north (maybe Robert Walker was right in his plan to annex Canada) and the South moving into Mexico and Central America. Two great nations. Would the Confederacy and What's-Left-of-the-Union eventually become allies? The whole idea is too staggering, and yet if Robert Lee routs Pope—it's a good thing the South is not thinking of conquest.

"Come," said the Tycoon. "Time to eat crow."

We rode over to McClellan's house, accompanied by a sheepish Halleck whose hands appeared to have attached themselves permanently to his elbows. Six months ago, after an insolent rebuff, the President stopped calling on the Young Napoleon at home and summoned him to the White House for meetings. Here we are, knocking on the general's door again.

McClellan was having breakfast with his wife and his aides, Colonel Key and Lieutenant Custer, all the best silver gleaming on the table as if freshly polished for the occasion, and graciously invited us to join them. Nellie McClellan, my idea of an attractive matron, moved fast to set a few places. Lincoln asked for coffee because he doesn't eat much breakfast, and came to the point.

"Colonel Kelton, Halleck's adjutant general, has been to the front," the commander in chief informed McClellan. "The condition of affairs is even worse than you had represented to General Halleck yesterday." Lincoln looked to Halleck, who looked miserable but took the cue.

"Kelton says there are thirty thousand Union stragglers on the roads," Halleck said with a sigh, "and that the army was entirely defeated and falling back on Washington in confusion. It is Bull Run all over again. We are worse off than we were one year ago."

McClellan said nothing and looked at the Prsdt. Lincoln kept his eyes on Halleck. That unhappy general said, "I regard Washington as lost. Chase has the money on ships; Stanton has all the ammunition in the city ready to send to New York."

Nothing was said for a few moments. General McClellan ate his eggs. Key and Custer and Halleck and I contemplated our plates. I wished I had a head of hair like Custer's.

"I would, under the circumstances," the Prsdt said, "consider it a great favor to me if you would resume the command, George. Do the best that can be done."

Give him credit, McClellan did not dicker for conditions or titles. Without hesitation, he said, "I accept the command. And I will save this city—I will stake my life on that."

"That's impossible at this stage," Halleck said. "We do not expect miracles. But perhaps you will be able to make a defense that will allow most of the troops to escape."

"I will save the city," McClellan repeated matter-of-factly, in a tone of voice that you would use for "I will have some more eggs."

Lincoln did not subscribe to Halleck's pessimism, but he did not contradict him, either. "You are now in command of this city, General McClellan. Do your best. Your troops are those who fall back on Washington from the front. Collect the stragglers, place the works in a proper state, and go out and take command of the army when it approaches the works—and I understand they are approaching fast. I commit everything to your capable hands."

He searched for some statement that would tell McClellan that the general had become indispensable, without demeaning his own office. "I am deeply grateful that you are here at this moment in the life of the Union."

I was half-expecting some talk about dictatorship, but McClellan did not even demand Halleck's General-in-Chief job. He was all business.

"I understand Stanton ordered a war steamer to the naval base," he said crisp as bacon, "with steam up, to take you and the Cabinet to New York. I would make a point of telling Admiral Dahlgren that you do not intend to make use of it, and let that word get around." Lincoln nodded yes. "The contents of the arsenal, I understand, are now being put on board ship for New York, in accordance with orders of the Secretary of War. Please countermand that order immediately."

"It will be done," said the Prsdt. I think Lincoln was heartened, not merely by McClellan's readiness to take over without conditions, but by the general's evident confidence that he could defend Washington despite the willingness of Stanton and the rest to abandon it.

Nobody can say I am a McClellan enthusiast, but here was a classic case of not being able to beat somebody with nobody. Pope obviously is a nobody on a grand scale, foisted on the Administration by the radicals, Chase his particular champion. McClellan, though not a fighter, could at least turn others into fighters. He may not know the command for "attack," but he is the past master at defense.

"I will proceed immediately to the front," McClellan said, tossing his linen napkin on the table and dismissing us. Custer bolted out to get the horses. Nellie McClellan kissed her husband and said something about not packing the silver.

Lincoln, Halleck, and I went outside. Standing in the mud from the previous night's rain, Halleck told Lincoln that it would cause an awful scene if McClellan went to the front and summarily superseded Pope; Stanton, in particular, would take that as a personal insult. Lincoln reluctantly went along, and sent Halleck back in the house to tell McClellan that he was in command only of the troops returning to Washington, and only for the capital's defenses. That alone would rouse the radicals to great heights of fury, without adding insult to injury by putting McClellan back in charge of the whole Army of the Potomac. Halleck hemmed and hawed, wishing Lincoln would tell Little Mac himself that the command was limited to stragglers, but Lincoln knew what he hired Halleck for, and sent him on the bureaucratic errand. Certainly Halleck was not good for strategy or judgment; how could any judge of military talent let himself be talked into believing in Pope?

Lincoln consulted nobody in the Cabinet in choosing McClellan as savior. He knows that it might cause a mutiny, especially among those who have not cultivated a taste for humble pie. But he has to face one crisis at a time.

CHAPTER 7

A HALTER AROUND HIS NECK

Pinkerton could not find a horse of his own. He sat behind Armstrong Custer, holding the newly promoted captain round the slim waist, making a face at the strong smell of cinnamon in Captain Custer's whipping blond locks. They followed McClellan and Colonel Key across Chain Bridge to Virginia and toward the sound of the cannon. The four men on three horses came to a halt at Upton's Hill, the most advanced of the works protecting the capital.

"This is as far as I have authority to go," said the general, restrained by Halleck's insulting curtailment of Lincoln's orders.

Pinkerton wished he could have brought Brady and his Whatizzit Wagon along; either they were all going to get killed gloriously in the rebel attack on Washington or McClellan would accomplish a miracle deserving of historic record. The only trouble was that Little Mac was not in command of the troops now under fire, his was only the army of stragglers, semi-deserters, and others in retreat or pretending to be looking for their units.

The detective could see the remains of a regiment of defeated and dispirited infantry trudging back from the front. Most of the men had no guns, many were supporting wounded comrades. This ragtag assemblage was followed by part of a cavalry regiment surrounding Generals Pope and McDowell. The horses drew up and stopped at McClellan's post.

The rotund McDowell, who knew McClellan—and had wanted to reinforce Little Mac on the Peninsula—introduced Pope to him. The former

"Hero of the West" was plainly a beaten man, angry and rattled and despairing, no longer the willing issuer of Stanton-written statements or the scourge of rebel guerrillas. It occurred to Pinkerton that now his headquarters was truly in his saddle.

"What is the disposition of your army?" McClellan formally asked Pope.

"The straggling is awful in your regiments from the Peninsula," Pope half-replied. "Last to arrive, first to break."

McClellan held his big black horse stationary; Pope's horse moved his hooves about in the mud. "You are coming from the sound of gunfire," Mac said coldly. "What's going on there?"

Pope looked over his shoulder as if the matter no longer concerned him. "Probably an attack on our rear guard over that way. Sumner's commanding. Kearny and Stevens are dead."

"Is the enemy in close pursuit?"

"Probably."

"And you are leaving the scene." That was less a question than an accusation.

"Yes. Unless something can be done to restore tone to this army, it will melt away before you know it." That was not a task Pope had in mind for himself, obviously. Pinkerton assumed that the beaten general now only wanted a dry bed and a sympathetic Joint Committee on the Conduct of the War.

Pope asked McClellan: "Do you have any objection to our proceeding to Washington?" Pope's request for such permission could be construed as a transfer of field command. Pinkerton sensed it meant that McClellan could take over not only the loose change in the rear, but the leaderless army in front of him.

"You might do that if you want," McClellan said, reining his horse past them. "I'm going to the firing."

That brief meeting took place near Munson's Hill, which Pinkerton remembered uneasily as the place where he had been fooled by the rebel "Quaker guns"—logs—the preceding winter. The commander of a detachment of infantry accompanying Pope had a familiar face; Pinkerton recognized John Hatch, an old McClellan friend who had been stripped of his cavalry command by Pope the month before. Hatch gave a high sign to Pinkerton, who poked Custer on the front of the horse to get him to signal to McClellan to stop a moment. The detective could tell that some delicious humiliation was at hand.

With the retreating Pope and McDowell still within hearing distance, Hatch raced down the line of his infantry column yelling, "Boys, McClellan is in command of the army again! Three cheers!"

The effect of the commander's unexpected return crackled through the lines of defeated men. Caps sailed into the air, followed by knapsacks, as men who had been trudging behind a beaten general, away from glory and toward disgrace, took the news of Little Mac's reappearance as a sign of miraculous deliverance. As each platoon shouted, clapping each other on the back and joyfully prancing around, the next down the line picked up the message and the enthusiasm.

General John Pope

Pope and his small contingent, shaking their heads bitterly, rode back toward the Capitol, the half-finished dome of which could be seen from atop Munson's Hill. McClellan, wearing a yellow sash and riding as expertly as any man in the U.S. Army, picked his way among the troops, saluting, nodding, taking spirit from the men and infusing them with his confidence. At his signal, Hatch organized the troops to change direction.

Pinkerton could hardly contain his delight at this turn of Fortune's wheel. By nightfall of September 2, the shout of "Little Mac is back!" had traveled through all the Union lines. The spontaneous joy of the soldiers of the Army of the Potomac—certain their chief had been unjustly brushed aside—infected the others assigned to Pope's army, who were eager for a fresh leader. These men, who had never served in the Army of the Potomac, had heard and read that McClellan might not be a great winner, but he was surely no loser; every one of the Union defeats had taken place under other generals. The McClellan veterans assured them that their leader now would not march them around in circles or send them vainly into a hail of fire, as Pope and amateur commanders had. The Young Napoleon cared for his army; the troops knew it and cared for him.

The second retreat from Bull Run did not turn into a rout. On the contrary, with McClellan improvising intelligently and Lee's lines stretched, the

Union units hurt the advancing enemy in dozens of skirmishes. No counterattack could be mounted, but Jackson's advance was slowed and then stopped. From a few rebel prisoners, Pinkerton soon ascertained that General Lee, with his fearsome lieutenants Jackson and Longstreet, did not intend to attack the Federal capital with an assault across the Potomac the next day.

"Armstrong, inform the President that the troops are in position to repulse an attack," McClellan told Custer. "Tell him again to unload the money and the ammunition, and make sure every rebel spy in the capital knows it. Washington is safe."

Pinkerton slipped off Custer's horse and scurried from sector to sector to get a line on the Confederate order of battle. He reported to McClellan one worrisome fact: Lee had moved some of his forces north and was preparing to cross the Potomac into Maryland. The detective did not know if this meant the rebels intended to swing down and attack the city by land, or to bypass Washington and head toward Baltimore or north to Philadelphia. With both possibilities in mind, McClellan promptly ordered the Union forces he could muster to the Maryland side of the river above Washington, sending another messenger back to inform the War Department.

Captain Custer, riding hard from Washington to get back to the scene of battle, brought a message from General Halleck: "He wants to know which of our generals is in command of those troops going into Maryland, sir. Says that your authority is limited to the defenses of the city and that no decision has been made as to the commander of the active army in the field."

Pinkerton swore. Typical damned military-clerk Halleck, harassing the man actually saving the Union with pretenses of concern about usurpation of military power.

"Say I'll take over the defense in person," said the general, "if the enemy attacks in Maryland." McClellan was following Halleck's lead in playing military politics, Pinkerton knew, making it sound as if the deployment of the army in the field, following Lee northward, was still within his orders to defend the capital. He carefully datelined his orders "Headquarters, Washington"; Lincoln had not yet empowered him to issue an order from "Headquarters, Army of the Potomac." He was not authorized to attack, only to defend.

"They're preparing the charge for a court-martial," Pinkerton warned.

"I know that," McClellan said. "If I lose, they'll try me for exceeding my authority. I'm expected to operate with a halter around my neck. On the other hand"—he grinned—"if I lose, who will there be in Washington to try me?"

Pinkerton took off his derby, mopped the sweat off his head, and returned the hat to its position. "They're using you. The cabal is still out to get you, now more than ever. Frankly, I'm surprised Lincoln has let you assume this much authority. He must be desperate."

"He is." McClellan was curiously detached, not in the least vindictive. Pinkerton wondered at the change; had Lincoln affected him in some way the other morning at breakfast, by being so humble and fearful? Or did McClellan feel touched by some destiny that sustained him in the absence of any duly appointed authority? Or was he simply happy to be busy and with his men again? "The President might even understand Lee's plan."

"Ah, Lee's plan," said Pinkerton knowledgeably. What plan?

"General Lee and I know each other well," the general observed. "The reason I could confidently guarantee that Washington was safe last night was not due only to our defenses. It is because Lee sees a chance to win the war with a single blow."

Pinkerton nodded as if understanding.

"If Lee were able to take Washington now," the general explained, "the Union Government would pack up and move north and continue the war. But if he invades the North, gets an uprising in Maryland to support him, moves into Pennsylvania—that would break the Union back."

Pinkerton nodded, remembering the secesh mob in Baltimore. The approach of Lee's army would panic New York and cause a demand for immediate peace. "And our plan?"

"To move up River Road in Maryland," said McClellan matter-of-factly, "to stay with Lee until he is far from any source of support, and then to deliver the fatal blow."

"Of course," said Pinkerton, adding, "even though he outnumbers us."

"This army is not ready to move," the general said, as he had said so often when Halleck was haranguing him to get his men out of the Peninsula in time to support the unsupportable Pope. Then he said something that surprised his intelligence chief: "But we have no alternative, and so we will move."

"I'm more concerned about an ambush in Washington," said Pinkerton. Did his commander have any idea of the intensity of feeling his return to command—especially his assumption of wider command—would have on the men around the President? The cheers of the men in the field had heartened him immeasurably, and the confidence grudgingly placed in him by Lincoln must have buoyed his self-esteem, but the detective noticed a difference in Little Mac now: more serious, less exuberant, a little older.

McClellan nodded, acknowledging the warning of political backstabbing but curiously untroubled by it. "Lincoln will turn on me at the first opportunity. But until that moment comes, he needs me as much as I need him."

CHAPTER 8

CABINET COUP

Although Attorney General Edward Bates, at sixty-eight, was the oldest member of the Cabinet, it was Navy Secretary Gideon Welles who gave the impression of being the dean of Lincoln's advisers. With his great white beard —which, with the naval assignment, gave rise to the sobriquet "Neptune"— Welles cultivated the attitude of maturity. Unlike the others, he felt closely drawn to Lincoln as a man; Welles's wife was one of Mary Todd Lincoln's few friends in Washington.

Welles thought of Mary Lincoln as a tortured woman, unable even to wear black in memory of a dead brother lost in the rebel cause. On top of that, she was unwilling to let her oldest son serve in the army, thereby causing anguish for her boy and political embarrassment for her husband. Perhaps a naval commission for Robert, on some safe patrol—no, Welles shook his head, that would create controversy and bring discredit on the senior service.

His thoughts about the President's family were interrupted by the unexpected arrival of Salmon Chase. The Treasury Secretary, usually forthright and of moralistic bearing, today had the demeanor of a conspirator. He closed the door behind him and took a sheet of paper out of his pocket.

"Something has to be done immediately about treason in high places," said Chase.

Welles blinked; Chase was not usually given to dramatics.

"George McClellan has been deliberately spreading false rumors that twenty thousand stragglers from Pope's army are clogging the roads," the Treasury Secretary informed him. "As you know, that is wholly untrue—Pope is victorious, despite all that the Little Napoleon has done to deny him help. But McClellan is spreading alarm, causing military and financial panic."

"McClellan's movement north has certainly been dilatory," Welles allowed. He was unprepared to credit or refute McClellan's information about Pope.

"I have here a protest directed to the President," the agitated Chase said. He began to read: " 'The undersigned, as your constitutional advisers, recommend the immediate removal of George B. McClellan from any command in the armies of the United States.' "

Welles, startled by Chase's presumption, said nothing.

" 'By recent disobedience of superior orders and inactivity,' " Chase read on, his voice gaining resonance as he read, " 'he has twice imperiled the army commanded by General Pope. We are unwilling to be accessory to the destruction of our armies, and the overthrow of the government, which we believe must be the inevitable consequence of George B. McClellan being continued in command.' "

Chase laid the paper on the desk in front of Welles; the startling document was in Stanton's handwriting, a backhand scrawl familiar to the Navy Secretary, over the signatures of Stanton and Chase, followed by their official titles.

"Bates and Caleb Smith have told us they will sign too," said Chase. "Seward would, as well, but he is up in New York on some recruiting matter."

Welles gave an understanding grunt. Trust Seward to avoid a situation like this, and with a patriotic excuse for his absence. The Navy Secretary was fully aware that he beheld a document unparalleled in American history: a threat by the Cabinet, or at least its leading members, addressed to the President, to dismiss the commanding general or to suffer the mass resignation of the department heads. Welles, who held no brief for McClellan, was astonished at the audacity—no, it was worse, the outright insubordination—of Stanton and Chase. And of Smith and Bates, less audacious, who obviously needed one more Cabinet signature to bring them along.

"I am not prepared to sign this," Welles said firmly. "First of all, we are not his 'constitutional advisers.' The Constitution says nothing about the Cabinet. The President can ignore our advice with no offense to the Constitution."

Chase waved that aside as nit-picking. "The moment is urgent. McClellan deserves to be court-martialed and shot."

"I do not choose to denounce McClellan as a traitor, as you declare in this paper," Welles told him, surprised at Chase's sudden conversion to Stantonian summary judgment. Still, he believed the general deserved censure for his delay in coming to the defense of Washington—all the more so if, as Chase reported him to be saying, Pope was in great difficulty. Perhaps the same disciplinary end could be accomplished by more respectful means. "But I would say—and perhaps it is my duty to say—in a Cabinet meeting that his removal from command was demanded by public sentiment and the best interests of the country."

"Not enough," Chase pressed. "The time has come for the Cabinet to act with promptitude, together, forcefully, in a way the President cannot ignore. Either the Government or McClellan must go down."

"That's an ultimatum." How would Lincoln react to this stab in the back? Either he would fire the Cabinet, which would be bad, or he would accede to the radical demands and become impotent, which would be worse.

"You don't know the full story of what this evil man has done," Chase was saying. "If we were to show you copies of cables from McClellan to Democratic politicians in New York, hinting at his interest in their ideas of opposition to Lincoln, even to the point of dictatorship—"

"Certainly that should be brought to the attention of the President," Welles said, "in a general consultation." The more Chase pressed, the more Welles became convinced that propriety demanded a preliminary discussion with Lincoln, rather than a formal, written confrontation that would surely appear in the newspapers. The Cabinet's ultimatum would be widely seen for exactly what it was: a seizure of significant power from the President by the key members of his Administration. Not complete executive power; but Welles judged that the office of President would never be the same.

"After this document is signed," said Chase, "—and there would be five of us, a majority of the Cabinet, that's why your support is vital—we should certainly consult with the President immediately. This petition would add substance and urgency to our demands."

Welles pushed the paper away. "Your method of getting signatures without an exchange of views in council is repugnant to my ideas of duty and right."

A secretary knocked, and at Welles's order to enter, brought in a note: Montgomery Blair had arrived, another surprise visitor.

"Have you consulted with the Postmaster General, by the way?" Welles assumed Blair to be the last man on earth Chase would want to see. "Judge Blair is a West Pointer; surely his military expertness is important here. Let's consult him."

Chase's face took on a horrified expression; he could issue no spoken warning as Blair entered the room, but Welles took it that Chase did not want this matter discussed with Blair at all. The Navy Secretary decided to accommodate Chase for the moment and covered the mutinous document.

Blair was dropping in on his way elsewhere in the building and did not even sit down. Just a social call. He nodded to Chase, who gave him what Welles thought to be an especially sickly smile, exchanged pleasantries, and left.

When the Postmaster General had gone, Chase said gratefully, "It is best he should for the present know nothing of this."

Of course not; either Monty Blair or his father, Welles assumed, would go to Lincoln like a shot with the information that a coup by the Cabinet was under way. They would put heat on Smith or Bates to refrain from signing; Old Man Blair would also find a way through Thurlow Weed to bring Seward back from Auburn to face the music.

"I will redraft this to meet your objections," Chase said, taking the document back, ignoring Welles's prime objection to a written statement without general consultation as a Cabinet. He left hurriedly, coming back only to say, "Please, not a word to Blair. Or anyone else."

Welles stroked his beard and frowned. The nation faced a military crisis in the field; it was wrong, at such a moment, to precipitate a political crisis in the Cabinet.

Chase, furious at the rebuff, went back to Stanton's office. "I can't budge the old goat," he reported to the Secretary of War. "Any news from the front?"

"Pope reports casualties, but thinks he will win. That's as of last night, nothing from him this morning." Stanton looked worried about that, which boded ill. "McClellan is still poisoning the well with his claims of disaster. You know, we have to get Welles on the document or it's no good."

"You get him," Chase said, worried now that there might be something of substance to the rumors McClellan was gleefully spreading. "He's a stubborn one."

"He hates me," Stanton stated as a fact, which Chase knew to be true. Since the *Monitor-Merrimack* day, when Stanton had behaved less than heroically, little communication had taken place between the Secretaries of War and Navy. "Let's get Bates in on this, to get enough of the truth out of the document to let you sell Welles on signing it. Welles trusts you."

As well he might; Chase had never done anything to undermine Welles's authority, as Stanton had. Chase did not want to let Stanton dictate the strategy on this document to him, and insisted that they both go to Bates and then to Welles.

As Chase expected, the Attorney General changed "constitutional advisers" to "confidential advisers" to conform to Welles's opinion of the Cabinet. To induce Welles to sign, he removed both the charge of disobedience and the threat of mass resignation.

Perhaps the fact that the document was in Stanton's handwriting offended Welles. Chase told Bates to rewrite the petition in his own hand, which he readily did: " 'The undersigned, as part of your confidential advisers, do but perform a painful duty in declaring to you our deliberate opinion that, at this time, it is not safe to entrust to Major General McClellan the command of any army of the United States.' " The signatures of Chase, Stanton, Smith, and Bates were on this watered-down draft, with space left for Welles.

Chase and Stanton headed back to see the Navy Secretary with the new paper. Stanton drew his chair up close to Welles and whispered, "Chase tells me you've declined to sign our protest. Can it be that you don't want to get rid of McClellan, especially after his indifference to all your requests for cooperation with the Navy?"

"I don't differ on that point," said Welles, "and I was also impressed with what Chase has passed on about those 'contacts' in New York. The Young Napoleon is definitely politicking, and it is reprehensible, considering all we've done for him."

Chase braced himself for the "but" after these concessions. Sure enough: "But I think your approach does not look well—it appears to be a combination by two of you to get their associates committed, seriatim, in detail, by a skillful ex parte movement without general consultation."

"Nothing could be further from the truth," Stanton soothed, though Chase had to admit to himself that the one-at-a-time approach was exactly what was under way. "It's just that the Blairs are liable to ally themselves with McClellan, as they always have, and destroy an honest attempt to show the President the extent to which we see McClellan as a danger."

"This still appears to me unwise and injudicious," Welles said stubbornly. Chase felt like yanking his beard. "I think it is discourteous and disrespectful to the President."

At that, Stanton lost his temper. "I am under no particular obligation to the President! He called me to a difficult, an impossible, job. He imposed upon me labors and responsibilities that no man could carry!"

The War Secretary began wheezing and choking, staggering to his feet. "He burdens me further by fastening on me a commander who is constantly striving to embarrass me in the administration of the War Department."

Chase put that near-apoplectic outburst down to Stanton's resentment at Lincoln's imposition of Halleck, and the loss of the Secretary's own power it had entailed. "I cannot and I will not submit to a continuance of this state of things," Stanton choked. "I will resign."

"You have stated your case strongly," Welles replied in an unruffled way— the man, Chase thought, was unbearably pompous—"and the state of things is surely severe on you. But—"

Chase interrupted before Welles could make a statement closing the door. They needed the old fool. "There is no movement here against the President," he argued, and in his argument persuading himself of the rectitude of the petition. "Surely this new document, drawn up by the Attorney General to meet your excellent constitutional objections, is presented in a manner both respectful and correct. It is designed, quite simply, to tell the President that the Administration be broken up or McClellan dismissed."

"You do not consider that form of ultimatum unusual?"

"As our case is unusual, our course is unusual." It flashed in Chase's mind that his response was particularly well phrased, and that he would have to pass it along to Anna Carroll. This obstinate old Navy Secretary stood between assertion and abdication of authority by the Cabinet, and Chase strained to bring him along.

"The President has called us around him," Welles countered, "as friends and advisers with whom he might counsel and consult—not to enter into combinations to control him." Waiting for an opening that would enable him to agree rather than challenge, Chase let the old man ramble on. "Perhaps we have not been sufficiently intimate, impressive, or formal in expressing our views on some subjects. Perhaps not sufficiently explicit and decisive . . ."

"Exactly my point," said Chase. "Our Cabinet meetings have been much too informal, as you say. Your views, Welles—very sound views, indeed—are rarely put forward in the Cabinet sessions, because of your natural reserve."

"I take that as a compliment."

"As you should, and surely you are right to think that conversation with the President on matters of great import goes around in circles." Chase felt he had found a handle to steer the Navy Secretary around—a tiller, so to speak. "These Cabinet meetings ramble on, they are not organized to a purpose. Argument in such a setting is useless, like throwing water on a duck's back. How can a more decisive, explicit expression of our views be made to help the President? Only one way: in writing."

As Chase hoped, his appeal to efficiency apparently impressed the former editor from Connecticut. "As early as last December," Welles acknowledged, "I expressed my disappointment in McClellan. At that time, the general was everyone's favorite, and neither you, Chase, nor you, Stanton, nor anyone heeded my doubts and apprehensions."

"You were right and we were wrong," Stanton immediately admitted, pushing the revised document toward Welles.

"And now it is evident that there is a fixed determination to remove and, if possible, disgrace McClellan," Welles plodded on. "You, Chase, even suggested harsher treatment."

"If I were President," Chase said with what he hoped was no trace of equivocation, "I would bring him to summary punishment. He deserves to be shot." No less than any soldier who deserts under fire.

Welles crossed his arms. "I think he occupies himself with reviews and dress parades, drills and discipline. He hesitates and doubts and has no realization of the true state of affairs. I think McClellan is wanting in the essential requisite of a commander. He is not a fighting general."

Chase's hopes rose; was he coming around?

"Some statements of yours indicate delinquencies of a more serious character," Welles said ponderously, "but I have seen no proof that he is a coward or a traitor." He looked squarely at Chase, then at Stanton. "I will sign no written demands to the President for his dismissal."

Chase was crushed. Stanton moved quickly to reduce losses. "Then we will not present it at the Cabinet today. Since we have been talking all along in absolute confidence, do we have your word to say nothing of this to the President or anyone?"

"You do."

"And can we count on you," added Chase, "to speak up in the Cabinet against McClellan, branding him as the nonfighting general he is?"

"I will."

"Have you heard the rumor that Lincoln is thinking of rewarding his treachery with the command of Pope's troops?" Stanton asked.

Chase had not heard that until this moment, nor had Welles. When both expressed shock, Stanton asked Welles: "Can we depend on your outspoken support in Cabinet council to stop this abomination from taking place?"

Navy Secretary Gideon Welles

"If the rumor is true," said Welles, always careful, "I will express the view that I have just expressed to you."

They left before the Navy Secretary could amend his pledge. Chase knew that Stanton was seething with the same frustrated fury that engulfed him. Welles, with his reluctance to show disrespect to the President—his slavishness, really—had made it impossible for them to present him with the ultimatum for McClellan's dismissal or a breakup of the coalition Cabinet. Chase knew that Welles, in refusing to go along with a written demand, had thrown away the opportunity for the Cabinet as an institution to assume great de facto powers, much as the Supreme Court had done under Marshall and Taney.

But Chase also was aware that too much was at stake to permit this setback to affect the continuance of the pressure of the radicals on the vacillating Lincoln. Though weak on the conduct of the war, Lincoln was curiously stubborn about the powers of the Presidency. Chase wished it were the other way around.

"We won't let him get away with it," Stanton was muttering, as they were returning to their offices before the Cabinet meeting. "Bates is right—Lincoln has not the power to command. Lacks nerve."

The time was ripe to confront the President—to stiffen his spine on McClellan or to let him vacillate by himself, without the support of the Cabinet that had been so carefully chosen to reflect the political factions in the Union. Lincoln might have stolen the radicals' clothing in his emancipation ploy, but in the treason of McClellan, Chase was certain he found an issue to regain the radical Republican leadership.

To fail to shoot the treasonous McClellan was bad enough; but if Stanton's suspicion was well-founded, if Lincoln was actually thinking of reinstating him to save the nation from the defeat McClellan's own duplicity toward the gallant Pope had brought about—the people of the North would never stand for that. Chase would drive that point home in private council and, if need be, in public.

"Be at the Cabinet on time," Chase told Stanton. "It may be the last time this group gets together."

CHAPTER 9

I WILL ANSWER TO THE COUNTRY

"Something fishy is going on," Montgomery Blair told his father. "I went into Neptune's office this morning and found Chase there, showing him some draft of a document. Chase looked as if he had swallowed the federal treasury —never seen him so uncomfortable. They're plotting something, probably about McClellan."

"Welles doesn't lend himself to plots," opined the elder Blair. "He doesn't have that good a mind. Stanton plots. Seward plots all the time, even when he doesn't have to, which is probably the influence of Weed. Chase would like to plot, as befits a man of vaulting ambition, but he doesn't have a knack for it."

To cut short his father's woolgathering, the Postmaster General repeated, "I think the document was about McClellan."

"McClellan told Pinkerton, and Pinkerton told Miss Carroll, and Miss Carroll told me," said the old man, "that McClellan thinks the President is a coward, that Seward is vile, that Welles is an old woman, that Bates is a dithering fool, and that the only man of courage and sense in the Cabinet is Blair—and he doesn't altogether fancy Blair!" Francis P. Blair had a good chuckle over that.

Montgomery Blair nodded curtly and made ready to leave for the Cabinet session, which made his father serious again. "They're underestimating Lincoln again, Monty. The President's back is to the wall, and the radicals are trying to deny him the only man who can save the situation. They'd rather lose than win with a general who isn't simon-pure on slavery."

"The country is with them on McClellan," the son said. "He keeps losing."

"Not true; he just doesn't win. Little Mac doesn't like mass homicide, and neither do I. The place to win the war is in the West, where it's easy, not here where it's hard." The old man frowned. "And whether the country is with McClellan isn't the point. The army is with McClellan. It's the army, not the country, that's falling apart. Let McClellan handle the army and Lincoln will handle the country."

"And I'll handle the Cabinet?"

"If you're any good, you will," the old man said tartly. "I told McClellan he should stop shooting off his mouth about slavery, to leave the politics to politicians, and I think he'll listen from now on."

"What do I do when the whole Cabinet gangs up on McClellan?"

"Don't let that happen. Filibuster. Muddle everything up if you have to, but split that Cabinet. Shake Caleb Smith up with rumors of a scandal about Chiriquí land—he's up to his hips in it."

"Would have been helpful to have Seward here," Monty Blair put in. "Pity he's on vacation."

"Vacation, my eye. Seward tried to take over from Lincoln right at the start, and the President had to slap him down. Now old Billy Bowlegs thinks Chase and Stanton will do the dirty work for him, and William Henry Seward will come back as the grand conciliator. No, Lincoln's all alone, except for you, Monty. Protect his back, and there'll come a day that the President will protect ours."

"You really think he will, Father?" The younger Blair doubted it; Lincoln struck him as a man who stuck with the people who could help him, and was unswayed by sentiment.

"Look," the old man snapped, "if McClellan is driven out, he becomes a martyr and the Peace Democrats unite behind him. The radical Republicans will then rally behind Chase in sixty-four and Lincoln and the Blairs are out in the cold. Use your head—help Lincoln keep McClellan in."

Montgomery Blair accepted that good advice—when the old man concentrated, there was nobody like him—and crossed the street to the Executive Mansion. The President was not yet in the Cabinet Room, nor was Stanton; the others were milling around. He spotted the young secretary, John Hay, across the hall, motioning to him.

"Pope and McDowell have come back beaten," the President's aide said quietly. "This morning the President went over to McClellan's house and offered him command." When Blair's eyebrows shot up, the young man added hurriedly, "Just of the defense of Washington, not the whole army."

"Who's in command of the army in the field?"

"That's the rub," said Hay. "Nobody. We expect McClellan to move into the vacuum, but the President doesn't feel he can appoint him, public sentiment being what it is. He hopes you will support him on that today."

"You've never been much of a McClellan man, Hay." Blair teased the young man, who was known to be a most vociferous critic of the general at Washington's dinner parties.

"I'm a Lincoln man, which means that today I'm a McClellan man. The trick is to get through today."

Blair nodded and took his chair in the Cabinet next to Bates. Frederick Seward, the Secretary of State's son and aide, was sitting in his father's chair to the right of the President's. Chase and Smith were present; Stanton had not yet arrived.

After some talk that Blair considered desultory, the Secretary of War burst into the room, breathing heavily as if he had run all the way across the street.

In a suppressed, trembling voice, Stanton said, "I have been informed by General Halleck that Lincoln this morning gave command of the army to McClellan. Treachery has been rewarded."

"God help the country," said Chase. "The reinstatement of that incompetent is a national calamity."

As dismay and shock were being expressed by all but Blair and young Seward, who wisely said nothing, Lincoln came in, favoring his left foot, and sat down. "Sorry I'm late. Not seeing much need for a Cabinet meeting today, I have been talking over at the War Department, and McClellan's headquarters, about the war."

"Is it t-t-true?" Caleb Smith asked what was uppermost in everyone's mind. "Have you reap-p-p-pointed Mmm . . . mmm . . ."

"McClellan!" Stanton shouted.

"Did I reappoint him General-in-Chief?" Lincoln rephrased the question so he could answer it in the negative. "No, I'm satisfied with Halleck. He and I did go and call on General McClellan this morning. We set him to putting the returning troops into the fortifications about Washington. I believe he can do that sort of thing better than anybody."

Blair marveled at Lincoln's composure in undertaking what everyone in the room knew to be a deliberate deception. But the President evidently understood his immediate problem. If McClellan were given command of the army in the field facing the rebels under Lee, the Cabinet majority might resign en masse, ending the coalition so painstakingly built, and thereby split the North. By couching his decision in the most limited of terms—pretending he had made no dramatic decision to switch commanders in hopes of saving the capital—Lincoln evidently thought he might ameliorate the radicals.

"Investing the fortifications with returning troops could be done just as well," said Chase with scorn, "by the engineer who constructed the forts. The truth, Mr. President, is that putting McClellan in command for this purpose is equivalent to making him second in command of the entire army."

Stanton did not wait for Lincoln to try to wriggle off Chase's truthful hook, which Blair thought was fortunate. The War Secretary let loose with a petulant outburst: "Now nobody is responsible for Washington's defense. Certainly not me—I don't give orders now that you have Halleck here. Not Halleck—he never gave the order to McClellan, you did." Stanton slammed some papers down on the Cabinet table in fury. "Should everything go wrong, McClellan will shield himself under Halleck, while Halleck could and would disclaim all responsibility for the order you gave."

Blair had to admit to himself that Stanton had a point. The command structure was now incredibly confused, and blame for the disaster might easily fall on the man who was quick to claim to be the "organizer of victory." But that was because Lincoln wanted the chain of command to appear vague, and there might be political design in the military fuzziness.

"No order putting McClellan in command of the forces around Washington has been issued by the War Department," Stanton made very clear.

"I have done what seemed to me best," Lincoln replied calmly, almost too calmly, "and I will be responsible for what I have done, to the country. Halleck agreed to it."

"You rammed it down Halleck's throat," Chase charged.

"Halleck is just as responsible as he was before," the President said blandly, using as his buffer the cerebral soldier who had been urged on him by the radical faction. "I repeat, the scope of the order is simply for McClellan to put troops in the fortifications and command them for the defense of the city."

"In this situation," Chase pressed his point again, "that is equivalent to making McClellan commander in chief for the time being—and it will prove very difficult to keep him from taking command of all operations in the field."

"He has the slows," Lincoln replied obliquely, because what Chase said was true. "I know his infirmities full well: he is not an affirmative man. For an active fighting general, I am sorry to say he is a failure. He's never ready for battle, and never will be. He's good for nothing for an onward movement."

That was no way, thought Blair, to justify placing the country in his hands at its moment of greatest peril.

"But McClellan, we can all agree," Lincoln went on, having disarmed the jury with his stipulation of the charge most frequently made against his client of the moment, "is good at defense; if anything, that's his specialty. He is a good engineer, all admit. He knows this whole ground; there is no better organizer."

"God help us," said Stanton, eyes rolling upward.

"He can be trusted," Lincoln insisted, "to act on the defensive."

Blair saw the moment to drive a wedge in the Cabinet's anti-Lincoln solidarity. "You're all overlooking the most significant military fact staring us in the face," he said. "George McClellan is the only general who has the confidence of the men in the field. The men can't be fooled for long—I've been saying here that Pope is a liar and a braggart, and you can hear the men returning from the field saying the same thing. Those glorious dispatches of Pope's about victory—the work of an imbecile or a liar." Blair knew that everyone present knew that Stanton wrote many of Pope's dispatches. "McClellan may not be the most energetic commander," Blair followed Lincoln's lead in conceding, "but he's the best we have—and the only one capable of rallying the troops."

Into a chorus of angry denunciation, Lincoln seized Blair's point: "That's what Halleck says too. You all wanted Halleck at my side, good Republican, right on slavery. Well, he's with me on this; ask him." Obviously, Halleck was not going to be useful to Stanton and Chase at the moment; Lincoln had neutralized him by bringing him along to the pre-Cabinet meeting in which he asked McClellan to defend the city.

"Giving the command to George McClellan," Chase said slowly, impressively, "is equivalent to giving Washington to the rebels."

"I would *prefer* the loss of Washington to the rebels," Stanton added, "to giving that traitor the command. One way we lose a city; the other way we lose the war."

"That's a lot of wild talk," Blair put in. Stanton had gone too far, and Blair saw a way to take advantage of his excess. Now, too, was the chance to take a more extreme position on the other side, giving Lincoln the opportunity to be the mediator. "McClellan has never been defeated; his last fight at Malvern Hill was superb. Even in retreat from the Peninsula, at the President's orders, he inflicted more casualties on Lee than we received. I am not wholly unfamiliar with military affairs"—Blair thought it would be good to remind them that he, alone of those in the room, had attended West Point—"and I propose that McClellan be given command of the troops beyond the capital, to go after Lee in Virginia, and to follow him into Maryland if need be."

"Never." Chase took the floor. "McClellan came to the command last year with my most cordial approbation and support. He possessed my full confidence, until I became satisfied that his delays would gravely injure our cause. Even after I urged the President to put another in command"—Blair noted that the Treasury Secretary avoided mentioning Halleck and Pope—"I supported him, raising the means to wage war and the money to pay his troops. But his omission to urge troops forward this weekend, his countenance of the criminal delay by Porter's corps, evinced a spirit which renders him unworthy of trust."

"Criminal is a strong word, Governor," Blair protested.

"George McClellan does not deserve a command," Chase said deliberately, "he deserves a firing squad."

That hung in the air for a moment. Blair did not think it was wise for him to step in; that was Lincoln's job now.

Unfortunately, Chase held the floor. "What say the others? Bates?"

Blair shot an alarmed look at Lincoln; was he going to let the Cabinet be polled? The President was impassive.

"I am very decided against McClellan's competency," Bates replied.

"Smith?"

"C-c-catastrophe."

Now the key man. Chase fixed his eyes on the Navy Secretary. "Welles?"

"I would not go so far as to court-martial, until examining the facts around the unconscionable delays in getting reinforcement to Pope," Gideon Welles said laboriously, in what Blair assumed had been in rehearsal when he interrupted the tête-à-tête in Welles's office, "but I am generally of the same judgment."

"Against McClellan," put in Stanton, to nail it down.

"Yes."

That was it: five members of the Cabinet opposed, one for, one absent, on the most momentous decision Lincoln had to make since the relief of Fort Sumter.

"It distresses me exceedingly," said Lincoln, "to find myself differing on such a point from the Secretary of War and Secretary of the Treasury." By omission, he dismissed the others, including Welles; did he realize the concerted move against McClellan was primarily a Stanton-Chase plot? "If I saw a better way, I would gladly resign my plan."

The last word was indistinct. Did the President say "resign my place"? Was Lincoln offering to quit? Blair said incredulously, "Resign your what?"

"Resign my plan to put McClellan in charge of local defenses," Lincoln said distinctly, to Blair's relief. "But I do not see who could do the work as well as he. McClellan has acted badly in this matter—unpardonably—but we must use what tools we have."

"General Hooker," Chase put in instantly, "or Burnside. Either could do the job better."

Lincoln, who until then had comported himself like a confident lawyer in a hostile courtroom, suddenly looked stricken, as if wrung by the bitterest anguish. "I don't doubt your sincerity, Chase. In fact, that is precisely what distresses me so—all of you are so obviously earnestly sincere." He drew a deep breath. "I'm almost ready to hang myself."

Blair did not like that abjectness on the part of the President. "Hooker could be impetuous," he said sharply to Chase, "like your man Pope. Remember how certain you were that Pope was our salvation?"

"Pope was done in by McClellan's deliberate delay," Chase shot back, looking to Stanton for corroboration. Stanton nodded his agreement; that was to be the radicals' story.

"I am alarmed for the safety of the city," said Lincoln, still too morose for Blair's taste. "I've been talking with General Halleck, and he tells me that Pope's army is demoralized. Said that if Pope's army came within the line of our forts as a mob, the city would be overrun by the enemy in forty-eight hours."

Bates, no military man, was the one to explode at that point. "If Halleck doubts his own ability to defend this city, he ought to be instantly broken! We have fifty-thousand men here—enough to defend it against all the power of the enemy. If Washington falls, it will be by treachery of our leaders and not by any lack of power to defend."

"Hear, hear," said Blair, urging him on. Chase and Stanton were all too ready to abandon Washington.

"The damn shame is," the Attorney General went on, "we are on the defensive instead of adopting an aggressive policy. Now, above all others, is the time to strike out at the enemy. General Lee is a long way from home."

Lincoln stopped looking so distressed and sat up in his chair. By supporting McClellan vigorously and attacking his attackers, Blair had tried to give the President a second extreme, opening the way to his favorite position: the middle way. But the Blairs were outcasts; now Attorney General Bates had unexpectedly contributed the notion of a forceful campaign against Lee's

threat, presumably hitting the rebels as they massed for an assault on Mary-
land and northward—assuming Lee did not see fit to try to seize the White
House in Washington. Blair saw support for his alternative to the dumping of
McClellan beginning to emerge: to give Little Mac command of the whole
Army of the Potomac and send him out to strike Lee before the rebels could
move.

"McClellan is a known quantity," the President said with deliberation.
Hooker, Burnside, and the others were not. Then, as Blair had expected,
Lincoln took the middle position. "We've only put him in command of the
local defenses." Looking sternly at Blair, not at Chase, he added, "Not as you
suggest, Judge." Blair knew, as did the others, that Lincoln was directing his
"no" to Blair, but he was really saying no to Chase.

"I give up," Chase said, shutting his eyes and shaking his head.

Blair suppressed a smile at the way the President had outmaneuvered the
radical members of his Cabinet. Although Chase and Stanton might have
been able to kindle a blaze of outrage with the return of the hated McClellan
to full command of the entire Army of the Potomac, the radicals would be
unable to whip up much indignation at the obviously sensible use of an experienced defender at the head of a small force to help protect the local environs
of Washington. Chase and his friend Stanton, the expensive lawyer, had the
facts on their side, but they had been outlawyered by Lincoln. Blair found
that amusing.

"Unquestionably, McClellan wanted Pope to fail," Lincoln admitted, "and
that is unpardonable, but he is too useful just now to sacrifice. We must use
what tools we have." That was carrying manipulation to excess, Blair
thought; "too useful just now to sacrifice" was an implicit promise to sacrifice
McClellan at an opportune time; Lincoln did not have to placate Chase and
Stanton to that extent.

"Most of our troubles," the President said sadly, "grew out of military
jealousies. If the Administration erred in discarding McClellan and putting
Pope in command, the country should not have been made to suffer, nor our
brave men been cut down and butchered. Pope should have been sustained by
McClellan, but he was not. These personal and professional quarrels came
in."

Blair scowled; Lincoln was going much too far in placating Chase and
Stanton, but nobody else in the room said a word in the field general's defense. Welles was looking down at the table and making notes.

"It is humiliating," the President continued, "to reward McClellan and
those who failed to do their whole duty in the hour of trial, but so it is.
Personal considerations must be sacrificed for the public good."

"The army is with McClellan," Blair put in, to change the emphasis.
"Maybe the soldiers know something that we don't know."

"I must have McClellan to reorganize the army and bring it out of chaos,"
Lincoln went on, evidently more concerned with placating his angry Cabinet
members than doing justice to his general. "There has been a design, a purpose in breaking down Pope, without regard to the consequences to the country, that is atrocious."

"Shocking," Chase growled.

"Yes, it is shocking to see and know this, but there is no remedy—at present," Lincoln agreed, leaving implicit that there would be a remedy soon enough. "As Judge Blair says, McClellan has the army with him."

Blair did not like the judgment expressed—a summary judgment of treason, with no trial or examination of contradictory evidence—and feared for Lincoln's belated reaction when the time came that he did not feel compelled to back his general. But he felt better when he looked at Stanton. The War Secretary was looking dully at the Cabinet table, mouth open, as if in a state of shock.

Chase rose and tossed a few tax appointments on the table in front of the President. "If you like these men, sign the appointments. If not, don't."

"I'll sign them all right now," Lincoln said mildly, "no questions asked." He did so and handed them to his Treasury Secretary with a small smile.

CHAPTER 10

THE CHIROPODIST

"How come nobody talks about peace?" Isachar Zacharie wanted to know. "Only war, how we're going to wipe out the rebels. Never a word about negotiations."

"Sha!" barked his patient, his naked foot on the table, leaning back in a chair, "they'll call you a copperhead."

"Clement Vallandigham is wrong," the chiropodist said. That Ohio Democrat was agitating for peace, to the extreme distaste of loyal Union men, who gave the peace talkers the name of a poisonous snake. "He would have us just give up. The North will never do that, not unless General Lee comes marching up here toward New York. No, I mean a sensible arrangement, the way wars end in Europe, with everybody's honor satisfied."

Dr. Zacharie, a British-born Jew, had been practicing his surgery on feet throughout the United States for fifteen years. He always asked for testimonials from famous patients, and on the walls of his office at 760 Broadway were letters from Senators Henry Clay, Lewis Cass, and John Calhoun, as well as the governor of Virginia and a group of distinguished citizens of Sacramento, California—proving, he was aware, more about the itinerant nature of his calling than about his abilities.

Other physicians accepted the presence of a practitioner of chiropody so long as it was temporary; the disdained "toe-cutter" would have to move on once the crop of corns was cut. The fact that he was a Jew—Zacharie guessed he was one of perhaps sixty thousand in a nation of twenty-three million people—added to the nomadic and outcast nature of his life. He would come to a town, take an advertisement parading his testimonials in the newspaper, and point out that he was the author of *Surgical and Practical Observations on the Diseases of the Human Foot with Instructions for Treatment to Which Is Added Advice on the Management of the Hand.* That was true enough, although he had borrowed some of it—actually, most of it—from an English doctor. If anybody asked for a medical degree, he would produce a diploma from the Academy of Medicine at Havana, which was fake but impressed some people and was impossible to dispute.

"Lee could be on his way," said the patient, also a Jew, "and it says in the *Herald* there's nothing between the rebels and New York but George McClellan."

"Don't criticize McClellan," Zacharie said, pulling a toe toward himself and using an instrument he had designed to probe a corn's subjacent tissue. "He's not bad for the Jews. Maybe not good, but not like those momsers Grant and Sherman. You heard about Memphis?"

The patient was more interested in his toe. "Something about Grant's father, I heard."

Zacharie changed position so that his back faced the patient's body and he rested his weight on the leg. The tissue around the corn was only slightly tumescent, enabling him to pare away the hard induration first. Reaching for his corn cutter, he squeezed the toe, cut along the plateau of the corn, and then paused to make his observation about the Union general.

"Grant's father, Jesse, is trying to make a dollar selling goods from Illinois to the Union army in Tennessee," the chiropodist said. "The old man is a terrible businessman, the same born failure as his son, so Jesse Grant gets a Jew as a partner and takes him to Memphis."

"Lots of business in Memphis these days. Careful, that hurts. With the army contracts, plenty of crooked business too. And I hate to say, but plenty of those peddlers—"

"Jews." Zacharie changed position again, facing his patient, and proceeded to place the sides of the corn in a clamp and gently jiggle it. "Well, it happens that General Grant gets wind of what his father is up to, and he's furious. He can't throw his father out of town, but he throws out his partner, the Jew. So today, no Jew, honest or not, can show his face in Memphis."

He stopped the jiggling, slipped a probe under the corn for leverage, and popped it out. "That's it, doesn't need a bandage. Other foot."

The other foot was more of a challenge. An ingrown toenail had discolored the big toe and was causing the man to limp. Dr. Zacharie elevated the foot and wrapped it in a cold, wet towel to lessen the flow of blood to the toe.

"What about Cesar Kaskel in Paducah?" the patient asked. Most Jews knew who was influential in each major city, and the Kaskels of Kentucky were a well-connected Jewish family along the border. "Can't he do anything about Grant? God knows, there's money being made with half the army running cotton North and medicine South, but it's not just the Jews. Could Kaskel get to Lincoln? Or Stanton?"

"Maybe it'll blow over," Zacharie said uneasily. He did not deny his heritage, but was not an observant Jew and thought open demands for fair treatment stirred up trouble. "We don't want to make too much of this, or of the way Sherman runs out Israelites. Nothing's been official, it's just these two generals letting off steam. We don't want to make a fuss."

"I wish we had a friend near Lincoln, all the same," said the patient. "Abe Jonas in Illinois was close to him, helped him in Whig politics, but Jonas is not in Washington. The North doesn't have a Judah Benjamin."

Zacharie nodded grimly, turned his back to the patient, bestrode his leg, and clamped the foot on the table. The scalpel's incision was quick, bloody, but he doubted that it was terribly painful; few patients ever hollered. With a scissors, he trimmed back the nail and then twisted the towel into a tourniquet; "I learned this technique from Sir Astley Cooper in London, the great English surgeon." Patients always appreciated that evocation of medical tradition, Zacharie knew; actually, Cooper died in 1841, when Zacharie was fourteen, but he had heard about it from one of Cooper's students, and the technique worked.

The chiropodist, still holding the towel tight, turned back to face the patient. "You have relatives down South?"

"Who doesn't?"

Zacharie nodded. "I have my father and sister in Savannah. They helped raise a Jewish regiment to fight for the Confederacy. I told them it was a mistake, it's better for the country not to be separate. I have a lot of friends in New Orleans, too, where General Butler is now."

"The Beast?"

"Not such a beast, I hear. Very good on sanitation, and he lets the Jews do business."

"Zacharie, listen to me. I have it on good authority, a member of my own family, that Butler goes around saying that the Lord has been trying to make something of the Jews for three thousand years and failed." The patient put his hand on the doctor's arm. "Butler says King John had the best way to deal with Jews—'fry them in swine fat.' My cousin heard this with his own ears."

"With his own ears?"

"He does business with Butler's brother."

Zacharie nodded his head with certainty. "That's what I mean. Butler says terrible things, but at the same time Butler does business. Like in Shylock, spit and borrow."

"Only because he has to. My cousin has some rebel friends in gold, and Butler needs a go-between."

That sent a thought through Zacharie's mind: the dealers in gold dealt fairly openly with financiers of both North and South. Jewish gold dealers were already accepted as intermediaries in trade; why not in greater matters?

A more exciting thought immediately followed: Who could better deal with such traders than one of their own religion? And who could pass through lines more easily than an itinerant foot doctor, with testimonials from patients North and South?

He bandaged the foot. "Stanton," Zacharie said aloud.

The patient tried to read his mind. "You ought to go see Stanton, there's a lot of footsore soldiers in the Union army. Not just corns, either—"

"Hammertoes, bunions," Zacharie agreed. "You know, many people joke about my profession. Physicians who should know better call it an unworthy surgical skill."

"But a real doctor sent me here."

Zacharie winced at the unintended derogation. "They even resist using the word 'chiropodist'—they call us 'toe cutters.' But I can tell you, my friend, that a pair of good feet will often carry a man out of a scrape, and that's what the nation needs."

"That's surely what soldiers need," said the patient, gingerly putting his foot on the floor.

The chiropodist nodded. He would send his book, with an accompanying letter, to the Secretary of War. He would volunteer to help the war effort, so that he could one day initiate a peace effort.

Zacharie, who had already promoted himself to the forefront of his profession, liked to think on a grand scale. Certainly an army marched on its feet, and healthy feet were the mark of a strong army. A corps of foot doctors, treating the soldiers of the North, would do a great deal to help win the war, and would surely raise the profession in the public eye. It was not too much to foresee the appointment of a chiropodist general.

He decided to write Stanton immediately. He would arrange to have his book and letter hand-delivered to Watson, Stanton's man, by a physician he knew in Washington. And he would not forget to suggest he treat any foot pains of the Secretary of War; that would get his attention. Everybody had foot trouble, and if the President of the United States stood over six feet four inches, as they said, with huge hands, then Lincoln very likely had big feet and big foot problems. Who better to treat Lincoln than the man who had cut the corns of his political idol, Senator Henry Clay?

Isachar Zacharie collected a greenback dollar with Chase's face on it and watched his patient limp out. If Lee struck north, New York and Philadelphia would be hit by panic and the war would be over; if Little Mac stopped him, there would be time for the right man to put himself in place for the beginning of talks between the sides. He closed the door and sat down to write.

CHAPTER 11

THE FORGOTTEN WEST

"You are the mysterious Anna Ella Carroll. I am Count Adam Gurowski."

Anna looked up to see a well-dressed gnome bowing formally to her. She was seated in the anteroom to the Secretary of War's office, waiting to see Stanton on a patronage matter, and was surprised at being addressed by this stranger, especially as "mysterious." She had heard of Gurowski, respectfully from Ben Wade, scornfully from the Blairs; he worked for Seward at State as an interpreter but the Polish exile had a reputation as a great busybody.

She rose and shook hands, saying nothing.

"Mr. Lincoln has become a myth," the count announced, as if in the middle of a conversation, confiding in her as an old friend. "His reality is only manifested by preserving slavery, by sticking to McClellan, by distributing offices, by receiving inspirations from Mr. Seward, and by digging the country's grave."

She did not want to be seen in the Secretary of War's outer office listening to that sort of talk. The city was still in imminent danger of an assault by Lee's troops; nobody knew what McClellan's status was, or if the rebels would now follow up their victory with a move to the north. But when she looked coldly and steadily at Gurowski, he took it as an invitation to continue. "Up to this day, the only man whose hands remain unstained is the last Roman, Stanton."

"I'm glad you think well of someone."

"Last night marked the inauguration of the praetorian regime. Have you heard? General McClellan has forced the President to postpone the investigation into the conduct of the slow and insubordinate generals who failed Pope —all three special favorites of McClellan's. Mutiny on the field of battle and McClellan prevents investigation! We are ruled by the *yanitschars* of a sultan."

Anna did not ask what a *yanitschar* was—she presumed it was a Polish word—but went directly to the only word that the count had said that was of interest to her.

"What makes you say I am 'mysterious'? My work is published, people know where I stand. You can find copies of my latest pamphlet, *An Address to Maryland*, here in the War Department and in the President's office as well. What's the mystery?"

He smiled conspiratorially, which Anna assumed was the only kind of smile in his repertoire. "How can a former Know-Nothing leader, not to mention a friend of Fillmore and Buchanan, be a confidante of Lincoln? How can one travel in the company of friends of the masses like Wade and Stanton —and then make herself at home in the Silver Spring mansion of the Blairs?"

The Count knew too much. And he had only scratched the surface of her paradoxical political life. She could have added a few questions of her own. How could a woman who argued against the Confiscation Act and an emancipation proclamation remain loyal to Lincoln? How could a woman who admired, respected, and even now felt a longing for John Breckinridge have flayed him in a pamphlet and helped to blacken his name in the North?

"That is not the mystery, of course," Count Gurowski hurried on. "We all have friends in different camps; it is impossible to agree with everybody on every issue. I am not accusing you of being what they call a 'trimmer.' I presume that is a nautical metaphor, from one who trims sails to catch the prevailing breeze."

She pulled her head back an inch as if she were examining a strange insect. "Frankly, Mr. Gurowski"—none of this foreign-title stuff for a daughter of Maryland—"your opinion doesn't interest me a bit."

"That is untrue, of course," he replied evenly, "but let us be friends. I admire your mind, and that is why I have presumed to speak so directly to you. Ordinarily I am quite circumspect. Do you forgive me? If I may," he went on before she had a chance to respond, "I will call you 'my dear lady,' as Stanton does. And now I will come to the true mystery of Anna Ella Carroll, to the question that nobody dares ask."

He paused, and she waited. If it had to do with her relationship with Salmon Chase, she would hit him with her large pocketbook.

"Where did a woman with no formal military training gain the knowledge to come up with the brilliant Tennessee plan?" His large eyes shone in wonderment. "The grasp of logistics, the understanding of high strategy, the incredible modesty that allows others to bask in the glory that your mind conceived—that is indeed a mystery."

What a perceptive man. She felt a surge of warmth for this controversial

Count Adam Gurowski

Polish nobleman, who was too often misunderstood or resented because of his candor. She had heard nobody else willing to credit a civilian, least of all a woman, with the strategy Grant had followed in the West. She put her hand on his arm and whispered, "I know something about the railroad business, my dear count. And I know which way the waters flow."

"Come in, both of you." It was Stanton, being peremptory. It occurred to Anna that he might have sent Count Gurowski out first to say the outrageous things about Lincoln that Stanton dared not say to anyone.

She stated her business immediately. "I bear a letter from Senator Garrett Davis recommending Joseph Breckinridge for a lieutenancy. The young man is presently serving as volunteer aide-de-camp to General George Thomas in Tennessee."

"That's a familiar name," said Stanton archly. Anna stiffened; if Stanton was going to suggest she was tender on the subject of Breckinridge, she would remind him that Stanton had supported Breckinridge in 1860.

"He is the son of the Reverend Robert Breckinridge, a longtime friend of my family's and mine. The Reverend Bob did more than anyone to keep Kentucky in the Union. Another Breckinridge, Mary Elizabeth, serves as a nurse for the Union Army in the West."

Stanton nodded. "Happens a lot in Kentucky, I know, but I cannot accommodate every senator who wants a friend made an officer."

"The endorsement on the letter is in President Lincoln's hand," she continued in a quiet voice, and began to read: "There are potent reasons why this young man should be made a lieutenant—"

Stanton snatched the paper from her, looked at it quickly, made a notation below the President's signature, and threw it in a box on his desk.

Count Gurowski smiled. "Now you owe Secretary Stanton a tremendous favor."

"What were the 'potent' reasons?" Stanton wanted to know.

"While all eyes here seem to be on General Lee's thrust into Maryland," she explained, "little attention is being given to the other invasion by the rebels across the Cumberland River into Kentucky. General Braxton Bragg is threatening Don Carlos Buell in the most strategic area of the war. McClellan is too far east to help, Grant is too far west. If we lose Kentucky—"

"We won't lose Kentucky!" Stanton barked.

"Where is Bragg right now?" asked Gurowski, more to the point.

Stanton looked sourly at him. "You're not the only one who wants to know." He rummaged on his desk and picked up a cable. "Here's a wire from the President to our man in Louisville: 'Where is General Bragg? What do you know on the subject?' And the reply is that we don't know anything. I suppose Lincoln's telegraph message was the result of your agitation about the importance of the West, my dear lady."

Anna Carroll did not deny it, though she had no way of knowing if her emphasis on the war outside the environs of Washington had affected the President. "If you were Jeff Davis, and had General Bragg's army ready to strike northward to invade Kentucky, what man would you send for to get the people of that state to rise up against the Union?"

"John Breckinridge, of course," Stanton replied. "Last I heard, he was at Vicksburg."

"I doubt whether Breck has reached Bragg yet," she said, and immediately wished she had not used the familiar form of the former Vice President's name. "He would probably refuse to take reassignment without his men, the Orphan Brigade."

"What brigade?" Gurowski asked. Anna knew he asked lest Stanton be forced to show any lack of knowledge about troops.

"The Kentuckians under Breckinridge are the only rebels fighting whose state remained loyal to the Union," she explained to Gurowski, with the Secretary of War listening intently. "They're orphans, no home to go to. Fought well at Pittsburg Landing. I imagine the traitor Breckinridge will want them with him to try to 'liberate' their state. That will take a few weeks. I would suggest that General Thomas in Tennessee needs reinforcements—"

"—and as many young officers named Breckinridge on his staff as we can appoint," observed Gurowski, nodding vigorously. "I would say that is a 'potent reason.' "

"We'll leave all that to Halleck," said Stanton gruffly, "he knows the West. I'm more interested, my dear lady, in what you have to offer the President on the Chiriquí tract. Has Caleb Smith readied his report on colonization? It's an urgent matter at this moment."

She drew a breath to tell him of her progress, but Gurowski broke in.

"Colonization is an absurdity," he announced, pronouncing the "s" in "absurdity" like a "z." "It is a display of ignorance or of humbug."

Anna tended to agree with him, but the Chiriquí tract in Panama was an assignment close to the President's heart, and she had to be careful. "Many people think," she hedged, "that it's the only answer to the question of what to do with the negroes once they are freed."

Gurowski made a loud noise inhaling through his nose. It was the first time Anna had heard someone actually snort in disgust.

"Do you know why the best Americans do not utter their condemnation of the colonization scheme? Because the President is to be allowed to carry out his hobby." The count could afford to be contemptuous, as Anna and Stanton could not. "The despots of the Old World envy Mr. Lincoln," the Polish exile went on. "Those despots can no more carry out their hobbies. *Le Roi s'amuse* had its time there, but it continues here."

"Ignore him," Stanton told her. "Lincoln feels he needs the colonization idea put forward in great detail in order for him to do what we need to do."

In an oblique way, Stanton was talking about the proclamation of emancipation that had been drafted by the President and was being kept secret. Anna looked at him quizzically and cocked her head toward the count, silently asking Stanton, "Does he know?" The Secretary of War, looking uncomfortable, shrugged as if he did not know.

Gurowski missed nothing of the byplay. "I am fully aware," he said more loudly than either Stanton or Carroll would have wished, "that when the President—urged by the noble Stanton here—was almost ready to sign a proclamation in the spirit of the law of God, Seward and Blair opposed it."

Anna winced inwardly; certain things, like the politics behind emancipation, were not to be spoken of widely, and certainly not discussed with a notorious gossip like Gurowski.

"Even the opposition of Seward and Blair was of no avail," the count went on. "Finally, Thurlow Weed was telegraphed, and he settled the question."

"Lincoln had his reasons," Stanton murmured, dissociating himself slightly from Gurowski's intimate knowledge of the inner workings of the Lincoln Cabinet.

"He has only the justification Seward and Weed gave him," the count declared, "which was that the President's proclamation would have evoked riots and counterrevolutions in the North." Gurowski lowered his voice to a level more befitting a conspirator. "I have informed Governor Andrew of Massachusetts about this, and urged that he call a convention of the governors and force upon the President a change in the Cabinet."

Anna was shocked at the thought of rallying the governors to pressure Lincoln, and more shocked at the willingness of Stanton to listen to such— she reached for the right words, not treason—personal disloyalty.

"Lincoln likes Seward and listens to Weed," was all she was willing to say. She respected Weed's political judgment and agreed with him about premature emancipation: it would split the North and unite the South. But maybe Lincoln knew best, and the President made the final decisions, and she was working for him. She had been given the chance to have her say on that; her advice was considered but not taken, and she would soldier on. Nothing counted as much as being in position to get across the message of the military importance of the West. That was where the war would be won, where the Confederacy would be strangled, and not in the games and maneuvers of McClellan and Lee near the capitals.

"Colonization is a great thing," said Stanton firmly, as if he believed it, "and it is nobody's hobby. That's the answer Lincoln must give to the Democrats in the Northern cities who say, 'What'll we *do* with them?' He's already said that the North need not take the colored in, but nobody believes that—the fear is that four million blacks will inundate the North. This Administration has to have an answer. Colonization is the answer."

"Absurd, a cruel deceit—"

"I don't give a tinker's dam if it is absurd!" Stanton exploded at Gurowski. "Lincoln doesn't think it's absurd, or at least he keeps a straight face about it, so we can all adopt the position that it is eminently practical. Later, we'll see. First, let's get the proclamation out of him." He turned to her. "I charge you, my dear lady, to come up with a report that even that dolt of an Interior Secretary can present with pride."

"I'll do that in good time," she promised. "Meanwhile, you'd better give some thought to the Northern reaction to emancipation, especially among the workingmen in the big cities. Weed could be right. There could be trouble."

Gurowski shook his head vigorously. "When emancipated, the Africo-Americans will at once make an excellent peasantry. Seward and his man Weed do not understand that. I've heard Seward say that both extreme parties will be mastered—both the secessionists and the abolitionists will give way to Mr. Lincoln and himself in the center. Seward and Weed are wrong."

Anna looked to Stanton, who understood more about American politics than the count. Was he blind to the likelihood of a lashing back at emancipation by white workers in the North?

"We'll be ready for a reaction," Stanton said ominously. "There will have to be two proclamations, not just one. I want to be able to slam into jail every rioter, every agitator who tries to use emancipation as a device to prevent recruitment. We will suspend habeas corpus with a vengeance, my dear lady, and let old Judge Taney scream. Your war powers paper will be put to the test again."

"Weed thinks that sort of suppression could cost you New York," she said. She agreed with the Albany editor but withheld her own opinion. "He says a combination of emancipation and a crackdown on the dissenters will defeat the Republican candidate in October. He says that Horatio Seymour—"

Stanton waved in disgust, and she desisted. But Anna had seen Horatio Seymour, the former Democratic governor of New York, in action. He was persuasive. Seymour would likely be nominated at the Brooklyn convention in a few days. He could capitalize on the resentment of whites against the 1 percent negro population of New York, and build his popularity among those incensed by Stanton's heavy hand crushing the right of dissent. The triumph of the peace party in New York, the biggest state, the source of so much money and so many men, was not even being considered here.

She stood frowning in thought. Anna was accustomed to men of power waving her arguments aside, or otherwise making a point of paying no attention. She would not press ahead, making a nuisance of herself, but she would not back away graciously either; a long, perturbed silence did her work.

"There is not a chance that the state of New York will be lost to the peace crowd," Stanton said at last. "I know that for a fact, my dear lady, just as I know we can brook no treasonable talk after we free the slaves. No agitation anymore—not when we need hundreds of thousands of recruits at the front."

The military draft—that was what was worrying Stanton. He had foolishly ended conscription in the spring, and by reimposing it, he would be admitting that the war spirit was flagging in the North. That was why he would jail every dissenter who interfered with recruitment. Anna guessed that he was thinking of taking the draft out of state hands, making it a national effort; that seizure of power might change the nature of the country, but the war was making the nation more national every day. A national draft would be "union" with a vengeance.

Stanton had confided in her as much as she thought he could; she could take her leave with dignity. "Think about the rebels under Bragg striking up through Kentucky," she cautioned, "and about Grant in Tennessee."

"Memphis is a hotbed of corruption," Stanton said, she thought irrelevantly. "I sent Dana out there to look into reports of rampant bribery among Treasury agents. He says that every colonel and quartermaster is in secret partnership with some operator in cotton, and every soldier dreams of adding a bale of cotton to his monthly pay. Nightmare of profiteering and trading with the enemy. If Grant can't clean it up . . ." He waved them off.

Gurowski bowed to let her pass, and they went out together. In front of the War Department building, within sight of Lincoln's bedroom windows across the way, he stopped and spoke in a low, urgent voice.

"Have you seen Lincoln's proclamation?" She had not; she doubted he had either. "It is an illogical, pusillanimous, confused half measure, written in the meanest and most dry routine style. Not a word to evoke a generous thrill, nothing for humanity. It is clear that it was done under moral duress, under the throttling pressure of events, and the writer had not his heart or soul in it."

She assumed Stanton had described it to him and the count was pretending to be more of an insider than he was. If his information and extrapolation were sound, it meant only that Lincoln understood that the measure had to be presented to conservatives as a necessity, not to abolitionists as a victory.

Anna poked her finger in his fancy vest. "I don't want to hear another word out of you about the President. Keep your thoughts about Lincoln to yourself. Scribble them down in a diary at night if you have to, but keep them to yourself. Only then can you and I be friends."

"You are in mortal fear of my honesty."

She breathed deeply. "Maybe so, sometimes. You can afford to shoot off your mouth like a cannon. I have to be careful, I have a goal in life, and women do not have that much leeway." She was irritated with him for pointing to her fear of frankness, because it was what she liked least in herself, but economic survival had its requirements. A woman could not stand in her own shoes if she took on every battle in the world. She tempered her irritation by reminding herself that the count was one of the few people who appreciated her Tennessee plan, and was a useful voice in radical circles.

She looked at the count appealingly. "So—will you behave yourself? At least when you're with me?"

He bowed. "The mystery of your influence deepens," he said dramatically.

CHAPTER 12

LIBERATING KENTUCKY

"You took your own sweet time getting here, Breckinridge."

"I have encountered every difficulty a man could meet," the Kentuckian responded, surprised at the reception. "Van Dorn didn't want us to leave Port Hudson. He said it would weaken him at Vicksburg."

General Braxton Bragg's eyes were icy. "He wanted only your brigade to stay. You could have come a month ago. I need *you* up in Kentucky, not your ragtag band of malcontents."

Breckinridge drew in his breath and looked down at Bragg. The man looked more like a chimpanzee than the leader of the Southern forces in the central theater. He had gained a reputation throughout the Confederacy as a capable tactician, but the rigidity of his discipline caused him to be viewed with distaste by most of his commanders and with an aversion bordering on loathing by the troops. Yet Jeff Davis trusted him with most of the late Albert Sidney Johnston's army, and Breck had to admit that Bragg had skillfully maneuvered his way up through Tennessee across the Cumberland River into Kentucky. Although Lee's invasion of Maryland was getting the headlines in the Richmond newspapers, it was Bragg's threat to conquer the key border state of Kentucky that Breck thought was more likely to force the North to talk peace.

"I fight at the head of the Kentuckians," General Breckinridge informed General Bragg. "Where I go, they go; that is my understanding with President Davis. And I wouldn't call them malcontents—"

"I would and do," Bragg snapped. "Their conduct is a disgrace. They are unpredictable in battle, and mutinous on the march. Don't defend them. You know I speak the truth."

Breck conceded nothing, though he had been having more trouble with the Kentucky Brigade than Bragg knew. Because they were not citizens of a state in the Confederacy, most of the troops did not consider themselves bound to orders from Richmond; because they were all volunteers, the Kentuckians showed open contempt for the conscripts in other units. However, their term of enlistment was ending. The struggle their leader faced was to get them to reenlist while Bragg's push was on to take Kentucky and they had the incentive of returning home in triumph.

"They fight well, General," Breckinridge replied, "and they'll stick with me."

"Your sentimentality may cost us the state," Bragg told him. The commanding general of the Army of Tennessee had come up from his headquarters in Knoxville for a quick look at supplies and reinforcements moving into Kentucky's state capital of Frankfort, recaptured a few weeks before. "I

General Braxton Bragg, C.S.A.

needed you in Kentucky for the past two weeks. Not as a general, but as a politician. You were a senator here, your name means something to the people. I've taken Frankfort, and General Kirby Smith—who is not under my command, for reasons known only to Jeff Davis—has taken Lexington. Now is the time for a popular uprising of Kentuckians still behind the Union lines."

"Who told you that would happen?"

"Colonel John Morgan, among others. He's a fine cavalry raider, driving Buell crazy by blowing up his bridges, and these Kentuckians are his people."

Breckinridge knew the man well; brave, resourceful, hotheaded. "John Morgan is no expert about Kentucky politics."

"Perhaps you forget, General," said Bragg, "that in the 1860 election Lincoln did not carry the state of Kentucky."

"Neither did I," Breckinridge countered ruefully. "It went to Bell because the people were confused. Kentuckians will cheer us on, and their hearts may be with the South, but they've pretty much decided the North will win. And they want to be on the winning side."

"Cowards." Bragg obviously cared little that Breckinridge was a Kentuckian to the core. "The people here have too many fat cattle. They're too well off to fight. They have to be made to see who will win this war."

"That's not what I meant," said Breckinridge hurriedly. "They don't—we Kentuckians don't—take well to being told what to decide. Whip Buell's army, General, but don't try to whip the Kentuckians. Show the people here which army wins battles, then let them decide to help us."

Bragg dismissed all that with a sharp hand gesture. "I want you out front," he ordered. "All along the line. Visit every camp. Talk to the newspapers. Tell them I'm here to save them from the Northern invaders, but if Kentuckians do not cooperate in throwing off the Union yoke, it will go badly for them."

"I'll do it my way," said Breckinridge. Bragg was in command, and a direct order in battle, no matter how sadistic, would call for instant obedience, but in political matters Breckinridge had some leeway. He suspected that Bragg had in mind to draft Kentuckians into his army; that idea would surely miscarry.

"And for God's sake, get some discipline in that brigade, or I will. I cannot have your mob contaminating my army. It's bad enough I have to put up with inferior generals who have friends in high places." Breck assumed that Bragg, who was known to complain about his colleagues in order to have somebody to blame in case of defeats, meant "Bishop" Polk and William Hardee, and not him. "First thing," directed Bragg, "is to get them to cut out drinking. Liquor doesn't belong in my army, Breckinridge. I would hope you would set the example for your men."

What did the little chimpanzee mean by that? Breckinridge was widely known to take a glass of Old Crow or two, or even three, but not in battle and not to excess. Never in public, at least.

"Don't let the good people of Kentucky hear you say that," he told Bragg. "Lot of good bourbon whiskey is turned out around here. If you want to get Kentuckians to harass the Union troops and not ours, you better start thinking about what sort of people you're dealing with."

He whipped around and left Bragg's headquarters in the State Capitol. It was good to be home, near bluegrass again, and he nodded kindly to a woman who recognized him on the street, but he was uneasy. The commanding general did not seem to have a realistic objective; the men in his own command were about to quit to go to their nearby homes; worst of all, he had no fix in his own mind about the worthiness of the Southern cause. There had to be more to fighting than a need not to be beaten. When he found himself wondering what the Southern cause was, he worried about his own political effectiveness in Kentucky on the impossible assignment Bragg had in mind.

His son Cabell was waiting outside with the horses and directions to General Breckinridge's new quarters.

"We're sharing a private house with General Cleburne, sir."

"The Irishman?"

"We met him at Shiloh."

Breckinridge liked Cleburne almost as much as he disliked Bragg. The only general of Irish descent in the Confederate Army, Cleburne was a hard man for anyone to forget. After Shiloh, on the retreat to Corinth, when the fighting had died down, Breckinridge and Cleburne had shared a bottle of whiskey and tried to figure out the war strategy. Patrick Ronayne Cleburne had failed the apothecary's test in Ireland as a young man, spent some unhappy time in the army, then came to America and settled in Arkansas as a druggist. When the war started, he organized the "Yell Rifles" and seized the Little Rock arsenal, launching his military career with gusto. Breck smiled at the thought of the rich brogue, which appeared in full when Cleburne was angry or excited, exhorting the Southerners and Westerners to charge.

"He's a big hero now," Cabell went on. "Couple weeks ago, he led a division under Kirby Smith that took Lexington. Our biggest single victory of the war, some say. At least the most lopsided."

Lexington was home; perhaps Cleburne had seen Mary Breckinridge. His long pace became longer and quicker.

"He took about five thousand Yankee prisoners, the rest ran away," the boy continued, long legs matching his father's stride. "Only about eighty dead on our side. Never been such a rout. That was while Lee was licking Pope at Bull Run, but Cleburne's victory was even bigger, scarin' the Yankees across the Ohio in Cincinnati."

"Pat's a courageous leader. Good man, too."

"They call him the Stonewall of the West. Wish to hell you could win a battle, Father, sir," Cabell observed. "Even when you win, you have to pull back in the end. It's been discouraging."

At the billet, Breck introduced his son to Pat Cleburne, who ushered them into a grand sitting room and found a couple of glasses. The Irishman had a bandage on his jaw but was able to smile through it and quickly give his new housemate an account of a visit to his headquarters the week before by Mary Breckinridge. He called her "Maureen," in the Irish way, and used that diminutive with Breck's name, calling him "Breckeen."

"The boy doesn't drink on duty," said Breck, toasting his host. "To your great annihilation of Yankees at Lexington."

"Sure, you should have been there." Cleburne pronounced the word "thayur" as he sipped the local product. "We captured two barrels of this stuff, but some lieutenant with no sense put a company of Irishmen to guarding it, and this bottle is all that's left."

"That wasn't all you captured."

"We came to the little suburb of Richmond, Kentucky—you know it? Of course you do, you probably stumped for votes there—and found six thousand raw Federal recruits in front of us. Kirby Smith, he's not like Bragg, he knows when to attack. Kirby gave me the sign, and my boys rolled right over th'm, grabbed the bunch. A few skedaddlers made it out to Louisville."

"Your wound?"

"I caught a ball in the cheek, passed right through—I spit it out, I think. Doc says it'll give me a charmin' dimple." Cleburne leaned forward. "You've dealt with this madman Bragg before?"

Breckinridge nodded grimly.

"Kirby Smith won't serve under him, has President Davis's promise to operate separately. Bragg established martial law in Chattanooga, did you hear? Had every Tennessean line up and list his occupation. Man's wild! Complains about his own generals all the time. Watch out, you'll get court-martialed before you know it."

"Let him just try that on Father," Cabell put in, then shut up.

Cleburne's bandage moved, suggesting a quick smile behind it. "I forgot, you've got connections. They say you turned down Secretary of War, Breck-een, is it true? Don't have to answer. But I have an idea for you next time you've got your feet up on the Cabinet table with the rest of the high and mighty."

"That won't be soon." Breckinridge did not expect President Davis to call him to the capital as long as Confederate fortunes were rising. With Lee striking into Maryland and Bragg into Kentucky, spirits were high in Richmond; if the populations of those border states treated the Southerners as liberators and turned on Union troops as the real invaders, the military situation might become untenable for Lincoln.

"Mine is a kind of a revolutionary idea," Cleburne was saying, "sort of thing you might expect from a politician like you, not a druggist like me."

Breck smiled. "We're in a revolution. Only if it fails will it be called an insurrection."

"What's our biggest problem?" Cleburne asked rhetorically. "As generals, what do we need most?"

"Men." Conscription was going badly in the South, especially after it had been called off in the North. Some men were just cowards, but others did not want to leave the farms in the hands of the women, in case the blacks were to stage a bloody uprising, as in Nat Turner's day. "The North outnumbers us better than two to one."

"Spoken like an old national candidate, my friend. Now if the war drags on much longer, and if our invasions don't succeed before this winter, the great advantage in men is going to swing over to the North, right?"

Breck nodded.

"And even presuming that one of our fine lads is worth two of the Yankees in a fight," the Irishman said, "sooner or later they'll overwhelm us by sheer force of numbers."

"Unless the Yankees get disheartened and force Lincoln to quit." To the

Kentuckian, that was the purpose of Bragg's thrust into Kentucky, and Lee's move into Maryland. He saw them as raids, not invasions, because they could not be sustained in enemy territory through a winter; unless Kentuckians and Marylanders rose to embrace their "liberators," the armies of Bragg and Lee would have to return to their Southern base for sustenance, and Breck saw little hope in a sudden popular surge in the border states for disunion. He knew Bragg disagreed; he hoped Lee was not similarly misled.

"We can hope for that in the next couple of months," said Cleburne, "but we can't count on it. In the end, the South will need men. Help in big numbers."

Breckinridge tried to guess what Cleburne was driving at. "Bring the British in? Judah Benjamin is working on that, and they're thinking of sending Rose Greenhow over through the blockade to appeal to English womanhood, but it's unlikely they'd send troops—"

Cleburne waved that aside. "The men we need are right here. Our Africans."

Breckinridge did not react. Evidently Cleburne was too wrapped up in his idea to remember to be a good host; the Kentuckian reached for the bourbon and poured the two of them a long drink. None for Cabell. He tilted his head back and drained the glass.

"Out of four million blacks," Cleburne went on, "there must be a million good fighting men. They're after knowing how to follow orders, and they're after working longer and harder than most of our soldiers."

Cabell broke in, disbelieving. "You suspect our niggers will fight for slavery?"

"Course not," replied Cleburne, who seemed almost merry in his excitement. "But they'll fight for the highest wages any people can be paid—their freedom." His eyes leveled on Breckinridge's. "Here is my idea: Offer freedom to those slaves who enlist in the Confederate Army."

The Kentuckian, from years in the Senate in Washington, knew better than to interrupt a man expressing a big, original, and controversial idea. Breck could see horrendous objections to the very thought of putting arms in the hands of slaves, or of enabling a million blacks to earn their freedom and thereby undermine the "peculiar institution." But he knew enough to wait.

"Faith, the choice is going to be made soon," the Arkansas Irishman continued, "about what we're fighting this war about."

"Southern independence," said Cabell.

"Slavery," corrected Breckinridge. He had never admitted it in the 1860 campaign, but he could not deny it anymore. Slavery was at the root of disunion, planted in the Constitution by the founders, his grandfather among them, who could not stop the slave trade then and there.

"You're wrong, Breckeen. Your son is right. How many men in your Kentucky Brigade are slave owners?"

Breckinridge looked at his son. "One out of four?"

"Not as many as that, sir. One out of six own slaves, or one slave. This brigade is not fighting for the plantation owners."

Breckinridge was surprised, not so much at the facts but at his son's point of view. He had always supposed Cabell, like himself, longed for the ultimate restoration of the Union. They were fighting against the domination of their state and region by a central despotism, with their aim to reestablish the Union as it was, with the sovereign rights of all the states reaffirmed. Now it seemed that his boy had other ideas.

"Tell your old man what you think about the draft," Cleburne urged.

"Maybe conscription is needed, but we don't much like the way it's being done," Cabell responded quickly, as if glad to tell his father about matters he had never been asked about. Breckinridge had worried about conscription, begun by the Confederacy in the spring; it brought into public view a long-hidden desperation about manpower. "There's talk of an exemption for any man with twenty slaves or more," the young man went on. "That's not fair. If it's slavery we're defending, why shouldn't slave owners be drafted?"

"They're needed to run the plantations," Breckinridge heard himself saying, not satisfied with his own response. "And when the North starts drafting men again, there's sure to be a money exemption. Money's needed as much as men, and the sons of the rich up North will buy their way out."

"Rich man's war, poor man's fight."

Cleburne slapped his thigh and shouted through his bandages, "That's right! That's what they're saying, North and South. For every slave trader like Nathan Forrest, there's five of us who never owned a slave and never will. Now, let's get down to the nubbin: if it isn't slavery you're fighting for, young man, what is it? The chastity of Southern womanhood? Military glory?"

Cabell looked straight at his father. "Independence, like I said. It's our revolution. We want to do things our own way." Breckinridge felt that implicit in what the boy said was another question: "Why did my father never ask me?"

"It's only you old fogies think slavery is all," Cleburne added to Breck. "The rank and file, even the high-born ones like your boy here—and he's a fine lad, Breck, you brought him up to speak his mind—the rank and file know better. You politicians used to talk about 'states' rights,' remember? What rights does a state have in the Confederacy? Richmond has mustered all the state troops into the national army. Martial law, and where's your habeas corpus now, my friend? Soon there'll be a national tax, same as in the North. And how'd you like to be a businessman—"

"I know, I know." Breckinridge didn't want to hear about any of that. The suspension of the rules against arbitrary arrest had shattered one of his fundaments, and as for central power—the Confederate Government owned or controlled all war production, and had issued rules about profits and markets that mocked the freedom of the entrepreneur. The Confederacy was already more centralized than the Union, and bid fair to become as repressive, though that was limited by the angry independence of Georgia and South Carolina.

"But these are temporary, emergency measures," he held. "It's wartime. This won't be the way it will be when the war is over." The former politician knew he was off balance, stunned at the way he seemed to be so out of touch with new ideas. He had been debating slavery and states' rights for his whole political life. Cleburne might be a wild Irishman, but if young Cabell Breckinridge thought this way, how many of the brigade did? How many of the Confederate rank and file?

"We're not fighting to save black slavery," pressed Cleburne, "we're fighting to stop white slavery—against becoming slaves to the government in

Washington. The Yankees are fighting for sectional superiority; they want to conquer the South and deprive us of our rights and liberties. Dr. Beecher as much as admitted the agitation about slavery was a guise, a device to inflame the North to take over the stubborn South."

"Independence is not our cause," insisted Breckinridge. He remembered his long arguments with Lincoln in the White House only a year ago. He had told the President, whose election Breckinridge as president of the Senate had personally certified, that the Southern "cause" was simply to be let alone. He had warned Lincoln not to strike at the institution of slavery, as the radicals were demanding. Even today, the Union could still come back together "as it was" if the offensives of Lee in Maryland and Bragg in Kentucky led to election victories in the late fall by the Peace Democrats. "Face the reality, Patrick—the difference between North and South is slavery. If we can keep it only where it was, we'll be back in the Union. One nation, each section respecting the other's rights."

"Is that what Jeff Davis thinks?" Cleburne shot back. "He sees himself as our George Washington, doesn't he? He put General Washington on the Confederate seal, didn't he? Forget Union, Breckeen, it will never come again unless we surrender."

"Heresy," declared Breckinridge. Cleburne was right about Davis, though —that good man saw himself as a military messiah, freeing his people from a distant tyranny as George Washington did less than a century ago. "Have you talked about this to anybody else?"

"I'm afraid to," said the hero of Lexington cheerfully, "they'd tar and feather me. But mark my words, that's what this war will come to—enlisting the blacks to fight with us."

"Would they fight?" Cabell asked.

"The helots of Sparta stood their masters in good stead in battle," Cleburne replied. "Paid with their freedom, the slaves will fight. More important, the passion will go out of the abolitionists in the North. And our present embarrassment will end with our dealings with the English—those foul blackguards could then recognize us."

"Could we spare the blacks from the fields?" Breckinridge found himself asking, as if the scheme were worthy of consideration.

"Enough slaves are administering to luxury alone," said Cleburne with some scorn, "to fill the places we need. After that, we could leave some of the skill at home in the fields and take some of the muscle to fight with. It would work. No, the real heresy is to admit that the slaves want to be free. That's something our Southern friends refuse to face. They spin a fairy tale about the slaves loving their present condition."

"He's right, sir."

Breckinridge shook his head; the idea, while eminently logical, could never be accepted by Southern firebrands. When Secretary of State Judah Benjamin secretly broached it to Jeff Davis, as a means of earning recognition of the Confederacy by Britain and France, he had been turned down immediately. Davis agreed only to consider drafting a force of slaves into the army to work as laborers, with no promises of freedom.

"Lincoln's getting ready to use blacks, you know," Cleburne added. "We could beat him to the punch."

"How do you know?"

"Butler the Beast, down in New Orleans, is training a regiment of Africans, supposedly for guard duty, but that's a lie."

Breckinridge had to admit that the prospect of the Federal Army's employing blacks, or of the Lincoln government's approving some form of emancipation for fugitives who joined Union ranks, gave weight to Cleburne's notion. If Lincoln tried to free the South's slaves, or even announced his intention to in some far-off future, that could be a blow to the South. It could turn many blacks actively against white masters. Emancipation might even force Jeff Davis to match the offer of freedom to potential black soldiers, no matter how the plantation owners protested.

"President Davis would have to be desperate to even entertain such an idea," Breckinridge concluded. "Patrick, I presume you told us this to get my political counsel."

"That I did, Breckeen. I can handle myself in an apothecary or on the field of combat, but politics was never mother's milk to me."

"It could be you're right and I'm wrong about independence now being more important than slavery," Breck allowed. "But if Lincoln thinks the cause of the Union is losing its force, he'll turn to abolition, and try to make the war about slavery."

"We mustn't let him, don't you see?" Cleburne's passion was infectious, but Breck did not want to be drawn into a conspiracy around an idea that would give Bragg a chance to come down on his neck and punish his brigade. "We're fighting for our own country. The Confederacy can expand down into French Mexico. To hell with the slave system if it's going to lose us the war."

Breck decided he would have to think about it some other time. He wished he could talk it over with Anna Carroll. "Just be sure, Pat, you don't let Braxton Bragg know what you're thinking."

"Then how do I gain support for the idea? Come on, now, man, this is your field, not mine."

"Talk it over only with men you trust." When an orderly came into the room with a pressed gray uniform, Breck stopped talking until the man left; Bragg was not above spying on his commanders. "Commit nothing to paper. In a while, if our advance continues into the North, or if sensible Democrats win up in New York in the election, you may want to forget you ever thought of it."

"But if things go sour," Cleburne posited, "if McClellan defeats Lee, or if Bragg gets us thrown back into Tennessee—"

"The moment might come to write a joint letter to a superior officer," was all Breck would say. He hated himself for being so tentative, but Cleburne was among the best soldiers of the South, and his career could be snuffed out by this foray into the most sensitive political issue. "Hand it personally to Hardee, or Polk—to be forwarded directly to President Davis. If I'm around Richmond," he added vaguely, "I'll talk to the President about it."

Cabell left to answer a knock at the front door.

"But what do you think of the chances, Breck?"

"Not good. At least not soon. It's just too big an idea to get your mind around. You really think Lincoln wants to use black troops?"

Cleburne nodded. "I have friends in New York—Irishmen. They say Greeley and the radical Republicans are screaming for it, and Lincoln can't resist much longer or he loses his party's backing."

"Freedom for the slaves cuts both ways," Breckinridge observed, "and a lot of your Irish friends don't want to see blacks flocking up there to take their jobs."

Cabell returned, papers in hand. "It's a petition from the men of the 5th Kentucky Brigade. They're almost home now. They've marched and ridden eleven hundred miles in fourteen days, switching to sever railroads; shoes are in short supply, and they demand to be discharged when their year is up. Which is next month."

"Sure and you've got a mutiny on your hands, General Breckinridge."

The Kentuckian despaired of the way Bragg would use this uproar against him and his men. He told his son to assemble the brigade along three sides of the parade ground and on the fourth set up a platform for him to speak. His task was not so much to incite the people of Kentucky to join the revolution against Yankee oppression as to keep the Kentuckians in his command from breaking up and going home.

"This means we won't be going home to visit your mother," he added to the boy. Again, Mary would have to wait. He thanked the Irishman for looking in on his family in Lexington and warned him again to keep his black freedom ideas to himself and a tight circle. Then Breck began to get his thoughts together for a fire-eating political stump speech. He had his own little election to worry about within the Orphan Brigade.

CHAPTER 13

THE RISE OF SEYMOUR

Anna Carroll had received a note from Thurlow Weed, sent by messenger from Secretary of State Seward's office, asking her to breakfast at Willard's. That was good news. She assumed he wanted some political favor done, requiring someone who had influence with Chase. Her influence with the capital's most eligible widower was never stronger; although he was seeing other women, Anna was certain there was nobody with whom the Treasury Secretary was more politically intimate. Other intimacy, she hoped, would soon follow. He was extraordinarily straitlaced, almost tortured, about giving way to his normal needs as a man. And his daughter continued to hover over him like his mother. She wished she could induce a phase of active courtship, but knew that any show of impatience would be fatal.

Whatever Thurlow Weed wanted, she hoped she could deliver it for him, because she wanted to enlist his support on an unpaid government bill in return. She told the messenger to tell the New York editor and political leader she would be there promptly at 8 A.M.

She arrived at seven-thirty, expecting to find a copy of the *Albany Evening Journal*, Weed's paper, at the Willard's newsstand, one of the best-stocked in town. The paper would be a few days late, but she knew it would be flattering for an out-of-town publisher to breakfast with a lady who took the trouble to read his editorials.

Sure enough, the man at the newsstand had a recent copy and a comment: "Mr. Weed makes certain his paper comes down on the same train with the *New York Tribune*, ma'am." She riffled through to get the drift of Weed's political positions.

Weed's *Evening Journal*, she was glad to see, expressed its gratification at McClellan's reinstatement. That unequivocal support of the man who was at that moment saving the Union from the predations of Lee in Maryland was in sharp contrast to the fury of Horace Greeley's *Tribune* at Lincoln for turning to "Little Mac" to defend Washington. Weed's Albany newspaper was also urging New York Democrats, whose convention would take place in a few days, to nominate General John Dix, a loyal War Democrat, rather than former governor Horatio Seymour. Anna noticed a low blow: Weed had dubbed Seymour the "Knight of the Sorrowful Countenance," a hint that Seymour might have been one of those who sympathized with the traitorous "Knights of the Golden Circle," the plotters of Southern insurrection.

"Your kindness and perspicacity in reading my newspaper are typical of you, Miss Carroll," he murmured, sinking heavily into the large chair. "I recommend the hominy grits here, if you are in the mood for porridge, unless you are watching your figger. Which, I am told, and meaning no offense, at least one former President has done."

"Two," she replied merrily. Washington in early September was still hot and humid, and she wore a dress that showed more neck and shoulders than fashion dictated for daytime, but her bosom was an asset she never hesitated to display. She folded her *Journal* and leaned forward to put it with her purse under the table. "You forget Fillmore."

"I can never forget Millard Fillmore," Weed said, looking at all of her with the frank admiration of a man too old to act but never too old to appreciate, "because his 'Silver Grays,' as the old-line Whigs now call themselves, are going for Seymour. And as governor of New York, Seymour would be a disaster for the Union."

"Can he be stopped?"

"That is where your intercession with Fillmore would help," he near-whispered, his soft voice always pitched to impart confidences. "You were influential once in providing him with the support of the Native American Party." Anna noted that Weed skirted the term "Know-Nothings," as if to spare her sensibilities. "A message from you and your many old friends of that persuasion, madam, which I would be happy to deliver, as I am going to Troy this afternoon—"

"Fillmore is an ingrate." She recalled the former President's pathetic maunderings at their last meeting in Rochester on her way back from the West. But she was in no position to turn Weed down; he might be able to help with her bill for $6,250 for her pamphlets, including printing, which the damnable War Department bureaucracy was questioning. The budget officer was writing to local lawyers to find if the fee was conscionable; paying a woman for anything was more than most disbursing officers could stand, and Tom Scott was no longer next door to Stanton to look out for her interests. "But I'll write the letter if it's important to you. Here's something you should find useful: the key to Fillmore and his supporters is Dean Richmond. If you could get to him—"

Weed nodded. She was talking about a fellow wirepuller, positioned across the political street, but not unreachable. Because she could not bring up the subject of her unpaid fee so soon, Anna changed the subject: "I notice you came around to supporting the Confiscation Act, Mr. Weed." Like her, he had originally opposed it as unlawful seizure of property.

"I was in England this summer, as you know," Weed replied. "Lincoln wanted me to buttress Ambassador Adams in talks with the Prime Minister and Foreign Secretary, who want to recognize the South. They fairly salivate for our permanent disunion. But the English workers are opposed to slavery. So we have to do what we can to show that the Union is fighting the extension of slavery. That's why I came around on the Confiscation Act."

"My own view of emancipation is changing," she said, treading carefully, "because the nature of the war has changed. What used to be a rebellion is now a full-scale war between two powers. Under the laws of war, slaves set free as a military measure cannot be deprived of their freedom after the war, any more than horses taken as booty or purchased by a prize court can be remanded to the original owner."

"Do not go overboard, my dear lady. Abolition would end all possibility of peace negotiations. It would mean a fight to the finish, unimaginable desolation, utter destruction. Moreover, the reaction of the voter to abolition would cost us the state of New York. The loss of New York to the Democrats would mean the loss of the war."

"I defer to your judgment on New York state politics. Maryland is my state."

"Will the people of Maryland, Miss Carroll, rise up to support Robert E. Lee when he comes to lift what he calls the Union yoke?" Weed was quick and to the point. General Lee was about to strike across the Potomac into her Maryland, where John Dix and the Union troops, by the most expeditious if undemocratic means, had only a year before prevented the legislature from seceding. If Marylanders welcomed Lee's Confederates, providing food and support to the rebel forces, not even McClellan could stop him. Philadelphia and New York City would be undefended; Lincoln would have to sue for peace.

"No," she said firmly. "The plug-uglies of Baltimore don't speak for Maryland. Lee will be disappointed. I've written to Governor Bradford to appoint Hicks senator, and he's popular with loyalists. No, the greater danger is Bragg and Breckinridge moving up into Kentucky."

That stopped him. "Tell me about Breckinridge."

She avoided that. "Kentuckians aren't like Marylanders—they'll go with whoever looks like the winner. The whole state of Kentucky could shift—"

"No, not the military situation. I mean Breckinridge as a political man. You knew him?"

How much did Weed know? "Our families were close. His cousin, the Reverend Robert Breckinridge, was my spiritual adviser." Uncle Robert was a loyal Unionist.

"I could have sworn Breck would be President one day," Weed mused. "Young, a gifted orator, strong for the Union, good understanding of patronage, everything going for him. Now John Breckinridge is branded a traitor, expelled from the Senate, a man without a state, ruined forever in politics." He added a phrase that was barely audible: "Unless they win."

She finished that thought for him: "And then he'd be the likely President of the Confederacy." That was the first time such a possibility had occurred to her, and if the recently beaten troops of the Army of the Potomac could not contain the triumphant Lee and Jackson, that might be a lively prospect. She wondered how Breck felt at the suspension of habeas corpus and other crackdowns on dissent by Jeff Davis; did he understand at last that, in the presence of arms, the laws fell silent?

"I can understand why men of power are attracted to you, Miss Carroll," the politician said in his most confidentially avuncular manner. "Why is it you've never chosen to marry?"

That was a nice way of putting the question so often asked of her. She decided not to take offense because Weed thought of all romance as a political game. She could hardly tell the truth—Fillmore was a cad, Buchanan never asked, Breckinridge was already taken, and Chase, perhaps on the brink, still hesitated—so she dissembled artfully.

"Most men of power want women who supplement their talents," she said. "I'm of an independent mind, and they see me as competition. It's too bad, in a way. I would like to have had children. On the other hand, being unattached has given me the freedom to do what few other women ever get a chance to do."

"I'm having great trouble with Chase," Weed said, seemingly irrelevant, finally to the point. "And now I come to my motive in inviting you to this sumptuous repast." He dropped a dollop of raspberry jam on a corn muffin and handed it to her, as if in outright bribery. "I don't know how well you know Chase, Miss Carroll—"

"I wish you would call me Anna, Thurlow." He knew precisely how well she knew Chase, which was why they were having breakfast.

"I would be grateful if you would drop two messages in Secretary Chase's ear."

He waited. Was she supposed to take out a pencil and make notes? She committed herself to nothing: "Go on."

"First, Anna, I would hope that Chase and Seward could get together on a suitable policy toward slavery and go to the President with it. Not abolition, by any means—just enough promises of abolition in the distant future to keep the English out of the war."

Anna wanted to tell him she knew about the proclamation of emancipation now sitting in Lincoln's desk, which Weed evidently thought he had stopped. But she was not about to confide in him more than he confided in her. She knew one fact that would have amazed Weed: that Chase was not as close to abolition as Lincoln was. Chase, to prevent Lincoln from seizing his radical following, would probably side with Seward in the Cabinet to restrain Lincoln from proclaiming emancipation personally.

"I'll do what I can to bring Chase and Seward together," she promised faithfully, since that temporary alliance was inevitable. "What else?"

"Tell Chase, for God's sake, to keep Greeley from running an abolitionist for governor of New York. Back John Dix for the Republican nomination."

Anna could not promise that; she was prepared only to ask Chase to do what he had already half-decided to do. To avoid having to turn him down, she asked, "Is Horatio Seymour that good a candidate? The Republicans carried New York by a hundred thousand votes last year."

"Seymour is not your usual politician," Weed said slowly. "He is very"—Weed searched for the word, which he pronounced with distaste—"high-minded. He is a man of intellect and principle, the sort Lincoln would like to debate. He would give respectability to those Irish ruffians who oppose abolition because they fear the African will come up and take their jobs."

"But he's a copperhead, like Vallandigham—"

"Ah, you underestimate the man. You will never hear him crying for peace at any price; on the contrary, he sounds like the voice of sweet reason. Seymour, with all his noble motives, could become the rallying point for those opposed to Lincoln on baser motives. I want you to get Chase to put the fear of Horatio Seymour into Greeley."

"Maybe Ben Wade is the best approach," she said obliquely, which was the best way to conclude a political conversation with Weed. Then she raised the matter of her unpaid bill at the War Department. As he hailed a hack to take him to the railroad station, Weed took out a notebook and jotted down the amount.

Horatio Seymour, nominee for governor of New York of the Democratic Party in convention assembled, had to remind himself to keep a straight face during the introduction.

He was seated on the jam-packed stage, in the middle of a crowd of running mates and party leaders, with the eyes of conventioneers, helpers, and hangers-on all upon him. The introducer spoke of a nominee carrying on a great family tradition of service to New York State; Seymour thought it was fair to recall the work of his legislator-father who helped build the Erie Canal, and knew that no introducer would add that Papa made a fortune in land speculation and shot himself in the Panic of 1837. The speaker shouting from the rostrum lauded the "family ties"; yes, it was nice that Mary Bleecker, his wife of thirty years, was of the Dutch landowning family. That had given him his estate and his chance to experiment with agricultural techniques, and to plant a great pear orchard with his own hands. Nothing would be said of the Seymours' profound disappointment at their childlessness.

Looking over the crowd, Seymour could see—in a flag-draped box, detached from the mob—the man who had cajoled him into acceptance of this nomination, Dean Richmond, an amiable wirepuller who would soon be lifted out of crass political dealing to fit Seymour's notions of high-minded campaigning. He spotted the massive form of Republican "dictator" Thurlow Weed in Democratic "dictator" Richmond's box, looking uncomfortable next to another journalistic guest, Horace Greeley of the *Tribune*, clothed as usual in the white suit that was supposed to stand for candor or purity. Seymour would suffer the slings and arrows of both men in the coming months; he was glad that they could hear his speech tonight.

The introducer was up to Seymour's days as governor in the early fifties, extolling the way he had wisely borrowed to widen and extend his father's Erie Canal. Nothing was said about his unpopular veto of the law passed in

Albany to prohibit the sale of liquor; Seymour believed that such prohibition was an unconstitutional invasion of the rights of local government, and the former governor was proud to this day of that veto, but it had earned him the reputation of being a drunkard and captive of the liquor interests.

Seymour, half-listening, was not in the least ashamed at having had the political temerity to invite the papal nuncio to a dinner with Protestant clergy, which brought down the wrath of Millard Fillmore and his anti-Papist Know-Nothings. In his campaign for reelection in 1856, these forces combined to drive Seymour out. It was a filthy campaign even by New York standards, and he had been happy to retire from politics to his Utica orchard.

Now here he was again, responding to the Democratic Party's call, preparing to campaign in a manner untried by any other New York candidate: he would stump the state from one end to the other, reaching out for votes in a systematic way that would shatter the tradition of professing nonchalance and giving out interviews from a rocker on the front porch. But he was not doing this in the spirit of party, or to line Dean Richmond's pockets; now he had a mission, a purpose beyond politics.

The speaker's last line, including the traditional "gre-a-a-t state of New York," was drowned in the hullabaloo of bands and shouts and cap-tossings. Seymour did not deny himself the moment's exhilaration. He knew why he was there, and why a voice within him wanted the nomination: he could be the nation's peacemaker.

"Two years ago at this convention," he called out, "we implored the new national Administration to submit some measure of conciliation which would save us from civil war. Our prayer was derided and denounced, and false assurances were given that there was no danger." Seymour was persuaded that Lincoln had not gone far enough to prevent the war; if the President had imagined then the horrors the nation knew now, he would surely have acted differently. Most voters knew that was true; the Lincoln intractability that led to bloody war was an exploitable weakness.

"Rottenness and corruption pervade the Executive department." He held up a clipping from a newspaper—the *Albany Evening Journal*—and, looking toward Thurlow Weed in the box, read with relish:

"Listen to the organ of the Secretary of State: 'Contractors have fattened on fat jobs, adventurers have found the war a source of private gain. Moral desperadoes have flocked about the national capital, and the scum of the land has gathered about the sources of power.' " Seymour grinned at the roar of the crowd at the discomfited Weed, and was glad that he had been able to find a similar diatribe in Greeley's *Tribune* to make a different point:

"And listen to this, from the *New York Tribune*, the organ of the founder of the Republican Party: 'The country is in peril. The rebels seem to be pushing forward all along the border line. They are threatening the Potomac and the Ohio. Through the timidity, despondency, or folly of the federal government, this simultaneous movement may become successful . . .' " Seymour enjoyed using *Tribune* pessimism to show that even Lincoln apologists could not hide the danger to which the Republicans had brought the country.

Before attacking further, Seymour wanted to reestablish his loyalty to the Union. "We charge that this rebellion is most wicked. Rebellion is not necessarily wrong. The rebellion of our fathers is our proudest boast, the rebellion of our brothers is our national disgrace." That establishes the loyalty of the opposition, Seymour reasoned; now to the disunity of the party in power.

"I have read to you the testimony of Messrs. Greeley and Weed, charging fraud, outrage, and incompetency. But bear in mind that the embarrassment of President Lincoln grows out of the conflicting views of his political friends."

Lowering his voice for emphasis—he had the crowd now, he no longer had to strain his voice—Seymour drove home a subtle point: "Mr. Lincoln's hands would be strengthened by a Democratic victory. We will relieve him of the pressures of those who thirst for blood."

Seymour had the proof: "In his communication with the loyal men of the border states, the President confesses he is pressed to violate his duty, his oath of office, and the Constitution, pressed by cowardly and heartless abolitionists who demand that those who have suffered most in this contest should have a new and further evil inflicted upon them by the hands of a government they are struggling to uphold."

Having lightly touched the tender subject of abolition, Seymour savaged "the brutal and bloody language of partisan editors and political preachers which has lost us the sympathy of the civilized world." Few politicians would dare to attack such powerful editors, but Seymour knew he had nothing to lose in taunting them; they would excoriate him anyway, and by attacking them, he attracted those voters who resented the rising power of the press lords.

Surely the Republicans would wrap themselves in the flag, imputing support of Lincoln's candidates to be support of the soldiers in the field. Seymour knew he had to chip away at that. "I went to the camp of our soldiers. Amid sufferings from exposure and want, I heard and saw only devotion to our Constitution." That was the week he had visited George McClellan, who he was certain had become his secret ally against the implacable Lincoln. "But a fanatical majority of Republicans in Congress make war on the Union men of the South and strengthen the hands of secessionists. Most of their time is spent in annoying our army, in meddling with its operations and embarrassing our generals."

The hall applauded this indirect support of McClellan. Having broached the issue of slavery, Seymour reminded his audience of the compromise struck by the Constitution's fathers and added, "Proclamations of emancipation are now urged upon the President, which could only confiscate the property of loyal citizens, for no others could be reached. You have been deceived. Who deceived you? Who stained our land with blood? The authors of our calamity now ask to adopt measures which they have heretofore denounced as unjust and unconstitutional. They cannot save our country."

The audience was attentive and enthusiastic, and Seymour felt he was doing for his cause what Lincoln had done at Cooper Union years before: impressing both the faithful and the undecided that at least here was a man who knew how to marshal the forces of his argument. He put in a ringing defense of the right of dissent, castigating the supposed patriots who were too quick to label as "traitor" anyone who stood for constitutional principle.

The nominee reached his peroration:

"Opposed to the election of Mr. Lincoln, we have loyally sustained him.

Governor Horatio Seymour

Differing on the conduct of the war, we have responded to every demand made upon us. We are pouring out our blood, our treasures, and our men to rescue our government from a position in which it can neither propose peace nor conduct successful war. We wish to see our Union saved, our laws vindicated, and peace once more restored to our land."

The reaction was better than he had expected and as much as he had hoped. No wild roars of racialist hatred or disunionist sentiment, no banners insulting the President or undermining the war effort; instead, long, sustained applause, as if the New York Democratic convention—having received his message and understood his campaign theme—was ready to join him in battle for a negotiated peace on the basis of the Union as it was, with slavery confined to the original slave states.

Now, for the first time, Seymour was looking forward to the campaign. He was not running for or against slavery. He was not running only for governor. He was running for peace.

In his box, Dean Richmond observed his guests with amusement. Weed wore a mournful look. Greeley's pink face mottled with passion, his shrill voice piping, "Traitor! He's nothing but a traitor! He'll be buried under the biggest avalanche of votes ever seen in the state of New York!"

Richmond, saying nothing, looked to Weed for the response. He knew the political adage that held it was folly to murder an opponent who was committing suicide. Weed said only: "Peace has an appeal, Horace."

"This idiot is advocating surrender! And he has the gall to suggest that his victory would *help* Lincoln!" Richmond had never seen the great Greeley so agitated; the Seymour speech must have been more effective than he at first thought. Perhaps the approach of Lee's rebel legions would make radical voters think twice about abolition.

"If any emancipation moves go forward," Weed said in a tone lower than his usual lowered voice, but one that Richmond could still catch, "Seymour will win on the peace issue."

"What does abolition have to do with delaying peace?" Greeley demanded. "It will hurry victory along, if anything."

"A proclamation would end all hope of a peace overture. It would mean a fight to the finish." Weed seemed quite certain of the future. "If peace is to be offered, if any negotiations are to take place, secret or otherwise, they have to be undertaken before any emancipation announcements. Striking at slavery crosses the Rubicon."

"It's the Potomac I'm worried about," Greeley rejoined. "As soon as Lee moves, McClellan will sue for peace. He won't fight. I cannot understand what got into Lincoln, reappointing that miserable ditherer. Hooker's the general, or Burnside. And if we should be taken to disaster by your McClellan, Thurlow, we are better off as two separate nations than as a Union incorporating the moral evil of slavery."

Richmond, out of a sense of political decency, turned as if to look at what was happening in an opposite direction. He heard Weed say, "No. The West needs the Mississippi River all the way down to the Gulf. The West will never let you permit the South to secede, because that would put the Mississippi in the hands of another nation. Before they'll let that happen, the West—all of it, Ohio, Illinois, Missouri—will accept slavery in the Union as it was. Think of the West, Horace."

"I have long recommended the frontier to our youth," the editor in the white smock and white hat said frostily. "I am getting the train to New York City. Troy always depresses me."

Richmond stepped out of the box and made his way through the crowd to the candidate's side, acknowledging nods from the politically cognizant. In a few minutes he was in the governor's suite, where he could report on the editors' reactions to Seymour's use of their editorials against them.

"Greeley is overconfident," the political leader reported to candidate Seymour in private. "He wants to humiliate Weed and Seward at their convention, and that will make Weed sit on his hands during the campaign. The radicals' hatred of Seward is fierce. You have a chance."

"I don't care about my election, that's not probable." Seymour was the first candidate to say that in Richmond's political experience; the political leader hoped the candidate was saying it only for effect. "But I want the opponents of the men who brought our country into its deplorable condition to be so much aroused as to make themselves felt and respected."

"You will have a great many people on your side, Governor, that you won't like. You realize that?"

"I want a strong, compact party that can defy violence and can keep fanatics in check," Seymour said. "Make certain you stay in touch with Barlow, and through him McClellan in the field. Mac is on our side; I know that for a fact. F'nandy Wood and I spoke to him. He's for peace, he doesn't want those fine men of his army butchered to satisfy some agitators."

"Casualties don't seem to worry Lincoln."

"True, he'd let the Union bleed to death, but remember—not a word by any of our supporters against Lincoln."

"The President is terribly unpopular—" Richmond did not want to lose a good target.

"He's a target for others, not for us. We attack only his advisers. If I met the man someday, I would not like to be burdened with the memory of personal attacks on him."

"He is tougher than he seems," Richmond said. Weed had told him how Seward had underestimated Lincoln's tenacity and stubbornness at first; the President was a man who used every kind of guile and Western folksiness to get his way. And he persevered. "I hear Lincoln is very good on patronage, but very hard on policy."

"We will attack that policy, but not the President personally," Seymour directed. "Stanton is the one who is waging war on the North with his arbitrary arrests. I will denounce the doctrine that Civil War in the South takes away from the loyal North the benefits of one principle of civil liberty."

The Democratic boss was pleased with his choice. "Use that idea of your victory helping Lincoln," Richmond advised. "I thought Greeley would turn purple when he heard it."

"In many respects, Dean, it was injurious to me to be nominated." Seymour smiled wryly: "I thought I had traded ambition for avarice. But now that I'm in the field, I want a sharp, bitter fight. If we save New York, we save the Union."

CHAPTER 14

JOHN HAY'S DIARY
SEPTEMBER 12, 1862

"How does it look now?" That was the message Lincoln sent to McClellan from the telegraph office across the street at 4 A.M. this morning.

The Prsdt is haggard, worried. He is limping around in his slippers because of his damned corns and now has a sprained wrist because of the damned runaway horse. He is not in a good mood. Two weeks ago Bates said after a Cabinet meeting that he looked as if he was ready to hang himself, and the Tycoon has not snapped back with his usual resiliency.

General Lee's invasion of the North has begun. The only force between him and Southern victory is George McClellan and the army recently whipped under John Pope. The Young Napoleon sent word back through Halleck that he is in Rockville, Maryland, looking for Lee. We think Lee is probably marching into Pennsylvania. Philadelphia is in a panic, and the governor of Pennsylvania is burning up our telegraph wires with horrific claims that 120,000 Confederates are streaming into his state.

Halleck says that McClellan wanted the garrison at Harpers Ferry to come and join his forces, insisting that the place is indefensible and he needs the troops to swell his ranks. Halleck disagrees, with Stanton probably egging him on, and won't send Little Mac those 12,000 men from Harpers Ferry. Lincoln said to send up Fitz-John Porter's 20,000 slow movers from the Washington area instead; McClellan likes Porter.

So all the archives, treasure, and bonds of Pennsylvania now in the capital at Harrisburg and at Philadelphia are being shipped up to New York. That doesn't help anybody's morale. We don't know which way Lee will head: he could aim for Philadelphia, or cut across Maryland for Baltimore, or double back here to Washington. The dismaying thing is that there is nobody to stop him from going clear to New York except McClellan, who is exceeding his authority by acting like the field commander of all our troops facing Lee, for which I suppose the Prsdt should be thankful. Lincoln does not have the backing to appoint McClellan to do what we expect him to do.

And that's only half the military problem. Bragg and Breckinridge, if not stopped, will overrun Tennessee and Kentucky and win the war that way. I ran a message across to the telegraph office from Lincoln to one of our more confused generals: "Where is the enemy which you dread in Louisville? How near to you?"

In the midst of all this commotion, with our armies having all this trouble finding the advancing enemy, a delegation from the Society of Friends trooped in. They want their coreligionists to be exempt from the draft. We passed a draft law for 300,000 men last month; now the papers are printing how many men are expected from each district in each state and the shoe is pinching. Adding to the general sense of desperation, a thousand old, grizzled squirrel hunters from the Ohio Valley sent word that they have formed a home guard in Cincinnati, in case Breckinridge or Bragg comes their way. The West as well as the North has invasion jitters.

I put on the Prsdt's desk the contract for shipping five hundred negroes to the Chiriquí Tract in Panama, and he signed it. But the government of Honduras is threatening to make trouble, as Anna Carroll warned; nobody wants our Africans, and they don't want to go to Africa. If we have this much trouble with shipping out five hundred, what will we do with the four million if the Tycoon goes through with the plan to set them free?

The Tycoon has tied together emancipation and colonization in his mind, and says he will not surrender the game leaving any available card unplayed. He is prepared to listen to the hollering of the blacks about being deported because he thinks that will quiet the hollering of the whites about freeing the slaves. And it's working: Frederick Douglass, whose black hand the Prsdt has shaken in the White House, reacted to the Tycoon's little chat with the cooperative colored leaders the other day with a blast at Lincoln's "inconsistencies, his pride of race and blood, his contempt for negroes and his canting hypocrisy." Douglass's disappointment soothes our conservative friends a bit. (Good turn of phrase, "canting hypocrisy.")

Speaking of hypocrites, Governor Sprague came in with an offer of three negro regiments raised in Rhode Island and Massachusetts. He knew, with the widespread white resentment about the draft, how hard it would be for Lincoln to say no. But the Prsdt is not willing to enlist black soldiers. Yet.

I do not like Sprague. He sees entirely too much of Kate Chase, slobbering over her in his stupidly drunken way, and she says she has to tolerate it because Sprague has a political hold on her father. I suspect Sprague must be offering to put his vast fortune at Chase's disposal to wrest the Republican nomination from Lincoln in '64.

Consider the position at this moment of the man trying to hold the country together: enemies in the field, on the march in two major offensives; enemies within the army, conniving to create a dictatorship or at least throw their weight to the Peace Democrats; enemies in the Cabinet, eager to supplant him at the next party convention; enemies in the Congress, plotting to snatch away his authority to run the war. Not to mention a wife crazy as a coot, now bringing in spiritualists to hold ghostly seances in the Mansion so she can speak to the dead Willie. Sometimes it seems that the Prsdt has to fight a half-dozen wars at the same time; who can blame him for looking as if he wants to hang himself?

CHAPTER 15

Antietam I
With Lee

General Thomas Jackson noted that his commander, Robert Lee, launched his invasion of the North while seated in an ambulance. Lee had fallen forward on his hands at the sudden move of a startled horse and had broken a bone in one hand and sprained the other wrist. With both hands in splints, Lee could not handle a mount, and was forced to lead his troops in a cart designed for transport of the wounded.

Jackson's back was aching from a fall of his own when his gray mare reared and toppled over backward. That would not have happened with his regular horse, Fancy, which his men liked to call "Little Sorrel." He found there was no accounting for nicknames, although he did not mind being called "Stonewall," the sobriquet universally applied after the first victory at Manassas. Jackson favored his regular horse, though others thought the reddish-brown animal ungainly and ugly, because Fancy was like himself: lean, angular, ascetic, not much for seems. The mare that nearly fell on him was all grace and beauty; the dour commander took that as a lesson.

Seated in pain on another mount, Jackson watched the Confederate Army on the march and did not like what he saw. The long columns of infantrymen were ragged and undisciplined. Stragglers frequently dropped off to the side of the road, pulling off their clothes to get at the "graybacks," the lice that kept even the sleepiest awake.

The men were unshaven and dirty, the butternut uniforms the color of road dust, shocks of hair sticking through holes in hats. Blankets, supposed to be tightly rolled and strapped to the back, were slung over the shoulder, as were knapsacks, tin cups, and canteens. As they walked, their general could hear the sound of flapping soles from those lucky enough to wear what was left of shoes.

Never in his military experience—West Point, the Mexican War, and just before the war an instructor at the Virginia Military Institute—had Jackson seen such a tatterdemalion bunch of tired men claiming to be an army. The ribbed, hungry horses and old artillery wagons with creaking wheels completed the picture of military dilapidation. This did not strike Stonewall Jackson as the picture of an invading army, come to liberate the oppressed people of Maryland; it seemed more like a bandit horde.

A. P. Hill's command, as usual, looked the worst; in his "Light Division," as the moody Hill liked to call it, the straggling and formlessness was so unmilitary as to be a disgrace to the Army of Northern Virginia. Jackson moved his horse forward and halted one brigade to allow it to re-form. The red-bearded Powell Hill, in his flamboyant red shirt, came galloping up and asked the brigade's leader by whose orders his division was being delayed. The brigadier motioned toward Jackson.

Hill glared at Jackson, unbuckled his sword, and held it out hilt-first to his

General Thomas Jonathan Jackson, C.S.A.

superior. "If you're going to give the orders to my men," he seethed aloud, "you have no need of me."

"Consider yourself under arrest," Jackson snapped back at the impertinence, "for neglect of duty."

"You're not fit to be a general," Powell Hill told him. Jackson, now burning with anger, did not trust himself to reply; he stared down "Little Powell" until that erratic and insubordinate officer turned and rode away.

That made two generals Jackson had under arrest; General Hood, whose Texans were among the fiercest fighters in Lee's army, had already been removed from command for insubordination. The tensions of invasion were at the breaking point in the highest echelons of the army, but Jackson considered discipline in the ranks and subordination in command above all. Powell Hill was unreliable; Jackson wished he could have a stiff-backed organizer like Braxton Bragg with them now, but Bragg, at Lee's suggestion to President Davis, had been chosen to lead the invasion in the West.

"Li'l Powell is one of them army lawyers," said Jackson's aide-de-camp. "He'll be demanding a written statement of charges."

The paperwork was a burden. "Only if I decide on a court-martial," Jackson said. "Tell Hill to remain with his division."

In the city of Frederick, before a small gathering in the town square, Jackson stood near Lee as the commanding general read a proclamation. It struck Jackson as a strange way for a conqueror to act, but Lee must have had his reasons, and Jackson trusted Robert Lee as he had no other man.

"The people of the Confederate States," read Robert Lee in his quiet voice, which could barely be heard by the small crowd, "have seen with profound indignation their sister state deprived of every right and reduced to the condition of a conquered province. Your citizens have been arrested and imprisoned upon no charge and contrary to all forms of law." That was a reference to the arrest of Merryman, Jackson recalled; Lee would probably cite Chief Justice Taney's opinion, so widely hailed in the South until the necessary suspension of habeas corpus there.

"The faithful and manly protest against this outrage," read Lee in this effort to make friends with the local population, "as made by the venerable Marylander, to whom in better days no citizen appealed for right in vain, was treated with scorn and contempt."

Jackson saw much nodding in the crowd; that was when Lincoln ignored Judge Taney's decision on habeas corpus, and later ordered the Maryland legislature arrested before the state could secede. Jackson figured he would have taken the same direct action in Lincoln's shoes.

"The people of the South have long wished to aid you in throwing off this foreign yoke, to enable you to again enjoy the inalienable rights of free men," Lee was concluding, as some of his soldiers looked longingly into the window of a shoe store. "Marylanders shall once more enjoy their ancient freedom of thought and speech. We know no enemies among you, and will protect all, of every opinion. This army will respect your choice."

A band played "Maryland, My Maryland," to the tune of the German Christmas carol "O Tannenbaum." A group of Southern stalwarts sang out the new lyrics:

> The despot's heel is on thy shore, Maryland, my Maryland!
> His torch is at thy temple door, Maryland, my Maryland!
> Avenge the patriotic gore, That flecked the streets of Baltimore,
> And be the battle queen of yore, Maryland, my Maryland!

Jackson, the stern Presbyterian, was not one for music, but hoped that the song would influence some local residents to hand out shoes and clothing.

After the crowd dispersed, Lee called a council of war. Jackson pointed out the need to demand local supplies and food; living off the land in enemy country was a traditional way of war. Lee differed; his was to be a liberating army, treating the population respectfully, in sharp contrast to the repression practiced by General Pope in Virginia.

"But what about food?" Jackson asked. "The hand of the quartermaster has never fallen on these Maryland valleys. We don't have the money to buy supplies, and if we try to press Confederate money on storekeepers, they'll say it's a form of confiscation."

Lee shook his head; they would have to put the strategy of winning the hearts of the residents ahead of the needs of the soldiers. James Longstreet, the other corps commander under Lee, had an answer: "In Mexico, I remember we lived for days on corn and green oranges. Here the corn is ripening in the rows, tassels everywhere. They're called 'roasting ears.' The men will get tired of corn, but they won't starve."

Jackson said nothing more; his men were doubled over with diarrhea, soiling the underclothes they marched in, because of their diet of corn and apples, apples and corn. Perhaps they would get used to the diet or, better yet, get better fed in Philadelphia.

"I have a motive in my proclamation, and in my concern for the sensibilities of the population in the North," Lee told them. "I have suggested to President Davis that we make a proposal of peace."

Lee's lieutenants looked at each other, then at their commander. Had they come this far to give up? Jackson was first to speak: "Is it for the South now to sue for peace?"

"In no way could it be regarded as suing for peace," Lee replied. "Being made when it is in our power to inflict injury upon our adversary, it would show the world that our sole object is the establishment of our independence and the attainment of an honorable peace."

"Lincoln will reject it," said Longstreet. For once, Jackson agreed with him.

"That would prove to the country who is responsible for the war," Lee argued. "An election is coming next month in the North. The proposal of peace would enable the people of the United States to determine whether they will support those who favor a prolongation of the war, or those who wish to bring it to a termination."

Jackson had not realized before that Lee considered himself to be a diplomat—showing all the world who wanted peace—or a politician, appealing to public sentiment in order to influence a coming election. Jackson's goal was simpler: winning the war. There lay the answer, he was certain, not in "settlement." When Lee said he would transmit his ideas about a peace offer to President Davis first, Jackson stopped worrying; like Lincoln, Jeff Davis thought only in terms of victory.

Longstreet rolled out the maps on the table in the tent, and they waited for Lee to explain his campaign.

The Southern commander obliged by pointing one of his crippled hands to a spot on the map that must have been most familiar to him: Harpers Ferry, Virginia, at the junction of the Shenandoah and Potomac rivers. Jackson knew that in 1859, it was at that arsenal and armory, where rifles were made and stored, that abolitionist Kansan John Brown made a raid that infuriated the South and delighted the anti-slavery partisans of the North. At that time, Colonel Robert Lee of the United States Army, with Lieutenant Jeb Stuart as his cavalry aide, was sent to the Harpers Ferry arsenal to put an end to the insurgency. Lee stormed the barricaded enginehouse, freed Brown's hostages, and brought the abolitionist to justice. Created quite a stir when they hanged the fanatic, Jackson recalled; the Yankees marched to a song about how his body was a-moldering in his grave.

"That is the crossing," Lee was saying, tapping his splint on the map, "of the Baltimore and Ohio Railroad, and is held by a Federal garrison of perhaps twelve thousand men. As you remember, Thomas, mountains on three sides."

"Foolish to try to defend," Jackson observed. "Harpers Ferry is more of a trap than a fort." When the war began, the Confederates controlled that arsenal, with Jackson in command of the dismantling of its machinery. He had shipped as much as possible to Richmond before slipping down the Shenandoah Valley to join Lee's main forces. Unless the garrison at the rivers' junction held out heroically, the position could be taken fairly easily, and with it a much-needed store of supplies and guns. "Pope's been replaced by McClellan, the papers say. I would think that McClellan would remove that garrison and bolster his own army."

"That would be the intelligent thing to do," Lee agreed, "but perhaps McClellan, by all odds their best man, is not in total command. At any rate, the prize is there. I propose to send you, General Jackson, to capture that garrison."

Jackson smiled his assent, but Longstreet demurred: "Divide our forces, here in the North, with a Federal army waiting to attack us? I don't think that's a good idea."

"That's how we beat Pope," said Jackson. Dividing the army was always a risk—perhaps it could not be reassembled in time to counter an enemy attack —but war required that sort of audacity. Longstreet was always too cautious; to Jackson's mind, the willingness to risk all made the Southern forces under Lee far more effective than the Northern army, under its series of generals.

"The second objective—General Walker's assignment—is the wrecking of the aqueduct of the Chesapeake and Ohio Canal at Monocacy," Lee continued. "The final objective is here, about sixty miles beyond Hagerstown: the bridge at Harrisburg, Pennsylvania, where the railroad crosses the Susquehanna River. General Longstreet, you and I will undertake that. In achieving these three objectives, we will isolate the Federal East from the Federal West." It was the same strategy, Jackson realized, behind the Federals' "Tennessee plan"—to cut the South in two along the Charleston to Memphis railway.

"Reinforcements for McClellan would thus be cut off," said the strategist. "After that, I can turn my attention to Philadelphia, Baltimore, or Washington, as may be best for our interests."

That would end the war; no need for peace proposals. Longstreet, however, was shaking his head.

"You doubtless regard it as hazardous," Lee said, finally addressing his concern, "to leave McClellan practically on my line of communication, and to march into the heart of the enemy's country. Are you acquainted with General McClellan?"

"Haven't seen much of him since the Mexican War, sir," Longstreet replied.

"He is an able general, but a very cautious one," was Lee's assessment. "His enemies among his own people think him much too cautious. His army is in a very demoralized and chaotic condition, and will not be prepared for offensive operations—or he will not think it so—for three or four weeks. Before that time I hope to be on the Susquehanna."

Jackson returned to his headquarters. He was not troubled, as Longstreet was, by the notion of splitting into separate units the Confederate force of about sixty thousand men. McClellan's larger Union force would be cautious for good reason: a tactical blunder might cost Lee his invasion, but a similar mistake by McClellan would cost the North the war. A losing Lee could always withdraw and defend the South; a losing McClellan would have no alternative but to tell Lincoln to sue for peace, and such a prospect would surely increase the caution of a cautious man. The only move that Lee feared, Jackson knew, was a McClellan thrust by water into the Peninsula to take Richmond. Fortunately for the Confederacy, Lincoln was not likely to let him do that again.

He awaited the delivery of Lee's written order, outlining the complex campaign assignments to each of the Confederate generals. When Special Order No. 191 arrived, Jackson studied it closely; the detailed plan showed extraordinary boldness in dispersing Lee's army for separate assignments in the presence of a stronger enemy army.

Trusting no aide to read the highly secret document, he made a copy in his own hand and sent the copy to his brother-in-law, General Harvey Hill, who was serving with Longstreet. Harvey was the solid, reliable General Hill; "Little Powell" was the troublemaker. Thomas Jackson dispatched the copy under seal, prepared mentally to recross the Potomac to strike the garrison at Harpers Ferry, and turned to his evening prayers.

CHAPTER 16

ANTIETAM II
WITH McCLELLAN

Corporal Barton Mitchell, Company E of the 27th Indiana Volunteer Infantry Regiment, United States Army, was persuaded that the citizens of Frederick, Maryland, were fine people and loyal Unionists and the women were good cooks.

"You sure you got the pie?" he asked First Sergeant John Bloss.

"I got the pies—apple and peach—and the fruit and the milk," said the sergeant, next to him in a rank of four men. They were walking route step on the road out of Frederick, forty miles northwest of Washington. "You better have the ham, and the chicken legs, and the bread, and everything else."

"Fine people, Marylanders," said the Hoosier corporal. "Yesterday Bobby Lee and his rebs was here, speechifyin' and proclaiming how they was lifting the yoke of oppression, and the people looked at 'em sullen-like. And as soon as the secesh moved out last night and we got here, all them same nice ladies in the streets with the food, the men in the windows with the Stars and Stripes, kids jumpin' up and down, made you feel good to be on our side."

"Be nice to eat this real food," said the sergeant. "Beats hardtack and salt horse."

"Can't bitch about McClellan chow," corrected the corporal. "Sure picked up after Pope got kicked out. Little Mac knows how to take care of his boys." He trailed along behind the sergeant for a few minutes, then added, "Except for tobaccy. I could go for a good smoke." He thought back dreamily to the time, before the Seven Days, when he had enjoyed a cigar.

"Here's a good patch of grass, an' a run of water." The sergeant raised his voice and hollered to the platoon behind them, "Fall out! Stack arms! Take a break!"

"Looks like secesh had the same idea," said Corporal Mitchell. The chosen campsite showed signs of recent use: fruit rinds lay about and spots in the earth showed where tent pegs had been ripped up not long before. No matter; a good site was useful for whatever army was passing by, and a nearby brook answered sanitation needs.

He built the triangle of rifles and lay on the grass near a sycamore tree. He remembered the leaf from Indiana hikes. "S'pose we're gonna catch those rebs, Sergeant?"

"Hand over the ham. They got a general with a red beard, went to West Point with Little Mac. The two of them were sweet on the same gal, and McClellan won out, married her. The feller who lost out, A. P. Hill—'Li'l Powell'—was sore as hell, swore he'd get even. Ever since, whenever McClellan and Lee face up, like in the Peninsula, there's A. P. Hill charging our lines like crazy, taking out his old grudge."

"S'pose that's a true story?"

"Everybody knows it. Last time he hit us, Malvern Hill, I think, the colonel yelled out, 'My God, Nellie, why didn't you marry *him!*' "

Corporal Mitchell had a good laugh at that. Only a week ago, he remembered, it had been hard to smile: he was a member of a beaten army under that tyrant Pope, and all he could think of was getting home alive. Now spirits were up; McClellan was in charge again. Colonel Silas Colgrove told them that Little Mac had never lost a battle, which was true, and some of that dread was gone. The corporal was not looking forward to catching up with the rebels, but if a battle had to be fought, better it should be under a general who knew what he was doing and thought about keeping his men alive.

After the peach pie and the milk and a hearty belch, he looked for a slope to stretch out on. The rest of the regiment had filed into the open field and the place was getting a little crowded, but the comfort-conscious Corporal Mitchell found a spot, not far from the sergeant, fit for generals. In fact, from the fairly fresh holes in the ground, it appeared that a headquarters tent had been on that spot. He sat down, wishing he had a smoke, and his eyes lighted on a large white envelope.

He reached over, picked it up, opened it, and his heart almost stopped. As if in answer to a prayer, three big, beautiful, fragrant cigars were inside, wrapped in a sheet of paper. Unbelieving, he inhaled the odor: the cigars were the best quality. He rolled them gently in his fingers; they did not crinkle, they were fresh, which brought forth a vision of hours of surcease from the rigors of war.

Some rebel general must have left behind his packet of cigars. These were not enlisted men's smokes. Corporal Mitchell looked around quickly to see who had seen him make the find. Sergeant Bloss, ten yards away, was looking at him. That meant two for himself, one for Bloss. He nodded to the sergeant, who came over.

"Go get some matches," said the corporal. When in possession of cigars, a corporal could give a sergeant orders. While Bloss was hunting up the light, Mitchell glanced at the document in which the cigars were wrapped.

"Headquarters, Army of Northern Virginia, Special Order 191" was written across the top. Rebel orders. "The army will resume its march tomorrow," it began. At the bottom was "By command of General R. E. Lee: R. H. Chilton, Assistant Adjutant-General."

Good memento; he would take it home to Indiana after the war was over, to remind him of this day and his good fortune with the cigars. Reading farther into the orders, he noted the specific place-names of towns and mountains in that area: Jackson to Harpers Ferry; Longstreet to Boonsboro; McLaws to Maryland Heights, Walker to Loudoun Heights. The rebel generals seemed to be marching off in all directions.

The sergeant came back with the matches, and Mitchell handed him one of the cigars, showing the paper to him. Sergeant Bloss read the whole document, put the matches back in his pocket, and inexplicably reached over and took the two cigars out of Mitchell's hands. He rolled all three up in the order, and put cigars and paper back in the original envelope. "We'd better take this to the company commander."

In ten minutes the captain had taken them to the colonel, who examined their discovery, gasped, and raced toward McClellan's headquarters. The corporal thought it amazing how three cigars could go from an enlisted man clear up the chain of command to the commanding general in less than an hour. Mitchell and Bloss returned to the rest area, where the regiment was unstacking weapons and getting ready to march.

"I'll see you get a commendation or something," said the sergeant.

"We could have just passed up the paper in the envelope," Mitchell objected. "You never should have given up them cigars."

CHAPTER 17

ANTIETAM III
AT DAYBREAK IN THE MORNING

Allan Pinkerton found it hard to believe what his eyes beheld. On a single sheet of paper handed to him by Captain Armstrong Custer, the aide-de-camp who smelled of cinnamon, was the battle plan of the enemy.

If authentic, and not some elaborate trick by a rebel out to embarrass him, this document would be the greatest piece of military intelligence in all the world's history. In terms of its effect, possession of this single sheet of paper could decide the coming battle and secure victory for the Union and immortality for George McClellan. The detective reached for a comparison. When Rose Greenhow provided General Beauregard with the expected movements of Federal troops before First Bull Run, that had been enormously helpful to him, but never had there been a discovery of the most intimate secrets of a campaign just before the battle.

"Chilton is Lee's adjutant, and he would sign the order," Pinkerton said. "But how do we know this is Chilton's authentic signature?"

Custer signaled the two colonels who had brought in the document and introduced them to "Major Allen, our chief of the Secret Service." One of the colonels, from the 27th Indiana, told how the document had been found, and showed the cigars. The other, Pittman, adjutant of the XII Corps, had what Pinkerton judged to be the necessary corroboration: "Chilton and I served together in Detroit before the war, Major Allen. I've seen his signature on orders a thousand times. That's his handwriting, I'll swear to it."

The thought occurred to Pinkerton, as he pocketed the cigars, that if this were a rebel trick, the same trickster who concocted the orders would have had the sense to have Lee's adjutant-general put his signature on them. But he did not want to think that; such suspicion undermined the chance to use military intelligence as it had never been used before. He handed Lee's order back to Custer, and the four of them hurried to McClellan's headquarters in a local Frederick house. A delegation of local citizens was present, but this news could not wait.

"Found by one of our men in the bivouac area used last night by General Hill," Custer reported.

"Powell Hill?"

"No, Harvey Hill. According to that set of orders, sir, A. P. Hill is with Jackson attacking Harpers Ferry right now."

McClellan read the paper quickly, then over again slowly, his astonishment giving way to delight. In the presence of the colonels and the local citizens, he cried, "Now I know what to do!"

When Pinkerton shot him a warning look, McClellan told the locals he had pressing military business to attend to, and Custer ushered them out. One of the visitors, Pinkerton noted suspiciously, seemed in a hurry to go; what was his rush? General Jubal Early, the damnably daring rebel cavalry leader, was undoubtedly in the area, reconnoitering; if this lost order was so important, the news of its finding should be protected. Pinkerton began to wish he had waited to see McClellan alone with the find. What could be done now? He would look foolish if he demanded the most distinguished local citizens be held in custody, and the detective in this moment of high drama hated above all to look foolish. He let it go.

McClellan was addressing him. "Do you suppose this is a *ruse de guerre?*"

Pinkerton wished the general would not use foreign languages in these crucial situations. That unfortunate habit came from having all those foreign princes around headquarters as observers. The Secret Service chief pulled his derby down tighter and scowled, as if in thought.

"It's not a trick," Custer put in, rashly as usual. "Pittman here vouches for the signature. He served with Chilton."

McClellan dismissed the colonels and sat down, reading the document again. "Here is a paper," he said with a mixture of deliberation and excitement, "with which, if I cannot whip Bobby Lee, I will be willing to go home."

"It doesn't give the size of the various forces," Pinkerton cautioned. "I estimate the total Confederate army at one hundred and twenty thousand. If Lee sent Jackson and Hill off to Harpers Ferry with half of them, we still face sixty thousand seasoned men behind South Mountain."

"Now that Porter's arrived, I have eighty thousand present for duty, and I have the other side's plans. It is as if I sat in at Lee's staff conference." He rose, folded the paper, and acted without the caution that Pinkerton always associated with him. "We'll strike through Crampton's Gap across South Mountain at daybreak in the morning."

"There's still time this afternoon," Custer suggested.

"Daybreak in the morning," McClellan repeated. "My general idea is to cut the enemy in two and beat him in detail. First Lee tomorrow, then Jackson the next day."

Pinkerton never saw such a commotion around a McClellan headquarters as followed that decision. Everything became *now*. The Army of the Potomac was moving out, not proceeding in its stately, well-organized custom, but with the first sense of urgency that Pinkerton remembered did not come from fear of impending disaster. Supply wagons were packed, the men were told "three days' cooked rations and forty rounds" in each knapsack. The horses were fed and readied for a long march across South Mountain, more of a long ridge of land running roughly parallel to the Potomac farther west. The rebel armies, now known to be split up into three or more units in that long wedge of land between the mountain range and the Potomac, made such an inviting target that alacrity rather than caution was the order of the day.

Pinkerton picked up a telegraph message on McClellan's desk and noted, "The President is asking his favorite question again." The plaintive telegraphed query read, "How does it look now?" Pinkerton thought that it would be wiser to keep the blabbermouths in Washington in the dark about the discovery of the lost order.

The general decided otherwise. He dashed off an excited message dated "Frederick, September 13, twelve noon" that Pinkerton thought was unlike any other sent by McClellan to Lincoln. "I have the whole rebel force in front of me, but am confident, and no time shall be lost. I think Lee has made a gross mistake, and that he will be severely punished for it." The general paused, then plunged ahead: "I have all the plans of the rebels, and will catch them in their own trap. Will send you trophies."

Pinkerton shook his head as the telegraph operator came in for the message. The detective read it and passed it to him, with a peremptory "Send this immediately, and show it to nobody else. Bad enough that Stanton will see it."

"Castiglione will be nothing to it," McClellan said to nobody in particular, as if still in wonderment at his good fortune. Pinkerton made a mental note to check up on Castiglione, whoever he was. Possibly another one of those foreign princes.

"This order confirms my estimates of rebel strength," said Pinkerton, lest his commander get carried away by his unaccustomed euphoria. "No numbers are in it, but eight commands are spoken of. Figure fifteen thousand men in each command, that's their average. Makes one hundred and twenty thousand men." He was pleased when McClellan nodded agreement. "Our forces may say eighty thousand on duty, but when you figure the cooks and quartermasters, and all our stragglers, that's maybe sixty thousand fit to fight. Even cut in half, Lee's forces are formidable, General; our cavalry scouts confirm this."

The general lost some of his euphoria. "And if we should be so unfortunate as to meet with defeat," McClellan added, sounding more like himself, "our country is at their mercy."

"Lincoln is holding fifty thousand men in reserve in Washington that should be here to fight this battle," Pinkerton said, deliberately touching his commander's most exposed nerve.

"If I lose, I'll be court-martialed and shot," McClellan said, now fully himself again. "I still have no authority beyond 'the defenses of Washington.' Wade and his committee, and that blackguard Stanton, will say I lost on purpose."

Pinkerton expressed his worry that the order might be a fake. The general waved that aside: "No matter, I'll whip Lee here and now. He is not a general to be trifled with, or carelessly afforded an opportunity of striking a fatal blow." He thrust the paper into Pinkerton's hand. "Here, take this to Colonel Key to be copied. I have to stir the utmost activity in my generals, Burnside especially. I cannot understand what has happened to Burn, he's loyal to me but he's been paralyzed in the movement of his troops. Go, quickly."

Pinkerton jammed one of the cigars found with the order in his mouth— the secesh had better tobacco than the Federals, never mind that they were ill equipped otherwise—and headed for Colonel Thomas Key's office across the hall. Nobody was more closely trusted than Key, officially the judge advocate but in reality McClellan's political adviser, and Key had a source of information that was invaluable to Pinkerton: his younger brother, Major John Key, worked as a lawyer for Halleck at the War Department.

Key had a couple of civilians in his office. The detective started to back out, but the colonel from Ohio waved him into the meeting. Pinkerton casually slipped Lee's order inside his jacket pocket for transmission to the colonel in private.

"Mr. Smalley and Mr. Paige of the *New York Tribune*," Key introduced them, "this is Major Allen, who supplies us with information about the enemy." These reporters, too, were the enemy, in Pinkerton's opinion—Horace Greeley's men, from the journal that was after McClellan's scalp. Why was Colonel Key seeing them? It must be at McClellan's behest. Smalley was a regular journalist, but Paige was a Washington lawyer who only pretended to be a war correspondent.

"I've been telling them of the plot, or talk of a plot, that we uncovered the other night," said Colonel Key. Pinkerton caught on; Key was sending Lincoln and the radicals a message through Greeley that McClellan was unwaveringly loyal to the Union.

"It's amazing—and frightening," said Paige.

"Some members of the staff of the Army of the Potomac," Key went on, "approached me last night with a scheme to turn and march on Washington, and to"—he searched for the word—"intimidate the President."

Pinkerton nodded; Colonel Key had come to his room with the information late last night. "General McClellan knew absolutely nothing about this, you understand," the judge advocate said. "He knows nothing of it even now. He is too much occupied with turning back Lee's invasion to be bothered with the idle talk of a few misguided officers."

"What is it that these officers wanted to intimidate Mr. Lincoln about?" asked Smalley.

"They wanted him to abandon his interferences with slavery," Colonel Key replied, "hoping that the war could be settled on the basis of 'the Union as it was.' They claimed to have heard that an abolition move was in the works in Washington. They wanted to take a substantial force down there to impress the President with the army's unwillingness to stand for that."

"Are you prepared to tell us who they are? They should be cashiered forthwith," said Paige.

"No, it was in the nature of idle talk," said Key. "I told them to abandon all such ideas, and they said they would. Now is hardly the moment, on the eve of battle, to strip this army of its field-grade officers because of a crazy idea."

"Why are you telling us this, then?" Smalley was a bit of a dandy but sharp, Pinkerton noted; a man to be careful with.

"To let you know the sort of thing we're up against," Key answered smoothly. Pinkerton knew the point the judge advocate was implanting. If McClellan and other loyalists were not on the scene, the largest Union force near Washington might be tempted to turn on Lincoln and take over the government, as the military did so often in other countries. The very possibility of a coup should give the radicals pause in their campaign to vilify McClellan. "It should be no secret to you gentlemen that some staff officers speak of our highest officials in Washington as 'those old women.' The irrational hatred of Lincoln, Stanton, and Halleck is rampant."

"Appalling," said Paige.

"What will stop this talk once and for all," Pinkerton put in, "is a victory. We're heavily outnumbered—I trust you've seen the messages from the governors of Pennsylvania and Maryland, estimating rebel troops in their states as over two hundred thousand?—but General McClellan is determined to give them a licking soon. That will stop the foolish talk in the camps."

"Let's hope so," said Paige, who would surely carry the story to Greeley or to Stanton. "Colonel, I do not doubt the entire accuracy of your account. Shocking."

"I trust nothing of this will appear in your newspaper," Key said, lawyer to lawyer. Paige nodded his assurance and Smalley looked dismayed, but went along. "But I thought it would be something for you to understand as you write about the fighting to come." The political fighting for McClellan's scalp was what he meant, Pinkerton knew; he had to admire Judge Key's adeptness.

On the way out, Smalley said, "I would like to put in a word for Alexander Gardner, the photographer. He would like to be attached to the army next week."

Colonel Key looked at Pinkerton, who said, "No. Mathew Brady is the Army of the Potomac's photographer." So much for that; the detective did not want Brady's competition wandering around the camps. If Brady's ungrateful employees wanted to set up for themselves, they would have to do so without access to battlefields. Pinkerton would be loyal to his friend.

When the *Tribune* men left, Pinkerton brought out the lost order of Lee's and enjoyed Key's amazed reaction.

"You were a genius to find this," the colonel said. "Thank God the general has a Secret Service like yours."

Pinkerton said nothing; he felt he had helped verify the information, and a truthful denial of all participation was not in him. With what he hoped was some mystery, he asked, "Does the name Castiglione mean anything to you?"

"That was a battle of Napoleon's, in 1796," Colonel Key answered instantly. He snapped his fingers. "Yes, yes, that's a perfect analogy—Bonaparte divided an overextended Austrian army and beat it in detail. I had no idea you were such a student of tactics, Pinkerton. You're absolutely right."

The detective tried to look modest.

CHAPTER 18

ANTIETAM IV
LEE'S OLD WARHORSE

James Longstreet was "Old Pete" to his troops, "my old warhorse" to General Lee. The forty-one-year-old South Carolinian could not figure out why everyone called him old.

Maybe it was because he inspired trust; if so, he had let them all down at Fair Oaks and Seven Pines. Longstreet blamed himself for the mistakes that caused those operations to fail. Overall, he must have performed well in the Peninsula, because Lee had rewarded him with command of the wing containing half the Confederate infantry. But at Second Manassas, Longstreet let down his commander again by not attacking quickly enough to complete the rout of Pope's Union troops. He was dependable enough, went Longstreet's self-assessment, but not bold enough. Why did Lee put him at his right hand, superior to all but Stonewall Jackson? Longstreet supposed it was because Lee had all the audacity he required and felt the need for a restraining mind nearby.

Longstreet was with Lee in Hagerstown, Maryland, worried about the Confederate forces being spread all over the map, as Special Order 191 had laid out. Thirteen miles away, at South Mountain, Harvey Hill was plugging the gaps in the long ridge with his rear guard. Even farther away, Stonewall Jackson was headed for Harpers Ferry on what Longstreet thought was an unnecessarily dangerous expedition; Jackson had A. P. Hill with him, released from arrest in view of the impending battles.

Old Pete, as he was beginning to call himself, was uneasy. On the other side of South Mountain, possibly preparing to pounce on the separated elements of the Confederate Army, was McClellan with at least ninety thousand fresh Federal troops, well-equipped, close to home, and with more and better artillery. General Lee had taken the terrible risk of dividing his army this way because he was certain of McClellan's caution, but the Young Napoleon was acting with uncharacteristic energy lately. Did McClellan somehow know he outnumbered Lee's total forces nearly three to two? Did he sense that Lee was risking all by sending Jackson and Powell Hill off to reduce the garrison at Harpers Ferry?

Pacing in front of the headquarters house, wondering if he should bother the commander again with his doubts about leaving the Southern forces so

General James Longstreet, C.S.A.

scattered, Longstreet made way for a hard-riding cavalryman. The man dismounted and announced he had a message for General Lee from General Jubal Early. Early's cavalry provided eyes and ears for Lee's forces. Longstreet nodded and led the man to the commander's office; it was 10 P.M., but Lee had not yet retired.

The general could not open an envelope with his bandaged hands. Longstreet did it for him, handed it over, and stood behind him to read it over Lee's shoulder.

He caught his breath. A Frederick citizen loyal to the South had been with McClellan when a messenger arrived with important information, which caused much excitement at the Union headquarters. Did the Union know of Special Order 191? Whatever had come in, McClellan had responded with a great flurry of activity, quite uncharacteristic of him. The citizen had reported to Early that an attack was likely through several of the mountain gaps at daybreak, and the cavalry leader passed it to Lee with urgency.

Lee dismissed the messenger. "Pete, you'll have to march back to South Mountain at first light. Harvey Hill cannot hold the Federals for long."

"What if McClellan knows we're spread out all over Maryland?" Did Lee realize the enormity of the damage done by the betrayal of his secret plans?

"We'll meet him at South Mountain with the men we have," the commander said softly. "Jackson and A. P. Hill will reduce Harpers Ferry and join us as soon as they can."

Longstreet was convinced Lee was making a mistake. "We're not prepared to make a stand in the mountain gaps. After a four-hour forced march, my men won't be ready for a major battle. We'll be outnumbered two to one, three to one."

"We've been outnumbered before."

"But this time McClellan knows it—he'll come at us with all he has. Let's try to get Jackson's men back in time, and to hell with Harpers Ferry."

Lee listened patiently, then ordered, "Get your men there. Make a stand at the mountain passes."

Longstreet swallowed his objections and left. With McClellan in probable possession of the Confederate battle plan, he felt naked. At the least, Lee should take advantage of the knowledge that he knew that McClellan knew—and change his plans radically.

He lay down on the cot in his tent, could not sleep, then wrote a note to General Lee with an alternative plan. Let South Mountain go, bring Harvey Hill and his five thousand men back to the town of Sharpsburg, and move Longstreet's men to that position as well. There, on the banks of the Antietam—not a very deep stream, but one that offered some sort of natural defensive position—they could organize a new defense that would await the arrival of Jackson and Hill from Harpers Ferry. Would Lee listen to reason? Did he have no respect for a rejuvenated Union army under a suddenly active commander? This deep in enemy territory, prudence required consolidation, if not withdrawal. He sent his note to Lee and waited for a reply.

Just before dawn, Longstreet gave up waiting and let sleep come. General Lee had given his order and expected it to be carried out. Old Pete, glad he had at least expressed his reservations in writing, set out with his men to try to stop McClellan, or at least to delay him, at the place of the Young Napoleon's choosing.

CHAPTER 19

ANTIETAM V
AN ARMY WITH BANNERS

Corporal Mitchell felt for the first time that he was part of a great enterprise. Sunrise on Sunday morning, September 14, 1862, the hills of Maryland pink and green, leaves just starting to turn, and the Army of the Potomac was on the move. Times before, he thought only of his platoon plodding along, with little idea about where the rest of the regiment was, and less idea of the grand plan.

This time was different. Three vast columns were forming to march down the western slope of the Catoctins, into a long valley, then up into the gaps in the long ridge known as South Mountain, where the Johnnies were.

Marching in cadence down into the valley, looking back, a soldier could get a picture of all he was a part of. The columns trailed back up into the hills like blue-black snakes, moving imperceptibly—and in clear view of the rebels —on the far ridge. What must they be feeling, Mitchell wondered, as we come at them with all the power and majesty of the Union in train? He remembered a phrase in his Bible, "terrible as an army with banners." A sight like this could make a man tremble.

A shout went up from the troops in front of him. There, astride his famed "Dan Webster," sat the man who put all this into action, Major General George Brinton McClellan, looking like a grand equestrian statue, reviewing the troops—*his* army, and Corporal Mitchell was proud to be a part of it—as it marched to war. As his platoon passed the general, the corporal saw Mc-Clellan raise his arm and point to the gap in the mountain ridge where the firing had begun. Corporal Mitchell knew he would never forget this moment as long as he lived, even if that went long past the impending battle; there, bestride his horse, was a real general, a leader who lifted a soldier's heart. This was what war should be like, Corporal Mitchell decided, not all home-sickness and dread of death, but being part of the greatest adventure of the age. He raised his cap to join his platoon in a thrilling "huzzah!"

CHAPTER 20

AT BRADY'S GALLERY

"Let me go out there, Mr. Brady," Gardner pleaded. "This may be the final battle of the war."

"I'll go myself. I'll take Foons. You stay in the studio."

Foons, the black who was a wagon driver and camera operative, knew whose side he was on in the dispute between Mathew Brady and Alexander Gardner. Foons was one hundred percent for Brady.

Not for the money, that was for certain: he had not been paid since the first of the year. He ate Mr. Brady's food and slept on a mat in the back of the studio, glad for shelter and scraps, more than most runaway slaves pretending to be freedmen could count on.

He had not been singled out for nonpayment; nobody had been paid, not even the men who thought wages a natural thing. Business was terrible and Mr. Brady was not much for keeping accounts. Gardner and his brother, along with Gibson and Tim O'Sullivan—especially the fiery O'Sullivan—all had horrendous fights with Brady that nobody could win. Foons was well aware that Brady's eyes were failing fast and he needed his operators to run the studio and photograph the war; but the operators needed Brady just as much, because the owner of the studio seemed to have a stranglehold on the rights from the War Department to go into the field and make war photo-graphs. As a result, Brady's studio had become a little war zone all its own.

"Brady, you goddamn pigheaded fool," O'Sullivan roared his way into the argument, "you and that skinny little nigger can't go out on a battlefield and you know it! You can't see your hand in front of your face and he'd get his black ass blown off by the rebs as a runaway slave, which he probably is."

"Irish scum," said Brady, which was all he ever said to O'Sullivan anymore. Brady was of Irish stock, too, but made it a point that he had been born in New York. Foons thought O'Sullivan a bully, but knew that Gardner considered him to be the best photographer of all of them, especially after seeing the pictures of the bridge destroyed at Second Bull Run, with the amazing texture of the water. His portrait of a derailed locomotive in the wake of Pope's defeat made the machinery look like a dead elephant.

"Tim, stay out of this, please," said Gardner, "you never do us any good with him. This time it's too important."

"Credit-grabber!" Sullivan shouted as he stormed out. "Cheap bastard!"

"I apologize for my colleague, Mr. Brady," said Gardner wearily. "He shouldn't insult you. And he shouldn't try to scare you, Foons; I'm sure you're safe here."

Foons knew he was safe in the studio, provided the South didn't win the war, but he knew also that O'Sullivan was right about being caught on the battlefield by the secesh. They did not take kindly to colored men who seemed to be working for the Union troops, and all this talk about abolition coming soon made them even madder. Foons was suspicious of what the politicians were saying about emancipation, especially when they added "colonization"; he did not want to be sent to Africa to become a slave again to some tribal leader. Besides, none of this freedom talk would mean much if McClellan got whipped by Lee. Where would he hide if the South took Washington and the Fugitive Slave Act was no protection?

"Mr. Brady," Gardner was saying in his most reasonable voice, "you have done more than anybody alive to make possible the photographic coverage of the war. I realize that."

"Who persuaded the Secretary of War, and McClellan and Pinkerton, that photography was an asset in mapmaking?" Brady demanded.

"You did, to your eternal credit, Mr. Brady. Generations of photographers yet unborn will revere your name."

"That is not what is important, Alex. I'm not a credit-grabber, as your Irish scum friend says." Foons had heard this lecture before. "But the name 'Photograph by Brady' is what gives a picture importance, and makes it possible for us to go into the field and record history."

"I've never disputed that."

"Ingratitude," muttered Brady, slamming around the empty plates on the table.

"I'm grateful for your bringing me here from Scotland," Gardner recited, "for the opportunity to use my knowledge of chemicals in this new art."

"You're lying," Brady declared. "If you meant it, you wouldn't keep threatening to leave and take all my help with you."

"All I want to do is what you wanted to do once," Gardner pleaded. "Set up for myself. Get the recognition that every artist deserves."

"Go ahead, do it. Leave today! Close up the shop on your way out, for Foons and I will be in Frederick, Maryland, with McClellan."

Now Mr. Brady had him, Foons judged. That was Gardner's weak point. The desire of the men who worked for Brady to cover the war made them no more than slaves to the man who was master of the military passes in the Whatizzit Wagon.

"You know I can't leave now," said Gardner, "any more than you can go to the front in your condition. We're at an impasse, Mr. Brady." Long pause. "I have a proposition for you, sir."

"I know what it is." Brady opened the medicine cabinet and took out a bottle of lavender lotion to slap on his face. "You want to go to the front and take the pictures of the last great battle, and bring the horror of war to every home in the North. And all you want is the credit—'photograph by Gardner' —and you'll let me have half the proceeds from the sale. Go to hell."

Gardner started to breathe deeply, and seemed to Foons to be near tears. "Hell, then, is where I will go. I'll take a wagon and go to the front without a pass and if I get arrested, so be it."

"Do that!" Brady slammed the chest shut. "Good luck."

Gardner crumpled. "You know I can't. Go ahead, Brady, you do the job yourself. You go to the last great battle of the war. If your eyes fail, if you miss the shot, if Foons cannot get the colloids ready just at the moment needed, or the pictures developed within ten minutes, then photography can wait until the next war."

After a long silence, Brady said, "Now I have a proposition to make to you. I'll get you a pass from Stanton and give you the wagon and equipment —stereos mainly, some eight by ten plates. I'll give you Gibson as your assistant." Good choice, thought Foons, who was just as glad not to have to go; as O'Sullivan had guessed, he had no freedman's papers. Gibson had done some fine work in the Peninsula.

"And it will be 'Photograph by Brady' as usual," said Gardner, thankfully but helplessly.

"The album card will say 'Brady's Album Gallery' in big letters," said Brady. "Along the lower edge of the print, in lettering too tiny for me to see, it can say 'Photograph by' whoever."

"And I'll have the copyright."

"Or Gibson will, if he took it."

"Fair enough. More than fair, Mr. Brady."

"The proceeds of all sales, of course, go to Brady and Company," the boss added. "You're on salary, if and when the money comes in."

"I'll leave within the hour," Gardner nodded, as if the money were not important. "Homer Bates in the telegraph office says that the fight has already begun at a ridge near Sharpsburg, about six hours' ride in the wagon. McClellan's never been so aggressive; he's forced his way through the gaps and told the President he's on the verge of a great victory." Foons had never seen Gardner show such excitement.

"And what did the President say?"

"He invoked God's blessing on the troops, and said, 'Destroy the rebel army if possible.' "

"Sounds like Lincoln, all right," said Brady. "Get going before the war is over. Shoot faces, not houses."

Gardner bolted out. Brady took off his thick glasses, folded them and put them in the pocket of his long chemise. He leaned forward and held his head in his hands.

"That man owes you a lot, Mr. Brady."

"He says it but he doesn't mean it. He'll take the great pictures and open his own place and drive me out of business if he can."

"Why do you let him, then?"

"Ah, Foons, they'll be great pictures. He has the eye." Brady sighed and added bitterly, "And he has the eyes."

CHAPTER 21

ANTIETAM VI
DESTROY IF POSSIBLE

South Mountain's gaps had been forced. As George McClellan had expected, the Confederates under Harvey Hill put up a fierce fight, emulating the Greeks at Thermopylae, delaying the Union advance a full day before falling back into an obviously prearranged defensive position behind a rust-brown, meandering creek called the Antietam near Sharpsburg. McClellan welcomed Lee's choice of battlefield; the Southerners would have a narrow stream in front and the wide Potomac at their back. It was as if Lee, unconcerned about a line of retreat, dared him to attack.

The Federals had at last won a battle, and for the first time since May were following up the fighting with a general advance. After notifying Halleck that Lee had been "shockingly whipped" at South Mountain, McClellan could not resist sending a telegraph message to old Winfield Scott, in retirement at West Point, saying: "R. E. Lee in command. The rebels routed, and retreating in disorder." So much for Scott's first choice to head the Union forces.

The Gorilla had been heard from: "Destroy the rebel army if possible." McClellan put that exhortation from Lincoln in his pocket with a wry smile: for the first time since he had reassumed command, and only as a result of his victory at South Mountain, the Union Army's general had an order making legitimate his very presence in the field. It seemed to him that whenever he succeeded, he was said to be carrying out orders; but if he failed, he would be prosecuted for exceeding his authority. He felt as though he were fighting with a noose around his neck.

The general scribbled out a message to Nellie, who he knew would be worried: "the army has gained a glorious victory. We are pursuing with the greatest rapidity, and expect to gain great results." He could almost hear her telling him to rein in his enthusiasm. Plenty of fight was left in Lee, and Pinkerton was certain that even this split portion of the South's forces outnumbered his own. It was a risky business, attacking 90,000 rebel troops behind a natural water barrier, with only 80,000 men of your own, with maybe 20,000 out sick. But if he was going to strike at all, McClellan knew he would have to strike quickly before Jackson's corps, including A. P. Hill's division—30,000 more Confederates—could return from their victory at Harpers Ferry to join with Lee's main force behind Antietam Creek.

The bad news was that Harpers Ferry with its 12,000 defenders had promptly fallen, proving McClellan right and Halleck a dolt. Still, McClellan had to grant that the garrison and all its supplies had served as bait, causing Lee to make himself vulnerable by splitting his force.

"Is the headquarters to your liking, sir?"

He nodded approval to Colonel Key and Captain Custer. They had chosen a two-story brick house on high ground about a mile from the Creek. Camp chairs, telescopes, and a flagpole had been unloaded from the wagons and set up in the front yard, augmented by armchairs belonging to the house's owner, a man named Pry. The general had an unobstructed view of the long slope to the river, where his army was slowly assembling. He would have a panoramic view of the battle.

He put his eye to the telescope on the lawn. Three bridges across the stream were visible. At the south end, to his left, a substantial stone bridge invited crossing. In the center, another stone bridge was heavily defended by artillery; that was where the rebels evidently expected the main attack. A mile and a half northward, to his right, a third bridge would be sheltered from rebel artillery fire by a dip in elevation; still farther upstream, the creek appeared shallow enough for Federal infantry to ford.

A plan of battle formed in his mind. Joe Hooker was his most energetic leader, especially with Burnside fretting about his authority these days; he would send General Hooker's division across the north bridge toward the white building he could see through the glass, dominating the high ground.

"What's that white building?"

"That's a Dunker church," said Captain Custer.

"A what?"

"The Dunkers. They're a religious sect, against war," Colonel Key explained.

McClellan grunted. "Why no steeple?"

Custer deferred to Key, who said, "I suppose they think it's arrogant to have a steeple. None of the Dunker churches do."

He would send Hooker and his men there to make a sharp left southward parallel to the stream, and then roll up the rebel defense line. At the same time, at the stone bridge farthest south he would send Burnside's corps across, which would prevent Lee from swinging his forces over to stop Hooker. He would hold Porter's men in reserve, and if needed apply the crusher with a thrust into the center. Or, if the battle went badly—if Jackson's force had already arrived back from Harpers Ferry and the rebel army was united—and Lee counterattacked across the Antietam, Porter and his 11,000 men would be there to make the stand to save Washington.

"Where's Burn?" McClellan was irritated at Burnside: he had been four hours late getting into position two days before, and McClellan had to send a sharp message calling him to account.

"He feels slighted and he's sulking," said Custer. "Thinks he should have the command you gave Hooker."

McClellan gave a small groan. Burnside, with his odd-shaped cheek whiskers, was a man whose reputation McClellan had been saving all his life. First at West Point, helping him with his examinations; later, in civilian life, hiring him for the Illinois Central Railroad because Burnside couldn't succeed as an inventor. And now, when Burn seemed gripped by some mental paralysis, he would have to carry him again.

"I have Jake Cox under him," McClellan said. "Get word to Cox to get the Ninth Corps into position to take the bridge as soon as Hooker attacks in the north." Lee had the advantage of interior lines, but a coordinated attack could defeat him; the settlement of the war would follow.

"Will that be today, sir?" Custer asked. "Hooker's ready now, it's not yet noon."

McClellan was torn: on one hand, there was the need for speed, with the rebel forces at Harpers Ferry finishing their job of paroling the Union prisoners and heading back to join Lee. On the other hand, he felt the constant tug of the need for better preparation: his artillery pieces were not yet properly positioned to take full advantage of his firepower. Burnside needed time to reconnoiter the stream around the southmost stone bridge; maybe it was fordable.

Another doubt assailed him: was he right to attack at all? Lee's invasion of the North had been stopped at South Mountain; the Gray Fox no longer seemed to be in the mood for an offensive.

He thought of Lincoln's order in his pocket: "Destroy the enemy, if possible." It was surely possible, and despite Lincoln's mistake in withdrawing from the Peninsula, the President did understand the need for a grand, pitched battle between the armies preparatory to any sort of settlement. His troops scented victory.

McClellan decided to carry the battle to the enemy. Honor as well as politics demanded that the invader be forcibly repelled, and not permitted to withdraw without punishment. The general was aware that the decision he had just made was the most important of his life. It would put to rest all false charges of treasonable timidity. He would strike the superior rebel force where it awaited him.

But not impetuously, not foolishly. To Custer's question about an attack on this day, he replied, "Tell Hooker to put an advance party across the creek upstream this afternoon." He would delay the attack until the morning. "Tomorrow," he declared, "tomorrow we fight the battle that will decide the fate of the Republic."

CHAPTER 22

ANTIETAM VII
TO THE DUNKER CHURCH

George Smalley was aware of Stanton's order banning all correspondents from battlefields. Accordingly, the *Tribune* reporter sought out the general most likely to be in the thick of the fight to offer his services as a volunteer aide-de-camp.

His choice was "Fighting Joe" Hooker. Smalley dressed properly for the occasion of meeting the general, setting aside his linen jacket and lavender pants for a blue suit that could easily be adapted to a Union uniform. He rode up to the general at dusk as Hooker prepared to launch a reconnaissance in force across the Antietam and briefly introduced himself, not so much as a correspondent as a volunteer. Smalley assumed that anyone who encouraged the sobriquet of "Fighting Joe" was eager for all the recognition he could get, and this judgment was confirmed when the general gave him all the credentials he needed with a casual "Come along with me."

The cavalry, in the lead, splashed across the creek far upstream, led by Hooker on a white horse, two divisions of infantry following in water no deeper than their knees. Smalley was instantly as thrilled by Hooker as he had been disappointed earlier in McClellan. Hooker played the game of war as the youngest member of a football team plays football, showing a joy of impending battle that the reporter had never observed in McClellan.

Hooker's countenance glowed when the battle began. Rebel muskets flashed at them in the gathering darkness, backing Hooker's lead cavalry, including Smalley, into the Federal infantry in the rear.

"If they had let us start earlier, we would have finished them tonight," the general muttered, freely criticizing his commander's decision to wait until the next day for a general attack. But even Hooker could not fight an unknown foe on unknown terrain after dark. The Union troops lay down on the ground within a stone's throw of the rebel skirmish line. Smalley slept with his horse's bridle wrapped around his arm.

At four in the morning, as soon as a man could see the sights on his rifle, a sergeant roused Smalley with a kick on the soles of his boots. The reporter did not have time to shave before the battle of the Antietam, or the battle of Sharpsburg—Smalley did not know what to call it yet—began.

Three divisions abreast, Hooker's corps drove the rebel pickets back toward the white Dunker church, taking a withering fire along the thousand yards. Smalley saw the puffs of smoke and heard the bursts that indicated the source of most of the rebel fire as coming from an adjoining cornfield. Hooker reined in his horse and with his sword waved at his batteries of artillery. Thirty-six Union fieldpieces began blazing canister and shell into the standing corn, chopping it—and the rebels firing from within—like a long scythe. From across the creek, longer-range Federal guns joined in the barrage. After five minutes of the worst artillery hell Smalley had ever heard about, General Hooker called a halt to the firing and led his infantry forward.

They were met by a new sheet of rifle fire; the Federal barrage had not dislodged the rebel infantry. An officer in front of Smalley dropped off his horse, the animal bolting forward until it, too, stumbled and dropped. He could hear the hail of bullets, and realized why it was called "hail"—the lead was whizzing through the air before thudding into flesh or dirt. Military formations were lost as the two armies grappled man to man. His eyes smarted from the smoke, his ears were deafened by the boom of nearby guns. Some crazed artillerymen were firing into the engaged infantry as if not caring which side's men were being killed and maimed.

But Hooker's troops kept on, swarming ahead toward the objective, a whitewashed church now pocked with rifle fire. The Confederate line at last broke, soldiers in butternut gray-brown trying to scramble over turnpike fences and being impaled as bullets caught up with them. Northern voices were roaring as the tide of battle seemed to turn.

Then the Texans hit them. The yelps of the countercharging rebels sent a shiver through the ranks as Hood's troops emerged from the woods, pulled up short, and at point-blank range decimated the Union ranks. In horror,

The Dunker church

Smalley saw men falling all around him, felt himself in the vortex of blood and death. He fought back a sudden urge to evacuate his bowels.

"The enemy are breaking through my lines!" Hooker shouted. "Fall back!"

Smalley's horse took a bullet in the neck, reared backward, and the reporter slipped out of the saddle before the horse collapsed on him. He ran to the rear with the others, all the way back to where the Federals had begun the charge a thousand yards and two thousand casualties ago. General Hooker, seated against a tree, looked dazed, one foot oozing blood, the fight gone out of him. But the massed Federal artillery saved the day: when the Texans whooped and charged again, Union canister ripped into their ranks and the rebel line melted away.

Hooker could not bring himself to assemble his men to mount a new charge. Some had deserted, others were separated from their units, thousands were dead or wounded; his corps was shattered. Another Union general came by, a white-haired man—Smalley assumed it was old Mansfield—and the bleeding Hooker waved him and his fresh troops ahead toward the Dunker church.

The terrible slaughter began again, without the mercy of a lull, the two armies stepping on their own and each other's dead, attacking and counterattacking. In the end, about noon, a gray-faced force of bluecoats held the ground around the church, too exhausted to press their advantage. The men in gray farther down the slope, many firing from the cover provided by corpses, were too whipped to throw more bodies into the carnage.

Longstreet rode down the line from the north. Stonewall Jackson, newly arrived from Harpers Ferry, having ridden far in advance of his own infantry, had helped stop the Federal assault, thanks to Hood's Texans.

"Where are your men?" Longstreet asked General Hood, who replied, "Dead on the field." The Texan had started fighting with nine hundred; three hundred were left. In all, the force under Jackson must have lost five thousand men that morning, probably more than the Federals.

Longstreet knew they could not afford that; in all, Lee had fewer than forty thousand men at Sharpsburg, not half of what he presumed to be the effectives available to McClellan. The gray line was a wisp, shuttling men up and down the interior line to meet the uncoordinated Yankee thrusts. Luckily the southernmost bridge had not been seriously attacked; Longstreet could not understand why McClellan's favorite, Burnside, was holding back, but he was thankful that all the attackers did not come at once.

Suddenly the center was in crisis. A sunken road had offered the Confederates a natural entrenchment, and from that cover the gray troops had been picking off any Yankees who dared come up the middle. But a Yankee force had outflanked the long trench and started blazing into it with enfilade fire. Longstreet looked down into the position and for the first time in his military career wanted to be sick. Bodies of Southern boys lay next to each other, on top of each other, scores of corpses shot in the bloody lane, as if prepared for mass burial.

Slightly to the north of the center, not far from the remainder of Hood's Texans, a force of bluecoats was pushing back a regiment of North Carolina men. Longstreet signaled for them to get back into line and return fire, but a

Confederate colonel held up an empty rifle helplessly. His men were out of ammunition.

Two artillery pieces were standing idle, no gunners to man them. The general dismounted and told his three aides to follow him and bring the cannons into line against the oncoming charge. Longstreet held the reins of the four horses and walked forward to call the shots. When the Yankees appeared, they were met with a roar of canister from one gun, then in a few seconds from the other. Longstreet signaled for the otherwise useless North Carolina men to stay in line and wave their colors; he was determined to make it seem as if the position were defended by ammunition-laden infantry backed up by artillery.

General Chilton, Lee's adjutant general, came riding up moments later and asked, "Where are the troops you're holding the line with?"

Longstreet pointed to his three aides, firing faster than they had ever done in artillery school, and to the flag wavers. "Over there, but they don't have a cartridge." Chilton's eyes widened; he struck spurs to his horse and sped to Lee for reinforcements. Longstreet knew the southern part of the line could spare them; he silently blessed Burnside for delaying his attack.

Arms folded, contemplating the stone bridge a hundred yards ahead of him, Ambrose Burnside turned over in his mind the advisability of sending his men charging across.

"An order from General McClellan," called Colonel Key, dismounting. That was unlike Mac; he rarely interfered with the decisions of his field commanders once a battle had begun. Burnside doubted that Hooker, Mac's new favorite, was being similarly harassed. "Push across the bridge," went the order, "and move rapidly up the heights."

"Great loss of life involved," Burnside warned.

"Carry the bridge at the point of the bayonet, if necessary," Colonel Key insisted; "sacrifices must be made." That did not sound like McClellan at all. Still, Key was the commanding general's right-hand man, which was probably why McClellan had chosen him to be the carrier of such an unlikely order. "Every moment is of the utmost importance."

"McClellan seems to think I am not trying my best to carry this bridge," General Burnside told Colonel Key. "You are the third or fourth one who has been to me this morning with similar orders." He waved him off.

For seven hours, Burnside had been probing the defenses around the stone bridge. Perhaps he should have sent a man ahead the night before to test the depth of the stream; if it was fordable, he could send his fourteen thousand men swarming across and overwhelm the rebels sniping from the other side. Burnside had been determined to get his men across dry-shod, thus better able to carry the battle up to higher ground, but Key's visit could not be ignored: He took a deep breath and ordered two regiments to rush the bridge, never mind the casualties.

The charge, to his surprise, was successful; for some reason, the rebel defenses were weaker than he had anticipated. With that bridgehead secured, Burnside ordered another division to attempt to ford the creek farther downstream, if it was not too deep. To his chagrin, the men did so with ease; they could have been across and in the fighting first thing in the morning.

Instead of pressing ahead against the thin Confederate ranks—it seemed that most of Lee's men were defending the other two bridges, in light of the relative inactivity at Burnside's position—the Union force stopped just over the bridge. A colonel came running back to him with embarrassing news.

"We're out of ammunition, General. The men have been shooting at snipers all morning, and we didn't realize that when we put them across the bridge."

"Ah," said Burnside. He could count on nobody.

When he said nothing else, the colonel asked, "Can we get the cartridges across to them?"

"No, bring that division back. Send up another division equipped to fire."

That took two more hours to do. Burnside was still irritated at the way he had been treated by McClellan; it struck him that Mac unaccountably favored that sneaky military politician Hooker in this campaign. He was further annoyed by, and refused to respond to, messages of urgency from the command post in the Pry house. By midafternoon he had put only three thousand of his fourteen thousand New Yorkers and Pennsylvanians across the stream and into the fighting, but could not see why his steady deliberation should be cause for McClellan's haste. He wondered if his old friend Mac had been panicked by the relentless pressure from Stanton and Halleck into attacking a superior force.

Lee did not let it show, but he knew he was witnessing the development of a catastrophe.

He had no reserves. His left, the northern position under Jackson, could not withstand another Union assault; accordingly, he ordered Jackson to deliver an attack of his own. His center was evidently being held by Longstreet's staff aides manning a cannon and a few unarmed men with flags. His right, which had been stripped to a skeleton force to strengthen the left against Hooker and those who followed him, now was under pressure as Burnside's well-rested thousands were pouring across the stone bridge. He needed a few thousand men to stop Burnside's belated move but could draw them from nowhere. A. P. Hill's light division was seventeen miles away in Harpers Ferry, but Lee did not know whether his message to drop everything and join the battle had made it to him.

"General, are you going to send us in again?" The voice of a cannoneer, ordered with his comrades to join Jackson in his attack, was familiar. It was his son, Robert.

"You must do all you can to drive those people back," the general replied. The boy was in the ranks, as he should be, with no privileges. He was proud of him.

His right began to cave. Blue flags could be seen on the ridges above, almost a mile up from Burnside's brigade; they could soon come around and cut off his line of retreat to the Potomac. In the distance, he could see two columns of troops in blue uniforms marching along separate sections of the ridge line. If they were Burnside's men, he might have to consider the possibility of surrender. Longstreet had been right: Lee should not have divided his army in the presence of McClellan, because Little Mac was not the easily confusable Pope. Lee did not dwell on those thoughts; if this army was going to lose, it would lose in glory, and he would take the ragged remnant home to fight again another day. Only heroes would be left.

"Whose troops are those?" he asked an artillery lieutenant. The officer offered him his binoculars. "Can't use it," Lee said, showing his bandaged hands. "Those troops there—whose are they?"

"They are flying the United States flag, sir."

Burnside's men, to cut him off. "And whose troops are those?" he pointed to the other column approaching from the southwest.

The lieutenant focused his glasses. "Those are blue uniforms, I'm sorry to say, General."

Lee did not permit himself a groan. The gamble had been his own, against Old Pete's prudent advice, and he would bear the responsibility not only for the terrible losses, but for the defeat.

"They're Union soldiers, I think, sir, but they have our flags." The spotter seemed confused. "Virginia and Confederate colors, General, maybe captured from us."

Hope surged in Lee. The colors were not captured, the uniforms were— taken along with shoes from the captured Union garrison and worn by the captors on their forced march to the battle.

Lee nodded calmly, as if that was what he expected. "It is A. P. Hill from Harpers Ferry." He was not finished yet.

CHAPTER 23

ANTIETAM VIII
A MASTERPIECE OF ART

"In ten minutes the fortunes of the day seem to have changed," wrote Smalley, kneeling, his notepad on his knee. "It is the rebels now who are advancing, pouring out of the woods in endless lines, sweeping through the field which their comrades had just left . . ."

The Confederates were wearing blue Federal uniforms, the *Tribune* man noted, part of the loot captured at Harpers Ferry, along with boots and rifles in such short supply. The Rhode Island and Connecticut regiments were confused—men in blue shooting at them?—and held their fire. A couple of Ohio regiments were rushed over to help Burnside's men but A. P. Hill's angry rebels were not to be stopped.

Powell Hill had apparently whipped his men seventeen miles in seven hours, over rugged terrain, losing two thousand of his five thousand by the wayside, but the men who arrived, no matter how tired, knew what their mission was. Their first volley dropped four hundred Connecticut men and drove the rest to cover. Burnside's line sagged and broke. Bursting shells set fire to haystacks where men were hiding or resting; their screams mingled with the sound of musket fire and the yip-yip-yip of rebel yells.

Was the battle over? Who had won? Smalley faced the twin problems of figuring that out, compounded by the challenge of finding a telegrapher to send his copy back to the New York *Tribune*.

General Ambrose Powell Hill, C.S.A.

A brigadier on McClellan's staff rode up to him. "Smalley! You're a friend of General Hooker. Ride to him now, tell him to rally his corps and lead it back onto the field. He can save the day—and save the Union!"

"Hooker is injured," the correspondent replied. "He took a bullet in his foot."

"Let him get into an ambulance, for God's sake, and drive back onto the field." McClellan's man, a general who said his name was Wilson, was insistent that Smalley and nobody else carry the message. "We need Hooker now, to take command. The men need a leader."

What was this general suggesting? That Hooker seize command from McClellan, or merely take command of his own men—now under George Meade —and rejuvenate them? He chose to interpret the suggestion as well-intentioned rather than mutinous. "Hooker will go back in action," he responded with enthusiasm, "I'll answer for it."

He rode back to the farmhouse field hospital. General Hooker was seated with his bandaged foot elevated on a chair.

"General McClellan wants to know how you are," said Smalley.

"In pain. What news from the battlefield?"

"Our side is no longer fighting," Smalley said. "Burnside cannot get his troops into the battle. Porter's reserves have not been committed and may never be. The rebels have suddenly been reinforced, and there's every chance that Lee will escape across the Potomac."

"All a waste, all those gallant men dead."

"Unless—" Smalley let the word hang. Here was this man's opportunity to become a genuine hero, since McClellan's caution and Burnside's ineptitude had created a vacuum.

"You need not go on," Hooker said hastily. "You see I cannot move."

The correspondent's shoulders sagged. He left, not knowing whether he had carried a message from McClellan, or from a group of insubordinate officers who wanted a fighting general to replace McClellan. Smalley wondered for a moment if a newspaperman should be carrying that kind of message, then reminded himself that he had wangled his way onto the field as a general's aide.

But now he had to write and file his story, whether or not the battle was finally over. No other correspondent was likely to have seen as much as he had seen. He made a note to remind himself of the critical mistake: "Burnside hesitated for hours in front of the bridge which should have been carried at once by a *coup de main* . . ."

As darkness began to add to the smoke in making observation difficult, Smalley hurried to McClellan's headquarters at the Pry house. The battle was stalemated; Lee's men had held at all three bridges. Were the Confederates exhausted, weak, ready to collapse at one more blow from fresh troops—such as those reserves under Fitz-John Porter that McClellan had saved for this critical moment? Or was Lee playing possum, holding back thousands of hidden troops of his own, waiting for McClellan to commit his last offensive reserve so as to strike back hard, win the battle and the war?

He looked at the men gathered on the lawn in front of the Pry house and made notes on the relevant details: "McClellan's glass for the last half hour has seldom been turned away from the left. He sees clearly enough that Burnside is pressed—needs no messenger to tell him that. His face grows darker with anxious thought." Nobody else would have these details.

"Looking down in the valley where fifteen thousand troops are lying," Smalley scribbled, "he turns a half-questioning look on Fitz-John Porter, who stands by his side, gravely scanning the field. They are Porter's troops below, fresh and only impatient to share in the fight.

"But Porter slowly shakes his head, and one may believe that the same thought is passing through the mind of both generals: 'They are the last reserves of the last army of the Republic; they cannot be spared.' "

McClellan, with Fitz-John Porter at his side, Captain Custer and Colonel Key at hand, stepped away from the telescope. Burnside's attack downstream had been a disaster. He should have followed orders and had fourteen thousand men across that bridge at 7 A.M. The strangely lackadaisical, probably fearful Burnside had finally put a fourth of his force across in midafternoon, but the delay had allowed Lee to concentrate on stopping Hooker to the north; now, the portion of Burnside's Federals who had crossed were met and stopped by A. P. Hill's men in their new Union blue coats.

Little Powell's relatively small force, coming just at the wrong moment, had effectively stemmed the Union tide; Nellie would find that ironic. It occurred to McClellan that if he had gone into action a day earlier, Lee would not have been able to reassemble his divided army. He put that troubling thought out of his mind; today's real problems were caused by the failures of Burnside and Hooker.

In McClellan's eyes, "Fighting Joe" had received a bullet in the foot and taken himself out of the action on the most important day of his nation's life —not much fight in Joe. McClellan reminded himself that Albert Sidney Johnston had died from neglect of a similar wound, but a corps commander's place in battle was at the head of his troops, unless he was seriously disabled.

He stepped back from the eyeglass to take in the panorama of the battle: Federal shells were bursting over and in the Confederate lines, as his artillery outgunned Lee's; the smoke from cannon and muskets obscured the fields where men were yet grappling in the dusk. Most of the flashes came from his left, downstream, where Burnside's men were being stopped; to the right, what was left of Hooker's old command was still putting pressure on the rebel lines.

Now was the moment, McClellan knew, to gamble all with a charge of Porter's fresh reserve troops up the middle. If such an attack succeeded, Lee might well be routed, the war won, McClellan recognized as the worthy successor to Napoleon.

"Robert Lee has always come up with the troops needed to stop us," said Porter, reading his thoughts. McClellan rested his arm on the telescope and looked at the ground; Fitz was the one general he could depend upon. He had courage and judgment. If McClellan called on him, Porter would lay down his life, if need be, in breaking that rebel center.

But what Porter had observed about Lee was true: somehow, at every stage, the aggressive Confederate commander, when forced on the defensive, had come up with enough troops at the right place to stop the Union thrusts. McClellan was certain that Lee had more forces than he was showing. How strong were his reserves? If Porter's men charged the center, would Lee then commit Longstreet and his corps, who had probably been held secretly in reserve, to stop them? And if Longstreet did stop the charge, as the rebels had done all this uncoordinated day, what then?

The overcommitted Union Army would have no way of stopping Lee's counterattack across Antietam stream. The Union commander put himself in Lee's shoes: Let McClellan exhaust his reserves attacking us all day, and then —with typical audacity—throw in Longstreet's fifteen thousand to drive the Union from the field. Nothing then would stand between Lee and Washington, or Baltimore, or Philadelphia. With an army of only fifty thousand men, he could humble the North and end the war.

"How many men do you have for a charge, Fitz?"

"I had eighteen thousand to start. We've been feeding them in slowly all afternoon, left and right. About four thousand infantry ready to go now."

That decided it for McClellan; the reserve was not great enough to carry the day on a charge, but it might be strong enough to make a stand and hold fast if Lee threw in his reserves in the next hour. McClellan could not properly take the gamble. His historic assignment was to stop Lee's invasion,

General Fitz-John Porter

which he had done; his task was not to risk total Union defeat on the possibility of total Union victory. No commander had the right to gamble for personal glory with his nation's existence.

"We'll hold your men here to stop Lee if he attacks," McClellan decided. Yesterday and today, he had taken the offensive; he won a victory yesterday and fought Lee to at least a draw today. The dead and wounded were heaped on the field in numbers that staggered the mind; the moans of the wounded could be heard behind the roar of artillery. Enough—the day's battle was over, the Republic saved; nobody could ask more of this army.

"Today's battle was a masterpiece of art," Porter assured him.

McClellan agreed. "My only mistake was not in giving to you the command I gave to Burnside."

He put his eye to the glass and watched the battle slowly become history. McClellan had found the enemy army, driven it to bay, and attacked a force that everyone agreed was much larger than his own. His fine army had bled and caused the enemy to bleed, as never before on this continent. He had captured a dozen guns and scores of enemy colors, losing, to his knowledge, none of his own. Plenty of trophies. He had been on the offensive all day; tomorrow, let Lee take the burden of the offense. McClellan would not leave the bloodsoaked field; when Lee learned that, he would have to withdraw.

"You'll be criticized by Lincoln and Stanton," Porter reminded him, "for not being aggressive enough."

That would be the next battle—with the second-guessers in Washington. But who in that crowd, with bags packed for evacuation, could dispute the fact that he had saved the country? "I'm going to insist that Stanton be removed and that Halleck shall give way to me as commander in chief."

"General-in-chief," Porter corrected him. "Lincoln is—"

"I will not serve under Halleck, the incompetent fool." He thought of the twelve thousand Union troops captured at Harpers Ferry, thanks to Halleck's stupidity and Lincoln's agreement—a force that could have been charging the rebel center right now. "Stanton must leave and Lincoln must restore my old place to me. Unless those two conditions are fulfilled, I will leave the service."

"They cannot refuse you that."

"I have done all that can be asked, in twice saving the country." That was the nub of it: McClellan had never campaigned to crush the South and subjugate its people. His mission had been only "the defense of Washington," but he had interpreted that as "to seek out and confront the enemy and save the country," and that is what he had done this day, here on the banks of the Antietam. He had demonstrated that neither side could conquer the other; now was the time for sensible statesmen to work out a settlement to restore the Union as it was.

With Stanton and Halleck out of the way, he could deal directly with Lincoln, who was not a bad sort when well advised. McClellan promised himself to keep the President better informed in the future; he was entitled to know grand strategy, just as McClellan, if he succeeded Lincoln as President, would expect to be informed by his subordinates.

He looked through the telescope again at the seemingly vulnerable center. Who knew how many men Lee had in reserve? The General straightened, and to Porter shook his head; there would be no gamble.

George Smalley looked again at the speculative line he had written, placing words in the mouth of one or the other of the Union generals: "They are the last reserves of the last army of the Republic; they cannot be spared." Was it fair of him to put that last part in quotations? It was only an observer's educated guess at what had been said, but perhaps the reader would think Porter actually was overheard using those words. Smalley liked it; he left it in quotes. Poetic license. Let the generals deny that was what they were thinking.

What about his lead? The *Tribune*'s readers would want to know who won, but he could not tell them because the battle was not over. Who would withdraw tonight or tomorrow? Would the exhausted armies, more than decimated by casualties, simply accept a stalemate and go home?

He could start with the casualties: "George McClellan, whose concern about casualties has caused him to be charged with timidity, today led the Union Army into the bloodiest single day of the war. Preliminary estimates are twenty-five thousand men killed, wounded and missing, evenly divided between the armies despite the South's advantage of interior lines and of being on the defensive all day . . ." The reporter rejected that before his editor could; irony did not belong in a lead.

Smalley began again. "Battlefield of Antietam, Wednesday evening, Sept. 17, 1862 . . . Fierce and desperate battle between two hundred thousand men has raged since daylight, yet night closes on an uncertain field." That was safer and better. "It is the greatest fight since Waterloo, all over the field contested with an obstinacy equal even to Waterloo . . ."

Hungry, bone-tired, afflicted with the urge to unburden himself of all the unreported information cramming his head, Smalley commandeered his colleague's horse—Paige started to object, but Smalley snatched the reins out of his hands—and raced for Frederick.

The Union forces had outrun the telegraph cable, which could only be strung at a mile an hour. Smalley had heard that McClellan had sent back a few cryptic messages to Stanton that a great battle was raging, perhaps the greatest in history. Those had been sent by rider to Frederick, Md., and then telegraphed to Washington, which would be the *Tribune*'s method of filing.

Smalley whipped his horse like A. P. Hill driving his troops but arrived at the telegraph office too late. The door was locked and the office dark. Nobody in the upstairs apartment knew where the telegraph operator lived; the correspondent would have to wait until seven in the morning.

Smalley sat on the front step of the telegraph office and started to compose his copy. If Bennett's man on the *New York Herald* had gone up to Hagerstown and found the telegraph open there, the *Tribune* would be beaten and editor Sydney Gay would never forgive him. Should he ride north? What if he got lost, or the horse stumbled, or the *Herald* had some unsuspected method of filing near Frederick? Smalley decided not to move; he would write his story where he sat, sleep on the telegrapher's doorstep, and file at daybreak. Covering some battles, a reporter often had to operate with no knowledge of the competition's resources.

Abraham Lincoln and son Tad

BOOK NINE

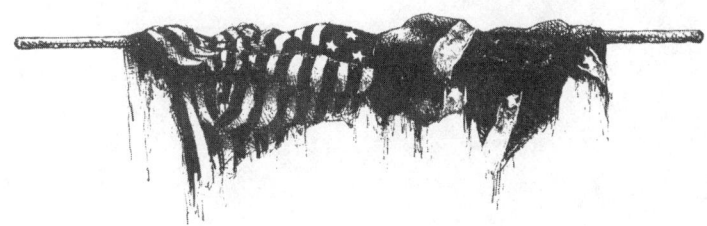

Abraham Lincoln

CHAPTER 1

Two Proclamations

No news from the front in Maryland. Lincoln fretted in his office for a time, then bolted over to the telegraph office, but the only word Stanton had received from McClellan was a brief message relayed through Baltimore because the Union forces had outrun the telegraph line. "We are in the midst of the most terrible battle of the war—perhaps of history."

He weighed McClellan's adjective: not the "greatest" battle, but the "most terrible" battle. What did that mean—more casualties than at Shiloh? Typical of McClellan to think of the hair-raising terror of a battle and not the opportunity to deliver the blow to save the Union and end the war. Lincoln had sent him eighteen thousand men with Fitz-John Porter; had that been enough? Had he been prudent, or criminally timid, to hold back fifty thousand for the defense of Washington? Certainly those fifty thousand could not hold Washington if McClellan lost to Lee north of Frederick. Lincoln began to have second thoughts about not giving McClellan all the reinforcements he sought before "the most terrible battle."

Lincoln had to give McClellan credit for unaccustomed audacity: for the past two weeks he had been acting like a fighter. What had changed him so? Lincoln assumed his reappointed general had been aroused to action by the sort of snubbing he got after Pope's angry charges against him. Certainly Little Mac had performed well a few days before at South Mountain, the first real victory the Union could claim since Grant at Donelson more than half a year ago. If he won today at Sharpsburg, capturing Lee's army, McClellan would pose a new and different problem: the victorious commander, with the army personally loyal to him, demanding that his views of peacemaking be carried out by the President.

On the other hand, if McClellan lost, the war was lost. The government would have to evacuate Washington and sue for peace on terms of disunion. Lincoln closed his mind to that; it was not in McClellan's nature to lose decisively, as he had shown on the Peninsula. If this day at Sharpsburg went against him, the Young Napoleon would retire in good order, defending Washington, holding fast to his professional reputation, husbanding the remains of his beloved army. At least he could be depended on not to lose.

That, of course, might be accounted for by more than his cautious nature; Lincoln suspected that the never-losing, never-winning pattern was part of the ambitious general's political-military design. Word had reached him of the talk in the army of stalemate, and negotiation between officers on both sides who knew and admired each other. And Stanton had reported the communication between McClellan and the Democratic leaders in New York. Such insubordination was really intolerable—the President slammed a sheaf of telegraph messages down on Major Eckert's desk at the thought of it—but what could be done? No McClellan, no army.

He could do nothing about that internal threat in this dark and doubtful moment. But Lincoln resolved, at the first opportunity, to rid himself and the nation of the determinedly irresolute general, and of the element in the officer corps whose heart was not in the war. The clearing of that particular hard acre, roots and stones, could not take place after a defeat, when McClellan would still be needed to defend Washington; nor could it be after a victory, which would make the general's removal appear to be politically inspired and might stimulate an army revolt.

Lincoln pondered a third possibility: the ambiguity of a draw. What if the result of today's battle turned out to be mutual bloodletting and exhaustion, as at Pittsburg Landing, with no clear victory for either side? In that case, Lincoln suspected that the pressure from Wade and Sumner and Greeley would make it expedient to take important command from McClellan soon. But not too soon; elections were coming and the Peace Democrats needed a dramatic issue to rally 'round. The second dismissal of McClellan, especially after any sort of achievement at Sharpsburg, would provide them that issue. Election Day in most states was only six weeks off; Lincoln could wait until then, but was determined not to wait a day later.

Meanwhile, if his generals could not win the war, Lincoln knew of one powerful political action he could take to strike at the secession.

Favoring his sprained left wrist, which was swollen and aching, Lincoln strode down the long War Department hall to Halleck's office. Senator Reverdy Johnson of Maryland, a good War Democrat, was there with a Union captain in tow, obviously dropping some bad news on the general-in-chief. Halleck was slouched behind his desk, clinging to his elbows the way he did when he was too scared to give a recommendation. He rose when the President walked in and told the captain to tell his story again.

"I just rode in from Harpers Ferry, sir. Our cavalry escaped."

"And the rest of the garrison?" Lincoln, as he asked the question, dreaded the answer.

"Surrendered. Colonel Miles wouldn't put up a fight. He just saw those rebels up on the heights and he ran up the white flag. Got killed doing it, too —cannonball."

Lincoln dug his hands into his hair; twelve thousand men captured at a time when the draft was producing no men at all! Tons of supplies now in the hands of the rebels, when they needed boots and rifles as never before to supply their invasion of the North. The garrison had been under the command of an officer convicted of drunkenness at First Bull Run, and this sudden surrender smacked to Lincoln of cowardice or treason.

"Other Union officers were there," Halleck said to the captain, as if it were all his fault. "Did they all turn tail when Miles wanted to give up?"

"Almost all tried to argue him out of it, General." The captain was near tears. "But Colonel Miles kept saying he was not going to be party to a massacre. We told him that McClellan had sent a relief column, and that we ought to try to hold out a while if only to tie down General Jackson's men, but he wouldn't listen."

"It's true he was outnumbered," Halleck said weakly.

"That's when the cavalry made our dash out. We didn't want to spend the war on parole or in prison."

"You did well to do that," Lincoln told him. The cavalry would have done better to dash toward McClellan's forces in battle rather than run home to Washington.

Lincoln shook his head in disgust. He told Halleck he was going out to the Soldiers' Home for the night, and to send a rider immediately with any telegraphed word from McClellan. He could not help the war by waiting in the telegraph office, but he could work on a second draft of one of the proclamations in Silver Spring.

"Stanton asked me to remind you about the proclamation on internal security," said Halleck miserably. "He expects riots about the draft, and he may be right if things go badly at Sharpsburg."

Lincoln nodded and walked outside to his horse. Hill Lamon handed him the reins, and followed him on the forty-minute journey to Silver Spring. The heat had let up; a thunderstorm appeared to be brewing. The well-armed Lamon was a comfort, even though Lincoln liked to say he had no need of a bodyguard.

He could think on the horse. Lincoln tried to direct his mind away from the battle in Sharpsburg because there was nothing he could do about that now. He had two proclamations to consider, both of them presidential actions that would surely affect the outcome of the war. The papers were in his plug hat, where he had been accustomed to carrying important papers as a lawyer riding circuit.

One proclamation was the suspension again of habeas corpus, this time on a much broader and more official basis. Stanton, who had lifted a milder order when he took over at the War Department, now felt it absolutely necessary. Agitators were everywhere, sowing disloyalty and disunion, undermining the recruitment of needed troops. When the commanding general at Cairo, Illinois, tried to find jobs for confiscated slaves sent North—overriding the Illinois law against bringing free negroes into the state—there had been a terrible ruckus. Lincoln judged the courts incompetent to handle such widespread anti-Union activity.

The other proclamation was general emancipation, leapfrogging the provisions of the Confiscation Act. He would work on that first, having wrestled with it for months, ever since that dismaying session with McClellan at Harrison's Landing, coming back from the Peninsula, when he'd had to suffer instruction from his military commander on political goals.

Seward, Weed, Blair and the rest of the conservatives would continue to counsel against it, and Lincoln granted the soundness of their expectation that emancipation would harm some Republican chances in the elections that fall. But he also knew that emancipation cut both ways: Sumner needed such an act to help him win in pro-abolition Massachusetts. And Stanton was denying General Wadsworth combat command because he wanted him to run for New York governor against the Peace Democrat Horatio Seymour; Stanton said Greeley was sure Wadsworth and emancipation would win, no matter what Thurlow Weed said.

On the whole, it was Lincoln's political judgment that this fall's elections would not be damaged as badly by an emancipation edict as Weed and the Blairs warned. Abolition would hurt the Republicans in Illinois—his friend Leonard Swett would have a hard time—but it would be good to have Wade and Tad Stevens and the rest of the radicals in Congress, along with Stanton and Chase in the Cabinet, enthusiastic about the Administration's policy. The abolitionists were still a minority in the country, but Lincoln sensed that their view had become dominant in the Republican party.

And emancipation would be an answer to all those in the North, like August Belmont and that money crowd, who kept demanding something decisive. Lincoln could declare that it was "my policy to have no policy," and claim to be driven by events, but a real policy was what people wanted— many of them only to be able to oppose that policy. Drift was the worst thing; with the military initiative now in Lee's hands, Lincoln could ill afford the appearance of political drift.

Walking his horse, reins in his good hand, holding his throbbing wrist high to alleviate the pain, Lincoln was aware that he was making a case for issuing the two proclamations right away. Still, the blatantly unconstitutional seizure of property troubled him: of the Founders, Adams and Jefferson had been abroad when the slavery compromise was made at the Constitutional Convention, but Washington and Madison were present; was it now for Abraham Lincoln, elected by forty percent of the people, and after having solemnly promised in his Inaugural not to strike at slavery where it already existed, to break that compromise?

Yes, he reckoned it was, because otherwise the Union would dissolve. The governments of England and France were fixing to recognize the Confederacy —Gladstone, Chancellor of the Exchequer, had said as much recently. That would give Jeff Davis the means and method to buy arms, to break the blockade, to set up in business as a country. But by freeing the South's slaves, Lincoln would embarrass the British government in the eyes of its own people. Prime Minister Palmerston might have to stay put, at least for another year.

More important, he reasoned, the threat of abolishment would hurt the enemy where he lived, in the South, on the plantations. He had to hurt them, and keep hurting them, until they realized that secession cost too much in lives and treasure. Emancipation might cause hundreds of thousands of blacks now producing the South's food and cotton to run away. A good number of young whites would have to be kept at home in fear of a servile revolt—which, of course, Lincoln did not intend, but which would be recognized as a danger.

On top of that, he could use Africans in the U.S. Army, first as noncombat helpers, later as soldiers. By letter from New Orleans, General Ben Butler reported that he had met with a black delegation and assured him that they would be excellent fighters.

Of course, there was the plain morality of emancipation: if anything was wrong, slavery was wrong. He had spoken out against its extension to free soil all his adult life: it was a monstrous practice, and those who deny freedom to others deserve it not for themselves. But that moral argument was not controlling in this case: he had pledged time and again not to interfere with the peculiar institution where it lay, provided only the Union would stand. And if the Southern states would come back today, he could not insist that their peculiar institution be abolished. Beyond the moral argument, legally—constitutionally—Lincoln knew he did not have a leg to stand on. The only justification that would hold up in the court of public sentiment was military necessity. On that basis, anything could be done.

The unconstitutional nature of abolition by fiat did not overly bother him: the Southern leaders had warred upon their flag, unforgivably calling into question the central idea of majority rule, and that had to cost something. That it should cost them the profitable institution of slavery was not all that distressing.

Lamon was humming. The brawny marshal from back home knew a lot of songs, both sweet and sad, which he would sing to the rhythm of the horses' steps. Lincoln asked him to sing "Picayune Butler," a comic ditty he always enjoyed, as they approached Silver Spring. Lamon obliged, and the President went back to his thoughts.

The counsel for the defense of the Constitution—a voice in Lincoln's mind as he was making the case for emancipation—had asked, Was this lawful? The attorney prosecuting the preservation of the Union, another voice in his mind, had a ready answer: Constitutional, no, but lawful, yes—as a war power needed to preserve the Constitution itself.

So military necessity is the justification, said the defense counsel—but is military necessity the real reason? Isn't the ulterior motive purely political, that you are losing your basic constituency in your party, and that without appeasing your radical Republicans you will not be able to fight on for Union?

Good question, Lincoln, sitting as judge, said to defense counsel, and looked to the prosecutor of the war for reply. Stipulated, conceded that fierce Unionist, surprisingly: let us grant that military necessity is merely a subterfuge, enabling the President to justify the political act of holding on to his noisy core supporters. By so doing, the prosecutor argued ingeniously, the President rebuilt the political backing needed to carry on the war—which transformed that politically motivated action into a *military* necessity.

Lincoln nodded approvingly. The prosecutor's argument seemed to be the embodiment of hypocrisy and sophistry, but it was happily freighted with common sense. Rallying the radicals was a political necessity; if it required the guise of military necessity, that guise became reality—because the war could not be fought without the new war spirit that only abolition or military victories would bring. The victories were not forthcoming; the action at Sharpsburg would probably not destroy Lee's army because that destruction was not McClellan's way; that left only the weapon of abolition.

The Constitution's defense counsel would not give up. What of Blair and Weed, the best political minds in your party? Don't they warn you that emancipation would be a political liability, that it would lose congressional seats in the North to Peace Democrats? Come on now, Lincoln—aren't you really doing this to satisfy some long-held moral imperative against the cruelty of slavery, or to trigger a slave uprising that would draw rebel troops back to the plantations, or to make impossible a negotiated peace that preserved slavery?

In the courtroom of his mind, still playing all the roles himself, the presiding Lincoln swung his glance over to the prosecutor, wondering how he would handle that.

Weed and Seward and the Blairs are mistaken, was the reply. Oh, you may lose some votes and offend a few pro-slavery generals, but not to act is worse than to act. Not to act against slavery is to play along with your conserva-

Ward Hill Lamon

tives, who will ultimately want to join the Democrats to make peace on Southern terms of disunion if the war drags on. Not to act means to lose your radicals and become another impotent Buchanan. By acting now to strike at slavery, you encourage the growing radical minority that can keep the war for Union going.

It is a *coup d'état*, declares constitutional defense counsel. No, it is counter-revolutionary, concludes the prosecutor of the war.

Lincoln the judge came down on the side of counterrevolution. Yes, he could analyze his political motive, the moral imperative, the diplomatic need, the military advantages, but the overriding reason had to do with crystalliz-ing public sentiment to fight to win.

He would take this desperate step of abolition, necessarily accompanied by a despotic step of suppression of rights, because it was the only way he knew to stop losing the war. The cause of Union, which was at the core of his political being, was being paid lip service by almost everyone else. But after the disasters at First and Second Bull Run, after the North had good reason to fear invasion by the South, after an onerous tax on income had been imposed on the people, after dissent had to be brutally suppressed, the cause of Union was losing its appeal. A more exciting cause was needed. Slavery had brought on the war; the abolition of slavery would have to reignite the war spirit of the North.

The rain came in long, sweeping sheets, but as long as it was this warm, he could afford to get wet. He could not fool himself: emancipation would mean a fight to the finish. The abolishment by proclamation would bury what few loyalists remained in the South and end their peace hopes. It would send an unmistakable message to Richmond and the world that all possibility of com-ing to terms was gone forever.

That troubled him most. Was there not a way, first, to use the *threat* of emancipation—to predict the action to come, and then offer the Southern leaders an honorable way out? In fact, no—an ultimatum would certainly be rejected—but in near-fact, maybe: at least he could demonstrate that his central idea was Union, and that abolition was a weapon to enforce Union.

In the prison camps, he had heard, there was a "deadline"—a line drawn near the prison wall, beyond which a prisoner could not step without being shot dead. Could there not be a similar demarcation for ending the state of insurrection, beyond which slavery would be abolished?

That was the way to do it: not to emancipate immediately, but to announce his intent to emancipate at some future date certain, which states in rebellion could avoid by rejoining the Union. By acting before the deadline, the South-erners could keep their slaves, just as loyal border states like Kentucky could keep slavery. The South would not do it, of course—Jeff Davis was hardly likely to treat this deadline as an incentive—but it would show the North that abolition was intended to be a military act, not a betrayal of past promises and a surrender to the moralizing of the radicals.

He would have to prepare both proclamations—on emancipation, and on suspending habeas corpus—for issuance in quick succession. One would cause explosions of protest that the other would have to cap.

He and Lamon, drenched and dripping, drew up in front of the Soldiers' Home in the verdant Maryland countryside. Lincoln looked back down the road to see if any messengers from the War Department were on the way with news from Sharpsburg. So much was beyond his control. No messenger; he slid out of the water-slick saddle.

Tad came running out and Lincoln lifted him up with his good arm, kissed him, and followed the boy inside. He limped in, wondering when he could get proper attention for his aching wrist and toes, wondering why news of the greatest battle in history, taking place not fifty miles away, should be withheld from the President of the United States.

At dinner, Mary told him of a wondrous new medium who could make contact with the beloved dead, and asked him to join her at a seance that night. He declined; Lincoln would not ridicule her belief if it gave her comfort in her extended bereavement, but he was not much for spiritualism.

Before they finished the spare meal, Homer Bates came racing in, suitably out of breath, from the telegraph office. He handed Lincoln a long yellow sheet.

"From General McClellan?" Mary asked.

"No," said Lincoln, looking at the paper in puzzlement, "from a man named Smalley."

"It's an intercepted cable, sir," the telegraph operator explained. "It was sent from Frederick, Maryland, to the *New York Tribune,* but the telegrapher in Baltimore didn't relay it to New York. Instead, he sent it to the War Department here."

Lincoln nodded; those were Stanton's orders. "This fellow Smalley says the day's battle ended with an uncertain field," he summarized as he read, "greatest since Waterloo . . . it seems that it's a standoff. Awful casualties. Lee's invasion has been stopped, at least."

Washington was probably safe. He took a deep breath; the war was not going to be lost today. It appeared that the bloody struggle at Sharpsburg was not yet a great victory, but at least no defeat. Nobody could gainsay the fact that Lee had failed in his object of invading the North; perhaps today, right this moment, McClellan would be attacking again, pinning Lee's forces against the Potomac. Little Mac was now in the attacking habit, though the great cost in lives must be torturing him; a thrust now, really hurting the enemy, could be decisive.

All eyes would soon be on the triumphant McClellan, who would surely press for his Harrison's Landing terms of unpunished reunion, "the Union as it was." That settlement, bearing what Lincoln had come to believe were the seeds of future renewal of the conflict over slavery, was no longer acceptable. Lincoln, the dispatch from the correspondent Smalley in his hand, saw as urgent the need to accompany the news of victory with a stunning action by the President to force the Southern leaders to come to the negotiating table with hats in hand.

A proclamation of threatened emancipation would do that. End the insurrection now or I will free your slaves. On top of the loss of Lee's army, that threat might crush the rebellion; in the more likely event that Lee's army would be stopped and turned back but not destroyed, the proclamation would inspirit the North and dispirit the South.

Lincoln dismissed young Bates with a nod and a smile; there would be no message to McClellan until the general reported to him.

What if the tide turned, if Lee drove the Federals back? Then he would forget about proclamations and fight on with another general, hoping to achieve reunion without abolishment. What if McClellan failed to attack again, if Lee's army escaped intact? In that case, Lincoln decided, he would go ahead with his proclamations, extending the deadline for ending the rebellion for sixty days, or perhaps to year's end. The political-military pressure would come from him; the President, not the Congress or McClellan and his army clique or the Peace Democrats, would frame the terms for peace.

In that regard, a notion formed in his mind to visit the battle scene soon; it was not McClellan's army, it was the Union Army, and it would do for the commander in chief to be with the troops. It would also do to set certain requirements for quick action which, if not met, would be the basis for relieving George on the day after elections.

He went to his plug hat and pulled out the drafts of the two proclamations aimed at enemies North and South. The proclamation suspending habeas corpus needed no further editing: "Be it ordered, first, that during the existing insurrection and as a necessary measure for suppressing the same, all Rebels and Insurgents, their aiders and abettors within the United States, and all persons discouraging volunteer enlistments, resisting militia drafts, or guilty of any disloyal practice shall be subject to martial law." Surely it was sweeping—"any disloyal practice" could be construed to mean anything—but times were hard and recruitment vital. He would sign it as Stanton had drafted it.

The other proclamation, of emancipation, needed work. He could see what was wrong with it instantly: in the first draft, written in the telegraph office and read to the Cabinet in July, he had been trying to hide behind Congress's Confiscation Act. "In pursuance of the sixth section of the act" was no way to begin a supreme assertion of executive authority; this was not a case of the President's carrying out the will of the Congress, but of the President's seizing the lead in infuriating the Southern rebels.

He brought a quill pen and a bottle of ink to the dining room table and began to write: "I, Abraham Lincoln, President of the United States of America, and Commander-in-chief of the Army and Navy thereof . . ." That was more like it.

Before threatening to free the slaves of the states in rebellion, he would make absolutely clear that his primary purpose was not abolition, but union: ". . . do hereby proclaim and declare that hereafter, as heretofore, the war will be prosecuted for the object of practically restoring the constitutional relation between the United States and each of the states, and the people thereof, in which states that relation is, or may be suspended, or disturbed."

He would never admit that a state had left the Union. Secession was not possible; the so-called Confederacy was never to be treated as a nation, lest that encourage foreign recognition. He paused, quill in mid-air. So much depended on the outcome at Sharpsburg. That was where the South could make a nation. He wondered if George McClellan realized how much the American experiment in self-government rested on his ability to hurt the rebel army. Not merely to make a stand, to stop Lee's advance, but to inflict such pain on the rebels that they would come to understand that the rule of the majority was the unshakable political religion of the land.

He returned to the document at hand. The rhythm of the drafted words threatening to change the status of slaves held by rebels—"shall then, thenceforward, and forever, be free"—did not sit well with him. He moved the "be" up to follow the "shall," lending strength to the concluding phrase.

CHAPTER 2

AFTERMATH AT BLOODY LANE

The Whatizzit Wagon of the Brady studio, with Alexander Gardner in charge, assisted by James Gibson, reached McClellan's headquarters overlooking Antietam Creek on Friday morning the nineteenth. Gardner thought it would be wise to seek out Pinkerton before the detective heard about the presence of the wagon.

"Is the battle over, Major Allen?" Gardner could hear no sound of firing. Wednesday had been the day of the great battle; yesterday, he had been told, both battered and bloody armies had stared at each other across the field, neither willing or able to mount an offensive.

"The pursuit of the beaten rebels has begun," was the way Pinkerton put it, in the accent Gardner recognized as Glasgow. "Lee pulled his army out last night, slipped across the Potomac into Virginia. The field is ours. Great victory."

"Lee has escaped, then?"

"General McClellan sent Porter's corps after him." Pinkerton evidently did not like the tone of Gardner's question; the photographer knew he should not have allowed a hint of criticism to slip into his question. "What are you doing here instead of Brady, anyhow? I said yes to Brady, no to you."

Gardner silently handed him an envelope addressed to "Major Allen" in Brady's fluid script; Pinkerton unsealed it and read the contents. Satisfied that Gardner was still working for his friend rather than in competition with him, the detective said, "You can set up right over there."

"We'd like to go out into the battlefield, if we can."

"No, the burial details are just setting out," Pinkerton said. "You can't make pictures of the Federal dead; it would start a panic in the North."

"How about just the dead rebels?" Gardner had a notion that the essence of this battle was its cost in human life. It was being said that this had been the bloodiest day of the war, worse even than at Shiloh. Gardner thought of himself as less a photographer of events than an artist interpreting universal suffering, which set him apart from Brady and the others.

Pinkerton shrugged. "I hope you have a strong stomach. Does your wagon horse know how to pick his way around bodies? It's no pretty scene out there."

The practical Gibson asked Pinkerton to point out the landmark scenes in the battle. The detective took them to a telescope in front of headquarters, near the flagpole.

"Burnside's bridge was important," Pinkerton explained. "If Burn had crossed it in the morning when Mac ordered him to, at the same time Hooker was charging from the other side, Lee's retreat would have been a rout." It seemed to Gardner that the McClellan staff was expecting criticism and had defenses ready.

Pinkerton swung the glass around. "The Dunker church. Be more famous than Shiloh."

"The what?"

"Dunker," Pinkerton repeated slowly. "They're Germans. The word has to do with the way they baptize their babies—they just dunk 'em in."

Small arms fire erupted in the distance. "That's Fitz-John Porter's men, chasing what's left of A. P. Hill's brigade," the detective said. "We're destroying the enemy. Tell that to your newspaper friends, Gardner. And take my advice, stay away from Bloody Lane."

"What's that?"

"You can't see it from here, because it was a sunken road. Sesesh used it as a trench—Lee isn't much for digging trenches—and it's like an open grave now." Pinkerton removed his derby, mopped his head with a red handkerchief, and replaced the hat. "If you want to see dead rebs in stacks, that's the place. You're welcome to it."

Gardner and Gibson climbed back aboard their wagon. The dour detective turned away, then back. "Wait, you two—I have a trophy for Brady." He reached in his inside jacket pocket and took out a cigar. "It's a secech cigar. Don't smoke it yourself, be sure to give it to him—I'll ask Brady if he got it later. Had something to do with the battle." He carefully wrapped the cigar in the envelope Brady had addressed to him and handed it over.

A cavalryman raced in with bad news: Porter's pursuing force had been caught at the Potomac and smashed by A. P. Hill's rear guard. Maybe three hundred dead Federals, many floating downriver. Nor was Pleasonton's Union cavalry doing much better; the new rifled guns taken by the rebels at Harpers Ferry were all too accurate. The infantry now had an advantage over cavalry.

Gardner did not wait for the reaction from McClellan headquarters because he did not want any changing of minds about the approval to photograph the battlefield. He told Gibson to make for the Dunker church first. They crossed one of the stone bridges and followed the pointed fingers of the gaunt-faced men seated on the ground staring at one another. Gardner was not new to scenes of battle, but this landscape was like nothing he had seen. Every vista was dotted with death. The stench of decaying bodies, humans and horses, fouled the air, relieved only occasionally by the smell of the residue of gunpowder and clinging smoke.

"Make the wet plate," Gardner ordered, taking the reins. Gibson, as soon as the wagon stopped, slipped back into the darkroom in the back; he coated a sheet of glass with collodion, the guncotton dissolved in alcohol and sulphuric ether mixed with a little bromide and iodide of potassium they had compounded the night before. Gardner trusted the careful Gibson to allow the plate to dry to the proper tackiness.

Gardner set up the camera in front of the church. Odd, a house of worship with no steeple. Gibson appeared from the back of the wagon with the wet plate in its lightproof holder and together they inserted it into the camera. Gardner ducked his head to the eyehole, moved the camera, tripod and all, six inches back to get a dead horse in the composition, and removed the lens cap. He counted to ten, covered the lens, and Gibson pulled the plate out and raced back to the wagon to develop it. In this hot, humid weather, the entire operation had to be completed within ten minutes or the plate would be spoiled.

Gibson came out into the light and signaled that the plate was okay. Gardner nodded, picked up the camera, loaded it onto the wagon, and they set out for the Burnside Bridge. Halfway there, in what had been the center of the rebel line, the horse refused to step forward. Gardner stood up to see what was causing the horse to shy and then sat back abruptly.

"Bloody Lane." The sunken road offered a stark spectacle he was certain he would not forget as long as he lived: hundreds of corpses neatly lined up in rows. The bodies in butternut brown had been fighting men before they were mowed down by the enfilade fire. He tied the wagon securely to a tree lest the horse bolt at the stench. He went through his picture-taking routine with Gibson once again, both eager to get away but unable to hurry.

In one half hour, they took three photographs of the heart-stopping sight. The burial detail was far away. A couple of Federal soldiers came and looked at the carnage, but would not stand still, and Gardner knew they would be blurred in the last photo.

"Let's get out of here," said Gibson finally.

Forty yards from the Bloody Lane, a cluster of corpses in blue uniforms were lying, obviously shot trying to storm the rebel position when the sunken road had offered a potent defense. Gardner, obeying Pinkerton's rule about Union bodies, passed them by until he heard a moan. He pulled back his reins. One of the Federal soldiers on the mound in front of the sunken road was alive.

"We'd better bring him in," he called to Gibson, who had heard the sound from the back of the wagon.

"Not our job," said Gibson. "When we get back, we'll tell them to send an ambulance."

"Just this one," said Gardner. The man could die in the time it would take for doctors to arrive. They rolled the moaning man over. He had taken a bullet in his upper leg, but the blood and his uniform material had clotted into a kind of bandage, and his eyes were focused.

"Thought you'd never get here," the man whispered hoarsely as they lifted him into the wagon, alongside the plates. "What in hell kind of ambulance is this?"

"We're war photographers," said Gardner.

"Like Brady?"

"We work for Brady."

The wounded soldier thought about that. "You gonna take a picture of me?"

"No, we're just going to take you to the field hospital. Can't waste plates." Gardner looked at the man's sleeve. "Where you from, corporal?"

"Twenty-seventh Indiana Volunteers. We beat the Johnnies, didn't we?"

"The rebels have left the field, pulled back across the river," Gardner told him. "Lee's invasion is over."

"We beat 'em. You know why? We knew every move Lee was going to make. Thank God for Little Mac," said the corporal.

They rode in silence for a few minutes, the bumping surely causing the soldier pain. He said what struck the photographer as a curious thing: "Lordy, what I'd give for a good cigar now."

Gardner couldn't say no. He took out the envelope with "Major Allen" written on it and handed over the cigar meant for Brady.

CHAPTER 3

JOHN HAY'S DIARY
SEPTEMBER 22, 1862

Any number of rumors are flying around about the McClellan conspiracy. Some say he plans to play the man on horseback, riding to Washington in triumph to take over the country, which may seem farfetched but you never can tell.

I have been passing these rumors on to the Prsdt, of course, only slightly embellished, but this morning I was told of a new and most disturbing one from the Tycoon himself.

"I heard of an officer who said that the army did not mean to gain any decisive victory," Mr. Lincoln told me, "but to keep this running on so that they, the army, might manage things to suit themselves."

I asked him what he planned to do about such treason. He said, "I will have the matter examined and if any such language had been used, his head should go off."

That's the spirit. The cabal around McClellan is a danger to the Republic. Certainly his decision not to pursue the rebel army fits in with that plot to let the war run on until Little Mac can take over or make a deal to split the country peacefully, under a Democratic administration in the North with himself at the head.

Big success for me this morning. The Prsdt has been limping in pain because of his corns. Stanton's assistant, Watson, sent me a note about a man who performs wonders on the feet. At my urging, Lincoln today saw the corncutter, who calls himself a "chiropodist." The fellow has been seeing Stanton about organizing a corps of foot doctors to work on the army's feet (which I understand are in terrible condition), when the Young Napoleon ever gets around to giving the order to march.

The doctor, if you can call him that, is an Israelite born in England and speaks in a cadence that I have never heard before. I scheduled Isachar Zacharie a half hour with the Tycoon this morning before the Cabinet meeting.

"They tell me you have a testimonial from Henry Clay," the Prsdt said in greeting. "He was my idol when I was a Whig."

"Hammertoes," said Zacharie, shaking his head in recollected sympathy. I had heard Henry Clay described many ways, but never as one who suffered from hammertoes. "Very painful. He could hardly stand up in the Senate to make a speech. I fixed it."

"Your idol had feet of Clay," I observed, which drew a hearty laugh from the Tycoon. My best line of the day.

Lincoln sat in his desk chair, took his shoes and socks off and at Zacharie's direction placed his giant feet gingerly on his desk. The doctor took out a towel and a little black bag and asked me to bring a pan of water. Forewarned by Watson at the War Department, I produced the medical equipment instantly.

"General Banks says you're an old friend of his," the Tycoon made conversation as Zacharie massaged one of his feet, which is presumably the way a foot doctor gets acquainted with a new patient. Nate Banks had been Governor of Massachusetts, but had not fared as well as a general against the unpredictable Stonewall Jackson. Lincoln knew Banks to be a capable administrator, scrupulously honest, and appointed him to command the troops remaining around the military district of Washington when McClellan took the army up to reach a stalemate with Lee. (Little Mac now claims those troops should have been with him, but he thinks of reinforcements as mother's milk.)

"Good man, fine family," said Zacharie of Banks.

"I'm thinking of sending him down to New Orleans," said the Tycoon, "to replace General Butler."

That was news to me; "Beast" Butler had been drawing plenty of criticism from people in the North about corruption and arbitrary arrests, and election time was drawing near. Sending Banks down there would placate Democrats in Massachusetts and might even calm things down in Louisiana, now a liberated state.

"Butler? Not such a good man," Zacharie opined, "if you'll pardon my saying so."

"You know him?"

"I have relatives in the South, mainly Savannah. And there are plenty of Jews in New Orleans, trading, banking. What I hear about Butler is not good."

"Give me specifics," Lincoln said, wincing but not looking away as a tender corn was touched by the surgeon's blade. It surprised me that he was talking of such confidential matters with a man he hardly knew, but perhaps direct contact with the foot engenders intimacy.

"Messer, Hyde and Goodrich are the principal jewelers in New Orleans," said Zacharie matter-of-factly. "They made out a check to a relation for five thousand dollars, the proceeds to be paid to clerks for salary. General Butler intercepted the mail and found the check. He made the relation cash the check and give Butler the cash. He claims he gave the money to the poor, but I doubt it."

Lincoln was interested in that. A specific charge is always more useful than accusatory generalizations, which is all we'd been hearing. He grunted when Zacharie finished with one toe, put that foot in the pan of water for more soaking, and took out the other foot, knotting the towel around it tightly. No blood; I supposed that spoke well of his skill at chiropody, if that is the word.

The corncutter changed the subject, with a line of patter that kept his patient's attention from focusing too intently on his foot. "You did us a favor the other day, Mr. President. I see in the papers you appointed the first Jewish chaplain, Frankel of Philadelphia. I know him, know the whole family."

I confess that I had primed Zacharie to say that. Fewer than 150,000 Israelites can be found in the whole country, North and South, two thirds of them piling in during the past decade. Those in the United States Army don't always identify themselves as such, so they don't really need a chaplain. But the law called for chaplains to be of some "Christian denomination" and some Jewish leaders didn't like that. Vallandigham, the copperhead, had taken up this issue in Congress, making it seem as if religion was being unconstitutionally established. So the law's wording was changed to "religious denomination" and the Tycoon appointed this fellow Frankel as a uniformed chaplain the other day. Zacharie, who is the first Israelite I have met, apparently sees the appointment as most significant—the first time his people got something they wanted from the Federal government. (It was easy enough; Lincoln never turns down anybody who wants to get into uniform.)

"Abraham Jonas was one of my earliest political supporters," said Lincoln, in oblique response to the mention of the chaplain appointment. "He came from Kentucky, as I did, and we met in Quincy back in thirty-eight. Like you, born in England. I appointed Jonas postmaster of Quincy last year."

The Israelite gave a that's-nice smile and stopped chatting because he came to some important part of his operation on the left big toe. "This is some big foot," was his only observation.

Zacharie switched the position of the feet in the pan and the towel. "You know, a lot of our soldiers have this same kind of trouble, even worse, Mr. President. I talked with Mr. Stanton about attending to the feet of our boys. I told him we could organize a corps of chiropodists to go from camp to camp to cut corns and treat diseases of the feet."

"Foot soldiers," the President said before I could.

"You make jokes," said the Israelite in reproof, "but I hear Lee's army had a terrible problem with stragglers in Maryland. Why? Because their feet were killing them, they couldn't keep up. Hill's division, seventeen miles in seven hours from Harpers Ferry to Sharpsburg. Could you imagine yourself, with a heavy pack and gun on your back, marching that far that fast on these feet?"

Lincoln looked impressed with Zacharie's specific instance again. Few people brought him hard facts to buttress their arguments. "I'll talk to Mars about that after the Cabinet meeting. Dr. Zacharie, something you said earlier interests me. You said you had relatives down South, and you obviously know a great many people in trade."

"My profession has taken me to every major city in the nation, Mr. President. My office is in my bag."

"Do the Israelites generally stay in touch with one another, more than most?"

"I know what you are getting at, Mr. President. I have friends and relations everywhere."

"New Orleans? There are a great many of"—he searched for an inoffensive word "—your co-religionists in that city. As you know, it is the only major Southern city that we occupy."

"Jews are in soft goods there, and in the money business. Although General Butler, like General Grant, doesn't have much use for us. Couple of rotten apples among our people spoil the barrel. But given the chance, we could do a lot for the cause of reunion. We know how to deal with both sides."

Lincoln wriggled his toes in thought. "The time may come for that. I have a proclamation in work that might bring about the need for some informal communications. You're finished? Is that all there is to it?"

"Step down on the towel."

Lincoln put his feet on the towel, gingerly at first, then more confidently. "That feels better. By jings, that feels pretty good."

"The test is with the shoes on," said the doctor. "No, not the slippers, try on leather shoes." He examined the canalboats that passed for Lincoln's shoes, and said he would recommend a shoemaker who made different shoes for each foot, but signaled for the President to go through what was always the painful process of encasing his feet.

The Prsdt drew on his socks and inserted his feet in his rarely used shoes. He stood up, always a slow, unwinding process.

"It doesn't hurt." He took a few steps, then walked back. "The terrible pressure is off. These old feet haven't felt so good in years." He gave one of those great grins that light up the countenance so rarely. "Zacharie, you're remarkable."

"It would be a great honor, and helpful to me in my profession, Mr. President, if you put something like that down on a piece of paper."

The Prsdt did not hesitate. He walked, almost skipped, to his desk and wrote out a brief testimonial: "Dr. Zacharie has operated on my feet with great success, and considerable addition to my comfort. A. Lincoln."

Zacharie read it and beamed. "I'll come back this afternoon? After you've talked to Mr. Stanton?"

"You have to see Seward, too—not about your foot soldiers, about his feet. He has the same trouble I had. I'll tell him about you."

After the good doctor marched out, Lincoln stood in the middle of the room, rocking on his heels. Though his wrist was still swollen, with his feet miraculously cured of the dread corn affliction, he was not in such bad shape for a man of fifty-three. "When Dr. Zacharie comes back, I think I'll ask him about my wrist, too."

Since he was in such a good mood, I handed him a copy of a new book that had been sent by Charles Farrar Browne, the humorist whose *nom de plume* is "Artemus Ward." His face lit up even more, and he sat down and immediately started reading it.

Fifteen minutes later, I came back in and he was chuckling away. It's not a good idea to interrupt the Tycoon when he's having a good time—those times come so infrequently these days—but I had something of importance to impart.

"Allan Pinkerton is in my office, fresh from the front," I said. "He came to see me, thinks I'm his source of inside information about all those nasty fellows around here out to get his revered general. He wants to pump me, but he most especially does not want to see you. Shall I drag him in?"

"I'd be pleased to receive him," the Prsdt nodded solemnly.

"Cabinet meets at noon," I reminded him. "You have about twenty minutes."

The Tycoon nodded from the couch where he'd been reading Ward and set the book aside. He was already thinking about the questions to be put to McClellan's man Pinkerton. That worthy gentleman, if he ever heard the words "McClellan conspiracy," would think not of the army's disloyal officer corps and its desire for a *coup d'état*, but just the opposite—of a cabal of elected officials out to unhorse his idol. It is in the ambitious McClellan's interest to make much of the affair at Antietam; it is in the nation's interest to minimize the victory, to treat it as the mere overture of the grand symphony to be played out at Cabinet today.

CHAPTER 4

MAJOR ALLEN'S INTERVIEW

Pinkerton forced the smile of the pursuer pursued. The head of the Secret Service of the Army of the Potomac had hoped to pry information out of young Hay without having to undergo interrogation from the President in the next office. That gamble failed, but not all was lost: Perhaps Lincoln, in his line of questioning, would reveal the truth about the cabal's intentions toward the man who had just saved the nation.

"How are the plums and nuts today, Pinkerton?"

"Heh-heh. You remember that still, Mr. President."

That damned coded message would haunt him all his life. It's only saving grace, he told himself, was the way it reminded the President that Pinkerton's vigilance had saved his life in Baltimore on the way to the Inauguration.

"I want you to tell me all you know about the movements of General McClellan's army," the President said. "And whatever I ask, I ask not in the spirit of criticism. Please understand that."

That sounded suspicious; beware of questioners who protest that no criticism attaches to their questions. Pinkerton had done that often enough himself.

"South Mountain, Antietam—those were great and decisive victories, achieved under great difficulty," the President said. "General McClellan has accomplished all he set out to do. He's pushed the rebels out of Maryland and freed the capital from danger."

Pinkerton relaxed a bit. "I wish everybody understood that as well as you do, sir."

"The nation owes him a deep debt of gratitude," Lincoln went on, "and I personally owe him more—he took command of the army at a time of great peril, when the army was suffering great defeats, and he took that army out to meet the foe. We can never repay him for that, Pinkerton."

The secret service chief nodded enthusiastically; this was just what he

Lincoln and Allan Pinkerton

wanted to hear. He decided he would not ask the President to refer to him as Major Allen, in the light of Lincoln's unfortunate amusement at code names. He took out a pencil and paper to make notes, so that the general would have the well-deserved praise as it came from the President's lips.

"I'm desirous of knowing a few things, which—I suppose from all the pressure on the general's mind—he hasn't advised me about, or perhaps thinks of minor importance. If your duty to General McClellan permits it, and if you know the answers, I'd like to ask you about them."

"The general relies on having the full confidence of the President," Pinkerton began, "and so relying, often does not deem it necessary to burden you with detail that—"

"The surrender of Harpers Ferry. Had everything been done to relieve the garrison there promptly?"

Pinkerton brightened. He had a good answer for that. "I happen to have right here in my pocket a copy of a dispatch from General McClellan to the commander of Harpers Ferry. Here, read it."

Lincoln did so and expressed his relief: "Many have tried to impress me that the general might have done more than he did for the relief of the garrison. Yes, this breathes his spirit, and I recognize the signature. At Antietam, what were the number and condition of the opposing armies?"

Pinkerton was certain about that one, too; he began to think he was wise in coming to the Mansion that day. Perhaps some detective's sixth sense had drawn him to Lincoln's office. "Enemy strength one hundred and forty thousand, ours ninety thousand, one army as eager to fight as the other."

"I believe the rebels have that many. I would estimate our strength at one hundred thousand," Lincoln observed, "but you're probably right. Tell me about the battle."

Pinkerton described his patron's strategy and bravery. Lincoln kept nodding—Pinkerton assumed that meant he agreed—and almost in passing wanted to know, "Why didn't the army fight on Thursday?"

Pinkerton explained the exhausted condition of the army Wednesday night, and the presence of the enemy in line of battle all day Thursday. No general short of a butcher could fight a battle on top of the very bodies of the dead and wounded, which had to be cleared from the field; long-range artillery ammunition, which had given McClellan the greatest advantage the day before, was in short supply; there was great need for caution lest the enemy, with its larger forces, counterattack and gain final success.

The President launched into praise of McClellan's skill, repeating that his questions were in no way evidence of criticism, rather of averting the criticism of others. Pinkerton felt much better about the man: it could well be that the cabal had not taken charge of the mind of the President, as he had feared.

"I wonder if you could tell me, without betraying General McClellan's confidence, how come the rebels escaped across the Potomac?"

Pinkerton assured him that the general wanted him to know the facts. That on Thursday night orders were given to bring on a general engagement the next day. That the stage of the water level made it easy for Lee's infantry and cavalry to cross the river anywhere. "I accompanied Captain Custer on a cavalry patrol Wednesday afternoon," he was able to add, "and had my sorrel horse shot out from under me."

At the President's praise of his personal bravery, Pinkerton made a deferential gesture. Lincoln wanted to know why, if the water was so easy for Lee to cross, it had been so hard for our troops to cross in pursuit.

"Oh, on our side, time was needed to probe enemy positions, to bring up ammunition, and to care for the wounded," Pinkerton explained. "Even so, on Friday, after Lee had crossed the river, General Porter's brigade pursued him into Virginia with great vigor and rapidity."

From the expression on Lincoln's face, the Secret Service chief got the distinct impression that he had put the President's mind at ease. He allowed himself a small smile as he jotted down Lincoln's commendation of McClellan's caution, along with the President's mild-spoken request that the general keep him more fully informed. "For example," said Lincoln, "I knew nothing of the position of Antietam Creek in relation to the two armies until I read about it in the newspaper."

Pinkerton promised to tell the general of the importance the President attached to seemingly insignificant details of minor skirmishes.

Secretary Stanton entered the President's office. Lincoln said something about being grateful for what sounded to Pinkerton like the corn cuttings, and asked him to sit down. The Secretary of War took one look at Pinkerton, said he supposed the President wanted to see Major Allen alone, and left. The detective suspected that Stanton felt uncomfortable about him, perhaps because he knew that Pinkerton knew about the Secretary's hidden support of the unconscionable release of Rose Greenhow.

Hay came in and reminded Lincoln of a Cabinet meeting in a few minutes. The detective, satisfied that Lincoln was not nearly as disaffected as the general feared, put on his hat and took his leave. He heard Hay ask if the President needed any papers for Cabinet that day.

"Couple of proclamations," the President replied, pulling some papers out of his desk drawer and inserting them in his plug hat. Pinkerton stood respectfully waiting for him to walk out the door first, which Lincoln started to do, then snapped his fingers and came back. "I'll take the Ward book, too. Cabinet will get a kick out of it."

CHAPTER 5

THE YOKE OF OXEN

Edwin Stanton, Secretary of War, could not believe his ears. Here was the President of the United States of America, his nation rent by civil war, casualty lists stunning the cities of the North after the bloodiest day of that war, traitorous agitators undermining the military draft, the Union Army's officer corps a snake pit of conspiracy to subvert the Confiscation Act and seize executive power, his Treasury nearly empty, Congress fed up with his vacillation, and his Republican Party support threatened by the looming elections— and what was he doing? Preparing to read a comical book to his Cabinet!

"The chapter I was reading just after I had my corns cut," Lincoln was saying, "—and Stanton, I want to talk to you about making the talents of this fellow Zacharie available to our men in the field—is called 'High-Handed Outrage at Utiky.' Ward is really very funny. Listen:

" 'In the Faul of 1856, I showed my show in Utiky, a trooly grate sitty in the State of New York.

" 'The people gave me a cordyal recepshun. The Press was loud in her prases.'

"The spelling is humorous, too, which you're missing," said the President, as the Secretary of War writhed in his chair, awaiting the discussion of a proclamation imposing martial law. "But let me go on," Lincoln continued, and did. Stanton thought it would never end.

Toward the end of this exercise in dialect humor, Lincoln broke out laughing, slapped his leg, removed his glasses to wipe his eyes, and returned to finish: " 'The young man belonged to 1 of the first famerlies in Utiky. I sood him, and the Joory brawt in a verdick of Arson in the 3rd degree.' "

The Secretary of War pointedly did not join in the chuckling around the Cabinet table. Not for him to participate in such sycophancy; he despised Seward, the toady, for laughing out loud. Of the others, only Chase maintained his dignity in the face of this foolishness by the Chief Executive. Stanton glared his disapproval.

"Gentlemen, why don't you laugh?" Lincoln looked suddenly sorrowful. "With the fearful strain that is upon me night and day, if I did not laugh I should die. And you need this medicine as much as I do."

With that, Lincoln set the book aside and said in a grave tone, "Gentlemen." What now, Stanton wondered, a recitation of his confounded poem about the spirit of mortals being proud? A proclamation was on Lincoln's desk that would give the Secretary of War the power he needed to slam down the lid on agitation. "All persons discouraging volunteer enlistments," Stanton had written, "resisting militia draft, or guilty of any disloyal practice" would be denied the coddling of the civil courts and made subject to Courts Martial. It was the only way to stop the coming riots; what was he waiting for?

"I have, as you are aware, thought a great deal about the relation of this war to slavery," the President began. "You all remember that, several weeks ago, I read to you an Order that I had prepared on this subject—which, on account of objections made by some of you, was not issued."

Stanton looked sharply at Seward, who had scotched the proclamation of emancipation in July, supposedly because it might look like "the last shriek," as someone had called it, of a desperate nation in retreat. At that time Seward's henchman, Weed, had come in to give an abolition edict the *coup de grâce* with his political nervousness. Today's topic was a surprise to Stanton: instead of discussing the proclamation suspending habeas corpus, Lincoln was talking about emancipation.

"Ever since then," Lincoln continued, looking at his folded hands, "my mind has been much occupied with this subject. I have thought all along that the time for acting on it might very probably come. I think the time has come now."

A new vista opened to the startled Stanton: the defeat of Blair and Seward in the Cabinet on the paramount issue of the age, followed by the removal of McClellan and his clique from military command. An act of abolition now

would sweep away all talk of negotiations and compromise with the slavocracy. At last Lincoln was becoming a serious man.

"I wish it were a better time," the President was saying, "I wish that we
were in a better condition. The action of the army against the rebels has not
been quite what I should have best liked."

Stanton cautiously nodded agreement; as Secretary of War, he did not want
the vast engagement at Antietam to be considered another defeat, but at the
same time he was damned if he would credit the traitorous McClellan with a
victory. The emphasis in public had to be placed not on the salvation of the
North from Lee's invasion, but on the failure of McClellan to destroy Lee's
army. No gratitude could be shown the Young Napoleon, lest his set of
Democratic generals be encouraged to settle the war on terms that would
preserve slavery in the South. Lincoln was right in speaking of the recent
fighting as an "action" rather than a military triumph; Sharpsburg was to be
described as merely a modest victory, only a limited action, which under a
decent commander might have given the valiant Union troops a decisive
victory.

"But they have been driven out of Maryland," said the President, "and
Pennsylvania is no longer in danger of invasion. When the rebel army was at
Frederick, I made a vow—a covenant that if God gave us the victory in the
approaching battle, I would consider it an indication of Divine Will. I said
nothing to anyone, but I made the promise to myself," he said, and in an
aside Stanton could hardly hear, "and to my Maker."

Was Lincoln suddenly getting religion? Stanton wondered if all the spiritualism surrounding his wife had affected him, and promptly decided not; this
was a politician saying he was following God's will. Stanton did not care how
Lincoln explained his change of mind, so long as he did it.

Lincoln looked at Seward, seated to his right. "The time for the enuncia-
tion of the emancipation policy can no longer be delayed. Public sentiment, I
think, will sustain it, and many of our warmest friends and supporters demand it." He shifted his attention toward Chase, considered by all the most
overtly pious man in the room, adding, "And I promised my God that I
would do it. It might be thought strange that I submitted the disposal of
matters this way. The rebel army is now driven out, and I am going to fulfill
that promise. God has decided this question in favor of the slaves."

Chase listened impassively, annoyed at Lincoln's uncharacteristic evocation of divine guidance. The Treasury Secretary had hoped that Lincoln
would let the military business of freeing and recruiting fugitive slaves be
handled by military commanders in the field, as Frémont and Hunter had
tried to do. If the damnable McClellan had won overwhelmingly at Sharpsburg, no such emancipation edict by the President would have been justifiable
militarily. The lead in freeing slaves could have been taken by Congress or the
military commanders.

Now the President, a consummate politician, was raising emancipation to a
high moral plane, taking full credit for finally doing what enlightened Republicans had been clamoring for him to do for over a year. Chase fought down
the resentment rising in him, which he quickly deemed unworthy, at the
adept way the President was able to run off with the radicals' clothes; on the

contrary, he told himself, he should feel elated at the conversion of Lincoln to his cause.

"I have got you together to hear what I have written down," said the President with finality. "I do not wish your advice about the main matter— that I have determined for myself." Typical Lincoln, Chase bristled—treating a Cabinet like his personal rubber stamp.

"This I say without intending anything but respect for any one of you," Lincoln added, perhaps sensitive to Chase's frown, "but I already know the views of each on this question." He regarded the papers in front of him. "If there is anything in the expressions I use, or in any other minor matter"— Chase noted how he emphasized the "minor"—"which any one of you thinks had best be changed, I shall be glad to receive the suggestions."

Then Lincoln made what Chase considered a curious and gratuitous point: "I know very well that many others might, in this matter, as in others, do better than I can. And if I were satisfied that the public confidence was more fully possessed by any one of them than by me, and if I knew of any constitutional way in which he could be put in my place, he should have it. I would gladly yield it to him."

That same obsequious point again, Chase thought, remembering the last time Lincoln offered to "resign his plan" or place. Why does he have to insult us and then fawn on us this way? Why doesn't he read the proclamation and get on with it?

"But though I believe that I have not so much of the confidence of the people as I had some time since," Lincoln went on deliberately, "I do not know that any other person has more." Time would tell about that. "I am here. I must do the best I can." He looked at Chase, who looked back at him squarely; neither man's eyes wavered.

So he is finally going to take the plunge into the political unknown, Seward observed. The Secretary of State recrossed his legs and unsteepled his fingers. Pity that McClellan had not been able to score a more smashing triumph, which would have forced the British leaders to scrap their plans to recognize the Confederacy and run the Union blockade. Now it will be Lincoln's abolition of slavery, rather than the Union Army's destruction of the Southern armies, that will hold the British and French at bay: the sentiment of workingmen over there would now be firmly on the side of the North. Unless, of course, the slaves revolted and started raping white women; then Lords Palmerston and Russell, eager to manufacture the Southern cotton, would enter the war on the Southern side for what they would call humanitarian reasons.

Who was advising the President to do this? Not Chase, surely, who would lose much of his political following by it. Stanton? Yes, but Lincoln used him to absorb unpopularity in managing the war, and paid little attention to his political judgments—Stanton had his own foolish Democratic ambitions anyhow, which was why he so feared McClellan's success. Certainly not the Blairs, or Bates or Seward or Weed—all had counseled the opposite course.

Remarkably independent and strong-willed fellow, this Lincoln; this situation was similar to Sumter, where all the wise heads save Blair advised against precipitating a civil war, but Lincoln accepted war. Seward freely admitted his misjudgment of the man; at the start, he had been certain he could control the unsophisticated President, and rule while Lincoln reigned. That had been a mistake. He sighed profoundly as Lincoln proceeded to read aloud the draft of his proclamation.

"I, Abraham Lincoln, President of the United States of America, and Commander-in-chief of the Army and Navy thereof . . ."

If he's bound to do it, Seward conceded to himself, that's the way; as Bonaparte had advised, if you are going to take Vienna, then take Vienna. That assertion at the beginning was to call attention to his war power; as Lincoln read on, Seward approved of the way he unequivocally reiterated that the goal of the war remained preservation of the Union, which was intended to remind one and all that he had not changed the purpose to abolition.

"That it is my purpose to again recommend the adoption of a practical measure tendering pecuniary aid to states which may voluntarily adopt immediate or gradual abolishment of slavery . . ."

The familiar bow to the border states: Lincoln was going through his litany of gradual, compensated abolition. Seward assumed he would next put in the usual nonsense about deportation.

". . . the effort to colonize persons of African descent will be continued . . ."

Yes, there it was; Lincoln, in the midst of what surely was an unconstitutional *coup*, was nothing if not consistent about all his previous offers.

"Hold it," Seward interrupted. "Put in 'with their consent.' "

Lincoln nodded, wrote in those words on the draft, and continued: *"That on the first day of January in the year of our Lord one thousand eight hundred and sixty three, all persons held as slaves within any state, or designated part of a state, the people whereof shall be in rebellion against the United States shall be then, thenceforward, and forever free . . ."*

That dry legal tone was probably best for a coup, Seward judged, but showed a frown at Lincoln's next line: *"and the executive government of the United States will, during the continuance in office of the present incumbent, recognize such persons as being free."*

"That won't do."

Lincoln looked up and took off his spectacles, waiting for Seward's objection.

"Where you say, 'during the incumbency of the present President'—I'd strike that out. You're issuing a state paper, not a personal message." Seward thought, but did not say, that Lincoln's qualifier seemed to invite the next President to revoke the whole thing. Chase piped up to say he liked Seward's suggestion, as Seward had assumed he would; the Treasury Secretary would prefer the proclamation be issued by anybody but the incumbent.

Seward also saw the weakness in Lincoln's proposal: the President was merely personally "recognizing" freedom during his term without saying he would actually deliver it permanently. "Where you say that you 'will recognize such persons as being free,' I'd change that to 'will recognize *and maintain* the freedom of such persons.' " In for a dime, in for a dollar; if Lincoln was going to stage a coup, he should do it with firm resolve.

"I considered that," said Lincoln, "but it's not my way to promise what I am not entirely sure I can perform."

"You ought to take that ground," Seward told him with great assurance. *"Recognize* by itself isn't strong enough."

"I'm not prepared to say that I think we're exactly able to *maintain* this," said Lincoln dubiously.

"Seward's right," said Stanton, though Seward knew it must have pained him to go along with a Cabinet rival.

"Put in *maintain*," agreed Chase. "The Proclamation does not, indeed, mark out exactly the course I should myself prefer." Seward rolled his eyes at the understated truth of that; Chase would probably have preferred an anonymous whisper in the night. "But I am ready to take it just as it is written, and to stand by it with all my heart. I think the suggestions of Governor Seward very judicious, and shall be glad to have them adopted."

Lincoln looked around the table and agreed to go along with the change. He rewrote the phrase as Seward had suggested. He continued reading a section that Seward considered ballast—calling attention in laborious detail to the Fugitive Slave Act and the Confiscation Act, inserting in the proclamation the printed sections of the legislation. Why all that?

Seward's puzzlement ended with the reading of the final paragraph: *"And I do hereby enjoin upon and order all persons engaged in the military and naval service of the United States to observe, obey, and enforce, within their respective spheres of service, the act and sections above recited."*

Ah, that was why Lincoln felt the need to quote from previous acts of Congress: to send a message to George McClellan & Co.: in this Executive proclamation threatening to free the slaves of rebels, he was building upon laws duly passed by both Houses. By ordering McClellan to obey the laws passed constitutionally, and enumerating them, Lincoln apparently hoped the exhortation would slop over to his unconstitutional coup of the seizure of the property of everyone who lived in the South, rebel or not. Shrewd.

But it troubled Seward that a President should have to "enjoin" the nation's armed services to obey the laws; that was surely unprecedented. "Enjoin" meant "command" or "direct" in Seward's lexicon: possibly Lincoln was worried about a counter-coup by the army, feeling its oats after its achievement at turning back Lee's invasion, and he wanted to remind the sure-to-be-angered officers who had not signed up for abolition that the recent acts in that direction were swathed in constitutional legitimacy.

When the President was finished reading, Seward, who realized his comments had been peripheral, looked to Blair for the much-needed political rebuttal. Although Lincoln had said his mind was made up on the central question, surely he was not impervious to comment from his Cabinet on the substance of the move.

Blair, however, merely looked at the ceiling. Seward assumed the Postmaster General had been advised by his sagacious father that the Blairs should not be in the forefront of opposition to the shift in the center of gravity of the party—especially if Seward was willing to take on that onerous task.

Because nobody else was making specific suggestions on a fairly important document, much less challenging its basic wisdom, Seward said "colonization. Isn't the Attorney General working on something along those lines?" He knew that the redoubtable Anna Ella Carroll was working with Bates on a policy statement about the emigration of freed blacks. They would be sent out

as emigrants, not as colonists—without the protection of the mother country
—in order to make their arrival more palatable to the Central American
countries.

"I'll have that by the end of the week," said Bates.

"So where you say 'the effort to colonize persons of African descent will be
continued upon this continent, or elsewhere,' " Seward suggested, "add 'with
the previously obtained consent of the governments existing there.' That will
be the import of the Attorney General's memorial when it arrives, I understand, and it should conform with your proclamation."

Lincoln nodded and put it in, adding "That's an important point, Seward.
How come you didn't bring it up right away?"

Seward shrugged.

"You remind me," smiled Lincoln, leaning back, "of a hired man out West
who came to the farmer with the news that one of a yoke of oxen had
dropped dead. And after chewing the fat for a while, and hesitating, the hired
man said the other ox in the team had dropped dead, too. The farmer asked
him, 'Why didn't you tell me at once that both oxen were dead?' and the man
answered, 'Because I didn't want to hurt you by telling you too much at one
time.' "

Seward had not heard that one before; Lincoln seemed to have an inex-
haustible supply of tension relievers that were entirely apropos. He joined in
the laughter and then Stanton had his say.

"I want it known that I support this measure to the fullest," Stanton said,
without equivocation. "This brave act will infuse new spirit in the forces of
the Union, and it will strike fear in the heart of the rebellion. It will win the
war. It will set right a terrible wrong."

Stanton looked around the room fiercely. "This act is so important, and
involves consequences so vast, that each member of the Cabinet should be
called upon to give distinctly and unequivocally his own opinion of it."

"Some of us have spoken up," said Seward cheerfully.

"Two gentlemen," Stanton replied, glowering in victory, "have not been
sufficiently explicit, though they seem to concur. I refer to the Secretary of
the Treasury"—Chase looked startled and then offended, a sequence of reactions Seward thought he was especially good at—"and to the Secretary of the
Navy." That, thought Seward, was Mars getting even with old Neptune for
making him look like a fool in the abortive Cabinet coup last month. "And I
have in mind another member," Stanton added ominously, "with whom I am
not in full accord on many policies." That, Seward knew, meant him; he
airily waved it off.

"I must admit the subject came upon us unexpectedly," Chase expostu-
lated, on the defensive. "I was surprised. As you all know, I have long espoused the arming of blacks, and this proclamation goes a step further than I
had ever proposed. But I am prepared to accept and support it." Chase
looked to Stanton for approval, which was withheld, so he went on: "I am
glad the President has made this advance, which he should sustain from his
heart." Seward made no effort to conceal his amusement as the distraught
Chase, trying to cover his lack of enthusiasm, went on to make an impromptu
argument in favor of emancipation in the rebel states.

Stanton nodded; then, like a strict teacher demanding that his pupils recite their lessons, glared at Navy Secretary Welles.

"The President does not misunderstand my position, Mr. Secretary," Welles responded solemnly, "nor that of any other member of this Cabinet. I assent most unequivocally to his measure as a war necessity."

"I am an emancipationist from principle," Blair felt constrained to put in. "At some personal sacrifice, at a time when many who are now all-out for abolition were silent, I defended the slave Dred Scott in court. You will recall I helped John Brown get a fair trial after he was captured at Harpers Ferry."

Seward nodded; that established his bona fides, with a nice dig at the come-lately Stanton.

"But I have doubts of the expediency of this executive action at this partic-ular juncture," Blair said. At last; Seward was beginning to doubt if anybody would have the courage to stay Lincoln's hand from this blunder. "We ought not to put in jeopardy the patriotic element in the border states, already severely tried. Elections are coming in a month. As soon as this proclamation reaches the border states, it will carry over those states to the secessionists."

"I have considered that danger," Lincoln said, "which is undoubtedly seri-ous. But there are two sides to it. The difficulty is as great not to act as to act. For months I have labored to get those border states to move, in vain. We must make the forward movement, and they will acquiesce, if not immedi-ately, soon."

"Why?"

"Because they will realize that slavery has received its deathblow from slave owners," Lincoln explained, as if it had always been apparent to him that by seceding, the South had given up its constitutional right to perpetuate slavery where it existed. "Slavery cannot survive the rebellion."

That was a sweeping conclusion, Seward thought, but Blair was not fin-ished making his case against emancipation now. "There are also party men, politicians in the free states who are striving to revive the old party lines and distinctions. We're putting a club in their hand to smash the Republican Party."

"That does not carry much weight with me," said Lincoln. "Their clubs will be used against us, take what course we might."

"I would like to ask your leave," said Blair stubbornly, "to file a paper with you against this policy. Time, and the course of the war, and the elections, may cause you to change your mind."

"I have no objection to that," said Lincoln.

Seward, who had hoped earlier in the meeting that Blair would pose the necessary objections, now worried that he had held his ground too long; it would not do for conservatives to appear to be against emancipation, if that was to be the policy. The abolitionists would lacerate them for not jumping when Lincoln did. Did Blair mean to file his objections privately, or publicly? Privately would be meaningless; publicly would invite his dismissal.

"Think twice about filing written objections, Judge," Seward said smoothly.

"I am worried," Blair replied, "about the effect of this proclamation on the army."

"The First Reading of the Emancipation Proclamation Before the Cabinet," engraving from a painting by Francis Carpenter. Seated, left to right: Secretary of War Stanton, President Lincoln, Secretary of the Navy Welles, Secretary of State Seward, Attorney General Bates. Standing, left to right: Treasury Secretary Chase, Secretary of the Interior Smith, Postmaster General Blair.

Nobody said a word at this allusion to the unspoken fear in the Cabinet of a coup by McClellan, only one day's march away. Seward thought the moment propitious for the protection of the Blairs, his allies in the Administration, against the memoirs and diaries and backstabbings to the press of the radical faction. "But you are emphasizing your personal belief, Mr. Blair, that slavery should not be perpetuated, and that it should be struck down in the states in rebellion, and only in those." Seward leaned forward and held a finger up, to be certain Blair caught the political warning. "Your objection is purely on timing."

"Of course. Yes," Blair responded. "That is my position exactly. Let nobody misconstrue it."

Stanton harrumphed, got everyone's attention, and looked hard at Seward. The Secretary of State alone had not really tipped his hand, not counting Caleb Smith of Interior, who had been heard to say, "Th-th-there goes Indiana."

With a sense of the occasion, Seward rose to his feet. "I'll take that document," he said to the President, who obediently handed it to him. "And I shall have the formal phraseology of attestation added, along with the Great Seal. I'll have it back here early this afternoon for your signature, and it can be released to the newspapers for publication tomorrow morning." He flashed a big smile at Stanton, and the meeting began to break up.

"Stay a moment, Stanton," Seward heard the President say. "I want to go over the other proclamation with you. And I want to ask you," he added, "what are we doing about the ailments of our soldiers' feet? That fellow you sent over was amazing."

"Wait," said Chase, shuffling through a stack of papers in front of him, "I should like to discuss a plan for the central purchase of all cotton, sugar, tobacco and rice, in which a certificate would be given, redeemable at the end of the rebellion, to—"

"That's entirely too important for decision without reflection," Seward told him gently. "That should be the first item at our next meeting." Threatening to free the slaves in Secessia by New Year's Eve unless the rebellion ended, followed by assuming dictatorial powers of arrest, was enough for one afternoon.

CHAPTER 6

GETTING RIGHT ON EMANCIPATION

Old Man Blair took the lengthy memorial prepared by his son Montgomery and read it through. The handwriting was near-illegible, making it hard on the old man's eyes. The reasoning was typical of Monty, sound and lucid; the arguments themselves, taken one by one, he found persuasive. The Proclamation of Emancipation, if carried out as yesterday's preliminary proclamation promised to do come January 1, would transform the war in a way that Lincoln had said must never be permitted—by turning an answer to insurrection into "a remorseless revolutionary struggle." But now it was the North on the side of revolution.

"Brilliant," he pronounced. Monty looked pleased; Frank, who had hurried over from the House of Representatives to join them for lunch at the Blairs' Pennsylvania Avenue house across the street from the Mansion, smiled at his brother proudly. "Now, Monty," the Old Man said, handing the document back to his elder son, "tear it up."

The boys looked perplexed. "Tear it up, tear it up," the Old Man insisted. "Into little pieces. You never wrote it. No copies exist, do they? Good. You didn't pass this around for comment? Thank God."

"I feel strongly about this, Father," said the Postmaster General. "I was thinking of issuing my objections publicly. If you think that making it public is a mistake, I can understand—it might weaken the President's hand at a difficult time. But I see nothing wrong in handing it to him privately, so that the President will have the argument against emancipation at this time in front of him."

"What in hell good would that do? The decision's been made. The proclamation is in all the newspapers."

"But it is provisional. His plan will not take effect for a hundred days, and plenty could happen in that time. Lincoln might yet be dissuaded. At least I want my objections on file."

"Horseshit," said the old man. He picked up the *New York Tribune,* which Monty had brought over from the railroad station. The headline read: "God Bless Abraham Lincoln!" Greeley's editorial was ecstatic.

"But look at these," his elder son protested. "From the *New York World,* an abolitionist sheet which thinks that Lincoln did not go far enough: '. . . the President has purposely made the proclamation inoperative in all places where we have gained a military footing which makes the slaves accessible. He has produced emancipation only where he has no power to execute it.' "

That was the whole beauty of the thing. The elder Blair was irritated at Lincoln both for ignoring his advice and for not warning him in advance. But the way the President had done it was ingenious: threatening to free slaves only in those areas in rebellion, where he was unable to free any slave. The maneuver was designed to rally the radicals without permanently estranging the conservatives. The Old Man's mind wandered to a curious fact his son had noted: from the issuance of the proclamation to the date it was supposed to be carried out was one hundred days, the famous length of time in which the returning Napoleon Bonaparte drove the French king out of Paris. Did Lincoln plan it that way? Did he know that much about history?

"And from the other side," Monty was going on, "Bennett's *Herald:* 'a sop to the abolitionists.' "

Frank held up a telegraph message: "Here's the reaction from the South. The *Richmond Examiner* calls it 'more an act of malice toward the master, than one of mercy to the slave.' And Jeff Davis is quoted this way—'A restitution of the Union has been rendered forever impossible by the adoption of a measure which neither admits of retraction nor can coexist with union.' This means war to the bitter end."

"We cannot know where it will lead," the Old Man told his sons, "but emancipation is now a fact. A political fact." He asked himself: was it? Lincoln had left himself an out if the South agreed to surrender, but that was most unlikely. What about a peace probe, with terms calling for no emancipation in return for reunion? Possible, if McClellan went on to new victories; Lincoln had created a strong bargaining position, and had placed himself rather than his general in command of the ultimate resolution of the war. Smart. "And I do not want any Blair on record on the wrong side of the slavery issue."

"We don't want to ruin my chances for national office, Monty," said Frank sensibly. "Your memorial would be construed by our enemies as a Blair family stand against emancipation. You could put in all the qualifiers you like, but that's what people would say."

"Frank's right, Monty," the Old Man said. "We lost. For the time being, conservative Republicans will have to take a back seat to the likes of Greeley and Wade and Sumner. Good generals like McClellan and Porter, who want both Union and peace, will be under pressure from incompetents like Hooker and Hunter and poor Burnside, who want abolition and conquest. That's the way it is, son. Don't run from reality."

Monty's face and body sagged. "This is all wrong. Half emancipation is a compromise that won't bring peace, it will bring war to the knife. If Lincoln wants to abolish slavery legally, why doesn't he propose an amendment to the Constitution?"

"Because he doesn't have the votes," said Frank, who had been carefully taught how to count the House. "And after November, he'll have even fewer abolition votes."

"What's done is done, Monty," said the Old Man. "Now let's look ahead. First, we want to be on the right side. There's a serenade to Lincoln tonight outside the Mansion and a reception at Chase's afterward—I want both of you to be there, and not looking glum. Agreed?"

Monty nodded reluctantly, adding, "There's a crisis brewing in the army, Father. We suspect that this emancipation announcement may be the match needed to light a revolt. The army is fifty miles away and in love with its commander. If the troops move on Washington, are you for McClellan or for Lincoln?"

"We're for both," said the Old Man unhesitatingly, speaking for the three of them. He had worked out the politics of this in his head during a long talk with the President. "First, we are for constitutional government and the man the people elected, Lincoln. An army coup is anathema. I'd stand out there in front of the Mansion with my old musket and let them shoot me down first."

"What a way to go, for a Jackson man," Frank said admiringly.

"Next: we're also for McClellan because he is the best general in the army and because we're the only people close to Lincoln who don't want to see this war end with the bloody conquest of the South. A hundred years of hatred would be no reunion. So we have to persuade McClellan not to do anything stupid that would get him fired."

"He's a very angry man," said Monty. "Stanton and Halleck never so much as congratulated him. They're picking apart his victory, even spreading rumors that he secretly met with Lee to work out a stalemate. Mac has provocation."

"Then we'll just have to unprovoke him." A family of influence did not merely react to events, it took concerted action to shape them. "Little Mac wants to be President, doesn't he? In sixty-four, the Republican candidate will be Lincoln, if the North has won the war. But if the war drags on, Chase will challenge Lincoln for the nomination and that damned trimmer may just take it from him."

"Country would be sick of war by then," Frank agreed.

"Either way," the elder Blair concluded, "the Republican candidate will be greatly unpopular in the North. That means a Democratic victory, and Mc-Clellan can have the Democratic Party's nomination for the asking—if he behaves like a patriot now and not like a would-be dictator."

"We're for Lincoln," said Frank slowly, trying to get it straight. "But if the radicals—Chase, Stanton, Ben Wade, Tad Stevens, the whole abolitionist crowd—take over the Republican Party, then we switch over to McClellan and the Democrats. But what about Horatio Seymour? He's the Democrat I like."

"Each of us will decide for himself," said the Old Man piously, since Monty was showing signs of unfilial independence, "but Seymour would have to win Governor of New York this year, and that's a long shot even with all the resentment against abolition." He abandoned the pretense of individual action; the Blairs would stick together to put Frank in the White House. "Here's the family plan: step one is to warn McClellan away from trying to set himself up as dictator, which would probably fail and would ruin him in sixty-four. The President is stronger than the army, and Lincoln told me he means to show it."

"The suspension of habeas corpus," Monty nodded. "He'll have that proc-lamation tomorrow. Stanton wants the power to jail anybody who says any-thing against the war. To protect the draft, Lincoln is backing him up."

"Not that," the Old Man shook his head. It was true that the anti-dissent proclamation would add to the impression of a tough-minded president, but that was not the demonstration of authority Francis Preston Blair had in mind. "He's going to make an example of a disloyal officer here at the War Department. Lance the boil, challenge the crowd that wants McClellan to take over. Show 'em a strong President, like Jackson."

"The officer—anybody we know?"

"Have you heard of a major named Key?"

Monty frowned. "There's a Colonel Key, Thomas Key, who's the judge advocate for McClellan. More than that, he's Mac's right arm, drafted that Harrison's Landing letter. He must be at Antietam now."

"May not be the same man that Lincoln's after. But you run the Post Office, Monty. Get a letter off to McClellan tonight. Tell him we've been talking to Lincoln, which is true enough—that he's caught a major here in the War Department named Key who said that McClellan's plan was to hold back his troops to make a compromise with the rebels for Union with slavery. Going to make a public spectacle of the man. This might be a good time for McClellan to say something critical of slavery."

"He won't want to," said Frank. "Mac believed all that stuff about the war being for the Union and not for abolition. He's as much against 'subjugation' and 'conquest' as cousin Breckinridge ever was."

"Put it this way, write this down," the Old Man dictated to his older son. "'Even if you had the ambitions to be President, George, this would be the best course to adopt, for I can assure you that no appreciable portion of the nation will favor the continuation of slavery after this war is over.' Got that?"

Monty was scribbling fast. "You're certainly a President's man, Father."

"And when McClellan becomes President legitimately, I'll be *his* man. The Blairs are no dictator's men, though. Tomorrow, I'll write Mac a letter, too. End of the week, you do too, Frank. Don't hint that one of these days he may be getting a surprise visit in camp from Lincoln."

"Did the President say he'd do that, Father?" asked Frank.

"No, he's playing what he calls 'shut-pan' with me, but now I know how he thinks." Francis Preston Blair resolved not to be caught napping again by a bold Lincoln move to protect his power. The President no longer had any intimate advisers to influence him—not the Blairs, not Weed, not Browning or Swett or any of those he used to lean on; he was his own man totally, confiding in one man for one purpose, using another for something else.

The Old Man saw how Lincoln subordinated every interest to his central idea of majority rule, with terrible punishment to those who tried to subvert it. The man was now President in his bones, prepared to use everyone to help him coax public sentiment toward defending that noble but unrelenting end, with little regard for personal affection or political loyalty. Blair noted that leaders, as they matured, trusted themselves more and others less, and found themselves at their most effective unencumbered by the barnacles of gratitude.

Even as he hated to be edged out of what had been an innermost circle, Blair admired that implosion of confidence he could see in Lincoln. As a family, the Blairs, too, had a central idea—to put Frank in the White House, which the Old Man granted was not as high-minded as majority rule, but from which could flow great things for the Republic. Strength of character, he had learned, was always more important than brilliance of mind in a democracy, and he was sure his youngest son had the Blair character. He hoped the boy would develop, in time, the shrewdness Lincoln was showing in jabbing sharp elbows into the sides of all the political forces pressing in on him. Perhaps one day the leader of an embattled democracy would find a way to defend the system more democratically, but that seemed a long way off to the man who had watched Jackson and was watching Lincoln.

Intimacy was not all, however; more satisfying than to be told a secret was to figure out a secret. Blair saw Lincoln's view of his main problem as the impatience of radical support: that had been taken care of by the tentative proclamation of emancipation, with the angry reaction suppressed by a proclamation suspending habeas corpus. Now a new problem would be from an angry officer corps dominated by Democrats who disagreed with his approach to the war.

"Do you know what I would do if I were President?" He looked from one son to the other. "First I would challenge the disloyal element in the military by slapping down some loudmouthed staff aide, loudly and publicly. Show authority, that's what they understand." He would not like to be in the shoes of this Major Key, whoever he was.

"And then you would do some local politicking," said Monty, understanding. The Old Man wished Frank had caught on as quickly.

"Exactly. I would go right to the source of the trouble with a sudden review of the army in the field." Blair could see Lincoln at his most serious and kindly, visiting the wounded, praising the brave, urging on the generals, establishing by his presence the fact of civilian control to the troops, and the fact of his military control to the people. "It's Mr. Lincoln's army, you know —not McClellan's. Not yet, not till he's elected President. It's up to us to save Little Mac from unwise counsels." At Antietam, the young man had earned a second chance to lead the armies.

Frank reached for his brother's memorial to the President on the table and looked at it again. "What are you going to do with this, Monty?"

The Postmaster General took it from him, and to their father's great satisfaction, slowly tore it in half, then in half again. The President would be denied some excellent advice he did not want to get, and the Blairs would not run the risk of being seen as standing in the way of emancipation.

"See you both at the party tonight at the Chases'," the Old Man said proudly. "Remember to smile—it's a celebration."

CHAPTER 7

SERENADE

Kate Chase, fresh from an exhilarating month-long sojourn at the Saratoga spa, felt guilty about her lack of participation in the war. Most of Washington's women of note had something noble to do, from rolling bandages to visiting hospitals; she had no role to talk about in a self-sacrificial way, and she told her father it troubled her.

"But you do a great deal, Katie," he replied, glumly reading the God-bless-Lincoln editorial in the *New York Tribune*. She knew he had been in a stunned state ever since Lincoln's political masterstroke. "Your long talks with Lord Lyons have done more to keep England out of the war than anything Seward can claim."

"I'm a parasite," she murmured. That was what John Hay had called her and she hated him for it because it was true. Why did he want to hurt her? Probably because she paid too much attention to Major Garfield and when John objected, she had called him a draft-dodger.

"Parasol? You already have a dozen of them."

She sat on the arm of his chair and kissed his massive, balding head. Father and daughter read the newspaper together, as they often did. He pointed to an article about casualties in the battle for Maryland: more than 20,000 killed and wounded on both sides, not counting the captured. The bloodiest single day of the war.

"I thought McClellan prided himself on maneuvering, keeping casualties low," she said.

"Not at Antietam. Lost more men than Lee, I suppose because we were on the attack, for a change. They say the carnage there is unbelievable."

"Brady is going to show the pictures at his emporium here and in New York," she noted, from the paper. " 'Exhibit of the dead at Antietam.' I don't want to go." That was unworthy, to use her father's favorite word. "Perhaps we should visit a hospital today, together."

"Too horrible for you, Katie. And we'd only be in the way." He read further and changed his mind: "They say General Hooker is at the Insane Asylum, which has been taken over as a hospital for the wounded. That's not far from here. I want to meet Hooker. He may be our man to replace McClellan."

She pulled him to his feet. "We're off." After the serenade at the White House tonight, she was planning to bring back a dozen or so couples for a reception, reminding everyone that emancipation was a great Chase victory. Wine and cake in the late evening made an appropriate entertainment, and cost much less than a sit-down dinner. She wanted to have something provocative to report, and "Fighting Joe" Hooker, wounded at the battle, would surely have something to say. "You get our boarder," she said. "I'll get a bonnet and parasol. Or parasite."

The "boarder" was her father's houseguest, James Garfield of Ohio, a major in the Union Army. More important, the major was newly nominated to be a congressman. If elected next month—a certainty, in the most Republican district in Ohio—he would probably remain in the army and delay taking his seat, but he was guaranteed the role of delegate to the '64 Republican convention. Kate enjoyed the company of the mercurial, handsomely bearded Garfield, and had happily endorsed his move from the Willard to their home at Sixth and E; at thirty, he was almost her contemporary.

Kate and the moody major had already shared one intimate moment: returning from a ride in the Silver Spring countryside, she had broken through his reserve and listened to his complaints about his prissy wife back home and his love for a girl who had been his former schoolmate in Florida; it was deliciously complicated by the guilt he felt toward his wife after the death of their infant a few months ago. Kate flirted with Garfield out of habit, but her feeling toward him was comradely.

Major Garfield had no money, no connections other than in Ohio politics, and in her mind no great prospects, and he was already married, unhappily or not; still, he was a fine second man to have around the house this season. She liked to compare him to John Hay: brooding where John was sparkling, constrained and respectful where the younger man was lustful and irreverent, as easily drawn completely into Chase's orbit as Hay had been into Lincoln's.

She sent the servant up to fetch their houseguest for what she called "our mission to succor the wounded." When the major came down, her father bravely set the tone of the day by praising Lincoln for taking his advice on slavery at long last.

"Strange," said the major, "that a second-rate Illinois lawyer should be the instrument through whom one of the sublimest works of any age is accomplished."

She came only slightly to the defense of the President by recalling Wendell

Phillips's perfect characterization of Lincoln as "a first-rate second-rate man."

"No, I mean that," Garfield insisted, and related what he had heard from Edward Stanly, military governor of North Carolina, when that conservative had stormed into Washington to protest to Lincoln about the devastating effect of the proclamation on Union sentiment in that state. "The President told him that emancipation had become a civil necessity to prevent the radicals from openly embarrassing the government in the conduct of the war. Lincoln said he'd prayed to the Almighty to save him from this necessity, said he'd asked, 'Let this cup pass from me,' but his prayer had not been answered."

Chase blanched at that evocation of the Bible in a direction opposite from that taken by Lincoln in the Cabinet Room. But Kate refused to let them become surly on what was a day of public celebration; she took the arms of both men and they set out merrily for the Insane Asylum.

The general did not look like a wounded man to Kate. She presented him with a basket of grapes and peaches which she had arranged herself, after calculating what was the proper thing to bring to a wounded hero. General Joseph Hooker was not in bed but lying on a couch, his bandaged foot inside a large slipper.

The doctor was optimistic enough: "The general's wound is as little dangerous as a foot wound can be," he told them cheerily. "The ball passed through the fleshy part just above the sole and below the instep, without touching a bone."

"I would suggest trying Dr. Forsha's Balm," said Chase, trying to be helpful. To the general, Chase said: "General Hooker, if my advice had been followed, you would have been in command this summer when the Union Army stood before Richmond."

"If I had commanded," Hooker took the opportunity to reply, "Richmond would have been ours."

"What happened at Sharpsburg?" Garfield put in. Kate noted that he spoke not as a major to a general, but as a future congressman to a soldier.

"The tragedy was that I was wounded in the morning, leading the first attack. If I could have remained on the field three hours longer," Hooker spoke with certitude, "our victory would have been complete. I had already gained enough ground, and seen enough, to make the rout of the enemy sure."

"Who did McClellan replace you with?" asked Garfield.

"George Meade, a fine man, but—well, let me just say this. After I had been carried off the field, McClellan sent for me to lead an advance *in an ambulance*. That's how much that field of battle needed a fighting general."

Kate looked at the slightly injured foot and marveled at how little it took to change the course of a battle.

"McClellan is surely no fighter," her father said. "He and Stanton, they say, are like oil and water."

"McClellan is unfit to lead a great army," Hooker said. "He is timid and hesitating where decision is necessary. The Battle of Antietam was near being lost by his way of fighting it. If the attack had been simultaneous—with

General Joseph Hooker

Burnside's corps attacking along with me, and Porter in the center—the rout would have been complete. For God's sake, Governor—excuse me, Miss—our force in the battle exceeded the enemy's by thirty thousand men! McClellan lost the chance to finally defeat the enemy."

"There's some talk," Chase said carefully, "of elements in the officer corps urging McClellan to come to Washington to intimidate the government. Especially after the Emancipation Proclamation. Do you place any credence in that?"

"It's not true that he has the support of the whole army," Hooker said obliquely. "Just two corps, Porter's especially, and those men are indulged and protected."

Kate wondered how many men were in two army corps—enough to seize Washington? Hooker relieved her mind: "Besides, McClellan is not audacious enough for a coup," said the general with his foot in the slipper, obviously eager to show his contempt for a commander in disfavor with Chase. "He'd think that Lincoln had two hundred thousand troops defending the Mansion. McClellan is just not dictator material."

As they left, Chase stopped the doctor in the hallway of the Insane Asylum, jammed with moaning wounded attended by nurses who seemed not to know what to do. The doctor was a military surgeon who had considerable battlefield experience, her father had told her. "What is your estimate of the wound?"

"He'll be walking in a week."

"What's your estimate of the man as a general?"

"Brave, energetic, full of life."

Garfield asked, "Were you at Antietam?" When the surgeon said yes, the major asked, "Was General Hooker skillful on the field?"

"Yes." It was a tentative yes, with a "but" underneath. "Not comprehensive enough, perhaps, for the plan and conduct of a great campaign. But he is surely a better soldier than Burnside."

The surgeon went on to recommend a colonel for appointment to general, which Chase noted down. Everybody, Kate observed, wanted something; it made her feel justified in her own long list of wants. What her father wanted, having been so disappointed in John Pope, was a general capable of replacing McClellan right away; she knew that Burnside, the other main possibility, had turned down the command a month ago, pleading inadequacy. What General Hooker wanted was a political sponsor to press his cause when a Republican replacement for McClellan was needed. What the doctor wanted was a general's star for a friend, and perhaps a high place on Hooker's staff. What Garfield wanted was an introduction to Washington power, a whiff of Republican radicalism, a taste of sophistication. Coming full circle, what Chase wanted in Garfield was an active supporter in his home base for the Republican nomination against Lincoln, and in Hooker a general who would be obliged to him for his command.

And what did she want? In the carriage back to the Executive Mansion, where the President was to be serenaded by a crowd enchanted by his emancipation edict, Kate changed the "what" to "who": she wanted, first, her father. She wanted his unalloyed affection, shared to a slight degree with her younger sister, Nettie, but unchallenged by any other potential official hostess.

That meant Kate Chase would have to counter Addie Douglas, widow of Stephen Douglas, cousin to Rose Greenhow; she seemed to be connected in some way to everyone who counted in Washington. The mail to her father from Addie had stopped; that probably meant she was writing to Salmon Chase at his office, to avert Kate's interception of correspondence. Addie, however, was just a charming socialite; more ominous were the frequent visits of Anna Carroll, who was a political force operating on a level of intellect and influence that Kate had not yet reached. Miss Carroll was troubling because she was smarter than her father and did not let him know it. Did her father call on Miss Carroll? Did he write her letters in reply to her interminable political polemics? Kate did not know, but sensed that this woman—Miss Carroll must be nearly twice her age—could seize the prize position that rightly belonged to the elder Chase daughter.

Kate was prepared to make great personal sacrifices on the way to becoming what the newspapers had begun to call "first Lady." Calculation was central: when she learned that a crowd was planning to serenade the President at the Mansion that night, it was her idea that the crowd be encouraged to march over to the Chase house and serenade the Cabinet member who had persuaded Lincoln to take the step toward emancipation. That, in turn, led to the opportunity for a reception inside the house for the people who counted in Republican and military ranks.

General James A. Garfield

The prospect of a party with a purpose of sharing the credit for abolition excited her. Lord Lyons would be there, and Roscoe Conkling, and Governor Sprague, her three most public beaux; Major Garfield would be looking at her, as he always did, as if she were an especially ripe piece of forbidden fruit; and John Hay would come over with the crowd from the Mansion. Red wine was the suitable beverage; thirty people, by her estimate, would consume at least two cases on a festive occasion. Sprague, she sighed, would handle a couple of bottles by himself.

John Hay stood several paces behind the President and Mrs. Lincoln on the front porch of the Mansion. He positioned himself next to Ward Hill Lamon, whom the Tycoon had appointed marshal and who had promptly appointed himself presidential bodyguard. Like so many people from Springfield, Marshal Lamon and Hay were related by marriage: John Hay's uncle Milton was Hill's brother-in-law. The burly Lamon was looking out into the crowd at dusk, searching for unfriendly faces, but there seemed to Hay to be none. This was an exuberant crowd, mainly Republicans, some negroes, almost all men, orderly and with a core obviously practiced in the anti-slavery songs of the day.

The Hutchinson Family Singers were there at John Hay's personal invitation. This group had given a concert to the Army of the Potomac one night, and George McClellan had later ordered them out of the army lines permanently. Their sin had been to sing the song they were singing right now, to the tune of a Martin Luther hymn, the words by Whittier:

> *What breaks the oath*
> *Of the men o' the South?*
> *What whets the knife*
> *For the Union's life?*
> *Hark to the answer: Slavery!*

Those abolitionist words had been too provocative for McClellan. The Hutchinsons sang them with extra fervor tonight, with the hint of a threat of another army—not Lee's but McClellan's—hanging over Washington.

"Fellow citizens," the President began his response to the serenade. Hay was not surprised: when he had asked Lincoln if he was planning any remarks, the President had said no but his second secretary knew he would have to say something.

"I have not been distinctly informed why you do me this honor, though I suppose it is because of the proclamation." That brought a laugh and applause.

"I can only trust in God that I have made no mistake."

"No mistake, all right!" cried a voice.

"I shall make no attempt on this occasion to sustain what I have done or said by any comment."

"We understand," said somebody; Hay thought it sounded like a revival meeting. He also knew that the President's disclaimer meant he would have a thought to offer.

"It is now for the country and the world"—Hay hoped that reference would get to the correspondent of *The London Times*—"to pass judgment on it, and, may be, to take action upon it. I will say no more. In my position I am environed with difficulties."

"That's so," said a sympathetic voice. Hay marveled at the use of the word "environed"—a great, King James biblical, mysterious verb; he vaguely recalled Lincoln reciting some Shakespearean passage with the phrase "environed he was with many foes." Lincoln surprised him from time to time with his use of archaic language slipped into the modern tongue.

"Yet they are scarcely so great as the difficulties of those who, on the battlefield, are endeavoring to purchase with their blood and their lives the future happiness and prosperity of this country. Let us never forget them." (Long applause.)

"On the fourteenth and seventeenth days of the present month there have been battles bravely, skillfully and successfully fought." Lincoln then called on the crowd to give three cheers to "the good and brave officers and men who fought those successful battles." He did not mention the name of the general in charge.

Hay followed the crowd to the Chase house on E Street, a ten-block stroll on a lovely fall evening, marred only by the sight of ambulances coming back from Frederick behind tired horses on the way to local hospitals. As the singing began—a little more organized this time, after the practice at the

Mansion—the Secretary of the Treasury came out on the front lawn, accompanied by his two daughters. Hay swallowed at the sight of Kate dressed in dark green silk with a golden sash around a waist that his hands had held much too long ago.

During the singing, he spotted Anna Carroll at the edge of the crowd, standing with Senator Ben Wade and his wife, Caroline, waiting for the serenade to end before going in to the reception. Hay knew that Chase and Wade were rivals in Ohio, but allies of a sort in Washington in the badgering of the President to strike down slavery. He joined the group.

"Harrah for Old Abe and the proclamation," said Wade, not too enthusiastically. "You can tell him I said that, young fellow. About damn time. Not far enough, either, but I'm surprised Billy Bowlegs and the Blairs let him go this far."

Hay let that go; Wade was too important an ally, flaying McClellan as Chairman of the Committee on the Conduct of the War, to offend in any way.

"You think, Senator, that the Proclamation of Freedom will have the military effect the President intends?" That was innocuous enough, Hay thought; maybe diplomacy would be his future. He also wanted to see whether the grand-sounding "Proclamation of Freedom" would catch on.

"The country is going to hell," Wade said, "and the scenes witnessed in the French Revolution are nothing in comparison with what we shall see here."

"He's a little bloody-minded tonight," said his wife, as if to apologize for the senator's extreme hostility toward the South. "He's heard that the army officers are plotting to ease up on the rebels."

"The rebels must be made to feel the horrors of war," Wade growled. "They won't give up until they've lost their slaves, their homes, their sons. We need a general who knows that, and then we'll have peace."

Hay nodded vigorously and turned to Anna Carroll. "Miss Carroll, your plan on colonization will be issued by the Attorney General day after tomorrow," he complimented her, knowing that she had prevailed on Wade to support Lincoln on the shipment of freed slaves to Chiriquí. Hay thought the deportation scheme was a barbarous and hideous humbug, so he changed the subject promptly: "We have another proclamation to put out first, making it hot for agitators."

"Good," said Wade. "If there is any stain on this administration, young man, it is that you have dealt too leniently with these traitors at home."

"You'll like this proclamation, then," Hay assured him. "It is aimed at the Democrats who will say that they signed on for Union, but not for abolition. We expect they'll oppose the draft."

"Mercy for traitors is cruelty to loyal men," said Wade. "Remember that." Hay would; the senator spoke in epigrams.

When the serenade ended, the Treasury Secretary made an earnest speech about the proclamation of future emancipation. He did not have a way with the crowd such as Lincoln had shown—the stump debates with Douglas had long ago taught the President how to play off a crowd's reaction—but he gave an impression of gravitas and trustworthiness. Hay listened for any hints of personal disloyalty to the President, any suggestions that Lincoln had not gone as far as Chase preferred on emancipation—in fact, the truth was the opposite. But Chase's remarks could not be faulted; Hay flashed a smile and waved in the direction of Kate, hoping she would see him.

The crowd marched off to bellow their songs at the Attorney General's house down the street and to force Mr. Bates to say something. Hay took Anna Carroll's arm as they went into the Chase reception, partly because he admired the woman, mostly because it would irritate Kate, who had made him lonely when she skedaddled to Saratoga for an interminable month.

"Hello, abolitionist," Anna said to Secretary Chase, who first looked startled, then grinned at Wade and said, "That's what we are, aren't we?"

Gleefully, merrily, they all called one another abolitionists, not mere emancipationists or Free-Soilers, and it seemed to Hay that they enjoyed the novel sensation of appropriating that hitherto dreaded label. All those at the party seemed to feel a sort of new and exhilarating life; they breathed more freely; in a way, the President's proclamation had freed them as well as the slaves.

"This is the most wonderful history of an insanity of a class that the world has ever seen," Chase told them after a few glasses of wine, savoring the moment and his part in it. "No party, no public feeling in the North," Chase went on, "could ever have hoped to touch what the rebels have madly placed in the very path of destruction."

"Incredible," said Anna Carroll. She looked at him with the conspiratorial respect that Hay assumed had worked wonders on a couple of former presidents.

CHAPTER 8

JOHN HAY'S DIARY
SEPTEMBER 25, 1862

Isachar Zacharie has established himself with the top levels of this administration as no medicine man before. He was in today to affix a splint and bandage to the Prsdt's still sprained wrist, on the theory that if he can give relief to one appendage, he can give relief to all.

Mr. Lincoln sent him to Seward to cut that gentleman's corns. Now Dr. Z is the only doctor in the country with a second testimonial, this one signed by both the President and Secretary of State, saying, "We desire that the soldiers of our brave Army may have the benefit of the doctor's surpassing skill." As a result, Stanton has given him a pass through the lines for thirty days to cut his way through the vast cornucopia of Federal marching feet. The pass takes him from Fortress Monroe clear down around New Orleans, where it is intended that General Banks will replace General Butler. The Prsdt has had several long talks with Dr. Z, and I suspect that something more is afoot.

Chase was slightly troubled by the "other" proclamation this week. Thinks it may unduly bend the Constitution to set up a band of civilian provost marshals, as Stanton plans to do in the discouragement of dissent, to carry out the decree of martial law. In fact, Stanton now has unlimited power to create new offenses such as "constructive treason" and jail and prosecute offenders, subject only to the President's review. The Democrats are screaming, especially Horatio Seymour and a few other friends of McClellan and his West Pointers in New York, but they had better not scream too loud, lest they arouse Stanton's ire and into the hoosegow they go.

Chase furrowed his large brow at Lincoln about this: "We are doing more to destroy self-government by these arbitrary arrests and illegal punishments in the North," he pontificated today, "than the Confederates of the South in their attempt to wipe us out as a nation."

Our high-minded Treasury Secretary can assume that noble posture because he has only to raise money, not troops. The Ancient of Days did not let him get away with that:

"This thing reminds me of a story I read in a newspaper the other day. It was of an Italian captain who ran his vessel on a rock and knocked a hole in her bottom. He set his men to pumping and he went to prayers before a figure of the Virgin in the bow of the ship."

Lincoln, as he does when telling a story like this, grew all animated. Chase, at the sound of the word "Virgin," looked pained.

"The leak gained on them," continued the Tycoon. "It looked at last as if the vessel would go down with all on board. The captain, at length, in a fit of rage at not having his prayers answered, seized the figure of the Virgin and threw it overboard.

"Suddenly the leak stopped. The water was pumped out, and the vessel got safely into port. When docked for repairs, what do you suppose they found? The statue of the Virgin Mary was found stuck head-foremost in the hole!"

Chase frowned some more. He was mildly unhappy with the arbitrary arrest policy, but he must have been most unhappy not to get the joke. "I don't quite see, Mr. President, the precise application of your story."

"Why, Chase, I don't intend precisely to throw the Virgin Mary overboard —and by that I mean the Constitution—but I will stick it in the hole if I can. These rebels are violating the Constitution to destroy the Union, and I will violate the Constitution, if necessary, to save the Union."

"To give Stanton the power to imprison anyone for as long as he likes on mere suspicion of disloyalty," Chase persisted, sounding to me like a resuscitated John Breckinridge, "seems to be a terrible encroachment on individual rights. The Constitution says—"

"I suspect, Chase, that our Constitution is going to have a rough time of it before we get done with this row. But we can't fight the rebels with elder-squirts and rosewater."

CHAPTER 9

THE KEY EPISODE

"The witness is here, Mr. President," said George Nicolay. "You sent for him."

Lincoln looked up, pulled his chair in and sat up straight. "Send the witness in."

A nervous officer on Stanton's staff stood at attention in front of the commander in chief's desk. Lincoln did not ask him to sit down.

"Your full name?"

"Levi C. Turner, sir; Major, Judge Advocate Corps."

"I am informed, Major," said Lincoln formally, "that within the past week you propounded a question to Major John Key of General Halleck's staff." He picked up a slip of paper. "The question was, 'Why was not the rebel army bagged immediately after the battle near Sharpsburg?' Did you ask such a question?"

"Yes sir, that's what I asked him."

"And what did Major Key reply?"

"As well as I can remember, sir, that that wasn't the game. It was a private conversation, sir. I happened to mention it to the Judge Advocate, who passed it up the line, I suppose."

"Please just answer my question, Major," said Lincoln, "and try to be quite specific. What exactly did Major Key say to you? What were the words he used?"

"He said, 'That is not the game.' I think those were his very words, Mr. President."

Lincoln nodded encouragement to the witness. "And then what else did he say? Be specific."

"He said that the object is that neither army shall get much advantage of the other; that both shall be kept in the field till they are exhausted, when we will make a compromise."

Lincoln shook his head at what he knew to be a deliberate omission. "I am told there was more to it. You left something out of the conversation as originally related."

The nervous officer took a deep breath and began again. "Major Key said that the game was that both armies should be kept in the field till they are exhausted, when we will make a compromise and save slavery."

"Anything else?" Lincoln asked.

"That was the substance of the conversation, sir. We were just talking, sir, as friends, in my room late at night. I don't think he meant anything serious by it, it was just talk."

"Thank you, Major Turner. Keep yourself available in your office across the street."

The troubled officer saluted and left. Lincoln wrote down the incriminating statement by Major Key and addressed a letter to him, concluding, "I shall be

very happy if you will prove to me by Major Turner, that you did not, either
literally or in substance, make the answer stated."

He called in Nicolay, whom he preferred to have working on this serious
business than the easygoing Hay. "Make a copy of this, and deliver the
original to Major Key right away. When he has read it, bring him here."

Lincoln waited. He picked up a newspaper and read that the Confederate
Congress had authorized President Davis to conscript men between thirty-
five and forty-five; evidently his counterpart in Richmond was having the
same trouble as he was in squeezing the civilian population for troops. He
recalled that Jeff Davis had months ago applied martial law to areas of the
Confederacy, a good answer to those who claimed that his own proclamation
of military rule this week was unprecedented. That reminded Lincoln of his
arguments with Senator John Breckinridge over encroachments on individual
liberty that were required by national security.

Breck. He had heard that Breckinridge, now a rebel general, was back in
his native Kentucky with Bragg, threatening an invasion of Ohio; he wished
he could be more confident that General Don Carlos Buell could stop them.
Buell, heading the Department of the Ohio, was now evacuating central Tennessee, falling back to defend Louisville and Cincinnati. Even if successful in
defense, the cautious Buell would probably be content with stopping the
invasion, as McClellan had stopped Lee at Sharpsburg, without destroying
the rebel army. Such was the state of mind of all his generals, it seemed.

Was the Union Army's leadership loyal? Lincoln remembered George Mc-
Clellan's fury when he confronted him with rumors of his disloyalty. He
concluded that Little Mac thought he was loyal, but his allegiance was to the
people in general and not to their elected commander in chief. That was
dangerously wrongheaded—not traitorous in intent but treasonable in effect.
The clique of West Pointers and political officers, with their ties to old classmates and friends leading the rebel army, had infected George McClellan
with the notion that the army should have a voice in the settlement of the war
on the basis of "the Union as it was." McClellan's Harrison's Landing letter
against emancipation was an example of that presumption. Now the Union
could never be as it was.

McClellan's popularity with his troops worried the President. Lincoln had
to give the man credit where it was due: when the nation had a bone in its
throat and was on the brink of strangling, George had responded correctly:
the general had not flinched or sought deals or promises, or even the authority that his President could not give him, but instead had taken a hundred
thousand defeated, dispirited men (whose defeat his sulking had unforgivably
helped bring about, but that was another matter) and whipped them into an
army capable of finding and fighting to a standstill the best of Lee's veterans.
Those bloodied but victorious men were now his constituency; would they be
loyal, in a crisis, to their beloved commander in the field, or to the commander in chief who had just offended many of them by promising to free the
blacks?

Lincoln supposed that McClellan was now facing the choice of remaining a
patriot, subject to removal by civilian authority, or becoming the central
figure in a military *coup d'état*. But Lincoln also knew the man: caution was
his middle name. If George McClellan could be persuaded that the President

had no fear of the Federal officer corps, he would ask himself *why* the President had no fear; that would lead McClellan to wonder if Lincoln had some hidden strength, perhaps troops assembling near Washington. To help McClellan choose patriotism and civilian rule, Lincoln felt himself compelled to demonstrate executive authority in the most vivid manner.

Nicolay brought in the accused. Lincoln remained seated, returning the salute with a nod. He let the officer, a bookish-looking man in his early forties, stand in the middle of the office. "Now bring in Major Turner, Mr. Nicolay."

Both majors stood before him, looking straight ahead, not at each other.

"You have my letter, Major Key. Did you give the answer stated therein?"

"Sir, I have never uttered a word that might not have been addressed to you without giving offense," said Key. "The conversation held with Major Turner, in his own room, was with him as a friend—"

"Did you say," interrupted Lincoln, familiar with evasions in a witness box, "what you are accused as having said?"

"I have no recollection of the expression, as reported."

"Are you saying," said the interrogator, making his voice and eyes cold, "that Major Turner here is not telling the truth?"

"I have no doubt, Mr. President, that Major Turner so understood me."

"Then you do not deny the accuracy of the statement attributed to you?"

"Sir, I have often remarked," said Key, panic in his eyes, "that the rebels would never let this contest be decided—if they could help it—by a decided battle between us. It's true I've said that they hoped to protract this war, as they hoped to make a compromise in the end, and that they were fighting with that end in view."

"You're evading the question." Lincoln turned his eyes toward the accusatory witness. "Major Turner, please repeat what you told me before about the specifics of that conversation."

"As I remember, sir," Turner said with evident reluctance, "the conversation was, I asked the question: why we did not bag them after the battle at Sharpsburg?"

That was what Lincoln had asked Pinkerton the other day, and received a simpering reply from a man it was too easy to fool. "And what was Major Key's reply?"

"Major Key's reply, sir, was—that was not the game; that we should tire the rebels out, and ourselves, that that was the only way the Union could be preserved, we come together fraternally . . ."

Lincoln waited, looking at him.

". . . and slavery be saved."

The President nodded grimly; sometimes in court the best question was no question. "Major Key, I am going to give you the opportunity to cross-examine Major Turner. You may proceed."

Key, his career at stake, was rattled. With no opportunity to consult counsel or to examine the evidence against him beforehand, he was obviously unprepared to controvert or shake Turner's damning allegation. Lincoln was aware of the unfairness of his kangaroo court, but was hardly going to turn this over to the military for a court-martial and sure acquittal. The defendant was a lawyer. This was as fair an examination, he felt, as the mutinous situation warranted. Much more was at stake here than an individual's career.

"Major Turner," Key began haltingly, "have we talked often about—the current troubles?"

"Yes," Turner replied. "We've had many conversations about the war."

"And have I ever said anything that sounded disunionist to you?"

"No. I have never heard you utter a sentiment unfavorable to the maintenance of the Union."

"This particular conversation," asked Major Key, gaining confidence from the friendly witness, "was it intended to incite anybody to anything?"

"No, it was a private one. And I have never heard you utter anything which I would consider disloyalty."

Key looked to the judge behind the President's desk. "Mr. President, I don't know what else I can say." To Lincoln's silence, he hurriedly added, "I solemnly aver that if this war terminates in the entire destruction of the South —they have brought it on themselves."

Lincoln cut through the amelioration with, "Are you attempting to controvert the statement of Major Turner?"

"I don't see how I can, other than to say again, to assure you, that I am true to the Union. I have no recollection at all of talking about a 'game' . . ."

"If there was a 'game' ever among Union men," said Lincoln slowly, "to have our army not take advantage of the enemy when it could, it is my object to break up that game."

Lincoln reached for a quill, dipped it in the inkwell before him, and wrote out his verdict. He rose and read it aloud:

"In my view it is wholly inadmissable for any gentleman holding military commission from the United States to utter such sentiments as Major Key is proved to have done. Therefore let Major John J. Key be forthwith dismissed from the military service of the United States."

Key staggered; Turner's head dropped in dismay. Lincoln handed the paper out to Nicolay, with the words "To the Secretary of War. Good day, gentlemen." The secretary took them out.

Lincoln went to the window and thought out his next step. He would send for Montgomery Blair, McClellan's staunchest supporter in the Cabinet, and tell him of Major John Key's dismissal for speaking of a policy that some men around McClellan might be actively pursuing. Blair knew that the major's brother, Colonel Thomas Key, was McClellan's closest confidant—some said the "evil genius" behind McClellan's reluctance to destroy the enemy. Judge Blair would be the best person to interpret Major John Key's dismissal to the general in the field: that the President would brook no such disloyal "games" from his subordinates, and that he was making an example of Major Key for McClellan's benefit.

Nicolay put his head in. "Sir, Major Key started to leave, and came back. He wants another moment of your time." The secretary came to Lincoln's desk and added, "His son, who was a captain in the Fiftieth Ohio, with Buell in Tennessee, was killed the other day."

Lincoln braced himself against the appeal. "Send him in." He folded his arms and sat on the edge of the desk; when the still-stunned officer came in, he motioned for the major to sit down.

"Mr. President, sir, I just can't believe this is happening to me." He slumped forward in the big chair, head in his hands, then rose and made an effort to pull himself together. "Just by a dash of the pen, you've ruined my life. It's a terrible disgrace."

Lincoln nodded; it was.

"I come from a family, sir, of patriotic Americans. All of us are brought up that way. One of us wrote the poem, the 'Star-Spangled Banner,' another is married to the Chief Justice. My brother Tom just fought at Antietam, and we're told is ill from some disease contacted there. How can I face the people I love? My son Joe—" His voice broke.

"I sincerely sympathize with you in the death of your brave and noble son," the President said.

"I'm a loyal Union man, Mr. President, I have been all my life. I don't deserve this, being cashiered in wartime, disgraced forever—for what? For something I'm supposed to have said to a friend that may have been misunderstood? Please, sir, consider this again. You're ruining my life, you're shaming my whole family"—his voice broke, but he continued—"and I'm as loyal a soldier as serves in the United States Army."

"You misunderstand me," Lincoln said after the officer had composed himself. "I did not charge, or intend to charge you with disloyalty." Lincoln wondered whether this man, a pawn in a "game" other than the one he had unfortunately spoken of, deserved an explanation of the reasons of state in his punishment. He decided, especially in the light of the recent loss of his son, that the man did.

"I have been brought to fear, Major Key, that there is a class of officers in the army—and not very inconsiderable in numbers—who were playing a game not to beat the enemy when they could, on some peculiar notion as to the proper way of saving the Union." Lincoln had no way of knowing how many there were; he hoped it was not more than a small cabal.

"When you were proved to me, in your own presence, to have avowed yourself in favor of that 'game'—and did not attempt to controvert the proof —I dismissed you from the military service. I dismissed you as an example and a warning to that supposed class." The unfortunate fellow chosen to be made the example was entitled to the truth. "I bear you no ill will," he continued, rising from his chair, coming around and laying his hand on the younger man's shoulder, "and I regret that I could not have the example without wounding you personally."

"You could show some mercy," Key offered, "then you would have your example, and I would have the chance to die for my country on some honorable field."

Lincoln could not permit himself to dilute the lesson. "Can I now, in view of the public interest, restore you to the service—by which the army would understand that I endorse and approve that 'game' myself?" He shook his head, no. Mercy would serve the wrong purpose.

"But you know the punishment is unduly severe. At the very most, this rates a reprimand, not a dishonorable dismissal."

The major was a fair lawyer, Lincoln had to admit, and had attacked the weak point in the case: the unfairness of the severity involved in "making an example" of anyone with an unblemished record. But a stern judge could not concede the point. "If there was any doubt of your having made the avowal, the case would be different. But when it was proved to me, in your presence, you did not deny or attempt to deny it. On the contrary, you confirmed it in my mind by attempting to sustain the position by argument."

No use prolonging this. "I am really sorry for the pain the case gives you," Lincoln concluded. "But I do not see how, consistently with duty, I can change my mind. Goodbye."

When the shattered officer left, John Hay came in, looking pleased. "That was a trial as prompt as those of Saint Louis, dispensing justice under the oak at Vincennes," the secretary said. "You were judge and jury, attorney for the prosecution and for the defense, and on top of all that"—he pointed to the transcripts Lincoln was drawing up for the record—"you functioned as clerk of the court."

"I dismissed Major Key," the President told him, not taking the exposition of the drumhead court-martial as such a compliment, "because I think his silly, treasonable expressions were 'staff talk' and I wished to make an example."

"Little Mac is not pursuing Lee into Virginia," Hay remarked. "Do you suppose he's listening to that staff talk?"

"I begin to fear he is playing false—that he does not want to hurt the enemy." McClellan ought to be able to intercept the enemy on Lee's retreat to Richmond; Lincoln resolved to make that the test that would justify his replacement. He could not replace him until after the elections in November. Between now and then, he could call attention to his delays and suggest that the "staff talk" of Key and others might be behind his caution. George Mc-Clellan would have to go because his goal was not Lincoln's goal: the President wanted to win and reunite the nation on his own terms, while the general wanted to work out a compromise peace that would solve nothing.

Lincoln was certain that the message, however much it ill-used one officer, would get through to the officer class at Antietam, to their instigators and abettors in the Democratic ranks, and to George McClellan himself. At this critical moment, driving that message home—that no reluctance to destroy the enemy would be tolerated—was more important to the fate of the nation than the career of one major.

CHAPTER 10

SURPRISE VISIT

Alexander Gardner, seething at Mathew Brady's egotism and selfishness, snapped the reins at the horse pulling the Whatizzit Wagon.

"Not too fast," cautioned Gibson, his assistant, "you'll rattle the plates and stir up the chemicals."

"We have to get to the Antietam before Lincoln does," Gardner told him, "or else we won't make Mr. Brady famous again."

The photographs taken three weeks before at the battlefield were works of art; Gardner was certain that never before had the horror of war been captured as vividly on wet plates. Shrewdly, Brady had gone beyond the normal distribution to magazines and newspapers for engravings and woodcuts. To capitalize on Gardner's work, he had arranged for special shows in his galleries in Washington and New York, bringing crowds into Brady's studios, stimulating other Brady business, spreading Brady's fame. The *New York Times* wrote of the show in that city in words burned in Gardner's memory: ". . . there is a terrible fascination about the battle-field that draws one near these pictures and makes him loath to leave them."

The reportage of war would never be the same after Antietam, and Gardner knew that the battles to come would see photographers from North and South rushing to the scene. The artist and social reformer in him wanted to use his art to show the horror rather than the glory of war, even as his commercial sense told him there was money in horror.

Although the photographic impresario with the failing eyesight had kept to his agreement and permitted a credit line—in the smallest type—to the operators who had made the stunning pictures, the photos were presented as a Brady Gallery special event. The artists who composed the pictures, who took their lives in their hands to go to the front and accomplished technical miracles as well, were obscured in the general admiration for the man who staged the event.

"Are you sure Lincoln will be coming to the battlefield?"

"The President is going to Harpers Ferry first," replied Gardner grimly, "then he'll pay a surprise visit to the Army of the Potomac. McClellan doesn't know. The general doesn't tell the President his movements, so the President isn't telling McClellan."

"If it's going to be a surprise to the commanding general, how come we know?"

"Hay told me. He has some sense of the historic importance of the visit and wants the scenes recorded. Wants me to do it; didn't even tell Brady for fear Brady would send somebody else, or worst of all, come himself."

"I suppose he didn't want Brady to tip off Pinkerton, if it is supposed to be a surprise," Gibson observed.

Gardner understood from Hay that it was important the public know that the Army of the Potomac was Mr. Lincoln's army, not General McClellan's army. And it was urgent that the troops in the field feel the physical presence of the commander in chief, lest some officers get ideas about taking control of the direction of the war. No matter that Lincoln on a horse looked like a clothespin on a line; the country and the army had to know that their leader was the man in the black frock coat and not the man in uniform.

"We'll take a few pictures of the President with McClellan," Gardner said, "and one of Lincoln with Pinkerton, to help us get around. Be sure to call him Major Allen—he thinks he's fooling somebody with that—but most of the pictures should be of the President with the other officers and troops."

"Brady wants—"

"Don't concern yourself with what Brady wants. The pictures that are important to the Gardner Gallery are the ones Lincoln wants."

McClellan was at his desk in the Sharpsburg headquarters tent trying to puzzle out Montgomery Blair's scrawl in a letter just delivered. Pinkerton slipped in. Pinkerton never entered; he preferred to materialize silently beside one's elbow.

"I have information, General, that his Excellency the President is about to honor the Army of the Potomac with a visit."

McClellan frowned. The last time Lincoln had paid a visit to the front was in the Peninsula, and what followed the President's return to Washington was an order from Halleck to abandon the position.

"Who's he bringing? Halleck? Stanton?" That would mean greater trouble; when the President came under their sway, he was impossible, demanding actions so precipitate as to be suicidal.

"No, sir. Some politicians from Illinois."

That was good: he would probably have John McClernand in tow, a politician-general who posed no threat. But why would Lincoln drag Illinois politicians out to the battlefields in Maryland?

McClellan posed that question to his intelligence chief, who was ready with an answer: "He's worried about Illinois in the elections next month. If Lincoln's close friend, Swett, loses in his home district, then Lincoln might as well plan to skedaddle. His own party will have repudiated him." When the general nodded agreement, Pinkerton added, "The President even has a photographer coming. Same one as operated the camera last week, taking pictures of the rebel dead. Only the rebel dead, sir."

McClellan approved. Photographs at the field of victory served his purpose as well as Lincoln's; William Aspinwall, the source of much money and influence among Democrats, had written to say how impressive his victory looked to visitors at Brady's Gallery. "Here, you look at this letter, Major Allen," he said to Pinkerton. "See if you can decipher Blair's handwriting."

Pinkerton squinted at the letter, going to the window to hold it up to the light. The Blairs were his only friends in Lincoln's inner circle, McClellan knew, and he would value their counsel if only he could make it out.

"'The recent action of the President,'" Pinkerton read slowly, "—I suppose Blair means the Proclamation of Emancipation—'will undoubtedly incite the radicals to new efforts to secure your removal from command.' Next few words are hard to make out—you'd think the Postmaster General would write a letter that was readable—but here it says, 'If you could make known the opinion which I suppose you entertain in common with the whole country, that whilst you supposed the object of the war to be the maintenance of the Government, yet the natural result would be the extinction of slavery, I think you would head off your opponents very cleverly.' General, that's a big step he's suggesting. You've never accepted abolition as a goal of this war."

Blair's idea was clever, but worrisome; was it politic to go along with Lincoln on abolition? The likelihood was that the proclamation of emancipation, followed closely by the equally infamous declaration of martial law, would stiffen the South and protract the war. The officials and financiers from the Democratic Party, from Fernando Wood to William Aspinwall, had urged him to take no stand on slavery specifically, but to send a signal of his toleration of its existence by standing on preserving the Union "as it was." Blair's suggestion that he say a word against slavery might strengthen Mc-

Clellan with the conservatives in Lincoln's Republican Party, but might weaken him with Democrats.

"Ah, here's why Blair's writing this to you right now," said Pinkerton, pushing his derby back on his head to see better. " 'The President told me this morning that Major Key of General Halleck's staff, brother of Colonel Key of your staff, has said that the reason why the rebel army had not been destroyed at Sharpsburg was that the plan was to exhaust our resources' "— Pinkerton grunted in disgust—" 'so that a compromise might be made which would preserve slavery and the Union at the same time.' "

McClellan slammed his fist down on the table; to catch the younger Key in the act of speaking treason reflected on the elder Key, and on McClellan personally. He sent the orderly to get Tom Key from his tent nearby.

"Read that last paragraph from Blair again," the general said when Colonel Key came in, which Pinkerton did, and continued, " 'The President summoned Key,' Blair writes, 'who could not deny that he had used such language but protested his loyalty. The President left me saying that he intended Major Key's dismissal.' "

Judge Key slumped into a chair. "Oh John, you poor fool."

"Your brother deserves to be cashiered," said McClellan harshly, angered at the indiscretion that reflected on him. "Didn't we agree that just the opposite point was to be made known? Didn't you tell the correspondents that I was actively discouraging such talk among junior officers?"

"I did, I did," said Colonel Key. "But I never thought to tell my own brother to keep his mouth shut around Halleck. John is such an innocent. He was probably just gossiping with a friend—"

"Now Lincoln has me at a disadvantage," McClellan said coldly. "Read Blair's advice in that light."

" 'Even if you had the ambition to be President' "—Pinkerton read, "I wish Blair wouldn't put that sort of thing in a letter, General—'this would be the best course to adopt, for I can assure you that no appreciable portion of the nation will favor the long continuance of slavery after the war is over, or will tolerate any guarantee for its perpetuity as the price of peace.' Do you suppose Lincoln put the judge up to this?"

That drew the general up short: was Blair acting as Lincoln's agent or McClellan's friend? McClellan had to ask himself: Was slavery doomed, as even the conservatives near Lincoln now held, or was the Union doomed to years of war and possible separation if slavery became the central issue? Would it be politically wiser, as Blair suggested, to go along publicly with Lincoln on emancipation—or more prudent to stay above the partisan issue and act only as a soldier?

That decision would rest on the extent of Lincoln's support of him now. McClellan suspected that the President's purpose in coming to the front was to push him into a premature advance into Virginia. If Lincoln threatened him with removal again for not following that ill-advised plan to march before the Army was ready, McClellan might respond with pressure of his own.

"You recall, Judge, how the men crowded around me yesterday, breaking ranks to fill the air with cheers. They love me. What a power," he mused aloud, "that places in my hands."

"Tremendous power," nodded Pinkerton. "And we're less than fifty miles away from the capital."

"What is there," McClellan put it to Key as if rhetorically, "to prevent my taking the government in my own hands—to bring about peaceful reunion?" He was not being serious, of course; but it was interesting to turn the thought over in his mind.

Key—probably distracted, McClellan assumed, by the prospect of his brother's and his family's disgrace—seemed startled by the thought. "General, don't mistake those men. So long as you lead them against the enemy, they will adore and die for you. But attempt to turn them against their government, and you will be the first to suffer."

That was not what McClellan wanted to hear. By promoting widespread talk of such a possibility—followed quickly, of course, by shocked disavowals of any such disloyal intent, McClellan backers could combat the radical warhawks demanding his removal. It made sense to remind the world that he was refusing to be dictator, even as Caesar had. The people would remember that in the next campaign for President.

Irritated by his aide's obtuseness, the general strode out of the building and mounted his morning horse, Burns. An excellent mount, in some ways more responsive than his familiar Kentuckon Dan Webster, Burns had a habit of bolting for his oats at feeding-time in the afternoon, no matter what his rider had in mind; consequently McClellan rode him only in the mornings.

Key and Pinkerton came running along behind, organizing a party to go out and greet the President. McClellan told them to keep the group small; Lincoln had been heard to say that the Army of the Potomac was "only McClellan's bodyguard," and the general did not want too many in his entourage.

"Would you please take your hats off, gentlemen? I can't see your faces in the shadow."

Gardner had set up his camera directly in front of the commanding general's tent. The President and McClellan were seated inside the tent, a table between them, a stack of captured rebel battle flags to the left. At the photographer's direction, the two men had moved to the front of the tent, near the flap, which had been drawn back as far as possible to let in the light. Gardner ducked his head under the black cloth and told himself no: there was still not enough light to see the faces. The hats cast a shadow. At Gardner's urging, McClellan removed his military cap, Lincoln his stovepipe topper, which he placed upside down on the battle flags. The photographer had Lincoln in profile, McClellan three-quarter view, the tent pole dividing them starkly, which Gardner thought was nicely symbolic of the division known to exist between the two leaders.

Gardner, still under the hood, raised the angle of the camera to get as much as possible of the tent, removed the lens cap to the count of ten and replaced it. Gibson grabbed the heavy plate and ran with it into the wagon.

"We are going to take the same scene in stereograph," Gardner announced, remembering Brady's way of asking for another sitting by declaring his intention with great firmness. To his relief, the Brady technique worked; the Union's leaders were content to wait fifteen minutes for their next portrait.

The general's aides, and the Illinois party accompanying the President, remained well out of the picture-taking area. Gardner stood by his camera, waiting for Gibson to finish preparations of the plate in the Whatizzit wagon. The photographer could hear the conversation of his two subjects clearly in the tent. Lincoln's voice was high-pitched with a Western drawl, McClellan's resonant and brisk, like an Eastern railroad executive.

"You remember my speaking to you," Lincoln was saying, "of what I called your overcautiousness."

"And I did not accept that. My army is not fit to advance."

"Are you not overcautious when you assume that you cannot do what the enemy is constantly doing? Should you not claim to be at least his equal in prowess, and act upon the claim?"

"You people don't know what an army requires," the general countered. "The old regiments are reduced to mere skeletons, and are completely tired out. They need rest and filling up. The new regiments are not fit for the field. Cavalry and artillery horses are broken down. So it goes—"

"You are now nearer Richmond than the enemy is," said Lincoln, tapping his finger on a map on the table before them, "by the route that you *can* and he *must* take. Why can't you reach there before him? Unless you admit that he is more than your equal on a march—"

"That's enemy country," McClellan explained. "That is country where the inhabitants furnish to the enemy every possible assistance—food for men and forage for animals. They tell him about all our movements. In such hostile territory, we especially need cavalry to be our antennae—and the horses we have are sore-tongued and fatigued."

Lincoln half-rose. "Sore-tongued and fatigued? Will you pardon me for asking what the horses of your army have done since the battle of Antietam that fatigues anything?"

Gardner stood stock-still, trying to disappear. McClellan sat in silence for a moment, and replied slowly, "The cavalry was in low condition before this campaign began. While on Stuart's track, it marched seventy-eight miles in twenty-four hours. The cavalry has been constantly making reconnaissances, scouting and picketing, engaging the enemy frequently."

"I'm sure there have been things to do, but—"

"If you can find, Mr. Lincoln, any instance where overworked cavalry has performed more labor than mine since the battle of Antietam, I am not conscious of it."

"Stuart's cavalry has consistently outmarched ours."

"You are misinformed," McClellan told him. "On one raid, Stuart had two relays of fresh horses to none of ours, which is why he outmarched us. We need more horses. You do an injustice to our cavalry, its officers and men, which is just as efficient as that of the rebels."

Lincoln backed off in the face of McClellan's facts and defense of troops. "I intend no injustice to any. But to be told, after a period of inaction, that the cavalry horses were too fatigued to move presented a very cheerless, almost hopeless prospect for the future. It may have forced something of impatience into my tone."

"My plan is to secure Maryland, and then to pursue Lee down the Shenandoah. But we cannot race after him unprepared, inviting a counterattack that would change the course of the war."

McClellan's plan seemed to aim at Lee around Warrenton, Virginia, in a month; Lincoln's plan seemed to Gardner to involve an attack much sooner. The President offered the general more reinforcements if McClellan would position the army so as to protect Washington while he was attacking Lee; in turn, the general sought to get Lincoln to understand the urgency of rail communication as an army prepared for battle.

When the talk turned to politics, Gardner could feel the tension rising. McClellan said he hoped Lincoln would pursue a "conservative course," and objected to the proclamation of martial law, saying that it was an unjustifiable abuse of the Constitution. That criticism stung Lincoln, who explained that the measure was needed to stop obstruction of the draft, which McClellan of all people should appreciate.

The general then said something that Gardner did not quite catch, about an honorable armistice after the defeat of Lee's army, leading to a peace without humiliation for the South and without complete victory for the North.

Lincoln did not agree with that at all. He leaned forward and, motioning with his finger toward McClellan's chest, spoke most deliberately and distinctly: "I expect to maintain this contest until successful, or till I die, or am conquered, or my term expires, or Congress or the country forsake me."

"Success, as I interpret it, is the maintenance of the integrity of the Union," McClellan shot back, "not the achievement of abolition. If we can put down the rebellion and end the secession, we will have succeeded. You have said that yourself in your Inaugural, and a hundred times since."

"You may not make war on a government without being hurt," Lincoln replied. "Blood has been shed. A penalty is called for. We must rip up disunion like a dog at a root, so that this may never happen again."

Gibson ran up with the stereograph plates, which Gardner inserted into the camera. He could feel his subjects watching him fuss with the lens. When the President spoke again, his tone changed from the taskmaster to the supporter.

"I want to assure you, George, that I am fully satisfied with your whole course," the President said. "The only fault I can possibly find is that you are perhaps too prone to be sure that everything is ready before acting."

"That episode with Major Key—"

"—Was not intended to reflect on you personally. I had to set an example. I will stand by you against all comers."

"Stanton and Halleck want my scalp," said McClellan directly. "We saw the way they resented your decision to put me in charge of the defense of Washington, when they were preparing to surrender Washington. You'll stand by me? I can count on you?"

"I am entirely satisfied with you," Lincoln repeated. "You shall be let alone, and I will stand by you."

"On a personal note," McClellan's voice was lower, "I have a request." Gardner made an effort not to listen, but he could not help hearing, "My wife, Nellie. I need very much to visit her, to see her and the baby. We are nothing without each other. As I launch a campaign into Virginia when the army is outfitted, perhaps you would not consider it taking too much time from my duty—"

"Ready," said Gibson aloud.

"Take a breath," Gardner called out. "Now hold it, please. Hold it. Don't move. Little longer . . . not yet . . . thank you!"

McClellan rode with the President back through one of the passes in South Mountain toward the Frederick railroad station. Lincoln was good enough to say that he did not see how the Union had ever forced its way through that pass, and that had McClellan been defending it, Lee would never have carried it. McClellan felt better about the President's surprise visit. He knew he was being flattered now, after the initial prodding, but did not mind Lincoln's obvious changes in approach. It had been three weeks since the battle, and he expected to be able to move in another three, if Lincoln could prod Stanton to get Quartermaster General Meigs to send up the shoes and horses.

Then an unfortunate coincidence took place: just as McClellan was saying farewell to the President, who should come up the road toward camp but the last person he wanted Lincoln to see in camp: William Aspinwall, the New York Democrat. Lincoln greeted him cordially. McClellan was grateful the President chose to ignore the likelihood that the New Yorker had come to talk Democratic politics.

Armstrong Custer was pleased at having been asked by the general to join the group posing for a picture with the President in front of the headquarters tent. He stood separate from the group, the only one in a cavalryman's slouch hat, ignoring the photographer's imperious signal to move closer to the others. Captain Custer did not take orders from civilians.

Abraham Lincoln was not his idea of what a President should be. Old Abe was a laughable sight on a horse, second-guessed his commanders in the field, and withheld needed supplies and reinforcements from his fighting forces while dandying up his useless bodyguard in Washington. Worse, he showed no appreciation for the salvation of the country by a far greater man, George Brinton McClellan. Worst of all, the President had shocked the headquarters staff of the Army of the Potomac with his cruel disgrace of John Key, who was guilty only of saying what everybody was thinking.

Custer could not understand why Little Mac did not simply change front and seize power in Washington. The troops would be with him, no matter what Colonel Key said; Key was a strange man, inconsistent, hating Lincoln and most of the radicals but hating slavery too, wanting McClellan in the White House but wanting to wait two more years to go through the folderol of election. Armstrong Custer's mind was clear: his leader should denounce both presidential proclamations of last week, march to Washington and take over, whip Lee at Warrenton to prove which army was better, and offer the South terms that would end disunion forever.

After the President and his party departed camp, followed by the photographers in their conveyance that looked like a spiritualist's wagon, Custer was told to assemble the headquarters staff outside McClellan's tent to listen to the general's message to the army.

President Lincoln and General McClellan

Colonel Key, feverish from some ailment he had picked up a month before on the battlefield, stood next to Custer to hear General Order No. 163.

"The Constitution confides to the civil authorities," went McClellan's order, "the power and duty of making, expounding and executing the Federal laws. Armed forces are raised and supported simply to sustain the civil authorities, and are to be held in strict subordination thereto in all respects."

"I hope he says something about the President's meddling in running a war," whispered the captain to the colonel.

Key shook his head; Custer imagined he'd had a hand in the writing.

"The Chief Executive, who is charged with the administration of the national affairs, is the proper and only source through which the needs and orders of the Government can be made known to the armies of the nation."

And not through the commanding general in the field, bitterly added Custer to himself. He was disappointed in his hero; McClellan was not about to become a Caesar. "And what about your brother?" he whispered to Key.

"Discussions by officers and soldiers concerning public measures," McClellan's voice resonated, "when carried at once beyond temperate and respectful expressions of opinion, tend greatly to destroy the discipline of troops. There must be no substitution of the spirit of political faction for that firm, steady and earnest support of the authority of the government which is the highest duty of the American soldier."

"He's doing the right thing," said Colonel Key heavily.

"Damn," said Custer under his breath. "And what about all of us who didn't sign up to fight for abolition?"

"He listened to Aspinwall, not Blair. Not a word against slavery."

"The remedy for political errors," McClellan was reading out, "if any are committed, is to be found only in the action of the people at the polls."

The sweating Key took Custer's arm for support. "Lincoln will stab him in the back at the first chance," the colonel predicted, "but it isn't treason to run for President."

Custer shook his head. "If Lincoln tries that, I'll resign and go home. And so will half the army." But he did not know about half the army; the fickle troops had been proud to cheer Lincoln as they passed in review. He had a heavy feeling in his chest that the cadaverous politician, with all his promises of standing by McClellan against "all comers" of the abolition faction, had taken his general into camp.

CHAPTER 11

THE DREAM

"Whiskey? Wine?" Mary Lincoln threw up her hands. "What are we going to do with it?"

Elizabeth Keckley, seated at her sewing in Mrs. Lincoln's upstairs parlor, looked up with amusement. The President's wife was understandably perplexed; two expressmen had arrived from New York with twenty cases of liquor from an anonymous donor. "I suppose we could drink it," the modiste observed. "Not all at one time."

Mary Lincoln shook her head emphatically. "We do not entertain here, not since Willie. And if I accept it, people will say I'm a secret drunkard."

Keckley recognized the truth in that. The President's wife was variously criticized as a bumpkin or a social butterfly, as a rebel sympathizer and a spendthrift. All but the last were unfair; the President's wife did have difficulty with money affairs, and her dressmaker knew that bills were sometimes left for months to be paid, but the attacks on Mrs. Lincoln's loyalty—and her dedication to emancipation—were as unfounded as they were vicious. No wonder she was so often afflicted with sick headaches.

"I'll get Stoddard," Elizabeth Keckley said, and went to fetch him.

The sallow young man who was Lincoln's Third Secretary contemplated the array of boxes and said to the two bored deliverymen, "There's plenty of room in the basement."

"My husband will never permit that stuff to remain in this house," Mrs. Lincoln told him. "The first thing he wrote that was printed, when he was still a boy, was about the evils of whiskey. Can we send it back? No—whoever sent it would take offense, and then people would say I'm wasting money."

Keckley gave Stoddard a do-something-quick look, and the young man rose to the occasion. "Divide it into five lots," he told the men, "and take it to the head physician at five hospitals. Come with me, I'll give you the addresses."

Mrs. Lincoln, relieved, added, "Say it's for anybody in pain, from the Lincolns."

"And bring back the five receipts," added the modiste, who did not want the expressmen taking the liquor for themselves.

"I like Stod," Mrs. Lincoln said, back in her sitting room, the minor crisis resolved. "He opens and reads all my mail, you know." Keckley said she assumed much of it was cruel, and that intercepting the worst was a good idea, but was surprised to learn that was not Mrs. Lincoln's reason: "It's because they accuse me of corresponding with the rebels, Lizzie. I want all my mail read beforehand."

The dressmaker was not in the Mansion that afternoon to work on a gown; rather, she was present in her capacity of companion, to accompany Mrs. Lincoln to the seance scheduled for the early evening. Before Willie died, the President's wife occasionally went to a spiritualist, as did many of Lizzie

Keckley's clients and friends—as did Mr. Lincoln on occasion, more out of curiosity than belief, she suspected. Since the death of the boy, however, Mrs. Lincoln had made it a habit. She would see any medium who would put her in touch with the ghost of her Willie.

She knew Mrs. Lincoln to be a religious woman, probably more so than her husband. The first Lady had told her dressmaker how she took the sacrament in 1852, though Mr. Lincoln would not. He had not joined the church as she had—Lincoln was not a church member to this day—but he paid the dues for the family pew. And he read the Bible more than most, quoting from it a lot, especially of late.

Keckley remembered the time, only a month ago, when the President had met the delegation of preachers from Chicago who had come to tell him, first, to order his generals to observe the sabbath—which he didn't want to do—and, even more important, to carry out God's will by emancipating the slaves. She had been in the anteroom of his office with Mrs. Lincoln and Stoddard, and had been discouraged at the President's reply: "It is my earnest desire to know the will of Providence. These are not, however, the days of miracles, and I cannot expect a direct revelation. Good men do not agree."

The preachers told him, she thought rightly, that the Bible denounces oppression, and the nation was guilty, and the war was a just punishment. And he had answered, "What good would a proclamation of emancipation from me do? I do not want to issue a document that the whole world will see must necessarily be inoperative, like the Pope's bull against the comet." Then, when the preachers said the blacks would enlist to fight, he had told them how General Butler in New Orleans had been issuing more rations to fugitive slaves than to his white troops, adding cruelly, "They eat, that's all."

That had hurt. Freedmen had been flocking to Washington all that summer, fresh from benighted regions of the plantation, looking for freedom and had found instead a new bondage of poverty amid the hostile whites of the North. No perpetual sunshine, only cold neglect. The Africans, no longer fugitives but only legally free, soon discovered that Yankees looked on their helplessness as proof that they were members of an idle, dependent race. Negroes like Keckley could organize some help, prevailing on Mrs. Lincoln herself to set a public example by contributing, but what if millions came North? Half the whites were worried the blacks would lie around and wait to be fed, while the other half were afraid the blacks would take their jobs.

Lincoln had sent the Chicago clergymen away with little hope, saying only that he had not decided against emancipation. Preaching to the preachers, he had left himself room to turn around: "Whatever shall appear to be God's will, I will do."

What had happened to change his mind in a week? She wondered if it could be that he had deliberately misled them to protect the surprise he had in mind, or to get them angry so they would cry out more loudly to their congregations to push his countrymen along the abolition road ahead of him. She decided that he must have been afflicted with terrible doubts right up to the last minute, when the Divine will had indeed been revealed to him.

President Lincoln appeared in the upstairs parlor, ducking his head down to let his wife straighten out his spiky hair, listening to her tell proudly of how she had handled the challenge of the donated whiskey.

He nodded gravely and said "Madam Elizabeth" to her, but as this was the first she had seen of him since the glorious proclamation, she felt called on to say what was in her heart.

"Mr. Lincoln, in your proclamation you carried out God's will."

"God's will," he repeated, slumping down into the sofa in the small sitting room, taking a small Bible from a stand near the head of the settee.

"I'm glad you listened to those preachers from back home," Mrs. Lincoln agreed, extending their Illinois home clear up to Chicago, "and to Senator Sumner, and even to that uppity Greeley. I've never been so proud. The will of God prevails."

Lincoln shook his head, not so much in disagreement, Keckley suspected, but in not being sure. "In great contests each party claims to act in accordance with the will of God. Both *may* be, and one *must* be wrong."

He hefted the small book in his huge hand, opened it, and began leafing through. "What was that passage you commended to me, Mrs. Keckley?"

" 'Gird up thy loins now like a man,' " she recited, " 'I will demand of thee, and declare thou unto me.' " She had prayed that he would have the courage to strike down slavery, and the prayers had been answered. Or at least promised an answer: by year's end, unless the slave owners did the impossible and gave up, all her people in the South would be free.

"Book of Job," he nodded. After a moment, Lincoln ruminated: "In the present civil war, it is quite possible that God's purpose is something different from the purpose of either party—and yet the human instrumentalities, working just as they do, are the best adaptation to effect His purpose."

Elizabeth Keckley recognized that as the message of Job, a good man who could not fathom why God had singled him out for awful punishment. The Bible had taught her that Job could not know that he was the subject of a struggle between God and the devil over the issue of the strength of faith. Mr. Lincoln seemed to be saying that he could not fathom God's will and had accepted that he might be an agent of a change that he did not comprehend.

"I am almost ready to say this is probably true," the President said, "that God wills this contest, and wills that it shall not end yet. By His mere quiet power, on the minds of the now contestants, He could have either *saved* or *destroyed* the Union without a human contest. Yet the contest began." He closed the book and took a deep breath. "And having begun, He could have given the final victory to either side any day. Yet the contest proceeds."

He did not finish his argument. She assumed he meant that, like Job, he felt that God was trifling with him as part of some grander design. She wondered if that was not a little bit heretical.

He looked under the sofa and drew out a pair of overshoes.

"Where are you going, Father?" his wife asked.

"To the War Department, Mother, to try and learn some news. About Bragg coming up into Kentucky, which we cannot afford to lose. About Lee escaping to resupply in Richmond so he can attack us again."

"Don't go alone."

"I'm not a child, Mother; no one is going to molest me." He stopped in the middle of drawing on an overshoe. "It seems strange how much there is in the Bible about dreams."

"Mostly the Old Testament," said Mrs. Keckley.

"Sixteen chapters in the Old, four or five in the New," he specified; obviously he had studied the subject. "And if we believe the Bible, we must accept the fact that in the old days God and His angels came to men in their sleep and made themselves known in dreams." He returned to pulling on the shoe and pounded his foot on the carpet. "Nowadays dreams are regarded as very foolish, and are seldom told, except by old women and young men and maidens in love."

"You look dreadfully solemn," said Mrs. Lincoln. "Do you believe in dreams?"

"I can't say that I do," he returned, in one of those replies that Mrs. Keckley noticed could go either way. "But I had one the other night which has haunted me ever since. Like Banquo's ghost, it won't go down. 'To sleep, perchance to dream—ay, there's the rub!' "

"The one about being on a ship coming close to the shore, and you can't make out what's on shore? You've had that a few times."

"No, and not the one that's a welcome visitor—of the ship drawing away, badly damaged, and our victorious vessels in close pursuit. I dreamed that just before Antietam."

His face took on a stricken look. "In this dream, there seemed to be a deathlike stillness about me. Then I heard subdued sobs, as if a number of people were weeping. I went from room to room; every object was familiar to me, but why were all the people grieving as if their hearts would break? I kept on until I arrived at the East Room."

The President seemed to Mrs. Keckley to be reliving the dream in the telling; she worried about its effect not on him—he was strong in every way—but on Mrs. Lincoln's mind.

"There I met with a sickening surprise. Before me was a catafalque, on which rested a corpse wrapped in funeral vestments. Around it were stationed soldiers who were acting as guards. There was a throng of people gazing mournfully on the corpse, whose face was covered . . . then came a loud burst of grief from the crowd, which awoke me from my dream."

"That is horrid! I'm glad I don't believe in dreams," Mary Lincoln said sharply, "or I should be in terror from this time forth."

Elizabeth Keckley wondered why he had told the troubling dream to his wife, knowing how impressionable she was. Perhaps he could not stop himself.

"Only a dream, Mary. Let us say no more about it, and try to forget it. I am afraid I have done wrong to mention the subject at all, but somehow the thing got possession of me." He belatedly tried to make her feel better: "Don't you see how it will turn out? In this dream it was not I, but some other fellow who was killed."

Mrs. Lincoln shuddered and said she had to prepare for the seance. When asked if he wanted to join them, the President declined. He wasn't much for spiritualists.

Lincoln, at the head of the staircase, heard the sound of a grand march coming from the Red Room downstairs, where the seances were usually held. The piano was being played with great authority, and he kept step with the music until he reached the doorway. He debated with himself a moment about going in: if the medium was Lord Colchester, he would not have any part of it. Noah Brooks told him he suspected the medium was nothing but a mountebank. He had gone to one of his circles in Georgetown, and in the darkness, as the guests listened to the sound of drums and bells from the spirit world, the disbelieving reporter lunged for the source of the sound and caught the medium detached from the circle of hands, making his own noises. Unfortunately, this had not discouraged Mrs. Lincoln from visiting the spiritualist again.

Nettie Colburn was another matter. She was a delicate young woman with the voice and demeanor of a little girl, but when entranced came under the control of other personalities, including "Old Dr. Bamford," who spoke with an authentic Yankee twang and told salty stories. There was also her inexplicable trick with the waltzing piano: at one seance, Miss Nettie had levitated the grand piano, which remained three inches above the floor, tilting this way and that to the music, even after Lincoln and the journalist Forney sat on top of it. Lincoln had joked with those present about being part of "the weight of the evidence" of the little spiritualist's powers, but it certainly defied rational explanation. Lincoln had been moved to look over the new book, *Further Communications from the World of Spirits*, and while he remained skeptical, he would not deny his wife comfort in communication with Willie; besides, he knew he always did have a strong tendency to mysticism.

He pulled open the door and stepped inside. The pianist stopped playing.

"So this is our little Nettie, is it?" He walked over and took her hand, asked a few kindly questions about her mediumship, and saw her lose consciousness and seem to pass under the control of someone or something.

He did not join the circle with his wife; instead, he took an easy chair in the corner, throwing his leg over the upholstered arm, to listen to Miss Nettie relay, in a strong, masculine voice, her message from what could be presumed to be the upper country.

"You have begun to hear counsels against your Proclamation of Emancipation," said a stentorian voice coming from Miss Nettie. "You are being urged to delay the final act beyond the first of the year." True enough, but that pressure for deferral was known to every member of the Cabinet, and to more than a few newspapermen. Above the piano, which Lincoln was relieved to note was not moving this time, a portrait of Daniel Webster looked down on the group. "Liberty and Union," that senator's most famous phrase, was surely Lincoln's purpose as well, but one did not always help the other.

"In no wise heed such counsel. Do not abate the terms of its issuance," said, or relayed, the medium. "It is to be the crowning event of your administration and your life."

When the medium came out of her trance, he thanked her: "My child, you possess a very singular gift; but that it is of God, I have no doubt." He left before the others.

Trudging back up the stairs—wonderful, no pain in his toes even when shod, and his wrist was better, too—he wondered about the hundred-day deadline he had set the South and himself as well. If McClellan were to catch up with Lee and destroy his army, if Rosecrans, replacing the cautious Buell, should be able to smash Bragg and Breckinridge in Kentucky and Tennessee, the "military necessity" of emancipation would disappear. Pressure to defer,

on solid constitutional grounds and in the name of making peace with reunion, would surely increase.

That was the sort of worry he hoped to have. He would deal with any
alternatives to emancipation at year's end in a month, when he would have to
write his annual message to Congress. Certainly the threat of abolishment
was an important move, necessary to hold Republican support, diplomatically well timed, perhaps militarily useful. And slavery was plain wrong.
Next month's election would determine whether the proclamation had been
politically wise.

Was it possible that declaring the rebels' slaves free, when he was in no
position actually to free them, would turn out to be the central act of his
administration? He sat on the bed and turned that over in his mind. He
couldn't say that it would.

CHAPTER 12

JOHN HAY'S DIARY
OCTOBER 8, 1862

On the train back from Frederick, the Tycoon must have been stewing about
the meetings McClellan has been having with Democratic leaders. Irritation
will be expressed, however, not at his political flirtation but at the inexcusable
military inactivity of the Young Napoleon. I make this assumption because no
sooner had he returned than the Prsdt closeted himself with Old Brains.

The upshot of that confabulation was a red-hot telegraphed order from
Halleck at headquarters to McClellan in the field: "The President directs that
you cross the Potomac and give battle to the enemy or drive him south. Your
army must move now while the roads are good."

The uninitiated may ask: why, since Lincoln saw McClellan only yesterday, did he not tell him this himself? The answer is obvious to me: McClellan, in person, has a million good reasons for every delay, and the Prsdt
cannot argue military tactics with him at length. However, McClellan at the
other end of a telegraph line is a different being. He is a soldier to whom
orders are sent, to be obeyed.

Not only that: from the command post of the Executive Mansion, the
President can push Halleck and Stanton out in front of him. Halleck's telegraph ended, "I am directed to add that the Secretary of War and the General-in-Chief fully concur with the President in these instructions."

And who do you suppose directed Old Brains to 'fess up to that? The
Tycoon himself, of course, who wants the top brass on the record with him all
the way. Everybody knows that Halleck's order to McClellan to get off his
duff will be examined in due course by Wade's Committee on the Conduct of
the War. The telegraph message is proof that the word from on high to
advance on the enemy was clear and unmistakable, no matter what McClellan says Lincoln told him while the two were passing the time of day in his
tent.

Is this construction of a paper noose fair to the man at Antietam? Perhaps not, but the Ancient of Days has a strange ambivalence when it comes to George Brinton McClellan. Although the Prsdt is quite able to be harsh to somebody's face—see Jessie Benton Frémont or Major John Key for testimony to that—when it comes to this short (my height), young (thirty-five, only twelve years my senior) whippersnapper of a general, Lincoln is loath to crack the whip. Why?

The answer is one part personal affection; one part a concern with Little Mac's incredible sway over his troops; one part gratitude for organizing an army twice out of a beaten rabble without asking for a contract; one part guilt for holding back troops to sit around Washington when they might have been better employed in front of Richmond and at Antietam; and three parts not having any general of proven ability to turn to.

That is why, on the very heels of that telegraphed, official order which must have come as a bit of a shock to the fellow he was chatting with only yesterday, Lincoln sent a handwritten note to McClellan telling him it would be okay to slip back into Washington some night to see his wife.

To some, that act of kindness and sympathy following a sharp blow to the back of the neck would be an anomaly; to me, it is quintessential Lincoln. There is a curiously appealing personal side to McClellan, and I should record it here: he loves his wife with an admirable passion. He is not foolish to do so, because Nellie is intelligent, beautiful, and radiant with her one-year-old in arms. Tales have reached here of the way the general, no matter what the military pressure, steals time from sleep late at night to write her long, intimate letters. I cannot say this is a weakness.

The Prsdt finds this side of the Young Napoleon touching, which is why he permits him to skulk into town for a feverish embrace when he should be splashing his way across the river at the head of his vast and expensive army. Perhaps Lincoln wishes he had a feeling like that for the Hellcat. No impassioned letters for her. I recall my favorite correspondence from the Tycoon to Mrs. L in New York last summer: "I am here, and well. How are you? A. Lincoln." Hardly lyrical, but the Hellcat surely does not inspire all that the lovely Nellie McClellan does.

At any rate, we have to tolerate the insolence of epaulets only until November 4. On Election Day, the Young Napoleon meets his Waterloo. I have no doubt about his dismissal on the day after elections. It would be impolitic at this moment to feed the flames of Democratic ire in Pennsylvania and New York, both of which now feel some gratitude to McClellan for halting Lee before the rebels swept into those states, by firing their military savior. We are less worried about the border states, because Stanton has some hush-hush plans for troops to keep secessionist sympathizers away from the polls, but Thurlow Weed's whispered eruption about the effect of the Proclamation of Freedom in New York has stirred the Prsdt's concern. Better to play it safe by not firing McClellan yet—at least not until Greeley's Republican candidate rolls over the "peace candidate," Horatio Seymour, in New York.

The Democrats are mistaken to make a fuss about the two edicts of "proclamation week": on emancipation, the fear of a tide of black job seekers will soon recede, and on agitators, we think the sentiment of the North is swinging toward punishing the South and its sympathizers. The copperheads are foolish to say that the two proclamations prove that the war is being waged "for the freedom of the blacks and the enslavement of the whites."

Although the Prsdt, Stanton, *et al.* think Thurlow Weed and the Blairs are *alarmiste* on the possibility of copperhead gains in the Congress, we are attracted to Weed's idea of bringing Horatio Seymour down to the Mansion to let Lincoln get the measure of the man. After all, Seymour as much as anyone is the leader of the opposition now that Stephen Douglas is dead. Maybe a brief exposure to the reality of life in the President's office will have a salutary effect on Seymour's foot-dragging view of the war.

Nothing would keep me from witnessing that confrontation. Miss Carroll says she is an old friend of New York Mayor Fernando Wood—she calls him "F'nandy"—and she claims that the mayor is persuaded that Seymour has a chance of upsetting our man in the race for the most important governorship. Oh, ye of little faith. The Tycoon is serene: he thinks his two proclamations and his continued sufferance of McClellan will get him through the late autumn of discontent.

This war is hitting home. The Prsdt's salary warrant came in today for the month of September: it is $2,022.33, some $61 less than his previous monthly warrants. That is because 3% has been deducted as a result of the "income tax," an abomination perpetrated upon us by the father of the woman I know at Sixth and E. Even my pittance is being clipped; some birthday present! (I am 24 today.) An end to that nefarious practice of snatching money from salaries will be one of the blessings of peace. There is no reason why this government cannot continue to be run on the revenues from customs duties.

CHAPTER 13

PRISONERS

Commotion in camp: some Orphan Brigade skirmishers had brought back a pair of runaway slaves, a field hand and his daughter. Cabell Breckinridge, washing his jeans in a stream, wrung them out as fast as he could, jammed his legs in and raced to the circle of soldiers.

"Caught 'em headed up toward the Gap and Kentucky," one of the skirmishers said proudly. "They made a dash through the woods, but the girl fell down and the man had to come back for her and we grabbed him."

"Mean-lookin' buck, ain't he?"

"She's a cute one, though."

Cabell looked over shoulders to the runaways in the center. The man wore overalls and a dark green shirt and hat—clothing for escape through the fields, except for a leg iron, its chain broken. He was short, well muscled, purple-black, his chest heaving from what Cabell assumed to be either exhaustion or terror.

His daughter was in rags freshly torn by her run through the brambles; slim, with long, scratched legs, breasts beginning to bud, she must have been about thirteen. Every man in the circle was looking at her hungrily—it had been a long, lonely march these three weeks—but Cabell knew their normal lust had to be tempered by a reluctance to get satisfaction out of a slave girl that young.

A Confederate officer came up before any fun could begin and detailed Cabell and the sergeant to return the fugitives to the sheriff in Maynardville, three miles southeast of the camp. The Kentucky Brigade was not due to begin its march to Knoxville until morning.

The sergeant tied a rope around the girl's wrists, with a six-foot length to walk her by. The field hand needed no restraints, he explained to Cabell, because the pappy wasn't likely to run anywhere without the girl. You kept her, you kept him.

"Ain't gonna hurt you," Cabell told them both, "but if you run, we'll shoot you dead. That's orders, you hear?"

He knew he wasn't going to shoot either of them no matter what, but they didn't know that. The owner would be asking after his property, and if Cabell failed to do his duty, any such failure would be used by General Bragg against his father. Bragg really had it in for Father.

Walking down the hilly road, the two soldiers and two slaves came on the body of a dead Yankee. The morning before, a skirmish with some of the Iowa volunteers had taken place here, and the Federals had drawn off too quickly to take their dead.

"Take off his shoes," the sergeant ordered the field hand. The man obeyed; the shoes came off the corpse. The sergeant handed Cabell the girl's rope and sat down at roadside to try them on. He stood up and stomped around. "Not bad. Better too big than too small, hunh? I'll just stuff the tip with leaves."

"You want Billy Yank's jacket?" Cabell asked the girl. "Keep you warm, if you don't mind the bloodstains. You could wash 'em off."

She shook her head, eyes wide with fear. Cabell wondered what sort of life he was bringing her back to. The Breckinridge family seldom had truck with slaves, so he did not know if the stories about what they did with young slave girls was true. It was exciting to think about the terrible acts of the slave masters, but he was certain that the Yankee book *Uncle Tom's Cabin* was exaggerated—abolition talk just to whip up people who didn't know that nobody smart abused their property more than a normal lickin'.

"Why'd you run away?" Cabell asked the man.

The slave looked at him but silently plodded ahead.

"Speak up when a soldier asks you a question," the sergeant barked, clomping along in his new shoes. "Did you hear that 'Massa Linkum' set you free? Was that it?"

The man continued to walk, eyes on the ground. The girl, wanting to be obedient, said "We heared. But that weren't all."

"Well tell us, chile," said the sergeant.

The field hand spoke his first words. "Gwine shoot us in the back," he warned his daughter.

"No, only if you run," said Cabell. He began to feel badly about his threat. You had to be careful how you talked to slaves, especially runaways, he decided; they took anything you said to heart. In their minds, whites were capable of anything, and that kind of power made him uncomfortable.

It didn't trouble the sergeant. He stopped in his tracks, pointed his rifle at the man, and shouted, "Talk!"

J. Cabell Breckinridge

The man merely looked at the sky and awaited execution. He seemed past caring. The girl tugged on the rope in Cabell's hands, looked a plea at him; he let her go to him. She lifted her father's shirt to show the soldiers his back.

Cabell, who had seen his share of wounds at Shiloh, turned away. All the skin had been flayed off the man's back; black shreds hung from the red exposed muscles. The vicious beating must have been administered within the last twenty-four hours. Since then, the man's every movement must have been an agony.

"Okay, keep walking," said the sergeant, slinging his gun, subdued. "You ran away before, didn't you?"

The slave, walking, nodded.

"Shouldn't do that, you get punished," said the sergeant. "Massa Linkum up north, he can say you're free, but that don't make you free down here. Fact is, up home in Kentucky, he didn't free no slaves. Runnin' there won't help you. Only place you're 'free,' 'cording to Massa Linkum, is down South where you're slaves."

That wasn't quite true, Cabell thought; if rebel-state slaves ran into Union lines anywhere, he had heard the Union military now had new orders not to return the fugitives to their owners. Times were changing.

In a low voice, Cabell asked the sergeant, "What do you suppose the owner will do to him now? Can't hurt him much more than last time. Kill him, maybe?"

"Probably take it out on the girl," said the sergeant. "Be a waste, markin' up a nice young thing, but some folks get mean when they're crossed."

A few hundred yards further, Cabell said, "You know, we're pulling out in the morning, all the way down to Knoxville, Tennessee. Owner'd never know the skirmishers caught 'em."

The sergeant shot him a funny look. "And you the general's son?"

"I don't say we let 'em go," Cabell said carefully. "Just that if they run, we'd be wasting good ammunition to shoot. We're short on cartridges. Supposed to use the ammo on the Yankees, not on a nigger cripple and his kid." If it were a straight chase, without shooting, the sergeant would surely fall on his face in those oversized shoes, and Cabell was not going to be the one to catch them.

What would his father do? He was a former senator, a former Vice President of the United States, a general in the Confederate Army, a man of the law. Cabell's grandfather had served as Speaker of the U.S. House of Representatives, and with Thomas Jefferson had written the resolution denouncing John Adams's unconstitutional Alien and Sedition Acts. Cabell was bred to revere the Constitution—now both of them—which made it all right to own slaves. He had been taught to obey the law, and no law challenged the right of people to hold on to their own property. Not even Lincoln's proclamation had done that. Was it right and proper for Cabell Breckinridge, son of a candidate who opposed Lincoln on forbidding the extension of slavery, to look the other way when a law-abiding man's property was running away?

That dilemma came on top of his disillusion with Braxton Bragg, who seemed to be defending every Southern state except Kentucky. Disgusted with the unfairness of it all, Cabell Breckinridge snatched his butternut cap off his head and threw it in the dirt. He and the other fifteen hundred members of the Orphan Brigade, under the command of his father, had trudged over roads, and climbed on and off railroad cars, clear across the Confederate states from the Mississippi to Cumberland Gap, where the northeastern tip of Tennessee meets the southeastern tip of Kentucky. And now that they were finally about to set foot on native Kentucky soil, joining the Confederate troops holding it free from the Yankee invader, in came orders from General Bragg to fall back down into Tennessee.

"Just 'cause Bragg got whupped at Perryville," Cabell said bitterly, "he's givin' up on Kentucky."

The sergeant, from Bourbon County near Lexington, picked up the cap and chucked it at him. "More than that, Cabe. Bragg hates your pappy's guts, blames him for losing at Perryville 'cause the Orphans didn't get there in time. And the folks up home didn't hold no parades signing up for this army. Bragg is pure Mississippi—he thinks Kaintuck is way up north."

"If we ain't got no better generals than Bragg," Cabell agreed, "we're in a bad row for stumps."

It struck Cabell that wars sure turned around in a hurry. Couple of weeks ago, General Bobby Lee was roaring through Maryland, scaring Yanks clear up to New York. At the same time Bragg, Kirby Smith, and cavalryman John

Morgan had the Union on the run in the bluegrass. On top of that, Lincoln makes a grab for every Southern slave, riling up the people and the soldiers of Dixie with his proclamation, giving them a new determination to win. Even the mutinous members of the Orphan Brigade, with their enlistment times up and fixing to go home, agreed to stay on till the end of the war when they heard about Old Abe's abolition. From Shiloh in April right up until Sharpsburg last month, all spring and summer, the war had gone the right way for the C.S.A.

But the news from Sharpsburg worried the men: McClellan, a soldier's general, had turned Lee's men around and sent the butternuts home. And at Perryville, the Yankee general Buell and the first respectable Union cavalry commander, Sheridan, had fought Braxton Bragg to a standstill. Nobody had won that battle, Cabell had been told by his father—Bragg had not really been whupped—but when you're on a big raid and you don't win, you lose. Worried about being trapped too far North without a railroad or a river to supply him, Bragg—like Lee in Maryland—turned around and hightailed it out of there.

Now the Federals, east and west, in Virginia and Tennessee, were pulling together all the supplies and ammunition, horses and brand-new shoes they needed to invade the South again. It seemed to Cabell that as soon as one side got into the other's territory, the invader lost for not winning and had to pull out.

The girl on the other end of the rope stumbled and fell. Cabell reached for her, his hand accidentally cupping one of her little teats, just as the field hand turned and leaned down for her. The black man's face was about six inches from his own, and Cabell didn't want to get a look from anyone like that again. He backed away and pulled her up by the rope, like a dog on a lead.

His own father was in a sullen mood these days. Bragg was bothering him, harassing the Orphan Brigade, wiring complaints about Breckinridge as well as "Bishop" Polk to Jeff Davis in Richmond. His father was worried about Mother, too; she had malaria, and her letters came from a hospital where she was a patient rather than a nurse. Cabell would see him sitting up late in his tent, bottle of bourbon by the lamp, writing home, as if afraid the world after the war would all be different.

He was thinking hard of what General Cleburne had told his father about the idea of Southern emancipation when he heard a sharp command behind him.

"Halt! Drop your guns!"

Might be a trick; he looked over his shoulder, unwilling to disarm himself until he knew the man behind him was armed. Four men in blue uniforms were in the road behind them, two with guns leveled at them. As the sergeant and Cabell stood stock-still, other Yankees appeared on the side of the road and in front of them. The skirmishers of yesterday had returned. These were live Yankees.

Still holding the rope, Cabell slowly put down his gun. The sergeant did the same, murmuring, "Libby Prison, here we come."

Libby was the hellhole every Johnny dreaded, as filthy and disease-ridden as the South's own Andersonville. It made Cabell sad, too, to think that his parents would think he was dead. But he was relieved at not having to make the decision to break the law about the runaway slaves.

"You are hereby emancipated," he said to the girl, and dropped the rope.

CHAPTER 14

DEBATE

"You and I are substantially strangers," the President began, addressing Horatio Seymour, candidate for Governor of New York, in what he intended to be a mood of friendly formality, "and I have asked you here chiefly that we may become better acquainted. I, for the time being, am at the head of a nation which is in great peril, and you are a candidate to become head of the greatest state in that nation."

"I don't claim any superior wisdom," Seymour replied, "but I am confident the opinions I hold are entertained by one half of the population of the Northern states."

Lincoln cocked an eyebrow at that sally; the urbane New Yorker, carrying the demeanor of man of wealth and executive experience, was apparently unawed by his presence in the White House and was ready for a rhetorical scrap. Might be interesting; Lincoln's purpose was to take the measure of the leader of the political opposition as the election campaign heated up, and he was secretly pleased that Seymour obviously overestimated Democratic strength. The President shrugged and allowed as how the election in four weeks would provide the answer to the candidate's contention.

Seymour nodded with civility. "I intend to show those charged with the administration of public affairs a due deference and respect," he promised. "After I am elected governor, Mr. President, I will give you just and generous support in all measures you may adopt within the scope of your constitutional powers."

His careful qualification did not escape the President. "You have been asserting that certain military arrests," Lincoln said to draw the man out, "for which I am ultimately responsible, are unconstitutional."

"I say that your suspension of habeas corpus will not only lead to military despotism," Seymour replied coolly, "it establishes military despotism. This action of your administration will determine, in the minds of more than one half of the people in the loyal states, whether this war is waged to put down rebellion in the South, or to destroy free institutions in the North."

Lincoln was not going to let him get away with that. "May I be indulged," he returned mildly, "to submit a few general remarks on the subject of arrests?"

"You have shown that you think the Constitution is somehow different in time of insurrection and invasion," Seymour continued, not indulging the President at all. "I disagree. The safeguards of the rights of the citizen against the pretensions of arbitrary power were intended especially for his protection in times of civil commotion." As Lincoln shook his head, Seymour added: "You forget, sir, that these civil rights were secured to the English people after years of protracted civil war, and were adopted into our American Constitution at the close of the Revolution."

"Wouldn't your argument be better," Lincoln asked, "if those safeguards had been adopted and applied *during* the civil wars and *during* our Revolution, instead of *after* the one and *at the close* of the other? I, too, am devotedly for them *after* civil war, and before civil war, and at all times except—and here I quote the Constitution—'except when, in cases of rebellion or invasion, the public safety may require' their suspension."

Lincoln thought he had the better of that exchange, but Seymour conceded nothing. "You are quoting the portion of the Constitution dealing with the powers of the Congress, not the President. You tried to justify your usurpation of this power in the Merryman case last year by claiming the Congress was not in session. Well, Congress is in session right now. If it is so urgent that those who disagree with you be clapped into jail without a trial, why not call on Congress to pass martial law? Who are you to override the most sacred rights of free men—solely when you choose to say the public safety requires it? You were not elected dictator."

Lincoln recognized the debating tactic: goad your opponent to anger with a personal dig. "Divested of your phraseology calculated to represent me as struggling for an arbitrary personal prerogative," Lincoln said slowly, containing his temper, "your question is simply a question of *who* shall decide, or an affirmation that *nobody* shall decide, what the public safety does require, in cases of rebellion or invasion."

"Not so. The Congress can decide."

"The Constitution contemplates the question as likely to occur for decision, but it does not expressly declare who is to decide it," Lincoln corrected him. "By necessary implication, when rebellion or invasion comes, the decision is to be made from time to time; and I think the man who, for the time the people have, under the Constitution, made commander in chief of their army and navy, is the man who holds the power and bears the responsibility of making it."

"With no restraints? No checks and balances, no appeals? That, sir, is dictatorial power."

"If he uses the power justly," Lincoln said matter-of-factly, "the same people will probably justify him; if he abuses it, he is in their hands to be dealt with by all the modes they have reserved to themselves in the Constitution."

"Do you realize what you are saying?" Seymour uncrossed his legs and leaned forward. "You are saying, 'If you don't like my arbitrary arrests, impeach me—but I can arrest you for speaking out to demand my impeachment.' No despot ever seized more power to mete out punishment."

"The purpose of these arrests is not punishment," the President said patiently. He realized he was in a dispute with a lawyer who knew his case, but Lincoln had been writing thoughts for this session on little scraps of paper for days, putting each arguing point in a drawer to be assembled for his presentation. "You claim that men may, if they choose, embarrass those whose duty it is to combat a giant rebellion, and then be dealt with only in turn as if there were no rebellion. The Constitution itself rejects this view. The military arrests and detentions which are being made are for prevention and not punishment—as injunctions to stay injury, as proceedings to keep the peace. Hence, like proceedings in such injunction cases, they are not accompanied by indictments, or trial by juries, nor in a single case by any punishment whatever beyond what is purely incidental to the prevention."

"Not punishment? To be arrested for one knows not what; to be confined, no one entitled to ask where; to be tried, no one can say when, by a law nowhere known or established, or to linger out life in a cell without trial—you call that no punishment? That is a body of tyranny which cannot be enlarged."

Lincoln could just hear those words being used effectively in a political stump speech. It was demagoguery, he knew, but, like all effective demagoguery, contained a germ of truth: Stanton had already appointed a special provost marshal in Washington to carry out the arrests, with provost marshals in every loyal state with power to ignore local court rulings. That would strike fear in traitorous hearts, as Lincoln intended, but would also send a chill into the hearts of the loyal voter.

"Habeas corpus does not discharge men who are proved to be guilty of defined crime," Lincoln instructed Seymour in the law, "and its suspension is allowed by the Constitution on purpose that men may be arrested and held who cannot be proved to be guilty of defined crime. Arrests are made, not so much for what *has* been done as for what probably *would* be done—preventive, not vindictive. In crimes against the state, the purposes of men are much more easily understood than in cases of ordinary crime."

"Oh?"

"The man who stands by and says nothing," Lincoln said, "when the peril of his government is discussed, cannot be misunderstood. If not hindered, he is sure to help the enemy—much more, if he talks ambiguously: talks for his country with 'buts' and 'ifs' and 'ands.' "

Lincoln watched Seymour burn at that imputation of disloyalty, and as Seymour said nothing, awaited the question the candidate would have to ask. Sure enough, Seymour rose to the bait: "Can you not bear to wait until a crime has been committed before meting out punishment?"

He had him. "Wait until a crime has been committed? Let me give you an example. General John Breckinridge, as well as others occupying the very highest places in the rebel war service, were all within the power of the government once the rebellion began, and were nearly as well known to be traitors then as now. Unquestionably, if we had seized and held them, the insurgent cause would be much weaker. But no one of them had then committed any crime defined in the law. If arrested, they would have been discharged on habeas corpus, were the writ allowed to operate." The President made his point triumphantly: "I think the time not unlikely to come when I shall be blamed for having made too few arrests rather than too many."

The candidate for chief executive of the state Lincoln counted on most for men and money shook his head as if in disbelief. "The Constitution provides for no limitations on the guarantees of personal liberty, except as to habeas corpus. Even granting you the usurpation of that power from Congress, do you hold that all the other rights of every man throughout the country can be annulled whenever you say the public safety requires it? Freedom of speech, of the press—"

"The benefit of the writ of habeas corpus is the great means through which the guarantees of personal liberty are conserved and made available in the last resort," Lincoln conceded. "But by the Constitution, even habeas corpus may be suspended when, in case of rebellion or invasion, the public safety may require it." Through his power to suspend that essential right, the President held the key to all the other rights.

"Can you be unaware, Mr. President, that the suppression of journals and the imprisonment of persons has been glaringly partisan? Republicans have been allowed the utmost licentiousness of criticism, while Democrats have been punished for a fair exercise of the right of discussion. For supporters of mine, even to ask the aid of counsel has been held to be an offense."

Lincoln started to interrupt, but the New York candidate pressed on: "An attempt is being made to shield the violators of law and to suppress inquiry into their motives and conduct. I warn you, sir, this attempt to conceal the abuses of power will fail. Unconstitutional acts cannot be shielded by unconstitutional laws."

"Now hold on." He did not appreciate being warned. "In this time of national peril, I would have preferred to meet you on a level one step higher than any party platform. But not all Democrats have denied me this. The Secretary of War, on whose discretionary judgment the arrests are being made, is a Democrat, having no old party affinity with me. And from all those Democrats who are nobly exposing their lives on the battlefield, I have heard from many who approve my course, and not from a single one condemning it."

If Seymour caught the subtle import of his point—that those Democrats doing the complaining were not the patriots doing the fighting—he ignored it airily. "I shall not inquire what rights states in rebellion have forfeited, but I deny that this rebellion can suspend a single right of the citizens of loyal states. I denounce your doctrine that civil war in the South takes away from the loyal North the benefits of one principle of civil liberty."

Lincoln wondered if the man would go as far as to threaten the national authority, and was astounded when Seymour did: "In the event that I am elected governor next month, I will make it plain that it is a high crime to abduct a citizen of the state of New York. I will admonish my sheriffs and district attorneys to take care that no New Yorker is imprisoned or carried by force outside the state without due process of legal authority."

The man was a danger to the Union. Seymour was, in effect, promising insurrection of another sort: a "high crime" was an offense of state, and could lead to the arrest, impeachment, and imprisonment of the arresting federal officer. And New York's police forces, added to local militia, would be more than a match for the thin federal forces in that state. If elected governor, Seymour would have the military power on the scene to back up his threat to federal authority.

"I can no more be persuaded," Lincoln told him, hoping a practical argument would take hold, "that the government can constitutionally take no strong measures in time of rebellion—because it can be shown that the same could not be lawfully taken in time of peace—than I can be persuaded that a particular drug is not good medicine for a sick man because it can be shown not to be good for a well one. Nor am I able to appreciate the danger that the American people will, by means of military arrests during the rebellion, lose the right of public discussion, the liberty of speech and the press, the law of evidence, trial by jury and habeas corpus any more than I am able to believe that a man could contract so strong an appetite for emetics during temporary illness as to persist in feeding upon them during the remainder of his healthful life."

"I suppose those homespun metaphors go over well with juries, Mr. Lincoln, but ask yourself this: did you approve of President Polk's war with Mexico?"

Lincoln frowned, not getting his opponent's sudden shift of argument. He reluctantly shook his head. Like many good Whigs in the 1840s, he had faulted Polk for provoking the war at the behest of the Texans.

"During the war with Mexico," Seymour recounted, "many of the political opponents of the Administration thought it their duty to denounce and oppose the war. With equal reason as you give now, it might have been said of them that their discussions before the people were calculated to discourage enlistments and to induce desertions. Were these people, yourself included, 'warring on the military,' to use your own phrase, and did this give the military constitutional jurisdiction to lay hands upon them?"

"I dislike to waste words on a purely personal point," answered Lincoln, "but you will find yourself at fault should you ever seek for evidence to prove your assumption that I opposed, *in discussions before the people*, the policy of the Mexican War." Lincoln had privately spoken forcefully against the start of Polk's war, but had refrained from speaking out publicly for fear of jeopardizing his political career in those early days. He realized now that as a young congressman, he had been wise to stay silent; anti-war oratory would have come home to haunt him now. Nobody could make him feel guilty now about not speaking out then. Time for an anecdote.

"Seward says that one fundamental principle of politics is to be always on the side of your country in a war," Lincoln drawled. "I remember Butterfield of Illinois was asked, at the beginning of the Mexican War, if he was not opposed to it. He said, 'No. I opposed one war and it ruined me. I am now perpetually in favor of war, pestilence, and famine.' "

Unfortunately, Seymour was too worked up for Lincoln's attempt to reduce the animosity to have the desired effect. "Do you seriously think that arresting the outspoken opposition," asked the New York candidate, "is going to preserve the public safety? I think the opposite. I think all authority is going to be weakened by your repression. Government is never strengthened by the exercise of doubtful powers: it always produces discord, suspicion, and distrust. If that is what you feel you must do, Lincoln, that is what I must run against."

Lincoln fingered the mole on his cheek; although he had flushed Seymour out and learned the campaign strategy, he was unhappy with what he had learned. He rose from his couch and walked to the desk, half sitting there. "This civil war began on very unequal terms between the parties. The insurgents had been preparing for it more than thirty years." Anna Carroll had documented the activities of the Knights of the Golden Circle in her pamphlet exposing Breckinridge. "Their sympathizers pervaded all departments of the Government, and nearly all communities of the people. Under cover of 'liberty of speech,' 'liberty of the press,' and 'habeas corpus,' they hoped to keep on foot among us a most efficient corps of spies, informers, suppliers, and aiders and abettors of their cause in a thousand ways."

"I find it hard to believe that a President of the United States swallows such a—"

"Hear me out, Seymour. They knew that in times such as they were inaugurating, by the Constitution itself the habeas corpus might be suspended; but they also knew they had friends who make a question as to *who* was to suspend it; meanwhile, their spies and others might remain at large to help on their cause."

"The person who first raised that question was the Chief Justice of the United States," Seymour said hotly. "Are you accusing him of being a part of a conspiracy to—"

Lincoln kept on going. "Or if, as has happened, the Executive should suspend the writ, without ruinous waste of time, instances of arresting innocent persons might occur—as are always likely to occur in such cases—and then a clamor could be raised in regard to this, of service to the insurgent cause."

"For God's sake, Lincoln, what about the courts? I'm not talking about arrests of bushwhackers and guerrillas in a war zone, I mean arrests of dissenters in those areas where judges now sit, empowered to hear cases."

"Nothing is better known to history than that courts of justice are utterly incompetent to such cases," Lincoln held. "Civil courts are organized chiefly for trials of individuals, or at most a few individuals acting in concert, and this in quiet times. Even in times of peace, bands of horse thieves and robbers frequently grow too numerous and powerful for the ordinary courts of justice. But what comparison, in numbers, have such bands ever borne to the insurgent sympathizers even in many of the loyal states?"

"Why are you, a lawyer, afraid of judges and juries?"

"A jury frequently has at least one member more ready to hang the panel than to hang the traitor," the President shot back. "Thoroughly imbued with a reverence for the guaranteed rights of individuals," he went on, "I was slow to adopt the strong measures indispensable to the public safety. Remember, Seymour: he who dissuades one man from volunteering, or induces one soldier to desert, weakens the Union cause as much as he who kills a Union soldier in battle. Yet this dissuasion or inducement may be so conducted as to be defined as no crime in civil court."

"Your reverence for the rule of law is overwhelming, Mr. Lincoln. I take it that you believe all of us who strive to protect the right of dissent are weakening the cause of the Union. You have become so obsessed with holding the Union together that you have forgotten that the purpose of the Union is to preserve individual freedom."

"Your own attitude, therefore," said the President, unrelenting, eager to make clear the political danger in the line Seymour had been taking, "encourages desertion, resistance to the draft, and the like, because it teaches those who incline to desert and to escape the draft to believe it is your purpose to protect them, and to hope that you will become strong enough to do so."

"We have nothing further to discuss," said Seymour, rising. "Your pretensions to more than regal authority are contemptible. You claim to have found within the Constitution a germ of arbitrary power, which in time of war expands at once into an absolute sovereignty wielded by one man, so that liberty perishes at his discretion or caprice. I will stand for election in New York, sir, and refute you. The American people will never acquiesce in your extraordinary doctrine."

"We shall see." Lincoln judged this fellow to be stronger than he had thought, and no demagogue, but felt confident he could take him in debate in '64 if it came to that, just as he had taken Stephen Douglas in '58. If he felt like debating, that was a President's prerogative. Greeley was certain that Seymour had no chance of winning the governorship next month, but Weed was worried about the undignified and unprecedented way he was traveling all over the state of New York, running instead of standing for election in the traditional way. "We shall see. I'll just have to keep pegging away."

CHAPTER 15

THE GOLD ROOM

On the wide landing of the stairs, her hand resting on the railing, Kate Chase listened to the familiar voices in the library below.

"I congratulate you on the rise of your seven-thirties, my dear Cooke," her father was saying, "and now I want to be a borrower myself. Will you lend me two thousand dollars, in the shape of your draft on New York?"

"Of course." Jay Cooke was always accommodating; but the Treasury Secretary had made Cooke's Philadelphia firm the exclusive agent for the government's bond issue, Kate was persuaded, only because Cooke had proved himself to be the most effective salesman of bonds in the land.

"I want it to pay on the account of a store I am rebuilding on Katie's property in Cincinnati," her father explained.

"Say no more," Cooke told him; "I'll write the draft now."

Scratching of quill. Kate waited on the landing; now was hardly the time to make an entrance.

"I must remind you again," her father told Cooke sternly, "of the necessity of putting a little more form in the address of your letters to the Secretary of the Treasury. I don't like to have private and public matters mixed. Please commence all your letters on public matters to him with 'Sir.' Write separate letters on private matters, or those in which you are trusted as a confidential agent, with 'Dear Governor' or 'Dear friend' or as you will. But let those personal letters contain nothing on public business or vice versa."

"Of course," said Cooke again. "Here you are—I hope the store is a great success."

"The store? Oh, on Katie's property. Yes."

Humming "Picayune Butler" as she walked down the stairs, Kate entered the library and kissed them both.

She ensconced herself on the part of the couch that needed covering. "Tell me about the Gold Room," she said to Cooke. "I hear it's a terrible scandal, and you should be ashamed."

Kate had read that a group of brokers in New York had formed an exchange to set the price of gold, and she knew that Jay Cooke would find pleasure in explaining it to her. It would help Father, too, who was sometimes too proud to seek financial instruction.

"Early this year your father put out the greenbacks, remember? The paper dollar is supposed to be worth a dollar in gold—and so it is, for paying the new tax on incomes, but foreign countries insist on payment of their debts in gold. That makes a gold dollar worth somewhat more than a greenback."

"And the more greenbacks we print, the less the paper dollar is worth against gold," her father put in.

Cooke nodded. "In January, gold was worth one dollar and three cents. Today, it's one dollar and twenty-five cents in the Gold Room. Since the nation would rather borrow than tax, the paper greenback will buy even less gold next year."

"Well, why do you let those money changers in the temple—those gamblers —make all the money that we need to finance the war?" Good question: she'd worked on it.

The young financier, smiling, shook his head. "In gambling," Cooke explained, "an artificial risk is created. But in gold speculation, a genuine risk is inherent in the situation. Since the price of gold against the dollar is sure to go up and down, depending on the fortunes of the North in the war, somebody is needed to accept the risk. If it isn't the speculator, it has to be the importers and other businessmen who must use gold in trade. The speculators perform a service taking that risk, which is why they should profit from it."

She shook her head warily. "There must be politics in it. I hear the 'Copperhead bulls' sing *Dixie* right in the Gold Room on news of a rebel victory, and the 'Union bears' sing 'John Brown's Body' when the North wins a battle."

"The reason for that," Jay Cooke explained, more to the Secretary than his daughter, "is economic, not political. When rebels win, confidence in the U.S. dollar drops, which means it takes more dollars to buy gold—so the price of gold goes up. The 'Copperhead bulls' are betting that the rebels will win and the price of gold will shoot up."

"Lincoln doesn't understand that," said her father. "He thinks the tail wags the dog, that the gold traders put the price up because they want the South to win. He banged the Cabinet table the other day"—Chase banged the table and imitated Lincoln's high voice—"'I wish every one of them had his devilish head shot off!' "

"I'm sorry to hear that," said Cooke, no longer smiling. "If Lincoln tries to control that market, or put the gold speculators out of business because he thinks speculation is unpatriotic, he'll bring our foreign trade to a halt. And then goodbye to your revenues from customs duties."

"Fear not," said Chase. "He does that to show Thad Stevens and that bunch he's one of them, against the vile bankers with their diamond stickpins."

A servant came in to announce that Miss Anna Ella Carroll had dropped by and was waiting in the front parlor. Kate, who had expected to be out all day, seethed; she was glad now that she had changed her plans, and glad her father looked discomfited.

"Were you expecting her, Father?"

"No, but Miss Carroll is always—"

"You two continue your important business," she said to the men. "I'll see her first, and bring her in when you've finished."

"We're finished," said Cooke, being helpful, then catching Kate's glare added lamely, "well, there are a couple of confidential details left, I suppose."

"Don't let her go," said her father; "I want Miss Carroll's thoughts on next week's elections. We didn't do too well back home in Ohio this month in our early elections, except for Major Garfield." Turning to Cooke, he added, "that young man won by a two-to-one margin, you know. Ashtabula is the most Republican county in the state, of course, but it shows James Garfield has a great future."

"Will the major take his seat, or remain in the army?"

Chase looked uncertain; Kate said, "He'll stay in the army awhile, if he gets a decent assignment. He thinks a good war record is the most important thing in the long run, and, of course, he's right." She had talked with him intimately and at length on a recent horseback ride toward Annapolis. Garfield was an attractive, passionate, in some ways mysterious man.

"I have an assignment in mind for him first," Chase told Cooke. "Stanton is going to get Lincoln to approve the convening of a court-martial of General Porter, for his disgraceful conduct toward Pope at Second Bull Run."

"McClellan will never stand for that," said Cooke. "Porter is his pet." Kate nodded approvingly; she had explained that to Jay the night before. She taught him more politics than he taught her economics.

"McClellan is finished," said Chase with finality. "It is inexpedient for Lincoln to remove him before the elections, because that would be misconstrued by most conservatives as a sop to those of us who have long demanded an end to slavery. Come Election Day, McClellan will be removed."

"But if he's hot on the tail of Lee at the time—"

"No matter. That's not the point. His delays are dreadful, and that's an excuse for sacking him, but McClellan and his crowd must be removed because of all the compromising on slavery they stand for."

"I can see why Lincoln wants to wait past the elections," Cooke said. "The man did save the country at Antietam, a lot of people in Philadelphia think— we were certain that Lee was on the way."

"McClellan failed to win the war at Antietam," Chase said sternly. "And after he's been removed, the court-martial of his man Porter will commence. That's why it is important for an officer with political judgment to represent us on the court-martial board. Major Garfield will see that justice is done."

"The major is not as sanguine as you about the elections," Kate said. She hoped she did not seem to her father to know too much about Garfield's thinking; she knew better than he that Garfield as judge would come down hard on Fitz-John Porter and drive the last nail in the coffin of McClellan's reputation.

"The unfortunate results of the early elections in Ohio and Pennsylvania," pronounced her father, "were influenced by the fear of Southern invasion. November's elections will reflect the enthusiasm for the emancipation and the relief at the defeats of Lee and Bragg."

"That might help in New England," Kate said, eager to put forward her political thoughts before Miss Carroll had a chance, and to show Jay Cooke how well she had been informed by Major Garfield, "and in California."

"We'll pick up seats in Congress," Chase said confidently, "and governorships as well. Greeley assures us that his man Wadsworth will trounce the Peace Democrat, Seymour, in New York." A frown crossed his fine brow. "But Illinois, of all places, might prove a problem. Leonard Swett, Lincoln's close friend running in Lincoln's old district, predicts a close race. Strange. Maybe Miss Carroll knows why."

Anna did not enjoy being sidetracked, but she could not refuse a cup of tea in the parlor with the lady of the house while the financial conference was concluding in the library. Kate Chase appeared drawn, not the radiant center of attention of the levees. The young woman apparently had something to say and Anna let her take the conversational lead.

"I understand, Miss Carroll, that you have been approaching several members of the Cabinet with your claim that the government owes you money," Kate Chase said abruptly, silver teapot in hand.

Anna waited for her to go on.

"Six thousand, two hundred and fifty dollars," Kate specified, pouring the tea. "That's a great deal of money."

Anna had not mentioned the sum to her father. Had Bates told her? Stanton? John Hay? "Yes," she replied. "I laid a great deal of money out myself, in the production of pamphlets."

"I know this is a rude question, Miss Carroll, but are you a woman of means?"

"You're right, Kate," she said, using the younger woman's first name to assert her seniority. "That is a rude question."

"I felt free to ask it, because I'm not. Not a woman of means."

Anna sipped her tea.

"Many women," Kate went on, "many single women, assume that because my father is Secretary of the Treasury and deals in millions of dollars, the Chase family is rich. It's not true."

Anna's eyes roamed the walls of the elegant parlor, took in the paintings and draperies, pointedly noted the breakfront with the expensive china, and continued sipping her tea. The young woman certainly knew how to brew and serve a cup of tea; it was a talent Anna had never mastered.

"All this is a façade, Miss Carroll," said Kate after Anna's eyes returned from their tour. "I thought you ought to know. It is not something my father would confide in you, or in Addie Douglas, or in any of the women who have set their cap for him. But it is the truth. Salmon Portland Chase, once a wealthy man, is now as poor as—"

"A church mouse, the expression is."

"Thank you. In telling you this, I am taking you into my family's confidence. It would not do for the city of Washington to know that we have to scrimp and save to meet the bills. Because my father trusts you, I trust you."

"Your predicament will never pass my lips."

"It would therefore be advantageous," Kate continued, "for my father to marry a woman who can present a bill for six thousand, two hundred and fifty dollars to the government every now and then. It would pay for my winter wardrobe. Are you quite prepared, Miss Carroll, to help support the Chase family—there's Nettie, too, my sister—in the manner to which we are accustomed?"

Anna put down her cup and sat back. "Young woman, you seem to be suggesting, with some puerile drawing-room irony, that I am running after your father for his money."

"I am glad you took my point."

"You're young, you're possessive, and you're wrong."

"If you could see the house accounts—"

Anna waved aside the details. "Your pecuniary problems are of no interest. I believe you, that you're short on ready cash, and, yes, it's a surprise to me. But your problem is not in protecting your father from avaricious women. Your problem is to create a life for yourself independent of your father."

"How d—"

"I dare because I've always dared to stand in my own shoes. You're filled with fear because you've always stood in your father's shoes. Grow up and get out on your own."

"I have worked, Miss Carroll, and been charming, and fought, and scratched, and lied and spied and done damn-all for a chance to be hostess in the Executive Mansion, and no society widow, or, or"—she struggled for a suitable capsule of Anna Carroll—"concubine of past presidents who never wears a dress with a decent bodice is going to deprive me of it!"

Kate's face was flushed, her chest heaving. Anna remained cool, choosing to deal with the insults obliquely. "I was flat-chested, like you, when I was in my teens," she said pseudosympathetically. She breathed deeply and arched her back. "Be of good heart. Over the years, figgers change."

After a moment, Kate recovered. "I would like you to stop seeing my father," she was able to say calmly.

"That's natural," Anna replied. It was time to stop fencing with the girl. "I resented every woman who came into the house after my father was widowed. We were very close, and I was a great support to him, just as you are to the governor. But what you want for your father, and from your father, is not my concern. That is between you and him."

She felt like rising to make her point, but then Kate would rise and tower over her, so Anna remained seated. "Your father is a self-made man and I am a self-made woman. We admire each other. We like each other. We can be helpful to each other. Perhaps we will get together someday, perhaps not— that's as much my choice as it is his."

"But neither of you knew the other was poor."

"And do you know what that means, Kate? It means that we both know how to keep up appearances."

Kate neither dissolved nor started whining. "I will fight you. I am more worried about you than about the society ladies."

"Good, that says a lot about your father's sense of himself, and it shows you know where you are weakest."

Kate looked puzzled, probably because she did not want to disagree with a compliment.

"You can share his ambition," Anna went on, "but you cannot share his life. He has needs that go beyond those that can be supplied by an official hostess, and those needs it would be"—she paused for emphasis, knowing precisely the word to use—"unnatural for you to provide." He had not yet expressed that need to her in any of their meetings, which Anna was not about to tell his daughter; let her suspect the worst. From the tension of her last meeting with him, she had hopes the worst would come soon.

"You think of me as a belle of parties, Miss Carroll, the hostess of a *matinée dansante*. But I will surprise you. I am prepared to make sacrifices to reach my goal, and to help Father reach his. More sacrifices than you have ever made in your life."

"Let him go. Make your own way."

Kate rose. "I'll show you to the library."

"No, I'll wait here. If they're not finished with their bond issue in a few minutes, I'll go along." Since Kate did not offer more tea, Anna poured herself a cup. She wished it were a glass of wine. What in God's name was a *matinée dansante*? Dancing in the afternoon, with the drapes drawn, by candlelight? Is that what these people did after lunch?

As she expected, as soon as Kate withdrew, Chase and Cooke came in to join her, accompanied by Major Garfield, the Chases' houseguest. That was the sort of political man Kate should be seeing, had he been single; not Lord Lyons, a professional bachelor, or John Hay, a comparative boy she could manipulate at will. Kate needed a man to share both ambition and bed. Anna was prepared to admit that so did she, but at least she was aware of it.

"The President is afflicted with the notion that the way to take Vicksburg is to send General McClerland, an Illinois politician, down the Mississippi," Anna Ella Carroll told them. "That's ridiculous. Grant should attack the fort by land, from the rear; that's what the Tennessee plan had in mind from the start. If the subject comes up in the Cabinet tomorrow, Governor, here's my idea . . ."

CHAPTER 16

JOHN HAY'S DIARY
NOVEMBER 5, 1862

Yesterday was Election Day and the results coming in today amount to a national calamity.

I knew that political disaster was imminent. I was home in Illinois last week, partly for some unobtrusive sparking but mainly to help Leonard Swett and other family friends get organized to turn out the Republicans on November 4.

Away from the federal city, in touch with the West, I was able to read the signs. I wrote Nicolay to tell the Tycoon how badly the political currents were running in Illinois. With stunning prescience, I predicted that the inaction of McClellan and Buell and the ill success of our arms would have a terrible effect. I pointed out that all our energetic and working Republicans are in the army. The district "captains of ten" and "captains of 100," who have always done our best vote getting, are all soldiers in the field and not enough were furloughed. I warned that the State of Illinois was in great danger.

But even I, fresh from the grass roots, had no more than an inkling of what turned out to be the sad state of public sentiment in the nation.

With the Prsdt lounging on his couch, as he does when flirting with the hypo, and Tad and the kittens unable to shake him out of his gloom, it was my task to take in the messages brought over from the War Department telegraph office by William Slade, our trusty colored messenger.

New Jersey was the first shock. A Douglas Democrat took the governorship by 61,000 to 46,000 votes, an upset of staggering proportions; on top of that, Peace Democrats took four of the five House seats and gained control of the Jersey legislature. Then came Delaware, just as bad in a smaller way, following in the pattern dismayingly set by our defeats in Pennsylvania, Ohio, and Indiana.

Hoping to break the chain of bad news, I went across the street to the telegraph office to get the word from Michigan, where I was certain that old Zack Chandler would deliver. He did, and I forgave him for his dalliance with John Barleycorn as I started back with the one small piece of cheer in the dismal landscape.

In the hall of the War Department near Stanton's office I came across Major Garfield, Chase's house guest, who is sort of hanging around waiting for a military post that will enshrine him in the eyes of Ohioans, meanwhile playing chess with Chase and mooning after Kate. Since he was one of the few winners in the congressional races—it would be impossible for us to lose Ashtabula—I asked him for some more good news to take to the Prsdt.

Congressman-elect Garfield was no help. "The news is most disheartening," he said heavily. "Several of the most important states seem to have gone secession."

"Word from New York? The defeat of Seymour would be a good sign, if by a large margin."

"Not yet. But Roscoe Conkling lost his seat, that was unexpected."

I was of two minds about that; Conkling was another one of Kate's admirers, but was one of the President's stalwarts in the House from New York.

I hazarded the view that all was not going well.

"There will be a jubilee in Richmond," Garfield responded miserably, "the like of which has not been seen since the first battle of Bull Run. At this rate, we will be overpowered by treason at home."

Since he was in Chase's orbit, I asked the major's opinion of the cause of the calamity.

"Democratic generals," was the response. "Having failed to buy up his enemies by kindness, Mr. Lincoln has been driving away all his friends by neglect."

I said I presumed he meant that he and his radical allies in the army had not been given the positions they wanted. "Please tell the President this," he urged. "If these disastrous elections act as a spur to give him some motion, I shall welcome them as messengers of mercy though they come in the guise of terrible disasters."

I thanked Garfield for that solace and ducked back into the telegraph office for any late word from Illinois.

"Not good," said Homer Bates. "The legislature has gone Democratic."

That meant that Orville Browning, who had been appointed to the Senate after the 1860 election by the legislature, would lose his seat to some Peace Democrat. It also meant that he would be badgering Lincoln for a Supreme Court seat that Lincoln had in mind for David Davis, his 1860 campaign manager. Two intimate friends, both deserving, but only one job; that meant trouble.

I asked about Leonard Swett, known as Lincoln's best friend back home, running in Lincoln's home district.

"Defeated," said Bates. He handed over the dispatch from the correspondent of the *Chicago Tribune*. The voters in our own backyard have rejected Republicanism and Lincoln. The Prsdt would take that hard.

"Frank Blair won in Missouri," said Bates, to perk me up. That was a foregone conclusion: the Blairs owned the big newspaper in that state, in a season when most other newspapers were killing us. William the messenger arrived, looking for fresh returns; I told him to await new results in the telegraph office, especially from the governor's race in New York, while I hurried back to the Tycoon. He had gone down the hall to the Cabinet Room. I followed with my bad news.

CHAPTER 17

BE RELIEVED FROM COMMAND

"The defeat of the administration is your own fault," Carl Schurz was lecturing him, "You placed the army, now a great power in this Republic, in the hands of its enemies."

The election defeat a result of neglect of patronage? Lincoln refused to accept that. "I distributed to our party's friends as nearly all the civil patronage as any administration ever did. The war came. It so happened that very few of our friends were of the profession of arms." Even so, he added, "I have scarcely appointed a Democrat to a command who was not urged by many Republicans and opposed by none. It was that way with McClellan."

Carl Schurz and Stanton were in the Cabinet Room with him, not commiserating, but blaming Lincoln for the poor results. Schurz was the human rights leader who had been tossed out of Germany after the revolution of 1848, and who swung great weight with the German vote here; accordingly, he was listened to, and had been appointed Ambassador to Spain after Lincoln's election. Schurz was bored there, however, so a military command was found for him, in charge of German regiments, of course, near Washington.

Lincoln liked Schurz. Even if a bit ultra, he had been a thoroughgoing Lincoln man, unlike Wade and Stevens; on top of that, Lincoln was comfortable with a lively fellow who spoke his mind with a refreshing absence of guile unt der unmistakable accent.

"But you sustained those generals after they had been found failing," insisted Schurz, as Stanton nodded. "Am I wrong in saying that the principal management of the war has been in the hands of your political opponents?

McClellan, in eighteen months, has succeeded in nothing except the consumption of our resources with the largest and best appointed army this country ever saw."

"The Democrats in the country were left in a majority by our friends going to the war," Lincoln explained. "Our newspapers, by vilifying and disparaging the Administration, furnished them all the weapons to do it with."

"The President is right about the damned newspapers, Schurz," conceded Stanton. "Look at Iowa. The only reason we won in Iowa is that I put the two Peace Democrat editors in Fort Lafayette for seditious agitation. Should have done a good deal more of that."

The German, now a general, disagreed. "That some of our newspapers disparaged and vilified the Administration may be true. But however that may be, I ask you—what power would there have been in newspaper talk had the Administration been able to set up against it the evidence of great military success?"

Lincoln dug in his heels: "I certainly have been dissatisfied with the slowness of McClellan, but before I relieve him, what successor would be better?"

"One who sympathized with your political aims."

"I need success more than I need sympathy," Lincoln said heatedly.

"The people had shown confidence in you," Schurz pressed, "and reaped disaster and disappointment. They wanted change in military leadership, and yesterday sought it in the wrong direction."

Lincoln suddenly didn't much feel like arguing. "We still have a Republican majority in the Congress."

"I entreat you, Lincoln," said Schurz, "do not attribute to small incidents what is a great historical event. You appointed generals who have no heart in this war. See the fact in its true light: the election results were a most serious and severe reproof administered to the Administration."

The President would not take that slumped in his couch; now he felt a surge of resentment at the unfairness in the accusation. He had done all that the radicals had asked him to do about emancipation and more; that, and not a failure of patronage, was what had cost the party dearly at the polls. Blair and Weed had been proved right in their dire predictions, Stanton and Sumner and Greeley wrong in their easy assurances—and now the radicals, instead of accepting political responsibility for emancipation's unpopularity, were searching for arguments to blame Abraham Lincoln.

He rose up and struck back: "I certainly know if the war fails, the Administration fails, and that I will be blamed for it whether I deserve it or not. You think I can do better, therefore you blame me already. I think I could not do better, therefore I blame you for blaming me." He poked his long finger in the German's chest. "Believe me, my dear Schurz, there are generals who 'have their heart in this war,' as you put it, that think you are performing your part as poorly as you think I am performing mine."

The German started to say something, swallowed, turned and departed without another word. Stanton looked at the floor.

Distraught at the election results, angry at himself for lashing out at a loyal friend who happened to be mistaken, and whose continued political backing was important, Lincoln stood uncertainly in front of the open-grate fireplace.

Carl Schurz

He rocked back and forth in his gigantic morocco slippers until his testiness subsided, then he told Stanton, "Go bring him back."

When the Secretary of War ushered the troubled Schurz back into the room, Lincoln put his hands on the German's shoulders and shook him gently. "I gave it to you hard, didn't I? But it didn't hurt, did it? I didn't mean to."

Lincoln forced a laugh. "It's just that all the criticisms coming down on me from all sides chafed a little. You happened to be the one to sum up all the criticisms and offer me a good chance for reply. I know you are a warm anti-slavery man and a good friend to me." He shook the man's shoulders again until Schurz smiled.

At that moment William appeared with the latest from the telegraph office. Lincoln looked at the message, laid it down on the Cabinet Room table, went over to the window looking out on Pennsylvania Avenue, and crossed his arms. He heaved one of those profound sighs that seem to come up from the Mansion basement. The opposition now had a leader in a position to challenge his executive power.

Stanton picked up the message and read aloud: "Horatio Seymour has been elected Governor of the State of New York."

After a moment's silence, Schurz took his leave. Lincoln asked Stanton to stay and they went down the hall to the President's office. He pointed to the map and asked his Secretary of War for the latest on the whereabouts of McClellan and Lee.

"Our army has finally put all its units across the Potomac into Virginia," Stanton reported. "It's been seven long weeks since Antietam."

Lincoln nodded and asked for specifics. McClellan's headquarters was in now Rectortown, near Warrenton; the general was complaining of lack of shoes for his men, and wanted more carbines and muskets, but he was undoubtedly on the move to engage the enemy. Lee's army was again separated by the Blue Ridge Mountains, with Jackson's corps on the western side in the Shenandoah Valley and Longstreet's troops down at Culpepper Court House. Apparently McClellan planned to strike down the east side of the mountain range at Longstreet, driving him back on Gordonsville before Jackson could unite with him. From there, Mac could take the Fredericksburg route to Richmond or try to talk Lincoln into letting him try the Peninsula route again.

The President noticed something as Stanton was talking; strange, how maps could speak to you about armies. If Longstreet was in Culpepper, that meant he was in McClellan's front; no longer could Lincoln hope that the Federal forces could cut off Lee's army from the rear. A case could be made, then, and would readily be understood by the public, that Lee's army had "escaped." Although he could no longer relieve McClellan on the grounds that he was not actively pursuing Lee—indeed, McClellan seemed in the process of making a major attack—he could relieve the general on the grounds that he had allowed Lee to slip his army between McClellan and Richmond, to escape. The President could say that had always been his criterion for replacing his field commander.

Because replace him he must. The victory of the Democrats in the elections, combined with what Schurz rightly recognized was the West Point crowd's unhealthy dominance of the army, had flung down a gauntlet. Lincoln knew he faced a stark choice: either back away from emancipation, ease up on the Democratic dissidents, woo the Republican conservatives, and accept the policy laid down in McClellan's Harrison's Landing plan—or do just the opposite: ignore the election results, crack down on the agitators, lay a strong hand on the colored element by using them as soldiers, fire McClellan and root out the West Point mind-set in the army.

The President crossed to the desk, took out a quill and ink, rummaged in the drawer for paper, and composed a message.

"Take this to Halleck," he told Stanton, knowing the Secretary would approve without hesitation. "I want this under his signature, not mine or yours." That was what Halleck was for: professional military coloration.

Stanton read it aloud: "By direction of the President, it is ordered that Major General McClellan be relieved from command of the Army of the Potomac; and that Major General Burnside take command of that Army."

Stanton nodded vigorously. "Leave it undated," he said. "We want to give Halleck some discretion in sending it. It should be taken to Burnside first by a high-ranking officer, then to McClellan in person only after Burnside says he is willing to do his duty. I would not trust this to the telegraph; it may be that McClellan will listen to the traitors around him and try to march his army to take control of Washington."

Lincoln agreed, glad that Stanton had not tried to make an argument for Chase's choice, General Hooker; Burnside seemed more solid than the flamboyant "Fighting Joe." Also, McClellan was a longtime friend of Burnside, and that choice of a successor would be less likely to ignite an army coup.

Stanton gave Lincoln another suggestion: "Perhaps you should relieve Porter in the same order and give his command to Hooker. If Burnside gets an attack of modesty, Hooker and not Porter would be next in line to take command, and we need somebody like Hooker to stop what the West Pointers call 'a change of front to Washington.' And then I want to court-martial Porter for not supporting Pope back at Bull Run—that will break the back of the whole cabal."

Lincoln saw the wisdom in that and wrote it out: "That Major General Fitz-John Porter be relieved from the command of the corps he now commands in said Army; and that Major General Hooker take command of said corps."

That was the sort of tough-minded response to the election needed to whip the North into line. Lincoln knew it was not his usual way, of pushing others out ahead of him and appearing to be led in their direction, but sometimes a sharp blow needed a more forceful return blow.

Stanton said he would dispatch a general in his office to carry the secret order to Burnside, and then to McClellan, putting a new man in command of the 142,000 well-organized troops of the Army of the Potomac. "No one else is to know," Stanton sternly adjured him, "no other member of the Cabinet, Blair especially. This must not get out to McClellan through any source but the general I send to him."

Lincoln pledged absolute secrecy; it would be hard playing shut-pan with Old Man Blair, who was coming to see him that night at the Soldiers' Home, but it was clearly necessary.

"We'll have to inform Chase," Stanton said, adding with what struck Lincoln as an unfortunate note of vindictiveness: "Chase has an officer who will make sure we get the right verdict in the court-martial of Porter."

Lincoln was fairly sure that the only way to overcome electoral defeat— and a loss of thirty-two seats in the 179-man House was surely a defeat—was a show of renewed authority, followed by military victory. The place would be the gateway to Richmond, perhaps in the vicinity of Fredericksburg, and the man of the hour would be Ambrose Burnside.

CHAPTER 18

PLAYING SHUT-PAN

Francis Preston Blair drove his carriage the short distance from his Silver Spring home to the Soldiers' Home, where the President was staying. Lincoln, sitting on the porch in the crisp early winter evening, seemed curiously relaxed for a man whose party has just been trounced in an election. He congratulated Blair on his son's victory amidst the general Republican debacle in the House, and allowed as how the election result was largely caused by the absence of good Republicans who were away from home fighting the war, and the baneful effect of the newspapers.

The Old Man did not argue. Above all, he was determined not to become an I-told-you-so on the effect of emancipation in New York, where Greeley now looked the fool and Weed and Seward the wizards. Presidents, he knew, did not welcome advisers to tell them why they had been wrong. At times like these, presidents needed sympathetic listeners to the lame excuses, and men who could offer sensible advice as to what to do next to ameliorate the losses.

"I would like to make the case for retaining McClellan," he said at the appropriate moment. "Monty tells me you're on the verge."

"I have tried long enough," Lincoln replied, "to bore with an auger too dull to take hold."

"A certain torpidity of McClellan's must be infuriating at times," Blair admitted, rolling with the President's evident distaste toward the commander, "but consider the difficulty, as I am sure you must have, of finding any other general capable of wielding so great a force and so complicated a machine."

"He has got the slows, Mr. Blair."

"You're right. That is why it would be important to send some common friend of yours and his to reach an explicit understanding with him. Tell him what the President expected him to do and when, and tell him that absolute and prompt obedience was the tenure by which alone he held his command."

Lincoln looked at the night sky. It seemed to Blair that the President felt his talks with McClellan at Antietam obviated the need for an intermediary. Those talks had produced merely a six-week delay, at a time Lincoln needed a pre-election military victory.

"I'm not qualified to make the military argument," said Blair, he hoped disarmingly. "Maybe it took too long, but he's now across the Potomac, aggressively seeking out the enemy. He surely has a plan to divide the forces of Lee and Jackson and defeat them in detail, but I understand he has been unwilling to share that plan with you. That should be rectified right away."

"You're giving the military argument," Lincoln reminded him.

"Let's talk politics, then. What would be the political result of your superseding McClellan? You would be seen as yielding once more to the ultras in our party, and acting in defiance of the majority that just spoke in the election. That would weaken you at a time you cannot afford to be weakened."

"No doubt the bottom is out of the tub," the President said.

"If, on the contrary," the Old Man continued, "McClellan could be pushed hard now, on the line he has taken, and compelled to make a vigorous winter campaign, what political effect would that have?"

The President just listened. Blair took that uncharacteristic response to mean that Stanton and Chase had persuaded him to get even with the voters by ridding himself of McClellan. Why? It was illogical, on the basis of the facts in hand; the Old Man sensed that there must be another element in all this of which the Blairs were in the dark. Ever since midsummer, when Lincoln returned from his meeting with the general at Harrison's Landing, the Blair espousal of McClellan's cause had been met with a certain numbness. Had the general said anything insubordinate or overtly political?

"Consider for a moment what your strong support of McClellan would mean," he went on, squinting at the expressionless face of the President. "The Democrats in the Congress, who are in heart on the side of oligarchy and the South, would be compelled to make war on McClellan. In turn, McClellan would be compelled to take sides with you, bringing to your support in the Congress the real War Democrats."

"Interesting theory, Mr. Blair."

The former adviser to Jackson warmed to his theme. "After that, those trying to resuscitate the Democratic Party to carry the presidency in 1864 would necessarily take an anti-McClellan man for their candidate. That would split the Democrats and enable you to win again."

"And if, as a general, McClellan fails?"

"He fails as a Democrat and the Democrats fail with him. At least your cause would best be served by retaining him until he failed—and I do not believe he would, given a new impetus."

The President slowly shook his head. Blair, losing him, tried one last time: "If you replace him now, on the very eve of battle, and his replacement fails, then the Democrats will unite behind a formidable ticket in sixty-four: McClellan and Seymour. That could beat you, and everything we all stand for."

Lincoln seemed on the brink of confiding something, then held back. He rose, stretched his arms, and closed the discussion with, "I'm sorry to play shut-pan with you."

Let Lincoln keep his own counsel; it would not be the first time that advisers who had been all too accurate in their dire predictions were snubbed by a President stung by the consequences of not listening to good advice. On his way back to Silver Spring, the elder Blair focused on his goal: the best route for his youngest son to the vice-presidential nomination in two or six years—as either Republican or Democrat. A partnership with Lincoln would be best. If that did not work out, there was always the possibility of an alliance with Horatio Seymour.

CHAPTER 19

BLOODLESS WATERLOO

"Pinkerton reports a special train from Washington arrived at Rectortown a couple of hours ago," Colonel Thomas Key told McClellan abruptly, "with Stanton's aide, General Buckingham."

"Secure the flap," McClellan said, motioning toward the tent entrance, "the snow is coming in."

Key moved to the entrance, but backed away as Captain Custer struggled in out of the storm.

"Buckingham is not coming here," Custer added to Key's report. "He's ridden to Burnside's headquarters at Salem, about five miles from here."

"That's worrisome," Key told McClellan. "If Stanton is dealing directly with your corps commanders, it could mean a change of command is in the works."

McClellan nodded understanding. "Judge, I have been told about your young nephew's gallant death at Perryville. I've written to your brother John"—he interjected sadly—"the former Major Key. He must be doubly crushed."

Key took off his greatcoat before answering and moved near the stove for warmth. McClellan noted his pallor, and the film of sweat on his face; he was ill, perhaps the typhus, picked up just after the fighting at Antietam. "Sixteen, the boy was," Key replied. "Picked up a regimental flag and led a charge. I suppose that balances the family disgrace."

"Mightn't that change the President's mind?"

Key said with sadness that his brother's appeal, notwithstanding the death of the boy, had been turned down. Evidently, to President Lincoln, a lesson was a lesson: there could be no mercy in the setting of an example to the military.

"I can imagine what they're conspiring in Burnside's tent," said Custer, getting to the central issue. "But the army won't stand for it."

"Don't talk that way, Captain," Key snapped. "The Secretary of War has the right to send an aide to see any commander in the army. It's no conspiracy."

"Stanton is doing his best to sacrifice this army again," Custer replied hotly. "For God's sake, Colonel, just one week ago, Lincoln telegraphed how pleased he was with the movement of this army. Why is Stanton sending messengers to talk to Burnside behind the general's back?"

"It could be that we haven't taken Washington into our confidence sufficiently, General," Key said to McClellan.

"That isn't the problem," McClellan said. He felt at the peak of his powers —more sure of himself, satisfied with his line of supply from Harpers Ferry, no complaints about needed reinforcements—and confident, after Antietam, that he could defeat Lee again. He had won two in a row, counting the last battle on the Peninsula. He knew how to take advantage of Lee's rashness and over-reliance on Jackson.

"Halleck certainly knows how I intend to interpose my army between Longstreet and Jackson," he explained. "Mr. Lincoln may not agree with my strategy, but he surely knows what it is."

"Lincoln needed a military victory so he could win a political victory," said Custer flatly and, McClellan thought, accurately. "Simple as that."

"Just as we think the President wanted us to speed up the battle to take place before the elections," Key said carefully, "the radicals think we have been waiting until after Election Day to launch our offensive."

The general found some truth in that suspicion, too; it was easy to sit in Washington and order a tired and bloodied army of 140,000 men, short of shoes, to march immediately. Experienced generals knew that it took at least sixty days to reprovision and reorganize between major engagements.

"You don't understand," said Custer urgently. "They're planning to court-martial us all. The black Republicans cannot admit that their darling Pope lost at Second Bull Run, and that the man they hate won at Antietam. They have to prove that Pope's loss was our fault, and blacken our names forever. They'll court-martial McClellan, Porter, you, me—everybody who isn't a damned abolitionist."

Key's shudder told McClellan there was something in what Armstrong

Custer was saying: rumors were rife of a court-martial board aimed at Mc-
Clellan, Fitz-John Porter, and other unnamed "West Pointers" unsympathetic to abolition. Lincoln's personal cashiering of Key's brother John was a
deliberate signal; now that the elections were over, and the radical defeat
blamed on McClellan's "inactivity," Wade and the rest would be going after
the scalps of all those at the top of the Army of the Potomac.

But Burnside was exempt, as was Hooker, both outspoken abolitionists.
The charge of treason would probably be leveled at McClellan, surely at
Porter, and perhaps others who had failed to get Pope out of his scrape. Small
wonder, the general thought, that the reaction of a portion of the officer corps
to the beheading of McClellan's army would be to demand that McClellan
march on Washington. If the officers were to be denounced as traitors anyway, why not—as Patrick Henry once put it—make the most of it?

"Lincoln and Stanton and Halleck have fought you every step of the way,"
Custer was pressing on. "At the Peninsula, when reinforcements would have
enabled you to take Richmond from the rear, they brought McDowell's forty
thousand men back to sit in Washington to guard the Mansion."

The general nodded. "In the end, whoever is in command will have to
follow my plan," he predicted calmly. "From Gaines' Mill, Cold Harbor, the
Federal forces will have to move to the James River to make Richmond
untenable."

"Then they abandoned the only way to take Richmond," Custer said, "and
put their favorite abolitionist, Pope, in charge of a doomed campaign. And in
that disaster, not only do they blame you for not coming to his rescue but, by
God, Lincoln was willing to surrender Washington rather than give the command back to you!"

"Stanton, Chase, and Halleck," McClellan corrected him. "Not Lincoln.
Be fair."

"Halleck was wrong every step of the way toward Antietam," Custer went
on. "I have all the telegrams warning you against following Lee north into
Maryland. If you had listened to that nonsense, Lee would be in New York
today. You were the only one who could organize this army, and the only one
who saw where it had to move to stop Lee from defeating the North. Lincoln
and his crowd were all wrong, first to last. Now they want to disgrace and
maybe hang you, take the army into battle with a damned incompetent who
couldn't get his men across a bridge at Antietam all day long—and all because the damned politicians want to be sure you don't emerge the hero of the
war!"

"Take care not to talk treason," warned Key, mindful of his brother's fate.

"You know as well as I do what Stanton said to the radical senators,"
Custer shot back. "He said, 'It is not on our books that McClellan shall take
Richmond.' I say that is the real treason. General, the radicals hate you and
they fear you, and they are willing to sacrifice this army rather than see it
victorious under you."

McClellan looked to his older aide, a man of the law and a good Democrat,
albeit an abolitionist, to counter Custer's passion.

"Armstrong, we do not know what message it is that General Buckingham
bears, if any," said Colonel Key. "We also know that General Burnside, who

may be irritated at the moment because of our criticism of his inaction at Antietam, knows his limitations."

"That's fair to say," judged McClellan. "He turned down the command before, when they gave it to Pope. Burn knows better than anybody that he cannot command the entire army in the field."

"He'll follow political orders," disagreed Custer, "and take the Army of the Potomac to bloody disaster."

"Let's hope Burnside asks Buckingham for a delay," said Key, speaking his hopes. "We only need a few days, then we'll be out of telegraphic contact with Washington and into battle."

"We'll see," McClellan said. "I don't have to make any decision yet."

"General," Custer pleaded, "this army loves you. You have a responsibility to save tens of thousands of these brave men from certain death. Do not submit to an order that history will condemn as the most brazen injustice ever motivated by politics. Lead us, General—the Army of the Potomac will follow you."

McClellan studied the pen he had been using to write to his wife. The post-election dismissal of a general on the eve of battle—especially a general loved by the troops, to be replaced by one distrusted by the troops—would send a wave of anger through every corps and regiment. The army knew it was ready to fight, and about to fight, and the injustice, not to say the danger, of firing a commander on the pretext of not being ready or about to fight would profoundly affect the main body of troops. All it would take would be one moment of anger, and in twenty-four hours the *coup d'état* would be accomplished.

"History does not remember Cromwell kindly," Key said.

"It remembers Caesar kindly enough," countered Custer.

"This is the United States of America, a republic," Key said. "For nearly a century we have abided by a constitution, as no other nation in history ever has. General, do you want to be the man remembered as the one who shattered that tradition of political stability?" When McClellan remained impassive, Key put in a practical point: "Besides, Lincoln will never get Burn to agree to replace you."

The general, ever the tactician, smiled ruefully: "Unless he threatens to appoint Hooker instead. Burn couldn't stand that."

"I am unfit for the command," Burnside told Stanton's messenger unequivocally. "Do you have any idea what it is like to try to figure out what Bobby Lee and Thomas Jackson are about to do? And then to be responsible for the lives of thousands of men who trust your judgment, when you do not trust it yourself?"

In Ambrose Burnside's tent, snow swirling outside, Brigadier General Catharinus Putnam Buckingham began what he knew to be the only important military mission of his life: to persuade the man Lincoln had chosen to be commander of the Army of the Potomac to accept the assignment, clearing the way for the relief of George McClellan.

"I taught a little topography at West Point thirty years ago," Buckingham said. "Ever since, I've been a professor of mathematics at Kenyon College in Ohio. Couple of years ago, I built a grain elevator; that's my only accomplish-

Captain George Armstrong Custer

ment. I wear this star because Stanton thinks his adjutant should have one. I'm not a military man, sir. I can't answer your question."

Burnside sighed. "What does Stanton expect me to do that McClellan cannot do?"

"The Secretary of War has no confidence in McClellan's military ability."

"He's wrong. If he thinks I am a better general than McClellan, he's out of his mind. Ask the officers, ask the men. Ask me."

"Moreover," Buckingham carried on, "he has grave doubts about McClellan's patriotism and loyalty."

"Just as George doubts Stanton's, but that's a personal dispute between two men. Surely President Lincoln does not subscribe to the Secretary's harsh indictment of a loyal soldier's patriotism."

"The President doesn't take me into his confidence, General, but I know this: Mr. Lincoln has said that if McClellan permitted Lee to slip away, he would fire him."

"What the hell does that mean?"

"I was hoping you'd know."

"But that's nonsense."

Buckingham blinked. It seemed to make sense to most of those who heard it.

"Don't tell the President I said this," Burnside reasoned, "but that cannot be the reason he wants to remove McClellan. General Lee is not a fool. He is not going to let any Union army get behind him to attack Richmond. There has never been any chance of that—not right after Antietam, not now. Every time McClellan moves South to threaten Lee's communications, Lee retreats South. Pete Longstreet just isn't the sort to let us run around behind him. To think that is just—silly. Is that what Stanton expects the commander to do?"

"No," Buckingham said hastily. "Not now—that chance to stop Lee's escape has passed. Lincoln and Halleck have a plan to drive Lee down to the Rappahannock, cross on pontoon bridges, and strike him near Fredericksburg."

"McClellan has a better plan," said Burnside. "To catch Lee much sooner, near Gordonsville, with Jackson the other side of the Blue Ridge."

"Lincoln's plan would offer more protection to Washington," the mathematics professor said, "I think. But General, I cannot really argue strategy. I must know if you are willing to do your duty and accept command."

"I have always done my duty. Sometimes duty demands that you inform your superiors of a mistake."

"But you don't understand, Burnside—unless I have your agreement, I cannot deliver the order to McClellan relieving him of command."

"Why not?"

Buckingham decided that Burnside might just be as thick as he made himself out to be. "Because if we do not have a man immediately in place when we dismiss him, McClellan might just take the army to Washington tomorrow and proclaim himself dictator. That's why."

Burnside thought that over. "Lincoln complains that McClellan has the slows. And yet we are now on the eve of battle, if McClellan stays. If I were to take over, I would need at least a month to organize staff, to get into position. More likely six weeks before any major engagement."

"The President and the Secretary are aware of that. You won't be rushed."

Burnside frowned, stroking his strange whiskers. "Then delay is not Lincoln's reason either, is it?"

Buckingham was on the verge of giving up. He played his last card. "My orders, General, are first to obtain your agreement, and secondly, with you at my side, present General McClellan with his dismissal. But if you fail to accept your responsibility, my orders are to proceed to General Hooker and make the same arrangement with him. I am told he is sufficiently recovered from his wound to take command."

Burnside snorted. "Some 'wound'! If Joe Hooker had had the courage to stay and fight at Antietam, I would have carried that bridge early in the day and Lee would have been routed and the war over. Hooker's appointment would be a disaster."

"In effect, you are ceding the command to him."

Buckingham let Burnside agonize in silence. Finally Burnside said, "My appointment is merely a mistake. Hooker's would be a catastrophe." He sighed. "Let's go and tell George."

A half hour before midnight, as he was writing to his wife, McClellan heard a tap on the tent pole. He called out for whoever it was to enter, and was not surprised to see Burnside and Halleck's adjutant, the mathematics teacher.

He greeted them cordially, ignoring the solemn looks on both faces, and engaged them in conversation to show his lack of concern at their mission.

"I think we had better tell General McClellan the object of our visit," Buckingham told Burnside, who nodded glumly.

Stanton's adjutant handed over the orders signed by Halleck: "General: On receipt of the order of the President, sent herewith, you will immediately turn over your command to Maj. Gen. Burnside, and repair to Trenton, N. J., reporting on your arrival at that place, by telegraph, for further orders."

McClellan saw that both men, especially Buckingham, were watching him most intently as he read the order and the attachment making the removal official. The mathematics teacher in a general's uniform from Stanton's office surely knew McClellan had the power to reject the order, to protect himself and his leading officers from courts-martial and possible execution, and to make himself commander in chief. Poor Burn was probably hoping McClellan would do just that, saving him from the terrible choice of taking unwanted command or handing this fine army over to Hooker.

McClellan knew what he had to do because he had no doubt about what he was: an officer of the United States Army and a loyal American citizen. He handed the papers to his unhappy and fearful friend with a brief, "Well, Burnside, I turn the command over to you."

He said it as if no other course were thinkable; George McClellan hoped that never again would a military officer of the United States be faced with the temptation presented to him that night.

Buckingham closed his eyes and took a deep breath, as if the other course had been narrowly averted. Stanton had probably poisoned the man's mind, McClellan assumed, causing him to expect a loyal soldier to turn traitor and usurper.

"I will leave in the morning, Burn. You have been as near as possible to me on this march, and I have kept you closely informed on the condition of affairs. You ought to be able to take the reins in your hands without a day's delay."

McClellan had planned for this eventuality, assuming that Lincoln would turn to Burnside, who was acceptable to the radicals, rather than to the respected Fitz-John Porter, the only general other than himself capable of facing Lee. He wondered which of them would face court-martial, Porter or himself, or both. The trial of George McClellan would certainly be dramatic, but perhaps too divisive; the radicals would probably go after Fitz instead.

He had hoped for more from Lincoln, especially after that last message of encouragement. Surely the President knew the next battle would be decisive, and it was less than a week away. Had he shown the commander in chief the proper respect? On mature reflection, he had to admit not always, certainly not in the beginning. But now that McClellan was showing his willingness to work in tandem with the civilian side, his service was rejected. He could see an irony in that, a belated justice that became injustice.

"I beseech you," Burnside said, "stay a few days, settle the officers down. I need you to transfer their loyalty over to me, as much as possible."

"To stay a revolt," Buckingham put it plainly.

Poor Burn; again, McClellan would have to try to save him, at least long enough to stumble into an engagement planned by Lincoln himself. Staying on as the replaced commander would be painfully demeaning, but McClellan would do his duty. He consented. His two visitors shouldered their way out of the tent into the driving snow.

He took up his pen and continued the one comfort of his life in the field, a letter to Nellie. "Another interruption, this time more important. It was in the shape of Burnside, accompanied by Gen. Buckingham. They brought with them the order relieving me from the command of the Army of the Potomac. No cause is given.

"Alas for my poor country! I know in my inmost heart she never had a truer servant. Do not be at all worried, my dear Nellie—I am not. I have done the best I could for my country; to the last I have done my duty as I understand it. That I must have made many mistakes, I cannot deny. I do not see any great blunders, but no one can judge of himself. Our consolation must be that we have tried to do what is right."

What would have been wrong was to seize the presidency. What he had come to see was right was to challenge Lincoln legitimately, in two years' time, as the candidate of the Democratic Party.

CHAPTER 20

IN JACKSON'S CHAIR

Darkness fell early in late November and Lincoln nodded gratefully to William for lighting the gas lamp on his desk. Hill Lamon was running a political errand; Nicolay and Hay had gone to eat at Willard's.

William asked if he would be taking dinner at his desk and he nodded; Mrs. Lincoln was in New York on one of her shopping trips. Angry at him for refusing to appoint one of her most unworthy favorites to an undeserved position, for three days before she left for Boston and New York she had refused to sleep in the room next to his. These petulant moods of hers came and went.

Stoddard, the third secretary, came in with a couple of pins to put in the map on the table. The pins with blue sealing wax on their heads signified Union battalions. After both William and Stod left, Lincoln rose from his desk chair, studied the map, and was pleased to see that Burnside was moving south toward Fredericksburg where the Union troops could fall upon Lee's army.

Burnside, though not one to inspire confidence, at least did what he was told. A year ago, Lincoln had been intimidated by the general officers, particularly the West Pointers, persuaded by his ignorance of military maneuver to rely on them for decisions in the war. Now he felt that he knew as much as any of them, and Halleck—a first-rate clerk and nothing more—would serve to reassure the public that well-trained military minds were in charge. But he had concluded that military men never understood the political dimensions of military strategy. Sometimes action or just activity, even if premature in purely military terms, was needed to enable the government to spur the people to raise troops and money. Ambrose Burnside might cavil at a point of tactics here and there, but he showed a refreshing humility when it came to sharing plans and carrying out orders.

Rocking back and forth in his shoes, looking at the pins in the map, Lincoln was glad he had not been forced to choose Hooker to replace McClellan. Too rash, just as George was too cautious. Had he been wise to relieve the Young Napoleon on the eve of battle, after he had finally begun to move on Lee's army? Lincoln thought that over again and decided he had been right. With the elections over, the Peace Democrats who had been using McClellan, along with the West Point element that wished to settle the war, had to be dealt with firmly. Besides, the radicals were desperate for an excuse for the Republican election defeat, and McClellan's tendency to delay was as good a reason as any.

Lincoln could not deny a personal affection for George, despite the man's fits of arrogance. He felt a twinge of conscience when he recalled the way the young general had stepped forward to defend the capital when Stanton and the others were ready to evacuate, and the way the general had manfully accepted his dismissal, showing none of the mutinous inclinations that Stanton and the others had feared.

But McClellan's goal in this war was not Lincoln's goal, as the episode with Major Key had demonstrated; moreover, the Collector of the Port of New York, Hiram Barney, Chase's man, had reported to him the discussions McClellan had been holding with Barlow, the New York Democratic leader. Barlow had told Barney, and Barney passed it along to Lincoln and Welles, that General McClellan planned to pursue a policy line of his own, regardless of the Administration's wishes and objects. Lincoln, remembering, shook his head at such perfidy. Yes, the evidence was hearsay, but he believed it because it was of a piece with the Harrison's Landing letter.

Perhaps if George had taken on Frank Blair as his chief of staff, as old Francis Blair had wanted him to, communications between field headquarters and the Executive Mansion would have been much improved; but no, McClellan had seen that as an effort to put a Lincoln man in his tent, and had rejected the idea. In retrospect, Lincoln assured himself, firing McClellan after his organizational usefulness had ended was inevitable; the Union could not remain whole with a commander more inclined to peace than victory.

Grant, out West, had been a possibility as a replacement, but he had a way of being away from his troops at critical moments, and the drinking was a problem. Even Congressman Washburne, whose protégé Grant was, was now having his doubts: Chase had come in with a letter from Washburne's brother, a general in Grant's command, painting a disturbing picture of conditions at Grant's headquarters. Not merely drinking and carousing, but commercial corruption. Grant was a fighter, and Lincoln respected that, but he could ill afford to take a chance with the most important command in the nation. Burnside, whose only personal quirk was a pair of silly muttonchop whiskers, offered the least risk.

Thinking of Chase reminded him of a worry. He went back to his desk, reached in the drawer, and took out a new greenback. The signature of the Treasurer looked real; that was the trouble, it looked too real. Did that not suggest infinite possibilities of fraud and embezzlement? Lincoln had to sign every commission of every assistant paymaster for it to be legal, and his hand hurt from signing sometimes; he was aware, too, that all government bonds were signed by hand by the Treasurer. That the paper currency seemed to be so signed, but was instead engraved, troubled him. He would have to talk with Chase about that in the morning.

Nor did he relish the likelihood that the Executive Mansion would be accused of mismanagement of funds. "Honest Abe," he was called; he hated the "Abe" but he intended to keep the "honest" part. He wished he could fire Watt, the gardener, but Mother protected him fiercely; it was all Lincoln could do to keep the stationery fund out of his hands. And he was the one she had taken with her to New York.

He walked out of his office, through the anteroom that served as the office of Nicolay and Hay, across the dark hallway to Stoddard's mailroom, hoping to find the young writer from Springfield. Stod had lent a helpful hand in the early political campaigns. He was a bit on the stuffy side, but was a fair writer and a good listener; Lincoln liked to try out speeches and important letters on him. Nicolay and Hay treated Stod like dirt, so Lincoln compensated from time to time by taking him along at night to visit Seward across the park.

Nobody in the office. Lincoln turned up the gaslight and looked at the mountain of mail on the desk—mostly, he knew, from conservatives complaining about his dismissal of McClellan or from radicals complaining about his failure to dismiss Seward. "Billy Bowlegs" was the new target of the radicals, Wade and Chandler stirring everyone up, Stanton and probably Chase quietly encouraging them; to their taste, Seward was insufficiently abolitionist. To Lincoln's taste, his Secretary of State was just right on slavery, and had supported a gradual approach from the start. The radicals, having tasted blood on McClellan, were now lusting after Seward. Lincoln had been prepared to toss them McClellan for his own reasons, but he was not about to sacrifice the man he was most comfortable with in the Cabinet.

His gaze lit on Andy Jackson's chair. Placed near the fireplace in Stod's room was that strange-looking chair, unlike any other item of furniture in the Mansion. Designed for reclining, it sloped backward, the slender mahogany frame held together by finely tooled leather. The Mexican-made chair had been in the Mansion since it had been sent to President Jackson; Mother didn't like the looks of it, and Lincoln preferred his cushioned couch, so the historic chair had found its way into the third secretary's office. Lincoln decided to try it out. He sat his long frame in it, gingerly at first, and found to his surprise that it accommodated him nicely.

Perfect for contemplating the ceiling, the Mexican recliner was conducive to rumination. Wiggling himself comfortable, Lincoln concluded that Andrew Jackson must have used it rarely. Jackson, a military man of action, had known how to enlarge his powers to fit his responsibilities; that could have had much to do with the fact that he was the last American President to have been reelected. Strange that he should understand Jackson's needs now; for so many years, as a Whig, Lincoln like his political allies had denounced the monarchic hunger of "King Andrew the First."

"Oh, why should the spirit of mortal be proud?" he said aloud into the silence, stretching out as far as he could and preparing to recite the entire poem. Then he changed his mind: the lines that came to him were from Shakespeare's Richard II, and he closed his eyes to visualize the monarch's cry of despair:

> "For God's sake, let us sit upon the ground
> And tell sad stories of the death of kings:
> How some have been depos'd, some slain in war . . ."

Lincoln groped for the next lines, could not remember them, and skipped ahead:

> "All murder'd: for within the hollow crown
> That rounds the mortal temples of a king
> Keeps Death his court, and there the antick sits,
> Scoffing his state and grinning at his pomp;
> Allowing him a breath, a little scene,
> To monarchize, be fear'd, and kill with looks,
> Infusing him with self and vain conceit
> As if this flesh which walls about our life
> Were brass impregnable; and humor'd thus
> Comes at the last, and with a little pin
> Bores through his castle wall, and farewell king!"

Lincoln's fingers held the imaginary pin and twisted it through the castle wall to dispatch the king. That reminded him of the blue-headed pins on the map in his office; he frowned, breathed deeply, and allowed himself to feel guilty about avoiding work on his second message to Congress. He had to write his portion of that in the next week.

He would give the border states one last chance to join with the Democrats and conservative Republicans in preventing the drastic action contemplated in the proclamation of emancipation. The more he thought of it, the more that proclamation—to take effect five weeks from now unless the South relented—seemed not merely radical, but revolutionary. The Blairs and Weed had been right about the voters' reaction to an act that Lincoln knew was so clearly unconstitutional. He had struck back hard at that reaction, cleaning out the army and letting Stanton go to work on the disunionists in the North; now, having demonstrated his willingness to use the stick, perhaps it was time for the carrot.

He had little doubt that once carried out on January 1, the edict of emancipation would make impossible any negotiated settlement of the war. Jeffy D. would see that as the final challenge to the South, the political lunge for the jugular when the North's military campaign was not succeeding. But having issued the threat, could he now not offer a stay of its execution? There was no magic in the date of January 1, 1863; the date of final emancipation might just as well be January 1, 1900, provided everyone agreed the day of slavery's demise would surely come. He thought it only fair that the large portion of the body politic that was not represented by the radical Republicans had a final opportunity to embrace gradual, compensated emancipation.

Jackson's chair was growing uncomfortable but he did not want to change position while a new approach was forming in his mind. The only way to make abolition constitutional was by amending the Constitution.

The amendment he had in mind would put off the abolishment of slavery until the year 1900, which would mitigate the opposition of those who held slaves today. It would provide just compensation, with a bond issue to finance the purchase of freedom. And it would provide for voluntary deportation in congenial climes when new homes could be found for negroes in lands of their own blood and race. What could be more reasonable? If the Congress or the states in rebellion wanted to stop his emancipation edict set to come on January first, all they had to do was to adopt the amendment and then appropriate the money to buy up and manumit all slaves by the start of the next century.

He had worked out the figures: Since the revolution, the nation had been growing at the rate of 35 percent every ten years. By 1930, if the present trend of growing by one third every ten years continued, that American family would be over 250,000,000 people—greater than that of Europe, provided the nation did not split up or otherwise inhibit the natural growth of its population.

Nobody could say he had failed to try. The case, thus put, was new; perhaps the Congress, too long held in thrall by the slavery issue, could be made to see that it had to think anew and act anew. In giving freedom to the slave four decades hence, the amendment would assure freedom to the free in the meantime and after. By paying hard cash for every slave, it would not offend the Founders' compromise; by encouraging the freedmen to emigrate, it would not upset white workers.

Lincoln would have no trouble with the peroration of such a message: it should exhort the Congress to nobly save the last best hope of earth, lest inaction cause the Congress to meanly lose it. That thought could be put more positively.

He asked himself, as a practical politician: would the amendment idea be accepted or rejected by the Congress? As matters stood now, probably the radicals would holler that he had sold them out and the conservatives would still not seize their last chance, and the proposal would fail. But his conscience would be clearer in usurping property rights on the first of January—and more to the point, if Burnside was able to whip Lee's army at Fredericksburg, his amendment would suddenly look much more attractive to the states in rebellion, and the loyal slave states too.

With another Union military victory, and the path to Richmond opened, little "military necessity" for unconstitutional emancipation would exist. Instead, a political necessity might well be created to reunite North and South under terms that would guarantee the abolition of slavery, but by constitutional means and not until the next generation. Lincoln resolved to meet with General Burnside at Aquia Creek, near his headquarters, at dark tomorrow night. Nothing was more urgent than a triumph at Fredericksburg soon. He would go over every detail with the man; the army would have everything it needed this time.

Lincoln was pleased with his amendment alternative; it was a way to restate his central idea of majority rule, with a practical and absolutely constitutional solution to the matter that was more on the minds of the people. He slid down even farther in the Jackson chair—better for his back but his feet overhung the end. The chair, he decided, was better left here in Stod's office than moved to his own.

He saw the occasion to be piled high with difficulty. But it was surely as difficult for the Southern leaders, now faced with squabbling within the Confederate states as Georgia resisted the dictates of Richmond. Was he doing all he could to make it easier for voices of reason and reunion to be heard down there? The finality of his promised January 1 edict troubled him as that date approached all too quickly. He did not want to give at least half the North cause to criticize him for closing the door to peace: in New York, for example, Fernando Wood was passing the word that only an amnesty from Lincoln was needed to enable Southern leaders to return to the next session of the Congress. Did Mayor Wood and Governor-elect Seymour have any secret contact with like-minded men in the South, or were they making mischief?

Lincoln turned his shoes overhanging the chair inward and outward, as he could do without pain since his corns had been miraculously attended to.

Zacharie. The Israelite had family in the South, had volunteered to make contact with Southern leaders, and pointed out that Judah Benjamin was a co-religionist. Lincoln knew that General Nat Banks wanted the Israelite along in New Orleans when he relieved Ben Butler, to help with the unofficial gold exchange. It might seem slightly ludicrous to send Dr. Zacharie south to attend to the feet of the Union Army, and while he was at it, to see if the rumors about Southern interest in amnesty had any foundation—but it would do no harm. Certainly the corncutter would arouse no suspicion and his real purpose could readily be denied, even laughed off.

Generals Grant and Sherman, Lincoln was aware, believed fiercely that Jewish peddlers in their command were a cause of the army's corruption, and the President had heard that there was an unofficial ban on admitting any more Israelites to the area, but that would not apply to anyone with a pass from him. He strongly doubted that the men in Richmond would be ready to talk peace until Burnside was at the gates and Lee whipped, but he wanted to be sure.

Lincoln pulled himself out of Jackson's chair to return to his office and write out a pass. But more important than sending an unlikely agent on what was likely to be a wild-goose chase, it was time for him to get started on the draft amendment in the message to Congress. The beliefs of the past were inadequate to the present, he would exhort them; rewriting in his head, as he walked back through the dark hall to his office, he added "quiet" to the past and "stormy" to the present, for the emphasis of contrast. And "beliefs" did not have the negative connotation he sought; "dogmas" was the word.

CHAPTER 21

JEPHTHA'S DAUGHTER

A man Chase recognized as Lincoln's bodyguard, Marshal Lamon, showed up at the door of the house at Sixth and E before breakfast.

"The President is worried about the integrity of our financial system," the broad-shouldered Westerner told the Treasury Secretary. "He wants you to come as soon as you can."

Chase looked hard at the man. His portion of the annual message was not due until the next day. Was Lincoln trying something to make him look dishonest? Had anyone been poisoning the President's mind about the dealings with Jay Cooke? "I'll be in to see him before the Cabinet meeting."

"Sooner would be better," Lamon replied. "Right now would be best."

Chase turned to Kate, who appeared behind him. "The imperial summons."

"If Mr. Lincoln is so worried," she asked Lamon coldly, "why didn't he come over with you this morning?"

That irritating thought had crossed Chase's mind too; when Lincoln wanted to see Seward, the President did not send for him; rather, he strolled across Lafayette Square to the Secretary of State's house. Seward was evermore Lincoln's *éminence grise;* now that McClellan had been driven from the scene, the man who next needed removal was the Secretary of State.

"I'm sure the President knows I'm always available to him," Chase said through his daughter to Lamon. With a twinge of conscience troubling him, Chase did not want to appear to stand on ceremony; perhaps Lamon, who was as much crony and confidant to Lincoln as bodyguard, knew what the President had on his mind. On the ride over, Chase could frame the answers about Cooke's exclusive and lucrative representation of the Treasury in the sale of its notes.

Climbing into the carriage, Chase asked, "What's bothering the President?"

"The greenback currency. Up to last night, he thought that Spinner was signing each bill himself."

Chase rode to the Mansion in silence, relieved that the integrity being questioned was the system's and not his own. Surely Lincoln could not be so naïve as to think that old Spinner signed every single greenback issued; that was the way it had been done at the start, and the poor fellow had found himself scribbling his signature twenty hours a day. Engraving the signature was the only way to keep up production. Lincoln must know that; what was really going through his suspicious mind?

At the entrance to the Mansion, Lamon reined in the horse and turned the reins over to the black man at the door, offering Chase a hand down from the carriage. The Treasury Secretary declined the help.

"Chase, there are not sufficient safeguards to afford any degree of safety in the money-making department," Lincoln said at once, no offer of coffee or anything.

The President expressed his worry that some unscrupulous operators could run off thousands of greenbacks and no one would be the wiser until the day of redemption, when a huge fraud would be discovered and his administration would be covered with shame.

Chase tried to reason with him. "In the nature of things," he told the nervous Lincoln, "somebody must be trusted in this emergency. You have entrusted me, and I have entrusted Francis Spinner, the Treasurer, with untold millions. When he was a congressman, they called him 'the watchdog of the Treasury.' We have to trust our subordinates."

The President was not in a trusting mood. He wanted to know exactly how Chase was protecting the public from the counterfeit printing of millions in excess greenbacks. As Lincoln's words waxed warmer, Chase began to wonder about his own lack of concern; could Lincoln be onto something? Who was actually counting the money that was being printed?

"It strikes me that this thing is all wrong, and dangerous." Lincoln had never before taken such an interest in the Treasury operations. "I and the country know you and Mr. Spinner, but we don't know your subordinates, who have the power to bankrupt the government in an hour."

Chase was nonplussed; he had gone along with the idea of greenbacks at Lincoln's urging. Indeed, when he had expressed his reservations on constitutional grounds, the President had told him that he was prepared to violate the Constitution to save the Union. The idea of paper money had worked, amazingly so; public trust was such that the paper was treated like real money, and was in effect a huge, interest-free loan from the people to the government.

"Spinner has been hiring women," Chase blurted, so that he could not be accused later of concealing anything of moment from the President.

"As employees of the government?" Lamon was surprised.

"They're very good at counting money," Chase explained. "Nimble fingers, good on the close detail work, and they never miss a day's work. I am prepared to take whatever criticism the policy causes." Chase was well aware that the potential for scandal existed when men and women were placed in close proximity, with the advancement of the women employees in the hands of male supervisors, but skilled money counters were in short supply. Now the unprecedented employment of women was Lincoln's problem as much as his.

"Perhaps we can protect ourselves by involving the Congress," Marshal Lamon offered. Lincoln nodded, and urged Chase to talk it over with his friends in the Senate.

"Yes, in particular Senator Sprague," Chase suggested. "Very sound on this. And he can keep financial matters to himself, which we need." He added a warning about the matter that had originally triggered the President's concern: "Not a word of your worries about the engraving of signatures on greenbacks, Lincoln, must get to the public. Jay Cooke and I have enough trouble maintaining confidence. Don't you start a run on the bank."

The President, with a pained last look at his own face on a greenback, nodded agreement.

Chase took his leave and walked across the street to his Treasury office, satisfied that Lincoln's fears could be handled, but worried about discovery of his relationship with Cooke. He was also vulnerable to misunderstanding on his dealings with Hiram Barney, Collector of the Port of New York. What if Thurlow Weed and Seward, who resented the way Chase had snatched away their New York patronage, found out and made a fuss in the newspapers? His chance at replacing Lincoln on the Republican ticket in 1864 would be ruined.

It was awkward for a man in his position, dealing in millions, to be personally short of funds. Nor was the problem likely to disappear in years to come; if anything, it would grow worse with the need to entertain potential delegates and keep up appearances. And every time the President sent Lamon over on some silly worry, Chase knew his own too-sensitive conscience would afflict him with the fear that somebody was impugning his integrity. That thought depressed him further.

Kate was at the office when he arrived. He shook his head to the unasked question, saying only, "Just some foolishness about Spinner's signature being engraved on the paper. If Lincoln knows as little about military affairs as he does about finance, the country is in worse trouble than I feared."

She closed the door to the office and faced her father across his desk. "I suppose the time has come when we have to make some sacrifices."

"You've been very good, Kate, about making do with last year's wardrobe," he began, and would have gone on in a fatherly way, but her grim look told him she had more far-reaching sacrifices in mind.

"Bill Sprague and I had a quarrel last week," she said. "I didn't like the way he was drinking, and making a mess all over himself in public. I told him I wouldn't put up with it any more."

Chase winced, hoping his daughter had not pushed Sprague too far. His support was absolutely essential to their plans. The Rhode Island Legislature had accommodated its state's richest family by electing the former governor and general to be senator; Sprague now had control of future convention delegates, and his influence reached into Massachusetts. "I'm certain your good advice will encourage him to reform. He adores you, as you know. He's told me that often."

"He tells that to everybody when he's in his cups," Kate said sourly. "No, he won't reform. He's a drunkard and always will be. Let's not fool ourselves about the boy governor."

Chase's heart sunk; would she never see Sprague again? Would she throw herself away on the effete Lord Lyons or the defeated Roscoe Conkling, or indulge her desires with young Hay, or become scandalously involved with a married man like Garfield? Sprague had his faults, but there were compensations, and his redemption from an unfortunate tendency toward a reliance on John Barleycorn might be possible under the influence of a good woman.

Chase could not bring himself to say that. If Kate intended to put her selfish interests ahead of their mutual dream, he would not try to dissuade her. Any such suasion he judged to be morally wrong. He thought of the biblical general Jephtha, who vowed if he won a victory to make a burnt offering of the first living thing that came through his door; to his horror, his daughter and only child was first, and she expressed her love by willingly becoming his sacrifice. No—Chase told himself that Kate had her own life to lead; he had hoped their ambitions were parallel, but the painful compromises demanded by politics were better understood by those who had suffered as he had.

"I am aware," he began, drawing a deep breath, "that you have been brought up to enjoy the company of men of substance and temperance. Lord Lyons. Senator Sumner—"

"And Salmon Portland Chase, who has the strength of character never to make a fool of himself. Father, you've spoiled me for men the likes of Sprague."

He hardly knew what to say to that, except, "Perhaps you underestimate him."

"Bill Sprague is impossible to underestimate. John Hay is quite right—he's a small, insignificant youth who bought his place." She seated herself and looked at her father levelly. "When would the announcement be most advantageous?"

He had been looking at the portrait of Alexander Hamilton over the fireplace, thinking of the cruel shortening of the first Treasury Secretary's career. He did not quite comprehend the import of his daughter's question. "Announcement?"

"My betrothal to Senator William Sprague of Rhode Island," Kate said, seeming to test the words for a printed invitation, "savior of our nation's capital in the early days of the rebellion, gallant general in command of his state's fighting men, confidential adviser to the President and Treasury Secretary on financial affairs, darling of the social salons of Washington, and well-known drunkard."

"Kate, are you serious? If you are, you must not act in a spirit of hypocrisy. Marriage is a sacred covenant before God—"

"I am deadly serious, Father. Becoming President is a serious business, and I am prepared to make the necessary sacrifices. And never, never speak to me of hypocrisy."

He was torn between delight at her sensible decision and his dread of sacrilege. After a moment, Chase was able to dismiss the latter as unworthily judgmental; who was he to dismiss a long tradition of marriages of convenience, which so often led to warm lifelong companionships, based as they were on shared interests rather than youthful passion? His own first marriage, to the unforgettable Katherine, had been a love match that had ended with her death of childbed fever; his second wife was also the object of his love, and died giving birth to Kate; but the third time he had been more prudent, selecting a judge's daughter of strength and health and social background, who served as a fine, if necessarily stern, stepmother for seventeen years before her death. If Kate could show the maturity in her early twenties that it had taken him much longer to attain, so much the better.

"I'm very proud of you, Katie. I know you will be happy."

"I'll be happy as the official hostess in the Executive mansion," she said with what he felt was unnecessary calculation, "with the country in the hands of President Chase."

He hoped his expression bore the proper humility. She drummed her fingers on his desk. "The spring would be the best time. We have the household money to hold out till then. Sprague's mother is a smart old lady, and she

William Sprague and Kate Chase Sprague

likes me; I can talk to her about the finances of a big wedding without involving you or the boy gov."

"I do not think that a proper sobriquet for your chosen husband-to-be," Chase said disapprovingly. "He is familiarly known as Bill. Or you could now call him 'the senator.' And you should not go ahead with this with avarice in your heart, Katie, I won't allow anything of—"

"Don't tell me what should or should not be in my heart," she snapped. "It's not love and it's not avarice. I don't need fancy clothes and expensive furnishings, you know that. I want to amount to something, and I want you to be all you should be."

He nodded, understanding that her decision was, if not based on love for her prospective husband, at least rooted in love for her father. He reproved himself for thinking her at first selfish and later calculating. She was a good daughter and, he was certain, would make an excellent wife. He went around the desk, assisted her to her feet, and embraced her with pride and tenderness. "You have my blessing, Katie."

She hugged him tightly for a moment, the way she had when she was small and had fled from her stepmother, and then stepped back to look directly up at him.

"I want more than a blessing, Father. I want a promise. I'll do my part."

"And I'll do mine," he said, hoping she would not become specific.

"You know what I expect," she said.

He knew exactly: no more letters to the office from Adele Douglas, no more visits at home from Anna Carroll, no possibility of remarriage until after the presidency, if then. The sacrifice was real—prolonged celibacy would be new to him—and he could not avoid the feeling that her demand was somehow unnatural. But her own sacrifice was at least as great, and the thought of his dutiful and self-assured daughter as hostess in his White House appealed to him. Kate would be far better received than Mary Lincoln.

"I hope always to live up to your expectations, Katie," he said, hoping she would find a meaning in that beyond his words.

She kissed him lightly on the cheek and made ready to leave. She drew on a vest espagnole, which he presumed to be the latest fashion since he had seen Addie Douglas in one recently, and the black-embroidered Moresco cloak brought down the week before by Jay Cooke. She had adorned her bonnet with wood violets and ties of lilac ribbon. "Say nothing for the time being, Father. I have some loose ends to tidy up. Perhaps you do too. Wait a week, and then arrange for the—for Bill to be summoned to Washington."

As she left, it occurred to him that hers would be the most glittering wedding that wartime Washington had yet seen. He began to think of a guest list. Which of their acquaintances would be most likely to determine the delegates to the next Republican convention?

CHAPTER 22

JOHN HAY'S DIARY
DECEMBER 7, 1862

Dr. Zacharie, our favorite foot man, is back from a couple of months at Fort Monroe, where he says he operated successfully on the feet of 5,000 of our soldiers—or 5,000 individual feet, I don't recall which. After uprooting these vast cornfields, he has returned to Washington to check on the impedimenta of the President.

I should not make sport of his profession because he brought both the Prsdt and the SecState great relief. The Tycoon used to hobble about in the King of Morocco's huge gift slippers because he could not stand shoes. No more; thanks to his friend Isachar, with whom he has these extended conversations after his treatments, the Prsdt bounds about as I have never seen before.

The Israelite came into the office devastated that word of his ministrations to the President had leaked. The Israelite assured us that the editorial in the *New York Herald* last week was not of his doing, and was anxious lest the notoriety impinge on his confidential relationship. Isachar did not know his man. I had put the cutting on the Prsdt's desk, and he read portions aloud to the somewhat uncomfortable foot surgeon with great glee.

"Says here, 'we have a cornucopia of information' about your activities, Doctor," Lincoln grinned, reading on: " 'The President has been greatly blamed for not resisting the demands of the radicals; but how could the President put his foot down firmly when he was troubled with corns?' That's pretty good. Says the bickering in the Cabinet has been—here—'caused by the honorable Secretaries inadvertently treading on each other's bunions under the council board.' "

"Not a word of any of this came from me," Zacharie said, looking miserable.

Lincoln positively cackled at the editorial. " 'No human being could be expected to toe the mark under such circumstances, which originated not so much with the head as with the feet of the nation.' " The Tycoon gave one of his great hee-hee laughs, hardly able to finish with " 'Dr. Zacharie has shown us precisely where the shoe pinches.' By jings, that's all right."

Zacharie perked up as it became clear that the Tycoon was amused and not upset by the public notice of his corns. Foot doctors must be sensitive to the way people poke fun at their profession, but Zacharie, I am sure, is torn between fear of ridicule and desperation for recognition. Well, he has claim to fame now. He is without doubt the most famous Jewish foot doctor in the world.

I suspect the President is pleased with the publicity for another reason. He intends to use the Israelite as an agent to get information from the South. The corn cutting that all of us are so quick to mock has the virtue of removing all suspicion from his clandestine activities.

"I see that you are sending General Banks to replace Butler in New Orleans," Zacharie said. Lincoln nodded; Banks had been a better governor of Massachusetts than a general in the field against Stonewall Jackson, but Lincoln trusted Banks to manage our biggest Southern capture more honestly than "the Beast."

Zacharie looked at me, wishing I were out of the room, I suppose, and said, "I think the time is ripe for my mission." Since the Prsdt did not throw me out, I looked at the ceiling, and Zacharie went on with his half-concealed plans: "The sister of the gentleman in Richmond is in New Orleans now, and in some distress. I should intercede on her behalf with the new Union commander."

I presumed "the gentleman in Richmond" was Judah Benjamin, the rebel Secretary of State and Zacharie's co-religionist. I doubt that we are planning to get any military information out of Jeff Davis's Cabinet; could it be that Mr. Lincoln has in mind a roundabout exploration of the peace rumors? He wants to do something before January first.

"I'll need a personal letter from you to Banks," said Zacharie, "telling him to take me to New Orleans with him."

Lincoln nodded. "While there is nothing in this which I shall dread to see in history, it is, perhaps, better for the present that it should not become public." That was putting it mildly. Zacharie could pass the word broadside about his corn-curing prowess, but on checking into supposed peace probes, the Tycoon expected great discretion.

"The pass," Zacharie reminded him. Lincoln went to his writing table and wrote a note to General Banks. When he finished, he read it aloud to the two of us: "Dr. Zacharie, who you know as well as I do, wishes to go with you on your expedition. I think he might be of service, to you, first, in his peculiar profession, and secondly, as a means of access to his countrymen, who are quite numerous in some of the localities you will probably visit."

"There's the problem of the prohibition of my people," Zacharie put in. "Grant and Sherman—fine officers, don't misunderstand me, but they don't want any Jews in their area. They blame us for all the trading with the enemy —not true, I assure you, and not fair, but such a feeling exists. We all know it."

Lincoln was aware of Grant's policy to make it difficult for Israelites to come near his command. The Prsdt did not want to involve himself in the general's efforts to stem corruption, however, and as long as the anti-Israelite policy was unwritten, and unapproved by the President, it posed no constitutional difficulties.

He added in his note to Banks: "This is a *permission* merely, excepting his case from a general prohibition which I understand to exist." That acknowledgment of Grant's tacit prohibition may be putting too much in writing, but no other way presented itself.

"My desire is to serve you," Zacharie said, picking up the pass, "in such a manner that my services may redound to your honor." That was Old-World style, but Lincoln seemed to appreciate it. I took the doctor into my office, put the pass in an envelope, and while I was at it handed him the latest cutting from the *New York World:* "The President has often left his business-apartment to spend an evening in the parlor with his favored bunionist."

"Mr. Hay, believe me, I had nothing to do with this notoriety." Zacharie tucked the clipping in his wallet and set off on his perhaps impossible assignment. What is there in that fellow that makes the President want to spend long hours talking with him? What do they have in common? Mystifies me.

I went back in with some newspaper reaction to his annual message; most of the radical press, like the *Evening Post,* said that Lincoln's idea of freeing the slaves by installments was like cutting off a dog's tail by inches to get him used to the pain. The conservatives and Democrats pretty much ignored it; Browning says there's no hope for a two-thirds vote in the Congress for such an amendment. Curiously, this does not upset the Prsdt; he did what he felt he had to do to show his willingness to make a deal.

The Tycoon, feet on the desk, smiling at his shoes, waved off the tut-tutting about his message. The editorial in the *Herald* about the cornucopia was still tickling him. "I tell you the truth, John," he told me, "when I say that genuine wit has the same effect on me that I suppose a good square drink of whiskey has on an old toper. It puts new life in me."

The Tycoon is in fine whack. I have rarely seen him more serene and busy, managing the war, foreign relations, the rambunctious Cabinet, and the majority of the country that needs to be dragged along on emancipation. With McClellan gone, and a more loyal general now actively pursuing Bobby Lee, Lincoln is at last fully in charge. I remember his saying back before Antietam, "if what I feel were equally distributed to the whole human family, there would not be one cheerful face on the earth"; 180-degree turn. A. Lincoln would never be cocking an ear toward any peace talk if he weren't sure he was on the verge of a great victory. I think he senses a turning point.

He sent for Halleck. "I had a long conference with General Burnside," he told the general-in-chief, who was scratching only one elbow today. "He believes that General Lee's whole army is in front of him at or near Fredericksburg."

"He's right," said Halleck promptly. "Burnside has one hundred and ten thousand men to Lee's sixty thousand. Does he say he wants more men?"

Lincoln shook his head, "No, he could not handle them to advantage." That was a far cry from McClellan. "Burnside thinks he can cross the river in the face of the enemy. But that, to use his own expression, is somewhat risky. I wish the case to stand more favorable than this."

He suggested a plan of attack to Halleck that did not rely so much on a frontal assault. Lincoln's scheme was to delay an attack until a second force could cross the Rappahannock, and then a third force swing around via the Pamunkey River to cut off Lee's line of retreat toward Richmond.

Halleck listened to what seemed to me to be a brilliant maneuver, and shook his head. "We cannot raise and put in position a force behind Lee in time. If we don't strike him now, he'll get away. That's what Burnside thinks, too, I'm sure."

The Tycoon nodded uneasily. Curious; Lincoln was in the McClellan role now, not wanting to risk Union lives on a single assault across a river, preferring a three-pronged attack—not unlike Antietam, which might have been more successful if all three of our corps had attacked at the same time. Now it was Burnside and Halleck who wanted to strike massively, quickly, before Lee could get reinforcements.

"Can't waste time," concluded Halleck confidently. "You gave Burnside the command, his army is in fine shape. We can't fight the war from here."

The Prsdt nodded again; Burnside did not have the McClellan slows. "What news from Tennessee?"

Only a few months ago, with Lee invading Maryland and Bragg invading Kentucky, the war was one gigantic Union retreat. But after Antietam in Maryland and the standoff at Perryville in Kentucky, the tide turned. Bragg lost his nerve and pulled back.

"Bragg's army in Tennessee doesn't threaten Kentucky and Ohio anymore," said Halleck. "He's trouble for Grant out West, though, who cannot turn his back completely and attack Vicksburg, not with Morgan's raiders storming around his supply lines. Soon our forces under Rosecrans will move on Bragg's headquarters at Murfreesboro, on Stones River."

I asked why Bragg had wilted. Halleck shrugged that off with, "His commanders hate him, I hear, and only Jeff Davis backs him up. We should not underestimate Bragg. He cut loose from his base, marched two hundred miles and beat an army of ours twice the size of his."

Lincoln asked for a detailed plan on the Rosecrans move on Murfreesboro in Tennessee, but we could see that his mind was on the more important battle impending between Burnside and Lee at Fredericksburg. That could be decisive. The war could be over by Christmas and then the question of an emancipation proclamation might become moot.

Which reminds me that I had better think of getting into uniform before it is over and I have no heroic answer to "What did you do in the war, Daddy?" But Washington has its compensations: Kate has never been so warm and winning as she has been in the past week. I shall soon have to put out some feelers of my own to see what sort of family life I shall be building when the war is over.

CHAPTER 23

FIRING SQUAD

"You must not execute this boy, Bragg. He's no deserter."

General Braxton Bragg, standing at the window facing the courtyard where the execution of Corporal Asa Lewis was to take place, did not look at Breckinridge. "He had a fair court-martial. He deserted. The firing squad will send a message to every troublemaker in your brigade."

"He went home to help with the planting," Breck pleaded, "to put in next year's crop. He was coming back; he did the same thing last year."

"You should have shot him last year, then. Kentucky blood is a little too feverish for the health of the army."

Breckinridge, steaming, held his temper. He was certain that Bragg had been driven from Kentucky by his own lack of zest for battle. The Mississippian was a maneuvering general, a fine marching officer, a classic disciplinarian, but not a commander of men in battle. When the citizens of Breckinridge's state failed to welcome the Confederate troops, and even went so far as to deny them supplies, Bragg directed his hatred at all Kentuckians. Breck knew that Bragg bile was especially directed at him, because the little chimpanzee had assumed that the Breckinridge name would rally all residents of the bluegrass state to the Southern side. Now that Bragg was conscripting any Kentuckian who fell into his hands, he would soon have plenty of deserters for hanging.

"If you won't listen to me," Breck pressed, "General Cleburne has asked to—"

"Waste of time. Don't you belong out there when the sentence is carried out? They're your men."

The Kentuckian withdrew, mounted, and rode into the courtyard where the condemned corporal was being blindfolded. The tall boy declined the blindfold at first, but the lieutenant told him that the men of the firing squad preferred not to have him looking at them when they did their distasteful duty.

Breckinridge dismounted. He walked to the corporal and told him his final appeal had failed, but that all his Kentucky comrades knew he was no deserter. He suggested that the condemned man say something to the soldiers about to carry out an abhorrent order.

Corporal Lewis complied. "Do not be distressed," he called out from behind his blindfold. "I beg of you to aim to kill, it will be merciful to me. Goodbye."

Breckinridge, who had seen so much death in the past year, was swept by an unaccustomed sense of dread. He went back and remounted. General Pat Cleburne, muttering Irish curses, moved his horse next to him. The clicking of the hammers could be heard in the morning cold on the command of "Ready." The men of the Orphan Brigade, drawn up in three formations to the rear of the firing squad facing the condemned man, tensed. Breckinridge, sweating, shuddered in the cold.

As the order to fire was given, Breckinridge started to lose consciousness. He felt Cleburne's hand grabbing his arm as he was falling off his horse. His aide, the boy who had replaced Cabell, ran up and helped the commander of the Orphans to the ground. He leaned against his horse, breathing deeply, until consciousness returned. That had not happened to him before; only women fainted. Breck was mortified that it had happened in front of the entire brigade; at Cleburne's suggestion, he remounted and they rode off together.

"Bad business. Bragg's a vindictive fool," the Irishman said. "This will cause more desertions than it will discourage. You all right now?"

"I never saw us shoot one of our own before," Breck said. The corporal had given him his comb and pocketbook to pass on to his mother, and he could feel the presence of the dead man's effects in his pocket.

"No news about your son yet?" Cleburne was trying to change the subject with a duller, deeper pain.

"He isn't on any of the prisoner lists." Breck was fighting off the sense of certainty that the boy was dead. Cabell was about the age of the corporal just executed—in fact, the same height and build. He shook his head and gulped the cold air.

"There was a Yankee nurse named Breckinridge we captured in Lewis-burg," General Cleburne said, trying to be helpful. "I figured you all must be related, so I sent her up to Louisville to tell your Union relations to look out for him."

"Her name?"

"Margaret Elizabeth; said her father was Judge John Breckinridge."

That was Uncle Robert's kin; if the girl got to that famous Union loyalist with a question about Cabell, he would know to get in touch with Anna Carroll in Washington, and she would press General Dix to search the prison camps. The possibility existed that the boy was still alive, his memory shocked out of him; or perhaps he was afraid to reveal his identity as the son of a man condemned as a traitor by the U.S. Senate. False hopes, probably.

"You were right about Lincoln and the slaves, Pat. He's going to enlist them in his army, maybe hundreds of thousands."

"That's what we should be doing." The Irishman was off on his favorite forbidden subject. "Lincoln was willing to take a gamble, and stand up to the hollering of most of his own people. That's the difference between him and Jeff Davis."

Breck was not sure. Lincoln's proclamation promising emancipation to the slaves of rebels was a stunning political act, wiping out all hope of ending the war by compromise—if he went through with it at the end of the month. But maybe Lincoln was searching for an excuse to delay the edict: his message to Congress last week, reported with some interest by the newspapers in the South, mentioned the proclamation only as something to be stayed. Was he trying to elicit a peace offer?

"The question is," Cleburne was saying, "why is Lincoln gambling now? Is he convinced the North is losing, and he must enlist black troops—or is he convinced the North is winning, and he can afford to challenge us to a fight to the finish?"

That was the question that had been nagging at Breck ever since late September, when he had read the news of Lincoln's two proclamations freeing the slaves and jailing the dissenters. Was Lincoln acting out of weakness or strength? Was the reason what he said it was—military necessity, which would mean weakness—or was that a pose, and Lincoln's ulterior motive to whip up the war spirit in the North to subjugate the South once and for all?

He remembered his arguments with Lincoln in the White House eighteen months ago. The man was then torn between his disgust for slavery and his solemn promise not to strike at the peculiar institution where it existed. The stunning way he resolved that dilemma had surprised Breckinridge, who had thought of his former presidential rival as a born compromiser. This was a decision, coming down hard on one side.

The war must have changed Lincoln, made him more certain of his tentative ideas, just as it had changed Breckinridge, making him unsure of what he was fighting for, or why he was fighting at all. Not for independence—he had always opposed disunion; not slavery—that was no cause to inspire a willingness to die; and not even individual liberty, since Richmond was now just as eager to suspend habeas corpus in the name of national security as Washington ever had been. For Kentucky? The people of his state had just been given the chance to rise to greet its liberators, and had decided against that; their apathy or indecision was as authentic a plebiscite as could be conducted. His only certainty at the moment was that the picture would never leave him of a Kentucky firing squad killing a Kentucky boy for the crime of slipping away to do some planting. The Breckinridge family was on both sides, and so, in a sense, was he.

Cleburne brought him back. "Maybe we'll sound out some of the hi-muck-a-mucks about recruiting the slaves at the Morgan wedding." John Hunt Morgan, the hothead turned heroic cavalry raider, was to be married the following week. His forays behind enemy lines had disrupted Union logistics and provisioned Confederate soldiers with Yankee supplies, the leaders of the army and the government would assemble for that wedding. "He's the only Kentuckian who gets along with Bragg."

"They can have each other," Breck said sourly. "But maybe a good woman will settle John down."

"Or take the fight out of him."

"Is that why you're a bachelor, Pat? You want to keep your fighting edge?" When Breck was Cleburne's age—thirty-three—he had been married a dozen years. Breck now wished he had spent more time with Cabell. That notion was a dead weight on his line of thought and he shook it off.

"I'll find the colleen one of these days, but not when I have to worry about leaving her a widow every time the moment comes to lead a charge. You have to be a little crazy to be a good raider like Morgan or Forrest—bloodthirsty too. You suppose Jeff Davis will come to the wedding?"

Everyone in the command, including Bragg, assumed that Breckinridge knew the President's plans. The Kentuckian never disabused anyone of that thought, because it helped him stand off the insufferable martinet of a commanding general. He shrugged and said he hoped so.

"Sure and we could use a council of war here in Murfreesboro," Cleburne said, slipping deep into his brogue. "The new Union general, Rosecrans, is a tad more headstrong than Buell. He'll be coming after us, because if he doesn't he knows Lincoln will be coming after him. Bragg had better be ready to fight. He can't keep blaming us for his own damn cowardice."

"I hear Lincoln paid a visit one night last week to Burnside at the Virginia front," was all Breck could say.

Cleburne nodded. They left unsaid their feeling that the Yankee general might be getting the better advice and greater inspiration.

CHAPTER 24

THE PRESIDENT VISITS

Jefferson Davis was glad of the chance to get out of Richmond, even for a few days. The wedding of Colonel Morgan, the dashing cavalry raider (why was "dashing" the only word to apply to a horse soldier?) to a young woman known throughout Central Tennessee as the belle of Murfreesboro offered an occasion to reaffirm his support of his good friend, Braxton Bragg.

Such a visit would also show the men of the Army of Tennessee that their commander in chief in Richmond considered the Central theater every bit as important as the Eastern, despite the likelihood that a great battle was impending on the banks of the Rappahannock near Fredericksburg.

Even as he prepared to meet Bragg, President Davis found it hard to shift his concentration from Robert Lee in Virginia. General Lee wanted to fall back thirty miles, drawing the Union forces away from their water base at Aquia Creek, in hope of destroying Burnside's army completely if the Union attack failed; Davis had overruled that, recommending entrenchment on the heights overlooking the river, hoping to draw Burnside into a hopeless uphill charge.

The leader of the Confederacy did not believe it necessary to destroy the Army of the Potomac; at this crucial post-election time a decisive repulse, with heavy casualties, would be more than even the unreasonable Lincoln could stand. Copperhead sentiment was obviously on the rise in the North, and needed fuel for its orators' fire. A stunning defeat of the army that expected to march on Richmond, coming just after Lincoln had staked all on the removal of McClellan and taken personal responsibility for this campaign, might well trigger angry uprisings in the North. A military defeat coming on the heels of a vote of no confidence might finally convince the English people that the North could not win, and that the South, as Gladstone had said truthfully, had made itself a nation.

Davis had more in mind with this visit to the West than assuring the soldiers of the Army of Tennessee of the importance of their task. Earlier that year he had chosen February 22, birthday of George Washington, to be inaugurated as the permanent President of the Confederacy; like General Washington, Davis saw the need for military daring designed for political effect.

He was planning a mission for Colonel Morgan and his raiders that transcended the usual military tactics. Davis wanted to tell Morgan in person about that great raid, even as he promoted the gallant and fearless Kentuckian to brigadier general. The promotion would serve as a wedding present from the Confederacy in gratitude for the bridegroom's fervor in disrupting Union logistics by destroying railroads and bridges.

The Richmond that the President left behind was turning, he was sad to admit, into a cauldron of bickering interests. The newly revered Robert Lee was the one who had advised Davis to press for conscription to offset the weight of numbers in the North, but the blame for this extension of the power of central government had been placed on Davis. When the President recognized the need to have the power to impose martial law in those Southern cities in danger of attack, the treacherous—Davis did not feel that treacherous was too strong a word—editors of the Richmond newspapers had vilified him for imitating Lincoln in suspending the privilege of habeas corpus. He found that comparison odious: it should have been clear that Lincoln had seized the power of arbitrary arrest illegally while Davis had obtained it lawfully, by seeking it through an action of the Confederate Congress.

He had some constitutional advantages over his Federal counterpart: Davis was serving a single term of six years, no reelection permitted, which put him above the maneuvering to maintain control that must trouble Lincoln; and to counterbalance the South's presumed shift away from national authority, the Confederate Constitution gave the President the power to veto specific items within legislation. But there were disadvantages to rejection of central power:

Confederate President Jefferson Davis

Lincoln might have his critics in the North, Davis mused, but at least he did not have his Vice President stabbing him in the back at every opportunity. "Little Aleck" Stephens was becoming impossible. The President found it hard to believe that Stephens, that emaciated gnome, was giving public political support to the Governor of Georgia, a states' rights fanatic who not only had been resisting conscription but refused to run military trains on Sunday. Davis had been told, on good authority, that Vice President Stephens had been saying of the President of the Confederacy that he was "a man of good intentions, weak and vacillating, petulant, peevish, obstinate but not firm, and now I am beginning to doubt his intentions."

Davis remembered every slight from an opponent and every insult from the press. His wife Varina kept telling him that his inability to forget an insult was a flaw in a political leader, and Davis knew he was more thin-skinned than he ought to be, but such sensitivity to slights had been part of his character since he had been a boy in Kentucky and nothing could be done about it now. His daughter Maggie had the sunny nature that allowed her to smile away people who snapped at her; Davis marveled at the way she had the forbearance to turn away from the cats as well as the snakes, but such charity was not in him. He felt every jab and remembered everyone who wounded him, but the Confederate President consoled himself that he also remembered those who loyally spoke up for him in times of trial. His old Mexico comrade Braxton Bragg was one of those, especially when that French popinjay Beauregard tried to blame Davis for failing to capture the Federal capital after First Manassas.

Seated in the room of the Murfreesboro Hotel, preparing for the prereception visits of Bragg, Breckinridge, and the others, Davis wondered whether Lincoln was afflicted with the same sensitivity to criticism. Probably not; he and Lincoln had been born in the same Kentucky county within a year of each other, but the Davises were a distinguished and wealthy family, the Lincolns a poor and uneducated lot. Lincoln had campaigned hard for the presidential nomination, trading promises for support, and been elected by a minority of the people; in contrast, Davis had not sought the leadership of his nation, had even chosen not to attend the convention in Montgomery that selected him unanimously. Out of a sense of duty, he had accepted the responsibility to lead the seceded states.

To Davis's mind, there was a coarseness to Lincoln, part and parcel of an innate hunger to triumph over his betters. Davis was a West Point graduate, experienced in command in the Mexican War, Secretary of War in the Pierce administration, and could deal knowledgeably with military affairs; Lincoln's military background was practically nonexistent, and yet he presumed to consider himself a great strategist and was known to meddle in the planning of campaigns.

Worst of all, thought Davis, Lincoln's coarseness had turned to sheer savagery in the crucible of war. His toleration of General Pope's barbarism was indicative, but his proclamation of abolition revealed a man so desperate to keep his dominion over the states that he would actually seek to incite a servile rebellion. For drawing that weapon of *terrorisme*, Davis was certain the Union leader would be remembered in history as a man capable of the most monstrous acts.

Lincoln's sly recommendation to the Southern blacks "to abstain from violence unless in necessary self-defense" was particularly infuriating, since it was an unmistakable hint to encourage the assassination of their masters. Every slave being disciplined now had the "right" from the President of the United States to strike out at his owner. Davis detested Lincoln for putting forward the most execrable measure recorded in the history of guilty man, and was fearful that it might have the effect intended of setting slaves on a path of rapine and murder on thousands of undefended plantations. He was convinced that Lincoln's protestations of the past two years that he had no intention of striking at slavery where it existed were a sham; the man was an abolitionist at heart, determined to impose his ways on an independent people just as had George III on the American colonists.

Braxton Bragg was the President's first caller. Davis assumed that the general, in constant strife with his subordinates, wanted to be sure that the President understood his side of any disputes before he heard them from the likes of John Breckinridge. Bragg was an irritating fellow, Davis was aware— as U.S. Secretary of War, he had accepted Bragg's angry resignation—but when General Beauregard failed, it was the abrasive but effective Bragg that Davis had turned to, and the stern disciplinarian had justified that faith with his march northward into Tennessee and Kentucky.

"You have not been receiving the praise you deserve in Richmond, General," Davis told him, going to the heart of what must be bothering his friend.

"The venal press want you to remove me from command," Braxton Bragg announced. "The *Richmond Whig* says the Kentucky campaign turned out to be a fizzle."

"I ignore the press completely," said Davis, wishing he could.

"A fizzle is exactly what it was," said Bragg, surprising him, "thanks to Breckinridge. If he had been with me a month sooner, when he should have been, he might have helped with those damned Kentuckians. Selfish, miserable people, wouldn't volunteer a crust of bread to the army. And our Kentucky Brigade is a joke, thanks to Breckinridge's coddling."

"I was born in Kentucky," Davis reminded him. "We Kentuckians have an independent turn of mind." He suppressed his irritation with Bragg's congenital derogation of his own subordinates, because the unfortunate man's simian looks and dyspeptic demeanor denied him friends and followers. Certainly he had too few supporters in the press: in his invasion of Kentucky, Bragg had accomplished as much as Lee in his invasion of Maryland, at less cost, yet it was Lee who was hailed by his countrymen as a hero while Bragg bore the brunt of criticism as a retreater. The pity was that both Confederate generals had been forced to fall back; valor was no match for railroad lines of supply to bring up ammunition and new shoes.

As Bragg launched into a series of complaints about his other officers, Davis interrupted to ask whether there were any men in Bragg's command worthy of promotion. He had in mind that day's groom, who, Davis had been told, would be married by General Polk with a bishop's robes worn over his uniform.

Bragg submitted a list for promotion. Davis saw the name of a colonel, recommended for general of a brigade, who had recently written a letter critical of the Davis administration that had been published in the newspapers. He struck that name off the list, along with several others he knew to be overly outspoken. Bragg did not always understand that the need for discipline also had to include political reliability. He came to Patrick Cleburne's name.

"You like the Irishman?"

"Young and ardent, but sufficiently prudent," Bragg nodded. "A fine drill officer. Has the admiration of his command."

"So does Breckinridge," Davis observed, knowing it would get a rise out of Bragg. "Popularity with the troops does not always mean good generalship," he said, adding, "although Breck is a superb commander and, like you, a colleague of long standing."

"Breckinridge is soft," Bragg said. "And he drinks."

Davis frowned, not wanting to hear this, but Bragg would not desist. "He came into my tent the other night and I could tell he was drunk. Mumbling something about his damned 'orphans,' and tried to get me to pardon a deserter. He's been drunk in the presence of the troops, too. Fell off his horse at a formation, dead to the world, made a fool of himself. As far as I'm concerned, you can send him back out West, along with his brigade of riff-raff."

"I'm glad you can spare the troops," said Davis, ignoring the serious charge. "I want you to detach Morgan's raiders for a mission I have in mind."

"I cannot spare Morgan's cavalry," Bragg said abruptly. "He has five thousand fighters under him. I expect an attack from Rosecrans soon, and I need every man I can get, excluding the shirkers under Breckinridge. You should not split my command more than it is already."

"I must. You are to send one division," the President ordered, "full strength, ten thousand men, to Mississippi right away. We must stop Grant from taking Vicksburg."

Nothing was more important to Davis, not even the defense of Richmond, than the continued denial of the Mississippi River to the North. He fervently hoped that the importance of Vicksburg would not assume an overriding significance in Lincoln's war strategy. He counted on Lincoln to remain transfixed with the battles along the Potomac.

"And you're taking Morgan's cavalry," said Bragg. "That's quite a loss."

Davis knew what he was doing with Morgan's force. He would take Forrest's cavalry raiders from Bragg as well, to harass Grant in the West and thereby prevent an attack on Vicksburg, but that could wait a few days. "Fight if you can," he told Bragg, "and fall back if you must, beyond the Tennessee River." He drew himself to his feet. "I expect you to work together with Breckinridge and General Hardee. I will promote Cleburne to major general, as you suggest, and will promote Colonel Morgan to brigadier. We will now attend the festive occasion."

"They'll come at us right here at Murfreesboro," said Bragg. As Davis expected, the general did not argue further; it was for him to try to work out what he could do with the forces remaining with him. "We don't have much of a natural defense at Stones River, but if we can stop them here, we can chase them up past Nashville."

Davis liked that spirit, and resolved to protect this faithful soldier from the wolves of Richmond. He cautioned Bragg to use entrenchment whenever possible—neither Bragg nor Lee liked that device, thinking that it robbed the men of their warlike spirit and undermined their discipline, but Davis was persuaded that earthworks and trenches improved the prospects of successful defense.

"I must do all in my power," the President told him as they walked out together, "to overcome the impression that I am an austere and unfeeling person." When the general demurred, Davis pressed the point that pained him, but was true: "No, that is an unfortunate burden I bear. That is one reason for my coming to the wedding, General, to show the officers and the troops that I am not the cold and distant person I am made out to be in the press."

He was telling Bragg this not merely because it was true, but to suggest subtly that the general suffered from a similar reputation. Some political men could succeed without appearing warm and outgoing—George Washington was the outstanding example of one who had maintained his reserve and dignity—but on the whole, Davis felt, men like Bragg and himself were weakened as leaders by a modesty or taciturnity that made it hard for them to let their inner natures be seen by their countrymen.

"There's going to be a lot of drinking at this wedding," said the general, "and a temptation to become lax in discipline. Your presence here will counter that, Mr. President."

Davis sighed; Braxton Bragg would never understand human relationships. Better Bragg in command than Beauregard, however; the ambitious little Frenchman wanted to be President. Bragg had his sick headaches that crippled him for days on end, Davis knew—migraines, they were being called—and his relationships with his fellow officers left much to be desired, but he would not run out on his President. One thought troubled President Davis, however: "About General Breckinridge. You realize that he is a braver man than either of us."

Bragg looked up sharply, as Davis knew he would. "You are a resident of Louisiana," said the President, "a state that seceded legally from the Union. I am the former United States Senator from Mississippi, also a state that seceded. If we should lose this war—and we must recognize that our maximum strength has been mobilized, while the enemy is just beginning to put forth his might—you and I have an unassailable legal defense against vindictive charges of treason."

He let that sink in. "Breckinridge, on the other hand, is from Kentucky. That state, unhappily, did not secede. If we should lose this war, or if General Breckinridge fell into enemy hands in the course of battle, he would surely be tried as a traitor. The likes of Tad Stevens and Ben Wade would settle for no less than the most severe punishment. And the likelihood is that Mr. Lincoln would see him hang."

"That's a chance he takes," Bragg said coldly. "No excuse for drinking."

CHAPTER 25

THE BANDIT TAKES A BRIDE

Breckinridge could not understand what had come over John Hunt Morgan. The hothead of Lexington, the reckless risk-all raider, the Yankee-hating swashbuckler who had been loosely attached to the Orphan Brigade since the start had undergone a transformation. Morgan was moonstruck.

To be in love was a fine thing, Breckinridge conceded, and let himself recall the innocent early days with Mary and the later days in Washington jousting and loving with Anna Carroll, but none of those experiences had intrinsically changed him; Colonel Morgan, in contrast, seemed positively lovesick.

"You know what Mattie said last year, when a Yankee officer asked her name?" Morgan asked him, as he asked everyone on his wedding day. "It was a year ago, we hadn't met. She told him, 'Write down Mattie Ready now, but by the grace of God, one day I shall call myself the wife of John Morgan.' There's a woman for you."

"She knows her mind," Breckinridge said to the groom, "for someone that young. And she's a lot better-looking than some of those women you've been slipping into camp."

"At least all my men are men, Breck," the cavalryman responded merrily. Breckinridge smiled; in his brigade, as elsewhere in the army, there were more than a few young women masquerading as boys. These volunteers usually buddied up, concealing their sex from the officers but not from the men in the ranks, for whom they performed their services profitably and well. Some of the disguised girls even charged nothing, considering it their contribution to the Cause. In battle, these hardened young women in soldiers' garb were among the steadiest under fire, and the noncoms passed the word up the line that it would harm morale if their services day or night were withdrawn. Breckinridge pretended to know nothing about it.

He sloshed around some of the purplish fluid that had been put in his glass. "What kind of God-awful wine is this?"

"Scuppernong," said the cavalryman, "and over there you can find all the applejack and peach brandy you want. I suppose they can break out a little bourbon for you, Breck."

Morgan looked across the large reception room of the house of the bride's father at the figure of President Jefferson Davis—cadaverous, pale, almost at the edge of infirmity—entering at the side of Braxton Bragg. "I think I rate a honeymoon with this incredible girl," Morgan was saying in a lower tone, "but we've been told to be ready to set out on a raid right after the wedding."

He seemed sorry for himself; that was the first time Breckinridge could recall that Morgan had not approached action with the eyes of a man who loved war more than a man should. Morgan was not the only Southern hotblood who was becoming more sober about the game of war, Breck had observed; the fighting was lasting too long and the adventure was losing its piquancy. He could not fault Jeff Davis on that. His former colleague in the

General John Hunt Morgan, C.S.A.

United States Senate had warned of a long war from the start; Breck had agreed, remembering his conversations in the Executive Mansion with Lincoln, who was obsessed with what he insisted was "an oath registered in Heaven" to prevent Southern independence at all costs.

Breck stayed away from the bar, moving instead to a table laden with quail, doves, and roast pork. Supplies were plentiful in Murfreesboro, a city crowded with wives and sweethearts of officers. He wished Mary had been well enough to come; it would be good to be with her in this soul-wrenching time of uncertainty about Cabell. No word about the boy in a month; the longer there was no news, the more the likelihood of never seeing him again grew. His name had not appeared on any of the prisoner lists.

The gaiety of the party, the whooshing of silk skirts, and the laughter of Morgan's raiders oppressed him. How many of these reveling raiders would come home across the backs of their horses after the next foray, and how many brides and sweethearts would soon be searching for replacements, just as generals demanded replacements that so seldom came? That led to another thought: why was Morgan's force being sent on a mission when the likelihood was that Bragg would be called upon to defend this area any day now? Cavalry provided an army its eyes, and the talent of Southern horsemen in scouting and harassing an approaching enemy provided the Confederacy an edge of supremacy that sometimes made up for the Northern advantage in artillery. General Breckinridge hoped Davis had a good reason for stripping Bragg's army of Morgan and his men at a critical moment.

At a nod from President Davis, who seemed unusually convivial and attentive to the guests this afternoon, Breckinridge went into the study to await his audience with the leader of the South. He was surprised and glad to see Pat Cleburne waiting there already, poking the fire, complaining about the bone-chilling dampness of these rambling mansions.

"I'm either going to be promoted or cashiered," General Cleburne told him quickly. "I'm afraid I couldn't keep my Irish mouth shut, Breck. I didn't take your advice."

"You didn't put anything in writing about recruiting and freeing slaves, I hope."

General Cleburne shook his head as the President entered. Jefferson Davis took their hands and motioned them to chairs before the fire.

"My friends, with constant labors in the duties of office, and borne down by care, I have had such little opportunity for social intercourse," the President said—it seemed to Breckinridge stiffly, like a politician incapable of warmth even among his closest supporters. "I hope the time may come when, relieved of the anxieties of the hour, we may have more social intercourse."

"The war is not going well, then," Cleburne probed.

"On the contrary, I see nothing in the future to disturb the prospect of the independence for which we are struggling." Breck knew the President had been profoundly troubled by the setback at Sharpsburg, but knew also that Davis would brook no defeatist talk. "Have you spoken to the bride and groom? With such noble women at home and such heroic soldiers in the field, we are invincible."

"Sure and you're a man of great faith," Cleburne replied, "but we just lost Kentucky. And with all respect, Mr. President, our glorious invasion of the North, by both Bragg and Lee, is a thing of the past. If we're to win, we need some radical changes."

Davis blinked, rubbed his bad eye, and changed the subject. "Breck, first let me say I have nothing to report to you about your son. The official channels, through the exchange commission, say he is not listed as a prisoner."

Breckinridge nodded numbly and said he was grateful for his concern.

"We have an informal means of communication with the North," the President continued. "Judah Benjamin's sister in New Orleans is in touch with a doctor of some sort attached to the headquarters of the Union occupiers. Some inquiries are being made through that channel, which was initiated by Mr. Lincoln, I suspect, when he replaced that madman Butler. Perhaps he is coming under pressure to see if negotiations for peace are possible. We will telegraph you immediately if there is any news of your gallant boy. Our prayers—"

"Send news about peace negotiations, too," said the irrepressible Cleburne.

"The only basis for talks would be a recognition of the Confederacy's independence," Davis said with great firmness. "The possibility that the North is interested is encouraging. It may be a sign of weakness. Demands for peace are growing every day in the North."

But not in the South, Breckinridge noted, and wondered why. Possibly because the North was the aggressor, striking against an attempt at peaceful secession; the way Lincoln had goaded the South into firing the first shot had been a transparent trick. More likely, peace talk was muted in the South because it was equated with a suggestion to surrender. Life in the two sections was surely of a different character (lending some credence, Breck would grant, to the idea of independence), and part of that difference was the inclination of the Southerner to consider a defeat of his cause to be a loss of personal honor. If a Yankee thought of losing the war, he did not worry about the occupation of his land by Southerners; but every Southerner had to consider the personal humiliation in store when the Yankee overlords came down to see that the slaves were in the saddle.

And then Breck felt another, unstated, slowly smoldering reason that peace talk was not heard in the South: not every Southerner was partial to the peculiar institution, particularly when slavery did him no personal good. To talk of peace was to doubt the necessity for slavery, which was to attack the aristocracy, and you didn't do that if you knew what was good for you. But plenty of poor Southern soldiers resented having to fight to help the plantation owner keep his slaves; Cabell had taught him that. And Breck knew that at least some well-bred officers felt that slavery—which might be justified on abstract economic grounds, and was surely permitted by the writers of the Constitution—was not the sort of cause that made its justifiers proud.

"Independence, then, is the Southern cause," Cleburne was saying to Davis, "the very essence of the war and the reason for the glorious struggle. Not the preservation of slavery."

Davis nodded unhesitatingly. "Abolition is merely the excuse for the war on the part of some Northern zealots," he explained, as if this were a lecture he had given often. "The real design of most of the Yankee bankers and politicians is to subjugate the South totally, dominating our economy and imposing their culture upon our own. The abolition of slavery was merely their excuse, and a device to keep foreign nations from recognizing us."

"If they're not really fighting to end slavery," said the Irish-born general in seeming innocence, "and we're really fighting for independence and not to save slavery—then why don't we emancipate the slaves ourselves, and use negro troops to fight for our independence and their own freedom?"

"There's been some talk of that around," Breckinridge put in, to soften the sound of Cleburne's heresy. "It's not disloyal in any way, Mr. President. Just take it as a suggestion to help swell our ranks."

"How would we pay for it?" Davis asked. Breck blinked and Cleburne smiled; that practical reaction was a surprise. "The Confederacy would have to buy the slaves to use in the army, at eight hundred dollars a head for a good field hand, and then free those who served honorably. Where's the money for that? We hardly have enough to pay for ammunition, for shoes even, and could not think of affording a million slaves."

"Is that all that stands in the way?"

Davis smiled his bleak smile. "Tell me where to find eight hundred million dollars for the first million slaves. But of course that is not the only drawback to the scheme. Some of our states would try to secede from the Confederacy to protect the peculiar institution—Georgia, South Carolina."

"We're outnumbered in every battle, sometimes two to one," Breckinridge put in. "The North outnumbers us three to one in men of military age available for the draft." As an experienced politician, Breckinridge was not prepared to endorse Cleburne's idea at this early stage. But that the notion evidently did not trigger automatic rejection by the President of the Confederacy was encouraging.

"Until our white population shall prove insufficient for the armies we require, to employ the negro as a soldier would scarcely be deemed wise or advantageous. Certainly not now, and the less said the better," said Davis. "The notion is quite premature."

"But if recruitment fell off," Cleburne pressed, and Breck wished he would not keep assaulting the position, "and we really needed the men—"

Davis shrugged. "Should the alternatives be subjugation of the South or the employment of the slave as soldier, there seems no reason to doubt what should then be our decision. We are not, of course, faced with those alternatives."

Breckinridge was stunned. Here was the President of the Confederacy coolly facing the prospect of ending slavery in order to maintain an independent state. Hundreds of thousands of men were dying for what—for independence? He would have to think hard about the politics of that, because he had not departed the Senate of the United States, to be branded a traitor by his peers, because he favored disunion; on the contrary, he had done his damnedest to avoid disunion, short of war. Nor was he an advocate of the property rights that enshrined human slavery.

Then what was he fighting for? What was the "cause"? Was resentment at the Republicans' political insistence that slavery not be extended to the Western territories worth this fratricidal war? His young cousin Margaret, Uncle Bob's daughter, intruded on his thoughts. She was a nurse for the Union, swabbing blood off the injured in hospitals that no belles like the girl marrying the lovesick Morgan had ever seen. Margaret Breckinridge had a purpose, simple, clear—the abolition of slavery, the end of the degradation of a race, the fulfillment of the American revolutionary promise that all men were created equal. That was something to drive her to serve in ways that no well-bred Kentucky girl would ever have considered in peacetime. What opposing cause gave strength to John Morgan's bride? Resentment of the majority's iron rule? Independence from an already independent Union? It was understandable for proud and sensitive Southerners to despise the arrogance of individual Yankees, but something else entirely for Southerners to hate the Union their fathers had helped create.

As these thoughts crowded in, Breckinridge felt as if his roots were rotting. He wished he could have a long talk about the underlying motives of North and South with Anna Carroll, who might have the wrong answer but would at least understand the question.

"As general officers," President Davis was saying, "you are both undoubtedly concerned about my decision to remove men from this command in the face of an impending attack on Murfreesboro—why, particularly, I am sending Morgan north for a long foray. I realize that your relationship with General Bragg is not close, and he is unlikely to explain my rationale."

Breckinridge broke away from his disturbing line of thought and looked up sharply: had Bragg been complaining about him again? The leader of the Orphan Brigade felt a surge of anger at the martinet willing to trouble the President of the Confederacy with petty squabbles.

"The copperhead movement is gaining strength in the North," Davis explained. "Horatio Seymour has been elected Governor of New York, the largest state in the Union, on a pledge to end the war with 'the Union as it was.' Clement Vallandigham of Ohio has introduced a resolution in the House of Representatives accusing Lincoln of trying to establish a dictatorship. Rumors are rampant that Seward intends to negotiate a peace on the basis of separation—"

"How did Val's resolution do?" Breckinridge wanted to know.

"Voted down seventy-nine to fifty, strictly according to party lines," Davis said.

Breck was impressed; when the leader of the copperhead faction of the Democrats in Congress could impose party discipline to support a calumnious attack on Lincoln, that meant the opposition was hardening. The South had no such opposition in place; no two-party system had been given time to develop. That made the Northern political system stronger in the long run, in Breck's reckoning, but vulnerable now.

"This is the time to do all we can to contribute to copperhead sentiment in the North," Davis said, "particularly in the fertile Western ground—Ohio, Illinois, Kansas." The President lowered his voice, requiring his generals to lean forward to catch his words. "I have been visited by men hatching what they call the Northwest Conspiracy—a rising of the copperhead secret societies, a riot in Chicago, open agitation to free our prisoners and negotiate an end to the war. That is where Morgan, and perhaps Forrest in a few weeks, can fit in—striking north and west, making the message plain that the war cannot be won by the Union."

Breck looked at Cleburne; did Davis know something about Northern morale that they did not know? He had no feel for the depth of support of the peace movement in the North, but if the movement could turn out every Democrat in the House to denounce the President of the United States as a dictator, perhaps Davis's faith in the value of raids in the Northwest was well placed. He wondered if Lincoln would be rattled by an explosion of peace talk in Ohio and Illinois; somehow, he doubted it. He could not be wearied of making war, because he was sustained by his obsession with Union and majority rule. The only way to defeat Lincoln was to beat his army.

"This is the critical time," said President Davis. "Now, this month. Our victory could come not so much from our strength, but from weakness in the Northern will. Do you agree, Breck? You have a surer grasp of politics than I do."

"We need more than successful raids," was his judgment. "We need some victories in the field here in Tennessee, leading back up into Kentucky, threatening Ohio. And we need General Lee to crush Lincoln's army at the Rappahannock in the East."

"Defense is the key," the newly promoted Cleburne put in. "If there is anything we've learned, 'tis the effect of the rifled barrel on all warfare. The guns can start killing at over five hundred yards, not one hundred, and that means the attackers are at a terrible disadvantage against prepared positions.

That should be our strategy here, if you can get it through Bragg's thick skull."

"It is the plan of General Lee at Fredericksburg," said Davis, ignoring the slight to his local commander.

"That is the way to weaken Lincoln's resolve," Breckinridge concluded. "The removal of McClellan was all his doing. The next battle is his defeat or his victory, no matter who the Union general is. A military setback there, followed by a repulse of the Federals here, would force him to listen to the Democrats and settle the war. Only then would he make a deal for 'the Union as it was,' with slavery."

"Which I, of course," said Davis, "will never accept. We are two nations now."

The practical Irishman made Breckinridge's point. "First let's get him to make us an offer."

CHAPTER 26

ALONE AGAIN

Governor Chase had never before come to see her at her flat in The Washington House. Her lodgings, Anna Carroll assured herself, were respectable enough, and the bedroom-work office had a certain genteel seediness attributable to the war. Certainly the quarters were not as grand as he was accustomed to at the Chase mansion at Sixth and G, but her sitting room had been host to a parade of congressmen and office seekers. Not a month ago, she had made the final arrangements in this drab room with Senator Henry Wilson for the appointment of a middle-level assistant in Chase's Treasury Department, which did nothing to pay the rent but at least enhanced her reputation as a person of some influence. That reputation, in turn, led to writing assignments. She wished the War Department would pay the $6,500 she was owed, or at least made an offer to settle the bill.

Anna was flustered when the bellboy arrived at the door with the Chase calling card, but she was not about to waste the governor's time by plumping up the pillows or brushing her hair. She wished she had bought a Christmas wreath to put on the door to show her piety. She also wished she had not worn her high-necked blouse but now was no time to change. She sent the boy down to the desk clerk with word to escort the Secretary of the Treasury upstairs—she was eager for the management to know that her visitors were of the first rank—and ordered tea.

"I trust I am not coming at an inopportune time," Chase said formally, handing her his hat and heavy overcoat, damp from the snow. She was inclined to say that of course the time was inopportune, she and her apartment looked a mess, and she was glad to have him here in her own domain without his possessive elder daughter looking on. Instead, as she did whenever she felt nervous, Anna let herself pour forth a cascade of small talk about grand strategy.

She took his wet hat and coat and heaved them up onto the brass hatstand, chattering about the likelihood of a battle on the Rappahannock, which struck her as being blown out of all proportion by the war correspondents. "They should be out West with Grant, focusing attention on Vicksburg. Why is Lincoln sending John McClernand, a hack politician playing general if there ever was one, down the Mississippi with a force to assault Vicksburg from the river side? That's doomed. The fortress can only be taken from the back, on land, by siege."

"I'm sure you know more about that than anyone, my dear lady," he said heavily, sinking into the only chair in the sitting room suitable for a big man. "As you know, the war appears to be drawing to a successful close. Even Seward admits that."

That was news to her; Anna doubted this would be a war lasting less than two years. The emancipation policy had not worked, and Lincoln seemed to be backing away from it; Orville Browning told her he hoped a way would be found to delay the proclamation's effect past the New Year's deadline. Chase's hopes for a quick Northern victory seemed misplaced to her, but Anna did not want to argue; perhaps he had come on other business and was making preliminary conversation.

"With McClellan finally gone, and some new spirit finally in our troops," Chase was saying, "we should be in Richmond in a matter of weeks."

She wondered about his optimism; did Stanton agree? That was not what she was hearing from young Bates at the telegraph office. The operator reported that "Hosanna"—that was the Union code name for Jefferson Davis, although the operators were more accustomed to hearing Lincoln call his counterpart "Jeffy D"—was confident enough about the defense of Richmond to make a visit to Murfreesboro to attend a wedding. The thought of that Tennessee city reminded her of "Old Rosey" Rosecrans, the new Federal commander facing Bragg and Breckinridge there, and she was glad to be able to pass on a tasty piece of political gossip to Chase.

"Whenever the war ends, Governor, I hear the Democrats intend to run every general they can lay their hands on for every major office in the North."

"I've heard those rumors about McClellan for President—"

"I've heard the Democrats want Rosecrans for Governor of Ohio." She knew that thought would worry him; Ohio was home territory for Chase, his base of political power, and she had this information from no less an Ohioan than Senator Ben Wade. She sat back to hear what it was he had come for, telling herself to restrain her tongue and to remain self-possessed, as if proposals of marriage came regularly. The fact that the governor had come calling without notice was a hopeful sign; maybe he did not wish to hold back an overdue impulse.

"As the war ends, I must give serious thought to how best I can serve the nation," he said. "The Republican convention is no more than eighteen months away. Mr. Lincoln, happily, is not likely to be given much consideration for renomination. Seward must be stopped at all costs—he and the Blairs would subvert the cause for which the war has been fought."

She nodded, forcing herself to listen without comment to a dubious analysis, wondering what would bring him around to a more personal subject.

"As Senator Wade has undoubtedly confided in you," he went on, "there is talk of urging Lincoln to remove Seward. Perhaps of precipitating a resignation of the Cabinet *en masse,* and reconstituting it with myself as a sort of Premier."

She remembered that was what Secretary Seward had tried and failed to do at the start of the Lincoln administration. Didn't Chase realize that Lincoln was too smart, or too strong-willed, to permit anything of the sort? Perhaps he thought Lincoln had been weakened by two years of war. But now, evidently, a great victory on the road to Richmond was expected; the prospect of impending peace would hardly cause the President to panic and turn over the reins to his strongest Republican rival. Just the opposite: victory would end the military necessity for sudden emancipation, allow Lincoln to regain his popularity as a man of moderation, and ensure his renomination. Anna frowned at the flaw in Chase's analysis, then caught herself, lest a frown be construed as disapproval, and smiled brightly.

"Whatever happens, the next year or two will be a time of great political activity for me," he was saying, "and because of that, I am duty-bound to curtail all other interests and activities."

She nodded. A busy time it would surely be for everyone.

"Which means, my dear lady, that I will have to curtail all social activities," he said, shifting in his chair. "I will be working later than ever. I will be traveling more. I will not be able to avail myself of the comfort and the stimulation of social intercourse that other men may indulge in."

What was the man getting at? She looked at him sharply. "Say what you mean."

"What I mean is that we cannot see each other as often as before. It means also," he added, as if in reassurance, "that I will be seeing none of the other friends who, unlike you, have little interest in public affairs." Anna took that to mean that Adele Douglas and a few other women friends of Salmon P. Chase were to be cast aside totally, along with her. Small solace there.

"I would think that at such a time," she countered, "you would need more than ever the companionship and counsel of someone who cares for your future and cares for you."

He shook his handsome head gently but firmly. "I have always conducted myself as a man of honor. I cannot honorably suggest to any woman, especially one for whose intellect I have the greatest respect, the possibility of sharing a life that, in the end, cannot be shared."

She was about to engage that argument and then stopped herself. This was not a discussion in which intelligent refutation of an opposing position would do any good. He was announcing a decision, and it was not the one she had hoped for. She took a deep breath, gave him the benefit of the doubt, and said only, "I do not understand."

"Let me be frank, then. If we were to continue to see each other as in the recent past, we would surely reach the point of considering a more formal and lasting relationship."

She nodded for him to go on.

"Of course, I have no way of knowing what your decision would be to my suit, but I cannot honorably allow matters to go that far. I will let nothing— not my personal happiness in a life that has seen such grief in marriage— nothing cause me to swerve from my path of duty."

Chase had buried three wives, she knew; certainly that affected his thinking about marrying again. But couldn't he see that in her case, she would be a political help, not a hindrance—an active and useful ally, not a dead anchor? The thought occurred to her that his daughter Kate had pressed him to stop seeing his women friends, but celibacy was an unnatural state for a virile man, especially one determined to compete for power. She knew he wanted her completely, as she did him.

What path of duty was he talking about? He was strong enough to deal with a possessive daughter. Instead of analyzing all he said for some hidden motive, she told herself to consider another possibility: it could be that this man, unlike all the others she had known in political life, was being sincere in seeking not to hurt her as others had. She would feel better if that were the reason, and she badly wanted to feel better.

"I will support you in every way I can," she said, "and if that has to include not seeing you, so be it."

Well put, she said to herself; she had a lifetime's experience in farewells without acrimony. She would not let herself think his withdrawal from immediate contact was final. At least this was not a bitter occasion; after Chase succeeded and was President, or failed and was not, perhaps there would be time for being together. She had learned not to close doors; men in public life suffered great changes in fortune that caused greater changes in mind, or else they found other ways to redress their emotional wrongs.

"The Native American Party people—" he began, and she smiled that away.

"I'll talk to my old friend Millard Fillmore in New York," she said. "He hates Seymour and cannot work with Seward. I think you can count on our Know-Nothings." She put her finger alongside her nose and then touched thumb to forefinger, making a zero, the old signal for "nose-nothing."

After the Treasury Secretary left the room, a tender kiss on her forehead his only expression of regret, Anna Carroll shook her head in wonderment at the gentleness of her own reaction to her latest disappointment. She actually felt more sorry for the man than for herself. She would miss a great deal, but he would be missing more. The pity was, he might find out too late to do either of them much good.

She looked out the window at his carriage pulling away in the snow and hurried to put on her overcoat, the good one that Lizzie Keckley had designed three years ago. Since her job was now apparently to be her life, she had to plunge into it with new zest: the first place she wanted to visit was the War Department. Reverend Bob Breckinridge had written her with news passed on by his daughter, Margaret Elizabeth, the Union nurse who had been captured and released in Tennessee: John Breckinridge's son was missing in action and the family was looking for some word of the whereabouts of the body, if hope had gone that he was a prisoner.

Anna Ella Carroll was a personage in Washington, she reminded herself, one of the few women who knew whom to see and what could be done and how to ask for it. Being busy on important work always helped dispel disappointment, as would the realization that her loss of a married future was small compared to the loss being felt by the Kentuckian she had known so well so long ago.

JOHN HAY'S DIARY
DECEMBER 12, 1862

I could not believe the words I was hearing.

"Everything can be the same as before," she said, as if she had not just turned my world inside out. "We can remain friends, perhaps be closer than ever."

"You are becoming another man's wife," I told her, as if explaining a mistaken step to a child, "and you are doing it for money, nothing else. For the money, and the position that Sprague family money can buy. Nothing will ever be the same, for you or for me."

"And who are you to talk about selling your soul for an illustrious future?" she demanded, hating herself through me. "You're an able-bodied young man hiding behind your desk in the Executive Mansion while brave men your age are fighting and dying. You'll stick close to your beloved Father Abraham until the war is almost over, writing your little diary that you can use later to twist history to suit your ends and make your fortune. And when the rebels are on the run, then you'll rush into uniform, with a high rank and a safe job, so that you can pretend to your children you were in the War when the bullets were flying."

I told her, I regret to say, that my children would not be sired by a drunk who had bought his wife. In the heat of the moment, I thought she deserved my cruel riposte; she cannot compare her unnatural attachment to her father to my respect for a great man. But then she started to cry—not the sniffles and tears from a child, but great sobs from a woman unaccustomed to crying, shaking her head in mortification at her weakness, forcing herself to face her shame.

"It isn't so terrible," she insisted when she could speak again. "It's a marriage of convenience, to help the family; the French do it all the time. If you loved me, you'd understand the sacrifice I'm making."

I will give her credit for composing herself quickly, lest some of the passersby in Lafayette Park notice a blubbering young lady amidst the statuary of General Washington's foreign helpers; she extended her gloved hand and gathered what was left of her dignity to bid me goodbye. "I wish you success in your chosen profession," I said coolly, a remark as cruelly accurate as it was felicitously phrased. Now I wish I hadn't said it.

She walked eastward in the late December afternoon, with that gait of independence and grace that I will not soon forget, the heavy woolen skirt concealing the long, slim, muscled legs that some damnable sot will soon know better than I. I have the memories of the kisses and suppressed love cries, the sketches in my mind that one day I will transcribe to poetry or prose, and the comfortable weight of melancholy that only the savored experience of rejection can bestow. And what does Kate have? Sprague, servants, and a bite at the apple of discord.

I suppose I might have frozen to death, sitting on the bench in the park across from the Mansion for an hour or so of such wallowing in my misery, but for the sight of Anna Ella Carroll bustling along Pennsylvania Avenue past the Mansion on the way to the War Department. I hallooed and waved to her to join me; she hallooed back and pointed straight ahead. I ran to catch up to her.

"You always told me Kate was a shrew and a vixen, entirely unworthy of a boy from Illinois," I said, with an attempt at lightheartedness, "and I want you to know that I was wrong and you were right."

She immediately slowed her pace and listened to my news. It affected her more than I thought it would; evidently this fine woman has more of an affection for me than I had hitherto believed. Women are not universally betrayers; Anna Carroll is a good egg.

"When did you learn of her engagement to Governor Sprague?"

"The boy governor is now the boy senator. She told me the happy news of her engagement an hour ago."

The timing seemed to mean something to Anna. She smacked her gloved fist into her palm and muttered some imprecation that, had Miss Carroll been a man, I would have taken as "that son of a bitch!" I assumed she meant that Kate had been acting the bitch in heat, which was all too true, and I agreed that the young lady had used me badly.

We ducked inside the front entrance of the War Department and remained downstairs, out of the cold but in a spot where we could talk privately. I told her the only saving grace of this dismal experience was that it had happened behind a screen of discretion; at least nobody would know of my rejection when the world learned of Kate's infamous match. I had not even told Nicolay. Anna's response was curious: "Tell me how Kate broke the news to you. Was she cold, or genuinely upset? Could you tell?"

I recounted the conversation in some detail as I have put it down in this diary, perhaps with more detail about her looks because the pain was fresher in my mind. When I finished, Miss Carroll startled me with a wholly unexpected reaction.

"You'll get over this in a week, John—your pride is hurt, and that's not all bad—but my heart goes out to that poor young woman."

I stood agape, wondering if I had explained it all wrong, or left out the most important part.

"He's letting her do this for him," she said with great conviction. "The impetus comes from Chase. He needs the Sprague fortune, and he induced his daughter to do this."

When I suggested the idea more likely originated with her, and her father was merely the bystanding recipient of good fortune, Anna Carroll shook her head with the certitude that makes her difficult to argue with. "Kate is a bright, ambitious girl. But Governor Chase is a grown man who knows right from wrong. He could have stopped her from ruining her life for him. He chose to encourage this."

"How can you be sure it wasn't her doing?"

"I know exactly the bargain he offered." She did not reveal the information that might have been so fascinating, and I did not inquire. "John, it is really most important that President Lincoln know how desperately Chase is trying to undermine him. I know for a fact that Chase hopes to enlist the Senate in a push to make Chase the dominant force in the government."

"Mr. Lincoln likes to say that when the presidential grub gets in a man, it hides well," I told her.

"What's a grub?"

"Some sort of chigger, I think, gets under your skin and you can't get it out." (I hate it when people ask me to explain some of the Tycoon's Kentucky figures of speech and I don't know them.) I asked her if Chase had hinted when and how he would make his move for this rather unlikely coup.

"It will be aimed at Seward," she said slowly, "but Lincoln will be the target. Now that the radicals have McClellan's scalp, they want more. Essentially, they want Seward and the Blairs out, Lincoln turned into a eunuch, and Chase in charge. If you think the West Point clique around McClellan was a problem, you may find the radicals behind Chase a real threat."

Something about the way she spoke took my mind off my pain and gave the strange scheme weight. Miss Carroll is an intimate of the Wades, and had been close to Chase; she ought to know whereof she speaks about radical cabals. I resolved to tell the Tycoon about this right away, or as soon as he can get his mind off the battle he has caused to be joined at Fredericksburg. Of late, when we turn to talk of politics, he has been worrying about the peace movement on one flank more than the radicals on his other flank. His problem may be more Chase in his own backyard than Seymour up in New York.

"Tell the President that Seward took the blame for ending the Chiriquí deportation plan," she told me. Miss Carroll had been assigned to work on that scheme for months, to assuage the worry of Northern workers that Emancipation Day would inundate the North with blacks. "Seward elicited an objection from the ambassadors from Central America to the colonization there of our negroes, and wrote back to them saying the whole deportation plan was off. Lot of people are angry at his high-handed ways. Chase and Wade will use that."

Anna beckoned me to follow her upstairs to help on an errand, and I hoped it was not to present her bill for pamphleteering services rendered because I have been told to stay out of that. Fortunately, her quest was to find out whether some secesh soldier had been identified as dead by any of our grave details. I went in with her to one of Stanton's aides, and my presence led him to believe the Prsdt was interested in Miss Carroll's quest, but even in that cooperative state the lists he provided could corroborate nothing. She asked to see our prisoner lists, looked through the B's, found nothing. Nobody was much interested in helping, what with the battle shaping up at any moment in Virginia.

We walked back slowly and she left me in front of the Mansion. I told her of my gratitude for her understanding and her absolute confidence, and she had some advice for me.

"You're too quick to condemn women, John. You call Mrs. Lincoln 'the Hellcat,' and you may not mean to be cruel, but you are. She is a troubled woman who needs help, not scorn. And with Kate"—she saw my warning scowl and ignored it completely—"count yourself fortunate you never misled yourself into thinking that you and she might share a life together."

To make myself feel better, I said maybe Kate had been too old for me.

That may not have been the right thing to say to Miss Carroll, because she snapped, "Then it's for you to grow up. Stop feeling sorry for yourself, John, you're enjoying it too much."

We walked along in silence until she added, "And when you see Kate again, be a man. A boy can be mean, but a man should be kind. She will learn, in good time, that the husband she chose is a disaster, and the father she is throwing away her life for is a sanctimonious fraud. As she grows older, Kate will see your success, and that will be all the vengeance you need—and by then, if you're like a good strong man I used to know, you won't need any."

She said she had another idea about the prisoner lists and whirled around to return to the War Department, leaving me with food for thought: I really should withdraw my first-flush-of-anger oratory. Perhaps a nice note is called for, showing real maturity and wishing her well, which will remove my sense of petty recrimination even as it makes her feel worse. Good idea. Meanwhile, my new philosophy: the sins of the daughters shall be visited on the fathers.

CHAPTER 28

FREDERICKSBURG I
WITH LINCOLN

Lincoln was well aware that these last two weeks of the year could make or break the Union and his administration.

In sixteen days, if Burnside pushed back Lee and if Rosecrans pushed back Bragg, he would be standing in the East Room at the New Year's reception, shaking the hands of thousands of admiring countrymen, seeing in their eyes the approval that could come only from military success. Perhaps that success would be swiftly followed by some response to the proposal, in his annual message, to amend the Constitution to bring about abolishment by the year 1900, with full compensation to owners. In that case, he would have to consider postponing the January 1 emancipation edict to see if the South was ready to end the rebellion on suitable terms. With military success, his would be the whip hand.

Or that day that would begin 1863 might be draped in defeat. In that case, the gloom following setbacks in Virginia and Tennessee would be exaggerated by the holiday period if the generals he had hand-picked failed him and brought the wrath of public sentiment down on the head of the commander in chief. Following so soon on the rejection of his party at the polls, military defeat would cause conservatives to demand he postpone the date of effect of the proclamation for a different reason—lest the Northern resentment of his radical act topple the government and defeat his entire purpose. If he acquiesced to that and stayed the political blow at the South, he would be showing weakness everywhere, unable to carry the day in the field or carry out his threat in the political arena.

So much depended on at least a modest victory somewhere. To achieve his central purpose, Lincoln knew he had first to overcome the pervasive weariness of war; now as never before, he needed the infusion of optimism that only a military excuse for a political thunderbolt would bring.

Of that central purpose Lincoln was in no doubt. The nearly two years of war had shaken him, drained him, aged and hardened him, but he was dead certain that he was right in his basic idea: if the experiment of this republic was to work, the majority had to rule—all the time, with no exceptions. That was the essence of self-government. If a city, or state, or section that was in the minority on any question could just pick up and go when the majority ruled the other way, then there would be no hope for democracy here or anywhere in the world. And if democracy could not take root in the New World, where the people had shown they had the will to overpower kings, then government by the people would stand revealed as an absurdity. Constant subdividing would lead to anarchy, followed by a return to monarchs, dictators, and despotism. He was certain of that in his soul.

The success of the American experiment rested on the willingness of the minority to acquiesce in electoral defeat. True, the Republican candidate in 1860 had been the choice of a plurality and not a majority, but Abraham Lincoln had been duly elected according to the Constitution, and was bound by more than his oath to beat down the notion that the losers could set up shop for themselves. He was certain that if he failed to hold the Union intact, using its blood as its glue, not only would the dream of the nation's founders be dissipated, but the cause of human freedom throughout the world would be set back for centuries. The stakes in this struggle could not be higher or the core idea clearer: upon the outcome of this war of brothers hinged the ability of people to be their own masters.

He rolled out of bed, took up the pitcher, and poured it over his head into the basin. That need to enforce the rule of the majority, he reminded himself, justified bending the Constitution occasionally. That justified opposing abolition last year when such restraint helped win the war, or supporting abolition this year when such radicalism helped win the war.

He had plunged the nation into war to put the flag back, not to put down slavery. Last year, to have undertaken abolition would have smacked of bad faith and weakened the cause of the Union. He had told his closest supporters that abolition's thunderbolt would keep. Now he needed a thunderbolt to energize and save the Union.

Certainly it took a load off his mind to be able, finally, to use that thunderbolt in a way that served rather than harmed the central goal: now he was in the happy position of being able to advocate both the preservation of the Union and an end to slavery. His previous position of promising not to strike at slavery where it existed, merely to prevent its extension, had not overly troubled him—he had been carrying out the contract of the founders and his own campaign promises. But his preliminary proclamation had opened a new vista: he was at last persuaded that his personal wish to end slavery would advance and not retard the saving of the Union. After the disastrous elections and the rise of Seymour and the peace movement, however, Lincoln needed at least a modicum of military progress to be sure.

He finished dressing and straightened his hair with his fingers, ignoring the mirror. He thought about looking in on Mary in the bedroom across the hall and decided against it. She needed her rest, which came best in the mornings for her, and the sight of her ashen face these days with its pursed-lipped mouth made him sad.

He remembered back to the days in Springfield, when her women's problems that came just after the birth of Tad had ended their passion, such as it was, and they had agreed it would be safer and more comfortable to sleep apart. The year he ran for the Senate against Douglas, and lost, they had the house remodeled and separate bedrooms put in. In those days she would come in and wake him, sometimes with coffee; now he rarely saw her in the mornings, and he worried about what went on in her troubled mind after those late sessions with mediums and seers, or after the debilitating bouts with the sick headaches. Mary was usually a burden now, but not always; sometimes she was a source of strength, when he was afflicted with the hypo and could talk to nobody else. And he would not forget that when he was an awkward and woman-fearing young man, the well-bred Mary Todd had helped civilize and socialize him.

On the way down the hall to his office, the President banged on Nicolay's door; though it was not yet six o'clock, his first secretary was already half dressed. Lincoln told him to get a horse and ride down to Fredericksburg to see if General Burnside had finally got his pontoon bridge across the Rappahannock. The damned pontoons had been delayed and Burnside would not consider any other way of getting his men and wagons across the river.

Lincoln told his senior secretary he was worried that the general was going to be too busy to keep the War Department informed of the attack on Lee.

"Maybe Chase was right," said Nicolay, stuffing his shirt in his pants. "Maybe Joe Hooker would have been better."

"Burnside is better," Lincoln said with more certainty than he felt, "because he is the better housekeeper."

The expected look of puzzlement crossed Nicolay's serious face. Nicolay was better than young Hay when it came to predictable reactions. "Do you need a housekeeper or a general?"

"I tell you, Nicolay, the successful management of an army requires a good deal of faithful housekeeping. More fight will be got out of well-fed and well-cared-for soldiers and animals than can be got out of those that are required to make long marches with empty stomachs."

"Yes, Mr. President. I'll write a pass for you to sign."

Lincoln strode to his office and wrote the pass himself: "Major General Burnside, My dear Sir: The bearer, Mr. J. G. Nicolay, is, as you know, my private Secretary. Please treat him kindly, while I am sure he will avoid giving you trouble." He signed it and soon sent Nicolay on his way with an admonition to stay out of the line of fire. Lincoln hated these days when a battle was raging nearby and he had to depend on busy or uncaring generals to send him news. He would likely spend the day and night at the telegraph office, hearing nothing. If the newspapers could afford a correspondent on the scene, so could the President of the United States.

He put his fists on his hips and stretched his long body, wishing he could get some exercise. So much rested with Burnside, more daring than McClellan, more cautious than Hooker. He had chosen the fellow with the weird whiskers partly because he was known to be a McClellan man, not eager to replace Little Mac, and thus would be least likely to provoke an army coup.

Lincoln knew that Burn had had more than his share of disappointments in life; he had even brought a girl to the altar of marriage, only to hear her say "no" at the crucial moment; the President shook his head to clear it of doubt. He had provided Burnside with every available man and gun, more than he had ever done for McClellan. The Union force was said to be 170,000, more than double the size of Lee's army and, thanks to the preceding commander, far better equipped.

Lincoln could not put the Young Napoleon out of his mind; the ousted general had planned to attack Lee in a place that might have had Stonewall Jackson's division far from Longstreet's; Burnside preferred a direct assault across the river. Was that wise? Lee surely was aware of the impending attack, delayed by the damned pontoons, and might have ordered Longstreet to dig in on the heights. Lincoln shook that thought off, too: Burnside could be counted on to smash the rebels now, before the end of the year.

Nothing to do but wait for news from the front. He contemplated the papers on his desk. The Sioux had risen in the West, massacring white settlers; the order to hang three hundred warriors was prepared for his signature. He wrote a note to the general asking him to select only those Indians who had actually participated in the killing of innocents in a massacre. That way, he estimated, he would approve the hanging of only about thirty.

The North was poised for a victory. Halleck was confident; General Haupt, the quartermaster, was equally certain of victory, and had gone down to the front to observe the battle after promising to hurry back to Lincoln with news of the first decisive engagement. The rebels under Lee had already been beaten a few months ago; the Army of the Potomac had never been better prepared for the strike that would have them eating Christmas dinner in Richmond. Then, on New Year's Day, he would sign the proclamation freeing the slaves under his war power.

He looked in the outer office for Hay or Stoddard; neither was at work yet. Lincoln trotted down the stairs and went to the front door to see if the newsboy had arrived yet with the *Intelligencer*.

CHAPTER 29

FREDERICKSBURG II
NOT A CHICKEN ALIVE

General James Longstreet, on his horse atop Marye's Heights, looked through his telescope down on the city of Fredericksburg, now being invested and looted by Federal troops. Behind them was the Rappahannock, which the men in blue had crossed on a pontoon bridge, taking some casualties from Confederate sharpshooters. He could see flashes of artillery from a wide arc facing him, as the Federals laid down one of the largest and longest barrages of the war. The incoming balls were not doing much damage to the Confederate position, where the troops were properly entrenched, but the barrage announced that the Army of the Potomac was massing for an assault up a long, sloping field toward the butternut troops on the heights.

"Pete, does our artillery cover that field?" General Lee asked him.

"My artillery chief assures me, sir," Longstreet replied, "a chicken could not live on that field when we open on it."

Never had the Confederate forces been in a more advantageous position to punish an attacking force. On Jeff Davis's orders, Lee had ordered entrenchment; beyond that, a sunken road ran parallel to the expected line of attack, providing invisible cover for defending infantry. The field guns were ready with canister to inflict maximum casualties.

"That sure isn't McClellan over there," he observed to General Lee. They had seen the order relieving their old adversary, replacing him with Burnside. The inventor of the best saddle had been replaced by the inventor of the best breech-loading rifle, and it apparently made a big difference in the way the battle would be fought.

"In a way, I regret to part with McClellan," said Lee. "We always understood each other so well. I fear they may continue to make these changes till they find someone I don't understand."

"The men don't like digging in, sir. They think it's cowardly work, unfit for white men. They call you 'the King of Spades'."

"My army is as much stronger for these new entrenchments," Lee said evenly, "as if I had received reinforcements of twenty thousand men."

They would need that advantage, because the oncoming Union Army was a sight to behold, massing as the morning fog lifted, for the onslaught up the long hills. Longstreet did not need his spyglass to see the polished arms and bright blue uniforms in array, battle flags fluttering, as on a holiday occasion.

"They are massing very heavily," Lee said, which Longstreet took to be his commander's way of noting that the opposing army outnumbered the Confederate troops by two to one.

"If you put every man in the Union Army on that field," Longstreet replied, "to approach me over the same line, and give me plenty of ammunition, I will kill them all before they reach my line. Jackson over there may be in some danger, but not my line."

He wondered why Burnside would be so foolhardy as to step into this trap. McClellan would never have put himself in this position, and if he found himself there, would have had the good military sense to swing around and concentrate his assault on Jackson's position and then try to roll up the line. Burnside was coming straight ahead, the whole of his army against the whole of the Confederate line.

Maybe the Union general was acting under direct orders from Lincoln. If Jeff Davis ever gave him an order like that, Longstreet vowed, he would resign rather than try to force his men to commit suicide against the enemy in its stronghold. Or maybe Burnside was acting on his own, trying to make up for his indecision and delay at the bridge over the Antietam; whatever the reason, the result was command stupidity on a scale never before seen in this war.

"They're coming," General Lee said.

That was not an order to fire; Lee left such decisions to his lieutenants. Longstreet waited until the massed blue troops came forward into the open field, almost within range of the 2,500 men in Cobb's brigade, hidden in the sunken road behind a long stone wall. He raised and dropped his arm, ordering his artillery to open fire. A sheet of flame seemed to lash down the hill and the carnage began.

"It is well that war is so terrible," General Lee observed; "we would grow too fond of it."

Longstreet watched the decimated ranks of blue resolutely march forward, maintaining a steady step and closing up broken ranks with more determination than he had ever seen in battle, until they came within range of General Cobb's muskets. A storm of lead swept through the advancing ranks from Confederates hidden behind a long stone wall.

No army, no matter how valiant, could long maintain discipline in the face of such crossfire. The massed muskets and artillery blasting grapeshot were chewing up the Union front and flank, while other artillery was devastating the rear. Longstreet thought ahead; if the Army of the Potomac kept sending wave upon wave of men to their death, the war could be ended today; if they fell back, perhaps a Confederate bayonet charge down from the heights could pin the remaining Federals against the river behind them. He wanted to talk to Generals Hood and Pickett about that. It was just possible that Lincoln and his new general had, in a gamble against impossible odds, thrown away the war.

"I wish," he heard Lee say, in a kind of justification of the slaughter but also an offhand summary of his personal goal in the war, "I wish these people would go away and let us alone."

CHAPTER 30

FREDERICKSBURG III
WITH NICOLAY

John Nicolay was frightened. He had cheerfully accepted the assignment to come down to Fredericksburg to observe the battle and to keep the President informed, but he had not realized the extent to which it might mean risk of life. He was a lawyer, not a soldier, and was willing to risk his eyesight studying late nights for his admission to practice before the Supreme Court, but physical exposure to enemy fire was not in his line.

The city of Fredericksburg was in Union hands but that offered no comfort because rebel guns were in position on the heights facing the city. It was Sunday morning, gray and foggy, but no church bells were ringing: the churches were closed. Most of the Virginia city's inhabitants had fled, and many Federal soldiers not at the front were busy stealing valuables from Virginian homes. A bombardment could begin at any moment if General Lee saw fit to destroy Southern property occupied by Federal forces. Nicolay saw no need to stay for the shelling.

The day before, he had learned, a great battle had begun. Late Saturday night, when the President's secretary arrived at Burnside's headquarters from Washington, he had found it difficult to determine the outcome. The Federal opening attack had been beaten back, and the talk was of terrible losses on both sides, but General Burnside was undaunted, which Nicolay supposed augured well. The secretary wondered whether he should have sent a tele-gram to the President, who was probably famished for news, but Nicolay could not figure out, in all the confusion and disagreement at headquarters, who was winning. It had been hard to tell anything from Burnside's head-quarters, located north of the Rappahannock across from Fredericksburg and out of sight of the fighting. Better to remain silent, he had decided, than to transmit a wild guess that might later come back to haunt him.

When the thunder of artillery woke him at dawn, he had hurried to the telegraph operator to see what Burnside was reporting to Washington. The 4 A.M. dispatch was encouraging: "I have just returned from the field. Our troops are all over the river. We hold the first ridge outside the town, and three miles below. We hope to carry the crest today."

But at a pre-breakfast council of war that Burnside allowed the President's representative to attend, a wholly different picture emerged.

"Any movement to my front is impossible at present," General Franklin told his optimistic commander. "The truth is, my left is in danger of being turned."

Franklin had been a McClellan favorite, Nicolay knew, and was not one of the more aggressive generals. Eyes swung to General Hooker, but "Fighting Joe" had as little taste for more battle. "I lost as many men yesterday as your orders required me to lose," he said bitterly. "There has been enough blood shed to satisfy any reasonable man, and it is time to quit."

Nicolay had understood from Stanton that no love was lost between Hooker and Burnside, rivals for the command of McClellan's army. Nor was Hooker a Lincoln man—"Fighting Joe" was famous for his frequent calls for a dictator, and his visits to the Chase home. Burnside was unlikely to heed Hooker's advice, even when it was the opposite of rash.

The crushing statement came from old General Sumner, leader of the Third Grand Division of Burnside's force. He had been in the army when Burnside was a child, and his reputation as a joyous warrior was approaching legend. Nobody doubted his courage or zest for combat; Burnside, it was said, had ordered him to remain at headquarters the day before lest the old man get killed leading charges.

"General, I hope you will desist from this attack," said Sumner. "I do not know of any general officer who approves of it, and I think it will prove disastrous to the army."

That shook Burnside for a moment, but he evidently knew what Lincoln had appointed him to do. "Assemble my old brigade. They know me, they will follow me anywhere. I will lead them myself in a charge against the center, against the sunken road, and I will break Lee's line or die in the attempt."

That struck Nicolay as foolhardy, even crazy, but he knew it was more than bravado; Burnside made it clear he had not come this far for a standoff, and was willing to do what none of his subordinates was ready to do. The others disagreed with the commander's desperate plan, and Burnside agreed to reconsider; the council broke up with no decision made.

The telegraph operator came in with a message from Lincoln to Nicolay. Five stern words: "What news do you have?" With that impetus Nicolay summoned what personal courage he had and rode across the pontoon bridge into the city of Fredericksburg. The town had been badly battered, the streets streaming with men carrying the wounded on litters to the charnel houses that the schools and churches had become. Nicolay stayed long enough to ride through two of the principal streets and to find a place where he could observe the heights from below. An officer lent him a small spyglass and angrily pointed to the area in front of the sunken road and low stone wall. Nicolay, to his horror, saw a long mound of blue bodies, with rebel soldiers creeping among them, pulling shoes off dead men's feet.

The officer invited him into one of the larger houses, its roof partially caved in, for a cup of coffee with some of his comrades. Nicolay asked them what he should report to the President, hoping they would hurry and let him go before the bombardment began anew.

"Tell Lincoln we might as well have tried to take Hell."

"We've lost more than two men to their one," said a lieutenant from Ohio. "If we have to go up that hill again, we'll lose the whole damn army. At least with Little Mac, we had a chance. We were on the attack at Antietam, but Lee lost as many men as we did, and he had to leave the field."

"Lincoln doesn't give a hoot how many of us he loses," a man with a bandaged hand told Nicolay. "He figures there's more of us than of them, and after a few years we'll grind 'em down. Burnside's his boy, and he'll shovel us in again today or tomorrow."

"That's not the worst of it," said the first officer. "If Bobby Lee finds out the shape we're in, he'll send Jackson's division down here and catch us up against the river. The whole army will have to surrender, and there won't be a blue coat between here and Washington."

Nicolay nodded quickly and headed back across the bridge, past the heavy artillery emplacements near the headquarters, back to Washington. He decided against answering the President's telegram with one of his own, because he could not legitimately advise whether Burnside was crazy or the rest of the generals were, like him, afraid for their lives.

CHAPTER 31

FREDERICKSBURG IV
JOHN HAY'S DIARY
DECEMBER 14, 1862

Poor Nico got back from the front at dusk Sunday, much the worse for wear, to have the Tycoon bark at him, "What news do you have?"

My rattled associate brought forth some isolated details about the battle scene and some second-guessing of the military commanders by low-level officers in a bar that was about to be blown to smithereens by rebel artillery. Maybe he was not the right observer to send. I might not have been much better.

At times like these, the Prsdt is especially short-tempered because he thirsts for information. Strategy can be obtained in great dollops from Halleck, who is in his office at 16th and Eye street, scratching, always scratching, but specific information is supposed to come from the generals at the front. Lincoln has been to the telegraph office across the street four times today, and once in the middle of the night last night, to see if he could suck some news through the wires.

Earlier today, the Hellcat came in to my office. Since her husband did not want to go to church, she wanted Stod to send a carriage for Orville Browning. That defeated senator from the political disaster land we used to call Illinois needs not so much a ride to church but a ticket to a permanent place in government. Both Lincolns want him to stay in Washington, but it is getting difficult to appoint the hometown crowd to more of anything.

After church, Browning came by the office to express his worry about casualties in the rumors that were floating up from Virginia. He asked the Tycoon about the strength of our army, considering the losses we were supposedly taking.

"With Sigel's corps, which has just joined Burnside," the Prsdt told him, "it numbers 170,000 men." He sighed and added, "But that's darkie arithmetic."

When his friend asked what "darkie arithmetic" was, Lincoln interrupted his pacing to relax into a story. "Two young contrabands, as we have learned to call them, were seated together when one said, 'Jim, do you know 'rithmetic?' Jim answered no. 'It's when you add up things,' said the first. 'When you have one and one and puts them together, they makes two. When if you have two and takes one away, only one remains.' Jim replies, ' 'Tain't true den; it's no good. S'pose three pigeons sit on that fence, and somebody shoot one of dem, do t'other two stay dar? No, sar, dey flies away quicker'n odder feller falls.'

"And Orville, trifling as the story seems, it illustrates the arithmetic you must use in estimating the number of troops we have and the losses we are supposed to take in battle." He obviously hoped Browning would take back the point of the story to the worriers in Congress. "Don't believe the count of killed, wounded, and missing at the first roll call after a battle. It always exhibits a greatly exaggerated total, especially in the column of missing."

He may be cheering himself up, readying himself for the worst. It is true that many of the men at first listed as missing later return, and Lincoln carries around figures in his hat to prove it, but every attempt to prepare himself, his friends, and the public for bad news has failed.

I refuse to join the general gloom; perhaps I lack the necessary sense of foreboding. The Army of the Potomac, which has never scored a decisive victory, may yet find its first on the banks of the Rappahannock.

7 P.M.: My optimism, and Burnside's, may be misplaced. I have just joined the general gloom. No substantial word from the generals, but the first reports from the newspaper correspondents are coming into the telegraph office for censorship and Stod says that Homer Bates says it does not look so good. Most of the press is all too delighted to emphasize the negative, however; it makes one wonder which side they are on. I sent word to Homer to keep an eye out for any dispatches from the *Tribune*. Uncle Horace's journal, at least, did a fair-minded job at Antietam.

9 P.M.: Quartermaster General Herman Haupt, the railroad man who

makes the army's trains run on time—Stanton thinks of him as a logistical genius, and Anna Carroll agrees, so I guess he is—came in to the War Department from the battlefield and Stanton sent him over here.

"Extremely heavy losses," he reported solemnly, "with no substantial gains of the high ground to show for them."

Lincoln took him to the map table, and Haupt laid out in some detail the order of battle and the progress made so far. Lincoln pressed him on the counsel that Burnside was receiving, and on his state of mind. Haupt thought that the subordinate generals were wise in wanting to stop the slaughter, but that Burnside was determined to make a final, decisive assault, and that he was of sound mind and body—brave, too; ready to lead the men up the hill. Lincoln wanted specifics, and for the better part of an hour the quartermaster read from his notes on the disposition of our forces and the relative strengths of the rebel positions.

They were interrupted by Senator Henry Wilson, who came in to worry about what a defeat would do in the Senate. He fears that anti-Seward sentiment is growing in the august body in which he serves, and all those who would like to stick a thumb in the President's eye by going after his closest adviser are looking for an event to trigger a crisis. Wilson says that a big defeat at this point could topple the President, whatever that is supposed to mean.

"What makes you think we face defeat?" I asked, since neither Lincoln nor Haupt wanted to volunteer the bad news or register false optimism.

"I've just come from the bar at Willard's," he said, "Smalley of the *Tribune* is there. He's fresh in from the battlefield and sent his dispatch to New York only a few minutes ago. Says we took a terrible licking."

"Get his dispatch from the telegraph office," Lincoln said to me, and then told Senator Wilson to fetch the reporter from the bar at Willard's and bring him to the Mansion.

CHAPTER 3 2

FREDERICKSBURG V
WITH LINCOLN

Lincoln wondered why the *Tribune* dispatch had not yet been received at the telegraph office. Probably there was an interruption down the line in Virginia. Fredericksburg was only forty-five miles away, halfway between Washington and Richmond, and a man riding hard could make that in a few hours, beating his own dispatch.

Henry Wilson showed up with correspondent George Smalley in tow. The President did not let on that he had been searching for his message to the *Tribune* in New York, nor did he show his concern about a possible setback.

The *Tribune* man was in his battlefield dress, romantically grimy, smelling of tobacco and whiskey. He was obviously embarrassed about being dragooned into the presence of the commander in chief in such a state of dishevelment. Smalley looked to Lincoln like an aristocrat, unlike most of the war reporters who called themselves the Bohemian Brigade. He stood straight and tall in front of the President, weaving just a little, when Wilson presented him in the second-floor reception room.

"I am much obliged to you for coming," said Lincoln, pumping Smalley's hand heartily, "for we are very anxious and have heard very little."

When Hay said his dispatch had not yet arrived in Washington for censorship, Smalley looked a little guilty, hemmed and hawed, then finally admitted that it was his plan to avoid the telegraph entirely, since he had had so much trouble with that method of communication during the battle at Antietam. "I sent it by special messenger on the night train to New York," he confessed, "to make sure it got there in time."

Lincoln read the ulterior motive immediately: the correspondent wanted to circumvent Stanton's censorship. Smalley would have kept that from almost anyone on earth, but Lincoln had learned it was hard for most men to lie directly to the President.

"What is the news, then?" Senator Wilson pressed. "Have we won the fight?"

"Burnside is defeated and in a terrible plight," Smalley reported with certainty. "The worst of it is that he doesn't know it."

The President, who had learned not to accept the immediate judgments of newspapermen, would not let himself believe that. He asked the correspondent to say only what he knew from his personal knowledge, and to tell him in general outline what had happened. Smalley, from exhaustion and the drinks he had imbibed at Willard's after sending his dispatch, talked in a slurred voice but—Lincoln was dismayed to admit—with a vast command of the facts.

The three Grand Divisions under Hooker, Franklin, and Sumner had attacked the heights, which were defended by Jackson on the right and Longstreet in the center and left. Old General Sumner had struck hard and been repulsed with devastating losses, leaving nearly a third of his men dead or bleeding on the field in his retreat. General Franklin attacked feebly and soon withdrew. General Hooker had done all that bravery and devotion could do, Smalley said, having objected at first to the suicidal charge he had been ordered to make, but having followed his orders until the withering fire from the entrenched positions had driven his men back. "At the day's end," Smalley concluded, "we were back where we had started, thoroughly and bloodily repulsed."

"Casualties?" asked Wilson.

"I don't say in my dispatch," the correspondent stated carefully, "but for your private information, I should guess between twelve and fifteen thousand men. It was a slaughter."

"I hope it is not so bad as all that," said the President. He then proceeded to question the *Tribune* man in detail for more than a half hour. What were Longstreet's defenses? How vulnerable was the rebels' present artillery command of the town and river? What were the physical condition and morale of the Union troops before and after the fight? What were the chances of success of another attack from each wing? What was the feeling about a renewal of the attack among the general officers?

Smalley laced his answers with censure of Burnside, but Lincoln was careful not to imply criticism of the commander in any of his questions. He also discounted Smalley's praise of Hooker; Thurlow Weed had told him after Antietam that the *Tribune* reporters were mainly Chase-Hooker men.

"Mr. President," Smalley said, when the questioning was at an end, "it is not for me to offer advice to you, and the truth is that I am not feeling very well at the moment and may regret my presumption later."

Lincoln waited for him to say what was on his mind.

"It is not only my conviction, but that of every general officer I saw before and after the fighting, that success is impossible." Lincoln's judgment was that the man was sincere. "The worst disaster yet suffered by our forces in this war will befall the Army of the Potomac if the attack is renewed, and unless the army is withdrawn at once to the north side of the river."

Retreat. Did the reporter know what he was counseling? What would the country say? If Grant had listened to that despairing advice at Shiloh after the first day, the West would be lost today.

Lincoln thanked him, giving no hint of his opinion of the advice. Senator Wilson assisted Smalley out. Hay volunteered to get word to Horace Greeley to treat his correspondent's dispatch the way he had a similar report of disaster at first Bull Run—that is, by editing out the worst of the news, which otherwise might cripple morale in the nation's largest city and feed red meat to the Seymour forces.

At midnight, Hill Lamon brought in word that Governor Curtin of Pennsylvania had sent in word that he had just returned from a visit to his state's troops at Fredericksburg and wanted urgently to see the President. Lincoln lifted Tad off the couch in the office where the boy had been sleeping, handed him to Mrs. Keckley, and told Lamon to fetch Curtin. He knew the Pennsylvanian to be a cool and sensible Union man, among the most stalwart of the "war governers," a regular provider of troops.

Governor Curtin entered with General Haupt. "Mr. President, it was not a battle, it was a butchery," the governor said bluntly. He recited what he had seen in grim detail and this time Lincoln had no questions. The President, listening, felt his control of the war and the country slipping from him.

Lincoln sat on the couch, head in his hands, breathing deeply, in no mood to put up a brave front to General Haupt and Governor Curtin. This was his defeat, a bloody refutation of Abraham Lincoln's military judgment, and it would open the gates for all his enemies in the Congress and in the peace movement to move in for the political kill. The demands in the next few days for a negotiation to settle the war would be loud and strident, and they could not be ignored. If the disaster worsened, if Burnside's army attacked and failed again, if Lee counterattacked and took tens of thousands of prisoners— that would surely be the end. Everyone would say it could never have happened under McClellan, and to Lincoln the worst of it was—that was the truth. Even assuming the army could be withdrawn without further disaster and the extent of the losses could be concealed for some time, the political storm could not be averted.

He raised his red-rimmed eyes to look at Curtin, who had not realized that his harsh recital came as the culmination of a day of hammer blows. The governor sat on the couch next to the President, took his large hand in his, and made a belated effort to soften the blow. Lincoln had not felt so stricken

George W. Smalley

after Pope's defeat; this was of a different order of magnitude of despair, a wave of depression he had not felt since Willie died.

"I am deeply touched, Mr. President, at the distress I have caused you," Curtin was saying. "It may not be as bleak as I said—no doubt my impressions are colored by the sufferings I have seen."

Lincoln nodded, not looking up. He felt the shortness of breath, the pain in his head and chest that signaled the onset of the hypo.

"It could well be that matters will look brighter when later reports come in," the governor added. "I wish—I would give everything I have to rescue you and our nation from this terrible war."

Lincoln leaned back, jammed his fingers through his hair, and forced the blackness away from him. The trick to containing the fear and grief was to tell a story. "Reminds me, Governor, of an old farmer out in Illinois I used to know."

He told the hog story, about the man who bought a prize hog and put it in a pen. His two sons taunted the hog, who broke out of the pen and drove one boy up a tree and was closing in on the other boy. The only way the boy could save himself was by holding on to the hog's tail. "The hog wouldn't give up his hunt nor the boy his hold," said Lincoln, animation returning to his face in recounting the familiar story, "and after they had made a good many circles around the tree, the boy's courage began to give out, and he shouted at his brother, 'I say, John, come down quick, and help me let this hog go!' "

That was the hog story, and Lincoln added the point, in case anybody missed the need for Burnside to disengage from Lee's victorious army: "Now, Governor, that is exactly my case. I wish somebody would come and help me let this hog go."

Curtin forced a chuckle, which Lincoln appreciated, and took his leave. The President, slightly refreshed and determined not to slip back down, paced the corridor for a while and asked Haupt to walk with him to General Halleck's office. The general was sure to be there on the night of a great battle.

At Halleck's, the President told Haupt to repeat what he had learned at the battlefront, and to repeat the reports of Smalley and Curtin about the danger to the troops now under the rebel guns. When the precise engineer concluded, Lincoln said to his general-in-chief, "I want you to telegraph orders to Burnside right now to withdraw his army to the north side of the river."

"I will do no such thing," said General Halleck. Into the stunned silence, he spoke again: "If such orders are issued, you must issue them yourself. I hold that a general in command of an army in the field is the best judge of existing conditions."

Lincoln found the situation hard to believe. There they all were—in the middle of the night, with the fate of the army and the nation hanging in the balance—at an impasse. Lincoln made no reply to the insubordinate statement by this military clerk, whose only job it was to pass along orders couched in military language to the commanders in the field. As Lincoln had checked his depression by force of will, he now checked his impatience. He stood at the fireplace saying nothing, lest Halleck become a devastating witness before Wade's committee when all this was over.

Herman Haupt moved to resolve the tension. "Perhaps the situation is not as critical as we imagine it to be," he said, pointing to the limitations of the *Tribune* correspondent's view, and the relatively few people that Curtin had spoken to. Battles, he said, had their ebbs and flows; in the view of this afternoon's observers, the Federal forces had looked defeated, but tomorrow might be different. At any rate, Burnside was not a rash commander, no matter how he sounded to some of his men on this day; he could be trusted to act in character in the end.

"What you say," Lincoln sighed, "gives me a great many grains of comfort. Still . . ." Smalley had been accurate about Antietam. Curtin had a keen eye and a good head. He walked back to the Mansion three blocks away, gulping in the frigid air, wondering if he should intervene in the battle and order Burnside to get back across those damned pontoons.

Homer Bates, on duty through the night at the War Department telegraph office, looked up and saw the President in the doorway. He appeared more haggard than usual. Bates looked to see if any late dispatches had come in from Burnside, but found none that had not been sent to the Mansion earlier.

"Is there a message you wish to send, Mr. President?"

Lincoln sat down at Major Eckert's desk, where he had spent so much time working on his proclamation, and fiddled with a pen for a moment. After a while he put down the pen, rose and without a word walked out, down the hall, down the steps and across the street to the White House.

A few hours later, just before dawn, clacking came from the headquarters of the Army of the Potomac. Bates quickly worked out the cipher: Burnside had decided to use the cover of a storm to withdraw his army to the north side of the Rappahannock.

The telegrapher thought that important enough to run over to the Mansion himself. He found Lincoln sleeping on the couch in his office, hesitated a moment, then woke him with the news of the safe retreat. Lincoln read the telegraph message, smiled his sad smile, patted Bates on the shoulder, and went off to his room to go to bed.

CHAPTER 33

GET SEWARD

Anna Carroll darted under the scaffolding supporting the men at work on the Capitol dome and found her way to the office of the Chairman of the Joint Committee on the Conduct of the War. Ben Wade, his bulldog features seeming only slightly more ferocious than usual, skipped his customary warm greeting and announced: "Seward must go!"

She cocked her head in puzzlement: what had the Secretary of State to do with the debacle at Fredericksburg? In her opinion, if any Cabinet officers deserved blame, they were Chase and Stanton; those two radicals were responsible for the mistaken removal of McClellan and his replacement by an incompetent.

"Did you see this?" Wade went on, thrusting a sheaf of papers at her. She read the innocuous title page of the disbound government document: "Diplomatic correspondence of the United States, 1861." Wade jabbed a stubby finger at a paragraph circled in red.

"This proves where Seward's heart is," the senator stormed. "Can you imagine the gall of a man to write a thing like that at the start of the war, a week before Fort Sumter? And then to rub our noses in it by publishing it this week?"

Anna read the offending paragraph by Seward in a letter to an American diplomat abroad. The Secretary of State had held in April of 1861 that Lincoln was not likely to force the seceding states to remain in the Union. "Only an imperial or despotic government," Seward had written, "could subjugate thoroughly disaffected or insurrectionary members of the state."

"That was not the Lincoln policy at the time," she said mildly. That verified what Old Man Blair had told her: only the Blairs had supported the President in the Cabinet when the new President decided to provision Sumter. If put to a Cabinet vote, there would have been no war and no Union. "I guess the President overruled Seward and decided to defend the fort."

"Goddamn Buchananism, that's what it was!" Wade roared. "That viper Seward, who now rubs our noses in the proof he didn't want to fight secession, has been the power behind the throne for nearly two years. And look right here—see this drivel? This is why we haven't had a proclamation of freedom yet, and why we probably won't have one on New Year's Day."

The sentence that enraged the senator, and surely would release pent-up fury in the Joint Committee when it met, jumped out at her: "It seems as if extreme advocates of African slavery and its most vehement opponents were acting in concert," read the Seward letter of July 5, 1861, "together to precipitate a servile war—the former by making the most desperate attempts to overthrow the Federal union, the latter by demanding an edict of universal emancipation . . ."

Seward's statement was, to say the least, impolitic in equating the abolitionists of the North with the secessionists of the South, blaming both equally for bringing on the war. Anna could not understand Seward's reason for putting all this out at this time, when the anger of the divisions within the Republican ranks did not need further aggravation. She had agreed with Seward's anti-abolition sentiments at the time, but at least she had the good sense to keep her mouth shut about all that now. Times had changed; the center of gravity within the party was shifting; one did not admit now to what one had thought then.

"McClellan in the field and Seward in the Cabinet," said Wade, taking back the papers and plopping them on his desk, "have brought our grand cause to the very brink of death. Seward must be got out of the Cabinet. He is Lincoln's evil genius."

Anna shook her head; that was going overboard. If anything, the printed correspondence proved that Seward's influence over Lincoln was not nearly so great as most people in Washington believed.

Her demurral stimulated another outburst from her friend Wade. "Seward has been the de facto President. He has kept a sponge saturated with chloroform to Uncle Abe's nose all the while, except for one or two brief spells."

"During which Lincoln decided to fight a civil war, and to free the slaves. Come on now, Ben—you've been talking to Chase again."

He glowered, the tucks at the corner of his mouth making him look more pugnacious; that was the visage that made witnesses tremble. She mock-glowered back and he settled down a bit. "Some of us pushed Lincoln into doing the right thing from time to time," he said. "Has Stanton paid your bill yet?"

She shook her head; she had forwarded to the War Department letters from Edward Everett and Horace Binney, both respected lawyers, praising her war powers pamphlet. In a more subtle move, she had placed on the President's desk her memorial showing how his proposed emancipation edict could be justified by a loose interpretation of the war power; it was better than anything he would get from his Attorney General. But she was becoming resigned to the likelihood that she would not be paid until the war ended. Thurlow Weed had steered a paying assignment to her, and somehow she was able to make ends meet. At least, she told herself, she would not have to support poor Salmon Chase.

"That's not why I'm here," she said. "I want you to get the committee's attention away from this back-and-forth business between here and Richmond, and focus on where the war can be won."

He did not agree. "The real war this week is right here in Washington. Forget all your military logistics and strategy, my dear lady. Either the Congress runs this country or Lincoln does. This week, within forty-eight hours, there is going to be a showdown."

She could tell that the senator was serious, but there was a logical inconsistency in his present anger at the President. "He got rid of McClellan, as you wanted," she said. "He's freeing the slaves, as you demanded. What is Lincoln doing that you want to force a showdown about?"

"We're not to blame for Fredericksburg!" Wade replied sharply, and the alacrity of his response to an accusation she had not made startled her. Then the outline of political maneuvering began to come clear: The slaughter on the Rappahannock was being blamed on Stanton's War Department, and on the radicals' insistence on replacing McClellan; deservedly so. To take the heat off themselves, Stanton and Chase—with the active cooperation of the radical faction in Congress—were trying to direct the public dissatisfaction at William Henry Seward. She knew Stanton to be a master manipulator who once before had conspired with Chase to reduce Lincoln's power; Chase had told her all about that attempted coup that might have succeeded but for Navy Secretary Welles's refusal to go along.

Evidently Stanton and Chase had been visiting Wade, and probably Zack Chandler and Maine's William Fessenden too. Wade and the radical Republicans, embarrassed at the failure that followed their replacement of McClellan, saw that they would soon be placed on the political defensive unless they attacked again, reasserting their control of the war and its ultimate purpose. This time the anti-Lincoln forces in the Cabinet were joining with the anti-Lincoln radicals in the Congress, making the movement more formidable; and at a time of much greater turmoil, they had chosen a target much closer to Lincoln. The President had always been ambivalent about McClellan, but Seward was his closest confidant and political ally.

"You think you can force Seward out?" She was certain of her political analysis; it was now what she enjoyed most in life.

"Damn right, Anna. Billy Bowlegs is a lukewarm man. Lukewarm on the war, lukewarm on abolition. Do you really think he'll let Lincoln go through with the proclamation? Not on your life."

She had some firsthand experience that testified to Lincoln's genuine interest in emancipation. "The President feels pretty strongly that a military necessity exists for recruiting slaves. And he has the war power."

He waved that off. "Did you read that pusillanimous Message to Congress couple of weeks ago? Very big on oratory—'we cannot escape history' and all —but when it comes to action, maybe the slaves get freed in the year nineteen hundred. That weaseling was Seward's doing, I'm sure. Seward and Blair."

And Blair. The radical senators were going after the conservatives in the Lincoln Cabinet. "Not Bates?" she inquired.

"The Attorney General is lukewarm, too."

The senators wanted a wholesale cleaning-out of the Cabinet, the removal of all who opposed their views. That was an ambitious strike for supreme power. It meant the end of the coalition of Republicans that Lincoln had put together soon after his election. If successful, the pressure from the abolition senators would mean that they would be in the Republican saddle and Lincoln would become a figurehead, his power flowing to Chase along with the next presidential nomination.

"Who do you have in mind to replace Seward?"

"Fessenden." Wade added, "He may not know it yet. And if you tell anybody, I'll strangle your pretty neck with my bare hands."

William Fessenden of Maine, chairman of Senate Finance, was Chase's close friend. Cool, principled, eloquent, elegant—not roughhewn like Wade or Chandler, he had shown himself to be every bit as tough-minded. With Stanton and Chase in the Cabinet and some shrewd opportunist like Ben Butler to replace Blair, Fessenden would help the Cabinet dominate the President. The Senate Finance Chairman was known to favor a parliamentary type of government, in which Cabinet members served in the Congress. Anna was familiar with his often expressed view that votes taken in the Cabinet should determine executive decisions.

She decided to share Wade's confidence. She liked and admired Ben, and knew she could count on him if all others failed her, but Wade was on the wrong side of a fight that would weaken the presidency, perhaps bring about a division of the North, and most likely lead to a negotiated peace. That was an outcome neither of them wanted. "You know, Ben, this is not the first time Chase and Stanton have tried to take over from Lincoln."

He dismissed that with a shrug. "Not interested in palace intrigues. This is fundamental to our democracy. No President—especially not this one, elected by a fluke—can be allowed to flout the will of the people's Congress."

She believed that he believed what he said, and that his profound concern for human freedom outweighed all considerations of government structure or personal position. He was a good man with a good brain and good instincts, but that did not put him above ambition: Benjamin Franklin Wade was president pro tem of the Senate, and if the Senate became the preeminent force in American government, then Wade would be running the country.

She planted her feet squarely and pointed a finger at him. "I think you're wrong, Ben. It's for the President to set national policy." She knew that in the overheated state of public opinion after this bloody defeat, Wade and his powerful clique had a good chance of forcing Lincoln to accede to their wishes: a dominant Senate might not be so bad, but she was sure that a reconstituted Cabinet with Chase the leader would undermine the character of the country.

He shook his head. "It does not belong to the President to devise a policy for the country."

She was stunned at his conception of an impotent Chief Executive. "If you force Lincoln to appoint a Cabinet to the Senate's liking, you'll cripple the presidency forever."

"Better that than let him cripple the country," Wade replied solemnly. "First he tried to usurp the power of Congress to wage war, and I had to put a stop to that. You and your pamphlets, you egged him on, and now he thinks he can decide what this war is all about. No. He's not a dictator. Congress dictates."

"Nobody should dictate—" she began, but the senator would not be interrupted.

"I wouldn't mind his seizure of power if he used it to free the slaves," Wade said, "but he's using it to keep the damned status quo. He's getting set to back out of that proclamation, you'll see—his message last week was the signal. Nineteen hundred, my foot! He's weak, Anna—weak on the great moral issue of our time. He thinks the presidency is a balancing act. We have to knock him off balance, push him forward."

"You cannot get too far ahead of the country, Ben. The army won't fight for abolition; they'll pack up and go home."

"The Union Army will fight if it's led to fight!" He stood at attention. "The people will follow if they're led on the path of righteousness."

She put her hands on his shoulders and pushed him back to his chair. "The people just spoke in an election. We lost, remember?"

"We lost at the polls because we've been losing on the battlefield, can't you get that through your head? And the reason we're losing the damn war is that we've been led by scoundrels who want to appease the slaveocracy—they run the army and they run the President."

"So now you want to run the President, you and Chase and Stanton."

"If we have to do it, Anna, then, by God, we will. Our boys have not been dying by the tens of thousands for nothing. Lincoln has been pushed this way and that, giving us something, giving Seward and his ilk something, as if he's still at the Chicago convention. The politicking is over, Anna. Lincoln has to be one thing or the other. We're going to damn well see to it that he's going to fight this war to a finish and strike down slavery forever. No compromise."

"Who elected you, Ben Wade, to decide that the President of the United States cannot try for compromise?" He started to reply, but she rolled on. "You represent a minority. You have no call to demand your way or none. That's what the Southern traitors did, and that's what Seward meant when he wrote that the country was being whipsawed between you and them. Don't you go get purple in the face at me—I'm not calling you a traitor, I'm saying you're just as wrong as they are."

"Young woman, you are straining the bonds of our friendship—"

"Those bonds can take it, or they're not worth anything. Chase was in here bending your ear about Lincoln never freeing the slaves, whipping you up—don't look surprised, it's not such a secret—and now you're going to help him stage a coup. This democracy cannot take that kind of strain, Ben. If you cripple the presidency, if you make it the creature of the Cabinet or the tool of the Congress, you'll destroy this government."

"The form of this government is not as important as the cause of human freedom," he hurled back. "If freedom continues to be denied, this democracy will die. If we win this fight for the soul of this nation, then all your concerns about Cabinets and Presidents and Congresses won't amount to a tinker's dam."

She could not get through to him with reason, so she jabbed him where it most hurt. "Chase's puppet, that's what everyone will call you. And they'll be right. Chase and Stanton are using you to overturn the results of the 1860 convention and election. And you're too bullheaded to see it."

"I love you dearly," Wade said through gritted teeth. "Now get the hell out of here and shut up about what I told you."

Had she pushed Wade too hard? He was her main congressional protector, the source of what leverage she had with the other radicals and the cause of her employment by Weed and Blair. She needed his friendship. She knew, too, that Wade needed Chase's support in Ohio next month to be reelected senator by the state legislature.

She laid a hand on his arm and he pulled it away with a curt "Don't touch the puppet."

"Chase uses people," she warned. "Then he runs out on them."

"You don't have to warn me about him. Some causes are bigger than individual differences."

She thought the moment had come for her to leave. "If you do go ahead with this," she told him, "Ben Wade should not be in the lead." She did not want the coup to succeed, but if it failed, she did not want him to suffer.

"I have Jake Collamer for that. Nobody can call old Jake a radical."

That dismayed Anna further: the radicals' assault on Lincoln's authority was evidently well planned. If a conservative like Senator Collamer could be drawn in, perhaps on the issue of senatorial prerogatives, and persuaded to take a front position, the pressure on Lincoln would be infinitely stronger. Coming after the slaughter at Fredericksburg and the national disgust with the military and political leadership responsible, the plot to turn the President into a figurehead could not be better timed.

She saw the consequences clearly: if Chase and Stanton, working behind the back of the man who entrusted them with power, could lead the large senatorial bloc into forcing Lincoln to replace his Secretary of State, the President would be permanently crippled. If Seward's replacement were Fessenden, Chase's closest Senate ally, then Lincoln would be President in place, but Chase would be President in fact.

A clear and timely warning to the Blairs in Silver Spring would at least give Lincoln and his loyalists in the Cabinet a chance to plan a counter-coup strategy. She picked up her large bag and slung it over her shoulder.

"This has been a very successful year for you, Ben," she told him, looking for a way to regain favor without giving up principle. "The Homestead Act was yours, and history will remember you as the best friend the American farmer ever had."

"Be remembered for the Morrill Act," he growled.

"The Wade-Morrill Act is what it should be called," she agreed enthusiastically. "Thirty thousand acres to every state for every representative it has in Congress, to endow agricultural colleges. The federal government aiding education in America, first time, and Ben Wade's doing. What an achievement!"

"Pretty good for Chase's puppet."

"I only said that is what everybody else is going to think." She could not leave on that half apology. "You are a great man, Ben, but when a great man is wrong, he is greatly wrong. Think again, that's all I ask." Anna did not trust his political judgment, but she trusted him in everything else; he would be a friend through life even if she could do nothing for him, which was more than she would say about any other man she knew. She kissed him and invited herself to dinner at the Wades' that night.

"Eat with Caroline," he nodded, "I'll be late. Tonight, right after adjournment, the senators meet."

CHAPTER 34

SENATE COUP

Senator Ben Wade's considered judgment was that Lincoln meant well but lacked backbone.

To the senior senator from Ohio, Lincoln's emancipation policy seemed to promise immediate freedom one day, a delay to the end of the century the next. His crackdown on traitors was fiercely proclaimed one day and carried out languidly the next. The Old Capitol Prison and Fort Lafayette bulged with seditionists, as Wade thought it damn well should, but the traitorous likes of Clement Vallandigham and Horatio Seymour were permitted to hold public office as congressman and governor.

Worse, Wade suspected Lincoln was losing his determination to fight the war to the finish. The President was two-faced: he would assure good radical Republicans that no peace without union and abolition was possible, but tell some confounded conservatives to look into the peace feelers. As a result, Wade concluded, nobody seemed to be in command, the country was adrift, the war was being lost by incompetence if not by design, and something drastic had to be done.

Thus, with the army cowering on the banks of the Rappahannock and the President's chair occupied by a man afflicted with moral paralysis, it was up to the Senate of the United States, and to Benjamin Franklin Wade in particular, to take charge of the conduct of the war at a time of unprecedented peril.

Anna Carroll's point about crippling the presidency had troubled him for a few moments. But weakness in the institution of the presidency, such as it was since Andy Jackson left the office, did not necessitate weakness in the execution of policy set by the Congress; it simply meant that Congress would have more to do. The senator was certain that no special "war power" existed in the Chief Magistrate; the very thought was slavish and un-American.

Wade found his original conviction unshakable: Lincoln was little better than Buchanan. With the Executive floundering, the Legislature was forced to take control not just of policy but its execution. Let those of faint heart and pettifogging constitutionality call that extreme, but when the nation's life was at stake, extreme measures were necessary and became right. As Lincoln had written in his most recent message to Congress—the damnable back-tracking document setting up a postponement of the proclamation of freedom—"we must think anew and act anew, and then we shall save our country."

To Ben Wade, thinking anew meant extending the power of the Congress, especially the Upper Chamber. When the Executive branch was gripped by fear, the Legislative branch, with its constitutional power to advise, must advise the Chief Executive to throw out the lukewarm men around him. The time had come to turn to those with the passion to vigorously prosecute the war and to end the abomination of human slavery. Wade was sure that most members of the Senate agreed with him that Lincoln had failed. With the army falling apart in Virginia, and Bragg and the traitor Breckinridge in Tennessee likely to strike back up toward Ohio any moment, further delay meant disaster.

The Senate had to exert its inherent power. The President had demonstrated he would bend in the direction that the wind blew strongest. Wade had backed Lincoln into a corner on McClellan, and the President had acquiesced and belatedly fired the pro-slavery coward. Now the time had come to force him to toss Seward overboard.

Wade was confident his consecutive approach would work. First the army, then the Cabinet, and finally, if need be, the Senate would replace the vacillating elected leader with a temporary dictator. Ben Wade would not flinch from his duty: step by step, control in this emergency would devolve upon the institution dominated by the men who represented the best instincts of the American people.

In the high-ceilinged Senate reception room, Wade nodded to Lyman Trumbull of Illinois, chairman of Judiciary, who called the meeting of Republican senators to order. No helpers or reporters were present. This was a secret caucus.

Trumbull, lean, tall, with gold spectacles and a demonstrated willingness to denounce the automatic Lincoln supporters within Republican ranks as "courtiers" and "sycophants," was Wade's choice to take the lead. He was a better debater than Wade, came from Lincoln's state, and made no bones about wanting to subjugate the slavocracy. Wade recalled with satisfaction the way he branded Breckinridge a traitor and engineered his expulsion. Trumbull had a trick of tearing up little pieces of paper while listening, which disconcerted those debating him.

"This meeting has been called," said Trumbull, "to ascertain whether it is our duty to take any action with regard to the present condition of the country. As we all know, the terrible disaster at Fredericksburg has occasioned great excitement. Many of us believe that now is the time for the Senate to take some action to quiet the public mind."

Wade could count votes. In the Thirty-seventh Senate, Republicans held thirty-one seats, which he divided into seventeen radicals and fourteen conservatives, though some—old Jake Collamer of Vermont, for example, the best lawyer in the Senate—drifted between the camps. Some senators voted mainly on radical-conservative lines, where Wade's Committee on the Conduct of the War held sway; other Senate votes were influenced by sectional pressures, East against West, and Wade also chaired the pivotal Territories Committee. In the new Senate Chamber, the conservatives might ally themselves with Democrats to slow down the radical moves toward a war for human freedom, but here in the Republican caucus, Wade held the whip hand.

Deploying his senatorial troops like a general the Union Army never had, Wade signaled Wilkinson of Minnesota, a born pessimist, to express his feelings.

"In my opinion, the country is ruined and the cause is lost," he announced gloomily. "Maybe the Senate could save it, but I can't see us uniting on anything unanimously, and without unanimity we're stuck." He looked at his colleagues in dismay, started to sit down, caught Wade's glare, then added: "Of course the source of all our difficulties is obvious. The man who exercises a controlling influence on the mind of the President is Secretary Seward, who never believed in this war."

"The country is by no means lost," added Foster of Connecticut. "But no improvement can be made with Seward in the Cabinet. The answer is to get him out."

Not one of the conservative bloc in the ensuing discussion, Wade noted with satisfaction, had a good word to say for the Secretary of State. Not even Preston King of New York, a fat, waddling toady with hanging chops who made his home in Thurlow Weed's pocket, resisted the tide in the room. Wade caught the eye of Grimes of Iowa and indicated it was time to put in the first resolution, one he knew was too extreme to succeed. That down-the-line radical rose to offer a resolution "that the Senate expresses a want of confidence in the Secretary of State and advises that he be removed from the Cabinet."

Wade heaved himself out of his chair and raised his arm to call for recognition. "The way this war has been conducted is a disgrace. The President is directly responsible and there is no blinking that away. Lincoln has placed our armies under the command of Democratic generals and Southern sympathizers, who do not believe in the policy of the government."

His direct attack on their Republican President was more than this party caucus could swallow, he was well aware, and so was his next recommendation. But Wade pursued his strategy: by leaning hard to the radical extreme, which happened to reflect his true opinion, Wade would shift the center of gravity of his party over to the radical side. To take charge of the Executive, he needed more than a slim majority of Republican senators; he had to have a general consensus.

"What is needed now is a lieutenant general," he proposed, "of higher rank than any officer now in service, endowed with absolute powers to crush the rebellion and its pernicious institutions."

Wade knew that this group was not yet ready for a Republican general given emergency despotic power, but earlier that day, over in the House, Vallandigham of the peace movement had introduced a bill making it a high crime for anyone to propose to "clothe any federal officer with arbitrary or dictatorial power." This was his answer to that miserable little traitor. Wade restrained his fury and directed his point to the matter at hand.

"I do not believe it is advisable to strike directly at the President at this time." That, for Wade, was being the very soul of reason and patience. "However, we must tell him he must remove the evil genius of his procrastination. Seward must go!"

As arranged, Jake Collamer of Vermont followed Wade with a less impassioned speech. Collamer, at seventy, was regarded with respect and even affection by his peers; Sumner liked to call him the "Green Mountain Socrates." He was no firebrand and was known to harbor a genuine affection for the President.

"I believe, gentlemen, that the difficulty is to be found in the fact that the President does not have a Cabinet, not in the true sense of the word." Wade had to lean forward to hear Collamer's reedy voice. "Yet a real Cabinet council is traditional in both the theory and practice of our government." Collamer reviewed the development of the Cabinet system, concluding "it is notorious that this President has departed from that tradition. He does not consult his Cabinet councillors on important decisions. Indeed, I understand that he has said on occasion, 'My policy is to have no policy,' and to let each Cabinet member attend to the duties of his own department. This is unsafe and wrong. The Senate has a responsibility to set it right."

Bill Fessenden's turn. The Finance Committee chairman from Maine was an inside man, seldom in the newspapers but always in the most important Senate decisions. Wade could never warm up to the austere money expert, who liked to think of himself as a "moderate," but he knew him to be reliable when it came to the dominance of the Congress.

"The Senate can no longer content itself with the discharge of its constitutional duties," said Fessenden. "A crisis has arrived that requires an active interposition in the execution of the laws. I have been told by one member of Mr. Lincoln's Cabinet"—Wade and just about everyone in the room knew he meant his friend Chase—"that there is a backstairs influence which often controls the apparent conclusions of the Cabinet itself."

Howard of Michigan interrupted. "Is the name of that backstairs influence William Seward?"

"No name was given," said Fessenden. He preferred to remain mysterious about his source, although Chase had been using that same word picture, "backstairs influence," to describe Seward to most of the senators present. "At any rate," Fessenden continued, "I have no doubt that measures must be taken now to make the Cabinet a unity—to remove anyone who does not agree heartily with our views in relation to the war."

Wade looked for the opposition to the resolution from Seward's only supporter among Senate Republicans. Preston King promptly provided it.

"As a senator from New York," said the man who, Wade suspected, would soon rush over to Seward's house with the news of this caucus, "I must protest against this proceeding. It is unjust, unwise, hasty—and all predicated on mere rumors. Perhaps it would be wiser to appoint a committee to have an interview with the President."

Such a direct confrontation was precisely what Wade wanted. Orville Browning of Illinois, considered by Wade to be a contemptible pro-slavery friend of the President's, but without the courage to defend Seward to his fellow senators, seconded King's suggestion.

Wade looked at Browning's ruffled shirt with distaste. The recently defeated senator, grubbing for appointive office from the President, would not be missed in the Senate; he had been afflicted with fits of the constitutional ague when it came to stripping rebels of their property. Wade believed that even a Democrat would be better than Lincoln's resident bootlicker. He asked Browning if his proposal of a meeting of the Senate delegation with the President meant that he supported the retention of Seward.

Browning hastened to disavow such an unpopular intent. It was not a matter of purpose but of seemliness. Perhaps the caucus's goal could be

Senator William Pitt Fessenden

achieved in a way that did not embarrass the President. "This would be war between the Congress and the President, and knowledge of this antagonism would injure our cause greatly in the country. However, a deputation from the Senate to the President, as Senator Wade suggests, is in order."

Wade figured if the President's best friend in the Senate was that reluctant to defend the Secretary of State, it meant that the radicals had Seward on the run. But Wade wanted that deputation to have a written ultimatum to read and to place in Lincoln's hands. That way, the Senate's point could not be filibustered by the President with his interminable jokes.

"Let's vote on the resolution," said Fessenden.

Wade signaled no. The votes were not in his pocket for the extreme resolution, and Wade did not want to put anything to a vote that would lose. The resolution was grossly insulting as it stood. Now was the time to let the conservatives water it down enough to make them think they had won something for Lincoln.

"I have a substitute resolution," Ira Harris said. He had taken Seward's New York seat in the Senate when Bowlegs moved into the Cabinet. "We don't have to name names." To the accompaniment of Turnbull tearing slips of paper, he read it out: "Resolved, that in the judgment of the Republican members of the Senate, the public confidence in the present administration would be increased by a reconstruction of the Cabinet."

That picked up wider support, but John Sherman of Ohio, who had stepped into Chase's seat in the Senate, said he did not like it. "That could be construed as saying we want all present members of the Cabinet out. Nobody wants Mr. Chase to leave the Treasury. I say we march directly into the President's office and tell him what's wrong with his Cabinet and himself."

Wade shook his head again. He wanted to go into the President's office to present a united Republican Senate front in writing, which Lincoln could not wriggle away from.

Charles Sumner of Massachusetts, a special hater of Seward, pleased Wade with his prompt move to wed Sherman's march-in-there proposal to the Harris resolution to remake the Cabinet. "Resolved, that a committee be appointed to wait upon the President in behalf of the senators here present and urge upon him changes in conduct and in the Cabinet which shall give the Administration unity and vigor." Excellent. Lincoln was directed not just to throw out Seward, but to change his own conduct. "Unity" meant an end to the balancing act.

"Let's have the resolution amended," added Fessenden, "to 'partial' reconstruction of the Cabinet." That made sure Chase stayed in. The Harris and Sumner proposals were merged and the Fessenden amendment accepted. Wade then called for a vote, looking hard at Orville Browning, who averted his glance.

Twenty names were read out, and twenty said "aye." The twenty-first was Lincoln's friend Browning, who hesitated and said "aye." The twenty-third was Preston King of New York, who owed his place to Seward and could hardly be expected to vote for the resolution to ruin him. But King had already slipped out of the caucus room: He would not go on record as calling for his patron's resignation, but he could not spoil the unanimity of the caucus with a vote against the historic resolution. Collamer recorded him as "not voting."

Wade sighed his satisfaction; his caucus strategy had worked perfectly. In all, twenty-eight Republican senators cast votes to direct the President to end the coalition Cabinet and replace its conservatives with radicals satisfactory to the senators. Never in nearly a century of American history had there been such a bold move to shift executive power; all that remained was Lincoln's acquiescence to the inevitable.

Browning said he would take the written resolution to Lincoln immediately and bring back a time for the confrontation. Wade agreed to that; he thought it would be a good idea for Lincoln to learn of the Senate's new strength and resolve from one of his own wishy-washy friends.

"What's the matter, Henry?" Wade said to Henry Wilson of Massachusetts as they filed out of the Senate reception room. "You look sick."

"I'm glad you and Collamer and Fessenden and Sumner are the deputation," said the worried Wilson. "That's not a meeting I want to be part of. If Lincoln agrees, he's finished; if he doesn't agree, God knows what will happen next. Impeachment, maybe. Right in the middle of a civil war. What's to become of us?"

Wade told him to cheer up. He had never felt more sure of himself or the rightness of what he was doing. With more than a little gratification, he watched Browning race down the steps of the Capitol to his carriage.

Orville Browning had often seen Lincoln looking haggard and anguished, but never like this. In the days after Willie's death, the man was in despair, but now he seemed driven to distraction.

"What news from our army?" the senator asked. He instantly regretted the question, because the subject was hardly one to reassure the President.

"I don't know what is to become of it," Lincoln said hopelessly. "One hundred and seventy thousand men, including Sigel's corps. It crossed the Rappahannock, fought a battle with an entrenched enemy at great disadvantage, and with great loss." He dug his fingers in his wiry hair. "And without accomplishing any valuable result. Now it cannot advance, or even stay where it is."

"Senator Wade intends to visit General Burnside soon," Browning told the President, which seemed to deepen rather than diminish his gloom.

After a moment, Lincoln looked up at him. "Were you at the caucus?"

Browning was surprised that Lincoln knew of the secret session beforehand. He hoped nobody had revealed his failure to vote against the resolution. He said yes, he had been there. Lincoln was evidently waiting for his report.

"What do those men want?"

"I hardly know, Mr. President, but they are exceedingly violent toward the Administration." Browning felt the need to explain why he had gone along with the resolution. "What we did was the gentlest thing that could be done. We had to do that or worse."

He recounted the details of the secret caucus without minimizing the hostility of the senators toward Lincoln which was being directed through Seward. It pained Browning to deliver this harsh news to Lincoln in his current state of anguish, but the President had a right to know the force of his party's move against him. Browning concluded with a reading of the demand of the Senate Republicans to meet with Lincoln at once "for the purpose of getting him to change his policy and to reconstitute a portion of his Cabinet." One purpose, two actions.

"They wish to get rid of me," Lincoln said bitterly, "and I am sometimes half-disposed to gratify them."

"Some do, that's true, but—"

"We are now on the brink of destruction." Lincoln sat forward, hands limply hanging over his knees, staring at the floor. "It appears to me the Almighty is against us, and I can hardly see a ray of hope."

This was no time for Lincoln to sink into the hypo. If the President took that familiar emotional plunge—and it seemed to Browning that his friend was already on the way down into that emotional morass—that would take him out of action for at least three days. Lincoln could not afford three days of despair and numb resignation while the Senate seized his power.

"Do not let them drive you from your post," Browning told him. That was what the senators, led by Wade and Fessenden, secretly urged on by Chase and Stanton, were trying to do. "To relinquish the helm now would bring upon us certain and inevitable ruin." He did not add what it would do to his own hopes for appointment to the Supreme Court.

Did Lincoln, in his present state of mind, understand the danger? "Those men," as the President defensively called them, were staging a coup. They were trying to drive him out of the presidency, and Lincoln's only response was to say he was half-inclined to let them do it.

Browning was sure he knew the cause of it all. By appeasing Wade and his crowd with an emancipation proclamation, the President had won no surcease of radical pressure; at the same time, the attempt to placate the left had been rebuffed by the electorate. Now the same men, abolitionists he had appeased, were demanding more. "You ought to have crushed the ultras last summer," Browning told him. "You could have done it then and escaped these troubles."

Lincoln looked up at him in such visible pain that Browning was compelled to stop telling him how wrong he had been. The President did not need political instruction or recrimination at this point. Rather, he needed plain sympathy. "But that is past. Let us be hopeful," Browning said, hand on his friend's arm, "and take care of the future. Mr. Seward appears now to be the especial object of their hostility." Lincoln nodded numbly. "I believe Seward has managed our foreign affairs as well as anyone could have done," Browning went on, an opinion he knew he had failed to express in the caucus. "Yet some of them are very bitter upon him." He had to add, "And some of them very bitter on you."

"Why will men believe a lie," Lincoln cried, "an absurd lie that they could not impose upon a child?" He seemed not to be able to imagine why the senators held the conviction that Seward exercised a malign influence over him. "They cling to it and repeat it in defiance of all evidence to the contrary."

Browning felt it would be unkind to state the obvious: that the senators based their belief of Seward's malign influence over him on the testimony of Salmon Portland Chase, repeated over and over again, substantiated by Edwin Stanton. Chase was the instigator; if Lincoln did not know it, Browning was not going to be the one to break the news that a viper was nestled in his bosom. Certainly Lincoln must know it; the man was simply not strong enough, under the battering of the war, to admit the duplicity of Chase to anyone, including himself.

Worse, Lincoln seemed to miss the point. The supposed belief held by some about the "malign influence" was not the problem; that was merely the device that Lincoln's attackers were using to get at the President himself.

Browning rose to leave. Lincoln did not get up. He asked the President: "You will see the deputation of senators?"

"Not right away. Tomorrow night."

"Seven o'clock, then. Lincoln, I hope I have not distressed you by the account of the proceedings of the caucus. It is important you know the truth about the senators' state of mind."

"I don't want to talk about it. Maybe we can just keep things along."

"You can't keep them along," Browning told him. "The Cabinet will go to pieces."

"I have been more distressed by this," Lincoln said, at the end of his rope, not coming to grips with the danger, "than by any event of my life."

Browning bade him good night and left feeling helpless to prevent the destruction in store.

CHAPTER 35

Your Constitutional Advisers

Lincoln was startled by Nicolay's hand on his shoulder. "I knocked, sir, but you didn't hear. Senator King is here, with Secretary Seward's son, Frederick."

"What time is it?" He had dozed at his desk, not a habit with him, and he felt a clutch of guilt at escaping to sleep in the face of adversity. The gaslight was on; it was still night. "News from the front?"

"Ten o'clock, sir. No news from Burnside's headquarters, all quiet there. I told Preston King and Fred Seward you were about to retire for the night, but they said it was urgent. I can tell them to come back in the morning."

Lincoln rubbed his face, pushed his fingers through his hair, started to rise, then sat back again. "Send them in."

Seward's son was a serious-minded soul, with little of his father's sprightliness and self-assurance, but Lincoln liked him. He wished his own son Robert wanted to work closely with his father, but all that young man wanted was to get into uniform. He envied Seward for being able to weather these storms with his son at his side as Assistant Secretary of State. Other than Thurlow Weed, there were few men William Henry Seward could trust. Why did such a good man attract such a swarm of bitter enemies?

Pasty-faced Preston King was out of breath. Father Blair wanted King to replace Stanton at the War Department, and was pressing hard for such a switch, but that would tip the fine balance in the Cabinet over to the conservatives. Besides, Lincoln relied on Stanton as a lightning rod for criticism of military affairs, and never so much as now. Orville Browning had already reported to Lincoln about what had happened at the Senate caucus; what was King so excited about?

"I have just come from Secretary Seward's home," Senator King puffed, "where I told him of the perfidious action of my fellow senators."

Seward would surely keep cool about it all, Lincoln assumed; the Secretary had long since grown accustomed to the hostility of his fellow Republicans. "And what did he say?"

"My father said that in view of the current misfortunes," Seward's son put in, "the senators were thirsty for a victim. He said he was not going to let them put the President in a false position on his account."

Lincoln nodded; Seward was like a rock.

"He immediately wrote out his resignation," said King, "and told me to bring it to you." The senator handed the paper to Lincoln.

"He told me to submit mine as well," said Frederick Seward.

Lincoln was stunned. Just when he needed most the people he could trust,

Assistant Secretary of State Frederick W. Seward

the Cabinet member most trusted felt it a point of honor to remove himself. Maybe, like Lincoln, Seward was half-inclined to oblige his enemies. He read the paper: "Sir, I hereby resign the office of Secretary of State, and beg that my resignation may be accepted immediately."

There it was, in Seward's hand, but Lincoln could not grasp the import of what he read. "What does this mean?" he asked the two men.

"It means that he believes he can serve you best," said Senator King, "by going home, and taking some of the poison out of the air."

A fresh wave of desolation washed across Lincoln's general distress. He needed Seward's presence and counsel, especially now; he had come to trust the New Yorker as nobody else over the past eighteen months; after the rough beginning, they had worked out a relationship of mutual loyalty that could not be replaced. He would not permit the Secretary of State to quit any more than he would permit himself the luxury of standing aside.

Lincoln unwound from his chair, picked up his tall hat, and signaled to the others to follow him. Marshal Lamon fell in step behind as they headed across Lafayette Park to the Seward home.

William Seward was standing in front of the fire, elbow on the mantel, cigar in hand, making an effort to look his usual imperturbable self.

"What does this mean?" Lincoln repeated, holding out the resignation.

"It's to the point, and should be self-explanatory," Seward said.

Lincoln could see that his Secretary of State was inwardly in turmoil but was determined to present a façade of calm self-sacrifice. Not even New York politics, which Lincoln was prepared to concede were the most fractious in the nation, prepared a man for the sort of relentless vilification Seward had been taking. The President knew what it was to be patronized, held in contempt, dismissed as a bumpkin elected on a fluke; but Seward was seen as smart and sophisticated and evil by his rivals, which made him preeminently an object of hatred.

"Frankly, Lincoln, it will be a huge relief to be freed from official cares."

"Ah yes, Governor, that will do very well for you," Lincoln said, "but I am like the starling in Sterne's story. 'I can't get out.'"

Seward smiled tightly at Lincoln's literary reference; the President had read the story at Seward's suggestion. Lincoln could talk in a personal code like that with his Secretary of State; nobody else could supply that kind of intellectual intimacy.

"That," said Seward, pointing to the paper Lincoln held, "frees you from all embarrassment. It is a weapon you can use as you see fit, or be your peace offering to Senator Wade and his ever thirsty friends."

"I cannot accept this," Lincoln told him.

"You must. In my judgment, I am more an albatross around your neck than a help at this point. It is time to go. Frederick, look to the packing."

Lincoln did not try to argue. He was not reacting quickly anymore and needed time to think it over, just as Seward needed time to cool down. The trouble was that enough time was not available for deliberation or the natural ebbing of a man's anger. Events were crowding in at the worst moment for decisions. At this time, the commander in chief should be devising a way out for Burnside and the Army of the Potomac; and on the political front, the nation's political leader should be concerning himself with a way to contain the hurricane of public indignation certain to come when the still-censored correspondents made known the terrible story of Fredericksburg and its fourteen thousand boys lost for no gain. But Lincoln had no chance to marshal his thoughts. His instinct was to hold his Cabinet together.

Outside the Seward house, the President was surprised to find a carriage waiting, the horse breathing puffs of vapor into the December air. Father Blair was in the back, motioning Lincoln and Lamon in. There was no room for the corpulent Preston King, so they left him behind.

Lincoln was not surprised at the Old Man's presence. The Blairs had a network to alert them to high-level machinations, and Blair knew that Lincoln valued his judgment.

"What would your Jackson have done?" Lincoln grunted, jamming himself in the carriage seat and pulling the blanket across his lap.

"If confronted by a congressional challenge?" The elder Blair was certain: "Same thing he would have done with anybody who challenged his authority within the party. He would have shown the senators the door, told them to go straight to hell. That's what Andy Jackson would have done."

But President Jackson had not served in the midst of a civil war, losing battles on top of losing midterm elections. How would Old Hickory act in circumstances that afflicted Lincoln now? As if reading his thoughts, the Old Man added, "Of course, times are different now. You don't have the luxury of telling off the radicals. You have to outmaneuver them. Seward quit just now, didn't he?"

Lincoln nodded confirmation. The Blairs were no friends of Seward, with the roots of their political enmity running deep through the years, but they had been on the same conservative side of late, and in politics one's useful friends are one's current friends.

"I thought he would," Blair nodded, "he's too damn proud. But it will help you in the counterattack."

Lincoln made himself look interested. Although he was deeply troubled at the prospect of the loss of the key member of his coalition, and heartsick at the loss of a man who had become a confidant, he had to think ahead.

"First, take McClellan back to the Army of the Potomac." When Lincoln did not reject that advice out of hand, the Old Man continued: "We must look to the Army as a great political as well as war machine. The soldiers are to give us success in the field and at the polls. McClellan is dear to them. He can bring them to the support of the country and to you."

Hire McClellan again? After Burnside's failure? What a colossal admission of error that would be, making the President appear hopelessly indecisive, weakening him when he most needed strength. But the older Blair's counsel was usually sound; Lincoln did not know what to think.

"After that, get rid of Stanton. He has aligned himself with Chase and the ultras. Replace him at the War Department with Preston King, or, if you need a Democrat, John Dix."

Everybody was remaking his Cabinet, including members of the Cabinet and their families. Ultras like Chase wanted it remade their anti-slavery way, conservatives like Blair wanted it remade on a "Union as it was" basis. Lincoln wished—vainly, he now feared—that he could keep the Cabinet as it was. Up to now, he had been able to maintain control by playing each group against the other, all in his sight, easily watched, in balance. Now it seemed impossible to hold that position, with the country in an uproar and more bad news on the way; one side or the other had to triumph.

If the victors were Chase and Wade, they would effectively take over the government and put in somebody like General Hooker as dictator. If it were the Blairs and Seward, the same thing might happen in the other direction, with "McNapoleon" as dictator. Either way, if the momentum to break up the coalition became unstoppable—whether pushed by the senators led by Wade, or by the Blairs and others in their suggested counterattack—the result would be an end to civilian rule. That was as bad as an end to majority rule; it would mean that democratic self-government was indeed an absurdity, that the American experiment had failed. The bottom was out of the tub, the dirty water slopping over everything.

"Pardon my zeal," said the elder Blair as the carriage drew up in the snow in front of the Mansion. "It is love for the cause and you. No selfish promptings."

Lincoln took that with a grain of salt. Father Blair never plotted any strategy without considering how it could help his two sons.

Nicolay and Hay were waiting at the door. Lincoln thanked the Old Man for the advice, bid him good night, and went inside with Lamon. He felt bone-wearily alone. Nicolay had something for him to sign about putting off until after Christmas the execution of the Indians who had led the Minnesota uprising, and Hay had something about an order supposedly issued by General Grant about expelling all Jews from the area of his command. It was past midnight. He waved them away and stumbled upstairs, Lamon behind him. He stopped on the landing, hand on the wooden railing.

"I have a white elephant on my hands." That did not express his travail vividly enough. "I have a fire in my front and in my rear."

"Richelieu," said Lamon, a secret student of history. "It was said of him that he was the first man in Europe, but no hero in his own country."

"Far from it!" Lincoln argued, figuring he had it much worse than the French cardinal. "Richelieu never had a fire in his front and rear at the same time. He had a united constituency, which it has never been my good fortune to have." His own constituency was the United States, riven before he took office; his specific voting constituency was the Republican Party, of which the abolitionist half wanted to force his resignation and the other half was allied with the "Union as it was" Democrats. Cardinal Richelieu never knew what real trouble was.

He trudged up the stairs feeling sorrier for himself with each step. "This improvised vigilance committee to watch my movements and keep me straight," he said, the picture of Ben Wade's angry-bulldog face in front of him, "appointed by Congress and called the Committee on the Conduct of the War, is a marplot. Its greatest purpose seems to be to hamper my action and obstruct the military operations."

Now Wade, the chief marplotter, would go down to Fredericksburg and interview Burnside. Would the general admit that the frontal assault was his own idea, not Lincoln's? Probably. Burnside was good about accepting responsibility, which meant that Lincoln could not blame him for anything and would have to treat the disaster as an unavoidable accident. But the country would not hold still for that.

He hoped to find cessation of despair in sleep. This was no time for the hypo to descend on him, Lincoln reminded himself, not with the Senate coming down on his head the next evening. "This state of things shall continue no longer, Hill," he said with more assurance than he felt, "I will show them at the other end of the Avenue whether I am President or not."

But Seward had resigned and would have to be replaced. The Senate would confirm only the nomination of one of the ultras to head the State Department—the unctuous Sumner, probably, or that cold fish Fessenden—and that would mean the end of his coalition, followed by a general smashup.

Who could govern this country then? A military dictator was a solution as bad as the problem itself. What new coalition, what political deal? A thought crossed his mind that perhaps he should stop courting the radicals and reach out in the opposite direction—not merely to the conservative Republicans and War Democrats, but beyond them to the Peace Democrats. Perhaps he could make some sort of an arrangement with Horatio Seymour in New York to take the anti-war pressure off now in return for an orderly transfer of power later.

He paused with his hand on the doorknob of his bedroom. He still had a card or two to play. His support in the presidential election of 1864 was one; if he could not be king, he could be Warwick, the kingmaker. The Emancipation Proclamation was another card; if the radicals deserted him, or tried to seize his power, he could postpone the edict in return for support elsewhere on continuance of the war. Maintaining the Union came before everything—the slaves, his second term, the lives of tens of thousands of soldiers, everything. Whatever he would do must be done with that goal fixed in his mind.

A dramatic political deal across partisan lines began to take shape in his mind. For that, he needed the shrewdest deal-maker he could find, a man intimately acquainted with the state of New York, and someone who could keep a secret forever.

"Weed," he said aloud. "Hill, I want you to tell Nicolay to send for Thurlow Weed in Albany."

"Wasn't he on his way back to London?"

Lincoln nodded, and said, "But he's still in Albany. First thing tomorrow, send for him. Not directly from me, but in confidence through Nicolay—he knows how."

A few weeks before, Seward had intended to send Weed abroad again to help keep Britain and France from recognizing the Confederacy. The editor had packed his bags and gladly booked passage to London, but Greeley and his radicals had raised the roof about "Seward's wirepuller" abroad, which forced Seward—who had sensed impending weakness—to rescind the assignment. Thurlow Weed, grumpy about that rebuff from the same Republicans who lost the state of New York because they wouldn't listen to his advice, was still in New York.

Lincoln thought he might get Weed to prevail on Seward to stay. At the same time, perhaps the old wirepuller had a private wire of communication into the Seymour camp through the Democratic boss, Dean Richmond. Those two were not above doing a little business together.

Lincoln's hopes, rising at that thought, sank again. Weed could not get down to Washington before the confrontation with the senators. At best, even if he came and agreed to act as agent in a desperate scheme, what Lincoln had in mind was a long-range answer to what was an immediate emergency. Lincoln dreaded the meeting with the senators scheduled for the next evening. He had no powerful arguments, could call no surprise witnesses, and faced a hostile jury. The President of the United States could merely listen, and delay, and let the prosecution take its time making the case. Maybe then he could come up with an idea for the defense.

He bade Lamon good night. He had long since given up attempts to dissuade the bodyguard from sleeping at his door. Lincoln slept badly that night and wasted most of the next day worrying.

William Pitt Fessenden of Maine followed Jacob Collamer of Vermont into the presidential office promptly at seven in the evening, followed by Trumbull, Grimes, and Wade. Sumner made his entrance breathlessly a moment later.

At the President's cordial invitation, the deputation from the Senate Republican caucus sat themselves in the wooden armchairs around the long black walnut table in the center of the room. Fessenden noted the disarray of the office: maps and papers piled on the President's desk and on the sofa nearby. He fumed; that was not the way the nation's principal executive office should look. Then again, the present occupant was hardly an executive.

The President greeted each of them with what Fessenden thought was his usual urbanity. The senator counted Lincoln as a shrewd if limited lawyer and put no credence in the newspaper folderol about "Honest Abe," the country bumpkin. He counted on the President's good sense and practicality, especially in light of his seriously weakened position in the country, to resolve the crisis without undue acrimony. Lincoln's recognition of the locus of real power was painful but necessary if the Cabinet was to be remade and the war policy reset.

Collamer solemnly read the resolution that the Republican caucus had passed the night before. "The theory of our government is that the President should be aided by a Cabinet council," the Vermonter intoned, "and that all important public measures and appointments should be the result of their combined wisdom and deliberation."

Lincoln's eyebrows rose slightly, as if that theory was new to him. Fessenden was aware that such a reading rested on a brief discussion at the Constitutional Convention, a century before, of a privy council. Against that theory was the fact that the founders had put nothing about a Cabinet in the Constitution, and no presidents had heretofore been bound by majority votes of their principal aides. On the contrary, the tradition of arguing advisers was set by George Washington, who liked the creative tension that developed when he balanced Hamilton against Jefferson.

But such diversity was disruptive in wartime. In Fessenden's view, the American system of government was flexible enough to take the change from an advisory board to a directory board right now. Traditions had to have a beginning, and there was no time like a civil war to start one. In his eyes, much mischief could have been avoided if the founders had stuck to their original intention of having Congress appoint the Executive.

Fessenden watched Lincoln listen impassively to Collamer's unity charge. "The Cabinet should be exclusively composed of statesmen who are the resolute, unwavering supporters of a vigorous and successful prosecution of the war." It was well known that Seward was lukewarm; he had to go.

"In the present crisis of public affairs," Collamer concluded, with all the weight of the united majority party of the Senate behind his words, "the Republican senators of the United States—identified as they are with the success of your administration—believe that changes in the membership of the Cabinet should be made. This will secure to the country a unity of purpose and action."

Lincoln made no response. He sat in his chair at the end of the table, waiting for more.

Since the President seemed immobilized, Fessenden took the floor. He expressed the confidence of the Senate in the patriotism and integrity of the President, and disclaimed any wish on the part of the senators to dictate to him with regard to the Cabinet. He felt that such a disclaimer would make the fact of their dictation more palatable. Fessenden had no wish to unnecessarily humiliate a man who was, after all, being forced to give up a significant part of his powers.

"We are your constitutional advisers," he reminded the President. He was on unassailable ground with that; little could be done in appointing anyone to any executive office against the advice and consent of the Senate. "We claim the privilege laid down in the Constitution to tend you our friendly counsel when, in our judgment, an emergency of sufficient importance renders it necessary."

Now to the point. "A belief exists that you do not consult the Cabinet as a council. In fact, it is well known that many important measures are decided by you without the knowledge of its members."

He awaited a response on which he could build an argument; Lincoln just looked back at him. Fessenden became more specific: "It is believed that the Secretary of State is not in accord with the majority of the Cabinet. In fact, we believe he exerts an injurious influence upon the conduct of the war. Such is the common rumor." That was a grave charge to make in the midst of a civil war—he had given "injurious influence" much thought, short of imputing treason—but it did not get a rise out of the President.

"The war is not sufficiently in the hands of its friends," Fessenden said with greater severity, hoping to get through the seeming numbness of his target. "You have systematically disgraced every anti-slavery general officer in the Army. General Frémont, General Hunter are but two. It is time to change this state of affairs, and to let the war be conducted by its friends."

He knew he was making an effective case. The other senators were as one with him as he attacked the President to his face, but with the utmost respect and civility. "Let us face it, Mr. President, we are going to get no help in waging this war from the Democrats. General McClellan has been used by them for party purposes, and is even now preparing an attack on us in the court-martial of Porter—"

The mention of McClellan seemed to wake up Lincoln. With the immediate subject no longer Seward, the President rose and produced a large bundle of papers that was evidently his correspondence with the deposed general. Taken aback, Fessenden allowed Lincoln to develop the case, which was of great interest to Wade. That, he soon realized, was a mistake.

For close to half an hour, Lincoln read from this correspondence, showing how McClellan had been sustained by the government to the utmost. Fessenden knew what Lincoln was doing: changing the subject and pretending the attack was on his dealings with his already dismissed general rather than with his Cabinet. The President went on and on, defending a position which was not under attack.

Senator Sumner at last interrupted to refocus on Seward. He complained about the Secretary of State's correspondence. "He has subjected himself to ridicule in diplomatic circles at home and abroad," charged the chairman of the Foreign Relations Committee. "He has uttered statements offensive to Congress and has spoken of it repeatedly with disrespect in the presence of foreign ministers. He has written offensive dispatches which you, Mr. President, could not possibly have seen or assented to."

"It is Seward's habit to read dispatches to me before they are sent," said Lincoln mildly, "but they are not submitted to a Cabinet council, that's true."

"What of this infamous dispatch of July the fifth, of last year, in which—"

"I just don't recollect that one," Lincoln said, which Fessenden thought unbelievable; Seward's insulting equivalence of "abolitionist" with "secessionist" was hardly something he would forget. For the better part of three hours, the meeting dragged on, with the senators making the same basic accusation —that the Cabinet was divided, and that Lincoln had to fire the lukewarm members—and Lincoln ducking, changing the subject, arguing obliquely, playing for time.

Fessenden was certain that everyone in the room, including the evasive Lincoln, knew that the Senate's information was correct. It had been provided by Treasury Secretary Chase, who ought to know because he sat in the councils that were divided and had reported unequivocally that Lincoln overrode and often ignored the Cabinet's advice.

"You know why the Republican Party lost the election last month, Lincoln?" The harsh voice was Wade's. "I'll tell you why: you placed the direction of the war in the hands of bitter and malignant Democrats."

"That reminds me of a story," Lincoln began, but Ben Wade was having none of that.

"That's all it is with you—story, story, story!" Wade rose and leaned across the table to look Lincoln in the eye. "You are the father of every military blunder that has been made during the war. You are on your road to hell, sir, with this government, by your obstinacy. You're not a mile off the road to hell this minute!"

"A mile," said Lincoln softly. "Senator, that's about the distance from here to the Capitol, is it not?"

The attempted witticism drew no laugh. Wade snorted that the meeting was a waste of time, grabbed up his hat and cane, and slammed the door on his way out.

To the others, in the ensuing silence, Lincoln dropped his attempts at humor and said, "I will examine and consider very carefully the paper you have submitted. I want to express my satisfaction with the tone and temper of the committee."

The President was in trouble and he knew it, Fessenden judged. Wade should not have blown up, but that was Wade, and Lincoln had successfully provoked him. The Senate had made its case forcefully; Lincoln had stalled. Now the next move was up to him. Fessenden was hopeful that the rumors of Seward's resignation were true; that would demonstrate the party's power while saving the President's face.

Fessenden left with the others, gratified at a good night's work changing the nature of the relation between Congress and the President. Lincoln was proving to be a tougher bird than he had thought. The President gave you nothing, not even a loss of temper, to help your case. But this would be decided by the application of power, not argument, and the senators had the upper hand. At the next meeting, which Fessenden supposed would be the next night, the surrender of autocratic power would have to be tendered, and it would be graciously accepted. The President—soon to be primus inter pares, first among equals, the Chairman of the Council of State, but no longer

Chief Executive—would be treated with all due respect by the men who had stripped him of misused power.

George Smalley, at the *New York Tribune* office in Washington, had not felt so frustrated since he could not get his copy filed from Antietam.

"Seward has resigned, I'm sure of it," the correspondent fairly shouted at Adams Hill, the bureau chief, "and the whole Cabinet is splitting up. And we cannot move the story?"

"Telegraph censorship," said Hill. "Stanton is treating it like news of a battle."

"But the senators were in with Lincoln tonight telling him how to set up his Cabinet. The Administration is in crisis—hell, in extremis. They're administering extreme unction. Greeley will break out the champagne when he hears of Seward quitting. It's been his fondest wish for years."

"I've been at the War Office, the telegraph room," said Hill wearily. "I argued with Eckert. I told him this is not what military censorship was supposed to do, that this was political news—but when Stanton says no, it's no. They will not pass it."

Smalley did not know who was worse, the censors in Washington or his editor in New York. A few days before, his exclusive story about the debacle of Fredericksburg had been at first softened by the censor, then finally killed in New York. The *Tribune* editor—not newsman Sydney Gay, but the politician-editor Horace Greeley—had been at the forefront of the clamor for McClellan's scalp and could not bring himself to print a heart-stopping report on the disaster that had befallen his replacement.

"I'll take the story up on the train," Smalley volunteered. "The government is coming apart. At least Sydney Gay should know about it. Maybe he can talk Greeley into running something. This isn't our fault."

"They know about it in New York already, I'll bet," said Sam Wilkeson, another *Tribune* reporter who had sauntered in. "Seward probably sent word up last night. He'd tell Thurlow Weed right away."

"Why hasn't it been in the paper, then?" Smalley wanted to know. Some newspaper would be interested; if not the *Tribune*, then Bennett's *Herald*.

Wilkeson had a theory about that. "Soon as word gets out, stocks are going to drop," said the worldly reporter, "and the price of gold is going to shoot up. Lot of money can be made by people in the know on the news of an upheaval in the Cabinet. And if I know Seward and Weed, they're cashing in right now."

CHAPTER 36

ARRAIGNMENT

Chase had been given a full report from Senator Bill Fessenden, whom he trusted completely, of the confrontation between the Republican senators and Lincoln. He had heard from Stanton that the *New York Tribune* correspondent was trying to telegraph to Greeley the news of the resignation of Secretary of State Seward.

The Treasury Secretary had good reason to be pleased. The snowball he had given the first push to was gathering speed and weight. Seward was already out, and the senators were demanding more—it would not be long before Blair and Bates volunteered to step down, and finally it would be possible to force out Navy Secretary Welles, who seemed to put personal loyalty to the President before all common sense.

At that point, Chase was certain that with Stanton's help he would be in effective control of the Cabinet. That newly unified and rejuvenated Cabinet council would, by majority vote, determine the national policy. From there to the Republican nomination and the Presidency were only a few short steps. The nation would at long last be in firm and capable hands. The precedent of a council wielding executive power did not trouble him; as President, Chase would make sure to appoint as department heads those of like minds, who would reflect his own vision.

He was not surprised to receive the message from George Nicolay that the Cabinet was being called into extraordinary session at ten-thirty that morning. In the future, he was certain, Cabinet meetings on all important matters would be the order of the day. Lincoln, put in his proper place, would no longer be able to take action without the approval of the nation's governing council.

Chase showed up promptly and was gratified to see the Secretary of State's place empty. Chase prepared his face to greet any seeming revelations of news with innocent surprise.

"What I have to communicate," said Lincoln, looking more forlorn than usual, "should not be the subject of conversation outside this room."

The President reported to his colleagues that he had first received Secretary Seward's resignation, and had then been visited by a committee of senators. "While they said they believed in my honesty, they seemed to think that when I had in me any good purposes, Mr. Seward contrived to suck them out of me unperceived."

Montgomery Blair asked the President if Senator Wade and the committee had been looking for any more scalps beyond Seward's. Lincoln said no. "Some not very friendly feelings were shown toward one or two others," the President allowed, and Chase knew that specifically included Blair, "but no wish that any but Seward should leave."

Lincoln then read aloud the secret paper left by the Republican senators calling for a unified Cabinet pledged to vigorous prosecution of the war.

Chase knew it almost by heart; he and Fessenden had gone over it often enough, tempering Wade's fulminations until this reasoned document had emerged.

"A plural Executive is really not our system of government," Bates offered, but Chase and Stanton frowned him silent.

"What sort of mood were these senators in," Montgomery Blair wanted to know. "Angry?"

"Earnest and sad, I should say," Lincoln answered with what Chase considered an earnest sadness of his own. "Not malicious or passionate." That was not what Chase had heard about Wade's remarks from Fessenden. "See here," Lincoln added fervently, "I don't want any of you to take this as a hint to retire also. To be frank, I cannot afford to lose you. I don't see how I can get along with any new Cabinet, made of new materials."

Chase was almost embarrassed for Lincoln, at the way the man clung to the Cabinet he had begun with, as if the loss of Seward and the other lukewarm members would leave him disconsolate. The coalition Lincoln had so laboriously put together last year was finished, dead, a thing of the past, because it had always been inherently unstable. Why couldn't Lincoln adjust to the new reality?

"I told them how we have always gone on harmoniously," the President went on, with what seemed to Chase a pleading note in his high voice. "whatever had been our previous party feelings. I said I had been sustained and consoled by the good feeling and the mutual and unselfish zeal that pervaded the Cabinet. I do not see how it is possible for me to go on, if faced with the total abandonment of old friends."

Hogwash. If Lincoln could not get on without Seward and Blair and Bates, then he should step down right away. No; that would mean Hannibal Hamlin at the head of the table, and Chase preferred the tamed Lincoln. He looked portentously at Stanton, the other man in the room he knew agreed that this sentimental drivel about a harmonious Cabinet was an insult to what intelligence existed among the divided group around the table.

The President was floundering; it seemed obvious to Chase that the man simply did not know what to do next. He could not choose a new Secretary of State without the senators' advice and consent, and they would insist on a Chase-approved selection. Lincoln was neatly boxed in. Chase was beginning to enjoy the play of executive power.

After some desultory conversation, Lincoln suggested that the Cabinet should join him that evening in meeting with the committee of senators.

"No," said Chase abruptly. "I do not believe that would be appropriate at all." Better that the congressional pressure should remain directly on the President alone. This was a fight between the Senate Republican caucus and the Republican President; for the Cabinet to mix in would be unseemly and might help the President get off the hook. Because Lincoln had not used the Cabinet as an effective force to govern, he did not deserve its defense against those who demanded unified leadership. Let Lincoln face his critics in the solitude he had sought.

"I don't see that any good would come of our being there," agreed Bates. Chase nodded vigorously at this unexpected support from the Attorney General.

"I really think the President is right," Montgomery Blair said to Bates. "It would be well for all of us to be present when he meets the senators. Seward won't be there during the discussion, which will be largely about him, so there won't be any personal embarrassment."

Chase looked at Stanton to refute Blair, but evidently the Secretary of War did not see any harm in the department heads being present at the political capitulation of the Chief Magistrate. Chase did not like that, but he told himself he was being unduly wary. And he could not deny a lively interest of his own in seeing the long-arrogant Lincoln in the dock.

"If the President wishes us to attend, gentlemen," said Navy Secretary Welles into his long beard, "then it is our duty to do so."

Chase wondered if Lincoln had any tricks up his sleeve. Before he could think of a good reason to block the joint meeting, the distraught President said with feeling, "Good. Half past seven this evening."

The Postmaster General picked his way over the frozen mud of Pennsylvania Avenue to the Blair house opposite the Mansion to consult with his father. The Old Man kept pulling on his arthritic fingers, cracking his knuckles, listening to his son's summary of the Cabinet meeting. Monty Blair could not recall ever having seen his father so tense.

"The President stressed the need for secrecy," Montgomery said, "so maybe he thinks he can talk Seward into changing his mind."

"That's not the point," the Old Man snapped. "Seward wants to stay. He wants Lincoln to reject his resignation, but Lincoln can't do that, not now. He has to have a good reason to hang on to Seward, something that will satisfy Wade and his crowd, or something to make them back off."

"Why can't Lincoln just tell the Senate to go to hell?" Montgomery knew that was impossible in the weakened state of the government after the Fredericksburg debacle, but he wanted to hear the answer from his father, who liked to counsel presidents privately at times like this.

"They have the tickets," the elder Blair said, using the old word for "ballots"; he liked those archaic political terms. "At this stage, the radicals can cripple Lincoln, impeach him, free the slaves, do whatever they want. That's why he's being so nice and respectful. I bet he wanted to throw Wade out the window."

Montgomery added an afterthought about the Cabinet session: "We're getting together with the senators tonight."

The Old Man looked up sharply. "Whose idea was that? To have the Cabinet there."

"Lincoln's. I suppose he wanted company in the lions' den."

"Did anybody object? Stanton?" The Old Man seemed to pounce on what his son thought was a point not all that consequential.

"Stanton didn't say anything either way, Father." After a pause, he remembered: "Chase objected."

The elder Blair thought that over, as his son marveled at the essence of political calculation that appeared on the wizened features. When a grin finally crossed his face, the Old Man looked positively Machiavellian.

"I think I see the plan. Oh, Monty, he's a cunning bastard, is Honest Abe." The grin disappeared. "Now, son, here is your position in that meeting with the senators: the Cabinet is the soul of harmony, never any bickering. All is mutual respect."

"But you know that's not true, Father." When that objection did not seem to make an impression, he added: "I believe, and so do you, that the President rules, not the Cabinet."

"Sure, Monty, but sometimes it is important to deny a little reality in order to uphold a great institution. Remember—if Lincoln wants to preach harmony, you become part of the choir. Deny any dissension, cut the ground out from under the senators."

"It won't work, Father. They know the truth as well as we do."

"The truth has nothing to do with this!" His small father reached up and took his lapels in his hands and shook him. "I think the plan is to embarrass Chase, to flush out the sanctimonious bastard. To make him lie in front of his friends rather than take on Lincoln directly. Divide and conquer, the way the Lincoln men did at the Wigwam. Oh, that cunning bastard. I hope it works."

"Wade's the problem. He'll force the Cabinet division out in the open."

"You're right, Monty. Fessenden is the brains of the crowd, and Collamer has the necessary gray hairs, but that son of a bitch Wade has the backbone." He thought about that, pacing the room slowly. "Maybe we could get a friend of Wade's to urge him to go to the front immediately, to see General Burnside. I'll work on that. I don't want him in that meeting with Lincoln tonight. Remember, Monty—harmony. When they complain about disunity in the Cabinet, you give them the sweetest smile you can muster and say, 'What disunity?' "

Montgomery Blair enjoyed the startled expressions on the faces of the senators entering the room. They expected to be meeting privately again with the President, but found themselves facing Lincoln and his entire Cabinet. Only Seward, the ostensible target of their attack, was absent.

"I have asked the Cabinet to join us tonight," said Lincoln, taking his place at the head of the black walnut table and getting right to business, "to demonstrate to you its unity."

Blair was amazed and amused; Lincoln was prepared to profess that black was white, just as his father had predicted.

"The necessities of the times, of course," Lincoln went on, "prevent frequent or long sessions of the Cabinet, and not every question is submitted for detailed discussion. But although these men could not be expected to think and speak alike on all subjects, they have all acquiesced and come together once a matter has been decided."

Blair did not believe Lincoln could get away with this argument. The senators were lawyers, mainly; they had been in courtrooms, and seen defense attorneys spin a tale wholly divorced from the facts.

Jake Collamer was the committee chairman. He apologized for Ben Wade's absence, explaining that the chairman of the Joint Committee on the Conduct of the War had found it necessary to be with Burnside in the field. Blair wondered how his father had been able to arrange that, but was thankful that Wade was not present to bellow the truth back at the President.

"There is truth in the maxim," said Collamer, "that in a multitude of advisers there is safety. What we want is united counsels, combined wisdom, and energetic action. It is the feeling of my colleagues, Mr. President, based on—" he hesitated—"reports, that you do not employ the Cabinet in such a manner."

"Indeed," Senator Fessenden put in, "we have been informed by the most reliable authority"—Blair noted that he did not look in Chase's direction—"that the Cabinet rarely meets and is not consulted on the gravest questions of the war and of the abolishment of slavery. You take those decisions yourself."

"And what would be wrong with that?" Blair heard himself asking.

"Everything, as the management of the war has demonstrated," Fessenden replied, "and as the delay in abolishing slavery suggests. The President is not a monarch. He is *primus inter pares,* and he cannot presume to run the country single-handed. That is not our constitutional tradition."

Blair did not want to turn this into a debate if Lincoln's strategy was to appear conciliatory, but that unsupported assertion could not go unchallenged. "Where is the tradition that has the President answering to the Cabinet?"

"It was my honor to serve with John Quincy Adams in the House of Representatives," said Fessenden. "You will recall that he returned to the House after he had been defeated for reelection as President by Andy Jackson. A measure came up on the House floor that was passed during President Adams's administration, and he told me that the measure was adopted against his wishes and opinion, but he was outvoted in Cabinet council by Henry Clay and others. That was how the country was governed—by combined wisdom."

"Perhaps that was why John Quincy Adams was so readily defeated by General Jackson," said Blair. When Lincoln shot him a look of caution, Blair added, "Though in his later years in the House, Mr. Adams grew in stature opposing slavery." No sense offending the radicals on their favorite subject.

"Wait a minute," Trumbull interjected. "Lincoln here says the Cabinet is unified, and approves of all decisions. You say it isn't important whether the Cabinet agrees or not. Mr. Chase, tell us—does this Cabinet count in the President's deliberations or not?"

That put the fat in the fire. Would Chase testify to the deep division of philosophy in the Cabinet, and of the fiercely conflicting goals of the men who made it up, as he had been surely telling the senators all week—or would he loyally lie in support of the President and the Administration of which he was a part?

He did both. "I endorse the President's statement fully and entirely," the Treasury Secretary said ponderously, and then qualified that support with "though I regret that there is not a more full consideration of every measure in open Cabinet."

Some of the senators began to squirm. Chase was the instigator of this coup, and it was hard for them to believe he would refuse to take a solid position on the central complaint.

"That was not our understanding, Chase," said Trumbull ominously. "We were informed unequivocally that this Cabinet was split down the middle, and that it was treated with contempt when it came to making great decisions."

Chase reddened, showing both his embarrassment and annoyance. "I would not have agreed to come here tonight," he said, "if I had known I was to be arraigned before a committee of the Senate."

Blair thought "arraigned" was the perfect word. The meeting, sought by the senators to force Lincoln to bow to senatorial pressure, was turning into a preliminary trial of Chase's veracity. Arranging the full-dress confrontation had been a brilliant idea. Either Chase would have to back up Lincoln, agreeing that the Cabinet was carefully consulted and essentially unified—which was a lie—or disagree with Lincoln to his face, showing himself to be the disloyal Cabinet member, which Blair suspected Chase did not have the stomach to do.

Fessenden came to Chase's aid. "Nobody is being arraigned here. Indeed, Mr. President, it was no movement of ours that brought your Cabinet to this meeting. When you suggested such a meeting with the Cabinet the other day, we did not think it was a good idea. We did not suspect or come here for that purpose."

Lincoln remarked innocently how it seemed a good idea to him for everyone to get together. He looked at Chase, as if the Treasury Secretary had been rudely interrupted.

"I would answer yes, that questions of importance had generally been considered by the Cabinet," said Chase, choosing to be the loyalist, "though perhaps not so fully as may be desired."

"Unity?" Trumbull glared at him.

Chase swallowed as he thought about how to handle that. "There has been no want of unity in the Cabinet," he said finally. "We have generally acquiesced on public measures. Once the President has decided on a measure, no Cabinet member has opposed it. To that extent, there has been unity."

Lincoln moved in at that point, smoothly admitting, "There have been occasions in which important action was taken without consultation with my Cabinet." Blair liked the subtle use of the possessive in reference to his Cabinet, and the disarming way Lincoln conceded a point that could not be denied. "Placing the army under McClellan's command after his return from the Peninsula, for example. The Banks expedition, too."

The President had chosen to send General Banks to New Orleans, where he could help Grant pose a threat to the Mississippi River forts rather than reinforce the hapless Burnside in Virginia. Having failed so dismally in the East, Lincoln was now looking to the West—to Grant and Sherman around Vicksburg, to Rosecrans in Tennessee—to save the Federal Army's reputation. The President had said nothing to the Cabinet that Blair could recall about that sudden shift in military plans.

Chase, who normally sat upright, slumped in his chair as Lincoln embarked on a long speech about harmony in the Cabinet, about Seward's earnestness in the prosecution of the war, about how Seward and Chase had often worked closely together on official correspondence. He called on any Cabinet member to speak out if there had been any want of unity or sufficient consultation, and Blair noticed how Chase looked in suppliance at Stanton, who looked away. Not even Caleb Smith, who had flatly opposed the Emancipation Proclamation—"th-th-there goes Indiana!"—had a word to say after Chase had refused to wash the Cabinet's dirty linen in front of the Senate.

Though it was growing late, Lincoln went on and on, not rambling, never taking the slightest umbrage at what seemed so obvious to Blair was the Senate's attempted usurpation of executive power, but holding to the shaky hypothesis that the senators were misinformed about the lack of consultation or absence of unity. He refused to take up the real challenge, ignoring it as he construed the senators' complaints much more narrowly. He refused to dispute their presumption to dictate, preferring to correct their reasons for dictating.

The more Lincoln leaned on Secretary Chase's words, emphasizing the grudging "unity" admission and minimizing the qualifiers attached, the more Chase looked pained and Trumbull looked furious. Blair was glad that Wade was not at the meeting to thunder at the trickery of the President and the hypocrisy of the Treasury Secretary; had Anna Carroll persuaded him to visit the front that day?

"As for the proclamation of freedom," Lincoln concluded, "Mr. Seward had fully concurred in it after I had resolved on it. Isn't that so, Governor Chase?"

Chase was obliged to nod in agreement. "As a matter of fact, it was Seward who suggested amendments to strengthen the proclamation," he volunteered, "such as the pledge to maintain the freedom of those emancipated. 'Maintain' was Seward's word, and it gives force to the document."

Lincoln, in his long speech, had evidently worn Chase down; the Treasury Secretary was no longer trying to straddle honor and loyalty. In front of his Cabinet colleagues and the President, he could not be forthright to his senatorial friends about his true feelings. Chase's backstabbing was limited to small gatherings with Lincoln not present.

Fessenden, the intellectual leader of the party's Senate group, backed off slightly on one point after the President had finished. "I never said that the President was bound by any decision made by his Cabinet. I maintain only that all important questions must be discussed in Cabinet council."

Blair sensed the beginnings of senatorial retreat and thought of himself as harassing cavalry. "The Cabinet has no voice, and should have no voice," he said, "except when the President calls for it. Unlike you, we have no constitutional mandate. We are a creature of the presidency, an extension of him, deriving our authority from his powers and with no independent power."

Fessenden started to object but Blair was not finished. "He might require our opinion in writing—my father informs me that was what President Jackson preferred, Senator Fessenden—but he is under no obligation to defer to what we think. In a Cabinet vote, the only vote that counts is the President's."

Lincoln gave him no signal to stop, so Blair went on. "Now about Governor Seward. I have differed sharply with Seward over the years, as you all know, and I have my differences with him today. But I believe him as earnest as anyone in this war. The charge that he is 'lukewarm' is sheer nonsense. I think it would be injurious to the public service to have him leave the Cabinet, and with all due respect, gentlemen, I would add this: the Senate had better not meddle with matters of this kind."

Lincoln shook his head at that last point, and hastened to assure one and all he did not think the senators were meddling. Blair had said it; Lincoln could disavow it and remain conciliatory, but Blair was certain it would help Lincoln to have the Senate leaders know that their overreaching was recognized as such.

"Seward's presence is what is injurious," said Grimes.

Senator Sumner picked that up and launched into a condemnation of Seward as a diplomatist. "The correspondence he has had in the name of this administration is an abomination, and its publication was a deliberate insult to all of us who have stood foursquare for the Union and against slavery." Sumner spoke longer than Lincoln had, listing all of Seward's shortcomings. The theme of the meeting had changed from a general disapproval of the way Lincoln was executing his office to a specific demand for the ouster of the Secretary of State, who had already resigned.

"Not all the senators present have given me their opinions on that," said Lincoln, looking around the table.

"You have mine," said Grimes. "Out."

"I'm not prepared to say," Jake Collamer wavered.

Blair understood what the President was looking for: any lack of unanimity. He thought that taking a kind of vote on Seward was a tactical mistake, but at this stage Blair was willing to trust Lincoln's political sagacity.

"I studied law in Seward's office," said Pomeroy of Kansas, "but I've lost confidence in him. He ought to go."

"Considering the state of the parties in New York," said Ira Harris of that state, who was not a Seward man but who, Blair assumed, was worried about Democrat Horatio Seymour's leadership of the peace movement there, "and Governor Seward's popularity with the anti-Seymour forces, I'd have to advise against his removal."

Lincoln looked at Fessenden, who shook his head. "I do not think it is proper to discuss the merits or demerits of a member of the Cabinet in the presence of his associates."

Chase was out of his chair like a shot. "I think the members of the Cabinet had better withdraw."

Blair hated to leave, but Lincoln seemed in control of himself and his presidency now that Chase was exposed to his own allies as all too ready to flinch. The Postmaster General politely held the door for Chase, Stanton, Smith, and Bates, threw a half salute at the President, and closed the door on the senators.

Fessenden knew he had been outmaneuvered by the lawyer from Illinois. Chase had been placed in a near impossible position, and his understandable equivocation had weakened the force of the senatorial move. Sneaking the Cabinet in, unbeknown to the senators, was a trick, but Fessenden could not charge Lincoln with anything more than discourtesy.

"I wish to know," he said with the Cabinet members gone, "whether you, Mr. President, intend to follow the wishes of the Republican senators on the Seward matter, when ascertained."

Lincoln, to Fessenden's disgust, told a long and vulgar story that was not to the point. Its lengthy recounting served only to give the President a chance not to answer the question, and no Wade was present with the equivalent boorishness to shut him up. Fessenden did not laugh and nod sagely, as

Senator Charles Sumner

others did, when the President tried to show how the story applied to the situation at hand.

Fessenden then used the information he had not yet admitted he knew: that the decision facing Lincoln was not to oust Seward, but to accept the resignation Seward had already submitted.

"There is a current rumor that Secretary Seward has already resigned."

"I thought I told you last evening," said Lincoln disingenuously, "that Mr. Seward had tendered his resignation." Fessenden did not remind Lincoln he had told them no such thing. That highly relevant fact weakened the President's position, and he was giving the Senate nothing. "I have his resignation in my pocket but have not yet made it public. Or accepted it."

"The question, then," stated Fessenden, "is whether Mr. Seward should be requested to withdraw his resignation."

Lincoln did not evade the question. "Yes."

"As the fact of his resignation cannot be concealed," Fessenden told him, "and its cause will be well understood, then all the harm done in dividing the Republicans in New York has already been done. No withdrawal of his resignation will heal that breach. I strongly advise that you accept it."

Lincoln nodded, which Fessenden could not tell meant that he understood or agreed.

The senator from Maine played his last card. "Shall I canvass my fellow senators on whether you should accept Mr. Seward's resignation?" Lincoln had, after all, been canvassing the senators in this room tonight on whether to fire Seward, but he had been careful not to obligate himself to follow the views he had solicited. If Lincoln agreed to that casually made suggestion, Fessenden could take the question of accepting a Seward resignation to an advisory caucus vote which Lincoln would be forced to treat as a Senate decision. That not only would lock out Seward, but would establish a new order in the Senate's relationship with the President. And not just for now; perhaps for the life of the Republic. Fessenden was aware of the stakes.

"I think not." Lincoln's reply matched the informality of Fessenden's suggestion. Not a blunt "no," not some sort of indecisive evasion, but a casually decisive "I think not"—as if to say he would just as soon hold on to his power, if the senators and the Republican Party would not mind.

It was 1 A.M. Fessenden was convinced that nothing more could be extracted from this man. The President had seemed to gain strength as the night wore on, as the others faded in fatigue. Fessenden rose, aware of the senators' defeat. "I take it you will make no change in your Cabinet?"

"If I let Seward go, I have reason to fear a general smashup."

"And why is that?"

"Chase would withdraw too, and I cannot do without him at the Treasury."

Fessenden shook his head in wonderment. Now Lincoln was telling a group of senators, including the man known to be Chase's closest friend, that he was expecting a resignation from Chase. That would surely get around and put pressure on Chase to quit. Fessenden thought it would be a good idea to leave before Lincoln came up with any other tricks.

On the way out, Trumbull took Fessenden by the arm. "Your friend Chase sang a different tune when he was alone with us," he said bitterly. "How in hell could he sit there and say that all was sweet harmony in the Cabinet?"

Fessenden did not want to reply, but old Judge Collamer answered quietly for him. "He lied." Fessenden, who had until that night counted himself Chase's main ally in the Senate, could not disagree.

"I think I'll just tell the President that right now," said Trumbull, whirling and heading back toward Lincoln's office. Fessenden made no effort to detain him. Had Chase—and Stanton—proved brave and true, great good might have come of this, but the only good result of this long night's work, he told himself coldly, was that it unmasked some selfish cowards.

Navy Secretary Welles returned to the President's office next morning as soon as he thought Lincoln would be finished with breakfast. He wanted to say that he believed Seward should not be allowed to resign. Welles knew that the Secretary of State did not want to leave the Cabinet, regretted his impulsive act, and was piqued that Lincoln had discussed the resignation with the senators.

Chase and Stanton were already there, waiting for Lincoln. Welles told them what was on his mind: "To yield a presidential prerogative to the Senate would be an evil example. It would be fraught with incalculable injury to the government and the country."

His two Cabinet colleagues, standing in front of the fire, met this with sour looks, but Lincoln, walking in, said he quite agreed: "If I let the senators have their way, the whole government must cave in. It could not stand."

The President stood next to the fireplace, arm on the mantelpiece, alongside the disgruntled radicals, as Welles took a seat on the sofa near the east window, in the morning sunshine.

"The session last night," Chase complained, "was a harrowing experience. It had come as a total surprise to me," he said, which Welles knew was untrue, "and affected me most painfully." That part was true.

Lincoln offered no sympathy and waited for him to go on.

"In fact, I have even prepared my own resignation as Secretary of the Treasury."

Chase was not resigning, Welles noted; merely hoping to shock Lincoln by saying he had "prepared" a resignation.

Lincoln's face lit up. "Where is it?"

Chase was taken aback. "I brought it with me," he answered, tentatively taking a sealed envelope from his breast pocket but not offering it up. "I wrote it this morning, but—"

"Let me have it," said Lincoln eagerly. He reached his long arm across the fireplace and held out his hand. Chase was reluctant to hand it over. Lincoln fairly snatched the paper out of Chase's fingers, tore open the envelope, and glanced at the paper inside.

The President let out a whoop, slapped the letter on his leg, and turned to Welles. "This cuts the Gordian knot!" He plunked himself down in the chair, motioning for Chase and Stanton to sit. "I can dispose of this subject now without difficulty. I see my way clear."

Welles fully understood the reason for Lincoln's delight. All of Washington was reshuffling the Lincoln Cabinet, and Stanton's censorship could not keep it out of the newspapers much longer. He did not have enough public sentiment behind him to refuse Seward's resignation. But by inducing Chase to resign as well, he could refuse both—maintain his Cabinet without change and retain his position as the fulcrum of the contending forces in his party.

Welles observed the dismay on Chase's handsome face, and the contrasting total lack of concern on Lincoln's part for the pain he was causing the Treasury Secretary. Stanton, who, Welles suspected, was using Chase as a stalking horse, huffed, "I wish you, sir, to consider my resignation at this time in your possession."

"You may go to your department," the President said impatiently, since Stanton seemed to miss the whole point, "I don't want your resignation. This is all I want," he waved the letter in his hand. "I will detain neither of you longer."

That was as peremptory a dismissal as Welles had heard come from the President's lips since he had known him. The two trooped out.

"Now I can ride," said Lincoln with relief. "I have got a pumpkin in each end of my bag." Welles found that word picture amusing: a farmer riding to market with pumpkins in each saddlebag, balancing his load as Lincoln was balancing the interests of the factions in his administration. He would now publicly make known the two resignations, and refuse to accept either. Seward would be relieved and grateful, somewhat less imperious in the future, and even more of a Lincoln man; Chase might still be angling for the Republican nomination in 1864, but would be weakened with the radicals who had seen him wither under fire.

"A masterstroke," Welles told him without any hint of flattery.

"I do not see how it could have been done better," Lincoln agreed. "If I had yielded to that storm and dismissed Seward, the thing would have slumped over one way"—Lincoln dropped a shoulder and slumped to illustrate—"and we would have been left with a scant handful of supporters. When Chase gave in his resignation just now"—he held up the paper in triumph—"I saw that the game was in my hands. Now I have the biggest half of the hog."

He went to his desk to write out the two refusals. Welles was astounded at the way this man, assumed by all to have been politically devastated and in such a depressed mental state, could have shown such resilience in the face of a vigorous challenge from the assembled powers of his party. Native shrewdness, he supposed, combined with some hidden sources of strength and divine obstinacy.

The Navy Secretary was satisfied that the President could survive the political attacks from within his party, whether in Congress or in his Cabinet. He wished he could be as certain that Lincoln could survive the blunders of his generals, and the continued staggering losses to his forces in the field. Public sentiment had never been so low. Something had to be done to resist the rising pressure of the defeatists and copperheads, who were angrily clamoring for peace and were all too willing to pay its price of disunion.

CHAPTER 37

CHIROPODIST, PEACEMAKER, SPY

For Isachar Zacharie, in the most exciting time of his life, being a Jew was both a help and a hindrance. Seated in the New Orleans home of the merchant Martin Gordon, a fellow Israelite and an official enemy of the United States, the foot doctor looked at both sides of that coin:

Less than a month before, Lincoln had given him a letter to take to General Nathaniel Banks, who had taken command of the Army of the Gulf from Ben Butler. Although phrased as a letter of introduction, Lincoln's letter hinted at his assignment: "Dr. Zacharie, whom you know as well as I do . . . might be of service to you in his peculiar profession"—by that the President meant foot-doctoring, which Zacharie understood was merely a cloak for his other activities—"and secondly, as a means of access to his countrymen, who are quite numerous in some of the localities you will probably visit."

By "numerous countrymen," the President referred to the many Israelites long resident in New Orleans. What was left unsaid was the common knowledge that the most renowned Jew from Louisiana was Judah Benjamin, the Confederate Secretary of State.

Isachar Zacharie

That channel to the Confederate elite was the helpful part of being a Jew. He could establish contact quickly with family and friends in Union-occupied New Orleans, and then to their connections in Richmond, with the purpose of discovering if any possibility existed of a peaceful solution to the conflict.

The difficulty of being a Jew was alluded to in the conclusion of Lincoln's letter to Banks: "excepting his case from a general prohibition which I understand to exist."

That "general prohibition" the President had heard about was the result of General Ulysses Grant's hatred of Jews. Zacharie understood the cause of the general's animus: some Jewish cotton traders were stealing the Army blind. Gentile cotton traders were not doing badly at that business either, but the Jews always stood out. Worse, Grant's father, Jesse Grant had been in business with a Jew to take advantage of the Army quartermaster. Grant could not get even with his father, so he took it out, Zacharie supposed, on the Jew who was his father's partner, and, as so often happened, on Jews in general.

Six weeks before, in early November, Grant had issued an order to his transportation officer in Jackson, Tennessee, forbidding Jews from using any railroad in a southward direction. As a result, it had become common knowledge that Jews were unwelcome visitors to the Western theater of war. This would have made the coming of Isachar Zacharie to New Orleans, and his activities there, slightly difficult to explain—were it not, as Lincoln's note indicated, for his convenient profession. Every army needed a foot doctor.

Zacharie was not unduly troubled by the President's tacit understanding of Grant's policy or Lincoln's willingness to leave undisturbed the effect of Grant's detestation of members of the Hebrew race. Like most Northern Jews, he was embarrassed and angry at the predations of the salesmen of the reclaimed-wool material called "shoddy," and eager to dissociate himself from those rotten apples.

So long as the "general prohibition," as Lincoln described it, was unwritten and informal—strictly a personal act by one general taken on an emergency basis—and was directed at stopping Jewish traders from coming into the war zone rather than driving local Jews out, Zacharie felt he could live with the Grant policy. Harsh and unfair, yes, but making scapegoats out of Jews was nothing new, and Zacharie justified his own acceptance of the worrisome precedent by telling himself that everybody suffered in wartime.

Not that he liked it, he reminded himself, any more than he liked the wording of the Sabbath Order that Lincoln had issued about the same time to pander to the Christian clergy around election time. Over Stanton's objection that it would interfere with the conduct of the war, Lincoln ordered Sunday work in the Army and Navy reduced to strict necessity, to preserve "the sacred rights of Christian soldiers and sailors, a becoming deference to the best sentiments of a Christian people." Zacharie knew that Lincoln was no religious zealot, did not attend church on the Christian sabbath himself, and signed the order only to gather political support; still, he should not have made Jews feel like outsiders, guests of a "Christian people." The idea of mentioning that to Lincoln occurred to him at the time but was swiftly put aside; that was a matter for more self-conscious Israelites to bother their heads about. Zacharie was not about to jeopardize his professional and personal relationship with the President of the United States over parochial interests.

"I want you to mingle freely with people of all classes, especially with your own countrymen," General Banks had told him when formally explaining his assignment. Banks was a good man, a Massachusetts politician but not a radical like Sumner, self-made, like himself; the "Little Bobbin Boy" was his sobriquet, attesting to Banks's start in the cotton mills he now owned. Banks was an all-out Union man, dead set against secession; generally anti-slavery but not a wild-eyed abolitionist—much like Lincoln. The foot doctor thought that Banks would make an excellent President one day, and was resolved to help bring that happy event about by crediting him with making the peace between North and South.

That was another reason he could use for not taking offense at the general prohibition against Jews. Nathaniel Banks was not the sort to fuss about formal "rights" of individuals when it came to winning the war and saving the Union. With great pride, Banks had told Zacharie of the day in the secession summer of a year ago when the legislature of Maryland was scheduled to meet to vote their state out of the Union. Lincoln had ordered McClellan to arrest the secessionist members before they arrived to vote, and Banks and Dix had been given the command to carry out the President's order. As Banks related the episode to Zacharie, he had struck ruthlessly and effectively, and never mind "states' rights." Obviously, the foot doctor concluded, it would be foolish to complain to such a man about the inconvenience being felt by a few Jews; as Lincoln liked to say, you can't make an omelet without breaking eggs.

"You will ascertain and report the nature of public opinion here," was another part of his charge from the general. Easy enough. The people here were eager to pour their past troubles with "Beast" Butler into a sympathetic Northern ear. "You will pay particular attention to gaining information about the location and number of enemy troops, the extent of their supplies and ammunition, and whether his troops are conscript or otherwise." Not so easy; that was spying. If Zacharie's primary purpose was to establish contact with the Confederate Cabinet, the sideline of spying might undermine his peacemaking. Not to mention making it much more dangerous. A peace emissary could be rejected, but a spy could be executed. No matter, Zacharie thought, he could do it all.

"May victory be our reward," Zacharie had told the general with all due solemnity.

"Lose no time and spare no expense." Banks had handed him an envelope containing what Zacharie knew to be five thousand dollars in Confederate bills. He had resolved to account for every cent, but not in writing.

His contact with the Confederacy was to be Martin Gordon, a New Orleans merchant of some prominence in whose stately home he now was visiting. Gordon was registered as an official enemy of the United States. That status meant that Gordon's business dealings in New Orleans were sharply circumscribed, but he was not under arrest and could travel safely in the Confederacy.

"The time is not ripe for a peace offer," his host was saying. "Not after

Fredericksburg. They hear in Richmond that Lincoln's government is falling apart. Seward out, Chase—"

"That's not true, Martin. President Lincoln is a very determined man." Zacharie knew how important it was to send word to Judah Benjamin through his sister in New Orleans that the rumor of a breakup of Lincoln's Cabinet was just newspaper talk. "I discussed this with the President myself, for hours. He will hold his Cabinet together, he will hold the Republican Party together, he will hold his Army together, and in the end he will hold the Union together. Holding things together is very important to him, more important than anything."

"You and Lincoln talked for hours?" Gordon was not being sarcastic, but the doubt was in his voice.

Zacharie had never found it difficult to exaggerate, or even to make up stories completely when necessary. He knew he had a talent for making people believe his stories; why could he not persuade people that he was telling the truth when he told the truth?

He had spent long evenings in the President's presence, not counting the sessions cutting his corns, just talking about life, the world, families. Obviously Lincoln enjoyed his company; Zacharie laughed at his jokes, but, more important, the foot doctor had a keen eye for detail, a true ear for the way people were talking, a thorough grounding in the Old Testament, and—perhaps most needed by Lincoln—a capacity for understanding the suffering that some some strong men inflicted on themselves. But who on the outside would ever believe that the President of the United States spent time discussing the future with a Jewish corncutter? He pushed forward his only credential, the note written by Lincoln and countersigned by Seward attesting to his skills as a practitioner of foot medicine.

"It's kind of a code," Zacharie said conspiratorially. "You'll understand." At least the commercial endorsement proved that he knew the man and the man knew him. Gordon could not produce the same evidence of personal contact with Jeff Davis. Zacharie took back the precious document and returned it to his wallet.

Impressed, Gordon reported that Richmond thought it now had an excellent chance to win the war. "The British Parliament convenes next month, and Gladstone has already said that the South has made a nation. After last week at Fredericksburg, and next week at Murfreesboro, the desire of the European powers to recognize the South will be irresistible."

Zacharie reminded himself that spying was one of his jobs. "Murfreesboro?"

"Big celebration going on there now," Gordon told him. "It started at the wedding of one of the generals—Morgan, the cavalry raider, even Jeff Davis came—and it will last up to Christmas. Forrest's raiders are hitting Grant in the West and Morgan, the bridegroom, has just been sent on some secret raid northward."

Zacharie made mental notes; it would not do to take out a pencil. But the Stones River area of Tennessee, just south of Nashville, was familiar to him; bunions, mainly. "I hear that Lincoln is desperate after his defeat in Virginia," Martin Gordon told him, "and is demanding that his man Rosecrans go on the attack in Tennessee. If he comes after Bragg in Murfreesboro, the

Federals will get beaten again and the British will recognize the South. That's the best time to start the peacemaking."

"No." They did not understand Lincoln. He might compromise on emancipation, even delay his proclamation a few months or years if the South showed signs of coming around, but on secession Lincoln would never compromise. War to the knife on that.

"Isachar, my friend, be realistic. All they hear in Richmond is the glorious victory over the Army of the Potomac, and the call for peace by Seymour and Vallandigham, and the talk of Seward's being forced to resign. With all that in the air, Richmond will not hear of talk of peace without secession."

The time for his great effort was not ripe, Zacharie ruefully agreed. If Lincoln signed the Emancipation Proclamation in ten days, as scheduled, the South's leaders would be more inclined to fight on. Military fortunes would have to change—one way or the other—before his peacemaking move could be made. Zacharie's job now was to establish trust, to set up lines of communication between Lincoln in Washington—General Banks in New Orleans, and Secretary Benjamin in Richmond—which would instantly be used when one side or the other began to see the futility of further slaughter.

Murfreesboro could be important. He would pass what he had heard just now to General Banks for transmission to Rosecrans (sounded like a Jewish name) in Tennessee. It occurred to him that, with all the famous rebel cavalry racing off to other places, this might not be a bad time for the Union general to attack Bragg, but that was not really his business.

For the remainder of their meeting, he and Gordon did the sort of business that would be preliminary to any peace undertakings: trading that established trust. Gordon submitted a list of grievances of New Orleans families harassed by the previous Union occupiers, which Zacharie knew he could alleviate quickly, and asked for information about the whereabouts of General Breckinridge's son, missing in action and not reported captured. The chiropodist promised to forward that query to General Dix, and then wondered aloud about the drug traffic from New Orleans into the Southern lines.

"No Southern lady worth her salt would hesitate to take a bag of quinine under her bustle," said Gordon. "You can't search them all, and I'd advise Banks not to search any."

Zacharie turned to the business of exchange rates between Confederate and Union currency, which could never be formalized but had to be unofficially established if New Orleans merchants were to be able to do any business in the South. After some enjoyable dickering, Zacharie shook Gordon's hand on a fair deal. The foot doctor departed with the expectation that one day— perhaps not until a military stalemate was established, but one day—they could be conducting business on the highest levels.

On his arrival at his room at the military headquarters, the chiropodist was met by a delegation of ashen-faced members of the group that Gentiles would call his "fellow countrymen."

Zacharie had seen nervous Israelites before, and discounted their fears; he knew that whatever orders had been put in place by Ben Butler could be countermanded. He brought them into his office with a generous wave of the hand.

"Which is the foot that hurts?" he said cheerily.

"Show him the order."

He drew on his glasses and looked at the heading: from Grant's headquarters at Holly Springs, Tennessee, General Orders No. 11. "General Orders" meant it was important, a statement of policy to be carried out in every part of the army commanded by Grant. The document was dated December 17, three days ago.

A sense of dread entered his soul as he read the opening words: "The Jews, as a class . . ."

He went to the window and studied the order. "The Jews, as a class violating every regulation of trade established by the Treasury Department and also department orders, are hereby expelled from the department within twenty-four hours from the receipt of this order."

Expelled. Every Jew, whether or not engaged in trade. As a class. Banished from Tennessee, from sections of Mississippi, from every city and town under the control of the armies of Grant and Sherman. That was a third of the Union-controlled Union. Zacharie, unbelieving, read on: "Post commanders will see that all of this class of people be furnished passes and required to leave, and anyone returning after such notification will be arrested and held in confinement until an opportunity occurs of sending them out as prisoners . . ."

At that moment, Zacharie realized he was not an American, not a presidential agent, not a member of the medical profession, but merely a Jew, to be rounded up and shipped off at the whim of an angry man in uniform.

"There must be some mistake," he said to the others, trying not to let the dread in his heart show on his face.

"I've just come from Oxford, Mississippi," said a gaunt man. "They didn't let us sell anything or take anything with us. We were loaded on a cart and told to get moving. I'm not a cotton trader, I didn't do any business with the army. My son is serving with the army under Burnside. Nobody would listen. Orders are orders, they said."

"What next, Zacharie? Will General Banks order the Jews out of New Orleans? Where will we go then, back to Germany?"

He did not know what to tell them. Banks was no Grant, but this sweeping order could hardly have been issued without some approval from the War Department in Washington. He recalled how Charles Dana, Stanton's eyes and ears in the field, had returned with tales of the infamous speculation in cotton by army quartermasters and Jews, which had infuriated Stanton and Halleck.

"The President cannot know about this," said the man from Mississippi. "Lincoln would never permit it if he knew." On that, there was a general murmur of agreement.

But Zacharie knew that Lincoln did know—if not of the expulsion order, certainly of the "general prohibition" of Jews by Grant throughout his command. And if the President tacitly approved of the one, who could say he would not look the other way at the next step of expulsion? The foot doctor felt a terrible personal responsibility. When Lincoln had discussed Grant's problems with Jews, when he had written of the prohibition in his letter to Banks, Zacharie had not uttered a word of protest. He had said nothing. It must have seemed to Lincoln that he approved, and that individual loyal Jews would not be stricken with fear at the thought of being treated "as a class," to be arrested the way fugitive slaves used to be. His heart sank further at that thought. Fugitive slaves now had more rights within the Union lines than Jews who had lived there all their lives.

"You have to go to see Lincoln immediately, tonight, Zacharie. You say you know him. He trusts you. Get him to stop this right away."

Zacharie shriveled inside. He could not do it. He was the wrong man, having acquiesced without objection in the general prohibition to which he had been an exception. Why, he asked himself in anguish, had he gone along with such unfairness when he could have spoken up for his people? He knew why. He was slightly ashamed of his people, the crooked ones, and had not imagined the restriction against them would get out of hand.

On his conscience at that moment were all the suppressed doubts of the past few months at the way Stanton and his men had been hacking away at the freedom of loyal Northerners to complain about the government. He thought of the arrests of the editors, of the way they were shipped to jail in silence, and of how he had said nothing. He thought of Watson, Stanton's evil right-hand man, saying, "Let them prove themselves innocent." That was wrong, not the way of law in America. Zacharie had known how Stanton had sent General Stone to imprisonment at Fort Lafayette without trial, because he was McClellan's friend and to satisfy Senators Wade and Chandler. That was a terrible scandal, and nobody but a few copperheads like Seymour and Vallandigham had raised their voices against it.

Should Isachar Zacharie have said something, put a word in the President's ear when he was working on his foot? He had not wanted to become involved in other people's injustices, not because he was ignorant of them, but because that sort of involvement would get him branded a troublemaker, possibly disloyal. And if that reputation attached to him, he could never do the great work of making peace. That was how he had reasoned his way into silence. And now the sudden arrests, the terror of unbridled authority, was coming after his own people, "as a class." He was afraid not only of what could happen, but also of his own guilt in not having tried to stop it.

He could not go to Lincoln because Lincoln knew that Zacharie had proof in writing that Lincoln had known in advance of Grant's policy. The Jewish leader to see Lincoln would have to be someone who did not know this, who would believe that no President of the United States could tolerate such bigotry by an officer of the United States Army. Then Lincoln could profess ignorance, surprise, and countermand the order with no loss of dignity.

"Kaskel," he said with certainty. "Cesar Kaskel of Paducah, he's the man to lead a delegation to the President. And he can get there overnight by rail, whereas it would take me days to sail around the Gulf."

"But you can get right to the President—"

"This cannot wait. I'll get a message to the Kaskels by telegraph, and send another message to Lincoln's secretaries."

"We are not permitted to use the telegraph, Zacharie," said the gaunt man. "I tried to send a message to General Grant. They would not accept it from a Jew."

At least, Zacharie knew, he had access to the military telegraph. Cesar Kaskel was a strong man, the leader of a family that commanded respect among Jews and Gentiles in Kentucky and Ohio. Lincoln would see him, unless Stanton or Halleck blocked the way. And if Lincoln saw him, then—Zacharie would not let himself think about what might happen. Grant was a Lincoln favorite, despite his drunken rages, despite his strange behavior at Shiloh, because he was a fighter. Perhaps Lincoln would not want to interfere.

The foot doctor thought of sending a personal message to the President through John Hay but decided against it. Too presumptuous. If a Jew could be the one to help make the peace, he told himself, that lifesaving act would win more respect for Jews in America than anything else one man could do. Let Cesar Kaskel be the one to see Lincoln to stop the expulsion of Jews; his own mission, Zacharie persuaded himself, was even more important. Leaving to send a telegraph message, he hoped the feeling of shame would soon pass.

CHAPTER 38

OFFER TO SUCCEED

Weed was sitting in the Secretary of State's office after a poor night's sleep on the train, and he had not removed his overcoat. It was cold in Seward's office.

"Thurlow, you look positively grumpy," said Seward. "What took you so long to get down here? Washington is lovely at Christmastime."

Weed had good reason to be out of sorts. His political partner had impetuously and foolishly submitted his resignation as Secretary of State without consulting him. Weed well remembered moving heaven and earth, and the President-elect, to secure that post for Seward two years ago, and he did not consider it partnerly for Seward to jeopardize the post in such cavalier fashion. Luckily, Lincoln had been able to euchre a resignation out of Chase, making possible his simultaneous, triumphant turndown of both.

"It's true the swamp here doesn't smell so awful in the winter," Weed allowed, "but I prefer Albany. Or London."

That was another reason for his grumpiness. Seward had sent word to Weed only a month before to prepare for a mission to London and Paris at year's end, and Weed had made all arrangements for the voyage. He told all his friends of the vast importance of the mission. Then some criticism by Greeley and Chase of the use of the "king of the lobby" for wartime diplomacy had panicked Seward into canceling the trip. This profoundly embarrassed Weed by making it appear that he was being punished for not working hard enough to stop the election of Democrat Horatio Seymour as governor of New York. The Greeley crowd had thrown away the most important state in the Union, and now Weed was being blamed. Frankly, he was glad Seymour had won; teach the damn black Republicans a lesson.

"Sorry about London, Thurlow," said Seward, reading his mind as alter egos should. "And I apologize, too, for acting peremptorily this week. You should have had a voice in my decision. But it all happened so fast."

What also rubbed Weed the wrong way was an unjust accusation of corruption. Word was out in New York that Seward's friends had made a killing in

Secretary of State William Henry Seward

the Gold Room, acting on advance news of the breakup of Lincoln's Cabinet. Weed had not even been given enough advance warning by his political partner to make such a killing, and to be accused of doing what he had not time to do was especially galling.

"I cannot be angry at you for more than a few moments, my good friend," Weed said in candor. "It is like being angry with myself. And what of you— now that it's all over, are you all right?"

"I confess to having been somewhat disturbed at the time, Thurlow. Lincoln should never have taken my resignation under advisement—a true friend would have rejected it immediately. And he should never have allowed the senators to come in to vilify me, dignifying their anti-constitutional bid with a hearing. But he did. And it came out all right. Now, curiously, I feel refreshed." He inhaled and exhaled, patting his narrow chest. "The entire episode has not only proved harmless, but rather reinvigorating."

"And what of the President, Governor—did he find the Cabinet crisis reinvigorating too?"

"Only temporarily. He's a curious fellow. A few days ago, after the terrible news of Fredericksburg, he was on the verge of—I don't know what. Declaiming that idiotic poem about the spirit of mortals, quoting bloody scenes from *Macbeth,* reciting from the Book of Job, pacing around like a madman all night long, and then sleeping away the morning in his office. I feared for his sanity, Thurlow."

Weed wondered aloud how, in that condition, Lincoln had been able to cope with the assault of the senators.

"That was the most amazing part," Seward replied. "When his authority came under challenge, every bit of cunning and shrewdness and ruthlessness came to the fore. He rose to the crisis, met it squarely with no hint of the hypo showing, and showed them who is master."

"Like you, then, he's feeling his oats?"

"Oh, no, not a bit. Quite the contrary, Thurlow. Lincoln is gloomy, preoccupied. The euphoria wore off in a few hours. That's why he sent for you."

That did not square with what Weed knew. "He started sending for me before the Cabinet crisis. But I've been sulking for the better part of three days."

Seward grinned at his half apology. "Don't take off your coat, we're going to see the President now. Come along. Tell me what you know about Seymour. What sort of inaugural address do you expect from him in Albany?"

Weed observed how they both had stopped calling Lincoln "Lincoln" and between each other had begun to call him the "President." To the President's face, of course, he was still "Lincoln." They passed up the carriage and chose to walk to the Mansion. The mud had frozen and the footing in the snow was not slippery.

Lincoln shooed his secretaries out of his office, calling for Marshal Lamon to join him with Seward and Weed.

Weed was not accustomed to meeting with Lincoln except in private, and frowned slightly as he glanced at Lamon. The President explained that a point of contact might be needed on a mission he had in mind, and that he wanted Hill Lamon to know the details. Weed signaled he understood. Lamon was part bodyguard, part company-keeper and friend, trusted to sleep at the President's door or to do political errands, and to forget what might be embarrassing to remember. Not as clever as Hay or as organized as Nicolay, but more tight-lipped than both.

"Lincoln here was asking me about the man who will soon occupy my old chair in the governor's office in Albany," Seward began, legs crossed, toe turning, as if making idle conversation. "We both agree that you were right about Horatio Seymour from the start, Thurlow. Undignified campaign all over the state and the like. You saw the disaster coming, and you were the only one."

Weed, mollified, assumed that the governor was making a difficult subject easier for the President to broach.

"What will Seymour do about conscription?" Seward wanted to know. Weed had connections across political lines to Seymour through Dean Richmond, the Democratic leader upstate, and it was natural for Seward and the President to assume that Weed knew what the governor-elect was thinking.

"He'll oppose the draft," Weed told them. "Don't count on a big contingent of troops from New York." That was what came from basing a Republican campaign on abolition and social revolution, rather than sticking to the Union as it was, Weed thought.

"We need those troops," said Lincoln.

Weed was tempted to say he should have thought of that on September 22, and again on September 24. The first proclamation promised to extend black freedom in the South, the second immediately restricted freedom for whites in the North. As if on purpose, the pairing of the proclamations infuriated all but the minority of abolitionists.

"Do you suppose Governor Seymour would interpose state police and militia," asked Seward, "in order to block the effect of the President's habeas corpus proclamation?"

"I wouldn't try any disloyalty arrests in New York for a while," Weed replied. "Seymour made a big issue of that in the campaign, and the fear many people have of getting clapped into Fort Lafayette for speaking out against the war helped him win. You heard what Seymour had to say about dictatorship, Lincoln."

He knew the President would recall the hot words that had passed between the two men on the subject of the need to restrict each citizen's freedom to preserve the nation's security. The recent election showed that most New York voters agreed with Seymour—with what Breckinridge used to say, for that matter—that treating every dissenter as a traitor corrupted the basis of the Union and made it less worthy of blood sacrifice.

"Seymour and Fernando Wood are already talking about putting out lines for a negotiated settlement to the war. That means," Weed put it delicately, "pursuing the suggestions you made in your excellent annual message this month about gradual, compensated emancipation, rather than in the proclamation you have in mind for next week."

"We have some lines out that may be more useful than anything F'nandy Wood can come up with," said Seward abruptly. That was news to Weed, and grounds for hope. Perhaps Lincoln would return to reason, stop exaggerating the power of the radicals in the party, and start to settle the war without demanding the abject surrender of the South. "Tell us, Thurlow—what sort of governor will Seymour be?"

"He is an honorable man," Weed said after a moment's thought. "Seymour will support the war so long as its purpose is solely to maintain the Union, and so long as it's conducted within the limits of the Constitution. If it is not, he won't—simple as that. Frankly, I think that is being a good governor."

Weed thought he had surprised them with that candid, anti-abolitionist opinion, but was surprised himself by his partner's next question:

"What sort of President would he be?"

Weed wanted to be sure he was hearing correctly. "Did you ask what sort of President would Horatio Seymour be? Of the United States?"

"Yes, Thurlow, that's my question precisely."

"He'd be a Democratic President, and we're Republicans." Strange question. What was Seward, speaking for Lincoln, getting at? The President had obviously talked this over with Seward, and Weed knew how Seward's mind worked, but this line of questioning led into a dense forest. Weed knew Horatio Seymour to be the high-minded sort, burdened with principle, who could never be seduced into crossing over into the Republican ranks.

"Would he be inclined to preserve the Union," asked Lincoln, "and if so, would he be able to?"

Weed chewed that over in each of its parts. The President was evidently considering some far-reaching proposal, and Weed wanted to be sure to convey his best information. "The story that is making the rounds," he said at last, "is that the Peace Democrats in New York and the West would be willing to let the South secede. Then what's left of the Union would split up, with New York and the West joining the South in 'the old Union as it was,' and letting the abolitionists around Massachusetts have their own country."

"We've heard that story," said Seward. "Any truth in it?"

Weed shook his head. "Not as far as Seymour is concerned. I think he would resist that, and he's the one Democrat capable of resisting it successfully. He's pledged to hold the Union together, in all its sections, and I think he'd stick to that. Not with abolition, though."

Lincoln nodded agreement of that assessment. Seward seemed to wait for the President to say something and, when he did not, added a fact to what little Weed knew about secret communication between the opposing parties. "Our Democratic friend in New York, Barlow," said Seward, "sent a man in to see the President not long ago. We assume it was with Seymour's knowledge."

"Sam Barlow is a powerful Democrat." Weed did not add he was the man trying to persuade George McClellan to run for President on the Democratic ticket in 1864.

"He wanted the President to abate his emancipation policy, which Lincoln declined to do, but Barlow's man was told that military law might be made to relent if some national unity could be achieved." Weed knew instantly what Seward was getting at. Lincoln, with his own party split, wanted to blur the partisan lines between Democrats and Republicans.

"I said that issues are swept away so fast by overtopping events," Lincoln put in, "that no political party will have time to mature until after the war."

Having said that, Lincoln rose and went to the fireplace, poked the logs with a black fire iron until the flames shot up.

"Governor Seymour has greater power just now for good," said the President matter-of-factly, "than any other man in the country."

"More than you, Lincoln?" asked Seward, giving Weed the impression that the two of them had gone through this before.

"Yes. Governor Seymour can wheel the Democratic Party into line, and, because of that, he has the ability to put down the rebellion and preserve the government."

Long pause, deep sigh, and Lincoln took the plunge. "Weed, tell Seymour for me that if he will render this service to his country, I shall cheerfully make way for him as my successor."

Weed always thought that he himself had as good a poker face as any man, but that offer caused his jaw to drop. For someone already in the presidency to stand aside for another was the ultimate political sacrifice.

The Albany politician knew how Lincoln had longed to be the first President since Jackson to achieve reelection. And although the war news was dreadful and the party split, Lincoln had just demonstrated he was not the sort to fear Chase's bid for the Republican nomination in 1864. Nor was Lincoln the sort to worry about beating McClellan or whoever the Democrats put up against him in the next election. Weed assumed that Lincoln felt in his bones he could take on one after the other and win.

"However stunned my partner may look, Lincoln," Seward was saying, "the irony of the moment is not lost upon him. Only this summer a cabal in your Cabinet tried to seize power from you, an aborted undertaking that I am sure you knew about as well as I, and that was turned aside. A few months ago the military was on the verge of installing their beloved 'Young Napoleon' in your office, and somehow that never materialized. And only yesterday your party in the Senate gathered its forces in great array and assaulted your presidency, to no avail. If nothing else, you have proved you cannot be dislodged."

"And yet," Weed concluded, "having won all those battles over those who would replace you, you are now prepared to renounce your right to run for reelection."

"Beyond that," said Seward, delighting in the scheme's daring, "he is prepared to support the leader of the opposition party. That is something this republic has never seen. In effect, he is choosing his successor, because with Lincoln's support, the Democrat could not lose."

Instinctively Weed shied away. "I don't like it. It would say to the world that you cannot win the war without Seymour's help, and for that help you are willing to pay anything. Everything."

Lincoln nodded slowly. His offer had not been lightly made.

"Come now, Thurlow, it need not say anything of the sort," Seward cautioned. "The world need not know about it yet. The deal would be a gentlemen's agreement known but to the three of us, and to Seymour. Complete secrecy is essential."

"And if the proposition is declined?" Weed did not want to rush into such an unprecedented scheme. The Republican Party was only six years old and this would surely finish it.

"If Seymour declines," said Seward airily, "and I cannot imagine that any man in his right mind would decline, then we must be in a position to deny that the offer was ever made. That is why the President has chosen the most discreet political person in the nation for this assignment."

Weed remembered the day, thirty years before, when he rose to make his first speech in the New York State Assembly. He had found himself unable to talk—he was literally speechless—and in his humiliation and chagrin had vowed never to seek public office or make a public speech again for the rest of his life. He took that vow because he saw no other course open to him. But Lincoln, a most resilient political man who had rebounded from defeat to the House and defeat to the Senate, did not have to undertake an act of political self-immolation.

"There is another way," Weed said quickly. "Sweep Chase and Stanton and the other ultras out of your administration and rally the conservative Republicans. Bring back McClellan and dare Wade to impeach you. Give in to the Democrats on the arrests, and delay your emancipation edict until you can get a couple of Confederate states to adopt your December proposal—"

Lincoln shook his head. Weed looked to Seward, who could not possibly go along with this final crushing of any hopes left to him to be President one day. Seward said only, "It's a sacrifice. But it is Lincoln's considered judgment that only an alliance with Seymour and his peace movement will preserve the Union, and he is prepared to sacrifice anything for that."

"The conditions are substantially these," said Lincoln, getting specific about his offer and passing a quill and inkwell across the table to Weed to write them down. "Governor Seymour is to withdraw his opposition to the draft. Second, he is to use his authority and influence as governor in putting down any riots in New York against the war." He slowed down to let Weed's writing catch up. "Finally, the Governor of New York is to cooperate in all reasonable ways, including recruitment and financial assistance, with the Administration in the suppression of the Southern rebellion."

That, the Albany editor calculated, was asking a lot of Horatio Seymour. On the other hand, Lincoln was offering even more—nothing less than the presidency in 1864. The proposition boasted a symmetry of conflicting interests required for a sweeping political deal.

If Seymour went for it, the arrangement would certainly sustain a war of any length to maintain the Union. A reduction of partisanship in the North would surely discourage the leaders of the South, who were counting on rising internal bickering in the North to lead to war weariness and pressure to let the "wayward sisters" depart. No chance of that if Lincoln and Seymour came to an understanding about resolute prosecution of the war through this presidential term and the next as well.

"Seymour will accept, won't he?" Seward was trying to sound certain.

Weed put himself in Seymour's shoes, anticipating the governor-elect's questions when the proposition was put to him. "Does this mean he would have to go along with your suspension of habeas corpus in New York?"

Seward nodded. "As the President said, he would be committed to cooperate in all reasonable ways with the Administration's suppression of the rebellion."

That meant yes. The only leeway Weed was being given in the negotiation was in that hint sent to Barlow that, by degrees, the military edict of emancipation might be made into the gradual, compensated sort that Lincoln had long espoused. His instructions were clear enough, but Weed wanted to be absolutely sure before undertaking such a far-reaching political mission that Lincoln was not acting as a result of depression or miscalculation.

"Perhaps you are unduly shocked by the catastrophe at Fredericksburg," he wondered aloud. "It is true that we lost half again as many men as the enemy, and such bloodshed is being laid directly at your door. Still, there have been bloody battles before—"

Lincoln shook his head; that was not the problem. "If the same battle were to be fought over again, every day, through a week of days," the President said dispassionately, "the army under Lee would be wiped out to its last man, the Army of the Potomac would still be a mighty host, the war would be over, the Confederacy gone."

Seward uncrossed his legs uncomfortably and crossed them again at such a cold-blooded assessment of the carnage, but Lincoln went on: "No general yet found can face the arithmetic, but the end of the war will be at hand when he shall be discovered."

Weed had his answer. Lincoln was making this political decision clearheadedly, and was not panicked at the news of staggering military losses. He was prepared to accept the sacrifice of tens of thousands of men to foil secession; it should not be surprising that he was prepared to make a personal political sacrifice for the same end.

"I will put the proposition to him," said Weed finally.

"See if you can get Seymour to come down here," said Seward, "this week, right after Christmas, well before his inauguration." And before any proclamation on New Year's Day, Weed understood. "Put it to him at one of your breakfasts at Willard's, and then if he shows interest, bring him to the Mansion."

Lincoln directed Lamon to take Weed to the telegraph office across the street, to see that his message of urgent summons was sent immediately to Seymour, and to await a reply.

Weed followed the burly marshal to the War Department. He composed a telegraph message to Seymour at his temporary office in Albany, where the Governor-elect was preparing his inaugural address and choosing a Cabinet. The telegraph operator, a young fellow who, Lamon attested, was entirely discreet—which meant he would not show the message to Stanton—put the message through without delay. It called on Seymour to come to consult with Weed in Washington on a matter of the utmost urgency. Seymour would know that meant the President wanted him to know something that could not be sent in writing. Weed added that he awaited a reply at the telegraph office in the War Department.

A half hour later, the return message came through. Bates handed it to him. Weed read it and frowned. "Seymour says the distance from Albany to Washington is the same as from Washington to Albany," he muttered to Lamon. "I'll have to go see him there." He consulted the watch in his pocket. "We can catch the noon train to New York."

"The noon train will leave for New York as soon as we get to the station," said Lamon. Weed grunted his assent; that was presidential service.

THE PREACHER BRECKINRIDGE

Anna Carroll, on the river steamer *Charlie Bowens* from Memphis up to Louisville, consulted her list of things to do.

Get paid for her three pamphlets. That was always at the top of the list and was never crossed off. It amounted to $6,250 and Stanton's man at the War Department had told her the most they could pay without a warrant from Congress was $750. Could she take that without giving up her claim to the rest? She did not want to think about that now.

Memorial about Vicksburg. She was certain that the Confederate fort maintaining control of the Lower Mississippi was the single most important military objective of the war. She would write Lincoln about ignoring the river fortifications, abandoning all the costly and impractical plans for a waterside assault on the fort overlooking the river, and taking Vicksburg by land from the rear.

The third item was colonization. That project, duly authorized and contracted for, was the excuse for her current travels. With emancipation looming, the President wanted a report extolling the prospects for negroes in Panama. Some felt Lincoln was insincere about this, and Seward certainly had not helped matters with his abject acquiescence to the protests of Nicaragua, Honduras, and New Granada, who did not want an exodus of blacks in their direction. But to her mind, and to Lincoln's, there remained the clear need for evidence of serious activity to ship the future freedmen to more congenial climes. She liked that phrase, "congenial climes"; it implied that the temperate zone of North America was uncongenial to blacks. In furtherance of that, she was soon to see the Reverend Robert J. Breckinridge, the senior agent of the American Colonization Society, a voluntary organization that had been doing successfully in Liberia what Lincoln hoped could be done in Central America.

The next item, listed as "boy alive?" was one she could also discuss with the Breckinridge who was a Presbyterian minister. She had known him as Reverend Bob all her life. Twenty years ago, when he was preaching in Maryland, Anna had taken to him all her adolescent fears. Through her formative years, before his return to his native Kentucky, he had been her spiritual adviser. Nobody, not even her governor-father, had been closer to her or more of an inspiration. Robert Breckinridge had been the first of a line of much older men who had profoundly attracted her, and while there had been no romance between the preacher and the girl just beginning to stand in her own shoes, she had daydreamed about him as husband or lover. Years later, when his tall nephew John was elected to Congress, the Reverend Bob had commended the young politician to her; then the impossible daydreams of her youth had been redeemed in another Breckinridge.

The Reverend Bob met her at the landing in Cairo, Illinois, at the junction of the Ohio and Mississippi rivers, to drive her in his carriage to his house in nearby Paducah, Kentucky. At dockside were nearly five hundred "contrabands." The word had been coined by Ben Butler to make legitimate the freeing of runaway slaves and was now used in sarcasm to describe all newly free blacks. They sat in the rain, in four rows, wearing leg-irons but otherwise unchained, awaiting official permission to enter. They were ragged, silent, soaked, and shaking in the cold; many seemed ill. Anna knew that a month before, Illinois voters, fearful of losing their jobs to workers who would take any wage an employer offered, had passed a law to prevent the admission of more free negroes into the state. When the Federal military authorities ignored the state law, forcing Illinoisans to accept what many feared would be a wave of black migration, Lincoln's popularity had plummeted in his home state. Not even a man known to be one of his closest friends could carry Lincoln's old congressional district.

She had not expected the radical change in Robert Breckinridge's appearance; the twenty years had whitened his hair and wizened his face. They rode through the freezing rain almost as strangers. In bringing each other up to date on mutual friends, some long dead, he alluded to the special pain being felt in the Breckinridge family, split like their state into rebels and loyalists. He did not mention his nephew John, and she, though hungry for news about the man who so moved and infuriated her, felt it wiser not to ask.

At home, at a table in front of the great iron stove throwing off heat in the kitchen of the well-to-do preacher, the aging Breckinridge went to the heart of her ostensible reason for visiting him: "Colonization won't work."

"I just cannot understand that, coming from you," she said. "Your society started work colonizing Liberia forty years ago. You raised the money to buy slaves, set them free, and gave them a new life in Africa." When he shook his head, no, she pressed: "In his annual message a few weeks ago, the President praised the achievements of the Liberians, and only last week, he signed the treaty recognizing Liberia as an independent nation. You have every reason, especially now, to be proud of your life's work."

"Did you manumit your own slaves, Anna?"

"I did, and raised the money to buy the freedom of those who were mortgaged. You were the one who inspired me to do that, by the example you set." And I'm still trying to pay those debts, she added to herself.

"Did the slaves you freed want to go to Liberia, or Chiriquí, or Hayti?"

"Well, no, they had family in Maryland, and—"

"Forty years the Society has been colonizing Liberia, and do you know what we have to show for it? Maybe three thousand colonists, total."

"That's a beginning."

"That's the end. Those were people who were often savagely mistreated here, who had reason to hate their lives in America. They took colonization as the only hope of escape from unspeakable cruelty. But the slaves being emancipated now will be free here in America. What reasons do they have to rip up their roots and go across an ocean to find heaven knows what?"

She would not crumble in the face of that experience. Colonization had to be made to work. "The reasons would be to find work and to have a land of their own."

"White men's promises. Anna, I've seen what it is like, over a lifetime, to move a mere three thousand people from slavery here to freedom there." He leaned forward and held up three fingers. "You're talking about moving three or four million or more—a thousand times as many—from freedom here to possible starvation overseas. It is impossible. And once you understand that, as the President must, then to raise the hopes of frightened whites that the objects of their fear are going to vanish overnight—that is hypocritical."

"And if a little hypocrisy makes it easier to end a great crime and cruelty, is that hypocrisy such a great sin?"

Anna surprised herself with that retort; as a girl, she had taken instruction from him with absolute faith. Their relationship had changed, his unquestioned authority was gone; she felt no guilt for anything she was doing, from justifying the extension of the President's war powers to persuading conservatives that colonization was a solution. She knew what side she was on.

"The means, Anna, have a way of becoming the ends."

"Now you sound like your nephew." That was cruel, and she wished she could recall the words when she saw the pain in the eyes of her old mentor.

"My nephew is a traitor to his country," he said finally, "and I am not."

She hastened to assure him that many in Washington knew of Robert Breckinridge's staunch loyalty to the Union, and of the way he led his branch of the family to outspoken support of Lincoln in a state inclined toward the Peace Democrats. "And even though my pamphlet *A Reply to Breckinridge* reduced the position of your nephew to dust and ashes, I made it clear to everyone that many members of the Breckinridge clan were patriots." That was true; she hoped he would believe it. Nor, for that matter, had she dreamed that her widely read paper would contribute to the Senate passion that resulted in the expulsion of John Breckinridge from that body, branding him a traitor who would deserve a death sentence.

"Compose your soul, my dear girl. I know how fiercely you oppose my nephew's views, as I do." He adjusted his spectacles and looked directly at her. "But I also know how you feel about John himself."

That made her wonder if Breck had said anything to his uncle about the depth of their friendship. Not likely. The nephew knew that Robert Breckinridge was a stern moralist who would be angered by any relationship between a married man and an unmarried woman, especially if they were his favorite nephew and his spiritual ward. Anna was certain that nobody suspected any attachment of any kind—especially after her attack on him in print—yet the old man seemed serenely confident that she shared his closeness to, and fondness for, Breckinridge the traitor.

"I have been in touch with my young niece, Margaret," he explained. "She told me of your mutual quest."

That was it; Anna's concern subsided. If Breck's missing son had not been killed, there was a chance that he would have assumed another name in the Union prison camps. At the War Department, Anna had scoured the lists for the name Cabell, which she judged would be the most likely last name taken by General Breckinridge's son. She had found a prisoner named Cabell listed as being held at the Johnson's Island prison in Lake Erie.

"I needed the help of someone who would recognize the boy," she explained, "and someone who could move through the horror of those prison camps without fainting."

Margaret Breckinridge, in her early twenties now, had always been a gentle, frail young woman, but unlike any in her Kentucky family, she was a burning abolitionist. Her anger at slavery drove her to do as a field nurse what most women found too nauseating, and Anna admired that. "My old friend John Dix has been most helpful, as has Mary Livermore." Anna had fallen into the habit of mentioning the names of important people who would do favors for her. She knew it was a bad habit, but she did not have so many, and this one gave her pleasure. She hoped he knew that General Dix was in charge of prisoner exchange, and that Mary Livermore headed the army nurses in the Sanitary Commission. "Have you heard from Margaret?"

"Not for weeks. But you've given us hope," he added, "and perhaps the family grapevine has passed that hope along to John and his wife, who must be suffering."

"What news of your nephew?" She tried to make the question sound casual, not only to conceal the depth of her own interest, but also because she was aware that a family's communication with traitorous members often led to charges of treason. Mary Lincoln had not been able to mourn a nephew's death.

Reverend Bob reached over to the sink, pulled a couple of newspapers off the counter and pushed them across the table. *"Louisville Journal* says he was in Murfreesboro, with Jeff Davis, not long ago, celebrating Colonel Morgan's wedding. Now Morgan and his raiders are doing their own celebrating, driving up this way burning and looting, and making Grant look helpless."

Anna felt a sense of dread. At the War Department, she had heard Halleck and Stanton talking about an attack by Rosecrans in Tennessee. That would be against Bragg and Breckinridge, now devoid of eyes and ears as their cavalry went off marauding, delighting the hearts of copperheads. If Breck went into battle believing his cause was lost and his son was dead, he might well ride at the head of some suicidal charge and throw his life away. She read the newspaper article to the end. "What a waste," she sighed. "John Breckinridge could have been President one day."

"If the South wins," said his uncle bitterly, "he may yet be. But not of the United States."

"Why did he go wrong? Breck always said he stood firm for the Union, and I believed him."

"He was against disunion, Anna. Probably still is."

She shook her head, uncomprehending. "Then is he weak, or stupid? He's not fighting for slavery, he told me as much. And he's not fighting for independence, because he believes in one nation. What is he fighting for? Kentucky? Kentucky stayed in the Union. He seems to be fighting for the sake of fighting, just because his friends are fighting, but he's a man who hates to fight. Can you figure it out?"

"Did he tell you about his arguments with Lincoln, at the tea table, last year in the White House?"

She nodded wearily. "Yes. After every one, he recited the entire debate, both sides. And the more Breck described them, the more I agreed with Lincoln."

"Why? What persuaded you?"

"Lincoln had one single, great, overriding purpose: to prevent disunion. He was and is absolutely clear about that. Remember when Lincoln wrote the letter to Greeley? He wrote that if he could save the Union by not freeing a single slave, he would do it, and if he could save the Union by freeing all the slaves, he would do it. Well, the abolitionists pretend now that he didn't really mean that, he was only teasing Greeley, that he's really been for emancipation from the start. But the fact is—Lincoln was telling the truth. That's the way he thinks."

"I'm told he favors black freedom."

She waved that aside. "That's not the point. He'll stretch the Constitution, he'll usurp the power of Congress and the courts, he'll change the system from a collection of states to a national power, he will free or not free the slaves, he'll grab at every idea I can make up to justify greater war powers, all to one purpose: to block forever the ability of a minority to break up the Union."

"You make it seem his obsession, Anna."

She bobbed her head up and down; Lincoln was surely a man possessed by a single idea. "What else is democracy but majority rule? If secession succeeds, the majority does not rule. If democracy fails here, it will fail everywhere. Lincoln sees that, and he is willing to do anything to defend it."

"Any means."

"Yes, any means, including getting us all killed. Emancipation is a means, a military means, to save the Union. He makes no bones about that. He may be wrong, of course—Thurlow Weed and the Blairs think emancipation is a means to losing the war—but his purpose is pure, clear, unwavering. That's why I am with him." The logical extension of that occurred to her, and she spoke it aloud: "John Breckinridge was never able to say what his purpose was, except to complain about the way Lincoln was doing what he was sworn to do."

She tried to remember Breck's central theme, and could not; the Kentuckian was complex, tortured, halting, uncertain, a Hamlet who could never be king. Yet John Breckinridge was no Fillmore, certainly no Buchanan; he inspired others with confidence in his judgment; he held his own with the best in debate. It stung her to be so drawn to a man who could not clearly identify his cause, as Lincoln did, even when Lincoln had to cloak the cause of union in the garment of emancipation.

"Let me explain something about the family," said the preacher. "Do you remember my middle name?"

The Reverend Robert J. Breckinridge. "Jefferson," she remembered.

"My father—John's grandfather and namesake—was allied with Jefferson against John Adams and the Federalists. Jefferson and Breckinridge despised the notion of a powerful central government, believing it would subvert the people's freedom."

She shook her head. "A strong executive need not endanger any freedom."

"But in their lifetime, Anna, it did. In a time of great anger and loud dissent, President Adams proposed and the Congress passed the Alien and Sedition acts. A citizen could not criticize the government. In the name of preserving the public order, tyranny took root. At that moment, the first John Breckinridge put forward the Kentucky Resolutions, challenging and in effect nullifying the national government's odious attack on the Bill of Rights. He got away with it. And ultimately the Alien and Sedition acts withered and died."

He walked to the corner of the kitchen, drew out a ladleful of water, put it in a pan with ground coffee beans, and set it on the stove. "That was our proudest moment, but let me tell you a family secret, something my nephew John doesn't know. His grandfather never wrote those resolutions; he couldn't write that eloquently."

"Jefferson wrote them?"

"Exactly. And later, when Jefferson became President, he made the so-called author of those Kentucky Resolutions his Attorney General. So this Breckinridge family is bred to the bone in the tradition of Jefferson's democracy, in the revulsion toward what you call a 'strong executive' and what we call a tyrant."

With an effort of will, she did not respond; it was more important, this time at least, to understand than to refute.

"To young John, the way that a government governs, especially in an emergency, determines the kind of government it will always be. The procedure is sacred, the Constitution is a covenant. When anybody abuses that covenant, for whatever end—even when it seems to be for the noble end of saving the nation's life itself—then the government has broken faith with the people."

That was enough; that was sophistry. "There is a commandment that goes, 'Thou shalt not kill,' but murder is permissible before God in self-defense," she responded. "That is what secession is—the murder of a nation—and Lincoln's war is self-defense."

"Of course, you're right, my dear Anna," Robert Breckinridge assured her. He was, after all, a loyal Union man. "But I thought you wanted to know why John, who has never drawn a traitorous breath in his life, took the path that we all know to be treason."

She nodded. She was thinking less of the argument than of his evocation of the family lines. The Carrolls of Maryland included John Carroll, first bishop and archbishop of the Roman Catholic Church in the United States; his cousin was said to be the richest man in America, the only man to put his address next to his signature on the Declaration of Independence—"Charles Carroll of Carrollton"—so the king would know where to get him if the revolution failed. Charles Carroll served in the first Federal Congress as Maryland's senator and later became a sponsor of Henry Clay; her father became, as if by right, governor of the state. She knew that the Breckinridges could claim nearly as proud a heritage in the formation of the country. What a lost opportunity that two such clans could never be joined. She amended that thought quickly; in a way, they were joined, in a bond that she would not allow to weaken between her and both the loyal and disloyal Breckinridges.

Reverend Bob did not relent. "John saw the arrest of the Maryland legislators, the closing of the Kentucky newspapers, the presidential suspension of habeas corpus, the jailing of protesters, and he judged that the Union was being saved at the expense of the people's liberty. He thought that was too great a price to pay, and he refused. Others in the South and in the border states refused for ignoble reasons—for slavery, for separation, for spite, for the foolish glory of battle—and they tarnished his cause. I cannot forgive my nephew for becoming a traitor, but I can understand why he did it. I fight him, and I suffer with him, and I grieve for him."

"I love that man," Anna heard herself say. She added, ". . . as I love you and as I love Ben Wade. But I will not suffer for him. Wrong is wrong, and he chose the wrong side." That said, she continued, "And if you should see him again, or be in touch with him in some lawful way, tell him I said that. All of it, the loving him too. The truth is, I miss him, and you."

The preacher nodded and began to make the sounds of ministerial comfort, but Anna's attention turned to the newspapers on the table. Rosecrans was advancing on Bragg and Breckinridge south of Nashville; they could be sucking Rosecrans into a trap, and if the Union army in Tennessee suffered the same kind of defeat inflicted on Burnside in Virginia, Lincoln would have to either settle the war or agree to the appointment of a dictator. Her eyes fixed on a headline in the newspaper about Israelites. She asked, "What's this about Jews here in Paducah?"

"It's a terrible thing Grant is doing," said the Presbyterian minister. "Throwing them out of here, where families have been for generations— Cincinnati, Louisville, all the way downriver from Cairo to Memphis."

"What's the reason?" She knew Stanton's War Department, and suspected the reason.

"The predations of the few, taken out on the many," said the Reverend Breckinridge. "The classic scapegoat people. A friend of mine, an Israelite, asked for a day's time to sell his belongings, but Grant's headquarters said no. They confiscated his things and put him and his family on a wagon out of town. The only Jews left in Paducah are in the hospitals, because they cannot easily be moved, but I wouldn't give much for their chances of staying long either. I hope you won't think me disloyal, Anna, but it's a disgrace."

Anna looked at the newspaper masthead: the *Louisville Democrat,* the paper that took over the presses when the *Courier* was closed down for being pro-secesh. She read aloud: "It says 'the Order is certainly the most extraordinary, unwarrantable order we have ever heard of'—that is a Peace Democrat paper, isn't it?"

"Yes, but look at the *Journal.* It's Republican." He pushed the paper across the table to her. "Look: 'How many thousand patriotic soldiers of Jewish descent have laid down their lives upon the altar of this country? And is this miserable, ungrateful order to be the price of their blood?' That's from a pro-Union, pro-Lincoln editor."

"You can imagine what Seymour and the copperheads will do with something like this," she observed. She did not say what she knew: that Grant and Sherman were not alone in this sweeping decision, but that Halleck and perhaps Stanton had been encouraging them to go ahead with the policy. It would surely be taken by them as more evidence that the Constitution was being flouted by the Administration, that the war was corrupting the Union, and all the old Breckinridge arguments. Anna was sure that this had been slipped past Lincoln, much as some military orders on emancipation were put forward by generals in the field stimulated by mischievous politicians.

"What was the price of cotton," she asked, "when Grant's order went into effect?"

"Forty cents a pound. I wouldn't ordinarily know that, Anna, but it was widely remarked that the next day the Army lowered the price to twenty-five cents a pound."

"Meaning the Jewish cotton traders had to dump their supplies immediately, at a ruinous loss. Somebody must have made a lot of money on this."

"I hadn't thought of that. I was more concerned with the moral corruption of stigmatizing all the practitioners of one religion. It's not right. These people are Kentuckians."

"What are they doing about it?"

"I hear the Kaskel brothers, the merchants in Paducah and Cincinnati, have set out to see Congressman Gurley in Washington. I don't think they have much hope for changing the policy. Lincoln would not want to countermand an order of Grant's, would he? Grant is the only Union general who seems to win. If Lincoln can put up with his carousing, he can put up with this."

Grant's Jew Order would have repercussions in New York, she thought; the newly elected governor, a Peace Democrat, would seize on the issue. Unless the President reversed this policy quickly, real damage could be done by all those who delighted in calling him a dictator for the arrests and his seizure of property with the emancipation edict. But wouldn't Stanton and Halleck at the War Department resist the embarrassment of a commander in the field? The last time Lincoln forced a general to rescind an order, it had led to the Frémont uproar.

"Your friends the Kaskels should go directly to Lincoln," she advised. "This is surely a surprise to him. He won't put up with it."

He fidgeted in his chair, the way he had when she was a girl and he was trying to think of a way to come to a sensitive personal subject.

She knew what he wanted to know. "And what of you, my dear," she said in a mock-deep preacher's voice, "why is it that you never married?"

He stopped squirming and beamed. "I would never have asked that. But now that you brought it up, are you happy, Anna? Are you the woman you wanted to be when we used to talk at Kingston Hall?"

"What you want to know," she answered crisply but not unkindly, "is: Can a woman be happy and fulfilled without a husband, without children, without a real home and roots? Is it enough to be successful and respected, and listened to on important matters by important men, and financially independent?" She threw that last item in, not because it was true, but to round out the question.

The preacher smiled. "What I sought to know was only what I asked, but I am also interested in the answer you want to give to the question you have often asked yourself."

"Life is incomplete without a partner, no denying that, for a woman even more than a man." Having granted that, at this point in her prepared answer, she was to have made a strong case for standing in your own shoes, but she found herself going on into what she had never let herself think aloud.

"I get lonely. And most of the time I wish there was somebody to stand up for me—not part-time like Ben Wade, but all the time. And I know this sounds silly, but I'm little. I'm a small person, I get jostled in crowds, and I am frightened on the streets at night, so being alone is a real problem, a physical problem."

She told herself to stop before she mentioned other physical problems. Reverend Bob helped with a question that directed her to specifics. "But you've known some men well, I'm sure. A woman of your attraction cannot have been alone always. The choice of singleness was yours, was it not?"

"I am my father's daughter," she asserted, "and there are not many men like Governor Carroll. The kind of men who interested me, who still do, are engaged in great enterprises."

"Important men."

"Men in important jobs, I've found, are not always important men." She thought of presidents Fillmore and Buchanan. "Nor are they prepared to share the important part of their lives with their wives."

She thought of Lincoln, the only one of the three presidents she knew with whom she had no personal relationship, but who treated her with a mixture of condescension and affection. Then the tall figure of Chase loomed in her mind. "Recently I thought there was one man who needed me for what only I have to offer: political sagacity, powerful contacts, and a zest for accomplishment."

"As well as an upright moral character."

"Yes," she nodded, breathing deep, "and a good figger, too."

"And what happened to him?"

She groped for a way to put it. "He married for money." She laughed at that. "Look, Reverend Bob, you know me, I'm still the same free-minded woman you saw when I was such a trial to the family. I'm a lot happier living the independent life, standing in my own two shoes, doing man's work in a man's world, than if I had to be the sweet Maryland belle in the house of a domineering man."

"Pity it has to be that choice," he said, and put his finger on the problem: "The time is out of joint, as Hamlet said."

"There may come a time for an upstart, disrespectful, pushing, smart woman next to a great man," she said.

"You're not that way, Anna."

"And now," she said with a sudden rush of savage honesty, "you want to know if your nephew and I have ever been in love, and if I had illicit relations with a happily married man younger than myself, and if we ever think of each other as anything but loyalist and traitor—"

He put up his hands in horror. "Sometimes you *are* that way, Anna!"

CHAPTER 40

JOHN HAY'S DIARY
DECEMBER 28, 1862

Talk about tempests in teapots. You might think, with a battle we cannot afford to lose shaping up in Tennessee, and with Senators Sumner and Browning in and out of here every day telling the Tycoon to sign or not to sign the final emancipation edict, that trivialities would be brushed aside. But the whole of this dark and bitterly cold morning was spent pouring soothing syrup over the sensibilities of people in a snit about offenses committed by our generals in the field—officers who are, after all, trying to protect their backs as they face the enemy.

Our esteemed Attorney General, Mr. Bates, brought in a Missouri constituent, the irate pastor of a Presbyterian church in St. Louis, who had been kicked out of the state by the occupying military for his sympathy with the rebellion.

"Here is a military order from General Curtis," said Bates, because his friend the Reverend McPheters was too sputteringly outraged to know where to begin, "exiling this clergyman to the South because he is a Southern sympathizer."

"True?" Lincoln, reading the order, asked the man, who was purpling before our eyes.

"I have signed the Union loyalty oath, as required. I have constantly prayed in church for the President and the government, just as I did before the war. It is my position that my personal sympathies are none of the government's business."

The Tycoon did not dispute that. "I don't see that anything specific is alleged against you. The charges here are all general—that you have a rebel wife and rebel relations, that you sympathize with rebels, that you exercise rebel influence, whatever that means."

"Some Lincoln men in my parish demanded that General Curtis do something about a churchman who dared to express his yearnings for peace," McPheters charged.

"Frankly, I believe this fellow does sympathize with the rebels," the Prsdt said to Bates, "but the question remains whether such a man, who cannot be charged with violating his oath, can be exiled upon the suspicion of his secret sympathies."

"My opinion is that he cannot, on those grounds," said the Attorney General.

Lincoln agreed, and said he would write to General Curtis suspending the order. He did not go so far as to revoke the military order, but the general would catch the President's drift. "The U.S. Government must not undertake to run the churches," Lincoln said. "Let the churches take care of themselves."

Our Presbyterian friend left satisfied. Bates remained behind a moment to submit his written opinion on a proposal, pushed through the Congress by the Jacobins, to split off the northwestern part of Virginia—which we now occupy—and admit it to the Union as a separate state. At the instigation of Bates, Lincoln had asked each member of the Cabinet to submit written recommendations on this thumb in the eye to General Lee and his ilk. The Prsdt is especially anxious this week to impress the Senate with how thoroughly he consults the Cabinet. I imagine Chase and Stanton will be asked for more paperwork than they bargained for, and they might not like going on the record with every opinion.

"I advise a veto of the bill," said Bates. "I understand that Blair and Welles agree."

True, the three conservatives in the Cabinet stand as one in not infuriating the South with this punishment of Virginia. But I have the written opinions in hand of Chase and Stanton, who most vociferously urge the signing of the legislation setting up a new state of West Virginia. Seward, who knows he is hanging on to his job by a thread and cannot further offend the radicals, will side with Chase and Stanton. And Caleb Smith, stumbling out of the Cabinet to a judgeship next week, has no opinion. That leaves the vote in the Cabinet three to three, which shows how it would be to run the Executive branch by committee.

Lincoln will sign the bill if he decides to go ahead with the Proclamation. That's because the bill admitting West Virginia has in it a requirement that the state gradually emancipate all slaves within its new borders; no steady abolition, no statehood. This week, the trick is to ameliorate the abolitionists, who were rebuffed in their grab for power last week, while not riling up the Peace Democrats, who fear the Edict of Freedom will prolong the war. The business of soothing has become the be-all and end-all of government. He must calm public sentiment at both extremes to keep the rocking ship of state from capsizing.

"Public opinion is never spontaneous with the people," Bates retorted, "it is always a manufactured article." When Lincoln looked interested at that observation, one of the few original thoughts to come through that scraggly beard for some time, Bates continued, "I would hope you not be overly influenced by what some people—who claim to represent public opinion—might say if you vetoed West Virginia, or modified your Proclamation next week."

"If I refused to issue that Proclamation," the Prsdt said, "there would be a rebellion in the North, and a dictator placed over my head in a week." (The latest radical candidates for dictator, I am told by a gossipy but ravishing young woman who consoles me for my loss of Jephtha's daughter, are "Beast" Butler and "Fighting Joe" Hooker; while the conservatives and Democrats still like McNapoleon.)

"But these two blows at the South, taken together, will make negotiations impossible," warned Bates. He was aware of a letter sent to Lincoln that week from General McClernand in Illinois, reporting that a messenger from high officers in the rebel army had approached him seeking the restoration of peace. It's a good thing the Fernando Wood crowd in New York were not in touch with the McClernand people in the West to compare peace feelers, or that both did not know of the probing that the Prsdt has permitted General

Banks in New Orleans. Such a comparison of notes would make it appear that serious negotiation was in prospect, and that Seymour's honey would attract more Southern flies than Lincoln's vinegar.

Ah, but now was the time for the hint in the other, more accommodating direction. "Let the people of the South adopt systems of apprenticeship for the colored people," the Prsdt said, tossing in that familiar half promise to delay abolition, "conforming substantially to the most approved plans of gradual emancipation. Then, with the aid they can have from the general government, they may be nearly as well off, in respect to this, as if the present trouble had not occurred."

An awe-inspiring straddle. To those anti-abolition Peace Democrats rocking the boat because they want peace negotiations now, he offers subtle assurances that emancipation means merely a nominal "freeing" of slaves in rebel states who would then remain indentured apprentices until the end of the century, with money paid to every slaveholder by the federal government for property seized. Gentle evolution.

To those at the other extreme, the vindictive Jacobins who want to subjugate the damned secesh, he offers freedom for the slaves by virtue of military necessity and a lopping-off of a huge chunk of disloyal Virginia. Radical revolution.

And he is doing this balancing act at the moment of his greatest military and political weakness. Something for everyone; nobody happy, but nobody so unhappy as to bring about what the Tycoon likes to call the general smashup. (Good name for a general.)

"I hope to stand firm enough not to go backward," he told Bates, "and yet not go forward fast enough to wreck the country's cause." Bates left half-satisfied, which is the most we can do for anybody.

However, the soothing of the Presbyterian minister with treason in his heart, but only in his heart, was as nothing compared to the soothing needed to calm the storm that was raised by the next delegation waiting in my anteroom. General Grant, it seems, has the Hebrews upset. The Israelites, offended by his policy of excluding them from his area of military operations, have gone to the press and the Congress to complain.

"The *New York Times* calls this 'one of the deepest sensations of the war,' " I told the President as I passed him the paper. Whatever has possessed such a true-blue loyalist as Henry Raymond to run such stuff? His *New York Times* has supported us staunchly even when Greeley wavered. But this editorial borders on hysteria, perhaps reflecting the population of Israelites in that city, which, I am told, numbers over ten thousand. "It is a humiliating reflection that after the progress of liberal ideas even in the most despotic countries has restored the Jews to civil and social rights, as members of a common humanity, it remained for the freest government on earth to witness a momentary revival of the spirit of the medieval ages . . ."

A Rabbi Wise of Cincinnati had stirred up Ohio congressmen, and a House resolution was introduced by Congressmen Gurley and Vallandigham to censure Grant. Grant's sponsor, Washburne of Illinois, prevailed on Tad Stevens to stop it on a close vote, 56 to 53. In the Senate, Powell of Kentucky was angry at what had happened to his constituents in Paducah, and moved the same resolution, which Sumner was able to table. The voting pulled over

congressmen who ordinarily did not rise to the usual Seymour-Vallandigham
bait about arbitrary arrests. It gave the Peace Democrats a new weapon to
bludgeon us with—religious persecution.

I detect a delicious irony in all this, evidence of my advancing maturity.
There go Seymour and Vallandigham, who don't give a damn for the freedom
of blacks, taking up the cudgels for the rights of Jews. And there go Tad
Stevens and Charles Sumner, who want to abolish slavery and punish the
slaveholders, defending a general who treats Jews as having as few rights as
slaves. Says something about moralists.

Fortunately, the Prsdt was not on record as approving the Grant policy
banning Jews. We knew about it, of course, and turned a blind eye because the
cotton speculation was of real concern to Grant. When Stanton sent Charles
Dana down to Memphis, that roving Grant-watcher reported the corruption
of the army quartermaster corps was something fierce. I have his report here:
"Every colonel, captain, or quartermaster is in secret partnership with some
operator in cotton; every soldier dreams of adding a bale of cotton to his
monthly pay." Dana blamed Jews and Yankees for corrupting the military;
Grant has nothing against Yankees.

When Lincoln sent Zacharie, the foot doctor, down to New Orleans, he
referred to the "general prohibition" he knew to exist. Banks has the original,
and Zacharie has a copy of that letter, but they are good eggs and should
cause no trouble. It should not be hard to deny knowledge of the policy.
Certainly we did not know Grant was going to make a great public show out
of it. The only part of the policy that the Prsdt even tacitly approved had to
do with prohibition against entry of Hebrews, not expulsion of those Israelites
already in the area.

So here we are, with Congressman Gurley in the anteroom with Cesar
Kaskel, a merchant from Paducah. The Tycoon went out the door, greeted
them heartily with "I'm always glad to see my friends," and brought them in.

Kaskel is a tall fellow, not more than thirty, mustache and no beard, deep
voice, dignified, carries himself like a successful man. (Why isn't he in uniform? Why aren't I in uniform?) Quite a different sort from Zacharie, the
only other Hebrew I have ever met. The foot doctor is mercurial, filled with
visions and the excitement of being a presidential agent, eager to please. The
merchant is more distant, very serious, respectful but not obsequious.

"We sent you a telegraph message," Kaskel said after thanking the Presi-
dent for receiving him on short notice. "When we received no answer in
Paducah, my friends delegated me to come to the congressman here, and Mr.
Gurley brought me to you."

Lincoln looked at me; I had received no telegraph message. Could it be that
it was not forwarded by the War Department? That outfit was not at all
happy with the reaction to Grant's order, especially since it had been issued
with the knowledge of some people here. Probably Halleck, maybe Stanton.
That's irritating; it is not for Stanton to decide which telegraph messages
addressed to the President to deliver. Censorship is supposed to go the other
way.

Kaskel laid on Lincoln's table documents from leading Kentucky citizens,
including the Reverend Robert J. Breckinridge (the loyal Breckinridge, who,
Anna Carroll thinks, should be the next senator from Kentucky), from Re-

publican leaders and military authorities, attesting to the patriotism and war efforts of the Jews in Paducah.

As the President perused them, Kaskel read from the message that had not been delivered: "General Orders No. 11 expels all Jews without distinction. We feel greatly insulted and outraged by this inhuman order, the carrying out of which would be the grossest violation of the Constitution." He cleared his throat and went on. "The order places Jewish families as outlaws before the world. We are loyal, respectable citizens, and pray for your effectual and immediate interposition."

The Prsdt smiled. "And so the children of Israel were driven from the happy land of Canaan?"

"Yes," said Kaskel, nicely picking up the biblical tone, "and that is why we have come unto Father Abraham's bosom, asking protection."

"And this protection they shall have at once." Lincoln wasted no time writing a short note to Halleck, directing him to telegraph instructions to Grant to cancel the infamous General Orders No. 11. "I don't like to see a class or nationality condemned on account of a few sinners," he added to Kaskel, and told me to take Kaskel to General-in-Chief Halleck directly.

The Prsdt did not disclaim knowledge of Grant's policy, but he left the impression that it all had been news to him, and added specifically that he felt no prejudice against Israelites. The alacrity with which he acted to countermand the order showed his understanding of the need to defuse this issue before Seymour in New York or the Peace Democrats in Congress could turn it into more of a cause célèbre.

I took Kaskel and Gurley down to Old Itchy Elbows, who pretended to disbelieve that the order had ever been issued. Halleck looked at the paper from Grant's headquarters as if it were a forgery, and wrote to Grant the most begrudging recision imaginable. "A paper purporting to be General Orders No. 11, issued by you December 17, has been presented here. By its terms, it expels all Jews from your department. If such an order has been issued, it will be immediately revoked."

I gave a copy to Kaskel so he wouldn't be arrested on the way home. Later, Halleck sent another message to Grant in apology, which he had to show us since he laid the responsibility on Lincoln: "The President has no objection to your expelling traitors and Jew peddlers, which, I suppose, was the object of your order; but as it in terms proscribed an entire religious class, some of whom are fighting in our ranks, the President deemed it necessary to revoke it."

That Jew Order was impolitic of Grant, though I suppose he could be excused for going ahead with the expulsion after nobody complained about his general prohibition. They are a touchy bunch, the Israelites, and it seems they have influence in the press and in the legislature beyond what might be expected from their numbers. Grant's putting the policy in writing was the bad thing; many understandings are better left unwritten.

Among the things not to be put in writing are communications between this office and the leadership of the opposition party now taking office in New York. The Ancient of Days has been playing his favorite game of shut-pan with Nico and me on this subject, but something has been afoot with wily old Thurlow Weed as intermediary.

I suspect this because Hill Lamon received a telegraph message delivered personally by Bates across the street, an unusual procedure neatly circumventing Stanton, Nico and me. Lamon took it in to the Prsdt, who looked at the paper, exploded with an expletive, crumpled it in his large hand, and threw it angrily in the waste bucket. That was an uncommonly intemperate response for the Tycoon. He doesn't react that way when we lose elections or battles. Something of great moment had gone awry. Then he spent a couple of hours on the draft of the final Proclamation, inclining me to think he will sign it.

Later, after he had gone to dinner with the Hellcat, curiosity drove me to a depth of snoopery that I rarely display. I fished around in the bucket next to the Prsdt's desk and came up with a crumpled telegraph message that was so cryptic it had needed no encoding:

"Proposition declined. Weed."

After dinner, Mayor Opdyke of New York, a Seymour supporter and general political troublemaker, came by to see the Prsdt and made the mistake of demanding Seward's removal. Lincoln is a man with a temper, but he usually hides it; this time, he gave his temper full rein and literally threw the mayor out of the office. That will offend the Seymour Democrats; the Prsdt suddenly does not seem to care.

At the end of this strange day of smoothing-over and blowing-up, I asked the Tycoon about General Sam Grant, whom he has never met. Alexander McClure has been telling the story at dinner parties that when Grant's detractors told Lincoln of Grant's drinking, the Prsdt replied, "Let me know what brand of whiskey he drinks, and I'll send a barrel to my other generals."

Since I knew what the Prsdt's real response was when word came from a trusted newspaper source that Grant was a drinker (he sent a worried query to Congressman Washburne to find out how true the charge was) I asked the Prsdt if send-the-others-a-barrel was a story he had told.

He shook his head and spoke with his accustomed expertness about humor. "That's a hardy perennial, like most jokes. Dates back to King George III, who was told that General Wolfe, in command of the English forces in Canada, was stark raving mad. The king said he wished Wolfe would bite some of his other generals."

CHAPTER 41

STONES RIVER

Bragg was still incensed. The night before, on the eve of a great battle, his division commanders had refused to stop a display of maudlin sentimentality that would surely erode the discipline and fighting spirit of the troops.

It had begun with "Yankee Doodle." General Rosecrans's Federal troops, forty-five thousand of them—over ten thousand more than the forces Bragg could muster, thanks to the unfortunate decision President Davis made to send men west to defend Vicksburg—were encamped the night before on the north side of Stones River, just outside Murfreesboro. One of the bands, in the cold and fog, began playing "Yankee Doodle." In return, one of the Confederate bands replied by playing "Dixie's Land." Bragg was certain it must have been under Breckinridge's command, since he was the leader of the conspiracy to undermine Bragg's authority dating from the execution of the Kentucky deserter. Then another Union band took up "Hail, Columbia," and another on the Confederate side (too damned many men with instruments, who would better serve carrying ammunition) played "The Bonnie Blue Flag."

That sort of serenading was bad enough, revealing positions unnecessarily, but when a band in blue played "Home, Sweet Home," the bands in gray had joined in. Soldiers on both sides of the river could be heard bawling out the emotional "Be it ever so hum-ble, there's no-o place like home." It was enough to make a disciplinarian sick.

The battle would be won, he had decided then, by the army that attacked first. Bragg estimated that the Union general, currying popularity as "Old Rosey" with his troops, would probably allow his men breakfast before a day's fighting. Accordingly, Bragg had ordered the attack at daybreak.

Before breakfast, with the first light showing over the Tennessee hills, he sent Polk's and Hardee's divisions smashing into the Federal right. That was twenty minutes ago; he could hear the guns and screams but did not have a way to see the battle.

He held Breckinridge and his six thousand men in reserve. One reason was that Bragg distrusted the fighting quality of the "orphans," supplemented by the reluctant riffraff drafted in Kentucky. More to the point, but not to be admitted to anyone, he placed Breckinridge as his reserve because Bragg was confident of victory and did not want the Kentucky politician to share the glory. If Breckinridge were so much as on the field of battle, Bragg was sure the venal press would pour on him the sort of adulation ordinarily reserved for Robert Lee, while the dogs of detraction would be loosed on Braxton Bragg for not caring about the lives of his men.

Casualties would be heavy today. The months of maneuver were past. In the present order of battle, little of consequence could be accomplished without the expenditure of blood. He was glad that Jeff Davis understood that, if few others did. Certainly the pack of whiners who were the general officers in his command did not: "Bishop" Polk was an ass, "Old Reliable" Hardee could be relied on to move sluggishly, and even the newly promoted fearless Irishman, Cleburne, had been spending all too much time with the chief malcontent in the Confederate Army, Breckinridge. He trusted none of them; if the army lost on this day, Bragg was quite prepared to blame the result on his incompetent division commanders.

He could not, however, find fault with what remained of his cavalry. Although Forrest and Morgan had been sent elsewhere at Davis's orders, the horsemen left behind under Joe Wheeler had ridden clear around the oncoming Union Army, ripping up Rosecrans's communications, destroying his supply and ammunition trains, and capturing enough guns and ammunition to arm a brigade. His cavalry had returned in time to join the Confederate attack on a Union Army whose commander mistakenly thought he had time to take the offensive after breakfast.

A rider came up with good news. "The Federal right has caved, sir.

They've fallen back into a wedge-shape line, with the point at that round forest. Hardee's been assaulting the point of the wedge but is taking heavy casualties."

Bragg scowled. He would have to use Breckinridge on the other side to divert the Union strength from the point. He sent an aide to order a modest advance by the Kentucky and Alabama troops. In moments, the rider returned with word from Breckinridge that he had been told by cavalry that a strong force of the enemy was in his front.

The Kentucky politician was a damned coward, Bragg decided; he probably did not want to attack the Union Kentuckians under Crittenden, his boyhood chum, facing him across Stones River. Bragg switched a couple of Breckinridge's reserve brigades to Hardee for his attack on the Federal strong point, which was resisting furiously in a rutted, wooded area offering good protection for defenders. He sent word to Breckinridge to stay where he was.

Bragg decided that the round forest into which Union troops had been forced—his troops were calling it "Hell's Half Acre"—had to be taken at any cost. He watched as Hardee hurled his men in, wave after wave throughout the interminable afternoon, at more than acceptable loss of life on both sides, without dislodging the Federals. One of his generals—Cheatham, looking red-faced and drunk—shouted "Give 'em hell, boys!" every few moments, and Bishop Polk, the prissy old fool, echoed with "Give 'em what General Cheatham says, boys!"

Bragg then calculated that Breckinridge would be useful in wearing down the salient before darkness closed in; no time for a victory today, but time for mutual punishment. As Rosecrans began a Union counterattack from Hell's Half Acre, Bragg ordered in Breckinridge and Cleburne to stop it. The "orphans" held together well enough, to Bragg's surprise, pushing the Federals back into the cedars before stopping to regroup.

The Kentuckian came to him for permission to suspend the attack. On Bragg's orders, the Kentucky brigades had been fed into the battle piecemeal and had been chewed up one at a time. "The Federals are supported by numerous batteries, and we have no artillery we can wheel in there," Breckinridge reported. "Their lines have the protection of the railroad cut, forming an excellent breastwork. I deem it reckless to continue."

Bragg shrugged his assent; the battle was won, the majority of the field in Confederate hands, and he was just as glad that Breckinridge was not undertaking anything heroic; better that he should be quoted in the reports as having been overly cautious. By nightfall, the fog mingled with the smoke and the darkness made further attacks impossible. He could permit the exhausted men to bivouac.

"I expect the Yankees to abandon the field during the night," Bragg told his commanders triumphantly. "I have notified Richmond that Rosecrans has been driven from every position except his extreme left, and that tomorrow our Army of Tennessee will present a great New Year's gift to the Confederacy."

His commanders, characteristically, did not applaud or offer congratulatory toasts. Hardee looked disgusted, Polk exhausted, Cleburne glum. Breckinridge, probably still smarting at the loss of a few Kentucky conscripts—he had fussed about legal niceties when Bragg had pressed them into service—

made some remark about the screams of the wounded and his hopes of sending out rescue and burial parties in the early morning. He had the temerity to suggest that the Confederate commanders thought they had the battle won after the first day at Shiloh.

Not one of the sorry lot caught what Bragg knew to be the significance of his victory: it applied the crushing blow to Union hopes on the very weekend before Lincoln's desperate proclamation of abolition on New Year's Day. When news of this Confederate victory reached London, the British would be sure to recognize the South and begin active assistance. Let Old Abe "liberate" the western portion of Virginia and play the hypocrite by approving its secession from Richmond; as Bragg's forces moved north through Kentucky, that area would soon be back in Southern hands.

Bragg was certain that not a single one of these malcontents under him appreciated the genius of his decision to despise defensive positions and to attack the attackers instead, just an hour before their planned assault. These generals were all envious of him; in his report, he was determined to detail their weaknesses in carrying out his orders.

"When Rosecrans withdraws tomorrow, be prepared to march north to recapture Nashville, " Bragg announced. Too many of that city's inhabitants had welcomed the Yankee invaders; for those disloyal Southerners, the time for retribution had come. "I want no talk of tired men and burial details. We march."

To Breckinridge, he added with a certain glee: "President Davis informs me that next month he will suspend habeas corpus throughout this area. We will be able to arrest and hold the Northern sympathizers among the civilian population without the delay of courts."

Bragg grinned up at the tall Kentuckian. "He asked me especially to break that to you gently."

CHAPTER 42

TAIL OF THE ARMY

"This the river steamer to Aquia Creek?"

"That's our run, soldier," the riverboat captain replied. "From our nation's capital to General Burnside's headquarters, just a couple of hours from peace to war."

"I should be pleased to go with thee tonight," said James Stradling of Mechanicsville, Bucks County, Pennsylvania, sergeant in a New Jersey cavalry regiment.

"No room. You can see how we're loading up."

Stradling had not anticipated that possibility, and looked perplexed. "Here are my furlough papers," he said to the boat captain. "Thee will notice that my furlough expires tomorrow, on the first day of the New Year. I am anxious to get to my unit at the front."

"Should of thought of that beforehand. We have some brass coming on board tonight. They take up a lot of space. Can't help you."

"But if I remain over here in Washington," the sergeant explained patiently, "the provost guard will pick me up and hustle me off with a lot of deserters to the front, and I don't want to go that way."

The captain was as unyielding as he was unconcerned. With an effort, Sergeant Stradling resisted the impulse to think ill of him. He picked up his bag, walked awhile up to the Capitol, moved through that half-finished edifice with his neck craned to see the sights, came out the back facing Pennsylvania Avenue. He hefted his bag up on his shoulder and walked down the long hill, wondering what to do.

If he showed up a day late, his lieutenant would be very disappointed, and might even think he remained in Washington to take part in New Year's Eve revelries. Stradling had earned a reputation as a responsible soldier, which he did not want to lose because transportation to the front was hard to come by. The other Quakers in his regiment would be more severe than the officers, because his actions reflected on them.

He came to the white house where the President lived, and stopped. A thought struck him: why not see the President? He would knock on the door, and if the President was not in, Mrs. Lincoln would probably know how soon he would be back and would ask a soldier to come in and abide awhile until Mr. Lincoln returned.

At the front door, however, two policemen were on guard. He had not expected that and looked at them blankly, shifting his bag off his shoulder to the ground.

"Well, country boy, what do you want?"

"I want to see the President."

They nodded him into a large room filled with people. The sergeant was puzzled at the size of the crowd. He asked a man near him if the people had assembled to hear the President make a speech. The man said that the people were assembled to see the President, all right, but not to hear a speech. Everyone had to wait his turn for a personal interview. It was that day of the week.

The sergeant thanked him, and looked around to see if the crowd contained anybody he recognized. Presently he saw a tall soldier with flowing blond hair and a commanding bearing: that was General "Fighting Joe" Hooker. He recognized him from a parade. General Hooker went to a side door, knocked, and a guard opened it and passed him inside.

"Where do people land when they go in that side door?" the sergeant inquired of a guard.

"Why, greeny, that goes to the President's room."

"Well, look, I'm a soldier in distress. Can you help me? I've been home on furlough, and—"

"You want to get it extended, I suppose. I don't think the President will do that." Sgt. Stradling told him the dilemma. "Oh, that's an Indian of another skin," said the guard. Stradling asked him what that meant, and the guard said, "It's like a horse of another color. You are green, aren't you?"

"That's what everybody always says," Stradling admitted, "but if I can get a chance to put my case before the President, I bet I can get him to help me. All I want is to get to the front tonight."

"Damn all steamboat captains," said the guard, who, Stradling supposed, had had difficulty with them himself. He took the furlough papers and went through the side door.

There followed a long wait, something the Quaker sergeant was accustomed to, having served in the army almost a year. While he was waiting, a well-dressed, fierce-looking short man came to the side door, showed the guard his card, and was passed in. Stradling asked who that was and was told it had been United States Senator Ben Wade of Ohio.

In a half hour, a man about the sergeant's age with a mustache came out and said, "I'm the President's secretary. I gave your furlough to the President, with a note that you were trying to get to the front instead of away from it. We don't get many requests like that."

Stradling told him that the fact that the President was warmly inclined toward soldiers who remained in the army, and stayed near the front, had trickled down through the army. As the possibility of actually meeting Lincoln face to face began to become real, the sergeant began to feel queasy.

Another long wait, during which a couple of other generals slipped in—from Franklin's division, he thought, where most of the ruckus about Burnside was being kicked up. Just about everyone in the army knew there was a feud going on at the top, what with the court-martial of General Porter to make Little Mac look bad.

"The President will see you in a few minutes," said the pleasant secretary, who took him inside to what Stradling at first imagined must be the President's office. It did not look as grand as he thought it would. The secretary went into the other room, leaving the door open, and Stradling could hear the generals running down old Burnside, calling him incompetent and bungling; worse, Burn was planning an attack across the river again, which the generals thought would bring another disaster. It seemed to Stradling that they could well be right, but it didn't seem fitting for generals to sneak out of camp and talk to the President behind Burnside's back. He'd hate to have any of the corporals under him talking that way to the lieutenant.

"General," said a high, strong voice, "we shall expect to hear some good news from you soon. I shall take what all of you have told me under advisement, and give you my word that this shall be kept in confidence." That must have been the President himself speaking; Stradling's throat went dry. The secretary motioned him in as the others left. Stradling saluted them. They did not look at him.

"Take a seat," said the man with the beard behind the big table.

"I'd rather stand, if you don't mind, sir."

The President then rose, and Stradling did not think he would ever stop going up. He was the tallest man the sergeant ever saw. He came around the table and extended a hand that seemed to be fully three times as large as his own, with a grip on him like a vise.

"What can I do for you, my young friend?"

Stradling coughed, regained his composure, stated his business, and saluted. Lincoln took his furlough papers, and said aloud what he was writing across them: "To any steamboat captain going to the front, please give bearer transportation." He handed the papers back, with "If I have any influence with steamboat captains, that should take you to the front."

The sergeant turned to leave but the President told him to hold on.

"Wade," the President said to a fierce-looking little fellow seated in the corner of the room, "we have had the heads of the army here a few minutes ago, and learned from them all they cared to tell. Now we have here the tail of the army, so let us get from him how the rank and file feel about matters." He turned to Stradling, adding, "I mean no reflection on you, Sergeant, when I say the tail of the army."

"I understand what thee are driving at," he told the President.

"A great many men have deserted in the past few months," Mr. Lincoln told him. "I am endeavoring to learn the cause. There must be some good reason for it. Either the army is opposed to me, or to the generals, or to the Proclamation of Emancipation that is supposed to be signed tomorrow." He turned to the man he called Wade with an aside: "None of the generals desert or resign, and we could spare a number of them better than we can spare so many privates."

Stradling was feeling better about everything, and drew himself up to tell the President what the army thought.

"Mr. President, the army has the utmost confidence in thee, in thy honesty, and thy ability to manage this war." That was true, no flattery, and a good beginning. Well launched, he went to the heart of what the President had been discussing before. "The army has no faith in the ability of General Burnside. He appears to us as a general with no military genius whatever. He fights his battles like some people play the fiddly, by main strength and awkwardness."

"Were you there at Fredericksburg? Did you see much of the battle?"

The sergeant nodded vigorously, and reported: "When the fog lifted, you could see nearly the whole line. It was on a long and level plain, what they call in Virginia bottomland. The rebels were entrenched on the low hills looking down on the plain where we were. They had filled a sunken road full of sharpshooters. There was no way of our winning that battle, sir, but General Burnside launched Hooker's corps, the flower of the army, against those positions. You know the result, for I can observe the great gloom which still hangs around you on account of that battle."

"That great gloom comes from our fears about another fight entirely," said the senator in the corner, "in Tennessee. But at Fredericksburg, was there any excuse for such a blunder?"

"You really want my view?" Stradling did not want to get in trouble with the lieutenant.

"Go ahead," said the President, "this is very interesting to me, and to Senator Wade."

"It was open country," the sergeant recalled. "Both flanks of the rebel army were susceptible of being turned. An assault straight ahead was sure to fail. We knew about that sunken road, because we of the cavalry had been over that road with General Bayard a few months ago, and he must have told General Burnside about it. I don't see a whole lot of excuse for that blunder."

"And such a disaster that followed," said the President, "still makes my heart sick."

"Our duty is not to criticize," Stradling allowed, "but to obey even if we get our heads knocked off. Which is what happened."

The President passed his big hand across his face, then changed the subject:

"You have said nothing about how the soldiers feel toward the Emancipation Proclamation."

"I know how thy heart is set on issuing that document, sir. So far as I'm concerned, I'm all for it. I was born a Quaker, and we're just about all anti-slavery. When I was a boy, I attended two or three debating societies a week in Bucks County, and that's where I learned to become a full-blooded aboli-tionist."

"What about your comrades?" asked the senator in his gruff way.

"Most of them say that if they had known the war was to free the niggers, they never would have enlisted. That's why so many have deserted." When Wade made a humphing sound, Stradling added a fact he was sure the senator did not know: "Others say they won't desert, but won't fight, so they get in the ambulance corps or the quartermaster's department, to get out of fight-ing."

"And when the slaves are freed?" Wade asked. "How will that sit?"

Stradling did not know how to lie or even soften the hard truth. "When you issue that proclamation tomorrow," he told the President, "a lot more is going to desert. Between that and General Burnside having no respect, it's a wonder so many of us stays." The sergeant was a little surprised at the firm sound of his own voice, but he had been invited to the feast and he had his say.

Senator Wade humphed, and walked to the window, staring out angrily, hands clasped behind his back. Stradling looked toward the President. Had he gone too far?

"Sergeant, I am glad indeed to have your views. I shall take this opportu-nity to make a few remarks which I desire you to convey to your comrades.

"The Proclamation is, as you state, very near to my heart. I thought about it and studied it in all its phases long before I began to put it on paper. I expect you're right—that many soldiers who care nothing for the colored man will seize on the Proclamation as an excuse for deserting. But I do not believe the number of deserters will materially affect the army."

"On the contrary," Senator Wade put in, "the issuing of the Proclamation will probably bring into the ranks many who otherwise would not volunteer."

"I agree," said the President, who seemed to be talking as much to Wade as to the sergeant. "After I had made up my mind to issue it, I commenced to put my thoughts on paper, and it took me many days before I succeeded in getting it into shape so that it suited me."

He looked directly at Stradling, and the sergeant told himself this was important to remember, so that he could pass it on to the entire company.

"Please explain to your comrades that the Proclamation is being issued for two reasons," Mr. Lincoln said. "The first and chief reason is this: I feel a great impulse moving me to do justice to four or five millions of people."

Well, good for him. Man should do what he believes in, and people said that's what Lincoln wanted all along. Stradling prepared his mind to remem-ber the second reason because when he wrote all this in a letter to John Gilbert in Mechanicsville, his peacetime boss in the tannery, John would want to know exactly what the President said. It was a pretty big responsibil-ity, passing along to his comrades in the field and his friends at home what the President himself thought.

"The second reason I am issuing this Proclamation is that I believe it will be a club in our hands with which we can whack the rebels. In other words, I have faith that it will shorten the war by many months." He looked at Wade, who nodded enthusiastically.

The President extended that giant hand and said, "I trust you will reach the front in the morning. Remember: first, emancipation does justice; and, it will shorten the war."

Mr. Lincoln bade him farewell, and the sergeant thought how sad, woebegone, and gloomy-looking the President was. His face did not smile or lighten up once during the visit. Stradling felt proud that he had gone straight to the top, and would have much to tell his comrades, but at the same time could not rid himself of the impression he had been to a funeral.

"Sergeant, hold up." The President's voice caught him at the door. "How do you suppose your comrades would feel about our arming some of those freed slaves, and putting them in our army?"

Stradling frowned; that wasn't in the proclamation he'd read about a few months back. He couldn't see sleeping right next to black men on bivouac, and it might be, if they were supposed to be holding the flank next to you, they'd cut and run at the first sound of firing. To be truthful, that's what he had done the first time, but the second time he'd held his ground.

"My guess is that it would set well," he said, surprising himself. There was a tune the Irishers sang about it. "If this is going to be a fight for the nigger, sir, he ought to be in it getting kilt along with the rest of us."

At that, Wade got up and pumped his hand, escorting him outside the office before he could say anything else.

On the way downstairs, the sergeant thought it curious that the President's most important reason for freeing the slaves was to do justice to the black man, and his second reason was to end the war sooner. From all Mr. Lincoln had said before, that Stradling could remember reading, it was the other way around. Abolition was always presented as a practical matter, a military necessity, that just happened to be right, too. He thought it was a good thing that Mr. Lincoln thought it was right, first, and useful to boot. It struck him that if you are going to act justly, then it makes no sense to go around apologizing for it, even if a bunch of malcontents were going to use it as an excuse to desert.

The guard who had passed his request in was still on duty. "You need not call me 'greeny' anymore," said the sergeant, "for I have learned more today than many people learn in fifty years."

He hefted his bag and headed out to look for a food counter, to enjoy his last meal without hardtack for what would surely be a long while. After that, he walked to the boat and showed the captain his furlough papers with the President's notation on it.

The steamboat captain raised his eyebrows at the signature. "Git aboard," he said.

HELL'S HALF ACRE

General Pat Cleburne worried that his friend Breckinridge might not survive this battle for Tennessee.

Last night, Bragg had announced a great Confederate victory, but the Federals under Rosecrans had not crept away from Murfreesboro as they were supposed to. This morning, there they were, just across Stones River, wet and freezing, tending their wounded and digging in, waiting for Bragg to launch another assault.

Why? The word was about that Rosecrans had spotted some fires behind him, assumed he was surrounded, and had decided to make a last stand. Cleburne wished he could send a man over under a flag of truce to say the line of retreat was wide open, that those fires were set by a few mischievous cavalrymen, and would General Rosecrans kindly take his Union Army and leave.

Cleburne was concerned about Breck because the Kentuckian's troops had been selected by Bragg to bear the brunt of driving the Federals from their well-prepared positions. The order was to take the high ground to the left of Hell's Half Acre, and a bloody murderous charge it was sure to be. Cleburne had a theory that he called the Irish Theory of Luck in Battle: If you go into a battle fearful of being killed, or worse, hopeful of being killed, then killed is what you get; if you go in positive that you will live, or fiercely determined to live, then you live. The theory did not apply to everyone, but it had applied to him very well so far.

What troubled Pat Cleburne was that Breck had the look about him of a man who no longer gave a damn. Bragg's unnecessary execution of the Kentucky boy, intended to send a chill of fear through the Orphan Brigade, had bred lasting resentment instead, infecting Kentuckians clear up to their commander. Surely that had been a searing experience for Breck, associated in some way with the dimming of hopes that his missing son might be alive and a prisoner. The bleakness of personal and national prospects showed in the man's eyes; Cabell was the future, and Cleburne suspected that the Kentucky boy who was shot for desertion and the Kentucky boy who was missing had become fused in Breck's mind.

And the famed orator who would expound, after a couple of glasses of good bourbon, on the dastardly corruption of freedom under the despot Lincoln, to the edification and inspiration of his troops and friends, had fallen silent of late.

Cleburne knew why. First there had been the South's military conscription, even of men in occupied portions of Kentucky, a state that had chosen to stay in the Union. Then came the pervasive control of the economy, with Confederate Government ownership of the most important commodity, cotton, as the central government in Richmond declared itself capable of overriding the decisions of the states. And now the South was treating itself to arbitrary

General Patrick Ronayne Cleburne, C.S.A.

arrests of citizens by the military for the crime of thinking disloyal thoughts. All the despotic inroads on individual liberty that come under the abolition of habeas corpus, which Breck nearly alone had decried in the U.S. Senate, were coming to pass in the Confederacy. All that and slavery too.

Cleburne's personal cause was Southern independence, national freedom, which he was persuaded had an even chance of being achieved. He worried for his friend, whose family cause had always been resistance to tyranny. Personal freedom was not doing so well on either side during the war. How much freedom must citizens give up to preserve a nation dedicated to freedom? Not much, was Breck's answer; let justice be done though the heavens fall. Plenty, was Lincoln's answer, and Davis's too: a life is never wisely given to save a limb.

And once the President had war powers, wouldn't he have much-expanded peace powers too, taken from the people? No wonder Breck looked so distracted these days. He was not merely a statesman without a state, he had become a crusader without a cause. In adopting the methods of the Union to protect itself from the Union, the South had become in a crucial way the same as the Union, and the requirements of national survival had ground the bedrock of constitutional principle into shifting sand for men like John Breckinridge.

Cleburne walked over to the Bragg headquarters tent, where Breckinridge was arguing against the plan to send his division charging up Van Cleve's hill. With a stick in the dirt, the Kentuckian was trying to show how the assault could be blown out of the field by the Federal artillery placed alongside the planned route of the charge. Cleburne overheard it all and nodded agreement with the Kentuckian; such an attack would be suicidal.

"Their ground is higher than mine," Breck was saying, "and the Federal artillery is placed to hit any direct charge both in the front and in the flank. It's a trap. That is exactly where they are waiting for us to attack. It would be a disaster."

"Your division was chosen," Bragg pointed out coldly, "because it suffered so lightly in comparison with the others day before yesterday."

"I'm not suggesting somebody else undertake this," Breck pleaded, "I'm saying nobody should be forced to commit suicide. Two rows of infantry cannot charge fifty guns uphill across an open field."

"Sir, my information is different," Bragg replied. "I have given the order to attack the enemy in your front and I expect it to be obeyed. I expect you to lead the charge, General Breckinridge."

Cleburne stared mournfully at the lines scratched in the frozen dirt and came to the conclusion that Bragg wanted Breckinridge dead. He was surprised to hear his own name mentioned. "I am ordering General Cleburne to assist you because he has proved his bravery, and I want that hill taken."

Breck and he were in this together. When their eyes met, it was to acknowledge that the Union grapeshot would rip through a great many of their men before the attackers came within musket range of the Union lines.

"Polk will open an artillery barrage at three forty-five this afternoon, and fifteen minutes later you will begin the charge," said Braxton Bragg. His parting words were: "The signal will be a single shot from the center of my line."

Cleburne walked with Breck back to his headquarters, just in front of his own. The brigadier, a Kentuckian named Hansen, had a solution to their problem: "I'll go and kill Bragg. Then you can court-martial and shoot me. I'll be dead either way, but we'll save thousands of lives." The officer was serious. They refused to take him seriously.

Muttering a string of Gaelic curses, Cleburne returned to break the bad news to his command. He resolved to approach the charge as an action that, with luck and grit, and perhaps some heavy artillery support of the South's own, could succeed by virtue of its daring. It seemed to him to be the whole war in a nutshell: Southern courage against Northern iron, Confederate desperation to win quickly before Union advantage in men and arms could take effect. And on Emancipation Day, too; that was fitting. If Cleburne had had his way, the blacks would be fighting on the side of the South, but now Lincoln had beaten them to that vast source of manpower. Cleburne was angry at that but refused to let himself become embittered. He was not afflicted with Breck's curse; he had the cause of independence, freedom of the South and West, to carry him up the hill to Hell's Half Acre.

At his tent, he was met by a Wheeler cavalryman in charge of a group of forty blue-clad prisoners taken in a sweep behind the enemy lines.

"You're all paroled, ye lucky lads," Cleburne called out, as the Yankee prisoners broke into smiles at the good news, and at the surprise of a Confederate officer speaking in a brogue. "We have no facilities for prisoners here. Swear you won't take up service again, and be on your way home. War's over for you."

"Will you be servin' us lunch, General Paddy?"

"General Cleburne to you, former soldier, and there'll be no free food for the likes of Billy-boys. On your way—Nashville's thirty miles up that road."

The Union soldiers turned and started tramping up the frozen path, all but one. It was a woman, not masquerading as a man, but in the full skirt and apron of an army nurse under her open overcoat. She was tall, very pale, in her early twenties, and Cleburne judged she was on the verge of collapse.

"I will not take a parole, General. I am your prisoner."

"And why is that, dear girl?"

"I wish to be exchanged, and I will serve the Union again another day. The wounded need me, and this is my calling."

That captivated him. He looked closely at her face, with its prominent forehead, wide-round eyes, strong jaw. "Why do I think I know you?"

"I am Margaret Elizabeth Breckinridge. My traitor cousin John is in your camp."

"I will take you to him."

She shook her head, then swayed. He moved to her side and took her arm to hold her up.

"I am ashamed of him and what he has done to our family," she said when she could. "I do not want to see him. But I have news about his son, my cousin Cabell."

Cleburne brought the young woman into his warmed tent and sat her down. If her news was bad, he would keep it to himself and pass it along to Breck after the battle.

"Reverend Bob asked me to look for Cabell in the prisoner camps. I've been to Libby and the others," she said, shuddering from the cold or at the memory, "and a lady who is a friend of General Dix's sent me to Johnson's Island and I found him there."

"Is the boy well?"

"He took his first name and used it as his last. That's why it was hard finding him. I don't blame him, changing his name, after bringing disgrace on us all, him and his damned father."

"Nurse, spare me the family feuding, just say—is the boy all right?"

"He had the camp fever, and he's thin, but he'll survive. General Dix, who, I think, knows John, said Cabell would be part of the next exchange."

"General Dix served in the Buchanan Cabinet, when your cousin was Vice President of the United States," Cleburne told her, annoyed at her attitude even as he was relieved at her news. "A great many people that you respect, who disagreed with his choice of sides in this war, think of your cousin not as a traitor but as a good man."

She shrugged. "That's what Reverend Bob says, and he's loyal and for freedom, but I see Cousin John as the Breckinridge who stood for slavery in the election. He's leading the fight for slavery right now and I despise him for that."

Cleburne checked his temper. "But you agreed to search for his son."

"I agreed to help find the boy, because he was too young to know his own mind, and he's kin"—the young woman's face was as implacable as it was exhausted—"though I will never forgive John Breckinridge for betraying his country to keep human beings in chains."

A long war it would surely be. That decided him. The abolitionist Union nurse was not to be the bearer of the good news. Cleburne ordered an aide to let her use his bed and tent, which he would not need soon again. If victorious that afternoon, Bragg's army would break camp to pursue the enemy, and if not, the camp would be overrun.

Returning to Breckinridge's headquarters tent, Cleburne found the Kentuckian with General Gideon Pillow, the corrupt coward who slipped out of Fort Donelson. The dastard's political connections in Richmond kept him in service, if not in command of troops.

"General Pillow is with us in this charge," said Breckinridge, and laid out the order of battle assignments. Cleburne knew exactly what Bragg was doing. Pillow was a dishonored political troublemaker; Bragg wanted him permanently out of the way. This charge was to be an execution of generals who defied Bragg's authority or whom the commanding general considered incompetent. Cleburne considered his own inclusion in the group as a kind of honor, although he wished Pillow were not a part of it—that skedaddle artist would probably hide behind the nearest tree when the first bugle blew.

"Breck, I need to see you alone on a personal matter."

"And I you." They walked outside into the sunny, cold, all-too-clear January morning, the sort of weather artillerymen pray for.

Breck spoke first. "Pat, you were born lucky, and you're going to come through this with your honor brighter than ever, so there is something that I want you to remember." Breck looked out at the long slope up to the Federal lines, and Cleburne knew he could sense the enfilading fire that would come from the Union cannon on the left. "This attack is made against my judgment, and by the special orders of General Bragg. Of course we all must try to do our duty and fight the best we can. If it should result in disaster, and I be among the slain"—this was the first time Cleburne had ever heard his friend mention the possibility of death before a fight—"I want you to do justice to my memory. I want you to tell the people that I believed the attack to be very unwise, and tried my damnedest to prevent it."

"It's a lucky thing you're telling me this and not somebody else," said Cleburne, more heartily than he felt, "but it will sound pretty silly when we're standing at the top of the hill and the Yankees are running down the other side."

The Kentuckian smiled. "I'm glad you're with me, Pat, but I'm sorry for you that you were included among the orphans."

"Cheer up, lad, I have good news for you about your son. Some of Wheeler's boys brought in a bunch of Federals, including a cousin of yours who is an army nurse. She says she saw your boy at the prison in Johnson's Island, looking fine and healthy, and he'll be exchanged in a week."

"Cabell alive?"

"Not only alive but well, and his good health vouched for by a nurse who knows him." A slight exaggeration about the boy's condition, Cleburne felt, was called for. "General Dix sends his compliments, and Miss Carroll too. I think she had a hand in it. They'll get your son back in jig time."

Breck stood silent for a few moments. He walked over to a tall cedar, leaned against the trunk, and began to weep. Cleburne followed him over, standing close, to appear to be in military consultation to any lookers-on. Damn Bragg would probably consider it evidence of drunkenness or cowardice before a battle. Breck could not stop crying, and Cleburne punched him in the shoulder so he would get control of himself.

After a moment, he did. "Margaret Elizabeth—is she still here?"

Cleburne shook his head. "Fine lass, set on going back to her wounded, so I gave her one of my horses. Looks like you, she does, but in a nice way."

"Did she say anything about—" Breck stopped, started that again. "The other side of the family, what do they say about the Senate action?" He was the first Breckinridge to be officially branded a traitor.

"She said they disagreed with your decision to go South," he lied stoutly, "but that they all understand your reasons and there's not a man jack among them who won't defend your integrity. Is one of them a Reverend Bob? He's especially in your corner."

He would tell the man what he deserved to hear, what should be the truth rather than what was. After the war, with the South independent and slavery on the way out, the Breckinridge clan could all make up along those lines anyway. Cleburne had no doubt that Margaret's bitterness would fade, the Kentucky family's cleavage would heal, and one day she would feel the way Cleburne reported she felt in the midst of the war. He was not lying; he thought of it as merely getting ahead of the truth. The two great nations would be natural allies, and the border between the Confederacy and the Union would not separate families and friends.

"I want to send a messenger back to Murfreesboro to tell my wife," Breck said, signaling for an aide. When the man came running up, the general hesitated, then sent a message to one of Bragg's aides asking for more artillery

General John C. Breckinridge, C.S.A.

support at three forty-five. To Cleburne, he said, "Let's tell Mary after the battle."

The South's only Irish-born general understood. His friend wanted to be certain that the news to Mary would show that at least one Breckinridge male had come back from the dead.

CHAPTER 44

DAY OF JUBILEE

"Happy New Year, Mr. President."

The voice was William's, the spindly colored boy he had brought with him from Illinois to attend to his needs in the early morning. Lincoln opened his eyes, focused on the crack in the bedroom ceiling, then turned his head on the pillow to see William with the large tray. The bowl of hot water for shaving would be on the tray, along with the breakfast dish of warm corn pone, and the boiled cabbage. He took a deep breath to draw in the smell of the cabbage. Food didn't mean much to him but he did look forward to cabbage every day.

Lincoln rolled out of bed and slid his feet into the carpet slippers. It occurred to him that the Israelite corncutter, now in New Orleans with Banks, would find it difficult to locate any rebel leader willing to talk with him about peace after the event of today. He sat in his nightshirt for a couple of minutes, saying nothing, watching William set the bowls on the table and whip up a lather in a cup for shaving.

"This is the great day for my people," the young servant said cheerily. "Big jubilee everywhere last night, Jubilee Day today. You ain't changing your mind?"

"I am a slow walker," Lincoln said, yawning and combing his hair with his fingers, "but I never walk back. The signing will be right after the levee this noon, William. You can count on it."

He had put William Johnson on the Treasury payroll as a laborer for six hundred dollars a year. When the boy finished his service as a valet in the Mansion in the morning, he worked as a messenger at Treasury in the afternoon. Lincoln watched him lay a freshly pressed black broadcloth morning coat on the bed next to the underwear and shirt and silk tie. To properly impress the diplomatic corps, the Congress, the men in uniform, and just about everybody else who was passing through town, Lincoln had to dress carefully for the annual reception from eleven to noon that New Year's Day. That levee was one of the few national traditions, and it could not be avoided. Mary would still be wearing her black velvet mourning clothes, with the black gloves and fan, in memory of the light that had gone out in her life. He shook off the memory of the way Willie would race in and jump on the bed on New Year's morning, before that thought of happier times could take hold and ruin the day.

William had standing orders to wake him at six, so that he could be at the telegraph office to be in touch with General Burnside in Virginia, and with General Rosecrans in Tennessee before seven. This morning, Burnside was in

Washington to testify at the court-martial of Fitz-John Porter, and would be at the Mansion first thing, probably to complain about the way his generals were complaining about him.

Lincoln had some sympathy for Burnside, who had failed out of ineptitude. He had less for Porter, who had succeeded all too well in helping his friend McClellan undermine poor John Pope at Second Bull Run. Had he been wrong in replacing George on the day after the elections, just as the victor of Antietam was showing signs of shaking off the slows? He decided not. Despite the debacle at Fredericksburg that followed, the President had to establish the principle that the Army could not set up shop for itself. Orville Browning had been in the other day to seek clemency again for Major John Key; Lincoln's answer was again an unequivocal no. And the Porter court-martial would go forward, driving home the same lesson again. Only one man could be commander in chief.

More important than Burnside's visit would be any word from Rosecrans, whose army had finally moved from Nashville toward the rebel concentration at Murfreesboro. At this moment, with England eager to recognize the Confederacy, the Union could ill afford to lose another battle, but last night's reports about the fighting at Stones River were not encouraging. The newspapers, especially the *Times* and the *Tribune* in New York, had been preparing the nation for a great victory, to wash away the terrible taste of Fredericksburg. If disaster lay ahead today at Murfreesboro, public sentiment would turn even more sour on the war and the pressures to let the wayward sister states depart in peace would become unbearable.

New Year's Day. Horatio Seymour was being inaugurated as Governor of New York. In that smoldering state, the Union's prime source of men and money, a grand jury had been convened to consider the indictment of Secretary Stanton for breaking state law with his arbitrary arrests. The governor-elect had been going around saying that it was a "high crime" to abduct a citizen of New York, and he left no doubt he considered Stanton or Lincoln to be high criminals. That would be a crippling confrontation; he could not fight a civil war on two fronts.

William was ready to shave him but Lincoln did not move, thinking of the challenge from New York. Lincoln had done all he could to placate Seymour, offering a share of political power as no other American President ever had; what more did the man want? Seymour's peremptory rebuff transmitted through Weed—"proposition declined"—still stung.

These copperheads were not interested in a go-slow-on-abolition compromise to save the Union. Rather, Lincoln was convinced, they wanted to pretend that Jeff Davis was ready to restore the "Union as it was" if only he were allowed to keep slavery. But the copperheads did not know Jeff Davis. He was just as foursquare for independence, for disunion, as Lincoln was for union.

Independence, especially for Americans brought up to revere Washington and Jefferson, was always a more popular cause than union, which smacked of imposing a yoke on an unwilling minority. As the American colonists fighting the better-equipped British had demonstrated, wars were ultimately won or lost by public sentiment, by the fighting spirit of a people. Such public sentiment could be rallied only by a great cause. If an ideal was attractive enough, it would define not merely itself but the essence of the opposition. In that way, the Southern cause of independence was making the Union cause appear to be anti-independence, and would make Abraham Lincoln look like a modern George III.

That was why he had come to the conclusion during the summer that union, seen all too often as anti-independence, was not enough of a cause to sustain the fighting spirit of the North. By raising high the banner of emancipation, he would define the enemy cause as slavery. Most people, even many of those against abolition, were disgusted by slavery.

Lincoln knew that was why, little by little, he had let himself be led into the illegal seizure of property called emancipation. Never mind that a majority of the North was against it, as the elections showed; and never mind that too many of Sergeant Stradling's friends would desert rather than "fight for the nigger"; the political fact was that the most active and articulate faction of the North demanded an end to slavery with a fierceness and dedication that would resist all pressures for a settlement.

Time was what he needed, time to wear down the Southern forces by weight of numbers and mutual casualties. The newly embraced cause—not his original, central cause of majority rule, but the new rallying cause of human freedom—would bring that time. On the brink of being broken, when other gamblers were tempted to reduce losses, Lincoln was prepared to double the stakes.

He moved in his nightshirt from the bed to a chair, drew a sheet around him, tilted his head back, and stuck out his chin to let William begin the shaving. The Proclamation was on his mind; he had worked on it again yesterday, letting the Cabinet make final suggestions, accepting Chase's pious emendation invoking "the considerate judgment of mankind and the gracious favor of Almighty God"; that would please the folks who did not want the soldiers fighting on Sunday.

Lincoln had added his own "warranted by the Constitution upon military necessity" to satisfy, or at least palliate, those legal minds who doubted the edict's foundation in law. He admitted to himself that his call upon the freed slaves, all behind Southern lines, "to abstain from all violence, unless in necessary self-defense" was more than a little disingenuous; it could be read on Southern plantations as a call for slaves to defend themselves with violent means when threatened, as many of them so often were, by the lash. The step was short from such individual self-defense to a general uprising. He would not encourage such a race war, indeed would publicly deplore it; but if an uprising came, it would come, demoralizing the Southern troops at the front and shortening the time of bloodshed.

One final amendment had been his own surprising adoption of the Chase-Stanton position on arming freed blacks. In for a dime, in for a dollar. Just as he swallowed the principle of secession in breaking off West Virginia yesterday, he could stare down the objections of conservatives to the provision of guns to former slaves to fire at their former masters. With Seymour and his ilk hopelessly beyond reach of a deal, he had no more compunctions about using black men as soldiers. "And I further declare and make known," the final Proclamation read, "that such persons of suitable condition will be received into the armed service . . ."

His Emancipation Proclamation was a weapon, all right, to whack the rebels with. He would put a weapon in every freed black hand capable of carrying one. Jeff Davis would surely be drawn into issuing a furious counter-proclamation. Lincoln was ready to seize on the expected excessive language to suspend all prisoner exchanges. The exchange of prisoners favored the South, with its smaller population base. Up to now, he had to consider the opinion of relatives of captured Northern boys, but an intemperate reaction by Davis to his Proclamation—the Edict of Freedom, Hay wanted to call it—would give him the moral standing to make a cruel decision.

As he thought about it, Lincoln envisioned his Proclamation as more than a weapon to cause disruption in the enemy camp. It would be more, too, than a means of reinvigorating public sentiment in the North, more than a way to block international intervention, and more than a new source of manpower.

He granted that the hundred-day-long threat of emancipation had not succeeded in coercing the Southern leaders. He had a hunch, however, that emancipation as a fait accompli might have a mysterious power of its own. Lincoln sensed that the Proclamation—which he always knew would cause bitter controversy within the North, as it deepened the bitterness between North and South—might be of greater import than he had at first imagined. He no longer felt troubled or defensive about its illegality. An event that caused a biblical jubilee in the streets of the North, as well as fervent, if silent, exultation in the slave quarters of the South could have an extraordinary effect on people everywhere.

The act seemed to be taking on a life of its own. Lincoln could not gauge its effect through the land, but he realized he had underestimated its effect on himself. Surely carping would come from the right, holding that it was so unconstitutional as to be despotic, and the left would argue that it freed only those slaves that he could not reach, leaving the slaves in the border states still enslaved. Those arguments missed the point.

The point was that if the war was finally won, this single proclamation could turn out to be the most memorable act of his administration. The new birth of freedom might be remembered not merely as the means of gaining time to keep the Union together, vital as that device was, but as the reason that the Union had a right to be held together. Although he had to justify his unprecedented seizure of property in the stilted and formal language of military necessity, the freeing of millions of human beings from bondage was a moral justification for the terrible bloodletting. That was what the abolitionists like Garrison had been saying for years, as they heaped abuse upon the Constitution as "a covenant with death" because it permitted slavery. Those provocations and threats of abolition might have helped goad the South into rebellion, but now the fact of abolition was needed to put down that rebellion.

He opened his mouth and stretched his upper lip to aid William's shaving razor. He knew that his war power, by itself, was inadequate; he had no power to wage a war for the principle of national cohesion if the people grew tired of war. But the war power, as the key to unlock the shackles of the slave, could release a power greater than any President could claim to find in a Constitution. Right did make might if it disenthralled and inspirited the populace.

That took him a long way from his old Whig principles, Lincoln realized.

Henry Clay would never approve, and Jefferson would spin in his grave at this use of an incendiary issue to establish a strong central government—even to save the life of the Union itself. Lincoln's long political apprenticeship had been spent opposing Jacksonian high-handedness and the central-government philosophy of Andy Jackson's Democratic successors. But Alexander Hamilton, Lincoln concluded, had been right in *The Federalist* 23 to argue that the nation's war powers "ought to exist without limitation," over Jefferson's objections; and Andrew Jackson had been right to stretch the executive powers, the sainted Clay and his Whigs to the contrary notwithstanding.

Political kinship with the likes of the centralizing Hamilton and Jackson made the old-line Whig in Lincoln uncomfortable. As soon as public sentiment would permit, a constitutional amendment would be needed to build a foundation for emancipation less ephemeral than the presidential powers that disappeared with peace. It bothered Lincoln profoundly that the Democrats, in opposition, could win elections by embracing the Whig principle of defending the people from the power of their government—in plain words, from him.

Seymour would probably be telling his inaugural throng today that Lincoln was enslaving the whites to free the blacks. The President bridled at that unfair but effective catch phrase. He was not taking freedom from the whites to give freedom to the blacks; on the contrary, he was freeing the blacks to make it possible to hold the whites together. The issuance of the Proclamation later that day would give him a negotiating tool. The pace of emancipation was available for compromise, and seizure of slave owners' property could be changed to purchase at a fair price; the only thing that could not be negotiated was the dissolution of the Union.

Of course, he was using the issue of black freedom to subjugate white rebels, but there can be no freedom for any body politic without subjugation to the will of the majority; the slaves, when they became free in fact as well as in theory, would learn that. No independence would ever be possible for any nation that did not hold fast to indivisible union, just as no freedom could be maintained by any individual unwilling to put his personal sovereignty into the general pot. A government too weak to maintain its own existence would hardly be strong enough to maintain the liberties of its citizens.

When William stripped back the sheet, Lincoln washed and looked at his face in the glass. He looked awful. To cheer himself up, he told the young manservant the story of the fellow who once presented him with a fine-looking knife. The man who owned it said it had been given to him as the ugliest man in the world, and he had promised to pass it along if ever he met an uglier man, so he was giving it to Lincoln. William dutifully laughed, but then disagreed about the ugliness. In fact, Lincoln usually liked the way he looked, and took special pride in his height as well as the strength in his arms, but he had to admit that these days his face looked lined and sallow, old for a man of fifty-three.

Lincoln asked himself: If emancipation was such a cause for jubilee, and if the hunch was possessing him that it would stave off defeat and carve a niche for the Lincoln administration in the history of the republic, why was he burdened with worry and guilt about the New Year's Day ahead?

He told himself he was worried because too much rested on the Army of the Cumberland facing the onslaught of Bragg and Breckinridge in Tennessee. Why did Rosecrans not have the good sense to attack first? Why should so much depend on Breckinridge, of all rebels, a man he had failed to persuade in face-to-face argument here in this house?

He felt guilty because he had to deal with Ambrose Burnside this morning, who had turned out to be all too right in his modest assessment of himself as a commander, and had no support from his own generals in an attack he was planning. The guilt came less from seeing Burnside's insubordinate subordinates yesterday, behind the general's back, than from having to restrain the commander of the Army of the Potomac from doing what he had been sent to do in replacing McClellan. Lincoln felt ill at ease worrying about army morale and the effect of casualties, holding a general back when the man wanted to smite the enemy. In playing the cautious, wait-for-preparation role with Burnside, Lincoln saw himself acting like the general he complained of having "the slows."

He thanked William and walked down the hall to his office, where Generals Burnside and Halleck were waiting. One look at the bristling Burnside, fluffing out his muttonchop whiskers, told him nothing good was in store.

"I have attemped a movement upon the enemy," said the commander without so much as a New Year's greeting, "at your repeated urging, in which I have been repulsed."

Lincoln nodded; he needed no reminder of Fredericksburg. Burnside had at least taken full responsibility and not tried to blame him; for good and for bad, he was no McClellan.

"I am convinced that the army ought to make another move in the same direction," the general continued, "but I am not sustained in this by a single grand division commander in my command."

When Lincoln said he was aware of that, Burnside asked how he knew. Lincoln saw no harm in telling him frankly that several of his generals had come up to visit him yesterday to predict that Burnside's ideas about renewing the attack would lead to disaster.

Burnside looked stunned. "Since my subordinates now have direct access to the President," he said, "it is impossible to manage my command. I ought to retire to private life."

"Which generals were here to complain?" asked Halleck, siding with Burnside. Lincoln said he would not breach the confidence of the officers who came to him with their fears, which caused the general-in-chief to say, "They ought to be arrested and cashiered."

Lincoln waved that aside; niceties about the chain of command did not trouble him at the moment. "It is my wish that you go with General Burnside to the ground at Fredericksburg," he told Halleck. "Confer with the officers, and say that you approve or do not approve of his plan."

Halleck shook his head, no.

Lincoln realized this was not going to be easy. "Your military skill is useless to me," he pleaded, "if you will not do this."

"I request that I be relieved from further duties as general-in-chief."

The New Year was not starting well. Last week, the Cabinet resignations; now the heads of the Army. Lincoln told them abruptly he refused both their

General Ambrose E. Burnside

resignations and did not want to discuss it further, as he expected all of Washington in the White House in a few hours for the annual reception.

He could not afford another defeat and would not attack again with Burnside. He could not now depend on the Union army to give him a weapon with which to whack the rebels, nor could he depend on much of his Republican Party for political support, or the state of New York for troops or money.

Walking downstairs to find his wife, who would be distraught at this first levee since the loss of Willie, Lincoln felt a curious sense of relief mingled with satisfaction at one thing he would do this day. He would set free the rebels' slaves and invite some of them into the Union Army. That would stir the pot. The worse everything else became, the better that idea looked to him. Right made might.

If emancipation worked in bringing new hope to the North and new fear to the South, and if the military picture turned around in some way, the occasion would be remembered as historic. However it had to be wrapped in military necessity, setting four million human beings free was a noble and uplifting act. He would rather be remembered for that than for bringing on a war to avoid disunion.

If emancipation failed, however—if it unified the South and split the North —he would have no apologies for reaching beyond his powers. His countrymen would know that the sixteenth President of the United States had left no stone unturned to defeat the enemy.

CHAPTER 45

RECEIVING LINE

He crooked his arm for Mary, who was trembling, to take hold. He told Tad to stop poking Robert—their student son was down from Harvard for the holidays, and at least was trying to look dignified—and the Lincolns prepared, as a family, to enter the Blue Room for the annual reception.

He had not held so much as a ten-minute private conversation with his eldest son since coming to Washington nearly two years before. Lincoln persuaded himself that the absence of intimacy was the boy's fault, not his; Robert just never opened up to him as Willie had or Tad did. He was glad only that his son had not shown the traits of cruelty and ignorance he remembered in his own father. Robert might not warm up to his presidential father, but Lincoln was satisfied that the remote young man was at least being provided with the best education at a time when other boys his age were fighting and dying. He was determined the boy would have no cause to refuse to attend his father's funeral, as Lincoln had done so long ago.

His spirits rose as the first wave of guests pressed in. This was the diplomatic corps in full costume, medals twinkling, impressed with themselves and each other on the cold, brilliantly sunny morning. Lincoln enjoyed a good levee, just as he did his twice-weekly "public opinion baths," and thought it unfortunate that Mary's extended grief for Willie kept them from having more receptions at the Mansion.

Robert Lincoln

The New Year's greeting of Washington officialdom, however, to be followed by the open house to all the public at noon, was not an event that the first Lady, as the newspapers were calling her, could properly cancel. The house belonged to the people, and the people had a right to come in as the year began. Last night, the eve of the New Year, Mary had gone with old Isaac Newton to see a spiritualist in Georgetown, to commune with the ghost of their lost boy, and had brought back the spiritualist's prediction that the Cabinet would soon have to resign. Lincoln wished the spiritualists would stick to spirits.

He faced these hours of handshaking with equanimity; he would see faces he wanted to see, perhaps swap a few stories, pick up political gossip. The duty of receiving offered a respite from the war, from having to restrain Burnside in Virginia and to exhort Rosecrans in Tennessee—"Old Rosey," he feared, might be destined to preside over the final Union disaster in the field. Afterward, when the Pennsylvania detachment acting as provost guard shooed the last of the guests out of the Mansion, he would go upstairs and sign the controversial Proclamation. No special ceremony, no correspondents; just his necessary co-signer Seward, and whoever else was around.

The diplomatic corps was shepherded by Seward and his son into the Blue Room and formally introduced, each in turn, by Marshal Lamon. Lincoln knew his friend Hill liked the task, listening to the whispered names and booming them out, because it gave him a chance to show off his stentorian voice while enabling him to stick by the President's side as a mixture of friends and strangers moved through the house.

England's Lord Lyons, as Lincoln expected, stopped long enough to ask about the action in Tennessee, saying nothing about the effect of the proclamation of freedom on the abolition-minded British people. Lincoln did not enlighten him on the battle at Murfreesboro because he did not know the results himself, but he expressed confidence in Rosecrans and reminded the British ambassador that the rebel general, Braxton Bragg, had not done all that well hurling attackers at the Hornet's Nest at Shiloh. Lincoln was unabashed about anticipating victory; if "Old Rosey" managed to recover and at least not lose, a great victory was what Lincoln would claim. He could not do that after Antietam for fear of boosting McClellan, but he was unworried about making a hero out of Rosecrans. And his Proclamation could cause no military harm to Rosecrans in Tennessee; Lincoln had exempted the whole state from the edict. That in effect guaranteed Tennesseans that their property in slaves would remain untouched.

After the diplomats, the justices of the Supreme Court and of the Court of Claims filed in. Then the governors and military and naval officers came through the line, looking grimly optimistic. When Halleck came by, Lincoln gave him a frigid look and offered no pleasantry. Burnside did not appear.

Pumping away, drawing the person in front of him to his right to move the line along, the President met the unofficial guests invited in before the public. Elizabeth Keckley was the first of them to come through the receiving line. Mary, who had begun to sag, leaning her weight on his left arm, perked up and told the modiste that she expected to see a great many of her dresses on the ladies that day. The black hand he held far longer than a moment was strong and calloused; he liked that hand, and the woman who had been such a source of strength and comfort to his wife. He recalled how the tall colored woman had sat up with him some nights when he was afflicted with his hypo.

"We will never forget today," Mrs. Keckley said, looking at him directly, head high. "We will never forget what you have done."

He swallowed. Mary was saying something about the contraband relief association that Lizzie had formed, and it occurred to Lincoln that if more of her race had the intelligence and self-reliance of Mrs. Keckley, little need would exist for colonization. The opening of opportunity available to her had been narrow, but she had squeezed through; perhaps others of her race would as well. The sincerity of her gratitude affected him.

She introduced the man behind her as someone who was a contributor to her contrabands. Wendell Phillips was a name familiar to Lincoln. He was an early and outspoken abolitionist orator—an advocate, with editor William Lloyd Garrison, of separation from the South—and the source of the widely quoted comment that Lincoln was a "first-rate second-rate man." He bore the man no grudge for that; it was a well-turned phrase, although entirely wrong.

Phillips thanked him for the coming Proclamation, offering a half promise of political help: "If we see this administration earnestly working to free the country from slavery, we will show you how we can run it into another four years in power."

"Oh, Mr. Phillips, I have long ceased to have any personal feeling or expectation in the matter," Lincoln white-lied, "so abused and borne upon I have been."

"Nevertheless," persisted the abolitionist, "what I have said is true. We hope you will find a use for John Frémont in carrying out your proclamation in border states."

Lincoln remembered the unpleasant visit with Frémont's wife, and of the first Republican candidate's premature proclamation of freedom. "I have the greatest respect for Frémont and his abilities," he told Phillips, who struck him as a second-rate second-rate man, "but the fact is, the pioneer in any movement is generally not the best man to carry that movement to a successful termination."

Of course, that same principle could be applied to a second Lincoln term. The unofficial reception line was not yet long, so the President amused himself with a biblical simile. "It was so in old times, wasn't it? Moses began the emancipation of the Jews, but he had to make way for Joshua to complete the work. The fact is, the first reformer has to meet such a hard opposition, and gets so battered and bespattered, that afterward, when people find they have to accept the reform, they will accept it more gracefully from another man." That man, it occurred to Lincoln—the Joshua leading a reunited Union without slavery—could have been Horatio Seymour. Lincoln was glad now that the proposition of succession made through Weed had been declined, because this time Moses was going to be right there on the scene when his people entered the Promised Land.

He felt Mary grow rigid next to him, and guessed that the next person in line was either Adele Douglas or Kate Chase.

It was Kate, looking more defiantly lovely than ever on the arm of her fiancé, Governor—now Senator, once General—Sprague. She gave her usual fish-eye to Mary, which Lincoln thought was getting tiresome, and said to him, "The Proclamation is a step in the right direction, Mr. President. I hope you have retained, in the final draft, the reference to the Deity."

So Chase was spreading the word that the high-sounding words in the Proclamation were his own; soon the Treasury Secretary would be persuading everyone that he had pressed for its adoption all along. Lincoln recalled how lukewarm Chase had been in the first Cabinet discussion; no wonder, it took the wind out of his radical presidential sails. At the last minute, only yesterday, Chase had submitted an entirely new draft of the Proclamation, avoiding the statement about violence in self-defense on the grounds that it was too incendiary, and leaving out any reference to the military employment of blacks, which he had advocated for months. His new approach, Lincoln thought, would gut the message of practical, military meaning. Only Chase's nicely phrased line about the Deity would be in the document he would soon sign, and Lincoln assured his daughter it would be there.

A hundred handshakes later, Henry Raymond of the *New York Times* appeared, looking burdened with news. Lincoln always enjoyed skirmishing with him, because the editor-politician was strongly pro-Lincoln and anti-Seymour. Raymond's newspaper did not offset the damage being done to Lincoln in New York City by Bennett's *World,* nor did every word of his editorials weigh a ton, the way Greeley's did in the *Tribune,* but Raymond could be relied on. He halted the line and drew the publisher aside to hear the latest.

"I have been with the army in Virgina," Raymond reported urgently, "and Burnside's subordinates are standing in the way of a general advance, slandering their commanding general."

"I shouldn't wonder," Lincoln murmured. Slander or not, that army was not going to assault the heights above Fredericksburg again.

"Burnside has prepared an order dismissing from the service Hooker, Franklin, Baldy Smith, and six other generals." Lincoln felt his eyebrows rising; that was something that Burnside had failed to mention earlier that morning.

"Mr. President, the dismissal order is well grounded in military discipline. You have no idea of the disparaging way Hooker speaks of his commanding officer."

Lincoln put his hand on the publisher's shoulder and spoke close to his ear, returning the confidence: "That is all true—General Hooker does talk badly. But the trouble is, Hooker is stronger with the country today than any other man, including me."

The New Yorker looked aghast. "How long would Hooker retain that strength, if people knew his real character and conduct?"

"The country would not believe anything said against him," Lincoln replied. "They would say it is all a lie." Joe Hooker, the would-be dictator, the favorite of Chase, was everybody's answer to the failure of Burnside. And public sentiment could not be ignored in a military crisis.

"But when I told Burnside that Hooker might resist a dismissal order," said the journalist, "Burnside said he would 'swing him before sundown.' "

Lincoln blinked. "Burnside said that?"

"Yes. That means he'd hang Hooker for disobedience in the face of the enemy, and I believe Burn is just furious enough to do that. Beware the fury of a patient man, and all that. Do you realize all this is happening down there within a rifle shot of General Lee and his army? I admire your equanimity, Lincoln, but it really seems as if things are getting out of hand."

Raymond went his way shaking his head. He would be shaking it harder, Lincoln thought, if he knew that both Burnside and Halleck had just tried to resign, and that the government did not know what was happening to the other Union army under Rosecrans at Stones River.

Mary left his side to try to get Tad to stop playing near the huge punchbowl before the near-hysterical boy fell in. She staggered forward, swayed, and Lamon caught her before she fell. Fortunately, Elizabeth Keckley was in sight, and she came forward quickly to take Mrs. Lincoln to her room. The line moved on, the President and his son Robert greeting the guests.

"My dear lady."

Anna Ella Carroll, with her animated face and low-cut dress, pumped his hand. She was a persnickety woman, and a bother about money, but she produced better-written work than any woman he knew, and most men too, and he had to admire her for that. Her *Reply to Breckinridge* pamphlet had come just in time to counter all the talk about abuse of presidential powers, and her recent report on colonization was impressively voluminous. He complimented her on that, and added that he had signed a contract only the day before for the transport of five thousand freed slaves to Île à Vache, a dependency of Haiti.

"Will you refer to your colonization plans in your Proclamation today?"

He said no, explaining he could not very well ask negroes to join the Army and leave the country at the same time. As soon as he had decided to go all the way with the radicals, arming the freed slaves, the decision about colonization had taken care of itself. Maybe some would go, maybe not; he could not solve every problem at once.

She stood on tiptoe and beckoned for him to bend forward, which he did, glad that Mary was no longer there to glare at him for it. "I'm just back from the West," she whispered in his ear. "Grant's plan to use gunboats on the Yazoo River to take Vicksburg is a mistake. The rebels can put logs in those little streams and foil our gunboats easily. Have to take Vicksburg by land from the rear."

He nodded noncommittally; Grant would do it his own way, but if his river plan failed to break the rebel hold on the Mississippi fort, Miss Carroll's alternative would have to be explored. She had come up with some surprisingly good military ideas before, probably because of her background promoting railroads. Lamon introduced the man with her, a lanky former congressman from Texas named Lemuel Evans, hired by the War Department at Miss Carroll's suggestion to provide information about Southern plans. Her companion held her arm possessively, which she did not resist; Lincoln assumed the independent lady had found herself a man, if she wanted one.

The photographer Alexander Gardner came along, his boss Mathew Brady in tow. Lincoln was glad to see they were still together, though it was sad to see Brady's need for help in moving about. He had read somewhere that the German composer Beethoven had gone deaf late in life, and a comparison could be made to a photographer going blind. Hay had said something about Gardner and others striking out on their own, in competition with Brady; Lincoln could understand that, and would surely patronize Gardner, with whom he felt more comfortable. He hoped the parting had not been acrimonious.

The gun on the lawn boomed noon and the people who had crowded outside were allowed to pile in. The ebullience of the people on the bright, cold day and their obvious delight at being in the nation's house and shaking hands with the nation's Chief Magistrate infected Lincoln. He felt they were with him to a man—strong for Union, pleased enough at the Proclamation, optimistic about the coming year. Though his giant hand was beginning to numb, his feet did not hurt—thank you, Dr. Zacharie—and he was uplifted at the sentiments sometimes shyly expressed, sometimes boisterously voiced with a squeeze of the arm. Lincoln hoped Robert would absorb some of this strength, but he could not tell from the boy's expression whether he grasped the intensity of the moment or the meaning of the day. Robert made himself hard to know.

As the time neared for the reception to end, Lincoln extended his swollen hand to Colonel McKay, an old political ally friend from the West, whom Lincoln remembered as a good dialect storyteller. McKay said he had heard a new one, and Lincoln leaned forward to hear.

"Seems a darky preacher was trying to explain the Emancipation Proclamation to his congregation as being based on 'military necessity,' " the colonel related, "and an old patriarch with white kinky hair got up and said, 'Bredren, you jes' listen to me. Massa Linkum he eberywhar. He know eberyting. He walk de earf like de Lawd.' "

McKay waited for the laugh, but Lincoln did not crack a smile. "It is a momentous thing," he said as much to his son standing at his side as to his story-swapping friend, "to be the instrument under Providence for the liberation of a race."

CHAPTER 46

HEART IN HIS BOOTS

John Forney hurried to keep up with the President's long strides. The New Year's levee was ended. Before attending to the Proclamation, Lincoln wanted to know what was happening to the Army of the Cumberland fighting at Stones River, near Murfreesboro.

Forney followed Lincoln across the street to the War Department, with its big Maltese cross over the entrance, two objectives in mind: first, to find out what was happening to his traitor friend, John C. Breckinridge, who, he heard, was one of Bragg's commanders in the clash of armies in Tennessee. And then to get the President to undo an injustice done by General Grant.

"Why don't you get the signing out of the way first?" he asked, trotting to keep up. "All the morning papers want a copy for tomorrow's editions."

"Not because of any uncertainty on my part," Lincoln said, "but hours of handshaking is not calculated to improve a man's chirography." Forney had never heard the word "chirography" before, and assumed it meant penmanship. Why was Lincoln explaining away the shakiness of his handwriting?

In the telegraph office, Lincoln took what Forney knew to be his regular position at Major Eckert's desk, next to the window facing Pennsylvania Avenue. "This is where I wrote the Proclamation," he said, to the proud nods of the operator, Bates, and the cipher translator, Tinker.

"The South had fair warning," he told Forney sternly, "that if they did not return to their duty, I should strike at this pillar of their strength. The promise must now be kept. I shall never recall one word."

Forney—newspaperman, Senate clerk, President Buchanan's Pennsylvania crony, abolitionist for decades, and confirmed alcoholic—was not so befuddled by the four cups of wine punch served that morning as to keep him from observing how Lincoln felt the need for reassurance. Here was a man who turned back assaults on his power from the Cabinet cabal, from a near mutiny by the West Point clique in the Army, and from a majority of his party in the Senate; who was quite prepared to turn the Constitution on its head to harass his enemies; who changed his Union horse for an abolition horse in midstream rather than drown—but who was concerned about the way his signature would look on a document.

"What news from the front?" Lincoln's favorite question.

Bates shook his head. Nothing yet from Tennessee. The President tilted the chair against the wall and put his feet up on the table in the center of the room, a long reach, settling in for a wait.

"You mean we don't know anything," Forney asked, genuinely surprised at the lack of information in the nerve center of the war, "after two days' fighting?"

"As you see, the government is no better informed than you are about the results of Stones River," Lincoln replied, as if that were the normal state of affairs. The buoyant mood of the levee was gone. Now he seemed to expect bad news.

"Do you think we'll win?"

Lincoln startled him further with the lugubrious remark that "I cannot see how either of our plans, East or West, will succeed." He pulled out a map he kept in Eckert's desk and showed the plan of campaign against Richmond, which had been unsuccessful before. He pointed to Grant's position in the West, seeking to reduce Vicksburg by pushing big gunboats up small streams near the Mississippi. He said some of his trusted military advisers had told him the Yazoo approach would never work.

"If you feel so confident of disaster in these movements," Forney asked him, "why do you permit them to be made?"

"I cannot prevent it."

"You are commander in chief."

"My dear Forney, I am as powerless as any private citizen to shape the military plans of the government." Lincoln stared out the window at the throng still assembled on the White House lawn. "I have once or twice attempted to act on my own convictions and found it was impracticable to do so. I see campaigns undertaken in which I have no faith and have no power to prevent them. And I tell you that sometimes, when I reflect on the management of our forces, I am tempted to despair. My heart goes clear down into my boots."

Forney did not know what to say. Lincoln had hounded McClellan into fighting, then pulled him out of the Peninsula, then selected Burnside to march overland toward Richmond, and was now expected to replace him with Hooker. The President had involved himself more each month in every major military decision and now was claiming he had no control at all. Why? Were his top generals squabbling, or quitting, or letting him down at a time like this? If that were so, if the military situation was as bleak as the President painted it, then his Emancipation Proclamation was one enormous bluff. Forney wished he had a drink.

"Of course," Lincoln added, "we are speaking in confidence, as friends. None of this must get into print, or be repeated."

Forney nodded his assurance of secrecy. The President, in his despair, had said too much. He waited a moment, figuring how best to bring up the subject of Grant and the newsman, then jumped when he heard the telegraph machine start to clatter.

The operator said, "Rosecrans headquarters, Army of the Cumberland," and Lincoln's feet came down off the table. Forney knew it would take a few agonizing minutes to receive the message and decode it.

Forney thought of Breckinridge, and of his own prediction a year ago that his friend of such great promise would go South and never come back to the Senate. Breck had said the only reason he would cross the lines would be to retrieve his young son, who had run away to join the rebels. But Senator Breckinridge got caught up in the rhetoric of his Senate speeches, haranguing the war hawks about the protections guaranteed by the Constitution—when it was the desperate need to fight a war that had forced Lincoln to tramp all over civil liberty. Fate made the choice for Breck, Forney concluded; the big Kentuckian was doomed to follow the sound of his own voice. Now he was leading rebel troops on some cold and godforsaken battlefield, and the man whose election he had so dutifully certified was here waiting for news of the battle.

But Lincoln made his own choice. Which one made the right decision? Who had the higher cause? Lincoln did, of course, and the Union did; the loyal Forney had never any doubt of that, largely because Lincoln was so certain that democracy in the world depended on the fight here and now for majority rule, and that on occasion freedom could be freedom's worst enemy.

Then what could have attracted a good and intelligent man like Breck to fight against his country, even against most of his home state, just as Forney had gloomily foreseen? There must have been a reason. Perhaps Breck's reason had disappeared in the course of the war and left behind only the reluctance to fail one's comrades.

Into the wait for deciphering, Forney inserted his business: "Sherman arrested another correspondent, court-martialed him as a spy. Grant is going to throw him out of the war zone or put him in prison." When Lincoln said nothing, Forney added, "A committee of correspondents asked me to get you to revoke the court-martial sentence."

"I'm not on the spot to judge." Lincoln wanted no part of it. Forney did not back away; he knew that Lincoln liked most of the reporters he was acquainted with but had little respect for journalists as a class. In some ways, Breck had been right about Lincoln: with him, the Union was flesh and blood; the Constitution, shadow and spirit.

"It's Tom Know of the *New York Times.*"

That was different; Lincoln knew the man to be a responsible correspondent. The President pulled out a sheet of paper and wrote a message, showing the sheet to Forney. "I'm making this conditional on the approval of Grant," he said, "but he knows I'm interested."

Forney was satisfied; with Lincoln these days, except for his fixed idea of no secession, it was not so much the principle of the thing as it was the practical end accomplished. War had a way of knocking the corners off a man.

Bates had handed a take to Tinker for decoding, and the boy was working on it. "Just tell us," said the President.

"Rosecrans reports that General Van Cleve has turned back a vicious rebel assault on the hill he was holding." Tinker worked some more on the cipher. "Six thousand rebels under Breckinridge charged, about half were killed or wounded." The young man looked up, struck by the weight of his words; three thousand men cut down on a single charge. He continued: "Our Kentucky and Tennessee troops under Crittenden are investing the rebel positions."

"Our casualties?"

"Not as heavy as yesterday. Our artillery enfiladed the rebel charge and not many of them made it to our lines. Cannon wiped them away."

The clattering continued. Rosecrans reported his belief that Bragg's army would now withdraw, but that Federal forces were too exhausted to pursue them. Lincoln's face darkened at that.

"Any general officers lost?" Forney asked the operator.

"None of ours, sir. A rebel, Major General Cleburne, was reported killed in the charge."

"General Breckinridge—news of him?"

"It is thought that Bragg, Breckinridge, and Hardee are planning to set up a new rebel line, south, at Duck River."

"Cleburne is a big loss for them," said Forney, relieved at Breck's escape from the carnage. "They were calling him the 'Stonewall of the West.' Irishman."

"Breckinridge was a friend of yours," said the President. When Forney nodded, Lincoln said, "I was fond of John and I was sorry to see him take the course he did. I regret that he sided with the South. It was a mistake."

After a silence, Lincoln wrote a message to be transmitted to Rosecrans. "God bless you and all with you." He added: "You gave us a hard-earned victory, which, had there been a defeat instead, the nation could scarcely have lived over."

The President pulled himself up, squeezed Bates's shoulder, wished the cipher man a happy New Year, and led Forney back across the street.

CHAPTER 47

WITHOUT COMPUNCTIONS

Lincoln was pleased to see everything in readiness for the signing. All morning, through the meeting with the failing generals, through the hours of the reception, he had felt himself in the presence of an impending event of greater moment than he had at first imagined. A metallic sound seemed to be in his head, which could be the glorious striking of shackles or the terrible clash of bayonets.

Frederick Seward held a large portfolio under his arm. His father told him to spread the Proclamation sheet out on the Cabinet table for signature by the President and the Secretary of State. Stoddard, the third secretary, had already prepared a couple of copies at Lincoln's direction, one to have in the office and the other to give to the press.

With William Henry Seward at his side, and about a dozen people in the room, the President considered the document, flexing the swollen, thoroughly squeezed fingers of his right hand.

Seward examined the portion of the document that exempted specific counties of rebel states, now occupied by Union soldiers, from the decree. He remarked that the President's decision of the day before, to accept the western counties of Virginia as a separate state, meant that the slaves in that vast area would not be freed.

Lincoln nodded; he had approved the secession of part of a state from a state, which seemed to go against his principle of majority rule, but he saw a clear distinction between secession that helped keep the Union whole and secession that would break it up. His decision to go along with the dismemberment of Virginia pleased the punish-the-rebel crowd, while the loyal people in the western portion of that state were glad they could hold on to their slaves, because the emancipation decree did not run to loyal states. Something for everybody in that one.

He found himself gripped by a sense of the occasion. Lincoln had signed thousands of state documents, decrees and appointments and messages and pardons, but it struck him that not one had been nearly so far-reaching as this, despite the compromises. He picked up a pen, dipped it in the inkwell, held it a moment, tried to get his mind around the notion of four million actual people, and then removed his hand from above the document and dropped the pen on the table.

He stretched his fingers, rubbing his right hand with his left. "I never in my life felt more certain that I was doing right," he explained to the friends in the room, "than I do in signing this paper. If my name ever goes into history it will be for this act, and my whole soul is in it."

He massaged his right shoulder and upper arm. "But I have been receiving calls and shaking hands since nine o'clock this morning, and my right arm is stiff and numb, almost paralyzed. Now this signature will be closely examined, and if they find my hand trembled, they'll say, 'He hesitated, he had some compunctions.' "

What was he waiting for? Why was he making excuses for delaying the moment, he wondered. Here, with a stroke, he would set free—in theory, perhaps one day in actuality—four million human beings. But looked at another way, Lincoln knew he was also seizing more property than any despot in history, putting forward a bill of attainder that shook the foundation of common law, and perhaps inciting a wholesale massacre of innocent whites by blacks emboldened to vengeance that would make this act remembered in history as among the bloodiest and most monstrous.

Who could be sure of the consequences? He freely admitted to himself that this Proclamation abolishing the South's cherished institution was his counter-revolution taken at a time of desperation, his bomb of unknown power rolled into enemy territory. He knew it would be seen as a device to recapture the war spirit and would surely end the hopes of a negotiated peace. As the trial became ever more fiery, he was doubling the stakes with this Proclamation, lengthening the war, forcing a fight to the finish. At the time— nearly two years ago—of his decision to provision Fort Sumter, he had only a vague idea of the bloody consequences; but now, defying the Union's military weakness and proclaiming a revolution, he could see the Bloody Lanes filled with bodies stretching into infinity.

Why, then, was he not paralyzed, as he had pretended for a moment his fingers were? Why did he feel instead an unaccustomed serenity today, despite the crowding-in of disaster? The answer was on the table in front of him. He recognized that his extra-constitutional device, his seemingly empty threat of terrible vengeance, his grand subterfuge, was at the same time the greatest moral act of his life.

If human slavery was not wrong, nothing was wrong. The punishment for rebellion was the loss of slaves, and the ennoblement of the carnage would be the emergence of freedom for an entire race. If every drop of blood drawn by the lash had to be paid for by the sword, that was not the fault of the President of the United States but was the judgment of God. Lincoln knew he was risking more blood, years of conflict, permanent hatred, unimaginable divisions, and—he could not deny it—a temporary loss of personal liberty for many, to attain a fusion of great purposes: a permanent democracy in which every person would be free.

He placed his hands on either side of the document and looked it over for a last time. Its roots were not in the cool compromises of the Constitution, but in the heat and fervor of the Declaration of Independence. He was in the end at one with the revolutionaries of 1776, at odds with the compromisers of 1789. He had lived with the act of abolition, in all its permutations, for six months. He had been ready to abandon it at the first sign of some Southern submission to emancipation's threat, willing to delay the edict if the North's Peace Democrats were willing to coalesce in a compact to put first the fight against secession. The Proclamation's threat had failed; he could hope that its reality would not fail.

The key words leaped up at him: *"I do order and declare that all persons held as slaves within said designated States, and parts of States, are, and henceforward shall be free . . ."*

Not "forever free"; he had dropped the word "forever" in the final draft. That was not his phrase originally but had been in David Hunter's premature order; it was presumptuous, too—who could promise anyone freedom "forever"? Freedom would have to be reearned, perhaps fought for, down to the latest generation.

"Anyway, it is going to be done," he said to the small group around the table. He picked up the pen and dipped it into the ink again.

Slowly, he did his best to lay across the parchment a bold and clear signature, his whole first name reflecting solemnity. He looked at the freshly inked name, not completely satisfied—it seemed to quaver a little, but there were no second chances—then allowed a smile to light his face. "That will do."

UNDERBOOK
SOURCES AND COMMENTARY

Welcome to the underbook, where the author cites his sources, points out controversies that have aged and ripened for a century among historians, justifies his own judgments, and makes clear where reporting ends and imagination begins.

The primary purpose here is to separate fact from fiction. The reader of any historical novel asks, "How much of this is true?" Instead of frustrating that reader with the standard assurance—"mostly true, with a few facts rearranged for dramatic impact or clarity"—this underbook spells out the answer: Here is what we know happened or what was said, based on these firsthand sources or contemporary documents. This part is close to the way it happened, reconstructed on the basis of these specified letters or diaries. And this other part is fiction, a device that overrides the facts to keep the reader awake, or—when it works best—to get at the truth.

The Bibliography lists the sources in detail; in this underbook, the most frequently cited sources are referred to in brief, by author's last name. *CW*, the citation that most often appears, is the nine-volume *Collected Works of Abraham Lincoln*, Roy Basler, editor. *LDBD* is *Lincoln Day by Day*, the chronology published by the Lincoln Sesquicentennial Commission that seems to put the historian in Lincoln's lap on any given day, opening the door to a variety of sources that reveal the day's activity. *HayDi* is John Hay's diary—his real diary, annotated by Tyler Dennett—and should not be confused with the fictional diary in this novel. *Nicohay* is my shorthand for the nine-volume *Abraham Lincoln: A History* by Nicolay and Hay, and *Nevins* indicates *The War for the Union*, Vol. I, *The Improvised War*, and Vol. II, *War Becomes Revolution*, in the series entitled the Ordeal of the Union by Allan Nevins.

PROLOGUE (p. 15)

"When will they come?" in *Nicohay* IV, p. 152. My statement that "the capital was besieged and its connection with all the states cut off" is verbatim from an order of Stanton's cited in Randall's *Lincoln the President*, p. 157.

The opening scene with General Winfield Scott—"They are closing their coils around us"—is from a conversation between Scott and Colonel Stone, with Lincoln not present, recounted in Margaret Leech's 1941 *Reveille in Washington*, p. 65, which is also the source of Lincoln's wonderment at mistakenly thinking he heard a cannon shot.

The scene with the delegation of soldiers was originally reported in *HayDi* for April 24, 1861, but by the time Hay used his notes for his history twenty-five years later, he and Nicolay were willing to change subtly the plain statement of Lincoln. The anguished "I don't believe there is any North" in the 1861 diary was softened to "I begin to believe that there is no North" on p. 153 of *Nicohay* IV, lest readers believe the mythic Lincoln they sought to portray really had no faith in the ultimate triumph of the North.

The sergeant's words are fictional, based on the description of the Baltimore attack in Randall, *Lincoln the President*, I, p. 362. The President's rationale for going to war is based on his July 4 Message to Congress, *CW IV*, pp. 421–41.

The scene restraining General Winfield Scott from arresting the Maryland legislature is based on Lincoln's letter to Scott, *CW* IV, p. 344. The letter authorizing Scott to suspend habeas corpus was sent two days later, on April 27, 1861, *CW IV,* p. 347; Basler noted that Lincoln inserted the number of the day of the month.

The scene with Seward is fictional. Lincoln's comment seeking to justify the suspension of habeas corpus—"More rogues than honest men find shelter under it"—was in Lincoln's handwriting in the first draft of the July 4 Message to Congress, softened in later drafts. In the drafting of that document, the President's wish to distance himself from that decision is evident: he went through it all at the end, changing the active voice to passive. "I decided" became the bureaucratic "it was decided"; "In my opinion I violated no law" was changed to "It was not believed that any law was violated." *CW IV,* p. 430n.

As the war went on, Lincoln grew more easy with the use of dictatorial power. As we shall see, he later ordered the arrest of the Maryland legislature, and later used the first person freely in defending his suspension of the privilege of the writ of habeas corpus.

The central question of whether the principles of freedom prevent a free government from defending itself effectively and when that necessity is exaggerated and the power to suspend freedom is abused is addressed on pp. 58–67 of Arthur Schlesinger, Jr.'s 1973 *The Imperial Presidency.* Don E. Fehrenbacher, in the chapter on "The Paradoxes of Freedom" in his 1987 *Lincoln in Text and Context,* concludes that Lincoln "brushed aside too lightly the problem of the example he might be setting for future Presidents." He adds, however, that "in every civil war a certain amount of repression may be one of the unavoidable costs of victory." My position tilts away from the historians' traditional tolerance for Lincoln's excesses, but this observation of Fehrenbacher's illuminates the Lincoln dichotomy: "The transcendent humaneness of the man lent the Civil War much of its luster, but it was his inveterate toughness that helped determine the outcome."

BOOK ONE, CHAPTER 1: JUDICIAL DEFIANCE (p. 3)

"The name of Taney," said Senator Charles Sumner, opposing funds for a bust of the dead jurist, "is to be hooted down the pages of history." The radicals despised the Chief Justice primarily because of his 1857 decision in *Dred Scott v. Sandford* which held that a Negro, even if free, could not be a citizen of the United States and "had no rights which the white man was bound to respect." In that decision, often cited as the most profoundly wrongheaded in Supreme Court history, the Taney Court struck down the Missouri Compromise, which barred slavery from territories above an agreed-upon line.

Taney's defenders claim he was right on the law, that the Constitution recognized slavery—and that while individual states could abolish slavery within their borders, the Congress could not extend that prohibition westward into the territories, or permit one state to take away the property of a citizen of another state. However, few will deny that the political and social effect of the decision was catastrophic, enraging public opinion in the North, helping abolitionists recruit support, which in turn infuriated slaveholders and contributed to the tensions that led to the war.

Taney's narrow reading of the Constitution, and his refusal to consider the consequences of his Dred Scott decision, weakened the Court four years later, just when its influence in protecting civil liberty was most needed. Taney was abused as a meddlesome old man who cared for the letter and not the spirit of laws, and this reputation as a moral neuter made unequal his contest with Lincoln over civil liberty.

The physical setting of the scene in the courtroom in Baltimore, along with Taney's assumption that he would be arrested, are on pp. 451–54 of Walker Lewis's biography of Taney, *Without Fear or Favor*. The words of the marshal, clerk, and lawyer for Merryman, as well as the selections from Taney's opinion, are in Edward McPherson's *The Political History of the United States During the Great Rebellion*, pp. 155–56, and *Ex Parte Merryman*, 17 Federal Cases #9487 (1861), pp. 144–49.

The best source for the reasons behind the Lincoln-Taney clash is Robert M. Spector's *Lincoln and Taney: A Study in Constitutional Polarization*, in the July 1971 issue of the *American Journal of Legal History*, Vol. XV, pp. 199–214. "After all," Spector writes, "there was nothing in the Constitution that denied a state the right to depart. Putting it in twentieth-century terms, most Americans would be more than disturbed to discover that by joining the United Nations, the United States lost its right to withdraw if it so desired." Spector also cites on p. 211 Taney's view of "the evil of slavery . . . a blot on our national character" from his defense of an abolitionist.

Style-minded readers will note that the word "Negro" is capitalized in the underbook, reflecting today's style, and uncapitalized in the novel, to conform with nineteenth-century usage.

The presence of John Breckinridge and Anna Carroll in the courtroom is fictional.

BOOK ONE, CHAPTER 2: PRESERVED FOR THIS OCCASION (p. 8)

A description of Taney's appearance in the Baltimore court on May 28, 1861, is in Dean Sprague's *Freedom Under Lincoln*, pp. 41–42. Mayor George Brown (not Breckinridge, who is in the scene for fictional purposes) approached Taney after the decision was read; in a memoir by Brown, *Baltimore and the 19th of April*, Taney was quoted as saying he was preserved for this occasion.

Taney's views on "peaceful separation" were set forth in a letter from him to former President Franklin Pierce on June 12, 1861, quoted in David M. Silver's *Lincoln's Supreme Court*, p. 33.

Taney did not cite Lord Coke; that is taken from a speech praising Taney's courage by Professor William Mikell of the University of Pennsylvania Law School, referred to by Walker Lewis in *Without Fear or Favor*, p. 455.

The running Carroll-Breckinridge conversation is fictional. Anna Carroll's concern about traveling in Maryland at the time, as well as her fervor for the Union cause in Maryland, was expressed in a note from her to Chase on April 27, 1861, on Ebbitt House stationery, now in the Chase manuscripts in the Library of Congress: "My dear Gov: It seems I cannot get to Frederick except in a way to incur danger, so I am flooding the legislators—Heaven defend us from such—with letters."

BOOK ONE, CHAPTER 3: THE PLUG-UGLIES (p. 13)

"The Hon. John C. Breckinridge was a warm personal friend," wrote Anna Ella Carroll in 1891, at the age of seventy-six. "I saw much of him during his term as Vice President and felt an unaccountable interest in him . . ."

There is no evidence that this "unaccountable interest" amounted to a love affair. That is fiction, as is the encounter with the plug-uglies. Miss Carroll did, however, expect Senator Breckinridge to remain loyal to the Union: "I was present when he took the oath of office . . . Mr. Breckinridge looked up at me and saw me when he was sworn in, and I smiled approval of the act, which I then thought equivalent to an open declaration for the Union." (*Life and Writings of Anna Ella Carroll,* 1895, Vol. II, p. 17). Nor was this the fond afterthought of an old lady: "I have in the spirit of friendship," she wrote in August of 1861, "repeatedly repelled by my pen the charge of disunion heretofore made against him." They were close; she was furious at his continued espousal of the right of states to withdraw peacefully, and apparently at her inability to dissuade him.

Her opinion of the Taney decision in the Merryman case in this chapter is based on her pamphlet *A Reply to Breckinridge,* same source, p. 36: "Judge Taney . . . was as guilty as any private person who should have attempted to free [Merryman] by force . . . His extreme age and his known and cherished sympathies with the secession heresy (of which the Dred Scott decision furnished mournful evidence) prepared the public mind for that given in the present case." She cited a letter by Thomas Jefferson to J. B. Colvin in December 1810 to justify the Lincoln reach on habeas corpus: "To lose our country by a scrupulous adherence to written law would be to lose the law itself, with life, liberty, property . . . thus absurdly sacrificing the end to the means."

Who was right in the Merryman case, Lincoln or Taney? A Latin maxim says: *Silent enim leges inter arma,* "The law falls silent in the midst of arms." That, in my view, absurdly sacrifices the means to the end. In 1866, in *Ex Parte Milligan,* the Supreme Court, although dominated by Lincoln's appointments, decided that the federal government acted unlawfully in establishing military tribunals to try civilians in areas where civil courts were open. The principle in *Milligan* applied to *Merryman:* Taney's opinion was swiftly and decisively upheld, and Lincoln's action remains condemned to this day.

The best short assessment of Lincoln's decision to put national security ahead of guarantees of individual liberty is in Randall and Donald's *The Divided Union,* Chapter 16, pp. 293–309. They held that "In the treatment of 'disloyal' practices the government under Lincoln carried its authority far beyond the normal restraints of civil justice," but conclude that "Lincoln's practice fell short of dictatorship as the word is understood in the twentieth century." Most Civil War historians, notably Harold Hyman in *A More Perfect Union,* agree with this pragmatic view. "The continuing great debate on arbitrary arrests," writes Hyman, "should not obscure the fact that the President never suffered repudiation on Capitol Hill, at the polls, or in the nation's highest courts." This was because "in 1861 the treason and related criminal clauses of the 1787 Constitution did not serve the nation's needs as a deterrent against or a punishment for disloyalty or treason. As the sole weapon against disloyalty, the treason clause left authorities too lightly armed for effective home-front combat."

But disloyalty was not then (and is not now) a crime, for the excellent reason that one man's dissent and free expression is a government official's "disloyalty." In wartime especially, while civil courts sit the Chief Executive must restrain himself from using patriotic fervor and popular approval against people protected in their persnickety disagreement by the Constitution. Lincoln, though sorely tried and much provoked, and with no desire for the personal trappings of dictatorship, failed in this test and has been getting away with it for over a century. I think Taney was as right on *Merryman* as he was wrong on *Dred Scott;* Lincoln was as wrong on his conception of his power to crack down on dissent as he was right on his extralegal vision of the indissolubility of the Union.

Did Lincoln really consider arresting the Chief Justice? Hyman footnotes on p. 84:

"Francis Lieber noted that Lincoln contemplated Taney's arrest, and issued Ward Hill Lamon, marshal for the District of Columbia, permission to arrest him . . . If it was ever intended or considered, Lincoln did not allow the arrest to occur."

BOOK ONE, CHAPTER 4
JOHN HAY'S DIARY, JUNE 29, 1861 (p. 26)

"John Hay's Diary," which appears throughout this book, is a fictional device to show what is happening around Lincoln in the White House. It draws occasionally on Hay's real diary, which was published privately in 1908, and republished in 1939 with the blanks filled in by Tyler Dennett as *Lincoln and the Civil War in the Diaries and Letters of John Hay.*

In this fictional entry, the newspaper quotations are to be found in David Silver's *Lincoln's Supreme Court,* p. 22. The Lincoln quotations, "some of our Northerners seem bewildered" and "the central idea pervading this struggle," are in Hay's real diary of May 7, 1861 (Dennett, p. 19).

The young man's real diary is illuminating and infuriating. The insider's data, complete with direct quotes of Lincoln's comments, are invaluable; the disappointment is in Hay's failure to keep the diary regularly. No entries exist between May 12 and August 22, 1861; in this fictional entry for the end of June, the item about the visit to Lee's home in Arlington is from *Lincoln Day by Day* of May 31, based on a note from Nicolay to Attorney General Bates to obtain a pass to cross Long Bridge into Virginia.

The Cabinet meeting of June 29, rejecting Scott's warnings and planning what was to be the first battle of Bull Run, is recorded briefly in Nicolay and Hay's *Abraham Lincoln: A History* (from now on: *Nicohay*), Vol. IV, p. 360. Not one of the Cabinet diarists was doing history's job at the time: Bates and Hay were sporadic diarists in this early period, while Welles and Chase did not begin their diaries until late 1861. *Nicohay* says that "the President and the Cabinet, as political experts, intervened" to overrule Scott and support McDowell.

The gossip about "Miss Carroll of Baltimore" and Lord Lyons's valet and Mrs. Emory's maid is recounted in Hay's real diary of August 7, 1863. Hay quotes a once-removed source as saying, "Have you heard the dreadful story about Miss Carroll of Baltimore? Raped by a negro! What are we coming to?" and his informant, naval officer Henry Wise, snickering, "How did she appear to like it?" It is included here to show that "Miss Carroll of Baltimore" (presumably Anna Carroll, always identified with Maryland, but not definitely here), was the subject of gossip, and to offer a glimpse of the young Hay's flip attitude toward women.

BOOK ONE, CHAPTER 5: FAMILY MAN (p. 29)

This is a fictional scene, with no specific basis for dialogue, except Breckinridge's "Men are sometimes placed in a position where they are reluctant to act and expose themselves to censure they do not merit," quoted on p. 31 of William Davis's *The Deep Waters of the Proud.* That historian recounts the Davis-Douglas-Breckinridge dealings on pp. 28–32.

In Jefferson Davis's memoirs, *The Rise and Fall of the Confederate Government,* Vol. I, p. 52, the Confederate leader describes his meeting with Stephen Douglas, in which he told the Illinois Democrat that Breckinridge "authorized me to say he was willing to withdraw" in favor of a compromise. Douglas, wrote Jefferson Davis, "replied that the scheme proposed was impracticable, because his friends, mainly Northern Democrats, if he were withdrawn, would join in the support of Mr. Lincoln . . ."

Since it is certain that Davis made the proposal of mutual withdrawal to Douglas, the question is: was it a sincere attempt by Davis to unify the Democrats, or was it a stratagem to split the Democratic Party and ensure the election of the man who would trigger the secession of Southern states? To Davis, in his recollection, it was sincere; to Blair, at the time, it must surely have seemed a trick; to Breckinridge, it must have been an unanswerable question.

Whatever the motive, the confluence of circumstances that led to Lincoln's election surely fit in with Davis's hopes. Alexander H. Stephens, just before assuming the vice presidency of the Confederacy, told Lincoln that Southerners did not fear his general opinions about slavery any more than they had feared those of Washington or Jefferson; however, Southerners refused to allow their institution to come "under the ban of public opinion and public condemnation," which the election of Lincoln emphatically did. Said Stephens: "This . . . is quite enough of itself to arouse a spirit [not only] of general indignation, but of revolt on the part of the proscribed" (William Baringer, *A House Dividing: Lincoln as President*, p. 212).

Thus, Davis's maneuvering to announce the nomination of Breckinridge not only led to the election of Lincoln, but set off the chain of events that culminated in the secession of the South; Lincoln's insistence on no secession without war, vigorously supported by the Blairs, meant that war would follow. Had Breckinridge not run, would his pro-Union Southern votes have gone to Douglas, enabling him to be President? Or to Lincoln, giving him a majority mandate? Or to yet another candidate, John Bell? My opinion: without the moderate Breckinridge in the race, enough of his support would have gone to the other Democrat; Douglas would have won and the war would have been postponed or averted, with slavery continued. Davis knew what he was doing in making sure Breckinridge was on the ballot.

The warm relationship between Breckinridge and the Blair family is shown in William Ernest Smith's *The Francis Preston Blair Family in Politics;* on p. 273 of Vol. II, when forces under Breckinridge and General Jubal Early occupied the Blair estate at Silver Spring late in the war, the house was spared destruction. According to the elder Blair, General Breckinridge told a servant: "This is the only place I felt at home on this side of the Alleghenies."

Breckinridge and F. P. Blair's son Frank were classmates at the College of New Jersey. William Davis's biography of Breckinridge, p. 62, quotes correspondence from the elder Blair to the Kentuckian in 1852 suggesting ways to make himself more popular; on p. 63, Breckinridge's association with Stephen Douglas is cited. Lizzie's affection for her cousin John is mentioned in Elbert Smith's *Francis Preston Blair*, p. 224.

In the same book, Smith cites on p. 271 the elder Blair's advice to Lincoln to "resist the South Carolina movement . . . by exhibition of the superior power of the North." In the Fort Sumter crisis, writes Smith, Lincoln's "only official advice to hold the fort came from Montgomery Blair." In W. A. Swanberg's *First Blood,* the appointment of Montgomery Blair to the Military Academy at West Point by Andrew Jackson is cited, and the historian suggests the younger Blair remembered the declaration of President Jackson during the South Carolina nullification crisis: "The Union must and shall be preserved," a thesis that had no special constitutional sanction.

Navy Secretary Gideon Welles recorded in his diary that unofficial Blair advice, from the old man, was crucial in helping Lincoln decide to "hold, occupy and possess" the federal property, contrary to the advice of Seward. When the elder Blair, "in his zeal, warned the President that the abandonment of Sumter would be justly considered . . . as treason to the country," wrote Welles, "he touched a chord that responded to his invocation."

BOOK ONE, CHAPTER 6: I RISE IN OPPOSITION (p. 35)

No evidence has ever come to light that John C. Breckinridge was other than a faithful husband; although he knew Anna Carroll and Rose Greenhow, and was described as a favorite of Lizzie Blair, the romantic involvements here are fiction. He did have a reputation for hard drinking.

"Nothing I utter here will have the slightest effect" was from his speech to the Senate of July 16, 1861, titled "On Executive Usurpation."

Breckinridge's friendship with John Forney is recounted in *Anecdotes of Public Men* by Forney, Vol. I, p. 41: "I have always believed that he espoused the Confederacy, if not reluctantly, at least in the conviction that it would forever end his political career . . . He used to relate how Sam Houston, for whom he had great respect, would expatiate upon the dangers and evils of slavery; and it was not difficult to trace the operation of the same idea in his own mind."

The speech of July 16, "I rise in opposition," is summarized and quoted in Davis's *Breckinridge,* pp. 269–71; Davis reports that "as for the Administration, in a perfect example of those violations of freedom that Breckinridge had attacked, it would not allow the Associated Press to telegraph his speech over the wires."

BOOK ONE, CHAPTER 7: SUNDAY IS NOT THE BEST TIME (p. 40)

Rose O'Neal Greenhow's warning to Breckinridge is recounted by her in *My Imprisonment, and the First Year of Abolition Rule in Washington,* the memoirs published in London in 1863, p. 42. The arrest of the Kentucky senator may or may not have been planned in the event of a speech that could be characterized as treasonable, but it is a fact that Breckinridge was removed from Henry Wilson's Military Committee in July.

Mrs. Greenhow's story of her life and times should be read in conjunction with Allan Pinkerton's *The Spy of the Rebellion,* pp. 250–70; Pinkerton's account of this "Southern woman of pronounced rebel proclivities" strongly differs, but is equally florid and self-serving.

The history of Mrs. Greenhow's remarkably successful espionage operation is told more reliably in James Horan's *Desperate Women,* pp. 3–55, and the same author's *The Pinkertons,* pp. 81–97. The most complete account of Mrs. Greenhow's life is Ishbel Ross's *Rebel Rose.*

Henry Wilson's concern about fighting on the Sabbath, and his presence on the Bull Run field as a spectator that day are cited on p. 308 of an adulatory 1876 biography by Nason and Russell.

Was Senator Wilson the source of the information Mrs. Greenhow sent to General Beauregard, and which is widely regarded as having had at least some influence on the outcome of the battle? Mrs. Greenhow dropped hints that he was, both in her memoirs and her correspondence, and there is no doubt that he was a frequent visitor to her home, which was surely a great indiscretion: the head of the Military Committee had no business to be consorting often with a known Southern sympathizer.

However, it could be that the spy was irritated with Wilson for not helping her enough in her imprisonment, and sought to cast suspicion on him in revenge. Ishbel

Ross writes on p. 99 of her Greenhow biography that "seized Confederate papers point more convincingly to young John F. Callan, a clerk of the Senate Military Committee whom no one had suspected of complicity. [Mrs. Greenhow] was gratified when she heard that Wilson was questioned by his political peers after the battle . . ."

BOOK ONE, CHAPTER 8: FAMILY COUNCIL OF WAR (p. 43)

This is a fictional account of a probable family gathering at Silver Spring. Background on Lizzie Blair's marriage, and the clannishness of the political family, is from Elbert Smith's *Francis Preston Blair*, Chapter 13, "The Clan." The family relationship with Breckinridge is mentioned on p. 224, as is the personal alliance with Senator Charles Sumner, the abolitionist.

The elder Blair's "men who have the destiny of great nations in their hands" is from a letter he wrote to Lincoln just before his Inaugural. He may have been consulted on the address, although Seward's contributions in its drafting were more significant than Blair's.

Montgomery Blair's belief that the majority of Southerners were pro-Union but "overawed by armed marauders" who claimed to represent a confederacy was expressed by him in a letter to Governor Andrew of Massachusetts on May 11, 1861, cited in Allan Nevins's *The Improvised War*, p. 150. This misreading of the Southern mind underlay his strategy of fighting early battles to gain a quick victory and induce Unionist Southerners to forsake secession. After the setback to this approach at First Manassas, General Scott's quite different anaconda strategy, to seek to surround and blockade the Confederacy, prevailed for a time.

BOOK ONE, CHAPTER 9
JOHN HAY'S DIARY, JULY 18, 1861 (p. 50)

No record of a Lincoln-Breckinridge conversation exists. However, the Kentuckian was a visitor to the White House on several occasions when his "Cousin Lizzie" Grimsley was the Lincolns' houseguest, and it would be unlikely for Mr. Lincoln not to take the opportunity to lobby the most important senator of a pivotal state under such circumstances. Certainly Breckinridge, on those visits, would be likely to seek out the President to press his own views, and Lincoln was accessible.

The stories about Ben Wade are cited in Burton Hendrick's *Lincoln's War Cabinet*, pp. 271–72.

Breckinridge's comments to Lincoln are fictional, based on his speeches in the Senate. Lincoln's words, almost verbatim, are taken from his July 4, 1861, message to the Congress. This message, *CW* IV, pp. 421–41, was written with some assistance from Seward, who probably caused the draft to be changed into the third person. I use the first person here.

The $166 chandelier bill is cited in *LDBD* for July 19, 1861.

The interchange between Breckinridge, Mrs. Lincoln, and Mrs. Grimsley about staying in the White House under the Confederacy is taken from Elizabeth Todd Grimsley's "Six Months in the White House," *Journal of the Illinois Historical Society*, XIX, April 1926.

On p. 57, she reports that a sister of Mrs. Lincoln from Alabama visited the White House, received a pass through the lines from the President, and betrayed that trust when she "went through the lines, carrying her weight, almost, in quinine, a veritable

SOURCES AND COMMENTARY

bonanza to the Southern Army" and then told "with great vim the story of her outwitting her too credulous 'brother Lincoln.' "

The paragraph from the Grimsley memoir that establishes the presence of an outspoken Breckinridge more than once in the Mansion is: "My relative on the other side of the house, General John C. Breckinridge, was open and aboveboard. He called a number of times, before leaving Washington, and most complacently said to me, 'Cousin Lizzie, I would not like you to be disappointed in your expected stay at the White House, so I will now invite you to remain here as a guest, when the Confederation takes possession.' Mrs. Lincoln replied, 'We will be only too happy to entertain her until that time, General,' whereupon arose a seemingly merry war of words, but there was a perceptible undercurrent of storm and sting, as would naturally be the case, when two bright, quick, embittered brains and tongues wage a contest."

Mrs. Grimsley's memory is fallible—Breckinridge was not yet a general during the period of those visits, and Mrs. Lincoln could not have referred to him as such—but the Grimsley account is eyewitness history and must be given weight.

BOOK ONE, CHAPTER 10: PICTURE OF WAR (p. 55)

Brady covered the first battle of Bull Run. Roy Meredith's 1976 book, *The World of Mathew Brady*, p. 7, has an account of that day given by Brady to New York *World* reporter George Alfred Townsend in 1891. "My wife and my most conservative friends had looked unfavorably upon this departure from commercial business to pictorial war correspondence with much misgiving," Brady said, "but, like Euphorion, a spirit in my feet said 'Go' and I went." In *Mr. Lincoln's Camera Man,* written thirty years earlier, Meredith details the Bull Run episode on pp. 1–14. The photographer was accompanied by the artist Alfred Waud and several other friends. The conversations in the studio and along the way are fictional.

Brady was probably also accompanied by Timothy O'Sullivan, according to a more thorough and critical biographer, James Horan, in the 1955 *Mathew Brady: Historian with a Camera,* and the 1966 *Timothy O'Sullivan: America's Forgotten Photographer.* On p. 34 of the O'Sullivan book, Horan quotes from an 1869 *Harper's New Monthly* article by John Sampson about O'Sullivan: "The battle of Bull Run would have been photographed 'close up' but for the fact that a shell from one of the rebel fieldpieces took away the photographer's [O'Sullivan's] camera . . ." Horan's books have descriptions of the colloidal process of preparing plates.

William Howard Russell of the *London Times* was the object of much American criticism for his reporting of First Manassas, but his critics were mainly Union partisans angry at his merciless account of the rout. He was derided afterward as "Bull Run Russell," the Englishman who saw none of the actual fighting and who skedaddled at the first serious firing. However, his account of the battle in *My Diary North and South* is more lucid and exciting than most, and it was his disinterestness that stirred the derision. His description of his own withdrawal walked on eggs: "There was nothing left for it but to go with the current one could not stem. I turned round my horse from the deserted guns, and endeavoured to find out what had occurred as I rode quietly back on the skirts of the crowd" (p. 226). The dialogue with him is based on his diary.

The account of the Pennsylvania ninety-day men going home is given by Russell, p. 219. The action of Colonel Burnside that day, as well as the presence of Senators Henry Wilson and Ben Wade on the field, is given in William Davis's *Battle at Bull*

Run, the 1977 book on that first major engagement of the war. The presence of Breckinridge is fictional; I do not know whether he went to Virginia that day.

Controversy: how did Colonel Thomas Jackson get his sobriquet, "Stonewall"? The conflicting testimony is given by Douglas Southall Freeman in *Lee's Lieutenants,* and in greater detail in Harry Hansen's *The Civil War,* pp. 76–77, and in the Davis book on Bull Run, p. 196. Confederate Brigadier General Bernard Bee was reported by several firsthand sources as saying, "There stands Jackson like a stone wall," adding, "Rally round the Virginians!"; that would indicate Jackson's stand as heroic. Bee's brother-in-law, who was with him when he fell, reported that Bee was furious with Jackson for failing to move out of his position to come and support his men. Whatever Bee meant by his "stone wall" simile, the phrase was taken as a compliment and applied with affection by the Confederate Army.

How important was Rose Greenhow's information to the South's victory? Certainly the movement of General Joseph Johnston's force from Winchester to Bull Run via the Manassas Gap railroad was essential to the Confederate cause, and Mrs. Greenhow gave General Beauregard the intelligence that caused him to ask for the Johnston force quickly. Senator Wade's committee later blamed the Union defeat on the failure of the Federal commander facing Johnston to hold him at Winchester; that was true enough, but more basic causes of the defeat were the Confederate knowledge of the Union plans and the inclination of McDowell's untrained men, devoid of military discipline and unfamiliar with the sound and smell of gunfire, to walk off the field when the serious fighting began and to panic when the pursuit closed in.

According to Mrs. Greenhow's memoirs, Jefferson Davis later told her, "Without you, there would have been no Bull Run"; that was a self-serving recollection, but Davis never denied it.

The Brady Studio photographs of the scenes specified here are all in the Library of Congress collection. With his eyesight failing, Brady probably did not personally take the pictures, but without his enterprise no pictures would have been taken. The paragraph about picking up the Confederate wounded soldier on the way back is fictional. Upon his return to the gallery, Brady—aware of the historic moment—posed for a self-portrait in his white linen jacket and marked the plate with the date.

BOOK ONE, CHAPTER 11: THE WAKE OF BULL RUN (p. 66)

A good description of the return of the defeated Union Army to Washington is provided by Margaret Leech in *Reveille in Washington,* pp. 102–5.

The party at the Blairs' is fictional. Thurlow Weed's encounter with Ambrose Burnside at Willard's Hotel is recounted on p. 344 of Vol. II of Weed's memoirs. Edwin Stanton's comments after Bull Run were in a letter to his brother-in-law cited on p. 125 of Thomas and Hyman's *Stanton.* McDowell's message, from a captain of engineers saying "the day is lost," and Seward's informing Lincoln of the surprise bad news are in Vol. IV, p. 353, of *Nicolay.*

Brady's carrying wounded men back is fictional.

BOOK ONE, CHAPTER 12: WHAT DRIVES THE MAN? (p. 70)

Both Rose O'Neal Greenhow and John Cabell Breckinridge were reported to have visited the Confederate prisoners at Old Capitol Prison on the night of first Bull Run. Though they were friends and in all likelihood spoke that night, the conversation in this scene is fictional.

No evidence shows an attempt by Mrs. Greenhow to recruit Anna Carroll as a spy. Miss Carroll's reading of a tract by the Reverend Robert J. Breckinridge refers to a pamphlet, *Discourse of Dr. R. J. Breckinridge Delivered on the Day of National Humiliation, January 4, 1861, at Lexington, Ky.*, condemning secession. Both Carroll and Breckinridge were probably familiar with it, and in all likelihood Miss Carroll drew on some of its arguments in her pamphlet *A Reply to Breckinridge*.

In 1984, C. Vann Woodward and Elisabeth Muhlenfeld edited and annotated *The Private Mary Chesnut*, the unpublished Civil War diaries of an active and opinionated Southern lady who traveled in the highest Confederate circles. In later life, Mary Boykin Chesnut rewrote this diary for publication, but the private diaries not meant by her for publication were the source of "Breckinridge, Clay, and Preston have escaped from the Lincolnites—into the part of Kentucky which is true to the South. Breckinridge is too late—how much might he have done by an earlier and bolder stand" (p. 169, entry for October 3, 1861). That probably represents the view of the leaders of South Carolina at the time; Breckinridge was seen as vacillating rather than fighting for peaceful separation in the U.S. Senate. Both Mrs. Greenhow and Breckinridge appear frequently in her works, usually as personal friends and in an admiring light.

BOOK ONE, CHAPTER 13: OLD FUSS AND FEATHERS (p. 74)

Lieutenant General Winfield Scott is characterized in *Webster's American Biographies* as "the foremost U.S. military figure between the Revolution and the Civil War." Although he counseled against fighting to maintain the Union, he was right on most of his military advice: (1) it was a mistake to send an unprepared army into battle, (2) it was vital for Patterson to keep Johnston engaged at Winchester, and (3) no victory over the South could be won without a total war against the Confederacy's economy, which meant effective blockade of the Eastern ports and control of the Mississippi and the West.

Scott's understanding of the need to keep the Confederate forces from combining was shown in telegrams to Patterson admonishing him two days before the battle, "Do not let the enemy amuse and delay you with a small force in front, whilst he reinforces the [Manassas] Junction with his main body," which is precisely what Johnston was able to do. Again, as the battle began, Scott wired: "Has he not stolen a march and sent reinforcements towards Manassas Junction?" *(Nicohay* IV, p. 344). (The phrase "to steal a march," meaning "to begin unexpectedly," evidently is rooted in this military use.)

General Patterson then became the scapegoat for McDowell's defeat. The elderly Patterson was surely remiss, and by engaging promptly could have averted disaster, but the Bull Run setback would not have taken place if Union troops did there what they were trained to do later in the war: close ranks in retreat rather than break and run. The primary cause of the defeat was lack of discipline that came from throwing untrained civilians-in-uniform into battle.

Bull Run, a stream near Manassas Junction, was the name most Northerners gave the engagement; Southerners generally called it Manassas, though there was frequent overlap. This pattern was discernible throughout the war, as Northerners preferred the names of distinguishing landmarks, Southerners the names of the towns. Thus, Billy Yank would talk of Bull Run (stream), Shiloh (the church on the battlefield),

Antietam (another stream), and Stones River, while Johnny Reb would call the same battles Manassas, Pittsburg Landing, Sharpsburg, and Murfreesboro.

Lincoln did meet with his Cabinet in General Scott's office on that Sunday night, July 21, 1861. The words quoted as spoken by Lincoln—"it seems we were in possession of the field"—are based on Senator Orville Browning's diary (p. 485) account of what Lincoln told him about the battle the next afternoon. The telegrams from the field are quoted in *Nicohay* IV, p. 354.

General Scott's thoughts throughout the scene are fictional, as are the early quotations from Blair and Seward. The quotations of Scott calling himself a coward for not standing up to the politicians before the battle and Lincoln's "you seem to imply that I forced you to fight this battle" were recounted by Illinois representative William Richardson, who attended a meeting in the White House a few days after the battle at which that exchange occurred *(Nicohay* IV, pp. 358–59). Richardson's speeches in the House, reported in the *Congressional Globe,* are also the source of the reference to a Douglas Democrat vs. Breckinridge Democrat resentment.

The conversation between Lincoln and Scott is fictional, based loosely on their known positions. Lincoln's condemnation of Cameron as "utterly ignorant" and his characterization of Chase as "despairing" can be found in notes taken by John George Nicolay during or just after a meeting with Lincoln on October 2, 1861, reported on pp. 178–79 of Helen Nicolay's *Personal Traits of Abraham Lincoln.* That is also the source (p. 174) of the Lincoln quote, "sinners were calling the righteous to repentance."

The penciled memo of what to do after Bull Run is given by *Nicohay* IV, pp. 368–69, and is also in *CW* IV, p. 462. His secretaries report that the President rewrote his penciled notes in two stages: the first part rewritten July 23, a second part July 27. They suggest he did it alone, as he "lay awake on a sofa in the executive office" on the night after the battle, adding to it bit by bit. However, logic suggests that he would have discussed these plans with Scott, especially since the first point—"Let the plan for making the blockade effective be pushed forward"—was central to the anaconda plan, and the final point urging Frémont into action down the Mississippi was also part of Scott's strategy. It is my speculation that Lincoln's belated adoption of his general-in-chief's approach fitted in with Scott's willingness to bring in McClellan, who was soon to replace him.

Book One, Chapter 14
JOHN HAY'S DIARY, JULY 21 AND 22, 1861 (p. 82)

How did Lincoln react to his first military defeat and the sudden realization that he was faced with a long war? His secretaries go to some length to make him appear the soul of serenity. "In this first shadow of defeat," they wrote, p. 367, "President Lincoln maintained his wonted equipoise of manner and speech. A calm and resolute patience was his most constant mood . . ."

I wonder. None of the Cabinet diarists were as yet working on their journals—Bates, Welles, and Chase began theirs later, and even Hay was taking a hiatus—but Senator Zachariah Chandler, who came back from the battlefield to see Lincoln, must have given his friends a different picture. "He drove at once to the White House," write his 1879 biographers at the *Detroit Post and Tribune,* "where he found Mr. Lincoln despondent, exhausted with his labors, and greatly depressed by the defeat and the loss of life involved" (p. 211). Homer Bates in *Lincoln in the Telegraph Office,*

p. 88, reported, "Lincoln hardly left his seat in our office and waited with deep anxiety for each succeeding dispatch." He "lay awake on a sofa in the executive office" all night, according to his secretaries (p. 368), which is hardly evidence of equipoise. It seems more in character for him at this stage of his presidency to be, as Chandler's biographers characterized Lincoln, "despondent . . . depressed . . . anxious" and considerably agitated at the prospect of losing the capital and being interned.

The description of Chandler's visit on the night of First Bull Run is from his biography, which puts in quotations that he asked Lincoln to issue an order for the enrolling of a half million men "to show the country and the rebels that the government was not discouraged a whit, but was just beginning to get mad." The *Washington Intelligencer* of July 22 credited Chandler and Wade, along with Representatives Blake, Riddle, and Morris, with stopping the rout: "Some of the fugitives who were armed menaced these gentlemen. None, however, were permitted to pass until the arrival of the 2nd New Jersey Regiment, on its way to the battleground . . ." In A. G. Riddle's 1888 biography of Wade, a long footnote on p. 294 describes the episode, concluding: "Wade's exploit, so in character—seven citizens stopping a runaway army—was much talked of."

Lincoln's "I must have somebody," which was either the source or the result of the adage "You can't beat somebody with nobody," has been frequently cited. It can be found in Helen Nicolay's *Personal Traits of Abraham Lincoln,* p. 255, in a discussion between Wade and Lincoln about the replacement, not the installation, of McClellan, as used in this chapter.

The decision of Mrs. Lincoln to set aside General Scott's advice and remain with her husband after Bull Run was described on p. 179 of Katherine Helm's 1928 book, *The True Story of Mary, Wife of Lincoln,* based on the wartime diary and letters by Mrs. Lincoln's sister Emilie (Mrs. Ben Hardin Helm).

Horace Greeley's letter, "If the Union is irrevocably gone," dated "Midnight" on July 29, 1861, was written to Lincoln on what the editor called "my seventh sleepless night," and advised Lincoln: "If they [the rebels] cannot be beaten, do not fear to sacrifice yourself to your country" *(Nicohay* IV, p. 366).

Why didn't the Confederate Army attack the federal capital and win the war? "Give me ten thousand men," Colonel Thomas Jackson reportedly told Jefferson Davis, who had ridden to the scene of battle, "and I would be in Washington tomorrow." When Davis asked Generals Beauregard and Joe Johnston what forces were pursuing the enemy, he was told that the Southern troops were hungry and needed rest. "Davis was unwilling to reconcile himself to this," writes Shelby Foote in his 1958 *The Civil War: A Narrative,* "but presently a slow rain came on, turning the dust to mud all over eastern Virginia, and there was no longer even a question of the possibility of pursuit."

Had Jackson been in command, I think Washington would have been taken, and the North would have sued for peace. But the victorious Southern generals tended to think of the hardships being suffered by their men; besides, Beauregard was tired. Thus are victories thrown away, strategic opportunities negated by tactical worries, and wars prolonged; Davis's frustration presaged Lincoln's after Antietam.

BOOK ONE, CHAPTER 15: THE PRESIDENT'S BEST FRIEND (p. 86)

The Carroll-Breckinridge love affair is fictional.

The word-picture of Senator and Colonel Edward Dickinson Baker stretched out on the grass, with President Lincoln sitting against the tree and Willie playing close by, is from a book by Benjamin Rush Cowen, *Abraham Lincoln: An Appreciation by One Who Knew Him,* pp. 29–31.

Was Baker Lincoln's "best" friend? Lincoln was not a man to make many close friends, but the closest was probably Joshua Speed; Baker's friendship was certainly one of Lincoln's longest and closest, and a man does not name a child after a friend lightly. They met when they served together in the Black Hawk War in 1831. They served in the Illinois State Legislature. According to Milton Hay (John's father), when Baker was threatened with bodily harm while denouncing a group of Democrats as thieves, Lincoln ran up to the platform, seized a stone water jug, and said, "I'll break this over the head of the first man who lays a hand on Baker." In *My Diary North and South,* correspondent William Howard Russell poignantly describes the effect of the loss of Baker on the Lincoln family.

Congress did not approve Lincoln's assumption of the power of arbitrary arrest until the passage of the Habeas Corpus Act in 1863; Breckinridge's appeals directed to the loss of institutional power had a delaying effect.

On August 1, 1861, Lincoln's harness account was charged twenty-five cents for a "whip crack" (Lutz Account Book, cited in *LDBD* for that date).

Colonel Baker's capture of a Mexican position at the battle of Cerro Gordo, with both Grant and Lee serving under him, is recounted in *Lincoln's Constant Ally: the Life of Col. Edward P. Baker,* a 1960 biography by Harry C. Blair and Rebecca Tarshis. The Blair-Tarshis work is also the source (p. 15) of the above stone water jug threat, and cites an article by Edward B. Jerome, Baker's nephew who was serving in his regiment, writing in the May 1880 issue of *The Californian* about his uncle's demand for courtesy after the groans that greeted Breckinridge. Baker "sprang forward, almost ten feet, it seemed at a single bound, and said, with flashing eyes, and in a loud, commanding voice—'Men of the California regiment, I hope you will remember the courtesy due your commander's guest.'"

Baker's conversation with Breckinridge on that ride, which did take place, is imaginary, but his willingness to have Lincoln become a dictator was expressed in his Senate speeches. Did Baker, in those speeches calling for subjugation of the South, speak for Lincoln? Only Lincoln spoke for Lincoln, but he seems to have made no effort to restrain his close friend.

BOOK ONE, CHAPTER 16: I HAVE READ WITH PAIN (p. 93)

The scene is fictional.

Anna Carroll's pamphlet, *Reply to the Speech of John C. Breckinridge in the United States Senate, July 16, 1861* is dated September 9, 1861. It begins, as indicated, "I have read with pain" and details the secret efforts of John Calhoun's followers after 1849 to organize a "disunion party" behind Mississippi governor Quitman. She then charged: "I have it upon the authority of a senator who was present that Mr. Breckinridge united with the conspirators in their consultations and gave to them the influence and sanction of his high position [as Vice President]."

Miss Carroll refutes with some solid research Breckinridge's suggestion that General Washington operated without martial law. To counter a Jefferson reference in the July 16 speech, she cites Jefferson's letter of December 1810 to J. B. Colvin: "To lose our country by scrupulous adherence to written law would be to lose the law itself, with life, liberty, property, and all those who are enjoying them with us, thus absurdly sacrificing the end to the means."

Carroll's pamphlet defends the closing of a St. Louis newspaper, which Breckinridge complained about. The attack began on this personal note: "When I also witness the devoted patriotism of his great and gifted uncle [the Reverend Dr. R. J. Breckinridge] in the present struggle for constitutional liberty, I cannot but feel sorrow that one who has enjoyed under this government every degree of elevation but the presidency, and to whom so large a portion of the American people have hitherto looked with confidence and hope, should at last prove himself recreant to the Union's cause."

She was evidently infuriated by her former friend's speech and subsequent actions, as her conclusion shows: "It may be necessary to arrest traitorous senators and members of Congress, judges of courts, etc., who are in complicity with the rebellion, and treat them as public enemies. Instead of suppressing one press, extend it to all presses engaged in exciting and stimulating the treason."

BOOK ONE, CHAPTER 17: POLISHED TREASON (p. 98)

"In the history of the Senate, no more thrilling speech was ever delivered," wrote Maine senator James G. Blaine in his 1884 memoirs, *Twenty Years of Congress*, Vol. I, p. 345. The strongly pro-Union Blaine referred to Baker's speech, of course: "It is impossible to realize the effect of the words so eloquently pronounced by the Oregon senator . . . The striking appearance of the speaker in the uniform of a soldier, his superb voice, his graceful manner, all united to give to the occasion an extraordinary interest and attraction. The reply of Mr. Breckinridge was tame and ineffective."

"Perhaps the most dramatic scene that ever took place in the Senate Chamber—old or new—" wrote John W. Forney in his 1873 *Anecdotes of Public Men*, "was that between Breckinridge and Colonel E. D. Baker of Oregon on the 1st of August, 1861." Forney's book is the source of the description of Baker's entrance.

The debate took place as described, and the words used in the scene were—with minor changes—taken from the transcription of proceedings in the Senate that day published in the *Congressional Globe* of August 2. For dramatic impact, I have broken into the long speeches of both men to juxtapose their responses to each other's points; in the actual debate, each was reluctant to yield the floor until finished.

Senator Lyman Trumbull wanted the bill voted on that day, but after Breckinridge's attack on the bill and—mistakenly—on Sumner for Fessenden's Tarpeian Rock remark, Senator Sumner urged the postponement of its consideration. The bill was then gutted; portions passed later, but in the session in which Baker all but accused Breckinridge of treason, the legislation opposed by the Kentuckian as dictatorial was blocked.

BOOK ONE, CHAPTER 18: PEACE IS NOT THE GOAL (p. 106)

The *Congressional Globe* reporting the debates in Congress during the special session shows Senator Charles Sumner to be the one gently blocking Trumbull's bill until the session ended.

In this chapter, Breckinridge leaves for Kentucky immediately after his debate with Baker; in fact, he stayed until the session ended five days later. Part of the conversation with Forney is fictional, part based on the farewell between the two men cited in the William Davis biography of Breckinridge, pp. 278–79. Forney did predict "you will follow your doctrine into the Confederate Army."

In Forney's *Anecdotes of Famous Men,* he reports: "When Breckinridge discovered it was Fessenden and not Sumner who had given this response, he did not complain of the first nor apologize to the second."

On the title page of his 1873 book, Forney identifies himself in this bipartisan way: "Editor of the organ of the Democratic Party (the *Washington Daily Union)* from 1851 to 1855, and Editor of the organ of the Republican Party (the *Washington Daily Chronicle)* from 1862 to 1868."

This switch as propagandist from one party to the other is described less sympathetically in Christopher Dell's 1975 *Lincoln and the War Democrats,* pp. 84–85: "Lincoln wanted Democratic support . . . From the moment the *Chronicle* started publication, it surpassed the *Intelligencer* as an instrument of Unionist designs . . . before long Forney was labeled in Peace circles as 'Lincoln's Dog.' "

Did Breckinridge intend to return to the Senate in December? According to the report of his conversation with Forney, yes; other interpretations hold that by his toleration of secession, and ultimate advocacy of peaceful separation, Breckinridge talked himself out of it. It is likely that the Kentuckian was much less certain than his friends that he would go South.

The account of the split in the Breckinridge family North and South is in Boatner's *Civil War Dictionary* under "Brother Against Brother," which adds: "A Yankee Breckinridge captured his Confederate brother in the battle before Atlanta."

The scene in Anna Carroll's rooms is fictional. Anna's Latin quotation is from her pamphlet *The War Powers of the General Government,* published in December 1861: "It is unquestionable that the chief of any distinct military command must necessarily have the right to employ martial law . . . and thus the old maxim, *Inter arma, silent leges,* is as true now as it was the day when Cicero penned it." That quotation from Cicero is more accurately put: *Silent enim leges inter arma.*

BOOK ONE, CHAPTER 19: SECOND-STORY MAN (p. 113)

"Plums arrived with Nuts this morning"—with Plums standing for Pinkerton and Nuts for the President-elect—was the coded telegram Pinkerton sent to Norman Judd, a friend of Lincoln's, in Harrisburg, Pennsylvania, after the safe arrival in Washington. The message became the butt of jokes. Ward Hill Lamon, Lincoln's bodyguard, later discredited Pinkerton's claims about an assassination plot in Baltimore, but that was because Pinkerton referred to Lamon as an "egotistical idiot" in his journal; late in life, Lamon confirmed in his *Recollections* that the President's life had been in danger on his trip to Washington. A description of this episode is in James Horan's *The Pinkertons,* pp. 52–61.

Pinkerton did work for McClellan in railroading, which he describes in one of his books, *The Spy of the Rebellion,* as "intimately associated with him while engaged upon various important operations connected with the Illinois Central and the Ohio and Mississippi railroads, of the latter of which he was then president." In this and his other books written in ponderous-popular style, Pinkerton's trademark appears on the cover: a wide-open eye, with the legend "We Never Sleep," origin of the phrase "private eye."

The dialogue between Pinkerton and McClellan in this scene is mostly fictional; they surely talked often, and their relationship was probably that of sly hero-worshipper to candid hero. Even in the wave of adulation that followed Lincoln's assassination, Pinkerton remained a strong supporter of McClellan in print. I speculate here that the detective misled the general about his views on abolition, since McClellan was not anti-slavery and Pinkerton had been a good friend of abolitionist John Brown, who often spent the night in Pinkerton's home on Adams Street in Chicago. When Brown was awaiting execution in Virginia after his raid on Harpers Ferry, Pinkerton disguised himself as a Southern planter and learned the layout of the prison from a guard, Jubal Early, who later became a Confederate general. Pinkerton concluded he could not successfully extricate his condemned friend.

McClellan's "Our George" remark is from Clarence Macartney's *Little Mac*, p. 85, as is his "I have no such aspiration" to dictatorship. The story of the firing of the quartermaster is from a soldier's letter on p. 93. His "all deferring to me" wonderment is from a letter to his wife dated July 27, 1861, cited in his autobiography, *My Own Story*, and cited in Warren Hassler's 1957 biography, *General George B. McClellan: Shield of the Union*, p. 24.

I have added lurid fictional detail to what is known about Rose Greenhow's spying operation in her home at 398 Sixteenth Street, later known as "Fort Greenhow." Allan Pinkerton tells of the raid on her home, including the peeking in the windows, on pp. 252–70 of his *The Spy of the Rebellion*, but all he reported was "a whispered good night and something that sounded very much like a kiss." Mrs. Greenhow's visitor was a Union captain, not Senator Henry Wilson; Wilson was a frequent visitor and friend, but her later attempts to implicate him in her book, *My Imprisonment*, suggest that he was not a major source of her information.

BOOK ONE, CHAPTER 20
JOHN HAY'S DIARY AUGUST 22, 1861 (p. 120)

The opening two sentences are from Hay's real diary of the same date. As a diarist, Hay was remiss throughout the special session of Congress, Bull Run, and the retention of McClellan—dereliction of diary duty that is partial cause of the frustration of historians; though he won the confidence of Lincoln, who treated him more like a son than he did his own son Robert, "John Hay lingered longer than most young men on the threshold over which one passes from youth to maturity . . ." (Tyler Dennett's biography of Hay, p. 47.)

About the visit of the Kentuckians, he wrote that the President "told them that professed Unionists gave him more trouble than rebels," which I put in Lincoln's mouth as a direct quotation, along with "we want to go through the state," which Hay also paraphrased.

Hay's "bilious fever," which would now be called a flu, was described by him in a letter to Nicolay dated August 24.

The "same damn three fellers" story is recounted in Don Seitz's 1931 book, *Lincoln the Politician*, p. 333, attributed to Senator John Henderson of Missouri. The "three fellers" were Senators Sumner and Wilson, along with Stevens; I have substituted Wade for Sumner in this scene because Wade provides juicier quotes attacking Lincoln for dawdling on emancipation. Henderson is also the source of Lincoln's "the hour has not yet come."

Wade's "you are murdering your country by inches" is cited in Hans Trefousse's *The Radical Republicans*, p. 184, and his "You could not inspire Old Abe . . . with a galvanic battery" on p. 179. Stevens's "repeopling of half the continent" is from Fawn Brodie's *Thaddeus Stevens, Scourge of the South*, p. 159. His "silk glove" derogation is cited in T. Harry Williams's *Lincoln and the Radicals*, p. 37, based on a Stevens letter dated September 5, 1861.

Lincoln's "We didn't go to war to put down slavery, but to put the flag back" is attributed to Charles Edward Lester in Sandburg, Vol. I, pp. 356–57, as is "That thunderbolt will keep."

"Lincoln means well but has no force of character" and the slap at "old fogies" by Wade is from a letter he wrote to the American consul at Manchester, England, on November 16, 1861, cited on p. 180 of Trefousse.

Lincoln's "central idea pervading this struggle"—the "necessity to prove that popular government is not an absurdity"—was recorded by John Hay in his real diary, dated May 7, 1861, as a remark to Hay commenting on Orville Browning's notion to subjugate the South and establish a black republic in its place. I think it is the most important Lincoln remark recorded by Hay.

Stevens's crack about Cameron's not stealing a red-hot stove is on p. 148 of the Brodie biography, citing Samuel McCall's biography of Stevens as the source.

The suggestion that Lincoln sent Pinkerton to F. P. Blair with the dirt on Henry Wilson is fictional.

BOOK ONE, CHAPTER 21: TAKE IT TO BLA'AR (p. 124)

The scene is fictional, and there is no evidence that Wilson's relationship with Rose Greenhow was used by Lincoln supporters to influence his radical Republican views.

The justification for my speculation is tenuously circumstantial: Henry Wilson was embarrassed by his undoubted relationship with Mrs. Greenhow; she did try to "finger" him as her source in her *My Imprisonment* memoirs; letters to her signed "H," though probably not in Wilson's handwriting, were found; and most important, Senator Wilson, of all the radicals, and in a position as head of the Military Committee, did appear to resist the assault on Lincoln's conduct of the war. To suggest that he was blackmailed into cooperating is a dramatic exaggeration, especially since he was never as avid an abolitionist as some of his radical associates; however, the possibility is not remote that some coercion was applied to him to be more malleable. Surely he felt some relief, and possibly gratitude, that his connection with a rebel spy was not exploited.

Keeping in mind that Francis Blair's involvement in this possible pressure is purely fictional, many of the internal references are true: the account of the Peggy O'Neale Eaton affair can be found in Claude Bowers's *The Party Battles of the Jackson Period,* in the chapter "Mrs. Eaton Demolishes the Cabinet"; Mr. Blair's knowledge of the scandal and its political fallout (through his friend, Kentucky publisher Amos Kendall) is pointed out on p. 36 of Elbert Smith's biography of Blair. That book is also the source (p. xiii) of the Thurlow Weed serpent analogy.

The Eaton brouhaha did cost John Calhoun the succession to Jackson and changed the course of American history. Calhoun's "concurrent majority" argument, essentially propounding a government by consensus rather than majority rule, is explored in Professor Andrew McLaughlin's article, "Lincoln, the Constitution and Democracy," in the 1936 papers of the Abraham Lincoln Association. Mrs. Calhoun's social ostracism of Peggy Eaton cost the Southern leaders, as well as proponents of state sovereignty in the West, their most articulate voice in the White House; the point is made here to show that the unexpected impact of the personal element on political causes is rooted deep in the American experience.

The excoriation of the radical position by Blair is imaginary but in character for him and consistent with his anti-slavery, anti-elitist, pre-nationalist political philosophy. In *Lincoln and the Radicals,* T. Harry Williams writes: "The Southern action [in seceding] created a revolutionary situation. It brought to power in the national government the radicals, doctrinaires who if the South had not left would not have had power, political types who in American politics usually hover on the edge of power rather than being at its center."

Henry Wilson was overshadowed by his Massachusetts colleague, Charles Sumner, but the "Natick cobbler" has his defenders: "Wilson was an indefatigable worker," writes Allan Bogue in *The Earnest Men,* "the armies of the Union would owe him much, and along the way he struck more than one notable legislative blow at slavery as well." Wilson owed his election as senator to the Know-Nothings, but he soon led a portion of this anti-immigrant, anti-Catholic party into the new Republican Party, which he helped to found, and later expressed shame at the "native American" prejudice.

A tangent: I crossed paths with the ghost of Henry Wilson while working as a speechwriter in the Nixon White House. President Nixon was an admirer of President Woodrow Wilson, and requested that the "Wilson desk" in the storage room be moved into the Oval Office. In a speech draft, I referred to President Wilson "seated at this very desk," which President Nixon trustingly used; however, a zealous curator later pointed out that the "Wilson desk" actually had belonged to Henry Wilson, when he served as Vice President in the Grant administration, and not to Woodrow Wilson. I was forced to make the correction in a footnote to the presidential papers, and have waited all these years to get even.

The radicals have been portrayed in the older Lincoln literature as a troublesome faction, goading the President toward abolition and not understanding his need to seek compromise and to follow, rather than lead, public sentiment; John Hay used the word "Jacobins" with scorn. Their vindictiveness toward the South after the war further tarnished their reputation often to the point where it is forgotten that the principle that they agitated for—human freedom over property rights—turns out to be, in retrospect, ringingly right. More recent scholarship gives them more of their due: Without the Southern firebrands dedicated to carry out Calhoun's principles, the radicals of the North would not have had a chance for power; without the radicals, Lincoln would have settled for a Union with slavery intact for generations.

BOOK ONE, CHAPTER 22: "GENERAL JESSIE" (p. 132)

The scene between Frank Blair and Jessie Frémont is fictional. The information in it is based on William Ernest Smith's *The Francis Preston Blair Family in Politics,* Vol. II, pp. 71–89.

Frank Blair's estimation of Lincoln's Cabinet as apes and poltroons, with Cameron flummoxed and Seward cowardly, is in a letter to his brother dated October 7, 1861.

Frémont prepared his emancipation proclamation about the same time he was preparing to jail Frank Blair, at the end of August 1861. Lincoln must have been worried about Frémont's political clout in the West; in John Nicolay's memorandum of a conversation with Lincoln on October 2, printed in his daughter's *Personal Traits of Abraham Lincoln,* the top item on the agenda is "Frémont ready to rebel."

BOOK ONE, CHAPTER 23
JOHN HAY'S DIARY, SEPTEMBER 11, 1861 (p. 136)

The first two paragraphs, expressing Hay's irritation with the mail from Southerners and his disgust at the "leprous" nature of the South's infamy, are taken verbatim from John Hay's real diary dated April 24, 1861, when the capital was in danger of capture.

The remarks cannot be found in Tyler Dennett's *Lincoln and the Civil War in the Diaries and Letters of John Hay*. He left them out, I presume, because they reveal a peevishness and anti-Southern animus that Hay, in later life, would have found an embarrassment. These unpublished diary entries can be found in manuscript at the John Hay Library at Brown University (which hides nothing in the diaries) and are included here to show (1) Hay's sophomoric fury at those who dared to secede, matched only by his anger at the Republican "Jacobins" who dared advocate abolition, (2) the range of his vocabulary, from *epistolatory* meaning "letter-writing" to *feculence* from *feces* and meaning "shittiness," along with the natural poetry in "simmered glimmeringly," (3) the willingness of his biographer to protect his reputation by striking out sections that reveal too much of Hay's snobbier or shallower side, almost as Hay as Lincoln's biographer manipulated his raw material to minimize criticism of his hero.

The Hay diary in this novel is not intended to be an extension of Hay's real diary; it is a fictional device to move the story along.

The daily activity of William Slade, the steward, and William Johnson, the barber, are recounted in John Washington's *They Knew Lincoln*.

"Lincoln, along with the country, first heard of the proclamation through the newspapers," wrote Carl Sandburg, and his detailed account of the Frémont emancipation order *(The War Years,* I:342–48) is the source of Montgomery Blair's "like a painted woman quoting Scripture" simile. Lincoln's letter to Frémont about his proclamation's ruining "our rather fair prospect for Kentucky" is in *CW* IV for September 2, 1861, with a follow-up exchange of correspondence leading to Lincoln's "cheerfully" revoking Frémont's order dated September 11.

The bitter late-night confrontation with Jessie Frémont has one primary source that somewhat contradicts two secondary sources, and is supported by one three-word note. Mrs. Frémont's undated recollection of what for her must have been a traumatic episode is quoted in Allan Nevins's *Frémont, Pathmarker of the West,* II, pp. 516–18. By her account, Lincoln was unfriendly to the point of boorishness, and she italicized the words she said were "exactly those of the President": *"It was a war for a great national idea, the Union, and that General Frémont should not have dragged the negro into it . . ."* The past tense, of course, shows it to be a paraphrase, but evidence that the President was at least testy that night is in the peremptory note he sent to her to come over to see him after her long railroad journey: "Now, at once" *(CW* IV, September 10, 1861).

That's not how the President remembered their meeting. His recollection is noted by John Hay (who had made no contemporaneous notes of the meeting) in a diary entry of December 9, 1863. Lincoln came into a gabfest with his secretaries and Norman Judd and Interior Secretary John Usher, and talked first about the Blairs: "The Blairs have to an unusual degree the spirit of clan. Their family is a close corporation. Frank is their hope and pride." He said he sent Montgomery Blair to Frémont as a friend: "He passed on the way Mrs. Frémont coming to see me. She sought an audience with me at midnight [incorrect, if that "now, at once" summons is accurate] and taxed me so violently with many things that I had to exercise all the awkward tact I have to avoid quarreling with her . . . She more than once intimated that if General Frémont should conclude to try conclusions with me he could set up for himself." (In *Nicohay* IV, p. 415, Hay corrects this diary quote, changing "conclude" to "decide.") Another secondary source is quoted by Sandburg, p. 345: Congressman J. B. Grinnell of Iowa heard Lincoln's account of his meeting with Jessie Frémont and wrote that Lincoln said she came "opening her case with mild expostulations, but left in anger flaunting her handkerchief before my face, and saying, 'Sir, the general will try titles with you! He is a man and I am his wife.' "

Lincoln's version, repeated, showed him tactful and patient in the face of stormy provocation; Mrs. Frémont's version shows a cold and hateful President taunting what he contemptuously called a "female politician." Historian Nevins judges "her narrative is probably more accurate than Lincoln's casual conversation, some two years after the event, casually jotted down later by John Hay, for the interview must have been burned deep into her retentive memory." In the writing of the chapter, I leaned on her narrative for details and much dialogue, but added Lincoln's recollection of his subordinate's threat to "try conclusions and set up for himself"—that is, to go to the mat with Lincoln and run against him in 1864 or even to organize the Western territories into a third nation. Lincoln was probably crueler and more boorish than he remembered, and Jessie more irritating and provocative than she recalled, but the essence of the meeting was probably more truthfully narrated by her.

The radical's reaction to Lincoln's recession of Frémont's emancipation order (on grounds of the dictatorial nature of permanent seizure of property, an argument that was used against Lincoln when he later did the same thing) is reported in Nevins's *The Improvised War,* p. 340.

The interview with Wade is fictional, but Lincoln's dialogue is taken from his letter to Orville Browning, the senator appointed to take the Illinois seat vacated by the death of Stephen Douglas *(CW* IV, September 22, 1861). Lincoln made the explicit connection to the shifting balance of power in Kentucky, where Breckinridge was campaigning for neutrality. After writing "to lose Kentucky is nearly the same as to lose the whole game," Lincoln thought to add, "You must not understand I took my course on the proclamation [by Frémont] *because* of Kentucky," which strikes me as disingenuous.

The joke about the man whose horse stuck his foot through the stirrup is recounted in Sandburg, Vol. III, p. 602.

BOOK ONE, CHAPTER 24: TO SAVE THE CLAN (p. 142)

No prominent American family was more profoundly split by the Civil War than the Breckinridges of Kentucky. Uncle fought nephew in the political arena, and brother fought brother in combat.

The full-scale account of the family's place in American history is in James C. Klotter's 1986 work, *The Breckinridges of Kentucky,* and the Civil War period is covered on pp. 79–149. The best brief account of the family's travail is in Stephen Hess's 1966 book, *America's Political Dynasties,* pp. 239–71.

Long before the war, Breckinridge family members took stands on principle that lacerated relations between relatives. Robert Jefferson Breckinridge disapproved of music being played in church, and when he discovered that his brother William, also a

Presbyterian minister, had introduced an organ into his church, proffered charges against him in the synod.

In this chapter and next, the events in Kentucky in August and September of 1861 are telescoped. The best-known Breckinridges—Unionist uncle Robert and neutralist nephew John—were in fact the leading exponents of their conflicting points of view, but there is no record of their having met for a personal confrontation or debate at this time.

Anna Ella Carroll's presence in Kentucky during this period is fiction, as is her love affair with John Breckinridge throughout this book. Her mentor-protégé relationship with Robert Jefferson Breckinridge—"Reverend Bob," as she called him in correspondence—is well documented but was probably not romantic. She frequently described Robert in her papers as the spiritual guide of her youth, and he was undoubtedly one of the great influences of her life. He probably led her into Know-Nothing politics, and the preacher's early leadership of the movement to manumit slaves and send them to Liberia in all likelihood laid the foundation for her own espousal of manumission and colonization later.

The arrest of the crippled newsboy took place on September 13, stimulating anti-Lincoln orators to heights of passion; the episode is recounted in Dean Sprague's *Freedom Under Lincoln*, p. 1689, but John Breckinridge never used it in a speech.

The setting of a three-hour speech to a crowd of ten thousand is from a description in William Davis's *Breckinridge*, p. 282, of a rally at May's Lick in Mason County on September 9, 1861. The horrors-of-war quotation and "what more can I say?" were spoken there, and John C. (referred to in this book as "Breck," as he was often called by friends and political associates) attended the Frankfort Peace Convention the next day. The coinage of the phrase "holocaust of lives" was by railroad executive and pro-Union politician Robert Walker, a friend of Anna Carroll's.

That Lincoln's prompt revocation of John Frémont's emancipation order had a potent effect on public sentiment in Kentucky at that crucial moment is a fact; the suggestion that it was one of the central reasons for Kentucky's shift away from secession is my judgment.

BOOK ONE, CHAPTER 25: EVERY REBEL YOU KILL . . . (p. 146)

John Breckinridge did have the opportunity, early in the war, for high Union command. Not only did his friend John McClernand of Illinois and many other War Democrats receive commissions, but Breckinridge political supporter Ben Butler of Massachusetts successfully made the jump. After a given moment—probably early in the special session, certainly by the time of his debate with Baker—the continuance of Breckinridge's peacemaking attempts and his incessant criticism of Lincoln's infractions of civil liberty removed from him the luxury of a choice. He could not but "go South."

No conversation in this chapter took place, nor was Anna Carroll in Kentucky at the time. The circumstances of the family split are true, as is the reference to General Quitman's secession plotting described by Anna Carroll in her pamphlet *A Reply to Breckinridge*. The discussion about the Tennessee River strategy suggests that pamphleteer Carroll was given the idea by Breckinridge, which is fiction; the idea was probably her own.

The scene with Walter Haldeman is imaginary, but the *Courier* owner, along with Breckinridge, was the target of an arresting party of Union soldiers just after the invasion by General Polk and the revocation of neutrality by the state legislature. Had Breckinridge not fled, he would surely have spent the war in Fort Lafayette, or faced charges of treason. In fact, he was indicted for that capital crime by a Federal grand jury a month later.

The Breckinridge-Lane campaign poem is cited on p. 278 of the July 1976 issue of the *Filson Club History Quarterly*, which is also the source of the quotation from a *Courier* editorial denouncing the Douglas Democrats and plug-uglies for attacking defenseless immigrants in 1855 "to prevent the friends of Breckinridge from being heard." John Breckinridge was neither pro-slavery nor pro-immigrant, but his positions of anti-anti-slavery and anti-anti-immigrant placed him in conflict with his uncle on the two great issues of the day.

The analysis of the world of Louisville journalism is based on an unpublished thesis, *The Storm of Disunion Over a Border State: There Editors of Louisville in the Years of Indecision in Kentucky, 1860–61* by Charles B. Rice, Jr., of Louisville, a descendant of Walter Haldeman who made his research available to me.

Which side first violated Kentucky neutrality? A case can be made that the North did, with Lincoln's decision to arm and expand the Federal force at Camp Robinson, and with the massing of Grant's forces across the river from Paducah, but the weight of evidence points to the South. Whatever the provocation, the fact is that Bishop Polk did send his men into Columbus first. That turned out to be a blunder of some magnitude, encouraging Confederate General Zillicoffer's move to close the Cumberland Gap. Only then did Grant's Union force take Paducah.

The conversation with John Hunt Morgan is fictional; he was not the one who escorted Breckinridge to safety. The two Lexington men knew each other, and Breckinridge disapproved of Morgan's guerrilla-warlike preparations during his futile campaign for neutrality.

A portion of Breckinridge's farewell to the people of Kentucky is quoted in Frank Heck's *Proud Kentuckian*, p. 106; it was in a letter written on October 8, and I have placed some of Breckinridge's words in a more dramatic speech context in this chapter.

Evidence that Robert J. Breckinridge's argument against state sovereignty was the basis for a significant passage in Lincoln's message to Congress, and that he was at least talked of as a potential replacement for Cameron at the War Department, is presented on pp. 283 and 286 of William Townsend's 1955 *Lincoln and the Bluegrass*, which also describes the Breckinridge and Morgan activities in September.

The quotation about Simon de Montfort's slaughter of the Protestants ("kill them all—God knows his own") is from a Robert Breckinridge speech in Lexington in September 1864, cited on p. 255 of Hess's *America's Political Dynasties*. The quotation beginning "By every blow you strike, by every rebel you kill" is from Robert Breckinridge's speech to the National Union Convention in 1864 that renominated Lincoln. Senator James Blaine called it "the most inspiring utterance of the convention."

BOOK TWO, CHAPTER 1: THE SHEEP FROM THE GOATS (p. 159)

The scene took place, and the words spoken by Lincoln are almost all documented.

Anna Carroll was not present at the Rockville meeting of Lincoln, the Sewards, McClellan, and Banks; I have used her as the reporter here because she was steeped in Maryland politics.

The letter to Carroll from Mathew Brady, undated, was probably written before the war because it refers to a previous pamphlet; the original is in the Carroll papers at the Maryland Historical Association in Annapolis. She took him up on the offer because the engraving by J. C. Buttre, which appears facing page 157, says it is based on a daguerreotype by M. B. Brady. That engraving was used as the frontispiece of the short 1891 biography of Carroll by Sarah Ellen Blackwell, *A Military Genius*. No print of the daguerreotype has been found.

Her anti-secession activity in Maryland was considerable, with Blackwell citing the letter quoted in this chapter from Govenor Hicks on p. 42. The Greenbies' biography details her badgering of secessionist legislators in Maryland in 1861 on pp. 230–46 in a chapter enthusiastically titled "Anna Holds Maryland." Blackwell on p. 48 includes a letter to Carroll dated May 13, 1862, from William Mitchell, an Indiana Republican congressman, saying, "I will tell you what Mr. Lincoln said about you last night. I was there with some seven or eight members of Congress and others, when a note and box came from you with products from Central America. He seemed much delighted and read your letter out to us and showed the contents of the box. He said, 'This Anna Ella Carroll is the head of the Carroll race. When the history of this war is written she will stand a good bit taller than ever old Charles Carroll did.' I thought you might like to hear this."

Her analysis of Maryland politics and Hicks's secret desires for a central confederacy is based on William Wright's 1973 book, *The Secession Movement in the Middle Atlantic States*, pp. 40–73.

The gift of kittens to Lincoln from Seward is in the diary of Frances (Mrs. W. H.) Seward cited in the August 31, 1861, entry of *Lincoln Day by Day*. Of the four presidential candidates in 1860, Lincoln ran a poor fourth in Maryland, and Breckinridge won handily.

Now to Lincoln's trip to Rockville to stop the Maryland legislature from voting secession. The primary source is Frederick Seward, on pp. 175–78 of his 1916 memoir, *Reminiscences of a War-Time Statesman and Diplomat*, a short chapter titled "Why Maryland Did Not Secede." The key dialogue between McClellan, Lincoln, and his father repeated in this chapter is verbatim from his firsthand account. In addition, I have put in his father's mouth words based on his son's paraphrasing. "As few persons as possible would be informed beforehand" in Frederick Seward's narration becomes his father quoted saying, "Tell as few persons as possible beforehand."

Lincoln's opinion of Banks quoted during the carriage ride is from his interview with Sydney Gay of the *New York Tribune* published on August 13, 1862.

Anna's observation about Lincoln, McClellan, and Banks knowing each other from railroad days is based on McClellan's account quoted on p. 33 of Clarence Macartney's 1940 *Little Mac*. In Albert J. Beveridge's biography of Lincoln, I, p. 595, an episode is recounted of Lincoln in court on a railroad case. The judge asked, "Who is Captain McClellan, and why is he not here?" Lincoln responds, "All I know of him is that he is the engineer of the railroad, and why he is not here this deponent saith not." It is likely that McClellan's later account of occasional meetings before the war is correct. Both McClellan and Nathaniel Banks were vice presidents of the Illinois Central in the late 1850s.

The quotation from Jefferson beginning "a strict observance of the written law" is from his letter to J. B. Colvin in December 1810, and was cited by Anna Carroll in her Breckinridge pamphlet.

"The sheep from the goats" quoting Lincoln is direct from the Frederick Seward account: "The views of each disunion member were pretty well known, and generally rather loudly proclaimed. So there would be little difficulty, as Mr. Lincoln remarked, in 'separating the sheep from the goats.' "

The account was recollected in 1916, more than a half-century after the event, and is therefore suspect; but it is substantiated by two items in the *Collected Works*, Vol. IV, in entries dated September 15, 1861. Lincoln's statement that "the public safety renders it necessary . . . in no case has an arrest been made on mere suspicion," etc., is in response to a query from the *Baltimore American* about the arrest of Mayor George Brown and secessionist members of the state legislature on September 13 to 16, 1861. When the legislature met, no secessionist members were present, and no ordinance of secession was proposed.

A second document, the original of which has not been found, is accepted as authentic in *CW* and speculatively dated September 15, the time of the Baltimore arrests, with Lincoln apologizing for a break-in by troops supposedly looking for arms. "Our security in the seizing of arms for our destruction will amount to nothing at all, if we are never to make mistakes in searching a place where there are none. I shall continue to do the very best I can to discriminate between *true* and *false* men."

Lincoln did not in this place cite the Jackson precedent. That was in his letter to Erastus Corning, *CW* VI, dated June 12, 1863. It is presented in shortened form as dialogue here.

The material about the Wisconsin guards who spoke no English is from William B. Hesseltine's 1948 *Lincoln and the War Governors*, p. 214: "The military arrested members of the legislature, set a non-English-speaking Wisconsin regiment to guard them, and kept them prisoners until after the November elections."

BOOK TWO, CHAPTER 2
JOHN HAY'S DIARY, OCTOBER 25, 1861 (p. 167)

The poem "Mortality" is by William Knox, a fact Lincoln never knew; his frequent declamation of it is discussed by Stephen Oates on p. 70 of *With Malice Toward None*. That perceptive biography is also the source of Lincoln's letter to a newspaper editor praising the poem beyond its worth. In another stanza of his original poem, Lincoln reflects on "reason dead and gone," which the biographer believes to be revealing of Lincoln's lifelong fascination with madness. Hay's derogation of "Mortality" is fictional.

Colonel and Senator Edward Baker was killed in the battle of Ball's Bluff on October 21, 1861, in a brave but inept and rash attack across the Potomac. Federal casualties were 921 to the Confederate 149. Senator Wade and other radicals savagely blamed General Charles Stone for the debacle; he was arrested and imprisoned for six months without any charges ever being presented. Released, he served honorably for two years, but always under suspicion and surveillance; broken by this persecution, he resigned. Twenty years after the war, he became engineer in chief for the construction of the pedestal of the Statue of Liberty.

McClellan's assessment of Baker's attack as one that "violated all military rules and precautions" is in a letter he wrote on October 25, quoted on p. 171 of his memoirs, *McClellan's Own Story*. The point is made here because McClellan, who did not violate those rules of caution, was soon to be criticized as overcautious by the same senators who found spurious excuses for Baker's inexcusable lack of caution.

Lincoln's words in this chapter are fictional. The Blairs did have Wade and Chandler over that evening, and McClellan joined them later, I presume at Lincoln's suggestion: the general's account of that meeting, written an hour after midnight, is on p. 171 of his memoirs.

P. 147 of those McClellan memoirs, which includes remarkably revealing letters to his wife, is the basis of his account of the Maryland election arrests: "On the 28th of October I received from the chief of the Secret Service a report . . ." He runs the text of Secretary Seward's order, and the order to General Banks from McClellan's chief of staff, General Marcy; neither Lincoln nor McClellan appeared to want their names on a document suspending habeas corpus. At no point in the arrest of the legislators or in the arrests a month later of rebel-sympathizing voters did McClellan object to Lincoln's decision: "Their arrest was a military necessity, and they had no cause of complaint."

BOOK TWO, CHAPTER 3: THE YOUNG NAPOLEON (p. 171)

The description of fortifications around Washington and troop numbers are from Nevins's *The Improvised War,* p. 291.

McClellan's meeting with Wade and Chandler at the Blairs' is recounted in his memoirs, p. 171, in the post-midnight letter to his wife. A good rundown of what transpired that night is on p. 154 of Hans Trefousse's biography of Wade. The quotations from McClellan derogating Winfield Scott are taken from several of his letters at the end of October 1861. Since McClellan was not trying to mislead his wife and was not engaged in what a century later became known as "papering the file," we can assume he believed at the time that the aging Scott was unduly restraining him. "He is for inaction and the defensive;" McClellan wrote his wife, "he endeavors to cripple me in every way; yet I see that the newspapers begin to accuse me of want of energy."

This chapter sticks fairly close to fact. "The Jacobin Club, represented by Trumbull, Chandler, and Wade, came up to worry the Administration into battle," John Hay noted in his real diary for October 26. Lincoln passed on some of the heat to McClellan that evening but added, "you must not fight till you are ready."

The confluence of the completion of the transcontinental telegraph and the laying of the keel of the *Monitor* can be seen on p. 131 of Long's *Civil War Day by Day.* The machine gun and the balloon observation post were also being unveiled at about that time, demonstrating how the war hurried along technological development.

The exchange between McClellan and Lincoln on the central point of their understanding ("Don't let them hurry me"; "You shall have your own way in the matter, I assure you") is from *Nicolay* IV, p. 453, and "I can do it all" is from Hay's real diary of November 1, 1861.

BOOK TWO, CHAPTER 4: IT FLOWS THE OTHER WAY (p. 176)

The scene with Frank Blair and Anna Carroll is fictional. He was jailed by Frémont, and she did go to St. Louis at this time, but Anna was not involved with Frank's release, nor did she seek information from him about Elizabeth Keckley's son.

Blair's account that Jessie Benton Frémont had compared herself to the Empress Josephine is on p. 305 of Elbert Smith's 1980 biography of Francis Preston Blair, also the source of much of the Frémont-Blair detail herein.

The Tennessee River plan, and her original strategic conception of it, was described by Anna Ella Carroll two decades after the war, in the April 1886 *North American Review.* "Neither Mr. Lincoln nor his generals," she insisted, "knew or had in mind any plan other than that of forcing a passage down the Mississippi . . ." At the

Maryland Historical Society in Annapolis is her handwritten plan, dated November 30, 1861, which she transmitted to Assistant Secretary of War Thomas Scott. After the war, Mr. Scott wrote twice to congressional committees attesting to his receipt of the plan from her, as well as its transmittal to the Secretary of War and Mr. Lincoln.

Benjamin Wade, writing in 1876, stated unequivocally "You were the first to discover the importance of the Tennessee River in a military point of view, and were the first to discover that said river was navigable for heavy gunboats . . . which was shown to the President, which information and plan caused the immediate change from the Mississippi to the Tennessee River . . . solely due to your labor and sagacity."

The case for Miss Carroll's origination of the campaign was made in the Greenbies' 1952 biography, pp. 285–95, as well as in *My Dear Lady,* which preceded it. The case against was made by Professor Kenneth P. Williams in the September 1950 *Indiana Magazine of History,* which dismissed Senator Wade's testimonial because "the very intimate friendship that existed between Miss Carroll and his wife made him a biased advocate." As for the repeated testimony of Assistant Secretary Scott, who traveled throughout the Kentucky-Ohio-Missouri area that winter, the historian held with some acerbity that "Scott's letter falls completely to pieces when put against documents written in the last of January and the first of Febrary 1862—some by Thomas Scott himself." He finds most convincing the letter written by General Grant on March 22, 1867, to his friend Representative Elihu Washburne: "I see the credit of attacking the enemy by the way of the Tennessee and Cumberland is variously attributed . . . General Halleck no doubt thought of this route long ago, and I am sure I did."

So where is Truth? Was Miss Carroll denied her place in history by generals who would not admit that a civilian and a woman could come up with brilliant strategy, and by Establishment historians biased against women and huffy about the intrusion of amateur historians? Or has she been falsely touted and outrageously promoted by feminists and romantic novelists eager to place a mysterious character at the center of power, making her, in the Greenbies' phrase, "the great, unrecognized member of Lincoln's Cabinet"?

Suspend judgment for a while. We'll chew this over in the underbook as her story unfolds.

BOOK TWO, CHAPTER 5: FLUB-DUBS (p. 183)

Elizabeth Keckley's memoirs, *Behind the Scenes, or, Thirty Years a Slave, and Four Years in the White House,* ghostwritten by James Redpath, appeared in 1868 and is one of the best firsthand sources of the detail of daily life available to Lincoln biographers. Her reference to her fallen son was brief: "Previous to this I had lost my son. Leaving Wilberforce, he went to the battlefield with the three months troops, and was killed in Missouri—found his grave on the battlefield where the gallant General Lyon fell. It was a sad blow to me, and the kind womanly letter that Mrs. Lincoln wrote to me when she heard of my bereavement was full of golden words of comfort."

She regarded Mrs. Jefferson Davis highly: "I parted with Mrs. Davis kindly, half-promising to join her in the South if further deliberation should induce me to change my views." Mrs. Keckley soon became a confidante of Mrs. Lincoln.

The scene about the expensive rug was not recounted in her book. That episode— with its extensive dialogue—was recorded in a letter from Major Benjamin Brown

French to his sister-in-law dated December 24, 1861. Some details—"Tell Nicolay to come here," "it would stink in the nostrils of the American people"—offer snapshots of Lincoln in action that few other witnesses had the candor to put on paper.

In the *Dictionary of Slang and Its Analogues,* compiled by John Farmer and William Ernest Henley, in seven volumes issued from 1890 to 1904, *flub-dub-and-guff* is defined as "rhetorical embellishment," with a citation for this Americanism dated 1888. Lincoln's use, a generation earlier, shows the phrase in its original, shorter form; in the vivid context of French's letter, *flub-dubs* meant extravagances.

A good account of Elizabeth Keckley's life is in the 1942 *They Knew Lincoln,* by John E. Washington, pp. 205–44.

BOOK TWO, CHAPTER 6
JOHN HAY'S DIARY, NOVEMBER 24, 1861 (p. 188)

William "Bull Run" Russell's denunciation of the degeneration of democracy in wartime is from his *My Diary North and South* and is cited by Jay Monaghan on p. 149 of his 1945 *Diplomat in Carpet Slippers.* Monaghan calls the seizure of the legislators "tyrannical perfidy" and "dictatorial"; his 1945 work is the source for "one war at a time" and the analysis put in Hay's mouth of the rising tension between the Union and the European powers.

The Lincoln story about the witness who did not count his years in Maryland as part of life is from Vol. I, p. 607, of Thurlow Weed's autobiography.

Lincoln's remark about good and bad *Times* is in the November 14, 1861, entry in Russell's diary.

The $12 million overdraft is from Sandburg, Vol. I, p. 424, and the Welles telegram about the *Trent* affair is on p. 362.

Scott submitted Anna Ella Carroll's river plan to Lincoln on November 30; *LDBD* cites the source as Miss Carroll's 1886 *North American Review* article.

The four-paragraph section of this fictional diary that begins "I wish here to record . . ." and concludes with the words "etiquette and personal dignity" is a trick played on the reader. This is verbatim from John Hay's real diary entry of November 13, 1861. It is inserted here because it is a famous passage always quoted in studies of Lincoln and McClellan, showing McClellan in a bad light and the President suffering his insolence with great patience, and because I want to display the real Hay style: "insolence of epaulets" is a lively play on Shakespeare's "insolence of office." I have lifted a passage from Hay's real diary before, one that was cut from the Tyler Dennett published version, but I do not do this again; the "Hay diary" in this novel is not to be confused with the real diary of John Hay.

BOOK TWO, CHAPTER 7: THE THIRTEENTH PRESIDENT (p. 190)

President Millard Fillmore and Anna Ella Carroll had a long political relationship that was mutually profitable but ultimately embittered.

She obtained a sinecure for her father as Naval Officer of Baltimore from President Zachary Taylor in 1849, and concurrently cultivated his Vice President, Fillmore, with flattering letters. When Fillmore became President on Taylor's death a year later, he kept Thomas Carroll in his job throughout his tenure in office.

When Fillmore signed the Fugitive Slave Act, he postponed the Civil War but sealed his doom as potential Whig nominee in 1852. Instead of the sitting "accidental" President, the Whig Party chose General Winfield Scott, who was defeated by Democrat Franklin Pierce. Fillmore returned to Buffalo, but Miss Carroll stayed in touch; in New York to collect money to help mortgage her slaves, she took an assignment to write a promotional history for the Mutual Life Insurance Company and arranged for Fillmore to be made a trustee. Her political coup in his behalf was in arranging for the American Party—the Know-Nothings, divided on slavery but united on opposition to immigration—to nominate Fillmore for President in 1856, while he was traveling in Europe. He cheerfully accepted, campaigned vigorously on a platform of ethnic and religious prejudice, and came in last, carrying only Miss Carroll's Maryland. The defection of Know-Nothing and Whig Free-Soilers to John Frémont, candidate of the new Republican Party, made narrower the victory of the Democratic ticket of Buchanan and Breckinridge.

Miss Carroll saved only a few letters to her from Mr. Fillmore—she did "consign to the flames" many of the others, as she assured him—but Fillmore rarely threw correspondence away. A cache of about fifty of her letters to him was discovered in 1958 and now rests in the Fillmore papers at the State University of New York, Oswego. In the August 9, 1959, issue of the *Maryland Historical Magazine*, pp. 36–63, Charles McCool Snyder examined them all in context. "Anna Ella Carroll, Political Strategist and Gadfly of President Fillmore" is my main source for this chapter.

Mr. Snyder never concludes that Miss Carroll and President Fillmore had a romantic attachment. The mosaic he puts together from one side of a correspondence is that of an insistent, importuning, favor-wheedling woman intent on getting her political benefits from an association to which she made no mean political contribution. She went after him, asking him to come "about gaslight, or any hour after . . . always love me and feel for me the interest a daughter would give you," and he sometimes came over, but always in dread of publicity. My salacious inference that there might be more to the relationship than political-filial devotion is drawn from the constant assurance Miss Carroll gave him of confidentiality, suggesting places to meet "where I could have a talk with you without the observation of anyone." During the campaign of 1856, she wrote to ask for a rendezvous in Niagara Falls "in such a way as to create no observation or remark," and he replied, "Of course our meeting must not attract attention."

They were both single at the time, both in politics, on the same side—what was the reason for the extreme caution to avoid in being seen together? The possibility of hanky-panky, while not proved, cannot be dismissed, especially in view of Miss Carroll's furious letters about his ingratitude and insensitivity when he failed to show up. Fillmore referred to these letters as "spirited."

Much of the dialogue in this chapter is from their correspondence. The "Jeremy Diddler in petticoats" is rooted in a character in an 1803 English farce who did not repay his debts and was used in correspondence between Fillmore and one of his political friends about Anna Carroll, whom Fillmore seems to have professed hardly to know. The friend wrote that Miss Carroll had once been arrested for swindling. (The current slang verb, "to diddle," is either from the character in the play, or predates it in a meaning of "to digitate sexually"; its English meaning is "to swindle" and American meaning is "to string along deceitfully." I digress.)

The meeting between Carroll and Fillmore at the American Hotel in Buffalo took place on November 24, 1861, and one subject discussed was her Tennessee plan. In 1871, when she sought to establish her authorship of the strategy, Miss Carroll wrote to him describing that portion of their conversation and asking for his recollection. Fillmore evidently answered, but his letter has been lost. He may have replied fuzzily, because she did not use his letter in her presentation. It is also possible that Fillmore's name was anathema to radical Republicans like Wade, and Miss Carroll decided it would be better not to use him.

This quoted discussion about Lincoln's leadership qualities is fictional. Fillmore's relationship with social reformer Dorothea Lynde Dix, who led the campaign to improve conditions for the mentally ill, is inferred from a lengthy correspondence between the two.

"Whatever your opinion of me, I shall ever rejoice in your prosperity and fame" is from Fillmore's defensive letter to Carroll of August 9, 1859.

BOOK TWO, CHAPTER 8: "FIVE HUNDRED DOLLARS A HEAD" (p. 197)

Anna Carroll was assigned by Attorney General Bates to write a war powers pamphlet, did the research in St. Louis, and returned home via Buffalo, where she met with Fillmore. The Greenbies' biography traces those movements in some detail.

Lincoln, by the way, accommodated his predecessor's request for a minor military appointment for a relative. Sandburg, Vol. II, p. 218, has Lincoln telling the story of Fillmore shopping for a carriage and asking if it was fitting for a President to own a secondhand carriage, to which the salesman replied, "After all, you're a secondhand President."

Lincoln's term for his public reception of a line of visitors seeking short audiences, the "public opinion bath," is cited in Sandburg, Vol. II, p. 237, a conversation recorded by General Charles G. Halpine, the poet who signed himself "Miles O'Reilly."

Montgomery Blair's proposal to confiscate the estates of traitors and use the money to compensate loyal slaveholders for their manumitted slaves was in a letter to the President dated November 21, 1861, quoted on p. 195, Vol. II of William Smith's *The Francis Preston Blair Family in Politics*. He believed, like Browning in his diary entry of December 1, 1861, that slaveholders would agree only if some method of deportation of former slaves could be arranged. In this last week of November 1861, the idea of compensated emancipation and colonization was taking shape in Lincoln's planning.

The conversation between Lincoln and Carroll is fictional, but the draft bill for Delaware, with Lincoln's notes thereon, which are the basis for his quotes about the plan, are in *CW,* dated November 26, 1861.

The "conversation" between Lincoln and McClellan, which Anna Carroll did not overhear, is based on a letter from Lincoln asking the questions quoted, with McClellan's written replies in *CW,* for December 1, 1861.

The Hay-Carroll conversation has no basis in fact. The conversation with Assistant Secretary of War Thomas Scott was summarized by him in a letter to Congress years later: "The plan presented by Miss Carroll in November 1861 for a campaign upon the Tennessee River and thence South was submitted to the Secretary of War and President Lincoln, and after Secretary Stanton's appointment, I was directed to go to the Western armies and arrange to increase their effective force as rapidly as possible."

BOOK TWO, CHAPTER 9: DOUBLE CROSS (p. 206)

This is a fictional dinner party. Caroline Wade's "gatherings over food" and the details about her are from A. G. Riddle's 1888 biography, *The Life of Benjamin F. Wade.* The mood of Wade and his followers as Congress entered its regular session is described in T. Harry Williams's *Lincoln and the Radicals,* pp. 53–76.

Was Stanton a "duplex character," as Buchanan lieutenant Caleb Cushing described him? Both Montgomery Blair and Cushing later claimed that Stanton advocated secession while in the Buchanan Cabinet. The controversy is examined in the Thomas/Hyman biography of Stanton, pp. 114–16. Stanton spoke ill of Lincoln in early 1861; in *The Diary of a Public Man* (not a reliable source), the anonymous author says he ran into Stanton on February 25, who told him he found Lincoln "a low, cunning clown."

The etymology of "double cross" is accurate, but it entered the language about that time from England. Lord Lyons would probably be as likely to be familiar with the useful new term as the Americans.

Kate Chase and the bachelor Lord Lyons were frequent companions. The subplot about Anna helping Hay get to know Kate is fiction.

The line Anna attributes to Lincoln—"the struggle of today is not altogether for today—it is for a vast future also" is from the Lincoln message released a few days later, and one of the few revealing or memorable lines in it.

While Stanton was offering McClellan refuge in his house from "browsing presidents," so that he could show Lincoln he could work in harness with the general-in-chief, he was giving radicals like Wade the impression he agreed with them that McClellan was dawdling. "Duplicitous" is a fair description, and Cushing's "duplex" —with its accusation of complex hypocrisy—is even better.

BOOK THREE, CHAPTER 1: TO ORGANIZE VICTORY (p. 217)

Did Edwin Stanton "set up" Simon Cameron for Lincoln's wrath in order to get him fired, as this chapter unequivocally suggests? I think so.

John Forney, in his *Anecdotes of Public Men*, I, p. 76, reports a heated discussion with Cameron about the arming of slaves; the Secretary of War knew it was highly controversial. He reviewed his annual message with Forney and others, who advised him against putting in that paragraph. Years later, Cameron wrote: "[Stanton] read the report carefully, and after suggesting a few alterations, calculated to make it stronger, he gave it his unequivocal and hearty support."

In the 1962 *Stanton: the Life and Times of Lincoln's Secretary of War*, begun by Benjamin Platt Thomas and completed after his death by Harold M. Hyman, the authors lay out the circumstances on pp. 133–35, concluding charitably: "Wittingly or unwittingly, Stanton had prepared the way for Cameron's downfall." Why did the legal adviser press for inclusion of the advocacy of using black troops? The biographers suggest that Stanton might have believed in that position, or might have been fomenting a quarrel within the Lincoln Cabinet, as his potential law partner, New York Democratic leader Samuel Barlow, was urging him to do. This much they find certain: "If the opinion he set for Cameron reflected his true views, they were strikingly at odds with the opinions he was expressing to McClellan and his other Democratic friends, who did not learn until years later he was the real author of this part of Cameron's report."

In my view, the canny Stanton knew exactly what he was doing in putting the words in Cameron's mouth that would get him fired and out of Stanton's way. That was one reason he concealed his authorship at the time; he maintained silence on the issue, as Forney recalled. Another reason was that he was busily giving McClellan, his frequent houseguest, an entirely contrary impression on the subject of enlisting and arming fugitive slaves. McClellan intended to carry out the Fugitive Slave Act by sending back escaped slaves, which would infuriate Republican radicals.

"The imbecility of this Administration" was the subject of a letter Stanton wrote to former President Buchanan after Bull Run, on July 26, 1861. Quoted in Vol. I, pp. 223–24 of George Gorham's adulatory 1899 biography of Stanton, this revealing explosion of frustration and contempt is the source of the "ruin of all peaceful pursuits and national bankruptcy" reference, and his judgment that McClellan would have "cabinet intrigues, and Republican interference thwarting him at every step."

McClellan's description of being concealed at Stanton's to dodge all enemies in the shape of "browsing presidents" is in a letter to his wife dated November 1, 1861. The young general was being wooed by Stanton, who needed to show Lincoln he would be a Secretary who could work in harmony with the general-in-chief. To establish an intimacy with McClellan, Stanton derogated Lincoln and his policies, which helped drive a wedge between those two men; McClellan wrote much later, "I always regarded these extreme views as the ebullitions of an intense and patriotic nature."

Stanton's conversation with Cameron is fictional.

On the *Trent* affair, McClellan wrote his wife on November 17, 1861: "Our Govt has done wrong in seizing these men on a neutral ship . . . the only manly way of getting out of the scrape is a prompt release with a frank disavowal of the wrong . . ." But a visit to Stanton changed his mind: "I have just returned from Staunton's [*sic*] . . . I am rejoiced to find that our Govt is fully justified . . . we can afford to fight in a just cause."

BOOK THREE, CHAPTER 2: OF SLAVES AND GUNPOWDER (p. 223)

Charles Dana's 1902 book *Recollections of the Civil War* was ghostwritten by biographer Ida Tarbell. (Historian Paul Angle discovered that in 1963; at the turn of the twentieth century, ghosts were ghosts.) On p. 2, Dana gives his version of the reason that Horace Greeley fired him in April 1862: ". . . while he was for peace I was for war, and that as long as I stayed on the *Tribune* there was a spirit there which was not his spirit—that he did not like." Dana then went to work for Stanton at the War Department.

Karl Marx, a German émigré living in London, was retained by Dana in 1851 to write a series on conditions in Germany because the *Tribune* wanted to attract German readers then swelling the population of New York. Marx's reports continued until April 1862.

It is not known whether Greeley received advance notice from Gilmore or from Stanton of the news about arming slaves in Cameron's message, but the *Tribune* did publish the suppressed version despite protests from the Administration. This could have been the result of journalistic courage or political manipulation. The *New York Tribune* on December 14, 1861, reported from Washington that radical House leader Thaddeus Stevens had claimed at a Republican caucus that McClellan had gone to Lincoln and threatened to resign unless the offensive paragraph about arming the slaves was struck out of the Cameron message. Stevens offered no proof or source, but his use of the episode shows how all the radicals were prepared to pounce on Lincoln's forced public disavowal of the proposal to arm the slaves as ammunition against both Lincoln and McClellan.

Greeley ran the original Cameron message, and then a story about how it had been suppressed by the President, as did other newspapers, causing embarrassment and consternation in the Administration. Greeley did invite the President to his January 3, 1862, Smithsonian speech, at which Lincoln occupied a seat on the platform.

BOOK THREE, CHAPTER 3
JOHN HAY'S DIARY, DECEMBER 4, 1861 (p. 227)

Lincoln's reaction to the paragraph about arming slaves that Stanton encouraged Cameron to put in his message was reported by the artist Frank Carpenter in his *Six Months at the White House:* "This will never do!" etc. The episode is recounted in Sandburg I, pp. 435–36 and in much greater detail and with more insight by Nevins I, 400–3. "Why did Lincoln so lose touch with Cameron that the Secretary could pen this paragraph?" Nevins asks, and answers: "We cannot excuse his secretaries [Nicolay and Hay] for not reading the newspapers, listening to Washington talk, and seeing that he was warned betimes." The errant secretaries, in their history, Vol. V, pp. 125–27, treat this episode in such a gingerly way as to cast doubt on their candor.

The support of Chase and Welles for Cameron's paragraph, and their resistance to disgracing him publicly by suppressing his original message, are in the story in the December 4, 1861, issue of the *New York Tribune,* which Nevins thinks was inspired by Cameron or Chase. The Chase quote in this chapter is fictional but approximates his position. All sources agree that this incident led to Cameron's resignation.

The Willie Lincoln poem is on p. 121 of Ruth Painter Randall's 1956 *Lincoln's Sons;* I quote two out of the five stanzas, which appeared in the *Washington National Republican* of November 4, 1861.

Lincoln's letter declining the offer of "war elephants" is in *CW* for February 3, 1862.

LDBD for November 30, 1861, accepts Anna Carroll's assertion in her *North American Review,* CXLII, pp. 345–47, article that the Tennessee plan was submitted to Lincoln on that day. Wade's visit was described by him in a letter dated April 4, 1876, appended to the House Report 386 in 1881; I have fictionalized the dialogue.

The key point about Lincoln's not wanting to turn the insurrection into a "remorseless revolutionary struggle"—that is, not to turn it into a war over slavery—is in his annual message, *CW* December 3, 1861. It is otherwise a lackluster message, in contrast to his message a year later, when the Union fortunes were worse but Lincoln's self-confidence and sense of mission had improved.

The Hay-Chase subplot is fiction.

The Senate proceeding of December 4, 1861, expelling Breckinridge is from the *Congressional Globe* for that date. The specific information about Breckinridge at the head of a brigade in Bowling Green was inserted; otherwise, the colloquy between Powell and Trumbull was largely as recounted.

The recollection of the scene nearly a year earlier in which Breckinridge, as Vice President and President of the Senate, counted the electoral ballots and declared Lincoln the victor, is factual. William Davis in his Breckinridge biography, p. 258, reports a move by a Southerner to clear the hall of "General Scott's janizaries" and observes: "If Breckinridge saw fit to act on the point of order, an effort to eject Scott's guards might well have disrupted the session, an end much desired by the Southern elements in Washington." Breckinridge refused and the electoral count proceeded to its conclusion. Exactly a century later, in similar circumstances but with no tension in the chamber, Richard Nixon as Vice President declared his 1960 opponent John Kennedy the victor, and in 1969 Hubert Humphrey, as Vice President, declared Nixon—his 1968 opponent—the winner.

BOOK THREE, CHAPTER 4: "FORT GREENHOW" (p. 233)

In 1951, reporter and historian James D. Horan went to the State Department records in the National Archives, opened a gray steel box marked "Civil War Papers, 1861–65; Greenhow, Captured Correspondence" and later wrote: "To examine its contents is a fascinating experience. From the yellowing, charred and torn papers, emerges a strange woman of unbelievable power. These papers show her to be the confidante of a President, senators, congressmen, secret agents, blockade-runners, spies, adventurers and madmen." Most of the facts in this chapter are drawn from Horan's 1952 *Desperate Women,* pp. 25–40.

One of the packets of letters in the steel box was from Senator Joseph Lane of Oregon, Breckinridge's 1860 running mate, showing him passionately taken by Mrs. Greenhow. The visit to her room by Colonel Key and Stanton while she was under house arrest was described in Mrs. Greenhow's *My Imprisonment at Washington.*

The recollection of Stanton's petty humiliation at the McClellan dinner table is from David Porter's Private Journal #1, in manuscript in the Porter papers at the Library of Congress, cited on p. 138 of Thomas and Hyman's biography of Stanton.

The conversation between Pinkerton and Brady is fictional, based on the fact of Mrs. Greenhow's letter to Seward; the conversation with Stanton is also fictional, based on the facts cited in this source note.

BOOK THREE, CHAPTER 5: CALHOUN'S ROOM (p. 237)

Rose Greenhow tells the story of her transfer from house arrest to Old Capitol Prison on pp. 202–24 of *My Imprisonment.* Her book was propaganda, shot through with errors—she described Pinkerton, whom she called Detective Allen, as a German Jew, although he was a Scottish Episcopalian—but enough facts are included about her life in the jail to use it, with skepticism, as a source. The tapestry code is probably true, as was her desire to go to England to gain recognition for the Confederacy. She noted the coincidence of being located in the room in which she had nursed Calhoun until he died.

The other sources for the Greenhow story is Horan's *Desperate Women,* Margaret Leech's *Reveille in Washington,* pp. 148–54, and Ishbel Ross's 1954 biography *Rebel Rose,* all of which draw heavily on materials in the little steel box found in the archives by Horan, on her autobiography, and on Pinkerton's account of her activities on pp. 250–70 of his 1883 *The Spy of the Rebellion.* All conversations in this chapter are fictional, as is my assumption that she made a deal with protectors.

The passing reference to the offer of a major-general's rank in the regular U.S. Army to General Albert Sidney Johnston by Lincoln is based on a letter from Montgomery Blair to Johnston's son, on p. 267 of *The Life of General Albert Sidney Johnston,* published in 1878.

BOOK THREE, CHAPTER 6: GUARDING THE SACRED INSTRUMENT (p. 244)

One primary source for the Cabinet meeting on Christmas Day, 1861, is Bates's *Diary.* The Attorney General notes Cameron's tale of the "plot" to entrap the American captain into stopping the *Trent,* and Seward's introduction of Senator Charles Sumner into the meeting to read the correspondence from John Bright and Richard Cobden. (Sumner had at the start justified the seizure, but changed his mind.) A good secondary source is Frederick Seward, the Secretary of State's son, who in Vol. III, pp. 25–26 of *Seward,* relates Lincoln's remark about unsuccessfully attempting to frame the arguments for the other side.

William Seward was an early convert to Lincoln's one-war-at-a-time approach, having notified Ambassador Adams on November 30 to point out to the British "without indicating that we attach any importance to it" that "Captain Wilkes having acted without any instructions from the government, the subject is therefore free from the embarrassment which might have resulted if the act had been specially directed by us." *(Works of Seward,* V, p. 293). Ambassador Adams, without permission to admit the United States was in the wrong—as presidential envoy Thurlow Weed could do unofficially—did get across that the seizure was not a deliberate provocation.

The second primary source about this meeting is Chase's *Diary,* and the "gall and wormwood" quote was what the Treasury Secretary says was on his mind.

Lincoln's "a bitter pill to swallow, but after this war is over we'll be so powerful" quotation, along with the "mind that grudge still stands" anecdote, is from Sandburg I, p. 368, attributed to Horace Porter's account of Lincoln's recollection.

The discussion of greenbacks as legal tender and the cessation of specie payment was not noted by the diarists, but some discussion along these lines must have taken place that week, as the banks stopped paying in gold and silver coin on December 27, 1861. Chase reluctantly put forward the Legal Tender Act authorizing "greenbacks," which passed the Congress on February 25, 1862; after the war, as Chief Justice, he cast the deciding vote that declared portions of the act unconstitutional. (See Clarence Macartney's 1931 *Lincoln and His Cabinet,* pp. 222–26, which is also my source of the "silver and gold have I none" joke.)

The assurance by Lincoln to Chase that "I have that sacred instrument here in my desk" is frequently quoted, but rarely in context. The source is Donn Piatt, in an article in *North American Review* and later in his 1877 book, *Men Who Saved the Union,* pp. 106–9. Piatt, a Stanton intimate from Ohio and not a wholly reliable source, reported he heard this from David Taylor, an Ohio Republican and War Department employee, who in 1861 shuttled between Lincoln and Chase with an idea for interest-bearing paper currency not convertible into specie. The quotations from "he is running that end of the machine," the "sacred instrument," the Virgin Mary story, and Chase's "you will never hear from me any opposition" are all from Taylor via Piatt.

What was the Lincoln reaction to reports of Grant's drinking? The popular view is his suggestion that he send his other generals the same whiskey, but in fact the rumor must have worried him. This letter from the editor of the *Chicago Tribune,* attaching a letter reporting Grant as "perfectly inebriate under a flag of truce with rebels," resulted in a note dated January 4, 1862, from Lincoln to Cameron—"Bross would not knowingly misrepresent," and the direction to consult with Representative Washburne —which is printed in *CW Supplement,* published in 1974.

Cassius Clay, the colorful minister to Russia (who was, incidentally, an enthusiastic admirer of Anna Carroll), was not only playing around with the Tsar's favorite ballerina, but brought her back with him and Mrs. Clay to live with them in Kentucky.

BOOK THREE, CHAPTER 7: TURNING BACK THE CLOCK (p. 251)

A. K. McClure, in his 1892 *Abraham Lincoln and Men of War-Times,* wrote on p. 164: "In Nicolay and Hay's life of Lincoln (Volume 5, page 128) is given what purports to be the letter delivered to Cameron notifying him of the change . . . it is not the letter that was delivered to Cameron." The secretaries' history, as usual, presents the official, expurgated version of an incident, concealing events that show Lincoln to be petty, wrongheaded, or mistaken.

McClure's version is recounted in this chapter; a second, similar McClure version, in which Cameron is quoted accusing Lincoln of plotting "his personal as well as his political destruction," is printed in Ward Hill Lamon's 1872 *The Life of Abraham Lincoln from His Birth to His Inauguration As President.* (This book, according to Rufus Rockwell Wilson in 1945, was ghost-written by Chauncey Forward Black from materials assembled by William Herndon, and cannot be taken as Lamon's eyewitness story; a subsequent Lamon book, the 1895 *Recollections of Abraham Lincoln,* edited by Dorothy Lamon, is a much richer and more authentic source put together from his notes by Lamon's daughter.)

A second primary source is Chase, whose account is in his diary entry of January 12, 1862, written in pencil. Sandburg I, pp. 436–39, has the complete story of the episode using both McClure and Chase books.

"What have I done wrong?", a revealing reaction of an uncertain Lincoln to an aide coming to see him with a frown on his face, is from Welles's diary, Vol. I, p. 17, dated in early April, 1861.

The Lincoln skunk story was referred to in a piece by Edward Dicey, an English journalist, which I have lost.

Lincoln's conversation with Scott is fictional. His gloomy assessment of the real state of the Union as the year began, beginning with "the people are impatient" and concluding "the bottom is out of the tub" is cited on p. 405, Vol. I of Nevins's *The War for the Union,* the source being Quartermaster General Montgomery Meigs's article in *American History Review,* XXVI, pp. 292–93, and the manuscript Meigs diary entry for January 10, 1862, in the Library of Congress.

BOOK THREE, CHAPTER 8: "LITTLE MAC" (p. 255)

You cannot read or write a book about the Civil War and Lincoln without taking a position on McClellan.

We will deal with each of the controversies as they occur, but the first, in this chapter, addresses the question: Was the President right to grow impatient with him? Did the general invite distrust by the civilian leadership through his own cockiness and messianic sense of mission, or was he pushed into a natural resentment of Lincoln and especially the radical Cabinet members by their unfair treatment of him?

The first half of this chapter, narrated from the point of view of McClellan, is primarily based on *McClellan's Own Story,* pp. 155–60. He relates that Colonel Key brought him the news of Stanton's appointment during his illness; that Stanton immediately called on him and asked for his blessing, as recounted in the chapter, and told him of the secret examination of his generals, including "They are counting on your death . . ." and that he went quickly to the White House, where, he writes, "my unexpected appearance caused very much the effect of a shell in a powder-magazine."

The reference to the Hutchinson Singers is interjected, from Hendrick's *Lincoln's War Cabinet,* p. 287.

I have telescoped four meetings. The first was at 8 P.M. on Friday January 10, with all but McClellan; the second, Saturday night at the same time with the same participants; a brief one with Lincoln on Sunday January 12, with accounts conflicting about McClellan's presence; and the dramatic, longer confrontation the next day with the players as listed in the second half of the chapter, narrated through Montgomery Blair's eyes.

Why, if Stanton was secretly in the radicals' camp and planning to turn on McClellan as soon as he was confirmed and ensconced as Secretary of War, did he warn the general of the secret examination of his commanders? W. C. Prime, McClellan's editor in 1886, who prepared the general's memoirs for posthumous publication, supplies this suggestion in a footnote on p. 159: "Willing to be made War Secretary by Mr. Chase's intrigues, [Stanton] may not have been so willing to have McDowell, or any other general closely allied to Mr. Chase, placed in command of the army." Another possibility: Stanton may have been angered that it was Assistant Secretary Tom Scott who had been invited to the crucial meetings rather than the War Department counsel about to be named as Secretary.

McClellan wrote that he informed Chase of his general plan for a Peninsula campaign early in December, and thought he had the Treasury Secretary's radical opposition neutralized; he was disabused of that in the secret examination meetings. In Chase's diary for the twelfth: "At church this morning. Wished much to join in communion, but felt myself too subject to temptation to sin."

Chase, curiously, does not mention anything of these meetings in his diary. However, four good firsthand sources exist for that mid-January clash, and they agree in the main on what happened. *McClellan's Own Story* is one; another was General Meigs's notes quoted in the January 1921 issue of the *American Historical Review*, in which he says he whispered to McClellan not to be disrespectful and was told that McClellan did not want his plans to appear in the newspapers the next day. (He quotes McClellan as saying it would appear in the *Herald*, but that was a pro-McClellan paper; more likely, he would have suspected it would come out in the *Tribune*, the recipient of the radicals' leaks.) *LDBD* cites p. 292 of *General M. C. Meigs on the Conduct of the Civil War* as a source.

The third source is General Irvin McDowell, who wrote a long memorandum of his recollection of those meetings (he remembered them as January 10, 11, and 12, not the 13th) to Henry Raymond, editor of the *New York Times*, who was preparing *The Life, Public Services, and State Papers of Abraham Lincoln*, published soon after Lincoln's death in 1865. Raymond, in this instance a solid historian, sent the McDowell memorandum to Lincoln in 1864 for verification and received this reply: "I well remember the meetings herein narrated. See nothing for me to object to . . . except the phrase attributed to me *'of the Jacobinism of Congress'*, which phrase I do not remember using literally or in substance, and which I wish not to be published in any event." *(CW,* October 7, 1864). The complete memo is on pp. 772–77 of Raymond's history.

McDowell and McClellan, who despised each other, agree in their accounts on most of the details, though McDowell added the reply of McClellan about the need for action in Kentucky in the West. He also generously characterized as a "rejoinder" Lincoln's "I will adjourn this meeting" after McClellan said he had a date in mind to move his troops.

The fourth source, and the most objective and detailed, is Major General W. B. Franklin's account in a book available only on microfilm in the Library of Congress: *The Annals of the War Written by Leading Participants North and South*, published by the *Philadelphia Times* in 1879. At the first of the meetings, wrote Franklin, "The President was in great distress over the condition of the country. He complained that he was abused in Congress for the military inaction; that, notwithstanding the enormous amount of money which had been spent, nothing was doing East or West; that there was a general feeling of depression on account of the inaction; and that, as he expressed it, the bottom appeared to be falling out of everything. [As others reported, "the bottom is out of the tub."] . . . He was exceedingly sorry for the sickness of General McClellan. He was not allowed to see him to talk over military matters . . . He complained of the rise of gold, of the unreasonableness of Congress, of the virulence of the press, and in general, told us all that depressed him, in a plain, blunt way that was touching to a degree."

At the brief Sunday meeting, Franklin writes, "Suddenly Mr. Seward hurried in, threw down his hat in great excitement, and exclaimed, 'Gentlemen, I have seen General McClellan, and *he is a well man*. I think this meeting would better adjourn.'" Next day, reports Franklin, McClellan appeared, "looking exceedingly pale and weak." He is the source of the quotations, after McClellan declined to reveal his plans, of Lincoln asking if he had a plan, and then saying, "Then, General, I shall not order you to give it," and of Chase's subsequent observation, "He is a ruined man," but adds it might have been Blair who said that.

All evidence points to a depressed, worried President embarrassed by the appearance of his ill General in Chief, and a sullen, angry McClellan forced out of a sickbed to keep his command from being taken from him. Both men had every right to feel the way they did.

BOOK THREE, CHAPTER 9: A NOSE SLIGHTLY PUG (p. 267)

This chapter is straight fiction. The conversation never took place; the budding relationship is imaginary.

Greeley's "viper with its fangs now fastened in the national breast" is from his *Tribune* editorial of December 4, 1861; in his Smithsonian speech, which Lincoln and Hay attended, the editor kept the abolition pressure on the Administration.

The paragraph beginning "He knows . . . but he has to maneuver the country ahead of him" is based on John Hay's letter to William Herndon dated September 5, 1866, not in Dennett's edition of the diaries or his biography but available in a pamphlet in the Library of Congress and on pp. 307–78 of Emanuel Hartz's 1940 *The Hidden Lincoln*. Hay explained there why he thought Lincoln was not "a modest man . . . no great man was ever modest" and used the owl and the comet metaphor. The line about "I am . . . the keeper of the President's conscience" is cited in Dennett's Hay biography, p. 39, and was spoken in jest. Other quotations in this chapter are imaginary.

Nicolay's calling Mrs. Lincoln "La Reine," and some details of the planned substitution of large receptions for the traditional dinner parties is in Nicolay's letter to his fiancée, Therena Bates, dated February 2, 1862, in *CW Supp.*, p. 123.

The analysis of social customs, from *soirée conversable* to *matinée dansant*, as well as a description of a New Year's reception at the Chase house with General McDowell's wife as co-hostess, is based on pp. 111–13 of Mary Merwin Phelps's 1935 biography *Kate Chase, Dominant Daughter*.

BOOK THREE, CHAPTER 10: THE TEXAS RANGER (p. 273)

General John C. Breckinridge reported to Bowling Green in late 1861 to assume command of the Kentucky Brigade, about 5,000 infantry plus John Morgan's cavalry. Although this scene between him and General Albert Sidney Johnston is fictional, such strategic conversations probably took place. Breckinridge and Johnston were related by marriage, and formed part of an army clique that resisted the decision by Davis to listen to Lee and concentrate on the Virginia front.

The search for the son is fictional; however, Joseph Cabell Breckinridge, then sixteen, who had gone South long before his father, was part of B Company of the Second Kentucky Regiment, commanded by Captain Robert Breckinridge, his father's cousin, the son of the clergyman who had fought to keep Kentucky loyal. (See William Davis's biography, p. 297.) Cabell's father, John C.—called Breck in this book—joined the two of them in the Kentucky Brigade.

General Johnston's strategy, along with many details of his background such as casting his only vote for Zachary Taylor, are from *The Life of General Albert Sidney Johnston,* published in 1878 by his son, William Preston Johnston. His teasing of Breckinridge on his dalliance in Richmond before getting his musket is on p. 380. The assumption that Halleck would choose the Tennessee River is drawn from General Sherman's memoirs, Vol. I, p. 220.

Johnston was right about Federal intentions at the time. Eager for ammunition and small arms, he wrote the Adjutant General in Richmond on January 22, 1862, that "The enemy will probably . . . be content to hold our force fast in their position on the Potomac for the remainder of the winter, but to suppose, with the facilitie of movement by water which the well-filled rivers of the Ohio, the Cumberland and the Tennessee give for active operations, that they will suspend them in Tennessee and Kentucky during the winter months is a delusion." Even so, Richmond sent most of its supplies to the East.

Johnston did not defend Fort Donelson with all his forces because that would have left Nashville exposed to capture by Buell's army. But why did Johnston send substantial reinforcements to Fort Donelson if he thought it was likely to fall? Since the Crimean War ten years before, ironclad gunboats had been thought to have a strong advantage over forts made of earthworks, like Donelson and Henry. In his 1968 *The Battle of Fort Donelson,* James Hamilton criticizes Johnston's decision for having "foolishly violated the famous military dictum against dividing one's force in the face of the enemy by hopelessly separating the garrison from Nashville."

Johnston would argue that to abandon the forts without a fight would have been a shattering admission of weakness. Also, it was possible that the Union admiral and general would botch their jobs. Johnston's biographer-son writes: "If the line of the Cumberland could be maintained from Nashville to Donelson for even a few weeks, General Johnston hoped that the awakened spirit of the country would supply him with the long-demanded reinforcements." These are weak arguments; it seems to me that Johnston sent his men into an indefensible position because he had to make a stand somewhere, which would justify a withdrawal through two states before making his attempt to win the war by surprising and smashing the Union armies in detail at Shiloh.

Did he really have Pittsburg Landing in mind this far in advance? Colonel Frank Schaller, who was later Professor of Modern Languages at the University of the South in Tennessee, wrote to Johnston's son in 1863 with a vivid and detailed recollection of a moment in January 1862 at which he was present, when the general stood at a map in his Bowling Green headquarters, found a position marked by the engineers as Shiloh Church, "laid his finger upon this spot, and quietly but impressively pronounced the following words . . . *'Here the great battle of the Southwest will be fought.'* " Not every historian believes this.

Additional firsthand testimony about Johnston's willingness to suffer the "popular clamor" as described in this scene is on pp. 490–91 of his biography, but the assessments of other generals attributed to him are fictional. The instructions to hold the fort, but be prepared to retreat and escape, are based on Johnston's telegraph message to General Pillow of February 13: "If you lose the fort, bring your troops to Nashville if possible."

Walter Haldeman was publishing the *Louisville Courier* in Bowling Green at that time, and did publish misleading reports about reinforcements being on the way, apparently at the behest of Johnston. His presence in these scenes is fictional.

The incident about Breckinridge's support of the Kentucky private who refused menial work and told his captain to go to hell is true, recounted in Davis's *The Orphan Brigade,* pp. 54–55, but General Breckinridge's cousin Robert, who did command B Company, was not the officer involved.

Military historians differ sharply in their estimate of Albert Sidney Johnston. In *The Politics of Command: Factions and Ideas in Confederate Strategy,* a 1973 work by Thomas Lawrence Connelly and Archer Jones, Johnston's defensive strategy is criticized for spreading his meager strength along the western line rather than concentrating it, as suggested by Beauregard (sent by Davis instead of reinforcements, partly to get that critic of Davis out of Richmond). After Fort Donelson's loss, which they say was "totally unexpected by a stunned Johnston," Beauregard "assumed de facto command of the Western department" as "a dazed Johnston seemed close to mental collapse" (pp. 96–98). In this interpretation, Johnston was a misfit and the Shiloh concentration was Beauregard's doing.

Shelby Foote, in Volume I of *The Civil War: a Narrative,* credits Johnston with being a genius of psychological warfare, frightening Sherman out of his command and keeping the North from using its numerically superior forces to invade the South, until "Grant called his game of bluff on the Tennessee and the Cumberland, and the whole western house of cards went crash." Foote describes (pp. 191–93) Beauregard's suggestion to risk all in a defense of the forts, and the necessity of Johnston's painful decision to withdraw because "Johnston's army was all that stood between the Federals and the conquest of the Mississippi Valley."

Sidney Johnston's use of propaganda, which for so long kept the North from attacking, was the undoing of his own reputation, because his bluffing misled Southerners into thinking that he had a powerful force with which to defend the Western front; in reality Johnston was outnumbered three to one, many of his men being equipped with muskets (unrifled) from the War of 1812. The abuse he received in the press and from Richmond critics of the Davis government, and the "public clamor" at his retreat he bore with more patience than other generals, especially the sensitive Creole, Beauregard. "Calm at the storm center," writes Foote of Johnston, "he displayed still the nobility of mind and strength of character which had drawn men to him all his life."

BOOK THREE, CHAPTER 11: NERVE CENTER (p. 285)

The scene with Anna and David Homer Bates is fictional, but some of the information is based on Bates's useful book, *Lincoln in the Telegraph Office,* published in 1907.

Stanton's method of operation in his office, as well as the incident of the firing of the slow arsenal officer, is from Sandburg I, pp. 446–47. The visit of Anna Carroll and Ben Wade is fictional, though both visited him there. Wade urged the further persecution of General Stone in the Ball's Bluff affair, and Stanton gladly acceded to his wishes, imprisoning Stone without charges for six months, probably because this sent an ominous message to the military about civilian control.

Wade in 1876 wrote a letter to Anna Carroll (Greenbies, 470) saying "I was convinced that if placed at the head of the War Department, [Stanton] would have your plan vigorously executed, since he believed it was the only means of safety as I did." Miss Carroll later quoted Wade as saying to her that Stanton had said to him that she "did the great work that made others famous," but that is once removed and too self-serving to serve as a source.

"We saw ten generals afraid to fight," and the Stanton hand in the idea of Lincoln's General War Order No. 1, is from Thomas and Hyman's *Stanton,* pp. 170–71, as is the incident of the refusal to appoint his nephew, a facsimile of which faces page 166. During the last week of January, 1862, the new Secretary noted with pleased surprise Lincoln's agreement with him about McClellan's slowness. This was the time Stanton was writing Dana of the *Tribune* that "the champagne and oysters on the Potomac must be stopped."

Wade's comments are fictional.

BOOK THREE, CHAPTER 12
JOHN HAY'S DIARY, JANUARY 27, 1862 (p. 290)

Montgomery Blair called Stanton more than a "little black terrier"—he questioned his political and personal honesty, later accused him of accepting bribes and said he "would not be surprised to hear that he was in the pay of Jeff. Davis." At first deluded into thinking Stanton was McClellan's puppet, the Blairs soon realized that with the departure of Simon Cameron they had lost their influence at the War Department, and vowed "we will give it to Stanton someday" (Thomas/Hyman, *Stanton,* 150).

Stanton's speech to Mrs. Lincoln is from his letter of February 24, 1862, to his friend Nahum Capen; his admonition to Mrs. Lincoln, which probably took place, is not recorded. John Hay wrote in his real diary that he preferred a visit to a smallpox hospital to asking a favor of Edwin Stanton.

The scene with Elizabeth Keckley is fictional, but the information therein is factual.

The episode of the refusal at first to obey Lincoln's dubious order (which took place in 1864, not 1862) is recounted by A. K. McClure in his 1892 *Abraham Lincoln and Men of War-Times,* p. 185, based on a firsthand account by Provost-Marshal-General James B. Fry, who wrote about the incident in the *New York Tribune.* Lincoln felt he needed the votes against McClellan in certain districts and wanted the enlistment of prisoners of war counted against the draft quotas there, a political abuse of presidential power.

Stanton's participation in the conception of a War Order from the President to McClellan, calling for a land movement in Virginia, is from notes taken by historian Benjamin Thomas from a book containing notes by Stanton, who evidently trusted nobody at the War Department in his first weeks in office (Thomas/Hyman, p. 170). This was a slap at McClellan, whose plan—known to both Lincoln and Stanton—was to transport the army by water and attack Richmond from there. The purpose of the War Order (followed by a more detailed Special Order four days later) was to get McClellan to disclose his own plan in great detail, which he then did in a twenty-two-page letter.

The issuance of Lincoln's order on Washington's Birthday strikes me as Lincoln's attempt to emphasize the commander-in-chief element of the presidency.

BOOK THREE, CHAPTER 13
THE BALL WITH NO DANCING (p. 295)

Mrs. Lincoln's attempt to dominate the Washington social scene with a *grande levée* took place on February 5, 1862, much as described in this chapter. John George Nicolay wrote a few days later: "A very respectable if not a brilliant success. The East Room was filled with well-dressed guests looking very beautiful and the [midnight] supper was magnificent."

Background to the first scene is in Ellis Oberholtzer's 1907 biography *Jay Cooke, Financier of the Civil War,* Vol. I, pp. 178–88. Cooke was Chase's chief financial man outside the government, and sought to take care of the Chases with investments and purchases, which were not always turned down. At about this time, Chase was thinking of "casting off the responsibility" of Treasury to "go into your firm." An excoriation of the Chase and Sprague family operations is in *So Fell the Angels,* a 1956 book by Thomas Graham Belden and Marva Robins Belden.

The scene in the Lincolns' bedroom (one of their bedrooms, as they probably did not sleep together) is from Elizabeth Keckley's *Behind the Scenes,* pp. 101, 124. She uses "Mrs. D" for Adele Douglas and "Miss C" for Kate Chase.

Robert Lincoln's desire to enlist, and his parents' resistance, is told in Ruth Painter Randall's 1956 *Lincoln's Sons,* p. 147. "Mr. Lincoln was in a position where he had to place either his wife or his son in an almost intolerable situation," she writes, "and he chose to protect his wife." The Senator placed on the reception line in this scene was Ira Harris. Robert Lincoln's account of his rescue by actor Edwin Booth, elder brother of John Wilkes Booth, is cited on p. 152, based on an account written by Lincoln's eldest son in later years.

The Stanton-Dana scene is fictional, but grounded on what happened: Dana wrote a laudatory editorial about Stanton's appointment, and ultimately was dismissed by Greeley and hired by Stanton.

Keckley, whom Lincoln called "Madam Elizabeth," as well as "Lisabeth," did sit up with Willie on the night of the reception, according to p. 102 of her memoir. Her thoughts are fictional, based on her book.

The scene with Major French and John Nicolay is fictional, the information in it from the *New York Times* of February 9, 1862. Lord Lyons was at the party, the *Times* reported, and the point was made of his acknowledgment of Prince Albert's death in Mrs. Lincoln's black lace. The mind reading in this scene is fictional.

Anna Ella Carroll was probably at the large party, though I have no evidence of her attendance. The scene with Chase is fictional, but the tense exchange between Kate Chase and Mrs. Lincoln did take place. The scene with Stanton is fictional as well, but the intensity of Stanton's animosity toward McClellan immediately upon taking office is based on fact.

BOOK FOUR, CHAPTER 1: UNCONDITIONAL SURRENDER (p. 311)

Except for the use of young Cabell Breckinridge as a reporting device, this chapter is factual.

U. S. Grant's thoughts about the rejection of his plan by Halleck are on p. 287 of Vol. I of his *Memoirs;* his non-voting decision on Lincoln over Breckinridge is on p. 216; and his opinion about the abolition of slavery not yet being the goal of the war is from a letter he wrote his slightly larcenous father Jesse on November 27, 1861, cited on p. 100 of William S. McFeely's 1981 biography, *Grant.*

His belief that the Civil War was bloody retribution for the unjust Mexican War can be found in citations from his writings on pp. 19 and 20 of Matthew Arnold's 1887 study of Grant, republished in 1966 with a rejoinder defending Grant's writing style by the former President's publisher, Mark Twain. (Arnold, the belles-lettrist and poet, criticized Grant's use of the new verb "conscript," a back-formation from "conscription," and frowned on such phrases as "badly whipped," presumably because the enemy Grant was writing about was well whipped. Otherwise, Arnold hailed Grant as a general and as a man, but Twain took offense.) In one of his few metaphors, Grant wrote that he thought of himself as a verb, as revealing an insight as has ever been written by or about that stolidly purposeful man.

The only book about the battle of Fort Donelson is the 1968 book of that name by James Hamilton, which is the source of many of the details in this chapter. In his 1899 *Life of General Nathan Bedford Forrest,* John Allen Wyeth cites on p. 67 a report written by Forrest immediately after the battle describing the Floyd-Pillow-Buckner meeting, adding that he found "two thirds of our army could have marched out without loss." The dialogue in the scene discussing surrender, and the passing of authority to Buckner, are from Hamilton's careful reconstruction of a series of reports and memoranda in the Official Records, which he cites on p. 362. The origin of "unconditional surrender" is in Hamilton, and its predecessor "full capitulation" in Hattaway and Jones's *How the North Won,* p. 74. The report of the Confederate prisoners with three days' rations in their knapsacks, and the Grant quotation, "The one who attacks first now will be victorious," is cited by Shelby Foote, Vol. I, p. 208.

The point about Donelson was that Grant took the offensive on his own with results in question, nearly lost the battle when the Confederates counterattacked, refused to accept defeat, and prevailed—a pattern that became his style. If Buckner had had the same attitude as Grant and Forrest, the battle might have been inconclusive instead of the first significant Union victory.

The Civil War is not such ancient history to Americans. General Simon Buckner, C.S.A., who later became Governor of Kentucky, lived until 1914; late in life he had a son who bore his name, became a general in the U.S. Army, and was killed commanding the 10th Army on Okinawa in World War II where a fort was named after him.

BOOK FOUR, CHAPTER 2: ENFORCED ANONYMITY (p. 320)

The conversations in this chapter are fictional but not improbable, based on that week's events and the characters of Carroll, Scott, and Stanton.

The capture of Donelson was reported in the press on February 17, and the death of Willie Lincoln took place on the twentieth.

Stanton's quotation, "If I tap that bell over there, I can send anybody in the country to a place where they never hear the dogs bark," with "you" substituted for "anybody, they" is quoted in Shelby Foote, Vol. I, p. 245. It is strikingly similar to the Seward boast to Lord Lyons the year before.

The passing reference to the Homestead and Morrill legislation is to show that far-reaching events were taking place outside the military sphere at the time. Southerners, fearing the population of the West by anti-slavery settlers, had opposed the cheap sale of land; when the South left the Congress, Northerners passed the Homestead Act that encouraged many to move westward. In the same way, Southerners in Congress opposed land grants for colleges in the West, and President Buchanan vetoed the Morrill bill at their insistence. In 1862, however, with the opposition in secession, the great federal distribution of national wealth began in May and the most significant federal aid to education began in July, with Ben Wade in the forefront in the Senate in behalf of both. These were not Lincoln initiatives (though his support was crucial), but combined with the nationalizing effect of a national currency and a Union Army, they changed the character of governance in the United States from predominantly local to national. The secession may have speeded the process by a half century.

BOOK FOUR, CHAPTER 3
JOHN HAY'S DIARY, FEBRUARY 28, 1862 (p. 325)

William Lincoln was buried in the Carroll family vault in Georgetown, the arrangements made by Orville Browning, according to his diary entries of February 23 and 24, 1862. William Carroll, a descendant of Charles Carroll of Carrolton (who was a signer of the Declaration of Independence and one of the wealthiest men in America), was a distant relative of Anna Carroll. Browning knew Anna Carroll, citing meetings with her in his diary for July 27, 1862 ("At 5 P.M. made a call on Miss Carroll and gave her a copy of each of my speeches which she had requested"), and October 24, 1875. There is no evidence that she helped arrange the burial with her remote Washington kin.

The reference to Tad's sleeping with his father is from John Hay's revealing letter to William Herndon dated September 5, 1866, from the U.S. legation in Paris. "[Lincoln] did not sleep very well but spent a good while in bed. Tad usually slept with him. He would lie around the office until he fell asleep and Lincoln would shoulder him and take him off to bed."

BOOK FOUR, CHAPTER 4: SOURCE OF STRENGTH (p. 326)

The subtitle of *Behind the Scenes,* Elizabeth Keckley's 1868 book, is *Thirty Years a Slave, and Four Years in the White House;* it is hard to believe that during those four years in close proximity to Mr. Lincoln, especially at tragic family moments, she did not share with him some of the details of her thirty years in involuntary servitude.

The detail in this chapter, and much of the language in quotation, is from her book. The lunatic asylum reference is on p. 104, and is cited in many biographies of Mrs. Lincoln; the account of Mrs. Keckley's flogging and subjugation is in the chapter titled "Girlhood and Its Sorrows," pp. 31–42. The ghostwriting is stilted, but the testimony rings true; since she and Hay offer the few intimate glimpses into the Lincoln household, her memoirs are a prime source for every biographer.

The conversation must be listed as fictional, since she does not say it took place. The facts and her voice are true, if you believe her account. The reference to Ann Rutledge, which Lincoln is not known to have made to anyone, is based on a consensus of historians that he did befriend the nineteen-year-old New Salem girl, who was engaged to another man, and that man later broke the engagement; that she and Lincoln had at least a close platonic relationship, and that he was deeply upset at her death. William Herndon, his early law partner, who hated Mrs. Lincoln, tried to make Ann Rutledge the one love of Lincoln's life in his lectures and writings, but that was not substantiated. Herndon's romantic hypothesis, however, cannot be disproved. The point here is that Lincoln went into what we would now call a depressed period after her death, and he suffered similarly after the death of Willie.

Lincoln's description of the slave coffle in chains "like so many fish on a trotline" on the Ohio River is in *CW* I, p. 260, in an 1841 letter to Mary Speed, Joshua Speed's half sister, made the point that the slaves being separated from their families were "the most cheerful and seemingly happy creatures on board," and used the analogy "God tempers the wind to the shorn lamb." In 1855, in a letter to Joshua Speed, *CW* II, p. 320, Lincoln recalled that river trip they took together and the sight of the slaves in chains, but by that time his recollection was not of cheerful darkies: "That sight was a continual torment to me," he told his old friend, who opposed abolition, and added that slavery "has the power of making me miserable." But he saw no way to abolish slavery where it existed: "I bite my lip and keep quiet." That dislike of slavery was balanced by a conviction that the institution was the result of a constitutional compromise, and that abolition would lead to permanent dissolution of the Union. That balance began to shift in his mind in the spring of 1862.

BOOK FOUR, CHAPTER 5: EDGE OF THE CROWBAR (p. 330)

The relationship between John George Nicolay and John Hay has never, to my knowledge, been adequately explored. In Tyler Dennett's 1933 biography of Hay, a couple of paragraphs appear on p. 15 of the beginning of their association; and in Helen Nicolay's 1949 biography of her father, on p. 12, she writes of his having "dreamed of going to college with this brilliant young friend, but neither his strength nor his purse permitted him to do so."

Nicolay, the older, was the more introverted, and more trusted by Lincoln for confidential assignments. Hay, the more original and extroverted, was treated by Lincoln as a kind of substitute for his oldest son, Robert. In his real diary and letters, Hay displayed a fraternal affection for "Nico"; Nicolay, impressed always by the dazzling young man, was steadily moving toward being the junior partner in their lifelong collaboration. He referred to Hay in his writings not as his assistant, but as "Lincoln's assistant private secretary."

Wade's visit with Lincoln is fictional, though certainly such visits took place; his comments about "backbone" and "not even a galvanic battery could inspire any action in the Cabinet" are cited on p. 278 of Hendrick's *Lincoln's War Cabinet*. The relentless, impatient Wade also said that Lincoln's attitude toward slavery "could only come of one born of 'poor white trash' and educated in a slave state." Two quotes in this scene, "I am for inflicting all the consequences of defeat on a fallen foe in an unjust war," and the description of gradual compensated emancipation as "thin milk-and-water gruel," were said by Thaddeus Stevens, not by Wade.

Lincoln's "too big a lick" and some other quotations in this chapter are taken from an article by Stephen B. Oates in the December 1980 *American Heritage* magazine, titled "The Slaves Freed," which is the best short analysis I have found of the evolution of Lincoln's position on slavery.

The Lincoln comment that begins, "In my judgment, gradual and not sudden emancipation is better for all," is a condensation of several messages to Congress on this subject.

The sharp turnaround elicited by Lincoln of the *New York Times* is based on his letter to Henry Raymond of March 9, 1862, and Raymond's obsequious reply, both *CW* V, pp. 152–53. The writing of this letter is described by Nicolay in a note preserved by his daughter on p. 134 of her biography. The letter to Raymond says "consider whether there should not be another article in the *Times*," but Nicolay recalled Lincoln's saying more peremptorily, "Think of this, and let there be another article in the *Times*."

That Sunday, March 9, was an eventful day; "Hardly had Mr. Blair gone," noted Nicolay, "when Mr. Watson, Asst. Sec. War, brought in a dispatch from Gen. Wool, saying the *Merrimack* was out . . ."

BOOK FOUR, CHAPTER 6: TIN CAN ON A SHINGLE (p. 336)

Stanton's panic at the threat of the Confederate ironclad is recounted at length by Navy Secretary Gideon Welles in his diary, Vol. I, pp. 61–67: "The most frightened man on that gloomy day, the most so I think of any during the rebellion, was the Secretary of War. He was at times almost frantic . . ."

Welles was resentful at Stanton's attempt to take over the war, and was sensitive to the slights at the naval service by the imperious Secretary of War; his account may have been colored by his anger. However, Welles proved right in maintaining his composure and advising against the sinking of barges in the Potomac, and his delighted quotation of Lincoln's account of "Stanton's navy" being "as useless as the paps of a man to a sucking child" rings true.

The tension between Stanton and Welles is vividly described in John Niven's 1975 biography, *Gideon Welles, Lincoln's Secretary of the Navy,* Chapter 21, and the scene in the White House that Sunday morning, March 9, in Chapter 22.

Welles's suspicion about Stanton's claiming credit for everything is given weight by an entry in Browning's diary for that day: "They all seemed excited," he wrote of the Cabinet members present, adding that Stanton took him aside to confide "that he had telegraphed to New York to have an iron Clad boat, with a powerful Engine, immediately constructed, at whatever cost, to run down and sink the *Merrimack.*" In fact, Stanton had nothing to do with the construction of the ship, and was derisive about its chances.

The most detailed account of the battle is in William C. Davis's 1975 book, *Duel Between the First Ironclads,* from which most of my detail is drawn. Shelby Foote has an exciting narrative of the battle on pp. 255–63 of his first volume.

Welles was right to view March 8 as the gloomiest day of the war for the navy; the devastation of U.S. naval might wrought by the *Merrimack,* rechristened the *Virginia,* went unmatched until December 7, 1941.

Who won the battle the next day between the *Monitor* and the *Merrimack?* Tactically, it was a draw; strategically, it was a victory for the North, since battles not lost were battles won, as the fictional statement ascribed to Lincoln states. (Linguistically, the *Virginia* lost to the *Merrimack* in common usage, probably because of the alliteration with *Monitor.* At the Confederate Museum in Richmond, however, relics of the warship resolutely and properly called the *Virginia* are displayed with pride.)

Had the Confederate ironclad not been stopped, it could have blocked the transport of Union troops and supplies to the Peninsula leading to Richmond; or the *Merrimack* could have broken the blockade or undertaken any of the attacks on Annapolis or New York that Stanton feared. Although, as Welles points out, there is never cause for panic, there is sometimes reason for alarm.

BOOK FOUR, CHAPTER 7: COST OF LIVING (p. 345)

This chapter is fiction. Kate did manage the household bills, and the Chases were embarrassed about money; the loan from Hiram Barney, Collector of the Port of New York, was improper. Bray Hammond's 1970 *Sovereignty and an Empty Purse,* Chapters 6 and 7, is the best source about the legal tender issue.

BOOK FOUR, CHAPTER 8: JOHN HAY'S DIARY, MARCH 15, 1862 (p. 349)

The fictional diary alludes to Lincoln's General Orders No. 2 of March 8, 1862 and No. 3 of March 11, which reorganized the Army of the Potomac into four corps, putting forward the generals whom Stanton and Lincoln knew were not McClellan favorites (McDowell, Sumner, Heintzelman, and Keyes), and splitting off two other forces, under Banks and Wadsworth, for the local defense of Washington. McClellan did not oppose the idea of consolidating the divisions into four corps, but believed the timing was bad: he did not know which generals would turn out to be the best in battle, and the new setup would discombobulate his supply requisitions just as he was setting out.

The dispute between Halleck and Grant is described in McFeely's 1981 biography of Grant, pp. 104–8. Halleck was miffed at Grant's enterprise and his seeming refusal to keep in communication with headquarters; the fault, most military historians agree, was not Grant's, who reported dutifully to one of Halleck's aides. Grant, the north's only victorious general, was relieved of command, harassed by unfair complaints, and isolated; his corrupt father Jesse visited him and pressed him for money; he caught cold, suffered stinging headaches, and was depressed. He fought back by going over the army's heads to the White House, through his congressman, and wired Halleck "to be relieved from further duty until I can be placed right in the estimation of those higher in authority." Lincoln backed him up by demanding that Halleck prove his charges; Halleck backed down and Grant was reinstated to lead the Tennessee River campaign.

BOOK FOUR, CHAPTER 9: HAYLOFT (p. 350)

Pure fiction. The "icicle in the sun" image is from John Hay's *Pike County Ballads,* published in 1871:

"I really could not help it,—
Before I thought, 'twas done—
And those great gray eyes flashed bright and cold,
Like an icicle in the sun."

BOOK FOUR, CHAPTER 10: THE FAMILY LINE (p. 354)

This is fictional dialogue, based on the chapter on "Civil War Politics," pp. 195–207 in Vol. II of William Ernest Smith's *The Francis Preston Blair Family in Politics.* I occasionally use "the old gentleman" as my interpreter of Lincoln's moves as seen from the conservative wing of the Republican Party.

BOOK FOUR, CHAPTER 11: IN DURANCE VILE (p. 358)

No book has been published about Alexander Gardner, certainly one of the great figures of American photography, although Mark Katz of Gettysburg, Pennsylvania, is working on one. Gardner's relationship with Mathew Brady is mentioned in passing on p. 47 of Horan's 1955 *Mathew Brady: Historian with a Camera* and the same author's 1967 work, *The Pinkertons,* recounts Gardner's visit to the prison to photograph Rose Greenhow. In *Mathew Brady and His World,* 1977, Dorothy Meserve Kunhardt and Philip Kunhardt, Jr., briefly describe Gardner's break with Brady, adding "but to Brady, 'operators' were expendable; there were always replacements."

Gardner's own book, *Gardner's Photographic Sketch Book of the Civil War,* published in 1866 at $150 a copy, was reprinted in 1959 and is available in paperback. He scrupulously gives credit to each of his colleagues who took the pictures.

The most complete account of his life I have been able to find, thanks to Peter Galassi of the Museum of Modern Art in New York, is a June 1958 article by Josephine Cobb in *Image* magazine. Miss Cobb does not list her sources, and confuses Rose Greenhow with Belle Boyd, another Confederate spy, but has most of the information about Gardner's life on which this chapter is based.

The conversation between the photographer and his subjects is fictional, but some interchange must have taken place. The picture (p. 364) tells the story and the photo credit is accurate.

BOOK FOUR, CHAPTER 12: WHITE RABBITS (p. 365)

Mind-reading Lincoln is, of course, fiction.

Hay's objections to meeting Mrs. Lincoln's monetary demands are in a letter from Hay to Nicolay dated April 9, 1862, the week of this scene (Dennett, p. 41). In that letter, he refers to Ward Hill Lamon's libel suit as indicated in the dialogue; a reference to that suit, as well as Greeley's thanks to Lincoln for his "interposition in the libel case," are in Harlan Horner's 1953 *Lincoln and Greeley.*

Lincoln's letter to Greeley urging persuasion rather than menace in approaching emancipation is in *CW* V, p. 169, dated March 24, 1862, and his letter thanking the sender of the white rabbits is in *CW* V, p. 177, dated April 2. Greeley did warn of danger on the Tennessee River expedition, and the *Tribune*'s correspondents' dispatches were censored. Grant's message to Halleck assuring him of full preparation for an attack is cited on p. 249 of William E. Woodward's *Meet General Grant.*

Congress's Joint Resolution on gradual, compensated emancipation was approved by Lincoln on April 10, and he signed the "Act for the release of certain persons held to service, or labor in the District of Columbia" on April 16, 1862 *(LDBD,* pp. 106–7).

BOOK FOUR, CHAPTER 13
"THE IRREPRESSIBLE CONFLICT" (p. 368)

Fiction. Although Breckinridge commanded a reserve division of Albert Sidney Johnston's army at Shiloh, and the two surely spent some evenings together talking politics, this particular conversation did not take place.

Its purpose here is to set forth the two basic positions in the argument that will never be settled: was the Civil War inevitable, given the fundamental split over slavery, or was it the result of a "blundering generation," in historian James Randall's phrase?

At the time of the Civil War and during the three decades that followed, the prevailing view was that the war had been inevitable. That suited the historians who raised the Lincoln myth, because it absolved him of responsibility for not averting a war that cost one soldier's life for every six slaves freed.

In the 1920s this determinist view was bolstered by historian Charles Beard, who showed how the industrial North and agricultural South had become incompatible. Thus an economic schism was added to the issue of slavery to make the onset of war inexorable, and the two Presidents—Lincoln and Davis—could do nothing to stop it. This conclusion, enriched with an understanding of cultural divergence, infuses Alan Nevins's *Ordeal of the Union.*

An opposing school of thought arose. Historiographers (historians of historians) labeled it revisionist. As Breckinridge argues in this chapter, slavery was described as having reached its natural limits; it was on the wane, and its evils were much exaggerated. Thus the Civil War was a needless war, brought on by a combination of well-meaning and greedy Northerners who wanted to dominate the South. Some revisionists argued that war never settled anything desirably, and that fanatic and opportunistic politicians on both sides fanned the sparks of conflict until the nation was in conflagration. James G. Randall made the case that a "blundering generation" could have avoided the war and done away with slavery in time without bloodshed.

Anti-revisionists counterattacked (Arthur Schlesinger, Jr., advanced the logjam-needing-explosives metaphor) and held that revisionists were apologists for the Lost Cause, whatever that had been, and were trying to blame Lincoln and the radical Republicans for causing a war that could have been avoided by men of goodwill.

A subtle analysis of this unresolvable clash over the "irrepressible conflict"—Seward's pre-war phrase—can be found in Kenneth Stampp's 1980 *The Imperiled Union,* pp. 191–245.

I have tried to give both schools a fair shake in this chapter's argument between Breckinridge and Johnston. My own conclusion is that the two-culture, two-economy, two-nation argument is not compelling, and that war could have been avoided by skillful unionist leadership in the 1850s. (That, however, would have delayed emancipation and perpetuated a terrible injustice by a generation or two.) Breckinridge, in one point he makes in this chapter, is right about the failure of shortsighted men of his time to hold fast to the compromising, nationalist impulse of the Founders. But by the time Lincoln was elected, the die was cast: then, no man determined to hold the Union together at all costs could have prevailed without paying the price of war.

BOOK FOUR, CHAPTER 14
AMERICAN WATERLOO:
SHILOH (p. 374)

Students of the battle of Shiloh ask at least three questions: Were Grant and Sherman inexcusably surprised by a nearby army? Did the death of Albert Sidney Johnston make the difference between victory and defeat for the Confederates? Was Grant justified in gambling all on Sunday afternoon by refusing to withdraw across the river? My answer to all three is yes.

Despite all Grant's excuses in his memoirs, and despite Sherman's insistence later that no Union soldiers were bayoneted in their beds, it seems clear that the Union generals were derelict in their duty to be prepared for an attack from what they thought was a much larger enemy force.

Correspondent Whitelaw Reid (who signed his dispatches "Agate") launched what would now be called a fire storm of criticism at Grant, but surprisingly made a hero out of Sherman, the man he had previously branded as all but certifiably insane, for his coolness under fire. For the first time, public opinion about a battle was formed by newspaper reports, and the absent, tardy Grant bore the brunt of blame for the heavy Union casualties. He deserved it—Grant's excuse that he stayed at Crump's Landing to be closer to Buell when he arrived rings false, largely because he later claimed that he could handle the Confederates without Buell's help. An account of Reid's reporting appears in Appendix I of Nevins's *War Becomes Revolution,* pp. 541–43.

Johnston's death, in my view, did make the difference in the outcome of the battle, and therefore on the progress of the war. He understood that success depended solely on smashing Grant's force before it was joined by Buell's reinforcing Union army, and that Buell was dangerously close. Beauregard—in disagreement with the Johnston strategy, and running a debilitating fever—should have passed the command to Hardee or Bragg, who were prepared to carry out Johnston's plan, but he mistakenly believed it his duty to assume command. He ordered the cessation of the Confederate attack on Sunday afternoon, when the Federals under Grant were reeling and unsupported. That delay gave Buell's army time to link up with Grant and turn the tide the next day. Lew Wallace's force of seven thousand Federals, marching around in circles on Sunday, finally found the right road and contributed to the South's defeat; Grant, in an article in *Century Magazine* collected in *Battles and Leaders,* I, p. 476, pretended that he could have won with Wallace's arrival alone, but that was his way of begrudging Buell's help. If Johnston had lived—but that is one of those "ifs." Grant, in his memoirs, did not agree with such an assessment; he called Johnston "vacillating and undecided in his actions." (Grant was sometimes redundant in his writing.)

However, Grant, in extremis, bet on himself; bet on the way the fortunes of war could turn for the army that kept on fighting when everyone was exhausted; and probably gambled, despite his denial, on the imminence of reinforcements at the decisive moment. Most other generals, on both sides, would have sensibly withdrawn across the river after the first day's licking, the retreat covered by the second Union army. Grant's dogged "lick 'em tomorrow" attitude made possible a stunning recovery, and his refusal to accept what others would consider disaster was his finest hour.

This chapter sticks to the facts in most scenes. The opening episode is fictional: Cabell Breckinridge was present at Shiloh as his father's aide, but was not making ashcakes. The description of this delicacy is on pp. 103–5 of Bell Irvin Wiley's 1943 *The Life of Johnny Reb.* The incident of the soldier capturing his brother and being warned not to shoot at his father was true, recounted in Paul Angle's *Tragic Years,* p. 228, and in Sandburg I, p. 477.

The scene of the Confederate council of war, along with much other detail in this chapter, is from Wiley Sword's 1974 *Shiloh: Bloody April* (the council on pp. 106–8), and from Johnston's biography, pp. 566–68, source of Johnston's determined "I would fight . . . a million" and "I intend to hammer 'em." His speech to Breckinridge analyzing Grant and McClellan, as well as his old subordinate Lee, is fictional. Robert Lee served as Johnston's deputy in the U.S. Army in Texas until Johnston was assigned to put down the Mormon Rebellion in Utah.

The scene of Grant unburdening himself to Sherman is based on Bruce Catton's 1960 *Grant Moves South* ("Take your damn regiment back to Ohio," p. 219), and B. H. Liddell Hart's 1929 *Sherman: Soldier, Realist, American* ("I can endure it no longer . . . not a bit" p. 135). Grant's despairing plan to go back to St. Louis was confided to Sherman after, not before, Shiloh. Sherman's assessment of himself in relation to Grant is based on a Sherman letter quoted on p. 59 of T. Harry Williams's 1962 *McClellan, Sherman and Grant,* which is also the source on p. 92 of Grant's complacent "There will be no fight at Pittsburg Landing . . ." On Grant's drinking, Williams says, "The truth seems to be that he drank when unhappy or lonely and that he was quickly affected by a few drinks." Grant's reason for demanding unconditional surrender from Buckner at Fort Donelson is from a firsthand account of an interview with Grant by Colonel John Joyce, whom not all historians trust, in his 1896 *Jewels of Memory,* p. 49: "He spoke of his capture of Fort Donelson . . . stating that one of the impelling motives for demanding an immediate and unconditional surrender was the fear that General Halleck might do something to change his plans before the victory in sight could be scored."

Sherman's hatred of the press—"the most contemptible race of men that exist"—is recounted in John Marszalek's 1981 *Sherman's Other War*, source of Tom Scott's "Sherman's gone in the head" (p. 62) and the "Agate" quotations. He was the only general in U.S. history to court-martial a reporter, Thomas Knox of the *New York Herald*, which established the principle of military accreditation of the press. Much of the press labeled Sherman insane; though depressed and perhaps suicidal, he was not, but he became nutty in his hatred of the press, one of those characteristics that made him a man before his time.

Grant's view of the opening of the battle is from Catton's book, with detail added from pp. 216–19 of Sword's book. These sources continue into the section written from Breckinridge's point of view, which adds material from p. 360 of his biography by William Davis. The report of Johnston's stopping a lieutenant from plundering, and then directing the battle with a tin cup he picked up from the table in a captured headquarters is from Hattaway and Jones's *How the North Won*, pp. 167–68.

The death of Johnston is recounted in his son's biography of him, and in the appendix of Sword's book on Shiloh. My fictional mind-reading of his thoughts of a political future is based on Jefferson Davis's memoirs, Vol. II, p. 71, in which the former Confederate President wrote of his "wish I had the power, by resigning, to transfer to him [Albert Sidney Johnston] the Presidency of the Confederate States."

The account of the battle's suspension by Beauregard, through Breckinridge's eyes, is based on the Sword book; the scene with Sherman and Grant on the landing Sunday night is based on the Catton and Sword books; Grant's determined "Not beaten by a damn sight" was heard not by Sherman but by Colonel Horace Newton Fisher, cited in Sword on p. 368.

Cabell's thoughts in the retreat are fictional. Colonel Forrest, under Breckinridge, led the rearguard charge that discouraged Sherman from pursuing, described on pp. 348–9, Vol. I, of Shelby Foote's narrative.

Shiloh was the bloodiest shock to both sides of the year-old war, and helped turn it into a fight to the finish: "I gave up all idea of saving the Union except by complete conquest," wrote Grant about his thoughts after Shiloh. Grant's 42,000 men faced Johnston's 40,000, before the arrival of Buell's army; Northern casualties were 13,047, Southern 10,694. The engagement was called "the Waterloo of America" because it was a battle that both sides lost.

The North lost more men, but won the field; it could thus be said to have won the Battle of Shiloh. The great loss to the South, in what many claimed at the time was a stalemate, was in failing to win the decisive victory in its grasp.

But in the North, despite initial excitement caused by Lincoln's announcement of "signal victories," the nineteen steamboat-loads of casualties, with the local names printed on all front pages, turned public opinion to rage at reports of Grant's inadequacies. His misjudgment led to charges of drunkenness, inability to ride, unwarranted absence from the field; he was attacked not so much for being surprised, which he had been, but for being drunk, which he had not been. The criticism he deserved was obscured in the charges he probably did not deserve, and his subsequent resentment of the slanders led him to pretend even to himself that he had done nothing really wrong at Shiloh.

BOOK FOUR, CHAPTER 15
JOHN HAY'S DIARY APRIL 10, 1862 (p. 397)

This chapter sticks closely to the account of the interview, post-Shiloh, by Alexander McClure in his *Lincoln and Men of War-Times*, pp. 189–207. Although written in

1882, thirty years after the events described, McClure's firsthand account is widely taken to be truthful, especially regarding its central statement, the quotation from Lincoln about Grant: "I can't spare this man; he fights."

Also, this memoir is one of the few with the honesty to make the writer out to be quite wrong: McClure conceded in old age that he had panicked at the public fire storm around Grant, and that Lincoln had come up with a cagey plan to satisfy public sentiment without humiliating the general who fought the kind of bruising, bloodletting war Lincoln felt necessary to carry the consequences of secession home to the South.

In his three engagements, at Belmont, Donelson, and Shiloh, Grant hurt the Confederacy as no other Union general had. He took heavy casualties and inflicted them, and the tough-minded President knew that the North had the manpower to win a war of attrition. At this moment, with McClellan launching his maneuver by water to approach Richmond, Lincoln must have seen the clear contrast between a general who grimly accepted casualties—to the point of being called a butcher by his compatriots—and a general who sought to win by a brilliant maneuver that would minimize casualties, thereby winning the affection of his army.

In this episode, Lincoln skillfully found a way to keep Grant while mollifying a Northern public that wanted Grant's scalp. That saved Grant's career and made possible his later emergence.

McClure added a postscript that casts light on the Lincoln-Grant relationship: two years later, with Grant in command and Lincoln running for reelection, the result in the state of Pennsylvania was in doubt. McClure urged Lincoln to ask Grant to furlough five thousand soldiers to go home and vote. When the President hesitated, McClure recalled saying: "It can't be possible that Grant is not your friend; he can't be such an ingrate?" Lincoln replied, "Well, McClure, I have no reason to believe that Grant prefers my election to that of McClellan." They settled on getting Generals Meade and Sheridan—Lincoln knew both to be loyal political supporters—to furlough ten thousand Pennsylvania soldiers, and that "bayonet vote" ensured electoral victory in that state. When McClure asked Grant, long afterward, why he had been so lukewarm when Lincoln needed him in 1864, he said Grant replied, "It would have been obviously unbecoming on my part to have given a public expression against a general whom I had succeeded as commander-in-chief of the army." This shows why Lincoln was more successful as President than as military leader, and Grant was the other way around.

BOOK FIVE, CHAPTER 1: MUCH LIKE TREASON (p. 405)

You would think historians would love a man who loved his wife enough to write to her every night he was away from home. In those letters is historical treasure: the intimate thoughts of a man making history written contemporaneously, not in the retrospect that smooths out mistakes and settles old scores.

That is what McClellan did, but most historians have not been kind to him. That is because he became the Anti-Lincoln in the mythical version of the salvation of the Union. If Lincoln was to be protagonist and hero, an antagonist and villain was needed to explain why the conduct of the war went so poorly for so long. Nicolay and Hay set the pattern in this, excoriating McClellan as an arrogant, temporizing, ineffectual general, thereby presenting the President as a superior military leader whose judgment was stymied by a foot-dragging, slightly disloyal field commander.

This attempt to manipulate the condemnation of McClellan for the purpose of mythologizing Lincoln is documented in a letter from Hay to Nicolay dated August 10, 1885 (p. 139 of Tyler Dennett's *John Hay: From Poetry to Politics*):

"I have toiled and labored through ten chapters over him (McC). I think I have left the impression of his mutinous imbecility, and I have done it in a perfectly courteous manner. Only in 'Harrison's Landing' have I used a single injurious adjective. It is of the utmost moment that we should *seem* fair to him, while we are destroying him." Hay wrote "we ought to write the history of those times like two everlasting angels" but added a devilishly loyal "There will be one exception. We are Lincoln men all the way through." His postscript: "Destroy this letter. It would be too great a temptation to any reporter who should pick it up." (Nicolay did not, and it was.)

In blaming all military misfortune of the year from October of 1861 to October of 1862 on this "mutinous imbecile," Nicolay and Hay—hereafter in this underbook, "Nicohay"—had the active cooperation during the war and afterward of the radical Republicans, in wartime centered in Wade and Chandler's Joint Committee on the Conduct of the War. In the political canonization of Lincoln after his assassination, radicals and "Lincoln men" submerged other differences in making McClellan the scapegoat for not gaining a quick victory.

Anyone who writes about Lincoln and the Civil War, with politics and military operations intertwined, must work out a position on McClellan as the Anti-Lincoln. Nineteenth-century historians, sold by Nicohay, treated him as a mere "good organizer" incapable of leading troops into battle. Revisionists like James Randall sought to salvage his military reputation, but were soon swamped by counter-revisionists from Sandburg to Nevins. My own reading of the complex relationship will emerge in subsequent chapters.

To sources: In the McClellan papers at the Library of Congress, there can be found a large notebook labeled "Extracts from letters to my wife" in General George B. McClellan's handwriting. Some time after the war, McClellan examined the letters home that his wife had saved and "extracted" them, apparently removing some of the intimate passages. The letters themselves have not been found. When McClellan died in 1885, his memoirs not yet fully written, his literary executor, W. C. Prime, set out to counter the history by Nicohay; both their *Abraham Lincoln: A History* and *McClellan's Own Story* appeared in 1886. Prime put in his extracts of McClellan's extracts of letters home; they were the most revealing passages in the posthumous "autobiography."

A comparison of the letters printed in the McClellan book to the copied extracts in the general's handwriting in the Library of Congress manuscript room shows what is now called "sanitization." In 1886 it was permissible to attack Stanton in print, but not the martyred President; Prime edited out the direct criticism of Lincoln that McClellan, in copying, left in (or put in) and also left out some of the plaintive self-justification of a man always on the verge of being fired.

For example, the letter to Ellen Marcy McClellan dated July 10, 1862, is presented in *McClellan's Own Story* as "Rose a little before six . . . I do not know what paltry trick the administration will play next . . . I have honestly done the best *I* could."

The unexpurgated version, on p. 95 of the notebook: "Rose a little before six etc. I do not know what paltry trick the administration will play next. I do not like the President's manner—it seemed that of a man about to do something of which he was much ashamed—a few days will [word indecipherable] show, & I do not much care what the result will be. I feel that I have always done enough to prove in history that I am a General & that the causes of my want of success are so apparent that no one except the [Chandler Committee (?)] can blame me hereafter. My conscience is clear at least to this extent—viz: I have honestly done the best I could."

A question arises: Is the handwritten extract accurate, or did McClellan later want his letters home to reflect what were really afterthoughts? We will not know unless the letters themselves turn up, but enough self-revealing material is copied to suggest that what was put down is a faithful transcription of what he wrote. Stephen Sears, author of the Antietam book, *Landscape Turned Red,* who is writing a biography of McClellan and putting together a book of his letters, thinks the general a truthful man who simply wanted to excise matter too personal or too religious for other eyes. (He has doubts about McClellan's generalship, not his veracity.) In subsequent chapters, material from the letters used in dialogue ("The President is an idiot," etc.) will be from the complete notebook, not the version published in 1886.

In this chapter, the timing is out of synch by one month because I wanted to follow Grant to Shiloh in the preceding chapters. The angry meeting of Lincoln and McClellan about "an ugly matter" took place March 8, 1862, and is described by McClellan in some detail on pp. 195–96 of his memoirs. A more contemporaneous account by McClellan is on pp. 245–46 of William Starr Myers's 1934 biography, in which the general says he told the President to talk to all the general officers in his command about his Peninsula plan "and form his own opinion as to whether I was a traitor or not," which Mr. Lincoln did. In his memoirs, written after he had years to brood about the unfair charge, McClellan protests that "it is difficult to understand that a man of Mr. Lincoln's intelligence could give ear to such abominable nonsense" and quotes Lincoln, concluding with the remark that the accusation did look to him "much like treason."

Lt. George Armstrong Custer did not join McClellan's personal staff until May in the Peninsula.

A description of Lincoln's frustration and anger at the episode of the too-narrow locks is in Helen Nicolay's biography of her father, pp. 142–44; the President all but threw McClellan's father-in-law and chief of staff, General Marcy, out of the office at what Stanton called "a damned fizzle." McClellan's explanation is on p. 193 of his memoirs. That Lincoln-Stanton-Marcy meeting is also the source of "The impression is daily gaining ground that the general does not intend to do anything."

Lincoln's statement backing McClellan "against any general of modern times" is a direct quotation by William O. Stoddard in his 1900 *Lincoln at Work.* The third secretary then goes on to describe a meeting Lincoln had with Marcy and McClellan in the latter's home, where the President asserted his authority at length and the generals deferred to him; infuriatingly, Stoddard as usual contributes no substance of what was said.

"Stanton deceived me" is what McClellan charged on p. 194 of his memoirs, which I have paraphrased in this chapter; the general added that Stanton had asked him not to discuss the Harpers Ferry lock mistake with the President. "Rebels on the one side, and the abolitionists and other scoundrels on the other" is in McClellan's May 1, 1862, letter to his wife.

The meeting with Horatio Seymour is described sketchily by Stewart Mitchell in his 1938 biography, *Horatio Seymour of New York,* pp. 243–44; Seymour was urged by Peace Democrats to see McClellan, lest radicals who had gained control of the Cabinet also achieve control of the army. This was realistic military politics: Lincoln and Stanton, without McClellan's advice, reorganized his army into four corps, with each corps headed by a Republican general, elevated over a dozen division commanders, all Democrats. Seymour (probably without Fernando Wood, who went later) visited McClellan in camp, ostensibly to see New York troops, and Mitchell writes "Lincoln got wind of the meeting and spoke of it with suspicion a year or more later."

Was McClellan, as early as April, 1862, beginning to play politics that would ultimately lead to his nomination as the Democratic challenger to Lincoln? I think so; he was convinced that the way to end the war was to conduct it in a way that could lead to peace terms, without seeking conquest and subjugation of the South. That was a political-military policy, just as political as Ulysses Grant's judgment after Shiloh that the war could only be ended by conquest. Lincoln agreed with Grant's approach, expressed in that general's grim desire to fight, and suspected accurately that McClellan lacked the killer instinct. That was why the President defended Grant after Shiloh and constantly second-guessed McClellan in the Peninsula.

BOOK FIVE, CHAPTER 2: LADY MINE (p. 410)

"The President is an idiot" is from the expurgated portion of McClellan's extracts of letters to his wife, p. 12, probably written in September of 1861. "Original Gorilla," p. 30, mid-November; everything McClellan says in this chapter, with the exception of a few transition lines, is directly from his handwritten copy of letters to his wife.

Source of the A. P. Hill–Ellen Marcy–George McClellan marital contest is William Woods Hassler's 1962 *A. P. Hill: Lee's Forgotten General,* pp. 17–25. The Hill "my ticket" quote is in a letter from Hill in the McClellan papers at the Library of Congress, which is also the source of a letter from Joseph E. Johnston beginning, "Beloved McC."

Francis Blair's "visit" was a letter to McClellan dated April 12, 1862, copied out in the extracts and quoted in full on p. 281 of *McClellan's Own Story.* McClellan, who was late getting his military campaign started, was evidently grateful for any advice urging caution and expressing concern about casualties.

BOOK FIVE, CHAPTER 3: SOME LAWFUL PURPOSE (p. 413)

Here comes trouble: do I suggest that Lincoln was on the take, or what?

The first aspersion cast in this chapter is that he accepted some money from Thurlow Weed the week after his nomination for President. That is not known to be a fact, but is the inference I draw from these two entries in *Lincoln Day by Day* Vol. II, p. 281, reprinted here in their entirety:

"May 24 [1860]. Thurlow Weed, political boss of New York and William H. Seward's 'manager,' visits Lincoln. *Register,* May 25.

"May 25. Lincoln deposits $500 in his bank account. *Marine Bank Ledger.*"

Nothing conclusive about that, or dishonest even if Weed was the source of the money Lincoln deposited: no campaign expenditure laws requiring disclosure offered any impediment to a candidate: taking contributions from anyone, and the income tax was not yet on the books. It is mentioned here to show that a strong possibility exists that Lincoln had turned to Weed for money before his presidency. The sum was not paltry, not what politicians came to call "walking around money": five hundred dollars in 1860 had a purchasing power of over six thousand dollars in 1987 dollars.

The fifteen-thousand-dollar payment is documented with certainty. A detailed account of the episode appears in Vol. II, pp. 434–35, of the 1883–84 *Life of Thurlow Weed* by his grandson, Thurlow Weed Barnes, who assembled materials dictated to

Harriet Weed, the lobbyist's daughter. The note in Lincoln's handwriting—"The matters I spoke to you about are important; & I hope you will not neglect them"—with the names of the contributors and "$1,000" next to all the names, with the fifteenth and sixteenth bracketed, is in the University of Rochester Library along with the other Weed papers. The indisputable facts are: The telegram was sent by Nicolay to Weed to come; he went to Washington and received the handwritten note from Lincoln; he raised the money in New York and each contributor signed his name to the President's note. No proof exists that Lincoln received the money or passed it along, but there is no reason to doubt that all the preceding activity led to that.

Lincoln's veiled fund-soliciting note is dated February 19, 1863, ten months ahead of my story. Roy Basler, in his *Collected Works of Abraham Lincoln* for that date, runs the letter, lists the names and business affiliations of the donors, and adds in a footnote that Weed "is quite specific about everything except the purpose for which the money was needed, but quotes Lincoln as follows: 'Mr. Weed, we are in a tight place. Money for legitimate purposes is needed immediately, but there is no appropriation from which it can be lawfully taken. I didn't know how to raise it, and so I sent for you.' It is more likely that the money was raised to finance party machinery than that it was needed for purposes of government."

As Basler's footnote points out, Welles noted Weed's presence in Washington on February 10 in his *Diary:* 'He has been sent for, but my informant knows not for what purpose. It is, I learn, to consult in regard to a scheme of Seward to influence the New Hampshire and Connecticut elections . . .''

In the Robert Lincoln papers in the Library of Congress is a letter from Weed to Lincoln dated March 8 saying that "The Secession 'Petard,' in Connecticut has probably hoisted its own Engineers. Thank God for so much. Governor Buckingham was reelected over Democrat Thomas H. Seymour by a 2,000 majority."

Digging further, let us examine an earlier draft of that Weed quotation of Lincoln, which appeared in the *New York Times* on February 18, 1870, fourteen years before the publication of the two-volume autobiography and memoir, under the heading "An Incident of the Rebellion/One Thousand Dollar Autographs/A Leaf from Mr. Weed's Autobiography."

Two changes were made between the first-person recollection by Weed and the rewritten recollection by his daughter and grandson. I will put the matter excised years later in italics. In 1870, Weed quoted Lincoln as saying, "We are in a tight place. *Some* money for a legitimate *war* purpose is needed immediately. There is no appropriation from which it can be lawfully taken. *In this perplexity the Secretary of War suggested that you should be sent for.* Can you help us to $15,000?"

Weed at first remembered this as a "war purpose," buttressed by Lincoln's statement that Stanton had suggested Weed be called in. Fourteen years later, it became "for legitimate purposes" and the reference to the Secretary of War was left out.

Something is fishy about the first version, which Weed's heirs probably figured out: if the money had been for any war purpose, Stanton would have been able to get an appropriation. Weed's early attempt to cover up the fact that it was for a non-war purpose—probably political—is transparent. That war-purpose story would not hold water, and Stanton's role would raise questions. Therefore the first-person memoir was changed to a third-person account of general "legitimate purposes." Weed was now less specific in quoting Lincoln as claiming the money was not to be used for some shady or illegal purpose. Stanton, in the edited memoir, was left completely out.

A century later, historian Basler—who, bound by his stern standard of completeness, could not ignore an embarrassing transaction that biographers have overlooked —quotes Welles as attributing the purpose of the Weed visit to a scheme by Seward, whom Welles despised. In *LDBD,* editor-in-chief Earl Schenck Miers notes Basler's inclusion of the note to Weed in *CW* and summarizes the Basler footnote with: "Probably raised to finance party machinery."

That speculation is as good as any, but the question arises: if the political problem was in Connecticut, and Welles was in the Cabinet to take care of Connecticut's claim, why was this a Seward operation? Also, if Seward was the planner of some political fixing or payoffs in New England, why would he not have discussed it that morning at breakfast with Weed, the man who shared his most intimate political secrets all his life? Also, if Weed was told to raise the fifteen thousand dollars to take care of a political matter outside of Washington, why was he not told to collect the money and pay it out himself—why did he have to send it back to Lincoln? (In the oiling of party machinery, the fewer hands touching the grease the better.)

If we were dealing with Presidents Grant or Harding, rather than with a Chief Executive whose probity is near-mythical, the suspicion would be that the money was needed to pay for personal bills run up by an unstable wife, or to cover up discrepancies in the White House accounts. The sum is substantial—in today's dollars, allowing for inflation in the early Civil War years, over $150,000—but no questions have ever been asked, which raises a larger question about Lincoln historiography. Why has no learned monograph been written about this? Who got the money from Lincoln? If, as Weed reported, Lincoln felt the need to claim that the purpose was legitimate, what was the money for? Assuming the best—that the purpose was to pay off New England politicians who could help elect men pledged to support the war to preserve the Union —how did Lincoln feel about personally setting up the deal?

The detail in this chapter about the cash sent back by Weed being the new greenbacks is speculative; the irony of the political bundle featuring ten-dollar bills displaying Lincoln's photograph and the dollar bill featuring Chase was attractive.

The description of the presidential office in Civil War time is from the Revised (1977) Edition of *The White House: An Historical Guide,* p. 73, which quotes C. K. Stellwagen, an artist who made a sketch of the room in 1864, that the wallpaper was "dark green with a gold star," the carpet "dark green with a buff figure in diamonds," and the upholstery faded.

The conversation between Seward and Weed at breakfast is fictional, based on the anti-abolition positions expressed by Weed in his autobiography and in a January 1978 *Lincoln Lore* by Mark Neely, Jr. Lincoln's preparations to veto the 1862 Confiscation Act is in *CW* V, p. 328.

BOOK FIVE, CHAPTER 4
JOHN HAY'S DIARY, APRIL 9, 1862 (p. 419)

Did Lincoln act prudently in making certain Washington was well defended, or did he —by holding back McDowell's corps of forty thousand men—undermine by his timidity McClellan's ability to capture Richmond?

That is one of the greatest military controversies of the Civil War. My judgment is that Lincoln should have followed McClellan's strategy to throw the full Union force at Richmond. That is what the South feared, and why Lee later sent Stonewall Jackson into the Shenandoah Valley—to frighten Lincoln, and thereby to keep McDowell from joining the main force threatening Richmond. However, there can be no assurance that McClellan, who tended to seek excuses for not engaging, would have used the full force aggressively.

An argument can be made that Stanton did not want McClellan to be the hero of the war, and dragged his foot in this campaign; no similar case can be made against Lincoln. McClellan wanted to win gently, thinking of reunion and "the Union as it was"; Lincoln wanted to win decisively, thinking of asserting the authority of majority rule for all time; Stanton wanted to win punitively, rooting out slavery and destroying the society that produced it.

Most military judgments of this controversy ignore the political aims. In my view, each man acted militarily in accordance with his own political goal. The questions then arise: did the commanding general have the right to put his political judgment ahead of the President's? Was the President right to second-guess, and fail to adequately supply, his military commander? Those will be addressed in subsequent chapters.

The correspondence between Lincoln and McClellan in this chapter is from April 6 and April 9, 1862, in the *CW*. "But you must act" was a letter, not a telegram.

The Blair position is loosely based on Vol. II, p. 136, of Smith's *The Francis Preston Blair Family in Politics*. The family power waned as the war dragged on. Frank Blair did apply for a post on McClellan's staff, was rebuffed, and joined Grant, where he made a record as a loyal and effective subordinate general; McClellan made a political mistake in not granting his application.

John Hay's derogation of McClellan facing the Confederates at Yorktown (eleven thousand men under Magruder, a much smaller force but not a "handful of men") is from a Hay letter to Nicolay dated April 9, 1862, in Dennett's *Lincoln and the Civil War in the Diaries and Letters of John Hay* (p. 40).

Stanton's spiritual transformation at that time is described in Thomas and Hyman's biography of him, p. 186. A critical account of his War Order No. 33 closing recruiting is in Hassler's McClellan biography, p. 86. Lord Charnwood, in his admiring biography of Lincoln, called this "the one first-rate blunder of Lincoln's administration."

Stanton's view of McClellan's being influenced by Jefferson Davis is in Browning's diary entry for April 2, 1862, but was spoken out of Lincoln's earshot; never in our history, before or since, has a Secretary of War questioned the loyalty of the leading general. Browning's entry of that day is also the source of Lincoln's report that McClellan shed tears denying imputations of disloyalty. McClellan's memoirs reported no tears, but this second source lends credence to the scene in an earlier chapter of the two men discussing, with much emotion, the charges of treason being made against the general by the radicals and transmitted, perhaps ambiguously, by Lincoln. It does not confirm McClellan's account that Lincoln accused him of being a traitor.

The mention of Colonel Thomas Key as "McClellan's evil genius" was not in fact by Stanton, but by the pro-Stanton, anti-McClellan Cincinnati journalist Donn Piatt, on p. 293 of his 1887 *Memories of the Men Who Saved the Union*. (The muckraking Piatt provoked criticism when he wrote that Lincoln "while good-natured in manner, was not remarkable for kindness of heart.")

The ironic analysis of Stanton's motives at chapter's end is not Hay's, but the author's.

BOOK FIVE, CHAPTER 5: FOR SERVICES RENDERED (p. 424)

This chapter sticks fairly closely to fact. Bates's "The President paid you a very handsome compliment" was in a letter to Miss Carroll from the Attorney General dated April 15, 1862, the same day she wrote a long memorandum to the President urging him to veto the bill emancipating slaves in the District of Columbia. (Greenbies' biography, pp. 327–28, citing House Miscellaneous Document 58, p. 28.) She held that "the Union men of the South" were still a substantial number, eager to end the war, and would be driven into active rebellion by evidence that the war was really over slavery. A draft of the memo, in her handwriting, is in the Carroll papers at the Maryland Historical Association in Annapolis, with the notation "This letter was not received by the President until after he had signed the bill—A.E.C."

The details about Willard's Hotel are from Margaret Leech's *Reveille in Washington*, p. 38. The meeting with Browning is based on the same House Document, p. 36, and a letter to Miss Carroll from Orville Browning dated June 24, 1862, in the Carroll papers.

The scene between Lincoln and Carroll almost certainly took place. The dialogue about the possible veto of the Confiscation Act is taken from the argument she put forward in her most cogent pamphlet, extensively titled *The Relation of the National Government to Revolted Citizens Defined. No Power in Congress to Emancipate Their Slaves or Confiscate Their Property Proved. The Constitution as It Is, the Only Hope of the Country.* It appeared in Vol. II of Sarah Blackwell's 1893 *Life and Writings of Anna Ella Carroll*, p. 99, with the introductory note by Miss Carroll: "The subjoined document was written after a conversation with President Lincoln, who dissented from several remarks made in the Senate at the time, and to whom the pamphlet was presented for examination immediately after it was written by the author, and he gave it his full and unqualified indorsement. It was at once distributed in both branches of Congress." It was reprinted in Frank Friedel's 1967 *Union Pamphlets of the Civil War*, Vol. I, p. 357.

Many of Lincoln's statements in the scene are from his draft veto message, *CW* July 17, 1862, including the line deleted from the draft, "When you extinguish hope, you create desperation . . ."

A further discussion of the legal imperfections in the bill, central to the development of Lincoln's emancipation policy, is in *The Civil War and Reconstruction,* the 1961 edition by James G. Randall and David Donald, pp. 372–73.

The description of the scene of Lincoln exploding at Carroll for her exorbitant monetary claim is from an irate letter to him from her following the episode, which took place in early August 1862. Together with a note to Carroll from Bates, her letter is in the Garfield papers, and is printed on p. 382, Vol. V, of *CW*. Toward the end, she writes: "When you said to me, that my proposition [']was the most outrageous one, ever made to any government, on earth,' I remarked, that, the difference between us, was in our views, upon the value of intellectual labor . . ."

BOOK FIVE, CHAPTER 6: NOT BY STRATEGY ALONE (p. 432)

Fiction. This is what I think Lincoln was thinking in late May, 1862.

BOOK FIVE, CHAPTER 7: THE GATES OF RICHMOND (p. 435)

Mathew Brady did not cover the Peninsula campaign; the Brady photographer sent was James Gibson, whose panoramic views of the Army of the Potomac encamped at

Cumberland Landing on the Pamunkey River give a remarkable impression of military power unused. Thus the conversation between Brady and others in this chapter is fictional.

A. B. Foons, a freedman who may have been the world's first black photographer, is referred to on p. 57 of *Mathew Brady and His World,* by Dorothy Meserve Kunhardt and Philip B. Kunhardt, Jr. This Time-Life book has a good account of the Brady-Gardner tension; it is disputed by Gardner biographer Mark Katz, who finds no evidence of angry disagreement.

Pinkerton's concern for his undercover agent caught in Richmond is cited in his *The Spy of the Rebellion;* Timothy Webster was hanged on April 29, 1862.

The messages between McClellan and Lincoln are accurate, but did not take place on the same day; they are to be found in *CW* and in McClellan's memoirs in May and June, 1862.

"Lincoln men" have clashed for over a century with a small band of McClellan supporters over the reasons for the failure of this campaign.

Did McClellan have a sound strategy in approaching Richmond by water, rather than fighting to get there overland? Yes; Lincoln's reluctance to approve the Peninsula campaign and his lukewarm support of it were mistakes. McClellan's major military oversight was the failure to see the potential for the use of sea power to terrify and harass Richmond.

Was McClellan right about the Jackson feint, and was Lincoln wrong to deny him the reinforcements under McDowell? Yes; the President miscalculated and vacillated, and his timidity about throwing all the available troops into the attack on Richmond was a factor in the Union's failure to take the enemy capital.

Did McClellan need the reinforcements to take Richmond? No—the army opposing him, which he thought to number nearly 200,000, was less than half that; the men in the Union force on hand outnumbered the defenders of Richmond. We now know he was badly misled by Pinkerton's estimates, which exaggerated his own fears for the loss of "his" army. If McClellan had attacked with what he had, using his plan of slow advance supported by artillery, he would probably have taken Richmond.

Thus Lincoln was wrong to snatch back the army of 40,000 which was not needed to defend Washington; McClellan, who did not realize the enemy weakness, was wrong to refuse to attack without the reinforcements he did not really need.

The criticism of slowness, heard in Washington at the time, was not justified if considered in the light of McClellan's goal: not to punish the enemy or to trade casualties, but to take his capital by the slow movement forward of well-defended heavy artillery. Lincoln's purpose, however, was to inflict maximum pain on the rebels until that agony of war forced them to surrender.

Partisans of Lincoln or McClellan as military strategists tend to overlook the basically different purpose of the two strategies. Lincoln's aim was to win decisively, making permanent the impossibility of overturning the result of an election; after victory was the time for magnanimity. McClellan's aim, and that of many of the officers around him who had lifelong friends on the other side, was to demonstrate the superiority of Northern arms, and then to find a compromise that would restore "the Union as it was"—with slavery in the South as permitted in the Constitution, but without the extension of slavery into the territories.

In the light of their quite different aims, both men acted sensibly and in character. Lincoln pressed for military action that would grind down the rebel forces, while

McClellan preferred action to place the Confederacy in a position where compromise would be more acceptable than protracted war.

The prevalent notion of the cowardly McClellan dawdling at the gates of Richmond while a despairing President urges him on, but retains enough forces to defend Washington, is simplistic and misleading. McClellan, guided by Thomas Key, was applying military pressure while seeking peace negotiations to find a basis for reunion; Lincoln, guided by his central idea of majority rule, was seeking clearcut military victory, after which he would try to reunite the jubilant victors and sullen vanquished.

A long-missing element in this hypothesis of McClellan's motivation has been an overt peace feeler. In Joseph P. Cullen's 1973 *The Peninsula Campaign 1862,* pp. 68–76, the author—who derogates McClellan as "more interested in politics than in fighting the war"—cites the Key-Cobb meeting, which has been ignored by historians since 1884, in the compilation of the official records, Series I, Vol. XI, pp. 1053–60. That is the basis of the next chapter.

At the root of the Lincoln-McClellan controversy is a political, far less than military, difference. The general's essential challenge to Lincoln's authority was neither in failing to keep him informed of battle plans nor in disagreeing about strategies for taking Richmond. His real insubordination was in presuming to set national goals and to try to bring the war to an end to accomplish those goals. Fighting a war is a general's job (in which Lincoln was wrong to interfere in detail, and he refrained from doing so after putting Grant in command); but deciding on terms for ending a war is a President's job, and Lincoln knew there could be only one President at a time.

BOOK FIVE, CHAPTER 8: SUBMISSION AND AMNESTY (p. 441)

Lieutenant George Armstrong Custer first came to the attention of General McClellan on May 25, 1862, after the twenty-two-year-old member of the 5th U.S. Cavalry showed courage in leading a reconnaissance across the Chicahominy. Custer's first mention in the 130-volume *Official Records* was by a topographical engineer who returned with him from this foray into enemy territory, and who reported that Custer "was the first to cross the stream, the first to open fire upon the enemy, and one of the last to leave the field." This is cited on the first page of John Carroll's 1977 *Custer in the Civil War.*

Previous mentions of Custer in this novel are fictional. McClellan, on p. 364 of his *Own Story,* tells of meeting the "slim, long-haired boy, carelessly dressed" soon after his reconnaissance and promptly appointing him to his staff. "In those days Custer was simply a reckless, gallant boy, undeterred by fatigue, unconscious of fear; but his head was always clear in danger . . . I became much attached to him." Writing in 1886, ten years after General Custer was killed in an ambush at the Little Big Horn by Chief Crazy Horse, McClellan added a poignant note about the criticism of Custer for being too rash that revealed his abiding resentment of criticism that he himself had been too cautious: "Those who accused him of reckless rashness would, perhaps, have been the first to accuse him of timidity if he had not attacked."

It is not known whether Custer was in the cavalry escort that accompanied Colonel Thomas Key from McClellan's headquarters to the first peace meeting of the war. Their conversation, though accurate about J.E.B. Stuart's ride and General Lee's suddenly enhanced reputation, is fictional. Key's exposition of the official excuse, or reason, for possible failure in the Peninsula, beginning "The McClellan plan was to turn Yorktown" is taken from "The First Great Crime of the War," an article in the

1879 *Annals of the War* by Major General W. B. Franklin, one of McClellan's most personally loyal corps commanders.

In that piece, Franklin also provided another first-person account of the confrontation the feverish general had with Lincoln and the Cabinet recounted in a previous chapter, and reported that Frank Blair, chairman of the House Committee on Military Affairs, told McClellan after First Bull Run that "if you do not feel that you are today king of this country, you do not appreciate your position." In many ways, "the Young Napoleon" was tempted to think of himself more as a national savior than a mere general.

The story of the first significant peace feeler of the war lay unremarked by historians for more than a century in the *Official Records* (Series I, Vol. XI, Chapter 23, pp. 1052–61) until spotted and written about by Joseph Cullen in his 1973 *The Peninsula Campaign 1862.* Cullen's judgment of McClellan and Key was severe: "To him there was nothing inconsistent in that fact that he, a known Democrat with presidential ambitions and Democratic friends in and out of Congress, without authority sent an officer to confer with the enemy on the terms of surrender and to explain to that enemy the policies and objectives of a Republican administration." The historian was especially critical of the phrase, "the President, the army and the people," which he took to be a misreading of the centers of power in a democracy.

Evidently McClellan felt it was part of his job to conduct the war in a way that he could end the war. He made a point of filing Key's complete report, on which this chapter is based, to Stanton with a request to lay it before the President. The Secretary of War replied coldly that he had done so, remarking, "it is not deemed proper for officers bearing flags of truce in respect to the exchange of prisoners to hold any conference with the rebel officers upon the general subject of the existing contest . . ."

As Key was assuring the South that Lincoln intended no strike at the institution of slavery where it existed, the President was beginning to give thought to precisely such a dramatic strike. Nothing further about peace or slavery was discussed between McClellan and the President until their June meeting at Harrison's Landing, where McClellan again was to reach into political affairs. But Lincoln did not forget Key's name, or what he must have considered Key's presumption, as a subsequent chapter will show.

BOOK FIVE, CHAPTER 9: ROSE ON TRIAL (p. 447)

Rose Greenhow's trial before Dix and Pierrepont took place in mid-March 1862, not mid-June as this chapter indicates, but the setting and circumstances are factual.

Allan Pinkerton and Colonel Thomas Key visited John Dix in mid-April to plead for intercession in the execution of Timothy Webster, according to Pinkerton's 1883 *The Spy of the Rebellion,* pp. 546–47. As a result, Stanton sent a message to Jefferson Davis with what Pinkerton says was "the decided intimation that if the rebel government proceeded to carry their sentence of death into execution, the Federal government would initiate a system of retaliation . . ." But Webster was hanged at the end of April, with Mrs. Greenhow still in Union custody. I have no direct evidence of this being used as pressure on the female Confederate spy, but it seems likely.

The conversation between Dix and Stanton at the opening of this chapter is fictional. Sources for the trial scene are Ishbel Ross's 1954 *Rebel Rose,* which quotes from the trial transcript, and Mrs. Greenhow's self-serving version in her book, *My*

Imprisonment. Dix had a longstanding social relationship with Mrs. Greenhow, and Pierrepont's line, "General, you know this woman. Why don't you talk to her privately?" is from the transcript, but hints of an involvement with either Dix or Stanton are unsubstantiated.

Most of the trial dialogue between Dix and Greenhow is from the transcript; about half the interchange between Pierrepont and Greenhow in this chapter is fiction.

My view of Dix's purpose—to get some face-saving confession or parole that would permit Stanton to ship her South—is a fair interpretation of the transcript and is buttressed by subsequent events.

The reference to Dix's proclamation "to prevent the ballot-boxes from being polluted by treasonable votes" is from his message to the U.S. Marshal of Maryland dated November 1, 1861, from p. 339 of *The Memoirs of John Adams Dix.*

BOOK FIVE, CHAPTER 10: JOHN HAY'S DIARY, JUNE 19, 1862 (p. 453)

From mid-June to mid-July, 1862, Lincoln arrived at the decision to emancipate the slaves in rebel hands by presidential proclamation. In both the novel and this underbook, we will follow the details of likely motives and outside pressures.

June 19 was the day Lincoln signed the bill sent him by Congress to abolish slavery in the territories, laying to rest for good the issue of "popular sovereignty." Lincoln was being pressed by the radicals on abolition; Wade, Chandler, and Trumbull were showing, with the success of their second Confiscation Act, that the mood of the Republican majority was shifting their way; the President must have realized that if he did not take action on emancipation soon, Congress would seize what he considered his prerogative.

Sumner's visit, in which Lincoln was reported to have called a presidential emancipation proclamation "too big a lick now" took place on July 4; their conversation was reported in a letter from *Tribune* correspondent Adams Hill to Sydney Gay five days later. In a footnote on p. 147 of Nevins's *War Becomes Revolution,* Sumner is cited as the source for Lincoln's "half the officers would fling down their arms," a quote that concludes "and three more States would rise."

Wade, who visited Lincoln from time to time, preferred that abolition be a congressional initiative, and on the floor of the Senate on July 16 dared the President to veto the Confiscation bill, calling his behind-the-scenes efforts to water it down "utterly illegitimate." Nicohay wrote later that the bill should be called "an act to destroy slavery under the powers of war."

The man the radicals suggested to replace McClellan was General John Pope; the "headquarters in the saddle" line, with its subsequent "where his hindquarters ought to be" was a natural joke and often attributed to Lincoln. In the Cabinet, Chase was a particular partisan of Pope. Stanton, throughout the spring, had been secretly encouraging General David Hunter in his plan to arm negroes; "Silence on the part of Stanton" write biographers Benjamin Thomas and Harold Hyman, "after he had received Hunter's Fort Leavenworth letter and his request for scarlet pantaloons, might very well have been interpreted by the general as implied consent to go ahead."

Lincoln's chief senatorial agent in opposing the Confiscation bill at this time was Orville Browning, who reports in his diary of July 1, 1862, a talk alone with Lincoln about the Confiscation bill at which the President read him a paper "embodying his view of the objects of the war." One of those objectives, according to the anti-abolition Browning, was: "Congress has no power of slavery in the states, and so much of it as remains after the war is over will be in precisely the same condition that it was before the war began, and must be left to the exclusive control of the states where it may exist." Senator Browning, the President's closest friend in the Senate, who often served as the private audience for Lincoln's poetry reading, wrote contemporaneously: "His views coincided entirely with my own."

Browning records making a call on Anna Carroll on July 27, 1862, "and gave her a copy of each of my speeches which she had requested." She agreed with him on vetoing Confiscation, and had probably been working with him on speeches that summer. She received a compliment from Lincoln at about that time: his note to her is cited in *CW* for August 19, 1862, and reads: "Like everything else that comes from you I have read the address to Maryland with great interest. It is just what is needed now and you were the one to do it." This Lincoln note, sent by her to President Garfield years later, is copied in her handwriting and the original has not turned up; it is accepted as authentic because Attorney General Bates's covering note, in his hand, says: "The President sends you a brief note of thanks." It evidently patched up the quarrel over money.

At the same time Lincoln was urging Browning to keep Congress out of the emancipation business and was telling Sumner abolition was "too big a lick now," he was telling visiting Quakers urging abolition that he had "sometime thought that perhaps he might be an instrument of God's hands of accomplishing a great work" (*CW*, June 20). And according to Charles Hamlin's 1899 biography, *Life and Times of Hannibal Hamlin*, Lincoln read his Vice President a draft of the Emancipation Proclamation on June 18.

I think the Hamlin report is in error on the date. As we shall see, Lincoln probably began drafting the proclamation just after the Seven Days' battles, which ended July 2. He was moved to this action by a combination of (1) congressional moves to seize control of an issue he wanted to determine himself, (2) what he believed was the severe setback in the war and the probable subsequent loss of recruitment and funds, (3) the failure of the border states to respond favorably to his plan for compensation, and (4) his personal inclination to do "a great work" in righting a great wrong.

BOOK FIVE, CHAPTER 11: COUNTERATTACK (p. 457)

Fiction subsumes fact in this chapter. Breckinridge was promoted to major general after Shiloh; at this stage of the war, he and his Orphans were at Vicksburg. I have brought him to Richmond (where he later spent months, with some of his social activities recounted by diarist Mary Boykin Chesnut) to serve as a fictional "reporter" for the mood of the Confederate capital just before Lee's breaking of the siege of Richmond and the series of battles known as the Seven Days.

President Davis's opening quote is taken from his memoir, *The Rise and Fall of the Confederate Government* II, 135: "It would almost seem as if the Government of the United States anticipated, at this period, the failure of McClellan's expedition." Davis believed that by creating an army under Pope to protect Washington, Lincoln wrote off McClellan's chances for taking Richmond. Confederate leaders considered Jackson's forays to be diversions designed to play on Lincoln's fears of an attack on his capital; Lincoln fell for the ruse. Whether McClellan, if supported by McDowell's army, would have been able to resist Lee's counterattack will never be known. I think McClellan, who was just resuming forward movement when Lee attacked, would have forced the Confederates out of Richmond. That would not have ended the war.

The conversation with Judah Benjamin is fictional, but Burton Hendrick, in his 1939 *Statesman of the Lost Cause,* pp. 212–13, attributes the sorry state of Confederate finances to a "monstrous blunder" of a cotton embargo and suggests that Benjamin opposed it. In vainly trying to coerce Europe into extending recognition, the South lost the resources it needed to finance a long war.

Davis's trip out Nine Mile Road to the Mechanicsville front and his frigid reception there by Lee is told on pp.131–32 of Volume II of Douglas Southall Freeman's 1934 biography, *R. E. Lee.* His comment to Breckinridge about not being like Lincoln, as shown by his willingness to risk the capital on a countermove by McClellan south of the Chicahominy, is fictional, but the case as stated is factual, drawn from Freeman's research.

The words attributed to Lee are almost all taken from the written record. J.F.C. Fuller's 1933 *Grant and Lee,* pp. 110–13, contains the quotations and their sources for Lee's remarks on slavery, on leaving the outcome of battle in the hands of God, and the story Lee recounted (in a letter to his son Curtis) of the Puritan legislator in the eclipse.

Although Breckinridge was over a thousand miles from the Richmond scene at the time, Davis may have been considering him for the Cabinet, as later events showed.

BOOK FIVE, CHAPTER 12: THE NEWSPAPER WAR (p. 468)

Telegraph messages, newspaper stories and headlines quoted in this chapter are all factual. The collection and evaluation of the news is dramatized conjecture, but on the basis of the documents and supporting correspondence is probably close to what happened.

Adams Hill's relationship with Greeley and Gay, the hiring of Page, Wilkeson's calling the local office a "bureau" and other details are from pp. 114–27 of Louis Starr's 1954 *Bohemian Brigade.* Starr also refers to Lincoln's arrest of Fulton, which is more fully covered on pp. 154–59 of Robert Harper's 1951 *Lincoln and the Press.*

Lincoln telegraphed Seward in New York on the night of June 29 that Charles Fulton of the Baltimore *American* had been his only source of news of the battle that afternoon, and that "I think we had the better of it up to that point of time." When he read Fulton's telegraph advisory to editors promising a report of his talk with the President as well as a report on the battle, Lincoln had the editor arrested. That reaction was excessive on the President's part, not to be excused on the grounds that he was worried about the army in the field. Stanton added to Lincoln's message to Seward that "my inference is, that General McClellan will probably be in Richmond in two days." Fulton's original advisory to editors was printed in the *New York Times* on June 30.

Hill's conversation with Bates is fictional. His private message to Gay about "the bluest day since Bull Run" is in the Gay papers.

A. P. Hill attacked Fitz-John Porter's corps at Mechanicsville on the first of the Seven Days' battles, but Stonewall Jackson, perhaps exhausted from two nights in the saddle, did not join the attack, and Hill's key charge failed. Porter, seeing his communications threatened, fell back to a prepared position near Gaines' Mill, and McClellan promptly ordered a change of base from the Pamunkey River to the James, where he would have the protection of Federal gunboats.

On the second day, June 27, with Jackson again failing to get into action, Porter inflicted severe losses on the Confederates, who finally broke his line, but he was able to move to join the main body of McClellan's army, its wagon trains and herd of cattle, toward the James. Lee's attack was uncoordinated and costly, but it was an attack, and McClellan's retreat was masterly, showing contingency planning, but it was a retreat.

The next day, with fighting temporarily abated as the army moved toward its new base at Harrison's Bar, also called Harrison's Landing, McClellan wrote his angry telegram to Lincoln about "You have done your best to sacrifice this army." As recounted in *CW* for June 28, Colonel Sanford deleted these inflammatory lines from the copy sent to Stanton and the President. The full message did appear in McClellan's official report, and the deletion was recounted in David Homer Bates's 1907 *Lincoln in the Telegraph Office.*

BOOK FIVE, CHAPTER 13: JOHN HAY'S DIARY, JULY 4, 1862 (p. 476)

About this time, physical strain was beginning to tell on Lincoln, up to then a man of muscle and stamina. According to Commander Dahlgren's diary for July 5, reported in *LDBD,* Mrs. Lincoln in the carriage on her way to the Soldiers' Home told him that the President frequently passed sleepless nights. Senator Browning's diary for July 15 characterized Lincoln's condition on that morning as "weary, care-worn and troubled."

The Marcy "capitulation" remark and meeting with Lincoln was on that July 15 and recorded by Browning, who got it from Lincoln. I have attributed remarks in that scene to Lincoln taken verbatim from his telegraph messages to McClellan on July 2, 3, and 4, and Marcy's comments based on McClellan's responses as listed in *CW* for those dates.

Anna Carroll prepared both a *Reply to Sumner* and a letter to Lincoln urging veto of the Confiscation Act as originally proposed; a draft of her letter dated July 4, from which part of her end of the fictional dialogue is taken, is in her papers at the Maryland Historical Society in Annapolis. She used the word "revengeful" rather than "vengeful," which was probably not an error at the time.

The "whose boots did you think I blacked?" line was spoken by Lincoln to Senator Sumner, not Anna Carroll, and is cited on p. 333 of Don Seitz's 1931 *Lincoln the Politician.*

The story told by Lincoln at the chapter's end is in Sandburg I, p. 495; his source was p. 288 of Ward Hill Lamon's *Recollections of Abraham Lincoln.*

BOOK FIVE, CHAPTER 14: HELL OF A FIZZLE (p. 481)

"One of the strangest episodes of the Civil War" was the way historian David Donald characterized the letter McClellan handed to Lincoln at Harrison's Landing. "Often treated by historians as an incredible aberration on McClellan's part," he wrote on p. 95 of his 1956 *Lincoln Reconsidered,* "or as a political document designed to win him the next Democratic presidential nomination, the letter was, in fact, merely a statement of what McClellan thought to be [Marshal] Jomini's principles; he believed that war ought to be fought by soldiers on the battlefield."

Alan Nevins sharply disagrees. "Lincoln was trying to be patient with McClellan . . . But McClellan put an intolerable tax on his forbearance when he handed the President a letter, dated July 7, expressing all his innate arrogance." He singles out in a footnote on p. 160 of his 1960 volume *War Becomes Revolution,* "one especially offensive sentence: 'A declaration of radical views, especially upon slavery, will rapidly disintegrate our present armies.' As Nicolay and Hay say, it had probably been prepared weeks before, and marked the beginning of McClellan's distinctively political career."

Nevins (and Sandburg, and most Lincoln biographers) adopt that Nicohay line, while Donald (and very few others) take the revisionist view of James Randall in his 1945 *Lincoln the President*, II, pp. 100–4. Randall slams *Nicohay*'s "quite inadequate account of the President's visit to McClellan's army"; he argues "the whole twisted context in Nicolay and Hay suggests that because the enemy was not planning to attack, therefore the army ought to be removed far to the rear and its commander reduced to a minor role." He reminds us of Hay's private letter to Nicolay expressing an ulterior motive: "It is of the utmost moment that we should *seem* fair to him [McClellan], while we are destroying him."

Most military historians hold McClellan in contempt; Kenneth Williams calls him "not a real general . . . merely an attractive but vain and unstable man, with considerable military knowledge, who sat a horse well and wanted to be President." But in *The Lincoln Nobody Knows* in 1958, Richard Current, examining the legend of Lincoln as a military genius, makes an objective case first for one, then for the other; in my judgment, the most telling point in both is the motive suggested for Lincoln's refusal to give McClellan the support the general thought he needed: "The Radical Republicans . . . did not want hostilities to end too soon for emancipation, nor did they welcome victory at the hands of a general whose glory would redound to the advantage of the Democratic Party. Better years of defeat than a quick success for McClellan . . ."

I do not believe Lincoln shared this view, and would have delighted in a quick success, but he was influenced by men (like Stanton and Wade) who believed this passionately. Hindsight shows that Lincoln was wrong to see Jackson's movement in the Valley as "a general and concerted one" and McClellan was right in seeing it as Lee's diversion intended to keep aid from moving toward the Army of the Potomac in front of Richmond.

Strategically, McClellan was on target with his summation plea after the President left Harrison's Landing: "Here, directly in front of this army, is the heart of the rebellion; it is here that all our resources should be collected to strike the blow which will determine the fate of the nation." Two long and bloody years later, under Grant, who saw the same opportunity but who had Lincoln's trust, that was the course taken.

But here is the stickler for any defender of McClellan: if Lincoln had sent reinforcements, would his general have moved on Richmond? If that answer is yes, which I think it is, would McClellan then have struck hard to destroy Lee's army as the Confederate Government moved to Montgomery? I think not, because his view of the war's purpose was different from Lincoln's.

In reaching this judgment, we now have fresh information about the state of McClellan's mind. Historians have drawn on the letters to Ellen Marcy McClellan published in *McClellan's Own Story*, which McClellan copied into a notebook later, some of which W. S Prime selected for inclusion in that memoir published after McClellan's death. However, the original notebook (not the original letters, which have not been found) in the Library of Congress contains unpublished material that is revealing.

In the letter to his wife in this chapter, drawn from this source, the general admits "I have not done splendidly," which to some degree shows that he knew his public claims of a brilliant change of base were, after all, excuses for lack of success. More important is his rationale for God's denial of his victory: "If I had succeeded in taking Richmond now, the fanatics of the North might have been too powerful, and reunion would be impossible."

This "new" information about his belief about his fate shows, first, that McClellan had a cockeyed view of the trend of public opinion in the North, which in reality was moving toward agreement with "the fanatics,"—in fact, his delay in taking Richmond played into abolitionist hands. Second, when viewed in conjunction with his earlier peace overture, this statement shows that negotiated reunion rather than destruction of enemy forces was his clear priority. Lincoln's route to reunion was through winning the war.

Thus the Harrison's Landing letter, though not intended by the writer (McClellan and Thomas Key) as an insubordinate or presumptuous incursion into politics, was read correctly by the President as expression of political-military opposition. No wonder he decided to pull McClellan back, and to begin to make the moves in the abolition area—directly contrary to McClellan's advice—that would both hurt the South and leapfrog the Confiscation Act.

In this chapter, the conversation between Stanton and McClellan is drawn from the general's recollections in his memoirs. My mind reading of Stanton is fictional, unkind, and I think accurate. Lincoln's brief address to the troops is in Sandburg I, p. 496, drawn from a *Harper's Weekly* account, and his examination of the generals is taken from Lincoln's extensive and lawyerly notes in *CW* from July 8 and 9 of 1862. McClellan's discussion of the goals of the war are taken verbatim from his Harrison's Landing letter, p. 487 of his *Own Story;* Stanton was probably not present when McClellan made these points to Lincoln, first orally, then in writing.

Stanton's conversation on the boat back with Lincoln is fictional; his fear that McClellan was a rival for his job is cited on the Thomas-Hyman biography, p. 212. The canalboats were called "Stanton's navy," and it is likely that Lincoln knew it. The running-aground at Kettle Shoals and the presidential swim are cited in *LDBD* for July 10, the source the *Boston Transcript* the next day.

In the final scene, the writing is from the unpublished notes. The particular meeting with Custer and Key is fictional, although they met with McClellan all the time; the line about letters urging a move to take over the government in Washington, attributed here to Custer, is from the McClellan notebook. The blast at Stanton is also verbatim from the notebook, deleted in the correspondence published in the memoirs. The final note to his wife about the baby is not in the notebook for that date, but was inserted in the memoirs by Prime, presumably from a letter in Mrs. McClellan's possession.

BOOK FIVE, CHAPTER 15: FIRST DRAFT (p. 488)

When did Lincoln decide to start writing an emancipation proclamation?

The best clue is in David Homer Bates's 1907 *Lincoln in the Telegraph Office.* On p. 138 the telegrapher quotes his former boss, Major Thomas Eckert: "Upon [the President's] arrival early one morning in June, 1862, shortly after McClellan's 'Seven Days Fight,' he asked me for some paper, as he wanted to write something special. I procured some foolscap and handed it to him."

That cannot be quite accurate: the Seven Days ended on July 2. Either Eckert was in error about "one morning in June," or "shortly after McClellan's 'Seven Days Fight.'" Since events make more of an impression on the memory than dates, the likelihood is that the day Lincoln came into the telegraph office to work on the Proclamation was during the first week in July.

What's significant about that? It tells us, first, that Lincoln made the decision after the bad news of McClellan's retreat from the gates of Richmond, and before he went down to Harrison's Landing. Thus, he was working on the draft of the Emancipation Proclamation at a time when his primary general was telling him he had better not do it lest the army disintegrate.

It also tells us that Lincoln, while seriously contemplating a veto of the Second Confiscation Act—the radicals' proposal to seize the property of rebels and liberate their slaves immediately—was preparing to take action on his own along similar lines.

He was being pulled away from abolition by the army, pushed toward it by a forceful minority in the Congress; he could no longer avoid history.

The quotation about colonization is from his appeal to the border state representatives, *CW* for July 12.

BOOK SIX, CHAPTER 1: SMALL CHANGE (p. 495)

When the value of government paper declined against precious metals in 1862, after hopes for a Union victory dimmed, stamps were used for small change. A good account of the phenomenon of public acceptance of the paper money is in Wesley Mitchell's 1903 *History of the Greenbacks,* pp. 90–101.

This chapter is fiction; no account of this conversation exists, and no romantic attachment between Hay and Kate Chase or Salmon Chase and Anna Carroll is known.

Thoughts about the vast changes about centralization of power, attributed to Chase's rumination, are my own, based on James Rawley's 1973 *The Politics of Union,* pp. 64–68.

Chase's description of Cabinet meetings as meetings of department heads (rather than as a committee to decide high policy) is cited in Burton Hendrick's 1946 *Lincoln's War Cabinet,* p. 373. John Nicolay later described Chase's attitude toward Lincoln as one that "varied between the limits of active hostility and benevolent contempt."

Kate Chase was sent to Miss Haines's boarding school in New York for six years, throughout her teens, where she received letters from her father mainly about sin, death, morality, and why it would be better if she did not come home for Christmas. Her resentment at this exile is suggested by several biographers, typically in the opening chapters of Alice Hunt Sokoloff's sympathetic 1971 *Kate Chase for the Defense.* "A daughter ought in all things to respect a father's feelings," Chase wrote her once, "and if wishes conflict and no moral principle is compromised by yielding, she ought to yield gracefully, kindly, cordially. You will easily remember instances in which you have tried me pretty severely by not doing so" (p. 73).

Charles Sumner visited Kate at school when in New York, and frequently wrote to Chase about his "intelligent daughter." Chase and Sumner were closer than indicated in this chapter; a portrait of Sumner hung in Chase's study, above a portrait of Charles Carroll.

The widower Chase's romances with Adele Douglas and Carlotta Eastman are recounted by Ishbel Ross on pp. 112–14 of the 1953 *Proud Kate;* Miss Ross includes among Chase's most frequent correspondents Grace Greenwood, Lizzie Pike, and Anna Ella Carroll. To avoid problems with Kate at home, the Secretary of the Treasury arranged for mail delivery at the office "like an amorous schoolboy." When Chase called on Mrs. Douglas one day and she was not in, he left a torn dollar greenback with his face on it for a calling card.

BOOK SIX, CHAPTER 2: JOHN HAY'S DIARY, JULY 12,1862 (p. 501)

We are now into a sequence of events that casts a light on Lincoln's state of mind and motives as he moves toward emancipation; accordingly, we will stick closely to the facts.

John Hay's real diary has no entries for the crucial three-month period of May through July, 1862; perhaps that section of his papers was lost or destroyed. The description of Lincoln's state of mind as unusually troubled and distracted is taken from Orville Browning's diary of that first two weeks of July.

Lincoln met with the border-state delegation on July 12, as this chapter says; he wrote out his remarks beforehand, and they exist in *CW* for that date, with a footnote on the Marylanders and Kentuckians present, and their cool reception to his suggestion. This scene is a shortened version of what was said, if Lincoln stuck to his prepared statement.

Preparing written remarks, and reading them to the visiting delegation, was certainly an unusually formal practice for Lincoln. Why did he do it? One reason could be that he considered what he had to say so important that he would not take the chance of ad-libbing; another is that he wanted a written record of the meeting so that its report could not be shaded by any of the participants. A third reason is that Lincoln knew that acceptance of his offer by the border states was unlikely, and wanted proof at hand that he had given the loyal slave owners their last chance.

The colloquy with John Crisfield is from p. 290 of Ward Hill Lamon's *Recollections of Abraham Lincoln*. Lamon wrote that Crisfield, a warm friend of Lincoln, was in Congress when "the proposition was made for gradual emancipation in the border states by paying the loyal owners for their slaves. Mr. Crisfield was on the committee that was to draft the reply to this proposition." Presumably this was the group that met with Lincoln on July 12. "When he was at the White House one day in July 1862," Lamon continues, "Mr. Lincoln said: 'Well, Crisfield, how are you getting along with your report, have you written it yet?' Mr. Crisfield replied that he had not. Mr. Lincoln—knowing that the Emancipation Proclamation was coming, in fact was then only two months away—said, 'You had better come to an agreement. Niggers will never be higher."

Carl Sandburg, in citing this episode from Lamon on p. 582 of Vol. I of *Lincoln: The War Years,* quoted Lincoln as saying "Niggers will never be cheaper." Either Sandburg mistranscribed the Lamon quote, or thought that Lamon had it mixed up, and corrected the source. However, it seems to me that Lamon had it right: Lincoln was saying that the time to sell slaves to the government was now, as the price offered was high, and it would be unwise of slave owners to await a higher price. Lincoln had a proclamation of emancipation of rebel-held slaves in mind, if the loyal border states did not accept compensated emancipation; the price of their slaves would surely fall—ultimately, as those slaves, too, were freed, to zero.

The word "nigger" is now a highly offensive racial slur, especially when spoken by a white; in 1862, it was still a slur, but much more commonly used and not considered so offensive. Lamon, a Virginian, would have used the word without thinking and might have attributed it inaccurately to Lincoln. Or he might have remembered the sentence vividly.

BOOK SIX, CHAPTER 3: THE TIME HAS ARRIVED (p. 503)

Hard evidence of the first inkling Lincoln gave to any of his Cabinet members that he was contemplating a proclamation of freedom is in Gideon Welles's diary, published in 1911. Inserted after Welles realized the historic import of the episode, the entry does not have the weight of a note written the day it happened—but Welles has a good recollection of detail (Seward was accompanied by his daughter-in-law, not his wife) and is considered a reliable witness by most historians.

I have turned into dialogue these sentences, among others: "This was, he said, the first occasion when he had mentioned the subject to any one, and wished us to frankly state how the proposition struck us. Mr. Seward said the subject involved consequences so vast and momentous that he should wish to bestow on it mature reflection before giving a decisive answer, but his present opinion inclined to the measure as justifiable, and perhaps he might say expedient and necessary. These were also my views."

Twelve years later, however, in 1874, after a memorial address by Charles Francis Adams emphasized Seward's contribution to what Welles thought was the detriment of Lincoln, the incensed former Navy Secretary wrote a series of articles in *Galaxy* magazine, later expanded into a short book, *Lincoln and Seward*. Welles recollected the same ride to the graveyard in a quite different light: "The time, [Lincoln] said, had arrived when we must determine whether the slave element should be for or against us. Mr. Seward . . . was appalled and not prepared for this decisive step . . . Startled with so broad and radical a proposition, he informed the President that the consequences of such an act were so momentous that he was not prepared to advise on the subject without further reflection." He does not add that "those were also my views."

Which Welles do you believe? I am inclined to go for the sober second thought in this case, not my usual practice, because (1) the first entry was not written the day it happened, and (2) Welles may have been flushed into a greater degree of frankness by what he considered an injustice done the memory of Lincoln. Also, as we shall see in subsequent chapters, Seward consistently counsels delay while his alter ego, Weed, advises against the emancipation policy. My judgment is that Lincoln's closest centrist adviser—the old "irrepressible conflict" Seward, now turned gradualist—leaned against the emancipation decision, making it all the more a bold Lincoln move.

The part of the conversation about arming the slaves is fictional; it was probably adverted to on that ride, since it was central to the argument at the time, and Lincoln's position is taken from Orville Browning's diary entry for July 1, less than two weeks before this scene: "He read me a paper . . . he had sketched hastily with the intention of laying it before the Cabinet . . . At present none [of the escaped negroes] are to be armed."

Seward's disagreement with Lincoln's interest in colonization is based on a letter he wrote to the U.S. minister to Brazil on July 21, 1862, a week after this scene, replying to the "finger of God" suggestion, including the phrase that republican governments do not "provide prematurely for future but not imminent emergencies" (Vol. V, p. 334, *Works of William H. Seward*, published in 1884).

At this point of time (to use a phrase Lincoln favored), the President was considering, and actually drafting, both his emancipation proclamation and his veto of the Confiscation Act. I think he did not have his mind made up about either.

BOOK SIX, CHAPTER 4: DYING SOMETIME (p. 508)

The opening scene is fiction based on documented sources. Orville Browning notes once in his diary that he visited Anna Ella Carroll; a decade later, she would urge him to run for President; they thought along the same conservative lines in politics.

Her remarks are taken from her letters to Lincoln of July 4 and 11, 1862, in her papers at the Maryland Historical Association in Annapolis. She vigorously opposed the confiscation bill on technical grounds as an unconstitutional blood attainder, and more generally as a divisive shift in the purpose of the war. Her remarks about Fessenden and Chase are fiction.

The scene at the Executive Mansion is based on Browning's diary for July 14 and 15, 1862. His contemporaneous account of the careworn President's "I must die some-time" rings true, and demonstrates Lincoln's melancholy state of mind during this active final week of the congressional session. Browning's role in this period, as Lincoln's closest personal friend and his emissary to the Senate on some but not all matters, is explained by James Randall in a footnote on p. 561 of the Diary, Vol. I.

Consider the events crowding in on Lincoln in that mid-July period, and his reactions to them: the visit to Harrison's Landing after the military disappointment and McClellan's warning about the army reaction to abolition; the beginning of drafting the emancipation proclamation, and the first discussion of it with Seward and Welles at Stanton's child's funeral; the passage of the Confiscation Act, seizing the slavery issue from the Executive branch; the preparation of the rare veto, and the legislative legerdemain described in the next chapter. Lincoln evidently let himself get depressed but did not let that stop him from responding cagily and vigorously to the challenges to his authority.

BOOK SIX, CHAPTER 5: NOT SO FAR TRUST ME (p. 512)

Although the conversation is dramatized, this is essentially what went on in the Senate that day, as Lincoln tried to head off having to veto legislation he considered too harsh. Lincoln's letter to both Houses of Congress is in *CW* for July 15, 1862, as well as Solomon Foot's reply, and Lincoln's answer chiding the Senate for not trusting him.

Fessenden's role in the shaping of a compromise, including his resentment at Wade's charge of "mousing around," is detailed on pp. 146–47 of Charles Jellison's 1962 *Fessenden of Maine.* Fessenden wrote to Hamilton Fish at the time that he suspected Lincoln would veto the legislation as it stood when passed, which "I fear will dishearten the country. He seems to be very much in the hands of the Philistines in this. Well, we have what we bargained for, a splitter of rails, and have no right to complain."

Wade's words quoted here about "I have no scruples about the property of his" and "The President cannot lay down and fix the principles upon which a war shall be conducted" and "we ought to have a committee on vetoes" are cited on p. 164 of T. Harry Williams's 1941 *Lincoln and the Radicals.* His speech on the floor of the Senate blasting Fessenden for suggesting what he considered truckling to Lincoln is on p. 3382 of the *Congressional Globe* for July 16, 1862.

Wade and Chandler, like Lincoln, were aware that the fight over the control of policy toward slavery embodied in the Confiscation Act was central to control over the terms of peace. That is why Lincoln, who wanted no bloodbath of Southern leaders afterward, wanted Congress's bill softened; he had his own approach to emancipation in his pocket. That is also why Wade, who wanted blacks to be given full rights as citizens in the South, believed it necessary to punish the rebellion's leaders and thereby break the Southern aristocratic establishment. Lincoln and Wade were right not to trust each other in the unprecedented jockeying to soften the bill's effect, because each had different goals. Wade foresaw the century of denial of black civil rights, while Lincoln put first the immediate need for reconciliation of whites in the warring sections.

BOOK SIX, CHAPTER 6: THE VETO THAT WAS NOT (p. 516)

According to Browning's diary, Lincoln went to the Capitol office set aside for the President on the day of the extended session, to be present at the convenience of the Congress. On that July 17, the explanatory resolution was passed, the President signed both the Confiscation Act and the resolution watering it down to meet his objections, and submitted his mooted veto message as a kind of "this is what I would have done if."

We do not know what happened in that office that day. The scene with Blair riding to the Congress is fictional, the political interpretation attributed to the old man my own. The scene with Thaddeus Stevens is fictional, though the chances are good that Stevens would have seen the President in the Capitol that day.

The remarks of Stevens in this chapter are drawn from Fawn Brodie's 1959 *Thaddeus Stevens, Scourge of the South*, pp. 157–59, and from Ralph Korngold's 1955 *Thaddeus Stevens, A Being Darkly Wise and Rudely Great*, pp. 164–65. The reference to Wade's saying the country was going to hell with Lincoln in the White House is in Williams's *Lincoln and the Radicals*, p. 166.

"How I wish the border states would accept my proposition" was directed to Representative Owen Lovejoy, not Stevens. "I am going to sign . . . since they are substantially one" is in *CW* for July 17, in his message to Congress.

Korngold's thesis is that Lincoln tried to block the second Confiscation Act in three ways: by substituting his bill for gradual compensated emancipation; then by the plea to border state leaders to act on his bond-financed buy-back plan; and finally by issuing the Emancipation Proclamation, which rendered confiscation of slave property (and emancipation) inoperative for the remainder of the year. Lincoln's hope, according to this theory, was that this pressure of an abolition deadline at year's end would cause the border states to accept his gradual, compensated plan, which might then also serve as an attraction for some of the seceded states.

My own guess is that Lincoln was going through the motions with his gradualist plan, protecting himself from charges of radicalism, making emancipation appear to be his last resort after reasonableness did not work. His watering-down of the Compensation Act with the "explanation" ploy left the President, not the Congress, in charge of the slavery issue and kept him in the center of public sentiment.

Since he was to spring the news of emancipation on his Cabinet within a week, the main reason for his half-veto of confiscation of rebel slaves seems clear: he wanted the weapon to use as a military act in defeating the South and preserving the Union. First things first. Union before anything.

BOOK SIX, CHAPTER 7: AN INSIDE SOURCE (p. 521)

Fictional scene, based on fact. Greeley's expectation of a "higgling" execution of the Confiscation Act was in the New York *Tribune* on July 19, cited in Ralph Fahrney's 1936 *Horace Greeley and the Tribune in the Civil War*, p. 125. Greeley's demand for a "brief, frank, stirring proclamation" was in the *Tribune* July 25.

Gay's quotation of the *New York Times*'s remarkably timely and accurate speculation about Lincoln's emancipation thinking is from the *New York Times* of July 17, 1862. (Stylistic reminder: New York was hyphenated at that time, but not in this book.)

James Gilmore, who used the pen name Edmund Kirke, is not a trustworthy source, since he "cooked" a letter supposedly written by Lincoln to substantiate his story of being an intermediary—he later admitted he "re-created" it from memory—and you always have to watch out for novelists, but he is better than no source at all. There is probably truth in the arrangement Gilmore described in his 1898 *Personal Recollections of Abraham Lincoln and the Civil War*, pp. 75–85.

BOOK SIX, CHAPTER 8: SURPRISE SUPPORT (p. 525)

Stanton knew all about General Hunter's premature proclamation of emancipation and plans for enlisting and possibly arming fugitive slaves when protests from Treasury agents managing plantations in his area were forwarded to the Secretary of War by Chase. A more vivid clue was in Hunter's letter to Stanton of January 29, 1862, requesting fifty thousand scarlet pantaloons, "and this is all the clothing I shall require for these people."

Lincoln's denial that Stanton was aware of Hunter's plan is in his letter to James Gordon Bennett of the *New York Herald* in *CW* for May 21, 1862.

Francis Brockholst Cutting's meetings with Stanton and Lincoln took place on July 22, before the historic afternoon Cabinet meeting. This chapter dramatizes some of what was probably said, based on pp. 238–39 of the Thomas-Hyman biography of Stanton, in turn based on a letter reviewing the events of that day from Cutting to Stanton dated February 20, 1867, in the Stanton papers.

Cutting also met with Lincoln after the Cabinet meeting, and wrote Stanton that Lincoln gave him the impression he planned to issue the proclamation the next day, which suggests that the decision at the meeting was to go ahead, not to delay the timing until after a victory, as was commonly believed. But that gets ahead of our story.

BOOK SIX, CHAPTER 9: THENCEFORWARD AND FOREVER (p. 528)

This chapter seeks to reconstruct what actually happened in the White House on July 22, 1862, at one of the most significant Cabinet meetings in American history.

The reader is entitled to a close look at the primary sources. Each recollection reflects a personal or political bias; not one should be taken as a fair summation of what went on in that room that day; but taken together, and fleshed out with what we know are the written positions of some of the characters present, we can get an idea of the interplay. We can also get an insight into who wanted to be remembered for what.

Were any notes taken at the meeting itself? Probably. These raw notes were in Edwin Stanton's handwriting and quoted in full—"reproduced as nearly as the types conveniently permit"—by Nicolay and Hay in Vol. VI, p. 128 of their history:

Tuesday, July 22.

The President proposes to issue an order declaring that, all slaves in States in rebellion on the _____ day of _____ _____ _____

The Attorney-General and Stanton are for its immediate promulgation.

Seward against it; argues strongly in favor of cotton and foreign Governments.

Chase silent.

Welles _____

Seward argues _____ That foreign nations will intervene to prevent the abolition of slavery for sake of cotton. Argues in a long speech against its immediate promulgation. Wants to wait for troops. Wants Halleck here. Wants drum and fife and public spirit. We break up our relations with foreign nations and the production of cotton for sixty years.

Chase _____ Thinks it a measure of great danger, and would lead to universal emancipation _____ The measure goes beyond anything I have recommended.

Nicohay published this with some glee, since the last lines showed that "the member who opposed the measure as a whole . . . was the anti-slavery Secretary of the Treasury, Mr. Chase . . ." The secretaries noted that "the omissions in this bit of historical manuscript are exceedingly provoking, but some of them are supplied by the President's own narrative, recorded and published by the artist, F. B. Carpenter, whose application for permission to paint his historical picture of the signing of the Emancipation Proclamation called it forth."

The secretaries promote the Carpenter account as "the President's own narrative," but was it? The direct quotation was recorded later by a visitor who was not making notes. Reprinted later in almost every biography of Lincoln, this unsupported recollection of the portrait artist's, even if he had a tape-recorder memory, "recorded" the President's recollection two years after the event. Read it remembering it is Carpenter's recollection of Lincoln's recollection:

"It had got to be," said he [Mr. Lincoln], "midsummer, 1862. Things had gone on from bad to worse, until I felt that we had reached the end of our rope on the plan of operations we had been pursuing; that we had about played our last card, and must change our tactics, or lose the game. I now determined upon the adoption of the emancipation policy; and without consultation with, or knowledge of, the Cabinet, I prepared the original draft of the proclamation, and after much anxious thought, called a Cabinet meeting upon the subject . . ."

At that point, the secretaries put an ellipsis and skip these lines that show the fuzzy nature of the artist's account: "This was the last of July," continues Lincoln as quoted by Carpenter, "or the first part of the month of August, 1862. (The exact date he did not remember.)" It was July 22. "This Cabinet meeting took place, I think, upon a Saturday," says Carpenter's Lincoln. July 22 was a Tuesday.

"All were present excepting Mr. Blair, the Postmaster-General, [Nicohay-Carpenter-Lincoln continue] who was absent at the opening of the discussion, but came in subsequently. I said to the Cabinet that I had resolved upon this step, and had not called them together to ask their advice, but to lay the subject-matter of a proclamation before them, suggestions as to which would be in order after they had heard it read. Mr. Lovejoy was in error when he informed you that it excited no comment excepting on the part of Secretary Seward. Various suggestions were offered."

Nicohay skips the next sentence without ellipsis, lest it reflect well on the Cabinet member they want to portray as no friend of the negro: "Secretary Chase wished the language stronger in reference to the arming of the blacks." That unmarked omission can only have been deliberate, and demonstrates their willingness to slant their story. The secretaries pick up Lincoln-Carpenter with:

> "Mr. Blair, after he came in, deprecated the policy on the ground that it would cost the Administration the fall elections. Nothing, however, was offered that I had not already fully anticipated and settled in my own mind, until Secretary Seward spoke. He said in substance, 'Mr. President, I approve of the proclamation, but I question the expediency of its issue at this juncture. The depression of the public mind, consequent upon our repeated reverses, is so great that I fear the effect of so important a step. It may be viewed as the last measure of an exhausted Government, a cry for help; the Government stretching forth its hands to Ethiopia, instead of Ethiopia stretching forth her hands to the Government.' His idea," said the President, "was that it would be considered our last *shriek* on the retreat. (This was his *precise* expression.)"

A question should be raised at this point: Whose precise expression was it? The construction is ambiguous: the parenthetical remark is within the quote attributed to Lincoln, so a good case can be made it was Carpenter quoting Lincoln quoting Seward; but it could also be Carpenter's own parenthesis, describing the precise expression Lincoln used, but not quoting Seward. I have chosen the latter, but that is a coin flip.

> " 'Now,' continued Mr. Seward, 'while I approve the measure, I suggest, sir, that you postpone its issue until you can give it to the country supported by military success, instead of issuing it, as would be the case now, upon the greatest disasters of the war.' " Mr. Lincoln continued: "The wisdom of the view of the Secretary of State struck me with very great force. It was an aspect of the case that, in all my thought upon the subject, I had entirely overlooked. The result was that I put the draft of the proclamation aside, as you do your sketch for a picture, waiting for victory."

Maybe that is Lincoln's recollection, reported nearly verbatim, maybe not; if so, maybe it is the way Lincoln wanted to remember the event. Certainly that is the story put forward by *Nicohay* and accepted by most biographers, though the secretaries did not want Chase's version registered. Later in his book, *Six Months at the White House,* pp. 87–88, the painter asked what would now be called a follow-up, ignored by *Nicohay:*

> I remember to have asked him, on one occasion, if there was not some opposition manifested on the part of several members of the Cabinet to this policy. He replied, "Nothing more than I have stated to you. Mr. Blair thought we should lose the fall elections, and opposed it on that ground only." "I have understood," said I, "that Secretary Smith was not in favor of your action. Mr. Blair told me that, when the meeting closed, he and the Secretary of the Interior went away together, and that the latter said to him, if the President carried out that policy, he might count on

losing *Indiana*, sure!" "He never said anything of the kind to me," returned the President. "And what is Mr. Blair's opinion now?" I asked. "Oh," was the prompt reply, "he proved right in regard to the fall elections, but he is satisfied that we have since gained more than we lost." "I have been told," I added, "that Judge Bates doubted the constitutionality of the proclamation." "He never expressed such an opinion in my hearing," replied Mr. Lincoln. "No member of the Cabinet ever dissented from the policy, in any conversation with me."

In the Carpenter version, the decision not to issue a proclamation of emancipation was not occasioned by doubts nor was the decision subject to review; only the timing was at issue. Certainly that is the *Nicohay* preference, showing a resolute President awaiting only a victory to avoid seeming desperate, and it has been accepted by most historians.

Not all, however. Thomas and Hyman, on p. 240 of their 1962 Stanton biography, write "there is evidence to indicate that Lincoln left the meeting undecided, chiefly because of Chase's opposition; that after giving the matter further thought he decided to issue the proclamation the next day; and that the delay afforded Seward an opportunity to bring a new influence to bear upon Lincoln in the person of Thurlow Weed."

Part of that evidence is a letter from Stanton's brother-in-law and aide, Christopher Walcott, to his wife Pamphila (Stanton's sister) dated July 27, presumably based on what Stanton told him about the Cabinet meeting: "The President is growing. The other day he proposed in Cabinet to issue *now* a proclamation setting free on the first of January next, all the slaves within states then under control of the rebels. All the Cabinet concurred save Seward who opposed, and Chase who doubted, saying 'it was a larger step than he ever contemplated!' " I am indebted to Norine D. Cashman of Brown University, a Stanton descendant organizing Stanton letters for donation to the Ohio Historical Society, for a copy of this letter, from which Thomas and Hyman quoted the remainder, which applies to the next chapter of this book: "We all plied him [Chase] so vigorously, that he came round next morning, but Seward had worked so industriously in the meantime that for the present, at least, that golden moment has passed away and *Chase* must be held responsible for delaying or defeating the greatest act of justice, statesmanship, and civilization of the last four thousand years."

Another source, also secondary, is a letter from Francis Cutting in the Wolcott papers stating that Lincoln told Cutting that afternoon he intended to issue the proclamation the next day, but that night Thurlow Weed got to the President and talked him out of it on the basis that it was an empty gesture that would unduly offend border states.

A third secondary source is abolitionist Count Gurowski, the State Department translator and diarist, who in an August 5 letter to Massachusetts governor John Andrew relates angrily that the proclamation of freedom for the slaves had just been shunted aside by the malign influence of Weed.

Thus, the widespread assumption that only a need for victory held up the issuance of the proclamation is at least challengeable; more likely, fierce jockeying on substance took place both in and after that Cabinet meeting.

Now back to primary sources. Attorney General Bates, who kept a diary, did not consider the day's events noteworthy enough for an entry, and John Hay's diary is silent throughout the entire summer of 1862; apparently both he and Nicolay were kept out of observing the decision-making at the time. But Salmon P. Chase recognized the significance of emancipation developments and saw the historical-political need to play up his plan to arm slaves and to play down Lincoln's plan to free slaves. Here is the entry from the Chase diary that reveals the remarkable message from Colonel Thomas Key, which must have angered Lincoln, and covers the Cabinet meeting that day:

July 22, Tuesday. This morning, I called on the President with a letter received some time since from Col. Key, in which he stated that he had reason to believe that if Genl. McClellan found he could not otherwise sustain himself in Virginia, he would declare the liberation of the slaves; and that the President would not dare to interfere with the Order. I urged upon the President the importance of an immediate change in the command of the Army of the Potomac . . .

The President came to no conclusion, but said he would confer with Gen. Halleck on all these matters. I left him, promising to return to Cabinet, when the subject of the Orders discussed yesterday would be resumed.

Went to Cabinet at the appointed hour. It was unanimously agreed that the Order in respect to Colonization should be dropped; and the others were adopted unanimously, except that I wished North Carolina included among the States named in the first order.

The question of arming slaves was then brought up and I advocated it warmly. The President was unwilling to adopt this measure, but proposed to issue a Proclamation, on the basis of the Confiscation Bill, calling upon the States to return to their allegiance—warning the rebels the provisions of the Act would have full force at the expiration of sixty days—adding, on his own part, a declaration of his intention to renew, at the next session of Congress, his recommendation of compensation to States adopting the gradual abolishment of slavery—and proclaiming the emancipation of all slaves within States remaining in insurrection on the first of January, 1863.

I said that I should give such a measure my cordial support, but I should prefer that no new expression on the subject of compensation should be made, and I thought that the measure of Emancipation could be much better and more quietly accomplished by allowing Generals to organize and arm the slaves (thus avoiding depredation and massacre on the one hand, and support to the insurrection on the other) and by directing the Commanders of Departments to proclaim emancipation within their Districts as soon as practicable; but I regarded this as so much better than inaction on the subject, that I should give it my entire support.

The President determined to publish the first three Orders forthwith, and to leave the other for some further consideration. The impression left upon my mind by the whole discussion was, that while the President thought that the organization, equipment and arming of negroes, like other soldiers, would be productive of more evil than good, he was not unwilling that Commanders should, at their discretion, arm, for purely defensive purposes, slaves coming within their lines.

Mr. Stanton brought forward a proposition to draft 50,000 men. Mr. Seward proposed that the number should be 100,000. The President directed that, whatever number were drafted, should be a part of the 300,000 already called for. No decision was reached however.

Chase indirectly admits dragging a foot, though he puts his lack of enthusiasm in the best radical light. It was more important to arm the slaves that came into their lines, and any emancipation should be done by commanders in the field on a military basis, not by the President on a political basis.

Let's see how Gideon Welles handled that meeting in his diary. Although he promptly recorded the first mention of the proposal in his diary the day of the funeral of Stanton's child, the Navy Secretary did not record his impressions of the July 22 meeting until October 1.

> It was pretty fully discussed at two successive Cabinet meetings [July 21 and 22], and the President consulted freely, I presume, with the members individually. He did with me. Mr. Bates desired that deportation, by force if necessary, should go with emancipation. Born and educated among the negroes, having always lived with slaves, he dreaded any step which should be taken to bring about social equality between the two races. The effect, he said, would be to degrade the whites without elevating the blacks. Demoralization, vice, and misery would follow. Mr. Blair, at the second discussion, said that, while he was an emancipationist from principle, he had doubts of the expediency of such a movement as was contemplated. Stanton, after expressing himself earnestly in favor of the step proposed, said it was so important a measure that he hoped every member would give his opinion, whatever it might be, on the subject; two had not spoken,—alluding to Chase and myself.
>
> I then spoke briefly of the strong exercise of power involved in the question, and the denial of Executive authority to do this act, but the Rebels themselves had invoked war on the subject of slavery, had appealed to arms, and they must abide the consequences. It was an extreme exercise of war powers, and under the circumstances and in view of the condition of the country and the magnitude of the contest I was willing to resort to extreme measures and avail ourselves of military necessity, always harsh and questionable. The blow would fall heavy and severe on those loyal men in the Slave States who clung to the Union and had most of their property in slaves, but they must abide the results of a conflict which we all deplored, and unless they could persuade their fellow citizens to embrace the alternative presented, it was their hard fortune to suffer with those who brought on the War. The slaves were now an element of strength to the Rebels,—were laborers, producers, and army attendants; were considered as property by the Rebels, and, if *property,* were subject to confiscation; if not property, but *persons* residing in the insurrectionary region, we should invite them as well as the whites to unite with us in putting down the Rebellion. I had made known my views to the President and could say here I gave my approval of the Proclamation. Mr. Chase said it was going a step farther than he had proposed, but he was glad of it and went into a very full argument on the subject. I do not attempt to report it or any portion of it, nor that of others, farther than to define the position of each when this important question was before us. Something more than a Proclamation will be necessary, for this step will band the South together, make opponents of some who now are friends and unite the Border States firmly with the Cotton States in resistance to the Government.

Who else was in the room? Interior Secretary Caleb Smith, who left no record of his impressions; Secretary of State Seward, who kept no diary and wrote no reminiscence of this; and Montgomery Blair.

As the testimony of others shows, Blair—the volunteer lawyer for runaway slave Dred Scott—was the most outspoken voice against the Proclamation. (Stanton's notes

1056

FREEDOM

make no mention of Blair's presence, which suggest they were written before he entered the room.) His point of view has not been adequately represented in analyses of this meeting because the memorial he said he would send the President (memoranda were then called memorials) was misfiled for a century in the Chase papers.

The Blair memo offering his views, dated July 23, is the basis for the quotations attributed to him in this chapter. His memo runs twelve hundred words and most of it has never been published but is available in the Chase papers at the Library of Congress. After dutifully giving Lincoln the most effective way to sell the idea—for its effect abroad—Blair concludes: "I verily believe it [the Proclamation] will prove ineffective in securing negro insurrection or any material support from that populations which we will not secure without it. And I am not sure that insurrection, which is the only aid we can hope from it, would not damage our cause rather than aid it."

From these materials is this chapter drawn. Although the scene may not have actually played in history as written here, it must have been close, and leads me to believe that the decision to postpone emancipation that afternoon was not final. Such far-reaching decisions are rarely made by presidents in Cabinet, and the Nicohay exaggeration of the Chase opposition is as false as the Lincoln-Carpenter profession of no real opposition at all. I think Chase twisted and squirmed, Welles leaned against, Stanton pressed hard for, Blair opposed on political and military grounds, and Seward won a delay so as to change Lincoln's mind overnight. No inexorability was apparent at the time, and with a sharp turn in the fortunes of war, no "military necessity" would have existed for emancipation. The delay was a much more difficult and controversial decision than it now seems.

BOOK SIX, CHAPTER 10: SECOND THOUGHTS (p. 541)

Though Chase and Carroll were acquainted, the stirrings of romance in this chapter and the presence of Anna Carroll at the meeting that evening of Chase, Stanton, and Cutting (which did take place) are fiction. The Greenbies biography is the source of the biographical information about her. The Chase visit to Charles Carroll, when he was the last surviving signer of the Declaration of Independence, and the presence of the painting of Charles Carroll in his study is in Ishbel Ross's *Proud Kate*, pp. 14 and 27.

Ben Wade's scornful assessment of Chase is on p. 270 of Hendrick's *Lincoln's War Cabinet*. Stanton's praise of Carroll is cited on p. 432 of Greenbies. The "spigot . . . twice as big as the bunghole" is a Chase remark made in May 1864, on p. 18 of David Donald's edition of the Chase diary.

The substance of what Cutting reported to Stanton is in the letter cited in the commentary on the previous chapter. The pressure Stanton brought to bear on Chase after the July 22 Cabinet meeting is in Thomas/Hyman, p. 240, with Stanton's brother-in-law writing to Stanton's sister "we all plied him [Chase] so vigorously, that he came round next morning . . ."

Anna Carroll, though a fictional reporter in this scene, would have remembered the Breckinridge-Cutting episode. Cutting was a pro-slavery Democrat allied with Breckinridge in repealing the Missouri Compromise, thereby allowing territories to decide for themselves about slavery, as the South wanted. The challenge to a duel when Cutting switched at the last minute is recounted in James C. Klotter's 1986 *The Breckinridges of Kentucky*, pp. 107–9, and is found in detail in Ben Perley Poore's 1886 *Perley's Reminiscences*, pp. 439–42. The enmity was fierce, with Breckinridge taking umbrage at the charge of "skulking," and Cutting charging he was libeled in "the most violent, inflammatory, and personal assaults that had ever been known upon this floor." Poore, Washington columnist for a Massachusetts newspaper, says that President Frank Pierce interceded and had the seconds stop the duel.

Anna Carroll's instruction to Chase about the way emancipation would change the nature of the war to revolution is not hers; I have taken it from Philip Paludan's 1975 *A Covenant with Death*, in his chapters about Harvard law professor Joel Parker's contemporary theories about the Civil War and the law of nations. Paludan makes a point of connecting the two proclamations of late September, emancipation and the crackdown on dissenters; Professor Parker feared the tyranny that Lincoln's "revolution" might bring.

BOOK SEVEN, CHAPTER 1: WIZARD OF THE LOBBY (p. 555)

Thurlow Weed, known to New Yorkers as the "Wizard of the Lobby," actively intervened with Lincoln on the night of July 22 to dissuade him from issuing the proclamation the President had in mind. Evidence of this activity is cited in the underbook for the previous two chapters, and is supported in general by Weed biographer Glyndon Van Deusen's description of the positions taken by Weed in public and private in that period (p. 300, *Thurlow Weed: Wizard of the Lobby*, 1947).

The conversations in this chapter are fictional, often drawing on quotations at other times. Seward's description of the policy being a coup d'état is on p. 333 of Van Deusen's 1967 biography of Seward, along with his story of the liberty pole. Seward kept no diary, but his opinion of the proclamation was expressed to Orville Browning and noted in that diary on January 22, 1863: "[Seward] regretted the policy of the Administration—thought the proclamations were unfortunate, and that we would have been nearer the end of the war and the end of slavery both without them . . . Said it was not alone the abolition clamor at home that induced the President to issue them, but that he was farther influenced by the wishes of foreign Nations . . ."

Lincoln's comments are a pastiche of quotations, from the frequently cited "the bottom's out of the tub" as an expression of despair to the equally frequent "justice to all" evasion, cited on p. 61 of Carman and Luthin's 1943 *Lincoln and the Patronage*. His assertion that he wrote the proclamation without help is in Carpenter's account cited in the previous chapter notes. The "sit on the blister" observation is on p. 42 of Vol. III of the papers of the Abraham Lincoln Association, in an article by Benjamin P. Thomas analyzing Lincoln's humor, also the source on p. 46 for the "elder-stalk squirts charged with rose water".

Now we come to Lincoln's statements about slavery and his answers to the taunts about abolition leading to the equality of the races. If the quotes are read in the light of today's standards, Lincoln can be shown to be a racist, as some in the 1960s tried to demonstrate. This is unfair, as a man's opinions should be judged in the context of his time. The fact that "tolerance" is not enough today does not diminish the courage it took to be tolerant a century ago.

Lincoln was a gradualist and an emancipationist, turning from persuasion and compensation early in the war to coercion later, as times and sentiments changed. He was consistent during the years of controversy in opposing the extension of slavery into the territories and unhesitatingly signed the bill freeing the slaves in the city of Washington.

On the other hand, the Great Emancipator was also the Great Would-be Colonizer.

His views on colonization were too consistent and frequently expressed to be sloughed off as a smoke screen. To suggest that his series of statements on sending the freed slaves to "congenial climes" in Africa and Central America were deliberate lies to calm the fears of white workers in the North attributes a degree of duplicity to Lincoln that I am unwilling to accept. The most charitable and thorough treatment of this usually avoided subject is in Gabor Boritt's 1975 article in Vol. 37 of *The Historian,* pp. 6199–30, in which the historian at Gettysburg College (who, incidentally, helped comb through this book for errors) attributes this aberration in Lincoln's thinking to the psychological technique of "avoidance." The President could not figure out what to do about the three or four million slaves, so he clung to this notion of sending them overseas rather than facing up to the problem at the time.

"I have no purpose to introduce political and social equality," cited ever since by white supremacists, is from *CW,* August 21, 1858; "Make them . . . our equals?" from *CW,* October 16, 1854; "I can just leave her alone" from *CW,* June 26, 1857; "We were constantly charged with seeking an amalgamation" from *CW,* February 28, 1857; "Fudge! etc.," from *CW,* September 6, 1859.

"If I take this step without the argument of military necessity" is from a letter to Chase a year later, about applying the proclamation to parts of states previously exempted, *CW,* September 2, 1863; the President's awareness of the Weed-Blair argument is in his conclusion "Would it not lose us the elections, and with them, the very cause we seek to advance?"

The famous line, "If slavery is not wrong, then nothing is wrong" was not written until April 4, 1864, to a Kentucky editor. Even then, eighteen months after the preliminary proclamation, Lincoln was careful not to make the moral case the basis for his act. His anti-slavery statement was accompanied by "I felt that measures, otherwise unconstitutional, might become lawful, by becoming indispensable to the preservation of the Constitution, through the preservation of the nation . . ." He insisted, to this border-state leader, that the motive of the action was military: "I was, in my best judgment, driven to the alternative of either surrendering the Union, and with it, the Constitution, or of laying strong hand upon the colored element. I chose the latter. In choosing it, I hoped for greater gain than loss; but of this, I was not entirely confident."

Helping to make him less than confident at the time was Weed, whose conversation in this chapter is fictional but probably close to what he was urging that night.

BOOK SEVEN, CHAPTER 2: PHOTOGRAPH BY BRADY (p. 562)

Alexander Gardner, his brother James, Timothy O'Sullivan, and other photographers left Mathew Brady's employ in the spring or summer of 1862, taking with them some of their photographic plates. Gardner later published many prints of these, with credit given to the camera operator and developer, in his 1866 *Gardner's Photographic Sketchbook of the Civil War.* This chapter is a dramatization of what might well have been an angry parting.

The details of Brady's studio, and the competition down the street, is in *Mathew Brady and His World,* pp. 52–55, by Dorothy Meserve Kunhardt and Philip B. Kunhardt, Jr. (daughter and grandson of Lincoln collector Frederick Hill Meserve) published by Time-Life Books apparently without a copyright page. They speculate, perhaps wishfully: "It may have been, too, that an unheralded young black man named A. B. Foons, who often drove the wagon when Brady himself went out, also helped operate the camera." I have taken that fancy and made Foons the camera operator, with Brady the compositor, of the photo of Lincoln that appears on p. 101 of *The Face of Lincoln* by James Mellon, with the caption *"Carte de visite* printed from one frame of the lost original multiple-image stereographic negative made by an unknown photographer at Mathew Brady's gallery in Washington, D.C., about 1862. Mellon Collection."

The letter from Brady to Anna Ella Carroll, undated, is in the Carroll papers in the Maryland Historical Association in Annapolis; the stationery suggests it was sent in the late 1850s.

A good early source for detail on the life of Alexander Gardner is in an obituary published in the March 1883 issue of *The Philadelphia Photographer,* to which I was referred by Jerry Maddox of the Photographic Division of the Library of Congress.

The remark by Lincoln to Ward Hill Lamon about playing every card is from a letter Lincoln wrote on July 25, 1862, to Reverdy Johnson, in the *CW* for that date.

BOOK SEVEN, CHAPTER 3: MAN OF AUDACITY (p. 570)

After Colonel Thomas Key's presumptive peace negotiation with General Howell Cobb, Lincoln moved to take the business of prisoner exchanges out of McClellan's hands. Stanton, at the President's direction, wrote: "The President's instructions respecting any further effort at exchange will be speedily communicated to you"; on July 12, after meeting with Dix at Fort Monroe, Lincoln told the New Yorker to handle these negotiations, taking care to avoid any recognition of the Confederacy.

On July 18, Dix met with General Daniel H. Hill, who was substituting for the ill Cobb; their "Cartel" is printed in William Hesseltine's 1930 *Civil War Prisons,* pp. 32–33, and identified both sides only as "the authorities they represent." Next day, Dix sailed up to Washington and met on the night of the nineteenth with Lincoln, according to a letter from Stanton the day after in the McClellan papers. In this chapter, I have placed that meeting a week later, after the Emancipation Proclamation Cabinet argument on July 22. Avoiding de facto recognition of the South as a separate warring nation affected Lincoln's planning in both exchanging prisoners and freeing slaves in whole states.

David Silver's 1956 *Lincoln's Supreme Court,* pp. 83–93, is the source for the speculation about the court-packing ideas I have placed in Dix's mind. A bill providing for a tenth justice from the far West was introduced by radicals in early 1863; the *New York Times* praised adding "one to the number which will speedily remove the control of the Supreme Court from the Taney school."

General Pope's anti-guerrilla order, and the South's bitter reaction to it, is described in Nevins II, p. 155, and Williams's *Lincoln Finds a General,* p. 253, for which Williams says "there was not justification at all in the recognized rules of warfare"; it surely complicated the prisoner negotiations. Pope's "I find it impossible" complaint to Lincoln is on p. 254. Lincoln, who did not want a "soft war," did nothing to ameliorate Pope's order, which had been submitted to him beforehand. In failing to strike it down, the President acted shamefully.

The "audacious man" story is from a Herndon note of February 27, 1891, printed in Hertz's 1940 *The Hidden Lincoln.* Wrote Lincoln's law partner: "It is a good story to show the power of audacity, self-possession, quick-wittedness, etc., and as such it pleased Lincoln admirably. The nib of the thing was what Lincoln was after. I have heard him tell it often and often."

BOOK SEVEN, CHAPTER 4: FAIR EXCHANGE (p. 574)

General John Dix accompanied Rose O'Neal Greenhow by boat from Fort Monroe to her release on June 1, 1862, not at the end of July as recounted in the novel. Their conversation is imaginary, though several points are rooted in fact: Dix was a friend of Breckinridge in the Buchanan administration; his statement that "there can be but two sides" and that neutralists were deadweight is from a Dix letter of September 9, 1863, printed on p. 344, Vol. II of the *Memoirs of John A. Dix,* compiled in 1883 by his son, Morgan Dix.

Rose's statements are a mosaic from her 1863 *My Imprisonment and the First Year of Abolition Rule at Washington* and other sources. Assistant Secretary of War Watson's "Let them prove themselves innocent" is from p. 317 of Nevins II. Mrs. Greenhow's remarks to her daughter—"You have shared the hardship of my prison life"— are taken from the inscription in her hand in a copy of the book that she intended to give to her daughter, which is now in the Rare Book Collection of the Library of Congress.

Dix's points in reluctant defense of repression of dissent, which are the purpose of this chapter, are not his, although they fairly represent his point of view; he appeared more stern than he was. The ameliorating argument that it was amazing what was *not* done to ignore the Constitution during civil war—especially in not suspending elections—was made by James Randall and David Donald in *The Civil War and Reconstruction,* pp. 307–9, and directly to the author by Professor Harold Hyman. "Lincoln's practice fell short of dictatorship as the word is understood in the twentieth century," write Randall and Donald. ". . . No undue advantage was taken of the emergency to force arbitrary rule upon the country or to promote personal ends. Lincoln half expected to be defeated in 1864 . . . The Constitution was indeed stretched, but it was not subverted." My view is that it need not have been stretched as much as it was; too much understanding has been shown and not enough outrage expressed.

Dix did not leak any hint of troop movements to Mrs. Greenhow, nor did she know of plans to block his nomination for governor of New York. I suspect that Stanton and Chase were in league with Horace Greeley and other New York Republicans in blocking the Seward-Weed choice, but I know of no record of this.

Rose did prepare the Confederate flag in prison and concealed it in the lining of her shawl (*My Imprisonment,* p. 321) but did not display it, she wrote, lest other female spies for the South still in jail lose a means of deception.

BOOK SEVEN, CHAPTER 5: JOHN HAY'S DIARY, AUGUST 1, 1862 (p. 580)

Fiction. In his real diary, Hay wrote about a girl on August 29, 1862, "Stoddard is quite spoony about her, while I am languidly appreciative" and on March 31 described a girl as "a first-class woman every way," but his flirtation with Kate Chase in this novel has no basis in fact.

The reference to the new pressures on the prisoner cartel arranged by John Dix is true: Long's *Civil War Day by Day* for July 31, 1862, has President Davis's charge that Pope had "commenced a practice changing the character of the war, from such as becomes civilized nations into a campaign of indiscriminate robbery and murder."

The "chin fly" story, which Lincoln told often about Chase, is referred to on p. 54 of Dennett's Hay diary. The quotation about newspaper articles, "I know more about that than any of them," and Hay's assessment that "No great man was ever modest" and the sentence that follows is from Hay's extraordinarily frank letter of September 5, 1866, to William Herndon, on p. 307 of Hertz's *The Hidden Lincoln*. When Lincoln's wallet was examined in the 1970s, it was found to contain favorable newspaper clippings. All the other introspection in this chapter is imaginary.

BOOK SEVEN, CHAPTER 6: BATTLE OF BATON ROUGE (p. 584)

The fighting in Baton Rouge on August 5 and 6, 1862, led to the withdrawal of Federal troops from the area and enabled the Confederates to fortify Port Hudson, south of Vicksburg. An account of the clash, with the scuttling of the *Arkansas,* and the nice detail of Union soldiers in hospital gowns joining the battle, is in Foote I, p. 580. This chapter telescopes the two days' action into one.

Breckinridge's speech to his men is quoted in Jefferson Davis's memoirs, II, p. 245, and the death of Ben Helms is on p. 320 of William Davis's biography of Breckinridge.

The father-son, general-aide relationship between Breckinridge and his son Cabell is described on p. 122 of James C. Klotter's 1986 family history, *The Breckinridges of Kentucky.* Nepotism was never charged; "I must not shield my son from the dangers of his comrades," the general was quoted as saying with some pain.

The analysis of the war strategy and the assessment of Lincoln placed in the general's head is fictional. I pick up the idea introduced in the previous chapter, of Lincoln as a man most influenced by the radical Declaration of Independence and Breckinridge as more the product of the conservative Constitution that followed. Jefferson's Declaration was bottomed on the philosophy of John Locke, stressing "natural" rights of man; the Madison-Morris Constitution accepted the fact of slavery in order to achieve the compromise necessary to union. The contrast is better made of Lincoln after 1862, but the idea is illuminating and is explored in the chapter on Herman Melville and Abraham Lincoln in John P. Diggins's 1984 *The Lost Soul of American Politics.*

BOOK SEVEN, CHAPTER 7: THE BEAST OF NEW ORLEANS (p. 590)

George Smalley started out rowing stroke oar for Yale, became a Beacon Hill lawyer in Boston, but turned to journalism before he turned thirty. He became famous for his *Tribune* reporting at Antietam, as we shall see.

He never went to New Orleans to Ben Butler. I use him as a fictional reporter in this chapter, drawing on facts about him in Emmet Crozier's 1956 *Yankee Reporters* and Louis Starr's 1954 *Bohemian Brigade*, to provide a dramatic setting for General Butler's reminiscences in *Butler's Book*, published in 1892.

Butler was almost as fierce as Sherman in his treatment of reporters. The ball-and-chain reference, on p. 277 of Starr's work, took place in 1863.

The Massachusetts general, in his sometimes reliable memoirs, cites his coal deal on p. 355 and the hanging of the rebel Mumford on 442. He refers to the Confederate general at Baton Rouge as "the victorious (?) General Breckinridge" and on p. 484 professes he never wanted to hold on to the capital of Louisiana anyway.

Butler deals with his infamous "women order" in delighted detail on pp. 414–21, which is the basis for his dialogue in this chapter. He takes a swipe at Lincoln's secretaries for saying the order was "indefensible as a matter of taste." The last word of the order—"plying her *avocation"* was a mistake; he meant "vocation."

The background on his father's service with Andrew Jackson in New Orleans and his habit of laying an (unloaded) pistol on his desk are in Howard Nash, Jr.'s, 1969 *Stormy Petrel.*

Butler's political flip-flop from Breckinridge candidate for governor in 1860 to canny abolitionist a year later is recounted in Hans Trefousse's 1957 *Ben Butler: The South Called Him Beast!* with a passage on the "native guards," also called "Butler's Corps d'Afrique," on p. 131.

Was he crooked? Judge Edwards Pierrepont, John Dix's partner in the Greenhow trial, thought so; as a lawyer representing a New Orleans banker, Pierrepont made a good case that Ben Butler illegally seized fifty thousand dollars in gold and used it for his own purposes. Northern sympathizers in New Orleans wanted a more humane and honest commander, and asked Lincoln to send John Dix or Nathaniel Banks; ultimately Banks replaced Butler there.

Of more lasting import than the debate over what the rambunctious politician considered honest graft, Butler's 1861 "contraband" legal creativity made possible the early freeing of many fugitive slaves. His plan in 1862 to re-create the "native guard" sped the inclusion of blacks in Union ranks.

BOOK SEVEN, CHAPTER 8: NATIVE GUARD, COLORED (p. 597)

In the 1154-page *Butler's Book* (the Civil War calls for long books), the memoirist recalls Lincoln's frequent "there's meat in that" on p. 298, derides Greeley as one "who had not strength enough to stand a political defeat in after years without going idiotically insane" on p. 289, and hoots at what he considered the treasonable presumptions of would-be dictators McClellan and Frémont on p. 570.

The letter from Chase is cited in J. W. Schucker's 1874 biography of Chase on pp. 375–76. The Secretary, writing to Butler on June 24, urges him to do diplomatically what General Hunter did without caring about the consequences: free the slaves in his military district. In that way, Lincoln would be denied the credit for emancipation; it is of a piece with Chase's recollection of the July 22 Cabinet meeting.

The dramatic scene with the twenty freemen, including the taunting of the blacks by a general who wanted to know why there had been no uprising so far in the war, may seem like fiction but is not. The dialogue sticks closely to the words quoted on pp. 492–93 of *Butler's Book.* It is unfortunate that General Butler did not identify the Negro leader, who comes across as a pioneer of black pride in America.

BOOK SEVEN, CHAPTER 9: BETTER THAT WE SEPARATE (p. 601)

The *New York Tribune* verbatim account of a meeting Lincoln held with a deputation of negroes on August 14, 1862, was considered authoritative enough by historian Roy Basler for inclusion in the *Collected Works of Abraham Lincoln.*

The group was probably selected for its submissiveness. Edward M. Thomas, the leader, wrote the President two days later: "We were entirely hostile to the [colonization] movement until all the advantages were so ably brought to our view by you . . ." A week later, however, the *Baltimore Sun* reported that the deputation was denounced at a gathering of less pliant negroes held at Union Bethel Church.

What was Lincoln's purpose in holding this first meeting of blacks in the President's office? Did he really expect to start an exodus of four million people to Central America by hinting at the development that would follow the building of what became the Panama Canal?

That is doubtful. Certainly one purpose of the meeting was to publicize his appeal to freedmen to leave the country; that was why he had a *Tribune* correspondent on the scene in the office, taking copious notes on the record, as if at a public speech. Horace Greeley's *Tribune* was chosen as the outlet because it reached radical Republicans, and because Lincoln wanted Greeley inside his tent on the colonization idea. I think that Lincoln, with a draft of emancipation in his pocket and a crucial gubernatorial election in New York coming up, was telling abolitionists: colonization is a way to sugarcoat the abolition pill to move conservative Republicans. Lincoln appointed a Commissioner of Emigration (James Mitchell, who arranged and attended this meeting) who published a pamphlet calling this lecture to blacks "one of the most important chapters in the history of the country." It may have soothed some Northern whites.

This suggests a degree of calculated political manipulation that not many will accept today. Gabor S. Boritt, in his seminal article on this much-avoided subject ("The Voyage to the Colony of Lincolnia: The Sixteenth President, Black Colonization, and the Defense Mechanism of Avoidance," *The Historian,* Vol. 27, 1975), puts forward a different hypothesis: that the ordinarily practical Lincoln's dogged pursuit of this inherently impractical notion was his psychological way of putting some of the consequences of abolition out of his mind. Lincoln would think through the details of this "solution" later; when that time came, he let the idea die. Avoidance has a sponsor in *King Lear,* one of Lincoln's favorite plays, in which the central character says, "I have no way, and therefore want no eyes."

Professor Boritt compares the way Lincoln scaled down his request from a hundred to fifty to twenty-five volunteers to the way the biblical Abraham bargained with the Lord about saving Sodom if only fifty, forty, even ten righteous men could be found in that sinful city. The historian writes that "Lincoln began to allow himself a glimpse of the fact that the idea of large-scale emigration was about as realistic as Abraham's saving Sodom." He concludes that the President's self-delusion that colonization was possible "permitted Lincoln to pursue his fight against slavery without having to break his head against the specifics of the problem of the freedmen in American society, a problem that perplexed him."

Was Lincoln fooling himself, as Boritt suggests? Or was he pandering to the outright racists who wanted the blacks out of the country en masse, as some writers in the 1960s were angry enough to argue?

In my view, Lincoln knew you could fool some of the people some of the time, and he deliberately chose to fool some worried whites in the North with the mirage called colonization. He spent only $38,000 of the $600,000 authorized by Congress on the project; although he was prepared to be less than intellectually rigorous in a good cause, he was not about to be dishonest with the people's money.

The most telling argument in support of the manipulative theory is this: he made a public call to freedmen to take the lead, which he must have known was surely doomed, when he could easily have made the offer to "contrabands"—slaves running into Union lines—with much greater success. He was going through the motions, blowing smoke, using this hope of the miraculous disappearance of a growing worry as his means of overcoming internal opposition to a move he was secretly planning that would help win the war. He probably said to himself: Who knows, maybe some of them will go down there and make a good life for themselves. You never can tell.

That is the conclusion I put in Anna Carroll's head in this chapter. She did write a memorial for Lincoln on the subject of colonization, supporting it, as the Blairs and Caleb Smith wanted (Greenbies, pp. 356, 365). Navy Secretary Welles did warn of dishonesty (see his diary, p. 151) and the resistance to the plan by the nations of Central America is summarized in Nevins II, p. 148.

Miss Carroll was not present at the meeting in this chapter; I have used her as my reporter for dramatic purposes.

BOOK EIGHT, CHAPTER 1: FATAL ERROR (p. 611)

Should Halleck have urged the reinforcement of McClellan and the attack on Richmond from the Peninsula? Yes; that was the route to victory taken by Grant years later. The reinforcements, though not needed by McClellan to take Richmond, were needed to get him moving. Jackson's maneuver was a feint to hold Union troops up North, as McClellan argued to no avail.

Should McClellan have attacked with the men he had, especially soon after the bloody repulse of Lee's troops at Malvern Hill as the Seven Days battles ended? Yes; he was wrong about his estimate of Lee's strength. Should he have bargained with Halleck when the hint of some reinforcements was put forward? No; that proved he was more inclined to procrastinate than attack.

Now to the most controversial question about McClellan's career: did he deliberately delay the withdrawal from the Peninsula in the hope that Pope would lose, or, in McClellan's poorly chosen phrase, "get out of his scrape"?

If so, that would be treason. Fitz-John Porter was court-martialed on the charge that his delay had been intentional, and Lincoln approved the court's condemnation. A generation later, President Grant disagreed, and Congress overturned the conviction and restored Porter to his rank. The story is told at length, taking Porter's side, in Otto Eisenschiml's 1950 *The Celebrated Case of Fitz-John Porter: An American Dreyfus Affair*. My judgment is that Porter tried to get to Pope's aid desultorily at first and more seriously later, the result not clear enough for a court-martial verdict against him, but with enough evidence presented to suggest he did not try hard enough.

With that said, however, John Hay's letter to Nicolay revealing his historical slant should be remembered in a wider context: "As to my tone toward Porter and McClellan—that is an important matter. It is of the utmost moment that we should *seem* fair to him, while we are destroying him. The Porter business is a part of this. Porter was the most magnificent soldier in the Army of the Potomac, ruined by his devotion to McClellan."

McClellan had the motive to let Pope fail; failure is what happened, and Pope's defeat led to what McClellan hoped for. On that basis, I accept Lincoln's judgment and make McClellan the villain in this chapter. Historians still find it debatable, and Little Mac was careful to cover his tracks with telegrams demanding transportation and reporting his obedience to orders, but a close reading of the record—and the way he "papered the file"—inclines me to fault McClellan for putting his own long-range view of the nation's interest ahead of his immediate duty to his commander in chief.

The quotations in the scene with Halleck about the "heart of the rebellion," as well as Halleck's "the President expects," and "I want to strike square in the teeth of all John Pope's infamous orders" are from *McClellan's Own Story*, pp. 497, 498, and 463; the "monkey" reference is on p. 464. The conversation with Porter is fictional.

McClellan's assessment that Halleck was a man "whom I know to be my inferior" is in a letter to Samuel Barlow of July 23, 1862, cited in James McPherson's 1982 *Ordeal by Fire*, p. 254. Halleck's logical comment "If it is true that Lee outnumbers you two to one, he could smash you here and then turn north and defeat Pope" is on

p. 160 of Bruce Catton's *Mr. Lincoln's Army.* Halleck's "A week ago, I wired you
. . . what have you been doing?" was dated August 3 and is in Foote, p. 595.

BOOK EIGHT, CHAPTER 2: JOHN HAY'S DIARY, AUGUST 19, 1862 (p. 616)

The Hay-Chase flirtation is, as usual, fictional.

On August 6, Lincoln did try to paper over the differences between McClellan and
Stanton in public, as presidents always do between high aides, by blaming overly
enthusiastic supporters of both. *CW,* V, p. 359.

The letter forwarded by Sydney Gay, and Lincoln's invitation in response, is in *CW*
for August 1. Sydney Gay of the *New York Tribune* visited Lincoln on August 12,
1862, *LDBY.* (A note on style: leading New York newspapers at the time treated the
name of the city as a compound adjective modifying the name of the newspaper; they
also had the word *Daily* in their mastheads; hence, *The New-York Daily Tribune, The
New-York Daily Times.* I do not use the full names in this book, preferring the anach-
ronistic *New York Tribune* or "Raymond of the *Times.* ")

The scene with James Gilmore and Robert Walker is from Gilmore's 1898 *Personal
Recollections of Abraham Lincoln and the Civil War,* pp. 77–85. Gilmore is a novelist
(under the name Edmund Kirke) and once represented a letter as having come from
Lincoln when it was his own paraphrase, but much of this part of his account rings
true. His quotation of Greeley on p. 85, that the Emancipation Proclamation represented "a change of front of the universe," has been widely quoted, and appears in the
following chapter.

Robert Walker, propagandist, balloonist, and senator from Mississippi who turned
anti-slavery, was Gilmore's partner in the *Continental Monthly.* He was probably the
first to use the word "holocaust" in its present sense, predicting "a holocaust of lives,
rivers of blood . . . with the stain of slavery wiped from the country." Walker favored colonization (to Mexico) because "there is a union of sentiment between the
masses, North and South, both opposing the introduction of free blacks."

In James Shenton's 1961 *Robert John Walker: A Politician from Jackson to Lincoln,*
p. 189, the historian attributes the lack of a widespread moral urgency to "the selfish
belief of free white yeomen that the new Western territories belonged to them alone."

The wording of Greeley's open letter in this chapter is accurate, though "the Prayer
of Twenty Millions" is abridged, and can be found following Lincoln's letter to him in
CW for August 22, 1862.

The excision of the "broken eggs cannot be mended" from the letter was explained
by James Welling in a footnote on p. 168 of Vol. CXXX of the *North American Review*
for 1880, which is also a source for the reasoning behind Lincoln's half denials of
determination to emancipate while he was planning to do so.

" 'Broken eggs cannot be mended, and the longer the breaking proceeds the more
eggs will be broken'—was erased," wrote Welling, "with some reluctance, by the
President, on the representation, made to him by the editors, that it seemed somewhat
exceptionable, on rhetorical grounds, in a paper of such dignity." Why, then, reveal
the line that was cut? "But it can do no harm, at this late day, to reveal the homely
similitude by which Mr. Lincoln had originally proposed to reinforce his political
warnings."

BOOK EIGHT, CHAPTER 3: UNIVERSAL CHANGE OF FRONT (p. 622)

The conversation between Greeley and Gay is imaginary, though they obviously talked frequently and the substance here is based on fact.

The objections of the rival newspapers to the *Tribune*'s "Prayer of Twenty Millions" is found in Robert Harper's 1951 *Lincoln and the Press,* p. 173–75. The *Times* on August 23 reported that Lincoln read a friend a rough draft of what appeared later in the letter to Greeley and "had thought of getting before the public some such statement of his position on the slavery question in some manner and asked the opinion of his friend as to the propriety of such a course and the best way to do it. The appearance of Greeley's 'Prayer' gave him the opportunity." Sour grapes, but probably true.

Greeley's assessment of Lincoln as a "bad stick" is from a letter written to Charles Sumner on August 7, 1862, cited in Sandburg II, p. 8. That is also the source of "Hell, continued."

The scene with Gilmore is from his reminiscences, cited in the underbook for the previous chapter.

The *Tribune*'s foreknowledge of the Emancipation Proclamation, corroborating the suspect Gilmore account, is detailed in a footnote in Allan Nevins's *Ordeal of the Union,* Vol. II, p. 233. In Adam Hill's letters of August 21 and 25, 1862, in the Gay papers, Nevins found that the *Tribune* editors were informed by Senator Sumner and Count Gurowski that (1) an emancipation proclamation had been discussed, and (2) it was suspended at the urging of Seward, Blair, and Thurlow Weed. Senator S. G. Pomeroy, pressing for adoption of the Chiriquí plan, had told correspondent Hill that the proclamation would be issued as soon as Lincoln had assurance that his colonization project could succeed. "Greeley must therefore have known," concludes historian Nevins, "that the proclamation was impending when he brought out his letter of minatory tone. Perhaps he hoped to end all hesitations." Or perhaps he wanted the credit for the policy shift.

George Smalley, then in the field with General Pope, was told by the general that Stanton and Halleck were issuing an order banning correspondents from the field. As he recounted on p. 118 of his 1911 memoir, *Anglo-American Memories,* Smalley "rode off to an outpost where I had a friend. The official notification may have been sent to my tent but never reached me." He added, in retrospect, "The business of a war correspondent is to be, not where he is ordered, but where he is wanted."

The Greeley commentary at the end of the chapter about the change in Lincoln are from *Greeley on Lincoln* by Benton, pp. 25, 42, 44, and 75.

BOOK EIGHT, CHAPTER 4: OUT OF THE SCRAPE (p. 628)

The conversation in this chapter is fiction.

The "spirit photos" are described in Louis Starr's *Bohemian Brigade,* p. 168. The telegrams between McClellan, Halleck, and Lincoln are cited on p. 192, Vol. I of Horace Greeley's 1866 *The American Conflict,* in a chapter titled "McClellan Marking Time," to show Greeley's disdain of McClellan's dilatory tactics in marching north.

Pinkerton's activity in behalf of John Brown is detailed on pp. 37–42 of James D. Horan's 1967 biography of the detective. The legend that Brown stopped off at Pinkerton's Chicago home on his way to the raid on Harpers Ferry is rooted in aid that the detective did give Brown and his accompanying fugitive slaves in the previous year, just before their raid into Missouri. The peroration of Brown's speech to the court, abridged here, is on p. 116 of James McPherson's 1982 *Ordeal by Fire*.

On p. 124, Horan cites a letter written by Colonel Key to Pinkerton in 1864 that "indicates that Pinkerton knew the contents of, or perhaps had helped McClellan to compose, the famous 'Harrison's Landing letter' . . ."

BOOK EIGHT, CHAPTER 5: SENDING OFF THE SILVER (p. 632)

Most of McClellan's words to Pinkerton and to Halleck in this chapter are from pp. 530–34 of his memoirs, as is the story of sending Colonel Kelton to the front; Pinkerton's responses are fictional but factual, Halleck's largely taken from the McClellan memoirs. The military situation is described well on p. 639 of Foote.

BOOK EIGHT, CHAPTER 6
JOHN HAY'S DIARY, SEPTEMBER 1–2, 1862 (p. 637)

This chapter draws heavily on John Hay's real diary for September 1, on p. 45 of Dennett's *Lincoln and the Civil War in the Diaries and Letters of John Hay*. I have quoted Lincoln directly where Hay paraphrased, as "The President said it really seemed to him that McC. wanted Pope defeated." He repeated this in his real diary entry of September 5, quoting Lincoln directly saying, "Unquestionably he has acted badly toward Pope. He wanted him to fail. That is unpardonable, but he is too useful just now to sacrifice."

The real entry's "The President seemed to think him a little crazy. Envy, jealousy, and spite are probably a better explanation" is reduced to a circular motion of Lincoln's hand and an internal thought from the fictional Hay. Same with the assessment of Halleck and the description of Stanton's wife.

Hay's real diary covers the two days in one; I have split them for clarity's sake, and to introduce testimony from McClellan's memoirs, p. 530, and his similar but later-written article in *Battles and Leaders,* Vol. II, pp. 549–50. The movements—from the Soldiers' Home on Sunday, September 1, to the telegraph office, to the Halleck headquarters, to the Stanton house, and to breakfast the next day at McClellan's house—are as described in *LDBY.* The mention of Stoddard's brother Henry coming in from the front by mule to report directly to Lincoln on what General Sumner and others knew to be happening is recounted in *Lincoln's Third Secretary,* the memoir published by his son, William O. Stoddard, Jr., in 1955. ("I have edited this material," wrote the son, "reducing his voluminous manuscript to this small book." I'd like to find that manuscript.)

Colonel Key and Lieutenant Custer are not recorded as present at the breakfast, though they might have been. Source of the President's urging of McClellan to have his friends support Pope, and the positive response, is the *Official Records,* Ser I., Vol. XII, Pt. 1, pp. 103–4.

I have attributed guilt feelings to McClellan in this part of the book for failing to move quickly northward; he never wrote anything of the sort, but I think he must have been torn between protecting his beloved men and letting Pope "get out of his scrape" at the cost of some Union casualties. I believe Lincoln's assessment, as reported by Hay, that McClellan was self-serving; I suggest some internal torment might be the cause of his uncharacteristic willingness to take on the responsibility for the command without the overall authority, but there is no documentation for this.

In *McClellan's Own Story,* p. 535, the general attributes despair to Lincoln at the breakfast in these terms: "He then said he regarded Washington as lost . . . Both the President and Halleck again asserted that it was impossible to save the city." I don't believe that; it would have been out of character for Lincoln to abandon Washington without a fight. Pro-McClellan biographers H. J. Eckenrode and Bryan Conrad, in their 1941 *George B. McClellan: The Man Who Saved the Union,* p. 157, can't quite swallow that either: "What appears to be true," they write, "is that Halleck, who was more alarmed than Lincoln, gave the color to the interview. Of Halleck's demoralization at this moment there can be no doubt, because he gave preliminary orders for the evacuation of Washington—orders that were canceled by McClellan. It was Halleck's panic that McClellan remembered when he wrote."

BOOK EIGHT, CHAPTER 7: A HALTER AROUND HIS NECK (p. 641)

Allan Pinkerton was close to McClellan during the period of his eclipse and sudden reemergence, and repeatedly warned of "a cabal in Washington," but my use of him as the reporter in this chapter is fictional.

The smell of cinnamon around George Armstrong Custer is from Jay Monaghan's description in his 1959 *Custer:* "his kepi over one eye, his cinnamon-scented curls on his shoulders . . ." He was called "Cinnamon" by some of his officer friends.

The allusion to Stanton's feeling about guerrillas—"let 'em swing"—is from the Thomas/Hyman biography of Stanton, p. 218. John Pope's quotation about restoring "the tone of this army" is from his message to Halleck cited in Foote, Vol. I, p. 645.

The source of the rest of the chapter is George McClellan's article in *Battles and Leaders,* II, pp. 550–52. Pope also has a detailed article nearby, but it is even more transparently self-serving, and is also grumpy—the flailings of a man who did not know what was happening to him at the time and never found out later.

Pinkerton's assessment of the change in McClellan is fictional; this is my view of what happened to McClellan after he was given his second chance. He became less political, less insufferable in his presumption that he had been anointed to save the Union, more inclined to give battle; he knew he was serving on borrowed time and it had a good effect. He had a better sense of what Lee would do than anyone, but not so good a sense about how little time he had borrowed from Lincoln.

BOOK EIGHT, CHAPTER 8: CABINET COUP (p. 645)

If you believe the facts presented in Gideon Welles's diary, as most historians do, this is fairly close to what happened on August 31 and September 1, 1862.

Some of my mind reading of Chase is fictional, and several meetings are telescoped into two, but on the whole the chapter is based on Welles's diary, I, pp. 93–95, 100–4; Chase's diary for August 31 and September 1, 1862, pp. 116–18; and on Burton Hendrick's vivid account in *Lincoln's War Cabinet,* pp. 306–14. "Had the ultimatum succeeded," writes Hendrick, "Lincoln's whole plan of a coalition cabinet would have gone adrift."

Chase writes: "On the suggestion of Judge Bates, the remonstrance against McClellan, which had been previously signed by Smith, was modified . . . Welles declined to sign it, on the grounds that it might seem unfriendly to the President,—though this was the exact reverse of its intent."

That night, after the petition was aborted, and on the eve of the tensest Cabinet meeting of the Lincoln presidency, Chase wrote: "a rumor pervaded the town that McClellan was to resume his full command. Colonel Key called at my house and told me that he supposed such was the fact." Evidently Thomas Key was keeping his Ohio political lines open to Chase, trying to lessen his opposition to McClellan—or was playing McClellan false.

Did Lincoln know this challenge from within was brewing? Welles recollected in his 1874 *Lincoln and Seward* that "The President never knew of this paper," but that stretches credulity. He went on to write that Lincoln "was not unaware of the popular feeling against that officer [McClellan] in which he sympathized, and of the sentiments of the members of the Cabinet, aggravated by the hostility and strong, if not exaggerated rumors sent out by the Secretary of War."

BOOK EIGHT, CHAPTER 9: I WILL ANSWER TO THE COUNTRY (p. 652)

This chapter, like the preceding one, draws principally on the memoirs of Welles, both in his diary recorded contemporaneously and his book written a dozen years later. Dimension is added by Chase's diary, a note from Bates, and Hay's real diary.

Historian James Randall wrote on p. 112 of Vol. II of *Lincoln the President* that "The historian would give a good deal for an adequate report of that meeting: from the fragments we have, given by Chase and Welles, it is evident that Chase and Stanton vigorously took issue with Lincoln in his determination to restore McClellan." Professor Randall also examines the controversy over the words "place" and "plan," a clerk's transcription of what Chase said Lincoln said; Randall disagrees with biographers Warden and Sandburg, and comes down for "resign my plan."

This chapter is a reconstruction of what probably happened in that Cabinet meeting. About Lincoln's mood: Welles's diary describes him as "greatly distressed," but his 1874 book changed that to "deliberate, but firm and decisive. His language and manner were kind and affectionate, especially toward two of the members who were greatly disturbed; but every person present felt that he was truly the chief . . ." I have him both ways in the scene, drawing also on the characterization by Bates below, and incorporate some quotations from a talk he had with Welles "on the succeeding Friday, when only he and I were present" from pp. 197–98 of Welles's book, *Lincoln and Seward.*

The Blairs' conversation is fictional, but Francis Blair's report of McClellan's estimate of the Cabinet is based on one of the general's unpublished letters to his wife, cited on p. 325 of Elbert Smith's 1980 *Francis Preston Blair.* That book is also the source, on p. 327, of Blair's blast at Pope as braggart and liar.

McClellan's Own Story, p. 545, cites Chase's estimation of McClellan's appointment as "a national calamity" (based on Welles's book, p. 194) and a letter from Montgomery Blair dated April 3, 1879, saying "Stanton and Chase . . . actually declared that they would prefer the loss of the capital to the restoration of McClellan to command."

Bates weighs in with a note cited on p. 486 of Vol. V of *CW.* Bates's draft of the petition to Lincoln was found in the Nicolay Papers, with a note in Bates's handwriting saying that Blair ("preserving a cautious reticence"), Welles ("for some reasons of etiquette"), and Seward ("absent") declined to sign, and adding: "The President was in deep distress . . . he seemed wrung by the bitterest anguish—said he felt almost ready to hang himself—in answer to something said by Mr. Chase, he said he was far from doubting our sincerity, but that he was so distressed, precisely because he knew we were earnestly sincere. He was, manifestly, alarmed for the safety of the city." Bates added a recollection of his own statement which is quoted in the chapter.

Chase's diary for September 2, pp. 118–20, is the basis for much of what he is quoted saying in this scene, though I have taken him beyond his diary entry's "I could not but feel that giving the command to him was the equivalent of giving Washington to the rebels. This and more I said."

BOOK EIGHT, CHAPTER 10: THE CHIROPODIST (p. 659)

Some contemporary accounts put the number of Jews in America during the Civil War as low as 60,000; Allan Nevins, in his introduction to Bertram W. Korn's 1951 *American Jewry and the Civil War,* accepts Korn's estimate of 150,000.

The Korn book is the source of much information about Dr. Isachar Zacharie, pp. 193–202, and the photograph of him is captioned "Chiropodist, Spy, Presidential Agent." The conversation with his patient in this chapter is fictional.

The reference to Grant's harsh treatment of Jewish traders is from p. 124 of William S. McFeely's 1981 *Grant,* quoting Grant contemporary James Harrison Wilson: "[Jesse Grant] came down into Tennessee with a Jew trader that he wanted his son to help, and with whom he was going to share the profits. Grant refused to issue a permit and sent the Jew flying, prohibiting Jews from entering the line."

For Zacharie's contribution as a podiatrist, the term that replaced chiropodist much as that word replaced corncutter, see William Scheibel's "The Podiatrist Who Became a President's Confidant" in the August 1962 *Journal of the American Podiatry Association,* and the same publication's May 1971 issue, with an article on Zacharie by Harry Bloch, M.D.

As years have gone by, Dr. Zacharie's medical reputation has improved. In a 1907 history of chiropody by R. H. Westervelt, he was not named but clearly referred to as "the most unscrupulous of charlatan chiropodists we have had in New York." British podiatrist J. C. Dagnall wrote in 1967: "Our good friend Isachar Zacharie . . . was an interesting personality but has a minor place in our history." Dr. Scheibel, however, wrote: "it must be admitted that the doctor did have 'something on the ball' . . . Nothing else can account for the President's implicit confidence in him. It is doubtful if the records can point to another podiatrist who ever filled and enjoyed a position comparable to the one achieved by Dr. Isachar Zacharie."

More to this chapter's purposes, the following letter, from Assistant Secretary of War Peter H. Watson to "John Hay, Esq., Private Sec., etc.," on War Department stationery and dated September 19, 1862, is in the Hay papers at Brown University: "The bearer Dr. Zachary is a most skilful chiropedist and will remove a corn or cure a sore toe nail if you are unfortunate enough to have one in a twinkling and by the most delicate and painless manipulation. If you have any friend suffering from Corns, Dr. Z. will operate, at your request, without charge and perform an almost magical cure." The friend Watson had in mind was presumably Lincoln, who frequently took off his shoes and massaged his corn-ridden feet.

BOOK EIGHT, CHAPTER 11: THE FORGOTTEN WEST (p. 662)

Diary from March 4, 1861, to November 12, 1862 by Adam Gurowski, published at the end of 1862, is the source of most of the remarks attributed to him in this chapter. The scene is fictional; there is no record of Anna Carroll and Count Gurowski meeting.

"Mr. Lincoln has become a myth" is from p. 262 of the diary. The Lincoln endorsement on the request to Stanton for a commission for Joseph Breckinridge is in *CW* for March 11, 1862, but was not presented by Anna Carroll. Stanton's reading of Lincoln's telegram "Where is General Bragg?" is in *CW* for September 6, 1862.

"Colonization is an absurdity" is on p. 252 of the diary, and is analyzed on p. 234 of LeRoy H. Fischer's 1964 *Lincoln's Gadfly, Adam Gurowski*. The Polish count's prediction that African-Americans would make "an excellent peasantry" and other comments are on pp. 165 and 305 of the diary. The "pusillanimous measure" and his derogation of the writing in the Emancipation Proclamation are on pp. 277–81. The political discussion about New York's potential loss is fictional, though truthful. Stanton's reference to Charles Dana's report on corruption in Memphis is from the *Official Records*, I, LII, Pt. 1, p. 331.

Did both Count Gurowski and Anna Carroll, relatively minor characters in the cast around Lincoln, know of the Emancipation Proclamation before it was publicly revealed on September 22?

Yes. Adams Hill of the *New York Tribune*'s Washington office wrote managing editor Sydney Gay in New York that Gurowski and Sumner knew of an emancipation proclamation, just as Greeley was writing the "Prayer of Twenty Millions" editorial (Nevins, p. 233n.) More solid proof of Gurowski's foreknowledge (and of Weed's role in blocking it earlier) is in his letter to Governor Andrew of Massachusetts dated August 5, 1862, preserved at the Massachusetts Historical Society: "The President, urged by the noble Stanton, was allmost ready to sign a proclamation in the spirit of the law of God. Seward and Blair opposed to it, but even their opposition was of no avail; finally Thurlow Weed was telegraphed and he settled the question . . . Seward & Weed's justification of the opposition is: that the President's proclamation would have evoked riots & counter revolutions in the North."

With less certainty, we can assume Miss Carroll knew too. In a memorandum to Stanton on September 9, 1862, a copy of which is in her handwriting at the Maryland Historical Association, she warned of the possible breakthrough of Braxton Bragg in the West. The South's purpose was not to take Washington, she wrote, but to cut the North in two from the Ohio River to Cleveland. "They rely very confidently on a revolution in the great northwest," she wrote, meaning Illinois and Ohio, "and believe that through the emancipation proclamation they will succeed."

As the Greenbies point out on p. 363 of their Carroll biography, there was nothing generally known at that time as "the emancipation proclamation." Miss Carroll's taken-for-granted mention of it suggests strongly that she knew of it in advance and was worried about its effect in the West.

BOOK EIGHT, CHAPTER 12: LIBERATING KENTUCKY (p. 669)

To summarize the September-October campaign in the West in a single chapter, I have telescoped some of the action. Breckinridge did not reach Bragg's headquarters until October 16, after Bragg had suffered a setback at Perryville and began to withdraw from Kentucky into eastern Tennessee; their scene is fictional, though their animosity was not.

"Sickly, sour-tempered, and stooped," writes James C. Klotter in his 1986 *The Breckinridges of Kentucky*, "Bragg . . . did not move men in the way that the sight of Breckinridge did. Nor did Breckinridge's ties to powerful blocs in the army help the Bragg-Breckinridge association." General Breckinridge was related to Generals Wade Hampton, William Floyd, Joseph Johnston, and William Preston, and was one of the unifiers of the "Kentucky bloc" in the C.S.A., which despised Bragg as an anti-Kentuckian martinet. Breckinridge (like McClellan) was worshipped by his troops, and was considered a fine leader of men in battle, though not a major tactician. Bragg dodged blame by condemning junior commanders, and complained about "the dogs of detraction" in a "venal press." A sympathetic account of his generalship is Grady McWhiney's 1969 *Braxton Bragg and Confederate Defeat,* which notes on p. 335 that Lee retreated from Maryland with praise from Southerners while Bragg pulled out of Kentucky amid bitter criticism.

Breckinridge's "I have encountered every difficulty a man could meet" is cited on p. 123 of William Davis's 1980 *The Orphan Brigade: The Kentucky Confederates Who Couldn't Go Home.* Bragg's derogation of Kentuckians as having "too many fat cattle and are too well off to fight" is on p. 247 of Hattaway and Jones's 1983 *How the North Won,* which has a good account by General Joseph Johnston of Breckinridge's liking for whiskey, and his ability to handle it, on p. 676. The reference to Cleburne's capture of barrels of whiskey, and his irate reaction to putting Irish troops in charge of the booty, is from *Cleburne and His Command,* p. 117, by Captain Irving A. Buck, C.S.A., first published in 1908 and rescued from obscurity with a 1958 reprint by the McCowat-Mercer press in Jackson, Tennessee.

In his introduction to the reprint, Bell Irvin Wiley writes: "On the basis of his demonstrated superiority as a division commander, Cleburne should have been made a lieutenant general and he possibly would have attained that rank had he not made himself suspect by his early advocacy of making soldiers out of the slaves and freeing those who rendered faithful service in the ranks."

That theme was developed in Robert F. Durden's 1972 *The Grey and the Black: The Confederate Debate on Emancipation.* Early proposals in print for this are dated September 1863, and it is logical to assume the taboo subject was discussed in private earlier; however, my scene between Breckinridge and Cleburne discussing this as early as the fall of 1862 is fictional.

Patrick Ronayne Cleburne's emancipation arguments, and some of his words, are from the long memorandum ("memoir") he sent the commanding general of the Army of Tennessee (Joe Johnston, who replaced Braxton Bragg) on January 2, 1864. The memorandum (printed in full on pp. 54–62 of Durden's book) reached Richmond, and was ordered suppressed by Jefferson Davis: "Deeming it to be injurious to the public service that such a subject should be mooted . . . if it be kept out of the public journals its ill effect will be much lessened."

However, six months later Davis prepared the way for such a plan of enlisting black soldiers in an interview with writer James Gilmore (Lincoln's channel to Greeley) that appeared in the *Atlantic Monthly* of September 1864. "We are not fighting for slavery. We are fighting for Independence . . . [slavery] was never an essential element." On November 7, 1864, after the *Richmond Enquirer* urged the purchase of a quarter million slaves for army service, to be given their freedom in return, the Confederate President recommended to his Congress "a radical modification" of policy: "engaging to liberate the negro on his discharge after service faithfully rendered . . ." The Congress balked; in March 1865, with the war nearly lost, President Davis by executive regulation put in a recruitment of blacks "conferring . . . the rights of a freedman." Too late.

BOOK EIGHT, CHAPTER 13: THE RISE OF SEYMOUR (p. 678)

The Weed-Carroll meeting is fictional, though they had dealings during the war. Her bill of $6,250 is described in the Greenbies' biography, p. 365, and her changing view of the Confiscation Act on p. 374–75: in a war between two powers, and not merely an insurrection, property seized as booty need not be returned.

Thurlow Weed's views on the Confiscation Act—approving so long as it did not mean outright abolition—are cited on pp. 299–301 of Glyndon Van Deusen's 1947 *Thurlow Weed: Wizard of the Lobby,* That biography also describes his actions at the Democratic convention in Troy, where he tried unsuccessfully to promote the candidacy of John Dix.

The best short biography of Horatio Seymour is on pp. 266–85 of Irving Stone's 1943 *They Also Ran* and is the source of some of the information about him in this chapter. The meeting with Dean Richmond is imaginary, though one surely took place; the quotations from his speech to the meeting in Troy on September 9, 1862, and the convention in Albany the day after, baiting Weed and Greeley, are on pp. 78–90 of David Croly's 1868 campaign biography, *Seymour and Blair: Their Lives and Services,* with color drawn from Stewart Mitchell's 1938 biography, *Horatio Seymour of New York,* made accessible in a Da Capo reprint edition in 1970. "I want a sharp, bitter fight" and "I do not care about my election. That is not probable" is from a letter to his sister cited on p. 246.

BOOK EIGHT, CHAPTER 14
JOHN HAY'S DIARY, SEPTEMBER 12, 1862 (p. 688)

Lincoln's 4 A.M. "How does it look now?" to McClellan is in *CW* for September 12, 1862, the date of this fictional Hay diary entry. He followed it with another telegraph message advising that General Thomas Jackson, in Maryland, was crossing the Potomac "and probably the whole rebel army will be drawn from Maryland." The President was badly misinformed about Lee's threat, and helped mislead McClellan into believing the Confederate Army was headed for Pennsylvania.

The Union general, still operating without specific authority, replied that he held Frederick, Maryland, and "If Harpers Ferry is still in our possession I think I can save the garrison if they fight at all." However, out of cowardice or treason, the Union commander there, Colonel Dixon Miles, promptly surrendered, proving McClellan right and Halleck wrong about the wisdom of trying to defend that point. In his 1982 *A Matter of Hours,* Paul R. Teeter argues that the treason of Miles denied ten thousand needed Union troops to McClellan at Antietam, and that the subsequent court of inquiry corruptly covered up the treason in order to disparage McClellan and justify his relief.

Lincoln sprained his wrist on September 13, according to the *Washington Star.* His corns must have been troubling him because it was about this time Hay arranged with Assistant Secretary Watson at the War Department to see Dr. Zacharie on September 22.

Frederick Douglass's criticism of Lincoln for what he told the black leaders is on p. 312 of Stephen Oates's 1977 *With Malice Toward None.*

BOOK EIGHT, CHAPTER 15: ANTIETAM I: WITH LEE (p. 690)

In *I Rode with Stonewall,* the 1899 eyewitness memoir by Henry Kyd Douglas published in 1940, Thomas Jackson was described by an admiring Confederate as "the most awkward man in the army . . . General Lee, on horseback or off, was the handsomest man I ever saw . . . John C. Breckinridge was a model of manly beauty

. . . and Joe Johnston looked every inch a soldier. None of these things could be said of Jackson."

The details in this chapter are taken from that book, p. 354, and from Douglas Southall Freeman's *R. E. Lee,* II, pp. 352–58. The angry interchange with A. P. Hill is from Shelby Foote's narrative, I, p. 665.

BOOK EIGHT, CHAPTER 16: ANTIETAM II: WITH MCCLELLAN (p. 695)

"The Finding of Lee's Lost Order" is described by Silas Colgrove, who was the colonel commanding the 27th Indiana Volunteers, in *Battles and Leaders,* II, p. 603. "Within an hour after finding the dispatch," reported Colgrove, "General McClellan's whole army was on the move."

In his 1951 *Mr. Lincoln's Army,* Bruce Catton gives an account of the episode on pp. 218–19, promoting Private Barton Mitchell to corporal, citing as his source the sergeant, John McKnight Bloss, in *Papers of the Kansas Commandery,* as well as *B&L.* Adds Catton: "It is irritating, in a mild sort of way, that none of the accounts of this affair mention what finally happened to the cigars. Bloss wrote later that he and Mitchell simply forgot about them . . . Did anybody ever smoke them, in the end— these cigars that were so important in the history of the war?" An answer to Catton's question is suggested in fictional form in a later chapter herein.

The apocryphal story about A. P. Hill and Ellen McClellan—"My God, Nellie, why didn't you marry *him?*"—is from a firsthand account in *I Rode with Stonewall* by Henry Kyd Douglas, p. 178.

BOOK EIGHT, CHAPTER 17
ANTIETAM III: AT DAYBREAK IN THE MORNING (p. 697)

Although Pinkerton is used as the reporter in this chapter, and was present at the time in McClellan's headquarters, he played no recorded part in the transmission of Lee's lost order. McClellan's exultant "Here is a paper with which, if I cannot whip Bobby Lee, I will be willing to go home" was reported by General John Gibbons in his *Personal Recollections* published in 1928.

Did McClellan, in possession of the plans of the enemy, move quickly enough to take full advantage of the divided rebel army? His order to General Franklin to move "at daybreak in the morning," though redundant, seems to reflect urgency; most military historians say he should have marched that afternoon (at dusk in the early evening).

An equally pertinent question is: Were Lincoln and Halleck wise to withhold all available troops from McClellan's army facing Lee? "I am sending you all that can be spared," telegraphed Lincoln in dispatching a division of Porter's corps, but he did not; he compounded the mistake of putting twelve thousand troops at risk of capture at Harpers Ferry with the error of retaining some fifty thousand Federal soldiers in and around the capital. By having one army in the field and another in Washington, Lincoln in effect divided his force and invited defeat in detail.

The conversation between Colonel Thomas Key and Nathaniel Paige of the *New York Tribune* is cited in a footnote on p. 231 of Nevins II. The McClellan reference to Castiglione, where Napoleon defeated a divided enemy, is from General Gibbons's *Personal Recollections.*

The news of the finding of Special Order 191 was promptly reported to Lee by a Southern sympathizer who had been present when the order was brought to McClellan. Freeman at first disputed this in a detailed footnote on p. 369, II, of his 1935 biography of Lee. But in the 1943 *Lee's Lieutenants,* II, p. 715, Freeman gives a complete rendition of the discovery and significance of the Lost Order in Appendix I, concluding "the news reached [Gen. J. E. B.] Stuart early in the night of September 13–14, passed swiftly to Lee, and almost certainly reached G.H.Q. the same night . . ." Thus, Lee knew that McClellan had his plans in time to understand the unaccustomed alacrity of the Union general and to grasp the need for speed in reuniting Confederate forces.

BOOK EIGHT, CHAPTER 18: ANTIETAM IV: LEE'S OLD WARHORSE (p. 702)

Longstreet's self-assessment is based on the facts in his entry in Mark Boatner's *Civil War Dictionary*. Most of this chapter is based on his recollections in *Battles and Leaders,* II, p. 667, and on Foote's narrative, p. 676.

BOOK EIGHT, CHAPTER 19
ANTIETAM V: AN ARMY WITH BANNERS (p. 704)

The thoughts attributed here to Corporal Mitchell are those of David Thompson, recorded in a piece titled "In the Ranks to the Antietam," pp. 556–58 of Vol. II of *Battles and Leaders.*

BOOK EIGHT, CHAPTER 20: AT BRADY'S GALLERY (p. 705)

The character of Foons is built on a single speculative sentence on p. 57 of *Mathew Brady and His World* by Dorothy Meserve Kunhardt and Philip B. Kunhardt, Jr: "It may have been, too, that an unheralded young black man named A. B. Foons, who often drove the wagon when Brady himself went out, also helped operate his camera."

The dialogue in this chapter is fictional. Although most photographic historians agree that Brady's employees were angry at his low wages and refusal to let them take credit for pictures, no memoirs have been found to flesh out the story of the photographers of the war. We know that Brady did not cover Antietam, and that Gardner, Gibson, and O'Sullivan did. "Brady's Album Gallery" appeared on the pictures from Antietam, with the names of Gardner and Gibson in fine print as copyright owners on the lower front edge of the original album cards and stereo views. The exodus from Brady's firm began about two months later, with Gibson and O'Sullivan joining the Gardner competition.

Mark Katz of Gettysburg, Pennsylvania, in a forthcoming biography of Gardner disputes the theory that Brady's employees departed in anger. He cites the fact that Brady permitted his men to copyright their own negatives in the fall of 1862 and concludes that the parting was amicable. I can find no evidence otherwise, but logic suggests that when an employee announces an intention to set up shop in competition with the firm that gave him his start, and he goes after the same clients, tensions arise.

We do not know whether Gardner was on the field on the day of the battle, though he dates one of his photographs September 17: "Although I have reservations concerning the accuracy of this caption," writes William A. Frassanito in his 1978 *Antietam: the Photographic Legacy of America's Bloodiest Day,* "it is fairly certain that Gardner was on hand prior to the withdrawal of the Confederate army . . ."

BOOK EIGHT, CHAPTER 21: ANTIETAM VI: DESTROY IF POSSIBLE (p. 708)

"God bless you and all with you!" wired Lincoln on Sept 15, after McClellan's victory at South Mountain. "Destroy the rebel army if possible." The President's message, cited by McClellan in his *Own Story* on p. 583, was the first real legitimization of his command. It also points to a difference of purpose between Lincoln and his field general: the President wanted the rebel army literally "destroyed"—killed or captured. McClellan would gladly have accepted a capitulation, but his goal was to defeat the rebel army, to repel Lee's invasion of the North, and from that point seek to reunite the country.

Lincoln's purpose was to end all resistance to Federal authority and then to dictate terms, as he ultimately did; McClellan's purpose was to win a decisive battle and make a deal. Lincoln understood that no deal was likely to be made. The President's object served the cause of majority rule, and wiped out forever the notion of secession; the general's object was limited to restoring the Union with a minimum of bloodshed. The mistake commonly made is to judge McClellan's military strategy in Lincoln's frame of reference.

The dialogue in this chapter is fictional. "Tomorrow we fight the battle that will decide the fate of the Republic" is from James Wilson, *Under the Old Flag*, I, p. 106.

BOOK EIGHT, CHAPTER 22
ANTIETAM VII: TO THE DUNKER CHURCH (p. 710)

Anglo-American Memories, a 1911 book by George W. Smalley, is the source of the *Tribune* correspondent's ability to cover a battle forbidden to correspondents by Stanton (pp. 128–41). The general who took him on as a military aide was John Sedgwick, not Joseph Hooker.

The Gleam of Bayonets, a 1965 book by James Murfin, offers a scholarly account of the Battle of Antietam; in 1983, Stephen Sears published the more exciting *Landscape Turned Red,* its title taken from a figure of speech used by a stunned participant. This battle is getting a closer look by historians and, linked as it must be with the Emancipation Proclamation, may replace Gettysburg as the turning point of the war.

Chapter 6 of Sears's work is the basis for the opening of this chapter; General Stephen Longstreet's account in *Battles and Leaders,* II, p. 663, the source of the scene written from his point of view; the scene with Colonel Key and Burnside is based on General D. B. Sackett's letter on p. 609 of *McClellan's Own Story,* following McClellan's complaint of Burnside's "inexcusable delay" in storming the bridge.

Lee's interchange with his son is cited in Freeman's *R.E. Lee,* II, p. 397, and his cool announcment that the men on the ridge were with A. P. Hill is on p. 401.

BOOK EIGHT, CHAPTER 23
ANTIETAM VIII: A MASTERPIECE OF ART (p. 716)

Smalley's reports to the *New York Tribune* are quoted in Louis Starr's *Bohemian Brigade,* 143–46, and the account of his urging Hooker to get back into battle is in Smalley's *Anglo-American Memoirs.*

The reading of McClellan's mind is fictional, based in part on his *Own Story.* Porter's assessment of the battle as a "masterpiece of art"; McClellan's second thought that his only mistake was in not having given Porter the command entrusted to Burnside; his demand that Halleck and Stanton must go; and "I have done all that can be asked, in twice saving the country" are in his letters to his wife.

Smalley's telegraph copy was jinxed; the audience for his first story from the field was Lincoln, not the readers of the *New York Tribune*. He wrote the full account of the battle on the train from Baltimore to New York, not knowing the battle would not be resumed the next day, and arrived to announce "this is the sloppiest piece of copy you ever saw." Gay hardly edited it, ran six full columns, and the piece appeared in dozens of other newspapers, an example of war reporting at its best.

The great question about this bloodiest day in American history remains unresolved: why didn't McClellan throw in his reserves on the afternoon of the seventeenth, or at least relaunch the attack against Lee's exhausted and outnumbered army the next day?

Stephen Sears condemns the Young Napoleon as "so fearful of losing that he would not risk winning." The historian cites Lee's willingness to stand his ground the next day: to remove his wounded, to evacuate the captured supplies from Harpers Ferry, to rest and feed his exhausted men, "but contempt for his opponent was evident in his decision as well." In the eyes of most military historians, McClellan had all the lucky breaks and did not take advantage of them.

Yet Antietam was not a draw; it was a Union victory. McClellan, with an army that had just been routed and humiliated, and without authority to attack, took off after Robert Lee and his victorious troops. On the offensive, the Federal commander lost a sixth of his army while the Confederate commander, on the defensive, lost a quarter of his (about the same number of men, a cruel trade the North could afford and the South could not). After the unprecedented killing had ended, Lee left the field and retreated southward; his invasion of the North ended for that year.

Yet McClellan is judged not for what he did (he pulled together an army and stopped the raid that appeared to be an invasion, thereby saving the Union) but for what he did not do (he failed to destroy Lee's whole army and win the war at a stroke).

Of course George McClellan was mistaken in not moving faster when he found the Lost Order, in not throwing in his reserves on the afternoon of the seventeenth, in not renewing the attack against the equally exhausted rebel army the next day. But Lee was just as mistaken in dividing his army, in choosing a poor defensive position in Sharpsburg, and in underestimating the willingness of his foe to take huge casualties. Lincoln was more mistaken in pulling McClellan out of the Peninsula (Grant would follow that sensible plan years later) and in withholding fifty thousand troops from a battle forty miles north of the capital, when those troops could not have stopped a victorious Lee. Yet only McClellan's mistakes are remembered and recounted with relish; why?

One answer is that he was a petulant, arrogant, backbiting, military man unappreciative of Lincoln's central idea. Another is that he is the Northern Anti-Lincoln, the force against which the Lincoln legend had to be built by Nicolay and Hay and their followers. Also, because Americans like a winner, and McClellan was not-a-loser, in a time long before clearcut victories were considered not attainable and wholesale destruction of enemies thought less desirable.

McClellan's less than complete victory over Lee is derogated because the respite it offered was promptly used by Lincoln to turn the South's insurgency into the North's counterrevolution, in the escalation of the war's aim from "the Union as it was" to the Union as it ought to be. With the issuance that weekend of the Emancipation Proclamation, which McClellan deplored, Lincoln took control of the war from a soldier reluctant to wage it fiercely.

Book Nine, Chapter 1: two proclamations (p. 727)

This reading of Lincoln's mind during Antietam, as he rewrote and decided to issue the Emancipation Proclamation, is my assessment of what the President was thinking at that critical and surely most "historic" moment of his presidency.

The physical movements are from *LDBD*. On September 17, the day of the battle of Antietam, he was in Halleck's office in the War Department; Chase's diary for that date records the conversation with the captain from Harpers Ferry. It can be safely assumed that he was also in the telegraph office that day, and if painter Francis Carpenter's account can be believed *(Six Months at the White House,* p. 23), traveled late in the day to the Soldiers' Home in Silver Spring. He returned to Washington the next morning.

Lincoln read the first account of the battle from an intercepted Smalley dispatch, according to Starr's *Bohemian Brigade,* supported by a letter from Adams Hill to Sydney Gay dated September 18, 1862, in the Gay papers.

The first draft of the Emancipation Proclamation is in *CW* for July 22, 1862, the first paragraph of which "In pursuance of the sixth section of the act" was issued three days later, to show compliance with the Confiscation Act. Its concluding words are "then, thenceforward, and forever, be free." The last draft is in *CW* for September 22, and was written, according to Hay's real diary, on Sunday, September 21: "The President rewrote the Proclamation on Sunday morning carefully." I assume Lincoln wrote it from an interim draft prepared around the time of the Antietam battle, basing that (perilously) on Carpenter's recollection of Lincoln's recollection: "Things looked darker than ever. Finally, came the week of the battle of Antietam. I determined to wait no longer. The news came, I think, on Wednesday, that the advantage was on our side. I was then staying at the Soldiers' Home (three miles out of Washington). Here I finished writing the second draft of the preliminary proclamation; came up on Saturday; called the Cabinet together to hear it, and it was published the following Monday."

Carpenter misreported part of that, or Lincoln misremembered after two years. The news probably did come late Wednesday, and it is likely that Lincoln was spending those hot nights at the Soldiers' Home with his wife and Tad; but he came up every day, according to *CW* activity for the rest of the week, and did not discuss it at Saturday Cabinet, unless both Welles and Chase neglected to put it in their diaries for that day. The evidence suggests that Lincoln kept the rewriting (probably from an interim draft, never found) to himself all weekend, as the news from Antietam became clear, and sprang the edict on an unsuspecting Cabinet on Monday, September 22.

Book Nine, Chapter 2: aftermath at bloody lane (p. 736)

Alexander Gardner and James Gibson, along with Timothy O'Sullivan, photographed the scenes at Antietam. It has not been determined whether they arrived before the firing ended.

The scene with Pinkerton is fictional, as is the notion that they met the corporal from the 27th Indiana who discovered Lee's lost order. Corporal Mitchell was wounded at Antietam, and never fully recovered, dying three years later. The story of his destitute family's pension request is told on p. 603, II, *Battles and Leaders.*

BOOK NINE, CHAPTER 3
JOHN HAY'S DIARY, SEPTEMBER 22, 1862 (p. 739)

John Hay, in his real diary (Dennett, p. 51) wrote of the "McClellan conspiracy" the week after the general's victory at Antietam: "Last night, September 25, the President and I were riding to Soldiers' Home; he said he had heard of an officer who had said they did not mean to gain any decisive victory but to keep things running on so that they, the Army, might manage things to suit themselves. He said he should have the matter examined and if any such language had been used, his head should go off. I talked a great deal about the McClellan conspiracy . . ."

This was the first recorded reference by Lincoln to Major John Key, the officer accused of such "conspiracy" talk; he was Colonel Thomas Key's brother, working in the War Department, and apparently Lincoln was told that this was the mutinous talk going on around McClellan. The President's reaction, as we shall see, shows the seriousness with which he treated rumors of an army plot to settle the war short of victory, and demonstrates the difference of approach to the conduct of the war that was the essential source of the Lincoln-McClellan friction.

Dr. Zacharie did visit and treat Lincoln on the day the preliminary Emancipation Proclamation was issued. Assistant Secretary of War Peter Watson's note to Hay of September 19 calling attention to the doctor's "almost magical powers" has already been cited; Lincoln's holograph testimonial to Zacharie was signed and dated September 22, (*CW* for that date) and has been reprinted with pride in journals of podiatry (formerly chiropody).

The visit and testimonial are facts; the dialogue is fiction. Lincoln must have been pleased with his treatment, and his subsequent action using Zacharie as a presidential agent in a peace probe suggests that the subject may have been tentatively broached at the start. Three days later, Zacharie returned to treat Lincoln's sprained wrist, according to the September 26 *New York Herald (LDBD)*.

Allan Pinkerton also visited Lincoln that day *(LDBD)*.

BOOK NINE, CHAPTER 4: MAJOR ALLEN'S INTERVIEW (p. 743)

This chapter is based entirely on a long report from Pinkerton to McClellan written on September 22, 1862, the day of his interview with the President. It can be found in full on pp. 130–33 of James Horan's 1967 *The Pinkertons.*

I have put Pinkerton's third-person narrative into dialogue form. Thus he begins, "Lincoln was very friendly . . . He said that . . . in talking with me whatever he might say was not meant to criticize anything relating to Genl. McClellan . . . That in reference to the Battle of South Mountain and Antietam he thought those great and decisive victories—victories achieved under great difficulty and . . . you had accomplished all you set out to do viz—to push the Rebels back of Maryland and free the Capitol from danger." Since it is so detailed, and obviously written with notes at hand and while memory was fresh, it probably reflects most of what was said.

The Pinkerton report tells what the detective did not understand: that Lincoln was flattering, deceiving, mocking, and pumping him. Major Allen lapped up all the honey and unwittingly revealed in detail how he was being manipulated.

Lincoln was dealing with Pinkerton in this way, asking for damaging evidence "without betraying Genl. McClellan's confidence" at a time the President wanted it known he suspected the McClellan staff of not really wanting to win the war. Pinkerton was close to Colonel Thomas Key; the two disagreed only on the release of Rose

Greenhow. In 1864 Key wrote Pinkerton: "My friendship for McClellan, my hatred of Stanton and Lincoln, my Democratic views, my anti-slavery sentiments, my abhorrence of the war and the way it is carried on, all combined to separate me politically from everybody that I know but yourself."

BOOK NINE, CHAPTER 5: THE YOKE OF OXEN (p. 746)

Three primary and two secondary sources are brought to bear here on what took place in the Cabinet Room on September 22, 1862.

The most reliable is the draft of the preliminary Emancipation Proclamation, in Lincoln's hand, showing the changes he made; these are noted in the footnotes to the document in *CW* for that date.

Next is Chase's diary. He realized the importance of the event at the time, and quoted Lincoln directly and at length. He recorded the reaction to the reading of Ward's "High Handed Outrage at Utica": Lincoln "read it, and seemed to enjoy it very much—the Heads also (except Stanton) of course." His contemporaneous diary then begins its most significant passage: "The President then took a graver tone and said:—'Gentlemen: I have, as you are aware, thought a great deal about the relation of this war to slavery . . .'" Most of the direct quotations in this chapter are from this diary entry.

Welles's diary also covers that meeting, but was written later and inserted for that date, after it became apparent that the day was historic. On pp. 141–44 of Volume I of his diary, his recollections generally conform to Chase's. For example, Chase quoted the President as saying: "I made the promise to myself, and [hesitating a little]—to my Maker. The rebel army is now driven out, and I am going to fulfill that promise." Welles paraphrased Lincoln, writing: ". . . he had made a vow, a covenant, that if God gave us the victory in the approaching battle, he would consider it an indication of Divine will, and that it was his duty to move forward in the cause of emancipation . . . God decided the question in favor of the slaves."

Welles provided more details of what oppositon was expressed: "Blair remarked . . . he did not concur in the expediency of the measure at this time, though he approved of the principle, and should therefore wish to file his objections . . ."

Francis Carpenter's recollection in *Six Months in the White House,* pp. 22–24, of what Lincoln told him of that day is substantiated by one change in the manuscript: " 'When I finished reading this paragraph,' resumed Mr. Lincoln, 'Mr. Seward stopped me, and said, "I think, Mr. President, that you should insert after the word '*recognize*', in that sentence, the words '*and maintain*' I replied . . . it was not my way to promise what I was not entirely *sure* I could perform . . . But Seward insisted we ought to take this ground; and the words finally went in!' "

Carpenter quotes Chase as having told him Lincoln said, "I made a solemn vow before God, that if General Lee was driven back from Pennsylvania, I would crown the result by the declaration of freedom to the slaves." The quotation is secondhand. That is the most widely held theory, accepted without question by most historians, of the reason for the Proclamation, but I think it is sentimental and misleading. Although something like it was most likely said by Lincoln, my thesis is that he had more practical political and military reasons for emancipation at that time.

Another secondhand quotation is from Judge Hamilton Ward of Albany, cited by Don C. Seitz on p. 334 of his 1931 *Lincoln the Politician.* Ward quotes a lengthy account of the September 22 meeting supposedly told him by Stanton, who said that after the reading of the Artemus Ward chapter "I was considering whether I should rise and leave the meeting abruptly, when he threw his book down, heaved a sigh, and said: 'Gentlemen, why don't you laugh? With the fearful strain that is upon me night and day, if I did not laugh I should die, and you need this medicine as much as I do.' " After the Proclamation had been read and discussed, Judge Ward wrote, Stanton told him he said to Lincoln: "Mr. President, if reading chapters of Artemus Ward is a prelude to such a deed as this, the book should be filed among the archives of the nation and the author should be canonized . . . And Lincoln said to me in a droll way as I was leaving, 'Stanton, it would have been too early last spring.' " Maybe it's authentic, maybe not; I have used the "why don't you laugh?" line because it fit the situation and sounds like Lincoln.

The story attributed to Lincoln about the farmer's breaking the news slowly is placed by Carl Sandburg, I, p. 585, in this meeting but without a source mentioned. (Sandburg wrote that the proclamation was published "September 24, 1862, on a Monday morning," adopting the mistake that the Cabinet meeting about this was on the preceding Saturday; it was published in newspapers of Tuesday morning, which was September 23.)

The mind reading of Stanton, Chase, and Seward in this chapter is fictional, though Seward's lukewarm attitude is examined in Glyndon Van Deusen's biography on p. 333. Attorney General Bates's memorial on colonization, which was worked on by Anna Carroll, is in his own diary for September 25, 1862, and is as described in this chapter. In *Galaxy Magazine* for October 1873, Welles wrote in an aside about this meeting: "Mr. Bates desired that the deportation of the colored race be coincident with emancipation."

One source has been lost, or was destroyed by Nicohay, possibly at the request of Robert Lincoln. It is this maddening note in John Hay's real diary, written September 26, 1862: "the President wrote the Proclamation on Sunday morning carefully. He called the Cabinet together on Monday [September 22], made a little talk to them (see (a)) and read the momentous document. Mr. Blair and Mr. Bates made objections, otherwise the Cabinet was unanimous."

As Tyler Dennett observes in a footnote on p. 50 of his Hay diary, "There is in the diary nothing to explain '(see (a))'." Presumably it was a draft in Lincoln's writing of what he wanted to say in announcing the Emancipation Proclamation to his Cabinet. We may know more if and when attachment (a) ever comes to light.

BOOK NINE, CHAPTER 6: GETTING RIGHT ON EMANCIPATION (p. 755)

According to Chase's diary, at the September 22 Cabinet meeting "Mr. Blair then said that the question having been decided, he would make no objection to issuing the Proclamation; but he would ask to have his paper, presented some days since, against the policy, filed with the Proclamation . . . he was afraid of the influence of the Proclamation on the Border States and on the Army . . . He disclaimed most expressly, however, all objection to Emancipation *per se* . . ."

Welles's diary corroborates this, including Blair's "wish to file his objections," adding his warning that it would give partisans "a club . . . to beat the Administration." Portraitist Francis Carpenter quotes Lincoln's saying of this session, "Mr. Blair thought we should lose the fall elections, and opposed it on that ground only."

Blair did not file any objection; no record of a paper Chase says he "presented some days since" has been found, unless Chase meant the memo Blair wrote just after the

July 22 meeting and cited in that chapter. It appears to me that Blair said he would file his objections—a kind of minority report—and his family talked him out of it.

The quotations of reactions from newspapers can be found in Robert Harper's *Lincoln and the Press,* p. 177, and the Davis quotation is from Foote's *Narrative,* I, 708. Francis Blair's letter to McClellan, "Even if you had the ambitions to be President" is cited on p. 322 of Stephen Sears's *Landscape Turned Red.*

The curiosity of the hundred days was noted by Lincoln to Francis Carpenter: " 'It is a somewhat remarkable fact,' he subsequently remarked, 'that there were just one hundred days between the dates of the two proclamations issued upon the 22nd of September and the 1st of January. I had not made the calculation at the time.' "

BOOK NINE, CHAPTER 7: SERENADE (p. 760)

The opening conversation between Kate Chase and her father is fictional.

The basis for the information about Major James Garfield is from *The Garfield Orbit,* pp. 123–27, begun by the late Margaret Leech and finished in 1978 by Harry J. Brown. The derogation of Lincoln as "second-rate lawyer" is in a Garfield letter of January 2, 1863, and the attribution to Wendell Phillips of "a first-rate second-rate man" is in *The Diary of George Templeton Strong,* p. 246.

The man who would become the twentieth U.S. President did not, however, know of the report by the irate Governor Edward Stanly after his meeting with Lincoln on September 24; I have put into his mouth the words of Stanly quoting Lincoln as reported by James Welling, editor of *The Intelligencer,* in his article in the February 2, 1880, *North American Review.* In this quotation, Lincoln explains to a border stater (who considered himself double-crossed on abolition) that the proclamation was needed to keep the radicals from withdrawing their support of the war.

That is a far cry from keeping a promise to one's Maker, the reason given the Cabinet; did Lincoln really say it? The quotation is secondhand; Welling said he heard it from Stanly just after he left Lincoln's office, and the editor noted it in his diary, including the "let this cup pass from me" allusion. Stanly did see Lincoln that day *(LDBD* September 27; *CW* September 29) and it is likely that the President cooled him off with this purely political explanation. That does not mean it is the real reason, or the only reason, for the proclamation's timing—just that it is probable that Lincoln used the fear of defection of the radicals as his reason in talking to a useful conservative who felt betrayed.

The visit by Chase, his daughter Kate, and Major Garfield to the bedside of General Hooker in the Insane Asylum, as the hospital was still called, is a dramatization of the September 23 and September 25 entries in Chase's diary.

The Hay-Lamon relationship is specified in Harry E. Pratt's *Concerning Mr. Lincoln,* p. 91, published in 1944 by the Abraham Lincoln Association. The songs in the serenade at the White House are from Sandburg I, 560–61 and the President's remarks are in *CW* for September 24; a footnote adds that the serenaders then went on to the Chase house.

John Hay's real diary for September 26 (Dennett, 50) reports "the crowd was in a glorious humor" and after it left "a few old fogies staid at the Governor's and drank wine . . . . They gleefully and merrily called each other abolitionists, and seemed to enjoy the novel sensation of appropriating that horrible name." I have used some of his language in this chapter. That entry is also the source of the Chase quotation about "insanity of a class."

BOOK NINE, CHAPTER 8
JOHN HAY'S DIARY, SEPTEMBER 25, 1862 (p. 768)

The Lincoln-Seward testimonial for Dr. Zacharie is on p. 152 of the *Supplement to the Collected Works of Abraham Lincoln,* dated September 23, the day after he treated Lincoln and obtained the first testimonial. On that order that "we desire that the soldiers of our brave army may have the benefit of the doctor's surpassing skill," Stanton issued Zacharie a thirty-day pass (later extended to sixty days) to go to work on the troops.

The chiropodist went first to Fort Monroe, where he said he operated on the feet of 5,000 soldiers, and then to New Orleans, where 6,000 more received his ministrations. Later in the war, he operated on some 4,000 more in the Washington, D.C., environs, and after the war submitted a bill for $45,000 for these 15,000 patients. The Committee on War Claims ruled that the ailment was not service-connected, refusing to "establish the principle that the Government was bound to remove the corns and bunions from the feet of the soldiers of its Armies during the last war. And then . . . why not sailors; And if sailors, why not civilian employees? The petition is reported back with the recommendation that it do lie on the table."

The Lincoln story about the figure of the Virgin Mary thrown overboard is on pp. 108–9 of Donn Piatt's 1887 *Memories of the Men Who Saved the Union,* but Lincoln told it to Chase in connection with a proposal to issue paper money. I have used it here because Chase did belatedly object to the arbitrary-arrest proclamation, the quotation in this chapter from p. 119 of the Piatt book.

Did Lincoln, in the week he made history in extending human freedom, simultaneously encroach significantly on the rights of already free Americans?

In *The Civil War and Reconstruction,* James Randall and David Donald—no mythmakers—cite the 13,000 arbitrary arrests during the war and (even if new scholarship shows that figure to be exaggerated) their judgment of the Lincoln government bears weight: ". . . that it swerved from the course of democratic government and departed from the forms of civil liberty is obvious; that it stretched and at times seemed to ignore the Constitution is evident." But the harshness was tempered by leniency, say Randall-Donald: "in the suppression of anti-government activity the government under Lincoln was milder than that of Woodrow Wilson, though facing greater provocation."

In *Stanton,* Benjamin P. Thomas and Harold Hyman also refrain from judging harshly in retrospect. "Under an authoritarian policy abuses were inevitable, frequent, and sometimes tragic. Personal animosities, political ambitions, and excessive zeal . . . made innocent Americans suffer." The crackdown proclamation "served to stiffen the attitude of resistance, and as almost all the victims were Democrats, the cry arose that the administration was attempting to stifle criticism and to destroy the opposition party." But they conclude: "Yet although not hesitant to act sternly on mere suspicion of guilt, Stanton, except in moments of high excitement and crisis, acted with reasonable restraint."

I disagree. The argument that times were tough, and a few thousand dissenters clapped in jail were no big deal in the midst of insurrection, misses the point of democracy under stress: insofar as a nation departs from its guarantees of civil liberty, it is less of a democracy.

Granted that national security sometimes must override individual liberty in order to protect the nation that provides that liberty, especially when put by Lincoln as "a limb may be sacrificed to save a life, but never a life to save a limb". But the answer to the suspension of habeas corpus should be: when was it ever really necessary? If ever "necessity" seemed urgent, it was in Lincoln's time, with the nation rent by civil war. But the argument of necessity turns out to be false, the product of panic: the thousands of arbitrary arrests did not help Lincoln win the war, and may well have been counterproductive by aggravating resentment in the North. Some anti-democratic tricks worked—the arrest of the Maryland legislators and the furloughing of soldier-voters were two—but the arbitrary arrests were more valuable to the Peace Democrats as a rallying point than to Lincoln as a means of control.

Lincoln cannot be above criticism because he meant well, or because he freed the slaves while he was at the business of saving the Union, or he was lenient in applying his usurpation of the rights of the people. The purpose of hindsight is to draw a lesson. The lesson in this most extreme of cases is that it is never a proper time to ignore the Constitution in the name of saving the Constitution. To be tolerant of Lincoln's excesses is to encourage future abuses of power.

In March of 1863 Congress made a feeble effort to reassert its authority by legislating a compromise between the bench and the executive, assigning the President the power to arrest arbitrarily, but giving the civil courts the power to release political prisoners if a grand jury subsequently found no reason to indict. In the midst of war, the majority knew that majority rule had gone too far under Lincoln, and moved to curtail his reach.

In 1866, the war over, the Supreme Court under Chief Justice Chase struck down Lincoln's usurpation. In *Ex parte Milligan,* a man sentenced to hang by a military commission was freed because "Martial rule can never exist where the courts are open, and in the proper and unobstructed exercise of their jurisdiction. It is . . . confined to the locality of actual war." The justice who wrote that decision was Lincoln appointee David Davis, who was the Lincoln floor manager at the 1860 Republican convention in Chicago. ("Make no deals in my name," wired Lincoln; "Hell, we're here and he's not," replied Davis, making Cabinet deals, that Lincoln later honored, to get the nomination.) In *Milligan,* which in effect declared Lincoln's proclamation of military rule unconstitutional, the Court was saying, "We're here and he's not": martyred heroes come and go, but the rule of law wins in the end.

BOOK NINE, CHAPTER 9: THE KEY EPISODE (p. 770)

This harsh scene is documented in Lincoln's handwriting. It telescopes his "Record of Dismissal of John J. Key" in *CW* for September 26–7 (a confrontation that took place in Lincoln's office at 11 A.M. on the 27th) and an exchange of correspondence in *CW* for November 24, 1862, which was Key's appeal and Lincoln's written response.

I have turned all the letters into dialogue and incorporated them in the morning meeting, which was a kind of civilian court-martial, in the President's office. John Key's son Joseph was killed at Perryville between the verdict and the appeal, which Lincoln noted with sympathy but did not allow to affect his decision. Both Montgomery Blair and Senator Orville Browning made appeals for clemency, which Lincoln turned aside.

Lincoln apparently considered the matter important. He wrote out his notes of the dismissal proceedings on October 14 (misspelling "literally"). John Hay's real diary for September 25, 1864, records Lincoln's recollections of the event, and is the source for "I dismissed Major Key for his silly treasonable talk because I feared it was staff talk & I wanted an example," and "I began to fear he [McClellan] was playing false—that he did not want to hurt the enemy." Nicohay VI, 186–87 covers the episode in detail, since it was intended to lay a basis for the derogation of McClellan and to justify his removal, after a decent interval, despite his victory at Antietam.

An excoriation of Colonel Thomas Key as "George McClellan's evil genius" is in Donn Piatt's *Memories of the Men Who Saved the Union,* pp. 291–95.

BOOK NINE, CHAPTER 10: SURPRISE VISIT (p. 775)

The conversation between Gardner and Gibson is fictional. Brady's shows of Gardner's Antietam coverage were well attended and the *New York Times* review was in the October 20, 1862, issue, cited in William A. Frassanito's 1978 *Antietam: the Photographic Legacy of America's Bloodiest Day.* (It was the bloodiest day: 26,000 casualties, compared to 6,700 American dead, wounded, and missing on D-Day in World War II.)

The pictures described in this chapter and included in this book (Lincoln with Pinkerton, Lincoln and McClellan in the general's tent, the President with the general's staff including Custer on the far right) are described in detail in Frassanito's work. Gardner's contribution to photography as an art form and his break with Brady at about this time or early the next year, are discussed in E. F. Bleiler's introduction to the 1959 reprint of the 1866 two-volume *Gardner's Photographic Sketch Book of the Civil War.*

The Pinkerton-McClellan conversation is fiction. The letter from Montgomery Blair advising a few words against slavery (and reporting on the dismissal of Major Key) is in the McClellan collection at the Library of Congress. The Key-McClellan conversation is mostly fictional, but McClellan's speculation about taking the government into his own hands is from his letters to his wife at about that time, and Thomas Key's advice against it is quoted in Donn Piatt's *Memories of the Men Who Saved the Union,* p. 294.

Lincoln and McClellan did have lengthy conversations in the general's tent on October 2–4, but no notes were made. I have reconstructed the conversation using Lincoln's letter to McClellan of October 13, *CW* (the next day, he saw fit to write out the notes of the Key dismissal) and McClellan's recollections of that visit and other letters in *McClellan's Own Story* with Lincoln's assurances that he would stand by him on pp. 627–28. Lincoln's "fatigued horses" exasperation, McClellan's response, and Lincoln's apology are in *CW* for October 25, 26, and 27. McClellan's request to go home and see his wife and baby is inferred from *CW* for October 7, in which Lincoln says, "You wish to see your family, and I wish to oblige you."

The visit to McClellan by Democratic leaders became a campaign issue in 1864.

McClellan's General Order No. 163, suggesting that soldiers unhappy with the Emancipation and habeas corpus proclamations find a solution at the ballot box, thereby cutting short the talk of a march on Washington, is in 28 *Official Records,* 395.

Two days after Lincoln left McClellan's camp and left McClellan believing he had the President's support, Halleck sent a message saying the President directed him to "cross the Potomac and give battle to the enemy . . . your army must move now, while the roads are good." Either the general later lied about the President's assurances, or Lincoln softsoaped him in camp and upon his return to Washington immediately began building the record for his dismissal.

The mind reading of Custer is fictional, but his frame of mind just after Antietam is taken from Jay Monaghan's 1959 biography. He writes: "Whisky voices threatened to 'change front' on Washington and set McClellan up as dictator rather than see him deposed. Lieutenant Wilson remembered one thick-tongued braggart—and it may well have been Custer, though he didn't drink—who shouted, 'Dismiss McClellan and I'll serve Lincoln's government no longer. I'll resign and go home.'" That's speculation by Monaghan, but Custer's writings remained loyal to McClellan all his life, right up to Little Big Horn.

BOOK NINE, CHAPTER 11: THE DREAM (p. 785)

The episode of the redirected wine shipment, along with the reason for the screening of Mrs. Lincoln's correspondence, is in Stoddard's *Lincoln's Third Secretary*, pp. 112–14.

The flashback to the visit of the Chicago preachers is based on the detailed account of that meeting in *CW* for September 13,1862. The Lincolns' religious practices are described in Ishbel Ross's 1973 *The President's Wife*.

Lincoln's meditation on God's will was written in his own hand but not dated; it appears in *CW* for September 2, 1862, and is described in Nicohay in their earlier *Complete Works* as written "while his mind was burdened with the weightiest question of his life . . . It was not written to be seen of men." Although his secretaries dated the fragment September 30, Roy Basler judiciously places it in the weeks preceding the preliminary Emancipation Proclamation, just after Pope's defeat at Second Bull Run when Lincoln was described by Bates as looking like a man about to hang himself.

I have juxtaposed Elizabeth Keckley's description of Lincoln's Bible-reading one day, including her comment about Job and "Gird up thy loins" (pp. 119–20, *Behind the Scenes)* with the Meditation because they seem to fit. "Father, you should not go out alone" and his reply, "Mother . . . no one is going to molest me" are on pp. 120–21.

Lincoln's dream of death, and the description of Mrs. Lincoln's frightened reaction to its impulsive telling, is in Ward Hill Lamon's *Recollections of Lincoln,* pp. 112–18. The dream came not in 1862, but near the end of Lincoln's life.

The seance is well documented. Nettie Colburn Maynard, the well-known medium, wrote a book in 1891 entitled *Was Lincoln a Spiritualist?* in which she sought to portray him as such. During and after the Civil War, attempts were made by anti-Lincoln writers and cartoonists to portray him as under the spooky spell of spiritualists, duped by them at fraudulently supernatural "circles," which was intended to counter the claims of clergymen that Lincoln was a religious man. In the *Illinois State Historical Society Journal,* Jay Monaghan surveyed all the literature on the subject and laid the spiritualists to rest in his article "Was Lincoln Really a Spiritualist?"

Mary Lincoln was a believer in communication with the spirit world, and especially after Willie's death attended many seances. Some were with Cranston Laurie, a trance medium, and his daughter Belle Miller, a physical medium for whom a piano was made to appear to dance when she was "under control," and on which Mr. Lincoln apparently did sit to try to hold it down. Some were with the charlatan "Lord" Colchester, one of whose spirit rappings was broken up by Lincoln's later secretary, Noah Brooks, and described by him on p. 66 of his *Washington in Lincoln's Time.*

Mr. Lincoln went to at least one seance, probably a few. According to Monaghan, the best-documented seances with the President in attendance, with reliable witnesses like John Forney also present, were those organized by Nettie Colburn. The historian quotes Miss Nettie's book at length, from which I drew the scene in this chapter, and considers her account of what was said to be credible: "There is nothing in the whole dialogue that indicates that Abraham Lincoln did or said any more than any other President or politician would have done in the same situation."

The reading of Lincoln's mind in this chapter is my own, but the thought "I always did have a strong tendency to mysticism" is from a letter to his close friend Joshua Speed. The reference to Lincoln reading *Further Communications from the World of Spirits* is from a facsimile of the title page of that 1862 book on which is Lincoln's signature (perhaps authentic) which is in the appendix of the 1957 *Abraham Lincoln Returns* by Harriet M. Shelton. Miss Shelton, a spiritualist, also reported that messages from the spirit world, at seances she had attended, indicate that Mr. Lincoln's spirit is content.

BOOK NINE, CHAPTER 12: JOHN HAY'S DIARY, OCTOBER 8, 1862 (p. 790)

Halleck's order is cited on p. 628 of *McClellan's Own Story*. Lincoln's permission to visit Ellen McClellan in Washington is in *CW* for October 7. Lincoln's curt telegraph message to his wife is in the *CW Supplement,* p. 141. The salary deduction for income tax is in *LDBD* for October 6. The plan to arrange a meeting with Seymour is fictional.

BOOK NINE, CHAPTER 13: PRISONERS (p. 792)

The episode is fictional. The passage about Perryville and the decision by Bragg, soon after being joined by Breckinridge's Orphan Brigade, to move south out of a Kentucky as unreceptive to recruitment as Maryland, is accurate. General Breckinridge's son Cabell was not captured until 1863, a year later; according to the Davis biography, p. 400, Cabell was sent to the prison camp on Johnson's Island in Lake Erie. Libby Prison did not become infamous until late in the war.

"In a bad row for stumps" is a Louisiana farming expression quoted by Bell Irvin Wiley in *The Life of Johnny Reb,* p. 346, meaning "in a bad way" or in a modern vernacular, "in deep trouble."

BOOK NINE, CHAPTER 14: DEBATE (p. 797)

This scene never took place, but the quotations are genuine.

I have interspersed portions of Horatio Seymour's speeches in the campaign of 1862, taken from David G. Croly's 1868 campaign biography, *Seymour and Blair,* pp. 75–95, with Lincoln's later reply to the same and similar charges, notably in his letter to Erastus Corning and others, *CW* for June 12, 1863, and his follow-up letter to Matthew Birchard and others, *CW* for June 29, 1863.

Another source is a more direct interchange: Lincoln's letter to Seymour of March 23, 1863, and Seymour's response in *CW* for that date. Although Lincoln came to see Governor Seymour as most important to the war, as we shall see later, the two never met face to face. The anecdote about being for war, pestilence and famine, which Lincoln told in relation to Seymour, is found in Hay's real diary for August 13, 1863.

Lincoln was pleased with his long letter justifying harsh measures against dissidents to Corning and other New York Democrats, which followed the arrest of Clement Vallandigham. Congressman James Wilson of Ohio reported (Sandburg, II, p. 308) that Lincoln said: "When it became necessary for me to write that letter, I had it nearly all in there [Pointing to the drawer] . . . Often an idea about it would occur to me which seemed to have force and make perfect answer to some of the things that were said and written about my actions. I never let one of those ideas escape me, but wrote it on a scrap of paper and put it in that drawer . . . I am pleased to know that the present judgment of thoughtful men about it is so generally in accord with what I believe the future will, without serious division, pronounce concerning it." He was wrong about that; division still exists about the necessity or wisdom of his arbitrary arrests.

BOOK NINE, CHAPTER 15: THE GOLD ROOM (p. 803)

Jay Cooke's personal dealings with Chase are detailed in Ellis Oberholtzer's 1907 *Jay Cooke: Financier of the Civil War,* I, pp. 210–11; this includes Chase's written reminder to Cooke to commence public letters with "Sir:".

The drop in the gold price of greenbacks in 1862, and its political cause, are from William Davis's *The Deep Waters of the Proud,* pp. 229–31. A fine short analysis of gold and greenbacks is in Randall and Donald's *The Civil War and Reconstruction,* pp. 248–353.

Was Chase involved in egregious conflicts of interest? Thomas and Marva Beldon, in their 1956 *So Fell the Angels,* charged that Chase stooped to favoritism and even bribery, which David Donald countered in a footnote in his book was "based on insufficient evidence". We will have to wait for Harold Hyman's biography of Chase for a closer look, but it seems that Chase was involved in what we would today consider unethical behavior, or at least its appearance. (The Beldons chose an apt title, from Shakespeare's King Henry VIII: "I charge thee, fling away ambition: by that sin fell the angels.")

Fawn Brodie, on p. 175 of her 1959 biography of Thaddeus Stevens, describes the singing in the Gold Room; Lincoln's expressed wish that the traders would get their heads shot off is from Carpenter's *Six Months at the White House,* p. 84.

"McClellan is finished" is based on a letter from Chase to Hiram Barney of October 26, 1862, in the Chase papers, cited by Warren Hassler in his McClellan biography, p. 319, and summarized as, "it was inexpedient to remove McClellan before the elections, lest the motives be misconstrued as a sop to the Radicals." Together with Hay's diary entry of September 5 quoting Lincoln saying that radical feeling "will make it expedient to take important command from him . . . But he is too useful just now to sacrifice," this bolsters my thesis that Lincoln's root reason for the removal of McClellan was political, not military.

Kate Chase was jealous of all the women her father saw, which included Anna Ella Carroll on occasion, but the scene between them is entirely fictional as is the putative romance between Carroll and Chase.

The *matinée dansante,* candlelit afternoon dances pioneered by Adele Douglas in the 1850s, was adopted by Kate Chase, according to Mary Merwin Phelps's 1935 biography, p. 111, and was in such vogue at one point as to eclipse the *soirée conversable.*

BOOK NINE, CHAPTER 16
JOHN HAY'S DIARY, NOVEMBER 5, 1862 (p. 808)

Hay was in Illinois just before the election, and wrote to Nicolay on October 28, 1862, with political prescience that "things look bad around here politically . . . this State is in great danger," blaming impatience with the lack of military success and the absence of precinct captains. He did not detect a backlash from emancipation: "I have been astonished to hear so little objection to the proclamation." He missed something there.

The quotations from Garfield are from letters he wrote just after the election, excerpted in *The Life and Letters of James Abram Garfield* by Theodore Clarke Smith, I, 253–54.

BOOK NINE, CHAPTER 17: BE RELIEVED FROM COMMAND (p. 810)

Carl Schurz wrote to Lincoln on November 8 about the election results, and the sharp Lincoln reply is dated November 10 in *CW*. Schurz wrote back and received another long and testy riposte from the President on November 24. According to his 1907 *The Reminiscences of Carl Schurz*, II, pp. 395–96, the German-born human rights leader received a short note from Lincoln a few days later asking him to come in early some morning soon.

Schurz described "the little room up-stairs which was at the time used for Cabinet meetings—the room with the Jackson portrait above the mantel-piece—and found Mr. Lincoln seated in an arm chair before an open-grate fire, his feet in his gigantic morocco slippers. He greeted me cordially as of old . . ." That memoir is the source for Lincoln's "Didn't I give it to you hard in my letter? Didn't I? But it didn't hurt, did it?" paraphrased in this scene.

Some of the thoughts attributed to Lincoln about the reasons for the replacement of McClellan are based on his previously cited predictions (in Hay's real diary) of the general's replacement at a propitious moment. The official reason given, and accepted by most historians, is that Lincoln promised someone—perhaps himself—that he would replace McClellan if Lee's army "escaped". The thoughts attributed to him in this chapter are what I think he was thinking, based on the day-after-election timing of his decision—despite the obvious movements toward engagement of McClellan's army.

McClellan's plans to strike Longstreet first near Culpepper Court House are set forth in his memoirs, p. 645; his critics insist he would have found excuses to delay. The pro-McClellan case is made in the three articles by George Ticknor Curtis in the *North American Review* in 1880, especially the June issue. In the light of later events at Fredericksburg and Chancellorsville, it is clear that his removal at this moment turned out to be a costly military blunder; however, at the time the decision made political sense.

BOOK NINE, CHAPTER 18: PLAYING SHUT-PAN (p. 814)

Francis Blair met with Lincoln alone the night of November 6, 1862, at the Soldiers' Home, near the Blair house in Silver Spring. The next day he wrote his son Montgomery an account of the meeting, which included Lincoln's "auger too dull to take hold" and "he has the slows, Mr. Blair." A long excerpt is in William Ernest Smith's Blair biography, II, p. 144.

In his letter to McClellan enthusiast George Ticknor Curtis dated January 21, 1880, Montgomery Blair recalled that night when his father "spent a long time in arguing against that proposal [to dismiss McClellan] . . . telling Lincoln . . . that the opposition to McClellan came from Chase and Stanton, who were hostile to him [Lincoln]." Lincoln's Postmaster General explained why McClellan was a dead duck after Harrison's Landing: "It was manifest to me that there was something more than I

knew of, of which McClellan's opponents were availing themselves against him . . .
I did not know till McClellan visited me, while attending the Porter trial the winter
afterward, and read me his Harrison's Landing letter, what it was that made Lincoln
so deaf to my own and my father's efforts . . . it was that letter which enabled
Stanton and Chase to remove him."

McClellan's impolitic foray into political advice at Harrison's Landing had done
him in. The letter was used by Chase and Stanton "to make Lincoln look upon him as
a rival . . . while I believe Lincoln to be as unselfish as any man, he was yet a man,
and no man could be told day by day that another was making use of the place he gave
him to supersede him in his own place, without being afterward against him and ready
to believe that he was both unfriendly and unfit for his position."

The Blairs ultimately formed an alliance with Seymour. Frank Blair was Seymour's
running mate on the Democratic ticket in 1868.

BOOK NINE, CHAPTER 19: BLOODLESS WATERLOO (p. 816)

"The defeat of McClellan," wrote a still intensely loyal Major General George Armstrong Custer in the June 1876 *Galaxy Magazine,* just before his death at the Little Big
Horn, "was not the result of . . . the open opposition of enemies in his front, but the
half-hidden interference of foes in his rear, that succeeded in marring the complete
success of McClellan's combination for the suppression of the rebellion." The *Galaxy*
pieces are reprinted in John Carroll's 1977 *Custer in the Civil War.*

The dialogue in this chapter is fictional, but Custer's resentment of the radicals who
brought down his hero and patron is obvious: "At a time when McClellan was about
to engage the Confederate army [in the Peninsula campaign]," Custer wrote, "serious
changes tending to weaken his army were made . . . one . . . in reply to a remark
that the contemplated change would seriously embarrass McClellan's movements,
remarked, 'It is not on our books that McClellan shall take Richmond.' " Custer was
especially upset that a senator voting on his confirmation as a brigadier general in
1863 wanted to know "if you are what is termed 'a McClellan man'." He was.

General Buckingham's movements, first to Burnside and then McClellan, are factual, though his dialogue in both scenes is imaginary. His mathematics background is
in Boatner's *Civil War Dictionary.* Burnside's candor in admitting he was not suited
for major command was summed up in Grant's memoirs: "He was not . . . fitted to
command an army. No one knew this better than himself."

The scene of McClellan turning over his command without a fuss is described on
p. 651 of *McClellan's Own Story,* and his letter to his wife is on p. 660. My mind
reading of his understanding of the ironies of the timing of his dismissal is undocu-
mented guesswork. He was a more mature man in 1862 than he had been the year
before, and I think he knew that his political outlook was the reason for his dismissal
—especially since that took place the day after election, at a moment when he was
moving inexorably toward the action that Lincoln supposedly wanted.

Because the general was usually too cautious after overestimating enemy strength;
because he resisted emancipation, and was the anti-Lincoln candidate in 1864, he has
been held in contempt by those historians seduced by the Nicohay slant. But George
McClellan twice created and led the army that saved the Union, and at the end
strengthened constitutional government by submitting without question to ultimate
civilian authority; these were great deeds, and we need not revile the man in order to
revere his adversary. Like Lincoln in the beginning, McClellan was among the major-

ity of his countrymen who did not understand the urgency of rooting out the moral outrage of slavery. The President, for a complex set of reasons, saw the light in time; the general did not.

BOOK NINE, CHAPTER 20: IN JACKSON'S CHAIR (p. 823)

This fictional attempt to assess Lincoln's state of mind as he prepared his surprising annual message to Congress has certain bases in fact.

The passing reference to Mrs. Lincoln expressing her pique by not sleeping near him is from Don Seitz's *Lincoln the Politician,* p. 359, citing George Bancroft, the historian, as authority: "One morning in came Lincoln sad and sorrowful: 'Ah,' said he, 'today we must settle the case of Lieutenant ———. Mrs. Lincoln has for three nights slept in a separate apartment.' " This implies that the Lincolns ordinarily slept together, but Charles Strozier, in his 1982 *Lincoln's Quest for Union,* pp. 87–88, draws a contrary inference from the separate bedrooms built into the Lincolns' remodeled house in 1856, and Mrs. Lincoln's letter of May 2, 1868, to Rhoda White: ". . . for the past three weeks, I have been seriously sick. [Following words crossed out.] My disease is of a womanly nature, which you will understand has been [end of crossing out] greatly accelerated by the last three years of mental suffering. Since the birth of my youngest son, for about twelve years I have been more or less a sufferer." (Justin and Linda Turner, *Mary Todd Lincoln, Her Life and Letters* pp. 475–76.) Strozier surmises that after Tad's birth in 1853, sexual relations between the Lincolns ceased. After four regularly spaced pregnancies, the childbearing stopped; since there was no contraception and abortion was unlikely, a case can be made that the Lincolns were forced to refrain from intercourse by some injury or infection connected to the birth of Tad. The only evidence suggesting intimacy in the White House is that offhand jest quoted by Bancroft. (That's a lot of background on a passing reference, but perhaps it explains her jealousy and his resistance to it.)

The reference to McClellan's communications with Democrats is from Welles's diary entry of September 8. Frank Blair's efforts to become McClellan's staff chief are in Ward Hill Lamon's *Recollections,* p. 206, which is also the source of Lincoln's concern about engraving signatures on the currency. Congressman Washburne's worries about his protégé Grant's drinking was in a letter to Chase, in the Chase papers, cited by Wood Gray in his 1942 *The Hidden Civil War,* p. 128.

The story of Andrew Jackson's chair was told by William Stoddard in *Lincoln at Work,* p. 66. The recitation of the lines from Act III of Shakespeare's *Richard II* was done at least three times—in Springfield, in the White House, and at the Soldiers' Home, according to John Hay's recollection quoted in Helen Nicolay's 1912 *Personal Traits of Abraham Lincoln.*

The reasoning for his backtracking on emancipation is my own, based on what he did a week later. The Second Annual Message to Congress (*CW,* December 1, 1862) is usually treated in a gingerly fashion by Lincoln scholars, but it is a closely reasoned, hand-written retreat from his position before September 22. Either he was having second thoughts about the efficacy or constitutionality of emancipation, or he thought it wise to go to great lengths to suggest to people that he was having those second thoughts. The headline in the story of the message is "Lincoln Offers South Forty Years to End Slavery," and the subheads are "Amendment Proposed for Compensation of Slaveowners" and "Deportation of Freed Blacks Urged."

Perhaps he felt he was safe in making this far more attractive offer to the South;

since they were not likely to take him up on it, the threatened, or promised, January 1 emancipation edict would seem less a challenge to a fight to the finish. Subsequent to his December 1 message, on December 11 Lincoln received a letter from Fernando Wood about an approach made to him in late November suggesting that an offer of amnesty would result in Southerners returning to Congress; Lincoln replied the next day *(CW* December 12) that he would be glad to receive more information about this, adding significantly, "Such information might be more valuable before the first of January than afterwards."

In this chapter, I have Lincoln knowing about Wood's information as he wrote the annual message; I think it fair to assume that talk of peace feelers was in the air toward the end of November.

Lincoln wrote that week to General Banks, on his way to relieve General Butler in New Orleans, asking him to take along Dr. Zacharie: "I think he may be of service to you, first, in his peculiar profession, and secondly, as a means of access to his country-men . . ." Roy Basler footnotes this in his *Supplement to the Collected Works:* "Zacharie's several letters to Lincoln reporting on conditions in Louisiana, beginning January 14, 1863, show that Lincoln's evaluation of his service was well placed."

Thirty days from his announced Emancipation Day, Lincoln was evidently tortured by its possible effects on the war and the North's war spirit. He moved to protect his conservative flank. The irony is that he used some of his most memorable language in this message: "The dogmas of the quiet past are inadequate to the stormy present. The occasion is piled high with difficulty, and we must rise with the occasion. As our case is new, so we must think anew and act anew. We must disenthrall ourselves, and then we shall save our country."

His words are now quoted as if they applied to the Emancipation Proclamation instead of to its substitute, his proposed amendment to buy up slaves over the suc-ceeding forty years. "The fiery trial through which we pass will light us down, in honor or dishonor, to the latest generation . . . In giving freedom to the slave, we assure freedom to the free . . . We shall nobly save, or meanly lose, the last, best hope of earth . . ." Fortunately for the slaves then living, the gradualist plan these immortal words put forward was not given serious attention.

BOOK NINE, CHAPTER 21: JEPHTHA'S DAUGHTER (p. 829)

The episode of Lincoln's worrying about the engraved signature on the currency is described by Lamon in his *Recollections,* pp. 217–20. Background on F. E. Spinner, the Treasurer with the distinctive signature, and his twenty-hour signing days, as well as his pioneering hiring of women for government work, is in John A. Joyce's 1895 *Jewels of Memory,* pp. 67–8.

The conversation between Chase and his daughter in this chapter is fictional, but some tacit understanding for him to remain single, could have existed. Kate resumed seeing Sprague about this time after several months of estrangement; they became engaged in May of 1863. I have moved it forward in order to have it take place during the time covered by this book. "Jephtha's daughter" was a characterization of her in this regard made by Henry Adams, and the John Hay assessment of William Sprague as a youth who had bought his place is from his real diary. The fashions draped around Kate are from *Godey's Lady's Book and Magazine* for November 1862.

BOOK NINE, CHAPTER 22
JOHN HAY'S DIARY, DECEMBER 2, 1862 (p. 835)

The newspaper citations deriding Dr. Zacharie's work on Lincoln's feet are from William Scheibel's article, "The Podiatrist Who Became a President's Confidant" in the *Journal of the American Podiatry Association,* August 1962.

Lincoln's letter to Banks is dated November 25 in the *CW Supplement;* its toleration of Grant's anti-Semitic policy is discussed in a later chapter. "Nothing which I dread to see in history" is from a Lincoln letter to Fernando Wood, *CW* for December 12, about a supposed peace feeler. The "new life" from a witticism is in a Stephen Oates article in *Civil War Magazine,* February 1984. "The Tycoon is in fine whack" is from Hay's real diary, p. 76.

BOOK NINE, CHAPTER 23: FIRING SQUAD (p. 838)

The episode of the execution of Corporal Asa Lewis is recounted in William C. Davis's *The Orphan Brigade,* p. 149.

The conversation between Breckinridge and Cleburne, both commanders under Bragg at Murfreesboro, is fictional.

BOOK NINE, CHAPTER 24: THE PRESIDENT VISITS (p. 841)

Jefferson Davis turned his back on "states' rights" as soon as he was faced with mobilizing a nation for war. The opposition from his brilliant and persnickety Vice President is detailed in Chapter XVII of E. Ramsay Richardson's 1932 *Little Aleck: A Life of Alexander H. Stephens.* In 1971, Emory Thomas summed up the ironies and anomalies in the need for union while fighting against the Union in *The Confederacy as a Revolutionary Experience:* "Goaded by the demands of 'modern', total war, the Confederate government abandoned the political system it was called into being to defend. The Confederacy raised a national army, conscripted troops, employed martial rule, managed the economy, and even interfered with Southern stills."

A comparison of the two Presidents is in Irving Werstein's 1959 *Abraham Lincoln vs. Jefferson Davis* (from which the Stephens quotation blasting Davis is taken, p. 241); the allusion to Davis's sunny daughter is from Cass Canfield's *The Iron Will of Jefferson Davis,* p. 83; and Davis's fury at Lincoln's "sly" recommendation that blacks abstain from violence unless in self-defense is in Russell Hoover Quynn's 1959 *The Constitutions of Abraham Lincoln and Jefferson Davis,* p. 19.

The *Richmond Whig*'s characterization of the Bragg Kentucky campaign as a "fizzle" is from p. 325 of Grady McWhiney's 1969 *Braxton Bragg and Confederate Defeat;* Bragg called them "the dogs of detraction" in a pre-Agnevian bit of alliteration. On p. 345 is Davis's instruction, "Fight if you can, and fall back beyond the Tennessee."

Davis admired and was friendly with both Bragg and Breckinridge, and must have tried to ameliorate the animosity between the two, but there is no record of it. In Hudson Strode's biography of Davis, there is a reference on p. 307 to the President's pessimism just after Antietam: "Our maximum strength has been mobilized," he told his Secretary of War, "while the enemy is just beginning to put forth his might." But like Lincoln, Davis had a resilient spirit in the face of adversity, and bounced back before Fredericksburg.

BOOK NINE, CHAPTER 25: THE BANDIT TAKES A BRIDE (p. 848)

The dramatic elements in this scene are fictional. President Davis did take the opportunity offered by the Morgan wedding to visit the troops in Murfreesboro at that time, and the cavalry raider was described as transformed by his newfound love; his swash never again buckled. But Cleburne, newly promoted to major general on Bragg's recommendation, did not make his argument on offering freedom to the South's slaves in return for army enlistment directly to President Davis. Nor was Cleburne's proposal officially submitted until January 2, 1864, just over a year after the Morgan wedding. As Robert Durden points out in his 1972 *The Grey and the Black: the Confederate Debate on Emancipation,* pp. 47–48, this idea percolated at the state level during 1863, with "indirect evidence" showing some slaves being mustered into state militias on the tacit understanding that they would be freed and given a patch of land after the war.

Davis's remarks on "little opportunity for social intercourse" and "we are invincible" are from Foote, II, pp. 105–6, and his comments on recruiting slaves are factual but drawn from 1864, when the military picture was quite different. His unfortunate military decision to detach Morgan's cavalry force from Bragg's army, just before the battle of Stones River, was rationalized as an attempt to disrupt Rosecrans's communications, but Howard Swiggett, in his biography of Morgan, pp. 94–97, posits that Davis believed in the usefulness of a plan, later known as the Northwest Conspiracy, to encourage an uprising of copperhead secret societies in connection with a raid by Morgan's cavalry. A description of a meeting with Davis on this is in the Maule papers in the Western Reserve Historical Society.

The interior monologue imputed to Breckinridge is my own, drawing on ideas in Kenneth M. Stampp's *The Imperiled Union* and Emory Thomas's *The Confederate Nation.* It goes beyond biographical license, but seems to me in character for Breckinridge—who despised Bragg, had no strong pro-slavery feelings, and had never been a disunionist before secession—to be thinking this way.

BOOK NINE, CHAPTER 26: ALONE AGAIN (p. 854)

Fiction. Miss Carroll's papers at the Maryland Historical Society show that she helped Senator Wilson get some patronage from Secretary Chase. The references to "Jeffy D" and the political future of Rosecrans are from Homer Bates's *Lincoln in the Telegraph Office,* pp. 160, 205.

BOOK NINE, CHAPTER 27
JOHN HAY'S DIARY, DECEMBER 12, 1862 (p. 858)

Fiction. As the quasi-romance between Salmon Chase and Anna Carroll is imaginary, the flirtation between Kate Chase and John Hay is equally without any foundation in fact. Each of the four surely had romantic attachments—but with other people. The purpose of making these two fictional connections is to provide a prism through which to examine their characters and a hatrack on which to hang other information, as well as to entertain the fact-laden reader and author.

BOOK NINE, CHAPTER 28: FREDERICKSBURG I: WITH LINCOLN (p. 861)

This is what I believe Lincoln was thinking on the eve of Fredericksburg, a fortnight from the deadline for the Emancipation Proclamation. Such mind reading is speculative; a contrary case is more often made that Lincoln was resolute and unwavering about issuing the Proclamation, and that his eloquent annual message, with its delay of emancipation by thirty-seven years, was a kind of smoke screen.

The estimate of Burnside as a better housekeeper than Hooker is from William Kelley's firsthand account in Rice's 1886 *Reminiscences of Abraham Lincoln by Distinguished Men of His Time*, p. 278. The letter introducing John Nicolay to Burnside is in *CW* for December 12, 1862.

The sources for the reference to separate beds can be found in the notes to Chapter 20 of this book. The order to hang only thirty Indians, with their names, is in *CW* for December 6.

BOOK NINE, CHAPTER 29
FREDERICKSBURG II: NOT A CHICKEN ALIVE (p. 864)

Source for Longstreet's internal monologue, as well as his conversation with Lee about McClellan, is his long memoir in *Battles and Leaders*, Vol. II.

Shelby Foote's narrative, II, p. 41, cites Lee on entrenchments, and General Edward Stackpole's 1957 *The Fredericksburg Campaign* assigns most of the blame for the Union disaster to Burnside's poor judgment.

BOOK NINE, CHAPTER 30: FREDERICKSBURG III: WITH NICOLAY (p. 866)

Burnside's telegram to Lincoln is in Foote, II, p. 41, and Sumner's advice on p. 39. Hooker's "enough blood" is in Nevins, *War Becomes Revolution*, p. 350.

John Nicolay did go to Fredericksburg that Sunday. His daughter's biography says he went because he was "curious to see the results," but it is a fair assumption that Lincoln sent him with a letter to Burnside for a firsthand report. On p. 158, Helen Nicolay prints an excerpt from a letter from her father to her mother that day that is my basis for the scene: "The place was within easy reach of the rebel batteries, and as there was a reasonable expectation that they would begin shelling it at almost every moment, I only stayed long enough to ride through two or three of the principal streets and get off and drink a cup of coffee with some of the officers who were lunching in one of the houses."

BOOK NINE, CHAPTER 31
FREDERICKSBURG IV: JOHN HAY'S DIARY, DECEMBER 14, 1862 (p. 868)

Browning's visit is in his diary for the fifteenth, not the fourteenth. The "darkie arithmetic" is in Rice's *Reminiscences*, p. 288. Haupt's report is described in Francis A. Lord's 1969 *Lincoln's Railroad Man: Herman Haupt*, pp. 180–81.

BOOK NINE, CHAPTER 32: FREDERICKSBURG V: WITH LINCOLN (p. 870)

The scene with the *New York Tribune* reporter brought to Lincoln from Willard's bar by Senator Wilson is documented, but the reporter was Henry Villard, not George Smalley. I have substituted Smalley (who after an attack of "camp fever" was assigned by Greeley and Gay to write as an editorial assistant in New York) because I did not want to introduce a new character.

The account appears in the 1904 *The Memoirs of Henry Villard*, pp. 390–91. After recalling "the sickening story of the appalling disaster for which Ambrose E. Burnside will, to the end of time, stand charged with the responsibility," Villard went on to fault Lee for not finishing off the Federals: "[Lee's] dispatches, during and immediately after the action, to the Richmond Secretary of War prove that he not only did not know the physical and moral disability wrought among our forces, but believed that there had been only a preliminary trial of arms, and that the battle would be renewed at daylight the next morning." Lee took much of the same criticism that had been directed at McClellan after Antietam: that he had not followed up his victory by wiping out the enemy.

The *Tribune*'s Villard later became a railroad magnate, formed the predecessor company to General Electric, and bought the *New York Evening Post.*

The visit of Curtin, and Lincoln's call on Halleck's headquarters that night accompanied by the efficient Haupt, are described in Sandburg I, pp. 629–30. The President's military dilemma that week was outlined gloomily in a note Haupt wrote to Lincoln on December 22: "We cannot advance; to stand still is ruin. To withdraw the Army and send it to the Peninsula would proclaim to the world that the evacuation of August was a mistake. We must go back substantially to the military position of May last when the Army of the Potomac was on the Peninsula and the Army of the Rappahannock at Fredericksburg, but General Halleck cannot, consistent with his former action, order this; and you cannot order this in opposition to him without assuming great responsibilities before the nation and losing perhaps proper cooperation from your present advisors." General Haupt, who could rebuild a bridge better than anyone, was suggesting a great mistake had been made in firing McClellan that was too embarrassing to rectify by first admitting it. "General McClellan's friends are numerous and powerful, but you cannot place him in position without offending opposing factions."

BOOK NINE, CHAPTER 33: GET SEWARD (p. 875)

With the exception of Wade's description of the comparative powers of the President and Congress (Hans Trefousse, *Benjamin Franklin Wade,* p. 193), this scene is fiction. I think it reflects Wade's views and his character, which include a vindictive humanitarianism, employing whatever means were necessary to achieve good ends (popular education, land for work, abolition).

Wade and his wife Caroline were good friends to Anna Ella Carroll, who disagreed with them on war powers and emancipation, for the rest of her life. In supporting her postwar claim to credit and compensation for creating the Tennessee plan, he testified unequivocally: "President Lincoln informed me that the merit of this plan was due to Miss Carroll." His steadfastness was backed by the testimony of Assistant Secretary of War Thomas Scott, and her case was championed by feminists like Sarah Ellen Blackwell, the woman's suffrage leader, but all this achieved little: Miss Carroll's bill was never paid.

This is a good place to assess the real Anna Ella Carroll's place in American history. I have idealized and softened her in the novel because she is, after all, my heroine, and has served me faithfully in reporting on, provoking and reacting to other real people whose characters are more factually portrayed.

She was born in 1815 to a wealthy, genteel Maryland plantation family. Her father served in the legislature and became governor when she was fourteen; the teenage girl was attracted to politics. She wrote for the press under a nom de plume, especially in political support of Thomas Hicks, a friend of her father, who later said he owed his own election as governor to Miss Carroll. She became a pamphleteer and propagandist, a force in the Native American (Know-Nothing) Party, and a friend or acquaintance of many of the powerful in nearby Washington, D.C., including Robert and John Breckinridge, Weed, Chase, Browning, and Jefferson Davis.

Her case as a "military genius" was taken up by Miss Blackwell and other feminists decades after the war, and was helped along by those who wanted to derogate Grant. But two problems got in the way of heroine-hood: she had put in writing words that we would now call bigoted, espousing the Know-Nothing line against immigrants; although she had manumitted her own slaves, she was on the record as an opponent of the Emancipation Proclamation, which became an ikon of freedom after Lincoln's assassination. She would have a tough time getting right with history.

But, in a way and for a time, Anna Ella Carroll did. Marjorie and Sidney Greenbie rediscovered her after World War II, and became her posthumous advocates. They touted her as the "great, unrecognized member of Lincoln's Cabinet," which was silly, but they also did some excellent historical legwork in finding and making available her papers. Their books, cited often herein, were a basis for a novel, Hollister Noble's 1948 *Woman With a Sword.* (The Greenbies sued the novel's publisher, Doubleday, for infringement of copyright and plagiarism, and lost.) This publicity attracted debunkers, and several historians gleefully debunked the role claimed for her in the Civil War.

How significant was she? Historian E. B. Long, known as Bruce Catton's "fact man" and the author, with Barbara Long, of *The Civil War Day by Day,* was the expert witness for Doubleday in the Greenbie lawsuit, and in July 1975 wrote a piece for *Civil War Times Illustrated* entitled "Anna Ella Carroll: Exaggerated Heroine?" He concluded she "was not a 'hidden' figure of history, maliciously hidden, that is, by chauvinist historians. She was and will remain a minor figure with a fascination all her own, but with slim importance."

I corresponded with Professor Long in 1979 about Miss Carroll (this novel was not produced overnight) and in a helpful letter he added: "Yes, I suppose I am the leading authority on the lady . . . Miss Carroll was very capable, intelligent, and able, though warped. She would probably be a lawyer or lobbyist were she alive today. However, her claims to have had something to do with the Tennessee-Cumberland River Campaign of the Civil War are, in my view, pretty much hogwash. . . . She was a good propagandist, was violently prejudiced (see her Know-Nothing writings), and for the day a capable writer." He dismissed the Greenbies' view with, "Rest assured that there has been no 'conspiracy' to downgrade Miss Carroll."

Having worked around a White House, I would not dismiss her claim of having called the Tennessee plan to Lincoln's attention as hogwash: although many people may have the same idea, the one who puts it in front of the President deserves some credit when it is adopted. And she was in fairly frequent contact with Lincoln, Bates, and Stanton: the Lincoln note to her is accepted as authentic in *CW,* the scene with Lincoln about the money almost certainly took place, and Browning mentions her in his diary. Reading her voluminous correspondence and draft pamphlets, one is struck by a daring, opinionated, short-tempered, vulnerable, and gutsy woman. No other woman, to my knowledge, in the nation's capital in that time thought as profoundly as Anna Carroll about public affairs, or took the active part in fixing, influencing, and manipulating issues and men. (Rose Greenhow and Kate Chase matched her in the manipulation department, but had no political philosophy of their own and did not write.)

Considering the way doors were closed to women in the political world at that time, and the financial obstacles she had to overcome, Anna Carroll's career—with all its disappointments—was remarkable. She showed what a combination of pluck and brains and drive and necessity can do for a person in any time.

Roy P. Basler, editor of the *Collected Works* cited so often herein, wrote in the 1979 *The Public and Private Lincoln: Contemporary Perspectives,* pp. 45–49: "No other American woman or man of the nineteenth century was more politically oriented or better trained in the law than Anna Ella Carroll." He explained her attraction to the Native American, or Know-Nothing, Party in this way: ". . . she became strenuously anti-Catholic, possibly because of the increasingly tight control of Democratic politics in Maryland by the influential Catholic slavocracy in collaboration with the Irish Catholic immigrants who were undercutting the native American laborers and craftsmen in Baltimore." Basler considers Lincoln's rebuff of her monetary claim "understandable, but scarcely justifiable . . . Miss Carroll had a right to be indignant . . ." and adds: "Professional historians have been even more ungenerous than Lincoln, for they have almost totally ignored her just claim [of recommending the Tennessee plan], and left the writing of her biography to amateurs and novelists who perhaps go too far in seeking to redress her wrongful treatment . . . Her full story needs yet to be told without either laudatory synthetics or the deprecatory male bias which . . . seem to lean over backward to disallow her achievements."

BOOK NINE, CHAPTER 34: SENATE COUP (p. 881)

This chapter is largely factual. In *The Diary of George Templeton Strong,* for December 18, 1862, the New York lawyer and treasurer of the Sanitary Commission wrote: "The general indignation is fast growing revolutionary . . . If things go on, we will have pressure for [Lincoln] to resign and make way for Hamlin . . ." A week later, he reflected the general uncertainty about emancipation: "Will Uncle Abe Lincoln stand firm and issue his promised proclamation on the first of January, 1863? Nobody knows . . ."

The secret caucus of Senate Republicans was recorded in detail by William Pitt Fessenden and his detailed summary appears in the biography by his son Francis, I, pp. 231–40. Browning's diary of December 16 and 17 describes the caucus, which took place over the two days. Browning's notes generally agree with Fessenden's, but he also describes "partisans of Chase" as "denouncing the President and expressing a willingness to vote for a resolution asking him to resign."

The political interpretation placed in Wade's mind in this chapter is my own, based on what I believe Wade to have been thinking, based in turn on the analysis of voting records and descriptions of the players (Turnbull's habit of tearing paper, the ruffled shirt of Browning) in Allan G. Bogue's 1981 *The Earnest Men: Republicans of the Civil War Senate.*

The scene with Browning and Lincoln is from Browning's diary entry of December 18, an entry that contains more direct quotation of Lincoln than most.

BOOK NINE, CHAPTER 35: YOUR CONSTITUTIONAL ADVISERS (p. 889)

The visit to Lincoln of Senator Preston King and Assistant Secretary Frederick Seward is described in Welles's diary for Friday December 19, and also in Attorney General Bates's surprisingly vivid diary entry for that day. They both relate what Lincoln told the Cabinet that day about the events of the night before. An exciting amalgam in narrative form of the two diaries, plus the Browning diary and the Fessenden memoir, is in Burton Hendricks's *Lincoln's War Cabinet,* pp. 331–48. (Chase stopped keeping a diary in October 1862 and did not begin again until August the next year. Hay's real diary also lapsed from November until April. Irascible Count Gurowski was fulminating during this period but was not on the inside. "Senators waking up to their duties," he wrote on December 18, "and to the consciousness of their power. These patriots have said to Seward, *Averte Sathanas*, [Behind me, Satan] and overboard he goes, after having done as much evil as only *he* could do.")

The scene with Francis Blair is fictional, but the dialogue is based on Blair's letter to Lincoln of December 18, in the Lincoln papers at the Library of Congress. It begins: "I propose to commune with no one but yourself on the subject on which I spoke yesterday," which suggests Blair was advising the President on the day the Senate coup took shape; the letter also warns of the potential formation of an anti-abolition party of Democrats and disaffected Republicans. Browning's diary also has Blair recommending King to replace Stanton, while Browning wanted Senator Collamer to replace Seward. Everybody was enjoying the reshaping of Lincoln's Cabinet.

The scene with Marshal Lamon is based on Lamon's *Recollections*, pp. 181–84, about Lincoln's reaction to the cabal out to "displace Mr. Lincoln . . . by the appointment of a dictator." This includes "I will show them at the other end of the Avenue whether I am President or not!" as well as other Lincoln quotes, including the reaction to Lamon's comparison with Cardinal Richelieu. On p. 185 is the interchange between Wade ("Yes, it is with you, sir, story, story!") and Lincoln ("the distance from here to the Capitol").

The final scene in the *Tribune* office is based on Wilkeson's letter to Sydney Gay, dated Friday night, December 19, in the Gay papers. It is cited by Nevins in a footnote, p. 355. I have used Smalley here for continuity's sake, but the *Tribune* reporter complaining bitterly to Adams Hill, and suggesting insider trading by Weed, was Wilkeson.

BOOK NINE, CHAPTER 36: ARRAIGNMENT (p. 899)

With the exception of the conversation between the Blairs, this chapter is well documented. The sources here are much the same as those cited in the previous chapters about the Republican senators' attempt to gain control of the Lincoln administration.

Bates's diary (p. 270) suggests the Cabinet was not surprised to see the senators that night; Welles's diary, with the best account of the proceedings (pp. 195–203), says: "The President requested that we should, with him, meet the committee. This did not receive the approval of Mr. Chase . . . I thought it a duty for us to attend." Nicohay, in an otherwise excellent report of the series of meetings in VI, pp. 264–72, which includes the "pumpkins" metaphor, inaccurately state that "each party was greatly surprised to find the other there." Only the senators were surprised; apparently Chase did not think to alert Fessenden to Lincoln's maneuver or to warn Wade of the full-dress confrontation ahead.

Collamer's blunt "He lied" is from Browning's diary for December 22. Fessenden's embittered assessment of "some selfish cowards" is from a letter to his family cited in Hendrick's *Lincoln's War Cabinet*, p. 342. The scene of Lincoln snatching Chase's resignation out of reluctant hands is from Welles's diary, p. 202.

Bates summed up: "The attack of the extreme senators (for such it was) failed—the thing *dribbled out*." Nicohay say: "By placing Mr. Chase in such an attitude that his resignation became necessary to his own sense of dignity, he [Lincoln] made himself absolute master of the situation . . ."

BOOK NINE, CHAPTER 37: CHIROPODIST, PEACEMAKER, SPY (p. 910)

Zacharie went to New Orleans under the cover of chiropody to help Banks with currency negotiations and to establish some links within the rebel government as described in this chapter.

The letter from Lincoln to Banks showing his knowledge of Grant's anti-Jewish move is in *CW Supplement* dated December 2, 1862; Grant's earlier restriction of Jews on railroads headed South is cited in Bertram Korn's *American Jewry and the Civil War,* p. 143. Lincoln's sabbath order is in *CW* for November 15, 1862; Jewish reaction to it is described in *Lincoln and the Jews,* an article by Isaac Markens in Vol. 17, p. 112, of the 1909 Publications of the American Jewish Historical Society.

The quotations from Banks to Zacharie are in a letter from Banks dated January 1, 1863, in the Banks papers. A letter from Zacharie to Banks dated October 9, 1863, from Washington shows that the doctor was able to meet with Confederate Secretary of State Judah Benjamin in Richmond, and on his return to the White House "on my first arrival Mr. Lincoln detained me four hours, locking his doors . . . he seemed to be delighted with my revelations . . . The subject has been brought before the Cabinet and bitterly opposed by Mr. Chase." Zacharie was used as an early prober for peace offers, but his efforts were unsuccessful.

The scene with Martin Gordon is fictional, based on the Zacharie letters and the account of Zacharie's life in the Korn book, with my political discussion added. The scene with the other Jews calling on him to do something about Grant's expulsion order is fictional; it is not known what Zacharie did or felt during that difficult moment for Jewish Americans.

BOOK NINE, CHAPTER 38: OFFER TO SUCCEED (p. 918)

I think the events in this chapter took place; not many historians agree, or give weight to the evidence about them. But if Lincoln, through Weed, made a serious offer to the leader of the Democratic opposition to support him for the presidency in return for support of the war, that offers an insight into (1) Lincoln's desperation and (2) his willingness to sacrifice everything to the cause of union. If true, the unprecedented succession offer was a major political calculation and would have been part of a reexamination of emancipation after Fredericksburg.

But Nicohay mention the approach to Seymour only to minimize its significance and cast aspersions on its source. Carl Sandburg, B. P. Thomas, and Stephen Oates ignore the offer, and Nevins gives it a couple of noncommittal sentences on p. 394; only Gore Vidal, in his 1985 novel *Lincoln,* p. 401, devotes a full page to the subject.

The first primary source is Thurlow Weed, from Vol. II, p. 428, of his 1884 memoirs edited by his grandson, Thurlow Weed Barnes: "One evening in December 1862, Mr. Weed was sitting with the President, when Mr. Lincoln said, 'Governor Seymour has greater power just now for good than any other man in the country. He can wheel the Democratic Party into line, put down rebellion, and preserve the government. Tell him for me, that if he will render this service to his country, I shall cheerfully make way for him as my successor.' Mr. Weed delivered this message to the governor, and urged him to accept the suggestion. Their conversation occurred, of course, before the governor was inaugurated. When the [New York State] legislature met, in January 1863, the governor sent in a partisan message, dealing largely with the 'rights of states.' And thus Horatio Seymour, not rising to the level of the 'War Democrats,' though subsequently a candidate, never became President." Weed's son adds, without corroborative detail, that six months later "Mr. Lincoln made almost identical over-tures to General McClellan, Mr. Weed again acting as mediator."

Is Weed to be believed? Lincoln's secretaries, in Vol. VII, pp. 10–13, of their his-tory, print a March 1863 exchange of letters between Lincoln and Seymour showing the President "desirous on public grounds to secure the cordial cooperation in war matters of the state administration in New York" and the governor responding "with the narrowness of a bitterly prejudiced mind . . ." Nicohay adds: "In an article [New York Times, August 18, 1879] published with his sanction many years afterwards, he [Weed] is represented as expressing his conviction that at the time of this correspon-dence there was a conspiracy of prominent Republicans to force Lincoln out of the White House; that the President was aware of it, and that this was 'the cause of the anxiety which he displayed to be on intimate friendly terms with Mr. Seymour.' " An examination of that edition, which featured a long obituary of Seymour, shows that conspiracy described not by Weed but by Simon Cameron; the former Secretary of War, returned from his Moscow assignment and presumed to be hostile to Lincoln, was invited to what he said was a meeting of prominent men whose "object was to find means by which the President could be impeached and turned out of office." Cameron said "it would be little short of madness to interfere with the Administration."

Thus, it can be assumed that, contrary to Nicohay, Governor Seymour's mind was not warped with "partisan bitterness and suspicion"; we now know that there was pressure to reduce Lincoln's power or even replace him with a dictator. Nicohay then derogates Weed's account as the maunderings of an old man: "Thurlow Weed is quoted as saying in his later years that Mr. Lincoln, after Seymour's election and before his inauguration, authorized Mr. Weed to say to him . . . Mr. Lincoln would cheerfully make way for him as his successor . . . It is probable that Mr. Weed, as is customary with elderly men, exaggerated the definiteness of the proposition . . ." Note that Nicohay does not deny the offer but only says its definiteness is probably exaggerated.

"In his later years" and "as is customary with elderly men" does not wash. Weed recounted the episode contemporaneously: the New York Standard and Statesman denounced him on April 12, 1864, for spreading a story that made Weed seem impor-tant enough to send Seymour to the White House. According to Stewart Mitchell's 1938 biography of Seymour, p. 274, this story appeared in the Albany Evening Journal about that time over the initials "T.W.": "Soon after the election of 1862, Mr. Lincoln remarked to me that, as the governor of the Empire State and the representative man of the Democratic Party, Governor Seymour had the power to render great public service, and that if he exerted that power against the rebellion and for his country, he would be our next President. I think Mr. Lincoln authorized me to say so, for him, to Governor Seymour. At any rate, I did repeat the conversation to him." That was Weed being very careful with the story during Lincoln's lifetime.

Then came corroboration in detail from Ward Hill Lamon when his Recollections of Lincoln was published in 1911. "His [Lincoln's] love of country was his paramount incentive," wrote the devoted aide (or his daughter, from his notes) on p. 215. "One instance in which this sentiment led him to propose an extraordinary act of self-immolation is deserving of special mention." Although reelection as Chief Magistrate of a reunited country "was the darling aspiration of his heart . . . he subjected this ambition to the promptings of a Roman patriotism, and proposed upon certain condi-tions a frank, full, and honest renunciation of all claims to the presidency for a second term; and in declining, under any circumstances, to be a candidate for reelection, he would cordially throw his entire influence, in so far as he could control it, in behalf of Horatio Seymour, then governor of New York, for President."

Lamon laid out the conditions for the deal: "Governor Seymour was to withdraw his opposition to the draft, use his authority and influence as governor in putting down the riots in New York, and cooperate with the Administration in the suppression of the Southern rebellion. This proposition was to be made through Mr. Thurlow Weed." He then describes how the Albany editor was summoned, and writes: "After a lengthy interview with the President and Mr. Seward, Mr. Weed telegraphed to Governor Seymour requesting him to come to Washington on business of urgent importance. This the governor declined to do, adding, in his reply, that the distance to and from Washington and Albany was precisely the same, and if they wanted to confer with him, to come to Albany, where he would be glad to meet them."

That detail, not mentioned by anyone before, adds a ring of authenticity. Lamon concludes: "Mr. Weed, upon this, left for that city, and after making a very brief stay there, returned to Washington and reported 'Proposition declined.' The answer was not expected by Mr. Lincoln, especially in time of civil war, and from the governor of the great and influential state of New York; and it was with sincere and manifest chagrin that the President saw himself deterred from making the magnanimous self-sacrifice proposed."

(Corollary evidence can be found: Stanton wrote to Seymour on May 23, 1864: "Would it be possible for you to come to Washington immediately to enable me to confer with you personally on some matters of great personal interest? Please answer." Seymour, said by one *New York Morning Herald* writer to be Stanton's choice for President, did not reply. The two uses of "personal" suggest that Stanton wanted to talk of matters more political than official.)

I think Weed's contemporaneous and later accounts are persuasive, especially in the light of his use by Lincoln in a secret fund-raising effort recounted herein; Weed was politically trusted. When overlaid by Lamon's recollection, long after the Nicohay attempt to pooh-pooh the offer appeared, the evidence becomes convincing. Many of Lamon's anecdotes and accounts of conversations have been used uncritically by historians, especially psychohistorians; yet this political revelation is ignored.

Seymour, as keynoter of the 1864 Democratic convention, said of emancipation: "[Lincoln] thinks a proclamation worth more than peace. We think the blood of our people more precious than edicts of the President." My guess is that if he had responded to Lincoln's offer in December with a proposal that the Proclamation be delayed along the lines described in the President's annual message, Lincoln would have gone along. Lincoln's priority was always union. When abolition hindered union, he resisted the Northern radicals, and would have double-crossed them by supporting Seymour; but if he decided abolition was needed to destroy the rebellion, his genuine anti-slavery feeling made him even more prepared to "lay a strong hand on the colored element."

Lincoln, to shore up support in his party and to threaten the South, moved suddenly left toward the radicals in the fall of 1862; when that led to election defeat and a mini-rebellion of radicals, and combined with military defeat to endanger union, he offered to move sharply rightward toward Peace Democrats in December. When that was rebuffed, he swung left again.

Sources for other items in this chapter: Van Duesen's biography of Seward cites "reinvigoration," p. 348; Nevins, p. 336, on the Barlow approach and the suggestion that military law might relent on emancipation; Hudson C. Tanner's 1888 *The Lobby from Thurlow Weed's Time,* p. 405, on Weed's inability to make a speech in public; and Sandburg, p. 632, citing Stoddard quoting Lincoln on the need for a general who can "face the arithmetic" of mutual losses.

The Lincoln biographer who treated the Seymour-Lincoln relationship with the significance it deserves is James G. Randall, in his 1953 *Midstream: Lincoln the President,* pp. 292–314. "To contemplate such an 'extraordinary political movement' was not unlike Lincoln," Randall writes, suggesting that declining war fortunes may have made a nonpartisan President desirable. ". . . Lincoln felt that he and Seymour had much in agreement in that they had the same stake in keeping the government going."

BOOK NINE, CHAPTER 39: THE PREACHER BRECKINRIDGE (p. 926)

This scene is fiction. The Reverend Robert J. Breckinridge was indeed Anna Ella Carroll's spiritual adviser in her youth, and was a formative influence; I assume he introduced her to his nephew when John came to Washington. Robert, one of the founders of the colonization movement, was also "the loyal Breckinridge" along with that branch of the split family, ultimately becoming one of the nominators of Lincoln in the 1864 "Union Party" convention. But Miss Carroll did not meet with him during the war; the purpose of this chapter is to record my own assessments of John Breckinridge's political motives and Anna Carroll's personal views of her single life. Her concern for the captured Cabell Breckinridge is fiction (though his capture is fact) and all quoted conversation is imaginary.

The background on the families is factual, although the reason given for Charles Carroll's inclusion of his address on the Declaration of Independence may be apocryphal: he may have added "of Carrollton" to avoid confusion with a relative, Charles Carroll of Annapolis.

The move by Seward to reassure Central American nations that blacks would not be shipped to their shores without permission is in *Diplomatic Correspondence: Papers Relating to Foreign Affairs,* Part II, 1862, pp. 900–10, GPO. The Illinois law to prevent free negroes from coming into the state is cited in Nevins, p. 371. The newspaper quotations regarding Grant's General Orders No. 11, and the information about the drop in cotton prices and the Kaskel brothers' visit to Washington is from Korn's *American Jewry and the Civil War.*

BOOK NINE, CHAPTER 40
JOHN HAY'S DIARY, DECEMBER 28, 1862 (p. 935)

The Bates visit with Dr. McPheters, and Lincoln's disposition of the case, is in a letter to General Curtis dated January 2, 1863, in the *CW,* referring to visit on December 29 and concluding "let the churches as such, take care of themselves."

Attorney General Bates's opposition to the bill creating West Virginia, and the Cabinet split about it, is in his diary entries for December 20 and December 30. A central issue was secession: how could Lincoln condone the secession of part of a state from that state, if he denied the right of states to secede from the Union? His answer, in the *CW* for December 31: "The division of a state is dreaded as a precedent. But a measure made expedient by a war is no precedent for times of peace . . . there is still difference enough between secession against the Constitution, and secession in favor of the Constitution." That was a weak answer, but he wanted to punish Virginia at that point and to set an example for his preferred emancipation.

John George Nicolay, who wrote the Civil War section of *The Cambridge Modern*

History, Vol. VII, just before his death in 1901, illustrates the significance to emancipation of the state's admission on pp. 594–95 of that work. On the tenth of December, the House passed the bill requiring gradual emancipation as the price of admission to the Union, along the lines of the President's annual message; the last week of the year, it was debated in the evenly divided Cabinet and Lincoln signed it on the thirty-first. (West Virginia went along with the requirement, was admitted in June of the next year, and the gradual emancipation was superseded by the Thirteenth Amendment.)

"If I refused to issue that Proclamation" is a remark of Lincoln's quoted in Browning's diary of December 30. He had evidently decided by then to issue the Proclamation; I presume it was after the rebuff by Seymour.

The suggestion that Lincoln threw New York mayor George Opdyke out of the office is based on Hay's real diary of October 30, 1863, quoting Lincoln's recollection of the Senate assault on Seward, which, if he had tolerated it, "the thing would have slumped over one way"; Lincoln added: "When I had settled this important business at last with much labor & to entire satisfaction, into my room one day walked D. D. Field and George Opdyke and began a new attack upon me to force me to remove Seward. For once in my life I rather gave my temper the rein and I talked to those men pretty damned plainly." It is my supposition that this uncharacteristic losing of his temper took place after his desperate overture to Seymour through Weed was declined. Lincoln would have had little patience then for New York Peace Democrats. (Finding Weed's message in the waste bucket is fictional; according to Lamon, Weed returned from Albany with that message in person.)

The visit of Cesar Kaskel protesting Grant's "Jew Order" is from *The Israelite,* IX, No. 28, p. 218, January 16, 1863, and from pp. 117–19 of the Markens article and pp. 121–44 of the Korn book already cited. Congressman Washburne's defense of Grant on the House floor is in the *Congressional Globe,* 37th Congress, 3rd Session, pp. 184 and 222. The quotation from the *New York Times* is from the edition of January 18, 1863.

How could Grant have issued such an order? Running for President in 1868, he explained in a letter to Representative I. N. Morris of Illinois that "It would never have been issued if it had not been telegraphed the moment it was penned, and without reflection." Bertram Korn, who makes a close study of the episode in *American Jewry in the Civil War,* refutes this by quoting from two previous Grant orders and a complaint Grant wrote to the War Department: "The Jews seem to be a privileged class that can travel everywhere." He proposed to buy up cotton and ship it North; "then all traders (they are a curse to the Army) might be expelled." Korn writes: "One is entitled to conclude that Grant himself was the author of General Orders No. 11 and that it would never have been withdrawn if Cesar Kaskel had not organized the pressure campaign against it."

Although Korn absolves Lincoln of all blame, commending him for promptly revoking the order when it was brought to his attention, we now know from the Zacharie pass that he was aware of the "general prohibition" in effect. He struck it down when it was put in writing, expelled non-traders, and became a political issue in Congress—and when Kaskel came and confronted him with it.

Lincoln's explanation of the origin of the Grant drinking joke, a McClure story wrongly attributed to him, is from Homer Bates's *Lincoln in the Telegraph Office,* p. 197.

BOOK NINE, CHAPTER 41: STONES RIVER (p. 940)

"Both the opposing commanders determined to take the offensive on the morning of the same day," writes Stanly Horn in his 1941 *The Army of Tennessee,* "and both planned to pursue identical tactics—an assault in force by the left wing against the enemy right." Bragg was wise to get up earlier; it was his best move of the battle.

Horn's book, p. 199, recounts the serenading on the eve of the fighting, which I have presumed would not meet the approval of a martinet like Bragg. The mind reading of Bragg throughout this chapter is fictional but in character for a resentful man who later complained about his commanders in great detail. The "dogs of detraction" phrase, directed at the Richmond press, is from a Bragg letter quoted on p. 325 of McWhiney's biography.

This account of the battle is drawn from those books, from Foote's narrative, II, pp. 86–93 ("Give them what General Cheatham says, boys!"), and from pp. 318–21 of Hattaway and Jones's *How the North Won.* Breckinridge's quote about deeming it "reckless to continue" is from McWhiney, p. 361.

The battle known as Stones River in the North is the Battle of Murfreesboro in the South, following the pattern of Northern focus on landmarks or natural features and Southern familiarity with place names (Shiloh vs. Pittsburg Landing, Antietam vs. Sharpsburg). Casualties during the two days of fighting at Stones River–Murfreesboro were as high as at Shiloh or Antietam, twenty-four thousand in all, divided almost evenly between North and South, and a third of those in combat. It was not until 1980 that this huge engagement was recorded in a book of its own, *Stones River: Bloody Winter in Tennessee,* by James Lee McDonough.

The first day of the battle was December 31, 1862; the second day saw no action, as Bragg waited for Rosecrans to withdraw, which he did not, partly because the Union commander mistakenly thought he was surrounded; and the final day was January 2, 1863, on which Rosecrans (like Grant at Shiloh) made his comeback. I will bring the second day ahead to January 1 so as to conclude the novel's action on Emancipation Day, but the only reliable news that Lincoln would have had about the battle that day was not good.

BOOK NINE, CHAPTER 42: TAIL OF THE ARMY (p. 943)

Sergeant James Stradling recounted his visit to the President in a letter to his peacetime boss, John Gilbert, dated March 6, 1863. "I give his exact words, as near as I can remember them," he concluded. "To have the President of the United States talk to me, and to be allowed to talk to him, was such an event in my life that I may be pardoned, I think, if I did feel 'a little set up,' as it were."

The Stradling letter was published in 1922, six years after he died, as *His Talk with Lincoln,* by Houghton Mifflin's Riverside Press with a preface by Lord Charnwood, the Lincoln biographer, and an introduction by Leigh Mitchell Hodges. Its information is cited in Sandburg, II, p. 84. Hodges rightly says: "As a historical portrait it speaks for itself, marking its author for one day, at least, a great reporter."

Stradling reported that Senator Wade was present along with two other men he did not know. I have moved the date of the meeting back from early March 1863 to December 31, 1862, to fit in the time span of my novel, but since both dates fall between the defeats of Fredericksburg and Chancellorsville, the gloomy mood is suitable. This means that I have changed the tense of references to the Emancipation Proclamation, but the central point—that Lincoln considered emancipation's "justice" ahead of being "a club with which we could whack the rebels"—remains valid and revealing. Lincoln in other conversations later came to see it that way, but this was early evidence that his moral reasoning was in the fore so close to the issuance of the edict.

The only significant addition I have made to Stradling's account is the question and answer about arming the freed slaves, which would have been on Lincoln's mind on December 31. At the urging of Chase and Stanton, he put that surprise in his final Proclamation; at that point, he did not care how he infuriated the rebels, and would have been concerned only about the Proclamation's reception by Union soldiers.

BOOK NINE, CHAPTER 43: HELL'S HALF ACRE (p. 949)

After a day of rest on New Year's Day (skipped over in the novel) the Battle of Stones River resumed on January 2. The South had failed to complete its victory on the first day because Breckinridge's reserve brigades were fed into the battle piecemeal; on the second day, when ordered to assault Hell's Half Acre in the face of fifty-eight pieces of artillery massed on a bluff west of the river, Breckinridge protested vigorously. His objections, quoted here, are from the Davis biography, pp. 341–42. In *Pat Cleburne, Confederate General*, a 1973 biography by Howell and Elizabeth Purdue, Cleburne's report of his own warning is on p. 177: "I feared, if my single, and now reduced, line was pushed on the enemy in his fortified position, the result would prove very disastrous . . ."

It was. Both Breckinridge and Cleburne, who participated in the charge, survived; General Pillow hid behind a tree and survived also; eighteen hundred Confederate soldiers were killed or wounded, mainly by artillery fire. The attack failed and that night Bragg decided to withdraw. As at Antietam, although neither side "won," the South withdrew from the field, and the result could be interpreted as a defeat. Bragg blamed his generals; Hardee conferred with Cleburne and Breckinridge and wrote Bragg that all three agreed a change in command of the army was necessary, but President Davis decided to keep Bragg in command.

Why didn't Bragg follow up his first day's victory with the immediate pressure that would have driven Rosecrans from the field? "He believed in attacking first," writes Joseph B. Mitchell in the 1955 *Decisive Battles of the Civil War*, "but if he was not immediately successful he became dispirited and lost his temper, blaming his subordinates for things that went wrong . . . he was an intelligent, skillful planner but, in the execution of his plans, was his own worst enemy."

The mind reading of Cleburne is fictional; the analysis attributed to him of Breckinridge's ordeal is my own, partly drawn from the chapter "The Paradoxes of Freedom" in Don E. Fehrenbacher's 1987 *"Lincoln in Text and Context."* Cleburne found himself in a similar situation under General John Hood at the battle of Franklin, Tennessee, on November 30, 1864; he said, "If we are to die, let us die like men," and did.

The scene with Margaret Elizabeth Breckinridge is imaginary. She was a Union army nurse and died of illness during the war but is not known to have condemned her cousin John; his son Cabell was captured, imprisoned at Johnson's Island, and exchanged in 1863. Another son, Clifton, was with General Breckinridge in Murfreesboro.

Bragg's failure of nerve after the first victorious day, like that of Beauregard at Shiloh, was mirrored by the unexpected tenacity of the surprised opposing Union general: Rosecrans at Stones River, like Grant at Shiloh. Because "Old Rosey" refused to quit, the North was spared another devastating defeat. If only, after the crushing disaster at Fredericksburg, the Union forces in Tennessee had been defeated, the war spirit in the North might well have been broken. It is one of those "if onlies" that tortured Southerners for years.

Lincoln acknowledged that in a letter to Rosecrans on August 31, 1863: "I will never forget, whilst I remember anything, that about the end of last year and beginning of this, you gave us a hard-earned victory, which, had there been a defeat instead, the nation could scarcely have lived over."

BOOK NINE, CHAPTER 44: DAY OF JUBILEE (p. 956)

The description of William Johnson, the young manservant Lincoln brought with him from Springfield, is from John E. Washington's 1942 *They Knew Lincoln,* pp. 127–34. He is not to be confused with William Slade, the White House steward; Slade was of olive complexion, well spoken, a member of Washington's black free society; Johnson was coal black, uneducated, and ill treated by others of the White House staff. The conversation is fictional, but Lincoln's "I am a slow walker, but I never walk back" is cited in William H. Townsend's 1929 *Lincoln and His Wife's Home Town,* p. 344, from the June 16, 1864, *Lexington Observer and Reporter.*

Horatio Seymour was inaugurated Governor of New York on January 1, 1863; the quotations attributed to him are from his first message to the legislature on the seventh, pp. 92–93 of David Croly's 1868 campaign biography.

The scene with Burnside and Halleck is based on their recollections of the meeting with the President that morning cited in *CW* for that day, and on Burnside's testimony to the Joint Committee on February 7, quoted in Charles Segal's 1961 *Conversations with Lincoln,* pp. 233–34.

The mind reading of Lincoln, as he prepared to sign the Proclamation later that day, is speculative.

BOOK NINE, CHAPTER 45: RECEIVING LINE (p. 963)

On June 6, 1865, less than two months after his father's assassination, Robert Lincoln wrote to biographer J. G. Holland, explaining why he could not be of much assistance, but unwittingly revealing the sad truth of the father-son relationship: "During my childhood and early youth he was almost constantly away from home, attending courts or making political speeches. In 1859 when I was sixteen and when he was beginning to devote himself more to practice in his own neighborhood, and when I would have had both the inclination and the means of gratifying my desire to become better acquainted with the history of his struggles, I went to New Hampshire to school and afterward to Harvard College, and he became President. Henceforth any great intimacy between us became impossible. I scarcely even had ten minutes' quiet talk with him during his presidency, on account of his constant devotion to business." That unvarnished account of the distance between father and son can be found on p. 499 of Rufus Rockwell Wilson's 1945 *Intimate Memories of Lincoln.*

Mary Lincoln's visit to a spiritualist on New Year's Eve is cited in Browning's diary for January 1; the President's wife told him the medium "revealed that the Cabinet were all the enemies of the President, working for themselves, and that they would have to be dismissed . . ."

I found four accounts of the 1863 New Year's Day reception. Welles's diary for that day describes "a bright and brilliant day" but dismisses the levee as "the usual formalities." The *Evening Star* reported that day: "About a quarter to twelve the officers of the Army and Navy left the Presidential Mansion, and a few moments later the gates were thrown open, and the 'sovereigns' gained admittance. One grand rush was made . . . After paying their respects to the President, the visitors proceeded to the East Room and out again through one of the large windows, and across on to the sidewalk over a substantial platform. Coverings were spread over the elegant carpets as a protection from the mud . . ." The police protection was said to be mainly for the crowd's sake, "to protect the visitors from the operations of the light-fingered gentry."

The *Intelligencer* for January 3 reported "the members of the Diplomatic Corps, in full costume" greeted President and Mrs. Lincoln, followed by the Supreme Court justices and officers of the Army and Navy in full dress. "The ceremony of introduction was performed by Marshal Lamon. The President received his numerous visitors with great affability, giving each a cordial grasp of the hand, and occasionally dropping a few pleasant words to some of his more intimate friends." The short-lived *Washington Chronicle* of January 2 also observed Lincoln's "availing himself of every opportunity to drop a pleasant word" to his visitors; "this pleasant ceremony lasted more than two hours."

The mind reading of Lincoln in this chapter is fictional. It is fair to assume that many of the characters in this book came to the White House that day to shake his hand. Kate Chase would have accompanied her father (not Sprague, to whom she was not yet engaged), who did submit his own draft of an emancipation proclamation, of which Lincoln used only the felicitous closing reference to Divine Providence. In all likelihood, Miss Carroll would seize this opportunity to have a word with the President, as would Brady and Gardner.

Wendell Phillips's presence is fictional, but the conversation quoted took place three weeks later, quoted in Segal's *Conversations with Lincoln*, p. 238. That valuable compilation is also the source, on p. 236, of Henry Raymond's journal entry of the first week in January, describing his meeting with Mr. Lincoln in a "great crowd," probably the New Year's levee, when the President replied to his report about the backstabbing of Burnside with "[General Hooker] is stronger with the country today than any other man." In that journal entry, printed in full in *Scribner's Monthly*, No. 19 (1880), pp. 703–6, Raymond goes on to describe how Burnside threatened to "swing him [Hooker] before sundown" if that officer resisted his dismissal.

The talk with Anna Carroll is fictional. Between the time of his annual message in the beginning of December and the Emancipation Proclamation at the end of that month, Lincoln discarded his emphasis on colonization. It was stricken from his earlier drafts of the final Proclamation, I think, when he decided to recruit and arm slaves. (However, as Nicohay write in VI, p. 359, he signed a deal for $250,000 to colonize five thousand negroes on Île à Vache near Haiti on December 31, an experiment that soon soured.) The approach to Vicksburg by land from the rear was her frequently stated view. At that time and later, Miss Carroll was seeing Judge Lemuel Evans, the former Texas congressman, and the Greenbies believe that he was the main love of her life.

The account of the dialect story told by Colonel McKay, and Lincoln's sober-sided reaction about being "the instrument under Providence for the liberation of a race," was unearthed from the McKay papers in the Illinois State Historical Library by Jay Monaghan and printed in his *Diplomat in Carpet Slippers,* p. 273. The conversation took place during the first week of January 1863, and suggests clearly that Lincoln's assessment of his act of emancipation was that it was far more than a military necessity.

BOOK NINE, CHAPTER 46: HEART IN HIS BOOTS (p. 969)

The times of some of the events and quotes in this chapter have been changed for narrative purposes, so that the signing of the Emancipation Proclamation on New Year's Day can conclude the novel.

Lincoln went to the telegraph office in the evening of New Year's Day, according to Bates's *Lincoln in the Telegraph Office,* pp. 143–46, "with a number of others who had dropped in to learn if there was any news from Rosecrans, who was then engaged in what at that time seemed almost a death struggle with Bragg." The news would have been about the first day of the battle, on December 31, which went badly for the Union forces; the reports of the failure of Breckinridge's charge at Murfreesboro on January 2 could not have come in until the evening of that day or the morning of the third. John Forney is my reporter in this scene because he was present at both the big levee and the small signing ceremony, and because he was a friend of Breckinridge's. Observations and notes made by him and others at about that time are attributed to him for dramatic simplification.

"Not calculated to improve a man's chirography" is a Lincoln explanation of the shakiness of his signature made to Schuyler Colfax on the evening of January 1, according to Francis Carpenter's *Six Months at the White House,* p. 87. The painter also quotes on p. 269 from a speech made by Colonel John Forney in 1865, in which the newsman-politician recollects the signing event he attended; that is part of the basis of the next chapter.

Lincoln's "heart in my boots" quotation, as well as his careful intercession with Grant on the arrested newsman, and the admonition "none of this must get into print," is from a memoir of a meeting on January 4, 1863, by John M. Winchell, a *New York Times* reporter. Winchell was a Chase man (author of the subsequent "Pomeroy letter" criticizing Lincoln in hopes of getting the 1864 nomination for Chase) but, like many, got right with Lincoln soon after the assassination. His memoir was published in *The Galaxy* for July 1873 and reprinted in R. R. Wilson's *Intimate Memories of Lincoln,* pp. 508–13.

The message to Rosecrans from Lincoln is from a letter in *CW* dated August 31, 1863.

Lincoln's recollection of Breckinridge, "I was fond of John," was said in February 1865 to John Bullock, a fifteen-year-old nephew of Breckinridge's, who came to the President to plead for the parole of his brother, a Confederate lieutenant. It is quoted in William H. Townsend's 1955 *Lincoln and the Bluegrass,* p. 347.

General Patrick Ronayne Cleburne's death in battle did not occur at Stones River, but at the head of an unnecessary charge ordered by General Hood at the battle of Franklin, Tennessee, on November 30, 1864.

BOOK NINE, CHAPTER 47: WITHOUT COMPUNCTIONS (p. 972)

Frederick Seward described the ceremony of signing on p. 227 of his *Reminiscences,* which conforms closely to Forney's recollection in Carpenter's book cited in the previous source note. Their quotation of Lincoln's concern that his signature not show "compunctions" is similar. No record was made of who was in the room besides

Lincoln, the two Sewards, and Forney. The internal Lincoln monologue is mine, though some phrases are drawn from his works.

The German historian Leopold von Ranke rejected the task usually assigned to history—that of judging the past, and of instructing the present for the benefit of the future. He labels as presumption that objective, professing to seek "only to show what actually happened *[wie es eigentlich gewesen]*."

That goal, of course, is a far greater presumption, demanding some way of filling the gaps between even the most provable facts. Von Ranke, writing in the nineteenth century of events before that time, looked at history from the top down, unconcerned with social currents and economic forces, but he had an insight that still stimulates and troubles historians: "Fact has a spiritual content . . . It is our job to recognize how it really took place . . . intuition is required."

The purpose of this long book has been to present the conception of a novelist up front and a pundit out back of "what actually happened."

As the reader of this underbook has seen, this historical novel relies on informed guesswork to come to conclusions that the known facts alone cannot fully sustain. When a few events are presented out of sequence (Weed's raising of fifteen thousand dollars for an unknown purpose, Greenhow's release) or romances imagined (Hay and Kate Chase, Anna Carroll and John Breckinridge), the author's conscience has been cleansed by full disclosure here in the back of the book, where the fully participating reader has a road map to see how far fact is departed from to get at truth.

The Lincoln presented here is not Herndon's sly Lincoln, or Sandburg's saintly Lincoln, or the modern consensus Lincoln. He is especially not a Lincoln endowed with twentieth-century hindsight. The accounts herein of his handling of the mutual endangerment of individual liberty and national security, his use of the means of damnably bloody war to achieve the blessed end of majority rule, and his discovery that the means of abolition was as central as the ends of union are my idea of the real Lincoln.

Reverence is a barrier to appreciation. Every scholar, buff, and active reader should have a different "real" Lincoln, arrived at by personal judgment of the man who proved that democracy was not an absurdity.

ACKNOWLEDGMENTS

At Doubleday, editor Stewart Richardson in 1979 first saw the potential in a Lincoln novel based on the theme of how much personal freedom must be sacrificed to maintain a free government; two years later, Kate Medina wrote a penetrating critique of the first draft that became my blueprint for turning a message-laden tract into a story with characters; and in recent years, Sally Arteseros and publisher Nancy Evans have helped boot this long-distance runner home. Alex Gotfryd creatively grasped the need for the graphic dimension in a work of fiction; cartographer Rafael Palacios provided the endpapers, and copy editors Chaucy Bennetts and Glenn Rounds saved a pop grammarian from innumerable embarrassments. (I have left in a few grammatical errors and one egregious misspelling as a test for readers.)

My lifelong friend, lawyer, and agent, Mort Janklow, who negotiated a contract with Sandy Richardson based on a single sentence describing the proposed work, never reminded me of slipped deadlines or panicked at the expanding scope; at that office, unsung Jerry Traum gets a song here, as do Joan Reckleff and Anne Sibbald. Ann Elise Rubin, my assistant at the *New York Times,* found spare time to be a source of help and ideas for research. Jeff McQuain was among those who helped me transcribe copy from paper to disk.

All photographs herein are courtesy of the Library of Congress and the National Archives, excepting John Cabell Breckinridge, p. xxii, Kentucky Historical Society Library; Anna Ella Carroll, p. 156, Louis A. Warren Library and Museum (where Mark Neely is always responsive to queries); Alexander Gardner, p. 566, E. Marshall Pywell; J. Cabell Breckinridge, p. 794, Catherine Breckinridge Prewitt, Prescott Collection; Isachar Zacharie, p. 913, American Jewish Historical Society; General Patrick Ronayne Cleburne, Museum of the Confederacy, p. 951. At the Photographic Division of the Library of Congress, Jerry Maddox was most helpful on research and guidance. Shirley Green helped me track down specific photos.

Librarian of Congress Daniel Boorstin was both inspiration and help; John Broderick and Oliver Orr were among the many at that valuable institution who made research easier. Professor Harold Hyman of Rice University disagreed with me usefully in my approach to Stanton and to Lincoln's record on civil liberty; Professor Gabor Boritt of Gettysburg College vetted the manuscript for factual errors, and argued with me to the end on judgments about Lincoln, some of which he does not share; the late Professor E. B. Long was generous with his experience on the subject of Anna Ella Carroll when I first approached him in 1978. Jennifer Lee at the John Hay Library at Brown University made available Mr. Hay's real diary for my perusal. The Abraham

Lincoln Bookstore in Chicago, first under Ralph Newman and now managed by Dan Weinberg, tracked down hard-to-find materials. Thanks also are due Mark Safire, who organized my computer's hard disk in a way that enabled me to summon characters from the vasty deep.

BIBLIOGRAPHY

A bibliography of Civil War material can go on forever. The books, pamphlets, and articles listed herein are cited in the Notes to this novel or directly bear on its conclusions.

Anderson, Dwight G. *Abraham Lincoln: The Quest for Immortality.* New York: Alfred A. Knopf, 1982.

Angle, Paul, and Earl Schenck Miers. *Tragic Years,* 2 vols. New York: Simon & Schuster, 1960.

Anonymous. *The Old Capitol and Its Inmates, By a Lady Who Enjoyed the Hospitalities of the Government for a "Season."* New York: E. J. Hale & Son, 1867.

Anonymous. *The Diary of a Public Man,* Prefatory notes by F. Lauriston Bullard. New Brunswick, N.J.: Rutgers University Press, 1946.

Baringer, William. *A House Dividing: Lincoln As President-Elect.* Springfield, Ill.: Abraham Lincoln Association, 1945.

Barnes, Thurlow Weed, ed. *The Life of Thurlow Weed,* Vol. I, Autobiography, Vol. II, Memoirs. Boston: Houghton Mifflin Company, 1883–4.

Basler, Roy P., ed. *The Collected Works of Abraham Lincoln.* The Abraham Lincoln Association, Springfield, Ill., New Brunswick, N.J.: Rutgers University Press, 1953.

———. *The Collected Works of Abraham Lincoln Supplement, 1832–1865.* Westport, Conn.: Greenwood Press, 1974.

Bates, David Homer. *Lincoln in the Telegraph Office.* New York: The Century Company, 1907.

Bates, Edward. *The Diary of Edward Bates 1859–1866,* Howard K. Beale, ed. Washington, D.C.: U.S. Government Printing Office, 1933. Published as Volume IV of the *Annual Report of the American Historical Association* for the year 1930.

Battles and Leaders. *See* Johnson, Robert Underwood.

Beldon, Thomas, and Marva Robins. *So Fell the Angels.* Boston: Little, Brown, 1956.

Belz, Herman. *Emancipation and Equal Rights: Politics and Constitutionalism in the Civil War Era.* New York: W. W. Norton, 1978.

Bestor, Arthur. "The American Civil War as a Constitutional Crisis," paper of May 3, 1963, to the Mississippi Valley Historical Association.

Beveridge, Albert J. *Abraham Lincoln, 1809–1858,* 4 vols. Boston: Houghton Mifflin Company, 1928.

Blackwell, Sarah Ellen. *Life and Writings of Anna Ella Carroll,* Vol. II. Washington, D.C.: Judd & Detweiler, 1893.

———. *A Military Genius: Life of Anna Ella Carroll of Maryland.* Washington, D.C.: Judd & Detweiler, 1891.

Blaine, James G. *Twenty Years of Congress.* Norwich, Conn.: Henry Hill Publishing, 1884.

Blair, Harry C., and Rebecca Tarshis. *Lincoln's Constant Ally: the Life of Col. Edward P. Baker.* Portland: Oregon Historical Society, 1960.

Bleiler, E. F. *Gardner's Photographic Sketch Book of the Civil War.* New York: Dover Publications, 1959 edition of 1866 book.

Bloch, Harry, M.D. "Issachur Zacharie (1827–1900) A Chiropodist of the 19th Century." *Journal of the American Podiatry Association,* May 1971.

Boatner, Mark. *Civil War Dictionary.* New York: David McKay, 1959.

Bogue, Allan G. *The Earnest Men: Republicans of the Civil War Senate.* Ithaca, N.Y.: Cornell University Press, 1981.

Boritt, Gabor S. "The Voyage to the Colony of Lincolnia: The Sixteenth President, Black Colonization, and the Defense Mechanism of Avoidance." *The Historian,* Vol. 27; 1975.

———. *Lincoln and the Economics of the American Dream.* Memphis, Tenn.: Memphis State University Press, 1978.

Bowers, Claude. *The Party Battles of the Jackson Period.* Boston: Houghton Mifflin Complete, 1922.

Boykin, Edward. *Congress and the Civil War.* New York: The McBride Co., 1955.

Brodie, Fawn. *Thaddeus Stevens, Scourge of the South.* New York: W. W. Norton, 1959.

Brooks, Noah. *Abraham Lincoln and the Downfall of American Slavery.* New York: G. P. Putnam's Sons, 1895.

———. *Washington, D.C., in Lincoln's Time.* New York: The Century Company, 1896.

Browning, Orville, diary. *See* Pease and Randall.

Buck, Irving A., and Thomas R. Hay. *Cleburne and His Command;* and, *Pat Cleburne: Stonewall Jackson of the West.* Jackson, Tenn.: McCowat-Mercer Press, 1959.

Butler, Gen. Benjamin F. *Butler's Book.* Boston: A. M. Thayer, 1892.

Canby, Courtlandt, ed. *Lincoln and the Civil War: A Profile and a History.* New York: George Braziller, 1960.

Carman, Harry J., and Reinhard H. Luthin. *Lincoln and the Patronage.* Gloucester, Mass.: Peter Smith, 1964.

Carpenter, Francis B. *Six Months at the White House.* New York: Hurd and Houghton, 1864.

Carroll, Howard. *Twelve Americans.* (includes life of Horatio Seymour, pp. 1–47). New York: Harper & Brothers, 1883.

Carroll, John M. *Custer in the Civil War.* San Raphael, Calif.: Presidio Press, 1977.

Catton, Bruce. *Mr. Lincoln's Army.* Garden City, N.Y.: Doubleday & Co., 1951.

———. *Grant Moves South.* Boston: Little, Brown, 1960.

Chambers, William Nisbet, and Walter Dean Burnham. *The American Party Systems: Stages of Political Development.* New York: Oxford University Press, 1967.

Chase, Salmon P. *See* Donald, David.

Chesnut, Mary Boykin, diaries. *See* Woodward, C. Vann.

Clymer, Kenton J. *John Hay: The Gentleman as Diplomat.* Ann Arbor: University of Michigan Press, 1975.

Coffin, Charles Carleton. *Drum-beat of the Nation.* New York: Harper & Brothers, 1888.

Connelly, Thomas Lawrence, and Archer Jones. *The Politics of Command: Factions and Ideas in Confederate Strategy.* Baton Rouge: Louisiana State University Press, 1973.

—— and Barbara L. Bellows. *God and General Longstreet.* Baton Rouge: Louisiana State University Press, 1982.

Cowen, Benjamin Rush. *Abraham Lincoln: An Appreciation, by One Who Knew Him.* Cincinnati: R. Clarke, 1909.

Cox, LaWanda. *Lincoln and Black Freedom: A Study in Presidential Leadership.* Columbia: University of South Carolina Press, 1981.

Croly, David G. *Seymour and Blair: Their Lives and Services.* New York: Richardson & Co., 1868.

Crozier, Emmet. *Yankee Reporters, 1861–65.* New York: Oxford University Press, 1956.

Cullen, Joseph P. *The Peninsula Campaign 1862.* New York: Crown Publishers, Bonanza Books, 1973.

Current, Richard Nelson. *The Lincoln Nobody Knows.* New York: McGraw-Hill, 1958.

——. *Speaking of Abraham Lincoln: The Man and His Meaning for Our Times.* Urbana: University of Illinois Press, 1983.

Curtis, George Ticknor. "McClellan's Last Service to the Republic." Parts I, II, III. New York: *North American Review;* D. Appleton & Company, 1880.

Dana, Charles A. *Recollections of the Civil War.* New York: D. Appleton & Company, 1898.

Davis, Cullom; Charles B. Strozier; Rebecca Monroe Veach; Geoffrey C. Ward, eds. *The Public and Private Lincoln: Contemporary Perspectives.* Carbondale: Southern Illinois University Press, 1979.

Davis, Jefferson. *The Rise and Fall of the Confederate Government,* 2 vols. New York: D. Appleton & Company, 1881.

Davis, William C. *Breckinridge: Statesman Soldier Symbol.* Baton Rouge: Louisiana State University Press, 1974.

——. *Duel Between the First Ironclads.* Garden City, N.Y.: Doubleday & Company, 1975.

——. *Battle at Bull Run.* Baton Rouge: Louisiana State University Press, 1977.

——. *The Orphan Brigade: The Kentucky Confederates Who Couldn't Go Home.* Garden City, N.Y.: Doubleday & Company, 1980.

——. *The Deep Waters of the Proud.* Vol. I of *The Imperiled Union.* Garden City, N.Y.: Doubleday & Company, 1982.

——. *Stand in the Day of Battle.* Vol. II of *The Imperiled Union.* Garden City, N.Y.: Doubleday & Company, 1983.

Dell, Christopher. *Lincoln and the War Democrats: The Grand Erosion of Conservative Tradition.* Rutherford, N.J.: Fairleigh Dickinson University Press, 1975.

Dennett, Tyler. *John Hay: From Poetry to Politics.* New York: Dodd, Mead, 1933.

——. *Lincoln and the Civil War in the Diaries and Letters of John Hay.* New York: Dodd, Mead, 1939.

Diggins, John P. *The Lost Soul of American Politics.* New York: Basic Books, 1984.

Dix, Morgan, ed. *The Memoirs of John Adams Dix.* New York: Harper & Brothers, 1883.

Donald, David, ed. *Inside Lincoln's Cabinet: The Civil War Diaries of Salmon P. Chase.* New York: Longmans, Green, 1954.

——, ed. *Divided We Fought: A Pictorial History of the War, 1861–1865*. New York: The Macmillan Company, 1956.

——. *Lincoln Reconsidered*. New York: Alfred A. Knopf, 1956.

——. *Charles Sumner and the Rights of Man*. New York: Alfred A. Knopf, 1970.

Donovan, Frank. *Mr. Lincoln's Proclamation*. New York: Dodd, Mead, 1964.

Douglas, Henry Kyd. *I Rode with Stonewall* (1899 memoir). Chapel Hill: University of North Carolina Press, 1940.

Draper, John William. *Thoughts on the Future Civil Policy of America*. New York: Harper & Brothers, 1865.

Dunning, William A. *Essays on the Civil War and Reconstruction*. Intro. by David Donald. New York: Harper Torchbooks, 1965.

Durden, Robert F. *The Grey and the Black: The Confederate Debate on Emancipation*. Baton Rouge: Louisiana State University Press, 1972.

Eaton, Clement. *Jefferson Davis*. New York: The Free Press, 1977.

Eckenrode, H. J., and Bryan Conrad. *George B. McClellan: The Man Who Saved the Union*. Chapel Hill: University of North Carolina Press, 1941.

Eisenschiml, Otto. *The Celebrated Case of Fitz-John Porter: An American Dreyfus Affair*. Indianapolis: Bobbs-Merrill, 1950.

Fahrney, Ralph. *Horace Greeley and the Tribune in the Civil War*. Cedar Rapids, Iowa: Torch Press, 1936; Da Capo Press reprint, 1970.

Farmer, John, and William Ernest Henley. *Slang and Its Analogues,* 7 volumes, 1890–1904. New York: E. P. Dutton & Co., 1905.

Fehrenbacher, Don E. *The Changing Image of Lincoln in American Historiography*. London: Oxford at the Clarendon Press, 1968.

——, ed. *The Leadership of Abraham Lincoln*. New York: John Wiley & Sons, 1970.

——. *Lincoln in Text and Context*. Stanford: Stanford University Press, 1987.

Fessenden, Francis. *Life and Public Services of William Pitt Fessenden*. Boston: Houghton Mifflin, 1907.

Fischer, LeRoy H. *Lincoln's Gadfly, Adam Gurowski*. Norman, Okla.: University of Oklahoma Press, 1964.

Foote, Shelby. *The Civil War: A Narrative,* 3 vols. New York: Random House, 1958, 1963, 1974.

Forgie, George B. *Patricide in the House Divided: A Psychological Interpretation of Lincoln and His Age*. New York: W. W. Norton, 1978.

Forney, John W. *Anecdotes of Public Men,* Vol. I. New York: Harper & Brothers, 1873.

Franklin, John Hope. *The Emancipation Proclamation*. Garden City, N.Y.: Doubleday & Company, 1963.

Franklin, Maj. Gen. W. B. *Annals of the War* (journal); "The First Great Crime of the War" (article). Philadelphia: Times Publishing Co., 1879.

Frassanito, William A. *Antietam: The Photographic Legacy of America's Bloodiest Day*. New York: Charles Scribner's Sons, 1978.

Freeman, Douglas Southall. *Lee's Lieutenants: A Study in Command,* 3 vols. New York: Charles Scribner's Sons, 1944–47.

——. *R. E. Lee,* 4 vols. New York: Charles Scribner's Sons, 1936–47.

Friedel, Frank. *Union Pamphlets of the Civil War,* Vol. I. Cambridge, Mass.: Belknap Press of Harvard University, 1967.

Fuller, J.F.C. *Grant and Lee*. London: Eyre & Spottiswoode, 1933.

Furniss, Harry. *My Bohemian Days*. London: Hurst & Blackett, 1919.

Gardner, Alexander. *Gardner's Photographic Sketchbook of the Civil War*. 1866; reprint, New York: Dover Publications, 1959.

Garrison, William Lloyd. *Discussion on American Slavery Between George Thompson Esq. and Rev. Robert Breckinridge Holden in the Rev. Dr. Wardlaw's Chapel, Glasgow, Scotland*. Boston: Isaac Knapp, 1836.

Gilmore, James (pen name: Edmund Kirke). *Personal Recollections of Abraham Lincoln and the Civil War*. Boston: L. C. Page & Co., 1898.

Gorham, George C. *Life and Public Service of Edwin M. Stanton*, 2 vols. Boston: Houghton Mifflin Company, 1899.

Grant, U. S. *Personal Memoirs*, 2 vols. New York: Charles Webster Co., 1885.

Gray, Wood. *The Hidden Civil War: The Story of the Copperheads*. New York: Viking Press, 1942.

Greenbie, Sydney, and Marjorie Latta (Barstow) Greenbie. *Anna Ella Carroll and Abraham Lincoln*. Manchester, Maine: Falmouth Publishing, 1952.

Greenhow, Rose. *My Imprisonment and the First Year of Abolition Rule at Washington*. London: Richard Bentley, 1863.

Greeley, Horace. *The American Conflict*, 2 vols. Hartford: O. D. Case and Company, 1864.

———. *Autobiography, or Recollections of a Busy Life*. New York: E. B. Treat, 1872.

Grimsley, Elizabeth Todd. "Six Months in the White House." *Journal of the Illinois Historical Society*, Vol. XIX, April 1926.

Gurowski, Adam. *Diary from March 4, 1861, to November 12, 1862*. Boston: Lee and Shepard, 1862.

———. *Diary from November 18, 1862, to October 18, 1863*. New York: Carleton & Co., 1864.

Hamilton, James J. *The Battle of Fort Donelson*. Cranbury, N.J.: Thomas Yoseloff, 1968.

Hamlin, Charles. *Life and Times of Hannibal Hamlin*. Cambridge, Mass.: Riverside Press, 1899.

Hammond, Bray. *Sovereignty and an Empty Purse*. Princeton: Princeton University Press, 1970.

Hansen, Harry. *The Civil War*. New York: New American Library, 1961.

Harper, Robert. *Lincoln and the Press*. New York: McGraw-Hill, 1951.

Harrington, Fred H. *Fighting Politician: Major General N. P. Banks*. Philadelphia: University of Pennsylvania Press, 1948.

Hart, B. H. Liddell. *Sherman: Soldier, Realist, American*. New York: Frederick A. Praeger, 1958 edition of 1929 book.

Hassler, Warren W., Jr. *General George B. McClellan, Shield of the Union*. Baton Rouge: Louisiana State University Press, 1957.

Hassler, William Woods. *A. P. Hill: Lee's Forgotten General*. Chapel Hill: University of North Carolina Press, 1962.

Hattaway, Herman, and Archer Jones. *How the North Won: A Military History of the Civil War*. Urbana: University of Illinois Press, 1983.

Hay, John, diaries. *See* Dennett, Tyler.

———. *Pike County Ballads*. Boston: James R. Osgood & Co., 1871.

———. *Lincoln & The Civil War in the Diaries & Letters of John Hay.* New York: Dodd, Mead, 1939.

Heck, Frank H. *Proud Kentuckian: John C. Breckinridge, 1821–1875.* Lexington: University Press of Kentucky, 1976.

Helm, Katherine. *The True Story of Mary, Wife of Lincoln.* New York: Harper, 1928.

Hendrick, Burton J. *Lincoln's War Cabinet.* Boston: Little, Brown, 1946.

———. *Statesmen of the Lost Cause: Jefferson Davis and His Cabinet.* Boston: Little, Brown, 1939.

Herndon, William H., and Jesse W. Weik. *Abraham Lincoln: The True Story of a Great Life,* 2 vols. New York: D. Appleton & Company, 1906.

Hertz, Emanuel. *The Hidden Lincoln.* New York: Blue Ribbon Books, 1940.

Hess, Stephen. *America's Political Dynasties.* Garden City, N.Y.: Doubleday & Company, 1966.

Hesseltine, William B. *Civil War Prisons.* New York: Frederick Ungar Publishing, 1930.

———. *Lincoln and the War Governors.* New York: Alfred A. Knopf, 1948.

Horan, James D. *Desperate Women.* New York: G. P. Putnam's Sons, 1952.

———. *Mathew Brady: Historian with a Camera.* New York: Crown Publishers, 1955.

———. *The Pinkertons.* New York: Crown Publishers, Bonanza Books, 1967.

———, and Howard Swiggett. *The Pinkerton Story.* New York: G. P. Putnam's, 1951.

Horn, Stanley. *The Army of Tennessee.* Indianapolis: Bobbs-Merrill Co., 1941.

Horner, Harlan Hoyt. *Lincoln and Greeley.* Urbana: University of Illinois Press, 1953.

Hyman, Harold M. *A More Perfect Union.* New York: Alfred A. Knopf, 1973.

———, and William M. Wiecek. *Equal Justice Under Law: Constitutional Development, 1835–1875.* New York: Harper & Row, 1982.

Jellison, Charles A. *Fessenden of Maine.* Syracuse, N.Y.: Syracuse University Press, 1962.

Johnson, Robert Underwood, and Clarence Clough Buel, eds. *Battles and Leaders of the Civil War,* 6 vols. New York: The Century Company and D. Van Nostrand Company, 1884–1888.

Johnston, William Preston. *The Life of Gen. Albert Sidney Johnston.* New York: D. Appleton & Company, 1880.

Jones, Virgil Carrington. *Ranger Mosby.* Chapel Hill: University of North Carolina Press, 1944.

Joyce, Col. John A. *Jewels of Memory.* Washington, D.C.: Gibson Brothers, 1896.

Keckley, Elizabeth. *Behind the Scenes, Or, Thirty Years a Slave, and Four Years in the White House.* New York: Carleton & Co., 1868.

Kinsley, D. A. *Favor the Bold: Custer: The Civil War Years.* New York: Promontory Press; Holt, Rinehart, & Winston, 1967.

Klement, Frank. *The Limits of Dissent: Clement L. Vallandigham & The Civil War.* Lexington: University Press of Kentucky, 1970.

Klotter, James C. *The Breckinridges of Kentucky, 1760–1981.* Lexington: The University Press of Kentucky, 1986.

Korn, Bertram. *American Jewry and the Civil War.* Philadelphia: The Jewish Publication Society of America, 1951.

Korngold, Ralph. *Thaddeus Stevens, a Being Darkly Wise and Rudely Great.* New York: Harcourt, Brace, 1955.

Kunhardt, Dorothy Meserve, and Philip B. Kunhardt, Jr. *Mathew Brady and His World*. New York: Time-Life Books.

Lamon, Ward Hill. *The Life of Abraham Lincoln*. Boston: James R. Osgood and Company, 1872.

———. *Recollections of Abraham Lincoln, 1847–1865*. Cambridge, Mass.: The University Press, 1911.

Leech, Margaret. *Reveille in Washington, 1860–1865*. New York: Harper & Brothers, 1941.

———, and Harry J. Brown. *The Garfield Orbit*. New York: Harper & Row, 1978.

Lewis, Lloyd. *Myths After Lincoln*. New York: Harcourt, Brace & Company, 1929.

———. *Captain Sam Grant*. Boston: Little, Brown, 1950.

Lewis, Walker. *Without Fear or Favor: A Biography of Chief Justice Roger Brooke Taney*. Toronto: T. Allen, 1965.

Lincoln, Abraham. *The Collected Works of Abraham Lincoln*, Roy Basler, ed. New Brunswick, N.J.: Rutgers University Press, 1953.

Long, E. B., with Barbara Long. *The Civil War Day by Day*. Garden City, N.Y.: Doubleday & Company, 1971.

Lord, Francis A. *Lincoln's Railroad Man: Herman Haupt*. Rutherford, N.J.: Fairleigh Dickinson University Press, 1969.

Macartney, Clarence Edward. *Lincoln and His Cabinet*. New York: Charles Scribner's Sons, 1931.

———. *Little Mac: The Life of General George B. McClellan*. Philadelphia: Dorrance & Co., 1940.

McClellan, George Brinton. *Letters of the Secretary of War Transmitting Report on the Organization of the Army of the Potomac, And of Its Campaigns in Virginia and Maryland, Under the Command of Maj. Gen. George B. McClellan from July 26, 1861, to Nov. 7, 1862*. Washington, D.C.: Government Printing Office, 1864.

———, W. C. Prime, ed. *McClellan's Own Story: The War for the Union*. New York: Charles L. Webster & Co., 1887.

McClure, Alexander K. *Lincoln and Men of War-Times*. Philadelphia: The Times Publishing Co., 1892.

McDonough, James Lee. *Stones River: Bloody Winter in Tennessee*. Knoxville: University of Tennessee Press, 1980.

McFeely, William S. *Grant*. New York: W. W. Norton, 1981.

McKitrick, Eric L. "Party Politics and the Union and Confederate War Efforts," in William Nisbet Chambers and Walter Dean Burnham's *The American Party Systems: Stages of Political Development*. New York: Oxford University Press, 1967.

McLaughlin, Andrew. "Lincoln, the Constitution and Democracy"; 1936 papers of the Abraham Lincoln Association, Springfield, Ill.

McPherson, Edward. *The Political History of the United States During the Great Rebellion*. Washington, D.C., 1865.

McPherson, James. *Ordeal by Fire: The Civil War at Reconstruction*. New York: Alfred A. Knopf, 1982.

McWhiney, Grady. *Braxton Bragg and Confederate Defeat*. New York: Columbia University Press, 1969.

Mahony, D. A. *The Prisoner of State*. New York: Carleton Publisher, 1863.

Marshall, John A. *American Bastile: A History of the Illegal Arrests and Imprisonments of American Citizens in the Northern and Border States, On Account of*

Their Political Opinions, During the Late Civil War. Philadelphia: Thomas W. Hartley & Co., 1883.

Marszalek, John F. *Sherman's Other War: The General and the Civil War Press.* Memphis, Tenn.: Memphis State University Press, 1981.

Marx, Karl, and Friedrich Engels. *The Civil War in the United States.* New York: Citadel Press, 1961.

Mearns, David C., ed. *The Lincoln Papers,* 2 vols. Garden City, N.Y.: Doubleday & Company, 1948.

Mellon, James. *The Face of Lincoln.* New York: Viking Press, 1979.

Meredith, Roy. *Mr. Lincoln's Camera Man, Mathew B. Brady.* New York: Charles Scribner's Sons, 1946.

———. *The World of Mathew Brady: Portraits of the Civil War Period.* Los Angeles: Brooke House Publishers, 1976.

Meserve, Frederick Hill, and Carl Sandburg. *The Photographs of Abraham Lincoln.* New York: Harcourt, Brace, 1944.

Miers, Earl Schenck, ed. *Lincoln Day by Day: A Chronology, 1809–1865.* Washington, D.C.: Lincoln Sesquicentennial Commission, 1960.

Milton, George Fort. *Abraham Lincoln and the Fifth Column.* New York: Vanguard Press, 1942.

Mitchell, Stewart. *Horatio Seymour of New York.* Cambridge, Mass.: Harvard University Press, 1938; Da Capo Press reprint, 1970.

Mitchell, Wesley. *A History of the Greenbacks.* Chicago: University of Chicago Press, 1903.

Monaghan, Jay. *Diplomat in Carpet Slippers.* Indianapolis: Bobbs-Merrill, 1945.

———. *Custer: The Life of General George Armstrong Custer.* Boston: Little, Brown, 1959.

Murfin, James. *The Gleam of Bayonets.* Cranbury, N.J.: Thomas Yoseloff, 1965.

Myers, William Starr. *A Study in Personality: General George Brinton McClellan.* New York: D. Appleton-Century Company, 1934.

Nash, Howard P., Jr. *Stormy Petrel.* Rutherford, N.J.: Fairleigh Dickinson University Press, 1969.

Nason, Elias. *Life and Public Services of Henry Wilson, Late Vice President of the United States.* Boston: B. B. Russell, 1876.

Nelson, Paul David. "From Intolerance to Moderation: The Evolution of Abraham Lincoln's Racial Views," article in the *Register of the Kentucky Historical Society,* Frankfort.

Nevins, Allan. *Frémont, Pathmarker of the West,* 2 vols. New York: Frederick Ungar, 1939.

———. *The War for the Union: The Improvised War, 1861–1862.* New York: Charles Scribner's Sons, 1959.

———. *The War for the Union: War Becomes Revolution, 1862–1863.* New York: Charles Scribner's Sons, 1960.

Nicolay, Helen. *Personal Traits of Abraham Lincoln.* New York: The Century Company, 1912.

———. *Lincoln's Secretary.* New York: Longmans, Green and Company, 1949.

Nicolay, John. *The Cambridge Modern History,* Vol. VII: *The United States.* London: Cambridge University Press, 1901.

Nicolay, John G., and John Hay. *Abraham Lincoln: A History,* 10 vols. New York: The Century Company, 1890.

Niven, John. *Gideon Welles: Lincoln's Secretary of the Navy.* New York: Oxford University Press, 1973.

Noble, Hollister. *Woman with a Sword.* Garden City, N.Y.: Doubleday & Company, 1948.

Oates, Stephen B. *With Malice Toward None.* New York: Harper & Row, 1977.

———. *Our Fiery Trial: Abraham Lincoln, John Brown, and the Civil War Era.* Amherst: University of Massachusetts Press, 1979.

———. *Abraham Lincoln: The Man Behind the Myths.* New York: Harper & Row, 1984.

Oberholtzer, Ellis. *Jay Cooke: Financier of the Civil War.* Philadelphia: George W. Jacobs & Co., 1907.

Paludan, Philip. *A Covenant with Death.* Urbana: University of Illinois Press, 1975.

Parrish, William E., ed. *The Civil War: A Second American Revolution?* New York: Holt, Rinehart and Winston, 1970.

Pease, Theodore Calvin, and James G. Randall, eds. *The Diary of Orville Hickman Browning,* Vol. I, 1850–1864. Illinois State Historical Library, Springfield, 1925.

Perkins, Fred B. *The Picture and the Men, Being Biographical Sketches of President Lincoln and his Cabinet; Together with an Account of the Life of the Celebrated Artist, F. B. Carpenter, Author of the Great National Painting, the First Reading of the Emancipation Proclamation Before the Cabinet by President Lincoln.* New York: A. J. Johnson, 1867.

Phelps, Mary Merwin. *Kate Chase: Dominant Daughter.* New York: Thomas Y. Crowell, 1935.

Piatt, Donn. *Memories of the Men Who Saved the Union.* New York & Chicago: Belford, Clarke, & Co., 1887.

Pinkerton, Allan. *The Spy of the Rebellion.* New York: Carleton & Co., 1883.

Pollard, Edward A. *The Lost Cause.* New York: E. B. Treat & Co., 1866.

Pollard, James E. *The Presidents and the Press.* New York: The Macmillan Company, 1947.

Poore, Ben. Perley. *Perley's Reminiscences of 60 Years in the National Metropolis,* Vols. I & II. Philadelphia: Hubbard Brothers, 1886.

Potter, David M. *The South and the Concurrent Majority.* Baton Rouge: Louisiana State University Press, 1972.

Pratt, Harry E. *Concerning Mr. Lincoln.* The Abraham Lincoln Association, Springfield, Ill., 1944.

Purdue, Howell, and Elizabeth Purdue. *Pat Cleburne, Confederate General.* Hillsboro, Tex.: Hill Junior College Press, 1973.

Quarles, Benjamin. *Lincoln and the Negro.* New York: Oxford University Press, 1962.

Quynn, Russell Hoover. *The Constitutions of Abraham Lincoln and Jefferson Davis.* New York: Exposition Press, 1959.

Randall, James G. *Constitutional Problems Under Lincoln.* Urbana: University of Illinois Press, 1926; revised edition, 1951.

———. *Lincoln the President, Springfield to Gettysburg,* 2 vols. New York: Dodd, Mead, 1945.

———. *Lincoln and the South.* Baton Rouge: Louisiana State University Press, 1946.

———. *Lincoln the Liberal Statesman.* New York: Dodd, Mead, 1947.

———. *Midstream: Lincoln the President*. New York: Dodd, Mead, 1953.

———, and David Donald. *Lincoln the President: Last Full Measure*. New York: Dodd, Mead, 1955.

———, and David Donald. *The Civil War and Reconstruction*. Boston: D. C. Heath, 1961.

Randall, Ruth Painter. *Mary Lincoln: Biography of a Marriage*. Boston: Little, Brown, 1953.

———. *Lincoln's Sons*. Boston: Little, Brown, 1955.

Rawley, James. *The Politics of Union*. Hillsdale, Ill.: Dryden Press, 1973.

Raymond, Henry. *The Life, Public Services, and State Papers of Abraham Lincoln*. New York: Derby & Miller, 1865.

Rice, Allen Thorndike, ed. *Reminiscences of Abraham Lincoln by Distinguished Men of His Time*. New York: North American Review Publishing Company, 1886.

Richardson, E. Ramsay. *Little Aleck: A Life of Alexander H. Stephens*. New York: Grossett & Dunlap, 1932.

Riddle, A. G. *The Life of Benjamin F. Wade*. Cleveland: Williams Publishing Co., 1888.

Ross, Ishbel. *Proud Kate: Portrait of an Ambitious Woman*. New York: Harper & Brothers, 1953.

———. *Rebel Rose: Life of Rose O'Neal Greenhow, Confederate Spy*. New York: Harper & Brothers, 1954.

———. *The President's Wife: Mary Todd Lincoln*. New York: G. P. Putnam's Sons, 1973.

Russell, William Howard. *My Diary North and South*. T.O.H.P. Burnham, Boston, New York, and Toronto, 1863.

Sandburg, Carl. *Abraham Lincoln: The War Years*, 4 vols. New York: Harcourt, Brace and Company, 1939.

Scheibel, William. "The Podiatrist Who Became a President's Confidant," article in the *Journal of the American Podiatry Association*, August 1962.

Schlesinger, Arthur M., Jr. *The Imperial Presidency*. Boston: Houghton Mifflin, 1973.

Schuckers, J. W. *Life and Public Services of Salmon Portland Chase*. New York: D. Appleton & Company, 1874.

Schurz, Carl. *The Reminiscences of Carl Schurz*, 2 vols. New York: McClure Company, 1907.

Sears, Stephen W. *Landscape Turned Red: The Battle of Antietam*. New Haven, Conn.: Ticknor & Fields, 1983.

Segal, Charles, ed. *Conversations with Lincoln*. New York: G. P. Putnam's Sons, 1961.

Seitz, Don C. *Lincoln the Politician*. New York: Coward-McCann, 1931.

Seward, Frederick W. *Reminiscences of a War-Time Statesman and Diplomat, 1830–1915*. New York: G. P. Putnam's Sons, 1916.

Seward, William H. *Works*, ed. by George E. Baker. Boston: Houghton Mifflin Company, 1884.

Shelton, Harriet M. *Abraham Lincoln Returns*. New York: Evans Publishing, 1957.

Shenton, James. *Robert John Walker: A Politician from Jackson to Lincoln*. New York: Columbia University Press, 1961.

Sherman, William T. *Memoirs*. Foreword by B. H. Liddell Hart; 2 vols. Bloomington: Indiana University Press (Centennial Series), 1957.

Silver, David. *Lincoln's Supreme Court*. Urbana: University of Illinois Press, 1956.

Smalley, George. *Anglo-American Memories*. London: Duckworth & Co., 1911.

Smith, Elbert B. *Francis Preston Blair*. New York: The Free Press, 1980.

Smith, Theodore Clarke. *The Life and Letters of James Abram Garfield*, 2 vols. New Haven: Yale University Press, 1925; Archer Books reprint, 1968.

Smith, William Ernest. *The Francis Preston Blair Family in Politics*, 2 vols. The Macmillan Company, 1933; Da Capo Press reprint edition, 1969.

Snyder, Charles McCool. "Anna Ella Carroll, Political Strategist and Gadfly of President Fillmore." *Maryland Historical Magazine*, August 9, 1959.

Snyder, Joel. *American Frontiers: The Photographs of Timothy H. O'Sullivan, 1867–1874*. Philadelphia Museum of Art, 1981.

Sokoloff, Alice Hunt. *Kate Chase for the Defense*. New York: Dodd, Mead, 1971.

Spence, James. *The American Union; Its Effects on National Character and Policy, With an Inquiry into Secession as a Constitutional Right*. London: Richard Bentley, 1861.

Sprague, Dean. *Freedom Under Lincoln: Federal Power and Personal Liberty Under the Strain of the Civil War*. Boston: Houghton Mifflin Company, 1965.

Stackpole, Gen. Edward. *The Fredericksburg Campaign*. Harrisburg, Pa.: Stackpole Co., 1957.

Stampp, Kenneth M. *The Imperiled Union*. New York: Oxford University Press, 1980.

Starr, Louis M. *Bohemian Brigade*. New York: Alfred A. Knopf, 1954.

Stephens, Alexander H. *A Constitutional View of the Late War Between the States; Its Causes, Character, Conduct and Results*, 2 vols. Philadelphia: National Publishing Co., 1868.

Stillwell, Lucille. *Born to be a Statesman: John Cabell Breckinridge*. Caldwell, Idaho: Caxton Printers, 1936.

Stoddard, William O. *Inside the White House in War Times*. Boston: Charles Webster Co., 1890.

———. *Lincoln at Work*. Boston: United Society of Christian Endeavor, 1900.

———. *Lincoln's Third Secretary*. New York: Exposition Press, 1955.

Stone, Irving. *They Also Ran* (includes biography of McClellan and Seymour). Garden City, N.Y.: Doubleday & Company, 1943.

Stradling, Sgt. James. *His Talk with Lincoln*. Boston: Houghton Mifflin Compa? 1922.

Strong, George Templeton. *Diary of the Civil War, 1860–1865*, Allan Nevins, e? York: The Macmillan Company, 1962.

Strozier, Charles. *Lincoln's Quest for Union*. New York: Basic Books, 198?

Swanberg, W. A. *First Blood: The Story of Fort Sumter*. New York: Char? Sons, 1957.

Swierenga, Robert P., ed. *Beyond the Civil War Synthesis: Political F? War Era*. Westport, Conn.: Greenwood Press, 1975.

Swiggett, Howard. *The Rebel Raider: A Life of John Hunt M? Bobbs-Merrill, 1934.

Sword, Wiley. *Shiloh: Bloody April*. New York: William Mc?

Tanner, Hudson C. *The Lobby from Thurlow Weed's Time? ald, 1888.

Teeter, Paul R. *A Matter of Hours: Treason at Harper'? leigh Dickinson University Press, 1982.

Thomas, Benjamin P. *Abraham Lincoln: A Biography.* New York: Alfred A. Knopf, 1952.

———. *Portrait for Posterity: Lincoln and His Biographers.* New Brunswick, N.J.: Rutgers University Press, 1947.

———, and Harold M. Hyman. *Stanton: The Life and Times of Lincoln's Secretary of War.* New York: Alfred A. Knopf, 1962.

Thomas, Emory. *The Confederacy as a Revolutionary Experience.* Englewood Cliffs, N.J.: Prentice-Hall, 1971.

———. *The Confederate Nation.* New York: Harper & Row, 1979.

Townsend, William H. *Lincoln and the Bluegrass.* Lexington: University of Kentucky Press, 1955.

Trefousse, Hans L. *Ben Butler: The South Called Him Beast!* New York: Twayne Publishers, 1957.

———. *Benjamin Franklin Wade.* New York: Twayne Publishers.

———. *The Radical Republicans: Lincoln's Vanguard for Radical Justice.* Baton Rouge: Louisiana State University Press, 1968.

Turner, Justin, and Linda Levitt Turner. *Mary Todd Lincoln, Her Life and Letters.* New York: Alfred A. Knopf, 1972.

Van Deusen, Glyndon. *Thurlow Weed: Wizard of the Lobby.* Boston: Little, Brown, 1947.

———. *William Henry Seward.* New York: Oxford University Press, 1967.

Vidal, Gore. *Lincoln: A Novel.* New York: Random House, 1985.

Villard, Henry. *The Memoirs of Henry Villard.* Boston: Houghton Mifflin Company, 1904.

Von Ranke, Leopold. *The Secret of World History,* ed. by Rogers Wines. New York: Fordham University Press, 1981.

Ward, William Hayes, intro. *Abraham Lincoln: Tributes from His Associates.* Boston: Thomas Y. Crowell, 1895.

Washington, John E. *They Knew Lincoln.* New York: E. P. Dutton, 1942.

Weed, Thurlow. *See* Barnes, Thurlow Weed.

Welles, Gideon. *The Diary of Gideon Welles, Secretary of the Navy under Lincoln and Johnson,* 3 vols. Boston: Houghton Mifflin Company, 1911.

———. *Lincoln and Seward.* New York: Sheldon & Co., 1874, based on *Galaxy* magazine October 1873 article.

Welling, James. "The Emancipation Proclamation," pp. 163–85, in *North American Review,* Vol. CXXX. New York: D. Appleton & Company, 1880.

Werstein, Irving. *Abraham Lincoln vs. Jefferson Davis.* New York: Thomas Y. Crowell, 1959.

Wheeler Richard. *Sword Over Richmond: An Eyewitness History of McClellan's Peninsula Campaign.* New York: Harper & Row, 1986.

Whiting, William. *War Powers Under the Constitution of the United States.* Boston: Lee and Shepard, 1871.

Wilbur, Henry W. *President Lincoln's Attitude Towards Slavery and Emancipation.* New York: Biblo & Tannen, 1970 reprint of 1914 book.

ïley, Bell Irvin. *The Life of Johnny Reb/The Life of Billy Yank: The Common Soldier.* New York: Bobbs-Merrill, 1952.

liams, Kenneth P. *Lincoln Finds a General,* 2 vols. New York: The Macmillan Company, 1949–56.

Williams, T. Harry. *Lincoln and the Radicals*. Madison: University of Wisconsin Press, 1941.

———. *McClellan, Sherman and Grant*. New Brunswick, N.J.: Rutgers University Press, 1962.

Wilson, Edmund. *Patriotic Gore*. New York: Oxford University Press, 1962.

Wilson, Henry. *History of the Anti Slavery Measures of the Thirty-Seventh and Thirty-Eighth Congresses*. Boston: Walker, Wise, and Company, 1864.

Wilson, Rufus Rockwell. *Intimate Memories of Lincoln*. Elmira, N.Y.: Primavera Press, 1945.

Woodward, C. Vann, ed. *Mary Chesnut's Civil War*. New Haven: Yale University Press, 1981.

———, and Elisabeth Muhlenfeld. *The Private Mary Chesnut: The Unpublished Civil War Diaries*. New York: Oxford University Press, 1984.

Woodward, W. E. *Meet General Grant*. New York: Horace Liveright, 1928.

Wright, John S. *Lincoln and the Politics of Slavery*. Reno: University of Nevada Press, 1970.

Wright, William C. *The Secession Movement in the Middle Atlantic States*. Rutherford, N.J.: Fairleigh Dickinson University Press, 1973.

Wyeth, John A. *Life of General Nathan Bedford Forrest*. New York: Harper & Brothers, 1899.

Zornow, William Frank. *Lincoln and the Party Divided*. Norman: University of Oklahoma Press, 1954.